KV-603-081

Contents

Introduction

Welcome to the tenth edition of this book. As regular users will notice, this edition now contains information on the top 400 trusts rather than 300. This expansion is due to the minimum eligible annual grant total for each trust being reduced from £400,000 to £300,000 (there are a couple of exceptions whose grant total may increase significantly in the next financial year). As well as several newly operational trusts, the trusts new to this book were previously featured in the companion Guide to the Major Trusts Volume 2 (which has also itself expanded). We hope you will find this new format even more useful.

As well as being a practical and useful resource for those seeking grants, it is also intended to be an independent review of the work of the UK's largest trusts and foundations.

Though most of them have now got used to this, and very many are positively helpful, we still get occasional but vigorous objections when we express views that are not shared by the trust itself, or even as a result of wishing to publicise what they do. For example: 'If your organisation chooses to print the proposed text we will respond with a legal challenge and seek damages using the full power of the law'. Such attitudes are a remarkable survival in an age when just about every other kind of public institution and charitable trust is indeed a public institution, not a private one, and recognises the need to take external scrutiny and criticism on board.

Our main challenge has always been to get trusts to say who they give their money to, and what for. The first part of this battle is largely won, though there is still considerable mopping up to do. The law requires disclosure of 'a sufficient number of grants to convey a proper understanding of the charity's grantmaking activities'. The SORP (Statement of Recommended Practice for charity accounts), which in these respects is backed by statutory regulation, further states that 'disclosure should cover at least the 50 largest grants or any other larger number which is necessary for the proper understanding of the charity's grantmaking activity'. Few charities now fail to name the top 50 recipients, but in some cases this is not enough to meet the further requirement to 'convey a proper understanding'. For example, whole funding programmes, worth over £1 million in some cases, can be hidden if they do not feature any of the larger individual grants.

The form of the disclosure can also be used to obscure rather than to convey understanding. Stating that St John's received £50,000 is not helpful. 'St John's Community Centre, £50,000' is not much better. A long, raw, alphabetical list of this sort, on its own, is a challenge. Trusts are also required to supply 'an appropriate analysis and explanation' of their grants. Here, compliance is much more patchy and the Charity Commission should not be as accepting of the absence of this as they seem to be at present.

Finally, the trustees' report should 'explain what the charity is trying to do and how it is going about it'. Here, many trusts simply report that they made grants. However making grants is not in itself a charitable purpose. Grants are simply a means of achieving some further charitable purposes, and it is these purposes, and success in achieving them, that must be explained and reviewed.

In all these requirements, some trusts still seek to meet the letter rather than the spirit of the law. Recalcitrants, therefore, continue to be named and, we hope, shamed in the following pages.

Overall, however, we generally see a growing willingness, even an enthusiasm, by trusts to explain what they are doing. There are now a substantial number of trusts whose entries in this book are almost entirely in the form of quotes from their own materials. Many large trusts and some of the smaller ones now have websites which provide full information on their activities, guidelines and examples of projects or organisations that have been funded. This further demonstrates their willingness to be open about what they do, and also shows the realisation that it is better to provide full information to potential applicants in order for them to make informed decisions on whether or not to apply, instead of remaining a closed shop and receiving 'sacks full' of ineligible applications each week. It is perhaps this realisation that has been partly responsible for a greater willingness to help us write fuller entries (although some have been doing this all along). We are very grateful for the help which we are given.

Frequently asked questions

How do you get your information?

In general we write and ask for the annual report and accounts and for any further information available from the trust. If there is no reply, we use the copy of the report and accounts on the public file at the Charity Commission. We then write a draft entry and send it to the trust, again inviting suggested additions as well as corrections or comments. New information provided by the trust, and not generally available, is usually put in the form 'The trust notes that . . .' In cases where the trust or foundation has a website containing full information on their activities, including downloadable annual reports and accounts, this is the first port of call. The draft entry is then sent to them in the usual way. One unfortunate aspect of tracking down information about trusts for this edition was the all too often situation of examining the public files at the Charity Commission only to find that the most recent annual report and accounts for an individual trust had not made it to their file for inspection, even though it had clearly been received from them (as indicated by an up-to-date income and expenditure figure on the Charity Commission's online database). Where this is the case it is highlighted in the entry.

Do you print everything the trusts say?

Generally yes, but there are a few exceptions, of two kinds. First if what the trust says is purely formal and could be said equally of most of the other trusts in this book, we do not feel it needs repeating. Secondly, a very few of the largest trusts now produce literature on such a scale that it has become impossible to reprint it all; the Lloyds TSB foundations or the Esmee Fairbairn Foundation would be the extreme examples. Provided it is available there, we now sometimes refer to the availability of further material on the trust's website.

Do you investigate further when the information from a trust is inadequate?

No, we just report the fact. We also try to ignore hearsay and anecdote, positive or negative.

A Guide to the Major Trusts

2005/2006 edition

Volume 1
The top 400 trusts

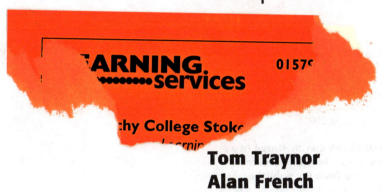

Tom Traynor
Alan French

WITHDRAWN

WITHDRAWN

DS006134

CORNWALL COLLEGE

DIRECTORY OF SOCIAL CHANGE

A Guide to the Major Trusts
Volume 1
2005/2006 edition

Published by
Directory of Social Change
24 Stephenson Way
London NW1 2DP
Tel: 020 7391 4800; Fax: 020 7391 4804
e-mail: info@dsc.org.uk
www.dsc.org.uk
from whom further copies and a full publications list are available.

Directory of Social Change is a Registered Charity no. 800517

First published 1986
Second edition 1989
Third edition 1991
Fourth edition 1993
Fifth edition 1995
Sixth edition 1997
Seventh edition 1999
Eighth edition 2001
Ninth edition 2003
Tenth edition 2005

Copyright © Directory of Social Change 2005

All rights reserved. **No part of this book may be stored in a retrieval system or reproduced in any form whatsoever without prior permission in writing from the publisher.** This book is sold subject to the condition that it shall not, by way of trade or otherwise, be lent, re-sold, hired out or otherwise circulated without the publisher's prior permission in any form of binding or cover other than that in which it is published, and without a similar condition including this condition being imposed on the subsequent purchaser.

ISBN 1 903991 55 2

British Library Cataloguing in Publication Data

A catalogue record for this book is available from the British Library

Cover design by Keith Shaw
Designed by Lenn Darroux
Typeset by Tradespools
Printed and bound by Page Bros., Norwich

361.7632 TRA

What is our policy on telephone numbers?

We normally print the telephone numbers of trusts, when we know them, and even if the trusts don't want us to, provided it is an office rather than a home number. Where a trust has said that it does not wish to receive telephone calls from potential applicants, or to have its number listed, this is noted in the text of the entry. However when the available telephone number is simply the head office of a big professional firm that acts as a postbox for the trustees, we leave it out.

Do you edit the 'applications' information?

No and Yes. The content of this section comes from the trust and we will reproduce whatever they give us. However we sometimes edit it to achieve a reasonable level of consistent presentation from one entry to another. This is why it is not printed as a 'quote' although it may still be written in the first person.

Why do you leave out the letters after trustees' names?

There are so many of them, and we try to present the entries in as simple and straightforward a way as we can. Besides, where do you draw the line – Captain the Honourable A Anthony, DSO, MBE, D Phil, AMCEEE and so on? Should we change? The additional information might be helpful in identifying one A Anthony from another. However we do see more and more trusts using simpler systems themselves, Arthur Anthony being more often happy to appear as such. However we do give titles – Lord, Lady, Dr, Professor and so on.

We are also sparing with capital letters. We use this minimalist style in the interests of clarity, but it does annoy some trusts, which go to considerable effort to try to change our usage back to what they see as proper. But reading about Trust after Foundation after Guideline after Application Form can get tiring.

Why don't the figures in the entries always add up?

There are a number of reasons, such as unclear distinctions between grant commitments and grant payments; the fact that grants lists and totals are often created by trusts quite separately from their audited figures; the fact that values for returned grants are included in some totals and not in others; and the existence of small undisclosed grants. If the discrepancies are large, we go to some effort to clarify the situation, but where they are small, well, we are not accountants, the figures are normally for illustration rather than being the basis for further calculation, and resources spent on seeking perfect numerical consistency would have to be taken from the more useful task of trying to find out and reflect clearly what the trust is doing. Grant figures given in the entries are also rounded up or down, which sometimes means that there may be a slight discrepancy between figures given individually and sum totals given elsewhere.

What's in a name? Trusts, Foundations, Funds, Charities, Settlements, Companies, Appeals; are they all the same?

The book covers organisations, usually charitable, that give grants to other charities. They may use almost any name; we judge them by what they do rather than what they are called.

Which trusts are in this book?

Roughly, all those that give, or could give £400,000 or more in grants each year. Smaller trusts are covered in volume 2 of this book (now expanded from 700 to 1,200), as well as in the local and specialised grant guides published by the Directory of Social Change (DSC).

Why are some grantmaking charities omitted?

This book does not seek to cover the following grantmaking charities.

- Company trusts. If they are operated by company staff on company premises, we will usually regard this as a channel for giving by the company, to be reported in our Guide to UK Company Giving.
- Specialised grantmakers, operating in a narrow field where they are likely to be well known and accessible to most applicants. Examples include trusts only funding research on specific medical conditions (these are generally accessible through the excellent website of the Association of Medical Research Charities, www.amrc.org.uk), or only supporting projects designed by themselves.
- Trusts or charities only making grants for work overseas. These are covered in the companion International Development Directory or The Major Charities – many of them operate on a large scale, like Oxfam or Christian Aid.
- Statutory funders, awarding public money.

What about lottery grants?

We have difficulties, and make compromises. We include the Big Lottery Fund but, despite its size, give it only a brief entry. The same goes for the admirable Awards for All small grants scheme. But we do not cover the arts councils, the sports councils, the Heritage Lottery Fund or the New Opportunities Fund. Although all lottery grants are part of public expenditure, subject to review by the National Audit Office and the Public Accounts Committee of the House of Commons, in many ways the Big Lottery Fund looks and acts like a grantmaking trust, and a particularly big and interesting one at that.

...and community foundations?

The local community foundations are a rapidly developing part of the voluntary sector. Originally the idea was that they would build up endowments which would enable them to become important local grantmakers. They are still doing this, but only a handful have generated enough income from their endowments to earn them a place in this book. However most of them have also developed two new streams of income. First they have become a vehicle through which local philanthropists make their donations, usually using a named subsidiary fund. But this is still on a modest scale in most cases. More importantly, they have become the vehicles for distributing government money, particularly the Local Network Fund for Children and Young People but also for a range of other local government funding initiatives. We have included brief entries for those giving grants of £300,000 or more, even when most of this is coming from such statutory sources. Contact details for all community foundations registered with the Community Foundation Network can be found at the back of this book.

What about the Landfill Tax Credit Scheme?

We have not included organisations such as the Lancashire Environmental Fund or the Gloucestershire Environmental Trust that are funded primarily through these tax credits. The scheme is covered in DSC's Guide to Funding from Government Departments and Agencies.

How to use this guide

The trusts are listed alphabetically, with indexes at the back of the book. As well as an alphabetical index, there are subject and geographical indexes which will help you to identify the trusts working in your field and area.

At the front of the book (from page xiv) we have ranked the trusts by the amount of money they give. This list also shows their main areas of interest. If you are looking for grants for your charity, we recommend that you start with this listing and tick the boxes of those trusts which might be relevant – starting with the biggest.

When you have ticked enough to be getting on with, read each trust entry carefully before deciding to apply. Very often a trust's interest in your field will be limited and precise, and may demand an application specifically tailored to its requirements – or, often, no application at all.

Remember to cover all parts of the guide; do not just start at the beginning of the alphabet. It is surprising, but still true, that trusts near the end of the alphabet receive fewer applications.

It is particularly important to show awareness of all the information available from the trust, to acquire up-to-date guidelines where possible, and to target your applications with respect to each trust's published wishes where such information exists. Inappropriate and ill-considered approaches, especially those that show you have not read the published guidelines, antagonise trusts and damage your organisation's reputation. Of course, many trusts publish nothing useful; here, you are on your own.

We have included a chart to help with the timings of your applications (see page xi). It shows, for over 100 trusts, the months when trustee meetings are usually held, and when applications need to be submitted.

For those new to raising money from trusts, the box on page ix is recommended as a starting point.

Classification

Serious applicants who will be fundraising from trusts in the long term do best, we believe, if they go to the most promising entries in this book and try to establish specific links between what the trust seems to be interested in and what their organisation is trying to do. The indexes and summary headings in this book are not likely to be enough on their own to identify the trusts that are most likely to have matching interests with a particular charity.

Notes on the entries

The entry headings

Grant total and financial year

The most up-to-date information available is given here. In a few cases the grants commentary in the main text is for the preceding year, as this information for the most recent year was unavailable or it was supplied at the last minute, too late for inclusion in this guide. Sometimes the information received on a particular trust dates from two different years – for example, most of the entry may contain information from the latest published annual report, but may also include very recent, as yet unpublished information gained from consultations directly with the trust.

The main areas of funding

These categories have been chosen by the editors from an analysis of the trusts' funding. They are indicative rather than definitive, and useful in a preliminary trawl through the guide. They are no substitute for a close reading of each entry.

The correspondent

The lead person. (Sometimes they are solicitors or accountants handling trust affairs solely on a 'postbox' basis.) Other useful administrative contacts may also be given in the 'applications' section, or within the main body of text.

Beneficial area

The area/s within which the trust operates, when this is restricted, either legally or as a matter of policy or practice. When a trust with a UK-wide remit shows an interest in a particular locality, this is noted. While the information usually comes from the trust itself, it may also arise from a pattern of grantmaking seen by the editors. Where this heading does not appear, the area of benefit is unrestricted.

Information available

This section notes the information available directly from the trust. If there is a website, this is usually the best starting point for information.

The main body of the entry

A summary of the trust's grantmaking usually prefaces the text. Trusts' policy notes and guidelines for applicants, where these exist, are normally reprinted in full. However, there are a few instances in which these are so lengthy that some abridgement has had to be undertaken. More trusts now analyse their own funding in their annual reports and, where available, this material also will usually be quoted in full. In general, however, analysis has been carried out by the editors based on grants lists accompanying the accounts.

Comment

The expansion of this edition and the increase in the amount of information on more trusts has meant a little less focus on analysis. The departure of Luke FitzHerbert from the production of this book, after nine editions and nearly 20 years, means that his extensive knowledge and experience in such matters has been redeployed. Comment in this edition tends to focus on factual matters such as the availability of information. We hope that the increase in information is an acceptable trade-off.

Exclusions and Applications sections

These reproduce, where possible, the trusts' own information or comments, though edited to suit the format of this book.

Editorial comment

The Directory of Social Change has been writing about grantmakers for many years. It has developed its own views of what it believes is entailed in good grantmaking, and of how it hopes that grantmakers will operate. Both explicitly and implicitly, it celebrates the many grantmakers who meet or exceed its expectations, and criticises those who fall short of them. These expectations are not complicated.

First we expect to see a demonstrated respect for applicants and beneficiaries. The issue has been put well by Jacob Neusner: 'those who receive are not less than or different from those who give. They have not only needs, but also feelings. They welcome not only our beneficence but also our respect. So when we engage in the act of giving we must do so in such a way that the equality of the giver and the receiver is acknowledged'.

From this point of view we are depressed, for example, by those who let it appear that fluency and accuracy in written English is a starting requirement for applicants. We dislike it when trusts say 'no telephone enquiries' without saying why or leave applicants in the dark about whether they will ever receive a response to their letters, be it positive or negative. For those who cannot, or do not wish to reply to applicants, a simple statement that there will be no response to unsuccessful applicants is surely a minimum courtesy.

Generally, we are saddened by funders whose style of work can leave applicants, even successful ones, close to tears.

On the other hand there are many grantmakers from whom applicants report receiving unending encouragement and support, even when no grant is made – 'they want to help', is a frequent comment. And this need not take extra time or money; the short postcard, with the right tone, is no more expensive than the typed letter of formal refusal (on writing paper of a quality and expense that most operating charities could only dream of). Indeed many grantmakers have little idea of the strength of the emotions, favourable or otherwise, that surround dealings between those with a lot of money and those in urgent need of just a little.

Secondly, more or less anonymous and unfocused grantmaking – 'all applications will be considered on their merits' – seems to us to be the weakest form of the art, even though it may often be popular with professional trust fundraisers, proud of their application drafting skills. The foundations that set out to make positive use of their money to achieve carefully considered aims seem to us to get better value for their money (and we therefore defend grantmakers who have to disappoint previous beneficiaries because they have decided to narrow and focus their grantmaking). Some trusts have worked this way for many years; the Carnegie UK and the Sainsbury family trusts are good examples (with Carnegie

UK now ceasing its grant programme to focus on funding long-term projects). We continue to be appalled by the clear and continuing bias in trust expenditures in favour of London and the Home Counties, though we welcome an increased consciousness of the issue, especially from the excellent Association of Charitable Foundations. We are uncomfortable with trusts that, even though unrestricted by their legal objects or published policies, allow their giving to be concentrated in the most prosperous areas of the country – especially when they justify this by saying that these are the areas whose problems are best understood by their trustees. In our view, such trusts need some new trustees. Sticking pins in a map to show grants clustering around the country homes of the trustees was regarded as a low trick when we first did it – we are happy that such practices are becoming uncommon, as are large grants to trustees' former, generally fee-paying independent, schools (or those of their children). But are we still right in thinking that few trustees are to be seen in the poorest and most depressed parts of our country? We seek out and celebrate any indication to the contrary.

We share the conventional view that trustees, and those connected with them, should not be remunerated except where 'there is no realistic alternative' (to use the Charity Commission's words). This is not solely to do with grantmaking – we hold this view in respect of all charities. But it is something we have long commented on, and regretted, in this series of guides. It is not a matter of law with any of the trusts that we describe, and there is no suggestion that the practice is in any way improper; it is simply our view of how charities are best organised.

And finally, we think that the effectiveness of grantmaking is multiplied when trustees are personally and intimately involved in the issues which concern the organisations that they fund. Being an active supporter is on a different level of commitment to being solely a funder; this can be seen when we contrast, say, the active engagement of the Tudor Trust's trustees and staff to the depressing situation where the administrators, a firm of solicitors or accountants often at a most expensive central London address, tell us simply that 'the trustees meet twice a year to review applications and award grants'. Though based on experience, these are simply our opinions. We welcome other views, and try to quote them positively and in full if they come from a trust. The mere fact that such a trust has had the energy to formulate another point of view marks them out from the many trusts that simply appear to believe that there are no issues to disagree about, and that good grantmaking is easy. It is not; it is difficult and demanding. It is also important and needs more critical examination than it usually gets.

How to apply to a trust

Although there are complete books on this (for example, *Fundraising from Grant-making Trusts and Foundations* and *Writing Better Fundraising Applications*, both published by the Directory of Social Change), there is no need to be daunted by the challenge of making effective applications. If your charity's work is good, and of a kind supported by the trust in question, a very simple letter (of one uncrowded page or less, and backed by a clear annual report and set of accounts) will probably do 90% of everything that can be done.

If there is an application form and detailed applications requirements, just follow them. But because they make it so easy, such trusts tend to get a lot of applications and you may have even better chances with the others.

1 Select the right trusts to approach
If they fund organisations or work like yours, and if you genuinely fit within any guidelines they publish, put them on your list.

2 Ring them
If the entry makes this sound sensible, ring them to check that the guidelines in this guide still apply and that the kind of application you are considering is appropriate for them.

3 Send in an application
Unless the trust has an application form (most don't), the main part of this, we suggest, should be a letter that fits easily on one side of a sheet of paper (back-up materials, such as a formal 'proposal' may be necessary for a big or complex project, but are usually, in our view, secondary). We suggest that the letter contains the following:

- A summary sentence such as: 'Can your trust give us £10,000 to develop a training programme for our volunteers?'
- The problem the work will address: This should normally be the beneficiaries' problem, not your charity's problem: 'Mothers of children with learning disabilities round here get very little help from the statutory services in coping with their children's day-to-day needs.'
- What you are going to do about this: 'Our volunteers, who have been in the same situations themselves, support and help them, but the volunteers need and want better training, especially on home safety.'
- Details of the work: 'We want to commission an expert from sister charity Home Start to develop and test suitable training materials that we will be able to use.'
- Information about your charity: 'We attach one of our general leaflets explaining what we do, and a copy of our latest Annual Report and Accounts.'
- Repeat the request: 'We will be very grateful if your trust can give us this grant.'

And that is all. Keep the style simple and informal. Where you can, handwrite the date, salutation and signature. A charity is not a business and does not impress by trying to sound like one. The best letter comes from a person involved in the proposed activity.

Making the letter longer will often reduce rather than increase its impact, but attaching compelling material is fine. You are not saying they have to read it through. A letter of endorsement might also be nice: your local bishop saying your work is wonderful, or whatever.

Appearance matters. It is a great help if you have a high quality letterhead on something better than photocopy paper, and if your report and accounts and literature are of appropriately high quality for your kind of organisation.

Good luck.

Dates for your diary

A = the last month for the receipt of applications

X = the usual month of trustees' or grant allocation meetings

Please note that these dates are provisional, and that the fact of an application being received does not necessarily mean that it will be considered at the next meeting.

	Jan	Feb	Mar	Apr	May	Jun	Jul	Aug	Sep	Oct	Nov	Dec
1989 Willan Charitable Trust			X			X			X		X	
29th May 1961 Charitable Trust			X			X			X			X
Sylvia Adams Charitable Trust		A		A		A		A		A		A
Ajahma Charitable Trust			A		X				A		X	
Milly Apthorp Charitable Trust			X			X			X			X
Architectural Heritage Fund			X			X			X			X
Baily Thomas Charitable Fund				A		X			A			X
BBC Children in Need			A								A	
Percy Bilton Charity			X			X			X			X
Britten-Pears Foundation	X			A	X				A	X		A
Bromley Trust			A	X					A	X		
Burdens Charitable Foundation			X			X			X			X
Clara E Burgess Charity	A	X		A	X		A	X		A	X	
William A Cadbury Charitable Trust					X					X		
CfBT Education Services			X			X			X			X
Church Urban Fund			X			X			X			X
Cinderford Charitable Trust		A	X									
City Parochial Foundation	XA			XA			X	A		X	A	
Clothworkers' Foundation and other Trusts		X			X		X				X	
Richard Cloudesley's Charity				X							X	
Colt Foundation					X						X	
Colyer-Fergusson Charitable Trust			X							X		
Ernest Cook Trust	A		X					A		X		
Baron Davenport's Charity			A		X				A		X	
Dulverton Trust	X				X		X			X		
Dunhill Medical Trust			X			X			X			X
Englefield Charitable Trust			X						X			
Eranda Foundation	A		X	A		X			A		X	
Essex Community Foundation	A							A				
Eveson Charitable Trust	X		X			X				X		
Allan and Nesta Ferguson Charitable Settlement	X					X						
Sir John Fisher Foundation					X						X	
Fishmongers' Company's Charitable Trust		A	X			A	X			A	X	
Four Acre Trust	X	A	X		A	X			A	X		A
Joseph Strong Frazer Trust			X							X		
J Paul Getty Jr Charitable Trust			X			X			X			X
G C Gibson Charitable Trust										A		

	Jan	Feb	Mar	Apr	May	Jun	Jul	Aug	Sep	Oct	Nov	Dec
Simon Gibson Charitable Trust			A		X							
Goldsmiths' Company Charity	X	X	X	X	X	X	X			X	X	X
Goshen Trust			X			X			X			X
Great Britain Sasakawa Foundation		X	A		X			A		X		A
Grocers' Charity	X	A		XA		X			A		XA	
Gulbenkian Foundation			X			X					X	
Lennox Hannay Charitable Trust		A	X									
Kathleen Hannay Memorial Charity		A	X									
Charles Hayward Foundation	X			X			X			X		
Help a London Child						A			A			
Help the Aged			X			X			X			X
Lady Hind Trust		A	X			A	X			A	X	
Sir Harold Hood's Charitable Trust									A	X		
Housing Associations Charitable Trust (Hact)		X		X		X			X	X		X
HSA Charitable Trust			X			X			X			X
John James Bristol Foundation	A	X		A	X		A	X		A	X	
Jewish Child's Day	A		X				A		X			
Elton John Aids Foundation			A				A				A	
King George's Fund for Sailors							X				X	
Ernest Kleinwort Charitable Trust			X							X		
Lambeth Endowed Charities	A		X	A		X		A		XA		X
London Marathon Charitable Trust								A				
John Lyon's Charity	A		X	A		X			A		X	
Mackintosh Foundation					X						X	
MacRobert Trust			X			A				XA		
Marshall's Charity	XA			XAA			XA			XA		
John Martin's Charity	X	X	X	X	X	X	X	X	X	X	X	X
J P Morgan Foundations	X		X				X			X		
National Art Collections Fund		X	X	X	X	X	X		X	X	X	X
Frances and Augustus Newman Foundation				A		X				A		X
P F Charitable Trust	X	X	X	X	X	X	X	X	X	X	X	X
Dowager Countess Eleanor Peel Trust			X									
Pilgrim Trust	X		A	X		A	X		A	X		A
Polden-Puckham Charitable Foundation		A							A			
J E Posnansky Charitable Trust					X							
Queen Mary's Roehampton Trust				A					A			
Rank Foundation			X			X			X			X
Joseph Rank Trust		A	X		A	X		A	X		A	X
Christopher H R Reeves Charitable Trust			X		X		X		X		X	
Robertson Trust		X	X		X		X		X		X	
Rose Foundation			A									
Joseph Rowntree Reform Trust Limited		A	X		A	X		A	X		A	X
Saddlers' Company Charitable Fund	X						X					
Francis C Scott Charitable Trust			X				X				X	
Sheffield Church Burgesses Trust	X			X			X			X		
Archie Sherman Charitable Trust	X	X	X	X	X	X	X		X	X	X	
Henry Smith Charity			X			X			X			X
South Yorkshire Community Foundation		A			A			A			A	
W F Southall Trust		X									X	
Steel Charitable Trust	X			X			X			X		

	Jan	Feb	Mar	Apr	May	Jun	Jul	Aug	Sep	Oct	Nov	Dec
Sir Halley Stewart Trust		X				X				X		
Stoller Charitable Trust		A	X		A	X		A	X		A	X
W O Street Charitable Foundation	X			X			X			X		
Trust for London	A		X	A		X	A		X	A		X
Douglas Turner Trust	A	X		A	X		A	X	A	X		
Wates Foundation			X				X				X	
Westminster Foundation for Democracy	X			X			X			X		
Will Charitable Trust	A		X					A		X		
Wixamtree Trust	X			X			X			X		
Woodward Charitable Trust	X				X		X					

The major trusts ranked by grant total

Trust	Grants	Main grant areas
☐ Big Lottery Fund	£650 million	Community, young people, welfare
☐ Wellcome Trust	£395 million	Biomedical research, history of medicine, biomedical ethics, public engagement with science
☐ Sainsbury Family Charitable Trusts	(£55 million)	See the entries for the individual trusts
☐ Awards for All	£53.7 million	General
☐ Football Foundation	£45 million	Grass roots football, community, education
☐ Garfield Weston Foundation	£36 million	General
☐ Comic Relief	£35 million	Community-based UK charities, Africa
☐ Gatsby Charitable Foundation	£33.3 million	General
☐ Wolfson Foundation	£31 million	Medical and scientific research, education, health and welfare, heritage, arts
☐ BBC Children in Need	£30.5 million	Welfare of disadvantaged children
☐ Esmée Fairbairn Foundation	£26 million	Social welfare, education, environment, arts and heritage
☐ Leverhulme Trust	£25 million	Scholarships for education and research
☐ Coalfields Regeneration Trust	£24.1 million	General, health, welfare, community regeneration, education, young people, older people
☐ Tudor Trust	£22.1 million	Welfare, general
☐ Lloyds TSB Foundation for England and Wales	£20 million	Social and community needs, education and training
☐ Northern Rock Foundation	£19.3 million	Disadvantaged people
☐ Henry Smith Charity	£19 million	Social welfare, older people, disability, health, medical research
☐ Wales Council for Voluntary Action	£18.8 million	Local community, volunteering, social welfare, environment, regeneration
☐ Bridge House Trust	£16.4 million	Welfare in London
☐ Shetland Charitable Trust	£14 million	Social welfare, art and recreation, environment and amenity
☐ Health Foundation	£12 million	Health care and public health research, training and development
☐ Sigrid Rausing Trust	£10.3 million	Human rights, women's rights, minority and indigenous rights, social and environmental advocacy
☐ Peter Moores Foundation	£10 million	The arts, particularly opera, social welfare
☐ Mercers' Charitable Foundation	£10 million	General welfare, elderly, conservation, arts, Christian faith activities, educational institutions
☐ City Parochial Foundation	£8.9 million	Social welfare in London
☐ Lloyds TSB Foundation for Scotland	£7.3 million	Social and community needs, education and training, scientific, medical and social research
☐ Jack Petchey Foundation	£7 million	Young people in east London and west Essex
☐ Linbury Trust	£6.5 million	Arts, heritage, social welfare, general
☐ Help the Aged	£6.4 million	Welfare, for older people
☐ Laing Family Foundations	£6.1 million	General
☐ Community Foundation for Merseyside	£6 million	Community development, general
☐ Paul Hamlyn Foundation	£6 million	Arts, education, India
☐ Robertson Trust	£6 million	General, in Scotland
☐ Stewards' Company Limited	£5.8 million	Christian evangelism, general
☐ Nuffield Foundation	£5.6 million	Education, child protection, family law and justice, access to justice
☐ P F Charitable Trust	£5.6 million	General, particularly arts/heritage, health, welfare, education

☐ Community Foundation Serving Tyne & Wear and Northumberland	**£5.6 million**	Social welfare, general
☐ Foyle Foundation	**£5.1 million**	Learning, arts, health
☐ Shirley Foundation	**£5 million**	Autism
☐ LankellyChase Foundation	**£5 million**	Social welfare, community development, arts, heritage, penal affairs, mental health
☐ Joseph Rowntree Charitable Trust	**£4.9 million**	Peace, democracy, racial justice, corporate responsibility
☐ Rank Foundation	**£4.8 million**	Christian communication, youth, education, general
☐ Joseph Rowntree Foundation	**£4.7 million**	Research and development in social policy
☐ Parthenon Trust	**£4.5 million**	Humanitarian assistance, third world development, medical research, treatment and care, assistance for the disadvantaged, general
☐ Clore Duffield Foundation	**£4.5 million**	Arts/museums, Jewish charities, education, elderly and disadvantaged
☐ ARK (Absolute Return for Kids)	**£4.4 million**	Child welfare
☐ National Art Collections Fund	**£4.4 million**	Acquisition of works of art by museums and galleries
☐ Allchurches Trust Ltd	**£4.3 million**	Churches, general
☐ Arbib Foundation	**£4.3 million**	Not known
☐ Freshfield Foundation	**£4.1 million**	Environment, general
☐ Jerwood Foundation and Charity	**£4 million**	The arts
☐ Foundation for Sport and the Arts	**£4 million**	Sport, the arts
☐ Action Medical Research	**£4 million**	Medical research
☐ Mayfair Charities Ltd	**£4 million**	Orthodox Judaism
☐ Elton John Aids Foundation	**£3.8 million**	HIV/AIDS welfare and prevention
☐ John Ellerman Foundation	**£3.4 million**	Health, welfare, art and conservation, for national organisations
☐ Tubney Charitable Trust	**£3.3 million**	Conservation of the natural environment, welfare of farmed animals
☐ Barrow Cadbury Trust and Fund	**£3.3 million**	Inclusive communities, offending and early intervention, global exchange
☐ Monument Trust	**£3.2 million**	Arts, health and welfare (especially AIDS), environment, general
☐ South East London Community Foundation	**£3.2 million**	Community activities
☐ Dulverton Trust	**£3.1 million**	Youth and education, welfare, general
☐ John Lyon's Charity	**£3.1 million**	Children and young people in north and west London
☐ Baily Thomas Charitable Fund	**£3.1 million**	Learning disability
☐ Headley Trust	**£3.1 million**	Arts, heritage, welfare, development
☐ Dunhill Medical Trust	**£3.1 million**	Medical research, elderly
☐ Community Foundation for Northern Ireland	**£3.1 million**	Community development, social welfare
☐ Wolfson Family Charitable Trust	**£3 million**	Jewish charities
☐ Charles Wolfson Charitable Trust	**£3 million**	Medical research, health, education, Jewish charities, general
☐ Clothworkers' Foundation	**£3 million**	Clothworking, general
☐ Keren Association	**£3 million**	Jewish, education, general
☐ Westminster Foundation for Democracy	**£3 million**	Strengthening democracy overseas
☐ Rachel Charitable Trust	**£3 million**	General, Jewish in the UK and Europe
☐ AW Charitable Trust	**£2.9 million**	Jewish causes, general
☐ Gosling Foundation Limited	**£2.8 million**	Nautical and service charities, general
☐ Birmingham Foundation	**£2.7 million**	General
☐ 29th May 1961 Charitable Trust	**£2.7 million**	Social welfare, general
☐ Jerusalem Trust	**£2.7 million**	Promotion of Christianity
☐ Church Urban Fund	**£2.7 million**	Welfare; Christian outreach in disadvantaged communities in England
☐ Lord's Taverners	**£2.7 million**	Minibuses and sports equipment for people with disabilities, cricket
☐ Variety Club Children's Charity	**£2.6 million**	Children's charities

☐ **Sobell Foundation**	**£2.6 million**	Jewish charities, health and welfare
☐ **Childwick Trust**	**£2.6 million**	Health in the UK, education in South Africa, Jewish and bloodstock charities in the UK
☐ **Community Foundation for Greater Manchester**	**£2.5 million**	General, in Greater Manchester
☐ **Football Association Youth Trust**	**£2.5 million**	Sports
☐ **Gannochy Trust**	**£2.5 million**	General
☐ **Allan and Nesta Ferguson Charitable Settlement**	**£2.4 million**	Peace, education, overseas development
☐ **CHK Charities Limited**	**£2.2 million**	General
☐ **Equitable Charitable Trust**	**£2.2 million**	Education of disabled/disadvantaged children
☐ **Baring Foundation**	**£2.1 million**	Strengthening the voluntary sector
☐ **Robert and Lisa Sainsbury Charitable Trust**	**£2.1 million**	Sainsbury artistic institutions, general
☐ **Sir John Cass's Foundation**	**£2.1 million**	Education in inner London
☐ **Gulbenkian Foundation**	**£2.1 million**	Education, arts, welfare
☐ **County Durham Foundation**	**£2 million**	Tackling social disadvantage and poverty, general
☐ **Diana, Princess of Wales Memorial Fund**	**£2 million**	Children and young people in the UK, overseas
☐ **Historic Churches Preservation Trust**	**£2 million**	Historic churches
☐ **Rufford Maurice Laing Foundation**	**£2 million**	Nature conservation, sustainable development, environment, general
☐ **Goldsmiths' Company Charity**	**£2 million**	General, London charities, the precious metals craft
☐ **UnLtd (Foundation for Social Entrepreneurs)**	**£2 million**	Social enterprise
☐ **The Queen's Silver Jubilee Trust**	**£2 million**	General
☐ **Hunter Foundation**	**£2 million**	Education, children
☐ **Eveson Charitable Trust**	**£1.9 million**	Health, welfare
☐ **Trusthouse Charitable Foundation**	**£1.9 million**	General
☐ **Army Benevolent Fund**	**£1.9 million**	Service charities
☐ **Royal British Legion**	**£1.9 million**	Service
☐ **Prince of Wales's Charitable Foundation**	**£1.9 million**	General
☐ **Djanogly Foundation**	**£1.9 million**	Education, arts, Jewish charities, general
☐ **Charles Hayward Foundation**	**£1.8 million**	Welfare and health, medical research, overseas
☐ **King George's Fund for Sailors**	**£1.8 million**	The welfare of seafarers
☐ **Sir Jules Thorn Charitable Trust**	**£1.8 million**	Medical research, medicine, small grants for humanitarian charities
☐ **Peacock Charitable Trust**	**£1.8 million**	Medical research, disability, general
☐ **Lolev Charitable Trust**	**£1.8 million**	Jewish
☐ **Maurice and Hilda Laing Charitable Trust**	**£1.7 million**	Promotion of Christianity, relief of need
☐ **John and Rosemary Lancaster Charitable Foundation**	**£1.7 million**	Christian causes
☐ **The King's Fund**	**£1.7 million**	Health and health care, especially in London
☐ **Cadogan Charity**	**£1.7 million**	General
☐ **Westminster Foundation**	**£1.7 million**	General
☐ **Joseph Rank Trust**	**£1.7 million**	The Methodist Church, Christian-based social work
☐ **Sutton Trust**	**£1.6 million**	Education
☐ **Lisbet Rausing Charitable Fund**	**£1.6 million**	Humanities and social science research
☐ **Pilgrim Trust**	**£1.6 million**	Social welfare, art and learning, preservation of buildings
☐ **Wates Foundation**	**£1.6 million**	'Support of the disadvantaged', especially close to south London
☐ **Archie Sherman Charitable Trust**	**£1.6 million**	Jewish charities, education, arts, general
☐ **Lloyds TSB Foundation for Northern Ireland**	**£1.6 million**	Social and community need, education and training, scientific and medical research
☐ **Grand Charity of Freemasons**	**£1.5 million**	Social welfare, medical research and hospices
☐ **ShareGift**	**£1.5 million**	General
☐ **Euro Charity Trust**	**£1.5 million**	Relief of poverty, education
☐ **Greater Bristol Foundation**	**£1.5 million**	General
☐ **Bernard Sunley Charitable Foundation**	**£1.5 million**	General
☐ **Eranda Foundation**	**£1.5 million**	Research into education and medicine, the arts, social welfare
☐ **Shlomo Memorial Fund Limited**	**£1.5 million**	Jewish causes

☐ J Paul Getty Jr Charitable Trust	**£1.5 million**	Social welfare, conservation to a limited extent
☐ Clydpride Ltd	**£1.5 million**	Jewish charities, general
☐ Tees Valley Community Foundation	**£1.5 million**	General
☐ Northwood Charitable Trust	**£1.5 million**	Medical research, health, welfare, general
☐ Impetus Trust	**£1.5 million**	General, social welfare
☐ Community Foundation for Calderdale	**£1.4 million**	General
☐ Patrick Charitable Trust	**£1.4 million**	General, with a particular interest in Muscular Dystrophy
☐ Kirby Laing Foundation	**£1.4 million**	Health, welfare, Christian religion, general
☐ Zochonis Charitable Trust	**£1.4 million**	General
☐ Unemployed Voluntary Action Fund	**£1.4 million**	Voluntary projects engaging unemployed people as volunteers
☐ Burdett Trust for Nursing	**£1.4 million**	Healthcare
☐ Rayne Foundation	**£1.3 million**	Education, medicine and health, the arts, social welfare, general
☐ Porter Foundation	**£1.3 million**	Jewish charities, environment, arts, general
☐ Stratford upon Avon Town Trust	**£1.3 million**	Education, welfare, general
☐ Derbyshire Community Foundation	**£1.2 million**	Social welfare
☐ Peter Harrison Foundation	**£1.2 million**	Children, young people, people with disabilities, people who are disadvantaged
☐ Manifold Trust	**£1.2 million**	Historic buildings, environmental conservation, general
☐ Ernest Kleinwort Charitable Trust	**£1.2 million**	General
☐ Francis C Scott Charitable Trust	**£1.2 million**	Disadvantaged young people in Cumbria and north Lancashire
☐ M & R Gross Charities Limited	**£1.2 million**	Jewish causes
☐ CAF	**£1.2 million**	General
☐ Lord Ashdown Charitable Trust	**£1.2 million**	Jewish education, general
☐ Hurdale Charity Limited	**£1.2 million**	Jewish
☐ John James Bristol Foundation	**£1.2 million**	Education, health, older people, general
☐ Lennox Hannay Charitable Trust	**£1.2 million**	Health, welfare, general
☐ Barbour Trust	**£1.2 million**	Health, welfare
☐ London Marathon Charitable Trust	**£1.2 million**	Sport, recreation and leisure
☐ Performing Right Society Foundation	**£1.2 million**	Music
☐ Hadley Trust	**£1.1 million**	Social welfare
☐ Jane Hodge Foundation	**£1.1 million**	Medicine, education, religion, mainly in Wales
☐ Sheffield Church Burgesses Trust	**£1.1 million**	Church, general
☐ HSA Charitable Trust	**£1.1 million**	Healthcare, medical research
☐ CfBT Education Services	**£1.1 million**	Education
☐ Leathersellers' Company Charitable Fund	**£1.1 million**	General
☐ Kennedy Leigh Charitable Trust	**£1.1 million**	Jewish charities, general
☐ Dunard Fund	**£1.1 million**	Classical music, the visual arts
☐ South Yorkshire Community Foundation	**£1.1 million**	General
☐ Souter Charitable Trust	**£1.1 million**	Christian evangelism, welfare
☐ Camelot Foundation	**£1 million**	Social welfare, disability
☐ Beatrice Laing Trust	**£1 million**	Relief of poverty and distress
☐ Albert Hunt Trust	**£1 million**	Welfare
☐ Mrs L D Rope Third Charitable Settlement	**£1 million**	General
☐ Hobson Charity Ltd	**£1 million**	Social welfare, education
☐ Lloyds TSB Foundation for the Channel Islands	**£1 million**	General
☐ Waterside Trust	**£1 million**	Christian causes, welfare
☐ Hugh Fraser Foundation	**£1 million**	General
☐ Laidlaw Youth Project	**£1 million**	Children and young people
☐ Gederville Ltd	**£1 million**	Jewish, general
☐ Alice Trust	**£993,000**	Conservation and education
☐ Kennedy Charitable Foundation	**£982,000**	Roman Catholic ministries, general, especially in the west of Ireland

☐ Kay Kendall Leukaemia Fund	£978,000	Research into leukaemia
☐ Samuel Sebba Charitable Trust	£961,000	Jewish causes
☐ Alan Edward Higgs Charity	£954,000	Child welfare
☐ Joseph Rowntree Reform Trust Limited	£954,000	Political reform, social justice
☐ Trust for London	£951,000	Social welfare in London
☐ Steel Charitable Trust	£950,000	Health, welfare, general
☐ Rose Foundation	£939,000	Grants for building projects
☐ Hedley Foundation	£929,000	Youth, health, welfare
☐ Sir James Knott Trust	£926,000	General
☐ Network for Social Change	£926,000	Third world debt, environment, human rights, peace, arts
☐ Medlock Charitable Trust	£920,000	Education, health, welfare
☐ Campden Charities	£902,000	Welfare and education in Kensington, London
☐ Fishmongers' Company's Charitable Trust	£889,000	Education, promotion of fisheries, relief of hardship and disability
☐ Sir Halley Stewart Trust	£875,000	Medical, social and religious research
☐ Stobart Newlands Charitable Trust	£875,000	Christian causes
☐ Isle of Dogs Community Foundation	£866,000	Regeneration, general
☐ Scottish Community Foundation	£862,000	Community development, general
☐ Lambeth Endowed Charities	£859,000	Education, welfare
☐ Itzchok Meyer Cymerman Trust Ltd	£850,000	Jewish Orthodox education, other Jewish organisations
☐ Millennium Stadium Charitable Trust	£850,000	Sport, the arts, community and the environment
☐ Cumbria Community Foundation	£826,000	Improving the quality of community life
☐ Marchig Animal Welfare Trust	£825,000	Animal welfare
☐ Drapers' Charitable Fund	£816,000	General
☐ Huntingdon Foundation	£807,000	Jewish education
☐ Joy Cohen Charitable Trust	£800,000	Jewish, general
☐ SPARKS Charity	£797,000	Medical research
☐ Märit and Hans Rausing Charitable Foundation	£795,000	National heritage, children, medical research, nature preservation
☐ Sutton Coldfield Municipal Charities	£794,000	Relief of need, education, general
☐ Rubin Foundation	£787,000	Jewish charities, general
☐ Entindale Ltd	£778,000	Orthodox Jewish charities
☐ Robert Gavron Charitable Trust	£774,000	The arts, policy research, general
☐ Blatchington Court Trust	£770,000	Education of people under 31 who are blind and partially sighted
☐ David Tannen Charitable Trust	£769,000	Jewish
☐ John Moores Foundation	£756,000	Social welfare in Merseyside and Northern Ireland, emergency relief overseas
☐ Charity Association Manchester Ltd	£754,000	Jewish charities
☐ MacRobert Trust	£754,000	General
☐ Reta Lila Howard Foundation	£750,000	Children, arts, environment
☐ Spring Harvest Charitable Trust	£750,000	The promotion of Christianity
☐ Sheepdrove Trust	£750,000	Environment, education
☐ Essex Community Foundation	£747,000	General
☐ Heathcoat Trust	£740,000	Welfare, local causes
☐ Levy Foundation	£736,000	Young people, elderly, health, medical research, Jewish charities
☐ Help a London Child	£731,000	Children and young people
☐ Goshen Trust	£731,000	Christian
☐ EBM Charitable Trust	£730,000	Children/youth, animal welfare, general
☐ Jacobs Charitable Trust	£725,000	Jewish charities, the arts
☐ D'Oyly Carte Charitable Trust	£724,000	Arts, medical welfare, environment
☐ Charitworth Limited	£712,000	Jewish causes
☐ Cash for Kids - Radio Clyde	£712,000	Children
☐ Maurice Hatter Foundation	£703,000	Jewish causes, general

☐ Glencore Foundation for Education and Welfare	**(£696,000)**	Education and welfare
☐ John and Lucille van Geest Foundation	**£694,000**	Medical research, healthcare, general
☐ Ernest Cook Trust	**£680,000**	Education in environment, rural conservation, arts and crafts
☐ Ridgesave Limited	**£660,000**	General, education
☐ J J Charitable Trust	**£659,000**	Environment, literacy
☐ Cripplegate Foundation	**£654,000**	General
☐ Ashden Charitable Trust	**£650,000**	Environment, homelessness, sustainable regeneration, community arts
☐ Three Guineas Trust	**£639,000**	Autism
☐ Sir Siegmund Warburg's Voluntary Settlement	**£619,000**	Medicine and education
☐ St James's Place Foundation	**£615,000**	Children and young people with special needs
☐ H D H Wills 1965 Charitable Trust	**£613,000**	Environment, general
☐ G C Gibson Charitable Trust	**£613,000**	Churches, health, welfare, medical research, wildlife, agriculture, general
☐ Mulberry Trust	**£608,000**	General
☐ Richmond Parish Lands Charity	**£606,000**	General, in Richmond, Surrey
☐ Edward Cadbury Charitable Trust	**£606,000**	Religion, general
☐ Vardy Foundation	**£606,000**	Christian causes, education in the north east of England, general
☐ Wixamtree Trust	**£602,000**	General
☐ Heart of England Community Foundation	**£600,000**	General
☐ Yorkshire Dales Millennium Trust	**£600,000**	Conservation and environmental regeneration
☐ Housing Associations Charitable Trust (Hact)	**£600,000**	Housing and related social need
☐ Tolkien Trust	**£600,000**	Christian - especially Catholic, welfare, general
☐ United Trusts	**£598,000**	General
☐ Tedworth Charitable Trust	**£595,000**	Parenting, child welfare and development, general
☐ Sir James Reckitt Charity	**£594,000**	Quakers, general
☐ John Martin's Charity	**£589,000**	Religious activity, relief-in-need, education
☐ Haramead Trust	**£580,000**	Welfare, children, animals, health education
☐ Percy Bilton Charity	**£580,000**	Disabled, disadvantaged youth, older people
☐ Allen Lane Foundation	**£580,000**	Unpopular causes
☐ Severn Trent Water Charitable Trust	**£579,000**	Relief of poverty, money advice, debt counselling
☐ Glass-House Trust	**£572,000**	Social housing and the urban environment
☐ Devon Community Foundation	**£571,000**	General
☐ British Record Industry Trust	**£570,000**	Musical education
☐ Architectural Heritage Fund	**£569,000**	Building preservation
☐ Four Acre Trust	**£567,000**	Respite care and holidays, vocational guidance, health disability, social housing
☐ Mr and Mrs J A Pye's Charitable Settlement	**£564,000**	General
☐ Milly Apthorp Charitable Trust	**£561,000**	Health, older people and youth in north west London
☐ 1989 Willan Charitable Trust	**£558,000**	General
☐ Marshall's Charity	**£550,000**	Parsonage and church improvements
☐ M B Foundation	**£550,000**	General
☐ Lord Leverhulme's Charitable Trust	**£548,000**	Welfare, education, arts, young people
☐ Grocers' Charity	**£542,000**	General
☐ David and Frederick Barclay Foundation	**£542,000**	Medical research, welfare
☐ SHINE	**£539,000**	Education of children and young people
☐ Tompkins Foundation	**£538,000**	Health, welfare
☐ Alice Ellen Cooper Dean Charitable Foundation	**£536,000**	General
☐ Kathleen Hannay Memorial Charity	**£535,000**	Health, welfare, Christian, general
☐ H B Allen Charitable Trust	**£535,000**	General
☐ Sherburn House Charity	**£532,000**	Welfare and the relief of need
☐ Frances and Augustus Newman Foundation	**£530,000**	Medical research and equipment
☐ J P Morgan Foundations	**£529,000**	Education

☐ Welton Foundation	**£524,000**	Medical research, music, general
☐ William A Cadbury Charitable Trust	**£520,000**	Local welfare and disability charities, Quaker churches, penal reform, overseas
☐ Colyer-Fergusson Charitable Trust	**£518,000**	Community activity (often through churches), environment, arts
☐ Colt Foundation	**£518,000**	Occupational and environmental health research
☐ J E Posnansky Charitable Trust	**£515,000**	Jewish charities, health, welfare
☐ John Beckwith Charitable Trust	**£515,000**	Youth, general
☐ Norwich Town Close Estate Charity	**£514,000**	Education in and near Norwich
☐ Hertfordshire Community Foundation	**£512,000**	General
☐ Mike Gooley Trailfinders Charity	**£511,000**	Cancer research, general
☐ Pilkington Charities Fund	**£511,000**	Welfare, health
☐ Central Church Fund	**£511,000**	Church of England
☐ Rothschild Foundation	**£507,000**	Arts, culture, general
☐ Band Trust	**£505,000**	Health, welfare, general
☐ Valentine Charitable Trust	**£500,000**	Welfare and the environment
☐ Oglesby Trust	**£500,000**	General
☐ Charities Advisory Trust	**£500,000**	General
☐ Mary Kinross Charitable Trust	**£500,000**	Mental health, community development, penal affairs
☐ Tajtelbaum Charitable Trust	**£500,000**	Jewish, welfare
☐ Henry Moore Foundation	**£499,000**	Fine arts, in particular sculpture, drawing and printmaking
☐ Bedford Charity (Harpur Trust)	**£498,000**	Education, welfare and recreation in and around Bedford
☐ Execution Charitable Trust	**£493,000**	Social welfare
☐ Kreitman Foundation	**£486,000**	Education, culture, the environment, health and welfare, Jewish charities
☐ Donald Forrester Trust	**£485,000**	Health, medical research, disability, welfare, general
☐ St Katharine & Shadwell Trust	**£482,000**	Education, training, general
☐ Jones 1986 Charitable Trust	**£482,000**	General
☐ Queen Mary's Roehampton Trust	**£480,000**	War disabled ex-service people and their dependants
☐ H C D Memorial Fund	**£475,000**	The relief of need
☐ Stone Ashdown Charitable Trust	**£472,000**	Equality and discrimination
☐ Sylvia Adams Charitable Trust	**£468,000**	Disability, welfare, poverty, children and young people
☐ Stoller Charitable Trust	**£468,000**	Medical, children, general
☐ Woodward Charitable Trust	**£467,000**	General
☐ Barnwood House Trust	**£465,000**	Disability charities in Gloucestershire, medical research
☐ Alliance Family Foundation	**£464,000**	Jewish, general
☐ Simon Gibson Charitable Trust	**£464,000**	General
☐ Dowager Countess Eleanor Peel Trust	**£462,000**	Medical research, general
☐ Sir Harold Hood's Charitable Trust	**£457,000**	Roman Catholic
☐ Triangle Trust (1949) Fund	**£455,000**	Health, welfare, education
☐ Balint Family Charitable Trusts	**£452,000**	Jewish charities, general
☐ Childs Charitable Trust	**£450,000**	Christian
☐ M K Charitable Trust	**£450,000**	Jewish charities
☐ Schreib Trust	**£450,000**	Jewish, general
☐ Carole & Geoffrey Lawson Foundation	**£450,000**	Jewish, child welfare, poverty, arts, education
☐ Will Charitable Trust	**£449,000**	Environment/conservation, cancer care, blindness, mental disability
☐ Debmar Benevolent Trust	**£448,000**	Jewish
☐ Maud Elkington Charitable Trust	**£446,000**	Social welfare, general
☐ Schroder Charity Trust	**£442,000**	Medical, international relief, social welfare, heritage, environment, arts
☐ Nemoral Ltd	**£439,000**	Orthodox Jewish causes
☐ Roald Dahl Foundation	**£434,000**	Haematology, neurology, literacy
☐ Baron Davenport's Charity	**£430,000**	Almshouses/hospices/residential homes, children and young people

☐ Sir John Fisher Foundation	£430,000	General
☐ William Leech Charity	£429,000	Health and welfare in the north east of England, overseas aid
☐ Staples Trust	£425,000	Development, environment, women's issues
☐ Milton Keynes Community Foundation	£425,000	Welfare, arts
☐ Hampton Fuel Allotment Charity	£418,000	General
☐ Al Fayed Charitable Foundation	£417,000	Children, health and general
☐ Girdlers' Company Charitable Trust	£415,000	Welfare, medicine, education, youth, heritage, environment, religion
☐ Hilden Charitable Fund	£412,000	Minorities, overseas, penal, homelessness, general
☐ Harold Hyam Wingate Foundation	£412,000	Jewish, medical, research, education, the arts, general
☐ Douglas Turner Trust	£411,000	General
☐ Sir John Eastwood Foundation	£409,000	Social welfare, education, health, in Nottinghamshire
☐ Underwood Trust	£408,000	General
☐ Burdens Charitable Foundation	£406,000	General
☐ Basil Samuel Charitable Trust	£404,000	General
☐ Stevenson Family's Charitable Trust	£401,000	Education, mainly Oxford and Cambridge universities, general
☐ Trustees of Tzedakah	£400,000	Jewish, welfare
☐ AIM Foundation	£400,000	Integrated preventative medicine, community development, environment
☐ Joffe Charitable Trust	£400,000	Development policy, projects in developing countries
☐ Teresa Rosenbaum Golden Charitable Trust	£400,000	Medical research
☐ Rowan Charitable Trust	£397,000	Overseas aid, social welfare, general
☐ Mackintosh Foundation	£385,000	Performing arts, general
☐ Audrey & Stanley Burton Charitable Trust	£381,000	Health, arts, Jewish charities, welfare, third world
☐ Alan and Babette Sainsbury Charitable Fund	£376,000	General
☐ Sandra Charitable Trust	£376,000	Health, social welfare, animal welfare
☐ Jewish Child's Day	£369,000	Jewish children in need or with special needs
☐ Great Britain Sasakawa Foundation	£362,000	Links between Great Britain and Japan
☐ John S Cohen Foundation	£358,000	General, arts, education, music, environmental
☐ Sovereign Health Care Charitable Trust	£354,000	Health, Disability
☐ Leigh Trust	£353,000	Drug and alcohol rehabilitation, criminal justice, asylum seekers, racial equality
☐ Englefield Charitable Trust	£349,000	General
☐ Golden Bottle Trust	£348,000	General
☐ Kobler Trust	£346,000	Arts, Jewish, medical
☐ Comino Foundation	£346,000	Education
☐ Talbot Village Trust	£345,000	General
☐ Richard Cloudesley's Charity	£343,000	Churches, health, welfare
☐ Alchemy Foundation	£342,000	Health and welfare, famine relief overseas
☐ Community Foundation for Wiltshire & Swindon	£341,000	Community welfare
☐ Achiezer Association Ltd	£338,000	Jewish
☐ Cinderford Charitable Trust	£336,000	Health and welfare, arts, environment
☐ Joseph Strong Frazer Trust	£332,000	General
☐ Isle of Anglesey Charitable Trust	£331,000	General, in Anglesey
☐ North British Hotel Trust	£331,000	Welfare, health
☐ Booth Charities	£330,000	Welfare, health, education, in Salford
☐ Ajahma Charitable Trust	£330,000	Health and social welfare
☐ Charles and Elsie Sykes Trust	£328,000	General
☐ Christopher H R Reeves Charitable Trust	£326,000	Food allergies, disability
☐ Adint Charitable Trust	£325,000	Children, medical and health
☐ Balcombe Charitable Trust	£325,000	Education, environment, health and welfare
☐ Enid Linder Foundation	£323,000	Health, welfare, general
☐ Merchant Taylors' Company Charities Fund	£322,000	Education, church, medicine, general
☐ Mental Health Foundation	£322,000	Mental health and learning disability research

☐ Peter Kershaw Trust	£318,000	Medical research, education, social welfare
☐ Jordan Charitable Foundation	£317,000	General
☐ Viscount Amory's Charitable Trust	£315,000	Welfare, older people, education
☐ Lady Hind Trust	£315,000	General
☐ Essex Youth Trust	£311,000	Youth, education of people under 25
☐ Clara E Burgess Charity	£310,000	Children
☐ Britten-Pears Foundation	£306,000	Arts, particularly music by living composers, Britten and Pears, education, the environment and humanitarian causes
☐ Starfish Trust	£304,000	Sickness, medical
☐ Saddlers' Company Charitable Fund	£303,000	General
☐ Polden-Puckham Charitable Foundation	£300,000	Peace and security, ecological issues, social change
☐ W F Southall Trust	£300,000	Quaker, general
☐ W O Street Charitable Foundation	£300,000	Education, disability, young people, social welfare
☐ Jim Marshall Charitable Trust	£300,000	General
☐ Bromley Trust	£300,000	Human rights, prison reform, conservation
☐ Lotus Foundation	£250,000	Children and families, women, animal protection, addiction recovery, education
☐ Nuffield Trust	£243,000	Research and policy studies in health
☐ Balance Charitable Foundation for Unclaimed Assets	New trust	General
☐ Reuben Brothers Foundation	New trust	Healthcare, education, general
☐ Carnegie United Kingdom Trust		See entry
☐ Spitalfields Market Community Trust		See entry

The 1989 Willan Charitable Trust

General

£558,000 (2002/03)

Beneficial area Worldwide, but mainly the north east of England.

8 Kelso Drive, The Priorys, Tynemouth, Tyne & Wear NE29 9NS

Tel. 0191 258 2533

Correspondent A Fettes, Trustee

Trustees *Miss E Willan; P R M Harbottle; A Fettes; F A Chapman.*

Charity Commission no. 802749

Information available Annual report and accounts were on file at the Charity Commission.

The trust has general charitable purposes, with a preference for the north east of England. It particularly aims to:

- advance the education of children and help children in need
- encourage the study of animals and birds and their protection for the benefit of mankind
- benefit people with physical or mental disabilities and alleviate hardship and distress either generally or individually
- further medical research.

In 2002/03 it had assets of £11 million, which generated an income of £566,000. Grants totalled £558,000.

There were 178 grants distributed during the year. The largest were £25,000 to Community Foundation and £20,000 to the MEA Trust. There were six grants of £10,000 each to the Alnwick Garden Trust, Community Foundation, Greggs Trust, Oxfam, Save the Children Fund and Unicef UK.

Remaining grants were in the range of £500 to £5,000. Beneficiaries included Hornsea Rescue and Motability (£4,000 each), Advocacy & Information Foundation, Beamish Open Air Museum, Brinkburn Music, Children's Heart Foundation, Darlington Association on Disability, the Eyeless Trust, NSPCC, Tyneside Challenge and Water Aid (£3,000 each), GAP, Links Overseas Exchange, Project Trust – Sri Lanka and World Exchange (£800 each) and NEMLAC and Seghill County First School (£500 each).

Exclusions

Grants are not given directly to individuals. Grants for gap year students may be considered if the individual will be working for a charity (in this case the grant would be paid to the charity).

Applications

In writing to the correspondent. Grants appear to be given four times a year, in March, June, September and November.

The 29th May 1961 Charitable Trust

Social welfare, general

£2.7 million (2002/03)

Beneficial area UK, with a special interest in the Warwickshire/Birmingham/Coventry area.

c/o Macfarlanes, 10 Norwich Street, London EC4A 1BD

Tel. 020 7831 9222 **Fax** 020 7831 9607

Correspondent The Secretary

Trustees *V E Treves; J H Cattell; P Varney; A J Mead.*

Charity Commission no. 200198

Information available Full report and accounts, and a separate grants list, were provided by the trust.

Summary

Around 300 grants are made each year, ranging in size from hundreds to hundreds of thousands of pounds; most are between £1,000 and £5,000. About half appear to be for work in the Coventry and Warwickshire area. Most grants are now on a three-year basis and will not be renewed without at least some interval.

General

The policy of the trustees is to support a wide range of charitable organisations across a broad spectrum with grants for both capital and revenue purposes. Some grants are one-off, some recurring and others spread over two or three years. The majority of grants are made to organisations within the UK and preference is given, where possible, to charities operating in the Coventry and Warwickshire area.

Grants for 2002/03

In 2002/03 the trust had assets of £67 million, which generated an income of £3.1 million. The costs of administration, support and generating funds were high at £404,000.

Grants were made to 290 organisations totalling £2.7 million, broken down geographically as follows:

International	£17,000
London and the South	£758,000
Midlands	£1,513,000
National	£763,000
North	£5,000
Northern Ireland	£2,000

Grants were further broken down as follows:

Social welfare – 109 grants totalling £509,000

There were 57 grants for £3,000 or more totalling £440,000 and 52 small grants totalling £62,000.

Beneficiaries included: Heart of England Community Foundation towards the administration of the foundation and the provision of small grants in the Coventry and Warwickshire area (£48,000); Birmingham Settlement towards running costs (£25,000); Lady Catherine Leveson Foundation towards the cost of refurbishing an almshouse in Warwickshire (£20,000); Buttle Trust towards the funding of a national child support scheme helping children living in poverty and facing disadvantage (£15,000); Action for Young Carers towards the cost of employing an educational liaison worker in Nottingham (£10,000); Childline towards the cost of providing a telephone helpline for children and young people (£6,000); British Wireless for the Blind Fund towards the cost of radio and cassette recorders for blind people nationally, Devon Community Foundation towards providing small grants for the local community and Universal Beneficent Society towards the cost of supporting people over the age of 70 (£5,000 each); Holy Cross Centre Trust towards the cost of various centres in King's Cross, Rehab UK towards the cost of a pilot programme in Birmingham to help young people with brain injuries and Westminster Pastoral Foundation towards the cost of a national network of counselling centres (£3,000 each).

Leisure, recreation and youth – 72 grants totalling £508,000

There were 37 grants for £3,000 or more totalling £450,000 and 35 small grants totalling £58,000.

The main beneficiaries during the year were Coventry & Warwickshire Awards Trust, which received £100,000 towards the running costs of a sports centre providing facilities for underprivileged communities, the Federation of London Youth Clubs, which received £69,000 for general running costs, and Midlands Sports Centre for the Disabled, which received £55,000 towards the running costs of an existing sports centre and the preparatory costs for a new sports centre.

Other beneficiaries included: Warwickshire Association of Boys Clubs for running costs (£25,000); Family Holiday Association towards the provision of holidays (£15,000); British Wheelchair Sports Foundation towards the cost of rebuilding a sports centre at Stoke Mandeville (£10,000); Kidsactive towards running costs of adventure playgrounds in London (£8,000); Country Trust for educational visits for young children from inner city areas and Trefoil House towards the cost of holidays at an adventure centre for the disabled in Edinburgh (£5,000 each); Bag Books for story books for people with profound learning difficulties and Theodora Children's Trust towards the cost of providing entertainment for children in hospital (£3,000 each).

Arts and museums - 19 grants totalling £450,000

The largest grant made during the year was £200,000 to the University of Warwick towards the general running costs of the Arts Centre. The University also received a further £12,000 in sponsorship for the Coull Quartet.

Other beneficiaries included: National Portrait Gallery towards the refurbishment of the Regency Galleries (£50,000); Martin Musical Scholarship Fund towards the provision of scholarships for young musicians (£42,500); Thinktank Trust towards the general costs of the Birmingham Museum of Science and Discovery (£25,000); National Art Collections Fund toward the general fund and Sir John Soane's Museum toward the restoration of No.14 Lincoln's Inn Fields (£10,000 each); Almeida Theatre Company towards the cost of refurbishing the theatre and Torquay Museum Appeal towards the cost of a major redevelopment (£5,000 each). Three small grants were also made totalling £5,500.

Employment, education and training - 22 grants totalling £413,000

Two large grants of £100,000 each were made to the London Business School towards the cost of refurbishing the

careers facilities, and the University of Warwick towards the cost of widening access to the university.

Other beneficiaries included: Coventry Day Care Fund for People with Learning Difficulties towards the cost of providing work experience for people with disabilities in Coventry (£65,000); Caldecott Foundation towards the cost of providing education and welfare to severely disadvantaged children (£20,000); Project Fullemploy towards the cost of projects aiming to stimulate activity in disadvantaged ethnic minorities (£10,000); St Mark's College Trust towards the cost of providing bursaries for disadvantaged people to attend a school in South Africa (£5,000); Gateway Technology Centre to provide free training for unemployed people in IT in London (£4,000); and Monte San Martino Trust towards the cost of providing bursaries for young Italians to study in the UK (£3,000). Four small grants totalled £6,500.

Homelessness and housing - 28 grants totalling £388,000

Beneficiaries included: Crisis towards core costs (£50,000); Depaul Trust towards the running costs of providing accommodation for homeless young people nationally (£35,000); Shelter towards the funding of the Shelterline telephone service for the homeless (£30,000); London Connection towards running costs (£25,000); Cardinal Hume Centre towards the running costs of a centre for homeless people in London (£10,000); Penrose Housing Association towards the running costs of providing support and accommodation for homeless people leaving prison and St Martin in the Fields Social Care Unit for running costs (£5,000 each); Exeter Homeless Action Group towards the running costs of a rent and repair guarantee scheme and Young Homeless Project towards the running costs of a project working with young homeless people in Warwickshire (£3,000 each). Two small grants totalled £4,000.

Medical - 21 grants totalling £221,000

The two largest grants of £50,000 each were made to Cancer Bacup for core funding and Moorfields Eye Hospital towards the cost of establishing the International Children's Eye Centre.

Other beneficiaries included: Alzheimer's Society towards core costs and Demand towards the cost of designing and manufacturing equipment for people with disabilities (£10,000 each); Ataxia

towards the cost of a touch therapy programme for parents of children with ataxia, and the Royal Marsden Hospital Appeal towards new facilities for cancer care and research (£5,000 each); and the Sequal Trust for the cost of providing aids for people with disabilities. Two small grants totalled £4,500.

Offenders - 14 grants totalling £115,000

Beneficiaries included: NACRO for core costs (£30,000); Prison Education Trust towards the provision of grants to enable prisoners to take educational courses (£20,000); Women in Prison towards the cost of an educational programme (£10,000); Howard League for Penal Reform towards the cost of providing support to teenage girls and young women in prison, and SOVA towards the cost of rehabilitation and the resettlement of offenders, ex-offenders and their families (£5,000 each).

Conservation and protection - 10 grants totalling £93,000

Beneficiaries included: St Paul's Cathedral Foundation towards the cost of cleaning and restoration (£50,000); Royal Geographical Society towards the Unlocking the Archives appeal (£10,000); and Culpeper Community Garden towards the cost a full-time worker to maintain the garden in North London (£3,000).

Exclusions

Grants only to registered charities. No grants to individuals.

Applications

To the secretary in writing, enclosing in triplicate the most recent annual report and accounts. Trustees normally meet in March, June, September and December.

Achiezer Association Ltd

Jewish

£338,000 (2002/03)
Beneficial area Worldwide.

132 Clapton Common, London E5 9AG
Tel. 020 8800 5465
Correspondent David Chontow, Trustee

Trustees *Mrs J A Chontow; D Chontow; S S Chontow; M M Chontow.*

Charity Commission no. 255031

Information available Accounts were on file at the Charity Commission.

This trust mainly supports Jewish organisations; in previous years a few small grants have also been given to medical and welfare charities. In 2002/03 it had assets of £1.4 million and an income of £515,000, most of which was from donations received. Grants ranging from £50 to £31,000 were made to 150 organisations and totalled £338,000.

12 organisations received grants of over £10,000 each. Beneficiaries were: Achisomoch Aid (£31,000); MYS (£25,000); JET (£24,000); Torah Teminah Trust (£23,000); MGS (£15,000); Beth Jacob Grammar School (£14,000); Torah Ohr (£13,000); and Yeshiva Michonois Yaacov (£10,000).

Other grants included those to Beis Yaacov Seminary (£9,200), Beenstock Home (£2,000), Edgware Yeshive (£1,000), Gateshead Talmudical College (£700) CML (£250) and Nightingale House (£50).

Applications

The trust states that funds are already committed to existing beneficiaries for the next two years. Unsolicited applications are therefore very unlikely to be successful.

Action Medical Research

Medical research

Approximately £4 million (2002/03)

Beneficial area UK.

Vincent House, North Parade, Horsham, West Sussex RH12 2DP

Tel. 01403 210406 **Fax** 01403 210541

Email info@action.org.uk

Website www.action.org.uk

Correspondent Dr Tracy Swinfield, Head of Research Administration

Trustees *Stephen May, chair; Ian McNeil; Paul Biddle; Prof. David Delpy; Prof. Mark Gardiner; Ms Val Hammond; Mike Hapgood; Colin Hunsley; Mrs Karen Jankel; Mrs Petronella Keeling; Prof. Neil McIntosh; Prof. Sandy McNeish; Terry*

Mansfield; Rupert Pennant-Rea; Lord Rea of Eskdale.

Charity Commission no. 208701

Information available Information was taken from the charity's website.

Support is given to a broad spectrum of research with the objective of (a) preventing disease and disability (regardless of cause or age group), and (b) alleviating physical handicap. The emphasis is on clinical research or research at the clinical/basic interface. The trust supports university departments, hospitals and research institutes for specific research projects.

Project grants are given for up to three years duration in support of one precisely formulated line of research. A one page outline of the proposed research is required before an application form can be issued.

There are two types of project grant round:

1) a general round, covering the whole remit. Outline applications began to be accepted for this general round in December 2004/early January 2005.

2) a themed round, covering part of the remit and supported by a specific fundraising campaign. The application closing date for the 'Touching Tiny Lives' grant round has now passed. Potential applicants should phone the office for information on future rounds.

Support covers salary costs, consumables and items of dedicated equipment essential for carrying out the work.

The average award we make is in the region of £80,000 and grants above £160,000 are unusual.

Grants are made to those in tenured positions in a university or institution. Research workers who require personal support from a project grant, and who have made a substantial intellectual contribution to the grant proposal, may be named as co-applicants with an established member of staff as the principal applicant.

Recent grants have included £131,000 to School of Biological Sciences, University of East Anglia for a project into cartilage repair, £110,000 to Department of Ophthalmology and Addenbrooke's NHS Trust, Cambridge for research into blindness and retinal detachment, £74,000 to National Centre for Training and Education in Prosthetics and Orthotics and the Department of Mathematics, University of Strathclyde, Glasgow for research into artifical limb comfort for below-knee amputees and £38,000 to the University of Aberdeen in conjunction with the Orthopaedic Suite, Woodend Hospital, Aberdeen for a project into back pain and the link with posture control training.

Exclusions

Action Medical Research restricts its funding to direct support of medical research in the UK only. Other charities and members of the general public are not supported. Grants are not awarded purely for further education or medical electives, NHS audit work, or for service provision. Research into cancer, cardiovascular conditions and HIV/AIDS is not supported.

Applications

A brief one page written outline of the proposal for a project grant must be submitted before a formal application form can be sent. Applications are assessed by peer review (sent to experts in the medical/scientific professions). For the closing dates for completed application forms, please contact Action Medical Research or see the web page.

The Sylvia Adams Charitable Trust

Disability, welfare, poverty, children and young people

£468,000 (2002/03)

Beneficial area UK, and Hertfordshire in particular; Africa, the Indian sub-continent and South America.

Sylvia Adams House, 24 The Common, Hatfield, Hertfordshire AL10 0NB

Tel. 01707 259259

Email info@sylvia-adams.org.uk

Correspondent Kate Baldwin, Director

Trustees *R J Golland; E Harris; T J Lawler.*

Charity Commission no. 1050678

Information available Full accounts were on file at the Charity Commission.

Summary

This trust was set up using the income from the sale of works of art, following Sylvia Adams' death. The trust's aim is to improve quality of life of those who are disadvantaged, through the alleviation of disease, sickness and poverty. Both UK causes providing a national benefit, and causes local to

Hertfordshire are supported, as well as UK charities working overseas. Grants are made in the following categories:

- people with disabilities;
- children and young people;
- people living in poverty.

Grant making policies

The trust assesses project proposals looking at the strength of the organisation as a whole and the sustainability of the proposed project.

The trust has a policy of building relationships with the charities that it funds so that it can use its funds in the most meaningful way for the charity and so that it can learn how best to deliver charitable benefits to inform its other work. It has now entered into medium term relationships with nine organisations offering flexibility of funding in order to target its money where it is most needed. The trust is not prescriptive in its grant making and, whilst having a clear view of the work it wishes to fund, does not believe its own objectives should distort the work of the charities with which it works. It therefore considers requests for capital projects, revenue costs, capacity building and new developments, seeking to do that which is most meaningful for each charity.

The trust builds medium term relationships with a number of charities working in its key areas so that its can maximise the benefit of its funds and build knowledge within the trust. It recognises the compexity of the voluntary sector and that this requires a flexible approach from funders.

In order to develop these relationships ... the charity's grant making is based on visiting organisations, being involved in charity networks and frequent use of new technology to keep in contact at low cost both in the UK and worldwide.

Partnerships

In its 2002/03 annual report the trust listed nine partnership arrangments that were in place. Grants are generally made over a five year period but the trust reserves the right to end the arrangement at any time. Each year there is a significant, full and thorough review of the grant in order to ensure that the money is being used appropriately. This involves written reports and visits.

The partnerships active in 2002/03 were:

- Sense (five years at £25,000 per annum agreed 1999) for a peer mentoring project for people with Usher syndrome.
- National Autistic Society (five years at £25,000 per annum agreed 1999) for a helpline worker and the help

programme for the parents of late diagnosed children with autism in future years.

- Emmaus (five years at £25,000 per annum agreed 1999) for the UK national development fund.
- Motor Neurone Disease Association (four years at £25,000 per annum agreed 2001) to develop a new model of care for people with this disease.
- Deafblind UK (£200,000 over three years agreed 2000) for a national centre for deafblindness.
- Intermediate Technology Development Group (five years at £25,000 per annum agreed 1999) for a transport project in Sri Lanka and Nepal.
- Oxfam (five years at £25,000 per annum agreed 2001) for an education project in Tanzania.
- Sense International (five years at £25,000 per annum agreed 2001) to fund core costs.
- The Graham Layton Trust (£50,000 per annum over three years) to meet the running costs of an eye hospital in Multan – Pakistan.

Grant making

In 2002/03 the trust had assets totalling £7.6 million and an income of £823,000. Grants totalled £468,000, of which overseas donations amounted to £199,000.

A total of 28 donations were made in the UK. In addition to those described above, grants included: £25,000 to Bedford Child Development Centre (£15,000 towards equipping the autism room and £10,000 towards building an extension to provide a music therapy classroom); £10,000 each to Aspire for outreach IT work in Hertfordshire day centres for people with physical disabilities and DEMAND towards a skiing project for children with disabilities; £7,500 to Sound Based Studios Trust towards the costs of a youth inclusion worker; £5,000 to Muscular Dystrophy Campaign towards its information service; £4,500 to Link towards the cost of an LCD project for training for people with sudden onset profound deafness; and £500 each to Hitchin Shopmobility towards set-up costs and West Watford Community Association towards providing disabled access to the centre.

Overseas grants, in addition to those described above, included: £23,000 to Basic Needs UK Trust towards core costs; £11,000 to Esther Benjamin's Trust towards the purchase of a property in Bhairahawa to serve as a refuge for Nepal's 'jail children'; £10,000 to Action

Aid for disability work in Bangladesh; and £5,000 to the Resource Alliance for a 'training the trainers' workshop in Bangalore.

Exclusions

The trust restricts its support to the three key areas shown above. Grants are not given:

- to individuals;
- to charities only benefiting older people;
- to UK charities benefiting people with AIDS and HIV;
- for medical research;
- to animal charities.

Grants are not made in war zones or to emergency relief appeals, nor in Eastern Europe, the former Soviet Union or the Middle East.

Grants in the UK are not made to local charities outside the eastern region.

Applications

In writing to the correspondent. Guidelines for applicants are available from the trust, and are quoted below.

'You are encouraged to contact the trust before applying.

'Applications should be in your own words, showing why we should support the organisation and which work you would like us to fund. You should enclose:

- a budget for the work;
- your latest annual report and accounts.

'You are actively encouraged to contact the trust to see if the application is well targeted.

'Deadlines for UK applications are two monthly and applicants are normally advised of the decision within two months of the deadline.

Deadline	Decision by
28 February	30 April
30 April	30 June
30 June	31 August
31 August	31 October
31 October	31 December
31 December	28 February

'The trust is able to provide a swift response when an urgent need for funding arises. The urgency procedure will only be initiated if:

- the need is genuine and was unpredictable;
- a swift response enables and facilitates important long term planning.'

The Adint Charitable Trust

Children, medical and health

£325,000 (2002/03)
Beneficial area UK.

BDO Stoy Hayward, 8 Baker Street, London W1U 3LL

Tel. 020 7486 5888

Correspondent D R Oram, Trustee

Trustees *Anthony J Edwards; Mrs Margaret Edwards; D R Oram; Brian Pate.*

Charity Commission no. 265290

Information available Accounts were provided by the trust.

Most of the grants made by this trust are for £5,000 or £10,000 to a range of health and welfare charities, many concerned with children.

In 2002/03 the trust had assets of £5.5 million, which generated an income of £302,000. Management and administration costs were low at £9,500. Grants totalling £325,000 were made to 56 organisations, only seven of which were also supported in the previous year.

The largest grants were £15,000 to Shelter, £14,000 to Sheffield Children's Hospital and £10,000 each to Action Research, Age Concern, Alone in London Service, ChildLine, CRISIS, Macmillan Cancer Relief, Mental Health Foundation, PM Club, Radio Lollipop, Samaritans, Save the Children Fund and Sight Savers.

Grants of £5,000 each included those to A Nolan Memorial Trust, Arthritis Care, British Lung Foundation, Family Holiday Association, John Grooms Association for the Disabled, National Music for the Blind, Salvation Army, Shaftsbury Society and the Sequal Trust.

Other grants went to NALSVI (£2,500), UCL (£2,000), Woodland Trust (£1,000) and Anne Frank Trust UK (£500).

Exclusions

Grants can be made to registered charities only and in no circumstances to individuals.

Applications

To the correspondent, in writing only. There is no particular form in which applications are required; each applicant should make its own case in the way it considers best. The trust notes that it cannot enter into correspondence.

The AIM Foundation

Integrated preventative medicine, community development, environment

£400,000 (2002/03)
Beneficial area UK, with an apparent local interest in Essex, and overseas.

Whittle & Co, 15 High Street, West Mersea, Colchester, Essex C05 8QA

Tel. 01206 385049

Correspondent L C Tippett, Trustee

Trustees *L C Tippett; Ian Roy Marks; Mrs Angela D Marks; Charles F Woodhouse.*

Charity Commission no. 263294

Information available Full accounts were provided by the trust.

Set up in 1971 as the Ian Roy Marks Charitable Trust, this trust changed its name to the AIM Foundation in 1993. The trust stresses that grant-making policy is to be highly proactive in seeking out potential partners to initiate and promote charitable projects principally in the fields of healthcare, community development, youth and environmental matters both in the UK and overseas. Each year around, 25 grants for amounts over £1,000 are given to a range of charities that the foundation has proactively chosen to support, often over a number of years.

In 2002/03 it was noted by the foundation that due to the current difficult investment conditions, the level of grants made will be maintained, at least in the short term, with the hope that market conditions improve and thereby avoiding any depletion in the trust's capital.

In 2002/03 the foundation had assets totalling £5.7 million and an income of £442,000. Grants totalled £400,000 and were categorised by the trust as follows:

Healthcare – Grants totalled £65,000, of which the five largest were: £20,000 to Prince of Wales' Charitable Trust; £13,000 to Chelmsford and District MIND; and £5,000 each to Homeopathic Research in Ethiopia, Foundation for Traditional Chinese Medicine and Rayne Institutue St Thomas' Hospital. A total of £17,000 was spent on undisclosed grants for amounts of £2,500 or less.

Community development – A total of £107,000 was given, including eight grants for amounts of at least £3,000. These were: £42,000 to Essex Community Foundation; £20,000 to New Economics Foundation; £10,000 to Ashoka Ltd; and £3,000 each to Beat, Intract, Tools for Self Reliance, Winged Fellowship Trust and World Voices. A further £7,500 was spent on undisclosed grants for amounts of £2,500 or less.

Environment – A total of £21,000 was given with the largest donations of £10,000 going to Berkeley Reafforestation Trust and £5,000 to GAIA Foundation. All others were for £2,500 or less and totalled £6,100.

Youth (care and development) – Grants in this category totalled £134,000. The seven grants over £2,500 were: £30,000 each to NSPCC and Antidote; £25,000 to Variety Club of Great Britain; £20,000 to Bartletts Nacro Project; £10,000 to Youth at Risk; and £5,000 each to Caterham High School and NCH Loughton Family Centre. Grants under £2,500 totalled £9,000.

Miscellaneous – Nearly 90% of the money (£62,000) in this category went to the Network Foundation, as was the case in 2001/02. £10,000 was also given to The Funding Network and grants under £2,500, totalled £1,000.

Many of the beneficiaries had received grants in previous years.

Exclusions

No grants to individuals.

Applications

It cannot be stressed enough that this foundation does not wish to receive applications. Unsolicited requests for assistance will not be responded to under any circumstance.

The Ajahma Charitable Trust

Health and social welfare

£330,000 (2002/03)
Beneficial area Worldwide.

4 Jephtha Road, London SW18 1QH

Correspondent Suzanne Hunt, Administrator

Trustees *Jennifer Sheridan; Elizabeth Simpson; James Sinclair Taylor; Michael Horsman.*

Charity Commission no. 273823

Information available Full accounts and guidelines were provided by the trust.

The trust generally supports established charities. It aims to balance its donations between international and UK charities.

Grants are considered in the following areas:

- development
- health
- disability
- poverty
- women's issues
- family planning
- human rights
- social need.

It has also favoured applications from new groups, and those which may have difficulty finding funds from traditional sources are particularly encouraged.

In 2002/03 the trust had assets of £3.5 million and an income of £161,000. There were 66 grants, ranging from £2,000 to £38,000, totalling £330,000. Local Headway groups have continued to receive substantial support from the trust, with grants amounting to £38,000.

The largest grants went to Oxfam (£25,000), Womankind Worldwide (£20,000), CAMFED (£16,000), Child Brain Injury Trust (£12,000) and Alone in London, Education for Choice, Impact Foundation, Ockenden International and Prison Reform Trust (£10,000 each).

Other beneficiaries included Foundation for Assistive Technology, Maternity Alliance, Prisoners Abroad and Village Aid (£8,000 each), Uganda Society for Disabled Children (£6,000) and Allavida, Association of Visitors, Brook and Speakability (£5,000 each).

The Headway groups which received support, of up to £7,500, were Bath & District, Belfast, Black Country, Great Yarmouth & Warrery, Jersey, Milton Keynes, Norfolk & Waveney, North East Worcestershire and West Midlands.

Exclusions

Large organisations with a turnover above £4 million will not normally be considered, nor will applications with any sort of religious bias or those which support animal rights/welfare, arts,

medical research, buildings, equipment, local groups or overseas projects where the charity income is less than £500,000 a year. Applications for grants or sponsorship for individuals will not be supported.

Applications

In writing to the correspondent. Four copies of the application must be sent. The trustees meet in May and November; the closing dates for applications are mid-March and mid-September.

The Al Fayed Charitable Foundation

Children, health and general

£417,000 to organisations (2003)

Beneficial area Mainly UK.

5th Floor, Harrods Ltd, 87–135 Brompton Road, London SW1X 7XL

Tel. 020 7730 1234 **Fax** 020 7225 6872

Correspondent The Foundation Manager

Trustees *Mohammed Al-Fayed; A Fayed; S Fayed.*

Charity Commission no. 297114

Information available Annual report and accounts were provided by the trust.

In 2003 the foundation had an income of £485,000, almost all of which came in Gift Aid payments and donations. Management and administration charges for the year were very low at just £4,400, less than 1% of the total income. Grants were made totalling £491,000, of which £417,000 was given to organisations and £74,000 in total in grants to 13 individuals.

By far the largest donation was £129,000 to ACF Sevenoaks. Other grants over £10,000 each were £80,000 to West Health 2000, £60,000 each to Francis House and Zoe's Place, £24,000 to Mary Hare Grammar School and £12,000 to Macmillan Distribution Ltd.

Beneficiaries of smaller grants included Thailand Orphanage (£9,900), Mines Advisory Group (£5,000), Samaritans (£3,000), Chain of Hope (£2,000) and British Association for Adopting and

Fostering, Oxted Charity Pram Race and the Teenage Cancer Trust (£1,000 each).

Applications

In writing to the correspondent.

The Alchemy Foundation

Health and welfare, famine relief overseas

£342,000 (2003/04)

Beneficial area UK and overseas.

Trevereux Manor, Limpsfield Chart, Oxted, Surrey RH8 0TL

Correspondent Annabel Stilgoe, Trustee

Trustees *Richard Stilgoe; Annabel Stilgoe; Revd. Donald Reeves; Esther Rantzen; Alex Armitage; Andrew Murison; Holly Stilgoe; Jack Stilgoe; Rufus Stilgoe; Joseph Stilgoe; Dr Jemima Stilgoe.*

Charity Commission no. 292500

Information available Full accounts were provided by the foundation.

This foundation was established in 1985 as The Starlight Foundation. It receives most of its income from a share of the royalties from the works of Richard Stilgoe and changed its name in 1987. It provides support for all forms of welfare, ranging from the material, mental and spiritual welfare of children, older people and people with disabilities or mental, physical or terminal illnesses to assisting those affected by famine. It also supports medical research. It shares the same board of trustees with The Orpheus Trust, a connected charity, which regularly receives large grants from this foundation.

In 2003/04 the total income was £338,000, of which £263,000 came from donations received and £75,000 was generated from the assets, which totalled £2.1 million. Grants were made totalling £342,000 of which £320,000 went to the Orpheus Trust and £21,000 in other grants. Those listed in the accounts were £15,000 to Share Music and £1,000 each to Howard League and Surrey Care Trust.

Applications

In writing to the correspondent.

The Alice Trust

Conservation and education

£993,000 (2002/03)

Beneficial area Buckinghamshire.

The Dairy, Queen Street, Waddesdon, Aylesbury, Buckinghamshire H018 OJW

Correspondent Fiona Sinclair

Trustees *Lord Rothschild; Lady Rothschild; Sir Edward Cazalet; Peter Troughton; Hon. Beth Rothschild; SJP Trustee Company Limited.*

Charity Commission no. 290859

Information available Information provided by the trust.

The trust's giving is focused on its principal beneficiary – the preservation, protection, maintenance and improvement of Waddesdon Manor, its lands and its contents, for the benefit of the public generally, together with the advancement of education in matters of historic, artistic, architectural or aesthetic interest. Very occasionally grants are made to other organisations.

In 2002/03 the trust had assets of £49 million and it had an income of £1.2 million. All of its grant expenditure was taken up with donations to National Trust for Waddesdon Manor running costs, repair and refurbishment.

Applications

In view of the trust's commitment to its principal objective, it does not at present invite applications; however, any enquiries are acknowledged.

Allchurches Trust Ltd

Churches, general

£4.3 million (2003)

Beneficial area UK.

Beaufort House, Brunswick Road, Gloucester GL1 1JZ

Tel. 01452 528533

Email atc@eigmail.com

Website www.ecclesiastical.co.uk

Correspondent Mrs R J Hall, Company Secretary

Trustees *Viscount Churchill; M R Cornwall-Jones; Rt Revd D G Snelgrove; W H Yates; N Assheton; H F Hart.*

Charity Commission no. 263960

Information available A copy of the report and accounts, statement of policy and guidelines, and application forms are available on request from the correspondent.

Summary

The trust makes a large number of small grants each year. Around 600 are awarded to churches and cathedrals, and perhaps 50 go to other organisations, many of which also have Christian associations.

General

The trust's income is derived from its wholly-owned subsidiary company Ecclesiastical Insurance Office plc, which transferred over £4 million in gift aid to the trust in 2003, all of which was given in grants.

The trustees make grants to the Church and the Christian community. Grants will be considered in response to appeals in support of churches, church establishments, religious charities and charities preserving UK heritage. Grants will be in the form of single payments.

Over the last 15 years, donations from Ecclesiastical has enabled Allchurches Trust to distribute more than £43 million to dioceses, parishes and other charitable organisations.

Grantmaking

The trust allocated grants amounting to £4.3 million during 2003. They were distributed as follows:

The Anglican Church Dioceses and Parishes	(£3.8 million)
The Anglican Church Cathedrals	(£234,000)
Other church and charitable bodies	(£307,000).

In a recent survey of dioceses, grants were allocated as follows:

Supporting clergy	(41%)
Supporting parishes	(34%)
Funding for new initiatives	(10%)
Building work	(7%)
Other	(8%)

Recent donations in early 2005 included: £5,000 to New Start Dartmoor Prison – Devon towards the renovation of a derelict chapel at the prison to create facilities to allow for a greater number of men to attend Alpha and other Christian courses run by the prison chaplaincy; £3,000 to Byker Bridge Housing Association – Newcastle-upon-Tyne towards internal redevelopment of St Silias church – Byker. The adjacent site

being redeveloped to provide long term accommodation for single, homeless and vulnerable people; £2,500 to Royal School of Church Music in support of general works and refurbishment of the building; £2,000 to St Augustine with St John Kilburn – London towards structural repairs to the south chapel, transept vaulting and the south-aisle wall; £1,000 to Scripture Union – Inverness towards refurbishing the Christian holiday centre to enable the centre to provide a wider range of activities for young people and families to learn about the Christian faith; and £350 to Dalserf Parish Church – Lanarkshire towards major repairs and refurbishment to the church and hall, including new toilets and heating and a better worship area.

Exclusions

The trust is unable to support:

- charities with political associations
- national charities
- individuals
- appeals for running costs and salaries.

Applications cannot be considered from the same recipient twice in one year or in two consecutive years.

Applications

Applications forms can be downloaded from the charity's website.

The H B Allen Charitable Trust

General

£535,000 (2003)

Beneficial area Worldwide.

Teigncombe Barn, Chagford, Devon TQ13 8ET

Tel. 01647 433235 **Fax** 01647 433053

Email hballen.charitabletrust@btinternet. com

Website www.peter.shone.btinternet.co. uk

Correspondent Peter B Shone, Trustee

Trustees *Heather B Allen; Peter B Shone.*

Charity Commission no. 802306

Information available Annual report and accounts, extracts of which can be found on the trust's website.

Summary

Grants, for amounts between £5,000 and £25,000, are made to a wide range of charities, national and occasionally local. Most grants are to charities previously supported.

In 2003 the trust had assets amounting to almost £15 million. It had an income of £1.5 million, including £766,000 from donations. Grants to 69 organisations totalled £535,000.

General

The trust describes its work as follows:

This is a general grantmaking charitable trust. The trustees have no restrictions on them as to the kinds of project or the areas they can support, and are generally prepared to consider any field.

Intending applicants should note that the organisations that have received grants in the past should not be taken as indicative of a geographical or other bias. All applications are considered on their merits.

There is no typical grant size, though the trustees make a large number at £5,000. Grants can be recurring or one-off, and for revenue or capital purposes. The trustees give priority each year to those organisations to which grants have been made in the past.

Please note: following a trustees' meeting in January 2003, the trust is now planning to fund a major project in 2005/06, which makes it unlikely that they will be able to help new applicants before the end of 2006.

Grants in 2003 were broken down as follows:

Arts	£10,000	1 grant
Blindness	£10,000	2 grants
Carers/elderly	£20,000	3 grants
Children/young people	£30,000	4 grants
Deafness	£15,000	3 grants
Disabled	£25,000	5 grants
Education/schools	£5,000	1 grant
Environment/wildlife	£75,000	8 grants
Hospices	£65,000	6 grants
Housing/homelessness	£5,000	1 grant
Medical/research/hospitals	£95,000	12 grants
Mental disability	£15,000	2 grants
Mental health	£5,000	1 grant
Museums/galleries/heritage	£35,000	3 grants
Overseas aid/international	£65,000	7 grants
Village/community halls	£5,000	1 grant

The largest grants of £10,000 or more were: £25,000 each to the Rowans Hospice and Wildlife Conservation Research Unit; £20,000 to Hebridean Trust, Intermediate Technology, Institute of Orthopaedics and Water Aid; £15,000 to the Sobriety Project; and £10,000 each to the Brain Research Trust, Children's Hospice South West, Dermatrust, Fauna & Flora International, Macmillan Cancer Relief, Martha Trust, Mount's Bay Lugger Association, Parasol Theatre for

Children, Parkinson's Disease Society, the Prince's Trust, Save the Children and WRVS Solent Area.

Exclusions

No grants to individuals, organisations which are not UK-registered charities or gap-year students (even if payable to a registered charity).

Applications

In writing to the correspondent. Please note the comments in the general section.

The Alliance Family Foundation

Jewish, general

£464,000 to organisations (2002/03)

Beneficial area UK, with some preference for the Manchester area.

12th Floor, Bank House, Charlotte Street, Manchester M1 4ET

Tel. 0161 236 8193 **Fax** 0161 236 4814

Correspondent The Trustees

Trustees *Sir David Alliance; G N Alliance; Mrs S D Esterkin.*

Charity Commission no. 258721

Information available Annual report and accounts were provided by the trust.

This trust mostly supports Jewish causes and is concerned with the relief of poverty and advancement of religion, education and medical knowledge.

In 2002/03 the foundation had assets of £8.8 million and an income of £525,000. Grants totalled £536,000. The sum of £464,000 was distributed in 92 grants to organisations and £72,500 in grants to 42 individuals. Beneficiaries included Somerset House Arts Fund (£100,000), University of Manchester – Chair of Bioethics (£60,000), George Elias Charitable Trust (£50,000), Shield House (£29,000), United Joint Israel Appeal (£25,000), Community Security Trust and UJS Hillel (£10,000 each), Chaim Sheba Medical Centre (£8,000), British Israel Communications & Research Centre (£5,000), and Iranian Volleyball Association (£3,500). Most grants were for £5,000 or less.

The trust has also committed, but not yet fully completed provision of, charitable donations of £100,000 a year over a five year period to UMIST (University of Manchester Institute of Science & Technology) and The Weizmann Institute of Science in Israel.

Applications

The trust has previously stated that unsolicited applications will not be responded to.

Viscount Amory's Charitable Trust

Welfare, older people, education

£315,000 to organisations (2002/03)

Beneficial area UK, primarily in Devon.

The Island, Lowman Green, Tiverton, Devon EX16 4LA

Tel. 01884 254899 **Fax** 01884 255155

Correspondent The Trust Secretary

Trustees *Sir Ian Heathcoat Amory; Sir John Palmer; Mrs D Cavender.*

Charity Commission no. 204958

Information available Full accounts were provided by the trust.

This trust has a strong preference for organisations in Devon, many of which receive recurrent grants. Local organisations in the south west of England are also supported and a variety of UK charities. (Grants are also made to individuals; for further information please see The Educational Grants Directory, or A Guide to Grants for Individuals in Need, both published by DSC.)

In 2002/03 the trust had assets of £7.4 million and an income of £273,000, including £1,800 in donations received. Grants were made totalling £328,000, broken down as follows:

	No.	Individuals	Organisations	Total
Educational	113	£13,000	£168,000	£180,000
Religious	15	/	£11,000	£11,000
General	130	£470	£136,000	£137,000
Total	258	£13,000	£315,000	£328,000

The largest grants were £73,000 to London Sailing Project and £60,000 to Blundell's School, both had received donations in the previous year. Other large grants were £15,000 to Eton College, £10,000 to Sands School, £8,200 to Grenville College, £8,000 to Queen's College and £5,000 to Bolham Primary School.

The grants list included many educational establishments. These included: Exeter School (£4,400); Stonar School (£4,200); Edgehill College (£3,400); St Margaret's School (£3,300); University of Bristol and Wellington School (£2,600 each); Morrison's Academy and Plymouth College (£2,100 each); Tower House School (£1,700); West Buckland School (£1,500); Magdalen Court School (£1,300); and Park Community School and University College Dublin (£1,000 each).

Among the other beneficiaries were many organisations in Devon. These included: Heart of Devon Enterprise Agency (£4,000); Devon FWAG (Kingfisher Award) and Tiverton & Mid Devon Museum Trust (£2,500 each); Devon FWAG (Bronze Otter Trophy) (£2,300); and North Devon Hospice and St Georges Church – Tiverton (£1,000 each).

Other recipients included: Addaction (£2,000); Exe Valley Team Ministry (£1,200); and Canal Awareness Group, Motability and National Trust – Save Tyntesfield Campaign (£1,000 each).

Exclusions

No grants to individuals from outside south west England.

Applications

In writing to the correspondent, giving general background information, total costs involved, amount raised so far and details of applications to other organisations.

The Milly Apthorp Charitable Trust

Individuals as well as voluntary and charitable organisations concerned with health, older people and youth in north west London

£561,000 to organisations and individuals (2003)

Beneficial area North west London, mainly the London borough of Barnet.

Borough Treasurer's Department, London Borough of Barnet, Town Hall, The Boroughs, London NW4 4BG

Correspondent The Grants Unit

Trustees *John D Apthorp; Lawrence S Fenton.*

Charity Commission no. 284415

Information available Information was provided by the trust.

This trust was set up in 1982 and when its founder Mrs M L Apthorp died in November 1989 considerable further amounts were left to the trust. The role of the trust is to 'enrich the lives of the community' in Barnet, particularly amongst people who are young and/or disabled. Most of the grants are made through three specific programmes run for the trust by the London borough of Barnet: the Administered Fund; Apthorp Adventure Fund; and the Holiday Fund. A fourth general grants programme may stray over the boundaries of the borough since it makes grants from an unrestricted general income fund.

In 2003 the trust had assets of £10 million and an income of £627,000. Grants were made to organisations and individuals totalling £561,000.

Grants were broken down as follows:

Administered Fund

Youth (£196,000 in 65 grants)

Grants were given for character building activities, job training, combating drugs, and sport.

Sports (£7,200 in 4 grants)

Projects which have previously been supported included helping a local residents' association with a tennis court refurbishment programme; and the

provision of subsidised transport for a sports club for people with disabilities.

Illness and disability (£152,000 in 132 grants)

Previously, grants have been made to individuals for household goods and repairs, travel costs, wheelchairs and other specialised equipment. Grants to organisations have included those for supporting a wheelchair maintenance scheme; improving facilities for people with disabilities at a Salvation Army Centre; and supporting a pilot scheme to enable adults with learning difficulties to produce their own newsletter.

Elderly (£36,000 in 16 grants)

Support has previously been given to sheltered housing schemes and clubs for annual outings, events and equipment.

General community benefit (£85,000 in 44 grants)

Support has previously been given to: environmental projects; arts activities; residents' associations; outings for parents and toddler groups; and local churches.

Apthorp Adventure Fund

The object of the fund is to give 'opportunities for personal development and social education to adolescents'. Grants totalling £21,000 were agreed in the year to enable 160 individuals to 'enjoy adventurous expeditions and character building activities'.

Holiday Fund

The mission of this fund is to enable 'physically handicapped people and/or their carers and families to go on holiday'. In the year a total of £22,000 was distributed to help 32 families go on respite holidays.

General Income Fund

In the year five grants were made totalling £41,000.

Exclusions

The trust states that the trustees do their own research into areas of interest; 'unsolicited appeals are not welcome and no reply is given to unsuccessful applicants'.

Applications

No applications to the Milly Apthorp Trust are invited. Trustees meet in March, June, September and December.

Organisations and individuals in the area of the London borough of Barnet can apply for the three funds administered by the borough. Organisations must be a registered charity or other non-profit making body which provides a service for residents of the borough and its environs and will normally be based in the Barnet area.

Grants may be for either capital or revenue projects, which are designed to extend existing levels of provision or to develop new services, and which demonstrate a clearly defined benefit to local people. Awards will not generally be made to support existing activities alone. Projects will be monitored and close attention paid to how the grant awarded is meeting its objectives.

UK charities are not eligible to apply but autonomous local branches of UK charities may do so. Applications must be submitted in the approved format and accompanied by latest audited accounts, plus constitution of rules and most recent annual report if one is produced. Projects should not normally exceed three years, and at the end of the funding period should be self financing or have an alternative source of funding available. For fuller details and an application form, contact the Grants Unit, Borough Treasurer's Dept, London Borough of Barnet, Town Hall, Hendon NW4 4BG (020 8359 2092).

The Arbib Foundation

Not known

£4.3 million (2003/04)

Beneficial area Unrestricted, but with a special interest in the Henley area.

The Old Rectory, 17 Thameside, Henley-on-Thames, Oxfordshire RG9 1LH

Correspondent Carol O'Neill

Trustees *Sir Martyn Arbib; Lady Arbib; J S Kirkwood: Mrs P Nicoll.*

Charity Commission no. 296358

Information available Accounts were provided by the trust.

The trust's grantmaking policy is described as follows:

'The charity supports the philanthropy of Sir Martyn Arbib, one of the trustees, and his direct family. Much of the funds are donated to the River and Rowing Museum Foundation, but the charity also supports charities local to the

foundation's base in Henley and other charities with which the trustees have a connection.'

In 2003/04 the trust had assets of £4.1 million and an income of £1.4 million. Grants totalling £4.3 million were distributed to 47 organisations. The largest donations were as follows: £3.6 million to the River & Rowing Museum Foundation, £250,000 to the NSPCC, £100,000 each to the Institute of Cancer Research and the Woburn Centre for Conservation and Education, £50,000 each to the Barbados Community Foundation, Jewish Care and the Royal Marsden Hospital Appeal and £30,000 to the RNIB.

Other grants included £20,000 each to the Caldicott School Appeal and the Ramsbury Recreation Centre Project 2005 and £10,000 each to Help the Hospices and the Royal Veterinary College Animal Care Trust.

Applications

In writing to the correspondent, but 'funds are targeted to organisations with which the foundation or the trustees have an established connection'. The trust regrets that it cannot respond to unsolicited applications, except in the case of charities local to its address.

The Architectural Heritage Fund

Loans and grants for building preservation

£569,000 in grants in 2002/03; also £4.1 million in new loans.

Beneficial area UK.

Clareville House, 26–27 Oxendon Street, London SW1Y 4EL

Tel. 020 7925 0199 **Fax** 020 7930 0295

Email ahf@ahfund.org.uk

Website www.ahfund.org.uk

Correspondent Ian Lush

Trustees *Jane Sharman, chair; Colin Amery; Nicholas Baring; Robert Boas; William Cadell; Malcolm Crowder; Mrs Fionnuala Jay-O'Boyle; George McNeill; Merlin Waterson; Dr Roger Wools; John Pavitt; Roy Dantzic.*

Charity Commission no. 266780

Information available Excellent annual review, report and accounts; notes for applicants and detailed application forms; book on forming a building preservation trust; directory of funding sources for historic buildings in England and Wales; information sheets.

Summary

The fund promotes the permanent preservation of historic buildings in the UK. It does this by providing advice, information and financial assistance, principally in the form of working capital loans for projects undertaken 'for the benefit of the nation' by building preservation trusts and other charities. Each year 20 to 30 projects throughout the UK are completed with help from AHF, and over 25 years it has helped, or is helping, more than 750 projects.

General

The charity had an income of £1,184,000 in 2002/03, £516,000 of it in the form of interest on investments and loans outstanding and £634,000 in the form of government grants.

Low-interest loans are available to any organisation with charitable status for repair projects that involve a change in the use and/or the ownership of historic buildings (normally through their acquisition by the borrower). Project administration grants and project organiser grants are available only to Building Preservation Trusts (BPTs).

Only buildings which enjoy the statutory protection of being listed, scheduled or in a conservation area are eligible.

Loans are usually for a period of up to two years, subject to a ceiling of £500,000 per loan. Every borrower must provide adequate security. The AHF charges simple interest for the agreed loan period, currently 4%.

There were 180 building preservation trusts on this charity's lists at the end of March 2003. Approved schemes can also be supported by grants, both refundable and non-refundable.

Financial help from AHF

The AHF can help any charity intending to rescue an historic building. The building needs to be listed, scheduled, or in a conservation area, and the project must involve a change of ownership and/or of use.

Feasibility Study Grants

The AHF can offer any charity with an eligible project, grants of up to 75% towards the cost of an initial options appraisal. The study should take a first look at key conservation issues affecting the building, examine the options, and consider in outline the viability of the most beneficial option. The maximum grant is normally limited to £5,000, but in exceptional circumstances can be up to £7,500. In rare cases the AHF will offer grants for studies which examine feasibility of only one option, but the grant offered will then be a maximum of £3,000.

During 2002/03 the AHF made 52 feasibility study grant offers amounting to £216,000 and disbursed £167,000 for 35 feasibility studies. Grants offers amounting to £13,000 either lapsed or were withdrawn in the year, and 54 offers worth £262,500 were carried forward to 2003/04.

Refundable Project Development Grants

Once a feasibility study has shown that the project has a reasonable chance of success, the AHF can offer refundable grants, normally up to £15,000, for specific items of professional work to develop a project to the point at which it meets the application requirements of the AHF and other funding bodies. In exceptionally large or complex cases a further £10,000 may be available. If the project proceeds, the amount of the grant disbursed is expected to be repaid.

During the year the AHF offered 11 refundable project development grants amounting to £244,000 and disbursed £141,000 in respect of 15 projects. Undisbursed offers amounting to £305,000 were carried forward to 2003/04.

Loans and Working Capital Grants

Low-interest loans are available for working capital for projects undertaken by building preservation trusts and other charities. The recipient must normally have, or acquire, title to the historic building to be repaired. The AHF requires security for every loan, either in the form of a formal repayment guarantee or a first charge over any property to which a free and marketable title can be offered. Loans are normally subject to a ceiling of £500,000 and the usual loan period is up to two years. The AHF currently charges interest at 4% simple per annum, payable at the end of the loan period.

Where a project can be fully funded but there is insufficient security to cover the AHF's contribution to the working capital requirement, it may at its discretion offer a refundable working capital grant in addition to a loan. Such a grant must be repaid, with interest, before the loan security is released.

During the year the AHF offered three refundable working capital grants to the value of £415,000, and disbursed part of a refundable working grant to the value of £18,000. These quantities and amounts are included in the information for loans stated below.

During the year the AHF contracted 16 new loans with a value of £3,267,000. Fifteen loans with a contract value of £1,787,000 were fully repaid. Cash of £3,210,000 was advanced in respect of the 16 new loans and 5 loans contracted prior to 1 April 2002. The actual amount being repaid during the year amounted to £2,380,000.

In 2002/03 the AHF offered 19 new supplementary loans amounting to £4,093,000. Seventeen loan offers were withdrawn and the AHF ended the financial year with offers amounting to £3,369,000 in respect of 16 projects.

Loan commitments at 31 March 2003 were as follows:

Value of contracted loans	38	£8,310,000
Less part repayment	4	(£796,000)
Loans offered but not disbursed	14	£3,686,000
Overall commitments	54	£11,200,000

There are two grants available only to BPTs:

Project Administration Grants

Once a feasibility study has identified the best option for a building and the BPT has resolved to take the project forward, it is eligible for a grant of £4,000 towards its own non-professional costs in developing the scheme.

The AHF offered 8 project administration grants during the year amounting to £32,000 and disbursed instalments in respect of these and previous grants amounting to £16,000. Grant offers amounting to £11,000 either lapsed or were withdrawn in the year, and undisbursed offers of £32,000 were carried forward to 2003/04.

Project Organiser Grants

Project organiser grants enable BPTs to pay for the time of a suitable person to develop and co-ordinate a project and take it towards completion. The project organiser may be someone appointed for a fee from outside, or can be a temporary or permanent employee of the BPT. The grant, which must relate to one specific project, will usually be spread over more than one year and normally be up to a maximum of £15,000.

During the year, the AHF offered 28 project organiser grants amounting to £362,000 and disbursed instalments amounting to £112,000. Grant offers amounting to £61,000 either lapsed or were withdrawn in the year, and undisbursed offers of £430,000 were carried forward to 2003/04.

Projects completed or under development in 2002/03

The following list contains examples of projects supported by the AHF during 2002/03, taken from its excellent Annual Review:

- Poplar Public Library, Tower Hamlets, London – Heritage of London Trust Operations.
- Former Procurator Fiscal's Office, Tain, Highland, Scotland – Highland Buildings Preservation Trust.
- 110 Brixton Road, Brixton, London – The North Brixton Trust.
- St Margaret's Almshouses, Taunton, Somerset – Somerset Building Preservation Trust.
- Ince Manor, Ince, Cheshire – The Chester Historic Buildings Preservation Trust.
- Welsh Presbyterian Church, Toxteth, Liverpool – Heritage Trust for the North West.
- Cleadon Pumping Station Chimney Tower, Cleadon, South Tyneside – North East Civic Trust.
- St Mary's Rectory, Rotherham, South Yorkshire – South Yorkshire Buildings Preservation Trust.
- Union Chapel, Islington, London – Union Chapel Project.
- 31–33 Bridge Street, Lisburn, Belfast – Lisburn Buildings Preservation Trust.
- Former Belmont Primary School, Belfast City – Old Belmont School Preservation Trust.
- Former Fire Station, Barry, Vale of Glamorgan – Vale of Glamorgan Buildings Preservation Trust.

Exclusions

Applications from private individuals and non-charitable organisations. Applications for projects not involving a change of ownership or of use, or for a building not on a statutory list or in a conservation area.

Applications

Detailed notes for applicants for loans and feasibility studies are supplied with the application forms. The trustees meet in March, June, September and December; applications must be received six weeks before meetings.

ARK (Absolute Return for Kids)

Child welfare

£4.4 million (2002/03)

Beneficial area Unrestricted.

27 Queen Anne's Gate, London SW1H 9BU

Tel. 020 7222 9272 **Fax** 020 7799 5666

Website www.arkonline.org

Correspondent The Office Manager

Trustees *Arpad Busson, chair; Blaine Tomlinson; Kevin Gundle; Ian Wace; Paul Marshall; Paul Dunning; Jennifer Moses.*

Charity Commission no. 1095322

Information available Annual report and accounts, good website.

Summary

This is one of the first of the new 'venture philanthropy' initiatives to be covered by this research. Started by a group of people in the alternative investment industry, it is a fundraising charity that 'provides a relatively small number of significant grants focusing on specific areas where it can make a meaningful and measurable difference'.

ARK's mission is through the support of local and international projects, to transform the lives of children, who are victims of abuse, disability, illness and poverty.

This will be achieved by providing grants to charities and charitable projects whose activities have been comprehensively researched by ARK, and where ARK has a high degree of confidence that funds will be efficiently and effectively deployed.

ARK's activities are supervised by an international group of professionals from within the Alternative Investment Industry who apply the same principles and disciplines to managing the charity as they have done in their own businesses.

ARK aims to maximise the impact of all donations and as such, the board of trustees ensure that 100% of the costs of ARK are met so that all donations to ARK are used exclusively to help those in need; hence further expanding the opportunities for cost-effective giving.

Funding criteria

ARK discourages the submission of unsolicited proposals. Instead, we research an issue or theme before we look at specific projects.

We consider it vital to look at a range of possible solutions, their costs and potential for long lasting impact. Comparing different approaches reveals variations in both cost per child and efficacy, neither of which could be picked up by sifting through project applications.

Armed with this contextual research, we are ready to evaluate potential projects and proposed management teams. We always conduct extensive due diligence and develop grant agreements including targets and drawdown dates.

When assessing projects, we consider:

Potential impact: the cost of achieving the outcome versus the size of impact, and the scale, looking for the optimum balance of high impact relative to cost.

Quality of execution: the management team, project risk and potential for getting matched funding from other sources or similar financial leverage.

The ARK portfolio: the fit with ARK's criteria including measurability of outcomes, ability to have adequate control as well as how well a given project complements those we are already funding.

Relationships with partners:

Start-up:

We will provide support to develop ideas or organisations (such as our UK pregnancy prevention project) or even start them ourselves (for example anti-HIV therapy in South Africa). This support might include developing a business plan, help with recruitment, sales and marketing, or expansion.

Growth:

When the organisation is experienced, ARK adds value through grant management and monitoring, problem solving, and helping with strategic planning (see child protection in Romania).

Mature:

ARK will provide specific operational funding to mature organisations (e.g. UK families in crisis). The relationship, while close, is primarily focused on monitoring. We also try to facilitate the sharing of expertise between grantees at different stages of development.

ARK projects:

ARK's trustees select a number of project areas in which to focus activities. Each project area must coincide with ARK's mission and all grants will be provided to charities or projects falling into a selected project area.

Current project areas:

- UK - Early intervention, education
- International - Victims of conflict, de-institutionalisation, HIV/AIDS

Chairman's report

What a year it has been! We have exceeded our goals, raising over £4.5 million in 2003. More importantly, we have invested the entire amount in new initiatives. Not only have we been able to keep our promise to triple our commitment to projects in the UK, but we have, at the same time, been able to launch substantial operations in South Africa.

We have remained true to our mission: to transform the lives of children who suffer from abuse, disability, illness and poverty. Moreover, we have not wavered from our focus: to ensure the effectiveness and impact of donations. Every pound you give is a golden pound, with undiluted impact in the field, because the trustees and patrons of ARK arrange to meet all administrative costs, meaning that 100% of your donations go directly to the good causes.

We all know that it is relatively easy to give money, but we also know that far too often this generosity does not achieve its intended goals. We at ARK are guided by the belief that the success of our philanthropic endeavours will be multiplied if we treat grants as we would an investment: constantly applying sound business principles, standards and ethics to ensure maximum impact. We are imaginative in seeking out opportunities. We research and evaluate them very carefully being sure to look at them from many points of view. And once we invest, we monitor regularly and are prepared to take action if things do not work out as hoped. The guiding criterion is impact analysis. We want to know not only to what extent the donation has transformed the lives of the kids, but also if it has generated a more far reaching benefit: a social return on investment.

We are united in our aim to take on challenging, hard-hitting causes. We are looking to give vital support to those children who are on the bottom rung of the ladder and who, with a helping hand from ARK, could go on to lead a fulfilling and meaningful life.

We believe that ARK responds to the philanthropist's need for effective giving by enabling donors to see the impact they are making on the lives of these children. Many of you have already supported us as donors and I thank you. There will be many ways in which you can be part of our new challenges and embrace the vision realised in ARK. Please continue to help us to transform the lives of these children who so need our support.

Applications

Unsolicited appeals will not be accepted or acknowledged.

The Army Benevolent Fund

Service charities

£1.9 million to organisations (2003/04)

Beneficial area Worldwide.

41 Queen Anne's Gate, London SW7 5HR

Tel. 020 7591 2000 **Fax** 020 7584 0889

Email sbrewis@armybenevolentfund.com

Website www.armybenfund.org

Correspondent Simon Brewis, Director, Grants and Welfare

Trustees *Gen. Sir Jeremy Mackenzie, chair; Maj. Gen. D F E Botting; N A Gold; M B Hockney; Maj. Gen. J Boyne; Sir Paul Newall; Col R R Barkshire; Col T A Hall; D J M Roberts.*

Charity Commission no. 211645

Information available Annual review was provided by the fund.

Support and benefit of people serving, or who have served, in the British Army, or their families/dependants.

The work of the [applicant] charity/service concerned must be of direct benefit to a number of soldiers, former soldiers or their dependants. Not only should this number be considerable but it must also comprise an appreciable portion of the numbers of people who benefit from the work or service of the charity.

In 2003/04 the fund had assets of £30.2 million and an income of £4.1 million from donations, legacies and investments. Grants to other charities totalled £1.9 million with £1.7 million to regiments and corps for the benefit of individuals.

Around 90 organisations benefited from the fund during the year. They included the Army Families Federation, Royal Commonwealth Ex-Services League, Officers' Association, Portland Training College, Royal Star and Garter Home, Thistle Foundation, Alexandra House, Wilton Memorial Trust and the Royal Hospital – Chelsea.

Applications

Individual cases should be referred initially to the appropriate Corps or Regimental Association. Charities should apply in writing and enclose the latest annual report and accounts.

The Ashden Charitable Trust

Environment, homelessness, sustainable regeneration, community arts

£650,000 (2003/04)

Beneficial area UK and overseas.

Allington House, 1st Floor, 150 Victoria Street, London SW1E 5AE

Tel. 020 7410 0330 **Fax** 020 7410 0332

Email info@sfct.org.uk

Correspondent Michael Pattison, Director

Trustees *Mrs S Butler-Sloss; R Butler-Sloss; Miss Judith Portrait.*

Charity Commission no. 802623

Information available Excellent annual report and accounts were provided by the trust.

Summary

This is one of the **Sainsbury Family Charitable Trusts**, which share a joint administration. They have a common approach to grantmaking which is described in the entry for the group as a whole.

This trust's main areas of interest are (with number and the value of grant approvals in 2003/04):

	No.	Approved
Environmental Projects UK	8	£156,000
Environmental Projects Overseas	6	£120,000
People at Risk	6	£136,000
Sustainable Regeneration	3	£85,000
Community Arts	9	£81,500
General	3	£23,000
Ashden Awards for Sustainable Energy	3	£96,000

General

Sarah Butler-Sloss (née Sainsbury) is the settlor of this trust and she has been continuing to build up its endowment, with donations and gifts in 2003/04 of £633,000. Total income during the year was £1.3 million including investment income. Its asset value stood at £19.4 million. Grants were paid during the year totalling £650,000.

Staff involved in its work include Michael Pattison, director of all the trusts in the group, Dr Patricia Morison, Victoria Hornby and Miss J Temple.

The following information about the trust's grantmaking in 2003/04 is taken from the annual report.

Environmental Projects UK

The trust initiates and supports work that looks for solutions in the areas of aviation and transport policy, climate change issues including energy efficiency and renewable energy technology, and sustainable agriculture.

In the area of aviation, the trust continues to identify activities or pieces of research which can inform policy making and feed into the public debate on the environmental impacts of aviation.

In the area of sustainable transport, the trust continues to support a range of cycling projects that represent best practice. In supporting cycling activities, the trust is interested not only in the environmental benefits, but also how such activities can bring about other social or economic benefits, such as increasing fitness, education, training, income generation etc.

The trust continues to be interested in the area of sustainable agriculture and has supported Forum for the Future's Land Use Strategy research project [£39,500]. A range of activities addressing the problems of climate change has been supported through the New Economics Foundation.

Beneficiaries during 2003/04 included: Green Alliance towards the Energy Entrepreneurs project (£30,000); Green Futures towards a joint supplement on renewable energy in the UK (£25,000); Centre for Alternative Technology towards its educational work with school children (£20,000 over two years); DEMOS towards the publication of a book on security and sustainability (£9,000); and Transport 2000 Trust towards the costs of its policy seminars.

Environmental projects overseas

The trust continues to support community-based renewable energy projects that aim to help people help themselves in an environmentally sustainable way. These projects help to alleviate poverty by using renewable energy technologies for the enhancement of income generation, agriculture, educational activities and health facilities.

The trust continues to build on its support for renewable energy in schools in Kenya, and this year made a grant to assist Renewable Energy Technologies Assistance Programme to expand a wood-lot development programme [£30,000 over two years]. This project aims to provide schools in the Mount Kenya region with the skills and capacity to grow their own sustainable sources of firewood for use in fuel-efficient stoves.

In addition to the schools programme, the trust has continued to support one-off projects that represent innovative approaches to the use of renewable energy or appropriate technology.

Beneficiaries during the year included: Student Partnership Worldwide to support technology dissemination projects in Mbale, Uganda (£24,500); Solarnet, Kenya towards core costs (£20,000); Kenya Schools Programme towards the provision of renewable energy technologies (£16,000); and Village Education Project for solar panel repairs (£750).

People at Risk (formerly Homelessness)

Grants are made to organisations that help homeless people to access emergency shelter and support, to secure permanent accommodation and to regain economic independence. The trust recognises that providing housing on its own is only part of the solution and is therefore interested in projects that provide a range of support needs (social, educational and economic) to help people once they move into independent accommodation.

Historically, nearly all the projects supported by the trust offer more than housing alone, and are pioneering approaches such as self-help and peer support groups, self-build housing and education and training projects, including provision for homeless people with mental health problems.

This year, the trust has continued to build on the *Dreams Deferred* report, supported by the trust and published last year, with a grant to Thames Reach Bondway to help the nationwide dissemination of good practice identified by the research.

Beneficiaries included: Alone in London Service towards a two-year pilot project to build a UK network of mediation services for young people and their families (£30,000); New Opportunities & Horizons Ltd towards the salary costs of a new co-ordination and development manager (£25,000); Honeypot Charity towards the provision of supported holidays for disadvantaged children (£15,000); and The Porch towards organic vegetable gardening and an accreditation project in Oxford.

Sustainable Regeneration (formerly Urban Rejuvenation)

Funding in this category aims to bring together the themes of social exclusion and environmentally sustainable developments in ways which can help local communities

make the most of their resources and develop new skills and competencies. In many cases projects will reflect the themes of the trust's environmental work, such as the promotion of cycling or sustainable agriculture.

Following work carried out by the London School of Economics, which identified the positive impact that cycling projects can have on social inclusion, the Cycling Project for the North West [£60,000 over three years] has been working with the community to deliver cycling activities, such as cycle repair and delivery schemes, which address issues of social exclusion. This has led to the provision of many other, locally-based cycling initiatives.

The Paddington Farm Trust [£15,000] is based in Wiltshire and is managed for the benefit of people who live in Paddington, London. It offers both accommodation and educational programmes and provides residents with the opportunity to learn about organic farming and to experience a different way of life.

Other beneficiaries include: Furniture Resource Centre Ltd Merseyside for the salary of a research assistant (£22,500); and Mull and Iona Community Trust towards a community project to develop local food initiatives such as a butcher's shop and produce market (£10,000).

Community arts

The trust's support is directed towards charities working in under-resourced areas and where relatively small sums have a large impact on the scope and quality of the projects they can undertake. The trustees are particularly sympathetic to arts projects which address environmental issues in imaginative ways. They like to help charities working in rural and isolated communities, where access to the arts is limited. Another strand is support for high-quality creative work which introduces young children and their carers to the arts. Support may also be given to projects which benefit the most marginalised groups within society, such as young carers, the learning disabled and those with more severe mental or physical disabilities.

The trust continues to develop its interest in environmental drama and has developed the Ashden Directory of Environment and Performance [£31,500 over three years]. The aim of this internet-based tool is to provide a practical resource to stimulate greater interest and high quality work in an area that remains relatively underdeveloped. The directory can be found at www.ashdendirectory.org.uk

Other beneficiaries were: Little Angel Theatre to develop the outreach programme for disadvantaged children (£16,000); Glasgow Repertory Company

towards project costs (£9,000 over two years); and Scottish Opera towards a further tour of a children's opera (£5,000).

Ashden Awards for Sustainable Energy

The Ashden Awards were created in 2001 by the Ashden Trust, originally under the umbrella of the Whitley Awards for International Conservation. The aims of the awards are to contribute to the advancement of education and relief of poverty for the public benefit in developing countries, UK and elsewhere by promoting the use of sustainable and renewable energy sources. The awards will do this through:

- raising awareness of small-scale sustainable energy projects in the UK and developing countries;
- demonstrating how best they can be put into practice, using the winners as best practice case studies;
- encouraging policy-makers, NGOs and other funders to incorporate small-scale sustainable energy into their agendas;
- providing financial awards to outstanding projects which are environmentally and socially beneficial.

The Ashden Awards 2003 comprised one UK award and three awards for work in developing countries in the areas of Community Welfare, Enterprise and Food Security. In addition, the judges awarded five runner-up prizes across the four categories. In total the Ashden Awards allocated prizes to the value of £157,500. The Ashden trustees, who approved a further grant of £96,000 in this year, are grateful for contributions for the 2003 Awards from the JJ, Mark Leonard, Staples and Tedworth Trusts [all of which have entries in this resource], which supported the major prizes and several runner-up prizes.

The trusts which fund this scheme have now established a company limited by guarantee and registered charity, the Ashden Awards for Sustainable Energy, which will further develop the scheme and in future will publish its own report and accounts.

General

Three grants were made in this category: They were to: Action for ME to enable the charity to work with patients, clinicians and service providers to develop best practice service models (£12,000); Resurgence towards a peace conference (£10,000); and East Tytherley Church towards running costs (£750).

Applications

See the guidance for applicants in the entry for the Sainsbury Family Charitable Trusts. A single application will be considered for support by all the trusts in the group.

However, for this as for many of the trusts, 'proposals are generally invited by the trustees or initiated at their request. Unsolicited applications are discouraged and are unlikely to be successful, even if they fall within an area in which the trustees are interested'.

The Lord Ashdown Charitable Trust

Jewish education, general, but see below

£1.2 million (2002/03)
Beneficial area UK.

Clive Marks and Company, 1st Floor, Lynton House, 7–12 Tavistock Square, London WC1H 9LT

Tel. 020 7388 3577 **Fax** 020 7388 3570

Correspondent Clive M Marks, Trustee

Trustees *Clive M Marks; D I Dover; A B E Marks.*

Charity Commission no. 272708

Information available Report and accounts on file at the Charity Commission.

For many years this trust has had two very different lines of activity, one concerned with Jewish education and welfare, and the other with social discrimination and exclusion. This situation has now been recognised with a three way division of the trust's assets. £4 million was granted to the *Stone Ashdown Trust* (which has its own entry) and £3 million to the *Chelwood 2000 Settlement*.

The trust will continue to honour its obligations to Jewish education, and to areas of great need and distress, by providing small grants between £250 and £500 each. The future development of the trust will be in the following areas:
• providing funds for qualified experts to advise on fundraising, technology and financial structure (cash flow) of charitable organisations. This is based on the requests that have been made to us for our expertise over the last five years;
• helping to set up international conferences, be they in the field of music, education or culture. To date, we have sponsored two major international conferences and are assisting in the

supervision of the resulting conference publication;
• helping to organise fundraising events, charitable cultural festivals, including fundraising dinners for those charities with which the trust has already been involved;
• assisting in the running and office management of other grant giving charitable trusts which do not require full-time staff;
• lecturing and providing lectures on many charitable trust matters.

Grants were broken down into the following categories:

Community	£763,000
Education	£234,000
Children/youth	£81,000
Inter-faith/race	£26,000
Students	£16,000
Arts	£8,500
Individual	£8,000
Addiction	£500
Medical	£500

Small grants for less than £250 each totalled £23,000.

Grants in 2002/03

During the year grants were made totalling £1.2 million. As well as the larger beneficiaries listed, around 400 smaller grants were made, most of which are recurrent.

Community

Beneficiaries included London Jewish Cultural Centre (£190,000 in total), Belgrave-Behano Peepul Centre (£140,000), Yakar Educational Foundation – London (£115,000), Lubavitch Foundation – London (£77,000 in total), World Jewish Relief (£52,000), Jewish Memorial Council (£14,000), UK Jewish Aid (£11,500) and Encounter (£2,500).

Education

The largest grant was made to Yeshivas Shaarei Torah Buildings Ltd (£100,000). Other beneficiaries included Friends of the Hebrew University of Jerusalem – London Conference (£27,000), University of Southampton (£10,000) and Schools J-Link (£5,000).

Children/youth

Three beneficiaries were listed in this category as receiving grants of more than £1,000 each. They were Children of Chernobyl (£69,000), Norwood Ravenswood (£37,000) and British Friends of OHR Somayach (£19,000).

Inter-faith/race

Four beneficiaries were listed. They were Council of Christians & Jews (£15,000), International Council for Christians & Jews (£6,600), Parliamentary Committee Against Anti-Semitism (£2,500) and National Yad Vashem Charitable Trust – Holocaust Museum (£1,500).

Other beneficiaries included Amadeus Scholarship Fund (£2,500).

Exclusions

'The trust does not, save in exceptional cases, fund the mainstream arts, large well-established national charities, exploration or adventure projects, nor does it give grants to enable students to study overseas, support elective periods of medical students, or assist with fees at private schools.'

Applications

Due to the commitment of nearly all the funds available, the trustees are not likely to respond to unsolicited applications.

AW Charitable Trust

Jewish causes, general

£2.9 million (2002/03)
Beneficial area Worldwide.

66 Waterpark Road, Manchester M7 4JL
Tel. 0161 740 0116

Correspondent Aubrey Weis, Trustee

Trustees *Aubrey Weis; Mrs R Weis.*

Charity Commission no. 283322

Information available Accounts were on file at the Charity Commission.

The annual report is largely uninformative, as in previous years. However, the 2002/03 accounts do include a list of beneficiaries for the first time since 1991/92.

The trust describes its grantmaking policy thus: 'to consider all justified applications for support of educational establishments, places of worship and other charitable activities as allowed for under the objects clause of the trust'.

In 2002/03 it had an income of £8.1 million, mainly derived from assets worth around £70 million, and also from gift aid donations. Grants were made during the year totalling £2.9 million. There were 344 grants made to 47, mainly Jewish, organisations. Although some received a single grant during the year, most received numerous payments.

The largest grants were to TET (£785,000 in 10 payments), Mosdos Toldos Aharon (£279,000 in total), Asser Bishvil (£200,000 in total), Tzedoko Vochessed (£106,000 in total), Community A/C Kil Rinoh Syn (£96,000 in 36 payments), Oneg Shabbos (£65,000 in total), Etz Chaim School (£61,000 in total), Kehal Toras Chaim of Vishnitz (£60,000).

Other beneficiaries included Sayser Charity (£57,000 in 76 payments), UTA (£52,000 in total), Beis Ruchel Girl's School (£31,000 in total), British Committee of Bnei Berak Hospital (£25,000), Yetev Lev Jerusalem (£20,000), Rav Chessed Trust (£15,000), Yeshiva Horoma Talmudical College (£11,000 in total), Keren Association (£10,000) and Bersam Trust (£8,500).

The trust also purchased a former nursing home in North Wales for £313,000, with the intention of establishing a convalescence home on a non profit making basis.

Comment

There was again no response to repeated written requests for a copy of the most recent annual report and accounts, despite the legal requirement to provide these on demand.

Applications

In writing to the correspondent.

Awards for All (see also the Big Lottery Fund)

General

£53.7 million throughout the UK (2003/04)

Beneficial area UK.

Tel. 0845 600 2040

Website www.awardsforall.org.uk

Information available All information is accessible through the website above.

Summary

This is the small grants programme for the Lottery as a whole. The aim is to fund projects which involve people in their community, bringing them together to enjoy arts, sports, heritage and other community activities.

The programme has recently been reviewed as part of the general Lottery overhaul. It has been decided that the maximum grant will be raised to £10,000, probably, but not certainly in summer 2005. 'We give grants to small local groups in a quick and straightforward way.' The 12-week turnaround time in England has now been reduced for most applicants to eight weeks.

Most activities can be funded except ongoing regular running costs, such as rent or salaries. Projects must meet one of the Awards for All aims to:

- extend access and participation by encouraging more people to become actively involved in local groups and projects, and by supporting activities that aim to be open and accessible to everyone who wishes to take part;
- increase skill and creativity by supporting activities which help to develop people and organisations, encourage talent and raise standards;
- improve the quality of life by supporting local projects that improve people's opportunities, welfare, environment or local facilities, for example through voluntary action, self-help projects, local projects or events.

Grants are generally, but not only, for organisations with an income of less than £20,000 a year, and can now be for amounts up to £10,000. There is a simple application process.

Success rates are very high. Most groups, though not all, that can manage to submit an eligible application, obtain a grant. Applications where there is no element of self-help in the project in the form of either cash or volunteers time, are the least likely to be supported.

Awards for All can sometimes fund statutory authorities, and community groups which support them, but only for activities which are new and not already supported by mainstream funding. They must also be able to show how the project will benefit the wider community.

The arrangements for Awards for All in Wales are slightly different, where the Welsh arts and sports councils have their own 'small grants' programmes (not covered here).

Obtaining further information

Most applicants need do no more than obtain, complete and send in their application forms. Although each region has some areas of special emphasis it wishes to focus on (details on the relevant regional website) these do not generally mean that grants outside them are less likely to be funded. Only if there is an excess of eligible applications are they used as a tiebreaker, and in most areas, most of the time, the scheme is well enough funded for this not to be necessary. These priorities are mainly used, in practice, to enable Awards for All to focus its local publicity.

For the minority of potential applicants who need further information, the contact points will normally be the appropriate regional office in England, or the country office in the rest of the UK, as follows (with details of some of the staff involved):

Awards for All – England
Ground Floor
St Nicholas Court
25–27 Castle Gate
Nottingham
NG1 7AR
Tel: 0115 934 9350

Director: Mike Wilkins
(mike.wilkins@awardsforall.org.uk)

Awards Officer – England: Janet Thompson
(janet.thompson@awardsforall.org.uk)

Awards for All in England operates through these nine regional offices:

Awards for All – North East
6th Floor
Baron House
4 Neville Street
Newcastle upon Tyne
NE1 5NL
Tel: 0191 255 1111

Senior Awards Officer: Pat Lowes
(pat.lowes@awardsforall.org.uk)

Awards Officer: Ruth Clark
(ruth.clark@awardsforall.org.uk)

Awards for All – North West
Ground Floor
Dallam Court
Dallam Lane
Warrington
WA2 7LU
Tel: 01925 626 800

Senior Awards Officer: Karen Rylance
(karen.rylance@awardsforall.org.uk)

Awards Officer: Neil Fairhurst
(neil.fairhurst@awardsforall.org.uk)

Awards for All – Yorkshire and the Humber
3rd Floor
Carlton Tower
34 St Paul's Street
Leeds
LS1 2AT
Tel: 0113 224 5345

Awards for All – East Midlands
Ground Floor
St Nicholas Court
25–27 Castle Gate
Nottingham
NG1 7AR
Tel: 0115 934 9350

Senior Awards Officer: Yvonne Ellison
(yvonne.ellison@awardsforall.org.uk)

Awards Officer: Caroline Watson
(caroline.wilson@awardsforall.org.uk)

Awards for All – West Midlands
8th Floor
Edmund House
12–22 Newhall Street
Birmingham B3 3NL
Tel: 0121 200 3511

Senior Awards Officer: Tina Costello
(tina.costello@awardsforall.org.uk)

Awards Officer: Pamela Phillips
(pamela.phillips@awardsforall.org.uk)

Awards for All – Eastern
Elizabeth House
2nd Floor
1 High Street
Chesterton
Cambridge
CB4 1YW
Tel: 01223 449009

Senior Awards Officer: Barry Griffiths
(barry.griffiths@awardsforall.org.uk)

Awards Officer: Sonja Harrow
(sonja.harrow@awardsforall.org.uk)

Awards for All – London
9th Floor
Camelford House
89 Albert Embankment
London
SE1 7UF

Senior Awards Officer: Oliver Dawson –
020 7587 6644
(oliver.dawson@awardsforall.org.uk)

Awards Officer: Joy Kinghorn – 020 7587
6645 (joy.kinghorn@awardsforall.org.uk)

Awards for All – South West
Beaufort House
51 New North Rd
Exeter
Devon EX4 4EQ
Tel: 01392 849705

Senior Awards Officer: Steve Barriball
(steve.barriball@awardsforall.org.uk)

Awards Officer: Eleanor Dowling
(eleanor.dowling@awardsforall.org.uk)

Awards for All – South East
3rd Floor
Dominion House
Woodbridge Road
Guildford
Surrey
GU1 4BN
Tel: 01483 462943

Senior Awards Officer: Philip Stevens
(philip.stevens@awardsforall.org.uk)

Awards Officer: Catherine Moffat
(catherine.moffat@awardsforall.org.uk)

Awards for All – Wales
For information about Awards for All
Wales use the contact details below:
Tel: 01686 611740
Fax: 01686 621534
Email:
enquiries.wales@biglotteryfund.org.uk

Awards for All – Scotland
4th Floor
1 Atlantic Quay
1 Robertson Street
Glasgow
G2 8JB
Tel: 0141 242 1400
Email: scotland@awardsforall.org.uk

Awards for All – Northern Ireland
1 Cromac Quay
Cromac Wood
Ormeau Road
Belfast
BT7 2JD
Tel: 028 9055 9090
Email: enquiries.ni@awardsforall.org.uk

Guidelines

Application forms

Application forms are available from the website in three formats:

- EAF (Electronic Application Form) – for PC users only
  The EAF allows you to complete your application and save your answers on your PC. Full guidance notes on using the EAF system and completing the form are included. When your form is complete, you can save your answers onto a floppy disk and send it to us along with any supporting documentation.
- Adobe PDF (Portable Document Format) form – for Apple Mac and PC users
  Both Apple Mac and PC users can use this version of the application form. The advantage of using a PDF form is that you can print out the form and write your answers on it, rather than having to order the standard paper application form.
- Request a paper copy of the application pack [the general telephone number for an application pack is 0845 600 20 40].

What to send with your application

The section below tells you what to send with your application. Look at each heading and decide which one applies to you. You need to send all the documents we ask you for.

Community group/club/society
- Constitution or set of rules;
- Annual accounts or statement of income and expenditure;
- Recent, original bank statement plus a photocopy.

Registered charity or exempt or excepted charity registered with the Inland Revenue in England
- Constitution or set of rules;
- Annual accounts or statement of income and expenditure;
- Recent, original bank statement plus a photocopy.

Parish or Town council
- Annual accounts or statement of income and expenditure;
- Recent, original bank statement plus a photocopy.

School
- Recent, original bank statement plus a photocopy or letter from the LEA confirming details of the bank account and that this award would be 'ring-fenced' for this project.

Health body
- Letter from the chief executive confirming status of your organisation;
- Recent, original bank statement plus a photocopy or a letter from the local authority confirming details of the bank account and that this award would be 'ring fenced' for this project.

Company limited by guarantee
- Memorandum and Articles of Association;
- Annual accounts or statement of income and expenditure;
- Recent, original bank statement plus a photocopy.

Dependent branch of another organisation
- Branch constitution or set of rules;
- Letter of endorsement;
- Annual accounts or statement of income and expenditure;
- Recent, original bank statement plus a photocopy.

What can be funded?

Awards for All can fund a wide range of projects and activities. Here are just a few examples:
- a crèche facility for a rural community;
- publicity materials for a group that recycles computers for use by the community;
- a training and activities programme to involve more disabled people in sport;

- a project to develop creative writing skills among young adults, to enable their work to be published and performed;
- materials for an exhibition and trail walk featuring buildings of local historical interest;
- play and sports facilities with qualified coaching for young people on an urban estate;
- a neighbourhood project to promote healthier eating of fruit and vegetables;
- a school which wants to create a wildlife garden;
- a project to introduce people to alternative cultures through participation in storytelling and drama;
- adapting a village hall to provide easier access for all members of the community;
- a project to set up a telephone helpline offering advice and support for people with cancer and their families;
- an historic pageant illustrating various periods of history and the rich cultural heritage of a community;

Here are some of the things that a grant could be spent on:
- putting on an event, activity or performance;
- providing training courses;
- setting up a pilot project;
- running a conference or seminar;
- improvements to community facilities;
- start up costs, including staff and premises;
- publicity;
- professional fees;
- research costs;
- equipment and materials;
- transport costs;
- volunteers' expenses;
- updating facilities/equipment for health and safety reasons.

We welcome applications for projects combining a range of community activities.

If you are not sure whether your project is something we can fund, please contact your regional Awards for All office.

Awards for All will not fund
- costs related to existing projects, activities or resources currently provided by your group, for example, ongoing staff costs and utility bills, regular rent payments, maintenance (including maintenance equipment) and annual events;
- items which only benefit an individual, for example, scholarships or bursaries;
- activities promoting religious beliefs;
- activities that are part of statutory obligations or replace statutory funding, including curricular activity in schools;
- endowments;
- loan payments;
- second hand road vehicles;
- projects with high ongoing maintenance costs – unless your group can show that you have the funds/skills to maintain

them once your Awards for All grant runs out.

National Criteria

The following criteria apply to all applications.

Your application will be assessed by one of our Awards Officers, who will look to see:

- how your group is set up and managed – by looking at your constitution;
- if the project is well organised and planned – whether you have the experience and skills to manage the project well;
- whether your application supports community activity, by meeting at least one of Awards for All's three aims;
- who in your community will benefit from the grant;
- whether the budget for your project is appropriate and realistic, and the project is an efficient use of funds – sending us quotes or costings might help to show this;
- what your group is contributing to the activity – we expect most groups to contribute to the project. This can be in cash, or 'in kind', or both. If your group has savings or 'reserves' of more than twelve months expenditure and is not spending any of this on the project, please explain why in question 13 on the application form.

When we are considering your application we may contact you for more information about your group or activity. We may also contact your referee.

When it has been assessed, your application will then be scored against the following criteria:

- what efforts the applicant group has made to ensure that under represented groups and those not normally involved in running a group are given the opportunity to do so;
- the applicant group's annual income;
- whether the applicant group has received National Lottery funding before;
- to what degree the application meets the aims of Awards for All;
- whether the total cost of the project is below £20,000;
- whether the project is a completely new activity for the applicant group;
- whether the application meets the Regional Focus (included with the application pack). The Regional Focus was produced following a consultation exercise within your region.

The score that we give your application will decide whether it is successful or not. The score that your application needs to be successful will vary depending on the

amount and quality of applications we receive, and the amount of money we have available at the time.

We will write to you to let you know if your application has been successful

If your application is successful we will send you a letter telling you how much the grant is and when it will be paid. The grant will be paid directly into the bank account you have given us in question 14 of the application form.

If we award you a grant you will have to keep to our terms and conditions. You will also have to comply with any relevant legislation affecting the way you carry out your project. By signing the contract on the back of the application form you are agreeing to keep to our terms and conditions and any relevant laws, if you receive a grant. Agreeing this beforehand does not guarantee that you will get a grant but it will help us pay any grant quickly. If you get a grant, you must use it only for the project you set out in the application form. You cannot give it to any other group.

You must spend the grant within one year of the date on our award letter. You will need to complete an End of Award report.

If your application is not successful we will tell you the main reasons why. This may help you decide whether to apply again.

Example of a regional focus – North West England

In the North West region we will score more highly those projects which:
- benefit disabled people.
  Disabled people may face a range of challenges and barriers to full participation in the community, and a lack of opportunities. We want to encourage projects which attempt to address such issues.
- benefit unpaid carers.
  Unpaid carers may face problems of isolation and a lack of opportunities to participate in their community. We want to encourage projects which attempt to address such issues.
- benefit black and minority ethnic communities.
  There is evidence that these communities experience barriers to accessing resources including consistently lower levels of Lottery funding than would be expected. Awards for All is attempting to redress this imbalance by supporting those projects which promote greater access to education and training, or support community activities and are in accordance with our national aims.
- help to tackle issues of deprivation and isolation in: Allerdale, Bury, Knowsley,

Pendle, South Lakeland, Barrow-in-Furness, Carlisle, Liverpool, Ribble Valley, South Ribble, Blackpool, Copeland, Manchester, Rossendale, Bolton, Eden, Oldham and Salford.

There is evidence to suggest that communities in these areas are affected by a lack of access to basic services, and experience barriers to accessing resources, including consistently lower levels of funding from Awards for All than would be expected. We want to encourage projects in these areas.

Grantmaking 2003/04

During the year Awards for All in England made almost 11,000 grants across the nine regions totalling £43.3 million:

	No.	Amount
North West	1,710	£6,875,000
London	1,573	£6,827,000
West Midlands	1,367	£5,655,000
South East	1,286	£4,965,000
Yorkshire & Humber	1,208	£4,739,000
South West	1,181	£4,340,000
Eastern	991	£3,532,000
East Midlands	881	£3,329,000
North East	795	£3,022,000

Grants for other UK regions during the year were:

Scotland: £5.6 million in 1,612 grants

Northern Ireland: £2.6 million in 755 grants

Wales: £2.2 million in 656 grants

Director of Awards for All England Mike Wilkins gives his review of 2003/04:

The past year has been both exciting and challenging for the team at Awards for All England.

We have continued to make grants of between £500 and £5,000 [although see above – ed] so that small, local groups can set up new activities or expand their work. And last year we made nearly 11,000 awards worth over £43 million – a total of £200 million to over 60,000 groups since we started making grants in 1998.

Our funding combines contributions from all the lottery distributors and our awards are designed to support a wide range of different projects – embracing heritage, arts, community, sports, environmental, educational and health initiatives.

We aim to improve the quality of life for communities, extend access and participation, and increase skills and creativity. Our closeness to local communities, through our regional offices, means we are able to fine tune our awards to reflect the concerns and needs of different regions – something which we continue to work on through our regional focus.

Updating our regional focus
Each regional office consulted on and updated their regional focus last year. The focus helps us make decisions on the awards that are the most appropriate in a particular area. Details of the different regional focuses are available on our website: www.awardsforall.org.uk

Reaching our 50,000th Award
Last November we made our 50,000th award. The grant was for a children's music project in the Eastern region, particularly aimed at children who come from families on a low income.

Improving the turnaround time for applications
Awards for All aims to be a quick turnaround and responsive grants programme. Last year, after a review, we introduced improved assessment procedures, scoring systems and decision-making by officers, reducing the average time taken to consider applications to eight weeks.

Remembering WW 2 veterans at home and abroad
We are a flexible grants programme and we've built up considerable expertise in handling requests for small grants for local projects. So last year we were asked to administer grant applications for Heroes Return, the grant scheme enabling World War 2 veterans to return to the places they saw active service and Home Front Recall, providing grants to commemorate the activities of the Home Front in the UK.

Why applications fail

The Yorkshire & Humberside region offers the following advice:

Around 70% of all applications have to be returned to applicants because they have not filled in the form correctly or they have not submitted the required documentation.

The top 3 reasons applications are returned are:

Documents missing: You must send in:
1. An original bank statement less than 3 months old. We cannot accept a photocopy.
2. Your constitution. This must be dated and signed as adopted (schools, parish councils and statutory health bodies are the only organisations which do not need to send a constitution).
3. Your accounts. These must be less than 12 months old. If you are a new group less than 12 months old you need to provide us with details of all your income and expenditure since you started, together with an estimate of income and expenditure for the next 12 months.

Documents submitted in different names
All the documents you supply must be in exactly the same name as the name on your constitution; i.e. the bank account name and the name on the accounts all must match exactly the name on the constitution. We are unable to make any exceptions to this requirement.

Referee not suitable or not independent
The independent referee cannot be a current or former member of your group. They should not be related to anyone who stands to benefit from the award. If your group works with children, young people or other vulnerable groups, the referee must be a person with a relevant professional qualification such as a teacher, social worker, child care or health professional.

Comment

This programme is one of the successes of the whole Lottery enterprise. Many thousand of grassroots projects have been funded throughout the UK, using small grants to achieve significant results. The success of the programme may have largely protected it from the apparent tinkering and government intervention that happened to the predecesors of the Big Lottery Fund.

Happily, the three-month response time for applications reported in the last edition of this book has apparently been reduced to eight weeks for most applicants in England.

Exclusions

Generally, organisations with an income more than £20,000 a year (though there are exceptions to this, particularly for projects coming through schools and similar bodies).

Also:

- costs related to existing projects, activities or resources currently provided by your group, for example, ongoing staff costs and utility bills, regular rent payments, maintenance (including maintenance equipment) and annual events;
- items which only benefit an individual, for example, scholarships or bursaries;
- activities promoting religious beliefs;
- activities that are part of statutory obligations or replace statutory funding, including curricular activity in schools;
- endowments;
- loan payments;
- second hand road vehicles;
- projects with high ongoing maintenance costs - unless your group can show that you have the funds/skills to maintain them once your Awards for All grant runs out.

Applications

All information is in the application pack available from the number above. The application form is simple, but the applicant organisation must be organised to the extent of having a constitution, a bank account and a set of accounts (unless a new organisation).

The Baily Thomas Charitable Fund

Learning disability

£3.1 million (2003/04)
Beneficial area UK.

Ernst & Young, 400 Capability Green, Luton LU1 3LU
Tel. 01582 643125 **Fax** 01582 643001
Email acooper1@uk.ey.com
Website www.bailythomas.org.uk
Correspondent Ann Cooper
Trustees *Charles J T Nangle; Prof. W I Fraser; Prof. Michael Gelder; Michael R Macfadyen; Mrs Ziva Robertson; Suzanne Jane Marriott.*
Charity Commission no. 262334
Information available Guidelines for applicants. Annual report and accounts, listing the largest 50 grants only.

Summary

This is the largest trust dedicated solely to the well-being of those with learning disabilities (it no longer covers mental illness). It combines one or two major funding programmes with an extensive programme of generally one-off medium and smaller grants. These are divided between revenue and capital costs, and seemingly without the common requirement for applications to be dressed up in 'project' form.

The fund says it is very over subscribed in terms of applications for grants.

General

In 2003/04 the fund had assets of £66 million and an income of £3.1 million. Grants totalled £3.1 million.

The largest grants were: £150,000 to Scotts Project; £100,000 each to Development Trust, Mencap – Huntingdon Support Association and National Autistic Society; £80,000 to

Mencap City Foundation; £75,000 to White Lodge Children's Centre – 'Space to be Me' project; £55,000 University of Edinburgh; £54,000 St George's Hospital Medical School – University of London; £53,000 to University of Wales College of Medicine towards a research project; and £50,000 each to Calvert Trust, Chailey Heritage School, Contact a Family, Guideposts Trusts, Mencap – Dartford & Swanley, Mencap – Falmouth & District Society and Pennyhooks Farm.

More typical grants during the year included £30,000 to Autism Cymru, £25,000 to The Mortimer Society and £20,000 each to Work-Link Project, Turning Point and Ruskin Mill Educational Trust.

Guidelines

[See separate guidelines below for research grants.]

The fund was established primarily to aid research into learning disability and to aid the care and relief of those affected by learning disability by making grants to voluntary organisations working in this field.

We consider under learning disability the conditions generally referred to as severe learning difficulties, together with autism. In this area, we consider projects concerning children or adults. Learning disability, thus defined, is our priority for funding. We do not give grants for research into or care of those suffering from mental illness or dyslexia.

Funding is normally considered for capital and revenue costs and for both specific projects and for general running/core costs.

Grants are awarded for amounts from £250 and depend on a number of factors including the purpose, the total funding requirement and the potential sources of other funds including, in some cases, matching funding.

Normally one-off grants are awarded but exceptionally a new project may be funded over two or three years, subject to satisfactory reports of progress.

Grants should normally be taken up within one year of the issue of the grant offer letter which will include conditions relating to the release of the grant.

The following areas of work normally fall within the fund's policy:
• Capital building/renovation/refurbishment works for residential, nursing and respite care, and schools
• Employment schemes including woodwork, crafts, printing and horticulture
• Play schemes and play therapy schemes
• Day and social activities centres including building costs and running costs
• Support for families, including respite schemes
• Independent living schemes
• Support in the community schemes
• Swimming and hydrotherapy pools and snoezelen rooms.

All applications to the fund will be subject to independent review.

A second application from an organisation will not normally be considered for a period of at least one year after completion of an initial grant or notification of an unsuccessful application.

Applications for research grants

We generally direct our limited funds towards the initiation of research so that it can progress to the point at which there is sufficient data to support an application to one of the major funding bodies.

Applications will only be considered from established research workers and will be subject to normal professional peer review procedures.

Exclusions

Grants are not normally awarded to individuals. The following areas are unlikely to receive funding:

• mental illness;
• hospices;
• minibuses, except those for residential and/or day centres for people with learning disabilities;
• advocacy projects;
• arts and theatre projects;
• physical disabilities unless accompanied by significant learning disabilities.

Applications

General
Applications (other than those for research) should be made in writing on the fund's four-page application form.

Applications will only be considered from voluntary organisations which are registered charities or are associated with a registered charity.

All applications will be subject to independent review.

A copy of the applicant's latest annual report and accounts should be submitted with the application form.

Do not send architectural drawings, plans or photographs. These are seldom necessary and will be asked for, if required.

Research applications
Applications should be made in writing in the form of a research plan to include a brief background and a short account of the design of the study and number of subjects, the methods of assessment and analysis, timetable, main outcomes and

some indication of other opportunities arising from the support of such research.

A detailed budget of costs should be submitted together with details of any other applications for funding which have been made to other funders and their outcomes, if known.

The fund does not expect to contribute towards university overheads.

A curriculum vitae will be required for each of the personnel actually carrying out the study and for their supervisor.

Evidence must be provided of the approval of the ethics committee of the applicant to the study and the approval of the university for the application to the fund.

An 80-word lay summary should also be submitted with the detailed research proposal.

Before submitting a full application, researchers may submit a one-page summary of the proposed study so that the trustees may indicate whether they are prepared to consider a full application.

All applications

Meetings of the trustees are usually held in June and early December each year and applications should therefore be submitted no later than 1 May or 1 October for consideration at the next relevant meeting. Late applications will not be considered.

The Balance Charitable Foundation for Unclaimed Assets

General

See below

Beneficial area UK and worldwide.

5 Chancery Lane, Clifford's Inn, London EC4A 1BU

Tel. 020 7936 4333 **Fax** 020 7410 0332

Email info@balancefoundation.org.uk

Website www.balancefoundation.org.uk

Correspondent Richard Compton-Burnett, Chief Executive

Trustees *Sir David Cooksey; Piers Le Marchant; Judith Portrait; Martin Thomas; Michael Webber.*

Charity Commission no. 1101333

Information available Information was taken from the trust's website.

Background

Many financial institutions hold unclaimed assets in policies and accounts that have lain dormant for many years. In many cases the identity or whereabouts of the owners of these assets are unknown, and they are likely to remain unclaimed indefinitely. The Balance Foundation was established in 2003 to 'unlock' these abondoned assets and use the resources charitably by making grants to other organisations for the benefit of the wider community. The two main roles of the foundation are summarised as follows:

- to work with current holders of unclaimed assets, advisors, authorities and industry bodies in order to secure the release of the unclaimed assets;
- to act as an independent charitable foundation through which the income from unclaimed assets will be paid to charity.

The initiative is backed by four large grant-making foundations: the Esmee Fairbairn Foundation, the Gatsby Charitable Foundation, the Paul Hamlyn Foundation and the Hunter Foundation.

General

The foundation has initially been focusing on unclaimed assets held by investment banks, with the scope expected to widen as the initiative becomes established. There are also procedures in place should the rightful owners of any assets come forward at a later date: 'It is intended that participating financial institutions will deduct a small percentage from the monies released to charity and use that money to purchase adequate insurance'. The foundation was expected to become operational late in 2004.

Grantmaking policy

At this early stage in the initiative there are still issues to be finalised, such as the application procedure and the definitive grant-making policy. At present, the foundation states the following about it's grant-making policy and how it expects it to evolve:

The foundation has the power to support any charitable work in the UK, or overseas work compatible with UK charity law. The

foundation plans to invest the assets released to it and distribute for charitable purposes its income after meeting overheads. The grant-making policy will be published and confirmed by the trustees once the full team is in place and there are funds available to distribute. The policy will evolve continuously, so that the trustees can support charitable work under several specific themes at any one time but can also support innovative ideas beyond those themes.

At present the initial trustees expect to concentrate on a wide variety of social exclusion issues, including educational disadvantage and financial literacy. They are likely to be willing to provide sustained support over extended periods for significant initiatives in the development of new services, recognising that these may take time to reach proof of concept and then evidence of viability. This could well include support for core costs during the development of such new initiatives. On the other hand the trustees do not see the foundation as a long-term source of core funding for individual charities.

The foundation may well receive some resources which will be held in restricted funds at the request of the institution which makes them available. The restrictions might, for example, require that the funds should be distributed within a particular region or to meet a particular type of charitable need.

The trustees will bring together small expert panels to advise on grant-making in specialist fields and to monitor the progress of the work they support. The trustees will aim for simplicity in the application process, encouraging web-based applications; transparency and speed in decision making; and recognition of changing needs in society for the spread of work they support.

It is expected that grant-making will commence during the last quarter of 2004.

Exclusions

No grants to individuals.

Applications

At the time of going to press the application procedure had not been finalised. Check the trust's website for up-to-date information.

The Balcombe Charitable Trust

Education, environment, health and welfare

About £325,000 (2002/03)

Beneficial area UK.

c/o Citroen Wells & Partners, Devonshire House, 1 Devonshire Street, London W1W 5DR

Tel. 020 7304 2000

Email jonathan.prevezer@citroenwells.co.uk

Correspondent Jonathan W Prevezer

Trustees *R A Kreitman; P M Kreitman; Mrs S I Kreitman.*

Charity Commission no. 267172

Information available Accounts were on file at the Charity Commission.

This trust generally makes grants in the fields of education, the environment and health and welfare. It only supports registered charities.

In 2002/03 it had an income of £222,000 and a total expenditure of £353.000. Grants were made totalling around £325,000. Unfortunately, no further information was available for the year.

Around 30 to 40 grants are made each year, with about half of the beneficiaries receiving recurring grants. Previous beneficiaries include Brook Advisory Centres, British Red Cross, ChildLine, Durrell Wildlife Conservation Trust, NSPCC, World Wildlife Fund UK, BACUP, Crisis, Parentline, Friends of the Earth, MIND, Princess Royal Trust for Carers, Samaritans and Who Cares Trust.

Beneficiaries of smaller grants included Body and Soul, British Trust for Conservation Volunteers, Galopagos Conservation Trust, Womankind and Youth Access.

Comment

Despite ample warning, and their obligation to the contrary, the Charity Commission were unable to give us sight of this trust's accounts.

Exclusions

No grants to individuals or non-registered charities.

Applications

In writing to the correspondent.

The Balint Family Charitable Trusts

Jewish charities, general

£452,000 (2003/04)

Beneficial area UK and overseas, especially Israel.

Suite A, 4–6 Canfield Place, London NW6 3BT

Tel. 020 7624 2098 **Fax** 020 7624 2076

Correspondent J K Olver, Administrator

Trustees *Andrew Balint Charitable Trust: Agnes Balint; Dr Gabriel Balint-Kurti; Roy David Balint-Kurti.George Balint Charitable Trust: Dr Andrew Balint; George Balint; George Rothschild; Marion Farkas-Balint.Paul Balint Charitable Trust: Dr Andrew Balint; Dr Gabriel Balint-Kurti; Paul Balint; Marc Balint.*

Information available Reports and accounts on file at the Charity Commission.

All the Balint Family Charitable Trusts operate from the same premises and are jointly administered. Two trustees of the Paul Balint Trust are also trustees of other Balint Family Trusts; the trusts are closely associated, with grants probably directed to similar beneficiaries.

The trusts' grantmaking capacity has diminished significantly since the previous edition of this guide, and at £452,000 in total grants in 2003/04, this may be the last time they are featured here. (In 1999/2000 the figure was £1.7 million; in 2001/02 it was £792,000.)

In 2003/04 the trusts had a total expenditure as follows:

Andrew Balint Charitable Trust	£270,000
Paul Balint Charitable Trust	£167,000
George Balint Charitable Trust	£152,000

The trusts have previously stated that no new grant applications were being considered. It may be the case that the trusts are simply fulfilling existing grant commitments.

Applications

In writing to the correspondent, but funds are fully committed.

The Band Trust

Health, welfare, general

£505,000 (2002/03)

Beneficial area UK.

Macnair Mason, Chartered Accountants, John Stow House, 18 Bevis Marks, London EC3A 7ED

Tel. 020 7469 0550 **Fax** 020 7469 0660

Email mm@macmas.co.uk

Correspondent R J S Mason, Trustee

Trustees *Hon. Mrs Nicholas Wallop; Hon. Nicholas Wallop; R J S Mason; B G Streather.*

Charity Commission no. 279802

Information available Annual reports and accounts.

Summary

The trust makes about 75 grants a year, about half of them for amounts of £1,000 or less, and seldom for more than £30,000, though exceptional grants up to £100,000 can be made. Large grants go principally, though not exclusively, to charities in the following fields:

- medical;
- children and young people;
- disabled.

Around one-third of grants in 2002/03, and more of the money, went to organisations that had been supported in the previous year.

General

The trust had an income of £621,000 in 2002/03, mostly from its investments worth £15.4 million. There was £555,000 in charitable expenditure, of which £50,000 was spent on scholarships and the rest went in grants.

The trust describes its policy as follows:

The trustees' prime objective is to aid residents of the United Kingdom who are in need of care, whether wholly or partially, including those who are ill, disabled or injured, old and infirm or children with special needs. Such aid includes the providers such as institutions, homes and equipment and the carers themselves, in particular the nursing profession.

Grants in 2002/03 were categorised as follows:

Disabled	£154,000
Medical	£100,000
Educational	£83,000
Children and young people	£76,000
Miscellaneous	£36,000
Elderly	£19,000
Arts	£18,000
Ex-employees	£18,000

Legal	£1,000
Total	£505,000

Examples of grants in the main categories are as follows:

Disabled

There were 16 grants in this category. Five grants went to organisations also supported in the previous year, including the largest grant – £30,000 to U Can Do It. Other previously supported organisations were Princess Royal Trust for Carers (£15,000), Papworth Trust (£10,000), League of Friends of Chelmsford Training Centre (£5,000) and Compaid (£3,000). Ten new beneficiaries received £84,000 or 55% of the funds in this category, including Broughton House Appeal (£10,000) and Winfield Trust (£5,000).

Medical

Of the 11 organisations supported in this category, seven received grants during the previous year. The largest grant was made to Blond McIndoe Research Centre (£35,000), which it also received the previous year. Other beneficiaries included: The Progressive Supranuclear Palsy Association (£15,000), Cancer Research UK (£10,000), Tapping House Hospice (£5,000) and Royal Hospital for Neuro-Disability (£1,000).

Educational

There were 10 grants made during the year, one of which was to the only recipient in the category in the previous year (Yorkshire Ballet Seminars – £7,500). Campaign for Stowe received the largest grant of £25,000. Other beneficiaries included: Tree House Trust (£10,000), Royal School for the Deaf – Manchester (£7,500), Newham Music Trust (£5,000) and Countryside Foundation for Education (£3,000).

Children and young people

Nine grants were made, ranging from £250 to £25,000, with six beneficiaries receiving grants the previous year. The largest grant was made to NSPCC, which received £25,000 as in the previous year. Other beneficiaries were: Home Start (£15,000), Royal Opera House Foundation and The National Association of Toy and Leisure Libraries (£10,000 each), Child Bereavement Trust, Volunteer Reading Help and Hornsey Trust – Children's Cerebral Palsy (£5,000 each), Kids Co (£500) and Children Nationwide (£250).

Miscellaneous

There were 23 miscellaneous grants, with all but two for £2,000 or less. The largest were £15,000 to Church Housing Trust and £5,000 to Regeneration Trust. Other beneficiaries included: Chelsea Festival (£2,000), Marie Curie Cancer Care (£1,500), Friends of Courtauld Institute (£1,000), Rose Road Children's Appeal (£500) and Centre for Lebanese Studies (£250).

Elderly

Three grants were made to Abbeyfield (Reading) Society (£10,000), Florence Nightingale Aid in Sickness (£5,000) and Dulwich Picture Gallery (£4,000).

Arts

Two grants were made to Grange Park Opera (£10,500) and Vivat Trust (£7,500).

Ex-employees

Two grants were made to former employees.

Legal

One grant of £1,000 is made each year to Barristers' Benevolent Fund.

Applications

In writing to the correspondent, for consideration at trustees' meetings three times a year. However, 'unsolicited applications will not normally be considered'.

The Barbour Trust

Health, welfare

£1.2 million (2002/03)

Beneficial area Mainly Tyne & Wear, County Durham and Northumberland.

PO Box 21, Guisborough, Cleveland TS14 8YH

Email edith.howse@barbour.com

Correspondent Mrs Audrey Harvey, Administrator

Trustees Dame Margaret Barbour, chair; Henry Jacob Tavroges; Anthony Glenton; Miss Helen Barbour.

Charity Commission no. 328081

Information available Exceptionally comprehensive annual report and full trustees' report and accounts.

Summary

This trust gives a large number of generally modest grants to local causes in the north east, as well as occasional larger support, usually in response to disasters at home or overseas. Applications from UK charities are only considered if they are carrying out projects within the area or have headquarters based in the north east of England. The trust also states that as in previous years, the same problems continue to persist in the area, namely unemployment and homelessness, particularly among young people. A substantial proportion of the grant total is in the form of clothing, rather than cash, supplied to the trust by the company at cost price. The trust has close working connections with the company, through which many of its applications are received.

General

This trust is endowed by Dame Margaret Barbour and her daughter Helen, whose fortunes derive from the remarkably successful clothing company of that name. The trust is endowed with shares in the company.

In 2002/03 the trust had assets of almost £4 million and an income of £403,000, down from £815,000 in the previous year. Grants totalled £1.6 million and were broken down as follows:

	Amount	Number of grants
Grants of £1,000 or more	£1.1 million	127
Grants less than £1,000	£47,000	346
Grants to individuals	£29,000	225

The three largest grants were £285,000 to Alnwick Garden, £250,000 to Centre for Children's Books and £99,000 to North East Discovery Trust for the Laing Art Gallery. Crisis at Christmas received two grants totalling £117,000.

Other grants of £10,000 or more were £30,000 to Northumbria in Bloom, £25,000 to Medical Sciences – University of Newcastle and £10,000 each to King George V School and Percy Hedley Foundation.

Other beneficiaries included Blyth Valley CVS – Second Chance (£7,000), Action Research, Cancer Research UK, National Probation Service and Refuge, North East Discovery Trust and Westminster Christmas Appeal Building Trust (£5,000 each), Barnardos (£4,000), Alzheimer's Research Trust and Whizz Kidz (£2,000 each), Age Concern, Durham Wildlife

Trust, Escape Family Support, RUKBA, Weston Spirit and Young Enterprise (£1,000 each).

Exclusions

No support for:

- requests from outside the geographical area;
- requests from educational establishments;
- individual applications, unless backed by a particular charitable organisation;
- capital grants for building projects.

Applications

In writing to the correspondent. The applications should include full back-up information, a statement of accounts and the official charity number of the applicant.

A main grants meeting is held every three months to consider grants of £500 plus. Applications are processed and researched by the administrator and secretary and further information may be requested.

A small grants meeting is held monthly to consider grants up to £500.

The trust always receives more applications than it can support. Even if a project fits its policy priority areas, it may not be possible to make a grant.

David and Frederick Barclay Foundation

Medical research, welfare

£542,000 (2003)
Beneficial area UK.

3rd Floor, 20 St James's Street, London SW1A 1ES

Tel. 020 7915 0915

Correspondent Lord Peyton, Chairman

Trustees *Lord Peyton of Yeovil, chair; Sir David Barclay; Sir Frederick Barclay; Lord McAlpine of West Green.*

Charity Commission no. 803696

Information available Annual report and accounts, with list of grants of £1,000 and above.

The foundation was established in 1989 by Sir David and Sir Frederick Barclay. The whole of the funds distributed have come from them. Donations received during 2003 amounted to £570,000. The trust usually makes around a hundred grants a year to organisations, and does not issue specific guidelines regarding applications. The following is taken from the 2002 report:

The general purposes of the foundation are to support medical research, give limited help to the young who are about to embark on their careers, and support charities whose purposes are to aid the old, sick and the disabled. Its practice is to distribute year by year the whole of the funds made available to it; it holds no reserves. Its practice is to avoid commitments which endure over a period of years; not only do these cause a loss of flexibility, but they take no account of the fact that the total funds available may and do vary from year to year.

In 2003 the foundation made 111 grants to organisations totalling £542,000.

The main focus of the foundation is medical research, with 16 grants made totalling £286,000. The largest grant made in this category was £200,000 to University of Glasgow. Other benficiaries included £17,000 in two grants to University of Southampton, £10,000 each to the British Neurological Trust, Harefield Research Foundation, Q Trust and St George's Hospital Medical School, £6,000 to Addenbrookes NHS Trust, £5,000 to Cambridge Arthritis Research Endeavor, £2,500 to National Society for Epilepsy and £2,000 each to Covent Garden Cancer Research Trust, Imperial College London and Multiple Sclerosis Nerve Centre Charity.

There were 27 grants totalling £109,000 made under the heading of 'help for the young'. Grants included £36,000 in two grants to Make-a-Wish Foundation, £20,000 to the Disability Partnership, £10,000 to Oxford Children's Hospital Campaign, £5,000 to Osteopathic Centre for Children, £3,300 in seven grants to Oxford Medical Students Elective Trust, £3,000 to Friends of Marlborough, £2,500 each to Book Aid International, Family Welfare Association and the Tavistock & Portman NHS Trust, and £2,000 to New Bridge.

Under the heading of 'aid for the old, sick and disabled', there were 16 grants totalling £108,000. Grants included £50,000 to Maggies Centre, £10,000 each to the Natural History Museum and St Martin in the Fields, £5,000 each to Kingston Hospital Cancer Unit and National Theatre, £2,500 to Chester Cathedral Development Trust and £2,000

each to Age Concern Somerset Holiday Care Service and Pets as Therapy.

Six individuals also received grants totalling £26,000.

Applications

Applications should be in writing, clearly outlining the details of the proposed project (if for medical research, so far as possible in lay terms). The total cost and duration should be stated; also the amount, if any, which has already been raised.

Following an initial screening, applications are selected according to their merits, suitability and funds available. Visits are usually made to projects where substantial funds are involved.

Decisions are normally made as soon as possible following receipt of application.

The trustees welcome information as to progress and require these on completion of a project.

The Baring Foundation

Strengthening the voluntary sector

£2.1 million (2003)
Beneficial area England and Wales, with a special interest in London, Merseyside, Cornwall and Devon; also UK charities working with NGO partners in developing countries.

60 London Wall, London EC2M 5TQ

Tel. 020 7767 1348 **Fax** 020 7767 7121

Email baring.foundation@uk.ing.com

Website www.baringfoundation.org.uk

Correspondent David Cutler, Director

Trustees *Tessa Baring, chair; Nicholas Baring; Martin Findlay; Anthony Loehnis; Janet Lewis-Jones; J R Peers; Dr Ann Buchanan; R D Broadley; C J Steane; Ranjit Sondhi.*

Charity Commission no. 258583

Information available Annual report was provided by the trust and guidelines for individual programmes were available from the trusts' website.

Summary

The main objective of the trust's work is to help build stronger voluntary organisations, both in this country and abroad. The foundation does so through its two grant programmes, of which it places a high priority on funding organisations through its core costs programmes, while also continuing to support smaller pieces of work through project funding.

- Strengthening the Voluntary Sector – Grants are for the organisational improvement, (including mergers) of national voluntary organisations working in England and Wales and local organisations working in London, Merseyside, Devon or Cornwall.
- International – This programme was closed for 2005. Details of international funding for 2006 were to be announced on the foundation's website in autumn 2005.

The foundation regrets that it will no longer be able to make Arts Project Grants. This decision is part of a general reduction in its grant-making due to reduced income. The foundation will continue to support arts organisations through its core costs grants and some strategic projects.

In 2003 the foundation had assets amounting to £58 million and an income of £1.6 million. Grants totalled £2.1 million.

General

Strengthening the Voluntary Sector programme – Guidelines for applicants

The objective of this programme is to improve the organisational effectiveness of voluntary organisations.

Who may apply?

This programme supports constituted not-for-profit voluntary organisations and provides funding for national organisations (in England and/or Wales) or in the local areas of:

- London (priority will be given to bids where the area of benefit is more than one London Borough; or providing second-tier support to other voluntary organisations in one London Borough)
- Merseyside (in the boroughs and districts of Liverpool, Knowsley, Sefton, St Helens and Wirral)
- Devon
- Cornwall.

This programme will also fund international development organisations based in England and Wales.

What may we apply for?

The foundation wishes to fund work which will lead to a significant and lasting change in the effectiveness of an organisation by improvements to its strategy, structure, systems or skills.

An application can either be for an organisation to improve its own effectiveness or to provide services to make other organisations more effective in these ways. For example:

- the introduction of organisational strategy and business planning or fundamental reviews of existing strategies and plans
- a new, more effective organisational or management structure
- introducing co-ordination and collaboration between organisations
- formal combined working or mergers
- improvements to essential systems such as information technology, finance, personnel and training
- the introduction of appropriate ways of assessing and improving the overall quality and effectiveness of an organisation
- introducing new skills or knowledge to organisations
- supporting the dissemination or replication of effective practice
- involving users or beneficiaries in planning and management for the first time or in a significantly better way
- making organisations more responsive to the needs of their users or potential users
- umbrella organisations can apply to administer a block grant that is used to enable exchanges of knowledge and skills between its members.

This list is not definitive: other work which is important to improving the effectiveness of an organisation will be considered. However, the foundation does not support the introduction of new or the expansion of existing services simply to increase the amount of work undertaken by organisations.

The foundation is flexible about how its money is used to achieve these sort of improvements. The ways in which its grants have been used include:

- freeing up the time of existing staff to undertake the work
- feasibility studies
- pilot schemes
- training
- buying in external advice and expertise
- meeting the costs of seminars or conferences
- exchanging skills and knowledge between individual organisations.

What will not be funded?

This programme will not fund:

- continuing running costs of an organisation, including salaries of permanent current or new staff
- cost of existing or increased services
- work already completed or currently taking place or due to start while the application is being considered

- repeat of an activity that took place in a previous year
- routine staff training
- costs of employing fundraisers
- general fundraising appeals
- purchase, conversion, refurbishment of buildings, gardens or playgrounds
- general office equipment including IT hardware
- vehicles
- medical research or equipment
- bursaries or scholarships
- expeditions
- religious activity.

How much can we apply for?

The foundation is prepared to consider applications for grants for up to £30,000 for work spanning up to two years. However, the great majority of grants will be for much less; the foundation's average grant in 2004 was £7,900 and only 20% of grants were for more than £10,000. The foundation is willing to fund a piece of work in its entirety or with a number of other funders.

How do we apply?

All applicants must complete the application form. This form is available to download in Word 97 format. Unfortunately, not everyone is able to view this format properly. If you have any problem downloading, please email us with your postal address and a paper copy will be sent to you.

Send the completed form to the foundation together with:

- a brief description of the current work and experience of your organisation including details of staffing, organisational structure and use of volunteers
- an outline description (using the following numbered headings and not exceeding 2 pages) of:

  1. what is proposed and will be achieved with the grant
  2. the need that will be tackled and how it was assessed
  3. how long the activity will take to be completed
  4. who will carry out the work and who will benefit
  5. why your organisation is equipped to carry out the work
  6. how the proposed activity will be documented and evaluated (a condition of any grant will be that a final report is made available to the foundation)
  7. why the proposed activity cannot be funded from elsewhere and what, if any, funding might be attracted from elsewhere if the initiative is successful.

- the detailed brief, if funding is requested to pay for a consultancy
- a detailed budget for the activity for which the grant is requested

- the income/expenditure projection of the organisation for the current year
- your organisation's most recent audited accounts or financial report required by the Charities Act (if the year covered by these accounts ended more than 12 months previously, an income/ expenditure report for the most recent complete financial year must also be included)
- your organisation's most recent annual report, if one is published.

Where an application concerns more than one organisation (e.g. one relating to a merger), it can be made jointly or by just one lead organisation. In the latter case, the foundation will need to know that the other organisations support the application and to have a copy of the accounts and annual report. In addition, one of the organisations will need to take on the role and responsibilities of the grant recipient.

In view of the sensitivity of some joint working or mergers applications, the foundation is willing to depart from its normal practice of publishing details of each grant it makes in its Annual Report. Please indicate on such applications whether you are prepared for details of any grant awarded to you to be made public.

When do we apply?

This grants programme has no deadlines; applications can be sent to the foundation at any time. The foundation's staff or advisers may need to telephone or visit the applicant organisation during the assessment process. Applications will be dealt with as quickly as possible but please bear in mind it could take up to 6 months. The foundation does not fund work that has already taken place or begun so please apply as far in advance of the project start date as possible.

Strengthening the Voluntary Sector Project Grants – 58 grants totalling £427,000

Grants were broken down into the following geographical areas:

National – England and Wales	£126,000	16 grants
National – England only	£43,000	5 grants
Cornwall and Devon	£15,000	2 grants
Cornwall only	£15,000	1 grant
Devon only	£18,000	3 grant
London	£151,000	21 grants
Mweseyside	£55,000	9 grants
UK NGOs	£4,000	1 grant

Grants were in the range of £2,000 to £15,000 and included: £15,000 to British Association Of Settlements & Social Action Centres towards the cost of developing collaborative arrangements for local community organisations to share services; £14,000 to Kids Club Network towards a searchable database and the first phase of a business consultancy for the Curiosity and Imagination initiative of Kids Club Network in collaboration with Demos and the Campaign for Learning; £13,000 to Westminster Advocacy Service for Senior Residents to pilot a national training and information network on advocacy with people with dementia; £12,000 to Westside Housing towards the cost of this West London Housing Association implementing an effective IT strategy to increase its efficiency and enhance services to clients; £10,000 to Caldecott Foundation towards the cost of installing new database management software; £9,500 to Field Lane Foundation towards a consultancy to document the model of care used by this London project in its work with homeless families; £9,000 to Little Hearts Matter towards the updating of information packs (£4,000) and the website (£5,000) to reflect the widened remit of the charity; £8,000 to West Devon Environmental Network towards the 'Communities in Action' project which will help build up the capacity of local groups to develop projects and find funding; £5,000 to Greenwich and Lewisham Congolese Welfare Group to enable the management committee and volunteers of this refugee group to undertake organisational training and develop a quality assurance framework; £4,000 to Womankind Worldwide towards five days of ICT consultancy; £3,000 to Welcare Community Projects towards the costs of a consultant to undertake a strategic review of this supervised child centre.

Exclusions

We do not accept applications from:
- appeals or charities set up to support statutory organisations
- animal welfare charities
- grant maintained, private, or local education authority schools or their Parent Teachers Associations
- individuals.

Applications

See the guidelines for specific programmes. Note that there is no provision for 'general' applications that lie outside the foundation's specific programmes.

'Applications will only be considered if all the supporting information and the completed datasheet are sent to the foundation.'

The Barnwood House Trust

Disability charities in Gloucestershire, medical research

£465,000 to organisations (2003)
Beneficial area Gloucestershire.

The Manor House, 162 Barnwood Road, Gloucester GL4 7JX

Tel. 01452 614429; 01452 611292 (grant enquires) **Fax** 01452 372594

Email barnwoodtrust@btconnect.com

Website www.barnwoodhousetrust.org

Correspondent Paul Guy, Director

Trustees *Mark Heywood, chair; David Acland; Keith Anderson; Richard Ashenden; Mrs Joan Barclay; John Colquhoun; Mrs Clare de Haan; Simon Fisher; Mrs Deborah Hutton; Roger Ker; Mrs Sara Shipway; Mrs Judy Whiteman.*

Charity Commission no. 218401

Information available Excellent annual report and accounts were provided by the trust. Full information for applicants available on the trust's website.

Summary

The trust makes grants to organisations supporting people with special needs in Gloucestershire, and, to a much lesser extent, for medical research.

Other than for medical research, grants are normally for amounts of less than £30,000 and the average such grant is for less than £4,000. They may be as low as £50. Grants are usually one-off and can not normally be repeated. The medical research grants are usually either pro-active, or made in co-operation with an appropriate 'clearing house' charity – often, in the past, Action Research.

General

The trust has five main activities, with grantmaking being but one:

- provision of a day home for elderly disabled people
- sheltered housing for elderly disabled people
- bungalows built to full wheelchair standard for families with a disabled member
- individual grants to people of Gloucestershire with special needs [Not covered here. For information on grants for individuals, see A Guide to Grants for Individuals in Need,

published by the Directory of Social Change.]

- grants to organisations caring for the welfare of people with disabilities and for medical research into the causes and treatment of disabling conditions.

The trust's grantmaking objectives are:

- Firstly, the relief of persons who have a mental or nervous disorder or a serious physical disability and who are sick, convalescent, disabled, infirm or in need, hardship or distress by relieving their condition or assisting their recovery. Preference is given to those who live or formerly lived in Gloucestershire.
- Secondly, the promotion of research into the cause, prevention and treatment of sickness associated with the above conditions and the publications of the results of such research.

In 2003 the trust had assets totalling £46.4 million and an income of £1.8 million. There were 137 grants made to organisations totalling £465,000.

Grantmaking in 2003

The trust gives the following review of its grantmaking activities during the year, and reflects on some recent developments on funding in the voluntary sector:

Overall the trust's grantmaking activity resulted in a lesser sum being committed for grants than in previous years. Nonetheless, 2003 was a busy year and resulted in new commitments totalling £608,000 for 2003 and future years. Taking all the grant commitments for 2003, including those made in previous years for 2003, these amounted to £717,000 (after cancellations) for grants to individuals, organisations and medical research – compared with a net total of £1,016,000 in 2002. In summary the breakdown is as follows:

Grants committee	£316,000
Individual grants	£252,000
Medical research	£138,000
Strategic projects	£10,000
Total	£716,000

The purpose of grantmaking within Gloucestershire remains the same – to help to meet special needs arising from serious physical or mental disability or exceptional needs which the person with a disability cannot afford. As well as supporting individuals in need [not covered here], grants are made to statutory and charitable organisations working with people with disabilities and for medical research into the causes and treatments of disabilities. The latter is carried out by making funds available to national medical research charities for selected projects of special interest to the trust. The work of each committee with

grantmaking responsibilities is described below.

It was anticipated that the amount of new commitments entered into and the numbers of organisations assisted would be less than in previous years. This was the outcome of (i) a reduced income (reflecting movement in the stock market and taxation changes), (ii) a temporary hiatus in grantmaking for medical research and special projects following the restructuring of committees in 2003, and (iii) the underlying trend of a decline in the level and numbers of applications to our reactive grantmaking programme. Our contact with the Gloucestershire Funders' Forum indicates that other grantmakers with a local bias are experiencing similar trends of reducing income and number of applications.

Whether or not the demand for grants from charitable organisations will continue to fall remains difficult to predict. It is becoming clear that in order to make their organisations more sustainable, the chosen path for some service charities is to enter the contract culture for delivery of public services. The trust prefers not to use its charitable funds to subsidise the start-up or running costs of delivering contracted-out public services by charities. Financial support for this activity is viewed as risky. This is because if public policy, priorities and funding streams change or are capped, contracts can be lost resulting in a failure of the 'investment'.

The Government has recognised charities' need for start-up capital (the Futurebuilders Fund announced by HM Treasury [in 2002] to build up 'not for profit' organisations needing capital in readiness for delivery of contracted-out public services will be an alternative source of finance, although it is not clear why this apparently unfair advantage is to be given to voluntary/community organisations who put themselves in direct competition with private or corporate providers). We hope that the introduction of new legal forms for charities as proposed by the White Paper 'Private Gain, Public Benefit', will make this activity (of delivery of public services) more transparent and accountable.

Apart from trust views on the risks for charities becoming involved in the contract culture, one of the trust's main concerns is that as more and more charities – encouraged by government as part of its 'modernisation' agenda – take on public service delivery, this may exclude people in need because they come with no 'dowry' of state support. This leads to questions about the future role for independent grantmaking trusts. Many have a special niche in assisting organisations that help those excluded from public services or for whom no service exists to meet their particular needs. 2003 saw the publication of the report by Anheiner and

Leat, 'From Charity to Creativity', and the re-publication of 'Voluntary Action', Barry Knight's thought provoking research for Centris. These have stimulated this debate within the charity sector, the Association of Charitable Foundations and our trustees in particular.

However, the trust has concluded that there will always be needs that the state cannot afford to meet and people in need who will find themselves outside the criteria for public services. The impetus of voluntary action to meet those needs will continue to require the support of independent funders.

Moreover, there will always be opportunities to assist the statutory sector by adding value to existing services, helping organisations manage change or test out new ideas and new ways of meeting the needs and aspirations of people who are disadvantaged by disability or other factors. An example of this is the 'social firm' which strives to provide employment to people with disabilities within a 'not for profit' self-sustaining income generating business. The trust will watch the development of this sector with interest.

We also support organisations through special projects, such as property purchase and lease back with commercial, soft or no rent requirements as appropriate. It is a particularly effective way of bringing forward new schemes for which its promoters would have spent years raising funds. Such activity is grantmaking of a different kind where the risk of the 'investment' is mitigated by retaining the value and freehold of the property concerned. During 2003 the trust purchased a former factory site in Cheltenham for lease to West Gloucestershire Primary Care Trust as a wheelchair centre and ultimately an independent living centre for the county [opened in 2004].

We continue to promote the trust's ability to help others through our website with clear information about our eligibility criteria, by sending mail-shots to local organisations, publishing features in other organisations' newsletters and magazines, the local print media and advertising in the Gloucestershire hospitals' in-house booklet which is seen by thousands of patients and carers.

Strategic Projects Committee (SPC)

This committee got off to an excellent start in the previous year (2002) by undertaking research into selected areas of indicated need which culminated in the commitment to grant over £114,000 to Gloucestershire Partnership NHS Trust for the start-up of an 'early intervention in psychosis' project for young people in Cheltenham and Tewkesbury. The target age group is 18 to 25 year olds and the work is based on Australian research that early intervention can improve the recovery outcome for young people with an emerging psychosis. The pilot project started in April 2003 and we await its evaluation in 2004.

Due to membership changes in the first half of 2003, this committee ceased to be viable and restructuring of grantmaking activity became necessary. SPC's prime functions, (i) to develop further the trust's understanding of need among the trust's beneficial group, and (ii) to encourage strategic projects to meet identified need, have now been embedded with the Policy Sub-Committee, while grantmaking for medical research has been transferred to the Grants Committee.

In early 2003, SPC was considering the theme of 'employment matters' and it is hoped this will develop further in the hands of the Policy Sub-Committee now chaired by Mr Roger Ker.

Grants Committee

The remit of this committee is to react to incoming appeals from organisations working with and for Gloucestershire people with disabilities and to make grants for medical research. The committee met four times during the year, committing a net total of £215,000 for 120 new grants to local organisations and £46,000 for a new medical research grant. The figure for medical research commitments for 2003 rises to £139,000 when grants agreed in earlier years for 2003 are included. Taking grants to local organisations and adding in the commitments for 2003 made in previous years, the net total rises to £316,000 for 131 grants, including those made under 'delegated powers'. This power enables the Chairman to award grants up to the value of £750. This is our 'fast track' scheme and our aim is to give a decision within 15 working days. A total of 30 requests were dealt with this way amounting to £13,500.

Over 75% of grant commitments to local organisations were for sums under £5,000. A significant number of applications were for less than £1,000 – for holidays, outings, weekend breaks and other recreational and therapeutic activities to a wide variety of voluntary and statutory organisations (schools, colleges, health and social care agencies) working hard to enhance the quality of life for children and adults with disabilities.

This well-spring of voluntary action by both volunteers and paid professionals is a very positive sign that voluntarism still thrives here in Gloucestershire. Another trend we have noted is for national charities to seek a donation towards their work here in Gloucestershire or their use by Gloucestershire people with disabilities. These services are managed nationally or

regionally, making the extent and value of their activities difficult to determine.

The trust was glad to renew its support for Forest of Dean Contact a Family (core funding of £35,500 over four years), The Orchard Trust (£11,000 for improvements to the education centre), Watershed Riding for the Disabled (£5,000 towards a replacement vehicle), Worcester House Day Centre (£2,500 for art sessions for service users), Young Gloucestershire (£1,000 to enable a young disabled woman to take part in the Prince's Trust volunteer programme), Children with Disabilities Service (£4,000 towards the salary of an OT assistant), Deafblind UK (£1,500 towards service costs in Gloucestershire) and Gloucester MS Information & Therapy Centre (£6,000 towards refurbishment of oxygen chamber).

Grants committed in a previous year for 2003 included £20,000 to Gloucestershire Partnership NHS Trust to start up an occupational therapy service in the healthcare unit of HM Prison Gloucester, £10,500 to Cafe Lynks, Stroud, for an extra staff member, £14,500 to Marie Curie Cancer Care for its home nursing service in Gloucestershire, £12,300 to RETHINK towards support costs at the Claremont accommodation project, £5,000 to Tewkesbury Volunteer & Help Centre towards lease rental, £5,000 to SHARE and £10,000 to Forest of Dean Crossroads for its palliative care service.

Responsibility for making grants for medical research was passed to the Grants Committee during 2003. The previous policy guidelines and practice have not changed. In particular the committee wanted to continue support for Research Training Fellowships (RTF) and was disappointed that the commitment made in 2002 to Research into Ageing (RiA) did not go ahead. This was because RiA was unable to find a suitable candidate and project. As an alternative, a new RTF through Action Medical Research was made in support of Dr Jane Warren's work at Imperial College on language impairment after stroke. This perfectly fitted the criteria that had been agreed by the previous committee as the focus for a new fellowship award.

Exclusions

Grants are only made for charitable work undertaken in Gloucestershire.

The trust would not normally provide core funding to a statutory body where the public sector had a duty to provide.

Grants are not normally made for delivery of health care or counselling services, for building or adapting public sector/social housing or to charities to start up or subsidise services contracted out to them by the public sector.

Grants to non-disability organisations to make community buildings more accessible to people with disabilities are only considered where there is evidence of substantial need or regular usage by a large number of people with disabilities.

A management charge applied to a project in order to underwrite core costs is not normally supported. Actual costs arising from a new project should be included in the project costs.

Applications

The trust advises potential applicants to ring before making an application. Grant application forms can be requested by telephone, email or by post. If a request is for less than £750, contact Mrs Christine Ellson (Tel: 01452 611292) as the trust may be able to consider it quickly under the fast track scheme. The trust also adds that even if a group or organisation has been helped before, it is always willing to consider fresh applications.

Please check with the trust as to when the next opportunity for grant consideration takes place, as the deadline to send in completed applications is six weeks before the meeting date. This allows the trustees time to visit the organisations and if necessary discuss requests in depth.

For information about grants for individuals, contact the trust, or see A Guide to Grants for Individuals in Need, published by the Directory of Social Change.

BBC Children in Need

Welfare of disadvantaged children

£30.5 million (2003/04)

Beneficial area UK.

PO Box 76, London W3 6FS

Tel. 020 8576 7788 **Fax** 020 8008 3177

Email pudsey@bbc.co.uk

Website bbc.co.uk/pudsey

Correspondent Sally Deighan, Chief Executive

Trustees *Prof. Fabian Monds, chair; Will Day; Simon Milner; Diane Louise Jordan; Neena Mahal; Beverley Tew; Terry Wogan; Tim Cook; Lorraine Heggessy; Yogesh Chauhan; Steve Wood.*

Charity Commission no. 802052

Information available Full information is available from the charity's website.

Summary

The charity makes around 2,000 grants a year in total, allocated in two rounds. Amounts range from a few hundred pounds to a normal maximum of about £100,000.

They are made for specific projects which directly help disadvantaged children and young people (aged 18 and under). About half of all applications result in a grant (though no doubt the success rate is higher for smaller applications and the amount given even in successful cases may often be less than the full amount requested).

Although most grants are for £5,000 or less, more than half the money goes in larger awards of over £35,000. Around half of its funds are given in one-off grants, the rest payable over two or three years.

Background

The charity, registered in 1989, distributes the proceeds of the BBC's annual Children in Need appeal (first televised in 1980). In 2003 the appeal raised over £30 million. (The appeal in 2004 raised £17 million on the night, with the final total likely to be several million pounds more.)

Guidelines for applicants

General

The appeal gives grants to organisations working with disadvantaged children and young people who must be aged 18 years and under, living in the United Kingdom.
    Their disadvantages will include:
- illness, distress, abuse or neglect
- any kind of disability
- behavioural or psychological problems
- living in poverty or situations of deprivation

The application should demonstrate how your project will change the lives of children for the better. It should be entirely focused on children. Where possible and appropriate it should take into account children's views and involve them in decision-making.

Advice to applicants

Organisations apply to us for a wide range of grants. The purpose and amount can vary enormously. From our experience we think that the following information might help an organisation to make a more effective application for a grant.

During the assessment of your application we will want to know more about:
- the background to your organisation and some knowledge of how it is governed
- how you work with other organisations and services in your area
- how your project was planned and what it hopes to achieve for children
- how you monitor/evaluate your work
- the child protection measures that are in operation
- job description(s), person specification(s) and expected salary level(s)
- the basis for costing equipment, services or activities
- the timing of other decisions with regard to multi-funding or complex projects.

The application form is designed to help us make an informed decision about your organisation and although some questions are probably easier to answer than others, you must complete the whole form otherwise we will not have enough information to make a decision.
    We are committed to making sure our grants bring about changes for the better in children's lives and we want to support work that can do this.
    The most important step in making a good application takes place before you even start to fill in the application form, and that is to plan your project well.
    Good planning means:
- identifying in advance what difference you want to make for children
- realistically defining how the project will achieve this difference
- knowing how you will recognise whether the project has made the difference you want to make.

If you are applying for staff salaries:
- please state whether a salary is for a new post or an existing one.
- make sure your costs include all the extras involved in employing staff e.g. recruitment, NI contributions, pension costs, inflation etc.
- enclose a job description, person specification, first year work plan and a completed Grant Breakdown form.
- new posts funded by BBC Children in Need (except short term or sessional staff) must be publicly advertised.
- during the assessment we will enquire about the organisation's skills to manage staff effectively.

(The application form itself has useful further guidance on completing individual questions. Ed.)

Grantmaking practice

Applications are assessed by a team of freelance assessors. Most of them are then considered, and grant decisions recommended, by advisory committees and staff at country or regional level.

The assessment reports cover five main areas:
- The eligibility of the application

    Are the children disadvantaged?

    Is the organisation charitable?
- The acceptability of the project

    Is it well organised?

    Does it take child protection into account?

    Does it involve children, where relevant?
- The organisation's ability to carry out the project

    What is the organisation's capacity?

    What is its track record?

    What are its linkages with others, especially the local authority?
- The organisation's finances

    Is the organisation adequately managed financially?

    Are the project finances sensible?
- The mission

    What differences will be achieved for the children?

    How will this be monitored/evaluated?

Grants in 2003/04

The charity provides information about its grants as the decisions are made, twice each year, and without waiting for the end of the financial year concerned. However some of the analysis has to wait for the year end, so some information, particularly statistical information on the number and value of grants, was unavailable at the time of writing.

The charity received 3,808 applications (representing requests for a total of £143.5 million), with 1,782 applications being successful (47%), though many grants will have been for less than the full amount requested. The total amount awarded during the year was £30.5 million.

The 2003/04 grants were categorised as follows:
- to provide family support, welfare and care for children living in poverty and deprivation (£8,191,000)
- to involve children, many with physical and mental disabilities, in activities such as sport, drama, music and play (£7,426,000)
- to provide family support, welfare and care for children suffering through

illness, distress, abuse or neglect (£4,159,000)

- to provide support and therapeutic services for children with disabilities, and advice or counselling services for children with special needs (£3,626,000)
- to help young people in trouble because of homelessness, drugs or solvent abuse, alcohol problems or eating disorders (£3,319,000)
- to playgroups, nurseries and other services for disadvantaged children under five (£1,935,000)
- to provide safe outdoor play facilities and holidays in the UK for children who need them (£1,135,000)
- to schools, hospitals and social services for activities and equipment for children which are in addition to those provided by the state (£743,000).

The charity notes that grants are targeted on areas of greatest need and the money is allocated geographically to ensure that grants are distributed in a balanced manner throughout the UK'.

The actual geographical distribution of the money is hard to report as the charity uses non-standard regional definitions for areas whose population is not given.

Grant allocation in 2003/04

England	(£18,081,000)
– South East	£6,159,000
– Midlands & East	£3,721,000
– North East	£3,012,000
– South West	£2,608,000
– North West	£2,581,000
Scotland	£3,879,000
Northern Ireland	£2,329,000
Wales	£2,328,000
UK-wide	£3,917,000
Total	*£30,534,000*

Examples of beneficiaries and projects supported include the following:

- Frank Buttle Trust: £789,000 for one year for small grants for disadvantaged children throughout the UK;
- New School at West Heath: £244,000 for two years for the salary of a full-time Director of Centre, part-time assistant, video production, course materials and equipment;
- Domestic Violence Intervention Project – London: £132,000 for three years for the salary of a specialist children's worker and funding for linked sessional work with children aged 5–18;
- Newham Autism Centre: £107,000 for three years for the full-time salary of a family services worker for a project offering advice, support and information to families, plus IT equipment;

- Renfield St Stephen's Church Centre – Glasgow: £98,500 for the provision of small individual grants for children in need;
- Mental Health Advocacy in Pembrokeshire: £91,500 for three years for the salary of a full-time Mental Health Advocate for children and young people;
- Haven House Project – Sheffield: £86,000 for three years for the salary of a full-time children's worker;
- Christ Church Youth & Community Centre – Bootle: £81,500 for three years for the salaries of four part-time project workers, resources, volunteer expenses and transport for an after-school activities project;
- Playback Trust – Midlothian: £81,000 for three years for the salary of a full-time trust development manager working with children with physical disabilities and other complex needs;
- Women's Aid Ynys Mon – Anglesey: £20,000 towards the salary of a part-time children's project worker;
- Swansea and Brecon Diocesan Council for Social Responsibility: £14,500 towards the salaries of a full-time play co-ordinator and a part-time play worker;
- Takeover Radio Children's Media Trust: £5,000 towards the costs of a radio training course for young carers;
- Brent Educational Tuition Service: £2,000 for the cost of providing a sensory tunnel, raised flower beds and constructing pathways;
- Coventry Youth Bowling Club: £500 for four lightweight bowling balls, training and transport to events.

Exclusions

The appeal does not consider applications from private individuals or the friends or families of individual children. In addition, grants will not be given for:

- trips and projects abroad
- medical treatment or medical research
- unspecified expenditure
- deficit funding or repayment of loans
- retrospective funding
- projects which are unable to start within 12 months
- distribution to another/other organisation(s)
- general appeals and endowment funds
- the relief of statutory responsibilities.

Applications

Straightforward and excellent application forms and guidelines are available from the website or from the following national offices:

England (and general helpline):
PO Box 76
London
W3 6FS
Tel: 020 8576 7788

Northern Ireland:
Broadcasting House
Ormeau Avenue
Belfast
BT2 8HQ
Tel: 02890 338221

Scotland:
BBC Edinburgh
Holyrood Road
Edinburgh
EH8 8JF
Tel: 0131 248 4225

Wales:
Broadcasting House
Llandaff
Cardiff
CF5 2YQ
Tel: 029 2032 2383

There are two closing dates for applications – 30 November and 30 March. Organisations may submit only one application and may apply on only one of these dates.

Applicants should allow up to five months after each closing date for notification of a decision. (For summer projects applications must be submitted by the November closing date or will be rejected because they cannot be processed in time.)

The John Beckwith Charitable Trust

Youth, general

£515,000 (2001/02)

Beneficial area UK and overseas.

Pacific Investments, 124 Sloane Street, London SW1X 9BW

Tel. 020 7225 2250

Correspondent Ms Sally Holder, Administrator

Trustees *J L Beckwith; H M Beckwith; C M Meech.*

Charity Commission no. 800276

Information available Annual report and accounts were on file at the Charity Commission.

In 2001/02 the trust had assets of £2.4 million and an income of £30,000, which was down significantly on the previous year (£1.1 million in 2000/01). Grants were made totalling £515,000. Unfortunately, no grants list was include in the accounts. The breakdown of the areas funded, however, was given as follows:

Sports	8 grants	£314,000
Arts	2 grants	£106,000
Social welfare	16 grants	£40,000
Education	1 grant	£35,000
Medical research	10 grants	£21,000

Previous beneficiaries include Youth Sport Trust (founded by John Beckwith), Institute of Sport – Loughborough University, Royal Opera House Development Trust, Harrow Development Trust, Colon Cancer Care, Helen Rollason Cancer Care Centre, Leukaemia Research Fund, Release, National Literacy Trust, Alzheimer's Society, Hearing Research Trust and Research into Eating Disorders.

In 2002/03 the trust had a total expenditure of £543,000, in 2003/04 its expenditure was £518,000.
Unfortunately, although submitted by the trust to the Charity Commission, the accounts for these years had not made it to the public files for inspection.

Comment

There was no response to repeated written requests for a copy of the most recent annual report and accounts, despite the requirement to provide these on demand.

Applications

In writing to the correspondent.

The Bedford Charity (The Harpur Trust)

Education, welfare and recreation in and around Bedford

£498,000 to organisations (2003/04)

Beneficial area The borough of Bedford.

Princetown Court, Pilgrim Centre, Brickhill Drive, Bedford MK41 7PZ
Tel. 01234 369500 **Fax** 01234 369505
Email grants@harpur-trust.org.uk
Website www.bedfordcharity.org.uk

Correspondent The Community Grants Executive

Trustees *The governing body consists of four university nominations; the nominees of the teaching staff and parents of the trust's four schools; ten co-opted trustees; and two nominees each of Bedford Borough Council and Bedfordshire County Council. Additional members with specific skills and experience are co-opted onto the grants committee.*

Charity Commission no. 204817

Information available Comprehensive annual report and accounts and an annual narrative booklet were provided by the trust. Full information is also available from its website.

This charity is one of the oldest described in this resource, and probably one of the oldest in the country:

The Bedford Charity, also known as the Harpur Trust, has been in existence since 1566 when it was founded by Sir William Harpur (1496–1573) a tailor from Bedford. William became Lord Mayor of London in 1561 and was knighted one year later.

In 1566, he and his wife, Dame Alice, executed a deed of gift creating an endowment to sustain a school he had already established in Bedford. This school had been granted 'letters patent' from King Edward VI in 1552 and later became what is now known as Bedford School. The endowment also made provision for the marriage of poor maids of the town, for deprived children to be nourished and informed, and for any residue to be distributed to the poor of the town.

The endowment originally consisted of some property and the schoolhouse in Bedford and, "...thirteen acres and one rood..." of water meadows in Middlesex. The latter being now part of Holborn, the endowment of the Charity has reached a valuation last year of over £45,500,000.

Today, the activities of the Charity are still inspired by the vision of William Harpur who saw the real value of education and the real needs to be addressed amongst the disadvantaged, poor and sick in his home town of Bedford.

There has been a review of its activities recently, with a strategic plan being approved by the trustees which will take the charity up to 2009, although its core objects remain the same.

The trustees' vision for the Bedford Charity in 2009 is:

The Bedford Charity will continue to serve the residents of the Borough of Bedford, first through an increasing, creative and constructive grants programme, which recognises the importance of education as a means of improving the life chances of all in society and in particular the disadvantaged.

Second, the Charity's schools will continue to provide excellent independent education, whilst widening access and enhancing their existing ethos of valuing public service. Third, the Charity will provide accommodation to cater for those whose needs can best be met by the Charity's almshouses.

Statement of Purpose

The Bedford Charity is a large, local charity which exists to apply the income from the endowment of Sir William Harpur, its founder, in pursuit of its three objects, which may be summarised as:

- The promotion of education
- The relief of poverty, hardship or distress
- The provision of recreational facilities with a social welfare purpose

This work will be undertaken largely within the Borough of Bedford but the Charity may pursue the promotion of education, which it defines in the widest terms, without geographical constraint.

The overall thrust of the plan is to shift resources gradually towards the community activities of the charity. The schools will remain fundamentally important to the charity and indeed be at the heart of much of the developing work. They are rich sources of expertise, enthusiasm and innovation and it is hoped that, combined with an active and growing grants programme, the schools will become an even more effective force for good in the area of benefit while continuing to deliver the extremely high standards of education for which they are justly known.

The trustees wish to pursue eight specific issues over the next five years, with the overall effect of releasing more resources for grant making and widening access to the charity's schools not only through bursaries but also other means, whilst keeping costs to parents of pupils at the school as low as possible. The plan will also place greater emphasis on the existing ethos of public service within the schools and seek to link, where appropriate, their charitable activities with those of our grant making programmes. The trustees will also develop a concept of 'Excellence in Education', which they intend to result in a coherent programme, involving both grant making and the expertise and resources of the charity's schools in cooperation with the maintained sector, to raise standards and enrich the experience of education enjoyed by people of all ages and economic staus in Bedford. The plan will be supported by a revised investment strategy and a communications policy to keep stakeholders informed and involved.

The plan will be taken forward through combined working groups of staff and trustees and implementation will be phased in over several years.

In 2003/04 the charity had assets of £85.5 million, held as school and almshouse property, and also including an endowment of £45.5 million. Income during the year totalled £42.5 million, mostly generated by school fees, and there was a total expenditure of £40.4 million, most of which was devoted to the welfare of pupils and the running of its five main schools. Grants were made totalling £498,000. Around the same amount is set aside each year for general grantmaking, although it is likely to increase as a result of the charity's recent strategic review.

Programmes and priorities

The promotion of education

The Bedford Charity since its inception has had a key role in developing and enhancing educational opportunities in the Borough. This interest is reflected in the educational programmes that comprise a major element of our community grants activities.

Our awards are generally made to support:

- collaborative projects, enabling significant numbers of young people in the Borough to have access to new and valuable learning opportunities.
- projects that focus on: enriching the educational experiences of younger people; enabling older people to remain active learners; provision for those with additional support needs to be able to access educational and training opportunities
- innovative and potentially replicable projects initiated by schools in the maintained sector, and other educational establishments, where there is no statutory obligation for funding
- educational projects where an award may help leverage in significant additional funding from other sources.

Relief

'The promotion of any charitable purpose for the relief of people who are sick or in need, hardship or distress.'

We will consider requests for staffing, running and capital costs for projects and core services. Competition for grants, however, is particularly fierce within this broad grants programme.

Through our own on-going research and consultation, locally and beyond the Borough, we continually develop our grant giving priorities to respond to emerging local needs and opportunities.

Our grant making activities aim:

- to help establish projects that can enable an organisation to prove the value of developing new, or enhancing existing, services to relevant audiences, particularly potential funders and other complementary service providers

- to encourage collaborative working between organisations to meet the needs of end beneficiaries. This may include our own involvement with developing funding partnerships at the early stages of a project's activities
- under exceptional circumstances, to assist established local organisations with short-term funding to enable continuity of their services until more sustainable financial support can be secured.

Recreation

'The provision of facilities for recreation and other leisure-time occupations in the interests of social welfare.'

Our grant giving under this programme has a strong emphasis on projects that aim to address the needs of young and/or disadvantaged people. How a project proposal will act 'in the interests of social welfare' will be carefully considered.

The focus of this programme is on people, and how a project will significantly improve their access to valuable recreational opportunities and experiences. Successful project requests generally include aspects that complement the objectives of our education and 'relief' programmes.

Grants in 2003/04

Beneficiaries receiving grants during the year and future commitments included Bedford Volunteer Bureau (£55,000 in total), Youth Action Bedfordshire (£48,000 in total), Bedfordshire Pilgrims Housing Association (£37,500 in total), Cecil Higgins Art Gallery and Bedford Museum (£24,000 in total), Ormiston Children and Families Trust (£20,000), Disability Resource Centre (£18,000), Mark Rutherford Upper School (£15,000), Autism Bedfordshire (£14,000), Bedford CAB (£12,000), Hinwick Hall College of Further Education (£10,000), Kempston Rural Playspace (£8,000), Bedford Creative Arts (£5,000), St Peter's Parochial Church (£4,000), Wildlife Trust (£2,500), Bedford and District Audio News (£1,000) and Distant Thunder Show Corps (£500).

Exclusions

No grants are made in support of commercial ventures. No grants can be made for any project that relates primarily to the promotion of any religion. With the exception of some very specific programmes under the education charitable object*[see the Educational Grants Directory, published by the Directory of Social Change]*, no awards are made to individuals.

Applications

Application forms are available from the trust. They encourage initial telephone enquiries and preliminary proposal letters. Trustees meet throughout the year. Guidance will be provided on the timescales for decision.

The Big Lottery Fund (see also Awards for All)

Community, young people, welfare

£600 million to £700 million each year

Beneficial area UK.

Tel. 08454 102030

Email enquiries@biglotteryfund.org.uk

Website www.biglotteryfund.org.uk

Trustees *Prof. Sir Clive Booth, chair; Dame Valerie Strachan; David Campbell; Roland Doven; John Gartside; Douglas Graham; Dugald Mackie; John Naylor; Esther Maria O'Callaghan; Anna Southall; Diana Whitworth; Dr Samuel Burnside; Paul Cavanagh; Breidge Gadd; Tom Davies; Taha Idris; Huw Vaughan Thomas.*

Information available All information on the various programmes will be found on the fund's website when details are finalised.

Summary

Launched in June 2004, the Big Lottery Fund was formed as a result of a merger between the New Opportunities Fund, which made grants for health, education and the environment, and the Community Fund, the main source of lottery money to the voluntary sector. It has also taken over the assets of the Millennium Commission and its role in supporting large-scale regeneration projects. The fund controls half of the 'good causes' money raised by the lottery, and it has stated that between 60% and 70% of its £1 billion of new funding each year will be distributed within the voluntary sector. This is expected to be the case until 2009.

The established Community Fund programmes will continue to operate until the end of May 2005. After that date they will be replaced by a range of 'demand-led' grant programmes to which a wide range of charities will be able to apply. The first of these, the Young People's Fund, was launched in 2004. Others are due to be announced in the summer of 2005.

They will be 'outcomes' based. The Young People's Fund, for which full information is available on the Big Lottery Fund website, is likely to be the model for many of these programmes.

There will also be further more narrowly restricted programmes, succeeding those previously operated by the New Opportunities Fund.

General

Although this is a statutory body responsible for spending most of the proceeds of the public's gambling through the National Lottery, one of its constituent parts, the Community Fund, has operated much like a grantmaking trust and is a member of the Association of Charitable Foundations; hence the appearance of the fund here.

There has been much controversy surrounding the launch of the Big Lottery Fund. The Community Fund previously operated via 'open-grants' programmes (for both medium and large-scale grants, which had their final deadlines for applications set for the end of May 2005). The Big Lottery Fund is to introduce new programmes based on themes and outcomes set by the government. These were announced by the government, not by the BLF, and before the relevant consultation period had ended, which led to fears that funds will be used to achieve government ends rather than those of applicant charities. It is also feared that some voluntary and community groups who were previously eligible for funding from the Community Fund may not now be eligible because their work does not fall within the outcomes chosen by the government.

One scheme that has already been introduced is the Young People's Fund. With an initial budget of £200 million in the first three years, the Young People's Fund aims to focus on projects that 'promote youth inclusion, particularly by providing facilities and activities, both after school and in holiday periods, for young people'. Much of the £200 million budgeted for the Young People's Fund is allocated to government schemes, such as the Out of Hours Learning/School Sports Partnership. £68 million is available to respond to bids from charities and community groups, £40 million for local groups and £30 million for larger-scale national projects.

In February 2005 the results of Phase One of the consultation process were published. The 'key messages' that emerged from the consultation were that:

- there was a strong view that the Big Lottery Fund should work more effectively with others to ensure that it delivers funding in partnership, and with greater co-ordination with other related strategies;
- there was concern about the need to focus on sustainability, both in terms of offering longer term and more flexible grants and in supporting organisations to develop exit strategies;
- respondents emphasised that funding should be additional to Government expenditure and should add value to existing programmes;
- there was strong support for a lightly prescribed, demand-led programme or programmes;
- it was widely felt that funding should not just prioritise new projects and exclude existing projects;
- respondents urged caution when targeting disadvantage based on geographical area, to ensure that pockets of deprivation and rural areas were not excluded.

It remains to be seen what will be taken on board by the fund after the consultation process has finished. A range of new programmes were to be announced after May 2005 to run alongside the Young People's Fund, the themes of which have already been decided. They include community learning and opportunity, community safety and cohesion and the promotion of wellbeing. What was made clear is that the consultation process would not change the government-decided themes and intended outcomes, which include people being better able to contribute to their communities through improved life skills, enhanced rural and urban environments and more physically active people and communities better able to make healthier eating choices.

Young People's Fund – England

Through the Young People's Fund, we aim to support projects that will improve local communities and offer more opportunities to young people.

We want young people to come up with ideas for projects and to be involved in making them happen. In particular, we want to encourage the involvement of young people from disadvantaged backgrounds.

Who can apply for funding?

We will be giving out three types of grant under the Young People's Fund:

- Grants to voluntary and community organisations to run local projects with and for young people;
- Grants to voluntary organisations to fund national projects;
- Grants to individual young people (or small groups of young people) to help them make a difference in their communities [guidelines for individuals are not covered here].

Guidelines for organisations (local projects)

Projects should be for young people aged 11–18. We can also fund projects specifically aimed at disadvantaged young people up to the age of 25 who find the transition to independent adult life difficult.

Grants are between £5,000 and £150,000 over a three-year period.

We expect projects to help disadvantaged young people to come together with other young people to enjoy and benefit from activities, and / or create a better understanding of disadvantage among young people.

It is also important that young people are safe from harm, so we need to know about what systems and procedures you have to make sure they are safe.

£40 million is available to fund voluntary and community organisations, (partnerships between voluntary and statutory organisations may also apply).

We will be funding projects that can achieve two or more of the Young People's Fund outcomes. They are:

- Being healthy: enjoying good physical and mental health and living a healthy lifestyle;
- Staying safe: being protected from harm and neglect and growing up able to look after themselves;
- Enjoying and achieving: getting the most out of life and developing skills for adulthood;
- Making a positive contribution: to the community and to society and not offending and behaving antisocially;
- Economic well being: overcoming socio-economic disadvantages to achieve their full potential in life.

Guidelines for organisations (national projects)

What we're looking for

We are inviting proposals for projects that achieve one or more of the Young People's Fund outcomes. We are particularly keen to see proposals for projects that address the 'being healthy' and 'staying safe' outcomes. This is because we expect that these outcomes may not be so well represented in other strands of the Young People's Fund.

The national programme has a two-stage application process. The deadline for the first stage of the process was December 2004, with only successful applications progressing to the second stage, which came to a close in May 2005. Contact the fund on 08454 102030 for information on future deadlines.

Young People's Fund – Wales

The Young People's Fund in Wales will help young people:

- Enjoy life and achieve their potential;
- Develop skills and contribute to their communities;
- Choose positive activities which discourage antisocial behaviour.

In Wales the Young People's Fund will give out grants worth £13.2 million between 2005 and 2009. The programme will focus on young people between 10 and 19 years old. It will have three strands:

- Make it Happen – small grants for projects developed and run by young people;
- Bridging the Gap – outreach and support services for the most disengaged and disaffected young people;
- Reaching Out – development projects that meet a clear gap in local services for young people.

The Young People's Fund was launched on 31 January 2005. Make it Happen opened on 31 January 2005, Bridging the Gap opened on 14 March 2005 and Reaching Out on 25 April 2005.

Make It Happen

Make it Happen will give out £1 million in Wales over the next three years for projects, activities and equipment that will make a difference to young people aged 10–19.

Make it Happen will operate throughout Wales and we welcome applications from all sectors of the community. Grants will be from between £500 to £5,000. We will not make grants to individuals.

Only groups working with young people can apply. They may be voluntary groups or statutory bodies, but the project or activity must have been planned and developed by young people. An application from a school or statutory youth club will have to show that the activity is beyond those that normally go on within the school or club. For legal reasons every group that receives a grant must have at least one person over 18 years old on their management committee or apply through another organisation.

All projects must meet one of the Young People's Fund aims. If we have more applications than we are able to fund, we will give priority to the following:

- Groups run by disabled young people;
- Groups run by young people from black and minority ethnic background small groups that have not had Lottery funding before;
- Groups of young people facing particular issues or disadvantage;
- Projects which promote integration between young people with different experiences or backgrounds.

We welcome applications for projects combining different activities. Some examples of what we could fund are:

- Trips to places that young people might not normally visit;
- Trying out adventurous activities;
- Events and festivals run by young people for young people;
- Community projects;
- Workshop activities.

We will pay for, among other things, travel, equipment, activity, staff costs and volunteer expenses. We will fund other activities but you should check with us on 01686 611700 before applying if you need a grant for something a bit different.

Information on the Bridging the Gap and Reach Out schemes had not yet been released at the time of writing. Check the website (www.biglotteryfund.org.uk/programmes/ypfw) for up to date information.

Mentro Allan – Wales

Mentro Allan aims to make the less active population of Wales more active by increasing their recreational use of Wales's natural environment. It will pay for schemes that will make the parks, waterways, coasts and countryside more accessible to people who might otherwise never use them.

The programme will be in two stages. In the first stage we will give a grant to an award partner to develop a range of schemes across Wales. We expect to announce who the successful partner is in June 2005, when the programme will be opened up to local organisations.

Active Futures – Scotland

Research has shown that the participation levels in physical activity among the 17–24 year age group declines sharply, suggesting people simply get out of the habit after leaving school.

If action is not taken, the substantial investment made to encourage school children to be more active could be lost and leave us with a legacy of unhealthy and unfit adults.

Through the £5.5 million Active Futures programme, we aim to support projects working together in partnership that target young women, disabled people, and/or people from black and ethnic minority communities.

We would expect projects to be able to demonstrate how they are able to encourage disadvantaged 17–24 year olds to become involved in regular sport and physical activities, or increase/sustain their participation levels.

Projects can apply for a minimum grant of £50,000 and a maximum of £500,000 spread over one to three years. However, applicants looking for more than £200,000 must contact the Enquiries and Information team to discuss this before they apply.

We invite applications from the following types of organisations:

- Voluntary/community groups;
- Registered charities;
- Sports clubs;
- Statutory bodies;
- Limited companies;
- Private sector organisations;
- Educational and training institutions/establishments;
- National bodies with a focus on sport and physical activity.

For more information and advice please contact our Enquiries and Information team on 0870 240 2391.

Community Sport: Active Lifestyles – Northern Ireland

In Northern Ireland, Active Lifestyles – valued at £2.1 million – aims to increase people's participation in physical activities.

Active Lifestyles aims to bring about the following outcomes:

- increased participation in physical activities by introducing new and creative solutions which will overcome barriers to participation in physical activities;
- increased provision of physical activities, creating new opportunities for people to get active and stay active;
- new working partnerships, and;
- new training and development opportunities for people such as coaches and voluntary workers.

Funding is available in two distinct grant sizes:

- Small grants of up to £1,000 are available to voluntary and community sector organisations to pay for local small-scale projects. You can apply for a small grant at any time up to 30 June 2006.
- Medium grants of between £6,000 and £30,000 are available to fund projects of up to two years. Applications for medium grants must be received by 31 July 2005 (for two-year projects) or 31 January 2006 (for one-year projects).

(The final deadline for the large grants programme was 28 February 2005).

Regional offices

Wales offices

2nd Floor
Ladywell House
Newtown
Powys
SY16 1JB
Tel: 01686 611700
Minicom: 01686 610205
Fax: 01686 621534
Email:
enquiries.wales@biglotteryfund.org.uk

6th Floor
1 Kingsway
Cardiff
CF10 3JN
Tel: 029 2067 8200
Fax: 029 2066 7275
Textphone: 0845 6021659

Scotland Office

1 Atlantic Quay
1 Robertson Way
Glasgow
G2 8JB
Tel: 0141 242 1400
Fax: 0141 242 1401
Textphone: 0141 242 1500
Email:
enquiries.scotland@biglotteryfund.org.uk

Northern Ireland

1 Cromac Quay
Cromac Wood
Belfast
BT7 2LB
Tel: 028 9055 1455
Minicom: 028 9055 1431
Fax: 028 9055 1444
Email:
enquiries.ni@biglotteryfund.org.uk

Strategic Grants Office – England

1st Floor
Chiltern House
St Nicholas Court
25–27 Castlegate
Nottingham
NG1 7AR
Tel: 0115 934 2950
Minicom: 0115 934 2951
Fax: 0115 934 2952
Email:
strategicgrants@biglotteryfund.org.uk

England regional offices

North East

6th Floor
Baron House
4 Neville Street
Newcastle upon Tyne
NE1 5NL
Tel: 0191 255 1100
Minicom: 0181 233 2099
Fax: 0191 233 2099
Email:
enquiries.ne@biglotteryfund.org.uk

North West

Ground Floor
Dallam Court
Dallam Lane
Warrington
WA2 7LU
Tel: 01925 626800
Minicom: 01925 231241
Fax: 01925 234041
Email:
enquiries.nw@biglotteryfund.org.uk

Yorkshire and the Humber

3rd floor
Carlton Tower
34 St Paul's Street
Leeds
LS1 2AT
Tel: 0113 224 5301
Minicom: 0113 245 4104
Fax: 0113 244 0363
Email:
enquiries.yh@biglotteryfund.org.uk

East Midlands

Lower Ground Floor
Chiltern House
St Nicholas Court
25–27 Castlegate
Nottingham
NG1 7AR
Tel: 0115 934 9300
Minicom: 0115 948 4436
Fax: 0115 948 4435
Email:
enquiries.em@biglotteryfund.org.uk

West Midlands

8th Floor
Edmund House
12–22 Newhall Street
Birmingham
B3 3NL
Tel: 0121 200 3500
Minicom: 0121 212 3523
Fax: 0121 212 3081
Email:
enquiries.wm@biglotteryfund.org.uk

Eastern

2nd Floor
Elizabeth House
1 High Street
Chesterton
Cambridge
CB4 1YW
Tel: 01223 449000
Minicom: 01223 352041
Fax: 01223 312628
Email:
enquiries.ea@biglotteryfund.org.uk

London

Camelford House
89 Albert Embankment
London
SE1 7UF
Tel: 020 7587 6600
Minicom: 020 7587 6620
Fax: 020 7587 6610
Email:
enquiries.lon@biglotteryfund.org.uk

South East

3rd Floor
Dominion House
Woodbridge Road
Guildford
Surrey
GU1 4BN
Tel: 01483 462900
Minicom: 01483 568764
Fax: 01483 569764
Email:
enquiries.se@biglotteryfund.org.uk

South West

Beaufort House
51 New North Road
Exeter
EX4 4EQ
Tel: 01392 849700
Minicom: 01392 490633
Fax: 01392 491134
Email:
enquiries.sw@biglotteryfund.org.uk

Applications

All application forms and guidance are available via the website or by calling 08454 102030.

Percy Bilton Charity

Disabled, disadvantaged youth, older people

£580,000 to organisations (2002/03)
Beneficial area UK.

Bilton House, 7 Culmington Road, Ealing, London W13 9NB

Tel. 020 8579 2829 **Fax** 020 8567 3650

Correspondent Wendy Fuller, Administrator

Trustees *W J D Moberly, chair; M A Bilton; J R Lee; W J Uzielli; S J Paciorek.*

Charity Commission no. 1094720

Information available Excellent annual report and accounts. Guidance notes for applicants, largely reprinted below.

Summary

Main grants are normally for building projects or for items of capital expenditure (though not for office equipment or furniture). They range from £2,000 up to a usual maximum, recently reduced, of £10,000 and are made to organisations working with:

- older people
- children or adults with learning or physical disabilities or learning difficulties
- children or young people who are socially or educationally disadvantaged or underprivileged

There is also a small grants programme that provides funding of up to £500 for small charities working with people who are disabled, older people and young people for furniture and equipment.

General

The annual report for 2002/03 gives the following review of activities during the year:

The charity's funding priorities were to support projects to provide day centres, care homes, sheltered accommodation or independent living schemes for older people and those with physical or learning disabilities or enduring mental health problems as well as the provision of educational and recreational facilities or supported living schemes for disadvantaged young people.

The charity ran two programmes for organisations, a main grants programme for donations over £2,000 and a small grants programme of up to £500 aimed at helping smaller organisations with immediate funding for equipment and furniture. A total of £580,000 (202 grants) was distributed to organisations under both programmes during the year. (£580,000 – 205 grants in 2001/02.)

Under the main grants programme, we supported both larger national charities whose work has recognised long term and widespread benefits as well as smaller regional specialist charities whose work has a more immediate effect. We gave grants between £5,000 and £10,000 to projects where we consider our donation could make a significant contribution. The number of deserving applications continues to exceed the funds available for distribution and we took the decision to help as many organisations as we consider practicable without substantially reducing the size of the average grant.

[...] we supported organisations throughtout the UK. Although London and the South East have received most funding, this is largely due to the greater number of applications from these areas. We assess all projects according to merit, considering their benefit to the end user and the feasibility of the scheme.

We continued visits to organisations to monitor the use of grants paid and evaluate the benefits and results achieved by the donations. This helped us also to understand the needs of such organisations and to analyse future applications (including those from other similar charities) in the light of information gained in discussions during such visits. It is also our practice to obtain written reports from organisations upon the completion of projects

To achieve fair distribution of funds, it remained one of our conditions that an organisation that received funding may not re-apply for a further grant within 12 months of receiving the first grant. Many applicants return for funding when this condition is satisfied and while it remains our policy to make single rather than continuing grants, we have assisted many eligible organisations with a number of grants over a period of years.

Guidelines for applicants

The trust states that applicants are welcome to contact the trust office for advice and guidance at any stage of the application process, by telephone or in writing.

We have two programmes for organisations:
- Large grants – one-off payments for capital expenditure of £2,000 and over: i.e. furniture and equipment; building/refurbishment projects. Please note that we do not fund running costs.
- Small grants – donations of up to £500 towards furnishings and equipment for small projects. This programme is more suitable for smaller organisations.

Amount of grant

The amount offered will usually depend on the number of applications received in relation to the funds available for distribution. You may therefore not receive the full amount requested.

Major appeals

In the case of major appeals please apply after 75% of the funding has been secured, as offers are conditional upon the balance being raised and the project completed within one year. We also require grants to be taken up within 12 months of the offer and you may wish to ascertain that your project is likely to be completed within this time scale before applying.

What the charity will fund

The charity will consider projects and schemes with any of the following primary objectives:

1. Disadvantaged/underprivileged young people (under 25)
- to assist with and alleviate problems facing young people who are educationally or socially underprivileged, disadvantaged or marginalised
- to encourage young people into education, training, supported living and employment away from crime, substance misuse and alcohol dependence, homelessness and unemployment
- to provide facilities for recreational activities and outdoor pursuits for young people who are educationallly or socially underprivileged or disadvantaged.

2. People with disabilities (physical or learning disabilities or mental health problems)
- to provide suitable facilities for residential, respite care, occupational and recreational establishments for children, young people and adults with physical or learning disabilities or enduring mental health problems
- to encourage those with the above disabilities to gain a greater degree of independence.

3. Older people (over 60)
- to provide day centres, nursing and residential homes, sheltered accommodation and respite care for the frail or sufferers from dementia or age related disorders
- to alleviate poverty and hardship, relief of isolation and loneliness among older people;
- to assist older people to maintain independent or supported living.

Grants in 2002/03

During the year the trust categorised its grants over £2,000 as follows:

Disabled – General	£161,000
Disabled – Youth	£134,000
Older People	£132,000
Disadvantaged Youth	£109,000

The following geographical breakdown of grants over £2,000 was also provided, but note that the apparent bias towards London and the South East is due to the lack of suitable applications from elsewhere, as noted above:

	No. of grants	Amount
London	19	£127,000
South East	20	£114,000
North East	12	£78,000
Midlands	13	£57,000
South West	12	£51,000
Scotland	8	£46,000
North West	9	£43,000
Wales	2	£15,000
East Anglia	1	£5,000
Northern Ireland	0	£0

Disabled – General

The largest grant in this category, and overall, was £17,500 to Butterwick Hospice – Stockton-on-Tees towards building work to convert a four-bedded ward into four single bedrooms at the hospice for adults with life-threatening illnesses.

Other beneficiaries in this category included: Society of St James – Southampton towards the purchase of property to accommodate seven people at any one time who are homeless (£10,000); Multiple Sclerosis Society – London for computers and telephone equipment for the Home Network Programme, to enable volunteers, all with multiple sclerosis to answer telephone calls to the MS helpline from their own homes (£9,000); Deafblind UK – Peterborough towards the construction of a National Centre for Deafblindness (£8,000); Rehab Scotland – Glasgow for computer equipment for the rehabilitation programme at the Spinal Injuries Unit of Southern General Hospital in Glasgow (£5,000); and Haven Banks Outdoor Education Trust – Exeter to purchase a safety boat to provide rescue cover for sailing activities on the Exe estuary for people with disabilities (£2,000).

Disabled – Youth

The largest grants were £10,000 each to the Elizabeth Foundation – Hampshire towards the conversion works at Ashtons in Hertfordshire, a family centre for pre-school deaf children and their parents, and Resources for Autism – London to refurbish the multi-sensory room within a new national resource centre for autistic children and their families.

Other beneficiaries included: Outlook Trust – West Yorkshire for an inflatable safety boat to provide rescue cover for boating activities with visually impaired people (£8,500); CASE Training Centre – Hull to refurbish the kitchen at the training centre which runs vocational and life-skills courses for young people with learning disabilities (£7,000); Springhead School towards an outdoor play area and sensory garden (£5,000); and Robert Owen Communities – Cornwall for animal handling equipment for Boscawen Farm, a new project providing livestock and agriculture based day services for young people with learning disabilities (£3,000).

Older People

The largest grant of £11,000 was made to Acredale House – Bathgate, Scotland to refurbish the kitchen of this day centre for older people including those suffering from dementia.

Several branches of Age Concern, including those in Edinburgh and Leigh, Kingsbridge, Kingstanding, Knaresborough, Pembrokeshire, St Helen's and Warwickshire, also benefitted from grants ranging from £4,000 to £10,000. The purpose of the grants included the purchase of a minibus, new building construction, refurbishments, kitchen and dining facilities and IT equipment.

Other beneficiaries included: Sudbury Neighbourhood Centre – Middlesex towards the refurbishment and extension of the centre, which provides day care for older people, especially those who are frail, housebound or disabled (£8,500); Hartlepool Alzheimer's Disease Trust towards furnishings and equipment for Marleborough House, a new day care facility in Seaham for older people with dementia (£5,000); and Abbeyfield North Downs Extra Care Society – Surrey for laundry equipment for David Gresham House (£3,000).

Disadvantaged Youth

The largest grants were £10,000 each to City Roads – London for the refurbishment of 352 City Road to provide additional short-stay accommodation for young drug users in crisis, and New Dragon Centre – Middlesex towards building works and fittings for the centre offering activities to disadvantaged young people in Hounslow.

Other beneficiaries included: Noah's Ark Children's Venture – Gloucestershire for building and refurbishment work at Bazley House (£7,000); Punch and Judy Family Centre – London for the refurbishment of new premises to provide more room for the work in Earls Court with disadvantaged young children, particularly from homeless and refugee families (£5,000); Manchester YMCA for IT equipment for an internet cafe to improve computer skills for disadvantaged young people who have been excluded from school as a result of behavioural problems (£4,000); and Emmaus Project – Hampshire for the installation of 6 new windows to replace old ones at the hostel for young people.

Exclusions

The charity will not consider the following (the list is not exhaustive):

- running expenses for the organisation or individual projects;
- salaries, training costs or office equipment/furniture;
- consumables (e.g. stationery, food and drink);
- publication costs (e.g. printing/distributing promotional information leaflets;
- projects for general community use even if facilities for the disabled are included;
- projects that have been completed;
- items that have already been purchased;
- provision of disabled facilities in schemes mainly for the able-bodied;
- general funding/circular appeals;
- play schemes/summer schemes;
- holidays or expeditions for individuals or groups;
- trips, activities or events;
- community centres or village halls for wider community use;
- community sports/play area facilities;
- pre-schools or playgroups (other than predominantly for disabled children);
- refurbishment or repair of places of worship/church halls;
- research projects;
- mainstream pre-schools, schools, colleges and universities (other than special schools);
- welfare funds or other grant making bodies for further distribution;
- hospital/medical equipment;
- works to premises not used primarily by the eligible groups.

Applications

If in doubt regarding the suitability of an appeal, contact the charity either in writing, giving a brief outline, or by telephone. If you have already received a grant, please allow at least one year from the date of payment before re-applying. However you can re-apply after 12 months.

How to apply for main funding

The charity does not provide application forms for grants to organisations. Please write on your organisation's headed note paper incorporating the following information in your appeal (business plans should only be sent as supporting information).

Please supply the following:

- a brief history and outline of your charity;
- a description of the project and its principal aims;
- details of funding (a) for equipment appeals, provide a list of items required with costs (b) provide a budget for the project, including details of funds already raised and other sources being approached (c) state cost or costs involved for building/refurbishment projects – please itemise major items and professional fees (if any);
- building or other plans – does the project have all relevant planning consents;

- dates when construction/refurbishment is to commence and be completed;
- whether the project has ongoing revenue funding;
- plans for monitoring and evaluating the project;
- a copy of your latest annual report and accounts.

We shall respond to all applications for main funding, normally within two weeks, and let you know whether your application can be considered by the board of directors and the date of the relevant board meeting. The directors meet quarterly to consider main funding applications, normally in March, June, September and December. It may therefore take up to three months for your application to be considered. Site visits or meetings may be required for certain applications.

For a small grant (£500 or less), please supply the following:

- brief details of your organisation;
- outline of the project and its principal aims;
- cost of the item/s required;
- (if your organisation is not a registered charity please obtain): a reference from a youth organisation that you work with or from the Voluntary Service Council;
- a copy of your most recent audited accounts.

Small grants are dealt with by a committee on an ongoing basis and we aim to let you have decision within two weeks.

The Birmingham Foundation

General

£2.7 million (2002/03)

Beneficial area Greater Birmingham.

St Peter's Urban Village Trust, Bridge Road, Saltley, Birmingham B8 3TE

Tel. 0121 326 6886 **Fax** 0121 328 8575

Email team@bhamfoundation.co.uk

Website www.bhamfoundation.co.uk

Correspondent Mr Harvey Mansfield, Director

Trustees R Taylor, president; D J Bucknall, chair; P Bache; M Ames; Revd Canon D J Collyer; P Graves; G Gould; Dr J Higgins; Cllr I McArdle; J M Munn; S Saville; C Trixson; T van Beurden; T Watts.

Charity Commission no. 1048162

Information available Annual report and accounts.

To meet the needs of people living within deprived and disadvantaged areas of Greater Birmingham, the Birmingham Foundation manages funds on behalf of businesses, individuals, families, the Government and Europe.

Priorities are however given to projects that:

- reach people who are disadvantaged or isolated through poverty, disability, age or culture
- regenerate and build communities;
- are small grass-root groups struggling to access other sources of funding.

The foundation aims to build up an endowment fund by encouraging local individuals, businesses and other organisations to give donations and consequently invest in the long-term future of their local community.

Like many community foundations, it administers individual funds which enable donors to direct their contributions to specific locations and/or target groups. The foundation also distributes money from statutory sources, such as the Local Network Fund for Children and Young People and the Community Chest.

In 2002/03 the foundation gave grants totalling £2.7 million.

Please contact the foundation for further information of funds that are currently open for application.

Applications

There is an application form which is available from the foundation and can be downloaded from its website. This has been designed to enable the foundation to match each application to the most appropriate fund. There is a seperate application form for some managed funds, however.

Grants are allocated on a rolling programme and there are no deadlines for the receipt of applications.

Blatchington Court Trust

Education of people under 31 who are blind and partially sighted

£770,000 (2002/03)

Beneficial area UK, preference for Sussex.

Ridgeland House, 165 Dyke Road, Hove, East Sussex BN3 1TL

Tel. 01273 727222 **Fax** 01273 722244

Email enquiries@blatchington-court.co.uk

Website www.blatchington-court.co.uk

Correspondent Dr Geoff Lockwood, Chair

Trustees Dr Geoff Lockwood, chair; Roger Jones; Richard Martin; Lady Helen Trafford; Bruce McCleod; Colin Finnerty; Ms Georgina James; Robert Perkins; Geoff Smith.

Charity Commission no. 306350

Information available Accounts were on file at the Charity Commission.

This trust's initial income arose from the sale of the former Blatchington Court School for people who are partially sighted at Seaford. Its aim is 'the promotion of education and employment (including social and physical training) of blind and partially sighted persons under the age of 31 years'. There is a preference for Sussex.

In fulfilling its objects, the trust's aims are to:

- develop as a distinct trust with a primary role of an independent facilitator
- focus its resources on clearly defined needs and to avoid any duplication of provision
- listen to, and further the interests of, people who are visually impaired relevant to its objects
- initiate and develop working partnerships with statutory and voluntary organisations concerned with the care of the young people who are visually impaired
- provide professional specialist service to people up to 31 years who are visually impaired
- make grants in pursuance of its objectives.

In 2002/03 the trust has assets of £7.4 million and an income mainly from investments of £420,000. Grants totalled £770,000.

The trust expends approximately £106,000 per year on professional support to young people who are visually impaired and £200,000 on grants directly to young individuals who are visually impaired.

The major corporate grants in 2002/03 were £350,000 to the Agape Trust for the provision for the residential unit for the young people who are blind in Hastings, and £150,000 to Liverpool Society for the Blind for the children's facilities in its new centre of excellence. Other grants included £15,000 to the National Library for the Blind, £10,000 to National Blind Children's Society, £1,500 to University of Sussex for its V. I. Support Officer and £500 to Talking Newspapers.

Applications

In writing to the correspondent from whom individual or corporate/charity grant application forms can be obtained. Applications can be considered at any time. An application on behalf of a registered charity should include audited accounts and up-to-date information on the charity and its commitments.

The Booth Charities

Welfare, health, education, in Salford

£330,000 to organisations (2002/03)

Beneficial area Salford.

Midwood Hall, 1 Eccles Old Road, Salford, Manchester M6 7DE

Tel. 0161 736 2989 **Fax** 0161 737 4775

Correspondent Mrs L J Needham, Chief Executive

Trustees M C Mowat; R P Kershaw; E S Tudor-Evans; R J Weston; E W Hunt; R J Christmas; D J Tully; R C Rees; W T Whittle; A D Ginger.

Charity Commission no. 221800

Information available Annual report and accounts on file at the Charity Commission.

The Booth Charities are two charities supporting disadvantaged people in Salford. Together they provide a wide range of support, including pension payments to individuals and grants to local charities and facilities. A large number of grants go to organisations which have a direct connection with the charities and a substantial number of these institutions bear the Booth name.

The trust's endowment, valued at £20 million, produced an income of £977,000 in 2002/03. Grants totalled £386,000 of which £56,000 went to individuals. It categorised its grantmaking as follows, shown with examples of grants:

Relief of aged, impotent or poor – £14,000 in 6 grants

Grants were £7,800 towards residents' Christmas parties, £4,000 to Salford Social Services; £1,100 to the Church of the Ascension – Lower Broughton; £500 to Precinct Area Forum – Jubilee Party and £150 each to Holm Court Tenants Association and Malus Court Tenants Association.

Relief of distress and sickness – £64,000 in 9 grants

The largest grant was £31,000 to the Humphrey Booth Clinical Research Fellowship. Other grants included £6,500 to Wood Street Mission, £3,000 to Hope Hospital – stroke services, £2,500 to British Red Cross – Greater Manchester branch and £2,000 to Children's Hospitals' Appeals Trust and £500 to the Humphrey Booth Lecture.

Recreation and leisure – £85,000 in 9 grants

Grants of over £10,000 each were £37,000 to Salfordian Trust, £20,000 to Salford Children's Holiday Camp and £16,000 to Lledr Hall – Salford City Council Activity Centre. Other grants included £6,700 to Ordsall Park Bowling and Social Club, £2,000 to St George's Handicapped and Able Bodied Club and £400 to 319 Squadron – Salford Training Corps.

Education – £61,000 in 8 grants

Grants were £29,000 to Salford Music Bursary, £19,000 to YMCA, £8,000 to Oakwood High Youth Club, £4,500 to Salford Endeavour – Africa Mission Possible 2002, £500 to Charlestown Community Primary School and £200 to Springwood Support Group.

Other – £106,000 in 16 grants

The five grants of £10,000 or more were £21,000 to Fairbridge Charity, £20,000 to Broughton House 'Fit for the Future Appeal', £12,000 to Agunda Youth Group and £10,000 each to the Broughton Trust and Mayor of Salford Charity Appeal. Other donations included £8,600 to the Salford Foyer, £2,500 to the Gaddum Centre, £500 to Bradshaw Family Centre and £100 to Lower Kersall Morris Dance Troupe.

A total of £56,000 was distributed to individuals, mostly for pensions.

Applications

In writing to the correspondent.

Bridge House Trust

Welfare in London

£16.4 million (2003/04)

Beneficial area Greater London.

PO Box 270, Guildhall, London EC2P 2EJ

Tel. 020 7332 3710 **Fax** 020 7332 3720

Minicom 020 7332 3151

Email bridgehousetrust@corpoflondon. gov.uk

Website www.bridgehousetrust.org.uk

Correspondent Clare Thomas, Chief Grants Officer

Trustees *The Corporation of the City of London. Membership of the grants committee: Patrick Roney; Sir Alan Traill; John Bird; Michael Cassidy; Richard Scriven; Wilfred Archibald; William Fraser; John Barker; Joyce Nash; Barbara Newman; Anthony Eskenzi; John Holland; Jonathan Charkham; Sir Clive Martin.*

Charity Commission no. 1035628

Information available Detailed annual report, accounts and guidelines are available from the trust or from its website.

Background

The purpose of the charity was, for very many years, to maintain the bridges connecting the City of London to Southwark. It has now been enabled (and is indeed required) to put its surplus revenue to charitable purposes for the benefit of Greater London, which it has chosen to do so far by making grants to charitable organisations.

It has done so in an unusually open way, with detailed grants schemes and in meetings that are open to the public. All assessment reports on applications are also in the public domain. They are in the form of a description of the proposed work and of the organisation putting it forward, and an indication of how it relates to the published criteria of the trust, but without a systematic ranking in comparison with other applications.

In 2003/04 the trust had assets totalling £579 million and an income of £34.4 million. There were 548 grants made totalling £16.4 million.

Main Grants Scheme

New policies and guidelines were published in June 2003, and as a result the grants programme has refocused into these five broad areas:

- access for disabled people;
- London's environment;
- children and young people;
- older people in the community;
- strengthening the voluntary and community sectors.

In the Main Grants Scheme, grants are large and the success rates are high – an unusual combination. Grants, though, are not necessarily for the full amount requested. The trust attributes the success rate to its willingness to discuss applications in detail before any formal consideration, as well as to a clearly defined geographical area of benefit, detailed guidelines and clear funding priorities.

The following guidelines and information is taken from extensive information available from the trust:

The trust makes both capital and revenue grants for the benefit of people living in Greater London. Usually, revenue grants can be made for up to a maximum of three years, although following the policy review, the trust has decided that projects of an exceptional or strategic nature can apply for a further two years, making five years in total.

The trust recognises that core costs are incurred in the delivery of good services and is willing to consider supporting such costs, provided that the work supported meets the trust's stated funding criteria, is not already funded from another source and cannot reasonably be found from existing resources.

The grants committee meets ten times a year and applications are accepted throughout the year. It takes about four months from receiving your application until a final decision is reached.

Normally we would only make one grant to an organisation at a time. If you receive a grant over three years, you can re-apply for a different purpose at the end of the period of the grant, when the work has been evaluated.

In the case of a capital grant a year must have elapsed since payment so that we can sensibly monitor the use made of the grant.

There are no minimum or maximum amounts of grant that can be awarded. However, the trust is unlikely to be the biggest funder of an organisation and therefore expects applicants to demonstrate they have other revenue funding in place. Very small organisations are advised to consider the Small Grants Scheme. Applicants for over £25,000 need to be accompanied by a more detailed proposal.

Some large multi-faceted charities can be supported with up to three grants; you are advised to speak to us if you think this might apply to your organisation.

Access for disabled people

Aims

We aim to reduce disadvantage experienced by disabled people of all ages by removing the barriers that prevent them from participating in society and by promoting a more inclusive society. Our definition of disability is that contained in the Disability Discrimination Act.

Objectives

- to increase disabled people's independence
- to increase disabled people's participation in society
- to improve disabled people's access to services
- to enable disabled people to access their rights and entitlements

Priorities

Access to transport:

- work which supports community transport schemes
- work which demonstrates maximum or shared usage of vehicles
- work which improves transport services through better co-ordination
- work which hires accessible transport from an appropriate source

When the request is for vehicle purchase, groups need to demonstrate:

- appropriate garaging and security arrangements
- evidence of planning for insurance, vehicle running costs and its eventual replacement
- capacity to ensure that drivers are trained in MiDAS (Minibus Driver Awareness Scheme) and PATS (Passenger Assistant Training Scheme) as appropriate and that all health and safety requirements can be met
- that there is no existing community or specialist transport service which can provide the level and nature of the required service
- that consideration is given to making the vehicle environmentally friendly e.g. using LPG or alternative fuel.

Access to buildings:

[This part of the programme was suspended at the time of writing – contact the trust or visit its website for up-to-date information.]

Exclusions

Not included is access to buildings that are principally used to deliver statutory services; churches and other religious bodies where the main activity is religious service, and large, national public buildings such as museums, galleries and arts venues. However, local and community resources and ancillary buildings to religious establishments offering community, non-denominational activity can be supported.
Access to opportunities:

- work which provides advice, information and advocacy support
- work which provides training for independent living
- work which prepares disabled people for employment
- work which offers arts, sports and leisure activities
- work which improves communication facilities, especially at a strategic level.

Principles of good practice

- involving disabled people in the planning, delivery and management of services
- collaborative working and sharing of best practice
- valuing diversity.

Exclusions

The trust is unlikely to fund employment projects that are able to attract significant funds from statutory sources.

Grants in 2004

Grants in this category included those to Rich Mix Cultural Foundation (£200,000), Young Vic Theatre Company (£150,000), English National Opera (£100,000), Kingston United Reform Church (£80,000), Good Shepherd Mission (£60,000) and Bromley Association for People with Disabilities (£30,000).

London's environment

Aims

We aim to maintain and improve the quality of London's environment and its sustainable development.

Objectives

- to increase Londoners' knowledge and appreciation of their local and global environment
- to improve the quality of the natural environment and encourage a healthy living environment
- to maintain London's biodiversity
- to broaden community involvement in improving London's environment.

Priorities

- work which delivers environmental education programmes
- work which increases Londoners' appreciation of the natural environment
- work which enhances London's natural environment and its biodiversity
- work which encourages waste minimisation, recycling and the efficient use of natural resources
- work which raises awareness of personal responsibilities around issues such as litter, rubbish dumping and domestic or office practices

- involves local people in the enhancement, management and sustainable development of their local environment.

Principles of good practice

- impacting positively on Londoners' quality of life and having indicators to demonstrate this
- contributing towards London's sustainable development
- involving people from marginalised and black minority ethnic communities
- promoting environment justice, so that all communities can have a good quality living environment
- collaborative working and sharing of best practice.

Exclusions

- animal welfare
- the capital or running costs of publicly-owned parks and open spaces (although we can fund community involvement schemes)
- education work which is clearly part of the core curriculum
- the repair, renovation or conservation of historic buildings
- general improvements to the built environment.

Grants in 2004

Grants included those to Forum for the Future (London Sustainability Exchange) (£300,000), Global Action Plan (£120,000), London Wildlife Trust (£93,000), Abney Park Cemetery Trust (£86,000), Paddington Farm Trust (£45,000), Thames Explorer Trust (£35,000) and Bexley Trust for Adult Students (£16,000).

Children and young people

Aims

We aim to redress imbalances in opportunities caused by poverty, disadvantage or circumstance and to encourage young people to fully participate in society.

Objectives

- to reduce the effects of poverty on young people
- to enable young people to make informed life choices
- to support parents, carers and families
- to support young people in crisis
- to break down barriers to opportunities for young people.

Priorities

Preventative work:

- work which reduces violence and the use of weapons amongst young people
- work which supports integration and better understanding between disabled and non-disabled children

- work that breaks cycles of abuse, violence, crime and discrimination against children and young people
- work that reduces conflict arising from cultural, economic or religious divides.

Enabling young people to realise their potential:

- work which enables young people to become active in their communities (e.g. inter-generational work or volunteering)
- work which enables them to support and help other young people (e.g. mentoring or peer-support)
- work which develops parenting and relationship skills (particularly amongst young men).

Helping young people in crisis:

- work which tackles substance misuse (e.g. drugs, alcohol or cigarettes)
- work which supports young carers
- work which provides support for young homeless people
- work which addresses depression and self-harm amongst young people
- work which supports young people as victims of crime.

Principles of good practice

- involving young people in the planning and delivery of services
- collaborative work and sharing of good practice
- valuing diversity.

Exclusions

- general under 5s, play or youth provision
- playschemes
- after-school clubs
- curricular activities.

Grants in 2004

Grants included those to Childline (£450,000), Home-Start UK (£127,000), YMCA Maze Marigold Project (£90,000), Kings Cross Homelessness Project (£70,000), Post-Adoption Centre (£52,000), Kids Club Network (£40,000), Tech4all Limited (£30,000) and Tower Hamlets Parents Centre (£15,000).

Older people in the community (those aged 60 or over)

Aims

We aim to improve the quality of life for older Londoners, particularly those disadvantaged by ill health or poverty and to enable older peole to take a full and active part in society.

Objectives

- to tackle poverty and the effects of poverty on older people
- to encourage health and fitness among older people

- to enable older people to make informed life choices
- to increase volunteering opportunities for older people
- to break down barriers which isolate older people from each other and from their communities.

Priorities

Active ageing:

- work which engages older people in volunteering
- maintains or improves health and fitness
- tackles poverty among older people, particularly through benefits and housing advice
- provides cultural, educational and social stimulus.

Reducing isolation:

- work which provides older people with advice, information and advocacy
- undertakes outreach to isolated older people
- tackles isolation by means of providing transport
- provides social and leisure opportunities.

Enriching life in residential care:

- work which enables those in residential care to participate in the wider community
- provides those in residential care with creative opportunities and social stimulus
- advocates for the improved standards of residential care, particularly for marginalised groups.

Principles of good practice

- involving older people in the planning and management of services
- respecting privacy and dignity
- valuing diversity
- the safety of older people who use services
- collaborative working and sharing of best practice.

Exclusions

- the capital or revenue costs of sheltered housing or residential care.

Grants in 2004

Grants included those to Age Concern London (£150,000), Shelter (£132,000), Harris Hospice Care (£100,000), St John's Palliative Care Centre (£77,000), Building Exploratory (£49,000), Cranford Good Neighbours Scheme (£30,000), 999 Club Trust (£20,000), Parkside Project (£10,000) and Theatro Technis (£5,000).

Strengthening the voluntary and community sectors

Aims

We aim to strengthen the voluntary and community sectors so that they can deliver effective, efficient and sustainable services helping reduce disadvantage.

Objectives

- to support second tier or membership organisation in the provision of services that strengthen voluntary organisations and help them to improve their organisational effectiveness
- to support second tier or membership organisations in helping volunteer-involving organisations improve their policies and practices in working with volunteers
- to support second tier or membership organisations in helping the voluntary sector to become more sustainable.

Priorities

Governance and accountability:

- work which improves the recruitment, induction, retention and diversity of trustees
- helps develop quality standards in the sector.

Resourcing the voluntary and community sectors:

- work which helps groups become financially more sustainable through funding advice
- supports groups in evaluating the impact of their work and its reporting
- develops new ways of resourcing voluntary and community groups (e.g. social enterprise, social venture capitalism, the development of asset bases and other alternatives to grant aid dependency)
- supports the ICT needs of the sector as a whole
- further collaboration and the sharing of facilities and resources
- supporting the black and minority ethnic voluntary sector.

Developing active communities:

- work which builds active communities and engages people in civil society through volunteering and active citizenship.

Development agencies:

- work which strengthens small groups
- work which delivers community accounting services.

Principles of good practice

- collaborative work and sharing of best practice
- involving users in the planning and management of services
- valuing diversity
- supporting and valuing volunteers.

Exclusions

- second tier or membership organisations providing training not related to organisational development
- groups applying for help with ICT solely benefiting their own organisation.

Grants in 2004

Grants included those to Women's Resource Centre (£122,000), Resource Information Service (£103,000), London Play (£93,000), Charities Evaluation Service (£75,000), Homeless Link (£60,000), School for Social Entrepreneurs (£56,000), Deptford Youth Forum (£30,000), Peel Institute (£22,000) and Volunteers Greenwich (£10,000).

Exceptional grants

Occasionally the trust will make grants outside the five priority areas. Applications will be considered from organisations which show that they are one of the following:

- demonstrably hard to fund
- have an innovative project
- responding to new needs or circumstances which may have arisen since the trust fixed its five priority areas (for example, a major catastrophe impacting on London)
- requiring short-term assistance to cope with unforeseen circumstances enabling them to change and move forward (however, need arising from poor planning will not be considered).

The trust states that only a small number of grants are likely to be made in this category.

In 2004 there were two grants made to Maytree Respite Centre (£100,000) and Sheriff's & Recorder's Fund (£30,000).

Small Grant Scheme

We aim to assist small voluntary and community organisations in order to strengthen their services and so improve the quality of life for Londoners.

The small grants scheme for 2003 onwards has been revised as part of the trust's recent policy review. Unlike the pilot scheme, the revised scheme is open to the whole of Greater London and there are no closing dates (applications will be processed within four months of receipt).

There are five priority areas for the small grants scheme:

- older people
- children and young people
- disabled people
- the environment
- community activity.

To be eligible for a small grant, your organisation needs to:

- be a suitably constituted voluntary organisation
- be undertaking charitable activity
- have a bank or a building society account
- have an annual income of under £50,000
- be doing work that benefits Londoners.

In 2003 grants included those to Amphitheatre of the Arts – Haringey (£5,000), Bethany Neighbourhood Link (£4,000), African Women Connexion (£3,000), Community Centre for Skills Development & People in Need (£1,500) and Brentford Lodge League of Friends (£500).

Comment

The experience of this fund shows that the assessment and award of grants can perfectly well take place in the public eye – all its grant meetings are open to everyone and any applicant organisations can ask to see their assessment report (or, within reason, those on the applications of others). Other trusts, especially those distributing money collected from the public, could well copy this admirable practice.

The annual report for 2002/03 shows 12 men and only two women on the grants committee. For any public body, but especially for one setting out to help those in need or suffering from disadvantage, this seems wholly inappropriate. However the structure of the fund makes this an issue that is particularly hard to address.

So far, the trust has seemed, to an outside reader of its reports, to be a primarily reactive organisation. In practice, it sees itself as a highly involved and responsive grantmaker, making many grants in response to extensive discussions with the organisations concerned and it has taken an active part in a number of policy initiatives.

On a particular issue, Bridge House appears from its guidelines and reports to make many grants to help with the running costs of service delivering charities, without making it clear what is expected to happen at the end of this period. In practice, the fund notes that issues of sustainability play a big though as yet unadvertised part in its assessment procedures.

Exclusions

The trust cannot fund:

- political parties;
- political lobbying;
- non-charitable activities;
- statutory or corporate bodies where the body involved is under a statutory or legal duty to incur the expenditure in question;
- grants which do not benefit the inhabitants of Greater London.

The trust does not fund:

- individuals;

- grantmaking bodies to make grants on its behalf;
- schools, universities or other educational establishments;
- other statutory bodies;
- medical or academic research;
- churches or other religious bodies where the monies will be used for the construction, maintenance and repair of religious buildings and for other religious buildings and for other religious purposes;
- hospitals.

Grants will not usually be given to:

- organisations seeking funding to replace cuts by statutory authorities;
- organisations seeking funding to top up on underpriced contracts.

Applications

There is a detailed eight-page application form, available from the trust or downloadable from its website. It includes a one-page summary which will be seen by members of the grants committee.

'If you need someone to talk to about your application, please get in touch with the Grants Unit. We will be happy to talk to you.'

For general enquiries and the Main Grants programme: 020 7332 3710

For the Small Grants programme: 020 7332 3705

British Record Industry Trust

Musical education

£570,000 (2003)
Beneficial area UK.

BPI, Riverside Building, County Hall, Westminister Bridge Road, London SE1 7JA
Tel. 020 7803 1302 **Fax** 020 7803 1310
Email brittrust@bpi.co.uk
Website www.brittrust.co.uk
Correspondent Maggie Crowe, Administrator
Trustees Sam Alder; Paul Burger; Greg Castell; Andrew Cleary; John Craig; Rob Dickins; Lucian Grainge; Peter Jamieson; Rupert Perry; Andrew Yeates.
Charity Commission no. 1000413
Information available Information was provided by the trust.

The trust was established in 1989 and is entirely funded by contributions from the music industry and related organisations in the UK. Its mission is 'to encourage young people in the exploration and pursuit of educational, cultural or therapeutic benefits emanating from music'.

In 2003 it had an income of £722,000, mainly from BRIT Awards Limited and Music Industry Trusts Limited, the principal funders of the trust. Several of the trustees are directors of these organisations, and several are also directors of organisations which received large grants. Grants during the year totalled around £570,000.

The two main beneficiaries of the trust each year are Brit School for the Performing Arts & Technology and Nordoff-Robbins Music Therapy, which receive about 80% of the grant total.

The trust also makes grants to several smaller trusts each year, some of which receive on-going support. Previously beneficiaries have included Drugscope, BRIT School Bursary, Heathfield Community College, Community Music East, British Performing Arts Medicine Trust, Black Arts Alliance, Irene Taylor Trust and Lenton Community Association.

In relation to new grants, the trust states that:

Each proposal must be relevant to the mission statement and requests are considered up to £5,000. The trust is limited to the amount of resources it can offer but endeavours to make its donations to those charities who may not be eagerly considered by the bigger music-related trusts.

Exclusions

No bursaries or grants to individuals. No capital funding projects are considered. Only registered charities are supported.

Applications

On an application form available from the correspondent or via the trust's website. Applications which match the trust's mission statement are welcomed.

The Britten-Pears Foundation

Arts, particularly music by living composers, Britten and Pears, education, the environment and humanitarian causes

£306,000 (2002/03)
Beneficial area UK, with a preference for East Anglia.

The Red House, Golf Lane, Aldeburgh, Suffolk IP15 5PZ
Tel. 01728 452615 **Fax** 01728 453076
Website www.britten-pears.co.uk
Correspondent The Trustees
Trustees Sir Robert Carnwath, chair; Dr Colin Matthews; Noel Periton; Hugh Cobbe; Peter Carter; Michael Berkeley; Mark Fisher; Stephen Oliver; Janis Susskind; John Evans.
Charity Commission no. 295595
Information available Information was provided by the foundation.

The foundation was set up 'to promote public knowledge and appreciation of the musical works and writings of Benjamin Britten and Peter Pears and the tradition and principles of musical education and performance developed by them.' It aims to promote the arts in general, particularly music, by way of grants to other charities or those whose objects are of charitable intent, for commissions, live performances and, occasionally, recordings and innovatory musical education projects. It also makes grants to educational, environmental and peace organisations. Grants normally range from £100 to £2,000.

The foundation owns and finances the Britten-Pears Library at Aldeburgh, and supports the Britten-Pears Young Artist Programme at Snape and the annual Aldeburgh Festivals in June and the autumn. Its annual income largely derives from the royalties from the performance worldwide of the works of Benjamin Britten, and is channelled to the foundation through its trading subsidiary, the Britten Estate Ltd, by Gift Aid.

In 2002/03 it had assets of £13 million (including property and manuscripts) and an income of £1.3 million. Grants were made totalling £306,000.

During the year the foundation made grants to Aldeburgh Productions totalling £205,000, regular annual grants of £34,000 and some 103 other grants amounting to £42,000. These figures exclude grants and expenditure on special projects totalling £26,000.

Exclusions

No grants for: general charitable projects; general support for festivals other than Aldeburgh; requests from individuals for bursaries and course grants other than for the Britten-Pears Young Artist Programme; travel costs; or purchase or restoration of musical instruments or equipment, and of buildings other than at Snape Maltings/ Aldeburgh.

The foundation does not consider applications for support for performances or recordings of the works of Benjamin Britten, of whose estate it is the beneficiary. Subsidy for works by Britten which, in the estate's view, need further promotion, can be sought from The Britten Estate Ltd, which is a subsidiary trading company.

Applications

In writing to the correspondent. Trustees meet in January, May and October. Applications should be sent for consideration by the middle of the preceding month. Five copies of any application should be sent.

The Bromley Trust

Human rights, prison reform, conservation

Around £300,000 (2004/05)
Beneficial area Worldwide.

5 Cressy Road, Hannibal Road, Stepney Green, London E1 3JE
Tel. 020 7790 1681
Email teresaelwes@thebromleytrust.org.uk
Website www.thebromleytrust.org.uk
Correspondent Teresa Elwes, Grants Executive
Trustees Anne Lady Prance, chair; Anna Home; Peter Edwards; Ann Lady Wood;

Anthony Roberts; Michael Ingall; Bryan Blamey.
Charity Commission no. 801875
Information available Information is available on the trust's website.

Established in 1989, the trust supports organisations in the fields of human rights, prison reform and conservation/ sustainability. The aims and objects of the trust, and the type of organisations it supports, are as follows:

Human rights

Charities campaigning for human rights under the Universal Declaration for Human Rights and those working to abate the consequence of the acute violation of these rights. These include charities working with individuals and communities that have experienced genocide, torture, rape, false imprisonment, oppression and abuse.

Prison reform

We are committed to the reduction of overcrowding in British prisons through the reduction of re-offending. We support both campaigning charities and service providers, particularly supporting charities that aim to reduce the cycle of re-offending by the furtherance of education and skill training helping the offender to engage more successfully in society on release.

Conservation and sustainability

The trust makes grants to charities involved in conservation with a particular focus on the preservation of the rainforests. We support charities that work in tandem with the rights of indigenous people whose way of life the trust seeks to protect. For the next 3 years the Bromley Trust has chosen the Mata Atlantica (Atlantic Rainforest) as a particular area of interest. The trust also supports charities in the UK that promote sustainability and help develop responsible knowledge and use of the world's resources.

Guidelines
- we only make grants to charities that fall within the remit outlined above;
- we support both campaigning organisations and service providers;
- we will support charities that we believe have merit even if they are unproven;
- we take advice from specialists in our fields of interest;
- we like to support smaller charities engaged in innovative work and filling a gap identified through experience in the field;
- we tend to give unrestricted grants though occasionally we will restrict the grant to a particular area of work or project;
- we are happy to join with other grant making foundations to support a particular initiative;
- grants are made bi-annually. We tend to make a grant for a period of two or three years but very occasionally a one-off grant may be made;
- the expedient use of funds is an important criterion in assessing all applications;
- we encourage charities to network with others working in the same field, in order to complement their work rather than see them as competitors for funds.

The trust's website contains full information on recent grants to organisations, many of which are supported on a regular basis.

Grants in 2004/05
Human rights

Redress (£20,000), Section of Trauma Studies of the Institute of Psychiatry – King's College London (£16,000), Amnesty International UK Section Charitable Trust, Anti-Slavery International and Survival International (£15,000 each), Detention Advice Service, Asylum Aid, Fair Trials Abroad and WomanKind Worldwide (£10,000 each) and Writers and Scholars Educational Trust – Index on Censorship Magazine (£5,000).

Prison reform

Hardman Trust, C-Far, Prison Reform Trust and Prisoners Education Trust (£10,000 each), Fine Cell Work and Koestler Award Trust (£5,000 each) and the Butler Trust (£3,000).

Conservation and sustainability

Durrell Wildlife Conservation Trust, Rio Atlantic Forest Trust (RAFT) and World Pheasant Association (£10,000 each), Tree Aid, Butterfly Conservation and Marine Conservation Society (£5,000 each) and Birdlife International (£3,000).

By far the greater part of the income goes to charities that are concerned with human rights; a comparatively small proportion is given to charities concerned with prison reform and the preservation of the world environment, although this may shift in the future. In general, conservation interests are limited to the preservation of rainforests and national and international conservation issues, not local projects. The trust has also recently established the Keith Bromley Awards and chose three prison reform trusts to receive additional support. One-off grants are occasionally made, but are infrequent. The trust prefers to give larger amounts to fewer charities rather than spread its income over a large number of small grants.

Comment

This well organised and focused trust also offers other organisations with similar interests and objectives the chance to participate in a network of like-minded groups.

Exclusions

Grants are only given to UK registered charities. No grants to non-registered charities and individuals, or for expeditions or scholarships, or anything outside the stated objectives.

Applications

The trust has a questionnaire, available on its website, with which potential applicants can make an initial approach. The trustees meet twice a year in April and October; applications should be received the previous month. Urgent appeals may be dealt with at any time.

Burdens Charitable Foundation

General

£406,000 (2002/03)

Beneficial area UK, but mostly overseas, with special interest in Sub-Saharan Africa.

St George's House, 215–219 Chester Road, Manchester M15 4JE

Tel. 0161 832 4901 **Fax** 0161 835 3668

Correspondent A J Burden, Trustee

Trustees *Arthur Burden; Godfrey Burden; Hilary Perkins; Sally Schofield.*

Charity Commission no. 273535

Information available Full report and accounts, with a list of the top 65 grants, were provided by the foundation.

The foundation was created in 1977 by Mr and Mrs W T Burden, who endowed it with shares in the business Mr Burden had created in 1929, WTB Holdings. This is a private company which employs about 1,000 people, many of whom also own shares in the company.

The application of the foundation's priorities has recently led to funds being distributed roughly equally between the UK and overseas to less developed countries where its aims, to relieve 'human suffering, impairment and economic deprivation', are most frequently encountered. The likely effect of the foundation's planned development is that UK grants will diminish quite substantially as a proportion of the whole in order to enable more to be distributed to, for example, Sub-Saharan Africa and India.

Priorities overseas are:

- the geographical area of Sub-Saharan Africa, although consideration will be given to projects in other parts of Africa and other less developed countries
- projects involving the provision of clean water, sanitation and combating visual impairment.

Priorities in the UK are:

- small local groups rather than large national/international charities
- social outreach projects of local churches
- groups where volunteers play a key role in the service delivered
- low-cost umbrella agencies designed to facilitate the above.

Grants can relate to core costs, salaries, capital assets and so on without any exclusions in principle, save only that they really do make a difference. Large charities/projects and causes using professional fundraising costs to any substantial extent do not generally score particularly well.

In keeping with the present policy regarding less privileged parts of the world, this tenet also applies within the UK. For instance the trustees perceive the south of England to be economically better placed than northern Britain, and London to have a resource of charitable grant-making trusts larger per capita than elsewhere. Whilst not always readily capable of precise measurement, the trustees endeavour to assist where the need is greatest and alternative resources are the least.

In 2002/03 it had assets of £12 million and an income of £377,000. Grants were made totalling £406,000.

The 62 largest donations were listed in the accounts. Beneficiaries included Hand in Hand (£10,000), International Foundation for Dermatology and National Library for the Blind – Books Around the World (£6,000 each), Armitage School – Gambia and Busoga Trust (£5,000 each), Harvest Help and Red R (£4,000 each), Ockenden International (£3,500), Methodist Church for Human Need and Water Aid (£3,000 each), Friends of Kaur, Impact, Project Trust and Uganda Society for Disabled Children (£2,500 each) and Fulshaind Village Trust, Gambia Young Offenders Project and Tools for Solidarity (£2,000 each).

307 other grants of less than £2,000 each totalled £39,000.

Exclusions

Causes which rarely or never benefit include animal welfare (except in less developed countries), the arts and museums, political activities, most medical research, preservation etc. of historic buildings and monuments, individual educational grants and sport, except sport for people with disabilities. No grants are made to individuals.

Applications

In writing to the correspondent, accompanied by recent, audited accounts and statutory reports, coupled with at least an outline business plan where relevant. Trustees usually meet in March, June, September and December.

The Burdett Trust for Nursing

Healthcare

Between £1.3 million and £1.5 million a year (planned)

Beneficial area Mostly UK.

SG Hambros Trust Company, 41 Tower Hill, London EC3N 4SG

Tel. 020 7597 3000 **Fax** 020 7702 9263

Email administrator@ burdettnursingtrust.org.uk

Website www.burdettnursingtrust.org.uk

Correspondent The Trustees

Trustees *Alan Gibbs, chair; Jeremy Soames; Sue Norman; Prof. Mary Watkins; Victor West; R P Baker-Bates; Prof. M Watkins; M Greenwood.*

Charity Commission no. 1089849

Information available Information was provided by the trust.

The Burdett Trust For Nursing is an independent charitable trust named after Sir Henry Burdett KCB, the founder of the Royal National Pension Fund for Nurses. The trust was set up in 2001.

The trustees aim to make grants to support the nursing contribution to healthcare. They hope to encourage applications from nurses and other healthcare professionals involved in a wide range of innovative projects. It will target its grants at projects that are nurse-led, using its funds to empower nurses and make significant improvements to the patient care environment.

All applications must be focussed explicitly on improving care for patients through nursing and may include multi-professional or team-working interventions. These interventions may involve clinical care, environment of care, social care, leadership, education and research. Applications should fit into one of the following eight categories:

- the rehabilitation of patients across the spectrum of mental and physical health;
- the care of older people;
- the transference of care from hospital to the home including maintenance of people in their own homes;
- risk assessment and risk management across all areas of health care;
- public health, for example, maintaining good health and preventing ill health;
- multi-professional and cross-agency team-working particularly in relation to care of older people, rehabilitation and public health;
- the development of nurse leadership;
- nursing contribution to healthcare policy.

The trust wishes to make a difference with its grants and, with this in mind, will give priority to applications that:

- lever in other funds;
- involve partnership and co-operation between organisations where this is feasible;
- offer maximum impact for the money spent and can demonstrate that impact. (The trust is concerned that, not only is its money spent for the intended purpose, but that its impact is maximized. Applications which include details of the intended impact and the evaluation process that will be used to demonstrate that impact, will be particularly welcome.)

The trust aims to make grants that meet the needs of a range of projects. In any year the trust will make a few large grants and a number of smaller awards. Whilst there is no ceiling on the amount that can be requested, those applying for larger grants will understand that the larger the amount sought, the more difficult it will be to obtain.

Grants will normally be made on a one-off basis although applications for

funding covering more than one year, up to a maximum of three years, will be considered. These will be on the understanding that funding beyond the first year will be subject to the satisfactory completion of regular agreed reviews of targets and achievements, and that the trustees may cancel or withdraw funding at any time if the review is not satisfactory.

The trust will accept applications from registered charities and other constituted charitable organisations. The minimum requirements are a constitution, a governing body, an annual report and a bank account.

The trust will not fund individuals directly. Where grants are available to support proposals originating from individual applicants, the application requires the direct support of a host institution.

Where applications are submitted by a consortia of two or more collaborating institutions, one must act as the lead applicant. Most applicants will be based in the UK. However, the trust will consider applications that involve international collaboration or promotion of a UK nursing initiative to assist another country.

The trust plans to be able to distribute between £1.3 million and £1.5 million a year in grants. Donations in 2004 included those to: St Mark's Hospital Foundation (£835,000); Macmillan Cancer Relief (£250,000); Foundation of Nursing Studies (£210,000); King's Fund (£175,000); Florence Nightingale International Foundation (£126,000); Nurses Welfare Trust (£60,000); and Napier University (£15,000).

Exclusions

The trust will not normally make grants to:

- general appeals;
- existing posts, although the trust will consider funding new posts directly associated with a project/initiative;
- overhead costs of academic institutions or statutory agencies;
- organisations closely aligned to government departments where funding should properly be provided from statutory sources;
- holidays or outings;
- retrospective funding;
- funding in lieu of statutory funding or as a replacement when it has run out or been withdrawn;
- significant capital appeals, for example building costs, minibus appeals.

The trust is not permitted to fund political parties, political lobbying or non-charitable activities.

Applications

The application process is different for large and smaller applications. Trustees will make decisions throughout the year in relation to smaller awards (up to £10,000) and will make a series of larger grants once a year at the end of their financial year in December. Application forms can be downloaded from the trust's website along with full details of the application procedure.

The Clara E Burgess Charity

Children

About £310,000 (2002/03)

Beneficial area UK and worldwide.

The Royal Bank of Scotland plc, Trust and Estate Services, Capital House, 2 Festival Square, Edinburgh EH3 9SU

Tel. 0131 556 8555 **Fax** 0131 228 9889

Correspondent The Administrator

Trustee *The Royal Bank of Scotland plc.*

Charity Commission no. 1072546

Information available Accounts were on file at the Charity Commission.

Summary

Registered in 1998, this trust makes grants to registered charities where children are the principal beneficiaries of the work. Grants are towards 'the provision of facilities and assistance to enhance the education, health and physical well-being of children particularly (but not exclusively) those under the age of 10 years who have lost one or both parents'. Within these boundaries grants can be made to the following causes: education/training, overseas projects, disability, social welfare, hospitals/hospices, medical/health and medical research.

General

In 2002/03 the trust had an income of £332,000 and a total expenditure of £432,000. Unfortunately, no more information was available for the year. Based on the percentage of total expenditure given in previous years in grants, grants during this year are likely to have been around £310,000. The trust has previously incurred substantial 'trustees fees'.

Beneficiaries previously supported include Winston's Wish, Cheltenham & Gloucester College of Further Education, After Adoption, St Francis Children's Society, International Care & Relief, Little Haven Children's Hospice, Barnardo's Orchard Project Newcastle, NCH Action for Children, Mildmay Mission Hospital, British Agencies for Adoption and Fostering, Save the Children Fund, The Royal Schools for the Deaf – Manchester, The Rainbow Trust Children's Charity, Le Jeune Clinic, BREAK, Sierra Leone War Trust for Children, The Royal Wolverhampton School, The Orphan Foundation, Hope & Homes for Children, The Rainbow Centre, Wigan Mencap, Richard House Trust – Children's Hospice, Acorns Children's Hospice, Family Service Units, Children's Aid Direct, Relief Fund for Romania and Wirral Autistic Society.

Comment

Despite providing previous accounts and annual reports, this editor was told that no information would be provided to compile a new entry for the trust, despite the requirement to supply this information upon request.

Unfortunately, we were unable to view the most recent accounts at the Charity Commission. Despite being requested in good time, there was a failure to make the public file available to view.

Exclusions

No grants to non-registered charities.

Applications

On a form available from the correspondent. The trustees meet to consider grants in February, May, August and November and applications should be received in the month before those meetings. The trust states that applications should be as brief as possible; the trustees will ask for any further information should they require it.

The Audrey & Stanley Burton Charitable Trust

Health, arts, Jewish charities, welfare, third world

£381,000 (2002/03)

Beneficial area Unrestricted, with a strong special interest in Yorkshire, especially West Yorkshire.

Trustee Management Ltd, 19 Cookridge Street, Leeds LS2 3AG

Correspondent The Secretary

Trustees *Audrey Burton; Amanda C Burton; Philip Morris; David Solomon; Raymond Burton; J J Burton:*

Charity Commission no. 1028430

Information available Annual reports and accounts were on file at the Charity Commission.

General

'Grants are normally made to cover health, arts, education and social needs. Preference will be given to charities in Yorkshire which have a specific aim or purpose.'

The trust has only a modest endowment and is financed mainly by transfers from an associated family trust. In 2002/03 it had an income of £393,000 and made grants totalling £381,000.

Grants in 2002/03

Grants during the year were broken down as follows:

Social and Welfare – 79 grants totalling £104,000

There were 28 beneficiaries receiving £1,000 or more listed in the accounts, with grants totalling £85,000; smaller grants totalled £19,000. The largest beneficiaries were Medecines Sans Frontieres (£20,000), Children in Crisis (£10,500 in total) and Emmaus Leeds (£10,000). Other beneficiaries included Medical Foundation (£5,000), Irene Taylor Trust (£3,000), CISV International (£2,000) and AbilityNet, Big Issue Foundation, Child Achievement Awards, Fortune Centre for Riding Therapy and Starlight Children's Foundation (£1,000 each).

Jewish and Israel – 42 grants totalling £80,000

There were 15 beneficiaries receiving £1,000 or more totalling £69,000. They included United Jewish Israel Appeal (£14,000 in total), Leeds Jewish Housing Association (£10,000), British Olim Society (£8,000 in total), Jerusalem Foundation (£6,000 in total), Donisthorpe Hall (£5,000 in total), British Technion Society (£2,500) and Council of Christians & Jews, Holocaust Educational Trust and Yoni Jesner Memorial Fund (£1,000 each).

Health – 36 grants totalling £78,000

There were 20 beneficiaries of £1,000 or more, the largest of which was Alzheimer's Research Trust, which received £27,000. Other beneficiaries included National Eye Research Centre and Scope (£10,000 each), Manic Depression Fellowship (£5,000), Sense (£3,000), Mencap (£2,000) and Brain & Spine Fellowship, Lady Hoare Trust, Prostate Cancer Charity and St Michael's Hospice (£1,000 each).

Education and Arts – 24 grants totalling £64,000

Sixteen beneficiaries received grants of £1,000 or more. Beneficiaries included Harrogate Theatre (£11,000), Leeds Grand Theatre Trust (£7,500 in total), Yorkshire Arts (£5,000), Live Music Now (£3,000), Highgate Literary Scientific Institution (£2,000) and Case Training Services and Halifax Learning Zone (£1,000 each).

Third World and Overseas – 13 grants totalling £56,000

Beneficiaries receiving £1,000 or more were Oxfam (£30,000), Save the Children (£15,000 in total), Action Aid, Children's Hearts and World Vision (£2,000 each) and Alzheimer's Disease International and Anti-Slavery International (£1,000 each).

Comment

The trust would not provide a copy of its latest annual report and accounts when requested, despite its obligation to do so.

Exclusions

No grants to individuals.

Applications

In writing only to the trust. Unsuccessful applicants will not necessarily be notified.

The William A Cadbury Charitable Trust

Local welfare and disability charities, Quaker churches, penal reform, overseas

£520,000 (2003/04)

Beneficial area West Midlands, especially Birmingham; to a lesser extent, UK, Ireland and overseas.

Rokesley, University of Birmingham Selly Oak, Bristol Road, Selly Oak, Birmingham B29 6QF

Tel. 0121 472 1464 (am only)

Email info@wa-cadbury.org.uk

Website www.wa-cadbury.org.uk

Correspondent Carolyn Bettis, Trust Administrator

Trustees *Brandon Cadbury; James Taylor; Rupert Cadbury; Katherine van Hagen Cadbury; Margaret Salmon; Sarah Stafford; Adrian Thomas; John Penny; Sophy Blandy.*

Charity Commission no. 213629

Information available Information on grants and guidelines for applicants were provided by the trust.

Background

This is described by the trust as follows:

William was the second son of Richard Cadbury, who, with his younger brother George, started the manufacture of chocolate under the Cadbury name. He came from a family with strong Quaker traditions which influenced his whole life. It was this Quaker ethos which underpinned his commitment to the advancement of social welfare schemes in the City of Birmingham. William Cadbury established the Trust soon after his two years as Lord Mayor of Birmingham from 1919 to 1921, wishing to give more help to the causes in which he was interested. One such was the building of the Queen Elizabeth Hospital, a medical centre with the space and facilities to bring together the small specialised hospitals scattered throughout Birmingham.

He did much to encourage the City Library and Art Gallery and a wide circle of Midland artists who became his personal friends. Through this charity, he also secured several properties for the National Trust.

As time went on, members of his family were brought in as trustees and this practice has continued with representatives of the next two generations becoming trustees in their turn, so that all the present trustees are his direct descendants.

General

The trust gives grants in the following fields:

Birmingham and the West Midlands

- Social welfare: community and self-help groups working with the disadvantaged (including young, old, ethnic and religious minorities, women, the homeless and the disabled), counselling and mediation agencies.
- Medical and healthcare projects including medical research.
- Education and training: schools and universities, adult literacy schemes, training for employment.
- The Religious Society of Friends (Quakers).
- Places of religious worship and associated social projects.
- Conservation of the environment including the preservation of listed buildings and monuments.
- Arts: music, drama and the visual arts, museums and art galleries.
- Penal affairs: work with offenders and ex-offenders, penal reform, police projects.

International

- Social welfare, healthcare and environmental projects.
- Sustainable development.

N.B. The international grant programme has recently been refocused on a small number of organisations with which the trust has close and well established links. Ad hoc applications for this programme are unlikely to be successful.

Ireland

- Cross-community initiatives promoting peace and reconciliation.

United Kingdom

- The Religious Society of Friends (Quakers).
- Penal reform.

Grants in 2003/04

Main grants were made to 211 organisations totalling £454,000 and were categorised as follows (there were also a further 121 small grants totalling £66,000 which were not categorised):

International – General: 3 grants totalling £96,000

By far the largest grant made during the year was a £90,000 annual grant made to Concern Universal, an international development and emergency relief organisation. The two other grants were made to Responding to Conflict for on-going projects (£5,000) and an annual grant to Achimota College (£1,000).

International – Social: 31 grants totalling £61,000

Grants ranged from £300 to £5,000, with beneficiaries including: Welfare Association Rehabilitation Programme – Gaza, United Nations Children's Fund Emergency Appeal – Democratic Republic of Congo and Mines Advisory Group – Kasese, Uganda for mine risk education (£5,000 each); Liberis – Romania for children's homes (£4,000); Ockenden International – Port Sudan for a water management project (£3,000); Ashram International – India for poverty alleviation projects (£2,000); Inter Care – Cameroon & Ghana for palliative care projects, Just World Partners for an emergency appeal and Canon Collins Educational Trust for Southern Africa for the Harare Shelter (£1,000 each); and Friends of Hope – India for projects in Nilgiri and Muslim Hands – Pakistan for a girls' primary school (£500 each).

Society of Friends: 21 grants totalling £50,000

Grants ranged from £300 to £15,000, with beneficiaries including: Quaker Peace and Social Witness for vocational training in Lebanon and projects in Israel (£15,000) and an annual grant of £5,000; World Gathering of Young Friends for the world gathering in 2005 and Woodbrooke Quaker Study Centre for centenary celebrations (£3,000 each); Claridge House for running costs and Quaker Social Action for the HomeLink project (£2,000 each); Quaker Council for European Affairs for a refurbishment and repair programme and an annual grant to the West Midlands Quaker Peace Education Project (£1,000 each); Settle Friends' Meeting House for meeting house improvements (£600); and the Quaker Tapestry at Kendal (£500).

Medical and Health Care: 16 grants totalling £37,500

Beneficiaries included: Artificial Heart Fund for artificial heart operations (£10,000); Birmingham Centre for Arts Therapies towards a general appeal and DEBRA – West Midlands for the EB nursing team (£5,000 each); WISH towards a general appeal for core funding (£3,000); Haven Trust – Herefordshire for the Haven Centre (£2,000); Royal College of Radiologists Research Appeal towards research projects (£1,000); City Hospital NHS Trust for the resuscitation unit (£500); and the Light House for counselling services (£300).

Penal Affairs: 9 grants totalling £31,500

The beneficiaries in this category were: Hibiscus – Female Prisoners' Welfare Project for a project worker (£10,000); Positively Women for a Drugs and Prison project and Wakefield Prison Visits Children's Play Facilities for running costs (£5,000 each); BEAT – West Midlands for a small business adviser (£4,000); Howard League for Penal Reform annual grant, Gloucestershire Community Chaplaincy and the Prince's Trust for pre-release courses at Stoke Heath Young Offenders (£2,000 each); HALOW annual grant (£1,000); and Warwick District Citizens' Advice Bureau (£500).

Community: 26 grants totalling £31,000

Most grants in this category were for £500 or less. Beneficiaries included: Gloucestershire Domestic Violence Project towards its Family Support Project (£5,000); ReCOM towards computer refurbishment for community groups (£4,000); Birmingham Money Advice & Grants towards a trust fund for asylum seekers (£3,000); Salvation Army annual grant (£1,000); Birmingham City Mission annual grant, Arab Women's Association for their Family Resource Centre and Asian Welfare Association towards a general appeal (£500 each); Kinghurst Community Care Centre for the Care Lunch Club and Birmingham East Victim Support towards counselling costs (£300 each); and Chase Drum and Trumpet Corps towards the purchase of new drums (£100).

Disability: 18 grants totalling £26,500

There were five larger grants made to: Worcester Snoezelen towards a music studio (£9,000); Tools for Self Reliance – Milton Keynes for workshop running costs and Sense – Oldbury for the relocation of the Garden Room (£5,000 each); Birmingham Focus on Blindness towards counselling services (£2,000); and Down's Syndrome Association for an information service for pregnant

women (£1,000). Grants of less than £500 included those to the Happy Society, New Horizons Fellowship for Disabled People, Kingstanding Pathfinders and Kinmos Drop-In Centre.

The Arts: 16 grants totalling £23,000

Four larger grants were made to: Birmingham Museums and Arts Gallery for the James Watt Collection (£10,000); City of Birmingham Symphony Orchestra for the School's Roadshow Programme 2004 (£5,000); Three Choirs Festival 2003 – Hereford (£2,000); and University of Birmingham Press for the publishing costs of the Feeney Family Book (£1,000). The remaining beneficiaries received either £500 or £300 each, and included Midland Youth Orchestra, Foursight Theatre, Sound It Out Community Music, Birmingham Contemporary Music Group and Birmingham Repertory Theatre.

Homelessness: 6 grants totalling £17,000

The beneficiaries were: St Basil's – Birmingham for the Educational Development Programme (£8,000); Oxford Homeless Medical Fund towards a building extension (£5,000); Nightstop UK – Tamworth (£2,000); St Paul's Hostel for the Worcester Rough Sleepers Project (£1,000); and Space Trust – Bristol for emergency funding and Birmingham Open Christmas (£300 each).

Church – Social: 11 grants totalling £16,000

Beneficiaries included: St Mary & All Saints Parish Church – Kidderminster for the Ring for the Future Appeal (£5,000); St Andrew's Church – Presteigne, Powys for the repair of a school hall and wall monuments (£3,000); Centre for Black Theology – University of Birmingham for student bursaries (£2,000); Our Lady of the Rosary towards a new community centre (£500); and St Nicholas Church for the church tower project (£300).

Environment and Conservation: 7 grants totalling £14,500

The beneficiaries were: Churchill Forge Trust – Worcestershire for the preservation of a small workshop, Birmingham Conservation Trust for 'Back-to-Basics Houses', Birmingham Botanical Gardens & Glasshouses for various projects and the Centre for Alternative Technology – Powys for an

education programme (£3,000 each); Feedback Madagascar for a birth assistant training programme and Fenland Archaeological Trust to improve visitor information (£1,000 each); and Agroforestry Research Trust for practical research projects (£300).

Education and Training: 5 grants totalling £12,500

The main beneficiary was the Edith Cadbury Nursery School, which received £10,000 towards a refurbishment and repair programme. Other grants were made to: Saltley School – Birmingham towards achieving Specialist School Status for science (£1,000); Templars Primary School – Coventry for a Relate counselling project and Selly Oak School – Birmingham towards a Duke of Edinburgh awards scheme (£500 each); and Koco Community Nursery – Coventry for toys and play equipment (£300).

Youth: 14 grants totalling £10,000

The two main beneficiaries were: Tall Ships Youth Trust for various projects (£3,000); and Fairbridge West Midlands for support programme costs (£2,000). Other beneficiaries receiving grants of either £500 or £300 included YWCA Birmingham, Vine Trust – Walsall, Westbury and Clayton Youth Club and Birmingham Boys' and Girls Union.

Children: 11 grants totalling £9,000

The two main beneficiaries were: Birmingham Settlement Community Nursery annual grant and Pre-School Learning Alliance for play and family areas within prisons (£3,000 each). Smaller grants included those to Woodside Pre-School Group, Children's Care Campaign, Home-Start Northfield and East Birmingham Family Service Unit.

Mediation and Counselling: 6 grants totalling £7,000

The main beneficiary was Relate Birmingham, which received £5,000 for counselling services and a £500 annual grant. The remaining beneficiaries were: Worcestershire Rape & Sexual Abuse Support Centre for training costs and an annual grant to Mission to Seafarers (£500 each); and Relate Sandwell and Dudley towards a general appeal and the Well Trust towards a new counselling centre (£300 each).

Ireland: 4 grants totalling £5,000

The two main beneficiaries were: Ocean Youth Trust – Belfast for various projects and Crossroads Caring for Carers (NI) Ltd for respite support. Small grants were made to Diocese of Connor and Glenanne, Loughgilly and Mountnorris CDA.

International – Environment: 4 grants totalling £4,000

The main beneficiary was the David Shepherd Wildlife Foundation for Asian conservation awareness. Three small grants were made to: Moon Bear Rescue, Forestry Fund and Christian Ecology Link.

Care for the Elderly: 3 grants totalling £3,800

The main beneficiary was Elizabeth Dowell's Trust, which received £3,000 to upgrade bathrooms in sheltered accommodation. Two small grants were made to branches of Age Concern in Weoley Castle and Warwickshire.

Comment

This energetic trust spreads its grants more widely in its local area than most other trusts. Most trusts simply support many of the same organisations each year, but this one finds new groups and projects to support all the time – showing that it can be done.

Exclusions

The trust does not fund:

- individuals (whether for research, expeditions or educational purposes)
- projects concerned with travel, adventure, sports or recreation
- organisations which do not have UK charity registration (except those legally exempt)
- overseas charities not registered in the UK.

'The trust receives many more applications than can be supported. Even if your project meets our requirements we may not be able to help, particularly if you are located outside the West Midlands.'

Applications

Applications to the correspondent in writing, including the following information:

- charity registration number
- a description of the charity's aims and achievements
- a copy of the latest set of accounts

- an outline and budget for the project for which funding is sought
- details of funds raised and the current shortfall.

'Alternatively you may fill in and submit a copy of our online application form. Please also forward a copy of your latest set of accounts to the above address.'

Applications are considered on a continuing basis throughout the year. Small grants (amounts not exceeding £1,000) are assessed each month. Major grants are awarded at the trustees' meetings held twice annually, normally in May and November. Applicants whose appeals are to be considered at one of the meetings will be notified in advance and asked to complete an application form.

Edward Cadbury Charitable Trust

Religion, general

£606,000 (2003/04)

Beneficial area UK, mainly in the West Midlands; overseas.

Rokesley, University of Birmingham Selly Oak, Bristol Road, Selly Oak, Birmingham B29 6QF

Tel. 0121 472 1838 **Fax** 0121 472 7013

Correspondent Sue Anderson, Trust Manager

Trustees *Charles E Gillett, chair; Christopher Littleboy; Charles R Gillett; Andrew Littleboy; Nigel Cadbury.*

Charity Commission no. 227384

Information available Full accounts were provided by the trust.

The trust makes up to 100 grants a year, many of them very small. However it also gives occasional large grants, of up to £500,000 or even more. A few grants are awarded to UK groups working overseas and to overseas charities. There are virtually no grants for local charities outside the west Midlands. It describes its grantmaking policy as follows:

To support where appropriate, the interests of the founder and the particular interests of the trustees.

- The voluntary sector in the West Midlands, including Christian mission, the ecumenical movement and inter-faith relations
- The oppressed and disadvantaged in the West Midlands
- The arts and the environment

'The size of grant varies, but most are between £500 and £5,000 and are usually one-off and of a capital nature for a specific purpose or part of a project. Ongoing revenue type funding commitments are rarely considered.

'The trust is unlikely to fund projects that have popular appeal/national high profile campaigns, or to fund projects that would normally be publicly funded.

As well as its usual grantmaking, the trustees seek large projects where a significant grant can make a real impact. These grants can be very large. A single award of £500,000 was made in 2001 and one of £4 million to Selly Oak colleges in 1994.

In 2003/04 the trust had assets of £21 million which generated an income of £676,000. Grants were made to 83 organisations totalling £606,000. Those over £2,500 each were listed in the accounts and broken down as follows:

Arts and Culture	1	£250
Community projects and integration	11	£91,000
Compassionate Support	42	£117,000
Conservation and environment	12	£56,000
Ecumenical and interfaith relations	3	£11,000
Education and training	11	£296,000
Research	2	£35,000

The largest grants were £244,000 to Woodbrooke Quaker Study Society and £60,000 to Lench's Trust – Birmingham

Other large grants were: £25,000 each to DEBRA and VSO – Regional Aid Initiative in Southern Africa; £22,000 to Responding to Conflict; £15,000 each to St John's of Jerusalem Eye Hospital and St John's Parish Church – Bromsgrove for it's 'Landmark' appeal and £11,000 to Malvern Priory Organ Fund.

Grants of £10,000 each went to Elizabeth Dowell's Trust, Police Foundation – 'Response to Terrorism' project, Queen Alexandra College – Birmingham, Stonehouse Gang – Birmingham and Women in Secure Hospitals – Midlands Branch.

Other beneficiaries included: Avoncraft Museum of Historic Buildings – Bromsgrove (£7,500); University of Birmingham – 'Religious and Citizenship Education for Muslim Pupils' (£7,200); National Deaf Children's Society (£6,000); Book Aid International, Deafblind UK – West Midlands, Plantlife, Turning Point – Birmingham Drugline and Transrural Trust (£5,000 each); International Childcare Trust, Malvern Priory Organ Fund, Rubery Youth Marching Band and Samaritans – Birmingham Branch (£4,000 each); and Fairbridge and St Andrew's Ecumenical Trust (£3,000 each).

Exclusions

Grants to registered charities only. No student grants or support for individuals.

Applications

In writing to the correspondent at any time, but allow three months for a response. Appeals should clearly and concisely give relevant information concerning the project and its benefits, an outline budget and how the project is to be funded initially and in the future. Up-to-date accounts and the organisation's latest annual report are also required.

Applications that do not come within the trust's policy may not be considered or acknowledged.

The Barrow Cadbury Trust and the Barrow Cadbury Fund

Inclusive communities, offending and early intervention, global exchange

£3.3 million (2002/03)

Beneficial area Unrestricted, but mainly UK.

25–31 Tavistock Place, London WC1H 9UT

Tel. 020 7391 9220 **Fax** 020 7391 9229

Website www.barrowcadbury.org.uk

Correspondent Sukhvinder Kaur Stubbs, Director

Trustees *Anna C Southall, chair; James Cadbury; Anna Hickinbotham; Roger Hickinbotham; Richard G Cadbury; Erica R Cadbury; Ruth Cadbury; Candia Compton; Thomas Cadbury; Helen Cadbury; Nicola Cadbury.*

Charity Commission no. 226331

Information available Guidelines for applicants, excellent report and accounts and interesting newsletter 'Barrow Cadbury Trust News' all available from the trust's website.

In April 2003 it completed a review of its portfolio and announced a new set of priorities, from which funding can be awarded from April 2004 (for applications received from February 2004 onwards).

The trust has long worked in close partnership with many of the organisations that it funds; accordingly most grants are to organisations already supported and a new application may need to be developed with the trust over a considerable period. For example, of the 19 organisations receiving grants in 2000/01 under the disability programme, 14 were also supported the following year. However the amounts usually vary and the grants cannot be seen as regular payments.

Grants are usually for salary or running costs and are typically for amounts between £10,000 and £35,000, though there are still a substantial number of smaller grants of up to £3,000 each.

The trust is interested in organisations and activities which provide the opportunity for active partnership. This means that it seeks to be engaged in campaign issues rather than simply issuing grants.

Guidelines for grants from April 2004

The trust's excellent website contains the following information:

The Barrow Cadbury Trust launched its new portfolio in April. Grants from the new portfolio will be available from April 2004. Detailed guidelines on how to apply will be published on [its] website from February 2004.

How we work

We look to develop partnerships with the many projects we support and these projects must fall within our objectives of promoting a fair, just, equal and democratic society.

We support long term funding relationships with many programmes. Our priority is to fund grassroots, user-led projects, usually operating at national level. When considering funding, we will favour those projects with a high impact on social change at a policy or practice level.

We look for visionary projects, often those that are catalytic or risky and we place great emphasis on projects that are backed by strong leadership. Our grants are mainly relatively small in size, usually in the region of £10–15,000. If you meet our criteria, we work with you to build an application to present to the Trustees. In many cases, this can take 6–18 months to develop. Decisions are made three times a year, when the Trustees meet to consider applications.

Decisions on the grants made are approved by a group of Trustees, who are descendants of the founders Barrow Cadbury and Geraldine Cadbury. The Trust operates independently and is not subject to the conditions affecting statutory funders. We are not bound by the same constraints as local authority and government programmes. This allows us to be flexible to needs of projects and reduce the burdens of administration placed upon them. We are, however, accountable to our Trustees and must adhere to the strict criteria as laid out in our Trust Deeds.

The grants policy also applies to the Barrow Cadbury Fund Limited, which is a registered company and is not restricted to grant making for charitable purposes. Grants are made in the same programme areas as the trust if there are grounds for assuming that the activity would not be deemed 'charitable' in the legal sense.

In response to the changing regulatory climate for the voluntary sector and heightened expectations of what independent grant-makers can do, the Barrow Cadbury Trust has been reviewing its own programme priorities. We have turned our focus towards the towns in the north of England and worked with local groups to consider what should be the appropriate response from statutory bodies. Our Trustees are conscious that drug misuse and violence threatens many communities and we will work with others to identify new solutions.

On key issues such as the conditions facing refugees and asylum seekers, the Trust has worked with partner projects to influence public debate.

We will continue to work with our partner projects to consider how we can add value to their work. We aim to spotlight best practice and develop partnerships and networks that help increase impact and lever additional funding. In future, we will seek out projects that demonstrate best practice and emphasise innovation and community benefit. By enabling project partners to find workable solutions, we aim to share with others that priceless asset–our accumulated wisdom and experience.

Descriptions

The Trust has now concluded its series of consultations on the new portfolio of programmes. We have consolidated our funding into three new programme areas:

- Inclusive Communities: focusing on mainstreaming approaches to equality.
- Offending and Early Intervention: addressing the rights of prisoners and protecting against criminalisation.
- Global Exchange: providing an international mirror to our domestic concerns.

In due course, we also propose to establish a funding stream to provide long term core support to strategically placed projects in our principal areas of interest. In all cases, our emphasis is on supporting community based organisations as a key component of civil society. The new criteria are designed to unlock practitioner knowledge and establish a systematic approach to the sharing of good practice.

Organisations that qualify for support

Grants are usually made to registered charities although, in exceptional cases, we can consider bodies that have not yet undertaken registration or organisations involved in political campaigning that may not qualify for charity status. The Barrow Cadbury Fund Limited, which is a registered company, is not restricted to grant making for charitable purposes. The fund makes grants in the same programme areas as the Trust if there are grounds for assuming that the activity would not be deemed 'charitable' in the legal sense.

We support national projects and in exceptional cases, local groups based in the West Midlands. Projects are usually England-based. We can also support international organisations.

The trust grants are relatively small— usually in the region of £10,000-£15,000, and some are small grants under £3,000. Trustees believe that their resources should be targeted on modest projects that have the capacity to generate considerable leverage for the users involved. Small grants are prioritised for activities that are important in the long-term but require a more rapid response.

Key Features of likely funded projects

- Our priority is for groups focusing on deprived communities or those operating from a position of disadvantage
- Operates nationally
- Visionary projects that are catalytic, risky or less popular
- Groups most likely to be successful will be those that have worked to engage the trust in their activities and whose work has come to be known to and respected by the trust. Often, this is through referrals from organisations we already support or through contact in the events and activities with which the staff are involved
- Track record of strong leadership
- Willing to work in partnership with the Trust based on mutual trust, shared values and thinking on how to achieve the objectives agreed
- High impact on social change at a policy or practice level.

If your organisation meets all these criteria, you will need to consider the programme areas we support and demonstrate how your proposed activity meets objectives of either one or more of the programmes.

2002/03 Annual Report

The most up-to-date annual report for this trust refers to the trust's previous grantmaking policies. The Chair's Report gave a good description of the relationship between the old and new policies, as follows:

Our focus during the year has been on the achievements and successes of groups we have supported over the years. Best Practice Pilots in two very different programme areas (Disability and Asylum, Immigration and Resettlement) alongside consultations in our other programmes revealed a wealth of activity. Many of the projects we support work away at local level after plugging the gaps in mainstream provision or challenging prevailing attitudes and systems. In all cases, they aim to improve equality, secure social justice and strengthen democracy. But these groups often work in relative isolation. Their understanding of barriers to effective implementation of policy and the solutions they provide to ingrained social problems go unnoticed by those in positions of influence.

As a result, the trust has decided to focus its limited resources on promoting and developing good practice. A number of special initiatives are being supported to enable policy makers to draw upon the experience of those who should ultimately benefit. A prime example is the initiative arising directly from our Best Practice Pilot on Disability. Developed at the behest of a wide range of disabled-led groups, this work will bring together senior officers from across Whitehall with disabled people to explore effective ways to bolster the government commitment to independent living.

In line with this approach and based on extensive consultation, the trust also consolidated its portfolio of programmes. The seven different programmes described in this report will in future become three; *Inclusive Communities, Offending and Early Interventions and Global Exchange*. A separate programme starting in 2005/06 will look to allocate longer-term funding for projects that do not neatly fit into these categories but rely on independent 'no-strings attached' income.

Barrow Cadbury will also develop its role as a regional funder. The West Midlands remains an important area of focus for our equalities work. Northern Ireland and the Middle East continue to be prime targets for our peace work. Both the North West and the South West are key regions for many of our disability projects. In the coming year, we will also open a London office. This will be more cost-effective in working with the dispersed groups we support and the national projects, many of which are based in the capital. It will also assist in enabling us to bring this wealth of activity to the attention of the decision makers.

We are confident that this more focussed approach will ensure that our limited resources are not dissipated, and that funds are being applied to achieve maximum leverage. Inevitably this will result in some shift in priorities but the programmes will stay true to the core values of the trust which are about being a risk taker with new initiatives, finding and backing good people, encouraging partnership working and supporting projects in more ways than simply providing grants.

The new portfolio provides a fresh start, releasing valuable funds for the type of pump-priming initiatives upon which we have built our reputation as a catalyst for social change.

Anna Southall
Chairwoman

During 2002/03 the trust had assets of £45 million, which generated an income of £1.7 million. Support cost amounted to £104,000 while management and administration totalled £221,000. Grants made to 91 organisations totalled £3.3 million, creating a deficit for the year of £1.9 million. There appears to be no realistic grounds for assuming that these figures should be significantly different in the coming years.

Grants were distributed during the year as follows (please note that as these are for the previous policies and under different programmes to currently running, they are not indicative of the sort of applications likely to appeal to and impress the trustees):

Asylum, Immigration and Resettlement

32 grants in this category totalled £494,000. The largest grants were £35,000 to Joint Council for the Welfare of Immigrants for project, core and running costs, £33,000 to Widows for Sudan – Birmingham for salaries and running costs and £30,000 each to Asylum Aid – London and Birmingham Asian Resource Centre. Other beneficiaries included Refugee Council for a parliamentary liaison and advocacy service (£28,000), West Midlands Anti-Deportation Campaign for salary and running costs (£25,000), Article 19 – London for research on refugees and freedom of expression (£15,000), Greater Manchester Immigration Aid Unit for an airport immigration/refugee advice unit (£13,000), Refugee Women's Legal Aid Group – Bristol for a conference on refugee and asylum-seeking women (£10,000) and Roma Rights and Access to Justice in Europe for development funds (£3,000).

Community Organising

A total of £705,000 was given in 41 grants. Citizen Organising Foundation in London received £250,000 for running costs whilst Community Resource and Information Service – Birmingham was given £100,000, also for running costs. Other beneficiaries included Chinnbrook Child and Parents Project for core costs (£25,000), Birmingham Heathlands Solihull NHS Trust for a research study (£15,000) and Leicester Tigers for a community development programme (£5,000).

Justice and Peace

28 grants were made totalling £726,000. The largest were £105,000 to George Bell Institute – Birmingham for running costs and fellowships and £100,000 to Committee on the Administration of Justice – Northern Ireland for running costs and an endowment. Other large grants were £60,000 to University of Exeter for awards and fees, £50,000 to VSO for a South to South volunteering programme and £40,000 to Kilcranny House – Coleraine for running costs. Smaller grants included £25,000 to Trust for Early Childhood, Family and Community Education for running costs, £20,000 to Middle East Budget for travel costs, £12,000 to Aktion Suhnezeichen Friedens-dienste – Berlin for a salary and £7,000 to Dhamaverdi Institute for running costs.

Disability

Grants to 27 organisations totalled £593,000. The largest grants were £100,000 to Crisis Network – Bristol and £88,000 to Parents for Inclusion, both for running costs. Other beneficiaries included Wargrave House Ltd for a building purchase (£50,000), Bolton Action Research Institute for salaries (£30,000), Independent Panel for Special Education Advice – Woodbridge for running costs (£20,000), Shaw Trust – Towbridge for research into effectiveness of joint action planning (£15,000), Minorities of Europe – Coventry for resource materials for schools as part of the International Year of the Disabled (£13,000) and WinVisible – London for the benefits take-up campaign (£7,000).

Gender

£458,000 was given in 21 grants. By far the largest, of £70,000, went to Women Acting in Today's Society – Birmingham for core costs. Other beneficiaries included Oxfam UK for salary and associated costs of the poverty programme (£38,000), All Saints

Women's Resource Centre – Wolverhampton for a salary and associated running costs (£30,000), St James Language Project – Birmingham for a women's support and health project (£22,000), Heart of England Community Foundation for a grant-giving scheme to local women's groups (£12,000), Clean Break Theatre Company for running costs (£10,000) and Pennell Initiative for Womens Health for staff and development costs of a pilot project.

Penal Affairs

Grants to eight organisations totalled £244,000. They were £87,000 to NACRO for a salary, £37,000 to Prison Reform Trust for running costs, £25,000 each to Frontier Youth Trust – Birmingham for a salary, Galleries of Justice – Nottingham for equipment and running costs and Prisoners Abroad for running costs, £20,000 each to Institute of Criminology – Cambridge for the Cropwood Fellowship and Fawcett Trust for the core costs of the Women's Commission on the Criminal Justice System and £5,000 to Leap Confronting Conflict for a conference on guns and gangs.

Racial Justice

Grants were made to 22 organisations and totalled £488,000. The largest were £95,000 to The 1990 Trust for salary and core costs and £74,000 to Asian Resource Centre – Birmingham for a salary. Other beneficiaries included Children's Society – Bristol for a salary in connection with the Right Track project (£36,000), Bangladesh Community Development – Birmingham for an outreach education project (£25,000), Early Years Trainers Anti-Racist Network – Reading for a salary (£20,000), Northern Ireland Council for Ethnic Minorities for administration costs (£15,000) and Association of Black Probation Officers for running costs (£5,000).

Exclusions
What we do not support

So much important work in the community requires support but our limited funds do not allow us to help everyone. Areas where we are not normally able to help include the following:

- Activities for which central or local government are responsible
- Activities which aim to collect funds to give to other charities or to individuals

- Animal welfare
- Arts projects
- Child abuse prevention projects
- Corporate subscription or membership of a charity
- Endowment funds (exceptional cases only where we have a long term funding relationship already established)
- Environment – conserving and protecting wildlife and landscape
- Expeditions, overseas travel, scholarships or gap years
- Fabric appeals for places of worship or other building renovation projects
- Fundraising events or activities
- Homelessness projects, referrals or individuals
- Hospitals and medical centres
- Loans or business finance
- Medical research
- Promoting religion
- Schools, universities and colleges, youth clubs
- Sponsorship or marketing appeals
- General appeals
- Overseas (we only fund those groups we approach ourselves).

Applications
Applying for a grant

New grants will be available from April 2004. Detailed guidelines will be available on [its] website from February 2004. In the meantime The Barrow Cadbury Trust will focus on the projects it already supports together with a number of special initiatives.

These initiatives will not only help us to learn more about the funding needs of projects but also lead to a tangible difference at community level.

We are sorry that we will not be able to respond to enquiries until a staffing structure is in place to support the new portfolio. One of the qualities that our partner projects have appreciated about Barrow Cadbury is the ability to talk through their projects rather than rely on lengthy and detailed applications. The new staffing structure will aim to maintain a level of contact with our partner projects, reinforce our regional focus and establish a proactive stance in identifying the projects meeting our criteria and objectives.

Please note that generally we do not use an application form as we prefer groups to set out their own priorities. However, the sort of points that groups may wish to consider when putting forward a proposal include:

- Information on your organisation and how it meets our qualification criteria.

- How your work meets the selected programme objective.
- Background about the issue you are working on – the scale of the problem, the gaps in provision, who else operates in the area.
- User involvement.
- Project leadership.
- Your partners and other bodies you would liaise with in order to deliver the work.
- Total budget and other funders involved.
- Timetable to start and complete project.
- Anticipated outcomes and how you will monitor your performance – including the desired external impact and methods of assessment.
- Any added value from advocacy, networking, promotion.
- Dissemination of the results for maximum effect.

The Trust prefers to provide smaller grants. Most grants are between £10,000 and £15,000 and some are small grants under £3,000. Trustees believe that their resources should be targeted on modest projects that have the capacity to generate considerable leverage for the users involved. Small grants are prioritised for activities that are important in the long-term but require a more rapid response.

GRANT APPLICATIONS

Please remember that it usually takes between 6 and 18 months before applications are ready to be considered by Trustees.

We recommend that you check [the trust's] website regularly for more information.

The Cadogan Charity

General

£1.7 million (2002/03)

Beneficial area UK, especially Kensington and Chelsea in London and Scotland.

18 Cadogan Gardens, London SW3 2RP

Tel. 020 7730 4567

Correspondent P M Loutit, Secretary

Trustees *Earl Cadogan; Countess Cadogan; Viscount Chelsea; Lady Anna Thomson.*

Charity Commission no. 247773

Information available Annual report and accounts.

Summary

There were five grants made of £100,000 or more in 2002/03, although most grants are for between £1,000 and £3,000 and go to a wide range of national organisations and some local ones in the Kensington and Chelsea area. About half the recipients have been supported in the previous year and the charity notes that 'contributions are given to a regular list of charities'.

General

The charity had an income of just over £1 million in 2002/03, mostly from its shares in the Cadogan Group Ltd then worth £10 million.

The trust notes that it has been inundated with requests and has to turn down very many. 'We have our regular list of charities to whom we provide support and we entertain as many others as we can but, generally speaking, these charities must be either Scottish or London based and in the latter case a request from a Kensington and Chelsea based organisation would stand more chance of success.'

Grants in 2002/03

Of grants made, only 15 were for amounts over £10,000: £500,000 to Inventure Trust; £250,000 each to Natural History Museum and Royal Hospital Chelsea Infirmary Building Appeal; £100,000 to Leukemia Research Fund; £75,000 to Pensioner's Mobility Fund; £65,000 to Laser Trust Fund; £50,000 to Downside Settlement; £13,000 to Animal Health Trust; and £10,000 each to Breast Cancer Care, Dockland Settlements, Guild of Pilots and Navigators, Oatridge Agricultural College, Spinal Injuries Association and West London Church Homeless Concern.

Most of the smaller grants were for between £1,000 and £3,000. Beneficiaries included: Royal Veterinary College (£7,500), Digestive Disorders Foundation, Magdalen College Development Trust, Scottish Wildlife Trust, Stroke Association and Worldwide Volunteering for Young People (£5,000 each), Barnardos and Colon Cancer Concern (£3,000) British Deaf Association (£2,500), Atlantic Salmon Trust, British Lung Foundation and SSAFA Forces Help (£2,000 each), AT Society, Suzy Lamplugh Trust, NCDL

and National Listening Library (£1,000 each) and British Stammering Association (£500).

Exclusions

No grants to individuals.

Applications

In writing to the correspondent, who states: 'Please note that contributions are given to a regular list of charities.'

CAF (Charities Aid Foundation)

See below

£1.2 million (2004/05)

Beneficial area UK.

Kings Hill, West Malling, Kent ME19 4TA

Tel. 01732 520334

Website www.CAFonline.org

Correspondent CAF Grantmaking

Trustees *Grants Advisory Council: Kim Lavely (Chair and CAF Trustee); Yogesh Chauhan (Chair of Minority Ethnic Fund); John Bateman (Chair of Short Term Assistance); Jackie Hurst (Chair of International); Gillian Crosby (Chair of Collaborative); David Landon (Medical Adviser); Christopher Phillips (Disability Adviser); Fiona Ellis (Consultancy).*

Charity Commission no. 268369

Information available Full information is available on the charity's website.

CAF is a charity offering financial services both to donors and to other charities. Technically, CAF makes grants worth over £150 million a year, but almost all of these are 'donor directed' payments where CAF handles the funds of other donors who are using its financial services. These include separate trusts set up within CAF by philanthropists seeking to use the administrative and grant payment services of CAF while keeping for themselves the decisions about where these grants should go.

On its own account, CAF has a separate grant programme. This was worth £1.2 million in 2004/05. Funds are allocated from a number of separate funds. As we were going to print in March 2005, it had yet to finalise its schemes and guidelines for 2005 onwards. Please consult its website for further information.

In 2004/05 grants were offered under the following schemes:

Support for training or consultancy needs

- Fast Track Fund – support for organisations seeking immediate funding for specific training to strengthen their organisation.
- Consultancy Fund – support for charitable organisations that do not have a chosen consultant and may need extra guidance and support to achieve the best possible results from their consultancy.

Support for immediate needs

- Critical Assistance Fund – support for organisations that are in a particularly difficult situation (including mergers, funding crises, relationships within organisations between trustee/ management committee and staff and/ or volunteers)

Grants in partnership with CAF:

- Collaborative Fund – support for organisations seeking to work in partnership with CAF. Funding is offered to up to seven organisations each year. Support is offered for initiatives that will strengthen the structure of an organisation and that of other organisations in the sector.
- Access Fund – CAF offers support in new ways to disadvantaged groups that have less access to support structures or increased needs for support for their own development.

There is also a Venturesome fund, offering loans, underwriting and, occasionally, share capital.

Applications

Please see the CAF website for further information.

The Camelot Foundation

Registered charities working with young parents or those at risk of becoming young parents, young asylum seekers, young people with mental health problems or who are disabled

£1 million (2004)
Beneficial area UK.

University House, 11–13 Lower Grosvenor Place, London SW1W 0EX

Tel. 020 7828 6085 **Fax** 020 7828 6087

Email info@camelotfoundation.org.uk

Website www.camelotfoundation.org.uk

Correspondent Julie Gilson, Grants Manager

Trustees *David Bryan; John Graham; Frances Hasler; Robert McGowan; Dot Renshaw; Anne Spackman; Dianne Thompson; Neil Wragg.*

Charity Commission no. 1060606

Information available Full information is available from the foundation's website.

The foundation was established in 1997 by the Camelot Group, the operators of the National Lottery in the UK, which provides an annual income of £2 million. Its funds are entirely separate and unconnected to any lottery money. It aims to give £1 million each year to around 50 organisations, and has one main grant programme for organisations:

Transforming Lives

The Transforming Lives programme is looking for small to medium sized organisations across the UK that :
- work with our priority groups (young parents or those at risk of becoming young parents; young asylum seekers; young people with mental health problems; young disabled people);
- have imaginative ideas for engaging young people in community life;
- share our values and commitment to change.

Guidelines for applicants

Before you submit a project proposal please read the guidance below in addition to the main guidelines. It will help you to decide whether what you want to do really matches what we are looking to fund. If you are still not sure whether to apply for a grant after you have read this information we strongly advise you to call the Camelot Foundation office on 020 7828 6085. We appreciate that it takes considerable time and resources to submit a proposal and a quick call to us can either help you strengthen your proposal to us or help you decide that another funder may be more suitable.

Key Reasons Why Proposals Fail To Reach The Shortlist:

Volume of Applications
Each year we have £1 million to award through the Transforming Lives grants programme and we receive just over 500 proposals. This means we are only able to shortlist about 1 in 12 proposals from which we can actually fund about a half of these and we are therefore unable to shortlist or fund many excellent proposals.

Innovation
The Camelot Foundation prides itself on funding innovative proposals and we are constantly amazed at the range and imagination of the proposals that reach us. We are looking for initiatives that seek to try out experimental ways of working. Often applicants are not shortlisted because although they are experimenting within their own organisation or region they are seeking to use an approach that others have already tried. An organisation may want to do this because the approach has been shown to work and could meet the needs of their clients, but it would not meet our wider definition of experimentation or innovation.

Proposals that are shortlisted will not only have shown that they will meet an identified need but will have explained how the approach they intend to develop is distinctive from others working in a similar field across the UK. For example, if you intend to develop a mentoring scheme, how would your scheme take the approach of mentoring somewhere different? If you want to provide basic skills training for your client group, how would you do this in a way that would be distinctive from the many basic skills courses which are already available?

The Voice of Young People
We want to fund proposals that provide creative opportunities for young people to influence, develop and in many cases lead projects. We are looking for evidence that you have explored the most appropriate and effective ways for young people to be involved in the work of the project you are fundraising for, and in your organisation more generally.

Minority Groups
If a proposal only states that it will work to an equal opportunities policy it will receive a low score. We want applicants to tell us how

they seek to meet the variety of needs of their target group. For example, if you are working with young disabled people, it is not enough to say that young disabled people are a minority group, we want you to tell us how you intend to meet the potential diversity within your target group of young disabled people.

Recent grants

Beneficiaries in this programme in 2004 included: 42nd Street, working across Greater Manchester, which received a grant of £90,000 to develop work with young disabled people who may either be at risk of developing mental health problems or who are experiencing mental ill health; Changing Faces, which received £89,000 to develop new initiatives; Youth at Risk, which received £85,000 to introduce a Performance Coaching programme model into a residential crisis recovery unit in North London. The model involves a young person working intensively with a volunteer coach who supports them to take small steps towards their goals; and Scottish Marriage Care, which received £54,000 to develop a comprehensive relationship education programme in Greater Easterhouse, Glasgow. This will help to support young people in the transition period of becoming a parent. The organisation will provide relationship counselling and young peer educators/mentors will deliver innovative modules and workshops.

Review 2003/04

The foundation offers the following review if its work in the context of wider issues within the sector:

During the year under review young people continued to move to the centre of the government's social policy concerns. The publication of the green paper Every Child Matters marked a watershed in efforts to co-ordinate a child and young person-centred agenda, setting out five key objectives to inform policy and practice across all services aimed at children and young people:

● Being healthy
● Staying safe
● Enjoying and achieving
● Making a positive contribution
● Securing economic well-being

At the same time, expert working groups continued to develop the National Service Framework for Children (NSF), due for publication in Autumn 2004. A ten year strategy, the NSF will set standards to improve delivery and quality of care, and reduce unacceptable variations in health. It will place an emphasis on the interweaving of responses to the needs of the whole child or young person, reinforcing expectations of working across boundaries between education, health and social care. New

integrated Childrens' Trusts mark a further commitment to joined-up working, and by the end of the year under review Childrens' Commissioners had been appointed in Wales, Scotland and Northern Ireland to safeguard the rights of children and young people. The expectation that young people will be consulted, and involved in, developing policy become a mainstream idea, backed by a half a million pound Consultation Fund announced by Margaret Hodge in July 2003.

On a less positive note, however, the extension of antisocial behaviour orders and the imposition of curfews for under 16s in some areas was criticised by human rights organisations as fundamentally undermining young people's basic human rights, including introducing an assumption of criminality or bad behaviour simply by virtue of being in a particular place at a particular time.

Nationally, pressure continued to build for the voting age to be reduced to 16, an argument which looked all the stronger in the light of the introduction of Citizenship Education as a statutory national curriculum subject in secondary schools in September 2002.

As we move into 2004/05 the transformation of services for children and young people continues to gather pace. The task for independent funders like ourselves who focus on the needs of vulnerable young people, remains to throw light on those issues that have not yet appeared on the government's agenda and to ensure that the benefits of social change are experienced by marginalised young people as well as by those young people who remain in the mainstream of UK life. We believe that our National Inquiry into Self-harm and our commitment to focusing on particularly vulnerable groups of young people in both the Transforming Lives and 4front Awards programmes [mainly for individuals] is evidence that independent funders have an important role to play in ensuring all young people have access to opportunities to make the most of their potential.

Plans for 2004/05

The challenges of the year ahead include:
● Publication of the first of a series of interim reports from the National Inquiry into self-harm among young people. The Inquiry Panel will continue to meet, take evidence and commission research into various aspects of this complex issue throughout 2003/04.
● Implementing a one-off programme of grants for organisations working in the field of self-harm. Our aim will be to fund work that will lead to a significant and lasting change in the effectiveness of the organisation. By strengthening organisations, we aim:

– to improve the support available to young people who self-harm
– to enable young people who self-harm to influence policy and practice developments at either local, regional or national levels.

● The second year of our 4front Awards programme, led by a new group of young people, determined to put their own stamp on this annual leadership programme. They are promising an equally memorable awards ceremony at the Ministry of Sound!
● The third year of our Transforming Lives programme, and the commissioning of an external review of the programme, to help the trustees' take stock and reflect on our impact as we approach the mid-point of our seven year life cycle.
● Consultation on the issue for our next strategic programme of work, in which we seek to focus attention on a specific issue within the overall field in which we are working.
● Launch of an annual policy forum, to surface the key policy issues emerging in the field in which we are engaged. We want to stimulate debate amongst key decision makers and leaders – and to surface the voice of young people in the debate.

Exclusions

The foundation will not fund work with children under 11 or people over 25; large national charities; projects where funding from local or central government has run out; work that is the responsibility of local authorities; capital projects; academic research that is not linked to a development project; overseas travel; playschemes; holidays; after school clubs; individuals; general appeals or any well-established or routine approaches.

Applications

For guidelines and a project proposal form send an A4 sae with 33p postage. Different formats, large print and audiotape are also available. There are usually four deadlines per year. Decisions usually take three months.

The Campden Charities

Welfare and education in Kensington, London

£902,000 to organisations (2002/03)

Beneficial area The former parish of Kensington, London; a north–south corridor, roughly from Earl's Court to the north of Ladbroke Grove.

27a Pembridge Villas, London W11 3EP

Tel. 020 7243 0551

Website www.campdencharities.org.uk

Correspondent C Stannard, Clerk to the Trustees

Trustees *Revd G W Craig, chair; Philippa, Viscountess Astor; D C J Banks; S Dehn; Cllr R J Freeman; Dr A Hamilton; Cllr S P Hoier; P Kraus; Ms S Lockhart; C S R Marr-Johnson; Hon. C McLaren; M J Mockridge; Mrs C Porteous; Cllr E P Tomlin; R T J Tuck; N B Wickham-Irving.*

Charity Commission no. 1003641

Information available Excellent annual report and accounts, included on the website.

The charity supports education and the relief of need in part of the present London Borough of Kensington and Chelsea – an area that, perhaps contrary to some stereotypes, contains extensive areas of inner city poverty as well as of exceptional affluence. The 2002/03 annual report described its approach to grant making thus:

The emphasis of trustees' grant-giving is to deliver the maximum benefit to individuals in need resident within the area of benefit. The focus of this policy is to move the funding closer to those who need additional support in addressing disadvantage. This has been either directly to impoverished individuals or families via the Individuals' Grant Committee or through the Organisations' Grant Committee to groups that directly address disadvantage or provide direct services for those on low incomes. Other organisations are supported only in so far as they support direct delivery organisations in their work.

Trustees' personal knowledge of the condition and needs of organisations within the area of benefit and of the individuals whom they serve is constantly updated through visits and through their own voluntary activities in the local community. Trustees, the majority of whom are local residents, have built up a picture of the needs and services as they are now and as

they have developed over the years. This enables the Campden Charities to be particularly confident and flexible in response to requests for financial support.

In 2002/03 it had assets of £54 million and an income of £2.2 million. Grants were made totalling £1.6 million, of which £544,000 was given for the advancement of education and the rest for relief in need. A total of £636,000 was given to individuals and £902,000 to organisations, broken down as follows:

Annual running costs

Grants were made to 53 organisations and totalled £585,000. Of this, 18 grants totalling £217,000 were for education and 33 totalling £368,000 for relief in need. The largest were £40,000 to Partnership of Supplementary Schools, £35,000 each to Kensington and Chelsea Preschool Learning Alliance and Venture Community Association, £25,000 to North Kensington Video/Drama Project, £23,000 to NHHT Furniture Store and £20,000 to Ilys Booker Under-Fives Centre.

Smaller grants included those to Family Service Unit – West London (£18,000), Rotalec (£16,000), Wornington Green Detached Youth Project (£12,000), Family Friends (£10,000), Kensington and Chelsea Carers (£9,300), Blenheim Project (£8,700), Kensington Day Centre (£6,500), Swinbrook Nursery Centre (£5,200), London Marriage Guidance Council (£2,300) and Junior Gateway Club (£1,800).

Holidays and outings

14 grants totalled £25,000, all for relief in need. The largest were £5,500 to Royal Borough Kensington and Chelsea Community Education, £5,000 to Kensington and Chelsea Summer Camp, £2,000 to Wornington Green Detached Youth and £2,000 to Immanuel Youth Group. Other beneficiaries included Salvation Army for children's holidays (£1,600), Piper House (£1,400), St Cuthbert's Centre for day trips (£1,000), Pepper Pot Club (£600) and Women's Pioneer Housing Association (£100).

Playschemes

13 grants totalled £56,000, all from the education budget. The largest were £10,000 to Kidsactive Acklam Playspace and £9,000 to Family Service Unit – West London. Other recipients included Earls Court Homeless Families Project (£6,000), Venture Community Association (£4,500), Pimento Project Education Scheme (£3,500), Eritrean

Support Group (£2,500), Ilys Booker Under-Fives Centre (£1,800) and Adventure Playday West London 2002 (£1,200).

Christmas grants

A total of £6,200 was given in 22 grants, all from the relief of need fund. The largest were £1,400 to St Mungo Association and £1,300 to Salvation Army. Other grants ranged from £50 to £350 each and included those to Pepper Pot Club (£350), St Clement and St James Community Project (£300), Response Community Projects (£200), Inkerman House and Longridge Road Under-8's Centre (£150 each), Whitchurch House (£100), T Block Peabody Estate Monday Club (£90) and Ormond Court (£50).

One-off grants

23 grants totalled £230,000, of which 14 were for education and totalled £177,000 and 9 were for relief-in-need totalling £53,000. The largest were £35,000 to Youth Enterprise Scheme for a capital grant, £30,000 to Barlby Primary School for a community library, £28,000 to Holland Park School for music equipment and £20,000 to Pepper Pot Day Centre for deficit funding.

Smaller grants included £17,000 to North Kensington Video/Drama Project for equipment, £15,000 to Ainsworth Nursery School for an extension, £11,000 to Air Training Corps 46th Kensington Squadron for a vehicle, £10,000 to Rotalec for a mobile classroom, £7,500 to St Cuthberts with St Mattias CE Primary School for IT equipment, £5,000 to Octavia Housing Trust Foundation for NVQ training (which also received £2,000 for the breakfast club), £1,600 to Magic Lantern for art workshops in schools and £300 to Boys' Brigade 146th London Company for parking fees.

Exclusions

No grants for:

- UK charities or charities outside Kensington, unless they are of significant benefit to Kensington residents;
- schemes or activities which are generally regarded as the responsibility of the statutory authorities;
- UK fundraising appeals;
- environmental projects unless connected with education or social need;
- medical research or equipment;
- animal welfare;

- advancement of religion or religious groups, unless they offer non-religious services to the community;
- commercial and business activities;
- endowment appeals;
- projects of a political nature;
- retrospective capital grants.

Applications

Initial enquiries from organisations should be made in writing or by telephone to the grants officer for advice and an application form which must be completed and returned with supporting information as required. Office visits are also encouraged to discuss complex applications, or staff may visit organisations.

The organisations committee, which meets 11 times a year, first considers applications and trustees may decide to visit organisations or invite them to present their requests in person. The committee's recommendations are subsequently approved by the board of trustees. This process can take up to two months.

Trustees' decisions are imparted to the applicant by letter, which stipulates the nature and size of the grant, date of payment and follow-up reports required from beneficiaries. Beneficiaries must ensure monies are spent only as intended. The charities' staff monitor grants made by studying annual or follow-up reports and by visits.

The Carnegie United Kingdom Trust

See below

See below

Beneficial area UK and Eire, with a special interest in Scotland.

Comely Park House, Dunfermline, Fife KY12 7EJ

Tel. 01383 721445 **Fax** 01383 620682

Website www.carnegieuktrust.org.uk

Correspondent Charlie McConnell, Chief Executive

Trustees *William Thomson, chair; Lady Anthony Hamilton; Paddy Linaker; Anthony Pender; David J Stobie; C Roy Woodrow; Millie Banerjee; Dr David Fraser; Jeremy Holmes; Dr David Smith; Bill Livingstone; Robin Watson; James*

Doorley; Angus Hogg; Bhupendra Mistry; Douglas Scott.

Scottish Charity no. SC012799

Information available Information was provided by the trust.

The following press release was issued by the trust in December 2004:

All change at Carnegie

Foundation shifts focus from grants to support for more sustainable change

The Carnegie United Kingdom Trust, one of Britain's oldest philanthropic foundations, is to re-target its resources to drive the agenda for sustainable change.

The Trust is shifting its strategic focus from reactive, short-term grant giving to supporting programmes that will make a real and sustained difference in people's lives.

The Trust will thus replace its grants programmes to the voluntary sector after March 2005 – and step up its investment in independent national inquiries, complemented by supporting larger scale action-research designed to influence public policy and deliver longer-term change for the benefit of the people of the UK and Ireland.

This new direction for the Trust builds upon the significant success that Carnegie has had in influencing public policy and statutory and non-governmental services around such areas as the Public Libraries, Social Work Services, the Third Age, the Voluntary Arts, Community Service and Youth Participation.

Announcing the change at its November 2004 Board, the Chair of the Trust, William Thomson, said, 'Carnegie has been involved in supporting communities and voluntary action for over ninety years, particularly through funding for libraries, village halls, national parks, youth projects, the arts and the environment.

'Whilst this support has provided a valuable source of funding for local social action, we have become increasingly concerned that our model of short-term funding, prevalent across the foundations world, has not been an effective way of addressing changing issues and needs.

'We believe that the time has come to focus upon a more strategic approach. As a foundation, we have managed an approach to grant giving that engages voluntary and community organisations in large amounts of time submitting complex applications for relatively small sums of money to Trusts like Carnegie. The reality is that over 90% of applications are rejected due to the competitive pressures upon our funds.

'We have taken the decision that the Trust will move away from this approach to grant giving to a more investment-led approach, linked to long-term and sustainable outcomes.'

In recent years, the Trust has been developing a more strategic approach to influencing public policy for the benefit of communities across the UK and Ireland. The most recent example is the Carnegie Commission for Rural Community Development chaired by Lord David Steel, launched in July [2004], which is already having a more systemic influence upon ways in which public and non-governmental agencies and local communities address sustainable change. Until 2003, however, only 25% of the Trust's capacity supported such initiatives.

This change of focus for the Trust is also underlined by what the Trust's Chief Executive, Charlie McConnell, highlights as a key feature of all the foundation's future programmes – working in partnership to secure long-term change.

'We shall be increasingly working with other foundations, statutory agencies, non-governmental organisations and the research community, both here and overseas. In doing this we shall in particular be enhancing our links with the over twenty Carnegie foundations worldwide to address the growing agenda of global issues that have an impact upon people's lives in the UK and Ireland'.

'This,' says Carnegie Vice Chair Millie Banerjee, 'provides Carnegie in the UK with unparalleled access to some of the best thinkers and civil society players worldwide, working in such areas as international peace, human rights, democracy building, the environment and education.

'Through the work of our Commissions and Inquiries and targeted action research, we shall be working with organisations here and overseas to influence change that brings a real and sustained difference in people's lives'.

The trust's new approach will involve working proactively with fewer organisations to achieve its aims and objectives. It is unlikely that this approach will involve unsolicited general applications from other organisations. All previously approved grants not yet paid will be honoured. The trust's final round of grantmaking was in January 2005.

Exclusions

See above.

Applications

See above.

Cash for Kids – Radio Clyde

Children

£712,000 (2002/03)

Beneficial area Radio Clyde transmission area, i.e. west central Scotland.

Clyde Action, 236 Clyde Street, Glasgow G1 4JH

Tel. 0141 204 1025 **Fax** 0141 248 2148

Correspondent Yvonne Wyper, Finance Manager

Trustees *Sir John Orr, chair; Paul Cooney; Robert Caldwell; Kirsty Archer; Sheena Bortwick*

Scottish Charity no. SCO03334

Information available Annual report and accounts were provided by the charity.

This is a Christmas appeal established by the radio station and CSV, a charity supporting media involvement in volunteering and in community support generally. The trust funds, via organisations such as playgroups, special schools or disability charities, small cash gifts for the benefit of individual children in need. Typically about 75,000 children benefit to the extent of £15 to £25 a head, or thereabouts. The trust seeks to 'reach those children who might otherwise face a bleaker Christmas'.

In 2002/02 the charity had an income of £891,000. Grants totalled £712,000. Only organisations receiving £1,000 or more are listed in the accounts. There were 39 of these in 2002/03. The list was headed by the Craighalbert Centre (£25,000), Ronald McDonald House (£20,000) and the Scottish Business Achievement Award Trust (£10,000).

Other beneficiaries included Sargent Cancer Care (£5,000), Dumfries and Stewarty Women's Aid (£4,000), Netherlea Short Break Services (£3,000), Southern Machars Playcare (£2,500), Children's Hospice Association Scotland (£2,000), Old Bridge Playgroup (£1,600) and Hamish Allan Centre Children's Fund, Penninghame Primary School and Princess Royal Trust for Carers (£1,000 each).

The report notes that for the first time a grant of £35,000 was paid to CSV, which runs the scheme jointly with Radio Clyde, for administration costs, although this was not included in the main grants list.

Exclusions

The trust does not fund trips in the summer or at Easter, equipment or salaries. Children benefiting must be aged 16 or under.

Applications

On a form available from the correspondent. 'To ensure proper stewardship of the funds raised, all nominations from those who believe the funds should be destined to a particular family or group have to be accompanied by a recommendation from an accredited body such as social work departments, Children 1st, head teachers, members of the clergy and community workers.'

Sir John Cass's Foundation

Education in inner London

£2.1 million to organisations (2002/03)

Beneficial area The inner London boroughs – Camden, City of London, Greenwich, Hackney, Hammersmith & Fulham, Islington, Kensington & Chelsea, Lambeth, Lewisham, Newham, Southwark, Tower Hamlets, Wandsworth, Westminster.

31 Jewry Street, London EC3N 2EY

Tel. 020 7480 5884 **Fax** 020 7488 2519

Email colincwright@hotmail.com

Correspondent Colin Wright, Clerk

Trustees *18 in all, of whom the following are members of the grants committee: M Venn; K M Everett; Revd Dr B J Lee.*

Charity Commission no. 312425

Information available Guidelines for applicants and good annual report and accounts, were provided by the trust.

Summary

Grants, usually for amounts between £1,000 and £40,000, are made to organisations for educational work with children and young people in inner London. The majority of grants are revenue funding for projects, though capital grants are occasionally made. The foundation has also supported a number of inner London schools in their bids for specialist school status.

Beneficiary organisations may be schools, organisations working with schools, or those with educational programmes outside school.

Grantmaking is only one of the foundation's activities. It owns a primary school in the City of London and a secondary school in Tower Hamlets, which receive regular support, and it also funds programmes at London Metropolitan University (Sir John Cass Department of Art) and City University (Sir John Cass City of London Business School).

There is also a substantial programme of support for individual students (£213,000 in 2003/04) with priority to those aged 19–24 [see the Educational Grants Directory, published by Directory of Social Change].

General

The 'Guidelines for Schools and other organisations' read as follows:

The foundation was established in 1748 to educate 'poor but worthy' children of the Portsoken ward of the City of London. Since that time the foundation's beneficial area has been extended to include the City of London, the City of Westminster, the Royal Borough of Kensington & Chelsea, and the London Boroughs of Camden, Greenwich, Hackney, Hammersmith and Fulham, Islington, Lambeth, Lewisham, Newham, Southwark, Tower Hamlets, and Wandsworth.

The foundation can only consider proposals from schools and organisations that will benefit young people under the age of 25, who are permanent residents of inner London.

The foundation will consider applications for time-limited projects where it is clear for what purpose and activities grant assistance is being sought.

Foundation governors wish to encourage and, where appropriate, support applications which:

- incorporate structured educational content related, where appropriate, to the teaching and learning of the relevant key stage(s) of the national curriculum
- demonstrate a realistic likelihood of continuing after the expiry of the foundation's grant
- are innovative, in the sense of identifying and meeting educational needs not met by other grant-giving bodies.

Within these parameters, governors particularly favour applications which:
- promote the teaching of science, maths, engineering and technology
- develop programmes that improve access to the curriculum and prepare beneficiaries for the world of work

- develop curricula or activities outside the normal school day.

Preference is given to original developments, not yet part of the regular activities of an organisation; to developments that are either strategic, such as practical initiatives directed toward addressing the root causes of problems; or seminal, because they seek to influence policy and practice elsewhere. Grants may be awarded for a maximum of three years, subject to monitoring and evaluation.

Due to the large number of applications in relation to the limited funds available, many good projects still have to be refused – even though they fit within the Foundation's general guidelines. The Foundation may also, from time to time, initiate new projects that do not fall into the priority areas for grants; in this fashion the Governors explore potential areas for involvement in the future.

Grants in 2002/03

During the year the foundation made 35 grants to 28 organisations totalling £2.1 million. Over half of this total (£1,250,000) was awarded to City University as the third instalment of a £5 million total award over four years. The grant provided capital funding for the new Cass Business School at City University. The university also benefited from a smaller grant of £14,000 towards a pilot project testing a new method of teaching degrees in computing that involves work within the industry.

Other larger grants included those to: London Metropolitan University (£111,000 in total) for various educational projects including workshops and outreach projects; Southwark Diocesan Board for Education (£104,000) towards the school governors' liabilities for building work; Hackney Education Action Zone (£100,000) for match funding for the third year of the EAZ for Hackney schools; London Diocesan Board for Schools (£80,000) towards the school governors' liabilities for building work; Camden Arts Centre (£66,000 in total) mostly for capital funding towards the centre's complete refurbishment; and Kobi Nazrul Junior Mixed Infants School (£61,000) for a phonics-based literacy programme running in six primary schools in Tower Hamlets.

Smaller grants included those to: Quality in Study Support (£22,000) for their Re-engaging with Learning programme; Children's Music Workshop (£17,000) for workshops in schools in Tower Hamlets; Billingsgate Seafood Training School (£15,500) for a schools programme promoting fish preparation

and cookery; Lady Margaret School (£7,500) for sponsorship of Specialist Schools' Maths and Computing College status; Prisoners' Education Trust (£5,500) for a bursary scheme for young offenders to obtain qualifications prior to release; London Coaching Foundation (£4,000) towards athletics coaching in six Tower Hamlets secondary schools; and Atlantic Council of the United Kingdom (£2,500) for its Partnership for Peace Appeal to run in secondary schools in the inner London area.

Exclusions

The governors will not fund:

- basic equipment or teachers' salaries that are the responsibility of the education authorities;
- the purchase, repair or furnishing of buildings;
- stage, film or video production costs;
- performances, exhibitions or festivals;
- independent schools;
- local youth and community projects;
- conferences or seminars;
- university or medical research;
- preschool, nursery education or toy libraries;
- establishing funds for bursary or loan schemes;
- supplementary schools or mother tongue teaching;
- retrospective grants to help pay off overdrafts or loans (nor will the foundation remedy the withdrawal or reduction of statutory funds);
- the purchase of vehicles, computers or sports equipment;
- research or publication costs;
- one-off music, drama, dance or similar productions, or the tours of such productions (nor does the foundation support ticket subsidy schemes);
- holiday projects, school journeys, trips abroad or exchange visits;
- school ground improvements;
- general fundraising campaigns and appeals.

Applications

To apply for a grant you should send an initial letter outlining your application to the correspondent. The letter should include some basic costings for your project and background details on your organisation.

If your proposal falls within the current policy and the foundation's basic criteria are satisfied, you will be invited to submit an application under headings that the foundation will provide, together with your latest annual report and audited accounts.

Upon receipt of the completed application, foundation staff will discuss your proposal with you and may arrange to visit.

Completed applications are then considered by governors, who meet quarterly.

Decisions are normally conveyed to applicants within seven days of a meeting.

Throughout the process, the foundation's staff will be happy to clear up any questions you might have and are available to receive initial telephone enquiries.

Applicants should note that an application is only finalised when all documentation has been received, a meeting has taken place and there are no further questions to raise. All this takes time and it is the applicant's responsibility to allow a reasonable length of time for this process.

Successful projects will include appropriate measures of performance, as the foundation is interested in evaluating the impact of funded activities.

The Central Church Fund

Church of England (see below) worldwide

£511,000 (2003)

Beneficial area Worldwide.

Church House, Great Smith Street, London SW1P 3NZ

Tel. 020 7898 1541/1767 **Fax** 020 7898 1558

Email ccf@c-of-e.org.uk

Website www.centralchurchfund.org.uk

Correspondent Rachel Lindley

Trustees *The Ven. David Woodhouse, chair; Michael Chamberlain; The Ven. George Howe; Mrs Carole Park; Revd John Patrick; Mrs Margaret Swinson; Prebendary Gill Sumner.*

Charity Commission no. 248711

Information available Accounts and guidelines were provided by the fund.

The Central Church Fund is an excepted charity but its trustee, the Central Board of Finance of the Church of England, is registered under the above number.

The fund is able to offer support where:

• 'there is clear evidence of parish/ project effort to raise funds and of firm commitment to realising and sustaining the project

• 'there is evidence of partnership(s) with the local community, statutory funders, other Anglican churches, ecumenical partners, other faiths etc

• 'a grant will help make the church accessible to the community

• 'a grant will unlock significant funding from other bodies, help complete the funding of a project or, especially in areas of particular need, give a message of encouragement

• 'there is evidence of strong diocesan support and, where appropriate, there is diocesan financial backing.'

The committee usually takes into account the relative needs of the applicant as expressed through the IMD 2000.

The fund has a limited capacity to make grants and its policy is to assist as many eligible projects as possible. Grants therefore tend to be below £5,000 and very rarely exceed £10,000. Loans are also offered.

In 2003 the fund had assets amounting to almost £15 million. It had an income of £590,000, mainly from investments. Grants paid totalled £511,000.

It is the fund's policy to spend only its income (except in exceptional circumstances) in order to preserve the fund as a permanent resource for parishes, dioceses and the national Church. The fund awards at least half of its annual grant-making budget to parish, deanery or diocesan projects. The balance is awarded as a direct grant to the Archbishops' Council with small direct grants to the two Archbishops' Discretionary Funds.

Exclusions

The fund will not support:

• 'projects that are essentially insular and inward looking

• 'the routine maintenance of or extraordinary repairs to the fabric of buildings, including churches, church halls, parsonage houses etc

• 'projects which are primarily about maintaining the nation's architectural heritage

• 'projects which are primarily about liturgical reordering

• 'restoration works to bells or organs

• 'research projects or personal grants

• 'the repayment of debts or overdrafts

• 'projects which are not directly connected with the Church of England, ecumenical or other faith

partnerships in which the Church of England element is small and projects which are predominantly secular in nature

• 'anything for which the Church Commissioners' funds or diocesan core funding are normally available, including stipend support

• 'feasibility studies (the fund is able to offer limited support towards the preliminary costs of projects, for example professional fees, but where a grant is awarded at this stage, no further funding will be available for the main body of the work).'

Applications

The committee meets four times a year to consider eligible applications. Full guidelines and application forms are available from the fund's website or from the secretary.

CfBT Education Services

Organisations involved in education, particularly those concerned with the development and management of schools, educational project management, teacher education, careers guidance, accountability and English language teaching.

£1.1 million (2003/04)

Beneficial area UK and overseas.

60 Queens Road, Reading, Berkshire RG1 4BS

Tel. 0118 902 1000 **Fax** 0118 902 1410

Email gen@cfbt-hq.org.uk

Website www.cfbt.com

Correspondent The Development Fund Manager

Trustees *Thelma Henderson; Dame Mary Richardson; John Webb; Iain MacArthur; John Harewood; Stephen Yeo.*

Charity Commission no. 270901

Information available Information was provided by the trust.

Support from CfBT follows the main theme 'Investments in Ideas' where support is given through: commissioned research and development projects; research awards by competition/tender; and funding for projects in response to applications and invitation. In 2004 the trust stated that 'approximately £1 million is available for donation each year'.

Applications that fall within one of the following themes are encouraged:

• the provision of schooling;

• managing and delivering effective learning and teaching;

• overcoming barriers to learning;

• projects involving communication, language and multi-lingualism.

Previous beneficiaries include High Reliability Schools Project, NPHA/ Queen's University, Banbury School/ University of Oxford, Special Needs Training Consortium, Warwick University – Improving Partnerships, Institute of Public Policy Research for Parents as Partners in Learning, Link Africa for Soshanguve Phase III and the Education Advisory Group.

Exclusions

The following are not funded: gap year sponsorship; professional development; loans; general appeals; grants to replace statutory funding; buildings or capital costs; projects which have only a local focus; research of a mainly theoretical nature; running costs; the arts, religion, sports and recreation; conservation, heritage or environmental projects; animal rights or welfare; expeditions, travel, adventure/holiday projects; educational exchanges between institutions; or staff salaries.

Applications

Applicants must first submit an outline proposal to the development fund manager who will advise them whether the proposal meets the criteria agreed by the trustees, and also on how to proceed. Full applications are considered at the meetings of trustees, in March, June, September and December.

The Charities Advisory Trust

See below

Around £500,000 (2003/04)
Beneficial area UK and overseas.

Radius Works, Back Lane, London
NW3 1HL

Tel. 020 7794 9835 **Fax** 020 7431 3739

Email people@charitiesadvisorytrust.org.
uk

Website www.charitiesadvisorytrust.org.
uk

Correspondent Hilary Blume, Director

Trustees *Dr Cornelia Navari; Dr
Carolyne Dennis; Prof. Bob Holman; Ms
Dawn Penso.*

Charity Commission no. 1040487

Information available Information
taken from the trust's website.

The Charities Advisory Trust is a registered
charity, which was set up 25 years ago
(originally under the name The Charity
Trading Advisory Group), with Home Office
funding, to provide an impartial source of
information on all aspects of trading for
charities.

The Trust is an innovative organisation,
concerned with redressing inequalities and
injustice in a practical way. It believes the
method of generating funds should reflect
the ethical concerns of the organisation.

The Trust is self-financing. It earns its
income through its activities. As a matter of
policy, at the outset of any initiative, the
sustainability of the venture is considered,
and a plan put in place to ensure viability.
Some activities are subsidised by others. The
Trust not only earns its income, it also gives
around £500,000 a year in charitable
donations.

Much of the Trust's work has been
directed to providing practical help to
charities to help them generate income
more efficiently. Most notably, perhaps,
through Card Aid, but also through the
establishment of the Charity Shops Group
(now independently constituted as The
Association of Charity Shops).

The Trust carries out research into all
aspects of charity trading with the aim of
providing reliable information on the sector.
It strives to provide practical help through
'benchmarking' and 'comparability', so that
charities can assess their performances and
set realistic targets. ('Trading by Charities: a
statistical analysis'–is a definitive study of the
performance of charity trading subsidiaries
produced every quinquennium.)

An important part of the Trust's work is to
provide an informed response to
Government and sector proposals,
particularly regarding income generation and
sector reform. These are usually posted on
the website.

Card Aid

Card Aid is the brand name of the Charities
Advisory Trust's charity Christmas card
activities. A trading subsidiary was set up
over 20 years ago to maximise the profits for
charity and upgrade the quality and image of
charity Christmas cards.

Card Aid produces Christmas cards for
charities to sell to their supporters. Card Aid
has been able to offer a tailor made service
for charities. It discourages over-ordering and
gives pragmatic advice.

Card Aid also supplies Christmas cards to
companies. The company can choose any
charity to benefit, and many companies
welcome the ability to support local charities.

The CARD AID chain of around 40 charity
Christmas card shops is the largest in
London, selling cards for nearly 300 charities
at locations as diverse as St Martin in the
Fields, Westminster City Hall, the Barbican
Centre and St Mary le Bow. There are also
shops in outer London locations and in
Cambridge, Oxford, York, Leeds, and
Guildford.

Good Gifts

Good Gifts Catalogue was launched in
autumn 2003. It is a radical new concept in
giving, using charity donations to buy
imaginative gifts, such as a 'goat for peace'
or an acre of rainforest.

Grant Giving

The Trust gives away over £500,000 a year.
Its grant giving policy is eclectic. Nearly all of
it is also pro-active: We find the projects and
people to work with, and develop the
projects with them.

Guidelines for applicants

We are willing to consider applications for
any charitable purpose: we have given
money to buy a canoe for young disabled
people in Wiltshire, and have bought a tea
plantation for tribal people in South India; we
have paid for books for village libraries and
supported research into early detection of
cancer.

In 2003/04, the main areas of interest to
which funds have already been committed
are:

– Peace and reconciliation projects,
  particularly in the Middle East
– The early detection of cancer through
  saliva sampling
– Research into the prevention and
  control of diabetes
– An ongoing programme of tree planting
  in cities
– Prevention of blindness
– Homelessness

Smaller amounts have been committed
to:

– The establishment of a fulfilment and
  warehousing project through a sheltered
  workshop
– Arts access, particularly for school age
  children
– Museums and galleries
– Help to refugees.

Exclusions

We do not consider grants to individuals in
need. Neither do we give to individuals going
on gap year trips to the developing world.

We rarely respond to unsolicited
applications for projects of which we know
nothing. In such cases where support is
given, the amounts are usually £200 or less.

We are unlikely to give to large fundraising
charities.

We do not give for missionary work.

Applications

We do not have an application form and we
accept applications throughout the year.
Nearly all our grants are made because we
have prior knowledge of the project or area
of concern. In most cases the idea for the
project comes from us; we work with
suitable organisations to achieve our
objectives.

We rarely respond to unsolicited
applications for projects of which we know
nothing. In such cases where support is
given, the amounts are usually £200 or less.

To apply simply send us details of your
proposal (no more than two pages in length)
in the form of a letter. You might try to
include the following information:

- the aims and objectives of your
  organisation;
- the project for which you need money;
- who benefits from the project and how;
- breakdown of the costs and total
  estimated costs;
- how much money you need from us;
- other funding secured for the project;
- a summary of your latest annual accounts.

If we refuse you it is not because your
project is not worthwhile–it is because we
do not have sufficient funds, or it is simply
outside our current area of interest.

Charitworth Limited

Jewish causes

£712,000 (2002/03)
Beneficial area UK.

Cohen Arnold & Co., New Burlington House, 1075 Finchley Road, London NW11 0PU

Tel. 020 8731 0777 **Fax** 020 8731 0778

Correspondent D Halpern, Trustee

Trustees *D M Halpern; Mrs R Halpern; S Halpern; S J Halpern.*

Charity Commission no. 286908

Information available Accounts were on file at the Charity Commission.

This trust was set up in 1983 and its objects are the advancement of the Jewish religion, relief of poverty and general charitable purposes. It is particularly interested in supporting religious and educational charities.

In 2002/03 the trust had an income of £518,000 and made grants totalling £712,000.

As in previous years, all beneficiaries were Jewish organisations. Previous beneficiaries include Cosmon (Belz) Limited, Friends of Beis Yaacov, Yeshiva Ohel Shimon Trust, Friends of Horim, Zichron Nachum, Dushinsky Trust, Mercaz Chasidei Buhush, Beth Hayeled Trust and SOFT.

Applications

In writing to the correspondent.

Charity Association Manchester Ltd

Jewish charities

£754,000 (2002/03)
Beneficial area UK and Israel.

134 Leicester Road, Salford, Manchester M7 4GB

Correspondent J Freedman

Trustees *David Ergi; David Newman; Howard Scawlabe.*

Charity Commission no. 257576

Information available Annual report and accounts on file at the Charity Commission.

The trust had an income of £711,000 in 2002/03 mostly from Gift Aid and covenants. Grants totalled £754,000. The seven largest donations over £10,000 each were £87,000 to Ahavas Chesed Trust, £72,000 to Sayser Charity, £58,000 to Academy for Rabbinical Research, £32,000 to Matono, £19,000 to Friends of Malchus Shomayim, £15,000 to North Salford Synagogue, £10,000 to North Talmudical Associates Ltd.

'Sundry' grants below £1,000 each totalled £292,000.

Applications

In writing to the correspondent.

The Childs Charitable Trust

Christian

About £450,000 (2002/03)
Beneficial area Worldwide.

2–4 Saffrons Road, Eastbourne, Eastbourne, East Sussex BN21 1DQ

Tel. 01323 417944

Email childs@charitabletrust.fsnet.co.uk

Correspondent D Martin, Trustee

Trustees *D N Martin; R H Williams; A B Griffiths.*

Charity Commission no. 234618

Information available Accounts were on file at the Charity Commission.

The objects of the trust are the furtherance of Christian Gospel, education, the relief of poverty and other charitable causes. The principal object is the furtherance of the Christian Gospel and the trustees are actively involved in supporting and encouraging Christian charities to achieve this goal. There is a preference for large-scale projects in the UK and abroad and ongoing support is given to some long-established Christian organisations.

In 2002/03 the trust had an income of £540,000 and a total expenditure of £492,000, an increase of about £120,000 on the previous year. It is likely that this increase has pushed the annual grant total up to around £450,000. Unfortunately, no further information was available.

Previous beneficiaries include Home Evangelism, Mission Aviation Fellowship, Latin Link, Echoes of Service, Mustard Seed Trust, Counties Evangelistic Work, Russian Ministries, Scripture Gift Mission, Words of Life Ministry, Medical Missionary News, Redcliffe College, Penhurst Retreat, East to West Trust, Sandhurst Baptist Church, Moorlands College and St Anthony's Church.

Comment

Unfortunately, we were unable to view the most recent accounts for this trust at the Charity Commission. Despite being requested in good time, there was a failure to make the public file available to view.

Applications

In writing to the correspondent. The trust has previously stated that its funds are fully committed and further applications are not welcomed.

The Childwick Trust

Health in the UK, education in South Africa, Jewish and bloodstock charities in the UK

£2.6 million (2003/04)
Beneficial area UK; South Africa.

9 The Green, Childwick Bury, St Albans, Hertfordshire AL3 6JJ

Tel. 01727 812486 **Fax** 01727 844666

Correspondent Karen Groom, Trust Secretary

Trustees *A R G Cane; J D Wood, chair; P G Glossop; Mrs S Frost.*

Charity Commission no. 326853

Information available Guidelines for applicants. Full accounts with a list of beneficiaries of £5,000 or more, and a limited trustees' report.

Summary

The trust makes a very large number of grants, most of them small. However about two dozen grants of £25,000 or more account for about half the grant total and most of these go to charities previously supported on a similar scale.

In 2003/04 it had assets of £54 million, an income of £2.2 million and gave £2.6 million in grants.

General

The trust was formed from the will of Jim Joel '... a bloodstock breeder of renown'.

The policies of the trust are described as follows:

The bulk of the grants awarded each year are made to charities that promote the health and relief of the disabled in the UK. The next largest proportion of grants goes to charities in the UK due to the links that Mr Joel had there. For similar reasons, charities connected with thoroughbred racing and breeding are next in line and Jewish charities follow close behind. These funding preferences were set by Mr Joel [...].

The types of grant made to charities depends entirely on the circumstances of the appeal [but] the majority of grants awarded are capital ones for medical equipment and for medical research.

The grants in South Africa are handled by the associated Jim Joel Education and Training Fund to which this trust transfers appropriate funds each year (£800,000 in 2003/04).

The grants in 2003/04 were classified as follows:

Health and associated causes, UK	48%
Education, South Africa	29%
Horse racing, UK	17%
Jewish charities, UK	6%

A total of 180 grants were distributed during the year, over 80 of these were for £5,000 or less. There is no indication from the trust of their purposes, beyond the statement noted above that most are for capital projects – though possibly this may apply mainly to the larger awards.

Beneficiaries of the four largest grants were British Racing School and Racing Welfare (£150,000 each), African Self Help Association (£137,000) and Thoroughbred Breeders Association (£100,000). Others in receipt of grants of £20,000 or more included Khululeka Community Education Development Centre (£75,000), Leonard Cheshire Home (£60,000), Read Education Trust (£59,000), Kings College Hospital (£45,000), Northwick Park Hospital (£40,000), Centre for Social Development – Rhodes University (£33,000), Sekhukhune Educare Project (£27,000), Animal Care Trust (£25,000), Centre for Early Childhood Development (£22,000) and Deafblind UK and Trinity Hospice (£20,000 each).

Other beneficiaries included Action Research, Cerebral Palsy Care, DEBRA, Dove Cottage Day Hospice, Early Learning Resource Unit, Faranani Trust, Fight for Sight, Friends of Marlborough School, Inspire Foundation, Jewish Care, Lifetrain Trust, London Catalyst, Peace Hospice, Rainbow Centre, Sense, Sunshine Centre Association, Step by Step, Toynbee Hall, United Response, Wellchild Research Centre and West Riding Blind Association.

Exclusions

The trust will not:

- fund statutory bodies;
- replace statutory funding;
- support students' individual education costs;
- participate in co-funding projects or match funding.

Applications

The trust does not issue application forms but provides the following information for applicants.

- Applications should be made in writing on the registered charity's official headed notepaper. Ideally, the appeal letter should be not longer than two pages of A4.
- Detailed costings or a budget for the project or projects referred to in the appeal letter should form a separate appendix or appendices to the appeal letter and should provide the fullest possible financial detail.
- The latest annual report of the applicant charity, together with the latest available full audited accounts, including a full balance sheet, should also accompany the written application.

During the course of the written application letter, applicants should endeavour to:

- introduce the work of the applicant charity; state when the charity was established; describe its aims and objectives; and define precisely what the applicant charity does and who benefits from its activities;
- comment upon the applicant charity's track record since its inception and refer to its notable achievements and successes to date; endeavour to provide an interesting synopsis of the organisation;
- describe the project for which a grant is being sought fully, clearly and concisely and comment on the charity's plans for the future;
- provide full costings or a budget for the project/projects to include a

detailed breakdown of the costs involved;

- give details of all other applications which the applicant charity has made to other sources of funding, and indicate precisely what funds have already been raised from other sources for the project.

Note that it can be beneficial for the applicant charity to concentrate on providing accurate and detailed costings of the project concerned, thereby enabling the trust to make its own judgement as to the level of financial support to be considered.

Applicants can greatly help their cause by concentrating on clarity of presentation and by providing detailed factual information. The trust will then do its utmost to ensure that the application receives the fullest and most careful consideration.

Acknowledgement of the trust's beneficiaries by means of loud publicity is discouraged, but publication of details of any grant is permitted if carried out in a discreet and unobtrusive way.

Applications for grants for South African beneficiaries should be sent to: The Fund Manager, The Jim Joel Education and Training Fund, Pastnet Suite 621, Private Bag X9, Benmore 2010, South Africa.

CHK Charities Limited

General

£2.2 million (2003/04)

Beneficial area UK, with a special interest in Gloucestershire, Oxfordshire and Warwickshire.

c/o Kleinwort Benson Trustees Limited, PO Box 191, 10 Fenchurch Street, London EC3M 3LB

Tel. 020 7475 6246

Correspondent Nick R Kerr-Sheppard, Secretary

Trustees *David Peake, chair; D A Acland; Mrs S E Acland; Mrs K S Assheton; Mrs C S Heber Percy; Mrs L H Morris; Mrs S Peake; Mrs J A S Prest; R Prest.*

Charity Commission no. 1050900

Information available Accounts were provided by the charity.

Summary

The charity (effectively one body) makes a large number of grants across a wide field. Outside the areas of local interest which account for about 15% of the grants by both value and number, few are for local organisations but nor is there much support for the largest and best-known national charities (or their local branches).

General

The charity was endowed by members of the Kleinwort family of the Kleinwort Benson bank and incorporates the former Cyril Kleinwort Charitable Trust. Particular support is given to charities operating in Gloucestershire and working in the fields of:

- education
- job creation
- conservation
- arts
- population control
- crime prevention
- youth development.

Assistance will be provided towards start–up or capital costs and ongoing expenses. This may take the form of a grant, for example, payable over three to five years, following which support may be withdrawn to enable the resources to be devoted to other projects. The charity makes donations across a wide field, of which about a dozen grants are for £25,000 or more, but most grants are for amounts between £2,000 and £5,000. About half of the recipients receive a similar amount as the previous year.

In 2003/04 the trust had assets of £54 million, an income of £1.7 million and made grants amounting to £2.2 million to a total of 251 organisations.

Grants in 2003/04

Grants were categorised as follows (with figures for 2002/03 in brackets):

Education – 31 grants totalling £697,000 (£235,000 in 2002/03)

By far the largest grant during the year was made to City University London, which received £500,000 in a single donation and also a further £21,000 in two small donations. Other larger grants were made to University of Cape Town Trust (£35,000 in two grants), British Museum (£25,000 in two grants), Dormer House School (Moreton-in-Marsh) School Trust Ltd (£20,000) and Kingham Primary School (£10,000).

Beneficiaries of more typical amounts included the Atlantic Council of the United Kingdom (£6,000), Ditchley Foundation, Institute of Economic Affairs and Tools for Schools (£5,000 each), Tate Gallery (£4,000), Balliol History Fellowships Campaign, Royal School of Needlework and Sir John Soane's Museum (£3,000 each) and Springboard for Children (£2,000).

Disabled/Handicapped Treatment and Care – 46 grants totalling £191,000 (£99,000)

The beneficiaries of the larger amounts in this category were the Unicorn Equestrian Trust (£17,000 in two grants), Demand, Pied Piper Appeal and Purley Park Trust (£10,000 each). More typical grants included those to Calvert Trust, Interact Reading Service and Stroud & District Mencap Homes Foundation (£5,000 each), 2Care and Handicapped Anglers Trust (£4,500 each), AbilityNet, Headway and Starlight Children's Foundation (£3,000 each) and Chernobyl Children Lifeline, Jubilee Sailing Trust and Whizzkidz (£2,000 each).

Youth Care – 38 grants totalling £162,000 (£241,000)

Beneficiaries included Army Cadet Force Association, Federation of London Youth Clubs, Girlguiding UK and National Association of Clubs for Young People (£10,000 each), Rhos-Y-Gwaliau Outdoor Education Trust Ltd (£9,000 in two grants), Athletics Youth Foundation, Everychild and Thames Valley Partnership's Young Citizens (£5,000 each), Centre for Adolescent Rehabilitation, Honeypot Home Charity and South West Adoption Network (£3,000 each), Joint Educational Trust, Oxford Youth Works and Woolaston Playgroup (£2,000 each) and Cricket Foundation and Unity of Children (£1,000 each).

Countryside Matters and Animal Welfare and Disease – 21 grants totalling £152,000 (£106,000)

Beneficiaries included the Global Canopy Programme (£50,000), Tusk Trust (£29,000 in two grants), Countryside Foundation for Education (£19,000), Wildfowl & Wetlands Trust (£10,000), Rural Regeneration Unit (£7,500), Game Conservancy Trust and Gloucestershire Wildlife Trust (£5,000 each), Borders Foundation for Rural Sustainability and Living Rainforest (£3,000 each), Museum of Garden History and Woodland Trust

(£2,000) each and Heythrop Hunt Charitable Trust (£1,000).

Miscellaneous – 11 grants totalling £120,000 (£104,000)

Two large grants were made, to Charities Aid Foundation (£68,000) and St John Ambulance (£20,000). Other grants went to Oxford House – Bethnal Green (£7,500), Gloucestershire Community Foundation, Gurkha Welfare Trust and St Luke's Hospital for the Clergy (£5,000 each), Complimentary Health Trust (£3,000), Food for All, Friends of War Memorials and Money Advice Trust (£2,000 each) and National Missing Persons Helpline (£1,000).

General Welfare and Social Problems – 6 grants totalling £113,000 (£73,000)

Most of the money in this category was awarded to Home-Start UK, which received £100,000. The other beneficiaries were Asylum Welcome (£5,000), Samaritans (£3,000), Friends of Citizens Advice Bureaux Trust and Family Holiday Association (£2,000 each) and Lydbrook Community Care (£1,000).

Artistic Causes – 18 grants totalling £106,000 (£118,000)

Beneficiaries included the Royal Shakespeare Company (£25,000), Chipping Norton Theatre Trust and Old Vic Theatre Trust (£10,000 each), Royal National Theatre (£8,000 in two grants), Cheltenham International Jazz Festival (£7,500), London Academy of Music and Dramatic Art, Royal Academy of Arts and Royal Academy of Music (£5,000 each), Guildhall School Trust (£4,000), Dancers' Trust and Pallant House Gallery Appeal (£3,000 each), Streetwise Opera (£2,000) and London Festival of Chamber Music (£1,000).

Other Medical Research – 9 grants totalling £102,000 (£60,000)

Beneficiaries were SPECAL (Specialised Early Care for Alzheimer's) (£50,000), International Spinal Research Trust and LEPRA (£10,000 each), Hepatitis C Trust (£7,000) and Alzheimer's Society, David Tolkien Trust for Stoke Mandeville National Spinal Injuries Centre, Health Unlimited, Restoration of Appearance and Function Trust and William Harvey Research Foundation (£5,000 each).

Homeless/Housing – 18 grants totalling £88,000 (£53,000)

Beneficiaries included Rural Housing Trust and YMCA (£10,000 each), Nightstop UK (£10,000 in two grants), Church Housing Trust, Field Lane Homeless Families Centre and St Basil's (£5,000 each), Community Housing and Therapy (£4,000), Haven Trust (£3,000) and Broadway (£2,000).

Conservation/Preservation – 11 grants totalling £78,000 (£55,000)

Two large grants were made, to St Paul's Cathedral Foundation (£42,000) and Gloucester Cathedral Trust (£10,000). Other beneficiaries included Christ Church – Cheltenham (£5,000), Georgian Group (£3,000) and St John the Baptist Church – Elmore (£1,000).

Employment and Job Creation – 7 grants totalling £73,000 (£52,000)

Beneficiaries were Prince's Youth Business Trust (£50,000 in two grants), Village Retail Services Association Educational Trust (£10,000), Gymnation (£5,000), Back to Work – Over 40's and Blind Business Association Charitable Trust (£3,000 each) and Computer Aid International (£2,000).

Research into Deafness – 5 grants totalling £73,000 (£17,000)

One large donation was made to Royal National Institute for Deaf People (£50,000). The other grants were made to Mary Hare Foundation (£10,000), Deafax Trust and Defeating Deafness (£5,000 each) and National Deaf Children's Society (£3,000).

Drug Prevention and Treatment – 2 grants totalling £70,000 (£41,000)

The two beneficiaries were Life Education Centres UK (£60,000) and Gloucestershire Life Education Centre (£10,000).

Hospital/Nursing Home Building and Equipment – 3 grants totalling £65,000 (£5,000)

The three beneficiaries were Oxford Children's Hospital Campaign (£50,000), St Bartholomew's and the Royal London Charitable Foundation (£10,000) and King Edward VII's Hospital Sister Agnes (£5,000).

Population Control – 3 grants totalling £62,000 (£40,000)

Beneficiaries were Margaret Pyke Memorial Trust (£52,000 in two grants) and Interact Worldwide (£10,000).

Research into Blindness – 10 grants totalling £44,000 (£45,000)

Beneficiaries included National Blind Children's Society and Telephones for the Blind Fund (£5,000 each) and British Council for the Prevention of Blindness and U Can Do I.T. (£3,000 each).

Crime Prevention – 7 grants totalling £28,000 (£45,000)

Beneficiaries were Crimestoppers (£10,000), Victim Support (£6,000 in two grants), Haven Distribution (£4,000), Gloucestershire Community Chaplaincy and Smart Criminal Justice Services (£3,000 each) and Be Your Best Foundation (£2,000).

Care of the Elderly – 4 grants totalling £23,000 (£41,000)

Beneficiaries were Notsey Trust (£18,000 in two grants), Universal Beneficient Society (£3,000) and Age Concern – Birmingham (£2,000)

There was also a donation of £7,500 to St Christopher's Hospice.

Comment

The information about how this charity works has improved; the relatively new practice of at least categorising the grants made is a useful advance. However the purposes for which they are made are still not disclosed, even when hundreds of thousands of pounds are given to a single organisation.

The trustees only meet twice a year, although there is a subcommittee for making grants of less than £25,000 in between these occasions.

Exclusions

No grants to individuals or to small local charities, such as individual churches or village halls, where there is no special connection to the trust. Appeals from local branches or offshoots of national charitable bodies are normally not considered.

Applications

In writing to the correspondent. The charity states that 'appeals will usually be considered within three months, but

may be referred for further consideration at board meetings which are held twice a year, normally in March and October.' Only successful applications are notified of the decision.

The Church Urban Fund

Welfare; Christian outreach in disadvantaged communities in England

£2.7 million (2004)

Beneficial area The most deprived areas of England.

Church House, Great Smith Street, Westminster, London SW1P 3NZ

Tel. 020 7898 1647 **Fax** 020 7898 1601

Email enquiries@cuf.org.uk

Website www.cuf.org.uk

Correspondent Fran Beckett, Chief Executive

Trustees *Peter Doyle, chair; Ven. Richard Atkinson; Richard Farnell; Ven. Granville Gibson; Chair of Grants Committee; Canon John Stanley; Patrick Coldstream; Dorothy Stewart; Rt Revd John Austin; Rt Revd Pete Broadbent; Michael Eastwood; Yvonne Hutchinson; Andrew Hunter Johnston.*

Charity Commission no. 297483

Information available Full information was provided by the fund.

Summary

The Church Urban Fund (CUF) makes grants, up to a usual maximum of £30,000, but usually about £20,000 in disadvantaged areas to groups that are part of, or have support from, local Anglican church structures.

To be eligible for a grant from CUF, a project must:

- be based in the 10% most disadvantaged areas of England
- be part of or have a working relationship with the local Anglican church
- tackle issues identified by the local community as important to them.

Background

CUF was established in 1988 following the publication of the report 'Faith in the City', commissioned by the Church of England. The report suggested that the Church should 'set up a fund to help churches work more closely with their local communities to help people tackle poor housing, poor education, unemployment and poverty'.

An initial capital sum was raised from what was presented at the time as a one-off appeal and income from this provides about half of the fund's present income. Most of the rest comes from continued donations and legacies.

As grants are being made at a level of about £3 million a year, well above the present annual income, it was necessary to decide whether the fund should simply exhaust its resources and then wind up, or whether it should have a continuing existence, probably involving renewed fundraising, or should simply continue operating at a much more modest level on the money earned by its existing capital.

The issue was contentious, as the fund represents in practice a very considerable financial transfer from congregations in prosperous parts of the country, themselves often struggling financially, to those that are poorest. However it has now been decided that the fund should have an ongoing existence and that fundraising should be renewed, starting in 2005.

Guidelines for applicants
Priorities and criteria for funding
The Church Urban Fund assists community-based projects that tackle issues of disadvantage, poverty and marginalisation in the poorest areas of England. The Church Urban Fund was set up in 1988 in response to the Faith in the City report a Church of England report that drew attention to the increasing levels of poverty in urban areas and to the widening gap between rich and poor.

Objectives
The Church Urban Fund's key objectives are to confront disadvantage and inequality in deprived communities and promote their economic, social and spiritual renewal. In particular we will support projects that:

• Tackle major problems in their area, such as poverty, unemployment, disaffected youth, lack of community facilities, loneliness and isolation, or housing and homelessness.

• Equip local communities to address local needs and issues, and encourage people to take control of their lives.
• Empower the faith community to take an active role in wider community development, particularly through interfaith and ecumenical developments
• Are innovative, will make a practical impact and can develop partnerships with other agencies.

Award level
Church Urban Fund is a first funder and many projects find that having Church Urban Fund funding enables them to lever significant funding from other sources. Church Urban Fund funding is limited and the maximum Church Urban Fund will award is £30,000 but this will be for those projects with the highest priority, in general awards are from £12,000 and £25,000. The Church Urban Fund never awards 100% funding.

Criteria
1. The project needs to be in the worst 10% of deprived areas in England.
2. The project needs to be based in the local community and to have local community involvement in identifying needs, initiating responses and running the project.
3. The project must be open to all regardless of faith, ethnic origin, disability, sex and sexual orientation.
4. The fund assists churches in deprived areas in their outreach to their local community. Projects do not have to be Anglican but there needs to be a strong link between the project and a faith group and the project needs to be endorsed by the Diocesan Bishop.
5. The project must have charitable purposes.
6. The project must be able to raise part of the required money from other sources.

Priority will be given to:
1. Projects with the greatest levels of deprivation in England.
2. Projects identified by dioceses as being key to the reduction of deprivation in their area.
3. Projects that by their nature are limited in the funds they can access so are in particular need of CUF funding.
4. Projects where CUF funding will make the greatest impact.

Church involvement
Whilst the fund is rooted in the Christian faith, grants are not restricted on the basis of religious belief. In carrying out its commitment to the teaching of Christ to 'love your neighbour as yourself', CUF recognises the importance of forming partnerships with ecumenical and interfaith projects. The fund welcomes applications from minority ethnic groups and from other faith groups and encourages such groups to apply.

Church involvement can range from being a wholly church owned project to one in which the church gives active support. Support should involve promotion, fundraising and/or volunteering by the church community. It needs to be more than the church being the landlord or there being a church member on the management committee.

The first point of contact for all applicants is the Diocesan Link Officer who holds the application forms and all application are first considered by the diocese who will select which project go forward to the Church Urban Fund. A letter from the Diocesan Bishop must support all projects.

Small Grants Programme
Small grants are divided into small initiative grants and project support grants. To be eligible for these grants, a project must demonstrate church involvement, be serving a deprived area and be engaged in urban regeneration.

All applications must be made on the appropriate form and submitted via your diocese along with relevant documentation and the recommendation of the diocesan bishop. For more information, contact your diocesan co-ordinator or contact the Grants Unit.

Grants in 2004
The largest grant was £100,000 to CTBI Racial Justice Fund. Other grants of £25,000 or more were: £40,000 to St Augustine's Community Works Project; £30,000 each to Gipton Arts Centre Ltd, St Stephen's PCC – Burnley and West Yorkshire Community Chaplaincy Project; and £25,000 each to Accross Communities, Ca14 Arts Project, Kairos Women Working Together, St dunstan's PCC – Bellingham, St Martin's – Byker and St Mary and St Chad – Longton.

Exclusions
• Projects outside England.

- Individuals.
- Projects not in the worst 10% of deprived areas.
- Direct support for other grant giving bodies.
- Publications and research.
- Revenue and capital funding for regional and national voluntary/community organisations, and public and private sector organisations.
- Replacement of statutory funding.
- Projects without faith links.
- Work that has already been funded by CUF for five years.
- Local ministry to those within the church, and overt evangelistic activity.
- Clergy stipends including Church Army posts.
- Internal re-ordering of churches for worship, church maintenance and repairs
- Work that does not increase the capacity of the organisation e.g. DDA compliance unless as part of a wider scheme.
- Organisations with significant reserves.
- Ongoing costs of Credit Unions.
- General appeals.

We will not give 100% funding. We never make retrospective grants, nor can we help pay off deficits or loans.

Applications

To help ensure that projects are rooted in their communities, the fund has developed a two-stage application process in which proposals are considered by the local diocese before being forwarded to our national office. So the first step is to contact the CUF officer in your diocese.

The officer will help you to determine whether your project meets the fund's criteria. He or she will also guide you through the process of securing a recommendation from the diocesan bishop, who prioritises all requests against the overall urban strategy for the diocese and forwards them to the fund.

When the application reaches our office, a member of the grants unit will contact the project to arrange an assessment visit. This visit usually lasts one to two hours, and gives us a chance to ask any questions that are not covered in the application form, clarify information and collect further documents if necessary. It is also an opportunity for applicants to ask questions and seek advice.

The application and the recommendation of the grants officer who has visited the project are then carefully considered by the grants committee, whose award decisions are ratified by our trustees.

The fund always receives more applications than it has resources to support.

Therefore, even if a project fits our criteria, it may not be possible to make a grant.

The CUF funding committee meets 4 times per year in the first week of March, June, September and December. Deadlines for applications vary between dioceses as each has its own assessment process prior to submission to the Church Urban Fund.

The Cinderford Charitable Trust (formerly the Ofenheim & Cinderford Charitable Trusts)

Health and welfare, arts, environment

£336,000 (2002/03)

Beneficial area UK, with a preference for East Sussex.

Baker Tilly, 1st Floor, 46 Clarendon Road, Watford, Hertfordshire WD17 1HE

Tel. 01923 657700

Correspondent G Wright

Trustees *R J Clark; R McLeod.*

Charity Commission no. 286525

Information available Full accounts were on file at the Charity Commission.

In May 2002, the trustees of the Ofenheim Charitable Trust transferred all of its assets to the Cinderford Charitable Trust, which it previously worked in conjunction with.

The trust makes donations to a variety of mainly UK causes, with some preference for East Sussex due to the founder's association with that area. High-profile organisations in the fields of health, welfare, arts and the environment are supported with many of the same organisations benefitting each year.

In 2002/03 it had assets of £8.4 million and an income of £296,000. Grants totalled £336,000.

Larger donations included: £12,000 each to Save the Children, Scope, Trinity Hospice and WWF (UK); £10,000 to Trinity College of Music; and £9,000 each to Children's Society, Elizabeth Finn Trust and Glyndebourne Arts

Trust. Smaller donations included: £5,000 each to Crusaid, Greater London Hospital for the Blind, Mildmay Hospital, St Wilfred's Hospice Eastbourne and Toynbee Hall; £3,000 each to Choir and Music Trust Fund and Hospice Care Kenya; and £2,000 each to Barn Owl Trust, Chaseley Trust, Greenwich, Deptford and Rotherhithe Sea Cadet Unit and Wallace Collection.

Applications

In writing to the correspondent. The bulk of the income is given to charities supported over a number of years and unsolicited applications will not be acknowledged. Trustees meet in March and applications need to be received by February.

The City Parochial Foundation (see also Trust for London)

Social welfare in London

£8.9 million (2003)

Beneficial area The Metropolitan Police District of London and the City of London.

6 Middle Street, London EC1A 7PH

Tel. 020 7606 6145 **Fax** 020 7600 1866

Email info@cityparochial.org.uk

Website www.cityparochial.org.uk

Correspondent Bharat Mehta, Clerk

Trustees *Ms Maggie Baxter, chair; Prof. Julian Franks; Peter Williams; Ms Elahe Panahi; Nigel Pantling; Charles Edward Lord; Ian David Luder; Peter Dale; Mrs Gillian Roberts; Prof. Gerald Manners; John Barnes; Miles Barber; John Muir; Mrs Jyoti Munsiff; Mrs Lynda Stevens; Albert Tucker; Ms Jane Wilmot; Cllr Raj Chandarana.*

Charity Commission no. 205629

Information available Grant guidelines; annual report and accounts; a review of policy for the years 2002–2006; an annual grants review and other publications.

Summary

The foundation gives grants, often towards salary or project costs, to a wide range of usually small or medium-sized charities working with, and often arising from, the poorer London communities. Grants are usually for amounts between £15,000 and £50,000 and often spread over up to three years.

From 2002 to 2006 grants will be concentrated on organisations tackling problems of discrimination, isolation and violence.

The foundation is also an active promoter of the voluntary sector in London generally, as far as the sector is concerned with the welfare of those in poverty.

The jointly administered **Trust for London** (which has its own entry) makes small grants in the same fields.

Background

The City Parochial Foundation (CPF) was established in 1891 as an amalgamation of the charities of most of the 112 parishes of the City of London. The trustees are appointed by various other bodies such as the Corporation of London, the Crown and London University. In 1986 the foundation also undertook the administration of the Trust for London.

In 2003 the foundation had assets of £158.4 million and an income of £12 million.

The foundation's mission is 'to benefit the poor of London. 'The poor' includes people who, for whatever reason, are socially, culturally, spiritually, environmentally and financially disadvantaged.

'The area our work covers is the Metropolitan Police District of London, which includes all 32 London boroughs, and the City of London. Every five years we review our grantmaking policies and issue new guidelines for those who want funding.'

General

The grant programmes are reviewed every five years and those described in this entry will be reviewed in 2006. Contact the foundation or check its website for up-to-date information.

The foundation notes that:

Throughout its history, the foundation has been guided by two major principles:

- an awareness of, and a need to guard against, the tendency for benefactions for the poor to fall into the hands of a somewhat higher income class
- a concern not to finance schemes which can be financed by local or central government so that the charitable funds are used, in effect, to subsidise the statutory authorities.

The foundation has a relatively large staff and often gets closely involved with the organisations that it supports. The foundation: 'has realised that organisations do not simply need money. In many cases – and particularly with small organisations which often have at most one or two members of staff – do not have internal resources for such things as training. And often activities that would normally be carried out by specialist staff, such as finance and accounting, are just among a host of things which have to be carried out by non-specialists.

This is why [the foundation has] adopted an approach best described as more than just funding or funding plus.'

Grant guidelines 2002–2006

These guidelines are largely reprinted from the last edition of this guide.

The types of organisation we fund

Generally, any organisation applying for funding should:

- be a registered charity (or have applied for charitable status), an industrial and provident society or a friendly society
- be open to all members of its community
- involve its service users as much as possible in the overall control and the management of the organisation
- be committed to sharing information, good practice and findings from its work with other organisations
- work jointly with other organisations as much as possible.

Our grant making priorities

We welcome grant applications from registered charities or charitable organisations that aim to

- tackle the causes of poverty
- help Londoners to cope with, and find ways out of, poverty.

We want to fund work which helps poor Londoners by reducing or overcoming
- discrimination
- isolation
- violence.

Groups of people we particularly want to target

We welcome applications from all organisations working with poor Londoners who are experiencing discrimination, isolation or violence, but we particularly encourage applications from organisations that work with, or are aiming to work with, the following:

- black, Asian and minority ethnic communities
- disabled people
- established communities, often predominantly white, in areas of long-term poverty
- lesbians and gay men
- refugees and asylum seekers
- young people aged 10–25.

Women are more likely to experience poverty, particularly through discrimination, isolation and violence, and so we especially welcome applications from women's organisations.

The work we will fund

We will fund the following types of work:

A. Organisations providing advice, information and individual advocacy – especially those organisations that are user-led or those that encourage user involvement, participation, and which lead to empowerment. For example:

- an organisation managed by parents to provide an independent advice, information and support service to parents of pupils from Black and minority ethnic communities who have been excluded (suspended or expelled) from school.
- an organisation working with benefit claimants who have a history of mental illness, to support them in applying for their benefits.

B. Organisations developing, promoting and providing education, training and employment schemes. For example:

- an organisation aiming to give refugees and asylum seekers access to IT training courses.
- an organisation seeking to promote training as mentors amongst middle-aged unemployed people in an area of long-term poverty.

C. Organisations that are attempting to develop initiatives that tackle violence and hate crimes against the target groups, for example:

- an organisation working with local people and the local police to tackle vandalism on an estate.
- an organisation providing support to victims of domestic violence, racist or homophobic harassment and violence.

We will consider applications for work with people who commit crimes and violence as well as work with the victims of crime or violence.

Core costs and management costs

Core funding for organisations led by or addressing the needs of the targeted groups can be difficult to secure. We usually encourage organisations to include a reasonable amount of management costs to cover their overheads when they apply for funding. In exceptional cases, we will consider funding the core costs of such organisations.

Other areas of interest

Work that aims to change policy

We welcome applications from any organisation that is working with the targeted groups to bring about policy changes relating to isolation, discrimination and violence and aimed at improving people's quality of life. For example:

- work that is led by disabled young people that results in greater provision of integrated services for disabled people in the area.

Second tier and infrastructure organisations

We believe that organisations led by or meeting the needs of the targeted groups need support and development. We will fund second tier and infrastructure organisations that want to provide such help to the targeted groups. For example:

- a Council for Voluntary Service that wishes to provide financial management training and consultancy for refugee community organisations.

Working with others

There can be advantages in organisations working with others to meet the needs of their members. We are particularly keen to fund such ventures amongst the targeted groups, for example:

- a refugee organisation and a lesbian and gay group working together on issues of community safety with the local police.

Small grants

Small one-off grants of up to £10,000 can significantly improve the efficiency of an organisation. We will consider applications for small grants from any organisation working with the targeted groups.

Exceptional cases

In exceptional cases we will consider applications for unexpected needs.

Foundation initiatives

Besides making grants in response to applications received, the foundation also undertakes initiatives of its own.

Two of these are still supported financially by this foundation.

Employability

This is an initiative of the City Parochial Foundation and a number of RCO and Refugee agencies. It was established as a registered charity in 2001. Employability exists to provide practical help to remove the barriers to employment that are frequently experienced by refugees in Britain.

The Evelyn Oldfield Unit

This was established in 1994 by a consortium of funding bodies and agencies which work with refugee community organisations, including City Parochial Foundation, Thames Telethon, London Borough Grants (now the Association of London Government), the Refugee Working Party and the Refugee Council. The aim is to develop specialist support for refugee organisations to enable them adequately to tackle the pressing needs of the communities they serve.

Review of 2003

The following information is taken from the 2003 annual report:

Incoming resources

Income from investment properties represented 43% of the foundation's incoming resources. The total income from investment properties fell from £5,230,000 in 2002 to £4,959,000 in 2003.

Bank and other interests fell to £869,000 in 2003 from £1,007,000 in 2002. Income from listed investments rose from £1,636,000 in 2002 to £1,869,000 in 2003.

Grants payable

Total grants payable in the year were £8,876,000 (2002: £7,235,000). Of this amount £5,092,000 was payable from the Central Fund and £3,784,000 was payable from the City Church Fund.

Grants made from the Central Fund

2003 is the second year of the present quinquennium 2002–2006 during which the trustees are allocating grants with the following priorities:

- organisations providing advice, information and individual advocacy;
- organisations developing, promoting and providing education, training and employment schemes;
- organisations that are attempting to develop initiatives that tackle violence and hate crimes against the target groups.

The trustees also appreciate the importance of back up or development work for the voluntary sector and fund the following:

- core costs and management costs;
- policy change;
- second tier and infrastructure organisations;
- collaborative responses
- alliance funding.

The trustees also have a Small Grants programme and may provide continuation funding for work funded by the foundation under the previous quinquennial policy.

In addition to the grants made from the Central Fund, a capital grant was made of £1.2 million to the Bellingham Recreation Project.

Analysis of grants by category (2002–2006)

Advice, information and individual advocacy	33%
Education, training and employment schemes	24%
CPF initiatives	13%
Schemes to reduce/tackle violence/hate crimes	9%
Core costs	9%
Second tier and infrastructure	8%
Policy change	3%

The policy of making mainly revenue grants was continued with 99% of the grants falling into this category.

The boroughs receiving more than £100,000 of grant money were: Barnet, Brent, Ealing, Hackney, Hammersmith and Fulham, Haringey, Hounslow, Islington, Lambeth, Merton, Southwark, Tower Hamlets and Westminster.

There were 205 grants made in total during the year.

Grants in 2003/04

The foundation's website provides information on more recent beneficiaries from 2003/04, with a description of the purpose of the grant.

Beneficiaries included: Bellingham Project, towards the cost of the project director, the project administrator and towards the production of a publication on the project's history (£150,000 over three years); Evelyn Oldfield Unit, towards the salary and on-costs of the director (£100,000 over three years); Croydon Housing Aid Society, towards the salary and promotion costs to establish a new housing advice project which will work with victims of domestic violence and racial and homophobic hate crimes (£50,000 over three years); Disability Advice Service Lambeth, towards a salary and running costs (£40,000 over two years); Tolerance in Diversity – Tower Hamlets, towards rent, running costs and community workshops (£30,000 over two years); Hampstead Theatre – Camden, towards the costs of an arts and drama project for people with disabilities (£20,000 over two years); Wandsworth and Merton Law Centre, towards the expansion of the education law team to develop services across south west

London (£15,000); Brentford Community Resource Centre to upgrade the current computers and for other IT-related expenses (£10,000); and Fitzrovia Neighbourhood Association, for salaries and costs (£7,000).

Exclusions

No grants for:

- endowment appeals
- individual members of the public
- major expenses for buying or building premises
- medical research and equipment
- organisations currently receiving funding from Trust for London
- replacing public funds
- trips abroad.

Applications

There are no application forms. The first thing you should do is read the guidelines and check that your organisation and the work that you want the City Parochial Foundation to fund fits into their grantmaking programme. If you feel that your work does fit the guidelines you should follow these stages.

Stage 1

Send written details of your planned work and funding needs (on no more than two sides of A4 paper) along with:

- your organisation's constitution;
- your most recent financial accounts;
- your most recent annual report.

Or

Telephone a field officer at the foundation to talk about your work and the funding you are looking for.

Stage 2

If CPF feels that your planned work fits their grantmaking criteria, a field officer will arrange to meet you and discuss it further.

Stage 3

Once you and the field officer agree about what you should apply for, you can apply by making a full written application on no more than three sides of A4 paper in a format that the field officer will give to you. Full applications must be received before the relevant deadlines listed below.

Stage 4

The field officer will present this application to the grants committee, which will make the final decision about funding your application.

Stage 5

You will be told about the decision in writing after the foundation's trustee board meeting.

If you would like to discuss your proposal before writing to CPF, you should contact them by telephone on 020 7606 6145.

When you should apply

You should contact CPF at least three months before the relevant deadline. The grants committee meets four times a years in January, April, July and October. The deadlines for receiving completed applications are:

    31 January for the April meeting
    15 April for the July meeting
    15 August for the October meeting
    15 November for the January meeting

An application is completed when you have had a meeting with a field officer, staff have no further questions to raise, and all the necessary papers have been received.

The Clore Duffield Foundation

Arts/museums, Jewish charities, education, elderly and disadvantaged

£4.5 million (2002)

Beneficial area UK, the larger grants go to London-based institutions.

Studio 3, Chelsea Manor Studios, Flood Street, London SW3 5SR

Tel. 020 7351 6061 **Fax** 020 7351 5308

Email info@cloreduffield.org.uk

Website www.cloreduffield.org.uk

Correspondent The Administrator

Trustees *Dame Vivien Duffield, chair; Caroline Deletra; David Harrel; Sir Jocelyn Stevens; Michael Trask; Sir Mark Weinberg.*

Charity Commission no. 1084412

Information available Excellent annual report. Good website with guidelines.

Summary

The trust makes a small number of main programme grants, though they can sometimes be very large, mainly in the fields of:

- the arts generally;
- health and social welfare, especially but not only to Jewish charities.

There is also a programme called Artworks for schools art education (up to £2,000). Another small grant programme is expected to be relaunched in 2005 focusing on performing arts education.

General

In 2002 the foundation received a total of 2,895 applications and made 123 donations, making the success rate around 1 in 24. Grants totalled £4,490,000, and ranged from £2,000 to £1,000,000.

The work of the foundation is comprehensively described in the annual report for 2002, as follows:

Introduction

This report covers the second full year of operation for the Clore Duffield Foundation, which was formed in December 2000, from the merger of the Clore Foundation and the Vivien Duffield Foundation. The Clore Foundation was established in 1964 by the late Sir Charles Clore. His daughter, Dame Vivien Duffield, became chairman of the foundation in 1979 and created her own in 1987. The priorities of the former foundations remain the priorities of the new foundation.

Grantmaking policies

Broadly speaking, the foundation concentrates its support on education, arts and museum education, cultural leadership training (new in 2002), the arts, health and social welfare. The foundation places a particular emphasis on supporting children, young people and society's more vulnerable individuals, through the charities which work to educate, inspire, empower or care for them.

The foundation does not adopt a rigid approach in terms of the criteria for its grantmaking. It does not fund individuals, but it can match lottery funding, fund capital redevelopments and provide project, programme and revenue funding. Its application procedures are straightforward and it is likely that the foundation will continue to maintain a balance between supporting large-scale projects with far reaching effects and small-scale local community endeavours.

The foundation balances its philanthropic work across reactive grant-giving and a more active, operational approach. When it sees a gap in provision, it will occasionally step in to put together a programme to address perceived need. This was the case when the foundation launched its Artworks Programme for schools (in 1999), and is currently the case with the foundation's new Clore Leadership Programme. Visual arts education and cultural leadership training are both areas of concern for the foundation and it has responded by acting to put in place specific initiatives to improve provision. In both instances, the foundation could not identify an appropriate independent agency to act as an intermediary so it has stepped in to support schools and cultural sector employees directly. This has been a new route for the foundation and one which has already borne fruit. It is likely that this approach will continue alongside the foundation's other donations.

Programmes and future directions

In 2002 the foundation managed three main programmes: a Main Grants Programme, a Small Grants Programme for Museum and Gallery Education, and the Artworks Programme (a visual arts education initiative through which grants are awarded to schools). All three strands of the foundation's activities are detailed in the Review of 2002 below. There [were] two changes [in] 2003: the addition of the Clore Leadership Programme (www.cloreleadership.org.uk), a new foundation initiative based at Somerset House; and the cessation of the Clore Small Grants Programme for museum and gallery education. The latter was launched in 1998 for a five-year period. [There will be no Small Grants Programme in 2004, although the foundation intends to relaunch it in 2005 with the focus being on performing arts education. The foundation's website will have up-to-date information when the details are finalised.]

Organisational structure

Dame Vivien Duffield is chairman of the foundation alongside five other trustees. A full-time staff of two – an Executive Director and a Secretary & Administrator – report to the Board. The trustees are advised by their investment managers and the staff of the foundation are advised by three Specialist Advisers assigned to specific programmes. All decisions are taken by the trustees. All investment decisions are taken by the trustees upon the advice of their investment managers.

Review of 2002

[Where appropriate grant values for new awards have been added in square brackets by these editors.]

Museums and galleries

2002 saw a continued emphasis on supporting museum and gallery education through both capital donations and programme funding and through both the Main Grants Programme and the Small Grants Programme. The foundation has always defined this sector broadly, so as to embrace science and discovery centres and children's museums.

The foundation commenced its support for the three Discovery Areas and two Study Areas within the British Galleries at the Victoria and Albert Museum [£500,000, the first instalment of a total donation of £1,500,000] and was gratified to see the extremely positive visitor feedback. The Galleries set a new standard for interpretation within museums, one to which the V&A must now aspire in terms of those of its galleries which have not been refreshed for some time. The foundation concluded its support for the Clore Educational Centre at Tate Modern [£1,000,000] and is pleased that the Tate have refurbished the space since opening to make it more inviting for students and their teachers. There were new donations for the Foundling Museum [£150,000] and the Museum of London [£300,000], to create Clore Educational Centres. Both of these are a long way off realisation and the foundation will view their evolution with interest, in the context of its research into creative learning environments in museums and galleries.

The trustees were particularly pleased to continue their support of the introduction of interactive exhibits into museum and gallery environments, with a donation towards the new Clore Natural History Centre at the redeveloped Liverpool Museum, opening in 2005 [£125,000] and further funding for the Clore Interactive Gallery at Manchester Art Gallery [£100,000]. This substantial space within the beautifully refurbished gallery has set new standards for hands-on approaches within galleries, providing a wonderful introduction to the collections for young visitors and their families. The trustees also continued their support for a new website for children – www.show.me.uk – as part of the very popular 24 Hour Museum website [£44,000, the second of three annual donations].

Not all donations were for capital projects. Dulwich Picture Gallery was granted funding in support of its education work [£10,000, first instalment of five annual grants], in recognition of its innovative and high quality programmes, and of their longevity. The foundation has supported the gallery's education work on several occasions since 1988, when very few galleries of a similar size had education staff or education programmes in place. The foundation also provided support for a conference for the UK network of science and discovery centres (ECSITE) and made a donation to support the education category of the Museum of the Year Award [£2,000].

2002 saw two rounds of donations (totalling 29 grants) through the foundation's Small Grants Programme for museum and gallery education. These spanned independent and local authority funded museums, art galleries, a community arts centre, and industrial heritage museums. The grants funded a range of projects, from the innovative to the very practical; these included the refurbishment of education facilities, theatre-in-education workshops, outreach activities, handling collections and discovery boxes, and workshops for young offenders and those at risk of getting involved with the criminal justice system, in a partnership project between the Galleries of Justice and Soft Touch Community Arts [£8,500]. The foundation has seen extensive evidence of the importance of making small grants available for small institutions which lack the resources of the national museums and galleries, and has been immensely gratified by the resulting projects. The trustees hope that this combination of large and small-scale funding for museum and gallery education will enable many more children and families to explore their cultural heritage in exciting and imaginative ways and within purpose-built spaces.

Whilst the majority of the foundation's support in this field focused on education, other donations included a donation to the National Portrait Gallery for the purchase of Sargent's portrait of Lord Balfour [£10,000] and further support for the Hermitage Rooms at Somerset House [£15,000].

Visual arts education

2002 saw the continued delivery of the foundation's major new visual arts education initiative. Artworks: Young Artists of the Year Awards is an annual initiative endorsed by the four Arts Councils and Qualification and Curriculum Authorities, Tate and other related agencies. The Artworks Programme aims to motivate and support teachers to develop ambitious and inventive teaching in art and design; to increase opportunities for children and young people to be inspired and challenged through learning about art; and to endorse the role that galleries and artists can play in the provision of high quality art and design education. There are three Award categories: Working with Artists, Working with Galleries and Working from Other Sources. Financial awards are available to schools and the award-winning projects are disseminated through the Artworks website (www.art-works.org.uk), as well as in an Artworks book which is sent to every school which enters the awards.

More than 550 schools entered the awards in 2002, their entries representing the work of around 37,000 pupils. The awards ceremony was held at Tate Modern on 20 June 2002, Children's Art Day with the award-winning schools represented by 200 children and teachers [29 schools received £2,050 each]. In addition to funds for art materials and trips, the winning schools, teachers and pupils all received a specially commissioned, signed, limited-edition print by internationally acclaimed artist Anish Kapoor. In addition, a donation of £25,000 was made to the National Association for Gallery Education (Engage), to fund a small grants scheme through which 53 galleries and museums were able to run events to celebrate Children's Art Day in 2003 on 3 July.

In addition to the awards and Children's Art Day, a further dimension to Artworks was added in 2001 when the foundation embarked upon an art education research programme. On 20 June 2002 the foundation published The Big Sink, the first-phase results of a two-year Artworks research project investigating art education spaces in schools, galleries and museums. The research was devised and funded by the foundation as part of its Artworks programme, and its findings are at the heart of the foundation's concerns, both as the founder of Artworks and as a funder of education spaces within galleries and museums throughout the UK. The project was developed in close partnership with Arts Council England, the Department for Education and Skills, the Heritage Lottery Fund, the Qualifications and Curriculum Authority, and other arts funding bodies.

The Big Sink is an investigation into the ideal spaces for creative, and specifically visual, arts exploration in schools, galleries and museums. In the course of consulting the users and managers of these spaces, it became evident that even the smallest details of space need careful consideration. One such small detail is the specification of sinks – their size, height and location, as well as what goes in and out of them; hence the title of the report.

The foundation was prompt to launch Artworks in response to the trustees' concern about the status of art in the curriculum. It will continue its commitment to Artworks and to the promotion of visual arts education, and will develop the scheme in partnership with the appropriate related agencies, over the coming years.

Performing arts

In the world of the performing arts, the trustees continued their funding of the National Theatre [£50,000] and the Royal Opera House [£40,000] (largely for the Clore Duffield Schools' Matinees Programme, enabling schoolchildren to attend opera and ballet performances at a fraction of the normal ticket price). New donations were made to the Friends of the Kirov Opera and Ballet [£40,000], and to the British Friends of the Israel Philharmonic Orchestra [£72,000].

2002 saw a number of donations to arts organisations to fund their work with young people, and particularly those who could only take part with financial support, such as participants in the Yorkshire Ballet Summer School [£5,000] and the Royal Ballet Summer School [£2,000]. The foundation also made a contribution towards the education work at Aldeburgh [£25,000, plus £5,000], and continued support for two organisations offering intensive residential conservatoire experience – the Samling Foundation in Cumbria [£20,000 final instalment] and IMS Prussia Cove in

Cornwall [£10,000 final instalment]. New support for Wigmore Hall in 2002 funded the educational work of the very impressive Belcea String Quartet [£12,000]. *The foundation will relaunch its Small Grants Programme in 2005 focusing on performing arts education.*

Education

Education support in 2002, beyond the arts sector, spanned initiatives to assist Jewish students and a scheme designed to inform secondary students about the realities of the situation in Israel and Palestine.

The trustees were pleased to continue support for the Women's Library in Whitechapel. Whilst the foundation has long supported education spaces within museums, it has rarely received such requests from libraries; the trustees were therefore delighted to fund the Clore Education Space and Seminar Room of the Women's Library, part of Guildhall University [£100,000]. This inspirational new library, built to house the Fawcett Collection – the UK's oldest and most comprehensive research library on all aspects of women in society, spanning suffrage and educational opportunities, fashion, cookery and a wide range of issues – is a model of good practice in terms of demonstrating how an archive and library can be opened up for exhibition and educational purposes. We hope to see more such proposals from specialist libraries.

Social welfare

Children and young people remained high on the foundation's agenda beyond the sphere of the performing arts, as did a concern for the quality of life for Britain's elderly population. The latter was reflected in support for research into Alzheimer's disease at Oxford University [£15,000]; the former was reflected in continued support of the Anna Freud Centre in North London towards their family support work [£10,000], in donations to Great Ormond Street [£10,000] and Chase Children's Hospice [£60,000], and in funding for holidays for children with asthma, organised by the National Asthma Campaign [£7,000]. The trustees were particularly pleased to provide support for Mencap's Gateway Clubs, to build a programme of creative arts activities for people with learning disabilities across the UK.

Looking ahead

Following a research and development project which commenced in January 2002 and drew to a close in December 2002, the trustees decided at the close of the year to move forward with a new foundation initiative to improve leadership training in the UK's cultural sector. The Rt. Hon. Chris Smith MP was subsequently appointed Director of the Clore Leadership Programme in April 2003 and in June he took up residence at Somerset House in London, where he was

joined by Deputy Director Sue Hoyle and Administrator Helen Acton. The programme will support in the region of 20 Clore Fellows a year, who will participate in a bespoke, modular programme involving secondments, mentor, a leadership course, bursaries to attend existing courses, university research fellowships and an annual conference. Full details of how to apply to become a Clore Fellow, published January 2004, are available at www.cloreleadership.org.uk.

Exclusions

No donations or grants to individuals, whether for education or any other purpose.

Applications

Applicants whose proposals fall within the foundation's defined areas of interest are advised to submit first-stage letters of application, on no more than two sides of A4 (enclosing an stamped addressed envelope and omitting any annual reports or other enclosures). There are no deadlines for submitting an application.

The Clothworkers' Foundation and other Trusts

Clothworking, general

£3 million (2003)

Beneficial area UK and overseas.

Clothworkers' Hall, Dunster Court, Mincing Lane, London EC3R 7AH

Tel. 020 7623 7041 **Fax** 020 7397 0107

Website www.clothworkers.co.uk

Correspondent The Secretary

Trustee *42 governors of the foundation.*

Charity Commission no. 274100

Information available Accounts and annual review with full grants list, analysis of grants/grantmaking, policy and guidelines. Good website.

Summary

Most grants are for amounts of between £1,000 and £50,000, although they can be for much larger amounts. They are mostly for capital costs which can include equipment and training directly related to a project.

Successful applicants cannot normally reapply for a grant for at least five years.

General

The Clothworkers' Foundation, and the associated trusts it administers (also covered by this entry), form the charitable arm of the Clothworkers' Company, one of the largest of the livery companies of the City of London. It is accessible in its grantmaking in both policy and practice and wishes to give 'the fullest possible help to potential applicants'.

'In March 2004, the Commission agreed schemes to restructure some of the remaining trusts to produce three subsidiary charities: The Clothworkers Charity for Education, The Clothworkers' Charity for Relief in Need and The Clothworkers' Charity for the Welfare of the Blind. This further rationalisation should help would-be applicants identify the charities' areas of giving.'

In 2003 the foundation had an income of £4.2 million in 2003, of which £2.0 million was donated by the Clothworkers' Company and subsidiaries. Grants totalled £2.2 million. The trusts had incoming resources of £700,000 and distributed grants of £800,000. At the end of 2003 the Foundation's assets increased to £55.6 million. The trusts' assets totalled £23.3 million.

Grantmaking policy and practice

Statement of objectives

The Clothworkers' Foundation aims through its funding to improve the quality of life, particularly for people and communities that face disadvantage.

As a major grant-maker with a permanent endowment, the foundation adopts a flexible and responsive approach to its giving.

Its primary objectives are:
- the promotion of technical textiles and preservation of the UK's textile heritage.
- the enhancement of the quality of life for the young and aged; the disabled and infirm; the disadvantaged, needy, abused and under-privileged.
- the promotion of skills by supporting education and training.

To a lesser extent, the foundation also looks to support:
- the promotion of the arts
- the work of the church
- the well-being of the national heritage and the environment
- the provision of aid to the under-developed world overseas
- the work of those organisations providing relief following international disasters

However, the foundation's grant-making policy is set in sufficiently broad terms to enable it to consider all areas of charitable giving.

Grantmaking policy

All appeals received from UK-registered charities are considered and, in so far as these are refused without direct reference to the trusts and grants committee, lists are circulated to the committee.

It is normally expected that a period of at least five years will elapse, from the date of payment of an approved grant, before consideration is given to further grants to the same charitable organisation. In the case of a grant spread over a period of years, the five year rule will apply from the date of the first payment of the first instalment.

Grants are made by means of single payments except in the case of more substantial grants, which may be made in up to five annual instalments.

The foundation does not accept invitations to appoint representatives to serve on controlling bodies or organisations and objects to which charitable assistance has been given.

Acknowledgement of the foundation's benefactions by means of loud publicity is discouraged, but publication of details of any benefaction is permitted if carried out in a discreet and unobtrusive way.

In general the foundation does not involve itself in directly financing research for which very substantial government funding and/or grants from a number of trusts are available. However, limited financial support is given for small specific projects (particularly those involving the provision of equipment) undertaken in various institutions and by certain specialist charitable organisations.

Preferential consideration is given to appeals received from self-help organisations and to charities requiring support to 'prime the pumps' for development and more extensive fund-raising initiatives. Also to appeals to textiles and kindred activities.

Normally the foundation does not support charities whose accounts disclose substantial financial resources and which have well established and ample fund-raising capabilities.

Occasional support is given towards the relief of world-wide natural disasters, such as earthquakes, floods, etc., but such support is normally channelled through the charity known as MERLIN (Medical Emergency Relief International Charitable Trust).

With certain limited exceptions the foundation does not involve itself in annual subscriptions or recurring grants to charities.

The foundation remains flexible at all times in its policy decisions, in order to preserve the breadth of its charitable endeavours.

Grantmaking practice

The foundation takes great pride in the fact that it welcomes telephone discussions between the foundation's staff and appeal officers when friendly, positive and helpful advice can be given as to what the foundation will or will not support, and as to how an application should be submitted to the foundation. Advice can also be given on the likely scale of competition for funds; how an application will be dealt with and approximately how long it will take for a decision to be reached. Experience has shown that providing help and guidance over the telephone is a highly cost-effective, efficient and helpful service to our applicants. As a matter of policy, grant interviews are rarely given in connection with fundraising since there would be insufficient time for all such interviews during each working day.

All applications receive the fullest and most careful consideration and are judged on merit and substance. Clarity of presentation and the provision of detailed factual information continues to be of the utmost importance.

All grant applicants are encouraged to seek funding from a wide range of sources and will be required to provide details of funds already raised in support of the applicant's appeal.

Clothworking

One of the foundation's primary objectives has been the 'development and evolution of Clothworking in general', reflecting the roots of The Clothworkers' Company.

The governors have been reviewing our grant-making strategy in this category, given the changes in the textile industry and the emergence of technical textiles. As a result, we plan to focus our textile-related giving on the following areas:
- academic institutions in the UK involving technical textiles, colour chemistry and needlework. This will involve the continuation of some existing relationships, as well as considering suitable appeals from other applicants.
- medical research using technical textiles, recognising that we shall have to be highly selective in projects we support.
- heritage appeals involving textiles, with particular emphasis on projects of national importance.
- grants to individual students pursuing postgraduate qualifications in textile-related subjects.

As a result, we have refined the objective to read 'the promotion of technical textiles and preservation of the UK's textile heritage'.

Grants in 2003

The charity provided the following breakdown of its grants.

Grants by sector

	Number of grants	Amount
Textiles	9	£392,500
Medicine and health	46	£990,000
Relief in need and welfare	30	£452,500
Children & youth	24	£270,000
Education and the sciences	7	£448,000
The arts	10	£97,000
The church	5	£49,000
Heritage and the environment	7	£84,000
Overseas	12	£300,000

NOTE: In the category 'Education and the sciences', 7 grants totalling £288,556 were paid to charities; 127 grants totalling £159,360 paid to individual students are excluded from this number.

Grants by size

£5,000 and under	40
over £5,000–£10,000	37
over £10,000–£25,000	46
over £25,000–£50,000	18
over £50,000	9
TOTAL	150

Geographical distribution of grants

National	32%
Greater London	13%
South East	24%
South West	6%
East Midlands	4%
West Midlands	3%
North West	2%
Eastern	1%
North East	1%
Yorkshire and Humberside	1%
Scotland	2%
Wales	1%
Overseas	10%

The charity commented that they were open to appeals from around the UK and made no distinction as to location of an applicant charity. 'In 2003, almost a third of our grant-making was to national charities, and a further 37% to beneficiaries in the South East. However such statistics can be misleading (for example, a South East-based charity may be serving people from all over the country), and we will continue to respond positively to suitable appeals regardless of geography.'

Grants approved in November 2004

Grants over £50,000 each were: £100,000 to St Paul's Cathedral Foundation for the textiles programme involving the creation of new vestments to celebrate the Cathedral's 300th Anniversary; £75,000 to CBA Projects Limited towards the capital cost of building a community resource centre which will provide enhanced facilities to support Sheffield Cathedral's social outreach, cultural and educational programmes; £60,000 to British Library Board for a conservation training bench and book conservation bench within the new British Library Centre for Conservation; and £50,000 each to Holly Bank Trust to

provide people with complex physical disabilities with a multi-activity centre and Sion Mills Building Preservation Trust for the restoration and regeneration of Herdmans Mill.

Other grants included: £40,000 to Institute of Cancer Research towards the capital cost of building a Genetic Epidemiology building to create purpose-built facilities where the causes of cancer will be investigated; £38,000 to Esther Benjamins Trust to meet the cost of a vehicle and bakery/training kitchen construction for their Circus Children Project, through which the charity is addressing the needs of the hundreds of children and people who have been trafficked from their homes in Nepal to become performers in Indian circuses; £50,000 to Queen Alexandra College towards the cost of creating a new learning centre for students with visual impairment and/or other disabilities at Queen Alexandra College, Harborne, Birmingham; £30,000 to Motor Waste Limited towards the cost of purchasing a suitable site in order to provide a permanent motor vehicle recycling centre, to provide training opportunities for disadvantaged young unemployed adults on Merseyside; £25,000 to YWCA England and Wales towards the cost of the refurbishment of a disused building in Kirkby, Merseyside to offer young disadvantaged women a much wider variety of programmes including alternative education, training courses, information, advice and guidance; £25,000 to British Archirectural Library Trust in support of a project to re-house over 1 million priceless architectural drawings, manuscripts and models at the Victoria and Albert Museum, London, thereby making them fully accessible to the public for the first time; £20,000 each to Groundwork Camden and Islington for environmental improvements of Bridgeway Street Estate and to Leeds Women's Aid for a new refuge for women and children who are experiencing domestic violence; and £15,000 each to Kemp House Trust for the conversion, refurbishment and equipping a new hospice resource in Kidderminster and Reigate and Redhill YMCA to equip and furnish a supported housing project for homeless and vulnerable young people in Surrey.

Grants of £10,000 each included those to Action for ME to assist with the expansion of a telephone support line for people with Myalgic Encephalomyelitis, Age Concern South Lakeland towards the cost of refurbishment of a newly acquired centre for older people in Cumbria, Beamish

Development Trust for improving the visitor access and interpretation at Home Farm in County Durham, Galapagos Conservation Trust for a project providing young Ecuadorean scientists the opportunity to study for professional qualifications in the UK, Institute of Cancer Research towards the capital cost of building a Genetic Epidemiology building, Thames Valley Hospice for the development of a therapeutic outpatient and day case centre and Sense – Scotland for an integrated resource centre for children and adults to support deafblind children, adults and carers in Scotland.

Exclusions

The foundation does not make grants to:

- non-UK registered charities;
- replace state or public funds;
- individuals;
- charities with ample resources or fund-raising capability;
- churches, schools, colleges or universities unless there is a close and long-standing connection with The Clothworkers Company;
- other grant-makers.

Applications are not considered from charities who have received a grant from the foundation, the initial instalment of which was paid within the previous five years.

Assistance to individuals for educational purposes is limited and is made through the associated Clothworkers' Charity for Education.

Applications

The Clothworkers' Foundation does not issue application forms. However, all applicants must complete a Data Information Sheet, which should accompany the written application/appeal. The foundation provides the following general guidelines for potential applicants:

Applications

- Applications from registered charities should be made in writing on the applicant charity's official headed notepaper. Ideally, the appeal letter itself should be no longer than two and a half pages of A4.
- Detailed costings or a budget for the project or projects referred to in the appeal letter should form a separate appendix or appendices to the appeal letter and should provide the fullest possible financial details.
- The latest annual report of the applicant charity, together with the latest available full audited accounts,

including a full balance sheet should also accompany the written application.

- POST the application. (We are unable to accept an application via fax or email. Faxed or emailed appeals will not be considered, however, if you are unable to contact us by telephone you may email paulinetester@clothworkers.co.uk with brief enquiries).

During the course of the written application letter, applicants should endeavour to:

- Introduce the work of the applicant charity; state when the charity was established; describe its aims and objectives; and define precisely what the applicant charity does and who benefits from its activities.
- Comment upon the applicant charity's track record since its inception and refer to its notable achievements and successes to date. Endeavour to provide an interesting synopsis of the organisation.
- Describe the project requiring funding fully, clearly and concisely and comment on the charity's plans for the future.
- Provide full costings or a budget for the project/projects to include a detailed breakdown of the costs involved.
- Give details of all other applications, which the applicant charity has made to other sources of funding, and indicate precisely what funds have already been raised from other sources for the project.
- All applicants are, of course, perfectly at liberty to request a precise sum of money by way of grant. However, it can be more beneficial for the applicant charity to concentrate on providing accurate and detailed costings of the project concerned, thereby enabling the foundation to make its own judgement as to the level of financial support to be considered.

The foundation's trusts and grants committee meets on four occasions each year, usually in February, May, July and November. For large grants, the committee's recommendations are then placed before a subsequent meeting of the governors. Accordingly, there is a rolling programme of dealing with and processing applications and the foundation prides itself on its flexibility.

The foundation's 'guidelines for grant applicants' clearly indicate the information required for use in the decision-making process.

Successful applicants are normally notified of the result of their application within days of the final decision being reached by the governors.

All unsuccessful applicants receive a written refusal letter.

Richard Cloudesley's Charity

Churches, health, welfare

£343,000 to organisations (2002/ 03)

Beneficial area North Islington only.

11th Floor, Beaufort House, 15 St Botolph Street, London EC3A 7EE

Tel. 020 7772 5830 **Fax** 020 7247 5091

Correspondent Keith Wallace, Clerk

Trustees *Appointed by the local council, the local Church of England churches, and co-opted. J F Durdin, chair; A L Chorley; the Mayor of Islington; Canon G Kings; Cllr Angela Brook; W G Carter; Mrs S V M Clark; Ms K Frenchman; R Goodman; P Haynes; Ms V Lang; B H March; R Perry; M Simmonds; D R Stephens; K A Streater; Cllr S Wright.*

Charity Commission no. 205959

Information available Annual report and accounts were provided by the trust.

General

The charity was founded in 1518 by the will of Richard Cloudesley. He left the rent from a 14 acre field in Islington, London to be used for the benefit of residents of Islington parish. The field was in Barnsbury and its centre was what is now Cloudesley Square. The charity still owns a number of the widely coveted Georgian terraces for which Islington is well known, however it anticipates that property will be sold as renting becomes less profitable.

Grants ranging from £100 to around £25,000 are given to Church of England churches and to charities benefiting the 'sick poor' in the 'ancient' parish of Islington. The charity also has a welfare fund to support individuals in need of financial and medical help in the area. There are perhaps only half a dozen new beneficiaries in a year, usually for amounts of less than £2,000. Most grants are given to charities previously supported, though the amounts are

clearly reassessed each year as they frequently vary.

In 2002/03 the charity had assets totalling £18.4 million and an income of £768,000. Grants were made to organisations totalling £343,000 (£485,000 in 2001/02).

Guidelines

Cloudesley money can only assist in activities in the Ancient Parish of Islington. This is the northern part of the modern London Borough of Islington – roughly everything north of Chapel Market and City Road.

Obviously enough there are few bodies that confine their work to a small area like the Ancient Parish of Islington. We are quite used to helping charities in Islington as a whole, or Islington and nearby London boroughs. What we ask is that you give us an assessment of the proportion of what you do that can be said to be related to people living in the Ancient Parish of Islington.

The geographic scope makes for difficulties in grant funds to nationally organised charities. Some of these have locally accounted branches – and others have locally identifiable projects – but without some restriction like this, we will be unable to assist.

Grants can only be made to benefit the sick poor. This means that both a medical and a financial need must be shown.

The Cloudesley trustees take a generous view on what is a medical need. As well as supporting bodies working with conventional medical conditions – strokes, arthritis, mental handicap, for example – grants have been made recently to charities dealing with:

- drugs
- alcohol abuse
- sex problems
- victim support
- bereavement counselling

The Cloudesley charities take the view that charities working in the medical field – in its wider interpretation – are supporting those in financial need. Pure medical research, though, would be outside the permitted ambit.

Often charities whose work is outside the medical field may be able to identify some aspect of what they do which can be viewed as medical.

Example 1. Cloudesley money can't be used for prisoners' welfare but it is given for facilities in Pentonville Prison hospital wing. Inmates in the wing are seen as falling within the 'sick poor' test.

Example 2. Charities helping the homeless are outside the scope but any medical or health services made available to homeless people can be the subject of grant assistance.

Grants in 2002/03

Twenty-one churches benefited from grants during the year, with grants ranging from £6,000 to £24,000. All are regular beneficiaries.

There were 78 grants to medical and welfare charities, ranging from £100 to £11,000, with around one third being made to organisations not supported in the previous year. Beneficiaries included CARIS (Islington) Bereavement Project (£11,000), Islington Community Contact (£8,000), Islington MIND (£6,000), St Mary's Neighbourhood Centre (£5,000), Union Chapel Homeless Project (£4,000), Freightliners City Farm, St Mary's Community Centre and Assisted Living Foundation (£3,000 each), Centre 404, Islington Relief in Need, Transcend in London, the Laundry and Islington Churches Cold Weather Shelter (£2,000 each). Recipients of either £1,000 or £1,500 each included In Touch Islington, Federation of Artistic and Creative Therapy, Asian Elderly Luncheon & Social Club and Marie Curie Cancer Care.

Over half of the medical and welfare charities received grants of less than £1,000 each. Recipients included the Elfrida Society, Pentonville Prison Board of Visitors, Rosemary School, Mildmay Pensioners Association, Highbury Roundhouse, Terrence Higgins Trust, Metropolitan Society for the Blind and Multicultural Counselling Centre.

The charity also made a grant of £164,000 to its Welfare Fund for further distribution to individuals in need in the Islington area [see A Guide to Grants for Individuals in Need published by Directory of Social Change].

Exclusions

Applicants must fall within the geographic and purposes scope of the charity.

Applications

The guidelines state:

'If you think your charity is going to be able to qualify for consideration of a grant, write first to the clerk to the charity. You will then get an application form.

'Applications should be:

- timely
- in writing
- supported by accounts.

'If you would like us to acknowledge your application, please send a self-addressed envelope. Otherwise, to save expense, we will not confirm safe receipt.

'Block grants are considered twice a year, around late April, and early November at a grants committee meeting.

'Recommendations are made by the grants committee at these meetings and are reviewed and authorised by the Cloudesley trustees as a whole two weeks later. The trustees normally adopt all the recommendations.

'We need to know what work your charity does, how it fits within [our] geographical scope and purpose scope and the purpose for which you are seeking a grant. So long as this is clearly set out, we do not need a great deal of detail.

'We place a great deal of importance on receiving the accounts of the charities we fund so please be sure to send these each time you apply.

'We will give brief reasons with any application that is not successful.'

Clydpride Ltd

Jewish charities, general

£1.5 million (2002/03)
Beneficial area UK.

1003 Finchley Road, London NW11 7HB
Tel. 020 8731 7744 **Fax** 020 8731 8373
Correspondent L Faust, Secretary to the Trustees
Trustees L Faust; D Faust; T Faust; A Faust.
Charity Commission no. 295393
Information available Accounts were on file at the Charity Commission.

The objectives of this charity are to 'advance religion in accordance with the Jewish Orthodox faith, relief of poverty and general charitable causes'. In 2002/03 grants totalled £1.5 million and were broken down as follows:

Orthodox Jewish education	£1.5 million (52 grants)
Relief of poverty	£48,000 (10)
Orthodox places of worship	£610 (5)
Medical	£600 (4)

Beneficiaries of grants of £1,000 or more were listed in the accounts and included Beth Jacob (£1.3 million in 10 grants), Gevurath Ari Torah Academy Trust (£100,000 in six grants); Notzar Chessed (£45,000 in four grants), Friends of Bnei Torah Movement (£15,000), Torah Vodas (£5,000), Achisomoch Aid Company (£2,500), Baer Jacob (£1,400 in four grants) and Gateshead Jewish Academy for Girls (£1,000).

Applications

The trust states that unsolicited applications are not entertained.

The Coalfields Regeneration Trust

General, health, welfare, community regeneration, education, young people, older people

£24.1 million (2002/03)
Beneficial area Coalfield and former coalfield communities in England (North West and North East, Yorkshire, West Midlands and East Midlands, Kent), Scotland (west and east) and Wales.

PO Box 97, Rotherham S63 7WX
Tel. 01709 760272 **Fax** 01709 765599
Email info@coalfields-regen.org.uk
Website www.coalfields-regen.org.uk
Correspondent Gary Ellis, Secretary
Trustees Bishop Alan Morgan, chair; Peter McNestry; Bill Flanagan; Ms Denise Tate; Cllr Eunice Smethurst; Ken Greenfield; Ms Paula Hay-Plumb; Hedley Salt; Peter Fanning; Ms Sylvia Wileman; Cllr Vernon Jones; Cllr Joe Thomas; Nicolas Wilson; Ms Dawn Davies; Wayne Thomas.
Charity Commission no. 1074930
Information available Annual report and accounts, with a list of main projects supported, were provided by the trust. Informative website.

Set up in 1999, the Coalfields Regeneration Trust is an independent charity dedicated to the social and economic regeneration of coalfield communities in England, Scotland and Wales. It was set up in response to a recommendation by the Government's Coalfields Task Force Report. The report highlighted the dramatic effects that mine closures had, and continue to have, on communities in coalfield areas.

The trust provides advice, support and financial assistance to community and voluntary organisations which are working to tackle problems at grassroots level within coalfield communities. It is closely connected with the areas it serves, operating through a network of staff based at offices located within coalfield regions themselves.

The trust is currently extending its work in Britain's coalfields, developing new programmes and supporting the work of existing groups. The trust's current main programme is Regenerate, which aims to draw attention to youth issues in coalfield communities and make an impact on the lives of the worst affected young people.

The Regenerate programme will be a main thrust of the trust's activity until March 2005 (contact the trust for up-to-date information thereafter). The programme has six aims:

- to identify and support projects around the UK that young people want to be part of, helping them to build confidence in their abilities, and improve their chances for a better future. This initial set of projects will be extended as the project progresses
- to raise funds over the next three years to support these key projects, and other schemes to help young people
- to bring opinion-formers, business and political leaders face-to-face with the issues faced by young people, in a series of 'reality' visits
- to give young people a voice by publicising their experiences of living in coalfield communities
- to commission some research into some of the issues surrounding youth work and youth perceptions in coalfields areas
- to increase awareness of coalfields issues, with the help of Regenerate Ambassadors, who lend their public support to the programme.

The trust has grown considerably since it was first established, and now handles around 1,000 applications each year. By 2001/02 it had a grant total of £7.3 million; in 2002/03 that figure rose to £24,103,000, distributed throughout coalfield areas in England, Wales and Scotland, although organisations in England received the largest share:

England	£21.4 million
Wales	£1.37 million
Scotland	£1.36 million

The following review of the trust's activities is taken from the 2002/03 annual report:

The principal activity [of the trust] is the promotion for the public benefit of urban or rural regeneration in areas of social and economic deprivation in the coalfield areas in England, Wales and Scotland.

In addition to, and in support, of, its grant-making activity the trust employs a network of Regeneration Managers across England, Wales and Scotland. This resource gives direct support to community groups and organisations working in coalfield areas.

The financial year to 31 March 2003 was the trust's fourth year of operation. It marked the first year of a three-year agreement with the Office of the Deputy Prime Minister for England and the first year of a two-year agreement with Communities Scotland, a division of the Scottish Executive. The trust entered into an interim arrangement with the National Assembly for Wales from April 2002 to March 2003.

Due to the relatively short term of our existing funding arrangements the first year of a new round of funding has resulted in a steep increase in grant awards compared with the previous year.

Net grant awards totalling £24,104,000 were made during the last financial year: awards in England totalled £21,374,000, awards in Wales totalled £1,367,000 and awards in Scotland totalled £1,363,000.

Total incoming resources amounted to £27,041,000, comprising of £23,539,000 from the Office of the Deputy Prime Minister, £1,571,000 from the National Assembly for Wales, £1,720,000 from the Scottish Executive and £16,000 from the Heritage Lottery Fund in support of its activities.

The trust has from the beginning always intended to be more than just another grant-making organisation. To this end the trust is heavily committed to providing direct and effective support to the coalfield communities via its Regeneration Manager network. This support comes in a variety of ways.

One of the trust's key objectives has been to invest in grassroots projects in the most needy coalfield communities. Unfortunately, as a recent study into the Heritage Lottery Fund showed, these communities can also be amongst the hardest to reach.

- In more deprived communities, where the community/voluntary sector may be underdeveloped, comparatively fewer people have experience of making detailed funding applications. This lack of experience can prevent applicants coming forward.
- Where good regeneration ideas do exist within the community, they may be in embryonic form, causing some funders to reject them as high-risk enterprises, which are likely to flounder, or fail to reach targets, and are therefore considered unsuitable for funding.

The Coalfields Regeneration Trust is structured to overcome these barriers.

- Each coalfield area has one or more Regeneration Managers. With their local knowledge and perspective, these managers provide an important direct link to communities.
- Regeneration Managers do not just provide assistance 'with the paperwork'. They are also able to work with the community groups and volunteers on the development and business planning of a project, before the funding application is submitted, to ensure that it is viable and is likely to succeed. In this way, the trust is able to support projects that other funders would not consider. Risk identification in the assessment process is used to highlight where additional support is required.
- Once a grant is given, the trust monitors each project throughout the life of the grant. Recognising that monitoring is part of the developmental process, grants staff are trained to take a problem solving approach to any difficulties that arise, using the trust's experience to help grant-holders to build their own capacity along the way.

The trust's model of on-the-ground staff has now been adopted by some other funders. However, the trust remains unique in its combination of development support and problem solving throughout all stages of a grant–from application to achievement of the project aims.

The trust realises that it is not enough to be reactive. In some communities and under some circumstances, a proactive, strategic approach is needed if we are to solve regeneration problems on the ground.

In recognition of this, the trust works hard to create and maintain links with other key agencies in order to keep coalfield issues on the agenda and stay abreast of country and regional priorities. The trust has also allocated a significant part of its funding to strategic interventions. This special budget, together with the trust's independent charity status, gives the organisation the ability to target 'cold spots', to work 'in the margins' and across local authority boundaries, and to initiate activities which may, in time, be taken on by other agencies, or by the community itself. Example of strategic interventions include:

- A project to upgrade and extend the activities of miners' welfare organisations, helping them to provide a more rounded service to the community.
- A project to fund training courses/reskilling for the Selby miners faced with redundancy. As a charity, the trust was able to provide this support before statutory agencies, which were unable to act until a redundancy notice had been served.

- The launch of the Coalfield Regen School – a hands-on practical school for social entrepreneurs and community activists, with mentors drawn from successful coalfields regeneration projects.
- The launch of SKILLSbuilder – a pilot initiative to reskill miners from recently closed or threatened pits, in preparation for a career in an industry with skills shortages. SKILLSbuilder: Construction – gas-fitting has already proved extremely popular with both miners and private sector employers, with a 100% employment rate at the end of the training period.
- The trust launched the first ever debt redemption scheme in Wales, which is exclusively funded by the trust and will be delivered by our key partner the Wales Cooperative Centre. This is a unique project and firmly builds on the trust's earlier commitment to fund credit unions.
- With partnership funding from the East of Scotland Objective 2 programme, the trust has made a grant to Scottish Business in the Community for three Business Support Groups for the voluntary and community sector. The Business Support Groups will provide the necessary infrastructure to enable groups to have direct access to various forms of business support and identify training needs. The aim is to provide a mechanism that will allow organisations to enhance and develop local projects by engaging companies to provide resources to meet identified needs.

Following on from the successful pilot run in Scotland, the trust has extended a new funding stream – Bridging the Gap – with a network of support to promote and administer it.

Bridging the Gap provides grants up to £10,000, with simplified paperwork, and a fast turnaround time from receipt of application to receipt of the funds. A review of its effectiveness has shown positive results.

The application criteria have been successful in deterring umbrella organisations and more 'professional' groups and attracting grassroots community and voluntary projects, ensuring that funding reaches these smaller groups.

An important spin-off from a successful Bridging the Gap application is helping to build capacity in groups, which may help community and voluntary organisations to access other funding streams.

Such is the developing track record of the trust's unique approach, that a major opportunity to contribute to the Selby Task Force was forthcoming. As a result, the trust has secured some £5 million plus over the next three years to assist those communities affected by the closure of the complex.

Working in partnership with other agencies, the trust is keen for it to be acknowledged that without input from the trust the level of wealth and quality of services achieved to date would not have emerged. This is due to the unique insight the trust has into the immediate, medium and long-term needs and aspirations of coalfield communities.

It is pleasing to note that those agencies working with the trust acknowledge the 'extra ingredient brought to the menu' which they are able to use to respond to the varying needs of individuals and communities.

Communications and Fundraising

The Communications and Fundraising team are effectively a new arm of the trust as it implements a strategy to assist it in a long-term development programme. This first full year of operation has concentrated on ensuring the case for support is robust, identifying where and how we can have the best impact, discussing our proposals with other key agencies and potential partners. This will ensure that we work in partnership with others, add value, and thereby meet our strategic objectives.

During 2002 the trust commissioned MORI to undertake what is believed to be the only dedicated poll of young people across coalfield communities of England, Scotland and Wales.

As a result of the poll, the trust launched Regenerate, a special programme to help at-risk young people from the most deprived communities. The themes of the programme address young people's concerns about the future. They are:
- 'somewhere to go, something to do';
- 'from leisure to work';
- 'my body, my future'.

Already the first wave of Regenerate projects has been identified, involving partnerships with organisations such as Sunderland Football Club Foundation, Turning Point, Cornerstone Housing Association, Weston Spirit and Scout Dike Activity Centre.

Whilst the trust has channelled some of its existing funding allocation to the Regenerate programme, this new strand of activity is being used to spearhead a fundraising effort, which will diversify the trust's current funding base. It is here where the trust's investment in creating a fundraising team is expected to attract private sector and statutory/trust funding into projects for young people in the coalfield communities.

The trust's 2002/03 annual report lists 67 beneficiaries in England who received grants of £100,000 or more totalling £12,500,000, 24 main beneficiaries in Scotland with grants ranging from £14,000 to £151,000 totalling £1,268,000, and 18 main beneficiaries in Wales with

grants ranging from £23,000 to £115,000 totalling £920,000. This leaves around £9,000,000 in grants to beneficiaries in England alone undisclosed in the accounts – enough in itself to make this one of the largest trusts described in this resource. A more comprehensive list is, however, available on the trust's website.

In May 2004 the trust announced a new fund worth almost £1 million, available for community projects in the North East of England. The new scheme is expected to run until the end of March 2005:

The CRT has grants of up to £25,000 available to community schemes in 63 wards across Northumberland, Sunderland, South Tyneside, Durham County, Derwentside and Sedgefield. In order to be eligible for funding, projects must be able to demonstrate that they benefit a coalfield region. This could be through improving the employability of local people, assisting community groups and charities or supporting the development of neighbourhood facilities. The grant can be used for a variety of purposes to enable people to participate in a broad range of projects that help individuals and wider community life.

Anna White, the North East Regeneration Manager commented: 'we urge any project in the [North East] to contact us now to make the most of the £1 million we have available'. See Applications for details of the North East office.

Grants in 2002/03

The trust states that it is 'always open to good ideas', but as a guideline projects usually fall into one of the following categories:

- providing community support and facilities;
- developing enterprise;
- lifelong learning;
- small, locally owned environmental improvement schemes;
- helping people into work through building skills and training.

The following information on beneficiaries and projects supported during the year is taken primarily from the trust's 2002/03 annual report, with additional information from its website.

England

The recipient of the largest grant in England (and overall) during the year was Sunderland Football Club Foundation for the Kickstart project, which received £473,000:

Kickstart is a major project of national significance demonstrating a serious commitment to the community. Kickstart aims to work with and make a difference to young people, aged between 5–19 across the whole district of the City of Sunderland. Using the power of football as a catalyst, it will develop an exciting partnership engaging with hard to reach young people in 5 identified core areas of basic skills, citizenship, health, environment and coaching. The project achieves this through three funded initatives–the Stadium of Light classrooms, an interactive multimedia resource and outreach delivery via a number of mobile classrooms offering a variety of learning experiences both on weekdays and weekends.

Other large grants of £300,000 and above were made to: Creswell Groundwork Trust – Mansfield for its Positive Futures for the Coalfields Unemployed project in areas of Derbyshire and Nottinghamshire (£398,000); SKILLSbuilder – Prince of Wales Colliery – Pontefract (£360,000); Groundwork Erewash Valley – Derbyshire for CRT Community Places ILM (£328,000); His Upper Room Trust – Derbyshire for the Alfreton Community Enterprise Incubator Hub at Genesis Enterprise Centre (£328,000); and The Community Regeneration Plan (£300,000).

Other beneficiaries included: West Cumbria Council for Voluntary Service for the South Whitehaven Regeneration Partnership (£253,000); Yorkshire Coalfields Resource Centre, Bold Miners Neighbourhood Centre and Grassmoor Community Centre (£200,000 each); Barnsley Credit Union development grant (£192,000); Bestwood Miners Welfare One Stop Shop Project – Harrogate (£178,000); Minsthorpe Charitable Trust – Wakefield for the Happy Days Children's Centre (£168,000); Isabella Community Centre (£142,000); St George's Community Project (£116,000); and Glasshoughton Community Centre Development and Marlpool Community Project (£100,000 each).

Scotland

Beneficiaries included: Business Support Partnership (£151,000); Coalburn Miners' Welfare Charitable Society for the Coalburn One Stop Shop and Cumnock & District Leisure Group for the Pool Project (£100,000 each); Tower House Community Centre Management Committee – Dunfermline for the Mad Cow Rock Music Group (£50,000); First Step Community Project – Musselburgh for its Family Support Service (£38,000); Midlothian Community Transport

Development Project (£31,000); Senscot Network Development (£22,000); and West Lothian Retired Miners Compensation Project (£20,000).

Wales

Beneficiaries included: Wales Cooperative Centre – Cardiff for their Debt Redemption and Money Advice Scheme (£115,000); Nantymoel Boys & Girls Club (£99,000); Troedyrhiw Boys & Girls Club – Merthyr Tydfil for an outside multi-purpose sports area (£66,000); Ynysybwl Regeneration Partnership – Rhondda Cynon Taff (£50,000); Amman Valley Enterprises – Ammanford for Steer Studios Development (£36,000); Torfaen Community Transport Group for the purchase of a minibus (£33,000); and Churches in Action for the Bargoed Youth Project (£23,000).

Exclusions

The trust will not fund private businesses.

Applications

'If you are thinking of applying for a grant and would like to talk through your idea, please contact your nearest trust office, where the Regeneration Manager can help you decide the best way forward.'

Local offices and contacts

England

North West
Caroline Broadhurst (Regeneration Manager)
CRT
Bold Business Centre
Bold Lane
Sutton
St Helens
WA9 4TX
Tel: 01925 222066
Fax: 01925 222047
email: caroline@coalfields-regen.org.uk

North East
Anna White (Regeneration Manager)
CRT
The Eco Centre
Room 9
Windmill Way
Hebburn
Tyne & Wear
NE31 1SR
Tel: 0191 428 5550
Fax: 0191 428 5005
email: anna@coalfields-regen.org.uk

Yorkshire (main office)
Andy Lock/Danny Buckley (Regeneration Managers)
CRT
PO Box 97
Rotherham
S63 7WX
Tel: 01709 765573
Fax: 01709 765599
email: andy@coalfields-regen.org.uk or danny@coalfields-regen.org.uk

Selby
Debbie Thornton (Administration Support Worker)
CRT
1st Floor
New Options Office
23 Finkle Street
Selby
YO8 4DT
Tel: 01757 212897
email: debbie@coalfields-regen.org.uk

West Midlands and East Midlands
Louise Winterburn (West Midlands) or Deborah Fraser (East Midlands) (Regeneration Managers)
CRT
1st Floor
42 High Street
Coalville
Leicestershire
LE67 3EG
Tel: 01530 510456
Fax: 01530 510678
email: louise@coalfields-regen.org.uk or deborah@coalfields-regen.org.uk

Kent
Mr Brinley Hill (Senior Community Development Officer)
CRT
White Cliffs Business Park
Dover
Kent
CT16 3PJ
Tel: 01304 821199
Fax: 01304 872004
email: brinley@coalfields-regen.org.uk

Scotland (West)
Ian McCormack (Regeneration Manager)
CRT
12 The Square
Cumnock
KA18 1BG
Tel: 01290 420262
Fax: 01290 422041
email: ian@coalfields-regen.org.uk

Scotland (East)
Yvonne Lord/Carol Bartholomew
(Regeneration Managers)
CRT
2/6 The e-Centre
Cooperage Way Business Village
Cooperage Way
Alloa
FK10 3LP
Tel: 01259 272127
Fax: 01259 272138
email: yvonne@coalfields-regen.org.uk or carol@coalfields-regen.org.uk

Wales
Alun Taylor (Regeneration Manager)
CRT
Unit 7
Maritime Offices
Woodlands Terrace
Maes-y-coed
Pontypridd
CF37 1DZ
Tel: 01443 404455
Fax: 01443 408804
email: alun@coalfields-regen.org.uk

The Joy Cohen Charitable Trust

Jewish, general

Around £800,000 (2002/03)
Beneficial area UK.

RSM Robson Rhodes, Centre City Tower, 7 Hill Street, Birmingham B5 4UU

Tel. 0121 697 6000 **Fax** 0121 697 6111/2

Correspondent R Hale

Trustees *Joy Audrey Cohen; Stanley Cohen; David John Brecher; Susan Rubin.*

Charity Commission no. 1065471

Information available Accounts were on file at the Charity Commission.

This trust mainly supports Jewish organisations, however support is also given to UK charities including a number of health and welfare organisations.

In 2002/03 it had an exceptional income of £1 million and a total expenditure of £854,000, most of which was given in grants.

Previous beneficiaries include Joint Jewish Charitable Trust, Maccabi Association, Jewish Culture Centre, British Wizo, Jewish Music Institute, British Heart Foundation, Holocaust Education Trust, Jewish Museum,

Samaritans, Save the Children, Shelter, UNICEF and World Jewish Relief.

Applications

In writing to the correspondent.

The John S Cohen Foundation

General, arts, education, music, environmental

£358,000 (2002/03)
Beneficial area UK and overseas.

PO Box 21277, London W9 2YH

Tel. 0207 286 6921

Correspondent Mrs Diana Helme

Trustees *David Cohen; Ms Imogen Cohen; Olivia Cohen; Mrs Veronica Jane Addison Cohen.*

Charity Commission no. 241598

Information available Full accounts were on file at the Charity Commission.

The objectives of this charity are general charitable purposes in the UK or elsewhere. A number of grants are made to charitable institutions overseas. The foundation is particularly active in supporting education, music, the arts and the environment both built and natural.

In 2002/03 it had assets of £6.9 million and income of £2.2 million, including a transfer of £1.7 million from the David Cohen Family a related charity with similar objectives and trustees. Grants totalled £3.3 million, including a transfer of £3 million to John and Golda Cohen Trust a charity registered in the State of Florida.

The remaining grants totalled £358,000, of which donations of £10,000 and over were £40,000 to Royal Academy of Arts, £15,000 each to National Gallery and Philharmonia Orchestra, £13,000 to Zoological Society of London, £12,000 to Cambridge Univeristy Library and £10,000 to Fitzwilliam Museum.

Smaller donations included: £7,100 to Dulwich Picture Gallery; £6,000 to London Symphony Orchestra; £5,000 each to Community Security Trust and Garsington Opera; £4,000 each to Aderburgh Festival and Festival of Jewish Arts and Culture; £3,000 each to Blackheath Conservatoire and Courtauld

Institute of Art; £2,500 to London String Quartet Foundation; £2,000 each to Bristol Catherdral, Jewish Book Week and Newmann Trust; £1,000 each to Burlington Magazine, Purcell School and Wiltshire Wildlife Trust; £600 to Grange Park Opera; £500 to Nightingale House and Southwell Minister; £250 to Music Therapy Charity; £100 each to Cavatina Camber Music Trust and Facial Surgery Research Foundation; £50 to Uganda Society for Disabled Children; and £25 to Springboard Concerts Trust.

Applications

In writing to the correspondent.

The Colt Foundation

Occupational and environmental health research

£518,000 to organisations (2003)
Beneficial area UK.

New Lane, Havant, Hampshire PO9 2LY

Tel. 023 9249 1400 **Fax** 023 9249 1363

Email jackie.douglas@uk.coltgroup.com

Website www.coltfoundation.org.uk

Correspondent Mrs Jacqueline Douglas

Trustees *Mrs Patricia Lebus, chair; Timothy Ault; Prof. David Coggon; Mrs Clare Gilchrist; Ms Natasha Lebus; Walter McD Morison; Alan O'Hea; Jerome O'Hea; Juliette O'Hea; Peter O'Hea, Prof. D Denison and Prof. A J Newman Taylor act as scientific advisors.*

Charity Commission no. 277189

Information available Report and accounts with grants list and narrative explanation of grants and grantmaking policy.

The foundation makes grants to support organisations and post-graduate students for research into occupational and environmental health. It is particularly interested in work aimed at discovering the causes of illnesses arising from conditions in the workplace. Donations to organisations vary from a few thousand pounds to over £100,000 and may be repeated over two to five years. Beneficiaries are well-established research institutes (awards to individuals are made through such).

In 2003 it had assets totalling £11.7 million from which £576,000 was

81

generated in income. After management and administration costs of £64,000, a total of 15 grants amounting to £518,000 were distributed and a total of £89,000 was awarded to an unspecified number of students.

Grants included those to University of Manchester (£145,000), National Heart and Lung Institute (£93,000), University of Edinburgh (£60,000), London School of Hygiene & Tropical Medicine (£45,000), University of Southampton (£44,000), Napier University (£27,000), Silsoe Research Institute (£22,000) and Defeating Deafness (£19,500).

Exclusions

Grants are not made for the general funds of another charity or projects overseas.

Applications

In writing to the correspondent. Trustees meet in May and November and applications may be submitted at any time.

Colyer-Fergusson Charitable Trust

Community activity (often through churches), environment, arts

£519,000 (2002/03)

Beneficial area Kent.

Friars House, 2 Friars Lane, Richmond, Surrey TW9 1NL

Tel. 020 8288 9101

Website www.colyer-fergusson.org.uk

Correspondent Jacqueline Rae

Trustees *Jonathan Monckton, chair; Nicholas Fisher; Simon Buxton; Robert North; Ruth Murphy.*

Charity Commission no. 258958

Information available Full accounts were provided by the trust, which are also available on the trust's detailed web site.

'The trust makes grants to registered charities (or those with registration pending) and churches working or based in Kent [that are] aiming to improve quality of life, tackle poverty, social isolation or exclusion and protect the

natural resources and heritage of the local areas for their inhabitants.'

The trust currently has the following priority areas:

- projects that are innovative or developmental and aim to tackle social isolation, exclusion or poverty as they affect the community;
- projects that involve the preservation of the natural environment and promote community access to these resources;
- projects that will use the arts to provide the community with a new creative experience or increase access to the arts in locations where access is limited;
- projects that involve the utilisation of church buildings or other church resources to the wider community and can demonstrate a practical need.

Extra consideration will be given to projects that: encourage self-help; involve users in their management; have built in evaluation procedures; and will use funds to lever funding from other sources.

In 2002/03 the trust had assets of £19 million and an income of £758,000. In this year the trust gave grants totalling £519,000 to the following priority areas:

Social isolation, exclusion or poverty	26	£360,000
Church buildings/resources	10	£93,000
Preservation of natural environment or heritage	2	£26,000
Community creative experience	4	£20,000
Exceptional grants	1	£20,000

Grants ranged between £500 and £40,000. The largest were as follows: Youthnet UK received £40,000 towards the cost of a journalist to underpin 'Ask-it'; Homestart South West Kent received £30,000 towards the cost of a project worker, three play workers and the set-up costs of two new groups for three years; Gingerbread received £29,000 towards the cost of a development worker; St Saviour's Church – Folkstone received £25,000 towards the cost of repairing the church floor; and The Romney Marsh Research Trust received £25,000 towards the cost of a web-based resource of geomorphological,

archaeological and historical data on Romney Marsh and its environs.

Other beneficiaries included: Caring All Together on Romney Marsh (Carm), Option 2, West Kent YMCA and The Thiepval Project (£20,000 each); Prince's Trust and Church on the Way (£15,000 each); Ashford & District Volunteer Bureau, Care Fund, Deptford St Paul and City of Canterbury Symphony Orchestra (£10,000 each); Deafblind UK, REACT and Live Music Now! (£5,000 each); Mystery Productions LTD and Fant Wildlife Group (£1,000 each); and The Friends of St John the Baptist – Harrietsham (£500).

Interestingly the trust provided a breakdown of the grants they made over the last three years as follows:

Size of grants	Number awarded
Under £5,000	21
£5,000 to £9,999	53
£10,000 to £19,999	30
£20,000 to £49,999	12
£50,000 or over	3
Total	119

Type of project	Total grants
Accommodation	£9,000
Access to the Arts	£68,000
Building costs	£30,000
Church – community initiatives	£265,000
Church – restoration and repairs	£70,000
Counselling, advice and mentoring	£389,000
Environment and heritage	£73,000
Health initiatives	£35,000
Independent living	£220,000
Literacy and education	£67,000
Respite and holidays	£40,500
Social welfare	£231,000
Other	£20,000
Total	£1.5 million

Type of beneficiary	Total grants
Carers	£20,000
Disabled people	£224,000
Ex-offenders	£40,000
Older people	£61,000
Visually/ hearing	£50,000
Homeless	£44,000
Isolated communities	£607,000
Vulnerable children/families	£330,000
Young people	£133,000
Medical conditions and illness	£10,000
Total	£1.5 million

Exclusions

No grants to churches and charities outside Kent. No grants to individuals or to the following:

- animal welfare charities;
- individuals directly;

COLYER-FERGUSSON CHARITABLE TRUST
Grants over the last three years

	Applications	Grants	Success ratio	Total awarded
Social isolation, exclusion or poverty	199	78	39%	£1 million
Preservation of environmental heritage	22	8	36%	£73,000
Community creative experience	30	9	30%	£68,000
Church buildings or resources	124	23	19%	£335,000
Other	19	1	6%	£20,000
Total	392	119	30%	£1.5 million

- research (except practical research designed to benefit the local community directly);
- hospitals or schools;
- political activities;
- commercial ventures or publications;
- the purchase of vehicles including minibuses;
- overseas travel or holidays;
- retrospective grants or loans;
- direct replacement of statutory funding or activities that are primarily the responsibility of central or local government;
- large capital, endowment or widely distributed appeals;
- applications from churches and charities outside Kent.

Applications

In January 2003 the trust moved from a paper-based to an on-line application form. It asks all applicants to apply via the web and highlights that access can be sought in local reference libraries, web cafes, CVS's and so on. In circumstances where this is not practical (which had occurred only once by September 2003), a paper-based form can be accepted. The trust states that they are happy to talk to anyone who is having difficulties with this new process, but stated in September 2003 that only positive feedback from applicants had been given.

The trust advises that applicants should visit the website for up-to-date information and guidelines. There is no deadline for applications and all requests for support will be acknowledged. Trustees meet twice during the year, usually in March and October, and decisions are usually processed within four to six months. All applicants will be notified in writing.

Comic Relief

Community-based UK charities, Africa

£35 million (15-month period ended September 2003)

Beneficial area UK and Africa.

5th Floor, 89 Albert Embankment, London SE1 7TP

Tel. 020 7820 5555

Minicom 020 7820 5570

Email red@comicrelief.org.uk

Website www.comicrelief.org.uk

Correspondent The UK Grants Team

Trustees *Peter Benett-Jones, Chair; Richard Curtis; Jana Bennett; Emma Freud; Matthew Freud; Mike Harris; Lenny Henry; Colin Howes; Claudia Lloyd; Laurence Newman; Eric Nicoli; J K Rowling; Albert Tucker; Nalini Varma.*

Charity Commission no. 326568

Information available Revised grant guidelines expected sometime after Red Nose Day, 11 March 2005. Financial statements with an inadequate report from the trustees and a simple grants listing was supplied. Little further information was made available to help in the writing of this entry.

Summary

Comic Relief runs three grants programmes. The figures in brackets are for total grants made in the 15-month period ended 30 September 2003 (due to the re-commissioning by the BBC of Sport Relief for July 2004 and 2006 the trustees changed the year end to end September). However, as the charity operates on a two-year cycle this can vary from year to year.

- UK (£12.8 million)
- Africa (£13.5 million)
- International, Children and Young People (£6.7 million)

This entry is concerned mainly with the UK grants (grantmaking overseas is covered in the International Development Directory, published by Directory of Social Change).

The charity receives its income from Comic Relief's Red Nose Day fundraising event, held every two years in partnership with the BBC, and the extent of the grantmaking depends entirely on the success of the preceding event.

In 2002, Comic Relief started a second initiative, Sport Relief. Half of its income goes to the International Children and Young People's programme, the other half to work with children and young people within the main UK grant programme.

There is also a smaller Robbie Williams' Give It Sum Fund (£400,000 in 2002/03) for community-based projects in his home area of North Staffordshire.

Programmes operate on a two-year cycle, each with several 'rounds' (or 'cycles' as they are called) of applications. Policies for 2005–2007 were under review when this book went to press and new guidelines were due to be published sometime after Red Nose Day, March 2005 (please check the Comic Relief website for details). The overall approach, however, will probably be maintained.

406 grants totaling £35 million were approved in the 15-month period ended 30 September 2003. The majority of the money is given in large grants. Many are paid over periods of up to three years.

There is also a UK small grants programme, for amounts of up to £5,000. Applications are dealt with through a fast-track process with a decision usually being given within three months of receipt of an application. These grants are only available to organisations with an annual turnover of less than £100,000.

Priority is given to applications for core costs and equipment costs and may be single payments or spread across up to three years. Comic Relief aims to reach the poorest and most disadvantaged communities to help them take control of their lives and find solutions to the problems they face.

The UK grant priorities from April 2003, until the guidelines for the next cycle are available in 2005, were:

- supporting young people;
- fighting for justice;
- domestic abuse;
- refugees and asylum seekers;
- local communities working for change.

There is also occasional funding for other specific issues. Recently they have included:

- racial harassment;
- complex needs;
- developing access to drug services for black and minority ethnic communities.

UK grantmaking

Comic Relief derives most of its revenue from the Red Nose Day fundraising event that it organises with BBC television every two years. In March 2003 over £61 million was raised. The charity does not have a separate endowment, but spends what it raises over each two-year cycle.

Grantmaking policy is also revised on a similar cycle, 'so the information in this entry about past practice is not necessarily a secure guide to future activity, but the charity has maintained consistent general policies for a number of years'.

The charity sets budgets for each of its programmes and seems generally successful in meeting them.

As this book went to print the next Red Nose Day was due on 11 March 2005. As a result, the following 2003/05 programmes have closed in anticipation of new guidelines being issued sometime following this date: Red Nose Day UK and Sport Relief UK (Red Nose Day Africa and the International Grants programmes have also closed).

However, applications are still open for The Robbie Williams' Give It Sum Fund and Small Grants for Gypsy and Traveller Projects, guidelines for both of which are given below.

The charity previously described its UK grantmaking in the 2003/04 edition of this guide as follows:

Every single project we support is helping poor and disadvantaged people in the UK, Africa or the world's poorest countries to turn their lives around and make positive changes in their communities.

Since Comic Relief began, we've made nearly 6,000 grants worth over £210 million.

Over 4,600 of those, totaling more than £75 million, have been to projects working across England, Northern Ireland, Scotland and Wales.

Over 1,200, totaling over £130 million have been to projects working in Africa.

Recently, we've also made 28 grants totaling over £2.6 million to projects working in some of the poorest countries around the world.

Around a third of the money Comic Relief raises in the UK during Red Nose Day is spent on projects working in the UK. The broad aims of our new UK grants programmes include:
- reaching some of the poorest and most disadvantaged people throughout the UK
- helping people to find solutions to the problems they face
- helping groups who face discrimination get their views heard and their needs met
- supporting groups that users are involved in running
- making the public more aware of the needs, hopes and rights of the disadvantaged people we support
- supporting work which influences social policy at national, regional and local levels.

We recognise that whilst the grants that we give to projects can and do make a huge difference to the people who need them, the amount of money we are able to give is small in relation to the needs across the UK. So we focus our grant making through programme areas in order to achieve the greatest impact.

Guidelines for applicants

This section gives excerpts from the guidelines for applicants for the 2003/05 cycle (due to be replaced in spring 2005). Applications under these guidelines will be closed by the time this book is in print; they are reproduced solely as the best available guide to the policies of the charity. The exceptions to this are the guidelines for the Give It Sum Fund and the Small Grants for Gypsy and Traveller Projects, which are both current as at 1 March 2005.

All guidelines are available in large print and, on request, in Braille and a range of languages.

There is a two-stage application process, with the cycle taking up to six months to complete. Applications for grants under £5,000 are processed within 3 months.

UK grants programmes – priorities for grant making 2003/05

The grants we make in the UK support the work of voluntary organisations to tackle poverty and promote social justice. Our aims are to:
- Reach the poorest and most disadvantaged people
- Help people find solutions to the problems they face
- Help groups who face discrimination get their views heard and their needs met
- Support groups which are user-led or which can show they want to move towards users running the service
- Make the public more aware of the needs, hopes and rights of the disadvantaged people we support
- Support work which influences policy at national, regional and local levels.

Who can apply?
We make grants to voluntary organisations and self-help groups in Scotland, England, Wales and Northern Ireland. We pay particular attention to parts of the UK which often miss out on funding, especially towns and cities outside London, and rural areas. We welcome applications from both small, local grassroots projects and larger organisations.

Any work we fund must be charitable. If your group is not a registered charity, but the work you are planning to do has charitable aims, we can pay funds through a registered charity. They will then pass on the grant to you.

Equal opportunities
We are especially keen to hear from groups, in the areas that we support, who are very disadvantaged or find it particularly hard to get funding. So we welcome applications that specifically benefit the following:
- People from black and minority ethnic groups
- Women
- Lesbians, gay men and bisexuals
- Older people

- Disabled people
- People who live in rural areas.

To apply, these groups must fall within one or more of our grantmaking programmes.

What type of grants do we give?
We give grants for both running costs and capital costs. We give building costs a very low priority. We have two different application processes depending on how much money you want to apply for. All applications must fit into one of our grant-making programmes.

Small Grants Programme
The Small Grants Programme is only open to small, local organisations with a turnover of up to £100,000. The most you can apply for is £5,000 and we will give priority to applications for core and equipment costs.

Large Grants Programme
The Large Grants Programme is open to any voluntary organisation that works within our grantmaking programmes. We can make grants for running costs for up to three years. The majority of grants approved are between £70,000 and £90,000. However the trustees might give more to projects which show new ideas or will make a major impact. If you would like to talk to someone before you apply, please get in touch with our Grants Team.

Give it Sum

(£400,000 in 2002/03 for community based projects in North Staffordshire)

Give it Sum is Robbie Williams' charitable fund which he set up in 2000 with the money he received from his Pepsi sponsorship deal. He asked Comic Relief to administer the Fund.

The Give it Sum Fund aims to make a positive difference to the lives of disadvantaged people living in North Staffordshire. Give It Sum is all about giving local people the chance to change their communities for the better. It aims to help them really tackle the poverty and disadvantage that hinders their lives.

Priorities for 2004/05
The fund will continue to work only in North Staffordshire. Robbie originally chose this area as he grew up there and wanted to put something back into the community.

The fund supports a broad range of self help projects, community groups and voluntary organisations (with an income of less than £150,00 a year) that address poverty, disadvantage and discrimination. We give priority to local community groups, but will also consider your application if you are a voluntary organisation which provides services to people in need. You will have to show clearly how your work has an impact on poverty and disadvantage in your local area.

Examples of work we will consider include:
- residents associations and self-help groups working to improve their local communities;
- projects offering help and support to those in need, for example, asylum seekers, young people with drug and alcohol problems, homeless people, single parents, older people, children and people from black and minority ethnic communities;
- projects that help people who are often left out, to have their say – for example, groups campaigning for better services and disabled people's rights groups.

Your project will need to show how you are involving the people who use your services and facilities in planning, running and reviewing your work.

You will need to clearly show how your work is serving the needs of a deprived community or that you are making a special effort to reach people who are excluded. If you meet these criteria, we will give grants for both running costs and capital costs.

Running costs, also known as revenue costs, are the costs you have to pay year after year such as rent, salaries, heating and lighting. There are two types of running costs:
- core costs which form part of the basic running costs of an organisation; and
- project costs which are the costs of carrying out a specific piece of work over a period of time.

Capital costs include the costs of buying equipment, for example computers and office furniture and building costs. Give It Sum does not usually make a contribution towards large capital schemes.

In addition, the Give It Sum fund gives very low priority to refurbishment and repair costs of village halls, but will consider applications from village halls that want money to pay for the very many worthwhile services they provide.

We can make grants up to two years. Grants will not usually be more than £15,000 each year. However, the trustees might give more to projects which show new ideas or are likely to have a major impact.

We will not fund activities that are the responsibility of any statutory agency, for example, a government department, a local council or health authority. And, we will not give grants to replace statutory funding.

You can only make one application or hold one grant at any one time.

The Give It Sum Fund also supports the Give It Sum North Staffs Community Chest which makes grants of between £50 and £500 to groups with an annual income of less than £10,000 addressing poverty and disadvantage throughout North Staffordshire. Further details can be obtained from Staffordshire Moorlands Council for Voluntary Service.

Small Grants for Gypsy and Traveller Projects

Gypsies and travellers face a whole range of serious problems, including a severe shortage of residential sites and legal stopping places, low literacy levels, poor access to education and health care, conflict with settled communities and racism and discrimination. There is a need for groups to work at national level to address some of the root causes of these problems, and Comic Relief is supporting the work of the Gypsy and Traveller Law Reform Coalition (the Coalition) in this area. There is also a need for smaller groups, working on a local level, to make sure that Gypsy and Traveller needs are recognised and that they can have an active role in decisions affecting them. These groups may be site based or cover a larger area. There are already some Gypsy and Traveller groups and more are needed to cover the whole of the UK.

Many small Traveller groups have little or no funding for basics like the cost of 'phone calls or attending meetings. The Small Grants for Gypsy and Traveller Projects programme will pay towards those vital costs that make running a group possible.

The programme aims to provide grants of up to £3,000 to small gypsy and traveller groups to help with setting them up and running them.

Any work we fund must be charitable. However, you do not have to be a registered charity, as long as the work you are planning to do has charitable aims and you have a constitution and a management committee. We give grants to groups throughout the UK.

The programme is aimed at small groups, so your annual income should be less than £50,000 a year.

We will give support to groups that are run by Gypsies and Travellers themselves as much as possible. Priority will be given to Traveller led projects, but we will consider other projects if they can show substantial involvement of, and consultation with, Gypsies and Travellers and that they are working towards the project being led by Travellers.

You can apply for core running costs including office and administration expenses, such as telephone, rent, insurance and heat and light; stationery and printing; sessional worker and volunteer costs; computer and equipment costs and, other costs of running your project. Your group may be doing any of the following or something similar:
- providing a link between Gypsies and Travellers and local partners and service providers to get Travellers' needs on the agenda;
- working with local residents to break down barriers;
- providing advice and information, advocacy and practical advice and help for individual Gypsies and Travellers and families so they can obtain basic rights and services;
- training such as in literacy and numeracy; youth projects to engage and empower young Gypsies and Travellers; or health initiatives around improving health and helping Gypsies and Travellers get access to health care.

We will not fund activities or services which by duty should be provided by a statutory agency, for example, a government department, a local council or health authority.

We will not usually fund organisations that have more than six months' annual running costs in unrestricted reserves (money which has been set aside and can be used for any purpose). This restriction does not apply to organisations with an annual *expenditure* of £15,000 or less.

Sport Relief

With new guidelines expected to be available in spring 2005, the following are reprinted from the 2003/04 edition of this guide solely as an indication of the policies of the charity.

Sport Relief is a fundraising initiative run by Comic Relief and BBC Sport. [It] brought together people from the world of sport to raise money for children and young people living in conflict or crisis here at home and in some of the poorest countries of the world. 50% of the funds raised are being spent through Comic Relief's International Programme for Children and Young People and 50% is being spent in the UK.

This grants programme is about [...] the power of sport to bring young people together to tackle tension and division in their communities.

There is growing evidence to suggest that although sport is rarely the sole solution to divisions in communities, it can be an important part of the solution. This is especially so for young people, and in particular where it is used not simply as a diversionary activity, but as part of involving young people in making real change within their communities.

The programme aims to support projects which use sport, activities and games to work with young people up to the age of 25 to tackle tensions and divisions within their local communities.

We especially want to support projects run and managed by the local community. You will be using sport as a way of making change, rather than as an end in itself. You will need to identify the tension that exists in your local community and show how the work you are doing will help to tackle this. We will be interested to see how you will consult and involve young people in the project.

Rather than give a lot of small grants, it is likely that we will make a bigger contribution to a smaller number of projects and put adequate resources into monitoring and evaluating the difference they make. We have a commitment to share this learning widely.

Examples of the types of projects we might fund are:

- A community project running a multi-racial football team, along with workshops and discussions, which has helped to bring young people together to reduce conflict and rifts between the Bengali and white communities.
- A project which has taken leaders of different gangs away together to take part in joint sporting activities, has helped participants develop skills in reducing conflict, fear and levels of violence back in their home areas.
- A group using basketball to bring together children from different 'sides' of the sectarian divide, which has given them the opportunity to mix with each other and take this positive experience back into their own communities.

We will fund voluntary organisations and self-help groups throughout all parts of the UK. We especially welcome applications from small, grassroots projects. Any work we fund must be charitable. If your group is not a registered charity, but the work you are planning to do has charitable aims, we can pay the grant through a registered charity. They will then pass on the grant to you. You can apply for a grant from the Sport Relief fund even if you are currently getting a grant from Comic Relief.

When we look at applications, we will want to make sure that we consider equal opportunities. We believe it is important that we consider everyone's needs - especially the needs of those who often miss out. [...]

We cannot fund statutory authorities. However, if you are a voluntary project and you are working with a statutory organisation, we may be able consider your request. Please discuss this with a member of the UK grants team before you apply.

It is unlikely that we will fund large capital projects (for example, building costs). Most of the funding will be given for revenue costs (running costs), although we will fund capital items such as office or sports equipment.

There is no maximum or minimum amount you can apply for. However, we are unlikely to make grants from this fund for less than £10,000 per year. You can apply for up to five years' funding, although in these cases, we are likely to reduce any grant during the last two years.

Recreation and play

Due to the limited funds available, we have to target our money carefully. We believe that we can make the most difference if we focus on one area of work. So, after considerable consultation, we have decided to limit applications to Sport Relief to those projects working through sport to reduce tension in communities.

Overseas programmes

With new guidelines expected to be available in spring 2005, the following are reprinted from the 2003/04 edition of this guide solely as an indication of the policies of the charity.

Comic Relief also has an extensive Africa and a more modest International Children and Young People's Grants Programme.

The Africa grants programme exists to help people in Africa who feel powerless to unite to improve their lives, make their voices heard and create a fairer society. The grants programme aims to tackle poverty and promote social justice across Africa. All the work we support is about helping people to make lasting, positive changes in their lives and their communities. Our 2001 – 2003 cycle considered applications that target one of the following.

- People affected by conflict.
- Women and girls.
- People living in towns and cities.
- Disabled people.
- Pastoralists – people who traditionally make a living from raising cattle, goats and sheep – and hunter-gatherers.
- People affected by HIV and AIDS.

We have developed an international grants programme [for areas other than Africa. Ed.] because we have started receiving money from all over the world from fundraising projects other than Red Nose Day. Sales of two special 'Harry Potter' books written by J K Rowling for Comic Relief have already generated several million pounds through world wide sales and it only seems right that this money should have a wider spread than just Africa. As a result, we will use this money to improve the lives of some of the most vulnerable children and young people in some of the poorest countries across the world.

Grants in 2002/03

The UK grants summary for the 15 month period ended 30 September 2003 (which may not be representative of other annual periods) show the following totals:

	Amount
Supporting young people	£1,547,000
Black young people and drugs	£81,000
Young peoples' participation	£770,000
Fighting for justice	£2,557,000
Complex needs	£145,000
Equality	£62,000
Racial harassment	£417,000
Refugees & asylum seekers	£959,000
Building community links	£5,000
Refugees online project	£376,000
Domestic violence	£1,018,000
Get connected	£1,000
Helpline project	£90,000
Supporting communities	£485,000
Self-organised drug and alcohol user groups	£263,000
Alcohol development work	£341,000
Human rights	£13,000
Travellers	£120,000
Sports Relief	£3,791,000
'Give it Sum' grants	£400,000
'Dish the Dosh' grants	£1,382,000

In the absence of a detailed breakdown of beneficiaries being made available to us, we provide some sample grants from 2001/02.

Grants for £100,000 or more included:

NSPCC	£555,000
Alcohol Concern	£300,000
Community Foundation for Northern Ireland	£180,000

Organisations receiving between £90,000 and £100,000 included:

Worcester and Malvern Women's Aid

Sunderland Refugee and Asylum Seekers Network

Bradford Lesbian, Gay and Bisexual Network

Irish Travellers Project

Oldham Race Equality Partnership

Partners of Prisoners and Families Support Group

A sample of those receiving more modest grants of £45,000:

St Peter's Community and Advice Centre

Senior Citizens Society

Bexley Womens Aid

Evelyn Oldfield Unit

Streetwise Youth Project

YWCA of Great Britain

As examples of small grants, the following received £3,000 each:

National Phobics Society

The Haven Wolverhampton

Trampoline

Kelty Toddlers Group

The African Community Development Foundation

Widows and Orphans International.

Comment

For some years this series of books has noted the limited information available about the work of this charity. It is the usual practice of these editors to base their entries on what is already publically available. An exception, however, was made for the previous edition of this guide and, following a meeting with the charity, further information was provided. For the current edition we again sought to rely on what was publically available but, unfortunately, this has proved to be less than comprehensive.

As a consequence of this we were unable to assess whether the charity's expectation of making a higher proportion of non-London grants during its most recent grant cycles was met.

Exclusions

In general, the charity does not fund the following (for UK grants):

- academic research;
- general appeals;
- schools, colleges and hospitals;
- individuals;
- promoting religion;
- trips abroad, holidays and outings;
- services run by statutory or public authorities;
- medical research or equipment;
- minibuses.

Applications

Give It Sum

How to apply

For grants up to £5,000 – Please use the application form for grants up to £5,000. We will consider all of those applications after each deadline (Cycle 3: 15 July 2005; Cycle 4: 11 November 2005) and if your application fits the criteria we will telephone to discuss your project in more detail. It is essential that you enclose all the information requested at the bottom of the form when submitting your application. The trustees will then make their final decision. We will not be able to accept applications after 11 November 2005.

For grants over £5,000 – Please use the application form for grants over £5,000 and remember to enclose all of the information requested at the bottom of the form. When we have received all the applications for each deadline (Cycle 3: 15 July 2005; Cycle 4: 11 November 2005), we will then decide which we are able to take forward. We will then visit each group we have selected to talk through the application in more detail. Please note that we will not be able to accept applications after 11 November 2005.

Depending on the size of grant you wish to apply for, the appropriate form is available from the address below.

Comic Relief
5th Floor, 89 Albert Embankment
London SE1 7TP
Phone: 020 7820 5555
Fax: 020 7820 5500
Minicom: 020 7820 5579
Email: giveitsum@comicrelief.org.uk

In returning your application please remember to mark the envelope 'Give It Sum'.

If you require help with your application a number of local development agencies within North Staffordshire are able to assist. Contact details are available from Comic Relief.

Small grants for Gypsy and Traveller Projects

How to apply

We consider applications for this programme at any time, while funds allow, and there are no deadlines. All you need to do is fill in the downloadable application form from our website, fill it in and send it to us. Make sure you send us everything on the checklist, or explain why if you do not have any of them.

We should give you a decision within three months of your application.

You can telephone the UK Grants Team at Comic Relief if you have any questions about applying for funding. Send your application to:

Comic Relief
5th Floor, 89 Albert Embankment
London SE1 7TP
Phone: 020 7820 5555
Fax: 020 7820 5500
Minicom: 020 7820 5579
Email: travellersfund@comicrelief.org.uk

Comic Relief UK grants

Small Grants Programme

A new cycle of this programme was expected to start in spring 2005.

Large Grants Programme

Applications had closed for the 2003–05 cycle when this book when to press. A new grantmaking schedule was expected in spring 2005.

The established procedures have been as follows:

At Stage 1 you will send in the summary form, giving basic details about your work. This will give us enough information to decide whether you should send us a full application or not As well as assessing whether you meet the requirements of the programme you are applying to, we will take the

following into account when we look at your application:

- the difference your project will make to the lives of poor and disadvantaged people;
- the numbers of people who will benefit from your project depending upon the type of service you are supplying;
- the size of your organisation – we want to fund both small and larger organisations;
- the benefit to groups who face particular disadvantage (women, people from black and minority ethnic communities, lesbians and gay men, people living in rural areas, disabled people and older people);
- how involved people using the project are in the planning and managing of the organisation;
- how the work influences policy or changes the lives of disadvantaged people;
- how we are spreading our funding throughout the UK.

Once we have received all the summary forms we will draw up a short list of applications for Stage 2. If your application qualifies, we will send you our full application pack. This will give you plenty of time to send us more details.

Sport Relief UK grants

There are two stages to the application process.

Stage 1

At stage 1 you will fill in the summary form, giving basic details about your work. We will need to know:

- the aims and activities of your organisation;
- a description of the area you are working in, clearly describing the tension in the community which young people experience;
- a summary of the work you want to do, making sure you tell us who you will be working with; and l how you hope the work will reduce the level of community tension and the difference you think it will make.

Please answer all the questions on the form but do not send any other information at this stage.

Stage 2

Once we have received all the summary forms, we will draw up a short list of applications for stage 2.

If you would like to talk to someone before you apply, please get in touch with our UK grants team: 020 7820 5555 Fax: 020 7820 5500: Minicom: 020 7820

5579 : E-mail: ukgrants@comicrelief.org.uk

The Comino Foundation

Education

£346,000 (2002/03)

Beneficial area UK.

29 Hollow Way Lane, Amersham, Bucks HP6 6DJ

Tel. 01494 722595

Email enquire@cominofoundation.org.uk

Website www.cominofoundation.org.uk

Correspondent A C Roberts, Administrator

Trustees *Anna Comino-Jones; J A C Darbyshire; Dr W Eric Duckworth; Mike Tomlinson; Simon Bailey; J E Slater.*

Charity Commission no. 312875

Information available Information was provided by the trust.

The Comino Foundation is an educational charity and has two main purposes:

- to promote awareness that industry and commerce produce the basic goods, services and resources on which wellbeing and quality of life depend;
- to promote a clearer understanding of the basic processes involved in getting results, and thus improve people's power and will to create opportunities and achieve their purposes.

The foundation's vision is: 'that people in Britain should live more fulfilled lives within a prosperous and responsible society. The foundation contributes to the realisation of this vision through its educational activities by:

a) 'encouraging and enabling groups and individuals to motivate and empower themselves and to develop progressively their potential for the benefit of themselves and others,

b) 'encouraging a culture which affirms and celebrates both achievement and responsible practice in industry and commerce.'

The trust meets these aims through its patented GRASP approach, which offers a structure for thinking in a results-driven manner through a greater pattern, design and method of thinking. Most of the funds are given towards centres which promote the GRASP approach. Further information on this can be gathered from a leaflet prepared from the trust or on their extensive website.

In 2002/03 it had assets of £5 million, which generated an income of £304,000. Grants were made totalling £346,000.

The largest were £61,000 to National Parenting Institute and £30,000 each to Black County Partnership, Institute for Global Ethics UK Trust, King Alfred's College – Winchester, Sheffield Hallam University, University of Warwick and Wigan Borough Partnership.

Other beneficiaries were PACE Centre (£18,000), Homeground Project – Liverpool (£16,000), Potential Trust (£14,000), Bailey Comino Scholarship (£12,000), RSA (£10,000) and Foundation for Science and Technology (£2,000).

Exclusions

No grants to individuals or general appeals.

Applications

By letter, including full details of the proposed project and finances. There is no formal application form. Applications are considered at four formal meetings of the trustees each year.

The Community Foundation for Calderdale

General

£1.4 million (2002/03)

Beneficial area Calderdale and, to a much lesser extent, West Yorkshire.

Room 158, Dean Clough, Halifax, West Yorkshire HX3 5AX

Tel. 01422 349 700 **Fax** 01422 350 017

Email enquiries@ccfound.co.uk

Website www.ccfound.co.uk

Correspondent Steve Duncan, Acting Director

Trustees *Mike Payne, chair; Mohamed Aslam; Malcolm Kielty; Ronika Cunningham; Ian Firth; Martin Olive; Kate Thornton; Brenda Hodgson; Les Lawson; Cllr Peter Coles; Kate Hinks; Ingrid Holdsworth; Alison Roberts; Rose Wheeler; David Roper; Carol Stevenson.*

Charity Commission no. 1002722

Information available Information was provided by the trust.

In 2002/03, Community Foundation for Calderdale saw a slight increase of about 6% in its grants total compared to that of the previous year. Grant funds carried over to be paid in the next financial year also increased by nearly £360,000 and included payments to other parts of West Yorkshire on behalf of the Local Network Fund for Children and Young People for West Yorkshire. Total grants paid through the foundation to Calderdale organisations amounted to around £593,000.

About three-quarters of the foundation's income in 2002/03 was from the government or other statutory sources, while the remaining quarter came from non-statutory sources, including the foundation's own endowment then worth £2.3 million.

The foundation runs a number of grantmaking programmes which includes the Local Network Fund, North Halifax Community Chest, SureStart Community Chest for West Central Halifax, A!CEE Bursary Fund, Global, Individual Fund, Urban 2 and the Foundation Main Grants Programme.

For the 'main grants schemes' run by the foundation and various private donors, grants can be for amounts up to £1,000. These are 'influenced strongly by donor preference', which are wide-ranging. The trust funds both capital and revenue projects, and says the larger projects it funds tend to be capital, though bearing in mind the normal grant maximum of £1,000. It is not necessary for applicants to identify which fund to apply to, as the foundation will allocate each application to the appropriate fund.

Government funded SRB grants can be for amounts up to £1,500 in North Halifax (SRB4). Whilst the Urban 2 European funded Action Halifax Community Chest will fund grants up to £10,000.

In 2002/03, grants were made to 428 organisations totalling £1.4 million. Grants were made to 97 individuals to 'alleviate personal need' totalling £7,400. Grants to organisations were categorised as follows:

	No.	Total
Local Network Fund (for disadvantaged children)	189	£938,000
Youth projects	89	£135,000
Community projects	137	£285,000
Sports, social and leisure projects	13	£12,000

Major Local Network Fund grants

There were 44 organisations in this programme which received the maximum grant during the year of £7,000 each, totalling £308,000. These included: The Cardinal's Wheelchair Sports Club, Chiraagh Newsletter, Three Crowns, Gan Yisroel Parents Association, The Video Group, Leeds African Women Project, Action 4 the Week, The Bradford South Girls Group, the Diwn Support Group, Sikh Youth Sports Association, and Cottingley Kidz Play Scheme. Other grants were made under this scheme totalling £630,000.

Major grants from other funds

There were 28 grants of £1,500 or more made from the other funds (youth, community projects and so on) totalling £232,000. These included those to: Kerbside (£33,000), Home – Start and Todmorden Youth Project (£25,000 each), Link Up Cafe and Cardiac Rehabilitation (£2,000 each), Calderdale National Childbirth Trust, Wheatley Pentecostal Church, Holy Nativity Toddler, The Halifax Learning Zone and Calderdale Strakonice Twinning Association (£1,500 each). A further £207,000 was given in grants to other organisations under this scheme.

Exclusions

The foundation will not fund the promotion of political activity or the direct promotion of religious activity. It will not fund projects or activities which replace statutory funding.

Applications

There is a single initial application process for all grants (except those for the Local Network Fund – telephone 0845 113 0161 for an application form). Application forms and guidelines are available from the foundation and its website. Applications are considered on a bi-monthly basis.

The Community Foundation for Greater Manchester

General, in Greater Manchester

£2.5 million (2002/03)

Beneficial area The ten boroughs of Greater Manchester, i.e. Bolton, Bury, Manchester, Oldham, Rochdale, Salford, Stockport, Tameside, Trafford and Wigan.

1st Floor, Beswick House, Beswick Row, Manchester M4 4LA

Tel. 0161 214 0945 **Fax** 0161 214 0941

Email enquiries@communityfoundation. co.uk

Website www.communityfoundation.co. uk

Correspondent Julie Langford, Director of Grants

Trustees *Dr Tom Manion, chair; John Sandford; Ian Wicks; Cllr William T Risby; Archie Downie; Gordon Humphreys; Chris Hirst; Melinda Beckett-Hughes; Esther O'Callaghan; Chris Woodcock; Cllr Tony Burns; Gary Newborough; Helen Morris; David Dickman; Simon Webber; Kathy Cowell.*

Charity Commission no. 1017504

Information available Full information is available on the foundation's website.

Summary

The foundation manages over 40 funds, ranging in size from £20,000 to £1.8 million. The total amount across all the available funds stood at around £4 million in 2004, which represents a significant increase over the past couple of years.

The money comes, as with many community foundations, from a range of mostly statutory sources and each fund has its own criteria and conditions.

We serve the Metropolitan Borough Council areas of Bury, Bolton, Manchester, Oldham, Rochdale, Salford, Stockport, Tameside, Trafford, and Wigan. This adds up to a total population of over 2.6 million and an estimated 20,000 voluntary and community groups operating throughout the area.

Our Mission
Our mission is to be the channel of choice for individuals, families and organisations who wish to provide sustainable and

effective financial support to improve the quality of life for local people and communities both today, and into the future.

Our research has shown that many small community groups lack the confidence to apply for funding because of the perceived complexities involved; therefore we have worked hard to make the act of applying for a grant as simple, accessible and transparent as possible.

Our Vision: to help local people do extraordinary things
By its nature, government, whether local or national, is prescriptive in its solutions to local problems. Very often, despite claims that policies are inclusive and reactive to local needs, the real needs and wishes of local people can be overlooked, discounted or even ignored.

Our role is to take calculated risks and invest money from the private sector into the local communities that make up Greater Manchester, encourage new ideas and provide lasting and sustainable support to the most effective projects.

Our Vision recognises that to make real change we must put our trust in the people who live their lives in these communities and who are best placed to truly make a difference.

Grantmaking in 2002/03

During the year the foundation made grants totalling around £2.5 million to local projects.

Its 'core business' is providing support to small, local, grassroots community and voluntary groups across Greater Manchester. Consequently the vast majority of its grantmaking activity, in terms of both numbers and monetary value of grants, has been directed to this objective. Excluding the major beneficiaries, 750 grants were made, with around 70% being grants of £1,000 or less and the remaining 30% between £1,001 and £7,000.

The largest grant during the year was made to Manchester Carers Forum, which received almost £130,000. Other recipients of larger grants were United Estates Wythenshawe (£23,000), Cervical Cytology (£21,000), Manchester Geomantics (£19,000), Big Life Company (£15,000), Weston Spirit and the Black Health Agency (£12,000 each), Central Manchester PCT, HTA Grant Development and the Monastery of St Francis – Gorton (£10,000 each), Benchill Ecumenical Services (£9,000), Minehead Resource Centre (£8,500) and St Mary's Home School Partnership (£8,000).

There were 71 beneficiaries listed in the accounts as receiving £7,000 each. They include Skye Children and Youth Group, Wacky Cleaners, Addison Community Association, Bridges Toy Library, Freedom Community Theatre, Hurdles, Peaceful Solutions, Harmony Youth Project, Moss Lane Community Outreach Project, Trax Resource Centre, Manchester Jewish Community Centre, Bolton East District Scout Club and Hope Carr Youth Club.

Current Programmes

We are keen to receive applications from small local community based groups or projects and community entrepreneurs that are involved in activities that help to regenerate and build communities across Greater Manchester. Please make sure that you meet the Community Foundation's basic applications criteria [see Applications].

Start by taking a look at the grant programmes listed below to see what current funding opportunities are available and the types of projects they will support. You will need to bear in mind that the grant programmes we offer will all have their own eligibility criteria, closing dates for making applications and minimum and maximum size of grant available.

Decide which fund you think you are eligible to apply to for a grant and then read through the more detailed guidelines.

Don't forget, we are always happy to discuss your ideas and to provide advice before you complete an application form. Call us on 0161 214 0940.

The foundation lists the following main programmes for 2005 (check with the foundation for up-to-date information on current and new programmes):

Small Grants Programme

[The programme aims] to support a great variety of people, groups and projects that want to have a positive impact on the community surrounding them. Grants of up to £2,000 are available to small local community or voluntary groups and individuals in the Greater Manchester area committed to tackling the effects of poverty, unemployment, crime, discrimination and social exclusion.

If your group or project provides a local service or activities that benefit people who face disadvantage or barriers in their daily lives, and you only need a small amount of funding to organise and run this, then we may be able to help with our Small Grants Programme.

We are here to support you if you are not quite sure how to complete the application or you need to speak to someone about your idea or project.

We would like to support new ideas as well as activities and projects that may seem

ordinary to others but are, in effect, a vital part in local peoples' lives.

Priority is given to groups and organisations who:

- are working to improve the circumstance of individuals and communities in economically, socially excluded or deprived areas;
- are locally run and have less than £10,000 in reserve, have no access to a professional fundraiser and experience difficulty in attracting funding from other sources;
- encourage involvement of local residents in improving, designing, identifying and implementing community activities;
- promote voluntary participation and inclusion as well as community involvement and self-help;
- meet an emerging or immediate need and serve to build the awareness of the community and its residents;
- do not duplicate an existing provision or service without good cause.

An application form is available for completion via the foundation's website, by ringing 0161 214 0940 or the Grants Hotline on 0161 214 0951 (24hrs). There are several deadlines throughout the year—call the foundation for up-to-date information.

Local Network Fund for Children and Young People

The aim of the Local Network Fund for Children and Young People is to help disadvantaged children and young people achieve their full potential, by investing directly in the activities of local community and voluntary groups working for and with children and young people.

Local community and voluntary groups working with children and young people can apply for grants to help with the costs of activities or services for amounts between £250 and £7,000 under any of the following four themes:

Aspirations and experiences

Projects that give children experiences, or help them achieve goals that more privileged children may take for granted.

Economic disadvantage

Projects that help families to improve their living standards and cope with difficulties that come from being on low incomes. Groups can organise activities that help children and young people achieve goals they'd otherwise be unable to achieve

Isolation and access

Schemes that help children that are isolated or alone, or have trouble accessing services.

Children's voices

Projects that give children and young people the chance to express their opinions and give advice on matters that concern them.

Please be aware that this fund cannot support organisations that benefit solely the users of statutory services, for example, Parent Teacher Associations or Friends of Schools or Hospitals, except where it can be demonstrated that the project engages with the wider community.

Application forms for this scheme are available from the Government's Children and Young People's Unit by ringing 08451 130161. Once the application form is completed, it should be returned to the Community Foundation's office at the address above. Each area within Greater Manchester has separate deadlines for applications and panel dates – contact the foundation for further details.

Community Champions Fund

The Community Champions Fund was set up by the Department for Education and Skills (DfES) to help people who can inspire others to get more involved in renewing their neighbourhoods through participation in community groups.

The Community Champions Fund supports individuals with ideas for exciting projects aimed at benefiting local communities. Priority is given to new projects, which involve skills development and educational benefits for the participants. The fund is available throughout Greater Manchester and has two schemes that you can apply to for funding.

If you need help deciding which scheme is right for you or you have any other questions regarding Community Champions, please contact us on 0161 214 0940. Applicants who are under 18 years of age will also need to complete and submit an underage consent declaration with their application.

Community Champions Project Grants

Grants up to £2,000 are available for projects that need more than a small financial investment to get them up and running. Applications will be assessed every two months by an independent grants panel and we aim to advise you of a decision 16 weeks after we receive an application.

Community Champions Fast-Track Grants

Fast-track grants have been designed to make small levels of funding available to the community as quickly as possible. Fast-track is right for you if you have an idea that you want to get off the ground quickly, or alternatively if you have identified some advantageous training that is happening soon. Applicants complete a shortened two page application form and submit it to the Community Foundation. This is not an emergency fund, instead it recognises the fact that a good idea should be acted on immediately. The most that can be requested is £400 and we aim to inform all applicants of a decision within 20 working days of receiving an application.

An application form is available for completion via the foundation's website or by ringing 0161 214 0940.

Dates for 2005

Deadline	Panel meeting
29th May	29th June
28th August	28th September
21st November	21st December

The Rainmaker Fund

Launched by Cherie Booth QC, this fund was established by founder members Jacqueline Hughes-Lundy, Carole Nash, Brigit Egan, Claire Howell and Carol Stewart. The fund aims to help women in Greater Manchester reach and fulfil their personal potential. The fund will support applications for up to £1,000 from women and community groups or projects working with women.

The Rainmakers Fund supports women who feel they need support to return to the work environment, require training to unlock their full potential or need help to work towards becoming self-sufficience.

This fund is for both organisations and individuals, and there is a separate application form for both. The priorities for applicant organisations are as follows:

- projects working with excluded women;
- projects working with women escaping from domestic violence;
- projects that are providing training in new skills to women;
- projects that are opening up new opportunities and experiences to women (especially those that can be described as excluded or socially or economically deprived);
- projects that are offering careers advice to women;
- projects that are helping women fulfil their potential;

- projects working with women from within deprived or excluded communities.

Most grants will be made for specifically costed items of expenditure on a non-recurring basis. This can include: training, equipment, publicity etc. Remember that we are looking for you to tell us what you need to fulfil your aims. Please make it very clear how the grant will be used. Applications that state that funding is needed to fulfil a certain objective, but do not give any information on what the money will be specifically spent on are unlikely to be seen as a high priority.

Because of the size of the fund, it is not likely that a single application will be given a grant of more than £1,000. In fact in many cases it may well be less than this. Please make sure that you ask for what you need and not just the maximum you can ask for.

An application form is available for completion via the foundation's website or by ringing 0161 214 0940.

As at January 2005 the deadlines for applications for this scheme had yet to be confirmed. Contact the foundation directly for further information.

Exclusions

The foundation will not support the following:

- requests for help from organisations outside Greater Manchester;
- statutory organisations such as local authorities, schools or colleges, or the replacement of statutory funding;
- activities that are intended solely to benefit the users of statutory services (such as primary schools);
- projects for personal profit–applications must have a charitable purpose;
- capital projects such as building or construction work;
- academic or medical research & equipment;
- projects involving overseas travel;
- political groups or activities promoting political beliefs;
- religious groups promoting religious beliefs;
- projects that have already taken place;
- sponsorship or fundraising events and contributions to major appeals;
- salary costs (unless short term or essential project costs).
- recurrent 'core' costs;
- holidays and social outings, except in cases of special disablement or psychological need;
- local branches of national charities/organisations, unless locally managed and financially autonomous;
- sports or arts projects with no community or charitable element;

- organisations intending to redistribute the grant.

Applications

The foundation has the following basic application criteria for all schemes:

- for groups that have made a successful application to any of the Community Foundation fund programmes, a period of twelve months must have lapsed before you will be eligible to submit a new application to the fund you applied to. You can however apply to any of the other funding programmes we manage as long as your application is for a new project;
- if your previous application(s) had been rejected you may submit another application at any time, providing it is for a different project or purpose;
- you must be a small charity, community group or local voluntary sector organisation operating in and benefiting the communities of Greater Manchester. The 10 Metropolitan Boroughs are: Bolton, Bury, Manchester, Oldham, Rochdale, Salford, Stockport, Tameside, Trafford & Wigan. Only certain fund programmes accept requests for funding from individuals, such as the Community Champions Fund and the Rainmaker Fund;
- your group must be locally run and have less than £10,000 in reserve, have no access to a professional fundraiser and have experienced difficulty in attracting funding from other sources;
- you do not need to be a registered charity but must be able to provide us with a copy of your group's constitution or set of rules when applying;
- when applying you must be able to provide us with your group's bank account details;
- you must be able to provide the details of an independent referee to support any application you make. This must be someone who knows you and your group and is able to recommend your application.

Application packs, which include the foundation's grants criteria and help notes on completing the application, are available from the foundation's office.

You make a single application to the Community Foundation using the form. Each application is matched to the most appropriate fund and submitted for consideration.

If you are applying for a grant for the first time, or if you would like advice before making an application, call the foundation on 0161 214 0940.

Applications will only be accepted if submitted on the foundation's application form. All sections of the form must be completed even if the information is supplied in the form of a report, leaflet and so on. We prefer not to receive applications by fax; so completed forms should be returned to us by post. The decision of the foundation's trustees is final and no discussion will be entered into. We will, however, try to provide helpful feedback to both successful and unsuccessful applicants.

Applicants are requested to provide copies of the constitution, and a copy of the latest, relevant annual accounts and the last two bank statements with their applications.

We aim to give you an answer to your application as soon as possible, almost always within three months but please don't hold us to this literally. The exact time will often depend on a number of factors and not just when the appropriate committee next meets.

One of our grants administrators may contact you for further information or to discuss your application with you. The Community Foundation operates a 24-hour grant line where application forms can be obtained at any time. The grant line telephone number is 0161 214 0951.

Community Foundation for Merseyside

Community development, general

£6 million (2003/04)

Beneficial area Merseyside and Lancashire.

c/o Alliance & Leicester, T169 Operations Block, Bridle Road, Bootle, Merseyside GIR OAA

Tel. 0151 966 4604 **Fax** 0151 966 3384

Email info@cfmerseyside.org.uk

Website www.cfmerseyside.org.uk

Correspondent John Rowe, Development Officer

Trustees A White; R Swainson; J Flynn; I Chapman; A McCombe.

Charity Commission no. 1068887

Information available Information was provided by the trust

This community foundation, formerly working under the name of Sefton Community Foundation, operates Merseyside-wide and increasingly in Lancashire.

It delivers a range of large grantmaking programmes. In common with most other community foundations, it makes grants on behalf of its donors and channels statutory funding to local groups, as well as carrying out a small grantmaking programme from its own funds.

The foundation provides a direct link between them and those who have the means to support them. A community foundation is unlike other trusts and foundations because it is independent, permanent, flexible and tailor-made for the needs of both the groups and the donors who would like to help them.

In 2003/04 the foundation had an income of £5.9 million, all of which was given in grants.

The number and type of grants available from the foundation can vary considerably over time.

In February 2004 the foundation was offering grants through the following funds, although please note, changes are always taking place.

Alliance & Leicester Fund

Grants of up to £5,000 are available to registered charities in Greater Merseyside, Manchester and Wigan. Applications for less than £500 should receive a decision within four weeks and larger applications will go to a separate panel, which meets monthly. Projects should be based around the themes of education and learning, health related or environmental projects.

Children's Voices Fund

Grants of up to £500 or more are available to Sefton-based groups working with children aged between 4–13 on projects that encourage them to have a say on their local community. The fund is targeted at specific areas of South Sefton and Southport.

Community Fund for Healthy Eating

Grants of between £50 and £400 are available to voluntary and community groups in Sefton to enable them to develop projects relating to food and nutrition.

Fylde Community Projects Fund

Grants of between £500 and £5,000 for groups that are based in Fylde, or work exclusively with people who live in Fylde. To be eligible for a grant you must be a locally managed voluntary, community or self help group and your proposed activity must aim to meet one or more of these objectives tying in with the Fylde Community Plan:

- help to create a more inclusive community within Fylde
- increase the enterprise in the area and/ or employment opportunities
- promote community safety
- protect and/or enhance the Fylde environment
- increase and promote lifelong learning in Fylde
- improve the health and social well being of the Fylde Community.

Local Network Fund for Children and Young People

This is a government Grants Scheme from the Department for Education and Skills for groups in Greater Merseyside and Lancashire. Grants of between £250 and £7,000 are available for projects aimed at the 0–19 age group which address: 'Isolation and access'; 'Aspirations and experiences'; 'Economic disadvantage' and 'Children's voices'.

Mersey Docks and Harbour Company 500 Fund

The Mersey Docks and Harbour Company already supports the local community through donations, the majority of which are made by the Mersey Docks and Harbour Company Charitable Fund. This fund offers grants of up to £500 and enables small organisations in Liverpool, Sefton or Wirral to access financial support.

Neighbourhood Renewal Community Chest

This is a government scheme, where grants of between £50 and £5,000 are available to support grass-roots projects that deal with local neighbourhood regeneration. Funding is available to groups in Greater Merseyside and Blackpool.

Neighbourhood Renewal Community Learning Chest

A government grants gcheme to fund activities to develop the skills and knowledge of communities participating in Neighbourhood Renewal at a local level. Grants of between £50-£5,000 are available to groups in Greater Merseyside and Blackpool.

Sefton Smartstars Developing Play and Community Activities Fund

The fund targets voluntary and community groups working with children under four and their families in areas of south Sefton not already covered by the existing Sure Start programmes. Available to groups working in specific areas of South Sefton to develop play and arrange activities for children under four years old. Grants of up to £500 for community activities and £750 for developing play.

Sport Relief

Community Foundation for Merseyside will be involved in the delivery of the Sport Relief grant programme throughout Merseyside and Lancashire over the next two years. More details are to follow but it is likely that organisations will be able to apply for small grants (between £250 and £5,000) for projects that encourage social inclusion etc. through sporting activity.

Applications

For more information on the grants available and application criteria contact the Grants team on 0151 966 4604 or visit the Community Foundation website.

The Community Foundation for Northern Ireland (formerly the Northern Ireland Voluntary Trust)

Community development, social welfare

£3.1 million (2002/03)

Beneficial area Northern Ireland and the six border counties of the Republic of Ireland.

Community House, Citylink Business Park, 6a Albert Street, Belfast BT12 4HQ

Tel. 028 9024 5927 **Fax** 028 9032 9839

Email info@communityfoundationni.org

Website www.communityfoundationni.org

Correspondent The Director

Trustee *Mary Black, chair and 17 others.*

Northern Irish Charity no. XN45242

Information available Annual report, separate guidelines for specific schemes.

The Community Foundation for Northern Ireland, formerly the Northern Ireland Voluntary Trust, was established in 1979 with a grant of £500,000 from government. This was accompanied by a promise to match pound for pound further funds raised independently by the trust. Recently the foundation received a further £3 million Challenge Grant from government.

The trust supports 'community development and peace building in the divided communities of Northern Ireland. We also encourage and support the difficult task of work between the communities. The foundation is non-partisan, non-sectarian and has no political affiliations. It is therefore in the unique position of being able to work across all the divisions within society in Northern Ireland.'

In financial terms, the foundation is primarily an independent distributor of statutory funds. Of the 2002/03 income of £6.2 million, just £259,000 was from

its own resources, with £5.6 million gained in statutory and other funding.

It is difficult to separate the foundation's own resources from other sources of funding, so this entry covers both. In 2000/01 the following strategic themes were agreed as priority areas for future grants programmes:

- peace-building;
- community development;
- social justice;
- cross-boarder development;
- active citizenship;
- social inclusion.

The foundation's website describes these broad areas as follows:

Supporting People

Through the last 25 years the Community Foundation has been supporting people through a variety of programmes, focusing on those who need help most and working for a more equal society.

- Ethnic minorities

  The advent of the EU Special Support Programme for Peace and Reconciliation enabled the foundation to develop a well resourced support programme for minority communities which fuelled unprecedented development within the communities themselves and enabled a new level of networking between those communities, and with the wider society.

- Women

  The Community Foundation has supported initiatives for women over a number of years. At grass roots level there has been a big increase in the number of women members in community based groups, in rural areas and in disadvantaged urban areas. It has recently established a rural women's fund.

- Young people

  During the last two years the Community Foundation has been involved in YouthBank, a pilot programme under which young people aged 16–25 have been acting as grant-makers for locally-based youth-led projects. YouthBank is now developing further.

Strengthening Communities

Helping communities develop is one of the largest areas of grant giving for the Community Foundation.

- Cross border

93

The EU Special Support Programme for Peace & Reconciliation enabled the Community Foundation to become involved in cross-border development for the first time. The programme made available substantial funding targeted at the development of the peripheral border areas and the promotion of the reconciliation and improved links in the border region and on a wider all-island basis. *[This programme is to continue. Ed.]*

- Rural communities

People in disadvantaged rural areas often lack economic opportunities. Voluntary activity can help to build community spirit and coherence as well as developing organisational and job related skills. Many rural initiatives have started with a single issue. Over time, they have grown into multifaceted organisations that might manage enterprise space or community care, initiate training for rural tourism and run annual festivals and cultural events.

- Building communities

For the past 25 years, the Community Foundation has supported efforts to tackle poverty and deprivation through community action and has stimulated community development activity in many areas and sectors. Helping communities develop is the largest area of grant giving for the Community Foundation.

Recently the foundation has focused its resources and experience on areas where community development has not yet been established or has not taken root.

Building Peace

The Community Foundation focuses its work on the grassroots and those who have suffered most from the conflict, to help them build a stable and enduring peace.

- Summer Emergency Fund

The Community Foundation secured £25,000 in each of the last four years to use as a rapid response programme during periods of heightened community tension. The intention of the fund was to make relatively small amounts of money available with the minimum of bureaucracy, where such funding could ameliorate or potentially prevent community conflict. It was the rapid response nature of this fund that made it effective.

- Areas of sectarian tension

The Community Foundation has resourced community development initiatives to support communities in many areas experiencing community tension. It is our belief that areas experiencing these tensions require new models of intervention and significant support [...] The Community Foundation will proactively develop a 'Communities in Transition Programme' in 10 areas experiencing weak infrastructure and tensions.

- Ex-prisoners

The Community Foundation considered that as a funder it should be prepared to take risks for peace. That included working with politically motivated ex-prisoners to reintegrate them into society. The needs of ex-prisoners that had served lengthy prison sentences was particularly pressing. Financial support was provided for welfare rights services, training initiatives and family support services. A self-help approach was adopted.

- Victims

The Community Foundation is committed to [...] supporting and giving resources to voluntary and community groups throughout Northern Ireland who work with victims/survivors. The foundation also brings victims together in a series of learning seminars and conferences, with the aim of helping this sector learn from each other.

In addition the foundation has a strong non-grant making role, through informing policy development, drawing on its learning from funded projects and activities which bring community sector representatives together (locally and internationally). It is currently leading a 'Foundations for Peace' network and won an award for its work with Youth Bank in the Balkans.

Specific grants programmes are listed on the website.

For how to apply, please see the 'applications' section below.

Applications

Most of the grant programmes do not have a set application form. Instead applicants should write a letter of request to the correspondent, who will forward it to the appropriate grants officer. This letter should detail:

- the name and address of your group and the lead contact person;

- background information about your group including
  - why you have set up
  - what your aims and objectives are
  - what activities you are currently involved in and
  - who your activities are for or with;
- a description of your proposed project including
  - where the idea for this project came from
  - what you hope to achieve through this project
  - why it is needed;
- how people who are often excluded from activities or programmes will be included;
- the costs of the project and how much is needed (if there are other funders supporting the work as well please say who they are and what they are giving);
- how you will record and assess the progress of your project.

You should also attach:

- a copy of your group's constitution;
- your latest annual report (if you have one);
- a copy of your most recent accounts or, for new groups, a current income and expenditure record.

Community Foundation Serving Tyne & Wear and Northumberland

Social welfare, general

£5.6 million (2002/03)

Beneficial area Tyne and Wear and Northumberland.

9th Floor, Cale Cross House, 156 Pilgrim Street, Newcastle upon Tyne NE1 6SU

Tel. 0191 222 0945 **Fax** 0191 230 0689

Email general@communityfoundation.org.uk

Website www.communityfoundation.org.uk

Correspondent The Trustees

Trustees *Joy Higginson, chair; Hugh Welch; Mike Worthington; John Josephs; Sally Black; Neil Brimer; Stephen Brown; Pamela Denham; Alan Ferguson; Roy McLachlan; Pummi Mattu; Richard Maudslay; John Mowbray; Chris Parkin; Trevor Shears; Michael Spriggs; John Squires; Dr Shobha Srivastava; Jane Streather; Bill Teasdale; Jan Worters.*

Charity Commission no. 700510

Information available Information was provided by the trust.

The foundation describes its grantmaking as follows:

The Community Foundation awards grants for charitable projects in Tyne and Wear and Northumberland. We welcome applications and will do our best to help your group. We're here to make grants so don't be afraid to ask!

Last year [2002/03] the foundation awarded over £5.5 million to more than 1,900 local groups. This means that the vast majority of our grants were for less than £2,500, but we also made a number of larger grants, sometimes for several years, of up to £100,000.

You'll find more detailed information about how to apply below, but before you read on, and at the risk of oversimplification, let's say that nearly all our grants are for social welfare purposes to help small voluntary organisations and most grants awarded are for

● one off sums up to £2,500
● equipment or specific projects
● development and training.

We always welcome applications for larger grants and you'll see examples of grants up to £100,000 over several years, but these are, as yet, few and far between. At this lower level, there are good odds on a successful application and we would like to see more good value, well targeted proposals.

We manage over 100 different funds which you will find listed (on the website). Some funds have much more specific and restricted criteria. For example, our largest fund, the Kellett Fund, is for people in the third age. We match each application to our most appropriate funds and submit it for their consideration. So don't worry.

General

Set up in 1988, this is one of the largest community foundations. In 2002/03 it had an income of £6.8 million and its endowment stood at over £21 million.

The foundation provides a service to individuals, families and companies who want to help the local community. Funds set up by our donors are invested to produce an annual income which supports a wide range of carefully chosen voluntary groups. Grants range from a few pounds to £150,000 but most are for £1,000 or less.

The foundation runs a variety of different grants programmes, some using statutory and others private sources of funds. Most can be applied for using the same form.

Grantmaking is described in more detail, as follows:

We prioritise projects which:
● help people in greatest need
● involve minority and disadvantaged groups
● are locally run and led
● use volunteers fully
● help the development of the voluntary sector

and

● the vast majority of our grants are under £2,500
● we make a small number of grants each year of between £5,000 and £15,000, and exceptionally of up to £50,000 or more
● most of our grants are one-off but we make a small number for two or three years
● we recommend a few proposals to a national grant making trust, Henry Smith's Charity. This covers the region from Berwick upon Tweed to Teesside
● we are keen to work with other funding partners but will consider 100% funding if there are no other options available
● we make grants to villages and neighbourhoods as well as supporting projects that work across our whole area, taking into account the different needs of urban and rural areas
● we make grants to individuals in certain circumstances – please enquire
● we receive many applications and are unfortunately not able to fund them all.

We make grants to a wide variety of projects and organisations, including:
● community associations, residents' and tenants' associations
● neighbourhood advice centres
● community regeneration projects
● organisations working with older people, encouraging active involvement in their communities
● a wide range of work with children and young people
● projects tackling homelessness
● projects run by and for disabled people, people from minority ethnic groups, carers and other minority groups
● community arts projects and informal education which may or may not be accredited

● we fund projects which help people to learn the necessary skills to get a good job, and/or support them through the process of finding work
● projects involving children
● small scale community environmental projects.

The website lists 16 funds for which there are separate guidelines and applications procedures. Further details can be found there. For details of how to apply generally, see the applications section below.

Grants in 2002/03

The foundation gave £5.6 million in grants, with over £1 million coming from the **Henry Smith Charity** (which has its own entry) for its grantmaking in the north east of England.

Recent beneficiaries across all funds included Rehab UK, Rowlands Gill & District Live at Home Scheme, Tyne & Wear Museums, Toby Henderson Trust, Success Through Quality, Cowpen Craft Club, Northumberland Wildlife Trust, North East Prison After Care Society, Finchdale Training College, Newcastle CVS, Wallsend Sea Cadets, Pelaw Youth Centre, Gateshead Crossroads, Iranian Centre North East, Redby Childminding Group, Gateshead Volunteering Forum, Burnside Community High School, Longbenton Youth Project, Grainger Park Boys Club and Newcastle Community Green Festival.

Exclusions

The foundation does not normally make grants for the following purposes:
● sponsorship and fundraising events;
● small contributions to major appeals;
● large capital projects;
● endowments;
● political or religious activities;
● work which should be funded by health and local authorities;
● projects outside our area (unless funding is made available by a supporter from funds they have contributed to the foundation).

Applications

'Applicants should obtain a set of the latest guidelines, available from the foundation and downloadable from its website. We recommend that you plan your application well in advance. It can be made at any time. You only need to make one application, which the foundation will match to the appropriate fund or funds. You are welcome to phone to discuss your application at any stage.

'The following should be enclosed with your application: up-to-date annual accounts; latest annual report; copies of written estimates or catalogue pages if asking the foundation to fund equipment or capital costs.

'Requests for over £7,000 should also include copies of the minutes of the last three management committee meetings; business plan, if there is one.

'Your application will be acknowledged within a week, so please contact the foundation if you do not receive an acknowledgement. You may receive a phone call from a member of staff requesting further information or a visit. A decision is normally made within three months.

'If you are applying for a grant for the first time, or if you would like advice before making an application, do give one of the grants managers a ring. There are also agencies to help you with grant applications and these are listed on the foundation's website.

'The grants staff include grants managers: Helen Hughes, Karen Griffiths, Kate Bradley, Francis Baring, Zahida Hussein and Karen Beumont.'

The Community Foundation for Wiltshire & Swindon

Community welfare

£341,000 (2002/03)

Beneficial area Wiltshire, Salisbury and Swindon only.

48 New Park Street, Devizes, Wiltshire SN10 1DS

Tel. 01380 729284 **Fax** 01380 729772

Email info@wscf.org.uk

Website www.wscf.org.uk

Correspondent Jen Wildblood, Programme Director

Trustees Phil Smith, chair; David Bousfield; Caroline Caunter; Clare Evans; Alan Fletcher; Carol Griffiths; Tom Harvey; Alastair Muir; John Rendell; Rhoddy Voremberg; Simon Wright.

Charity Commission no. 298936

Information available Information was provided by the trust.

The foundation was set up in 1991. It incorporates the former Wiltshire Community Trust and the Thamesdown Community Trust. The foundation works as a practical partnership between the public, private and voluntary sectors, with representatives from all three being involved as trustees, grants committee members and volunteers.

The foundation is keen to play a pro-active role in helping those in need and those in a position to support local causes. It supports voluntary and community groups in Wiltshire whose primary aim is to improve the quality of peoples' lives through social and community care provision. Funding priorities are based on the findings of research commissioned by the foundation, Communities in Crisis in Wiltshire.

Although the foundation retains a wide basis for its grant-making, its focus is on projects which will make the most difference to the lives of people in the greatest need. It is also committed to making the best use of limited funds so particularly welcomes applications from groups who might find it difficult to raise funds elsewhere. Projects that can use an award from the foundation as a lever for attracting grants from other funders are also welcomed, though match funding is not a formal requirement.

The foundation wishes to promote equal opportunities through its grant-making programme. This involves issues of access, community involvement and user representation within the project, as well as ensuring the project will be open to all members of the community.

Grants programmes are as follows:

Main Grants Fund

Revenue or capital grants to projects meeting the following criteria:

- Supporting Community Care – working especially with people who are older and disabled, and with carers such as those caring at home for elderly or disabled relatives.
- Tackling Isolation – working in particular to improve access to services and information, improve transport in rural areas and support minority groups.
- Investing in Young People – concentrating on issues such as homelessness, education, training and self development.

Grants are for up to £3,000 per year for up to three years. Groups that have previously received an award can apply again to support new developments.

Small Grants Fund

One-off grants to small groups working to charitable purpose with a set of rules or a constitution. Grants are for up to £500.

Donor Advised Grants

The foundation also works in partnership with other funders to deliver a programme of grants aimed at Wiltshire groups. Recent partners include John Paul Getty Jnr Charitable Trust, R J Harris Trust, Ian Mactaggart Charitable Trust and High Sheriff's Grant Fund.

Progress Fund (Global Grants)

Grants up to £10,000 are available to fund projects which support people who are unemployed and from particular disadvantaged groups with the aim of increasing employment opportunities.

Local Network Fund

Donations of up to £7,000 are available to enable organisations to tackle poverty in the 0–19 age group. Work must involve at least one volunteer and fit into one of the four categories below:

- helping children to achieve goals they would otherwise not achieve
- helping families to improve living standards or cope on a low income
- helping young people who are isolated or alone
- Giving young people the chance to make their voices heard.

(The later two funds are time limited and it is suggested that applicants should contact the trust for up–to–date information on the funds currently running.)

Any grant not taken up after 12 months will be reviewed.

Donations awarded between 2002/03 totalled £341,000 and were broken down as follows:

Central main grants – north Wiltshire, Kennet and west Wiltshire

Beneficiaries included: Action Pact, Wiltshire Music Centre and Revival (£3,000 each); Springboard Opportunity Group (£2,500); Kennet Friends, Soundwell Music Therapy Trust and Wiltshire Play Resource Centre (£1,500 each); Alzheimer's Support – West Wiltshire and Kennet Gateway Club

(£1,000 each); Prospect Foundation (£750); Pewshaw Youth Club (£600); and CVS North Wiltshire (£550).

Swindon main grants – Swindon

Recipients included: Millen Advice Point (£5,500); Parks Advice Point (£3,000); Swindon Counselling Service (£2,000); Swindon Ten–Eighteen Project and The Friday Group (£1,500 each); SMASH Youth Project (£1,000); Prospect Foundation (£750); and Well Woman Centre Swindon (£420).

Salisbury main grants – Salisbury and district

Beneficiaries included: Anchor Staying Put – Salisbury (£4,500); Greencroft Centre (£2,700); Army Families Federation (£1,800); Salisbury District Well Woman and Salisbury Trust for the Homeless (£1,500 each); Age Concern – Salisbury (£1,000); and Harnham Youth Venture (£500).

Wiltshire–Wide grant (That is projects that will benefit all of the three benefical areas)

Recipients included: Wiltshire Play Resource Centre (£3,000); Wiltshire Bobby Van Trust (£2,000); Wiltshire Children's Breakaway (£1,000); Wiltshire Access Consultancy (£750); and DIAL Wiltshire (£600).

Small grants fund

Beneficiaries included: All Seasons Club, Dogridge Estate Residents Association and Melksham PHAB Club (£500 each); Rudloe Community Centre and Wiltshire Countryside Activities and Access Group (£300 each); Devizes Wednesday Club (£250); and Corsham Knitting & Crochet Group (£200).

Donor Advised Grants

- Avon Rubber Fund – A fund to benefit groups operating in the West Wiltshire area. Carers Support West Wiltshire received a grant of £3,000.
- Community 2000 Fund – Set up by the Gazette & Herald, small grants benefiting groups operating in the G & H area. Beneficiaries included: Guthrie Playgroup (£170); 2nd Devizes Guides and 3rd Devizes Scout Group (£140 each); Bromham Youth Committee and Devizes & District Tuesday Handicapped Club (£100); and All Seasons Club (£80).
- First Great Western Fund – Small grants to benefit groups operating in the First Great Western region. Recipients of £500 each were: Berkshire Community Foundation, Cornwall Independent Trust Fund, Devon Community Foundation, Greater Bristol Foundation and Somerset Community Foundation.

- High Sheriff's Grant Fund – Small Grants for the High Sheriff Crimebeat awards, promoting community safety issues. Beneficiaries included: Literacy & Numeracy Mentoring Project (£1,000); Millennium Volunteers, Tisbury Youth Centre, Westbury Youth & Community Centre and YPSS Social Development Project (£500 each); A Helping Hand (£430); Atworth Youth Club (£150); Rowdeford School (£110); and Pewsey Platform (£100).
- Honda UK Manufacturing Fund – Grants to benefit groups working in health & social care in a 25-mile radius of the Honda plant in Swindon. Beneficiaries were Swindon People First (£600) and SCAMP, Stepping Forward (£300) and Working for Opportunities Trust (£300 each).
- Ian Mactaggart Trust Fund – Beneficiaries included: Carers Support West Wilts and Home-Start – Swindon (£5,000 each); The Bridge Project (£3,000); and Service Users Network Swindon (£1,000).
- J.P. Getty Jnr Fund – Recipients included: Threshold Housing Link (£7,500) and Elizabeth House Social Centre (£4,800).

Exclusions

No grants for:

- projects operating outside Wiltshire or Swindon;
- large UK charities without local management groups;
- individuals;
- sponsored events;
- medical research and equipment;
- animal welfare;
- general/large appeals;
- promotion of religion;
- party political activity.

The foundation normally only funds work with children and young people in the 12–25 age group, unless they have a special need or disability (please refer to the Local Network Fund criteria). Arts and environmental work is not supported unless its primary aim is to support, enable and include people in need.

Applications

Application forms and guidelines are available from the foundation. All potential applicants are asked to make early contact with the programme director, preferably by phone, to discuss their project, prior to completing an application form.

Details of main grants rounds, plus any other funding opportunities open during the year, are publicised via local Voluntary Action newsletters and the local press. Decisions on main grants usually take place twice a year in the autumn and spring.

Decision making – All applications are fully assessed, normally by an on-site visit from the programme director. An objective report is then prepared for committee members.

The foundation has three area grants committees covering Swindon, Salisbury and Central Wiltshire, each chaired by a trustee. These committees give grants, contribute local knowledge and expertise and help to raise the profile of the foundation in their area. To enable a speedy turn around, decisions on small grants are taken outside of meetings by a sub group of the main committees.

Monitoring – The programme director and area committee members are involved in monitoring grants, which takes place either through visits or by post, depending on the size and complexity of the grant. Payment of any subsequent monies will be subject to a satisfactory outcome of this monitoring. The foundation encourages groups to develop and implement suitable monitoring and evaluation systems, and applicant groups should be prepared to develop ways of measuring their progress against their projects' objectives.

Grant-aid is viewed as part of an on-going relationship. Organisations in receipt of a grant are asked to provide reports, updates, newsletters, to include mention of the foundation's grant in their annual report and accounts and to invite the foundation to their AGM. The foundation is also prepared to be involved in discussions on future developments.

The Ernest Cook Trust

Education in environment, rural conservation, arts and crafts, often with youth focus; research

£680,000 (2002/03)

Beneficial area UK, but with a special interest in Gloucestershire and in other areas where the trust owns land (Buckinghamshire, Leicestershire, Dorset and Oxfordshire).

Fairford Park, Fairford, Gloucestershire GL7 4JH

Tel. 01285 713273 **Fax** 01285 711692

Email grants@ernestcooktrust.org.uk

Website www.ernestcooktrust.org.uk

Correspondent Mrs Antonia Eliot, Grants administrator

Trustees *Sir William Benyon, chair; Sir S A J P Bosanquet; M C Tuely; A W M Christie-Miller; P S W K Maclure; T R E Cook.*

Charity Commission no. 313497

Information available Comprehensive information on grants and guidelines was provided by the trust.

The trust was founded in 1952 by the late Ernest Cook, a grandson of Thomas Cook, founder of the travel agency. The sale of the family travel business in 1928 generated enough wealth for him to direct his energies into the purchase and conservation of great houses and estates and the art works they contained. The trust's estates lie at Hatherop, Fairford, Slimbridge and Barnsley in Gloucestershire; Hartwell and Boarstall in Buckinghamshire; Little Dalby in Leicestershire; Trent in Dorset; and Filkins in Oxfordshire.

Any project supported by the trust must be clearly educational. However, the trustees are particularly interested in applications which provide opportunities for young people: these may encourage the latter to gain qualifications to further their employment prospects, or they may assist training in crafts which are in danger of dying out.

The trustees are also keen to support applications which educate people about the rural environment and the countryside. Grants are also awarded for projects which educate young people in the arts, particulary if such work is linked to schools and the National Cirriculum. In addition, a few research grants are awarded if the work covers areas of interest to the trustees.

Grants range from £100 to £3,000 in the small grants category, of which modest amounts for educational resources for small groups form a large part. At the two main meetings grants are mostly in the range of £5,000 and £10,000, with only a few larger awards for projects closely connected with the trust's land holdings and educational interests.

In 2002/03 the trust had an income of £2.8 million. A total of 242 grants were awarded, amounting to £680,000. Grants made were categorised as follows:

Arts and crafts – 80 grants totalling £197,000 were made, ranging between £175 and £14,000. The largest grants were given to Hopetoun House Preservation Trust towards the ICT equipment and resources to make it accessible for educational purposes (£14,000); Cotswold Museums Charitable Trust towards the redevelopment work being undertaken at the Corinium Museum (£13,000); Holburne Museum of Art – Bath to support the salary of the education officer, Chatham Historic Dockyard towards help with educational work and Watermill Theatre to continue the work of the Watermill Young Company and its schools' workshops (£10,000 each) and Arkwright Scholarships to encourage more people into the industry (£9,000).

Environment and rural – 60 grants totalling £237,000 were made, ranging between £300 and £20,000. The main beneficiaries included Farms for City Children to cover the salary of the education officer for the farm in Wales (£20,000); Royal Horticultual Society towards the training costs for a student on the Wisley Student Programme (£17,000); Friends of the Earth towards the ongoing scholarship programme designed to equip young people as leaders and decision makers in environmental issues, Soil Association towards the organic education work of the association and Wildfowl & Wetlands Trust – Barnes to help with the cost of training volunteers to enthuse the visitors in conservation and wildlife issues (£10,000 each).

Youth – 69 grants totalling £137,000 were made, ranging between £250 and £10,000. The largest grants included those to Life Education Centres towards the puchase of a second mobile unit, Operation New World to support increasing employment prospects for young people without a job, Shaftesbury Society to support the Reach Out Project and Teens in Crisis towards the contribution to the salary of the project manager (£10,000).

Research – 4 grants totalling £41,000 were made, ranging between £5,000 and £25,000. Beneficiaries included Wildlife Conservation Research Unit supporting the Mammal Monitoring Research Programme at University of Oxford's farm – Wytham (£25,000); Somerset Wildlife Trust towards research that will encourage participation in a daily stewardship scheme and then assess the

resulting environmental benefits for grassland farms (£6,000); and Kingfishers Bridge Wetland Creation Trust towards research into balancing tecniques for breeding success and sustained populations of flora and fauna and National Foundation for Educational Research towards research into the state of art education in primary schools (£5,000 each).

Other educational grants – 29 grants totalling £70,000 were made, ranging from £50 to £20,000. Beneficiaries included Farmor's School Fairford – Gloucestershire, towards its bid for special status (£20,000); Volunteer Reading Help towards training more helpers and to provide more book boxes as resources (£7,500); Calvert Trust towards funding towards information boards and leaflets which link in with the National Curriculum (£6,700); Community Service Volunteers towards the training of 20 student volunteers to work alongside 40 disadvantaged pupils in Gloucestershire primary schools (£5,000); and Whaddon, Lynworth & Priors Neighbourhood to help with the cost of educational classes run by the Cheltenham based project (£2,500).

Exclusions

Applicants must represent either registered charities or not-for-profit organisations. Grants are only awarded on an annual basis and will not be awarded retrospectively. The following restrictions apply, as grants will not be made to:

- individuals;
- agricultural colleges;
- education work which is part of social support, therapy or medical treatment;
- building and restoration work;
- sports and recreational activities;
- work overseas.

Support for wildlife trusts and for farming and wildlife advisory groups is largely restricted to those based in counties in which ECT owns land (Gloucestershire, Buckinghamshire, Leicestershire, Dorset and Oxfordshire).

Applications

Trustees meet in March and October to consider applications and additional meetings are held at more frequent intervals to consider requests for £3,000 or less. Applications for the two main meetings must be finalised by 31 January and 31 August. There is no set application form but applicants are asked to focus their request on a specific educational need and to present clear and concise proposals on a maximum of four sides of A4 paper. A simple budget for the project and a copy of the latest annual report and accounts should also be enclosed. Applicants are encouraged to contact the grants officer if they require further details.

The Alice Ellen Cooper Dean Charitable Foundation

General

£536,000 (2002/03)

Beneficial area UK, with a preference for Dorset and west Hampshire.

Hinton House, Hinton Road, Bournemouth BH1 2EN

Tel. 01202 292424

Correspondent Douglas J Neville-Jones, Trustee

Trustees *Miss S A M Bowditch; Rupert J A Edwards; Douglas J E Neville-Jones; Miss E J Bowditch; J R B Bowditch.*

Charity Commission no. 273298

Information available Annual report and accounts were provided by the trust.

This trust aims to relieve poverty, distress and sickness, and advance education and religion and other charitable purposes of benefit to the community. Donations are only made to registered charities, which includes UK charities, but primarily go to local organisations in Dorset. Grants usually range from £1,000 to £25,000 each.

In 2002/03 the trust had an income of £695,000 and gave 93 grants totalling £536,000. Its investments almost doubled on the previous year to £11.1 million.

There were 17 grants for £10,000 or more. Two exceptional grants of £40,000 and £30,000 were made to British Red Cross Zimbabwe HIV Home-based Care Project and the Chesil Trust respectively.

Other large grants included those to Hyped Ladders Project and the Wessex Autistic Society (£25,000 each), Leonard Cheshire Care at Home Service – Dorest and Wiltshire (£20,000), St Martin in the Fields Social Care Unit and UNICEF Afghan Children Appeal (£15,000 each)

and East Holton Charity and Tenovus (£10,000 each).

The majority of grants are for £5,000 or less. Beneficiaries included Army Benevolent Fund, Bournemouth Young Men's Christian Association, Colon Cancer Concern, Dorset Advocacy, Dorset Opera, Friends of War Memorial, Lady Hoare Trust, Motability, Salisbury Cathedral Trust, Sports Aid South West, Stroke Association and Youth Cancer Trust.

Exclusions

No grants to individuals.

Applications

In writing to the correspondent. The trust has previously stated that its funds are fully committed and that unsolicited applications have little chance of success.

County Durham Foundation

Tackling social disadvantage and poverty, general

Around £2 million to organisations and individuals (2003/04)

Beneficial area County Durham, Darlington and surrounding areas.

Jordan House, Forster Business Centre, Finchale Road, Durham DH1 5HL

Tel. 0191 383 0055 **Fax** 0191 383 2969

Email info@countydurhamfoundation. co.uk

Website www.countydurhamfoundation. co.uk

Correspondent Vikkie Wilkinson, Operations Manager

Trustees *Bernard Robinson, chair; Sir Paul Nicholson; Michele Armstrong; Peter Cook; David L Brown; John Clarke; John Hamilton; Andrew Martell; Lady Sarah Nicholson; David Watson; Mark I'Anson; Barry Keel; Mark Lloyd; Frances Bourne.*

Charity Commission no. 1047625

Information available Full information is available on the foundation's website.

The foundation is striving to build a permanent endowed fund for the benefit of local people. It currently manages endowments valued at around £3 million

and intends to boost this to £6.4 million by the end of 2005.

As at January 2005 the following programmes were active (the beneficial area for each programme is in brackets):

Community Action (County Durham and Darlington)

Grants of up to £1,000 for small organisations. Priority will be given to start up grants and applications from groups in Durham City, Chester le Street, Teesdale and Darlington, although groups in other districts can apply.

Neighbourhood Renewal Community Chests (Derwentside, Easington, Sedgefield and Wear Valley)

Up to £5,000 is available to groups working towards the regeneration of the stated areas. Priority will be given to local activities and services to address local need, that are user-led, involve volunteers and which will provide a lasting benefit.

Community Learning Chests (Derwentside, Easington, Sedgefield and Wear Valley)

Up to £5,000 is available for community groups to take part in learning activities which will improve their management, such as training courses, fact-finding visits to other projects or to purchase learning materials.

Local Network Fund – Children and Young People (County Durham and Darlington)

Grants of up to £7,000 (£12,000 over two years in exceptional circumstances) are available to initiatives which aim to make a difference to the lives of children or young people up to the age of 19. Projects must demonstrate that the children or young people benefiting are facing poverty or disadvantage, and that their views are heard and they are involved in decision making regarding the project. An application form is available from the Local Network Fund by ringing 08451 130 161.

Fair Share (Central and Northgate wards, Darlington)

A total of £250,000 over three years is available (minimum grant £5,000). It aims to ensure that a larger share of lottery funding is received in Central and Northgate wards. A sum of £800,000 will be awarded over ten years towards local regeneration, job creation and environmental improvements.

Previous grant recipients from various programmes include: Trimdon Station Residents Association, Tow Law Millennium Green Trust, Cotherstone Jubilee Committee, Friends of St Benets, Chester West Community Project, Wearhead Village Hall Association, Hilda Park Action Group, Community Enterprise Direct, Burnhall Residents & Friends, Jackass Youth Theatre, Willington Cricket Club, Durham City Centre Youth Project, Bearpark Youth Group, Elm Ridge Youth Group, Easington Welfare Youth Group, Phoenix Fun Club, Seaham & District Training Trust and Moveable Feast Gift Group.

The foundation also runs a number of grants schemes for individuals, not covered by this entry. Details of these programmes can be found on the foundation's website. Contact the foundation directly for up-to-date information on new programmes.

Exclusions

The foundation will not fund:

- projects outside County Durham and Darlington (but groups from Sunderland can apply for environmental grants);
- national or regional charities with no independent office in County Durham or Darlington;
- general contributions to large appeals (but specific items can be funded);
- groups that have more than one year's running costs held as free reserves;
- grants for more than one year (although the Local Network Fund for Children and Young People makes grants over two years in exceptional circumstances);
- projects which should be funded by a statutory body;
- school projects other than environmental improvements to land open to the public;
- improvements to land that is not open to the general public at convenient hours;
- building or buying premises and freehold or leasehold land rights;
- minibuses or other vehicles;
- overseas travel;
- animal welfare;
- political or religious activities;
- deficit or retrospective funding, i.e. no grants for activities that have already taken place.

Some of the programmes have other exclusions. If your project is at all unusual please contact the foundation to discuss your application before submitting it.

Applications

An application form is available from the foundation's website. Full guidelines, criteria and application details for each programme are also available from its website or by calling the foundation on the number below.

Cripplegate Foundation

General

£654,000 (2004)

Beneficial area The ancient parish of St Giles, Cripplegate, London, the former parish of St Luke Old Street as constituted in 1732 (broadly speaking, the southern part of Islington and the north of the City of London), and now extended to include the Islington Council wards of Barnsbury, Bunhill, Clerkenwell, Canonbury East, Canonbury West, St Mary, St Peter and Thornhill.

76 Central Street, London EC1V 8AG

Tel. 020 7549 8181 **Fax** 020 7549 8180

Email grants@cripplegate.org.uk

Website www.cripplegate.org

Correspondent Kristina Glenn, Grants Manager

Trustees *Grants Committee: Paula Kahn, chair; John Broadbent, Joseph Trotter,Barbara Riddell, Rachel Panniker, Laura Willoughby, Lucy Watt, SteveStevenson.*

Charity Commission no. 207499

Information available Information was supplied by the trust. Guidelines for applicants are available.

Summary

The Foundation gives up to £1 million a year to a wide range of organisations in the south Islington area of London and part of the City of London. Most grants are awarded to organisations working in south Islington. In 2004 grants of over £10,000 accounted for over 50% of the expenditure although many smaller grants were also made. The average grant was for £11,470. Grants can be made for any purpose, including core and capital costs. Three year grants accounted for over 57% of the grant expenditure.

Over 20% of grants were for the benefit of children or young people.

25% of grants were spent on community groups and voluntary sector infrastructure.

General

Guidelines

We provide grants which aim to:
- improve the quality of life in our area of benefit
- provide opportunities for local residents
- make a real difference to people's lives
- help local people in financial need
- contribute to the welfare of local residents.

We give grants both to organisations and to individuals.

We also distribute grants in Islington under the Government's Community Chest and the Community Learning Chest programmes.

The foundation's grant making is informed by:
- a knowledge of available funding streams
- its links with other funders
- a knowledge of and a long-term relationship with the local area.

This can mean directing organisations to more appropriate funding or providing match funding. The foundation ensures it is not replacing or duplicating statutory funding. Our grant making aims to help organisations meet their objectives. Our flexible reporting regime is informed by organisations' aims.

Programmes

Main grants programme

All applications are considered which benefit the local area. The foundation funds:
- core costs for key Islington voluntary organisations;
- project funding;
- salary costs;
- capital costs.

Schools programme

The schools programme aims to:
- raise achievement;
- enrich the curriculum;
- improve opportunities for young people and their families.

Each primary school in south Islington can apply for up to £10,000 over three years.

Each secondary school in south Islington can apply for up to £25,000 over three years.

Each special school in south Islington can apply for up to £25,000 over three years.

Learning the Lessons: A review of Cripplegate Foundation's schools programme was published in 2004. This gives information on the work which has been supported. The foundation works closely with schools and voluntary organisations to develop new programmes of work.

'Pro-active' programme

The foundation has a history of 'pro-actively' identifying and targeting important local needs that may not be reflected in applications. More than 30% of the foundation's funding is currently allocated this way. This is central to the foundation's approach to funding.

Over the past eight years the foundation has been involved in:

- establishing a detached youth work project in Finsbury in 1996;
- establishing a programme for funding work in schools in 1997;
- setting up and funding the South Islington Plus Bus in 2000;
- establishing the South Islington Advice Project to offer welfare rights advice to south Islington residents in Finsbury and Clerkenwell in 2000;
- encouraging funding applications and new services in the Kings Cross area in 2001/02;
- developing a mental health service for young people aged 16–25 in 2002;
- setting up a writers in schools project in 2003;
- extending the South Islington Advice Project to Kings Cross in 2004.

Grants to individuals programme

Grants to individuals programme the foundation provides financial help to individuals to relieve hardship and distress. All applicants are visited and offered a fullwelfare rights benefits check. There were 109 grants totalling £31,000 in 2004.

Neighbourhood Renewal Community Chest / Neighbourhood Renewal Community Learning Chest

These schemes aim to support small and new local community groups to contribute to the regeneration of their communities in Islington.

Grants of between £50 and £5,000 are available from both the Community Chest and Community Learning Chest to organisations. The Community Chest fund awards grants to groups with a turnover of less than £100,000, but with priority for groups with a turnover of under £50,000. The Community Learning Chest fund does not have an upper limit on turnover.

Decisions on applications are made by a panel of Cripplegate Governors and members of the Islington Community Network.

Grants of over £370,000 were approved in 2004 for organisations ranging from supplementary schools to mental health groups, tenants and residents associations and arts projects.

Grants in 2004

Grants to organisations were broken down as follows, shown here with examples of grants in each category.

Schools and work with schools – £174,000 in 37 grants

20 schools received grants with most receiving more than one. Support included those for artists and writers in schools projects, theatre and drama projects and school trips. Further organisations received support for work with schools, including Little Angel Theatre, Theatre Adad, Volunteer Reading Help and Writer in Schools Project.

Community groups and infrastructure – £270,000 in 9 grants

Islington Voluntary Action Council, the local CVS received £60,000 over three years towards core costs. The Peel Centre, a multi purpose centre received £80,000 over four years and the Claremont Project, a health and older people's centre received £20,000 over two years.

Work with young people – £89,336 in 5 grants

Kings Corner Project received £50,000 over three years towards running costs and salaries. Crumbles Adventure playground received £21,000 over two years to allow the playground open later and at the weekend.

Social welfare and advice

One grant of £3,000 was made to St Silas church towards the restoration of a church hall for community use.

Mental health – £44,000 in 3 grants

One grant of £30,000 over three years was made to the Maya Centre, which offers psychotherapy to women on low incomes, towards core costs.

Arts, leisure and environment – £64,200 in 3 grants

These were: £19,000 over three years towards the cost of a gardener at Culpepper Community Garden; £45,000 over three years towards the cost of a community projects manager at the London Symphony Orchestra Discovery project; and £200 towards the cost of a commemorative event organized by Upper Street Association to mark the 60th anniversary of the demolition of Highbury Corner by a doodlebug.

Education and training

A grant of £24,000 was made over two years to Refuge Education and Training Service over two years towards the cost of providing an advice and information service for refugee organisations.

A further £250,000 was distributed from the Neighborhood Renewal

Community Chest and £80,000 from the Neighbourhood Renewal Community

Learning Chest.

Exclusions

No funding given for:

- national charities and organisations, or organisations outside the area of benefit, unless they are carrying out particular pieces of work in the area of benefit;
- schemes or activities which would be regarded as relieving either central government or local authorities of their statutory responsibilities;
- grants to replace cuts in funding made by the local authority or others;
- medical research or equipment;
- national fundraising appeals or appeals to provide an endowment;
- advancement of religion and religious groups, unless they offer non-religious services to the local community;
- animal welfare;
- retrospective grants;
- commercial or business activities.

Applications

An application pack is available from the foundation and can be downloaded from the foundation's website.

Cumbria Community Foundation

Improving the quality of community life

£826,000 (2002/03)

Beneficial area Cumbria.

Unit 6b, Lakeland Business Park, Lamplugh, Cockermouth, Cumbria CA13 0QT

Tel. 01900 825760 **Fax** 01900 826527

Email enquiries@cumbriafoundation.org

Website www.cumbriafoundation.org

Correspondent Andrew Beeforth, Director

Trustees *Capt. John Green; Cllr Jim Musgrave; Arthur Sanderson; Bob Mather; Glyn Roberts; Henry Bowring; Ian Brown; James Cropper; John Dunning; John Fryer-Spedding; Keith Adamson; Mark Elliott; Michael Hart; Peter Hensman; Richard Simpson; Robin Burgess; Charles Woodhouse; Mrs Margaret Martindale; Mrs Suzie Markham; Ms Chris Coombes; Ms Shirley Williams; Ms Susan Aglionby; Stuart Young; L Victory; Dr J Stanforth.*

Charity Commission no. 1075120

Information available Annual report and accounts were provided by the foundation.

Established in 1999, this community foundation is concerned with 'improving the quality of the community life of the people of Cumbria, and in particular those in need by reason of disability, age, financial or other disadvantage'. The foundation has had much success in raising a permanent endowment, partly due to a scheme with Francis C Scott Charitable Trust (which has its own entry) whereby they gave £1 for every £2 donated, to a maximum of £500,000.

In 2002/03 the trust had an income of £1.4 million, with £942,000 from statutory sources and £397,000 in donations from businesses, trusts and individuals. Grants totalled £826,000. Following the 2001/02 focus on helping those affected by foot and mouth, the foundation has significantly increased its grant making with over £650,000 distributed in grants to 389 groups. This compares with 244 groups receiving £378,000 in 2001/02.

Grants in 2002/03 were broken down by the foundation as follows (with totals for 2001/02 in brackets). See table below.

The trust operates the grants programmes listed below:

Countywide

County grants

Grants of up to £1,000 for small organisations with an annual income of up to £25,000.

Beneficiaries in 2002/03 included Barrow St Andrew's Pipe Band and Epilepsy Action Cumbria Forum (£1,000 each), Alston Moor Sports Club, Cumbria Schools Cricket Association and Lindale Pre School Nursery (£500 each), Hutton End Village Hall Committee (£400), 5th/8th Kendal Scout Group (£300) and Dalton Community Association (£160).

Cumbria Key Fund

This is a countywide, European Union funded programme. Grants of up to £6,000 are available for organisations providing projects aimed at encouraging cooperation between members of the local community to carry out activities that improve the quality of life and the local environment.

Beneficiaries in 2002/03 included Silloth Childcare Initiative and Whitehaven Community Trust (£6,000 each), Cleator Moor Business Centre and Thomlinson Community Development Centre (£5,000 each), Tranquility Young Enterprise Company (£3,500), South

Cumbria Leisure Link (£2,500), Motability (£1,600), West Cumbria Trades Hall Centre (£1,000) and Lifelong Learning Project (£340).

Cumbria Local Network Fund

This is a government funded programme. Grants between £250 and £7,000 for activities targeting disadvantaged children and young people (0–19 years). Application packs can be requested from the national call centre on 0845 113 0161. Organisations are encouraged to contact the foundation before applying.

Beneficiaries in 2002/03 included Eden Carers, Family INC and Wigton Youth Station (£7,000 each), Carlisle Mencap (£6,500), Impact Housing Association Ltd (£6,000), Cumbria Alcohol and Drug Advisory Service (£5,000), Longthwaite Road Pre-school, Ousby Activity Committee and Penrith Methodist Church Bridge Project (£3,000 each), Barrow Cheerleaders (£2,500) and Barrow Borough Sports Council (£1,000).

Cumbria Drug Action Team

In April 2003 the foundation received £42,000 from the Drug Action Team for distribution to small-scale community based projects aimed at preventing the abuse of illegal drugs.

Community Champions

This fund is for individuals and gives grants of up to £2,000.

Cumbria Community Recovery Fund

This fund is aimed at those affected by the Foot and Mouth outbreak.

Allerdale area only

Allerdale Community Fund

Grants of up to £5,000 are available to small community and voluntary organisations located in the Parish councils of Allerdale.

Beneficiaries in 2002/03 included Portinscale Village Hall, Threlkeld Recreation Field Trust and Westfield Community Play Project (£5,000 each), Cockermouth Croft Bowling Club (£3,300), Lions Club of Cockermouth and Maryport Inshore Rescue Boat (£3,000 each), Crosby Youth Club and Little Clifton Playfield Group (£2,000 each), Abbeytown Pre-School/Playgroup, Prospect Village Hall and Westward Parish Room (£1,000), Dearham Junior Band (£500) and Velo Club Cumbria (£300).

CUMBRIA COMMUNITY FOUNDATION

Grants in 2002/03 (with figures for 2001/02 in brackets)

	No.	(No.)	Amount	(Amount)
Disabilities	39	(20)	£42,000	(£42,000)
Children under 14	105	(48)	£166,000	(£44,000)
Young people 14–25	74	(46)	£162,000	(£59,000)
Elderly	9	(10)	£16,000	(£7,000)
Homelessness	0	(1)	£0	(£5,000)
Community action	118	(75)	£173,000	(£131,000)
Local residents	34	(25)	£52,000	(£51,000)
Visitors and tourism	8	(10)	£18,000	(£20,000)
Local economy	1	(8)	£500	(£18,000)
Endowed Challenge Funds	3	(1)	£9,000	(£1,500)
Foot and mouth relief – Community groups	30	(313)	£122,000	(£783,000)
Foot and mouth relief – Individuals	71	(1,077)	£45,000	(£1,060,000)

Allerdale Neighbourhood Renewal Community Chest and Allerdale Neighbourhood Renewal Community Learning Trust

Grants of up to £5,000 are available to voluntary and community organisations in the most deprived neighbourhoods in Allerdale.

Beneficiaries in 2002/03 included Allerdale Disability Association, Crosscanonby Community Centre and Thomlinson Community Development Centre (£5,000 each), Workington Zebras Athletic Club (£4,000), Age Concern North West and Resolve Mediation Service (£2,000 each), Low Moor Pre School and St Bridget's Kids' Club (£1,000 each), Stonham Housing Association (£500) and Silloth Childcare Initiative (£250).

Allerdale Youth Bank

Grants of up to £500 are available to groups that provide activities for young people between the ages of 11 and 25.

Allerdale and Copeland areas

West Cumbria Coalfields Community Chest

Grants of up to £10,000 are available for revenue funding available to community groups and organisations in the Allerdale and Copeland area.

Beneficiaries in 2002/03 included West Cumbria Credit Union Development Project and Whitehaven Credit Union (£6,000 each), Cleator Moor Business Centre (£5,000), Great Clifton Village Hall Committee (£3,000), Moresby Primary School (£2,300), Greenbank Community Centre (£1,000) and Flimby School Association (£500)

Rockcliffe and Westlinton areas

Rockcliffe and Westlinton CWM Trust

This fund provides grant assistance to community groups and organisations for environmental projects within the parishes of Rockcliffe and Westlinton. Grants are available for up to £10,000 – although larger grants may be available in exceptional circumstances.

The website has full details of the criteria and application procedure for most programmes, and the foundation can be contacted on 01900 825 760 for further details.

Exclusions

Please contact the foundation for individual restrictions on each of the grant programmes.

Applications

For details on how to apply, refer to the foundation's website or contact the foundation on 01900 825 760.

Itzchok Meyer Cymerman Trust Ltd

Jewish Orthodox education, other Jewish organisations

About £850,000 (2002/03)
Beneficial area UK and overseas.

15 Riverside Drive, Golders Green Road, London NW11 9PD
Tel. 020 7272 2255 **Fax** 020 7272 5111
Correspondent I M Cymerman, Trustee
Trustees Mrs H F Bondi; I M Cymerman; M D Cymerman; Mrs R Cymerman; Mrs S Heitner.
Charity Commission no. 265090
Information available Annual report and accounts.

The objective of the trust is 'to advance religion in accordance with Orthodox Jewish faith and general charity'. Almost all funds are awarded to Jewish organisations, religious or otherwise. The list of beneficiaries changes very little from year to year.

In 2002/03 the trust had an income of £672,000 and a total expenditure of £868,000. Grants were made totalling about £850,000. There are around 50 grants made each year, mainly to the same beneficiaries.

Regular recipients include Centre for Torah Education, Gevurath Ari Torah Academy, Mepi Olelim, Telz Academy Trust, Girls' School – Zichron Ya'akov, Yeshiva Gedola Zichron Michael, Friends of Harim Establishments, Friends of Ohr Akiva, Mesivta Lezeirim, Russian Immigrant Aid Fund, Beis Yaakov Institutions, Torah Vechessed L'Ezra Vesaad, Mesilat Yesharim, Pardes Chana Institute, Beth Jacob Town, Central Charity Fund, Gur Trust Building Fund, Seminar Ateret Malkah, United Institutions of Arad and Yeshivat Dromah.

Applications

In writing to the correspondent.

The D'Oyly Carte Charitable Trust

Arts, medical welfare, environment

£724,000 (2002/03)
Beneficial area UK.

1 Savoy Hill, London WC2R 0BP
Tel. 020 7420 2600 **Fax** 020 7240 8561
Correspondent Mrs Jane Thorne, Secretary
Trustees Jeremy Leigh Pemberton, chair; Sir John Batten; E John P Elliott; Mrs Francesca Radcliffe; Mrs Julia Sibley; Dr Robert K Knight; Henry Freeland.
Charity Commission no. 265057
Information available Application form and guidelines, annual report and accounts were provided by the trust.

Summary

Grants, mainly one-off, start at around £500. The majority are for amounts under £5,000 although some can be for larger amounts. Awards are made in the following areas:

- arts;
- medical welfare;
- environment.

Most of the money goes to organisations under the first two headings.

General

The trust was founded in 1972 by Dame Bridget D'Oyly Carte, granddaughter of the founder of both the Savoy Theatre and the Hotel. Its distributable income increased significantly on her death in 1985, when it inherited her shareholding in The Savoy Hotel plc, and again in 1998 following the company's sale.

In 2002/03 the trust had an income of £973,000, from its investment then worth £27.2 million.

The trust supports general charitable causes connected with the arts, medical welfare and the environment. Certain charities in which the founder took a special interest continue to be supported on a regular basis.

Guidelines for applicants

In 2003 the trust reviewed its guidelines and priorities. For the period 2003 – 2006 the trust will focus on the following:

The Arts

- promotion of access, education and excellence in the arts for young people to increase their opportunities to become involved outside school and to build future audiences
- access to the arts for people who least have access to them
- performance development of graduates in the performing arts in early stages of their careers and to encourage their involvement in the community through performances and workshops for the benefit of those with special needs and those who would otherwise have no opportunity to hear or participate in a live performance.

Medical Welfare

- promotion and provision of music and art therapy to improve the quality of life for the elderly and the disabled
- promotion and provision of music and art therapy in the palliative care of children
- support for charities concerned with alleviating the suffering of adults and children with medical conditions who have difficulty finding support through traditional sources
- support and respite for carers with emphasis on the provision of holidays for those carers who would not normally have a break from their responsibilities – and with special emphasis on projects and schemes that allow young carers to enjoy being children.

The Environment

- preservation of the countryside and its woodlands – with emphasis on the encouragement of voluntary work and active involvement in hands-on activities
- protection of species within the United Kingdom and their habitats under threat or in decline
- conservation of the marine environment and sustainable fisheries
- heritage conservation within the United Kingdom based on value to, and use by, the local community – the trust favours projects that seek to create a new use for fine buildings of architectural and historic merit to encourage the widest possible cross-section of use. (The trust does not normally support major restorations unless a specific element of the work can be identified as appropriate to the aims of the trust.)

Most grants are one-off, 'although grants for up to three years are given occasionally, particularly in respect of bursary funding for educational establishments, mainly in the arts sector'.

Grants in 2002/03

During the year the trust made 168 grants totalling £724,000: the number and total value of grants has significantly reduced from the level seen in the previous year (282 grants totalling £1,425,000 in 2001/02). The trust's annual report includes this description of its grantmaking activities during the year:

The distribution of grants between the sectors continues to favour charities in the arts and medical welfare sectors, with less than 10% of the trust's income this year going to environmental charities. However, whatever the cause, the trustees always try to direct their funds to where they can make a material difference, and this aim steers them away from significant appeals.

This year again, the arts took the largest proportion of the trust's spending at £342,000 compared to £687,000 in the previous year, or 47.2% of the total. Spending on the medical welfare sector amounted to £314,000 compared to £567,000 in the previous year, or 43.4% of the total. In the third sector, the environment, £68,000 or 9.4% of the total was distributed compared to £170,000 in the previous year.

Arts

This year saw the conclusion of a significant three-year commitment by the trust to four national youth arts organisations – Music for Youth, the National Children's Orchestra, the National Youth Music Theatre and the National Youth Orchestra – vital core funding to assist them during a difficult period.

During the year, Music for Youth, the National Children's Orchestra and the National Youth Orchestra each received £50,000 in respect of the third and final instalment of the trust's commitment. The National Youth Music Theatre did not receive a grant in 2002/03 as the grant of £50,000 pledged to this organisation for that year was paid out at their request towards the end of the previous financial year.

The trustees are very pleased that their significant support has enabled these four organisations to continue to operate effectively by maintaining and enhancing performance opportunities and facilities for children and young people. Through this funding, amounting in total to £700,000 over three years, the trust has successfully helped them to 'bridge the gap' pending confirmation of the funding that all four organisations are now receiving through the National Foundation of Youth Music (Youth Music).

A further 61 grants were made to arts charities, involving a total distribution of £342,000 overall in this sector [a decrease of 50% from the previous year]. The average

grant in this sector was £5,300. The grants detailed below are the other grants that were above average for this sector this year.

- Royal Academy of Dramatic Art (£20,000), first instalment of new three-year commitment towards bursary funding
- Abbotsbury Music Festival (£15,000), second instalment of a three-year grant to promote access to professional arts in Dorset
- City and Guilds of London Art School (£10,000), first instalment of a new three-year commitment towards bursary funding
- Royal College of Music (£10,000), third and final instalment of three-year funding for two postgraduate scholarships
- Royal Northern College of Music (£10,000), first instalment of three-year commitment towards bursary funding.

The remaining grants in the arts sector were for between £500 and £5,000.

Medical/Welfare

During the year 83 grants were distributed to medical/welfare charities totalling £314,000, compared to £567,000 in the previous year.

The average grant in this sector was £3,800, and the grants detailed below are some that were above average for this sector this year.

- Haven Trust (£30,000), first instalment of new two-year commitment towards the salary costs of the medical director
- Help the Hospices (£15,000), first instalment of new three-year commitment towards the provision of training opportunities for hospice staff throughout the United Kingdom
- Breakthrough Deaf Hearing Integration [now DeafPLUS] (£12,000), towards setting up uniform recording and measurement systems
- Belfast Central Mission (£10,000), towards the salary costs of a part-time project worker to work with children with autism and their families
- Jesse May Trust (£10,000), to provide home respite care for children with terminal or life-threatening illnesses
- East Anglia Children's Hospice (£6,000), towards a bereavement support project for the siblings, parents or grandparents of terminally ill children in East Anglia
- Sobell House Hospice Charity (£5,000), towards annual running costs
- Youth at Risk (£5,000), towards the 'Coaching for Success' programme.

The smaller grants in the medical/welfare sector were in the range of £500 to £3,200.

The Environment

There were 19 grants made to environmental charities totalling £68,000, compared to £170,000 in the previous year.

The average grant in this sector was £3,600, and the grants that are listed below are those that were above average for this sector this year.

- Royal Botanic Gardens – Kew (£15,000), second instalment of current three-year commitment to support the Margaret Mee Fellowship Programme to train Brazilian botanists and illustrators to assist conservation, build biodiversity and sustainability
- Natural History Museum Development Trust (£10,000), second instalment of £5,000 of a two-year commitment and a further grant of £5,000 towards the underpinning of all activities in Wildlife Garden at the Natural History Museum
- Wildlife Trust Surrey (£10,000), towards the Save Bay Pond project to install a silt trap and reedbed filtration system
- Farming and Wildlife Advisory Group (£5,000), towards the continued delivery of services to farmers and landowners
- Tufton Charitable Trust (£5,000), towards the restoration of the Grade II Chapel at Dartmoor Prison
- Whale and Dolphin Conservation Society (£5,000), towards the volunteer researcher programme in the Moray Firth.

The remaining grants in the environment sector were in the range of £500 to £3,500.

Smaller grants to new beneficiaries across all three funding areas included those to Aberdeen International Youth Festival, Ataxia-Telangiectasia Society, Bracken Trust, Bradford Cancer Support, Cherub Company London, Chicken Shed Theatre Company, Conquest Art, Dyspraxia Foundation, Federation of Artistic and Creative Therapy, Gwent Association for the Blind, International Otter Survival Fund, Laza Kostic Fund, Live Theatre Winchester, Otakar Kraus Music Trust, Reach, Shared Earth Trust, St Giles Trust, Teeside Hospice Care Foundation, Willow Trust and Young Persons Concert Foundation.

Exclusions

The trust is unlikely to support the following:
- animal welfare;
- applications from individuals, or for the benefit of one individual;
- charities requiring funding for statutory requirements;
- charities operating outside the UK;
- conferences or seminars;
- exhibitions;
- expeditions and overseas travel;
- general appeals;
- large national charities which enjoy widespread support;
- maintenance of religious buildings;
- medical research;
- NHS Trust hospitals for operational or building costs;
- recordings and commissioning of new works;
- religious activities;

- schools, nurseries and playgroups (other than those for children with special needs);
- support and rehabilitation from drug or alcohol abuse.

Because of the volume of appeals received, the trustees have decided not to consider requests from charities that have had an application turned down until two years have elapsed after the date of rejection.

Applications

Potential applicants should write to the correspondent with an outline proposal of no more than two A4 pages. This should cover the work of the charity, its beneficiaries and the need for funding. Applicants qualifying for consideration will then be required to complete the trust's two-page application form.

The form should be returned with a copy of the latest annual report and accounts. Applications for specific projects should also include clear details of the need the intended project is designed to meet and an outline budget. The trust also requires applicants to provide information on how the work supported will continue after the trust's grant has been completed, with plans for monitoring and evaluation. The trust states that it is happy to discuss potential applications on the telephone.

The Roald Dahl Foundation

Haematology, neurology, literacy

£434,000 (2002/03)
Beneficial area UK.

92 High Street, Great Missenden, Buckinghamshire HP16 0AN
Tel. 01494 890465 **Fax** 01494 890459
Email admin@roalddahlfoundation.org
Website www.roalddahlfoundation.org
Correspondent Linda Lazenby, Deputy Director
Trustees *Felicity Dahl, chair; Martin Goodwin; Roger Hills.*
Charity Commission no. 1004230
Information available Guidelines for applicants. Exceptionally clear, complete and well-written annual report and accounts were provided by the trust.

This foundation aims to provide support to three areas that were of personal interest and significance to Roald Dahl: neurology, haematology and literacy.

Within these areas, its current policy and criteria are as follows:

Neurology and haematology

The Foundation makes grants to benefit children and young people up to the age of 25 years, who suffer from the following conditions:

Neurology
- Epilepsy

Acquired brain injury as the result of:

- benign brain tumour
- encephalitis
- head injury
- hydrocephalus
- meningitis
- stroke
- neuro degenerative conditions, defined as conditions in which there is progressive intellectual and/or neurological deterioration.

Haematology

Any chronic debilitating blood disease of childhood, excluding leukaemia and related disorders. Conditions include:

- sickle cell anaemia
- Thalassaemia
- haemolytic anaemia
- bone marrow failure syndrome
- haemophilia
- thrombophilia
- Von Willebrand's disease.

Specifically applications for grants to charities and hospitals will be considered for:

- Pump-priming of specialist Paediatric nursing posts where there is an emphasis on community care for a maximum of 2 years. We require information about the source of permanent funding at the end of the pump-priming period.
- The provision of information and/or support to children and young people, and their families.
- Specific projects within residential and day centres to benefit children and young people within the above-mentioned criteria.
- Small items of medical equipment, not available from statutory sources, to enable children to be cared for in their own homes.

Other projects which specifically benefit children and young people within the above mentioned medical criteria may be considered.

Grants to individuals

Small grants of up to £500 are available to children and young adults up to 25 years who meet the above mentioned medical criteria and whose families are dependent on state benefits or have a similarly low income. Grants are made to meet specific needs including household items, clothing, fuel bills, toys, stimulation equipment etc. No retrospective grants are made. Only in very exceptional circumstances will grants be made for holidays and then only in the UK.

All applications must be submitted on the family's behalf by a social worker or health care professional on the form available from the foundation.

Further information about applying for grants for individuals is given on the application form.

Literacy

Through its association with *Readathon*, the national sponsored reading scheme in schools, the Foundation is already involved in promoting literacy throughout the UK.

The Foundation recognises that for a wide variety of reasons some children and young people have not acquired full literacy skills. The Foundation welcomes applications from charities undertaking specific literacy work with children to improve poor literacy skills in out-of-school projects and also centres for young people aged 16–25 years. Projects working with families are also considered. Grants are made to meet project costs, including materials, books etc. and very occasionally to help towards tutor costs.

Applications are also considered for computer/technological assistance and adapted books to enable children and young people with a visual impairment or a head injury to access the written word.

N.B. Please note we do not currently consider applications concerning dyslexia. Before Roald Dahl's death a large sum was raised for the Dyslexia Institute through the gift of the copyright of the book The Vicar of Nibbleswicke, written by Roald Dahl and illustrated by the Foundation's President, Quentin Blake.

In general, the foundation aims to provide help to organisations to whom funds are not readily available. It prefers to help small or new organisations rather than long-established, large or national organisations.

The range of grants given is wide. Grants to individuals do not exceed £500.

Potential applicants are strongly advised to telephone the foundation to obtain a copy of the current guidelines, and to

discuss a potential application, before making an application for funding. Guidelines and application forms are also available on the foundation's website.

Grants in 2002/03

In 2002/03 the foundation had assets of £1.1 million and an income of £725,000 including £45,000 in general donations and £613,000 from the proceeds of the annual Readathon (whose proceeds are shared with Sargent Cancer Care for Children). Grants totalled £434,000 and were categorised as follows, shown with examples of beneficiaries:

Neurology – £249,000

There were 25 grants listed in this category, of which 11 were over £10,000, many of these represented part payments of grants of up to three years. Included in these grants were: £21,000 to Brighton and Sussex University Hospitals NHS Trust towards funding a Head Injury Support Nurse; £15,000 to Edinburgh Sitters towards a respite service for families of children with epilepsy; £14,000 to Royal Liverpool Children's Hospital - Alder Hey towards a nurse specialist in paediatric epilepsy; £12,000 to Child Brian Injury Trust towards core costs and development of support to children and families in Scotland and Northern Ireland; and £10,000 to Headway – Belfast towards running costs including salary costs.

Other grants included: £8,000 to Headway – Shrewsbury towards a kitchen for a new day centre; £5,400 to Encephalitis Support Group towards a Family Weekend; £5,000 to REHAB UK towards Basic Skills work for a new adolescent project at the Birmingham Brain Injury Centre; £1,400 to Snappy – York towards sensory equipment for children with epilepsy; and £700 to Bradford Epilepsy Parent Support towards set up costs for a new parent support group.

Haematology – £64,000

There were three grants listed in this category. Grants were: £27,000 part payment of a two year grant to fund the North Middlesex Hospital NHS Trust towards funding a Children's Home Care Nurse for children with Sickle Cell Disease; £14,000 to Brent Sickle Cell and thalassaemia Centre towards equipment for a neuro-psychological screening project; and £2,500 to the Sickle Cell Society towards the costs of payroll giving recruitment.

Literacy – £81,000

There were 21 grants listed in this category. The two largest grants made over £10,000 each were: £15,000 to Booktrust towards the 'Book Touch' project; and £12,000 part payment of a two year grant to Education Extra towards project costs of out of school learning schemes in Northern Ireland, Scotland and Wales.

Other grants included: £6,900 to the Children's Laureateship towards platform debates about children's literature at five literary festivals; £5,000 to Ogmore Centre Trust – Bridgend towards literacy courses for children; £4,500 to Learning for Life with Technology – London towards after school literacy clubs: £2,500 to Orana Family Support Group – Newry towards literacy work within an after school club; and £1,000 to Meridian Alternative Education – Sunderland towards books and literacy materials for a project for children excluded from school.

Small, unlisted grants, were distributed across the three categories to individuals and families totalling £73,000. Those distributed in the literacy category were given via Disability Aid Foundation.

Exclusions

The foundation does not consider grant applications for:

- general appeals from large, well-established charities or national appeals for large building project
- research in any field
- any organisations which do not have charitable status or exclusively charitable aims
- statutory bodies
- projects outside the UK
- school or higher education fees
- arts projects (although applications can be considered from arts organisations for specific literacy projects)
- core funding.

Applications

On the straightforward form provided, with a covering letter if necessary. Applications are considered throughout the year. Decisions on smaller sums can take as little as a few weeks. Applications for grants of several thousand pounds may take several months to be considered.

Baron Davenport's Charity

Almshouses/hospices/ residential homes, children and young people

£430,000 to organisations (2003)

Beneficial area The counties of Warwickshire, Worcestershire, Staffordshire, Shropshire and West Midlands.

Portman House, 5–7 Temple Row West, Birmingham B2 5NY

Tel. 0121 236 8004 **Fax** 0121 233 2500

Email baron.davenport@virgin.net

Correspondent Marlene Keenan, Charity Administrator

Trustees A C S Hordern; P A Gough; W M Colacicchi; J R Prichard; S Hughes.

Charity Commission no. 217307

Information available Report and accounts, now with a list of the largest grants, though without a narrative review, were provided by the trust.

Established in 1930 by Mr Baron Davenport, the charity now has invested assets of £24 million.

Of the income, 40% goes in grants for individuals, specifically for widows, spinsters, divorcees (of 60 years and over) and ladies deserted by their partners together with their children who are in financial need. Fatherless children are also included.

The remaining 60% of the income is distributed equally to:

- almshouses, residential homes and hospices
- organisations that assist children and young people, up to 25, who are disadvantaged or in need.

Many grants are made to organisations each year – 369 in 2003, most of them, inevitably, for amounts of £1,000 or less. With such a lengthy list of beneficiaries, some organisations are almost inevitably funded in consecutive years, but every grant must be separately applied for each year; there is no automatic renewal.

In 2003 the trust's assets generated an income of £829,000. Management and administration charges were fairly high at £84,500 (probably due to the large number of grants made to organisations and, especially, individuals, and the fact

that all applications receive a response), with a further £122,000 spent generating the funds. Grants to organisations totalled £430,000. A further £319,000 was given in total to 4,131 individuals.

The largest grants were made to Catherine Walkers' Almshouses and the Stonehouse Gang (£10,000 each). Other beneficiaries included Donna Louise Trust and Foundation of Lady Katherine Leveson (£7,500 each), St Richard's Hospice (£7,000), St Mary's Hospice (£6,000), Berrow Cottage Homes (£5,000), Myton Hamlet Hospice Trust (£4,000), Abbeyfield Sutton Coldfield Ltd (£3,000) and the Children's Society, Edward's Trust, Powell & Welch Almshouse Charity, St Giles Hospice and Westcroft Community Foundation (£2,000 each).

Exclusions

There are no exclusions, providing the applications come within the charity's objects and the applying organisation is based within the charity's benefit area, or the organisation's project lies within or helps young people who live in the benefit area.

Applications

In writing, accompanied by the latest accounts and any project costs. Distributions take place twice a year at the end of May and November and applications should be received at the charity's office by 15 March or 15 September. All applications are acknowledged and those not within the charity's objects are advised.

The Debmar Benevolent Trust

Jewish

£448,000 (2001/02)

Beneficial area UK.

3rd Floor, Manchester House, 86 Princess Street, Manchester M1 6NP

Tel. 0161 236 4107

Correspondent M Weisz, Secretary

Trustees M Weisz; G Klein; H Olsberg.

Charity Commission no. 283065

Information available Full accounts were on file at the Charity Commission.

Grants are given towards the advancement of the orthodox Jewish faith and the relief of poverty.

In 2001/02 the trust had assets of £2.1 million and an income of £798,000. Grants totalled £448,000. Donations made over £1,000 each, of which there were 44, were listed in the accounts.

The largest grants were given to Friends of Yetev Lev Jerusalem Trust (£33,000), Gevuras Ari Academy Trust and Telz Talmudical College (£28,000 each), Mifal Halbershaw (£25,000) and Beis Hamedrash Hachodosh (£16,000).

Grants of £10,000 each were made to 19 organisations including Beis Aaron Trusts, Chasdei Belz, Ohr Akiva Institute – Israel, Tomchei Shaarei Zion and Zichron Yaacov Girls School.

In 2002/03 the trust had a total expenditure of £499,000. Unfortunately, although submitted by the trust to the Charity Commission, the accounts for that year had not made it to the public files for inspection.

Applications

In writing to the correspondent.

Derbyshire Community Foundation

Social welfare

£1.2 million (2003/04)

Beneficial area Derbyshire and the city of Derby.

The Old Nursery, University of Derby, Mickleover, Derby DE3 5GX

Tel. 01332 592050 **Fax** 01332 592200

Email info@ derbyshirecommunityfoundation.co.uk

Website www. derbyshirecommunityfoundation.co.uk

Correspondent The Grants Team

Trustees Helen Bishop; Arthur Blackwood; Cllr Ian Eames; Sylvia Green; Mollie Kirkland; Nick Mirfin; David Moss; Lucy Palmer; Roger Pedley; Pat Taylor; Andrew Tomlinson; David Walker; Brig. Edward Wilkinson; Robin Wood.

Charity Commission no. 1039485

Information available Annual review provided by the trust. Information is available from the foundation's website.

The trust supports voluntary and community groups that work to tackle disadvantage. It operates the following programmes:

Derbyshire Community Foundation General Fund

Supports applications for awards of £100–£1,000. However, due to limitations of resources, applications of up to £500 are favoured.

Our own fund, which includes the named funds of a number of major donors, supports a wide range of projects according to the themes and priorities listed below:

- Supporting Family Life–Including: voluntary projects dealing with mediation and relationship counselling; debt counselling; combating domestic violence; parenting skills; supporting families under stress; respite care; social support; confidence-building; family literacy schemes; projects working with children and young people.
- Health and Wellbeing–Including: health-based self-help groups; projects promoting mobility and social contact for older people; work to tackle recognised local health problems; support across the range of physical and sensory disabilities, mental distress and substance misuse; independent living; housing advice; homelessness; promotion of healthy lifestyles.
- Education and Regeneration–Including: community enterprise and job creation; schemes providing training for jobs or further learning; community-based or culturally-appropriate training courses; projects designed to prevent crime or promote security; community development; projects with an economic focus, such as credit unions, local exchange and trading schemes, etc; environmental projects.
- Culture and Creativity–Including: group-work or projects enabling people whose access to arts is limited by any factor to take part in creative work of any kind: theatre and performance; carnival; music, classical and modern; dance; creative writing; plastic arts; visual arts etc; work which promotes understanding of the diverse cultures embraced by Derbyshire.
- Hutchinson Music–The Award has been made possible through an individual donation to the Derbyshire Community Foundation to support young people's music. In its first year of 2001, working with Derbyshire Advisory & Inspection Service, the Award supported three individuals with the cost of piano lessons and the purchase of new instruments.

- The Locko Fund–The Locko Fund supports disadvantaged children under the age of 12 in the Erewash and Chaddesden areas of Derbyshire and has been made possible through an individual donor. Two grants have been awarded this year to West Hallam Junior Cricket Club and to a Storysack Library at a primary school in Erewash.

Bridging the Gap in Derbyshire

Grants from £500 to a maximum of £10,000 (in exceptional circumstances) however we expect that the majority of grants approved will be for amounts less than £5,000. Up to 100% may be made available if no other funding is available to support your project.

We can also contribute to a larger project (of up to £100,000) as long as all other funding is secured.

If you are planning to do this, your application will be subjected to the Trusts 'free reserve test'.

Who can apply?

The fund is for small voluntary and community groups working in, or benefiting people within, the designated coalfield wards (see below for a list of the wards). These groups must

- Be not for profit organisations.
- Be fully constituted organisations.
- Have annual accounts, or for new groups a detailed budget with full operational costs.
- Have a bank or building society account, in the name of the applicant group, with at least two signatories.
- Be fully able to account for all funds in the bank, not being used to support this project.

Town, Parish and Community Councils are eligible to apply.

What type of project will we support?

Applications from groups, which promote regeneration in Coalfield communities by:

- Helping to develop or improve an eligible group/organisation.
- Helping to develop or improve a new/existing facility or service.
- Contributing to local strategies/development plans.

Bridging the gap wants to encourage communities which are:

- Self-reliant–activities which promote greater community involvement or improve facilities or resources
- Working–projects which help communities access employment
- Lifelong learning–activities which improve learning facilities or involve learning
- Enterprising–activities which promote or support local community business.
- Attractive–projects which improve the natural, or built, environment

As a regeneration charity, the trust needs to ensure that the projects it supports make a real difference to the quality of life of the people who live in our coalfield communities. Your project should add to what is already happening in your area and 'make sense' at a local and regional level.

What can we provide funding for?

- Revenue (e.g. salaries, room hire, running costs, insurance, publicity materials etc.).
- Capital (e.g. office equipment, computer equipment, building maintenance/refurbishment).

NB: If your project is seeking a grant towards capital works to land or buildings, including purchases; you need to own, have a lease or license for the property. For further details contact the Grants Coordinators.

- Feasibility studies and business plans.
- To develop or improve your group, existing activities and services
- To develop a new facility, service or activity

What we cannot fund

We are unable to make grants to:

- Individuals, profit making organisations or statutory bodies (excluding Parish, Town and Community Councils)
- Projects which promote religious or political activities
- National organisations
- Groups which do not provide benefit to Coalfield Communities
- Projects which are the responsibility of a statutory organisation

We cannot fund (in addition to the list above)

- Project management charges
- Fees for professional fundraisers
- Deficit or retrospective costs
- School fees
- Continuation projects
- Bank charges or depreciation.

Community Champions

Does your group have a training or development need? Do you have a new project you need funding to get underway?

If you can answer yes to either of the questions above, then maybe Community Champions fund is the answer for you.

Community Champions fund offers small grants of up to £2000 for individuals living in Derby or Derbyshire who want to do something that will improve their community. You may be new to community projects or have been running them for years, but you could be a Community Champion!

The grant aims to help you turn ideas into reality. Anyone can apply, whether or not you're part of a group as long as the project will benefit your community. The funding can be used to:

- Visit other communities or talk to someone already doing what you'd like to do
- Get specific training i.e. community work or project management skills
- Share and develop skills for the benefit of your community
- Put together a bid for a project
- Get support to set up a social enterprise
- Go to a conference to exchange ideas and good practice
- Make it easier for community residents to find things out for themselves
- Produce a community newsletter involving residents
- Travel and/or childcare costs whilst undertaking any of the above

Your project must be a new idea because you cannot get continuation funding from this source. Individuals can apply but grants have to be paid to the organization with which they're involved.

Unfortunately, Community Champions cannot fund:

- Core funding for community or voluntary sector groups
- Training for paid workers in your organizations
- Activities of a political or predominantly religious nature
- Continuation funding
- Provision that can be funded from other sources
- Large community purchases of equipment – more than £1,000.

Neighbourhood Renewal Unit– Neighbourhood Renewal Community Chest and Community Learning Chest

The Neighbourhood Renewal Community Chest Fund

This is part of the Government's National Strategy for Neighbourhood Renewal and will provide funding to stimulate and support community activity, so that more people may become involved in the regeneration of their communities and neighbourhoods.

This fund is open to all local community and voluntary groups whose project will help to meet at least one of the objectives below. Groups must be working within Derby City wards (there are 12 priority areas within the City wards) and its objectives are:

To encourage greater involvement in local community activities;
For example:

- providing childcare to allow parents and carers to take part in community group meetings and regeneration activities
- buying materials for a community art club or drama society
- funding a community festival or sports day
- printing a community newsletter

- hiring an interpreter or translating documents
- paying a new group to hire a room to hold a first meeting.

To improve the management of local communities and groups;
For example:

- buying basic IT equipment and the training to go with it
- paying for a training programme or learning opportunity for a group's committee or members
- paying for an exchange visit to a similar group in another town to share good practice
- designing and printing community group stationery or publicity materials

To help community groups to improve their local neighbourhood;
For instance through:

- renovating disused premises so they can be used as a community centre or as a group's headquarters
- the upkeep of a local community amenity – for example, a children's playground
- to help black and culturally Diverse communities explore their culture, history and traditions and through a better understanding of cultural diversity, promote racial harmony and community cohesion;
- to support any other activities by which local community and voluntary groups can contribute to the regeneration of their local area.

Applications will be welcomed from often marginalised communities such as:

- young people
- refugees
- faith communities
- black and culturally diverse communities
- travellers
- older people
- disabled people.

Community Learning Chest

This is now part of the Neighbourhood Renewal Community Chest Fund and was previously known as the Skills and Knowledge Fund.

Grants up to £5000 can be made to residents within the Neighbourhood Renewal Fund area i.e: Derby City, who do not have access to other funding. Residents will be able to take up learning opportunities to help them play an active role in neighbourhood renewal.

Examples of projects eligible for funding:

- Paying for a training programme or learning opportunity for a groups committee or members
- Paying for participation in activities which aim to develop community leadership
- Paying for an exchange visit to or from a similar group in another town to share good practice

- Accessing advice from regional advisors and residents consultancies
- Subscriptions to journals on neighbourhood renewal or similar issues
- Reasonable expenses incurred whilst participating in learning activities (e.g. care, travel)
- Paying for other sources of good practice such as reference books and current research
- Training to facilitate membership of Community Empowerment Networks and Local Strategic Partnerships
- Buying in-house training for members of groups
- Buying basic IT equipment and the training to go with it
- Covering conference and seminar fees (and associated attendance costs).

The Local Network Fund

This programme is delivered across the County by Derbyshire Community Foundation on behalf of the Department for Education and Skills (DFES). This government funding stream was set up to tackle disadvantage and poverty by giving local groups the chance to make a difference to the lives of children and young people aged 0–19 years old.

Grants range between £250 and £7,000 and are for projects that meet one of the following four themes:

- Aspiration and Experience – some children miss out on childhood experiences that others take for granted. Groups can organise activities and help children and young people achieve goals that they would otherwise be unable to achieve.
- Economic Disadvantage – schemes that help families improve their living standards and cope with difficulties that come from being on a low income.
- Isolation and Access – support and opportunities for children and young people who may feel isolated or alone; or have difficulty accessing services that are available to other young people.
- Children's Voices – giving children and young people the chance to express their opinions and contribute to improving policy and services on issues that concern them.

To be eligible to apply to this Fund (as set by DFSE):

- Your project must be a NEW activity or be start up costs for a new group/service
  - The fund will not support core running costs for existing projects
- LNF must be providing 70% or more of the funds for the project.
  - The fund was created by government to set up small-scale activities in local community areas.

The fund does not look favourably on refurbishment /building works and can only award in certain exceptional circumstances for more information please contact us on 01332 592050.

- Your activity must focus on children and young people between 0 –19 ONLY – we cannot fund activities that only benefit above this age. However, we can fund activities that help parents and families that improve children's lives.

  – Grants can be accessed for young people up to 25 where the beneficaires have learning difficulties.

- Most of the children and young people benefiting from your activity must be facing disadvantage or poverty.
- You need to be a small locally managed, voluntary, community or self-help group.

  – 'Small' according to LNF criteria is an annual turnover of under £100,000.

- Groups with a higher turnover than this must submit evidence that they are the only organsation/facility capable of delivering the proposed project in the area.
- You must have people volunteering to help with your activity, who are NOT part of your management committee.
- You must have written rules (Constitution) of the group.
- You must take steps to ensure that the children and young people taking part in your activity do not come to any harm while in your care, therefore you must have written procedures for keeping children safe – this will be needed as a condition of funding.
- Derbyshire Community Foundation can help any group create or update a policy simply and effectively please contact us for more advice.

In addition to the general exclusions [see below], this fund will not grant awards to:

- Very large projects where this is only a small part of the cost.
- Grant making bodies applying for funding to redistribute to individuals or groups.
- Organisations that already hold a grant from Local Network Fund – groups are only able to hold one grant at a time.

The Local Network Fund has its own application form available by calling 08451 130161.

Community Empowerment Fund

The Community Empowerment Network for Derby was launched in February 2003. The aim of the Community Network is to open up communication channels between groups and organisations in the voluntary and community sector to share experiences and ideas and to ensure that those normally excluded are given the full opportunity to participate. It will also provide opportunities for people within such groups to be aware of and participate in the development of locally informed regeneration policies.

The Community Network meets approximately 3 times a year and works closely with Derby City Partnership, providing two representatives to sit on the Local Strategic Partnership board to represent the voluntary and community sector within Derby.

If you apply to Community Chest and Community Learning Chest, you will automatically be entered on the Database for the Community Network and will receive regular information and updates about other voluntary and community groups within the city.

If you would like further information about the Community Empowerment Network, including details on how to become a member, please contact Linda Stone at Derby CVS on 01332 346266.

In 2003/04 the foundation had an income of almost £3.1 million and gave grants totalling £1.2 million.

Beneficiaries across all programmes included: Alfreton Shopmobility, to develop a business plan and undertake research for the start-up of this scheme (£9,500); South Normanton Community Church, to fund the salary of a project worker (£7,500); Derby Playhouse, to encourage active participation from disadvantaged young people both through drama workshops and audience participation, and Derby West Indian Community Association, to fund the running costs of a summer school (£7,000 each); Amber Brook Therapeutic Craft Group, towards equipment costs of setting up the group (£6,000); Multi-Faith Centre, to develop a forum of faiths in Derby (£5,000); Chapel Playgroup Association, to fund a variety of equipment and resources (£4,000); Rec Theatre Company, to fund rehearsal and production costs of an open air production of Midsummer Nights Dream (£3,500); South Wingfield Youth Club, for a series of visits and activities for the group (£2,000); and Derbyshire Chinese Welfare Association, to set up a pilot community forum (£900).

Exclusions

The foundation does not support the following: general and major fundraising appeals; individuals; statutory work in educational institutions; overseas travel or expeditions for individuals or groups; direct replacement of statutory or public funding; promotion of religious or party political causes; medical research and equipment; projects operating outside Derbyshire; animal welfare; large national charities (except for independent local branches working for local people); or work which has already been done.

Applications

New applications are invited on a rolling programme. Contact the foundation's office before making an application. Each application is carefully assessed and, where possible, is discussed with the applicant before they are submitted to the foundations panels for consideration.

The application form asks:

- what you plan to do,
- what need you will meet,
- how people will benefit, and
- whether your group is well-managed.

The form aims to help groups, especially small groups, to think through the questions they need to be asking themselves.

Decision-making

The foundation almost always has more applications than they can fund, so the process is competitive. The decisions are made by DCF's Local Panels–made up of people within the community–and supported by grants co-ordinators. There are four panels throughout the county, covering

- Derby City
- South Derbyshire (including Erewash, Amber Valley, and Southern Derbyshire Dales)
- North East Derbyshire (including Chesterfield, North East Derbyshire and Bolsover)
- North West Derbyshire (including High Peak and North Derbyshire Dales).

Timescale

Applications are accepted on a rolling programme, and have up to six deadlines every year. The foundation aims to make decisions within eight weeks of the deadline date and feedback is usually given to unsuccessful applicants. Successful applicants are asked to return quarterly monitoring forms detailing how their grant has been spent and the impact of their work.

Criteria

Unless otherwise stated all funding streams are open to 'not-for-profit' organisations. An applying group does not need to be a registered charity to apply for funds, as long as the organisation has charitable aims and has a structure in place to show it is properly run. The project must benefit people in Derbyshire and have a bank account with at least two signatories and be able to provide simple activity and financial reports to the foundation.

Devon Community Foundation

General

£571,000 (2002/03)

Beneficial area County of Devon.

The Island, Lowman Green, Tiverton, Devon EX16 4LA

Tel. 01884 235887 **Fax** 01884 243824

Email grants@devoncf.com

Website www.devoncf.com

Correspondent The Grants administrator

Trustees *E Bourne, chair; Sir Ian Heathcoat Amory; Countess of Arran; M H Gee; G Halliday; T Legood; N A Maxwell-Lawford; I Mercer; S Rous; J Trafford; N J Wollen; S Hindley; G Sturtridge; Dr K Gurney; P Thistlethwaite; Mrs M Garton.*

Charity Commission no. 1057923

Information available Information was provided by the trust.

The trust was established with the objective to support or promote any charitable purposes for the relief of poverty, the advancement of education (including training for employment or work), the advancement of religion or any other charitable purposes for the benefit of the community in the county of Devon.

In March 2002 the foundation learned it was to become the managing body for the Local Network Fund in Devon, a major government grant-making initiative to support children and young people. This had a dramatic impact on the grant total increasing from £85,000 in 2001/02 to £574,000 in 2002/03. The trust anticipates that in 2003/04 this figure will rise to £930,000.

In 2002/03 beneficiaries included: West Devon Sports Trust to purchase a new safety boat (£5,000); Babes 'n' Us to fund a worker to develop activities for young parents (£1,400); Cruse Bereavement Care in Plymouth towards core costs (£500); and Open Doors International Language School for straff training in running an interpretation course (£250).

Exclusions

No grants to individuals. No funding for religious causes, statutory agencies or responsibilities, party political activities, medical research, animal welfare, projects outside Devon or village appraisal groups.

Applications

Telephone calls are welcome. Application forms and current guidelines are available on request. A sae is not required.

The Diana, Princess of Wales Memorial Fund

Children and young people in the UK, overseas

Around £2 million (2004/05)

Beneficial area UK, including UK organisations working overseas.

The County Hall, Westminster Bridge Road, London SE1 7PB

Tel. 020 7902 5500 **Fax** 020 7902 5511

Email info@memfund.org.uk

Website www.theworkcontinues.org

Correspondent The Grants Department

Trustees *Christopher Spence, chair; Lady Sarah McCorquodale, president; Taheera Aanchawan; Douglas Board; Rt Hon. Earl Cairns; Michael Gibbins; Jenny McAleese; Caroline Whitfield; Roger Singleton.*

Charity Commission no. 1064238

Information available New grantmaking criteria and guidelines available early 2005.

The fund has had a difficult time over the last couple of years as a result of a lawsuit filed by Franklin Mint Company. All the fund's grantmaking activities were suspended as a result of the action, with several other large grantmakers stepping in to cover some of its outstanding grants to organisations, without which those organisations would have been unable to continue operating. In November 2004 a settlement was reached which has now enabled the fund to resume its activities:

The fund will immediately release £525,000 for projects:

- in the UK for work supporting prisoners' families, refugees and asylum seekers;
- in Tanzania, Zimbabwe, Uganda and Zambia for the care of people with life limiting illnesses and their families (palliative care).

The fund will shortly approve another tranche of funds for key projects:

- to improve services for bereaved young people;
- to tackle the needs of learning disabled people in the prison system;
- to improve palliative care for people in Africa, and to raise awareness of palliative care in the context of HIV care in developing countries.

The fund will be preparing to run a competitive grants round for both UK and international work in 2005. It will also launch a full consultation with the voluntary sector in 2005 on future grants.

In addition, the fund will in parallel begin the five-year international programme of humanitarian work announced in the joint statement with the Franklin Mint.

Andrew Purkis, Chief Executive of the Fund, commented as follows:

'The final settlement of this lawsuit means that we can get back to committing all our energy and money to our humanitarian work. We are immediately resuming our grants programme to support vital projects that aim to change the lives of some of the most vulnerable people.

Despite the difficulties of the last two years, we have been determined not to let down our existing beneficiary projects, all of which survived. We are very grateful to all those who rallied round to provide replacement funding so generously when our assets were frozen as a result of the lawsuit.

Our overriding desire has been to revive our full grant-giving and championing of humanitarian causes with renewed energy. Now we can. We believe that is the best way of honouring the memory of Diana, Princess of Wales.'

It was expected that new criteria, guidelines and application deadlines would be announced in January 2005. At the time of writing (February 2005) no final decisions had been made on either the UK programme or the international programme. Another press release dated 7 February announces the payment of grants held over from 2003, presumably made under previous guidelines:

The Diana, Princess of Wales Memorial Fund today announces nearly £1.5 million in grants to help disadvantaged people in the UK and overseas. These grants had been agreed in principle in 2003, before the fund's assets were frozen as a result of a legal dispute (now ended) and have now been updated, reassessed and approved for release.

In the UK the fund supports work with young people who find the transition to adulthood especially difficult, including, in this round, three new grants that will address the health and social welfare of young refugees and asylum seekers.

● fsu – Investing in families (Waltham Forest) £164,000
Providing sexual health education and welfare for young, unaccompanied refugees, many of whom come from areas seriously affected by HIV/AIDS, and who have missed out on vital personal, social and health education, to help them integrate into the wider community.

● The Black Health Agency £145,000
Funding a programme to engage with young refugee and asylum seekers. Assisting them in making informed choices about their health and well-being, and developing their skills and confidence to challenge the barriers that prevent access to health services, resources, advice and guidance.

● b arts £90,500
Funding a full-time youth worker at a drop-in centre to provide counselling on housing, health, education and finance issues for young asylum seekers and refugees in north Staffordshire.

● Young Voice £139,500
Supporting a self-advocacy project for young parents leaving custody. This will include creating a training pack for service providers beyond the prison service who come into contact with young parents leaving custody, their partners and children.
The fund's international grants programme aids work for the creation of safe and viable communities in post-conflict countries.

● BasicNeeds £300,000
Funding a project to address war trauma and other mental health problems in north Sri Lanka, including running community awareness sessions; holding community consultations; referring individuals for treatment and developing community-based solutions; lobbying for better mental health services; raising awareness through media campaigns about the effects of war on mental health and sharing this information on with other post-conflict communities worldwide.

● Jaipur Limb Campaign £224,000
Supporting an Angolan organisation of people with disabilities (LARDEF) to extend their activities/membership and to become the first organisation of people with disabilities in Angola to be involved in landmine awareness. The project aims to train disabled people to become activistas – community activists for mine risk

education and to support income generation projects for disabled people and their families.

● Landmine Disability Support £204,000
Providing education, skills training, and resources for some of the most vulnerable disabled people in the Kompong Chhnang province of Cambodia, and developing advocacy and livelihoods programmes so that they can sustain a better quality of life for themselves and their families.

● Mercy Corps Scotland £200,000
Funding to develop an income-generating project for disabled people living in Bosnia Herzegovina, including those affected by landmines and other explosive remnants of the 1992–5 war. The grant will also strengthen the capacity of Mercy Corps Scotland's Red Cross partners and raise awareness of the needs of disabled people in this area.

Contact the trust directly or check its website for up-to-date information on its new grantmaking criteria and guidelines

Exclusions

These exclusions are likely to remain when the trust's programmes have been reviewed.

The trust will not fund:

● projects outside its funding priorities
● individuals
● services run by statutory or public authorities*
● organisations that are mainly fundraising bodies
● arts and sporting activities which give little benefit in terms of social inclusion
● academic research
● schools, colleges and hospitals
● repayment of loans
● promotion of religious beliefs
● rapid response to emergency situations
● retrospective funding
● debts
● capital expenditure for religious institutions or buildings
● party political organisations
● fees for professional fundraisers
● major capital projects related to premises or buildings
● appeals.

*While the trust will not fund activities which are the responsibility of any statutory agency, for example a government department, local council or health authority, and it will not fund projects that are direct replacements of statutory funding, it welcomes applications for collaborative projects and those involving both the voluntary and public sectors.

Applications

Contact the trust for up-to-date information.

The Djanogly Foundation

Education, arts, Jewish charities, general

£1.9 million (2002/03)

Beneficial area Unrestricted, with a special interest in Nottingham and Israel.

8 Blenheim Street, London W1S 1LQ
Correspondent Mr Christopher Sills
Trustees *Sir Harry Djanogly; Michael S Djanogly; Lady Djanogly.*
Charity Commission no. 280500
Information available Report and accounts, with grants lists but without the required analysis or review.

The 2002/03 annual report stated the guidelines were as follows: 'The objects of the charity are to sponsor developments in medicine, education, social welfare and the arts. The charity also invites applications for funding of projects to relieve distress and to promote the welfare of the aged and the young.'

The grants list shows it usually makes large annual payments to academic institutions in Nottingham, as well as recurrent awards to well-known arts establishments, mostly situated in London. Most other grants are of up to £2,000 each (although there are no set limits) and support is given to a wide range of organisations, although there are preferences for Jewish and Nottinghamshire projects (but not at the expense of other causes).

In 2002/03 the foundation had assets of £21 million, which generated an income of £1.5 million. Grants were made to 72 organisations and totalled £1.9 million.

As usual, the largest grant went to University of Nottingham, which received £380,000. Other sizeable grants were £355,000 to Victoria and Albert Museum, £284,000 to Tate Gallery, £200,000 to British Museum and £139,000 to Nottingham City Technology College Trust.

There were 12 other organisations receiving grants over £10,000 each. Beneficiaries included Royal Ballet

School Trust (£81,000), Jerusalem Foundation (£76,000), National Portrait Gallery (£65,000), Somerset House Trust (£50,000), Royal Academy of the Arts (£30,000) and Jewish Care (£10,000).

Other beneficiaries included United Synagogue (£9,200), Norwood Ltd (£7,500), Royal National Theatre (£5,000), Wordsworth Trust (£2,000), Garsington Opera Trust (£1,800), Cancer Research UK and Camden Arts Centre (£1,000 each) and Almedia Theatre and Wellbeing (£500 each).

Applications

In writing to the correspondent.

The Drapers' Charitable Fund

General

£816,000 to organisations (2002/03)

Beneficial area UK, with a special interest in the City and adjacent parts of London and Moneymore and Draperstown in Northern Ireland.

The Drapers' Company, Drapers' Hall, Throgmorton Avenue, London EC2N 2DQ

Tel. 020 7588 5001 **Fax** 020 7628 1988

Email dthomas@thedrapers.co.uk

Website www.thedrapers.co.uk

Correspondent Miss Deborah J Thomas, Charities Administrator

Trustee *The Drapers' Company. Chair of the Charity Committee: P J Bottomley.*

Charity Commission no. 251403

Information available Report and accounts with full grants lists were provided by the charity.

Summary

This is a city livery company, one of those descended from the guilds of London, and has a trail of historical connections, the most important of which are with Queen Mary, University of London and Bancroft's School in Essex, but which also includes Adam's Maintained Comprehensive School in Wem, Shropshire and various Oxford and London university colleges.

The fund makes a large number of small grants. The few awards for £10,000 or more are generally to institutions with which the Drapers' Company has a long-standing connection. Following a review of the charitable criteria during 2002/03, the charity continues to have very wide objectives for which grants are currently made. They vary widely but fall into four broad categories:-

- 'the relief of need i.e. aid to the disadvantaged. In particular, initiatives aimed at improving the quality of life of those disadvantaged by poverty, ill health or disability, or aimed at counteracting the effects of disadvantage
- 'education and training
- 'where there is traditional/historic link with The Drapers' Company or one of its related organisations
- 'culture and religion.'

General

Our current Charitable Themes

The Company receives many appeals for assistance, the majority of which fulfil the main purposes outlined above. To further help the process of refining the variety of appeals to support in its grant making, charitable themes have been chosen which include geographic areas, specific areas of charitable activity or particular types of project. Where possible, the trust aims to direct a percentage of its overall funding amongst five main themes, outlined below:-

(i) Relief of Need 35%
(ii) Education 40%
(iii) Textiles 10%
(iv) Culture and Religion 5%
(v) Northern Ireland 10%

What will we fund?

Relief of Need:
- homelessness
- causes and effects of social exclusion among young people in inner city areas, predominantly in London and with an emphasis on education projects
- disability, with a preference for supporting adults and improving the quality of life
- prisoners
- retired servicemen and veterans.

Education:
- Drapers' schools
- associated universities and colleges
- outreach projects
- science
- student hardship at affiliated educational institutions.

Textiles:
- design
- conservation
- technical textiles.

Culture and Religion:
- City institutions/heritage
- Company linked churches.

Northern Ireland:
- Projects predominantly in Draperstown and Moneymore, preferably linked to other areas of the company's charitable themes.

Size and duration of grants

The average level of grant is between £1,000 and £5,000, however, from time to time, the trust aims to make occasional larger grants (£10,000–£25,000) where our support will make a marked difference to the success of a particular project. Grants are usually made on a one-off basis rather than recurrent. Further submissions will not be expected for at least two years after an initial grant has been made. Grants payable over a set term, i.e. two or three years grants, are occasionally approved by the trustee. In such cases, recipients will be required to provide feedback and a yearly progress report to confirm that satisfactory progress is being made. These grants are also subject to the continuing availability of funds.

In 2002/03 the trust had assets of £17 million and an income of £1 million. Grants totalled £816,000. They were broken down as follows:

Education – £391,000 in 20 grants to 15 organisations

Northern Ireland – £30,000 to 4 organisations

Social exclusion – £131,000 to 36 organisations

City of London/Drapers' company links – £63,000 to 20 organisations

Other charitable causes – £167,000 in 115 grants to 100 organisations.

The sum of £15,000 was distributed from designated funds. A further £17,000 was distributed in 32 educational grants to individuals.

Exclusions

Charitable causes/areas that are not usually supported:

- Projects supporting animal welfare.
- Local branches of national charities.
- Individuals with no Drapers' links, including applicants seeking individual sponsorship of fundraising events or activities.
- Individuals applying for support for expeditions or overseas travel.
- Overseas based projects.
- Medical research/relief and hospitals and medical centres.
- Loans or business finance.

- Organisations that are not recognised charities, are normally considered to be outside our guidelines.
- Promotion of religion.
- Major capital/building projects, where the fund's input would be barely significant.

Applications

There are no application forms. Written applications should be sent to the charities administrator in the form of one or two sides of A4, clearly outlining the purpose of the application, the level of funding required and details on how this will specifically be allocated, detailed budget of the project, targeted beneficiaries, details of other funders or grants secured and any other relevant information.

Applicants should also include any supporting literature together with a copy of the organisation's most recent audited accounts and annual report. Full guidelines are available on the fund's website. The trustees meet three times a year.

The Dulverton Trust

Youth and education, welfare, general

£3.1 million (2002/03)

Beneficial area Unrestricted. Mainly UK in practice. An interest in the Cotswolds, and in Scotland. Limited support to parts of Africa. Few grants for work in London or Northern Ireland.

5 St James's Place, London SW1A 1NP

Tel. 020 7629 9121 **Fax** 020 7495 6201

Email trust@dulverton.org

Correspondent Col. Christopher Bates, Director

Trustees *Col. David Fanshawe, chair; Christopher Wills; Sir John Kemp-Welch; Hon. Robert Wills; Lord Carrington; Lord Dulverton; Earl of Gowrie; Dr Catherine Wills; Richard Fitzalan Howard; Sir Malcolm Rifkind; Dame Mary Richardson.*

Charity Commission no. 206426

Information available Good reports and accounts with analysed grants schedule; leaflet outlining 'Policy and Practice'.

Summary

Grants were made during the year in the following categories, listed according to the value of grants with the greatest first:

- youth and education;
- welfare;
- conservation;
- miscellaneous;
- minor appeals;
- religion;
- Africa;
- peace and security;
- founder's subscriptions;
- preservation;
- local appeals.

The trust states that a number of grants fall within more than one category, making calculations approximate. Awards are seldom for more than £50,000 except to organisations that have established funding connections with the trust.

During 2002/03 the trust received 1,530 appeals for funding, 272 of which received a grant, making the success rate one in six. Though there are wide areas of 'exclusion' these can be funded if an application is recommended by a trustee. The grant total for the year was £3,105,000.

Background

This is one of the trusts deriving from the tobacco-generated fortune of the Wills family. It has an endowment worth about £65 million and a body of trustees which combines family members with others who have achieved distinction in public life.

The Dulverton Trust is unusual in saying that an application, outside its guidelines, may be accepted if it is supported by an individual trustee – most trusts say that their trustees decide their grantmaking intentions and policies first, and then stick to them.

Four of the trustees are from the Wills family, and the chairman David Fanshawe has an indirect family connection. There is a clear, reported family connection with the Cotswold area (though no longer apparently with Bristol, where many of the Wills factories were located). Sir John Kemp-Welch is a former Chairman of the London Stock Exchange and has been a patron of the National Portrait Gallery. Lord Carrington, as a former foreign secretary, brings expertise to the trust's minor area of interest in peace and security. Lord Gowrie is best known for his interests in the arts. Richard Fitzalan Howard is on record as an active member of the National Trust. Sir

Malcolm Rifkind, another former foreign secretary, is also president of the Edinburgh University Development Trust.

During the last financial year the trust had a staff of six, only four of them full time. The former director, Sir Robert Corbett retired in May 2003. The average salary, NI, health insurance and pension cost were £205,000, or £34,000 a head. The costs in support of grantmaking were 8.5% of the total distributed.

Investment management fees represented 7.3% of investment income.

General

Apart from a few special programmes described below, the trust makes one-off grants and will not normally consider further applications until a period of at least two years has passed. About one in five applications results in a grant, though not necessarily for the amount requested (but note that the trust, unusually, has been known to give more rather than less than the requested amount, when it has investigated the project concerned).

The following guidelines from the trusts are in general terms and there is clearly flexibility in their interpretation in practice.

The main work of the trust is conducted in two areas which the trustees consider of particular relevance. These are youth and education and general welfare. Other areas of priority are conservation and religion, in which the main emphasis is the promotion and development of religious education in schools, principally through the Farmington Trust in Oxford, followed by preservation, peace and security. Other causes considered by the trustees to have special merit may also be supported under the miscellaneous category. Limited grants are made to historic contacts and associations in east Africa, and occasional grants are made in response to appeals from South Africa.

To focus the work of the trust and to allow grants to be made on a worthwhile scale, some exclusions to the general remit have been applied. Therefore, grants are never made to individuals and are not normally made in the following areas unless the projects is recommended personally by a trustee, and is considered to be of special merit:

- from the broad fields of medicine and health, including drug addiction and work with the mentally and physically handicapped;
- historic building, museum, church and cathedral projects;
- the arts;

- projects for schools, colleges and universities;
- charitable projects based in the Greater London area, in Northern Ireland (except for a very small number of nominated charities) and overseas (except for occasional grants to Africa);
- expeditions.

Requests for grants are considered following an application to the director, who will examine each case in detail. He will discuss it with the applicant and usually, when time allows, one of the trust's staff will visit the project. Each application is treated on its merits and grants are made according to the worthiness of the cause, as presented. The final status of an application lies with the trustees who must confirm any recommendation by the director to reject an appeal.

There are currently 29 perennial grants made by the trust. In 2002/03 this represented 18% of the grant total. The trustees review them annually, with one year's notice of cessation, and they are now separately identified in the annual reports. The value of most of the grants has been slightly reduced over the past few years.

£225,000 is reserved for 'minor appeals' to a maximum value of £2,500. A further £25,000 is reserved to enable Lord Dulverton to respond to local appeals in the Cotswolds. A total of £30,000 goes regularly to nine charities listed in the 'founder's memorandum'.

Grants in 2002/03

The number and value of grants for 2002/03 were categorised as follows (2001/02 figures in brackets):

Youth and education	52	£1,184,000	(£1,035,000)
General welfare	33	£669,000	(£711,000)
Conservation	16	£286,000	(£386,000)
Miscellaneous	16	£256,000	(£320,000)
Minor appeals	117	£200,000	(£200,000)
Religion	5	£181,000	(£189,000)
Africa	8	£174,000	(£145,000)
Peace and security	5	£73,000	(£109,000)
Founder's subscriptions	9	£30,000	(£30,000)
Preservation	2	£27,000	(-)
Local appeals (Cotswolds)	9	£25,000	(£25,000)
Industrial understanding	-	nil	(£25,000)

A further table shows that over the last four years the value of grants for youth and education, welfare, conservation and Africa have increased, while miscellaneous, religion and preservation have generally decreased.

Examples of grants in 2002/03 were as follows:

Youth and education

This is the trust's largest area of activity and is concerned in the main with help for disadvantaged youth. The trustees are also keen to assist deserving youngsters who would otherwise be unable to achieve their true potential. In view of the enormous number of appeals within this category, priority will always be given to those which are open to all members of the community and are not aimed at any particular sector of society. The trustees are also concerned with promoting an understanding of the importance of industry and good industrial relations, and any such appeals will normally be considered in this category./Q>

This category represented 38.1% of the trust's grant total. There were 12 perennial grants made in this category, the most out of all categories. Beneficiaries included Oxford University Dulverton Scholarships (to be a continuing programme: £125,000), Atlantic College, for scholarships and bursaries (£42,000), Duke of Edinburgh's Award (£32,000 – a perennial grant), Voluntary Service Overseas (£30,000 – a perennial grant), Caldecott Foundation, Guide Association and Taste for Adventure (£25,000 each), Reading Matters for Life, St Mary's Cathedral Workshop Project and Wings South West (£20,000 each), Raleigh International (£17,000 – a perennial grant), Outward Bound Trust and Project Trust (£14,000 each – perennial grants), New Dragon Centre (£5,000) and Batsford Foundation (£3,000).

General welfare

Particular emphasis is placed upon those appeals which deal with the very young and the problems suffered by the increasing proportion of elderly people within the UK. Support for those caring for others, especially young carers, is an area of particular interest as is the importance of marriage and the problems encountered within the family in the 21st Century.

Some 21.5% of the grant total went on general welfare grants. The largest grant of £50,000 was made to ARC Addington Fund in connection with the aftermath of the foot and mouth disease outbreak. Other beneficiaries included Emmaus Bristol (£30,000), Police Rehabilitation Trust (£25,000) and Army Families' Federation, Community Self Build Agency and Samaritans (£20,000 each). Four perennial grants were made, to Age Concern (£16,000), Help the Aged (£15,000), Scottish Council for Voluntary Organisations (£14,000) and One Plus One (£9,000).

Conservation

General conservation issues within the UK are of prime importance with the emphasis being on the protection of wildlife habitats. Single species appeals are rarely considered.

The largest grants went to education centres at two botanical collections, Bedgebury Pinetum and the Sir Harold Hillier Gardens and Arboreum, both of which received £30,000. Other beneficiaries included UK Centre for Economic and Environmental Development (£23,000 – a perennial grant), Scottish Wildlife Trust (£20,000), Association of West Coast Fisheries Trust and Scottish Native Woods (£15,000 each), Royal Society for Nature Conservation (£10,000 – a perennial grant), Royal Society of Arts (£7,000 – a perennial grant) and Knoydart Forest Trust (£4,000).

Miscellaneous

This category embraces appeals considered to be of particular merit in areas normally excluded by the trust, if they are recommended personally by a trustee. It also includes a limited number of appeals from charities which provide services for the benefit of the charitable sector as a whole.

Beneficiaries included: Harefield Research Foundation (£40,000), Habitat for Humanity Great Britain (£30,000), Royal Life Saving Society UK (£20,000), Shakespeare Globe Trust (£10,000), Allavida (£9,000 – a perennial grant) and Marchant-Holliday School (£2,500).

Minor appeals

The sum of £225,000 has been set aside by the trustees. These grants are aimed specifically at charitable organisations, usually operating at local or county level, where a small grant, currently to a maximum of £2,500, would make a significant difference to their ability to operate. Competition for these awards is intense and priority will usually be given to charities working in areas of severe deprivation. Appeals can fall within any of the above categories but, at this level, they are more usually with the areas of youth and education, general welfare and conservation.

A total of 117 grants were awarded to organisations with an average value of £1,709. Grants were disbursed as follows: 28 grants in June 2002 totalling £50,000; 31 grants in September 2002 totalling £50,500; 28 grants in December 2002 totalling £47,500; 30 grants in March 2003 totalling £52,000.

Religion

This category of appeal is concerned predominantly with the teaching of religious education in schools, especially at secondary level.

The largest grant of £131,000 was made to Farmington Trust, which also received the same amount during the previous year. The four other beneficiaries in this category were Society for Promoting Christian Knowledge (£25,000), Atlantic College Launcelot Fleming Fellowship (£15,000) and Christian Education Movement and Spire Trust (£5,000 each).

Africa

Unless there are exceptional circumstances, assistance is given only to a very small number of organisations operating in east Africa, or occasionally South Africa, which have a long association with the trust.

The trust continues its interest in covering conservation, education and welfare, especially of children. The beneficiaries were Tusk Trust (£31,000), BookPower (£30,000), Hope & Homes for Children (£26,000), Book Aid International (£22,000 – a perennial grant), CARE International UK (£21,000 – a perennial grant), Rhodes University Trust and Zimbabwe Farmers' Trust Fund (£15,000 each) and Food and Agriculture Research Management (£14,000).

Peace and security

The trust provides very limited support in this category, mainly through the awarding of annual grants to organisations which have a high degree of expertise in this area of activity.

Grants were made to Royal United Services' Institute (£30,000 – a perennial grant), Royal Institute of International Affairs (£19,000 – a perennial grant), International Institute for Strategic Studies (£10,000), St Ethelburga's Centre for Reconciliation & Peace (£8,000) and Council on Christian Approaches to Defence and Disarmament (£6,000 – a perennial grant).

Founder's subscriptions

Awards continue to be made to the nine organisations, or their successors, which were nominated by the 1st Lord Dulverton to receive annual support from the trust

The beneficiaries were Church Army, General Welfare of the Blind and Salvation Army (£4,750 each), Gloucester Diocesan Board of Finance (£3,500), Family Welfare Association and National Association for the Care and Resettlement of Offenders (£3,000 each), NSPCC and Royal Hospital for Neuro-Disability (£2,500 each) and Gloucestershire Rural Community Council (£1,250).

Preservation

This is concerned with the preservation of heirlooms of outstanding historic and national importance. Whilst it occasionally includes support for churches and cathedrals, individual appeals can rarely be addressed due to the very large number of applications received.

Despite their only being supported 'very rarely', two historic building charities receive perennial awards: Historic Churches Preservation Trust (£16,000) and Scottish Churches Architectural Heritage Trust (£11,000).

Local appeals

Most of the nine grants that were made went to community centres and village halls in the Cotswolds, and ranged from £1,000 to £5,000. Recipients included Campden & District Peelers Trust, Redesdale Hall Trust, Sheepscombe Village Hall and Oddington Village Hall.

The trust notes that as a matter of policy it tends not to give grants in London or Northern Ireland (though there are occasional exceptions in each case).

Although a high proportion of grants appear to be made to charities based in the south of England, the trust points out that it is particularly keen to support projects in the more disadvantaged northern half of England and many of the grants made to national charities went to projects in the north.

Comment

Though this trust is one of the dwindling band of general grant makers, it is distinguished from some of the others by being adequately staffed. It is therefore better able to make careful and informed decisions than those which rely almost entirely on written applications with little personal follow-up.

The continued recruitment of distinguished public figures as trustees – Sir Malcolm Rifkind being the latest – for a trust working with charities in the relatively day-to-day fields of education and welfare is not obviously the best use of their time.

Exclusions

The trust does not operate within the broad fields of medicine and health, including drug and alcohol addiction and work with people who are mentally and physically disabled, although exceptions are made from time to time for the development of young people who are physically disabled. Also generally excluded are museums, galleries, libraries and exhibition centres, and individual churches, cathedrals and other historic buildings (except for limited support under the preservation category) or heritage projects. The whole field of the arts, including theatre, music and drama is excluded together with appeals from individual schools, colleges and universities. Appeals concerned with sport including sports centres and individual playing field projects are not considered. Award schemes are also not considered.

No grants to overseas charities, except for limited support in Africa. Grants are not made to individuals or for expeditions.

The trust very seldom operates within the Greater London area, or in Northern Ireland except for specific, nominated charities.

Unless there are exceptional circumstances, the trust will not usually provide funding for salaries, major building projects, including the purchase of property or land, endowment appeals or appeals which seek to replace statutory funding.

Applications

Applications should be made in writing to the director. Trustees meetings are held four times a year – in January, May, July and October (though decisions on small grants can be made more rapidly – if essential, very rapidly).

Initial enquiries by telephone, for example to establish eligibility, are welcomed.

Applications should, if possible, be restricted to a letter and maximum of two sheets of paper, and should include the applicant's registered charity number, a brief description of the background, aims and objectives of the charity, details of the specific appeal for which funding is sought together with the funding target, and the balance of funding outstanding at the time of application. Initial applications should always include a copy of the previous year's annual report and accounts.

All applications will receive a reply as soon as possible, although research and consultation may delay a response. All rejected applications will receive notification and an explanation for an appeal's rejection will be given.

The selection procedure can take between three to six months, so applicants are advised to apply in plenty of time if funding is required by a certain date.

Dunard Fund

Classical music, the visual arts

£1.1 million (2002/03)
Beneficial area UK, but with a strong interest in Scotland and the north of England.

4 Royal Terrace, Edinburgh EH7 5AB

Tel. 0131 556 4043 **Fax** 0131 556 3969

Correspondent Mrs C Høgel, Trustee

Trustees *Carol Colburn Høgel; Elisabeth Norman; Catherine Høgel; Colin Liddell.*

Charity Commission no. 295790

Information available Accounts were on file at the Charity Commission.

This charity, established in 1986, is not endowed but is funded annually by an unknown corporate benefactor.

The trust describes its grantmaking as follows:

The funds are committed principally to the training for and performance of classical music at the highest standard and to education and display of the visual arts, also at international standard. A small percentage of the fund is dedicated to environmental projects.

In 2002/03 the fund had assets amounting to almost £3 million. It had an income of £1.4 million and gave £1.1 million in grants to 54 organisations. Half of these were for less than £5,000, for which no further information was available. The other grants were categorised by the trust as follows, shown here with examples of grants:

Music – £368,000 in 12 grants

Beneficiaries included Scottish Chamber Orchestra (£105,000 in two grants), London Philharminc Orchestra Ltd and Trinity College of Music (£50,000 each), Royal Scottish National Orchestra (£40,000), Monteverdi Choir and Orchestra (£30,000 in two grants), Lamp of Lothian Collegiate Trust (£17,000), European Union Youth Orchestra (£10,000) and New Towns Concert Society (£5,000).

Culture and the arts – £604,000 in 14 grants

Beneficiaries included Edinburgh Festval Society (£349,000 in three grants), National Galleries of Scotland (£50,000), Scottish National Photography Centre (£50,000 in two grants), Academy of St Martin in the Field (£27,000), Brighton Festival (£25,000), Chelsea Festival (£15,000), Yehudi Menuhin Memorial Appeal (£10,000), the Queen's Hall (£6,500 in two grants), Aldeburgh Productions Bursary Fund (£5,000) and Festival City Theatres Trust (£1,500).

Humanitarian and environmental – £42,000 in 1 grant

The sole beneficiary was Waverley Care Trust.

The trust states that while there is no strict yearly quota, it aims for a 'liberal geographical distribution throughout the U.K.' of its grants.

Exclusions

Grants are only given to charities recognised in Scotland or charities registered in England and Wales. The fund says that it does not consider:

- unsolicited applications;
- applications from individuals.

Applications

Any applications should be in writing only to the Dunard Fund, but see exclusions above.

The Dunhill Medical Trust

Medical research, elderly

£3.1 million (2003/04)
Beneficial area UK.

I Fairholt Street, London SW7 1EQ

Tel. 020 7584 7411 **Fax** 020 7581 5463

Email info@dunhillmedical.org.uk

Website www.dunhillmedical.org.uk

Correspondent Claire Large, Administrative Director

Trustees *Ronald E Perry; Timothy Sanderson; Dr Christopher Bateman; Prof. Maurice Lessof; Sir Cyril Chantler; Ven. Christopher Chessun; Prof. Martin Severs.*

Charity Commission no. 294286

Information available Full annual report and accounts and guidelines available on the trust's website.

Summary

The trust makes a relatively small number of grants, some of them very large, mostly for medical or health care research connected with ageing. It presently funds 20 Dunhill Research Fellowships.

In 2003/04 it had assets amounting to £73 million generating an income of £2.8 million. The trust received about 300 applications during the year and made 48 grants and funded 17 fellowships. Grants totalled £3.1 million and were funded in the following areas:

Care of the elderly	30%
Fellowships	22%
Disabilities and rehabilitation	20%
Research – diseases & related issues of ageing	14%
'Unfashionable' issues	10%
Other	4%

General

Dunhill Medical Trust (DMT) has two primary charitable objectives:

- medical research and provision of medical care and facilities
- research into the care of the elderly and the provision of accommodation and care for the elderly.

DMT supports four main strands of work that fall within these charitable aims:

- the development of new and innovative projects
- projects with a low public profile that have difficulty attracting funding
- pump-priming major projects
- funding the unmet educational need in the scientific community through the funding of DMT Fellowships.

For all applications the trust seeks:

- evidence of true need and
- confirmation that the proposal sits securely within its strategic grant-making framework.

Presently expert reviewers advise the trustees on the merits of all research-based proposals.

In time this will evolve into a more formal structure of peer review. The present Government's NHS Research Governance Framework consultation will help to inform this process.

The UK trend is towards a more elderly population profile. The trust will mirror this by increasing support for:

- care for the elderly
- research into diseases and issues of ageing
- projects related to disabilities and rehabilitation in respect of the elderly.

The trustees wish to encourage approaches by charities and institutions that have not previously applied for funding which fall into the above priority areas.

They particularly welcome proposals that demonstrate original thinking and where the potential outcomes have a prospect of wide application within the community at large.

The trust will continue to support projects that are less likely to attract funding from mainstream sources.

Wherever possible the trust will support organisations directly rather than through third parties.

To achieve a better balance in its distribution of funds the trust may occasionally actively seek out projects for support.

The trust presently funds twenty Dunhill Research Fellowships. Dunhill will retain the present number of Fellowships but will develop the programme to widen opportunities.

Grants in 2003/04

Grants were broken down as follows, shown with grants in each category:

Care of the elderly – 9 grants totalling £903,000

Grants were £500,000 to Guild Care, the first payment of two; £300,000 to ExtraCare Charitable Trust, the second payment of three; £34,000 to Cancer Bacup, the second payment of three; £25,000 to Bethshan; £21,000 to Age Concern Solihull; £10,000 to Age Concern St Helens; £6,300 to Abbeyfield Eastbourne; £4,500 to Bentilee Volunteers; and £2,000 to the Respite Association.

Research diseases/issues relating to ageing – 8 grants totalling £440,000

Grants were: £70,000 to CEDAR; £67,000 to University of Central Lancashire, the final payment of three; £59,000 to King's College London, the final payment of three; £57,000 to Royal Brompton; £51,000 to Liverpool John Moores University, the second payment of three; £47,000 to University of East Anglia; and £36,000 to University of Liverpool, the final payment of two.

Disabilities and rehabilitation – 9 grants totalling £623,000

Grants were: £500,000 to Connect, the final payment of five; £30,000 to the Multiple Sclerosis Society; £28,000 to Independent Living Centre Semington – Wiltshire; £25,000 to 4Sight; £11,000 to InterAct Reading Service; £10,000 to West Sussex Association for the Disabled; £9,500 to Bath Institute of Medical Engineering; £7,500 to Multiple Sclerosis Society – Bognor and Chichester; and £2,000 to Chichester Stroke Club.

Unfashionable issues – 5 grants totalling £132,000

Grants were: £109,000 to University College London – Continence Technology Group; £100,000 to University of Southampton, the final payment of three; £50,000 to King's College London, the second of three

payments; £25,000 to Bristol Urological Institute; and £22,000 to Imperial College London, the final payment of two.

Other – 17 listed grants totalling £132,000

Grants were: £40,000 to the Brain and Spine Foundation; £25,000 to Fund for Addenbrooke's; £17,000 to University of Oxford; £12,000 to King's College London; £10,000 each to the National Centre for Epilepsy and StartHere; £3,600 to RAFT – Mount Vernon Hospital; £3,300 to St Wilfrid's Hospice; £2,000 each to Friends of Chichester Hospital, Friends of Guy's Hospital and Q Trust; £1,000 each to Florence Nightingale Museum Trust and St John's Ambulance; £970 to CARE at Walberton; £900 to Tissue Engineering and Medical Research; and £600 to Friends of Action Research. Sundry small donations totalled £500.

Fellowships

Fellowships were funded at 17 institutions around the country. These totalled £657,000.

Exclusions

The trustees will not normally approve the use of funds for:

- providing clinical services that, in their opinion, would be more appropriately provided by the National Health Service;
- sponsorship of individuals;
- organisations outside the UK;
- charities representing specific professions or trade associations;
- institutional overheads;
- travel/conference fees;
- hospices.

Applications

To the administrative director. Trustees meet in March, June, September and December.

The Sir John Eastwood Foundation

Social welfare, education, health, in Nottinghamshire

£409,000 (2002/03)

Beneficial area UK, but mainly Nottinghamshire in practice.

Burns Lane, Warsop, Mansfield, Nottinghamshire NG20 0QG

Tel. 01623 842581 **Fax** 01623 847955

Correspondent Gordon G Raymond, Chair

Trustees *Gordon G Raymond, chair; Mrs D M Cottingham; Mrs V A Hardingham; Mrs C B Mudford; P M Spencer.*

Charity Commission no. 235389

Information available Accounts were on file at the Charity Commission, or available from the trust for £15.

The charity makes grants to registered charities benefiting Nottinghamshire, although other applications are considered. Priority is given towards people with disabilities, older people and children with special needs.

The charity supports a number of registered charities on a regular basis by making donations each year to those particular charities. The prime target of the trustees each year is to ensure the continuance of these regular donations. Once these have been ensured the trustees consider special projects applications and then other individual applications. These are reviewed and donations made as the trustees deem appropriate out of surplus income.

In 2002/03 the trust had assets of £9.8 million and an income of £592,000. Grants totalled £409,000. Beneficiaries of larger grants included Portland College (£100,000), Oaklands Warsop (£25,000) and Newark & Nottinghamshire Agriculture Society (£10,000).

Smaller grants were given to Birklands Primary School (£6,000), Disabilities Living Centre, Hetts Lane Infant & Nursery School, Nottingham & Nottinghamshire Advocacy Alliance and REMIDI, Yeoman Park School (£5,000 each), National Heart Research Fund (£4,000) and Warsop United Charities (£3,000).

Grants of £1,000 or less included those to Sense and Zone Youth Project (£1,000 each), Motability (£750), DIAL Mansfield (£500) and PDSA (£200).

Exclusions

No grants to individuals.

Applications

In writing to the correspondent.

The EBM Charitable Trust

Children/youth, animal welfare, general

£730,000 (2002/03)

Beneficial area UK.

Moore Stephens, 1 Snow Hill, London EC1A 2EN

Tel. 020 7334 9191 **Fax** 020 7651 1953

Correspondent Keith Lawrence

Trustees *Richard Moore; Michael Macfadyen; Stephen Hogg.*

Charity Commission no. 326186

Information available Annual report and accounts were provided by the trust.

The trust gives around 30 grants a year for amounts between £1,000 and £200,000. Most grants are for between £10,000 and £50,000.

In 2002/03 the trust had assets of £27.7 million, which generated an income of £937,000. Grants were made to 26 organisations totalling £730,000.

The trustees' report, as has been the case in previous years, stated simply that 'beneficiaries included charities involved in animal welfare and research, youth development and the relief of poverty'.

The largest grants were made to the British Racing School and Fairbridge (£100,000 each), Covent Garden Cancer Research Trust (£65,000), Cambridge University Veterinary School Trust and SPARKS (£50,000 each), Chicken Shed Theatre Company and Youth Sport Trust (£40,000 each), Community Links (£35,000), Groundwork UK, Kidscape and Worshipful Company of Shipwrights Charitable Fund (£30,000 each) and Battersea Dog's Home and BBOWT (£20,000 each).

Other grants include those to Dogs for the Disabled, Macmillan Cancer Relief, New Astley Club and Sports Aid.

Applications

In writing to the correspondent, but the trust states that 'unsolicited applications are not requested' and 'the trustees' funds are fully committed'.

The Maud Elkington Charitable Trust

Social welfare, general

£446,000 (2002/03)

Beneficial area Northamptonshire and Leicestershire.

c/o Harvey Ingram Owston, 20 New Walk, Leicester LE1 6TX

Tel. 0116 254 5454 **Fax** 0116 255 3318

Email plf@hio.co.uk

Correspondent Mrs Paula Fowle, Administrator

Trustees *Roger Bowder, chair; Allan A Veasey; Caroline A Macpherson.*

Charity Commission no. 263929

Information available Full accounts were provided by the trust.

The trust has general charitable purposes in Northamptonshire and Leicestershire, giving a large number of small grants. In 2002/03 only 6 of the 227 grants were of over £10,000, 151 were of less than £1,000 each. Many of the grants go to organisations in Desborough, Kettering and Leicester and countywide branches of UK-wide organisations, although all types and sizes of organisations are represented in its grants list.

The trust had assets of £14 million in 2002/03, which generated an income of £454,000. Grants were made totalling £446,000.

The total management and administration charges for the year (including costs of generating the funds) were high at £67,000, although this may have been due to the large number of grants it made. However, it included £17,000 to a firm in which one of the trustees is a partner. These editors always regret such payments unless, in the words of the Charity Commission, 'there is no realistic alternative'. It is also regrettable that £10,000 was paid in trustees' renumeration, which equates on average to over £500 per trustee per meeting. Whilst this may, unusually, be permitted within the trust deed, it

appears to go against the principal of unpaid trusteeship. It has long been the opinion of DSC that it should be possible to find competent and knowledgeable trustees to undertake, free of charge, the agreeable task of giving away someone else's money, especially on this local scale.

The largest grants were £25,000 to SENSE – Kettering Development, £20,000 each to Kettering General Hospital Department of Medicine and Leicester Learning Zone and £16,000 to Northampton Care and Repair. Two large grants were made for disbursement to individuals; £39,000 to Leicester County Grammar School for bursaries and £19,000 to Northamptonshire County Council Social Services for payment to 59 individuals.

The grants lsit contained details of all grants of £1,000 or over. Among the beneficiaries in Desborough, Northamptonshire and Leicestershire were: Desborough Town Welfare Committee (£4,800), Leicester Charity Link (£3,800), Leicester Children's Holiday Centre – Mablethorpe (£3,500), Northampton and District Mind (£2,500), Northampton PCT (£1,800) and Northampton Social Services – Corby (£1,200).

There were many organisations listed in the grants list which did not have an identifiable location, although it is likely that the local branches were funded.

Exclusions

No grants to individuals.

Applications

In writing to the correspondent. There is no application form or guidelines. The trustees meet every eight or nine weeks.

The John Ellerman Foundation

Health, welfare, art and conservation, for national organisations

£3.4 million (2003/04)

Beneficial area Unrestricted.

Aria House, 23 Craven Street, London WC2N 5NS

Tel. 020 7930 8566 Fax 020 7839 3654
Email enquiries@ellerman.org.uk
Website www.ellerman.org.uk
Correspondent Eileen Terry, Appeals Manager
Trustees *Richard Edmunds; John Hemming; Sue MacGregor; David Martin-Jenkins; Vice-Admiral Anthony Revell; Lady Sarah Riddell; Mrs Beverley Stott; David Robinson.*
Charity Commission no. 263207
Information available Guidelines for applicants. Excellent annual report with analysis of grantmaking and a full list of donations.

Summary

This trust, which once made very many small grants, now makes about 70 new grants a year, with a minimum grant size of £10,000, to UK-wide or regional charities only. No grants are made to local charities.

The charity is happy to fund core or running costs, though on a short term basis, with most grants running for two or three years. It has a particular interest in funding innovatory work and supporting charities that are working together.

From the total 1,081 applicants in 2003/04, 68 received grants.

In 2003/04 the foundation had assets of £91 million, an income of £1.9 million and made grants totalling £3.4 million. Due to falls in investment markets over the period 2000–2003, the trust stated it would probably take another two or more years to return to spending levels of over £4 million a year.

General

The foundation describes itself and its work as follows:

The foundation was established by the late Sir John Reeves Ellerman in 1971. It is a general grantmaking trust distributing around £4 million each year. The foundation aims to support a broad cross-section of national charities doing work of practical significance in the following five categories:

- Health and Disability
- Social Welfare
- Arts
- Conservation
- Overseas

The foundation will only consider applications from registered charities with a UK office. Our resources allow us to give significant grants which we hope will enable charities to make a difference to the cause they serve. Our minimum grant is £10,000

and the average grant is higher. We aim to develop relationships with funded charities and are gradually moving towards making larger grants.

We have a general interest in supporting innovatory work, co-operation between charities and charities sustained by large numbers of volunteers. We incline towards helping front-line charities offering direct practical benefits rather than those working on policy or campaigning. We know core funding is still difficult to obtain and are open to receiving applications for this purpose. Charities which receive core funding will be expected to account for expenditure and identify what it has enabled them to do. Requests for a contribution to large capital appeals are not encouraged.

As a generalist grant-maker with a wide range of interests, we will only support UK charities making a genuinely national impact or with a UK-wide footprint. We believe other trusts and funders are better placed to fund individuals and/or local and regional charities. For this reason:

Applications are invited from charities working throughout the UK or England.

The foundation supports some overseas work but, for historical reasons, this is limited to applications from UK-based charities working in Southern and East Africa

Guidelines

The general guidelines and exclusions apply to all five categories.

Health and disability

Main focus
At present the focus of our funding is directed towards the following:

- organisations, including self-help groups, for the relief and support of those with serious medical conditions
- severe physical disabilities, including the deaf and the blind
- mental illness and learning disabilities
- carers, including nurses and the families of sufferers and hospices (currently funding for hospices is given solely through Help the Hospices).

Particular themes and concerns
The foundation is particularly interested in charities which can demonstrate all or most of the following:

- real benefits to patients/sufferers and the quality of their lives
- a particular commitment to the young and the old
- self help programmes, including the provision of acknowledged expert information and advice
- promotion of all aspects of healthy living.

Social welfare

Main focus
At present the focus of our funding is directed towards the following:

- disadvantaged children and young people
- needy parents and families
- elderly people.

Particular themes and concerns
The foundation is particularly interested in charities which can demonstrate all or most of the following:

- tangible benefits on a significant scale to disadvantaged/vulnerable people
- sharing of good ideas and collaborative work with other charities
- work collaboratively or share good ideas with others doing similar things
- encouragement of and motivation towards self-help and self-sufficiency
- employment and training of a broad base of volunteers.

In all the above groups we have a particular leaning towards charities which offer new experiences or learning opportunities to improve the motivation and self-respect of beneficiaries and improve their day to day quality of life.

Arts

Main focus
At present the focus of our funding is directed towards the following:

- music and opera
- museums and galleries
- theatre and dance.

Particular themes and concerns
The foundation is particularly interested in charities which can demonstrate all or most of the following:

- excellence within the field
- commitment to attracting new audiences and wider public access
- youth participation and motivation
- originality and creativity in design, production and/or presentation
- lasting impact.

Conservation

Main focus
At present the focus of our funding is UK based charities working throughout the UK and/or internationally in at least one of the following areas:

- protection of threatened animals, plants and habitats
- promotion of better understanding of and solutions to major environmental issues like climate change and biodiversity
- development and extension of conservation facilities/sites
- promotion of sustainable ways of living, including renewable energy technologies.

Particular themes and concerns

The foundation is particularly interested in charities which can demonstrate all or most of the following:

- practical and sustainable benefits of significant scale
- collaborative work with others and the open sharing of ideas
- effective operation with or alongside local communities and cultures
- recruitment, training and employment of a broad base of volunteers.

Overseas

In 2004/05 rather than continuing to provide grants abroad with funds from the other categories, the foundation has re-established a separate overseas category.

Main focus

At present our funding has three elements:

- Southern and East Africa (providing c. £250,000 a year and supporting UK-registered charities working in social welfare/development, health and disability in Kenya, Uganda, Tanzania, Zambia, Mozambique, Zimbabwe and Namibia)
- South Africa (providing c. £50,000 a year to continue to support charities set up by or closely connected with Sir John Ellerman)
- International Programme – Africa (providing currently £50,000 a year towards a joint programme in Africa with the Baring Foundation.

Particular themes and concerns

The foundation is particularly interested in charities which can demonstrate all or most of the following:

- focused help on a significant scale to the most disadvantaged/vulnerable people
- employment of key staff 'in country'
- collaboratively work with other charities in the field and generally share good ideas
- promotion of dignity, respect and self-sufficiency.

We have a leaning towards charities which galvanise the energy and skills of volunteers and enable them, whenever possible, to initiate or extend projects locally, regionally or internationally.

Grantmaking in 2003/04

Health and disability – 54 grants totalling £1.5 million

Grants were in the range of £10,000 to £60,000 and included: £35,000 to Prostate Cancer Charity the second of three payments towards funding a cancer specialist nurse to support patients through prostate cancer; £30,000 each to BBC World Service Trust, the second of two payments towards the cost of

developing new projects and implementing a fundraising plan for the trust, which promotes development and health through the effective use of the media and Muscular Dystrophy Campaign, the first of three payments towards the cost of recruiting and training volunteers to provide peer advice and support; £20,000 to L'Arche, the second of two payments towards the shortfall in the costs of the central office supporting local L'Arche communities and £15,000 to Action for M.E. a one-off payment towards the cost of developing the first clinical networks to share best practice.

Social welfare – 40 grants totalling £990,000

Grants were in the range of £10,000 to £65,000 and included £65,000 to Depaul Trust, the third of 3 payments towards the cost of the New Business Unit to promote new initiatives, co-ordinate mergers and acquisitions, and offer consultancy services to charities in difficulty; £50,000 to Emmaus UK, the third of three payments towards the establishment of a £5 million fund to start 10 new Emmaus communities providing accommodation and work for homeless people; £40,000 to Parents for Children, the second of two payments towards the cost of a full-time adoption manager to co-ordinate post-adoption support; £25,000 to Action for Prisoners' Families, the second of three payments towards the cost of the director's and administrator's salaries; £21,000 to National Children's Bureau, the first of three payments towards the shortfall required to claim a Community Fund grant for extending and improving the range of support services available to bereaved children in England; and £20,000 to Girlguiding UK, a one-off payment towards the cost of providing disabled facilities for new Group Adventure Houses at three National Leadership Training Centres.

Arts – 34 grants totalling £709,000

Grants were in the range of £10,000 to £50,000 and included £30,000 to SS Great Britain, a one-off payment towards the cost of providing full and equal physical access for all visitors; £25,000 to Academy of Ancient Music, the first of two payments towards the costs of development, including the establishment of residencies in Cambridge and Norwich; £20,000 each to Handel House Trust Ltd, the third of three payments towards the salary costs of the post of Director of the Handel

House Museum and Victoria & Albert Museum, a one-off payment towards the cost of the New Glass Gallery; £15,000 to English Chamber Orchestra Charitable Trust Limited the first of three payments towards the cost of employing an Outreach and Development Manager to implement the strategy for the 'Close Encounters' outreach programme; and £10,000 to Art Academy, the second of two payments towards the cost of improved management support for this new academy, which offers full and part-time training in all aspects of sculpture and painting.

Conservation – 12 grants totalling £265,000

Grants were in the range of £12,000 to £50,000 and included those to: £50,000 to Soil Association, the third of three payments towards the cost of employing a Business and Finance Director; £25,000 to BirdLife International, the first of two payments towards the costs of the Site Action Unit, which manages overseas projects and supports overseas partners; £20,000 to Friends of the Earth Trust, the second of two payments towards core costs of their environmental work; £15,000 to Plantlife International, the first of two payments towards support for the conservation volunteers programme, landscape scale management pilots, and other projects; and £12,000 to University of Stellenbosch -Ellerman Resource Centre, a one-off payment towards salary costs.

Exclusions

Grants are made only to registered charities, and are not made for the following purposes:

- medical research;
- for or on behalf of individuals;
- individual hospices;
- local branches of national organisations;
- 'Friends of' groups;
- education or educational establishments;
- religious causes;
- conferences and seminars;
- sports and leisure facilities;
- purchase of vehicles;
- the direct replacement of public funding;
- deficit funding;
- domestic animal welfare.

Circulars will not receive a reply.

The foundation cannot make donations to the continents of America south of the USA.

Applications

In the first instance, by letter – no more than one or two sides of A4, and include with it your latest annual report. This should tell us:

- about your charity–when registered, what you do, who your beneficiaries are and where you work
- about the need for funding – turnover, reserves, main sources of income, why funds are needed, and, if requesting funds for a particular project, rough costings.

All letters are studied by the Appeals Manager and at least one trustee who recommend whether a proposal is of sufficient merit to be brought to the attention of the full board.

Because of the volume of appeals received, the trustees have decided not to consider further requests from charities which have had an application turned down until at least two years have elapsed since the letter of rejection. Similarly, funded charities can expect to wait two years from the last grant payment before a further application will be considered by trustees.

The Englefield Charitable Trust

General

£349,000 (2002/03)
Beneficial area Worldwide, with a special interest in Berkshire.

Englefield Estate Office, Theale, Reading RG7 5DU

Tel. 0118 930 2504 **Fax** 0118 932 3748

Email benyon@englefields.co.uk

Correspondent A S Reid, Secretary to the Trustees

Trustees *Sir William Benyon; James Shelley; Lady Elizabeth Benyon; Richard H R Benyon; Mrs Catherine Haig.*

Charity Commission no. 258123

Information available Report and accounts with full grants list were provided by the trust.

In 2002/03 the trust had assets of £7.7 million and an income of £366,000. Grants were made totalling £349,000. Out of about 300 applications received in the year, a total of 108 grants were made to registered charities, most of them based in Berkshire. Grants varied from £250 to £30,000, with most in the range of £1,000 to £5,000. A wide variety of causes are supported including a number of Christian, health and welfare organisations.

In addition to grantmaking, the trust also provides low-cost and retirement housing. The latter cost the trust £56,000 during the year.

The largest grants were £30,000 to St Mary's Minster and £20,000 to Newbury Spring Festival. Other sizeable donations included Spire Trust and Chelsea Physic Garden (£11,000 each) and Douglas Martin Trust and The Willink School (£10,000 each).

Other beneficiaries included Hamble Court Refurbishment, Game Conservancy Trust, Newbury & District Agricultural Society, Parish of All Saints – Wokingham (£5,000 each); Voluntary Action Centre (£2,300); St Lukes Hospital for the Clergy (£1,000); Sparklers (£500); Reading Adult & Community College (£450) and St Bartholomew's Parents Association (£250).

Exclusions

Individual applications for study or travel are not supported.

Applications

In writing to the correspondent stating the purpose for which the money is to be used and accompanied by the latest accounts. All applicants should have charitable status. Applications are considered in March and September. Only applications going before the trustees will be acknowledged.

Entindale Ltd

Orthodox Jewish charities

£778,000 (2002/03)
Beneficial area Unrestricted.

8 Highfield Gardens, London NW11 9HB

Tel. 020 8458 9266 **Fax** 020 8458 8529

Correspondent Mrs B L Bridgeman, Secretary

Trustees *A C Becker; Mrs B A Sethill; Mrs B L Bridgeman; S J Goldberg.*

Charity Commission no. 277052

Information available Annual report and accounts on file at the Charity Commission.

This trust aims 'to advance religion in accordance with the orthodox Jewish faith'. In 2002/03 it had an income of £1.7 million derived mainly from rent on its properties worth £9.6 million. Grants were made to organisations totalling £778,000.

During the year, 134 grants of over £100 were made, with many grants probably going to previous beneficiaries. There were 21 grants of over £10,000, with the largest to: Menorah Grammar School (£100,000), Yeshivas Bnei Reem (£36,000), Society of Friends of the Torah (£35,000), Kehal Chasidim Bobov (£29,000), British Friends of Ohr Somayah (£28,000) and Atteress Yeshua Charitable Trust (£25,000). Many of the listed grants were for £3,000 or less, often much less. Grants of £100 or less totalled £1,000.

Comment

The was no response to a written request for a copy of the most recent annual report and accounts, despite the requirement to provide these on demand.

The annual report, viewed at the Charity Commission, is inadequate. Unfortunately there is no narrative review of the charitable activities, nor are the grants analysed and explained as the law requires.

Applications

In writing to the correspondent.

The Equitable Charitable Trust

Education of disabled/ disadvantaged children

£2.2 million (2002)
Beneficial area UK.

5 Chancery Lane, Clifford's Inn, London EC4A 1BU

Tel. 020 7320 6292 **Fax** 020 7320 3842

Correspondent Brian McGeough, Joint Managing Trustee

Trustees *Brian McGeough; Roy Ranson; Peter Goddard.*

Charity Commission no. 289548

Information available Annual report and accounts, with an excellent grants list.

Summary

Grants, usually for amounts of between £5,000 and £75,000, and often paid over three years, are made for both capital and revenue projects to schools and other educational projects and organisations concerned with the education of disadvantaged children.

General

The trust is financed by a commercial school fees prepayment scheme, now ended but whose existing commitments are still being met. Income is now diminishing year by year but the trust is accumulating a part of its income into a permanent endowment, so that it will continue to operate indefinitely, but on a reduced scale.

The trust is managed voluntarily by Brian McGeough, one of its trustees, who was formerly the treasurer of Smith's Charity.

'The trustees will continue to concentrate on the educational needs of disadvantaged children by making grants for specific projects to schools and other organisations catering for such needs. They will also fund interesting and innovative educational projects of all kinds wherever they can find them, especially if they are capable of being introduced into a large number of schools to supply needs not adequately met at present.'

The trust no longer makes grants for the purchase of computer equipment for use by disabled young people in connection with their education, nor does it support individual students in any other way.

In 2002 the trust made 98 awards, few of them for less than £10,000, with eight being for £50,000 or more. More grants were made in this year than in the previous year, however, they were generally for less. Overall, the level of grantmaking remains the same as in the previous year. Grants totalled just under £2.2 million. Larger grants are usually for work extending over three years.

The largest grants were made to:

- Voluntary Service Overseas – Zambia, as the second of two grants to support VSO's programme to build the capacity of community schools (£96,600);
- Winged Horse Trust – Andes, the first of three grants towards the cost of an educational project for young women in the High Peruvian Andes, teaching medicinal plant cultivation (£75,000);
- Fairbridge – Cardiff and Glasgow, the third instalment of a three year grant towards the Learn 2 Earn school exclusion programme for deprived young people from inner city areas aged 14 to 16 years old (£60,000);
- PACE Centre – Aylesbury, a single grant towards the cost of an outreach and follow-up department for young children with motor impairment in mainstream education, at the PACE Centre (£58,400);
- Caldecott Foundation – Surrey, a single grant towards the cost of building a senior school and multi-purpose hall at this special school for vulnerable excluded children and young people who have suffered extreme emotional, sexual and physical abuse (£50,000);
- Helen Arkell Dyslexia Centre – Feltham, a single grant towards the centre's outreach programme, educating disadvantaged young men with dyslexic-type learning disabilities at the Feltham Young Offenders Institution (£50,000);
- Hiltonian Society, Hilton College – South Africa, a single grant to be applied over three years towards the cost of the Hilton Vula outreach programme, providing education and IT training for local disadvantaged youngsters who are underachieving in mainstream schools (£50,000);
- Listening Books – National, a single grant towards the cost of extending the library's Sound Learning programme over two years, to provide educational audio materials for use in the classroom and at home for children with special needs (£50,000).

Other beneficiaries included Birds of Paradise Theatre Company – Glasgow (£30,000), Changing Faces – National (£25,000), St Basil's Birmingham (£20,000), Nexus Institute – Northern Ireland (£19,000), Youth at Risk – Nottingham (£15,000), Musical Keys – Norwich (£12,000), Greenmead Primary School – London and Toxteth Vine Project – Liverpool (£10,000 each), Nechells Association for Community Education – National (£8,000), Replay Productions – Belfast (£7,000), Sussex Lantern (£5,000) and Sophie Centre – London (£2,500).

Exclusions

No grants to individuals or LEA schools.

Applications

In writing to the correspondent. The charity does not use application forms but offers the following guidelines to applicants for grants:

Applications should be no longer than four A4 sides (plus budget and accounts) and should incorporate a short (half page) summary.

Applications should:

- state clearly who the applicant is, what it does and whom it seeks to help;
- give the applicant's status (e.g. registered charity);
- describe the project for which a grant is sought clearly and succinctly; explain the need for it; say what practical results it is expected to produce; state the number of people who will benefit from it; show how it will be cost effective and say what stage the project has so far reached;
- enclose a detailed budget for the project together with a copy of the applicant's most recent audited accounts (if those accounts show a significant surplus or deficit of income, please explain how this has arisen);
- name the applicant's trustees/patrons and describe the people who will actually be in charge of the project giving details of their qualifications for the job;
- describe the applicant's track record and, where possible, give the names and addresses of two independent referees to whom the Equitable Charitable Trust may apply for a recommendation if it wishes to do so;
- state what funds have already been raised for the project and name any other sources of funding to whom the applicant has applied;
- explain where the ongoing funding (if required) will be obtained when the charity's grant has been used;
- state what plans have been made to monitor the project and wherever possible to evaluate it and, where appropriate, to make its results known to others;
- ask, where possible, for a specific amount.

Please keep the application as simple as possible and avoid the use of technical terms and jargon.

The trustees are in regular contact with each other and deal with applications as and when received.

The Eranda Foundation

Research into education and medicine, the arts, social welfare

£1.5 million (2002/03)

Beneficial area UK.

New Court, St Swithin's Lane, London EC4P 4DU

Tel. 020 7280 5301

Correspondent Jennifrer Mitchell, Secretary

Trustees *Sir Evelyn de Rothschild; Mrs Renée Robeson; Leopold de Rothschild; Miss Jessica de Rothschild; Antony de Rothschild; Sir Graham Hearne.*

Charity Commission no. 255650

Information available Accounts with a brief report. No grants list.

In 2002/03 the trust had an income of £2.3 million, mostly from its investments, the value of which had fallen by £9 million to £57 million by the end of the year.

The 2002/03 report says that:

The foundation supports charitable work in the areas of:
- the arts
- health, welfare and medical research
- education.

The ongoing policy of the foundation is to promote original research and the continuation of existing research into medicine and education, fostering of the arts and promotion of social welfare.

Grants were categorised as follows:

	2002/03	2001/02
The arts	£202,000	£209,000
Health, welfare and medical research	£598,000	£525,000
Education	£714,000	£537,000
Total	£1,524,000	£1,270,000

The report goes on to note that 'a detailed list of the above grants is available from the secretary at the foundation's address'; however this was not provided for these editors despite numerous requests. The foundation says that it prefers to remain anonymous.

Applications

In writing to the correspondent. Trustees usually meet in March, July and November and applications should be received two months in advance.

Essex Community Foundation

General

£747,000 (2002/03)

Beneficial area Essex (including unitary authorities of Southend and Thurrock).

52a Moulsham Street, Chelmsford, Essex CM2 0JA

Tel. 01245 355947 **Fax** 01245 251151

Email general@essexcf.freeserve.co.uk

Website www. essexcommunityfoundation.org.uk

Correspondent Judy May Brandy, Programmes Director

Trustees *John Burrow; David Boyle; Gay Edwards; Peter Heap; Brian Hilton; Christopher Holmes; Joan Hutchison; Ian Marks; David Price; Annie Ralph; Colin Sivell; John Stranger; Jane Valentine.*

Charity Commission no. 1052061

Information available Full accounts and annual report was provided by the trust.

The foundation was set up in 1996 and manages funds on behalf of individuals, companies, charitable trusts and public agencies in order to give grants to voluntary and community organisations working to improve the quality of life for people living in the beneficial area.

In 2002/03 the trust had a total income of £1.2 million and an endowment of around £3 million. Grants totalled £747,000 and were distributed from various funds to suport all aspects of social welfare. Grants ranged from between £100 to approximately £10,000 each, with the average being £2,500.

Funds in 2002/03 included:

- Local Network Fund for children and young people
- Chiron Fund
- High Sheriffs' Fund supporting people and organisations tackling crime in their community
- Essex Crimebeat (set up in 2001 to encourage the participation of young people in addressing issues of crime)
- ESF Key Fund (part of a European Social Fund grants programme)
- Marsh Community Fund giving grants to organisations in Witham
- Royal London Community Fund giving grants to organisations in and around Colchester

- Southend Fund giving grants to organisations in Southend
- Women's Fund giving grants to organisations supporting women and their families
- Harlow Youthbank, a young people led programme supporting young people's activities in Harlow

In 2001/02 the foundation had assets of £3.8 million and a total income of £745,000. A total of 243 grants were made to voluntary and community organisations totalling £384,000. Grants ranged from £50 to £10,000, with the average being £1,500; 48 grants were made of £3,000 and over, 198 grants of less than £3,000 were made.

The largest grants of £10,000 each went to six organisations: Chelmsford Agency for Volunteering to fund the Youth Action Project which encourages and supports volunteering among young people aged 14 to 18; Essex Association of Boy's Clubs towards the costs of extending Project Respect aimed at young people at risk; Families in Focus to develop support work for families of children with special needs; Maldon (Essex) Mind – for costs towards recruiting and training young adult volunteers on BroSis mentoring scheme (the organisation also received a further £3,000 towards running the scheme); SWANS – Maldon towards day centre costs, IT training and other courses for people with disabilities; and Uttlesford Community Travel towards the cost of replacing a community vehicle.

Other beneficiaries included: Realife Trust (£9,000); Essex Disabled Peoples Association (£8,500) Uttlesford Carers (£6,000); Furniture Project Thurrock, Kingsway Hall, Bridge Counselling Service and Interact Chelmsford (£5,000 each); Churches and Refugees Together and Young Peoples Counselling Service (£4,000 each); Harlow and District Chinese Association (£3,500); and Ashoka, Teentalk Clacton, Humane Research Trust and Chelmsford Community Environmental Trust (£3,000 each).

Smaller grants included those to Rivenhall Friendship Club, Brentwood Club for Visually Impaired Persons, Harlow Well Women Centre, 4 Youth Drop-In Centre, Halstead Youth Initiative, Maldon University of The Third Age, The Braintree Foyer, 1st Wivenhoe Guides, Harlow CAB and Phoenix Youth Orchestra Brentwood.

Exclusions

No grants for projects outside Essex, political or religious activities, animal welfare, statutory bodies, general appeals or individuals.

Applications

Applicants can just apply to the foundation with a general application form. The foundation then finds the most appropriate fund. If in doubt, telephone calls are welcome.

Application forms are available from the foundation's office or can be downloaded from the website. Deadlines are twice a year; usually in mid August and mid January; please contact the trust for exact dates. Grants are awarded within three months of the deadlines. Trustees usually meet around the end of January, April, July and October.

The Essex Youth Trust

Youth, education of people under 25

£311,000 (2002/03)
Beneficial area Essex.

Gepp & Sons, 58 New London Road, Chelmsford, Essex CM2 0PA
Tel. 01245 493939 **Fax** 01245 493940
Correspondent J P Douglas-Hughes, Clerk
Trustees *Mrs Enid Edwards; Richard Francis Wenley; Thomas Gepp; Julien Courtauld; Michael Dyer; Raymond Knappett; Revd Duncan Green; Mrs G Perry; W D Robson.*
Charity Commission no. 225768
Information available Information was provided by the trust.

This trust comprises the four charities of The Essex Home School, George Stacey Gibson, George Cleveley and Adelia Snelgrove, all of which are accounted for together, with the exception of the last charity. In March 1998, the trust had a permanent endowment which amounted to £7.2 million.

The trust's objects are the education and advancement of people under the age of 25. Preference is given to those who are in need owing to 'being temporarily or permanently deprived of normal parental care or who are otherwise disadvantaged'.

In 2002/03 the trust had an income of £339,000 and gave grants totalling

£311,000. No further information was available for this year.

In 2001/02 it had assets of £7.3 million, an income of £370,000 and made grants totalling £325,000. Of the 67 applications received, 49 were agreed, 4 were deferred and 14 were declined. All grants made were a one–off donation. The report stated that 'the trustees favour organisations which develop young people's mental and spiritual capacities through active participation in sports and indoor and outdoor activities. As a result they are particularly supportive of youth clubs and other organisations which provide facilities for young people to take an active part in an assortment of activities as well as single activity organisations.'

Larger donations made in the year included: £49,000 to Cirdan Sailing Trust; £28,000 to Essex Boys' Club; £17,000 to Community Links; £15,000 to St Mark's College; and £10,000 each to Active Christian Trust, Cecil Jones High School and Open Door – Thurrock. Other donations included: £7,500 to Wellgate Farm; £6,300 to Barking and Dagenham Pupil Referal Unit; £5,900 to Centurions Youth Club – Colchester; £5,000 each to Brentwood Opportunities for Special Needs, Chelmsford Boys' Club, Essex County Scout Council and South East Essex Christian Hospice; £4,400 to Barking & Dagenham Befrienders; £4,000 to Chain Reaction Theatre; £3,000 to Belhus Park Amateur Boxing Club; £2,500 each to Bar–n–Bus and Teen Talk; £1,500 to 3rd Collier Row Scout Group; £950 to Parents of Autistic Children Together in Barking and Dagenham; and £500 to Dystonia Society.

Exclusions

No grants to individuals.

Applications

On a form available from the correspondent.

Euro Charity Trust

Relief of poverty, education

£1.5 million (2003)
Beneficial area Worldwide.

Unit M, Waterloo Road, Yardley, Birmingham B25 8AE
Tel. 0121 706 6181
Correspondent Afzal Majid Alimahomed, Chair
Trustees *Abdul Majid Alimahomed; Afzal Majid Alimahomed; Shabir Majid Alimahomed.*
Charity Commission no. 1058460
Information available Annual report and accounts, without a grants list or any information about actual grants made, on file at the Charity Commission.

The objects of this trust are listed as 'the relief of poverty, to assist the vulnerable and to assist in the advancement of education in the UK and the rest of the world'. The trust receives all its income from Euro Packaging Plc. Donations are made to both organisations and individuals worldwide.

Euro Packaging has grown from a small paper bag merchants into a large diversified packaging group. Paper bag production commenced in 1984 and today the firm is the UK's largest manufacturer. It has its own facilities for polythene bag manufacture, and also recycles both plastic and paper products.

In 2003 the trust had an income of £3.2 million and a total expenditure of £1.7 million. Grants appear to be consistently around the £1.5 million mark each year, although the trust does not include any information on beneficiaries. It is likely grants are made to organisations in the local area around Euro Packaging sites (in the UK in Birmingham and in Malaysia) and Malawi, where the settlor is originally from.

Applications

In writing to the correspondent.

The Eveson Charitable Trust

Health, welfare

£1.9 million (2002/03)
Beneficial area Herefordshire, Worcestershire and the county of the West Midlands (covering Birmingham, Coventry, Dudley, Sandwell, Solihull, Walsall and Wolverhampton).

45 Park Road, Gloucester GL1 1LP
Tel. 01452 501352 **Fax** 01452 302195
Correspondent Alex D Gay, Administrator
Trustees *Bruce Maughfling, chair; Rt. Revd John Oliver, Bishop of Hereford; J Martin Davies; David Pearson; Bill Wiggin.*
Charity Commission no. 1032204
Information available Annual report, accounts and very brief guidance notes for applicants were provided by the trust.

The trust was established in 1994 by a legacy of £49 million from Mrs Violet Eveson to support the following causes:

- people who are physically disabled (including those who are blind or deaf);
- people who are mentally disabled;
- hospitals and hospices;
- children in need, whether disadvantaged or physically or mentally disabled;
- older people;
- people who are homeless;
- medical research in any of these categories.

Grants are currently restricted to the geographical areas outlined above, as a policy decision of the trustees. The trust does not instigate programmes of its own, but responds to the applications which it receives (and the submission of which it actively encourages). Most of the larger grants appear to be one-off, though a higher proportion of the smaller awards are probably recurrent.

The trust has recently had a minor change of policy, deciding that from the start of 2004 it no longer considers applications for funding towards special facilities for people with disabilities to be installed in existing community buildings, village halls or churches. This includes buildings of organisations not specifically or exclusively working with people who fall within the remit of the trust. Previously, grants of up to £4,000 each had been made for this purpose.

In 2002/03 the trust had assets of £50 million, which generated an income of £2.1 million. Grants were made to 324 organisations totalling £1.9 million, broken down as follows:

Accommodation – 23 grants totalling £95,000

The largest grants were: £15,000 to Malvern Hills Homeless Young Adults for running costs; £14,000 to Taste for Adventure Centre – Hereford for facilities for people with disabilities; and £10,000 each to Dodford Children's Holiday Farm for a building project and Pioneer Centre for holidays for disadvantaged children.

Other beneficiaries included: Left Heart Matters – Birmingham for an activity weekend for children with hypoplastic left heart syndrome (£6,000); Stonehouse Gang – Birmingham for building improvements (£5,000); Camp Quality UK for holidays for children with terminal illnesses (£4,000); and Honeypot Charity for holidays for disadvantaged children (£3,000).

Health care – 24 grants totalling £345,000

The largest grants were £50,000 over two years to WellChild for the development of a Children's Research Centre at Birmingham Children's Hospital, £33,000 to University of Birmingham Institute of Cancer Studies for a research nurse involved in a study of pancreatic cancer and £25,000 each to Acorns Children's Hospice for running costs, League of Friends of Tenbury Wells Hospital towards a building development, Primrose Hospice – Birmingham for a building extension and Queen Alexandra College for the Blind – Birmingham towards a computer-aided training, education and communication facility.

Other grants included £20,000 each to Hereford and Worcester Advisory Service on Alcohol towards the conversion of a property into a residential crisis clinic and Sunfield Children's Home – Stourbridge towards new residential accommodation for children with autism; £16,000 to Birmingham Rathbone Society for furniture and equipment; £12,000 to Haven Trust for the running costs of the Hereford Support Centre; £10,000 to Elizabeth Dowell's Trust for improvements to the residential accommodation; £8,000 to Lisieux Trust – Sutton Coldfield for equipment; £6,000 to Edwards Trust – Birmingham for running costs; and £5,300 to Shaftesbury Society for equipment at a residential unit in Hereford for people with disabilities.

Social care and development – 277 grants totalling £1,630,000

Grants totalling £137,000 were made to 11 branches of Age Concern, including £25,000 each in Leominster for running costs and Malvern for the handyperson service; £18,000 in Hereford (City and Rural) for a mobile day centre's running costs; £12,000 in Droitwich Spa for home support and information services; £10,000 each in Worcester for a home support project and Wyre Forest for the helping hands project; and £7,000 in Ledbury for information services.

Other large grants were £45,000 to Barnardos for a three-year project benefiting children affected by sexual abuse in Birmingham; £36,000 to Voluntary Action North Herefordshire for a new minibus and the running costs of the Community Wheels project; £30,000 each to Droitwich Women's Refuge towards outreach and resettlement of women and their children and Riding for the Disabled – Herefordshire towards the purchase and development of a new centre; £28,000 to Workmatch for a new vehicle and its running costs in rural areas; £25,000 to Autism – West Midlands for running costs in Herefordshire and Worcestershire; and £20,000 to British Association for Adoption and Fostering for running costs over two years.

Other beneficiaries included: Terrence Higgins Trust for running costs in the local area (£18,000); Big Issue Foundation for running costs of providing drug/alcohol advice and a guidance service to homeless people in Birmingham (£12,000); Worcestershire Association for the Blind for a home visiting scheme (£10,000); Pre-School Learning Alliance – Worcestershire for running costs (£7,000); West Midlands Stroke Support Group – Wolverhampton for tricycles to loan to people with balance, coordination and mobility problems (£6,200); Mercia MS Therapy Centre – Coventry for running costs of the physiotherapy service (£6,000); MIND – Dudley for computer equipment for a day centre in Wordsley and Solihull Carers Centre for running costs (£5,000 each); National Gulf Veterans and Families Association for support of ex-service personnel in the area (£3,500); Community Action Malvern District for the Shoparound project (£3,300); Yemini Day Centre – Birmingham for running costs (£3,000); Wolverhampton Foster Care Association for equipment for a creche for children with special needs (£2,500); and Courtyard Audio-Description Association – Hereford towards audio-description facilities (£1,100).

Exclusions

Grants are not made to individuals, even if such a request is submitted by a charitable institution.

Applications

The trustees meet quarterly, usually at the end of March and June and the beginning of October and January.

Applications can only be considered if they are on the trust's standard, but very simple, 'application for support' form which can be obtained from the administrator at the offices of the trust in Gloucester. The form must be completed and returned (together with a copy of the latest accounts and annual report of the organisation) to the trust's offices at least six weeks before the meeting of trustees at which the application is to be considered, in order to give time for necessary assessment procedures, including many visits to applicants. Before providing support to statutory bodies (such as hospitals and schools for people with learning difficulties), the trustees require written confirmation that no statutory funds are available to meet the need for which funds are being requested. In the case of larger grants to hospitals, the trustees ask the district health authority to confirm that no statutory funding is available.

Where applications are submitted that clearly fall outside the grantmaking parameters of the trust, the applicant is advised that the application cannot be considered and reasons are given. All applications that are going to be considered by the trustees are acknowledged in writing. Applicants are advised of the reference number of their application and of the quarterly meeting at which their application is going to be considered. The decisions are advised to applicants in writing soon after these meetings.

The Execution Charitable Trust

Social welfare

£493,000 (2003/04)

Beneficial area UK.

Block D, The Old Truman Building, 91 Brick Lane, London E1 6QL

Tel. 020 7456 9191 **Fax** 020 7375 2007

Correspondent Jacky Joy, Trustee

Trustee *Jacky Joy.*

Charity Commission no. 1099097

Information available Information taken from website.

This new trust was established in 2003 by stockbrokers Execution Ltd as a means of distributing funds raised from their 'charity days', when all commission revenues generated on the day are donated to charity. The first such day in November 2002 raised £547,000, the second in November 2003 raised £840,000. The company intends to make the charity day an annual event, with all proceeds going to the charitable trust. It is likely the trust will distribute at least £550,000 each year in the future.

The trust is focusing on a Community Projects Programme, which aims to 'provide grants that are leveraged for the maximum benefit of those in desperate need of help, by supporting the work of successful community projects'. The trust has brought in advisors New Philanthropy Capital (NPC) to identify worthwhile projects to support, through its own research and also as a result of referrals from other agencies. The focus is on organisations and projects that work in disadvantaged communities.

The first round of distributions were made in 2003/04. NPC initially identified 14 organisations to support throughout the UK. Grants were made totalling £493,000 to:

- Absolute Return for Kids (£135,000), for various projects;
- Broxburn Family and Community Centre – Edinburgh (£43,000), over two years to fund the post of a youth worker;
- Bryncynon Community Revival Strategy – Wales (£43,000), over two years to fund the posts of a finance assistant and an IT worker;
- Cheltenham Community Projects – Gloucestershire (£40,000), over two years to fund the post of a training and education manager to support the Enhanced Curriculum programme;
- World's End Regeneration Trust, Kensington and Chelsea – London (£31,000), over two years to fund the organisation's core costs;
- Hull Community Church (Respect) – Hull (£30,500), over two years to fund 11 sessional workers, who will enable Respect to expand its services and activities to include youth and elderly clubs, summer sports activities and creative sessions;
- 999 Club – London (£30,000), over two years towards the core costs of running the group's Deptford centre;
- West Harton Churches Action Station Limited – South Shields (£24,000), to fund the post of a Community Development Manager to attract new users to the centre;

- Barry YMCA – Glamorgan (£23,000), to fund the post of a fundraiser/project officer for one year, to identify the unmet needs of the community and develop fundraising strategy which may lead to the construction of an additional community centre;
- Copperdale Trust – Manchester (£22,000), to fund the post of a Community Development Officer for one year;
- Family Action in Rogerfield and Easterhouse – Glasgow (£21,000), over two years to fund the post of a part-time office administrator;
- Safety Zone, Bargeddie – Glasgow (£18,000), to fund the post of a senior youth worker;
- Corner House Cross Community Family Centre – Belfast (£16,500), over one year, to fund the post of a youth and after-school worker to engage people under the age of 13 in the organisation's activities;
- Wishing Well Family Centre – Belfast (£16,000), to cover the insurance of the centre for two years.

Comment

This new trust appears keen to ensure that its funds are distributed to organisations in all parts of the UK. It also seems that it is willing to consider funding organisations in disadvantaged communities for almost any purpose, from core funding and salaries, to project costs and even insurance costs.

Please remember, however, that New Philanthropy Capital does its own research on potential grant recipients, and does not consider unsolicited applications.

Applications

New Philanthropy Capital has been appointed by Execution Ltd to seek out worthwhile organisations and projects to receive funding from the Execution Charitable Trust. The trust does not consider unsolicited applications for grants. The funding programme is based on New Philanthropy Capital's research into the voluntary sector. If you wish to be included on NPC's database, please send a copy of your annual report for future reference.

Contact details:
Claudia Botham
Execution Charitable Trust
c/o New Philanthropy Capital
3 Downstream
1 London Bridge
London
SE1 9BG
Tel: 020 7401 8080

Fax: 020 7654 7888
Email: cbotham@philanthropycapital.org

Esmée Fairbairn Foundation

Social welfare, education, environment, arts and heritage

£26 million (budgeted for 2004)
Beneficial area UK.

11 Park Place, London SW1A 1LP
Tel. 020 7297 4700 **Fax** 020 7297 4701
Email info@esmeefairbairn.org.uk
Website www.esmeefairbairn.org.uk
Correspondent Margaret Hyde, Director
Trustees *Jeremy Hardie, chair; Sir Antony Acland; Ashley G Down; Felicity Fairbairn; John S Fairbairn; Rod Kent; Kate Lampard; Martin Lane-Fox; Baroness Linklater; William Sieghart; Beverley Bernard; Tom Chandos; Andrew Graham.*
Charity Commission no. 200051
Information available Detailed guidelines for applicants and excellent annual report and accounts, all available on the clear and helpful website.

Summary

The foundation gives grants under four programmes, for which excellent guidelines are available, and for a small group of special initiatives. It gives grants of all sizes, for core or project costs, but very seldom for capital expenditure. However there are now few grants for under £5,000 – seven out of 206, for example, in the large social development category in 2003. Indeed, the average grant in 2003 was just over £38,000.

The foundation has developed rapidly over recent years as its income has greatly increased. It now has regional grants officers across the country as well as programme specialists in London.

The main programmes, with their grant budget for 2004 are:

- Social Development – £8.6 million
- Environment – £5.6 million
- Education – £5.6 million
- Arts and Heritage – £5.6 million

The foundation also operates its own initiatives, from the Adult Learners Initiative, a project to support the development of new strategies for engaging hard-to-reach adult learners in Barnsley and the Forest of Dean, to the Regional Theatre Initiative, a strategic initiative of the Arts and Heritage programme worth £450,000 that gives new theatre directors the opportunity to create work on the main stage in regional theatres in England and Scotland.

In 2003 the overall success rates for applications was 27% – for those that pass an initial screening for conformity with trust policies, however there are variations in the success rates between programmes.

This long entry starts with the parts of the guidelines that apply to all programmes and which give an excellent account of the grantmaking as a whole. Then each programme has a separate section in this entry, in which will be found the relevant guidelines for applicants, and examples from the grants that have been made. The entry ends with some recent information on grants made between January and June 2004. Please note that the grants made in 2003 were given under the previous guidelines.

Background

Ian Fairbairn established the foundation in 1961 (renamed Esmée Fairbairn Foundation in 2000). He was a leading city figure and his company, M&G, was the pioneer of the unit trust industry. Ian Fairbairn endowed the foundation with the greater part of his own holding in M&G, and in the early years the majority of grants were for economic and financial education.

His interest in financial education stemmed from his concern that most people had no access to stock exchange investment, and were therefore precluded from investing their savings in equities and sharing in the country's economic growth. It was precisely this concern that had led him into the embryonic unit trust business in the early 1930s.

The foundation was set up as a memorial to Ian Fairbairn's wife Esmée, who had played a prominent role in developing the Women's Royal Voluntary Service and the Citizens Advice Bureaux before being killed during an air raid towards the end of the Second World War. Her sons Paul and Oliver Stobart contributed generously to the original trust fund, as co-founders.

General

The foundation gives the following overall description of its grantmaking in its guidelines, which were reviewed in May 2004:

Esmée Fairbairn Foundation makes grants to organisations which aim to improve the quality of life for people and communities in the UK, both now and in the future.

We like to consider work which others may find hard to fund, perhaps because it breaks new ground, appears too risky, requires core funding, or needs a more unusual form of financial help such as a loan.

We also take initiatives ourselves where new thinking is required or where we believe there are important unexplored opportunities.

We are one of the largest independent grantmaking foundations in the UK. We make grants for charitable purposes across the UK in four programme areas:

- Arts and heritage
- Education
- Environment
- Social development

We receive many more applications than we can fund and each programme has specific funding priorities.

In 2004 we expect to make grants up to £26 million. Our grantmaking fund is divided between the four programmes as follows:
Arts and heritage (£5.6 million)
Education (£5.6 million)
Environment (£5.6 million)
Social development (£8.6 million)
In 2003 grants ranged in size from £726 to £450,000. We only make a small number of grants that exceed £100,000. Our average grant in 2003 was £38,254.

As well as making grants in response to applications we receive, we set aside funding for our own initiatives. Examples of these include: the Regional Museums Initiative, which supports regional museums to strengthen their exhibition programmes, and Rethinking Crime and Punishment, which [was] designed to raise the level of debate about responses to crime, and to identify credible alternatives to prison in the UK.

We also have a three-year pilot programme worth £3 million to make loans for charitable purposes in tune with our priorities.

Equal opportunities

The foundation wishes its policies and practices to support and encourage the development of a free, stable and socially cohesive society. We welcome applications for funding from all sections of the community.

Types of grants made

We make grants towards project and core costs. These include running costs such as staff salaries and overheads.

A full list of our previous year's grants is on our website www.esmeefairbairn.org.uk and included in our annual report. For a copy, please telephone our office.

Funding for posts

If you are applying to fund a post please include the job description and person specification for the post.

Size of grants

There is no maximum grant size and the amount you request should be the amount you need. In 2003 we made 623 grants of which less than 6% (38) were for over £100,000. The average grant size was £38,254.

Duration of grants

Grants may be for one year or for a longer period. Generally we do not make grants for longer than three years. We will sometimes consider a longer period or a repeat grant, for example to help a young organisation develop.

Workplans

A workplan may be a helpful tool in planning your project [see 2 in 'Points to cover' under Applications below]. There is an example of a workplan on our website or we can send you a copy of it.

When to apply

We do not set deadlines for applications and you can apply for a grant at any time. Trustees meet four times a year and you do not need to time your application to coincide with these meetings. We do not publish the dates of the trustees' meetings.

Programmes

You will need to nominate one programme that best fits your proposal. Making your work fit more than one programme will not increase your likelihood of receiving a grant, but please do let us know if your work genuinely fits more than one programme, and describe how it matches our priorities.

What happens to you application

We aim to send you an acknowledgement letter within one week of receiving your application. If your proposal is ineligible we will tell you in this letter. We will assess all eligible applications and may contact you for further information.

We aim to make decisions on grants of £20,000 and under within two months of receiving your application. Decisions on grants over £20,000 will normally be made within five months. If your application is likely to take longer than this we will let you know.

Applying again

If you have had an application refused, you can apply again 12 months after you sent us your last application. If you have received funding in the past you may apply again. If you are currently funded by the foundation and wish to apply for a grant to continue or develop your work, you should telephone us six months before the end of the grant to discuss the possibility of renewal.

Progress reports

If you receive a grant, you will be asked to complete a progress report for each year of the grant, telling us how your work is developing. We will send you advice on progress reports if you are offered a grant. This information also appears on our website.

Applying for a loan

For more information about our loans programme, please see our website www.esmeefairbairn.org.uk or telephone us for a leaflet on 020 7297 4700.

Grants in 2003

In 2003 the foundation had assets of £668 million, which generated an income of £33.3 million. It received 2,171 applications during the year, of which 623 (29%) were successful. Grants were made totalling £26.5 million.

The geographical breakdown of grants, based on the location of the ultimate beneficiaries of the grant rather than where the funded organisation is based, was as follows, based on pence per head in the region:

UK-wide	11p
England-wide	0.05p
Northern Ireland	81p
Scotland	35p
Wales	23p
North East England	36p
South West England	29p
London	27p
South East England	24p
Yorkshire	20p
North West England	18p
West Midlands	18p
East Midlands	12p
East England	11p

Social Development programme – guidelines for applicants

The Social Development programme aims to improve the lives of people and communities facing disadvantage. We prioritise those at greatest need, including those living in or on the edge of poverty.

Funding priorities

We want to invest in organisations which change people's lives. We will support community-based work which enables individuals to progress, enterprising activities, and initiatives which tackle more entrenched, structural problems. Applications may be for local, regional or national work which tackles disadvantage and meets the specific priorities in one of the following areas:

Independence

We are particularly interested in increasing independence in the following ways:
- new opportunities for individuals to become more economically independent, e.g. job coaching, work-related mentoring
- interventions at time of transitions or crisis which improve people's chances of long-term independence e.g. moving from prison, seeking asylum, leaving
- imaginative proposals to enable people to become more involved in their communities, e.g. by running their own organisations or playing a more direct part in decision making.

Enterprise

We want to encourage organisations to be more effective by:
- enabling social enterprises and social firms to improve their business or social performance
- supporting enterprising voluntary and community organisations to become more sustainable by making the most of their existing resources and developing new ones, e.g. by increasing earned income, trading for a social purpose
- strengthening enterprising organisations by developing leadership and talent.

Institutional change

We welcome creative proposals that tackle institutional barriers to change for those at greatest disadvantage, in particular those which:
- advance financial inclusion by increasing access to financial services
- encourage the wider community to become more involved with responses to crime and punishment, e.g. by developing people's understanding of the penal system, increasing the participation of local communities and others in prisons and community penalties
- promote greater social cohesion by enabling divided communities and people to work together
- find ways of encouraging public, voluntary and private institutions to become more responsive and accessible to those at greatest disadvantage.

Characteristics of the work we want to fund through the Social Development programme
We want to make grants which help promote and share good practice, so

129

applications should show how they will do all or some of the following:

- demonstrate quality from best practice to exemplary work
- add value such as levering other funding, showing good volunteer involvement
- have a wider impact by leading to changes in the law, policy or practice or developing new approaches which can be rolled out elsewhere
- bring about lasting change for people and communities facing disadvantage
- be inclusive through work which is user-led and engages people who have previously played less of a part in the community
- involve individuals who are talented and capable of achieving change
- prevent future problems rather than dealing with the symptoms.

What we are very unlikely to support in addition to the [standard] exclusions

A wide range of work can tackle disadvantage. Our limited funds are intended to complement and not subsidise or replace statutory provision and funding. Some work is already well supported by others or relatively widespread. We have therefore decided not to support certain kinds of organisations and activities unless the proposal is genuinely developmental or there is something exceptional about the circumstances:

- mainstream activities of local organisations which are part of a wider network of others doing similar work e.g. Age Concern, CABx, MIND
- arts projects
- childcare, nurseries, pre-school and after-school clubs
- citizen's advocacy
- community transport, unless it fits the priority on enterprise
- counselling and therapy
- drug rehabilitation services and drug education
- homelessness, e.g. drop-in centres, guarantee schemes, routine resettlement work
- information and advice services
- prison resettlement work
- recycling, unless it fits the priority on enterprise
- work which is primarily the responsibility of local government or health authorities
- vocational training, basic skills, ICT
- youth clubs.

If your organisation or work falls into one of the above categories and you still think it should be considered, please telephone us before applying.

Social Development grants in 2003

There were 206 grants made, totalling £8 million and averaging £39,000 each.

Of these, 145 were of over £10,000 and totalled £7.6 million, accounting for 70% of the grants and 95% of the total.

The largest grants went to:

- Council of Ethnic Minority Voluntary Sector Organisations (CEMVO) towards the costs over three years of rolling out the Capacity Building Programme for BME groups throughout England (£450,000 over three years)
- Justice Research Consortium towards the costs of research into the impact on sentencing restorative justice conferences, where victims and offenders meet and decide together how to deal with the aftermath of an offence (£200,000)
- Scarman Trust towards the costs over two years of rolling out the Can Do Exchange, a web-based resource and support facility for voluntary groups and individuals (£179,000)
- Community Development Finance Association towards the salary and running costs over three years of a Capacity Building Fund Manager to enable Community Development Finance Institutions to become more sustainable (£150,000)
- Mental Health Foundation towards the costs over three years of the Youth in Crisis programme, to develop appropriate and accessible mental health crisis services for young people (£120,000)
- Regen School North East towards core costs over three years to run a programme of mentoring and practical apprenticeships in regeneration for voluntary and community organisations in South Yorkshire (£120,000)
- Runnymede Trust towards the core costs over three years of an organisation whose remit is to promote a successful multi-ethnic Britain (£120,000)
- Apex Trust Scotland towards the salaries over two years of three Aftercare Workers, to improve housing and employment opportunities for young offenders (£101,000)
- Social Firms UK towards core costs over two years to provide support for developing social businesses across the UK (£100,000)
- Community Foundation for Northern Ireland towards the salary over three years of a Fund Development Manager to promote philanthropy within Northern Ireland and to engage in fund development activities (£100,000).

Other grants included those to: Prison Advice and Care Trust towards the salary over three years of a development worker and towards volunteer expenses, to continue the development of three family centres in prisons in Devon (£97,500); Spinal Injuries Association towards the salary and costs over three years of the Peer Support Development Officer of the Regain Project to work with spinal cord injured people to acquire the skills for independent living (£75,000); Yemeni Development Foundation towards the salaries and costs over two years of a development officer and community facilitator (£55,000); National Children's Bureau towards the cost over two years of SHAPE's Young Media Representatives project, to enable young disadvantaged people to influence the debate on youth crime (£45,000); Rhayader & District Community Support towards costs over two years to enable the organisation to maximise the facilities within its new building (£35,000); Royston Youth Action Glasgow towards the salary of a youth worker and expenses of six full time volunteers to deliver the 'Themed Youth Task Force' programme aimed at helping deprived young people to become community leaders in the future (£25,000); Kurdish Cultural Centre towards the cost of supporting dispersed Kurdish communities in South Yorkshire (£20,000); Findhorn Village Centre towards the salary of a community development worker in Findhorn, Moray (£15,000); and Manchester Jewish Community Centre towards the salary of an administrator to improve opportunities and quality of life for people in one of Manchester's most deprived areas (£11,000).

Small grants of £10,000 or less included those to Brecknock Carers Centre Association and Worldwide Volunteering for Young People (£10,000 each), Hope in the Cities (£9,000), St Cleopas 468 Urban Aid (£8,000), Domestic Violence Services and Parkside Project (£7,000 each), Liverpool Somali Women's Group (£6,000), West Plymouth Credit Union Ltd (£5,000), Service Users Network (£3,500) and Double Elephant Print Workshop (£3,000).

Environment programme – guidelines for applicants

Many environmental impacts are a consequence of growing resource consumption created by the global spread of industrialisation and affluence. Environmental improvement is therefore dependent on changes in public opinion and lifestyle choices. Our Environment programme seeks to support projects that prevent environmental degradation whilst recognising legitimate aspirations for housing, goods, transport and leisure activities.

Funding priorities

We welcome applications under the following headings:

Biodiversity and Marine Conservation

We wish to support work on fisheries and on less charismatic UK species and habitats under threat or in decline. Applications should focus on recovery and preservation work, for example through appropriate management or habitat protection.

Business, Consumers and Investors

We seek to work with the consumer driven economy to achieve environment improvement, including reduced carbon emissions. We are interested in exploring factors such as demand management through taxation and subsidy policy, eco labelling, certification and working with key groups such as purchasing and investment managers.

Community Living

We wish to support work that improves the quality of public spaces. This may include work on noise, pollution, traffic congestion, environmental improvements to run down areas or good management of woodlands, public gardens, allotments and other accessible 'green lungs'.

Sustainable Food Systems

We are interested in increasing local sourcing and distribution of food, organic or less intensive farming, and retaining money in the rural economy through increasing the skills and capacity of local food enterprises. We may also support lobbying work for the reform of environmentally damaging fisheries, farming or distribution systems.

Characteristics of the work we want to fund

Applications to fund routine work outside the funding priorities listed will not be considered. However we recognise that new issues arise constantly and that charitable grantmakers are best placed to respond to these quickly. We will therefore always consider applications for genuinely new areas of work related to the environment which further the foundation's aims.

The programme will maintain a balance between funding smaller projects and larger pieces of work. We will support projects that promote local and 'human scale' improvements as well as those that attempt to secure leverage and impact by engaging with Government and business.

Environment: what we are unlikely to support (in addition to the foundation's general exclusions)

- conservation of charismatic, well-supported species or of non-native species
- enhancement of habitat for sporting purposes where there are no clear wider conservation or education benefits
- expeditions, fieldwork outside the UK and postgraduate study
- horticultural therapy
- individual furniture, white goods, computer, paint, timber and scrap recycling projects
- individual playgrounds and school grounds improvements
- zoos, captive breeding and animal rescue centres.

Environment grants in 2003

There were 79 new grants made, totalling £4.2 million. Of these, 65 were of over £10,000 each which totalled £4.1 million, accounting for 82% of the grants and 98% of the grant total. The average grant size was £53,000.

The largest grants went to:
- Farming and Wildlife Advisory Group towards salaries and costs over four years to re-establish a Northern Ireland branch (£370,000 over four years)
- Federation of City Farms and Community Gardens towards the costs over three years of core regional and support staff to extend work in the regions (£240,000 over three years)
- British Butterfly Conservation Society towards the core costs over three years of implementing regional action plans and supporting an active volunteer network (£200,000 over three years)
- WWF-UK towards the costs over three years of engaging stakeholders to produce a comprehensive fish stock recovery plan for the waters of South West England (£180,000 over three years)
- The Woodland Trust towards the cost over two years of a major new programme to plant twelve million trees, one for each child in the UK (£160,000 over two years)
- Living Streets towards the costs over two years to enable the organisation to develop organisational capacity and become more self-sufficient (£140,000 over two years)
- The Ponds Conservation Trust towards the salary and costs over three years of a new director and setting up costs of this small development charity (£138,000 over three years)
- Institute for European Environmental Policy towards the continuation costs over two years of the Sustainable Fisheries programme (£135,000 over two years)
- Community Recycling Network towards the salaries and costs over three years of core staff to provide support to its national

network of recycling organisations (£120,000 over three years)
- Council for National Parks towards the salary and costs over three years of an officer to work on and inform the public inquiry into the proposed South Downs National Park (£116,000 over three years)

Other grants included those to: University of Newcastle towards the salary over three years of a project co-ordinator, and running costs for a programme of ecological research that will engage local communities in marine stewardship (£92,000); AccountAbility towards the cost over two years of promoting the development and take up of better standards of corporate sustainability (£75,000); Pesticide Action Network UK towards the cost over two years of a programme to minimise the environmental impact of pesticides (£68,000); Carplus The Car Club Network towards the salaries over two years of three project officers and seed funding for communities setting up car clubs in rural and urban areas (£60,000); Kent Wildlife Trust towards the purchase of 620 hectares of Blean Woods, a semi-natural ancient woodland between Canterbury and Herne Bay (£50,000); Amicus Vision towards the costs over two years of giving unemployed people the skills to maintain open spaces around areas of social housing in Hastings (£45,000); Whithall Allotment Society towards the installation of a land drainage system to prevent flooding (£34,000); Station Lane Area Residents Association towards regenerating a derelict site into a community park in County Durham (£20,000); and Treesponsibility towards the salary and costs of a project to plant new woodland to improve flood control, reduce erosion and raise awareness of sustainability and climate change (£15,000).

Small grants of £10,000 or less were made to British Naturalist's Association and Moorclose Community House Group (£10,000 each), Soho Green (£9,500), University of Newcastle (£7,000), Tresillian Garden Project (£6,000), Caol in Bloom and Institute of Agricultural Management (£5,500 each), BACARC, Duxford Allotment Society and Greater Turf Lodge Residents Association (£5,000 each), Berryhill Fields Centre Trust Limited (£4,000), Wirral Local Agenda 21 Forum (£3,500), Shirley & District Allotment Society (£3,000) and Friends of the Earth Kingston (£700).

Education programme – guidelines for applicants

The foundation's Education programme covers two broad areas of interest: 'new approaches to education' and 'hard-to-reach learners'. We look to support imaginative and flexible approaches to learning that are unlikely to be funded through statutory education sources. Where appropriate, we will support the costs of professional and curriculum development, research and evaluation.

New approaches to education

Aim:

To improve the quality, breadth and relevance of learning for young people (0–16) in pre-school and statutory education by testing new approaches to teaching and learning.

In this category, we will only consider work that is likely to have a lasting influence on education policy and/or practice. All applicants should contact staff on 020 7297 4722 for advice before applying.

In addition to proposals that match the following priorities, we occasionally consider other ideas that meet the aim of our 'New approaches to education' category.

Funding priorities
- improving the quality and relevance of preschool and statutory education (0–16) by giving young people, parents and carers more say in how, when, where and what young people learn
- improving motivation, behaviour and attainment in schools through strategies that promote young people's emotional, social and moral development (this does not include routine aspects of the citizenship curriculum)
- increasing the skills and confidence of primary school and early years' staff in teaching the arts (projects should be of regional or national significance and should not include routine residencies in schools by artists)
- improving the accessibility and relevance of learning for under fives, young people of exceptional ability and/or those with physical and learning difficulties.

Characteristics of the work we want to fund through new approaches to education
Applicants should specify:
- why the work cannot be supported through statutory education funding
- how the work is new or developmental
- how the work will have a wide and lasting impact on policy and/or practice
- how the work will involve partnerships between statutory education and other providers.

Hard-to-reach learners

Aim

To develop new ways of inspiring hard-to-reach learners to engage with education, primarily outside formal education settings.

Funding priorities
- helping young people (3–16) who are excluded from pre-school or school to value and re-engage with education (this

includes young people who are permanently excluded from school, and those missing mainstream education for other reasons including bullying, disability or family circumstances)
- inspiring hard-to-reach adults to engage with learning through imaginative and informal education programmes (this does not include routine work in basic skills or other courses that are eligible for statutory funding)
- giving hard-to-reach parents or carers the confidence to support their children's education and to learn for themselves.

Characteristics of the work that we want to fund through hard-to-reach learners
Applicants should specify:
- why the work cannot be supported through statutory education funding
- how the work will target hard-to-reach learners, i.e. those unable to take advantage of educational opportunities for reasons of background, culture or disability
- how the work is new or developmental.

Education: what we are very unlikely to support (in addition to the Foundation's general exclusions)
- applications which primarily benefit the independent education sector
- capital costs (i.e. building and refurbishment costs)
- computer training or ICT learning centres
- counselling or therapy
- equipment
- health, including drugs education
- local organisations which are part of a wider network of others doing similar work, e.g. Pre-School Learning Alliances
- rehabilitation or education assessment services
- routine arts or environment education proposals that do not match any of our specific priorities
- student grants and bursaries
- vocational or pre-vocational training including National Vocational Qualifications and training that is eligible for statutory funding.

Where work is exceptional and is likely to have a wide impact we occasionally make grants in the following categories. Potential applicants should telephone for advice before applying:
- education publications, websites, conferences or seminars
- individual pre-schools, nurseries, schools, out-of-school clubs, supplementary schools, colleges, youth clubs, toy libraries
- statutory education bodies, for example local authorities or early years' partnerships.

Education grants in 2003

There were 154 grants made totalling £4.5 million, at an average of £29,000 each. Of these, 93 were of over £10,000 and totalled £4.1 million, accounting for 60% of the grants and 90% of the total.

The largest grants went to:

- Open University towards the cost over three years of developing and piloting two professional development programmes in mathematics for non-specialist teachers in primary and secondary schools (£159,000 over three years)
- The Place to Be towards the salary over three years of the head of planning and development and costs to expand support for children transferring to secondary school (£155,000 over three years)
- Continyou towards the costs over two years of a project to develop active citizenship in primary schools (£150,000 over two years)
- The Dyslexia Institute towards the salary and project costs over two years of a co-ordinator to expand services and widen access to learning support for dyslexic children and adults in the south of England and Wales (£118,000 over two years)
- The Who Cares? Trust towards staff costs over two years to expand educational services for the 60,000 young people in care across the UK (£108,000 over two years)
- East London Schools Fund towards the salary and costs over three years of a training officer to support the national expansion of the fund's work with young people at risk of educational exclusion (£105,000 over three years)

Other beneficiaries included: U Can Do I.T. towards the salary over three years of the development officer to expand the education programme for adults with learning and physical disabilities across the UK (£90,000); Manchester Metropolitan University towards the project costs of a training programme for early years practitioners working with children under the age of three in Birmingham, Bridgwater, London, Manchester and Newcastle (£73,000); YWCA towards the salaries over two years of project workers and a research officer for a national programme to reintegrate young women aged 11–16 who are excluded from school back into full-time education (£60,000); Brathay Hall Trust towards the costs over two years of a project to improve the motivation and attainment of up to 1,440 young people aged 13–14 from schools in disadvantaged areas in

Cumbria (£50,000); Forum on Prisoner Education towards the salary of a co-ordinator to increase the effectiveness of the forum's activities in promoting the importance of prisoner education (£40,000); Liverpool Hope University College towards the cost of developing a community education programme for hard-to-reach adults in Everton, Liverpool (£30,000); North Derbyshire Childcare Clubs Network towards the cost of training coaches to provide support for 40 hard-to-reach adult learners studying for childcare qualifications (£18,000); and Nuneaton Women's Multicultural Resource Centre towards the salary and costs of childcare co-ordinator to encourage women from black and minority ethnic communities in Nuneaton to be actively involved in their children's learning (£13,500).

Small grants of £10,000 or less included those to Kirkgate Studios and Workshop (£10,000), Axis: Visual Arts Exchange and Information Service (£9,600), Ezer North West Ltd (£8,200), Music and the Deaf (£6,800), Brainwave Centre Limited (£5,000), Education Renaissance Trust (£4,000), Study Support (£2,000) and the Music Education Council (£1,300).

Arts and heritage programme – guidelines for applicants

The foundation allocates approximately 75% of its Arts & Heritage grants budget to the Arts programme, and 25% to the Heritage programme.

Arts programme

The Arts programme has two main areas of interest: Serving Audiences and Supporting Artists. We welcome proposals that fit the aims of both of these, particularly proposals that benefit audiences and artists outside Greater London.

Serving Audiences

Aim
    To expand high quality performing and visual arts provision in parts of the UK less well served than others.

Funding priorities
    To achieve this aim we will support proposals which do one or more of the following:
- sustain and/or create regional touring circuits and/or tour across UK national borders
- create opportunities for showing new work or second runs
- involve artform/s which tend to be less well funded
- reach new audiences.

Supporting Artists

Aim
    To support the professional development of talented artists throughout their careers.
    We do not accept applications from individual artists.

Funding priorities
    To achieve this aim we will support proposals which do one or more of the following:
- nurture artists at an early stage in their career
- help artists to develop new approaches to their artistic practice later in their careers
- enable the creation of new work
- develop the skills of curators and arts professionals who support the work of artists.

Characteristics of the work we want to fund
    In addition to our specific priorities above, we wish to support proposals that do one or more of the following:
- support innovation in terms of artistic practice and delivery
- add value such as levering in other funding
- have the potential to make a wider impact on policy, or have a significant influence on a particular area of the arts.

Heritage programme

Aim
    The Heritage programme aims to preserve and provide public access to our national heritage particularly outside Greater London.

Funding priorities
    To achieve this aim we will support proposals which do one or more of the following:
- preserve and provide public access to collections of historical significance
- preserve and provide public access to buildings of historical or architectural significance.

We are unlikely to support capital proposals where the total project cost exceeds around £500,0, or proposals from organisations with a large turnover.

Characteristics of the work we want to fund through the Heritage programme
    In addition to our specific priorities above, we wish to support proposals that have one or more of the following characteristics:
- is unusual or difficult to fund
- is a vernacular building of local value
- is significant to the local community
- involves heritage organisations working in partnership
- develops the creative skills of professionals in the heritage sector.

Arts & Heritage: what we don't support (in addition to the foundation's general exclusions)
    We are currently only able to support one in four proposals within the Arts & Heritage programme. To enable us to meet demands within our funding priorities, we are unable to prioritise other areas of work as follows:
- festivals – we do not support festivals
- education/young people – we do not support arts and heritage education proposals, or proposals involving young people
- initial training of artists – we do not support proposals for the initial training of artists in further or higher education
- websites/publications – we do not fund websites or publications
- conferences – we do not support one-off activities such as conferences or seminars
- religious buildings – we do not support the maintenance of individual religious buildings (including parish churches). The foundation currently supports such work through grants to a number of independent specialist conservation and preservation trusts, for delivery in line with their own guidelines
- arts and social inclusion – generally we do not support arts projects which contribute to wider social or community development programmes such as youth offending, crime reduction, or arts work in prisons; participatory arts in deprived communities with disadvantaged groups e.g. single parents; or arts activities in healthcare settings. However, there are rare exceptions and occasionally we support nationally recognised arts organisations which aim to tackle social exclusion.

Arts & Heritage grants in 2003

There were 152 grants awarded totalling £4.8 million, which averaged £31,000 each. Of these, 114 were for over £10,000 each totalling £4.5 million, accounting for 75% of the grants and 94% of the total.

The largest grants went to:
- Birmingham Contemporary Music Group towards the costs over three years of a rural touring programme and related evaluation (£113,000 over three years)
- National Art Collections Fund towards the costs of enabling museums in Northern Ireland to purchase works for their collections (£102,000)
- Council for the Care of Churches towards the conservation grants programme, which preserves historic furnishings and works of art in churches of all denominations (£100,000)

- Stephen Joseph Theatre – Scarborough towards the costs over two years of a rural touring programme and the development of new work (£100,000 over two years)

Other beneficiaries included: De La Warr Pavillion Charitable Trust towards the artists' fees and production costs over two years to create new work (£95,000); North West Play Resource Centre towards the salary over three years of a part-time producer, and commissioning and production costs, to produce new theatrical work in Northern Ireland (£85,000); St Magnus Festival towards the costs over three years of an annual arts festival in Orkney (£78,000); Swansea Print Workshop towards the salary over two years of a new studio manager, and Merseyside Dance Initiative Ltd towards the core costs over three years of developing dance through promoting performances and building audiences (£60,000 each); Chapter Cardiff Ltd towards the costs of a series of performing and visual arts projects touring Wales (£50,000); Eastgate Theatre & Arts Company towards the costs over three years of the recruitment , salary and training of a box office operator to expand performing arts provision in the Scottish Borders (£49,000); Music in the Round towards the costs of touring a programme of chamber music to regional venues (£30,000); Diversions Dance Ltd towards the artists' fees and costs over three years of touring four new dance works in Wales (£20,000) and Early Music Network Ltd towards the costs of touring the musical ensemble to six venues across England (£13,000).

Smaller grants of £10,000 or less included those to Belfast Print Workshop (£10,000), Perpetual Motion Theatre Ltd (£8,000), the Scottish Crannog Centre Limited (£7,000), Spacex Gallery (£6,000), Fold Gallery (£5,000), Catalyst Arts (£3,500), Collective Artistes (£3,000) and In Situ (£2,000).

Shared grants

22 grants, totalling £1.7 million, were made that were funded by more than one programme.

Beneficiaries included:

- Parenting Education & Support Forum towards the salary over three years of a co-ordinator to enable parents to learn skills, contributing to education and employment opportunities (£150,000 funded jointly from the Education and Social Development programmes)

- Clean Break Theatre Company towards the core costs over two years of a project to provide education, training and creative opportunities to women, including those with an offending or mental health background (£100,000 funded jointly from the Arts & Heritage, Education and Social Development programmes)
- Children's Music Workshop towards the cost of a programme to explore the challenges facing children and teachers in rural areas (£90,000 funded jointly from the Arts & Heritage and Education programmes)
- Bridgend People First towards the salaries over three years of the training co-ordinator and administration worker to expand the education opportunities of people in the Bridgend area (£59,000 funded jointly from the Social Development and Education programmes)
- Friends of the General Cemetery towards the salary over two years of a project manager to develop plans for the restoration of a Grade II* listed chapel for community use (£20,000 funded jointly from the Arts & Heritage and Environment programmes).

TASK grants

The foundation has a special category of grants known as Trustees' Areas of Special Knowledge (TASKs). These grants are made to organisations especially known to the trustees and in which they take a close personal interest.

In 2003 it was foundation policy to apply a cash limit of £825,000 on the aggregate spend of TASK grants. In 2003 actual spend was £824,000 which represented 3.1% of the foundation's total grant commitment.

123 grants were made during 2003, headed by £20,000 to Pallant House Gallery Trust and £17,500 to Handicapped Anglers Trust. There were 10 grants of £10,000 each including those to Crosslinks, NCH Action for Children, Somerset House Arts Fund and the Royal Horticultural Society.

Beneficiaries receiving less than £10,000 included Aberdeen International Youth Festival, Balliol College, Christ Church Edinburgh, Health Unlimited, Mary Hare Foundation, Scottish Amateur Music Association, Amar Appeal and Westminster Children's Society.

Strategic Initiatives

The foundation also operates its own initiatives where it feels new thinking is required or where it believes there are important unexplored opportunities.

There are nine initiatives in all, although at present the foundation is not accepting unsolicited applications for these programmes and one, Rethinking Crime and Punishment, is due to come to an end at the end of 2004.

Rethinking Crime and Punishment

Rethinking Crime and Punishment (RCP) was a three-year strategic grantmaking initiative launched by the Esmée Fairbairn Foundation in 2001 to raise the level of public debate about the use of prison and alternative forms of punishment. The grantmaking programme closed in the summer of 2004, but the initiative intends to continue to promote a wide-ranging debate about the role and impact of imprisonment and other forms of punishment, among the public, the media and policy-makers for the foreseeable future. Contact the foundation for up-to-date information, or telephone Rethinking Crime and Punishment directly on 020 7297 4738.

During the lifetime of the initiative, 55 projects were funded:

The 55 projects we have funded over the last three years are now producing valuable findings. RCP has begun to draw these together and communicate them to policy makers, sentencers and the media. The final and largest single project is the independent inquiry into alternatives to prison chaired by Lord Coulsfield. The Inquiry is scheduled to report in the autumn of 2004 [as of early October 2004 the Coulsfield Report had not yet been published. For further details or up-to-date information on the progress of the report, email the Inquiry Secretary Valerie Keating at valeriekeating1@btconnect.com]. The year saw five commissioners appointed, a successful launch event at the Royal Society for Arts, and well over a hundred submissions from interested organisations and individuals.

In the meantime RCP published 'Exploring Alternatives to Prison', a summary of work funded by the programme, and 'Tackling Crime in the Community', a ten-point plan based on emerging learning. Home Office minister Paul Goggins thanks us for our thought provoking ideas which he promised to consider carefully.

'What Can I Do?' produced jointly with the Prison Advice and Care Trust, lists opportunities for individuals to volunteer in criminal justice, and thus engage with the system, while the Rethinking Pack summarises key facts about how we deal with offenders in the UK.

Media perceptions are a critical element in the debate about crime and punishment. Two Rethink briefings dealt with how the media shape what we think about crime and with the specific problems posed by foreign national drug couriers who make up a sizable minority of the female prison population.

Four one-day conferences for grant-holders, each addressed by members of our supervisory board, have resulted in new levels of understanding and co-operation between these varied organisations who operate in the sector. Similarly and RCP-convened gathering of trusts and foundations operating in the criminal justice and penal fields showed enthusiasm for forging stronger working relationships.

RCP's chairman and director have spoken at more than 50 other seminars and conferences throughout the year. Politicians from the Labour, Conservative and Liberal Democrat front benches spoke at our three fringe meetings at the party conferences. The report by Patrick Carter 'Managing Offenders, Reducing Crime', published in early 2004, proposes measures to ensure that custody is reserved for serious, dangerous and highly persistent offenders. Mant of these resonate strongly with RCP's thinking.

Not only will 2004 see the outcome of Lord Coulsfield's inquiry but the culmination of the wider RCP initiative with a final report and evaluation of RCP's effect, a closing conference and a series of events to ensure that findings and recommendations are widely communicated within the criminal justice sector and beyond. In addition the foundation will wish to take on board any learning about strategic grantmaking and share it with the wider funding community.

RCP grants in 2003

There were 15 grants made during the year totalling £150,000. The two largest were made to: Fawcett Society towards the costs of a project to raise awareness of gender and justice among the general public and to educate decision makers (£40,000); and University of Central England towards the costs of a series of screenings of prison films and events to raise awareness and debate about the growth of the UK's prison population (£39,000).

The other grants were made to NCH Scotland (£13,000 in total), Penal Affairs Consortium, Powys Challenge Trust, Scottish Council Foundation, the Open University and Winchester RJ International Conference Committee (£10,000 each), Centre for Crime and Justice Studies (£7,300), Howard League for Penal Reform (£4,600), Revolving Doors Agency (£3,600), Diocese of Winchester (£3,000) and the University of Luton (£1,500).

The other strategic initiatives are as follows, but please note, no unsolicited applications will be accepted at present (telephone the foundation for up-to-date information):

Adult Learners Initiative

A £500,000 partnership between Esmée Fairbairn, Workers' Educational Association (WEA) and the National Institute of Adult Continuing Education (NIACE), under the Education programme. This project will support the development of new strategies for engaging hard-to-reach adult learners in Barnsley and the Forest of Dean.

Esmée Fairbairn Allotments Initiative

An initiative under the Environment programme worth £850,000 to develop 'how to' models for regenerating underused allotment sites or finding alternative ways of maintaining them as publicly accessible open spaces.

Esmée Fairbairn/Villiers Park Partnership

A research project under the worth £40,000 to identify new professional development opportunities for subject teachers in primary and secondary schools.

Esmée Fairbairn UK Biodiversity Programme

A programme under the Environment programme initially worth £500,000 to support the recovery of threatened UK species that are not benefiting from other funding sources.

HEARTS - Higher Education, the Arts and Schools

A joint initiative with a projected budget of £500,000 between Esmée Fairbairn, the Calouste Gulbenkian Foundation, the Teacher Training Agency and the National Endowment for Science and the Arts aiming to strengthen the position of the arts in schools.

Middle Managers Initiative

A £145,000 programme under the Education programme that aims to develop the leadership skills of middle managers in five schools in Birmingham.

Regional Museums Initiative

A strategic initiative of the Arts and Heritage programme worth £800,000 to support regional museums to strengthen their exhibition programmes.

Regional Theatre Initiative

A strategic initiative of the Arts and Heritage programme worth £450,000 that gives new theatre directors the opportunity to create work on the main stage in regional theatres in England and Scotland.

General grants in 2004

The following is a selection of grants over £10,000 that were made from January to June 2004 across all four main programme areas and some strategic initiatives:

Arts & Heritage

- The Sage Gateshead towards the costs over three years of commissioning, programming and touring work (£180,000)
- Live Theatre Company towards the salary over three years of a literary manager and a commissioning fund, and the costs of two new productions (£97,000)
- Look Ahead Housing & Care Ltd towards the cost over three years of a series of public art commissions (£60,000)
- Hebrides Ensemble Limited towards the salary costs over three years of the part-time general manager and the artistic director (£39,000)
- Norfolk & Norwich Festival towards the costs of producing and marketing a new opera (£18,000)

Education

- The Campaign for Learning towards the costs over three years of a scheme promoting the development of high quality family learning opportunities in England, Scotland and Wales (£240,000)
- Nippa – The Early Years Organisation towards the salary over three years of a project co-ordinator to establish cross community early years' services in Northern Ireland (£150,000)
- Children in Scotland towards the costs over two years of a development officer to research barriers to pre-school education for young people with additional support needs (£69,000)
- Liverpool Community Spirit towards the costs over three years of developing and delivering programmes for families and young people at the risk of exclusion (£30,000)
- Education Renaissance Trust towards the costs over two years of teacher training events to encourage new approaches to teaching religious education (£15,000).

Environment

- Marine Stewardship Council towards the salaries and costs over four years of the Fisheries Assessment Manager, International Policy Director, Accreditation Manager, European Sale Manager and Commercial Projects

Manager, to improve the integrity of the MSC label (£600,000)

- Soil Association towards the costs over two years of a project to achieve widespread adoption so sustainable agriculture and localised food network (£300,000)
- East Anglia Food Link Ltd towards the salaries and costs over three years of six county-level co-ordinators to convert schools and hospitals to sustainable food (£145,000)
- Carbon Disclosure Project towards core costs to create a dialogue between institutional investors and corporations on climate change (£80,000)
- Brecon Beacons National Park Authority towards the costs over three years to promote local biodiversity activities and assist local people to use natural resources (£25,000)

Social Development

- Forward Thinking towards the core costs of this new organisation which aims to improve understanding between British Muslims, the wider community and the establishment (£365,000)
- Centre for Adolescent Rehabilitation towards core costs over two years of a project to provide a residential alternative to custody (£200,000)
- CADI SPA Scotland towards the costs over three years of maintaining and expanding its work supporting local community groups in Scotland (£90,000)
- Kuumba Imani Millennium Centre – Toxteth, Liverpool towards the salary over two years of an operations manager to manage the centre and co-ordinate community programmes and activities (£35,000)
- Derbyshire Dales Careline towards the costs of the part-time deputy manager to improve the welfare of elderly, disabled and vulnerable people (£12,000)

Strategic Initiatives

Art & Heritage: Regional Museums Initiative

Beneficiaries included York Museums Trust (£96,500), Whitworth Art Gallery (£81,500), Royal Albert Memorial Museum (£20,000) and Sheffield Galleries & Museums Trust (£10,000).

Education: Adult Learners Initiative

The Sutton Trust (£17,300).

Education: Higher Education, the Arts and Schools

Faculty of Education – University of Plymouth (£197,000).

Environment: Esmee Fairbairn Allotments Initiative

Federation of City Farms and Community Gardens (£30,000).

Environment: Esmee Fairbairn UK Biodiversity Initiative

SAMS (£145,000) and Buglife (£139,000).

Staff

General

Margaret Hyde - Director
margaret.hyde@esmeefairbairn.org.uk

Tricia Brown - PA to the Director
tricia.brown@esmeefairbairn.org.uk

Arts & Heritage

Shreela Ghosh - Programme Director
shreela.ghosh@esmeefairbairn.org.uk

Finella Boyle - Grants Manager
finella.boyle@esmeefairbairn.org.uk

Alison Holdom - Grants Administrator
alison.holdom@esmeefairbairn.org.uk

Education

Hilary Hodgson - Programme Director
hilary.hodgson@esmeefairbairn.org.uk

Jo Rideal - Grants Manager
jo.rideal@esmeefairbairn.org.uk

Rachel Faulkes - Grants Administrator
rachel.faulkes@esmeefairbairn.org.uk
(also Environment - Grants Administrator)

Environment

Tim Keenan - Programme Director
tim.keenan@esmeefairbairn.org.uk

Helen Murray - Grants Manager
helen.murray@esmeefairbairn.org.uk

Social Development

Nicola Pollock - Programme Director
nicola.pollock@esmeefairbairn.org.uk

Danyal Sattar - Grants Manager
danyal.sattar@esmeefairbairn.org.uk

Laurence Scott - Grants Manager
laurence.scott@esmeefairbairn.org.uk

Sharon Shea - Grants Manager
sharon.shea@esmeefairbairn.org.uk

Rhona Clews - Grants Administrator
rhona.clews@esmeefairbairn.org.uk

Tania Joseph - Grants Administrator
tania.joseph@esmeefairbairn.org.uk

Rethinking Crime and Punishment

Rob Allen - Director
rob.allen@esmeefairbairn.org.uk

Frances Thompson - Project Officer
frances.thompson@esmeefairbairn.org.uk

Policy and Communication

James Wragg - Policy and Communications
james.wragg@esmeefairbairn.org.uk

Manager

Ellen O'Donoghue - Communications and
ellen.odonoghue@esmeefairbairn.org.uk

Information Officer

Finance and Resources

Ron Clarke - Finance and Resources Director
ron.clarke@esmeefairbairn.org.uk

Judith Dunworth - Foundation Secretary
judith.dunworth@esmeefairbairn.org.uk

Vandana Gopalji - Finance Manager
vandana.gopalji@esmeefairbairn.org.uk

Mark Jetten - Finance Assistant
mark.jetten@esmeefairbairn.org.uk

Bharat Naygandhi - Finance Assistant
bharat.naygandhi@esmeefairbairn.org.uk

Nikki Thompson - Administrative Assistant
nikki.thompson@esmeefairbairn.org.uk

Exclusions
What the foundation does not support

We will not accept applications for grants:

- that directly replace or subsidise statutory funding
- from individuals or for the benefit of one individual
- for work that has already taken place
- which do not have direct benefits for the UK
- for medical research
- for healthcare and related work, including complementary therapy
- for residential and day care
- for animal welfare
- for adventure and residential courses, expeditions and overseas travel
- for holidays and respite care
- for endowment funds
- for festivals, sport and leisure
- for the promotion of religion
- that are part of general appeals or circulars
- from applicants who have applied to us within the last 12 months.

What the foundation is unlikely to support

There are also categories of work or organisations that we are very unlikely to fund:

- large national charities which enjoy widespread support
- local organisations which are part of a wider network of others doing similar work, e.g. Age Concern, CABx or Mind
- individual pre-schools, schools, out-of-school clubs, supplementary schools, colleges or youth clubs
- websites, publications, conferences or seminars.

Each programme also lists work or organisations that they do not or are very unlikely to fund (see above).

Capital funding

The foundation does not make grants towards capital projects (i.e. buildings and refurbishment costs) unless they fall clearly within the priorities of our Heritage programme or our Environment programme. Items of equipment are also unlikely to be funded unless part of a wider proposal.

What the foundation occasionally supports

Research

Exclusions

We occasionally fund research where its aims match our priorities and where we consider that it is likely to have an impact, for example, by establishing good practice or changing the way that services are provided.

Exceptional projects

We may consider proposals of exceptional merit that are in tune with our wider foundation interests but fall outside our specific programme funding priorities. Such proposals will not be routine and will focus on important practical innovations or emerging issues. Our normal exclusions apply. In the first instance please telephone the enquiry number for whichever of our four programmes you consider most relevant to your idea.

Applications

Potential applicants are strongly advised to see a copy of the guidelines, available from the trust and downloadable from its website, from which the following information is taken.

1. Read the guidelines
   Please read these guidelines carefully to make sure that you are eligible to apply for funding, that your proposal fits our priorities and that you send us the information we need.

2. Check what we do not or are very unlikely to support
   Please check the exclusions (above) and what the foundation is very unlikely to support. Then check the details of the programme to which you are applying for information about what we do not, or are unlikely to, support within individual programmes.

3. Telephone us if applying for more than £100,000
   If you are intending to apply for over £100,000 please telephone us to discuss your proposal.
   Arts & Heritage 020 7297 4719
   Education 020 7297 4722
   Environment 020 7297 4722
   Social Development 020 7297 4727

4. Fill in the application cover sheet
   The application cover sheet [available at the back of the guidelines] helps us to deal with your application more quickly. The questions which limit you to a number of words will be entered on to our database. The detailed information we ask for must be submitted in a proposal document.

5. Write your proposal document
   Write your proposal document by following the 'Points to cover' [below].

6. Enclose supplementary information
   There is a checklist of information to send us [below]. You may send other documents that you think are relevant to your application, although we will not be able to read large amounts of additional information. Please make sure that all documents have your organisation's name at the top.

7. Post it
   Make a copy of the entire application for your records and send the original to:
   Grant Applications
   Esmée Fairbairn Foundation
   11 Park Place
   London
   SW1A 1LP
   We cannot accept your application by fax or email – you must post it.

Writing your application

Your proposal document
   Please cover the points (1–12) set out below in your application. Some points will be more relevant to your proposal than others, but please try to address them all.
   We generally expect an application for under £20,000 to be up to six sides of A4 and applications for over £20,000 to be up to and occasionally more than ten sides of A4.
   Points to cover

1. A brief description of your organisation
   This should include your aims, date established, size, structure, governing body, legal status, number of staff and volunteers, and the geographical area where you work. Also tell us briefly about your organisation's recent achievements.

2. What will our funding support?
   Please summarise the work you want to do. What activities are planned? Where will they take place? How long will they take? When will they be completed? You may find it useful to attach a workplan (there is an example of a workplan on our website or we can send you a copy). If you are applying for funding for a post, please enclose a job description and person specification.

3. What do you want to achieve through the work and who do you aim to reach?
   Please specify what the results of the work will be, and give numbers of beneficiaries and who they are, for example their ethnic origin, age, gender and whether they have any disabilities.

4. What is the need for the work and how have you identified it?
   Why have you decided to do this work? Who have you consulted about the project/proposal? What did this tell you? How will this work build on your previous activities? What are your links with other organisations doing similar work?

5. How does the work match the priorities of the programme you are applying to and the characteristics of the work we want to fund described [for each] programme [above].

6. How will you attract and involve the people who you aim to benefit (where applicable)?

7. Who will do the work and how will it be supervised and managed?

8. How will you evaluate whether your work achieved what it set out to do?
   Please explain how you will assess the progress of the work against the results described in point 3 and against your workplan (if you are using one).

9. What plans if any do you have to share the results of your work with others?

10. How will you continue the work after our grant has ended and how will this be funded?
    If you have no plans to continue the work, please tells us how it will be wound down.

11. Please provide us with the following financial information
    (a) An income and expenditure budget for the proposed work. This must show:
    - the itemised costs of carrying out the work you are proposing for each year, clearly showing the funding you are requesting from us
    - any income already secured towards the costs or expected from other sources; tell us what these sources are
    - other income still to be raised and from where you plan to raise it.

(b) The current year's summary income and expenditure budget for the organisation as a whole. If your application is for more than one year, please provide summary budgets for each of the years, where possible.

(c) Your most recent annual report

(d) Your most recent full accounts (if not for your last financial year, please let us know when these will be available).

Please label each document clearly.

12. If you are not a registered charity, please send us a copy of your constitution or set of rules. This should set out:

- the organisation's name and objectives
- how the governing body is elected or appointed
- what will happen to the assets if the organisation closes down
- the date the constitution or set of rules was adopted
- signature, name and position of Chair or other senior office holder.

Checklist of information to send us

We aim to let you know as quickly as possible whether your application has been successful. If you have not answered all of the questions and enclosed all of the requested information, it may take longer to deal with your application.

Please make sure you have included the following:

- A fully completed application cover sheet [included in the guidelines available from the foundation]
- A proposal document covering all the points [above]
- An income and expenditure budget for the proposed work
- The current year's summary income and expenditure budget for the organisation
- Your most recent annual report
- Your most recent full accounts
- Your constitution or set of rules (if you are not a registered charity)
- A job description and person specification (if applying for funding for a post)
- Equal opportunities policy, if you have one.

Please ensure that each piece of information has your organisation's name clearly at the top and you have made a copy of the application for your own reference.

Allan and Nesta Ferguson Charitable Settlement

Peace, education, overseas development

£2.4 million to organisations (2003)

Beneficial area Unrestricted, with a local interest in Birmingham and Bishop's Stortford.

Stanley Tee, High Street, Bishops Stortford, Herts CM23 2LU

Tel. 01279 755200

Email jrt@stanleytee.co.uk

Correspondent Richard Tee, Trustee

Trustees *Elnora Ferguson; David Banister; Anne Roff; Richard Tee.*

Charity Commission no. 275487

Information available Annual report and accounts were provided by the trust.

Summary

The Allan & Nesta Ferguson Charitable Trust was set up in memory of two generations of the Ferguson family to promote their particular interests in education, international friendship and understanding, and the promotion of world peace and development.

Most of the trust's grants go to local projects overseas, often in Africa. It also makes some very large grants, centred on the pursuit of international peace and understanding.

General

In 2002/03 the trust had assets amounting to almost £34 million generating an income of £593,000. Grants to organsations totalled £2.4 million with £314,000 going to assist postgraduate students.

Grants were categorised as follows, shown here with examples of beneficiaries:

Grants to educational bodies (£1 million)

17 beneficiaries were listed. The two largest donations went to Loughborough University (£500,000) and Multifaith Centre Derby (£200,000 in two grants). Other listed grants were in the range of £7,500 to £50,000. Beneficiaries included Coventry University (£50,000), Royal Shakespeare Company (£25,000), the Roy Trust, Save the Children Fund and

Weoley Hill Cricket Club (£20,000 each), Deafway (£18,000), Video Educational Trust (£15,000),World Federation of Neurology (£10,000) and NAM Publications and WWF UK (£7,500). Other unlisted grants totalled £140,000.

Overseas development (£1.1 million)

26 grants were listed. The three major beneficaries were Kaloko Trust (£200,000), Traidcraft (£150,000), Farm Africa (£100,000) and the Nepal Trust (£97.000). Other grants were in the range of £6.000 and and £69,000 and included those to Harvest help (£69,000), Africa Now (£63,000), Fairtrade Foundation (£45,000), the Karuna Trust (£24,000), Ecumenial Council for Corporate Responsibility, World Medical Fund and Zambian Ecumenical Link (£15,000), Computer Aid International and Mary Slessor Foundation (£10,000 each), Azafady and United Nations Association International Service (£8,000 each) and Sudan Self-help Foundation (£6,000). Other unlisted grants totalled £177,000.

Educational – projects encompassing the promotion of world peace (£142,000)

Seven beneficiaries were listed: Amnesty International (£25,000), the Gospel and Our Culture Network (£15,000), Arab Cultural Community, Biblelands and Christain CND (£10,000 each), Project Hope UK (£9,700) and Just World Partners (£9,300). Other unlisted grants toatlled £53,000.

Applications

On an application form available from the correspondent.

Simple applications are dealt with on a monthly or bi-monthly basis. More complicated ones are decided at trustees' meetings in January and July each year.

The Sir John Fisher Foundation

General

£430,000 (2002/03)

Beneficial area UK, with a preference for the Furness peninsula and Merseyside.

c/o 8–10 New Market Street, Ulverston, Cumbria LA12 7LW

Tel. 01229 583291

Correspondent Mrs D S Meacock, Trustee

Trustees *Mrs D S Meacock, chair; D P Tindall; R F Hart Jackson.*

Charity Commission no. 277844

Information available Full accounts were on file at the Charity Commission.

The trust states that it gives grants to charities concerned with the Furness peninsula and local branches of UK charities. Grants are also made to national and international groups concerned with the shipping industry, medicine, the navy or military and music or theatre.

In 2002/03 it had assets of £12 million and an income of £475,000. Grants totalled £430,000, broken down as follows:

Local – 110 grants totalling £282,000

Grants of £5,000 or more were made to 17 organisations, including Barrow Sea Cadets (£50,000), Hospice for Furness and Lancaster University – Sir John Fisher Chair (£25,000 each), Friends of Wordsworth Trust (£20,000), Lakeland Housing Trust (£15,000), Parish School of St John the Evangelist – Barrow (£7,500), Barrow CAB, Furness Drug and Alcohol Concern and Samaritans Furness (£6,500 each) and Cartmel Priory, Friends of Sandside School and Parkinsons Disease Society Complementary Therapy Clinic (£5,000 each).

Beneficiaries of smaller grants included YMCA Lakeside Centre (£2,000), Alzheimers Society – South Lakeland, MIND – Ulverston and Windermere Steamboat Museum (£1,000 each), Barrow Island Community Centre (£500) and Cumbria Rural CAB (£100).

Liverpool – 8 grants totalling £8,500

Beneficiaries were Merchant Taylor's School (£3,000), Frontline Project (£2,000), Claire House Children's Respite Hospice (£1,000) and Breast Cancer Campaign, Christ Church Centre – Netherley, Royal Mersey Inshore Rescue and Royal School for the Blind (£500 each).

National – 62 grants totalling £139,000

There were eight beneficiaries of grants of £5,000 each or over: Royal College of Physicians (£15,000), Anglo-Austrian Music Society Ltd, Cancer Research UK, Foundation of Coagulation and

Thrombosis and National Maritime Museum Cornwall (£10,000 each) and Marine Conservation Society and NSPCC (£5,000).

Beneficiaries of smaller grants included Prince's Trust (£2,500), Royal Star and Garter Home (£2,000), Family Welfare Association and Royal Merchant Navy School Foundation (£1,000 each) and Actor's Benevolent Fund and Barnardos (£500 each).

Exclusions

Grants are not given to students.

Applications

In writing to the correspondent. Trustees usually meet in May and November.

The Fishmongers' Company's Charitable Trust

Education, promotion of fisheries, relief of hardship and disability

£889,000 to organisations (2003)

Beneficial area UK, with a slight special interest in the City of London and adjacent boroughs.

The Fishmongers' Company, Fishmongers' Hall, London Bridge, London EC4R 9EL

Tel. 020 7626 3531 **Fax** 020 7929 1389

Email clerk@fishhall.co.uk

Correspondent Keith Waters, Clerk

Trustee *The Wardens and Court of the Fishmongers' Company.*

Charity Commission no. 263690

Information available Annual report and accounts were provided by the trust.

Summary

Over 200 grants are made each year to new beneficiaries, though a major part of the grant total is for the regular support of three charities closely affiliated to the Fishmongers' Company.

Grants, few for more than £10,000, are made within four main categories: education; fisheries; disabled and medical; and hardship.

General

In 2003 the trust had assets of £8.6 million and an income of £735,000 including £483,000 from donations. Grants totalled £987,000 of which £889,000 went to orgnisations. As in previous years, major grants to two charities with a close connection to the company received a large proportion of the money: Gresham's School (£323,000); and Jesus Hospital Almshouses (£195,000).

Grants were classified as follows, shown here with examples of beneficiaries:

Education – 27 grants to organisations totalling £408,000

This category included the major grant to Gresham's School, mentioned earlier. All but four of the grants for £1,000 or more went to organisations that had been supported with closely similar amounts in the previous year, probably because they were regularly established scholarship or bursary schemes, such as City & Guilds Art School (£26,000), Guildhall School of Music & Drama (£5,800) and Royal College of Music (£4,900). New beneficiaries were City & Guilds Institute, Voices Foundation, Joint Educational Trust and Tall Ships Youth Trust (£2,000 each).

There were 37 grants to individuals totalling £54,000.

Fishery grants – 21 grants to organisations totalling £80,000

The pattern here was different with only 5 of the 21 organisations receiving £1,000 or more having been supported in 2002. The largest grant to a new beneficiary was £6,000 to North Atlantic Salmon Fund. Other new beneficiaries included Marine Stewardship Council and the Soil Association (£5,000 each), Association of West Coast Fisheries Trusts (£4,000), City University (£3,000), Freshwater Fisheries of the Falkland Islands (£2,500), Albrighton Trust (£2,000) and Sea Safety Group (£1,500).

There were 19 grants to individuals totalling £35,000.

Disability and medical – 26 grants totalling £44,000

In this category, only one of the beneficiaries of grants over £1,000 had been supported in the previous year. The largest award was to Queen Elizabeth Foundation (£10,000). Other beneficiaries were St Joseph's Hospice (£2,200), Deafblind UK, Downs

Syndrome Association, Mary Hare Foundation and Q Trust (£2,000 each) and Blind Business Trust, British Dyslexics and Willow Trust (£1,500 each).

There were 9 grants for amounts of £1,000 or less.

Hardship – 36 grants totalling £321,000

A large proporton of the grant total in this category was accounted for by the grant to Jesus Hospital Almshouses mentioned earlier and the £87,000 to Harrietsham Almshouse. Not a registered charity, this is part of the Fishmongers' complex of benevolent institutions. Other beneficiaries were the Lord Mayor's Appeal (£7,500), Victoria & George Cross Memorial Appeal (£2,000) and Action on Elder Abuse and and Church Housing Trust (£1,500 each).

There were 27 further grants for amounts of £1,000 or less and 36 grants to individuals amounting to £9,000.

Heritage – 31 grants totalling £34,000

Only two of the beneficiaries had been supported in the previous year. The largest grant of £7,500 went to St Paul's Cathedral Trust. Other beneficiaries were City of London Archaeological Trust (£3,200), Museum of Garden History (£2,500) and Guildhall Library, SS Great Britain Trust and York Foundation (£2,000 each).

There were 24 further grants for amounts of £1,000 or less.

Environment – 1 grants totalling £1,500

The sole beneficiary in this category was Sustrans.

Exclusions

No grants are made to: individual branches of national charities; to regional or local charities, other than those in the City of London and adjacent boroughs; or to charities all of whose beneficiaries are outside the UK. No grants are awarded to individuals except for education. Educational grants are not awarded to applicants who are over 19 years old.

Applications

In writing to the correspondent. Meetings take place three times a year, in March, June/July and November, and applications should be received a month in advance. No applications are considered within three years of a previous grant application being successful. Unsuccessful applications are not acknowledged.

The Football Association Youth Trust

Sports

£2.5 million (2003/04)
Beneficial area UK.

Football Association Ltd, 25 Soho Square, London W1D 4FA
Tel. 020 7745 4589 **Fax** 020 7745 5589
Email mike.appleby@thefa.com
Correspondent Mike Appleby, Secretary
Trustees W T Annable; R G Berridge; B W Bright; G Thomson; M Armstrong.
Charity Commission no. 265131
Information available Information was provided by the trust.

The principal activity of the trust continues to be the organisation or provision of facilities which will enable pupils of schools and universities in the UK to play association football or other games and sports, including the provision of equipment, lectures, training colleges, playing fields or indoor accommodation. In addition, the trust has organised or provided facilities for physical recreation in the interests of social welfare in the UK for people under 21 who need such facilities. Schools and in particular, the English Schools' Football Association and the Universities and City Football Associations are major beneficiaries. A range of projects and events have been supported, an increasing number of which have been small donations to schools and clubs. Beneficiaries must be under 21 unless they are in full-time education.

In 2003/04 the trust had an income of £1.4 million, including a £1 million donation from the Football Association. General grants amounted to £827,000, with £1.6 million in total being spent on the TOP Sports Football Programme.

General grants were made to the English Schools Football Association, schools and universities. There were 96 grants to County Football Associations and 25 made through the Mini Soccer Scheme.

Applications

In writing to the correspondent. Grants are made throughout the year. There are no application forms, but a copy of the most recent accounts should be sent.

The Football Foundation

Grass roots football, community, education

£45 million (2003)
Beneficial area UK.

25 Soho Square, London W1D 4FF
Tel. 020 7534 4210 **Fax** 020 7287 0459
Email enquiries@footballfoundation.org.uk
Website www.footballfoundation.org.uk
Correspondent The Trustees
Trustees T D Brooking; D G Richards; R C Scudamore; G Thompson; Hon Ann Taylor; R Burden.
Charity Commission no. 1079309
Information available Information is available on the foundation's website.

The foundation was set up in 2000 to revitalise the grass roots of football. It also funds educational and community projects. In 2003 the Foundation had assets of £60 million with an income of £56 million and grants totalling £45 million

Funding is mainly coordinated through a grass roots advisory group and a community and education panel, their work is described here along with some examples of grants awarded.

The grass roots advisory group works at an infrastructure level to deliver modern facilities in parks, local leagues and schools throughout the country. Local football partnerships have been established to ensure that all relevant groups have a voice in how football is delivered in their communities. Members include representatives of the County FA, local authorities and local sports organisations.

Grants included £1 million each to Leyton Orient Community Sports Programme and Chippenham Town Council, £974,000 to Mark Hall Community School, £888,000 to

Northumbria University, £807,000 to Carlisle City Council, £798,000 to Birmingham City Council, £776,000 to Camborne Pool Redruth College, £679,000 to Pershore High School and £650,000 to Newcastle Under Lyme Borough Council.

The community and education panel aims to promote community and education initiatives and enhance football's role as a positive force in society.

Grants included £363,000 to Street League and £250,000 each to Bournemouth Borough Council, North Lincolnshire County Council, Cumbria County Council, Northamptonshire County Council, Rochdale Metropolitan Borough Council, Nottinghamshire Council and Oldham Borough Council.

The foundation also runs a Junior Kit Scheme. Grants are available for FA affiliated under-16 teams and can be used for the purchase of kit. The maximum award is £300 and the club would normally receive only one grant every three years. The grant will be given in the form of vouchers which can be exchanged with a nominated supplier. A total of £588,000 has been awarded to over 1,800 junior football teams and clubs.

In addition to its grant making activities the foundation has set up the Register of English Football Facilities. By creating a definitive database, it hopes to be able to identify the quality, quantity and demand for facilities in every part of the country and identify areas of need.

Applications

Application forms and guidance notes are available on request from the foundation's helpline (tel: 0800 027 7766) or on their website.

The Donald Forrester Trust

Health, medical research, disability, welfare, general

£485,000 (2002/03)
Beneficial area UK and overseas.

231 Linen Hall, 162–168 Regent Street, London W1B 5TB
Tel. 020 7434 4021

Correspondent Ms Brenda Ward
Trustees *Wendy J Forrester, chair; Anthony J Smee; Michael B Jones; Hilary J Porter.*
Charity Commission no. 295833
Information available Annual report and accounts on file at the Charity Commission.

Established in 1986, the trust's grantmaking is concentrated on helping sick and disabled people, particularly older people and children. It also makes a smaller number of grants in other areas, including to religious organisations and overseas aid. Most grants go to well known (and often, though not exclusively, national) charities.

In 2002/03 it had assets worth £7.6 million and an income £346,000, which included a Gift Aid payment of £300,000 from Films & Equipment Limited, of which two trustees, Wendy Forrester and Anthony Smee, are directors. There appeared to be virtually no income from investments. Management and administration costs for the trust were very low at £1,000.

During the year the trust made 90 grants totalling £485,000. With the exception of seven grants for £10,000 each, all grants were for £5,000. Due to financial constraints, the trust was not able to continue its practice of making several larger grants during this year.

Grants were listed in the accounts under various headings, including animals and birds, children and youth, hospices and hospitals, medical research and welfare, and many beneficiaries have been supported in previous years. This may explain the comment in the 'applications' section, whereby the trustees continue to fund organisations they already know.

The recipients of grants for £10,000 were: Guide Dogs for the Blind, NSPCC, Salvation Army, the Peace Hospital, St Kentigern Hospice & Palliative Care Centre, RNLI and Tearfund.

Recipients of £5,000 each included: Animal Defence Trust, Cats Protection League, Sense, Children in Crisis, Save the Children, Centrepoint, West London Mission, YMCA England, British Deaf Association, Trees for London, Latimer House, Action for Dysphasic Adults, British School of Osteopathy, Marie Curie Cancer Care, British Lung Foundation, Lupus UK, Samaritans, Contact the Elderly, International Care & Relief, Medecins Sans Frontieres, Water Aid, Leonard Cheshire Foundation, Prestatyn Parish Church

Bells Appeal, Royal British Legion and Police Dependants' Trust.

Comment

The was no response to repeated written requests for a copy of the most recent annual report and accounts, despite the legal requirement to provide these on demand.

The annual report for this trust, viewed at the Charity Commission, is inadequate. Unfortunately, there is no narrative review of charitable activities, nor are the grants analysed and explained as the law requires.

Exclusions

No grants to individuals.

Applications

The trust has previously stated that: 'regrettably, applications for aid cannot be considered as this would place an intolerable strain on administrative resources '

Four Acre Trust

Respite care and holidays, vocational guidance, health disability, social housing

£567,000 (2002/03)
Beneficial area Worldwide.

PO Box 48, Wotton-under-Edge GL12 7WZ
Tel. 01453 844129
Email info@fouracretrust.org.uk
Website www.fouracretrust.org.uk
Correspondent Rob Carruthers, Trustee
Trustees *Mary A Bothamley; Daniel Abel; John P Bothamley; Robert L Carruthers; Stephen Ratcliffe.*
Charity Commission no. 1053884
Information available Accounts were provided by the trust including a list of the top 50 grants.

The trust's Guidelines for Applicants state:

The Four Acre Trust makes grants under three specific categories:

- respite care and holidays for children and young adults – holidays, holiday centres, refuges, carer support and respite, subsidised holidays

- guidance in choice of vocation – counselling for work training, employment generation, foyer schemes, English teaching
- relief of health disability at low unit costs, especially abroad – cataract operations, prostheses, rehabilitation back into society.

Grants may be awarded for one year or phased. The trust is inclined towards support on a regular basis.

Grants may be made towards revenue, capital or project expenditure.

Retrospective grants are not made.

The trust always receives more applications than it has funds to support. Even if a project fits the trust's policy priorities, it may not be possible to make a grant.

Recently rejected lottery bids will be considered. Send an initial single page summary.

The trust was formed in 1995. A large part of the trust's income is derived from a company within the construction industry.

Grants

The trust provides grants up to £100,000 but most are between £2,000 and £5,000. Preference is given to projects that might substantially be enabled to happen with the trust's funding, rather than to projects where a grant would form part of a larger funding scheme. Local, district and smaller national organisations are particularly encouraged to apply.

The trustees consider that an operational charity should broadly spend all its income received on charitable works. They do not like to see charities amassing large investments. Prudent management of finances is essential and some reserves, of course, are necessary. Strict interpretation of financial and other statistics ensure that charities use their funds conscientiously. Our policy is to build long term relationships and fund on a regular basis. Charities with substantial investments of their own should not apply.

Please refer to the specific categories that we support.

The trust's guiding principles

- The purpose must be charitable and normally the trust will only consider applications from registered charities.
- The trust's area of interest is worldwide. The trustees aim to give particular attention to less advantaged areas.
- In general the trust favours projects which will contribute to the preservation and development of a free and stable society.
- There is a preference for projects which are innovative, developmental, designed to make a practical impact on a particular problem/need and reflect the principles of market forces. Especially in the case of local projects preference is given to those which demonstrate active local participation and support self-help.
- The trust attaches importance to the assessment and dissemination of the results of work it had funded, so that others might benefit.

The trust states that it has continued to support many recipients (114 in 2001/02), and does not necessarily restrict its funding to just three years. There is an emphasis on supporting small charities mainly operating in the UK.

In 2002/03 it had an income of £514,000 and gave £567,000 in grants.

In 2001/02 the assets totalled £2.8 million and the income was £412,000. This comprised £280,000 from donations and gifts, £125,000 property income and £7,000 from investments.

Direct charitable expenditure totalled £396,000, made up of £275,000 in grants and £122,000 in rental income foregone, with £23,000 in depreciation of property used for charitable purposes.

'A major project for the trust was the purchase of Ardale, a former community home, in Thurrock, Essex. This will be updated, converted and extended into a new community in partnership with a number of leading and local charities.'

The project aims to provide sites and buildings for registered charities at 'highly discounted prices'. The project has been delayed, it appears because of Thurrock Council taking a long time to deal with the planning application. The trust states that new guidelines by the Charity Commission (which the trust welcomes) make rural and urban regeneration and the relief of unemployment clearly charitable objects. The trust can now show the project's costs as charitable expense in future accounts. It states: 'A large part of the trust's expenditure in the coming year is likely to be made on this project as well as continuing support of other charities.'

The largest grants given were £25,000 each to Princess Royal Trust for Carers, and Young Carers Home Start; £10,000 each to Ashoka and Youth Hostels Association and £6,000 to Northam Lodge. There were six recipients of £5,000; Abel Charitable Trust, Alzheimer Scotland, Brittle Bone Society, Church Pastoral Aid Society, National Benevolent Fund for Aged and Raleigh International. Other beneficiaries of £2,000 or more included Belfast Central Mission, Disability Challengers, Green Space, Nepal Leprosy Trust, Ocean Youth Trust, Shepherds Bush Families Project, Stroud & District Mencap and Youth Hostels Association.

Exclusions

The trust does not support the following:

- animal welfare;
- arts;
- basic services (as opposed to imaginative new projects) for people who are disabled or elderly;
- branches of national charities;
- commercial publications;
- conferences or seminars;
- direct replacement of statutory funding;
- establishing funds for scholarships or loans;
- expeditions;
- general appeals;
- heritage;
- hospices;
- individuals;
- individual parish churches;
- large UK-charities which enjoy wide support, including local branches of UK-charities;
- medical (including research), general healthcare or costs of individual applicants;
- night shelters;
- overseas travel, conference attendance or exchanges;
- performances, exhibitions or festivals;
- projects concerning drug abuse or HIV;
- religious activities;
- science;
- sports;
- stage, film or television production costs;
- university or similar research.

The trust does not make loans, pay off deficits, replace withdrawn or reduced statutory funding or give grants retrospectively. Grants are not given towards any large capital, endowment or widely distributed appeal. It would consider a specific item, or project, making part of a large appeal.

Applications

In writing to the correspondent. Trustees meet in March, June, October and

January. Applications should be kept brief and received one month before the meeting. The trust does not welcome telephone calls.

The Foyle Foundation

Learning, arts, health

£5.1 million (2003/04)
Beneficial area Unrestricted.

Rugby Chambers, 2 Rugby Street, London WC1N 3QU

Tel. 020 7430 9119 **Fax** 020 7430 9830

Email information@foylefoundation.org.uk

Website www.foylefoundation.org.uk
Correspondent David Hall, Chief Executive
Trustees *Silas Krendel, chair; Michael Smith; Kathryn Skoyles.*
Charity Commission no. 1081766
Information available Annual report and accounts, with full grants list, were provided by the trust.

Summary

The foundation makes around 200 grants each year, most of which are for between £5,000 and £50,000, in each of three fields:

- learning
- arts
- health

The normal maximum for an individual grant is £500,000 in any one year; the trustees anticipate making no more than three to five grants a year that will approach this maximum. Large grants such as these may be payable over several years.

The decision that successful applicants for large grants will have to wait three years before another application can be made suggests that there is an intention to spread the grants as widely as possible.

The foundation was formed under the will of the late Christina Foyle. She was the daughter of William Foyle who, with his brother, founded the family owned bookshop Foyles in Charing Cross Road, London, which she continued to manage after her father's death.

Grantmaking objectives

The foundation describes its objectives in its three fields of interest as follows:

Arts

The foundation's aim is to widen the opportunity to enjoy and be stimulated by the arts and to foster creative endeavour. This will be achieved by helping to make the arts more accessible, developing new audiences, supporting tours, festivals, educational projects and by helping to develop new work. Building and infrastructure projects to construct new arts facilities, improve or re-equip existing venues will also be considered.

Learning

The foundation seeks to widen access to education and learning and to raise educational standards. This will include special educational needs, learning difficulties, improving literacy, numeracy and general education. Libraries, museums and archives will be considered. State funded schools may be supported for projects with direct educational impact that cannot be funded from statutory or other available funding. Skills acquisition for employment will not generally be supported.

Health

Applications that are linked to a known medical condition or direct healthcare provision will be supported. The foundation prefers to fund projects or core work that makes an active contribution to improves health care and is not keen on funding advocacy and general support services such as information and leaflet distribution or telephone helplines. The foundation will also support research projects from time to time.

Review of the year

In 2002/03 the foundation received 773 new grant applications, and as 146 applications were brought forward from the previous year, a total of 919 applications needed to be processed.

The trustees met five times during the year to consider applications and 186 new grants were approved totalling £2.9 million, some of which will not be paid out until later financial years. A total of 206 grants were paid out in the year amounting to £3.3 million (taking into consideration previous commitments made). Of the grants paid out, 90 were for the Arts totalling £1,357,000; 61 were for Learning totalling £1,264,000; and 55 were for Health totalling £661,000. In addition, commitments have been made to support a number of organisations in the future (subject to terms and conditions being met), with grants totalling £1,576,000.

Grants in 2002/03

Arts

Beneficiaries during the year included Unicorn Children's Centre – London (£100,000), English National Opera (£75,000), the Arvon Foundation Ltd (£55,000), Glasgow Cultural Enterprises Ltd (£50,000), Spitalfields Festival (£30,000), Chichester Festivities (£25,000), Quicksilver Theatre – London (£20,000), Music for Youth (£15,000), Brighton Festival (£12,000), Drake Music Project Scotland, Horse and Bamboo Theatre – Rossendale, Square Chapel Trust – Halifax and the Fruitmarket Gallery (£10,000 each), Cathedral Quarter Arts Festival (£7,000), Taigh Chearsabhagh Museum and Arts Centre – Outer Hebrides (£6,000) and Burbage Community Arts Festival, Common Ground Sign Dance Theatre – Liverpool, Snibston and Desford Colliery Band – Leicester, Firebird Trust – Lincoln and Woking Dance Festival (£5,000 each).

Learning

The largest grant during the year, as in the previous two years, was £500,000 made to King's College London. This is the third instalment of a £2 million commitment to the creation of the Foyle Special Collections Library in the former Public Records Office building in Chancery Lane. Another substantial grant was again made to the Royal Geographical Society, which received £100,000 during the year. Other beneficiaries included the British Museum Development Trust (£46,000), Nation Centre for Young People with Epilepsy (£25,000), Halifax Learning Zone (£20,000), National Literacy Trust (£15,000), Beamish Development Trust, Foundation for Conductive Education and the Welsh Initiative for Conductive Education (£10,000 each), Hengrove School – Bristol (£6,000), FACT – Liverpool, Milton Hall Primary School – Essex and the Rose Walton Centre (£5,000 each).

Health

Beneficiaries included the Institute of Cancer Research (£50,000), Motor Neurone Disease Association (£35,000), Hearing Research Trust (£25,000), North Devon Hospice (£20,000), Noah's Ark Children's Trust (£15,000), Bobath Children's Therapy Centre Wales and Listening Ear Merseyside (£10,000 each), Positive Vision (£8,000), First Steps to Freedom (£6,000), Elimination of Leukaemia Fund, Mental Aids Projects and Sunbeams Trust (£5,000 each) and

University College London Hospitals Charitable Foundation (£2,500).

Activities in 2003/04

The following review of 2003/04 was provided as this publication went to press:

The number of applications received has steadily risen. 890 new applications were received during this year and 168 applications were brought forward from the previous year. For the current year, if the latest trends continue, the foundation expects to receive up to 1,400 applications.

For the year 2003/04 198 new applications were approved totalling £5.1 million, some of which will be paid out in later financial years.

As shown on our website, 208 grants were paid out amounting to £5.1 million (up substantially from the £3.3 million paid out in the previous year). Of these grants paid out, 93 were for Arts totalling £1.6 million, 64 were for Learning totalling £1.5 million and 50 were for Health totalling £782,000. One special grant for £1.2 million [to the Royal Academy of Music to save the Menuhin Archive from imminent dispersal at auction] was made. The foundation had grant commitments of £1.5 million carried forward into the next year.

As awareness of the foundation has grown over the last three years, more and better regional applications have been received and the foundation was pleased to be able to increase the number of grants awarded to regional projects in this year whilst the total amount paid to London-based projects fell slightly from the previous year. We anticipate this trend to continue.

Exclusions

Once a major award has been made the trust will not normally accept any further applications from the same charity for three years.

No grants to individuals.

No retrospective funding.

Applications

Application forms are available from the correspondent and via the foundation's website, as are checklists and guidelines for applicants.

All applications will be acknowledged within two weeks and all eligible applications should be processed within four months.

The Hugh Fraser Foundation

General

About £1 million (2003/04)

Beneficial area UK, especially western or deprived areas of Scotland.

Turcan Connell, Princes Exchange, 1 Earl Grey Street, Edinburgh EH3 9EE

Tel. 0131 228 8111 **Fax** 0131 228 8118

Email enquiries@turcanconnell.com

Correspondent The Trustees

Trustees *Dr Kenneth Chrystie, Chair; The Hon. Miss Ann Fraser; Miss Patricia Fraser; Blair Smith.*

Scottish Charity no. SC009303

Information available Annual report and accounts are available for £10.

The foundation makes around 300 grants each year, with most for around £3,000. Most grants are said to be made in Scotland, but this has not been confirmed.

Grants are probably made in almost all fields of charity.

The trustees' description of their policy has changed in that it no longer says that 'applications from other parts of Britain and Northern Ireland are considered'.

The trustees' policy is to pay special regard to applications from the west of Scotland and applications from those parts of Scotland where the local economy makes it more difficult to raise funds for charitable purposes.

The trustees consider that grants to large highly publicised national appeals are not likely to be as effective a use of funds as grants to smaller and more focused charitable appeals.

The trustees also consider that better use of funds can be made by making grants to charitable bodies to assist them with their work, than by making a large number of grants to individuals.

The trustees are prepared to enter into commitments over a period of time by making grants in successive years, often to assist in new initiatives which can maintain their own momentum once they have been established for a few years.

The foundation makes donations to charities working in many different sectors, principally hospitals, schools and universities, arts organisations and organisations working with the handicapped, the underprivileged and the aged.

The trustees are nevertheless prepared to consider applications from charities working in other fields.

Elsewhere the trust reports that it makes grants principally for:

- medical facilities;
- medical research;
- the relief of poverty;
- assistance to the aged and infirm;
- education and learning;
- encouragement of personal development and training of young people;
- provision of better opportunities for the less privileged and vulnerable;
- encouragement of music and the arts.

Exclusions

Grants are not awarded to individuals. Major highly publicised appeals are rarely supported.

Applications

In writing to the correspondent. The trustees meet on a quarterly basis to consider applications.

The Joseph Strong Frazer Trust

General

£332,000 (2002/03)

Beneficial area England and Wales only.

Scottish Provident House, 31 Mosley Street, Newcastle Upon Tyne NE1 1HX

Tel. 0191 232 8065 **Fax** 0191 222 1554

Correspondent The Correspondent

Trustees *Sir William A Reardon Smith, chair; D A Cook; R M H Read; W N H Reardon Smith; W I Waites.*

Charity Commission no. 235311

Information available Annual report and accounts with no analysis of grantmaking.

Established in 1939, the trust has general charitable purposes, with broad interests in the fields of social welfare, education, religion and wildlife. Recipients are based all over England and Wales. It appears flexible in its ability to consider applications, with its grant making policy described as follows:

It is the aim of the trustees to support a wide number of good causes and charitable objects and make best use of its resources. Applications for grants are considered by the trustees and distributions are made where it is thought most appropriate and effective.

In 2002/03 it had assets of £9.2 million and an income of £4 million, mainly derived from its trading subsidiary The Great British Bollard Company Limited. There were 256 grants made totalling £332,000. These were categorised as follows:

	No.	Amount
Medical and other research	46	£65,000
Caring organisations	31	£42,000
Children	32	£41,000
Other trusts, funds and voluntary organisations	30	£37,000
Deaf and blind	18	£28,000
Hospitals and home (and connected activities)	18	£28,000
Disabled	15	£17,000
Leisure activities, animals and wildlife	11	£15,500
Maritime	12	£12,500
Youth	11	£11,000
Schools and colleges	6	£9,500
Old and infirm	6	£9,000
Mentally handicapped	6	£8,000
Religious bodies	7	£7,500
Armed forces	3	£4,000

Grants of over £2,000 were listed in the accounts, and went to 70 organisations totalling £141,000.

The largest grants were given to Children's Hospice in Wales Appeal Limited (£5,000), MHOSLJ Charitable Trust and Royal Merchant Navy School Foundation (£3,000 each) and Covent Garden Cancer Research Trust, Hill Homes, National Botanic Garden of Wales and Welsh College of Music and Drama (£2,500 each).

All other listed grants were for £2,000 each. Beneficiaries included Army Benevolent Fund, Boar Bank Nursing Home, Contact – London, Fairbridge, Hearing Dogs for the Deaf, Mencap, NSPCC, Partially Sighted Society, Reed's School, Scope, Sparks and Whitefield Development Trust.

A total of £191,000 was distributed in 186 grants under £2,000 each.

Exclusions

No grants to individuals.

Applications

In writing to the correspondent. Trustees meet twice a year, usually in March and September. Application forms are not necessary. It is helpful if applicants are concise in their appeal letters, which must include an sae if acknowledgement is required.

The Freshfield Foundation

Environment, general

See below

Beneficial area UK, with a preference for Merseyside.

2nd Floor, MacFarlane and Co., Cunard Building, Water Street, Liverpool L3 1DS

Tel. 0151 236 6161 **Fax** 0151 236 1095

Email paulk@macca.co.uk

Correspondent Paul Kurthausen

Trustees P A Moores; A Moores; Mrs E J Potter.

Charity Commission no. 1003316

Information available Accounts are on file at the Charity Commission.

The Freshfield Foundation was established in 1991. It was accumulating income in its early years and only began to make grants in 1997/98. In 2002/03 it had an income of £348,000 and a total expenditure of £4.2 million, an increase of over £3.5 million on the previous year. Unfortunately, no further details were available for this year.

Over the past five years the trust has received an income in excess of £10 million. It is perhaps the case that only a few large grants are made every other year. Previous large grants include £3 million to the Formby Land Trust for the purchase of land to house a swimming pool for local residents.

Comment

There was no response to repeated requests for a copy of the most recent annual report and accounts, despite the requirement to provide these on demand.

Despite ample warning, and their obligation to the contrary, the Charity Commission were unable to give us sight of this trust's accounts.

Applications

In writing to the correspondent.

The Gannochy Trust

General

£2.5 million (2003/04)

Beneficial area Scotland, with a preference for the Perth area.

Kincarrathie House Drive, Pitcullen Crescent, Perth PH2 7HX

Tel. 01738 620653

Correspondent Murdoch MacKenzie, Administrator

Trustees *Dr Russell Leather, chair; Mark Webster; Dr James H F Kynaston; Dr James Watson; Ian W McMillan; Stewart N Macleod.*

Scottish Charity no. SC003133

Information available Annual report and accounts, with a full list of beneficiaries were provided by the trust.

The trust concentrates on the needs of 'youth and recreation', but supports a wide range of causes. It had an endowment of £104 million in 2003/04, derived from the personal fortune of Arthur Kinmond Bell, whisky distiller, and produced an income of £4.2 million. It makes a large number of grants, 213 of them in 2003/04 totalling £2.5 million, of which 110 were for amounts of £5,000 or less. They were classified as follows, with the percentages referring to the value of the grants:

Arts	32%
Health	19%
Recreation	16%
Education	14%
Social welfare	12%
Environment	7%

Major grants were:

- £900,000 to Perth & Kinross Leisure – £800,000 by way of the final instalment towards the establishment of the new Perth Concert Hall, £100,000 towards the renovation and repair of community facilities in the Perth area and £90,000 towards sports coaching for young people.
- £300,000 to University of Edinburgh Research Institute for Medical Cell Biology Project towards the provision of an imaging suite.
- £250,000 to Kelvingrove Art Galley & Museum.
- £204,000 to the Royal Society of Edinburgh to cover the cost of establishing the Gannochy Trust Innovation Award.
- £135,000 to the Perth & Kinross Countryside Trust over two years for the development and upkeep of the

rural heritage of the Perth countryside.

- £132,000 to the Kincarrathie Trust towards refurbishment and maintenance at Kincarrathie Home for the Elderly – Perth.
- £100,000 to Perth & Kinross Heritage Trust for the upkeep and preservation of local heritage.
- £100,000 to the University of Glasgow – British Heart Foundation Cardiovascular Research Centre.

Other larger grants included £50,000 to Auchterarder Gymnastics Trust, £30,000 to Guide Association Scotland, £25,000 to Compass Christian Centre Ltd, £20,000 to Children First, £18,000 to DEBRA, £15,000 to Fairbridge in Scotland, £12,000 each to Portessie Public Hall and RSNO Junior Choir and £10,000 each to British Sports Trust, Craignish Village Hall, Leonard Cheshire Foundation in Scotland, Perth & Kinross Music Foundation, Scottish Motor Neurone Disease Association and Scottish Sports Futures.

Other beneficiaries included Scottish Huntingdon's Association (£8,000), Fife Folk Museum Trust (£7,500), Abbeyfield Ballachulist Society and National Youth Choir of Scotland (£7,000 each), Perth Choral Society (£6,000), Cornerstone Community Care and Move On Limited (£5,000 each), YMCA Coupar Angus (£4,000), Mull & Iona Community Trust (£3,000), Aberdeen International Children's Festival (£2,000), Kilmadock Development Trust Limited – Doune (£1,500) and Moray & Nairn Sea Cadets (£1,000).

Exclusions

No grants to individuals. Donations are confined to organisations recognised by the Inland Revenue as charitable.

Applications

In writing to the correspondent, confined to two pages of A4 including:

- a general statement on the objects of the applicant's charity;
- the specific nature of the application;
- the estimated cost and how this is arrived at;
- the contribution of the applicant's charity towards the cost;
- the contributions of others, actual and promised;
- estimated shortfall;
- details of previous appeals to the trust – whether accepted or rejected;
- a copy of the latest audited accounts.

It will be helpful to extract the following information from the accounts:

- income
- expenditure
- reserves
  – committed
  – uncommitted.

Auditors' reservations, if any, should be explained. 'It is the practice of the trustees to scrutinise accounts before making donations.' Time rarely permits visits either to the trust office or to the charity concerned. The trustees meet frequently, generally monthly, to consider appeals.

The Gatsby Charitable Foundation

General

£33.3 million (2003/04)

Beneficial area Unrestricted.

Allington House, 1st Floor, 150 Victoria Street, London SW1E 5AE

Tel. 020 7410 0330 **Fax** 020 7410 0332

Email contact@gatsby.org.uk

Website www.gatsby.org.uk

Correspondent Michael Pattison, Director

Trustees *Christopher Stone; Andrew Cahn; Miss Judith Portrait.*

Charity Commission no. 251988

Information available Excellent annual report and accounts were provided by the trust.

Summary

This is one of the Sainsbury Family Charitable Trusts, which share a joint administration. It supports organisations that aim to advance policy and practice within its selected areas, usually by means of practically-oriented research.

The foundation is proactive and seldom responds to conventional short-term applications – 'trustees generally do not make grants in response to unsolicited appeals' – but it does expect organisations to respond to its published long-term priorities: 'the trustees identify first the areas where they sense that something needs to be done. They hope organisations will respond to these priorities and propose projects.'

Specific areas of support, which are set out later in this entry, come under the general headings shown in the table (to which have been added the percentage of the foundation's funding over ten years from 1994 to 2004 and the value of grant payments in 2003/04):

	1994–2004	2003/04
Technical education	27%	£9,825,000
Plant science	15%	£3,962,000
Mental health	13%	£3,249,000
Disadvantaged children	11%	£5,308,000
Developing countries (mainly Africa)	10%	£3,973,000
Economic and social research	8%	£696,000
The arts	7%	£4,135,000
Cognitive neuroscience	4%	£1,536,000
General	3%	£28,000
Local economic renewal	2%	£871,000

There are big annual fluctuations in the size of its new awards each year to different categories of work because of the large multi-year funding commitments decided by the foundation.

Background

This is one of the largest and most interesting grantmaking trusts in the UK, with an income of over £20 million a year. It allocates large sums to long-term programmes and so the figure for yearly grant approvals fluctuates considerably.

The foundation was set up in 1967 by David Sainsbury, created life peer and Lord Sainsbury of Turville in 1997. He is now a Labour minister with the Department of Trade and Industry. He himself has never been a trustee of Gatsby but is still contributing massively to the endowment of the trust, and it is generally supposed that the trustees pay close attention to the settlor's wishes.

Most of the foundation's investments are in the form of shares in the Sainsbury company. While such a lack of diversity inevitably exposes the foundation to unusually high investment risks, these have been more than outweighed recently by the foundation not being affected by the recent stock market bubble and its pricing.

The staff of the foundation in 2004 included:

Michael Pattison, director (as of all the Sainsbury family trusts)

Peter Hesketh, deputy director

Dr Yvonne Pinto, executive

Matthew Williams, executive

Victoria Hornby, executive

Mr Williams is known for his involvement, no doubt among other things, in support for disadvantaged children. Victoria Hornby concentrates on social exclusion and overseas activities.

General

The work of the foundation is described in its annual report for 2003/04 which starts with an overview of its work. The grantmaking in the year is then reviewed.

Introduction to the Gatsby Foundation

From the annual report for 2003/04

This is a good moment to reflect on the roles which can and should be undertaken by privately endowed grantmaking trusts. They should be recognised as a mechanism through which philanthropy can be practised systematically, in a disciplined and businesslike way and within which expertise in the giving of money can be developed.

Our report this year has been prepared against the backdrop of parliamentary scrutiny of a draft Charities Bill. As we go to press, the Bill has been included in the Queen's speech for introduction in the parliamentary session beginning in November 2004. As matters stand, the draft Bill proposes considerably increased powers for the Charity Commission. It offers no new incentives, nor even encouragement, for our society to support philanthropy. Gatsby's Trustees are pleased to see that parliament's pre-legislative scrutiny committee has made a firm recommendation that this oversight should be corrected in the final version of the Bill.

Part of the context for this draft Bill is that government ministers are showing a keen interest in the scope for using service-providing charities to take over services which have not prospered in public sector management. There is merit in the idea that some charities can work closer to the ground than public sector agencies but also a threat in the idea that the unit cost for delivery of such services can continuously be driven downwards.

In the twelve months since our last annual report was published, the Trustees have observed the voluntary or compulsory liquidation of several charities which they had long supported. It is perhaps prescient that in one case we noted in an earlier annual report that the kind of success demonstrated by the charity carried with it 'direct costs which will always exceed the unit cost targets set by the main publicly funded bodies dealing with vocational education. It is a source of continuing frustration that such programmes cannot be costed through a model which considers the wider economic and social benefits of equipping someone to earn an independent living, even where the initial investment in this process is likely to be higher than the norm for people who have a better start in life.'

The Trustees continue to believe that the best role for grantmaking trusts in the area of service for disadvantaged people is:

- to test the boundaries of current assumptions about how to provide such service;
- to develop new models;
- to prove the concepts and, when that is achieved, to demonstrate how services can be scaled up.

Beyond that, it should not be the standard model that charitable funding supports the further development of services, which in most cases will be purchased through the public purse in some form or other.

If charities are to fulfil the role of testing models of service and new ideas, they need funding of a kind which can encourage those processes and which is not necessarily beholden to targets or even philosophy laid down by government. The Gatsby Trustees aim to be in a position to provide such funding. The testimonials included in this report from some of the Foundation's beneficiaries suggest that the Trustees have succeeded, in at least some cases. That is why Gatsby's Trustees believe firmly that there is a valuable role within civil society for independent funding which can be used to back interesting ideas put forward by, or developed in partnership with, a whole range of charities or people and organisations engaged in charitable activity. Yet the Trustees observe an increasing volume of reporting and compliance requirements which achieve little other than to distract them from their main role: testing new ways of meeting a whole range of needs in our society. Instead, they are diverted towards bureaucratic compliance requirements which seem to them to have marginal if any relevance to their main objects as charities.

Many of these requirements are undoubtedly driven by occasional experiences of poor practice or worse within individual charities, but usually in charities that are not remotely comparable with privately endowed grantmakers. Other compliance requirements seem to be driven by little more than the parochial interests of some of the professional groups, which define reporting and accounting formats showing total disregard for the underlying philosophies of trusts that are designed to put private funds to public service.

So while the Gatsby Charitable Foundation identifies some significant success by charities it has supported, in addition to some valuable work in testing ideas, even where those do not prove fruitful, the Trustees find that the climate of regulation around charities like Gatsby is becoming more and more challenging. Definitions of best practice multiply. Sometimes the imposition of these definitions have a statutory basis and on other occasions the best practice is used as a compliance test by regulators. Yet the very nature of a grantmaking charity with the kind of agenda adopted by Gatsby's Trustees is just that it should be willing to think and act unconventionally, not simply conforming to conventional definitions of best practice. Our judgement is that much of the supposed best practice is drawn up in the context of service-providing charities. Its one-size-fits-all application can be at least irrelevant and at worst positively harmful to the desirable objective of drawing more funds into charitable work through grantmaking trusts and foundations.

The Trustees recognise that privately endowed grantmakers have probably done too little to make their case for the value of their role in civil society and therefore for proper recognition that effective and proportionate regulation of their activities needs to be undertaken in ways which recognise their distinctive character by comparison with many other forms of charity. It is not surprising that this small group of charities has done so little to make its case. It is part of the British tradition that personal philanthropy has been a discreet activity on the part of most donors. This philosophy has been carried through into the style of trusts and foundations created by such donors. Those donors are often distinctly uncomfortable with a changed climate where donors are mistrusted if they do not wish to publicise their activity. Here again, regulators need to understand the origins of this philosophy and the grantmakers need to explain and justify.

The Gatsby Trustees can approach all this on the basis of a record as custodians of a charity which has given away well over £400 million in some 35 years. With over £100 million in additional funds already committed to beneficiary charities and medium-term plans to continue their existing programme areas, the Trustees hope to see many more grantmaking trusts growing in this country to improve on that record. They also plan to maintain and improve on their own record of giving in the decades ahead. They welcome newcomers who are already making a contribution but they sense a complete lack of understanding – and fear a lack of real interest – amongst the policymakers and regulators about how to create a climate to encourage the kind of generosity shown by Gatsby's own settlor.

Review of activities 2003/04

During the year grants were made totalling £33.3 million, with over £25.9 million more approved for payment. The following section includes excerpts from the review, to which have been added examples of payments in the year. Note that these payments are not the same as the total value of the grant or programme, for which payment will often be spread out over a number of years.

In the year under review, the trustees continued the policy of reinforcing their commitment to the major themes of their programme. The bulk of both payments and new awards underline their long-term commitment to work they have agreed to support. At the same time they increased their emphasis on drawing together the evidence generated by several programmes, and collaborated with opinion leaders to ensure that such evidence could be fed into the policy process. Their education programmes have been supplemented by work with the Royal Society's Education Committee and the relatively new Advisory Committee on Mathematics Education; their technology transfer work by a programme of analysis of the full range of this work through the Freeman Centre at Sussex University and Brighton University. Similarly, the trustees' programmes in sub-Saharan Africa have been widened to include partnerships with the Rockefeller Foundation and others to build on the success of Gatsby-funded projects over the past decade.

Elsewhere, the trustees have made new commitments for work in fields that have been identified as gaps in coverage within themes which are already part of their programme. In mental health, for example, they have funded a new project through the London Borough of Greenwich to look beyond the personal challenges faced by people with mental health problems and towards the impact on dependants and carers, in this case particularly the situation with children where a parent has a serious mental health problem.

The trustees have been concerned for several years about the apparent decline in non-statutory sources of funding for challenging work in fields where charitable funding can be relevant. They have therefore made a substantial commitment to helping to unlock one possible new source of funding, in the form of unclaimed assets held in a range of financial institutions. The work of the Balance Charitable Foundation *[which has its own entry here - ed.]* is a substantial response to an important opportunity, to set alongside other work recently funded by Gatsby on attitudes to philanthropy.

During the year trustees met eight times to make grants and twice to review investments. During this year trustees approved grants totalling £59.23 million. This is an increase of over £23 million or nearly 64% on the previous year and is the highest value of grants approved in a single year since the inception of the foundation. Grants approved but unpaid brought forward from the previous year amounted to

£77.96 million which taken together with those approved in this financial year totalled £137.19 million.

Grants paid during the year from the total above amounted to £33.35 million (2002/03: £30.83 million) leaving unpaid commitments at the end of the year of £102.43 million. The trustees expect to pay the majority of these grants from the income of future years. As in previous years, the size of grant approved varied widely from £50 to £12 million.

This is the third year in which the accounts have been prepared under SORP 2000. To comply with those requirements, trustees have accrued both the full unpaid balances of awards made with a binding legal commitment and the sums which, in their best judgement, will be paid in the next financial year from other awards. Although the majority of these payments will be made from future income streams, the accrual treatment required by SORP erases the balance of £5.42 million brought forward on the unrestricted fund producing in its place a negative balance of £9.5 million. In a similar vein, net current liabilities increased from £31.1 million to £53.99 million.

As a result of these accounting conventions, the overall net assets value of the foundation recorded in this year's accounts increased by just over £36 million, although investment values increased by £60.58 million.

Trustees have commented previously that this accounting treatment does not reflect the real financial strength of the foundation, nor their prudent management of the foundation's resources. At the year end Gatsby held cash and near cash investments on its income amounting to £50.13 million, in addition to its expendable endowment of more than £321 million.

Investment income was marginally ahead of 2002/03 at £19.15 million (2002/03: £18.89 million) and further generous donations from the settlor of £16.24 million increased income overall to £35.39 million. Support and administration costs reduced this to £33.55 million net available for grantmaking, a sum coincidentally very close to the payments made in the year. Many endowed charities have found it difficult or have been unable to maintain the level of grantmaking in real terms in the last few years. One of the reasons for this has been the staged withdrawal over five years of recoverable tax credits on UK dividends, the transitional scheme finally ending on 5 April 2004. Over 80% of Gatsby's investments are UK equities and, despite the loss of these credits, in this period the trustees have increased the value of grants awarded. The trustees have retained cash, in significant amounts, as a reserve against future payments.

The costs of running the foundation, comprising support and administration costs, amounted to 5.2% of total income. Last year the equivalent figure was 4.6%, but that figure only reflected the running costs for nine months in the leased premises from which the foundation now operates.

The foundation held shares in J Sainsbury with a market value of £275.81 million at the year end. On 26 July 2004, Gatsby received a special distribution in cash from the company following the sale of its US business. The distribution amounted to £35 million and this sum has been added to the foundation's expendable endowment. The trustees intend to use part of the distribution in their grantmaking programme and gradually to invest the balance as part of their diversification strategy. J Sainsbury also consolidated its shares on the basis of seven new shares for eight originally held. This consolidation is an important factor for the trustees to take into account in their planning assumptions on future investment income.

After the financial year end, J Sainsbury announced that its dividend would be reduced by 50% with effect from the interim payable in January 2005. Although Gatsby derives a significant proportion of its income from that source, trustees intend to maintain grantmaking at the average level of the past few years. Gatsby has substantial expendable endowment which can be used for grantmaking should the trustees decide to do so, as well as other sources of income.

Technical education: [39 larger grants. Total grants: £9,825,000]

'To support improvement in educational opportunity in the UK for a workforce which can better apply technology for wealth creation; and to encourage effective technology transfer from universities and other research centres to productive industry.'

The trustees seek to achieve this aim through programmes:

- to encourage good teaching and good materials in schools in mathematics, science and technology as an essential prerequisite to the health of the manufacturing base
- to encourage appropriate IT development which will enhance mathematics, science and technology in schools
- to ensure that the courses and the awards are respected and valued by industry, parents and students
- to encourage the most able technologists to enter manufacturing industry both at professional and technician level
- to encourage technology transfer between universities and industry.

The trustees have established a separate charity, Gatsby Technical Education Projects (GTEP) (www.gtep.co.uk), to develop and manage a range of projects designed to enrich and enhance learning through:

- subject support for initial teacher training courses;
- professional development for teachers in science, mathematics and technology; and
- curriculum support materials.

GTEP is funded by Gatsby to carry out a number of projects where the trustees have not identified a suitable outside agency. GTEP also administers Gatsby funding where the trustees have made grants to other organisations.

Sample grants included:

University of Cambridge (£2,514,000) – for the CMI Initiative, the Cambridge Foundation, the Faculty of Education and the Institute of Manufacturing.

Gatsby Technical Education Projects (£2,408,000) – towards the Teacher Effectiveness Enhancement, Science Enhancement, Mathematics Enhancement, Headteacher Enhancement, Headteacher Management, Early Years, Primary-Secondary Transition, Physics Enhancement and Gatsby Teacher Fellows programmes. Also for GTEP core office costs.

Royal Academy of Engineering (£1,160,000) – towards the Best programme: development of other training opportunities in engineering, science and life sciences programmes, and the Sainsbury Management Fellowship scheme.

University of Warwick (£1,012,000) – towards the Technology Enhancement Programme and the mathematics subject-enhanced PGCE course.

East Middlesbrough Education Action Zone (£124,000) – towards partnership funding for a school collegiate project.

University of York (£87,000) – towards the development of the Primary Science Enhancement Programme and participation in a Russian satellite initiative.

University of Nottingham (£81,000) – towards postdoctoral Business Science fellowships.

Grants of less than £50,000 each included those to University of Greenwich (£49,000), Science Engineering Technology & Mathematics Network (£40,000), University of Wales (£33,000), Imperial College (£25,000) and Biosciences Federation (£15,000).

Disadvantaged children: [21 grants totalling £5,308,000]

'To explore new approaches to early diagnoses of barriers to personal development.'

The trustees have three main interests:
- language and communication development
- exclusion from school or family life
- mental health.

Trustees believe that to test an idea thoroughly requires a long-term approach and therefore support is mainly directed to a small number of organisations for ongoing, evolving programmes.

Language and Communication Development

Since 2000, the trustees have supported an action research project to test a new, bottom-up approach to encourage communication development in pre-school children and get expert help more quickly and frequently. This is a national project based round a number of local parent-professional research partnerships. This year the project established itself as an independent charity in its own right, Big Wide Talk [£868,000 in 2003/04]. Through a series of national demonstration events, the project has developed a series of activities containing powerful and unobtrusive ways to assess individual children's communication development that can be run locally.

Exclusion from School or Family Life

The National Children's Bureau (NCB), to which the trustees give a substantial grant for a portfolio of work [£1,476,000] based around the Children's Residential Care Unit, Pupil Inclusion Unit and Research Department, published the evaluation of Taking Care of Education. This was the conclusion of a project run by NCB with three local authorities (Derby, Portsmouth and Harrow) to improve participation in school or further education by children in care of their local authority. The project showed that it is possible to achieve a focus on the education of children in public care across a whole local authority and that this improves children's educational opportunities and self-confidence. Trustees made a second round of grants to the three local authorities to embed the project work into their everyday business.

Trustees continued their core funding for the ACE Centre Advisory Trust, Oxford [£449,000], which provides multidisciplinary guidance to parents and professionals on supporting children who use mechanical and electronic devices to communicate. They also made a grant to ACE North, a sister charity based in Oldham, and grants to both ACE Centres to improve joint working on national policy and practice development

and co-ordination of their research and training portfolios.

Other beneficiaries included: I CAN towards extending programmes and starting more Early Years nurseries (£1 million), Foyer Federation (£245,000), Speech, Language & Hearing Centre (£100,000), Who Cares? Trust (£50,000), Auditory Verbal UK (£44,000) and Artswork (£15,000).

Plant science: [13 larger grants. Total grants: £3,962,000]

'To develop basic research in fundamental processes of plant growth and development and molecular plant pathology and to encourage young researchers in this field in the UK and to support improved introduction to the world of plants within school science teaching.'

The Sainsbury Laboratory

The Sainsbury Laboratory, located at the John Innes Centre on the Norwich Research Park, continues to be the major focus for the trustees' funding in this category [£3,089,000 in 2003/04]. Established some 16 years ago, and now a company limited by guarantee and a registered charity in its own right, it continues to undertake world-class research into the right interaction at the molecular level between plants and their pathogens.

At present six teams conduct research in a number of significant fields, including plant-fungal interactions, cell death signalling, key proteomic technologies, disease resistance gene function, plant symbiotic signalling and gene silencing.

In 2003, an international peer review of the third five-year research cycle confirmed the scientific excellence of the research, justifying the laboratory's worldwide reputation in molecular plant pathology.

Scottish Crops Research Institute

The trustees have supported a novel project on functional genomics of plant-cell organelles [£89,000]. This enables genes which are responsible for particular characteristics to be isolated, characterised and sequenced. The methods employed allow rapid screening of large numbers of genes and add wealth to our knowledge of the function of these genes within plant cells.

Plant Science Network

The trustees continue their support for undergraduate and postgraduate studentship programmes aimed at supporting students of the highest calibre to develop and sustain an interest in plant science research. Research areas include fundamental processes of plant growth and development and molecular plant pathology.

On the basis of success with the first Gatsby Interdisciplinary Research Fellowship, the trustees have agreed to support a second series [£52,000]. The aim is to support an outstanding research scientist who wishes to apply skills learned with other organisms to studies with plants.

The Annual Plant Science Network Meeting continues to be well attended by students, alumni, supervisors and advisers. This year's meeting, which was held in Magdalen College, University of Oxford, was attended by 28 students. Looking ahead, the trustees also agreed to support the first annual undergraduate summer school in 2005, which will be a week's residential course for up to 180 undergraduates at the end of their first year of research. The school will provide an introduction to new exciting areas of plant science and will allow a community to develop amongst plant science lecturers.

Science and Plants for Schools

SAPS works with teachers, trainee teachers and students to stimulate interest in the plant sciences and molecular biology [£276,000 in 2003/04]. The delivery of professional development courses is an important part of SAPS's activity and this year has seen a large increase (some 40%) in the number of workshops run throughout the UK. The activities are well received as evidenced by feedback from participants. Further information can be found at www.saps.plantsci.cam.ac.uk

Other grants included those to the universities of Glasgow (£33,000), Cambridge (£30,000) and Leeds (£19,500).

The arts: [6 grants listed. Total grants: £4,135,000]

'To support the fabric and programming of institutions with which Gatsby's founding family has long connections.'

The most important development in the period was the planning of a year's closure of the Sainsbury Centre for the Visual Arts at the University of East Anglia. This is in preparation for a project which will combine what is effectively a 25-year service of this innovative building with the addition of an important new architectural feature which will provide an integral link between the original main section and the later Crescent Wing. The building is, in practice, itself the principal object in the collection it houses, and the Trustees are please to join with the University of East Anglia and the Robert and Lisa Sainsbury Charitable Trust in this important renewal project [£47,500 in 2003/04].

Most of the money in this category, as in the previous year, was awarded to Royal Shakespeare Company (£3.2 million)

towards staff posts and project costs. Along with the Sainsbury Centre for the Visual Arts, other beneficiaries included Robert and Lisa Sainsbury Charitable Trust (£270,000), Chamber Orchestra of Europe (£250,000) and the Unicorn Theatre (£100,000).

Developing countries: [27 larger grants. Total grants: £3,973,000]

'To promote environmentally sustainable development and poverty alleviation through selected programmes aimed at supporting basic agriculture and other enterprise in selected African countries.'

Since the 1980s the trustees have supported a small number of targeted poverty alleviation programmes in selected African countries. The themes are support for small-scale enterprise in East Africa and Cameroon, the enhancement of education in South Africa, and the search for sustainable agricultural development in eastern, western and southern Africa. In all three themes the trustees seek to work through long-term relationships with organisations offering capacity to develop and deliver high-quality projects. In the case of small-scale enterprise support, four local micro-finance trusts have been established.

Small-scale enterprise support

Access to basic financial services still remains a problem for most people and small businesses in disadvantaged or isolated areas. Through their support for the development of four micro-finance trusts in Cameroon, Kenya, Tanzania and Uganda, the trustees have been able to contribute to the growth of many small businesses. The trusts themselves have been able to look broadly at the needs of people running small businesses and test out ways of helping them to ensure their long-term sustainability. In the early 1990s the Uganda Gatsby Trust pioneered the creation of technology transfer programmes for small entrepreneurs. This work, in collaboration with Makerere University in Kampala, is now being replicated by the other trusts, in varying forms and to the benefit of universities and small businesses alike.

Agricultural research

Gatsby's support for agricultural research is geared to increasing the physical yields of small farms, and the nutritional and market value of subsistence crops, in ways which are both valuable to low-income households and environmentally sustainable. The trustees aim to achieve this by supporting projects along a spectrum which includes applied research at institute level, extends to programmes for the dissemination of improved varieties and cropping systems and includes support for seed production and the propagation of improved planting material.

Over the past 15 years Gatsby has been fortunate to work with many gifted African institutions and individuals both in co-funding projects and in the development of entirely new initiatives. Earlier this year, trustees decided to formalise this experience and create an institution to able to build on the strengths and vision of African agriculturalists.

The Kilimo Trust

Over the coming year Gatsby aims to create a new charitable trust dedicated to the growth and progress of agriculture in East Africa. Like the micro-finance trusts, the Kilimo Trust will be governed and managed locally by people with outstanding vision and expertise. The Kilimo Trust will take responsibility for the continued progress of a number of the projects which the trustees currently support, such as the Maendeleo Agricultural Technology Fund, as well as developing new projects and programmes that will be able to address some of the most fundamental barriers to the success of agriculture in East Africa. Gatsby believes that providing the support for these initiatives to be led by African agriculturalists is an important step forward.

International Institute of Tropical Agriculture, Nigeria

Gatsby has had a long association with the International Institute of Tropical Agriculture (IITA) where it has supported research programmes on bananas, cowpeas, yams and rice over the past 14 years [£337,000 in 2003/04].

Some exciting developments have been the identification of molecular markers in cowpeas, which are associated with resistance to bruchid beetles, aphids, drought and Striga witchweed, which has enabled the development of practical tools for plant breeders to improve local cowpea varieties and their availability to farmers. Similar work to disseminate high yielding varieties of yams has been undertaken in partnership with a number of national agricultural research centres in West Africa.

Whilst much of the work has retained a crop-based focus, Gatsby has also supported the expansion of projects which concentrate on a holistic crop-livestock farming system which can make a significant and positive contribution to food security, health and nutrition, income generation and natural resource conservation. The trustees are currently supporting a programme focusing on cowpeas and livestock in the Nigerian states of Kano and Kaduna, which is proving highly successful.

South Africa

Trustees continue to support educational initiatives in mathematics and science in the Western Cape responding to the challenges of emerging educational policies. This support has primarily been realised through the Scientific and Industrial Leadership Initiative (SAILI) [£643,000 in 2003/04], which aims to increase the pool of individuals with access to tertiary education from disadvantaged backgrounds.

This year trustees also gave their support to the launch of the African Institute for Mathematical Sciences (AIMS) [£88,000], a collaborative initiative at the University of Stellenbosch, the Western Cape and with support from the University of Cambridge in the UK. The initial focus has been the provision of a postgraduate diploma in mathematics. The programme is open to both recent graduates and practicing teachers and particularly targets those from disadvantaged backgrounds. AIMS has attracted the support of some of the world's leading international mathematicians and lecturers and in the longer term hopes to offer both doctoral and postdoctoral programmes.

The trustees are advised on the African programmes by Mr Laurence Cockroft.

Other beneficiaries of large grants in this category were William Jefferson Clinton Presidential Foundation (£543,000), International Centre of Insect Physiology and Ecology – Kenya (£295,000) and the Legal Resource Centre – South Africa (£112,000).

Mental health : [10 grants totalling £3,249,000]

'To improve the quality of life for people with long-term problems by improved delivery of services.'

Sainsbury Centre for Mental Health (SCMH)

Under the leadership of Dr Matt Muijen, Chief Executive, SCMH has been at the forefront of innovation and reform in mental health policy and practice. The trustees strive to achieve this through three key themes:
- empowering service users;
- building a workforce; and
- designing better services.

Dr Muijen stepped down from his post in March 2004 and the trustees would like to express their thanks to him for his major contribution to the success and development of SCMH.

Empowering Service Users

SCMH developed, with the University of Warwick's Department of Philosophy and Medical School, a new learning and skills framework for values-based practice, including the groundbreaking workbook Whose Values?. This sets out how to make working with values a foundation stone for effective practice. In particular, how an appreciation of different values helps resolve tensions, promote recovery and social inclusion and deliver a better service.

Building a Workforce

A Mental Health Workforce for the Future, a 'how to' guide based on two years of research, set out a new, practical approach to workforce planning which matches staff skills and experience to the creation, with the National Institute for Mental Health, of a national unit to support workforce development.

Designing Better Services

SCMH set out for managers and practitioners how to plan, set up and run a high-quality early intervention service for people experiencing their first episode of psychosis. SCMH also highlighted the cost pressures preventing local service managers from meeting national targets for better mental health services, and showed that under-investment in mental health services costs us more as a society than the economic effects of crime.

Prof. Howard Goldman, National Institute of Mental Health (USA) advises the trustees on mental health.

The SCMH received almost £2.9 million from Gatsby in 2003/04. There were nine other grants made, including those to Mental Health Media (£94,000), University of Wales College of Medicine (£50,000), First Step Trust (£36,000) and the British Urological Foundation (£25,000).

Cognitive neuroscience: [5 grants totalling £1,536,000]

'To support world-class research in UK centres of excellence.'

The trustees continue to remain committed to the nurturing and expansion of cognitive and systems neuroscience in the UK, their main focus being the Gatsby Computational Neuroscience Unit (www.gatsby.ucl.ac.uk) and associated grants at University College London. This year, the unit's most important task has been the recruitment of an additional faculty to broaden and deepen the range of the Unit in theoretical neuroscience. The new faculty members cover two key, but under-represented areas: the analysis of neural spiking data and neural dynamics.

Gatsby Computational Neuroscience Unit received £969,000 in 2003/04. The other beneficiaries were University College London (£380,000), University of Cambridge Cavendish Laboratory (£141,000), University of Bristol Department of Psychology (£17,500) and Winchester Festival of Art and the Mind (£15,000).

Economic and social research: [7 larger grants were made. Grants totalled: £696,000]

'To support institutions and individual studies which can help us to understand and improve our society.'

This year trustees continued their support for several long-running beneficiaries. They also built up their commitment to promoting the wider cause of philanthropy in this country. For this purpose, they increased their funding for the Association of Charitable Foundation's Philanthropy UK project in its final year. This has now brought together a valuable, continuing network of people pursuing the subject and produced an important research publication in the form of Theresa Lloyd's book Why Rich People Give. The whole area deserves much more attention and encouragement if Britain is to retain a vibrant charitable sector.

In further pursuit of this aim the trustees were pleased to play a major part in the funding of the Balance initiative, a systematic effort to release unclaimed assets held in financial institutions with little prospect of rightful owners ever appearing to claim the assets. The subject has been examined from time to time over the years but the novelty in the Balance approach comes in the form of discussions with the insurance industry which have confirmed that potential future claims from legitimate owners can be handled by insurance, thereby removing any justification for holding these assets within the institutions in which they have lain dormant for some time. The first moves for release of some of the funds are in progress, and the initiative has had welcome encouragement from the Chancellor of the Exchequer, but much more remains to be done if the momentum generated so far is to be turned into a much-needed new flow of resources for charitable activity. [The Balance Foundation for Unclaimed Assets is now active and has its own entry here - Ed.]

The Balance initiative received £254,000 from Gatsby in 2003/04. Other beneficiaries include London Business School (£200,000), University of Cambridge (£150,000), Association of Charitable Foundations (£20,000) and Imperial College London (£15,000).

Local economic renewal: [8 grants totalling £871,000]

'To support innovative approaches to enterprise generation and address barriers to social exclusion which underlie chronic economic failure in specific communities'.

Combined Universities of Cornwall

In this context, trustees are particularly keen to explore the potential and catalytic roles of both HE and FE institutions. It was this motivation that led the trustees to make a

151

major capital contribution to the campus construction programme as part of the formation of the Combined University of Cornwall (CUC) [£500,000 in 2003/04]. Here the intention is to explore how both the intellectual and physical resources of CUC can be harnessed to provide an effective enterprise support programme in Cornwall, particularly in communities that have suffered from the demise of traditional industries. Trustees have recently commissioned further work with CUC to develop specific industry-sector based approaches.

Manchester College of Arts and Technology

Looking ahead and continuing the enterprise support theme, the trustees are interested in the specific challenges and opportunities of inner-city areas of chronic urban deprivation. On this they are supporting the work of Manchester College of Arts and Technology (MANCAT) to develop ideas focused specifically on the needs of three wards in north-east Manchester.

Impetus Trust

Alongside support for enterprise-led regeneration, the trustees have also chosen to explore how best the values and principles of enterprise can be applied to improving the impact and sustainability of the voluntary sector. To this end they have made a grant of £150,000 over three years to the Impetus Trust [which also has its own entry here - Ed.]

Trustees believe that the charity and voluntary sectors have the potential to make an even greater contribution towards both economic and social regeneration. However, the sectors are generally characterised by lack of available finance and their inability to attract high levels of management and operations expertise.

The Impetus Trust aims to be the first venture philanthropy organisation operating in the UK. The approach is to invest a package of infrastructure finance, management support and capacity building (delivered through volunteer associates) to support charities that have the ability and ambition to make a step change in their performance.

Other grants were made to Community Links (£100,000), National Tenants Resource Centre (£50,000) and Community Development Finance Association (£20,000).

General : [9 grants totalling £235,000]

'To support on occasion other charitable work which falls outside their main fields of interest.'

Just one grant was listed in this category during the year - £25,500 to the

Sainsbury Archive. Small grants were made to the value of £2,500.

Comment

This hugely impressive charity is the nearest that Britain has to the great US foundations such as Ford or Rockefeller which take a long term approach to major issues. Other trusts sometimes suggest that this is only possible because of Gatsby's great income, but, taken field by field, there is nothing it does that could not also be undertaken in a similar manner by a number of other organisations described elsewhere.

This foundation, though, is not immune from the general criticism about an over emphasis on London and south east England organisations that is made about the Sainsbury Family trusts as a whole in the entry under that title.

Exclusions

Generally, the trustees do not make grants in response to unsolicited applications or to individuals.

Applications

See the entry for the Sainsbury Family Charitable Trusts. A single application will be considered for support by all the trusts in the group.

The Robert Gavron Charitable Trust

The arts, policy research, general

£774,000 (2002/03)
Beneficial area UK.

44 Eagle Street, London WC1R 4FS
Tel. 020 7400 4300 **Fax** 020 7400 4245
Correspondent Mrs Dilys Ogilvie-Ward, Secretary
Trustees *Lord Gavron; Charles Corman; Dr Katharine Gavron; Jessica Gavron; Sarah Gavron.*
Charity Commission no. 268535
Information available Annual report and accounts, with 2002/03 grants list.

Summary

This is a personal and family trust, with no full-time paid staff, whose grants go mainly, though not exclusively, to charities already known to the trustees.

General

The annual report for 2001/02 gives the following account of the trust's policies:

The principal fields of interest continue to include the arts, education, social policy and research and charities for the disabled. The trust operates with minimal assistance, as reflected in the administrative expenses. In the absence of staff who can undertake extensive research, the trustees prefer to make grants to organisations they personally know and admire.

This does not mean, however, that charities unknown to the trustees personally have not received grants. One part-time associate visits and reports on new applicants to the trust and his reports are taken into account by the trustees when they make their decisions. This has led to a number of grants to new organisations during the past financial year. Some of the charities awarded grants for the first time are small charities working in areas which do not easily raise funds and without the resources themselves for professional fundraising. They include small local volunteer organisations, charities working with ex-offenders and some of the smaller charities working with disabled children and adults. The trust has also continued to help previously funded small charities which come into these categories.

In 2002/03 the trust made 92 grants totalling £774,000, with grants ranging from as little as £50 up to £200,000 for Institute for Public Policy Research, although most grants were for £5,000 or less.

Other major beneficiaries during the year were National Gallery Trust (£100,000, the fourth instalment of five), House of Lords Collection Trust (£55,000), London School of Economics Library Appeal (£50,000, the third instalment of five), Georgepiperdances (£50,000 in total), Barbados Cricket Association (£35,000), The Runnymede Trust (£30,000), and Royal Society of Literature (£25,000).

Grants of £5,000 or less included those to Hamlet Centre Trust, Royal Academy Trust and The Open Trust (£5,000 each), Bag Books (£4,000), African AIDS Action, Cheltenham Festival of Literature, Ferring Country Centre and Libri Trust (£2,000 each), Julia Polak Research Trust, Frank Longford Charitable Trust, Dyslexia Institute, Recycle, North London Action for the

Homeless, The Roundhouse Trust and Charlton Park School Fund (£1,000 each), Listening Books and The Dancers Trust (£500 each), Howard League for Penal Reform (£250), American Museum in Britain (£100) and ZSV Trust (£50).

Exclusions

The trust does not give donations to individuals or to large national charities.

Applications

In writing only to the correspondent.

Please enclose a stamped addressed envelope and latest accounts. However, the trust has said that it is fully committed to its existing areas of interest and the trustees would have difficulty in considering further appeals. There are no regular dates for trustees' meetings, but they take place about six times a year.

Gederville Ltd

Jewish, general

See below
Beneficial area UK.

40 Fontayne Road, London N16 7DT
Correspondent Y Benedikt
Trustees *Joseph Benedikt; C Benedikt; Jacob Benedikt.*
Charity Commission no. 265645
Information available Basic accounts were on file at the Charity Commission, without a list of grants.

The trust states that it works for the advancement of the orthodox Jewish faith and for general charitable purposes. The trust does not disclose its beneficiaries.

In 2002/03 the income and total expenditure of the trust increased significantly on previous years to £900,000 and £1 million respectively. Unfortunately, although submitted by the trust to the Charity Commission, the accounts for that year had not made it to the public files for inspection.

No further information is available.

Applications

In writing to the correspondent.

J Paul Getty Jr Charitable Trust

Social welfare, conservation to a limited extent

£1.5 million (planned 2004)
Beneficial area UK.

1 Park Square West, London NW1 4LJ
Tel. 020 7486 1859
Website www.jpgettytrust.org.uk
Correspondent Ms Bridget O'Brien Twohig, Administrator
Trustees *Christopher Gibbs, chair; Lady Getty; Vanni Treves; Christopher Purvis.*
Charity Commission no. 292360
Information available Excellent guidelines for applicants and exceptionally full annual report and accounts.

Summary

The trust funds projects to do with poverty and misery in the UK, and unpopular causes in particular.

Grants, usually for running or project costs, are often for three-year periods and can be for up to a usual maximum of about £30,000. There are also a large number of small grants of £2,000 or less.

Few projects are supported in London. The grants for heritage and conservation are few and small.

The trust has doubled its level of grantmaking, taking the view that it should start assuming a long-term level of total return on its investments that will ignore short-term fluctuations, especially in gains or losses of capital. Nevertheless the trust remains heavily oversubscribed, with a success rate of only about 15% even for eligible applications, no doubt the result of its own accessibility to those working in fields few others are interested in funding.

Background

The J Paul Getty Jr Charitable Trust started distributing funds in 1986. Since then over £26 million has been given to over 3,000 worthwhile causes all over the UK.

The trust was funded entirely by Sir Paul Getty KBE, who died in April 2003 in London, where he had lived since the 1980s. He took a close interest in the trust, but also continued to make major personal gifts to the arts and other causes in England

(£50 million to the National Gallery, £3 million to Lord's Cricket Ground, £17 million to the British Film Institute, £1 million towards the Canova Three Graces, £5 million towards the restoration of St. Paul's Cathedral). These were personal gifts and had no connection with this trust.

Nor has this trust any connection with the Getty Trust in the USA, to which J. Paul Getty Senior left his money, and which finances the J. Paul Getty Museum in California. These two trusts, one very large and one small by comparison, should not be confused by people who apply to us!

The trust, which now has capital of about £40 million, made grants totalling over £1.3 million in 2003.

Guidelines for applicants

The trust aims to fund projects to alleviate poverty and misery in general, and unpopular causes in particular, within the UK. The emphasis is on self-help and enabling people to reach their potential. The trustees favour small community and local projects which make good use of volunteers.

There are four main beneficial areas:
- social welfare,
- therapeutic use of the arts,
- conservation,
- environment.

Most of the funding is given to social welfare, as you will see if you look at the annual report. Please check under the headings below for details of types of projects funded in each category.

Grants are usually in the £5,000 to £15,000 range, for both capital and revenue. Those for salaries or running costs can be repeated on an annual basis for a maximum of three years. Some small grants of up to £2,000 are also made in between the quarterly trustee meetings.

Priority is likely to be given to projects in the less prosperous parts of the country, particularly outside London and the South East, and to those which cover more than one beneficial area.

Please read the *Exclusions* section [below] carefully first before applying, as it is possible that the particular aspect of your application, rather than the general purpose of your organisation, may be excluded.

Social welfare

Mental health in a wide sense. This includes projects for:
- mentally ill adults;
- drug, alcohol and other addictions, and related problems;
- support groups for people under stress, e.g. battered wives, victims of abuse, families in difficulties, etc.

Offenders, both in and out of prison, men and women, young offenders, sexual offenders.

Communities which are clearly disadvantaged and trying to improve their lot, particularly projects to do with helping young people in the long-term.

Homelessness, particularly projects which help prevent people becoming homeless or to resettle them.

Job creation projects or ones aimed at making long-term constructive use of enforced leisure time, particularly ones set up by unemployed people.

Ethnic minorities involved in above areas, including refugees, particularly projects aimed at integration.

Arts

Only the following will be considered:

- therapeutic use of the arts for the long-term benefit of the groups listed under Social Welfare;
- projects which enable people in these groups to feel welcome in arts venues, and which enable them to make long-term constructive use of their leisure.

Conservation

Conservation in the broadest sense, with emphasis on ensuring that fine buildings, landscapes and collections remain or become available to the general public or scholars. Training in conservation skills. Not general building repair work.

Environment

Mainly gardens. Historic landscape. Wilderness.

What are your chances?

We receive far more applications which come within these guidelines than the trust can afford to fund, so please do not feel too discouraged if we have to say 'No' to you. In 2003, we received over 1,500 new applications, and were only able to fund 107. A further 89 grants were paid to projects being funded for a second or third year.

We hope all this helps.

Annual report 2003

Summary of 2003 activity

	2003	2002
Number of new applicants	1,527	1,326
Number of new applicants supported	107	103
Value of new grants authorised	£971,000	£1,325,000
Average size of grants (excluding small grants)	£9,426	£10,420
New applicants granted support for more than one year	28	35
Total distribution	£1,356,000	£1,651,000
Number of grants paid	205	215

In view of the continuing uncertainty in financial markets and the consequent erosion in the capital value of our funds by the end of 2002, we felt we had no choice but to suspend our total return policy and set a reduced distribution target for 2003 of £1.3 million. After the invasion of Iraq and subsequent market revival, we decided this could be cautiously increased, and by the end of the year we had distributed £1,355,800, 18% down on the previous year. (Our initial distribution target for 2004 is £1.5 million.)

Much of the money available for 2003 had been already committed by way of 2-year and 3-year grants. Although we managed to maintain the number of new applicants supported, the average size of grant dropped, (from £10,420 in 2002 to £9,426 in 2003), as did the number of applicants supported for more than one year (from 35 to 28). The number of applications received was probably equivalent to 2002, but the number eligible for funding rose as those outside our criteria fell to 25%, the lowest level since the trust started. The number of Small Grants (£2,000 and under) increased, and we funded 1 in 11 of eligible applicants. We held to our decision to give priority to good projects seeking to cover their current running costs, over those seeking funding for developments which could wait for better days.

Early in the year we were one of a number of trusts represented at a meeting with the Chancellor of the Exchequer. This was at his invitation, to discuss the effects on registered charities of their losing ACT refunds, and to explore with officials possible ways of replacing the income lost. So far there has been little result, but at least the point has been made that with a reduced income charitable trusts will give lower priority to contributing to partnerships with statutory agencies which are, in effect, subsidising government policy.

The Addictions Adviser project, a joint initiative of this trust with the Rank Foundation and the National Addictions Centre to fund a new senior research post under Prof. John Strang, had a promising but not trouble-free first year in operation, and has had to be restructured. It got off to an excellent start with the appointment of Dr Jim McCambridge. Within months, however, he was awarded a Wellcome Fellowship (the first in the addictions field), and as a consequence the Rank trustees decided to withdraw. We are delighted that the Pilgrim Trust has now joined us as a funding partner, and Dr Peter Miller will be replacing Dr McCambridge in April 2004.

Valuable lessons have been learnt already on three fronts: out in the field with the

---

J PAUL GETTY JR CHARITABLE TRUST
Categories of New Grants Authorised in 2003

Categories	2003 no.	2003 total	2002 no.	2002 total
Community groups	13	£139,750	13	£134,000
Mental health	8	£54,800	8	£88,500
Family	6	£72,000	3	£29,000
Youth	18	£297,500	16	£381,000
Offenders	7	£104,000	2	£75,000
Drugs and alcohol	4	£51,750	7	£222,000
Homeless	9	£43,750	6	£80,250
Ethnic minorities	5	£114,000	5	£47,000
Women	3	£19,000	4	£112,000
Physically disabled	4	£16,000	6	£7,750
Heritage and conservation	17	£42,750	21	£135,500
Environment (gardens)	2	£3,000	2	£2,500
Miscellaneous	11	£12,500	10	£10,750
Total	107	£970,800	103	£1,325,250

J PAUL GETTY JR CHARITABLE TRUST
Geographical Spread of Grants Authorised in 2003

Area	2003 no.	2003 total	2002 no.	2002 total
Birmingham	9	£90,250	8	£161,500
Cumbria & North West	1	£20,000	1	£30,000
Devon & South West	5	£32,000	8	£89,500
East Anglia	5	£16,000	2	£32,000
Headquarters/National	16	£103,000	18	£201,500
Ireland	6	£53,300	4	£51,500
London & Home Counties	7	£33,950	15	£44,500
Manchester & Lancashire	6	£30,000	3	£28,500
Merseyside	1	£24,000	2	£90,000
Oxfordshire	5	£15,000	-	-
Newcastle & North East	5	£92,000	4	£81,500
Scotland	5	£64,800	5	£95,000
South	10	£55,250	8	£67,500
Wales & Bristol	8	£105,000	9	£161,000
Worcester & Hereford	1	£7,000	-	-
Yorkshire	17	£229,250	16	£191,250
Total	107	£970,800	103	£1,325,250

projects, on the research side, and in managing the relationship between the two trusts. The first two are positive, in that projects have been selected on a better informed basis. Some have welcomed advice, based on proven findings, to increase their effectiveness by changing their working practices. One has reluctantly had further funding withheld because it was found to be largely ineffective, and showed no signs of improving. The hoped-for two way process has also taken root, in that the field experience has fed into and altered approaches to research.

On the management side we look forward to developing the initiative further with the Pilgrim Trust. There is considerable potential in these joint initiatives, which in future might extend to more than one partner. What is clear, however, is that there must be commitment and clear agreement between the partners at all levels, and that it takes much time and application to nurse worthwhile developments through the early stages.

Comments on Categories

Following the trend of the past few years, the bulk of the funding has been allocated to projects working with disaffected, disadvantaged Young People. Three more new youth cafes aiming to provide a safe, cool place for young people to hang out rather than the streets were given grants towards salaries: CAN in Ashby de la Zouch (£10,000 x 3), the Oyster Bar in Arbroath (£14,000 x 3), and Knotted Note in Barton upon Humber (£10,000 x 3). They were also encouraged to share their plans with each other, and to visit existing youth cafes. Central Action Stirling (£11,000 x 3) and St. Paul's Trust in Liverpool (£8,000 x 3) both aim to give poorly educated young people a better chance of employment by offering practical training in areas likely to attract them: Central Action via IT and radio broadcasting, and St. Paul's Trust via boat handling skills. Projects for young people as usual overlap with those for Offenders and those addicted to Drugs and Alcohol. South Bristol Community Construction Company (£12,000 x 3) aims to train young offenders, many with addiction problems, in building skills. We are funding a mentor to provide the vital individual support needed to keep them going. Debt continues to be a major problem in poor communities, as much with families on low wages as with those relying on benefits. We have funded money advice workers in the Bridlington CAB (£10,000), Speak Easy Advice Centre in Cardiff (£7,000 x 3), and Taxaid (£10,000 x 3), which is based in London but provides free tax advice country wide to low-earning self-employed people and those encouraged to set up their own small businesses who then get into tax debt. Under the Environment and Heritage

headings, grants were made to Burn Valley Allotment Association in Hartlepool (£1,000) and the Hillier Arboretum in York (£2000). The John Rylands Library in Manchester received £10,000 towards its refurbishment, and St. John's College in Nottingham £5,000 towards the production of a fascinating CD Rom on Christian iconography for the benefit of younger generations of students of medieval literature, history and art history who are unable to interpret much of what they see and read.

Geographical Distribution

In line with our aim to give priority to applications from poorer areas outside London and the south East, the bulk of the funds has been distributed to projects in the North East and Yorkshire. Many are spread out in the market towns, former mining villages and outlying estates, rather than clustered in the larger towns and cities. The Cornforth Partnership in east Co. Durham (£10,000 x 3) and the Rookhope Inn (St. Aidan's Trust) (£10,000 x 3) in the fell country to the west are both trying to revive community spirit and provide a social focus for isolated young people in areas which have lost their source of employment. Bransholme Family Focus (£10,000 x x3) is on a straggling estate on the northern outskirts of Hull, and the Sobriety Project (£10,000 x 3), which is running a work training project for unskilled women including a large contingent from a prison, is on the canalside outside Goole. The Vale of Glamorgan MIND drop-in for people with mental health problems (£10,000 x 3) is on the outskirts of Llantwit Major. The Caddy Community Group (£10,000) runs the only community meeting place in a rural area in Co. Antrim in Northern Ireland.

The new office of the Inside Out Trust in Stratford upon Avon (£10,000 x 2) will facilitate negotiations for work projects inside prisons in the Midlands, and the North East Post Adoption Service in North Shields (£10,000 x x3) will be able to take on more casework helping adoptees through the difficult process of tracing their birth families. St. Wilfred's Day Centre in Sheffield (£2,000) cares for people with mental health problems, the Bradford Cyrenians (£2,000) and Harbour House outside Blackpool (£500) for homeless people. Projects for refugees were funded in Reading (Refugee Support Group £12,000 x 3), London (Detainee Support Group £10,000 x 3) and Bradford (Thornbury Centre £15,000 x 3).

Comment

This is one of the very few trusts where virtually the entire entry can be given in the trust's own admirably clear and interesting words.

Exclusions

Grants are not given for:

- the elderly;
- children;
- education;
- research;
- animals;
- music or drama (except therapeutically);
- conferences or seminars;
- medical care (including hospices) or health;
- medical equipment;
- churches or cathedrals;
- holidays or expeditions;
- sports or leisure facilities (including cricket pitches);
- residential or large building projects;
- replacement of Lottery or statutory funds;
- national appeals;
- grantmaking trusts or community foundations;
- individuals.

Headquarters of national organisations and 'umbrella' organisations are unlikely to be considered.

Past recipients are not encouraged to re-apply.

No applications for projects outside the UK are considered.

The project must be a registered charity or be under the auspices of one.

Priority is likely to be given to projects in the less prosperous parts of the country, particularly outside London and the south east, and to those which cover more than one beneficial area.

Please remember this trust has no connection with the Getty Foundation in the USA.

Applications

We only accept applications by post. A letter no more than two sides long is all that is necessary at first, giving an outline of the project, who will benefit, a detailed costing, the existing sources of finance for the organisation, and what other applications, including those to statutory sources and the lottery, have been made. Please also say if you have applied to or received a grant previously from this trust.

Please read the exclusions section (above) carefully first before applying, as it is possible that the particular aspect of your application, rather than the general purpose of your organisation, may be excluded. 25% of the applications we received in 2003 were outside our guidelines.

Please visit the website or telephone the office for the latest version of our guidelines before applying as they may be subject to change.

Please do not send videos, tapes or bulky reports. They will not be returned.

Annual accounts will be asked for if your application is going to be taken further.

Applications can be made to the administrator at any time. There are no 'closing dates', and all letters of appeal will be answered, we hope within six weeks. But please remember, only two sides in the first instance. And don't shrink it–edit it!

See contact details for where to send your application.

If a project is short-listed for taking forward for a grant over £2,000, it will also have to be visited by the administrator before an application can be considered by the trustees. This may mean a delay, as it is only possible to visit a small part of the country between each quarterly trustees' meeting.

The trustees usually meet around the end of March, June, September and December. There is a shortlisting process, and not all applications are taken forward. Not all those taken forward will necessarily be put to the next trustees' meeting as the administrator may not be visiting their area in that particular quarter. Three months is the least it usually takes to award a grant. Some small grants of up to £2,000 can be made in between meetings without a visit, but only for specific purposes.

The G C Gibson Charitable Trust

Churches, health, welfare, medical research, wildlife, agriculture, general

£613,000 (2002/03)

Beneficial area UK, with interests in Suffolk, Wales and Scotland.

Deloitte & Touche, Blenheim House, Fitzalan Court, Newport Road, Cardiff CF24 0TS

Tel. 029 2048 1111

Correspondent Karen Griffin

Trustees *R D Taylor; Mrs J M Gibson; George S C Gibson.*

Charity Commission no. 258710

Information available Annual report and accounts on file at the Charity Commission.

In 2002/03 the trust had assets amounting to almost £10 million and an income of £455,000. A total of £613,000 was donated to 155 charities during the year under the following headings:

- art, music and education
- health, hospices and medical research
- community and other social projects
- religion

The trust stated of its grant-making policy that the 'majority of donations have been made towards the annual expenditure of the charities concerned. Whilst the trustees will consider donations for capital projects, the average donation of £5,000 is more suited for meeting the revenue commitments of the donees'.

'Applications have been considered from charities working throughout the UK. Preference has been given to applications from charities who have already received donations from the trust as the trustees recognise the importance of providing recurring donations whenever possible.'

Grants were broken down as follows, shown here with examples of beneficiaries in each category:

Art, music and education – 25 grants totalling £113,000

By far the largest donation in this category was £25,000 to Royal Welsh College of Music and Drama. Other grants included £5,000 each to Cardiff Bay Chamber Orchestra, the Hollies School, Royal National College for the Blind – Hereford and Stefan Batory Trust, £3,000 each to Christ College Brecon Appeal Fund, St David's Hall Trust and St Michael's College – Landaff and £2,000 each to Cambridge & County Folk Museum, Farm Land Museum and Welsh National Opera.

Health, hospices and medical research – 46 grants totalling £194,000

Grants of £10,000 each went to Haven Trust – London, King Edward VII Hospital, St Michael's Hospice – Hereford and St Nicholas' Hospice – Bury St Edmonds. Other grants included £6,000 to Marie Curie Cancer Care, £5,000 each to the Alzheimer's Disease Society, Cancer Research Campaign Scotland, Cystic Fibrosis Research Trust,

Jersey Hospice Care, National Ankylosing Spondylitis Society, North Devon Hospice, Seeability, St Francis Hospice, Sue Ryder Old Palace Project and Winston's Wish, £3,000 to East Anglia Children's Hospice, Kidney Research Unit for Wales Foundation Appeal, Mental Health Foundation, National Society for Epilepsy, Starlight Children's Foundation and Hy Hafan and £2,000 each to the Arthritis and Rheumatism Council – Newmarket, Children's Hospital for North Wales, Headway, Muscular Dystrophy Group and Vision Foundation.

Community and other social projects – 64 grants totalling £240,000

The largest grant in this category was £10,000 to Weston Spirit. Other grants included £7,000 to the Wildfowl and Wetlands Trust, £6,000 to Astley Institute – Newmarket, £5,000 each to Appledore Lifeboat Crew Account, Bramford Road Community Centre, British Red Cross Society, Bury St Edmonds Volunteer Centre, Gwent Wildlife Trust, Kiloran Trust, Penarth Gymnastics Club, Salvation Army, Moorcroft Racehorse Welfare Centre, Relate, Royal Star and Garter Home and Shelter Cymru, £4,000 to Sail Training Association, £3,000 each to Age Concern Wales, Anti-Slavery Society, Bishopswood Village Hall, Cardiff Young Men's Christian Association, Kidsactive, Prospect Burma, Toynbee Hall and Worshipful Company of Farriers Charitable Trust and £2,000 each to Army Benevolent Fund, Blue Cross Animal Welfare Charity, Frontier Youth Project, Hertfordshire Association for Young People, NSPCC – Saundersfoot, Sailors' Children's Society and Wales in Trust and £1,000 to Hampshire Garden Trust.

Religion – 20 grants totalling £66,000

Grants included £5,000 each to Ely Cathedral Restoration Trust, Landaff Cathedral Restoration Appeal, St Mary's Church – Newmarket, £3,000 to Bishopswood Parish Church Council, Christian Children's Fund of Great Britain and Walford Parish Church Council, £2,000 each to Canynges Society and Scripture Union and £1,000 to St Mary's – Old Harlow.

Exclusions

No grants to individuals. Only registered charities are supported.

Applications

In writing to the correspondent by October each year. Trustees meet in November/December. Successful applicants will receive their cheques during January.

Organisations that have already received a grant should re-apply describing how the previous year's grant was spent and setting out how a further grant would be used. In general, less detailed information is required from national charities with a known track record than from small local charities that are not known to the trustees.

'Due to the volume of applications, it is not possible to acknowledge each application, nor is it possible to inform unsuccessful applicants.'

Simon Gibson Charitable Trust

General

£464,000 (2002/03)

Beneficial area UK, with a preference for Norfolk, Suffolk, South Wales and Cambridgeshire.

Wild Rose House, Llancarfan, Vale of Glamorgan CF62 3AD

Tel. 01446 781004 **Fax** 01446 781004

Email bryan@marsh66.fsnet.co.uk

Correspondent Bryan Marsh, Trustee

Trustees *Bryan Marsh; Angela Homfray; George Gibson.*

Charity Commission no. 269501

Information available Report and accounts were provided by the trust.

Following a review [...] in response to a substantial increase in the number of applications received, for the foreseeable future the trustees have decided to limit grants to national charities and local charities from areas with which the trust is associated [...] Suffolk, Norfolk, Cambridgeshire and South Wales.

Around 100 grants are made per year, usually ranging from between £3,000 and £5,000, but occasionally up to £50,000. Donations are made to charities in a broad variety of fields, including to welfare, children and young people, animal welfare, arts and culture and international organisations. Many of the donations made are recurrent.

In 2002/03 the trust had an income of £404,000 and made 109 grants totalling £464,000. Beneficiaries included Jubilee Appeal for Commonwealth Veterans (£20,000), Ely Cathedral Appeal Fund, Ewing Foundation, Prostate Cancer Charity, Save the Children Fund, St Nicholas Hospice – Bury St Edmonds and the Princes Trust (£10,000 each), Action on Addiction, Bookaid International, Harrow School Appeal, National Galleries of Scotland, Star & Garter Appeal and Suffolk Historic Churches Appeal (£5,000 each), Adopt a Minefield, British Heart Foundation, Civic Trust for Wales, Grange Town Community Concern, Orbit Theatre Company and Suffolk Youth Jazz Orchestra (£3,000 each), International Spinal Research Trust, Llancarfan Parish Church, Salvation Army and Welsh National Opera (£2,000 each).

Exclusions

No grants or sponsorships for individuals or non-charitable bodies.

Applications

In writing to the correspondent. Telephone calls should not be made. The trust has no application forms. It acknowledges all applications but does not enter into correspondence with applicants unless they are awarded a grant. The trustees meet in May and applications should be received by March in order to be considered at that meeting.

The Girdlers' Company Charitable Trust

Welfare, medicine, education, youth, heritage, environment, religion

About **£415,000** (2002/03)

Beneficial area UK, with a preference for City of London, Hammersmith and Peckham, overseas.

Girdlers' Hall, Basinghall Avenue, London EC2V 5DD

Tel. 020 7638 0488 **Fax** 020 7628 4030

Email margaret@girdlers.co.uk

Correspondent The Clerk to The Girdlers' Company

Trustees *C E Grace; Sir Gordon Pirie; D R L James; A R Westall; Sir David Burnett; Sir Michael Newton; N K Maitland; B D Moul; Dr D N Seaton; A J R Fairclough; Rt Hon. Viscount Brentford; I P R James; Capt. G M A James; T J Straker; P F D Trimingham; J S Maitland; P V Straker; Sir Thomas Crawley-Boevey; I W Fairclough; J P F Reeve; S V Straker; J M Westall; F M French; J O Udal.*

Charity Commission no. 328026

Information available Accounts are on file at the Charity Commission.

This trust prefers to give to small local less well-known charities, rather than to those that are large and well publicised.

In 2002/03 it had an income of £731,000 and a total expenditure of £434,000. Grants were made totalling around £410,000. Unfortunately, no further information was available.

Previous beneficiaries include London Youth, Surrey County Cricket Club Youth Scheme, Gordon's School, Stoke Manderville Research Nurse, Sports Aid London, London College of Fashion, St Paul's Choir School Foundation, Macmillan Cancer Relief, Dorothy House Hospice and Marchant Holiday School.

Comment

There was no response to repeated written requests for a copy of the most recent annual report and accounts, despite the requirement to provide these on demand.

Despite ample warning, and their obligation to the contrary, the Charity Commission were unable to give us sight of this trust's accounts.

Exclusions

No grants to individuals.

Applications

In writing to the correspondent.

The Glass-House Trust

Social housing and the urban environment

£572,000 (2003/04)

Beneficial area Unrestricted, but UK in practice.

Allington House, 1st Floor, 150 Victoria Street, London SW1E 5AE

Tel. 020 7410 0330 **Fax** 020 7410 0332

Email info@sfct.org.uk

Correspondent Michael Pattison, Director

Trustees *Alexander Sainsbury; James Sainsbury; Jessica Sainsbury; Elinor Sainsbury; Miss Judith Portrait.*

Charity Commission no. 1017426

Information available Excellent annual report and accounts were provided by the trust.

Summary

The trust is concentrating all its resources on housing design, with a big new initiative being developed by the Architecture Foundation and the National Tenants Resource Centre. Far fewer grants are now being made in another field of interest; parenting, family welfare and child development, although grants are now being made for art and architecture.

General

This is one of the Sainsbury Family Charitable Trusts, which share a joint administration. They have in common an approach to grantmaking which is described in the entry for the group as a whole. It is the trust of Alexander Sainsbury and three of the four other trustees are his brother and sisters, who each have trusts of their own.

Glass-House reported in their annual report for 2000/01 that a major policy change had been made:

[The] trustees have moved away from their traditional emphasis on parenting, family welfare issues and child development. The trustees still wish to support work aiming to bring about social change, but will concentrate on doing so via an emphasis on the importance of the built environment rather than uniquely via the promotion of psychological welfare. This has allowed the trustees to commit substantial funding to an initiative in the field of social housing[...]

In 2003/04 the trust made 11 grants, including part of the two-year grant to the Architecture Foundation and the National Tenants Resource Centre to allow them to establish the Glass-House Service to provide design advice for social housing tenants (£300,000).

The other grants were made to:

Art/Architecture

Pier Trust, towards core and project costs (£82,000); London Musicians Collective, towards Resonance FM's core costs (£30,000); Architecture Foundation, towards the Home Project to research the concept of 'desirability' as an aspect of housing design, social inclusion and regeneration (£20,000); Building Exploratory, towards the programme of adult education activities (£10,000); and Broomhill Trust, towards Broomhill Opera's appeal to fully restore Wilton's Music Hall (£8,000).

Parenting, Family Welfare & Child Development

Just one beneficiary, the Institute of Education in Hackney, received a total of £62,500, mostly for support costs for the A Space after-school project (£60,000), but also for fundraising consultancy and strategic support costs for the project (£2,500).

General

Transform Drug Policy Foundation received £50,000 in total towards core costs and the cost of employing an administrator; Ashden Awards for Sustainable Energy received £10,000 towards core costs.

Exclusions

Grants are not normally made to individuals.

Applications

See the guidance for applicants in the entry for the Sainsbury Family Charitable Trusts. A single application will be considered for support by all the trusts in the group. However 'proposals are generally invited by the trustees or initiated at their request'.

The Glencore Foundation for Education and Welfare

Education and welfare

$1.3 million (2003)

Beneficial area Mainly Israel.

c/o Glencore UK Ltd, 50 Berkeley Street, London W1J 8HD

Tel. 020 7629 3800 **Fax** 020 7499 5555

Email colin.smith@glencore.co.uk

Correspondent Colin Smith, Secretary

Trustees *Danny Dreyfuss; M D Paisner; L M Weiss; Colin Smith.*

Charity Commission no. 1041859

Information available Annual report and accounts (in US dollars) were provided by the trust.

The foundation's income was $2,602,000 in 2003 (2002 $570,000), almost entirely from donations. Grants were made during the year totalling $1,316,000, a decrease of $542,000 on the previous year. The foundation's review of activities for 2003 is largely unchanged from the previous year, except for the explanation that the charity's income is now derived from more than one Glencore company (previously just Glencore UK Ltd.

The foundation's review of activities for 2003, identical to that of previous years, stated:

The Glencore Foundation for Education and Welfare was established in 1994, for general charitable purposes, but the principal area of activity has been within the fields of education and welfare with particular reference to Israel.

The charity's annual income for 2003 derives from Glencore UK Ltd, Glencore Energy UK Ltd and Glencore Commodities Ltd. [...] The emphasis on education and welfare is likely to remain the principal policy of the trustees during the coming year.

In 2003, most of the 51 grants listed went to Jewish charities, and most recipients were based in Israel. The largest grant ($100,000) went to Sacta – Rashi Foundation, Madarom Programme for Education in the South.

There were some small grants of up to $3,300 to non-Jewish UK charities (including the Meningitis Trust, When You Wish Upon A Star and the Blue Cross).

Comment

The annual report of this foundation is inadequate, with the brief narrative review of activities seemingly remaining unchanged from year to year. The trust says 'the report remains unchanged year on year as the nature of the foundation's activities remains unchanged'.

Applications

In writing to the correspondent.

The Golden Bottle Trust

General

£348,000 (2002/03)

Beneficial area UK.

Messrs Hoare Trustees, 37 Fleet Street, London EC4P 4DQ

Tel. 020 7353 4522 **Fax** 020 7353 4521

Email enquiries@hoaresbank.co.uk

Correspondent The Trustees

Trustees *Messrs Hoare Trustees (H C Hoare; D J Hoare; R Q Hoare; A S Hoare; V E Hoare; S M Hoare; A S Hopewell.)*

Charity Commission no. 327026

Information available Basic accounts, with no list of grants or review of the trust's activities.

The trust was established in 1985 by C Hoare & Co. bankers, the oldest remaining private bank in the UK. With a customer base of 15,000, it has only two branches, in the City and in the West End of London. The trust is managed by Messrs Hoare Trustees and has general charitable purposes. It continues to receive most of its income from C Hoare & Co.

In 2002/03 the trust had assets of £3.9 million and an income of £635,000, including investment income of £113,000, and further donated income of £450,000. After administration expenses of just £3,500, grants were made totalling £348,000.

No grant information has been included in the trust's accounts since those for 1993/94. The 2002/03 accounts state that 'the trustees consider that disclosure of material grants may prejudice the furtherance of the purposes of the charity', although the trust could not explain how this might happen. Details of material grants had been provided to the Charity Commission, apparently seperate from the accounts and not available to the public.

The accounts also state that 'the activities of the trust remain satisfactory and the objects of the trust were acheived during the year', althought there is little indication of what these objects are or how they were acheived.

It is apparent, however, from information available elsewhere, that the trust does give to a wide range of organisations, causes and projects. Recent beneficiaries include the Arvon Foundation, National Manuscripts Conservation Trust, Treloar Trust, Whitchurch Silk Mill, St Ethelburga's Centre for Reconciliation and Peace, World Land Trust, Coram Family Children's Charity, EPRA UK pilot project, Natural History Museum, Royal Signals Museum, King's College London – for the conservation of items in the rare books collection and to the Chapel Restoration Fund, sponsorship of the 'London 1753' exhibition in the British Museum, National Literacy Trust, Marine Conservation Society, Museum of London 'Linking Lives' project, Whitley Laing Foundation, CancerBACUP, Chamber Orchestra of Europe, Soil Association, Island Trust and St Dunstan in the West Church.

Exclusions

No grants for individuals or organisations that are not registered charities.

Applications

In writing to the correspondent, who stated 'trustees meet on a monthly basis, but the funds are already largely committed and, therefore, applications from sources not already known to the trustees are unlikely to be successful'. This is presumably why the trust declined to provide details of its guidelines for donations.

The Teresa Rosenbaum Golden Charitable Trust

Medical research

£400,000 (2001/02)

Beneficial area UK.

140 High Street, Edgware, Middlesex HA8 7LW

Tel. 020 8952 1414 **Fax** 020 8952 2424

Email rross@regentsmead.com

Correspondent R A Ross, Trust Administrator

Trustees *T Rosenbaum; R A Ross; R M Abbey.*

Charity Commission no. 298582

Information available Excellent accounts were provided by the trust.

The trust produces an information leaflet, which states:

The T R Golden Charitable Trust makes most of its charitable donations to medical research, because it wants to support cutting-edge medical research over a wide spectrum of first-class projects. The trustees give preference to projects that offer a realistic prospect of practical results which will lead to new or improved therapies or drugs to benefit patients.

The trustees are completely independent, having no link with any pharmaceutical or other commercial company engaged in the medical field, and their objective in making substantial donations for medical research is the successful outcome of the research programmes, leading to effective practical treatments. Usually, the trustees start with relatively small grants, but as the reporting progresses and a good working relationship develops between the trust and the researchers these grants are steadily increased and over a period of years can build up to substantial sums.

In 2001/02 the trust had assets of £741,000. Total income was £886,000, of which £855,000 came from donations received. Grants were made totalling £400,000. After the costs of generating the funds, there was a surplus for the year of £468,000.

A large grant of £61,000 was given to The Tissue Engineering Centre at Imperial College – Chelsea, and Westminster and Hammersmith Hospitals to fund a researcher in a specific area of developing bone cells.

Other grants included: £25,000 to Research into Ageing for five different projects; £21,000 to Kings Medical Research Trust for a clinical trial into the treatment of advanced liver cancer; £15,000 to Oncology Trust at Royal Free Hospital into clinical trials in patients using new antibodies; £10,000 to Hearing Research Trust for research at Institute of Otology – London and Institute of Hearing Research – Nottingham into regenerating hair cells and understanding more about possible self-repair mechanisms by studying reptiles and birds; £7,000 to Muscular Dystrophy Campaign for a follow-up project into implanting skin cells into damaged muscles; £6,000 to MS Society for a project to carry out a comprehensive analysis of auto reactive T-cells in multiple sclerosis; £3,000 to Brain and Spine Foundation for a Belfast-based project to block enzymes thought to be responsible for the spread of brain tumours; and £2,000 to Lasers for Life for research into the use of lasers in the treatment and early diagnosis of cancer.

A number of organisations received more than one grant during the year.

Alzheimer's Society, for instance, received £10,000 for a fellowship studying the role of TAU protein in the development of tangles leading to the death of brain cells, £5,000 each for a fellowship studying the mechanism of cell death in specific areas of the brain and a fellowship studying protein accumulation and the death of brain cells, and £3,000 to a speculative research project to develop a saliva test to diagnose Alzheimer's disease. Similarly, Royal College of Surgeons received four grants of £2,500 each, for a study into chemotherapy and blood clotting and for fellowships into the role of bacteria in the non-healing of leg fractures following pinning, improvements in knee replacement design to enhance the beneficial effects of surgery and an investigation into how low temperatures could protect the gut in babies and children with severe digestive disorders.

Comment

Despite ample warning, and their obligation to the contrary, the Charity Commission were unable to give us sight of this trust's most recent accounts.

Exclusions

No support for individuals, or for non-medical research.

Applications

In writing to the correspondent. Applicants must complete a simple pro forma which sets out briefly in clear layman's terms the reason for the project, the nature of the research, its cost, its anticipated benefit and how and when people will be able to benefit. Proper reports in this form will be required at least six-monthly and funding will be conditional on these being satisfactory.

'The trustees are not medical experts and require short clear statements in plain English setting out the particular subject to be researched, the objects and likely benefits, the cost and the time-scale. Unless a charity will undertake to provide two concise progress reports each year, they should not bother to apply as this is a vital requirement. It is essential that the trustees are able to follow the progress and effectiveness of the research they support.'

The Goldsmiths' Company Charity

General, London charities, the precious metals craft

£2 million (2002/03)

Beneficial area UK, with a special interest in London charities.

Goldsmiths' Hall, Foster Lane, London EC2V 6BN

Tel. 020 7606 7010 **Fax** 020 7606 1511

Email the.clerk@thegoldsmiths.co.uk

Website www.thegoldsmiths.co.uk

Correspondent R D Buchanan-Dunlop, Clerk

Trustees *The members of the Court of Assistants of the Goldsmiths' Company.Charity committee: Lord Cunliffe, chair; S A Shepherd; Miss J A Lowe; Dr M P Godfrey; A M J Galsworthy; Hon. Mark Bridges; Revd D Paton.*

Charity Commission no. 1088699

Information available Exemplary annual report and accounts with a narrative exploration of grantmaking and a comprehensive grants list covering the amount awarded and the purpose of the grant.

Summary

The charity gives around 300 small grants, for between £1,000 and £3,000, to a wide range of national and London-based charities each year. Most of these are in response to applications received, and can be for almost any purpose, including supporting core costs. Capital costs seem less frequently supported than revenue ones. At least 50% of recipients receive grants for a period of three years, and about half of all applications received result in a grant.

The charity also gives about ten large grants annually, generally up to a maximum of £50,000. These are usually to organisations proactively sought out by the charity rather than as a result of applying for a grant.

General

John Perryn's Charity, the Goldsmiths' General Charity and the Goldsmiths' Charitable Donation Fund, which were already closely allied and had shared an annual report for a number of years, were merged into one single charity, the Goldsmiths' Company Charity in 2001.

The charities' combined endowment of £65 million produced an income of £2.4 million in 2002/03.

Grantmaking

The Goldsmiths' Company's grantmaking policies fall into three main areas, outlined by the charity as follows:

General charitable support

The largest area of grant-making is towards general charitable needs, ranging from the disadvantaged in society and general welfare, to the churches, heritage and the arts.

Support of the Goldsmiths' Craft

Support for trade training is given to higher and further educational establishments and to students and apprentices, to promote excellence in design and craftsmanship.

Education

The company sponsors a number of educational initiatives directed mainly towards primary and secondary education.

Grants in 2001/02

The charity gave 339 grants totalling just under £2 million in 2002/03; most were for between £1,000 and £3,000.

The charity's excellent annual report notes that the average grant (excluding grants over £5,000) in 2001/02 increased from £2,000 to £3,000. This figure is now likely to stabilise. The number of three-year grants awarded went down from 63% to 56%.

Total amounts spent on each of the three broad areas of grantmaking in 2002/03 were:

Support of the craft	£854,000
General charitable work	£793,000
Education	£341,000

Grants for general charitable work in 2002/03 were further categorised as follows:

General welfare (including housing, prisoners, drug addicts and alcoholics)	£366,000
Medical welfare and disabled	£139,000
Youth	£159,000
Arts	£79,000
Heritage	£42,000
Church	£9,000

In this area most of its grants were made in response to appeals.

General charitable work

General welfare

There were 120 grants made in this category, led by: £45,000 to Community

Foundation in Wales; £20,000 to Cornwall Independent Trust Fund; and £15,000 each to the London boroughs of Southwark and Tower Hamlets.

Other beneficiaries included Centrepoint Soho and Shannon Trust (£5,000 each), Ex-Service Fellowship Centres (£4,000), Hackney Community Law Centre, Oasis Charitable Trust and Refugee Arrivals Project (£3,000 each), Butler Trust and Family Trends (£2,500 each), West London Churches Homeless Concern (£1,500) and Action on Elder Abuse and Soho Family Centre (£1,000 each).

Medical welfare and disabled

There were 63 grants made in this category. Beneficiaries included Young Minds (£3,500), AbilityNet and British Blind Sport (£3,000 each), Merton Association of Disabled People for AIM (£2,500), British Brain and Spine Foundation and Refresh (£2,000 each), Action for ME (£1,500) and Listening Books (£1,000).

Youth

There were 67 grants in this category. Beneficiaries included Airbourne Initiative (£7,900), Federation of London Youth Clubs (£7,000), UK Youth (£5,000), Alone in London Service and Friends of Marlborough School (£3,500 each), Catholic Children's Society (£3,000), Stopover – Lewisham (£2,500), British Sport Trust (£2,000), Army Cadet Force Association (£1,000) and London Children's Flower Society (£500).

Heritage

The 17 beneficiaries in this category included Braintree District Museum and Study Centre (£3,000), Canal Museum Trust and Dr Johnson's House Trust (£2,500 each) and Museum of London and National Association of Decorative and Fine Arts Societies (£1,500 each).

Church

The three grants in this category went to St Mary's Church – Acton (£5,000), Historic Chapels Trust (£2,500) and Methodist Church Open Door Project (£1,000).

Arts

The 23 grants in this category were led by £19,000 to City Music Society and £10,000 to Orpheus Centre Trust. Other beneficiaries included Children's Music Workshop – Tower Hamlets, Dulwich Picture Gallery and National Opera Studio (£3,000 each), Islington Design Trust (£2,000) and Paintings in Hospitals Scotland and Royal Scottish National Orchestra (£1,000 each).

Education

Of the 41 grants made in this category 8 were for amounts over £10,000 each,

including £58,000 to Science for Society Courses, £38,000 for literacy projects in 8 primary schools, £26,000 to Education of the Children of London Clergy and £12,000 to Guildhall School of Music and Drama.

Other beneficiaries included West Dean College (£8,000), St Paul's Cathedral Choir School (£3,500), Parents for Inclusion (£2,800), Caldecott Foundation (£2,000), Phoenix Special Needs School (£1,000) and Mansion House Scholarship Scheme (£500).

Support of the craft

Grants went to Goldsmiths Arts Trust Fund (£916,000), Goldsmiths', Silversmiths' and Jewellers' Benevolent Fund (£26,000 in two grants), Goldsmiths' Craft and Design Council (£20,000). The sum of £91,000 was distributed towards 17 apprentice bursaries.

Exclusions

Applications are not normally considered on behalf of:

- medical research;
- memorials to individuals;
- overseas projects;
- animal welfare;
- individuals, except those who have been resident in certain inner London boroughs for at least ten years; these are made through Social Services or similar.

Applications from any organisation, including those previously successful, are not considered more frequently than once every three years.

Applications

Applications for general charitable support should be made on an application form available from the charity. This form requires detailed information about the purpose of the grant (including a budget for the proposed activity; the methods by which the success of the project will be evaluated; the income/expenditure projection for the organisation for the current year; other grantmaking organisations appealed to for the same project and with what result). The form should be accompanied by the following:

- a letter stating the aims and objectives of the charity, including an outline of the current work and details of staffing, organisational structure and use of volunteers;
- the specific purpose for which the grant is requested;

- the organisation's most recent annual report and audited accounts.

Trustees meet monthly except during August and September.

Mike Gooley Trailfinders Charity

Cancer research, general

£511,000 (2002/03)

Beneficial area UK.

Trailfinders Ltd, 9 Abingdon Road, London W8 6AH

Tel. 020 7938 3143 **Fax** 020 7937 6059

Correspondent Louise Breton

Trustees M D W Gooley; Mrs B M Gooley; T P Gooley; M Bannister.

Charity Commission no. 1048993

Information available Accounts on file at the Charity Commission, but without a full narrative report or a list of grants. The charity provided additional information about their grants on request.

The charity supports medical research, community projects which encourage young people in outdoor activities and armed forces veterans' organisations, particularly the Soldiers, Sailors, Airmen and Families Association - Forces Help.

In the period of 2002/03 the charity awarded substantial sums to medical research charities, fulfilling their pledge of donating £6.1 million to Cancer Research UK.

In 2002/03 the charity had assets of £4.7 million with an income of £850,000 and gave grants totalling £511,000.

Two grants were awarded in this period, with £500,000 to Cancer Research UK and £10,000 to Prostate Cancer Charity.

Exclusions

Grants are not made to overseas charities or to individuals.

Applications

In writing to the correspondent.

The Goshen Trust

Christian

£731,000 (2002/03)

Beneficial area North east England and overseas.

PO Box 367, Stockton-on-Tees TS16 9YR

Correspondent R Oliver, Administrator

Trustees *A G Dicken; P B Dicken; J R Dicken; A Dicken; R Oliver.*

Charity Commission no. 274910

Information available Accounts were on file at the Charity Commission.

The trust mainly supports Christian organisations with a preference for the north east of England. Christian mission works overseas is also funded.

In 2002/03 the trust had an income of £743,000 and made grants totalling £731,000. There were 43 grants made for £1,000 or more.

Beneficiaries during the year included King Bible College – Oxford (£100,000), Emmanuel Fellowship (£76,000), Emmanuel Christian Centre (£65,000), Cross Rhythms (£30,000), Mercy Ships (£25,000), Centre for Justice and Liberty (£16,000), Full Gospel Christian Centre (£12,000), Operation Mobilisation (£10,000) and Reach and Teach Ministries (£6,000).

Beneficiaries receiving £5,000 or less included Walk Through the Bible Ministries, Christian Friends of Israel, Make a Child Smile, On the Move Trust, Moorlands College and Fusion.

In 2003/04 the trust had a total expenditure of almost £2.8 million. Unfortunately, although submitted by the trust to the Charity Commission, the accounts for that year had not made it to the public files for inspection.

Applications

In writing to the correspondent. Applications are considered in March, June, September and December. An sae is needed if a reply is required. Initial applications should include minimum information as further information from potential beneficiaries will be requested.

This entry was not confirmed by the trust, but was correct according to information on file at the Charity Commission.

The Gosling Foundation Limited

Nautical and service charities, general

£2.8 million (2002/03)

Beneficial area UK.

21 Bryanston Street, Marble Arch, London W1A 4NH

Correspondent Miss Anne Yusof, Secretary

Trustees *Sir Donald Gosling; Ronald F Hobson.*

Charity Commission no. 326840

Information available Annual report and accounts on file at the Charity Commission.

Summary

About 150 grants are given each year to a wide range of charities, with naval and other army-related charities generally receiving substantial support. There are some grants for around £100,000 or over each year, while most are for £5,000 or under. Perhaps one-third of beneficiaries will have received a grant the previous year.

General

The foundation was established in 1985 by Sir Donald Gosling, co-founder of NCP car parks and former seaman. The foundation's endowment derives from his personal fortune. In 2002/03 had assets of £69 million and an income of £2.8 million all of which was given in a total of 134 grants.

Almost 75% of the grant total was made up by ten large donations of £100,000 or more. The beneficiaries were Fleet Air Arm Museum Appeal Fund and Royal Navy Submarine Museum (£500,000 each), Historic Royal Palaces (£350,000), John Groom Association for the Disabled (£200,000), Royal Naval Reserve 100 Project (£125,000), Britannia Association and Duke of Edinburgh Award Scheme (£103,000 each), Imperial War Museum, Outward Bound Trust and Parachute Regiment Central Fund (£100,000 each).

There were 23 grants for between £10,000 and £35,000, a number went to nautical organisations such as HMS Welfare Trusts. Most other grants were for amounts of £5,000 or under and went to a wide range of organisations.

Beneficiaries included Imperial War Museum, Rainbow Trust and Refuge (£5,000 each), Royal Horticultural Society and Variety Club of Great Britain (£2,000 each), Ocean Youth Club and RSPCA £1,000 each), Royal British Legion and Whizz Kids (£500 each).

Most general grants go to national organisations, although some local organisations are supported. There may be a particular interest in supporting London-based charities. Beneficiaries included City of London Police Federation Fund and London Youth Trust (£1,000 each), London Youth Clubs (£650), Royal London Society for the Blind (£500), City of London Development Trust (£200)

Applications

To the correspondent in writing.

The Grand Charity of Freemasons

Social welfare, medical research and hospices

£1.5 million in non-Masonic grants (2002/03)

Beneficial area England and Wales.

60 Great Queen Street, London WC2B 5AZ

Tel. 020 7395 9296 **Fax** 020 7395 9295

Email info@the-grand-charity.org

Website www.grandcharity.org

Correspondent The Chief Executive

Trustee *The council, consisting of a president and at least 26 council members, listed in the annual reports.*

Charity Commission no. 281942

Information available Annual report and accounts, with detailed grants lists, were provided by the trust.

Summary

Grants range from £500 to over £100,000 for national rather than local charities (many of which are supported by local Masonic lodges). Most of the money is spent on about 40 large grants to national charities. A few very large grants (over £100,000) are made each year, other grants in this category are often for about £25,000. Small grants are usually £5,000 or less. There is a separate programme for small grants to hospices.

General

The Freemasons' Grand Charity is the central charity of all Freemasons in England and Wales. It provides grants for three purposes:

- the relief of 'poor and distressed Freemasons' and their dependants;
- the support of other Masonic charities;
- the support of all other UK charities.

Geographic coverage

The charity makes grants to registered charities which operate nationally in England and Wales. Local or regional charities are not eligible for funding and should apply to the Provincial Grand Lodge of the region in which they operate (their offices are listed in telephone directories, usually under 'Freemasons' or 'Masons').

Size of grant

The charity gives grants ranging from £500 to £500,000. Grants, for core funding, will be made up to £5,000 only to charities with an annual income of £500,000 or less. Any grant greater than this amount must be for a designated purpose.

Policy areas supported

The charity gives grants principally in support of general welfare in the widest sense, especially of the young and the old. Its areas of support are broadly based and cover support for vulnerable people, health and medical research and opportunities for young people.

For grants greater than £5,000, the charity will only provide funding for a specific purpose. Projects should also contribute to the well-being of the wider community and be recognised and acknowledged publicly.

The charity also gives grants, normally for between £700 and £3,000, to hospices as part of a nationwide project.

Grants in 2002/03

In 2002/03 the trust had assets of £61 million. Total income was £13 million, mostly from donations, festivals and contributions from lodges. Grants were given to Masonic organisations totalling £50,000, individual Masons totalling £2.3 million and non-Masonic causes totalling

£1.5 million. Non-Masonic grants were broken down as follows:

Emergency grants for relief aid

Two grants were made; they were £15,000 to Algerian earthquake (via the Red Cross) and £5,000 to Cyclone Ami (via the south west Pacific group of lodges).

Designated grants

22 grants were made totalling £624,000. The largest was £120,000 to Northwick Park. Other beneficiaries of grants of £10,000 or more included Homestart (£65,000), Seven Springs (£32,000), Action on Addiction, Contact the Elderly and Implanted Devices Group (£30,000 each), United Response (£29,000), Cancer Bacup and Children's Fire and Burn Trust (£26,000 each), Imperial Cancer Research (£25,000), Bicycle Helmet Initiative Trust (£22,000), Rett Syndrome Association (£15,000), Help the Aged – Gardening Blitz Week Project (£13,000), Bliss (£11,000) and Changing Faces and National Society for Epilepsy (£10,000 each).

Hospices

Grants to 202 hospices throughout England and Wales totalled £500,000.

Grants over £10,000 each

Other beneficiaries were Headway (£80,000), Dial UK (£75,000), Colon Cancer and Downs Syndrome Education Trust (£20,000 each) and Living Paintings Trust (£10,000).

Grants of less than £10,000

The seven largest grants of £5,000 each went to ACT, Lansdowne House Alcohol Advisory Unit, Lymphoma Association, Miracles, Queens Nursing Institute, Starlight Children's Foundation and Thames Valley & Chiltern Air Ambuance Trust. Other beneficiaries included ASSIST (£4,000), Children with AIDS Charity (£3,000), Bendrigg Trust, British Dyslexics, JET and Operation New World (£2,500 each), Families and Carers Trust, Sequal Trust and Tripscope (£2,000 each), Harvest Trust and Matthew Trust (£1,500 each) and Soundabout (£1,000).

Exclusions

Local or regional charities are not eligible for funding.

Grants are not normally given to:

- individuals (other than for the relief of 'poor and distressed Freemasons' and their poor and distressed dependants);
- organisations not registered with the Charity Commission;
- activities that are primarily the responsibility of central or local government or some other responsible body;
- organisations or projects outside of England and Wales;
- animal welfare;
- the arts;
- the environment;
- charities with sectarian (religious) or political objectives.

Applications

Application forms are available from the charity office or from the website. This form must be completed in full, either typed or written in block capitals, and accompanied by a copy of the latest annual report and full audited accounts; these must be less than 18 months old.

Hospice grant applications are made on a separate form, available from either the appropriate Provincial Grand Lodge (listed in telephone directories, usually under 'Freemasons' or 'Masons') or the charity office.

Applications may be submitted to the office of the charity at any time throughout the year.

The Great Britain Sasakawa Foundation

Links between Great Britain and Japan

£362,000 (2003)
Beneficial area UK, Japan.

Dilke House, 1 Malet Street, London WC1E 7JN
Tel. 020 7436 9042 Fax 020 7355 2230
Email grants@gbsf.org.uk
Website www.gbsf.org.uk
Correspondent The Administrator
Trustees Council: Prof. Peter Mathias, chair; Hon. Yoshio Sakurauchi; Michael French, Treasurer; Baroness Brigstocke; Jeremy Brown; Baroness Park of

• GREAT / GREATER

Monmouth; Earl of St Andrews; Kazuo Chiba; Prof. Harumi Kimura; Yohei Sasakawa; Akira Iriyama; Prof. Shoichi Watanabe; Sir John Boyd.

Charity Commission no. 290766

Information available Accounts and report were provided by the foundation, including a full list of grants.

The Foundation's aim is to develop good relations between the United Kingdom and Japan by advancing the education of the people of both nations in each other's culture, society and achievements. It was established following a meeting in 1983 when the late Ryoichi Sasakawa, a shipbuilding tycoon, and the late Robert Maxwell met a number of senior British politicians to discuss Anglo-Japanese relations. The foundation was inaugurated two years later with a gift of £9.5 million from the Japan Shipbuilding Industry Foundation (now called The Nippon Foundation). It has offices in both Tokyo and London.

Support is given for activities in the following fields:

- youth exchanges;
- schools and education;
- Japanese language;
- arts and culture;
- humanities and social sciences;
- science and technology;
- medicine and health;
- environment;
- sport.

The foundation's awards are intended to provide 'pump-priming' and not core funding of projects, but even small grants have enabled a wide range of projects to reach fruition, such as:

- Visits between the UK and Japan by academics, professionals, creative artists, teachers, young people, journalists and representatives of civic and non-governmental organisations.
- Research and collaborative studies, seminars, workshops, lectures and publications in academic and specialist fields.
- Teaching and development of Japanese language and cultural studies in schools, Further Education colleges and universities.
- Exhibitions, performances and creative productions by artists, musicians, film-makers, writers and theatre groups.

In 2003 the foundation had assets of £17.7 million and an income of £666,000. Grants totalled £362,000. Examples of beneficiaries include: Institute for Ageing and Health – Newcastle (£20,000), GBSF Japan Experience 2003 (£16,000), Alzheimer's Disease International (£6,000), Royal Institute of International Affairs (£5,000), Community Action Network, Cross Culture Holdings Limited, 'The Sixteen', Royal National Theatre and Visiting Arts (£4,000 each), Centre for Japanese and East Asian Studies and Japanese Language Committee (£3,500 each), Edinburgh College of Art, Royal Armouries and Sainsbury Institute – Norwich (£3,000 each), Meiji Gakuin University – Tokyo and Tomlinscote School (£3,000 each), Japanese Business Language and Practice Project and Sadler's Wells Theatre (£2,500 each), Pestalozzi International Village Trust (£2,000), Global Books Ltd (£1,000), Bristol University (£500) and Association for Language Learning (£200).

In 2001 the foundation established The Butterfield Awards to commemorate the achievements of Lord Butterfield, a medical researcher, clinician and academic administrator, and former chair of the foundation. The awards aim to 'encourage exchanges and collaborations between researchers and practitioners in medicine and health'. Five awards were made in 2003.

Exclusions

Grants are not made to individuals applying on their own behalf. The foundation can, however, consider proposals from organisations that support the activities of individuals, provided they are citizens of the UK or Japan.

No grants can be made for the construction, conservation or maintenance of land and buildings.

The foundation will not support activities involving politics, legislation or election to public office.

Grants are not normally made for medical research.

Applications

In advance of formal applications, foundation staff welcome telephone enquiries or personal visits to their office to discuss eligibility. The awards committee meets in London in February, May and October. Applications should be received by December, March and August. Awards meetings in Tokyo are held in April and October, with applications to be submitted by February and September. Applicants should request an application form either from the London headquarters or from the Tokyo liaison office; however, the foundation expresses a strong preference for e-mailed applications. A form will be e-mailed on request, and is also available on their website. Applications should contain the following information:

- a summary of the proposed project and its aims, including its likely impact and long-term benefits
- total cost of the project and the amount of the desired grant, together with a note of other expected sources of funds, including estimated period for research projects, visits or study
- a description of the applicant's organisation and, where relevant, brief career details of the main participants in any project, and where appropriate the ages of those individuals who may be the recipients.

Applicants are expected to make a careful calculation of all costs of a project before seeking a grant. Where a grant is approved no application for an increase will be accepted after approval, except in very special circumstances.

The foundation will not consider making a further grant to an applicant until at least two years after a successful application. Organisations applying should be registered charities, recognised educational institutions, local or regional authorities, churches, media companies, publishers or such other bodies as the foundation may approve.

School applicants are requested to first file an application with Connect Youth International, Japan Exchange Programme, 10 Spring Gardens, London SW1A 2BN (which is part of the British Council), to which the foundation grants external finance, aimed at encouraging exchanges (both ways) for schools in Great Britain and Japan (their website is www.connectyouthinternational.com).

All applicants are notified shortly after each Awards Committee meeting of the decisions of the trustees. Those offered grants are asked to sign and return an acceptance form and are given the opportunity to say when they would like to receive their grant.

Greater Bristol Foundation

General

£1.5 million (2002/03)

Beneficial area Former Avon area – Bristol, North Somerset, South

164

Gloucestershire and Bath & North East Somerset.

Royal Oak House, Royal Oak Avenue, Bristol BS1 4GB

Tel. 0117 989 7700 **Fax** 0117 989 7701

Email info@gbf.org.uk

Website www.gbf.org.uk

Correspondent Helen Moss, Director

Trustees *Trevor Smallwood, chair; Will Bee; Norman Biddle; Gillian Camm; Steve Egginton; Jos Harrison; Alfred Morris; John Pontin; Simon Speirs; Tim Stevenson; Simon Storvik; Jay Tidmarsh; Heather Wheelhouse; Sir David Wills; Sam Allen; Eric Thomas; Peter Rilett.*

Charity Commission no. 1080418

Information available Guidelines and application form, annual report and accounts and annual review are all available.

Great Bristol Foundation is a community foundation, which manages and distributes funding on behalf of individuals, companies, charitable trusts and statutory agencies to meet needs in and around the west of England.

The trust runs its own programme, known as the Express Fund, which makes grants of up to £1,000 to small, local and community organisations in the former Avon area. Priority is given to cases where a small amount of funding can make a difference in the disadvantaged areas of the beneficial region. The trust is also sometimes able to make larger donations, generally up to £5,000, depending on an organisation's work and particular funding needs.

The trust also manages a range of other funds which have their own criteria, closing dates and maximum amount available. These funds are listed below under the geographical areas they support. Also listed are funds which support projects across the west of England.

Grants for Bristol city

- Arts Access Fund – Grants for artists with disabilities in the city of Bristol to help them develop their work. Grants of £1,000 are available for access issues and £3,000 for project work.
- Bristol Collection Box Scheme – Grants of up to £1,000 for organisations based in Bristol that support the resettlement of homeless people.
- Bristol Youth Community Action (BYCA) – a) Grants of up to £1,000 for community safety projects in Bristol led by young people. b)

Funding for groups providing summer holiday activities for young people in Bristol.
- GWR FM Bristol Kidz Fund – Grants of up to £2,000 to organisations based within a ten-mile radius of the centre of Bristol.
- Neighbourhood Renewal Community Chest and Community Learning Chest – Grants of up to £5,000 to community organisations in Neighbourhood Renewal areas, other pockets of need and communities of interest in Bristol city.
- Neighbourhood Renewal 'Pockets' Money Fund – Grants up to £10,000 to community organisations working in areas that address the following themes; educational attainment, health and crime and community safety.
- Safer Communities Fund – Grants of up to £2,000 to organisations in Bristol working to make their community safer.
- Social Economy Business Development Fund – Up to £15,000 to strengthen and develop social enterprises in Bristol.
- University of Bristol Students Rag Fund – Grants of up to £1,000 for organisations in Bristol that work with children, homeless people or support people with long-term illnesses.

Grants for Bath & North East Somerset

- Bath & North East Somerset Fund – Grants of up to £1,000 for small, local voluntary and community organisations in disadvantaged areas of Bath & North East Somerset. During 2003/04 the fund is particulary interested in supporting local community resources, such as meeting places and community art activities.

Grants for North Somerset

- North Somerset Fund – Grants of up to £1,000 for small, local voluntary and community organisations in disadvantaged areas of North Somerset.

Grants for South Gloucestershire

- Express Fund – Grants of up to £1,000 for small, local voluntary and community organisations in disadvantaged areas of South Gloucestershire.

Grants for all area in the west of England

- Bristol & West Group Charitable Fund – Grants of up to £1,000 to

organisations working in the south west of England that support the development of disadvantaged young people.
- Churngold Environment Fund – up to £5,000 to support environmental and educational projects.
- Local Network Fund for Children and Young People – Grants of up to £7,000 for community and voluntary groups in the former Avon area that provide local solutions to the problem of child poverty.
- Mall Fountain Fund – Up to £1,000 to small, local voluntary and community organisations which help people in need within a 25-mile radius of The Mall.

Each of the funds listed above has its own criteria, so the foundation should be contacted for further information (see 'applications').

In 2002/03 the foundation made 978 grants totalling £1.5 million. In the previous year had assets of £6 million and an income of £1.8 million. 836 grants totalling £1 million were made to local charities, voluntary groups and community projects working in the west of England (former Avon) region. It was also noted that grants made had an average size of £1,200.

In 2001/02, when grants totalled £1 million, beneficiaries were broken down as follows:

Helping people throughout the community – 32%

Beneficiaries included: Bristol East Side Traders for a training programme for local traders who want to develop a market stall and for a series of festival-type activities to run alongside a market being piloted in the inner-city (£10,000); North Somerset Volunteer Agency for a development worker to provide practical support and advice to local charities and community groups (£8,000); Avon Valley Railway Trust to improve public access and use of this site on the Avon Valley walkway (£5,000); Cycle West to install cycle stands at public buildings in North Bristol (£4,300); Avon Friends of the Earth to develop recycling services in Hartcliffe (£2,000); Stockwood Community Council for the costs of a newsletter and community survey in this isolated part of the city (£1,000); West Arts Festval for organising and running a short story festival (£800); and Castle Green United Reformed Church to improve the garden for groups using the church hall in Eastville (£600).

Young People – 31%

Organisations included: Basement Studio to run open radio and media training sessions for young people (£12,000); Central Bristol Youth Sports Forum to set up a coordinated programme of sporting opportunties and training for young people (£10,000); Young Bristol for a week of activities in Sea Mills and Fishponds (£1,000), to run a 5-a-side football tournament across the city (£1,800) and to run a series of taster days for young people interested in different kinds of volunteering (£7,300); Imayala for a community event giving young people training and skills opportunities (£6,500); No Way Trust for an awareness-raising session in schools about the reality of prison life (£1,500); Frith Youth Centre for repairs and Wick Skateboarding Group for equipment (£1,000 each); Ace Youth Theatre to allow young people from Lawrence Weston to visit The Old Vic Theatre, Bristol (£800); and Northavon Youth Theatre to produce a play written by young people (£700).

Families – 12%

Beneficiaries included: Bristol Children's Playhouse to create a garden and make environmental improvements (£5,000); Neighbourhood Centre Kids Club for equipment and an additional worker to run extra sessions (£2,000); Teyfant Community School to start a breakfast club for pupils and Colstons Primary School PTA for an adventure playpark (£1,000 each); Community Nutrition and Weight Loss for running weekly sessions promoting healthy eating for all the family and Copplestone Out of School Club for arts and craft equipment (£900 each); and Holy Cross PTA for out-of-school activities (£600).

Disabled People – 11%

Beneficiaries included: Knowley West Media Project/Brave New World for a multi-media IT project helping young people with disabilities people to explore their artistic capabilities (£5,000); Art and Power to enable a group of artists from Bristol to take part in a residency at Tate Liverpool and Infinite Blue Productions for the development of a film production (£3,000 each); Lifeskills for improved disability access (£1,000); and Woodspring Association for Blind People for equipment to help the user group embrace new technology (£700).

Elderly People – 6%

Beneficiaries included: Elderly People's Group for transport costs for this lunch club for older Chinese people (£2,000); Community Caretaking Project for caretaking services for older, vulnerable people no longer able to carry out their own repairs (£1,400); Age Concern Bristol for upgrading a computer system (£1,000); and Dementia Care Trust for sense-stimulating therapeutic equipment for a day centre and St Paul's Advice Centre for new chairs for the waiting area (£900 each).

Homeless people – 5%

Recipients included: Missing Link to develop a training and lifeskills project for people who are moving into their own accommodation after long-term homelessness (£5,000); Second Step Housing Association to provide grants for people who are moving into their own homes after a long period of homelessness, enabling them to buy basic household equipment (£1,700); Cold Weather Group for a volunteer co-ordinator's post (£1,000); and Bristol Methodist Church for a dishwasher (£700).

Black and minortiy ethnic people – 3%

Organisations included: SARI for operating costs (£10,000); Awaz Utaoh for trips for young people in need of support (£750), travel and volunteer costs for a drop-in project for Asian women (£1,000) and a cultural event for Asian young people (£3,000); YWCA for a research project into the counselling and support needs of young Asian women in south Bristol (£2,700); Somali Women's Group for computer equipment to develop the services (£2,600); and Displaced Youth Programme for activities for young refugees (£2,400).

Exclusions

The foundation's own grants programme does not fund:

- appeals outside the beneficial area;
- national organisations without a base in the beneficial area;
- individuals;
- large capital appeals;
- annual donations;
- overseas trips;
- promotion of religious causes;
- political organisations.

Applications

Application forms and full guidelines can either be downloaded from the foundation's website at www.gbf.org.uk or requested by telephone. Contacts are as follows:

Grants for Bristol City – Contact Ronnie Brown or Alice Meason on 0117 989 7700 or email info@gbf.org.uk

Grants for Bath & North East Somerset – Contact Jilly Edwards on 01225 443996 or email banes@gbf.org.uk

Grants for North Somerset – Contact Ronnie Brown on 0117 989 7700 or email northsomerset@gbf.org.uk

Grants for South Gloucestershire – Contact Ronnie Brown or Alice Meason on 0117 989 7700 or email info@gbf.org.uk

Grants for all areas in the West of England – Contact Ronnie Brown or Alice Meason on 0117 989 7700 or email info@gbf.or.uk

Please remember to include with your application:

- your most recent accounts or financial information. If your organisation has only recently started please include an estimated budget for your first year;
- a list of the names and addresses of the members of your management committee.

The Grocers' Charity

General

£542,000 (2002/03)

Beneficial area UK.

Grocers' Hall, Princes Street, London EC2R 8AD

Tel. 020 7606 3113 **Fax** 020 7600 3082

Email anne@grocershall.co.uk

Website www.grocershall.co.uk/charity

Correspondent Miss Anne Blanchard, Charity Administrator

Trustee *Directors of The Grocers' Trust Company Ltd (about 30).*

Charity Commission no. 255230

Information available Annual accounts; annual report with list of grants (for £1,000 or more), detailed narrative breakdown of grants/grantmaking and guidelines for applicants.

Summary

The Grocers' Charity was established in 1968, and has general charitable aims. The charity states:

Grant-making policy is reviewed periodically, which may result in different categories attracting a greater level of support. Currently, some 36% of the annual expenditure is committed to the field of education, by way of internal scholarships and bursaries at schools and colleges with which the Grocers' Company has historical links.

The charity's main interests are relief of poverty with an emphasis on young people, education, disability, medicine, the arts, heritage, the church and older people. The current emphasis is on the first two categories. Both capital or revenue projects are supported and grants are usually one-off.

Grantmaking

In 2002/03 the charity had assets of £8.6 million and an income of £507,000. Grants totalled £542,000. Of the 947 applications received, 126 were successful. Grants were broken down as follows:

Relief of poverty (inc. youth)	£85,000	16%
Education	£196,000	36%
Medicine	£34,000	6%
Disability	£99,000	18%
Churches	£27,000	5%
Heritage	£37,000	7%
The arts	£37,000	7%
Older people	£26,000	5%

The charity's annual report lists grants of £1,000 or more, and the amount of smaller grants and their total.

Relief of poverty/disadvantaged young people

There were 32 grants in this category. The two largest were £12,000 each to Fairbridge for core costs and Network East Foyers – Hackney Foyer. Other beneficiaries included VSO to sponsor five volunteers (£5,000), Emmaus South Lambeth, Hope and Homes for Children and St Botolph's Project (£3,000 each), Oasis Trust – Southwark Health Centre and Roots and Shoots – Kennington (£2,500 each), Book Aid International, British Red Cross and Seaview Projects – Hastings (£2,000 each), Army Benevolent Fund and Morning Star Trust (£1,500 each) and ARCC, Anti-Slavery International, Phoenix House and South and West Lancashire Food Bank – Skelmersdale (£1,000 each). Three donations of less than £1,000 totalled £1,600.

Education

A total of 25 donations were listed in this category. The company's schools at Oundle in Northamptonshire received a total of £112,000 to fund internal

scholarships and bursaries. Also the sum of £18,000 went to fund bursaries for children of freemen and others. Other grants included those to the Elms – Coldwall (£9,800), City and Guilds of London Art School – Bursaries (£6,600), St Paul's Cathedral Choir School (£5,500), Mansion House Scholarship Scheme (£5,000), City of London Freemen's School – Scholarships (£3,000), Guildhall School of Music & Drama Foundation (£2,500), Camberwell Choir School (£1,500) and Fitzwilliam Museum – Glanville Lecture (£1,000). Donations of less than £1,000 each were made to four organisations and totalled £1,900.

Medicine

The 17 beneficiaries in this category included Juvenile Diabetes Research Foundation (£5,700), Association of Post Natal Illness and Alzheimer's Research Trust (£3,000 each), Cancer Research UK (£2,500), International Spinal Research and Sight Savers International (£2,000 each) and Barts City Life Saver and Cancer Resource Centre – south west London (£1,000 each). Unlisted grants under £1,000 were made to two organisations and totalled just under £1,000.

Disability

Thirty four grants were made in this category, the two largest being £20,000 each to Scope – Camborne Project and the Enabling Partnership. Other beneficiaries included the Grange Centre – Bookham, Dame Vera Lynn Trust and SHARE Community (£3,000 each), University of Cambridge for equipment for a Disability Resource Centre and Prospect Hall – Birmingham (£2,500 each), Blind in Business, Eating Disorders Association, Headway Hurstwood Park building appeal, Shakespeare Link and Treloar Trust (£2,000 each), Aidis Trust and Families in Focus – Essex (£1,500 each) and Chichester Diocesan Authority for Family Support Work and Wiltshire & Bath Independent Living Centre (£1,000 each). Donations of less than £1,000 each were made to four organisations and totalled £2,000.

Churches

The annual contributions made in support of the Livings under the patronage of the Grocer's Company and the payments to the Parochial Church Councils of those parishes, accounted for £21,000. Other donations made in this

category were to churches having a close connection with the company.

Heritage

There were 34 beneficiaries in this category, the recipient of the largest grant being the Museum of London – Medieval Gallery which received £10,000. Other beneficiaries inlcuded the 1944 Trust, Charleston Trust – East Sussex and the Georgian Theatre Trust – North Yorkshire (£3,000 each) Guildford Cathedral Music Development Foundation (£2,500), Crossness Engines Trust and Heritage of London Trust (£2,000 each), the College of Arms towards book conservation (£1,500), Cathedral Cams, City of London Endowment Trust for St Paul's Cathedral, National Life Story Collection and Wild Camel Protection Foundation (£1,000 each). Three donations of less than £1,000 each totalled £1,600.

The arts

There were 17 donations in this category. Beneficiaries included Edward Barnsley Education Trust, Central School of Ballet, Yehudi Menuhin School – Surrey and Unicorn Children's Centre – Southwark (£3,000 each), Yvonne Arnaud Theatre – Guildford (£2,500), Bampton Classical Opera for Education Outreach, British Youth Opera and Lyric Hammersmith for the installation of an induction loop system (£2,000 each), English Touring Opera and London Festival of Chamber Music (£1,500 each) and Courtauld Institute of Art for book conservation (£1,000).

Older people

There were 9 grants made in this category, the largest being £11,000 to Age Concern Theatre Trust. Other beneficiaries included the Brendon Nursing Trust towards a new passenger lift (£3,000), British Commonwealth Ex-services League (£2,000), Silloth Nursing & Residential Care Home – Cumbria (£1,500). There was one further unlisted donation of £500.

Exclusions

Only UK-registered charities are supported. Individuals cannot receive grants directly, although grants can be given to organisations on their behalf. Support is rarely given to the following unless there is a specific or long-standing connection with the Grocers' Company:

- cathedrals, churches and other ecclesiastical bodies;
- hospices;

- schools and other educational establishments;
- research projects.

Applications

In writing to the correspondent on the charity's official headed notepaper. Full details of the project or projects referred to in the application and a copy of the latest audited accounts and annual report should be included. The receipt of applications is not acknowledged but all receive notification of the outcome. They are considered in January, April, June and November and should be received two months before the relevant meeting. Informal enquiries are welcome by telephone or e-mail to the correspondent.

Unsuccessful applicants are advised to wait a year before re-applying. Successful applicants should wait for at least two years before re-applying.

The M & R Gross Charities Limited

Jewish causes

£1.2 million (2001/02)
Beneficial area UK and overseas.

Cohen Arnold & Co., New Burlington House, 1075 Finchley Road, London NW11 0PU
Tel. 020 8731 0777 **Fax** 020 8731 0778
Correspondent The Trustees
Trustees Milton Gross; Mrs Rifka Gross; Mrs Sarah Padwa; Michael Saberski.
Charity Commission no. 251888
Information available Accounts are on file at the Charity Commission.

This trust makes grants to educational and religious organisations within the orthodox Jewish community in Great Britain and abroad. In 2001/02 it had assets of over £16 million and an income of £4.1 million.

There were 16 grants in total. By far the largest grant of £703,000 went to United Talmudical Associates, which receives regular support from the charities. Ardenlink Ltd received the second highest amount of £175,000. The other ten grants were all for amounts between the £60,000 to Kolel Shomrei

Hachomoth and the £2,500 for the Torath Chested.

In 2002/03 the trust's total expenditure had increased to over £2 million. Unfortunately, although submitted by the trust to the Charity Commission, the accounts for that year had not made it to the public files for inspection.

Applications

In writing to the organisation.

The Gulbenkian Foundation

Education, arts, welfare

£2.1 million (2003)
Beneficial area UK and the Republic of Ireland.

98 Portland Place, London W1B 1ET
Tel. 020 7636 5313 **Fax** 020 7908 7580
Email info@gulbenkian.org.uk
Website www.gulbenkian.org.uk
Correspondent Paula Ridley, Director
Trustee The foundation's Board of Administration in Lisbon. UK resident trustee: Mikhael Essayan.

Information available Good annual reports with full details of the foundation's thinking, policies and grants. Excellent if slightly slow website. A free leaflet 'Advice to Applicants for Grants' is also available. As the foundation is not a charity registered in Britain there are no files at the Charity Commission. There is also a free publications catalogue of its new and recent titles.

Summary

The foundation is organised around programmes in:

- arts (Siân Ede)
- education (Simon Richey)
- social welfare (Paula Ridley)
- Anglo-Portuguese Cultural Relations (Miguel Santos).

There is a small programme of modest 'director's grants' which may range rather more widely.

Grantmaking takes two forms: principally, making grants, usually for less than £10,000 but now with a number of grants for larger amounts (though seldom exceeding £30,000), for projects proposed by applicants; and to a

smaller extent, meeting the costs of projects and activities initiated by the foundation itself (and not covered by this entry).

The foundation has an expert staff and often works closely with the organisations that it funds.

In September 2002 the foundation announced the Gulbenkian Prize for Museum of the Year. This is a £100,000 prize to be awarded annually to one museum or gallery, large or small, in the UK. It is awarded for the most innovative and inspiring idea–be it an exhibition, new gallery, public programme or important new initiative. In 2004 the prize was awarded to the Scottish National Gallery of Modern Art in Edinburgh.

More information is available from www.thegulbenkianprize.org.uk

Background

This is described as follows by the foundation:

Calouste Sarkis Gulbenkian was an Armenian born in 1869. He became a British citizen, conducted much of his work in Britain, and finally settled in Portugal. The Calouste Gulbenkian Foundation was established in 1956, a year after his death.

The headquarters of the foundation are in Lisbon and consist of the administration, which deals with grant-giving throughout the world, together with a museum housing the founder's art collections, a research library, a centre for scientific research, concert halls, indoor and open-air theatres, exhibition galleries and conference halls, a centre for modern art, a children's pavilion, an orchestra, a choir and a ballet company. The foundation also maintains a Portuguese Cultural Centre in Paris, and a grant-giving branch in London for the United Kingdom and the Republic of Ireland [with which this entry is concerned. Ed.].

There is one resident trustee in London, but the UK branch operates with wide local discretion. However grants for more than £15,000 have to be referred back to Lisbon, a necessarily more complicated and time-consuming process.

Guidelines for applicants

The following information is from the foundation's excellent leaflet for applicants:

The UK Branch of the Calouste Gulbenkian Foundation has a reputation for recognising and initiating innovative ideas. The foundation focuses on a few specific grant priorities in any one year in order to do them justice – these change every two or three years. The 2005 priorities for the four programmes – Arts, Education, Social Welfare and Anglo-Portuguese Cultural Relations – are set out below.

As a general principle the foundation supports projects which are genuinely original in their field and also favours those which take place outside London.

The foundation is becoming increasingly proactive in inviting certain organisations to propose projects which meet its aims. It also commissions research and its own publications.

Applicants should note that the foundation very rarely gives grants towards core costs or salaries, and never does so in response to a general fundraising appeal. It cannot offer grants towards the simple continuation of existing services.

Current priorities

The four main areas the foundation supports, listed below, remain the same each year, but priorities within each of them change fairly frequently, at least every three or four years. Applicants are strongly recommended to check the website or call the foundation to request a copy of the most recent 'advice to applicants' leaflet.

Arts

Assistant director: Siân Ede

The Arts Programme is principally for professional arts organisations or individual professional artists working in partnerships or groups. Its purpose is to support the development of new art in any art form. It excludes activities which are linked to mainstream education.

Research and Development

The fundamental aim of the Arts Programme remains to provide early-stage support for experimental research and development activities for realisable professional arts projects. We are particularly interested in fostering unconventional and unusual ideas. Projects in which artists engage with science come within the scope of this programme. Individual projects are likely to attract grants up to £5,000. Larger grants may be offered to a select number of organisations after discussion initiated by the foundation.

Non-professional Arts Projects

The Foundation will make available grants to groups of non-professional participants outside the formal education and community sectors for the research and development of unusual experimental projects. Brief outlines of potential applications should be submitted to the Assistant Director for consideration at least three months before the start date of the project.

The Gulbenkian Prize for Museum of the Year

[2005] is the third year of the foundation's prestigious prize for museums and galleries in the UK. With one major annual prize of £100,000, the prize is awarded to the best and most imaginative initiative undertaken by a museum or gallery in the previous year. The winner of the 2005 Gulbenkian Prize will be announced in May.

For further information about The Gulbenkian Prize and how to apply see: www.thegulbenkianprize.org.uk or contact The Gulbenkian Prize Administrator: info@thegulbenkianprize.org.uk Tel: 020 7636 5365.

Education

Assistant director: Simon Richey

Educational Innovations and Developments

Helping Schools, Helping Parents

Assistance is offered:
- to primary and secondary schools, and those agencies that work with them, to enable them to provide educational opportunities for 'hard to reach' parents with particular regard to parenting skills;
- to primary and secondary schools, and those agencies that work with them, to enable them to offer support to all parents at significant stages in their child's development (i.e. transition from primary to secondary school, adolescence, etc.).

The Arts Included: Support for the Arts in Pupil Referral Units and In-school Learning Support Units

This programme is designed to encourage at a strategic level arts activities in PRUs and LSUs with a view to promoting pupils' personal, social and emotional development. In particular the programme aims to support the engagement of professional artists in these settings. Assistance is offered in the following categories:

Training initiatives that:
- help teachers in PRUs/LSUs initiate arts projects or residencies by artists/companies with greater confidence;
- help artists/companies develop a better understanding of the culture and needs of PRUs/LSUs.

Networks

Opportunities for teachers interested in promoting arts activities to develop networks that allow for the sharing of practice, the planning of joint initiatives, etc. Assistance could include help with the cost of cover, travel expenses, fees for visiting workshop leaders or speakers and, where appropriate, the payment of fees to allow for the co-ordination of such networks.

Dissemination

Help with the documentation and dissemination of effective practice whether through the printed word, visual displays, videos, websites, etc.

Evaluation

Help with the commissioning of evaluation studies by research consultants or educational establishments.

Exceptionally grants may be offered outside the above categories for projects considered to be of particular importance.

Social Welfare

Director: Paula Ridley
Grants manager: Ruby Cowling
Grants given under the Social Welfare programme will remain strongly focused on capacity building in local groups and neighbourhoods and exploring new forms of area management and service delivery, in particular:
- For community groups, in both rural and urban settings, which are developing new strategies for neighbourhood and area regeneration, including new forms of service delivery and social enterprise;
- For communities and professionals working together to develop effective skills in any of the following areas: neighbourhood management, housing management, neighbourhood services and employment;
- For research, by recognised organisations, which contributes to exploration and knowledge of new policy options to reduce social exclusion, including new forms of service delivery.
- The foundation will also consider projects offering sustainable solutions to local environmental issues. Of particular interest are projects which will encourage wider awareness of sustainability and personal responsibility.

Anglo-Portuguese Cultural Relations

Assistant director: Miguel Santos

This programme aims to help projects that promote contemporary Portuguese culture in the UK and the Republic of Ireland (British cultural projects in Portugal are the responsibility of the British Council). 'Cultural relations' are taken to include social welfare, as well as activities in the arts, crafts and education.

The programme includes:
- Activities and events concerned with Portugal or containing Portuguese elements – its language, culture, people. Unlike the other programmes, performances, exhibitions and festivals may be considered.
- Cultural and educational interaction between British or Irish and Portuguese people. This may include research and development visits to Portugal by professionals (festival and/or arts venue directors, managers, producers, etc.) who

169

are interested in presenting Portuguese arts in the UK and Ireland.

- The educational, cultural and social needs of the Portuguese immigrant communities (but not individual Portuguese immigrants or visitors).

But grants are not normally given for projects focused upon:

- sporting activities, tourism, holidays
- full-time teaching or research posts or visiting fellowships
- the maintenance, salary or supervision costs of researchers
- fees or expenses of individual students pursuing courses of education and training, or doing research
- UK cultural or other work in Portugal.

Grantmaking in 2003

The foundation is well known for the comprehensive accounts of its grantmaking in its excellent annual reports. That for 2003 is reprinted in part below, after the overall figures for the year.

Grant summary for 2003

Arts	£546,500
Education	£587,000
Social welfare	£568,000
Anglo-Portuguese Cultural Relations	£369,000
Total	£2,070,000

Director's Preface

During the past year, the United Kingdom Branch has been operating against a background of concern over the Government's plans to involve the voluntary sector—our clients—much more closely in the delivery of public services across the country. This proposal is driven by the need to improve service delivery, and to involve users more directly. There is no doubt that it is a very challenging proposition for the voluntary sector. Although some of the larger national charities are already service providers, there are huge implications for charities that need assistance with capacity-building in order to develop their ability to compete in these new markets. Both the Home Office and the Treasury are keenly engaged in agendas for change and support, though local authorities are considerably more cautious. While there are enormous issues to resolve, discussions have recognised the important role that charities can and do play. Government preference for the social enterprise model—long championed by this foundation—as one of the key delivery vehicles has been an interesting development. There is still a long way to go: questions not only of capacity but of procurement remain to be resolved (for example, meeting local needs while still abiding by European law). Our publication of John Pearce's *Social Enterprise in Anytown* in

March was well received as an important contribution to this debate.

The UK Branch has funded a number of other publications in these emerging policy areas during the year, amongst them *Public Interest: New models for delivering public services?* by the Public Management Foundation and *Replacing the State? The case for third sector public service delivery* by ACEVO (the Association of Chief Executives of Charitable Organisations). ACEVO has been much to the fore this year as issues of strategic direction and governance are becoming more current and critical, and we were pleased to support their publication.

Undoubtedly the highlight of 2003 was the award of the first Gulbenkian Prize for Museum of the Year. The foundation offers this annual £100,000 prize, the largest in Britain, for the most original new development in a museum or gallery anywhere in the UK. The prize is administered by an independent charity, The Museum Prize trust, chaired by Penelope, Viscountess Cobham, who worked tirelessly with her colleagues to ensure the success of the inaugural award. Six judges, chaired by Bamber Gascoigne, dealt with over 100 applications and a shortlist of 11 to select the winner—the National Centre for Citizenship and the Law at the Galleries of Justice in Nottingham. We were particularly pleased that the Chairman of the Foundation, Dr Emilio Rui Vilar, was able to visit London for the presentation of the prize by the Minister for the Arts, Baroness Blackstone. Our thanks go to all those involved.

Our own prize for enterprise and initiative must go to Miguel Santos, the UK Branch's Assistant Director in charge of Anglo-Portuguese Cultural Relations, and his assistant, Isabel Lucena, who between them ran the third year of the Atlantic Waves festival with even more success than before. Many concerts were sold out, the press coverage was extensive and friendly, and the profile of Portuguese music of all kinds was raised—the British suddenly acquired a fascination with Fado. In addition, Miguel's own programme continues to develop in reach and style.

The Arts, Education and Social Welfare Programmes also flourish. Sian Ede, Assistant Director in charge of Arts, pursues the Gulbenkian tradition of innovation, and is a prolific writer and traveller. Simon Richey, Assistant Director in charge of Education, is developing his work on arts activities for children who are excluded from school, and has launched a research project to test the effectiveness of this approach. Our Grants Manager, Ruby Cowling, assists me with the administration of the Social Welfare Programme. Refugees and asylum seekers were again a key focus, though we are

increasingly concerned with the elderly and the environment.

In 2003 the Director's programme supported, among many other projects, the provision of education facilities at Brading Roman Villa on the Isle of Wight [a grant of up to £15,000 to Oglander Roman Trust]; part of the restoration of the Reading Room at Rylands Library in Manchester [£20,000 towards the costs of providing signage, including Braille signage, in the Reading Room and throughout the building]; and the acquisition of a Paula Rego triptych by the Abbot Hall Art Gallery in Kendal [£5,000]. We also assisted a three-day forum held by the British Council in Wales to discuss the experiences of asylum seekers and how arts activities might be used to facilitate their integration into host communities [£8,500]; enabled five nineteenth-century Scottish newspapers to transfer their local heritage onto microfilm [£10,000 to the Newsplan 2000 Project]; and helped the Runnymede Trust with the costs of designing and evaluating a Black History Month Directory for use by schools, colleges and other organisations [£7,000].

Other beneficiaries in the various programmes included:

- National Foundation for Educational Research, which received a grant of up to £56,000 to research for the foundation and report on the impact of arts activities on young people's educational, personal and social development in Pupil Referral Units and in-school Learning Support Units;
- University of Plymouth, which received £25,000 towards the cost of establishing the HEARTS scheme, a fund established by the foundation to help teacher training institutions improve the quality of teacher education in the arts at primary level;
- Artangel, which received £20,000 towards the costs of facilitating the research and development for four new visual arts projects;
- Photoworks, which received £10,000 towards the costs of a one-off pilot project in which a documentary photographer and a creative writer will work with medical students at Brighton and Sussex Medical School to make documentary diaries of their first year's experience;
- ATD Fourth World, which received £10,000 towards the costs of a pilot project designed to involve families in the training of social workers, in order to increase the latter's understanding of poverty and social exclusion;
- Parity for Disability, which received £9,000 for an award scheme for art students to design a series of posters

which convey the meaning of profound disability;

- Listening Ear (Merseyside), which received £5,000 towards the costs of the first year of a project providing counselling for children aged 11–16 who have suffered a loss such as bereavement or parental separation;
- Connecting Youth Culture – North Yorkshire County Council, which received £2,000 to enable the Portuguese dance group 54E FunkyPhatBeat to take part in the Youth Arts Festival, Tadcaster in July 2003;
- King's College London, which received £800 towards the cost of The Sound Universe in Eca, a musical event which was performed in London and Oxford in April 2003.

Exclusions

The foundation gives grants only for proposals of a charitable kind, usually from organisations, which should normally be registered charities or otherwise tax-exempt.

It does not give grants for:

- the purchase, construction, repair or furnishing of buildings;
- housing;
- equipment, including vehicles or musical instruments;
- basic services or core costs (as opposed to imaginative new projects);
- the education, training fees, maintenance or medical costs of individual applicants;
- establishing funds for scholarships or loans;
- university or similar research;
- conferences or seminars;
- overseas travel, conference attendance or exchanges;
- performances, exhibitions or festivals;
- stage, film or television production costs;
- commercial publications;
- science;
- medicine or related therapies;
- religious activities;
- projects concerning drug-abuse or alcoholism;
- animal welfare;
- holidays of any sort;
- sports.

The foundation never makes loans or retrospective grants, nor helps to pay off deficits or loans, nor can it remedy the withdrawal or reduction of statutory funding.

It does not give grants in response to any large capital, endowment or widely distributed appeal.

Applications

Apply to the relevant programme director.

Please bear in mind the size of grant the UK branch of the foundation is normally able to make. At present there is a notional limit of £10,000 to £15,000 for any one grant.

Please apply in writing to the UK branch, not by telephone, e-mail nor in person.

There is no standard application form, nor does the foundation ask for any specified format or length (though succinctness is welcomed). Certain information, however, should be included.

- The exact purpose for which the proposed grant is sought and what difference a grant from the foundation would make.
- The amount required, with details of how the budget has been arrived at.
- Information about other sources of income, if any: those that are firm commitments as well as those you are exploring.
- Information about the aims and functions of your organisation and about its legal status. If your organisation is a registered charity, it is essential to send its charity registration number; if it has an official tax exemption number or letter, please send the reference. The foundation sometimes makes a grant available to an organisation which does not yet have charitable status through an organisation which does, when there is a suitable association between them. If you are uncertain, consult the foundation.
- Your last annual report and any available audited accounts.
- Any plans for monitoring and evaluating the work.

Please remember that preliminary work on a grant application may involve consultations and discussions, modification or development, and often an on-site visit, all of which takes time.

Fully-prepared proposals are considered at trustee meetings usually held in the first week of March, July and November. Papers have to be finalised six weeks in advance, therefore initial proposals need to be submitted at least ten weeks before the relevant trustee meeting.

H C D Memorial Fund

The relief of need

£475,000 (2002/03)

Beneficial area UK, Ireland and worldwide.

Reeds Farm, Sayers Common, Hassocks, West Sussex BN6 9JQ

Tel. 01273 832 173 **Fax** 01273 832 146

Email debenham@reedsfarm.fslife.co.uk

Correspondent Jeremy Debenham, Secretary

Trustees *Nicholas Debenham, chair; Bill Flinn; Dr Millie Sherman; Jeremy Debenham; Catherine Debenham.*

Charity Commission no. 1044956

Information available Brief annual report and accounts were provided by the trust.

Summary

Grants range from £2,000 to about £50,000; most are for amounts between £10,000 and £20,000. About half of the money, sometimes more, goes to international organisations with the rest going to charities in the UK and Ireland.

General

The trust has no permanent endowment. Its income in 2002/03, mostly from donations, was £536,000. Grants were made during the year totalling £475,000. This is a family foundation, with no employed staff and negligible administration costs.

The trust's guidelines are as follows:

Type of grant made

Mainly, grants are made for the relief of need, whether due to poverty, ill-health, disability, want of education or other causes. Areas of special interest specifically are:

Overseas

- Development aid, by way of appropriate technology
- Primary health care, to include training, water, hygiene and nutrition
- Education.

UK and Ireland

- Help for those who are homeless, excluded, isolated, disabled or otherwise disadvantaged, especially where there is an element of self-help.

Other criteria

The fund prefers projects which are small or medium-sized to large ones. It has a particular interest in cases which, without its help, might founder or not get off the ground.

The fund is prepared to take a risk in an appropriate case and go where other grant-makers might not.

The trust also says it prefers to focus on prevention by addressing the causes of problems rather than coping with the consequences of them. It makes grants for both capital and revenue purposes and is willing to support core costs.

Grants in 2002/03

The fund made 37 grants for amounts ranging from £1,000 to £65,000. As in the previous year, around two-thirds of the money went to international organisations. International recipients included those in Africa, Mexico, India, Bangladesh, Nepal, Belarus and France, and are involved in medical and relief work and education. Beneficiaries in the UK and the Republic of Ireland work with those who are homeless or disabled, and also social, educational and environmental projects. Many beneficiaries had received grants in the previous year.

International

The largest grant, as in previous years, was made to San Carlos Hospital in Mexico (£65,000). Other beneficiaries included ITDG, for technology-related projects and Impact Foundation – India and Africa (£30,000 each), Angels International – Belarus (£24,000), Concern America – Mexico (£20,000), Hope & Homes for Children – Sierra Leone (£15,000), St Michael's Community Centre – South Africa (£8,000), Hope Foundation – India (£7,000), Hospice of Hope – Romania (£5,000), Congregation of Josephites – Congo (£2,000) and Quaker Service Cape – South Africa (£1,000).

UK and Ireland

The largest beneficiary in the UK was St Mary's Convent & Nursing Home, which received £30,000. Other beneficiaries included A Rocha, a Christian conservation group, and St Patrick's Trust for work with homeless people (£20,000 each), Koestler Award Trust for work with prisoners, and Buckmore Park for work with young people (£10,000 each), St Cuthman's Light Centre for family support programmes, and Schools Outreach for educational projects

(£7,000 each), Lady Margaret Hungerford Charity to support almshouses (£5,000), Ashenground Community Centre (£2,000) and Alan Care Fishing Friends for work with people who are disabled (£1,000).

There were two beneficiaries in Ireland; these were the Arrupe Society, which received £20,000 towards work with people who are homeless, and the Nicky Donovan Memorial Fund, which received £1,500.

Exclusions

The following are unlikely to be supported:

- evangelism or missionary work;
- individuals;
- nationwide emergency appeals;
- animal charities.

Applications

In writing to the correspondent, although please note that the trust has a preference for seeking out its own projects and only very rarely responds to general appeals.

'Unsolicited applications are not encouraged. They are acknowledged, but extremely rarely receive a positive response. No telephone enquiries, please.'

Note that the trust does not have any employed staff.

The Hadley Trust

Social welfare

£1.1 million (2001/02)

Beneficial area UK, especially London.

Gladsmuir, Hadley Common, Barnet, Hertfordshire EN5 5QE

Email mail@hadleytrust.org

Correspondent Carol Biggs, Trust Administrator

Trustees *Mrs J Hulme; P W Hulme.*

Charity Commission no. 1064823

Information available Inadequate annual report and accounts, without a grants list or analysis of grantmaking.

The trust was established in 1997 for welfare purposes. In 2001/02 it had assets worth £61.7 million which generated an income of £2.1 million. The

total expenditure of the trust during the year was over £1.3 million, which included £1.1 million on grants to around 70 charities. The accounts show management and administration costs of £252,000, consisting of £26,500 in accountancy fees, £6,000 for legal, professional and audit fees and £219,000 on financial advice. The reason for the high costs are not explained. The trustees note that they 'have taken a conservative approach' to the trust's investments.

The trust's review of developments and activities consisted of the following:

The trustees consider that the performance of the charity in this period has been satisfactory. The trust continued to build on existing relationships. Over time the trust is becoming increasingly focused on a number of core interests within its general objects.

No beneficiaries were listed in the report and accounts.

In 2002/03 the trust had a total expenditure of £1.4 million. Unfortunately, although submitted by the trust to the Charity Commission, the accounts for this year had not made it to the public files for inspection.

Comment

The annual report and accounts fall far short of Charity Commission requirements and do not enable a full entry to be written about the work of this trust. Grants are not listed, let alone categorised and explained. The report does not say what the trustees were trying to achieve. There is no explanation for the high level of expenditure on financial advice.

Applications

In writing to the correspondent.

The Paul Hamlyn Foundation

Arts, education, India

£6 million (2003/04)

Beneficial area UK and overseas (mainly India).

18 Queen Anne's Gate, London SW1H 9AA

Tel. 020 7227 3500 **Fax** 020 7222 0601

Email information@phf.org.uk

Website www.phf.org.uk

Correspondent Faye Williams, Director

Trustees *Jane Hamlyn, chair; Sue Mitchell; Michael Hamlyn; Lord Gavron; Robert Boas.*

Charity Commission no. 327474

Information available Annual report, accounts and guidelines for applicants are all available on the foundation's website.

Summary

The primary concern of this foundation is to address issues of inequality and disadvantage, particularly in relation to young people, through the arts, learning and education. Grants are seldom large or recurrent. There is a usual maximum of £30,000, with an extensive small grants programme. There is an emphasis on widening participation in the arts and in society generally by young people who are disadvantaged.

The wealth of this foundation has been increased by further very large donations from the will of its founder, Paul Hamlyn. A complete rethinking of the foundation's work was completed early in 2003; detailed new policies and practices are described below.

In general terms the foundation will stay with its (and Paul Hamlyn's) primary concerns with arts and education for young people. The present relatively minor interest in India will also continue.

The big change has been that about half of the foundation's funds will be reserved for activities and projects that it has itself actively instigated or developed, leaving the other half for more reactive funding in response to applications received.

General

The foundation was established in 1987 and endowed with a personal gift of £50 million from the founder. After his death in 2001 the endowment was greatly increased through further provisions in his will. At March 2004 assets stood at £356 million.

In 2003/04 the trust received 1,147 eligible applications and made 572 awards totalling £7.6 million. These represented 31% of all applications received. Grants payable during the year amounted to just over £6 million. One hundred and forty-six grants were made through the foundation's small grants programme.

Grants to organisations in 2003/04 were categorised as follows

Arts	£2,271,000
Education	£1,906,000
Overseas	£256,000
Other	£1,613,000

Grants are normally one-off rather than recurrent, and only 12 were for more than £30,000.

Guidance

This section includes under each heading examples of grants in 2003/04.

These guidance notes set out the foundation's priority areas for funding and should help you to decide whether to make an application for funding. The foundation also runs its own special projects which focus on areas where there is an urgent need for positive change. These may lie outside the published priority areas.

We are happy to receive exploratory phone calls or letters describing your work before you consider making a formal application to the foundation. We are glad to comment on ideas at an early stage.

There is no standard application form, but applicants must address the questions on page 8 of our guidance notes (available by post from our office) and complete the Project Details Form which will be sent with the Guidance Notes.

The foundation welcomes applications from minority ethnic groups and from organisations based outside London.

The arts

Increasing access to the arts

The foundation is interested in supporting initiatives in all parts of the UK which address inequality of access and lack of opportunity to experience and enjoy the arts, particularly for young people. Priority is given to exemplary projects concerned with social inclusion and underachievement amongst young people, including those 'at risk', and young offenders.

Arts and learning

The priorities are:
- Imaginative partnerships between schools, arts organisations and other agencies which aim to develop the arts within formal education.
- Schemes which give teachers access to best practice in the performing and creative arts, thereby enhancing their own professional development and their pupils 'or students' learning experience.
- Informal educational experiences for children who are not currently well served.

Awards for artists

A Foundation Award for individual artists was launched in 1993. The award is currently for visual artists, with a strong emphasis on experiment, innovation and cross arts collaboration. Each year 20 nominators put forward names of artists who live or work in the UK and five awards are made by a panel of independent judges.

Musical Futures (A Paul Hamlyn Foundation Special Project)

The aim of this special project is to devise new and imaginative ways of engaging young people in music activities as an entitlement of all 11–19 year olds. Funds for this project are not available through open application.

What's the Big Idea? (A Paul Hamlyn Foundation Special Project in Northern Ireland)

This proactive project seeks out and encourages inspirational ideas and approaches which will enhance young people's experience and involvement in creative opportunities. The project has a particular but not exclusive focus on the arts. For further details please contact the foundation's advisers in northern Ireland, Shona McCarthy and Frances Cassidy on: phfenquiries@rubyblue.org.uk; tel: 028 9077 4399.

Grants in 2002/03 (150 grants totalling £2.2 million)

The three largest grants were: £187,000 to Royal Opera House; £127,000 to Tate Galley; and £116,000 to The Sage Gateshead.

Other grants included £57,000 to National Theatre; £49,000 to Royal Exchange Theatre Company – Manchester; £30,000 to Multi A – Bristol; £25,000 to Keys to Success – Nottingham; £20,000 to British Film Institute; £16,000 to the Hackney Music Development Trust; £15,000 to Escape Artists – Cambridge; £14,000 to Madcap Trust – Milton Keynes, £10,000 to the Unit for the Arts and Offenders – Canterbury; and £5,000 to DanceEast. Two arts bursaries were funded totalling £19,000. 89 grants totalling £291,000 were made for amounts under £5,000 each. Awards to individual artists totalled £191,000.

A total of 4 projects totalling £186,000 were funded under the Musical Futures programme and 11 projects totalling £313,000 under the What's the Big Idea? programme.

Education and learning

The foundation is concerned about young people who are affected by inequality and disadvantage. It supports initiatives which address these issues, or seek to combat disaffection and alienation in young people.

Priority will be given to:
- Projects which focus on issues of school exclusion and truancy.
- Applications from supplementary schools.

- Innovative educational projects concerned with young offenders.

The Reading and Libraries Challenge Fund (A Paul Hamlyn Foundation Special Project)

This new fund supports innovative national or local projects in the UK which aim to improve long term access to books, reading and library services for young people, and others, with limited access to books and reading. There are three streams:

- Right to Read – access to books and reading for children and young people in public care.
- Free with Words – access to books and reading for prisoners and young offenders.
- Libraries Connect – focused on communities, such as refugees and asylum seekers, which are not benefiting from the services which public libraries can offer.

Further information about the fund is also available from the website of the National Literacy Trust (www.literacytrust.org.uk/ phffund)

Fund for Refugee and Asylum Seeker Young People (A Paul Hamlyn Foundation Special Project)

This new fund is looking to support imaginative and practical projects and activities which encourage the integration of 11–18 year old refugees and asylum seekers in host communities in the UK, particularly in regions outside London

Publishing Training Schemes (Administered by the Publishing Training Centre)

Support focuses on:

- Making skills training available to small publishers (employing ten people or fewer) and freelance's who do not have access to the training that some large companies offer.
- Providing publishing training for the voluntary sector.

Further information and application forms available from: The Publishing Training Centre at Book House (www.train4publishing.co.uk).

Grants in 2001/02 (126 grants totalling £1.9 million)

The three largest grants in this category were: £80,000 to the London Borough of Merton for a Quality Leaders Project; £60,000 to Kids Company; and £59,000 to London Libraries Development Agency.

Other grants included: £45,000 to Keen Students School; £40,000 to Book Trust; £30,000 each to Feltham YOI Trail-Blazers, Teach First and Youth At risk UK; £20,000 each to Shaftesbury Homes and Arethusa and Youth Education Support Services; £18,000 to the Lighthouse Outreach – Bradford; £15,000 each to Habitat for Humanity Great Britain and Outside Chance; £13,000 to Writers & Scholars Education Trust; £12,000 to Museum of Childhood at Bethnal Green; £10,000 to the Total Learning Challenge – Newcastle upon Tyne; £7,500 to African Youths Initiative; £6,000 to One London; and £5,400 to Safer Cardiff. 52 small grants under £5,000 were made totalling £199,000.

Under the Reading and Libraries Challenge Fund, 19 grants were made totalling £509,000.

Under 'publishing training', support was provided for 91 small independent publishers, 85 freelancers and 3 voluntary organisations.

Two grants totalling £199,000 were made from the Fund for Refugees and Asylum Seeker Young People.

India

The foundation gives direct support to local projects in India, run by Indian organisations. It does not support UK organisations working in India. Focus is on the following areas:

- development schemes
- programmes to strengthen NGOs generally through training, information exchange and networking
- schemes which benefit disadvantaged children.

Initial consideration of applications is by the foundation's adviser in India, Ajit Chaudhuri, who can be contacted by e-mail at: achaudhuri@hotmail.com

Grants in 2001/02 (23 grants totalling £256,000)

There were 21 grants made to organisations in India. The largest of these, £37,000, was for Bhagwan Mahaveer Viklang Sahayta Samiti. Other grants ranged from the £28,000 for Delhi Council for Child Welfare to the £3,300 for Arpana Research & Charities Trust – Haryana.

There were to grants to overseas organisations outside India, including one of £19,000 for emergency relief programmes in Nicaragua.

Small grants programme

The foundation makes small awards, up to a maximum of £5,000, to support local schemes and initiatives that fall within its priority areas. Applications should be for specific projects rather than revenue or deficit funding. The grant requested should represent the major part of the funding required. Grants will be made for one year only and applications in the following year from the same organisation will not normally be considered.

Other grants

A substantial grant of £1.3 million was made to the Helen Hamlyn Trust. Other grants included: £160,000 and £47,000 to the Royal Marsden Hospital; £23,000 to National Film and Television School; £15,000 to Council for Assisting Refugee Academy and £10,000 to Thames Gateway London Partnership. Two small grants under £5,000 totalled £8,400.

Exclusions

'The foundation will only exceptionally consider applications which fall outside its declared areas of interest and priority. It only considers supporting staff posts as part of a project which falls within its priority areas. Funding from the foundation is normally for a maximum of three years.

'The foundation does not make grants for any of the following:

- general appeals or endowments.
- capital projects
- buying, maintaining or refurbishing property or equipment.
- support for individuals, except where the foundation has established a special scheme
- performances, production costs and exhibitions
- education projects concerned with particular issues such as the environment or health.
- large national charities
- medical causes
- applications for retrospective funding
- organisations which do not have charitable purposes.
- research'

Applications

If you still want to make an application:
– Talk to us first, or send an online letter.
– Complete the Project Details Form.
– Write not more than five single sides of A4 (unbound), with a further page for the budget and complete the Project Details Form. Supporting information may be supplied in appendices, but the main statement should be self-contained and provide the essential information required by the trustees.
'This should include:

- what sort of organisation you are;
- the general aim of the project and its specific objectives;
- how it is to be done and by whom;
- what problems you anticipate in doing it;
- whom it is intended to benefit and how many;
- when it will start and how long it will take;

- how much money you need and for what purposes – salaries, rent, administration and so forth;
- how other interested parties will be informed of the outcome;
- how you will know whether or not it has succeeded;
- which other funders you have approached and with what success;
- if you will need funding beyond the period of the grant, where it is to come from.

Please enclose with your application a copy of your most recent annual report and financial statements, and details of the management and staffing structure, including trustees.

Applications sent by e-mail or facsimile will not be accepted.

The foundation's procedures

Applications will be acknowledged when received, but it may take some time to assess them. This may involve correspondence and meetings between staff and applicants and will involve consultation with the trustees, advisers and independent referees.

Applications for sums of £5,000 or less are handled by a Small Grants Committee which meets monthly, except August and December. Grants will be made for one year only and applications in consecutive years from the same organisation will not normally be considered. Applications received by the first Friday of each month, except August and December, will be dealt with in the same month, otherwise the following month. Ideally, applications should be submitted at least two months prior to the commencement date of the project.

A second Grants Committee, which meets four times a year, deals with applications for sums from £5,000 to £30,000.

Applications for sums above £30,000 will be considered at the quarterly Trustees Meetings. Applications in excess of £100,000 will be considered in two stages: trustees will look at an application in principle at a first meeting and, if they wish to take it forward, the full application will be considered at their next meeting.

Although we endeavour to consider applications received by the given closing date of the next relevant meeting we cannot guarantee that applications above £5,000 will be considered at any particular meeting.

The exact meeting dates are available from the receptionist at the foundation.

Hampton Fuel Allotment Charity

General

£418,000 to organisations (2002/03)

Beneficial area Hampton, the former borough of Twickenham, and the borough of Richmond (in that order).

15 Hurst Mount, High Street, Hampton, Middlesex TW12 2SA

Tel. 020 8941 7866 **Fax** 020 8979 5555

Correspondent M J Ryder, Clerk

Trustees *Mrs M J M Woodriff, chair; Revd G Clarkson; R Ellis; G Hunter; Mrs M T Martin; J Mortimer; D Parish; J A Webb; Revd D N Winterburn; Mrs A Woodward;*

Charity Commission no. 211756

Information available Information provided by the trust.

Grants range from £500 to £50,000, although most are for under £10,000. Revenue and capital costs are supported; this includes many grants towards general running costs. Many recipients are supported year after year, although sometimes for different amounts and purposes.

Roughly three-quarters of applications received by the charity are successful.

As its name suggests, the charity was created (following the 1811 Enclosure Act) with a grant of land to produce a supply of fuel for the poor of the ancient parish of Hampton. The original ten acres was sold to Sainsbury's in 1988 and the sale proceeds form the financial base of the charity.

The charity's objects are:

a. the relief of need, hardship or distress of those within the area of benefit;

b. support for those who are sick, convalescent, disabled, handicapped or infirm;

c. promoting the education of children and young persons;

d. provision and support for recreation and other leisure-time occupations in order to improve the conditions of life in the interests of social welfare.

The trustees' current guidelines are as follows:

a. to meet a proportion of the fuel bills of individuals in need;

b. to provide essential equipment for individuals in need or distress

c. to support organisations which deliver services for those in need in the area of benefit;

d. to allocate the charity's income within the broad headings of:

1. support to individuals in need

2. hospitals and hospices;

3. organisations assisting those suffering from disability;

4. organisations engaged in social welfare including the elderly, youth, recreation and leisure;

5. organisations providing housing for those in need;

6. organisations providing additional educational support;

7. organisations engaged in community activities.

In 2002/03 it had assets of £38 million, which generated an income of £1.5 million. Management and administration costs, including the costs of generating funds, were slightly high at £217,000, although this may have been due to the large number of individual grants made. Grants totalled £1.1 million, of which £529,000 was distributed in nearly 2,000 grants to individuals and £418,000 in grants to organisations, broken down as follows:

Support of individuals in need

The only grant was £40,000 to London Borough of Richmond upon Thames Children with Disabilities for continuing support.

Hospitals and hospices

Five grants totalled £149,000. Teddington Memorial Hospital received two of these; £75,000 for the establishment of a digital x-ray unit through its League of Friends and £300 for the annual add-on costs of the TENS machines in the physiotherapy department.

The other beneficiaries were Kingston Hospital Cancer Unit Appeal towards establishing a new centre (£50,000), Princess Alice Hospice for regular activities (£15,000) and Radio West Middlesex to upgrade and relocate the hospital radio station (£7,500).

Disability

Grants totalling £107,000 were made to 22 organisations. The largest were £19,000 to Richmond Borough

Association for Mental Health for regular activities, Richmond upon Thames Crossroads Care for the costs of its services (£12,000) and Mencap – Richmond for ongoing and new activities (£10,000).

Smaller grants included £9,000 to Richmond Advice and Information on Disability for regular activities, £7,500 to Creative Educational Projects for projects involving people with special needs, £6,500 to Marie Curie Cancer Care for regular activities, £3,500 to Cancer Resource Centre – Wandsworth for running costs, £2,000 to Art and Soul for an arts event for people with mental health problems resulting in exhibitions at Orleans House Gallery, £1,800 to Maddison Centre Day Hospital for yoga and gardening groups for people with long-term mental health problems, £1,200 to Pod Charitable Trust for entertainers in the children's wards at Kingston and West Middlesex Hospitals and £400 to Parkinson's Disease Society for regular activities.

Social welfare – elderly

Grants to six organisations totalled £21,000. By far the largest of these was the £16,000 to Age Concern – Richmond upon Thames for regular activities. Others were £1,800 to Tangley Hall Day Centre for aromatherapy for people with dementia, £1,600 to Hampton Hill Old People's Welfare Committee for regular activities, £1,100 to WRVS Hampton Darby and Joan Club for social activities, £500 to Churches Together in Teddington for Christmas lunches for people who are lonely or otherwise in need and £130 to Sandown Court Residents' Association for Christmas lunches for older residents.

Social welfare – youth

A total of £84,000 was given in 17 grants. The largest were £15,000 to Richmond Youth Offending Team for regular activities, £12,000 to Off the Record for provision of regular counselling and advice services for young people, £10,000 to Conference of Voluntary Youth Organisations for a drugs project and £9,500 to St James's Primary School PFA and 2nd Teddington Scouts for a minibus for joint use.

Other beneficiaries included St Christopher's Fellowship for improvements at Rosslyn Road (£6,800), Cirdan Sailing Trust for a bursary scheme for young people from within the borough (£4,000), Strathmore Centre for summer activities (£3,000), 2nd Whitton Scout Group for the conversion of a store room into a training room (£2,000), Twickenham Brunswick Club for Young People for replacement fire doors (£1,500) and Hampton Community Mini-Soccer Group for running costs (£650).

Social welfare – recreation

Six grants totalled £31,000. Hampton Pool Limited received £20,000 for new pool lining. Other beneficiaries were Richmond Homes for Life Trust for a support programme for people with learning difficulties to access mainstream leisure and sporting opportunities (£4,000), Horse Rangers Association (Hampton Court) for the costs for riding for people with disabilities (£3,500), Hampton Choral Society for regular activities (£1,600) and Richmond upon Thames Arts Council for a young poets competition and drama awards and Richmond upon Thames Performing Arts Festival for the annual arts competition (£800 each).

Social welfare – other

£7,500 each went to Furniture Scheme – Richmond upon Thames for regular activities and Relate – Richmond, Kingston and Hounslow for counselling services. Other grants were £6,000 to Home-Start Richmond upon Thames (£6,000), Meditation in Divorce (£2,000) and Cruse – Bereavement Care – RuT branch (£1,800).

Educational support

13 grants totalled £131,000 of which £50,000 went to Hampton Junior School for the provision of arts space. Other large grants were £18,000 to London Borough of Richmond upon Thames Schools Targeted Assistance for schools' welfare funds, £17,000 to Richmond Music Trust to reduce fees for instrumental tuition and £10,000 to Hampton Hill Junior School to develop a garden scheme.

Other beneficiaries included Archdeacon Cambridge's School PTA for an 'early years' play area (£7,000), Hampton Community College towards gaining performing arts specialist school status and Whitton School Association to redevelop an area of land (£5,000)each and Richmond upon Thames Childminding Group for regular activities (£3,000).

Community activities

Grants to 18 organisations totalled £141,000. The largest were £46,000 to Richmond Citizen's Advice for regular activities, £20,000 to White House Community Association to restart the lunch club and alter the building and £15,000 to Vineyard Congregational Church for a shower, toilets and laundrette facility for clients of its drop-in centre. Smaller grants included those to Christ Church – Teddington for disabled access to the church hall (£8,000), Ethnic Minorities Advocacy Group for regular activities (£7,500), Richmond upon Thames CVS for a fundraising service for six months (£5,900), Holy Trinity Church and Parish Room – Twickenham to replace the heating system (£5,000), Fulmer Close Tenants Association towards a salary (£1,800), ACCOUNT for a photocopier (£1,600), BTCV for support costs (£1,000), Nation Court Social Fund for garden improvements for older residents (£600) and Richmond Borough Police for a Data Link emergency information service (£500).

Comment

The charity produces an excellent, comprehensive annual report. This includes a section disclosing all trustees' interests in the beneficiaries the charity supports–a commendable practice. (When an interest has been disclosed, the trustee(s) concerned do not take part in the final decision.)

Exclusions

The charity is unlikely to support:

- grants to individuals for private and post-compulsory education;
- adaptations or building alterations for individuals;
- holidays, except in cases of severe medical need;
- decoration, carpeting or central heating;
- anything which is the responsibility of a statutory body;
- national general charitable appeals;
- animal welfare;
- religious groups, unless offering a non-religious service to the community;
- commercial and business activities;
- endowment appeals;
- political projects;
- retrospective capital grants.

The trustees have decided for the present to limit grants towards major 'one-off' projects generally to £30,000. Applicants are advised to contact the clerk prior to formally submitting such applications.

The trustees are also reluctant to support ongoing revenue costs of organisations unless they can show clearly that within the area of benefit a substantial number of people are being charitably assisted. They also expect organisations to show that other support will be forthcoming and that the organisation will become self-reliant over an identified period of years.

Applications

The charity provides an application form for organisations seeking financial assistance.

On receipt of your application form the clerk to the trustees will review it and may wish to ask further questions before submitting it to the trustees for consideration. All eligible applications will be put before the trustees.

The general grants panel meets every two months and considers all project grants. For grants over £20,000, it makes a recommendation to a meeting of all the trustees. There is a meeting of the full trustees every three months. The clerk to the trustees will be pleased to inform organisations about the dates of meetings when their applications are to be considered. Organisations are advised to lodge their applications well in advance of meeting dates.

In the case of major capital or other large projects it may be that, on occasion, a small group of trustees is asked to discuss the scheme with your organisation and its advisers. This may also involve a site visit or an independent evaluation by an assessor appointed by the trustees.

A version of the application form is available in electronic form. Copies can be obtained by supplying a clean 3.5 inch diskette 1.44 MB. The version will be Windows 95, Microsoft Word 97. All applications must be submitted in printed form.

The Kathleen Hannay Memorial Charity

Health, welfare, Christian, general

£535,000 (2002/03)
Beneficial area UK.

c/o RF Trustee Co Ltd, Ely House, 37 Dover Street, London W1S 4NJ
Tel. 020 7409 5685
Correspondent G Fincham
Trustees *Enid A C Hannay; Simon P Weil; Mrs Christian A K Ward.*
Charity Commission no. 299600
Information available Full accounts were provided by the trust.

The trust supports a wide variety of UK and worldwide charitable causes. In furtherance of its objectives, the trust continues to make a substantial number of grants to charitable organisations both on a one off and recurring basis.

In 2002/03 the charity had assets of £12 million with an income of £278,000 and gave grants totalling £535,000.

The largest grants were £25,000 to Amnesty International UK Section, £20,000 each to Children's Fire & Burn Trust, Handel House Trust, Life of World Trust, NSPCC and Samaritans, £16,500 to Network Counselling & Training, £15,000 each to MENCAP and Disasters Emergency Committee, £14,000 each to Helen House – Hospice for Children and Wiltshire Air Ambulance Appeal, £12,000 each to National Schizophrenia Fellowship, Rethink Severe Mental Illness and Schizophrenia Association of Great Britain, £11,000 each to English Concert (PEC Concerts Ltd) and Childrens Aid Direct.

Other grants included £10,000 each to Barnardo's, Camphill Village Trust, ChildLine, Crossroads Caring for Carers, Ethox Foundation, Fight for Sight, Medical Foundation – Caring for Victims of Torture, SCOPE and Torch Trust for the Blind, £8,000 each to Church Mission Society and St Ethelburga's Centre for Reconciliation and Peace, £7,000 each to Save the Children and Red Hill Christian Centre, £6,000 each to African Evangelical Fellowship, Compton Bassett Parochial Church Council, Douglas House and Musicians Benevolent Fund, £5,000 each to Westcott House, St Mungo Community Housing Association, St John's RC School, Society for the Assistance of Ladies in Reduced Circumstances, Royal Blind Asylum & School, Order of the Holy Paraclete, Alcohol Recovery Project, Children's Society, Community Music East Ltd, Cruse Bereavement Care, Emmanuel Care Trust, Kennet Action for Single Homeless, L'Arche Inverness Community and MS Nerve Centre.

Exclusions

No grants to individuals or non-registered charities.

Applications

In writing to the correspondent. Applications need to be received by February as trustees meet in March.

The Lennox Hannay Charitable Trust

Health, welfare, general

£1.2 million (2002/03)
Beneficial area UK.

c/o RF Trustee Co Ltd, Ely House, 37 Dover Street, London W1S 4NJ
Tel. 020 7409 5685 **Fax** 020 7409 5681
Correspondent The Trust Manager
Trustees *RF Trustee Co Ltd; Walter L Hannay; Caroline F Wilmot-Sitwell.*
Charity Commission no. 299099
Information available Accounts and brief annual report, with full grants list.

This trust was established in 1988 by Walter Lennox Hannay for general charitable purposes, making both one-off and recurrent grants.

In recent years it's assets have increased due to the receipt of £15 million in cash from the takeover of Robert Fleming Holdings Ltd (in 2000/01). In 2002/03 assets stood at £20.2 million. Charitable expenditure has also generally increased, with £529,000 being donated in 2000/01, and £1,189,000 being donated in 2002/03 (although this figure is slightly down on 2001/02).

In 2002/03 the trust made 129 donations, broken down as follows:

	No. of grants	Amount
Sport & recreation	2	£505,000
Medical, health & sickness	44	£212,500
Disability	29	£155,500
Education/training	16	£101,000
Accommodation & housing	6	£68,000
Economic/community development	9	£39,000
Relief of poverty	8	£36,000
Overseas relief	5	£32,500
Environment & conservation	3	£16,000
Religious activities	3	£13,000
Animal welfare	3	£10,000
Art & culture	1	£500
Total	129	£1,189,000

Grants in 2002/03

Almost half the total grants during the year went to one organisation—Oxford University Boat Club Trust, which received £500,000 towards rebuilding its boat house.

There were a further 18 grants of £10,000 or more. These included grants to: Help the Hospices towards skills training for staff and volunteers (£50,000); Amber towards residential training courses for young out of work people (£40,000); Health Unlimited towards the provision of primary health care (£20,000); and a general donation to NSPCC (£17,000). Grants of £10,000 each were made to British Deaf Association, British Dyslexia Association, DEBRA, Drupka Trust, Fight for Sight, Game Conservancy Trust, National Autistic Society, National Missing Persons Helpline, Restoration of Appearance and Function Trust (RAFT), Save the Children Fund, Sense and St Dunstan's.

Almost all of the remaining grants were for £5,000 or less. Beneficiaries included Barnados, Calvert Trust, Children's Bereavement Trust, Coram Family, Dreams Come True Charity, Friends of Nettlebed School, Healing Foundation, Hopscotch, Kent Autistic Trust, Little Sisters of the Poor, Noah's Ark Trust, Refuge, RNIB, Soundaround, Terrence Higgins Trust and Winged Fellowship Trust.

Exclusions

No grants to individuals or non-registered charities.

Applications

In writing to the correspondent. Applications need to be received by February as trustees meet in March.

The Haramead Trust

Welfare, children, animals, health education

Around £580,000 (2003/04)

Beneficial area UK and overseas, with a preference for Leicestershire.

Park House, Park Hill, Gaddesby, Leicestershire LE7 4WH

Tel. 01664 840908 **Fax** 01664 840908

Correspondent M J Linnett, Trustee

Trustees S P Astill; Mrs W M Linnett; M J Linnett; R H Smith; D L Tams.

Charity Commission no. 1047416

Information available Accounts were on file at the Charity Commission.

The trust's objectives are:

- the relief of need, hardship and distress;
- relief of suffering amongst animals;
- children's welfare;
- advancement of health education.

In 2003/04 the trust had an income of £659,000 and a total expenditure of £593,000. Grants were made totalling around £580,000, a level that seems to remain fairly constant.

Previous beneficiaries include Catholic Fund for Overseas Development, British Red Cross, Leicester Children's Holiday Home, Catholic Children's Society, Marie Curie Cancer Care, DePaul Trust, Future Hope, LOROS, Menphys, Rainbows, Angels International, Cambodia Trust, Chicks, India Development Group, Soundabout and Winged Fellowship.

Applications

In writing to the correspondent. The trustees meet every couple of months.

The Peter Harrison Foundation

Children, young people, people with disabilities, people who are disadvantaged

£1.2 million (2003/04)

Beneficial area UK and south east of England.

Foundation House, 42–48 London Road, Reigate, Surrey RH2 9QQ

Tel. 01737 228 000 **Fax** 01737 228 001

Email enquiries@ peterharrisonfoundation.org

Website www.peterharrisonfoundation. org

Correspondent John Ledlie, Director

Trustees Peter Harrison, chair; Joy Harrison; Julia Harrison-Lee; Peter Lee.

Charity Commission no. 1076579

Information available Full accounts provided by the trust.

Summary

The trust was founded by Peter Harrison in April 1999. As a keen and active sportsman throughout his life, Peter Harrison believes that education and sport provide the key stepping stones to self-development, creation of choice, confidence building and self reliance. A pioneering and successful businessman, entrepreneur and sportsman himself, Peter wishes to share his success by making these stepping stones more readily available to those who may be disabled or disadvantaged and who may not otherwise have the opportunity to develop their self potential.

The creation of the foundation is the means by which Peter hopes that this may be achieved. In the first few years since its formation, the foundation has distributed over £5 million and has made grants to over 150 charities.

In 2003/04 the trust had assets of £30 million and an income of £1.2 million. Grants totalled £1.2 million.

General

The foundation only accepts applications from organisations that are:

- registered charities;
- friendly or industrial provident societies;
- recognised by the Inland Revenue in Scotland or Northern Ireland as having charitable status.

Grant Programmes

Opportunities through Sport (Nationwide)

This Programme is a nationwide one and applications are accepted from charities throughout the UK.

The trustees wish to support sporting activities or projects which provide opportunities for people who are disabled or otherwise disadvantaged to fulfil their potential and to develop other personal and life skills.

Grants will often be one off grants for capital projects. However, revenue funding will be considered for a new project or if funding is key to the continuing success or survival of an established project.

The trustees welcome applications for projects:

- which provide a focus for skills development and confidence building through the medium of sport ;
- that have a strong training and/or educational theme within the sporting activity;
- that provide sporting equipment or facilities for disabled or disadvantaged people;
- with a high degree of community involvement;
- that help to engage children or young people at risk of crime, truancy or addiction.

Special Needs and Care for Children and Young People (South East of England only)

This Programme is for charities in the South East of England and applications are accepted only from charities in: Berkshire; Buckinghamshire (excluding Milton Keynes); Hampshire; Isle of Wight; Kent; Oxfordshire; Surrey; East Sussex; and West Sussex.

The foundation does not accept applications from charities based in or operating in London, but may consider funding charities based in London for a specific project taking place in the south east area that meets our criteria.

The trustees welcome applications for projects:

- that work with or benefit disabled, chronically or terminally ill children and provide support for their parents and carers;
- that help to engage children or young people at risk of crime, truancy or addiction;
- organised for young people at risk of homelessness or that provide new opportunities for homeless young people.

Opportunities through education

The Trustees do not invite applications to this Programme.

This Programme supports education initiatives, primarily in the South East of England, which are of particular interest to the trustees. These include the Specialist Schools Programme.

Through this Programme the trustees also fund bursary places for children from the Reigate and Redhill areas in Surrey to enable them to attend Reigate Grammar School.

Trustees' Discretion

The Trustees do not invite applications to this Programme.

This Programme supports projects that are of particular interest to the trustees.

Grants in 2003/04

Shown here are examples of grants for the two programmes that are open to applications.

Opportunities through Sport – 25 grants totalling £591,000

Grants in this category ranged from £3,500 to over £60,000. The largest was £66,000 to Sailability for a continuation of their foundation level accreditation programme. Other larger grants included: £60,000 to the British Paralympic Association towards the team weekend for the British team; £50,000 to the Atlee Foundation in London to provide sports facilities for young people; £45,000 over three years to the Greenbank Project in Liverpool and Merseyside to fund seven new clubs aiming to increase participation by people with disabilities in sport; £30,000 to the Uphilll Ski Club to provide opportunities for people with disabilities to learn to ski; £25,000 to Southend Mencap to purchase sports equipment for a new sports hall; and £17,000 to the Calvert Trust, Kielder in Northumberland towards an adapted motor cruiser to allow people with severe disabilities an opportunity to experience water sports. Smaller grants included: £14,000 to Trojans Youth and Development Group in Derry, Northern Ireland to purchase football equipment; £5,100 to Rethink Disability in Suffolk to expand a project enabling supported swimming sessions for people with disabilities; and £5,000 to Barrow Farm Group (Riding for the Disabled) in Essex for a metal mounting ramp and a hoist.

Special Needs and Care for Children and Young People – 9 grants totalling £185,000

Grants in this category ranged from £3,900 to £50,000 and included: £50,000 to Queen Elizabeth's Foundation for Disabled People in Leatherhead towards the provision of a multi-purpose Culture and Activity Centre; £30,000 over three years to the British Institute for Brain Injured Children towards the cost of a new mobile clinic service; £18,000 over three years to Thedora Children's Trust to fund the provision of monthly 'Clown Doctor' visits to patients at the National Centre for Young People with Epilepsy; £15,000 to the Down Syndrome Education Trust to fund an additional Early Development Group for pre-school children in Hampshire; and £3,900 to Carousel in Sussex to fund a series of

drama performances in Special Schools as part of their national tour.

Other Programmes – 22 grants totalling £402,000

In addition, 13 grants totalling £195,000 were awarded through the Trustees' Discretionary Programme and 9 grants totalling £207,000 through the Opportunities through Education Programme.

Exclusions

- General appeals;
- retrospective funding;
- individuals;
- other grant–making bodies to make grants on its behalf;
- projects that replace statutory funding;
- projects that are the responsibility of the central or local goverment;
- holidays in the UK or abroad and expeditions;
- outdoor activity projects such as camping or outward bound expeditions;
- overseas projects;
- projects solely for the promotion of religion.

Applications

We strongly recommend that you telephone the foundation before making an application in order that we can advise you on the eligibility of your project.

If we feel that your project will be of interest to the trustees, we will invite you to submit a grant application. You must complete an application form–which may either be downloaded from our website or requested from the foundation–and send it by post to the foundation.

Application process

All applications are acknowledged. We aim to process your application as quickly as possible, but please be aware that the foundation receives a large number of applications and it may sometimes take up to six months for your application to be considered.

Applications are assessed by the foundation's staff, who will arrange either to visit your project or to conduct a telephone discussion with you about it. They then make a report and recommendations on your application to the trustees.

The trustees hold regular meetings to consider these reports. We will write to you as soon as possible after your application has been considered to let you know the outcome.

The foundation receives many more applications than we are able to support and we regret that we have to turn down many good proposals, even though they meet our criteria.

The Maurice Hatter Foundation

Jewish causes, general

£703,000 (2002/03)

Beneficial area Unrestricted.

1000 North Circular Road, Staples Corner, London NW2 7JP

Correspondent Jeremy S Newman, Trustee

Trustees *Sir Maurice Hatter; H I Connick; Jeremy Newman; Richard Hatter.*

Charity Commission no. 298119

Information available Annual report and accounts are available at the Charity Commission.

In 2002/03 it had assets of £7.3 million and an income of £617,000, comprising £421,000 from rent and £195,000 from investments. There were 45 grants made totalling £703,000 with some organisations receiving more than one grant.

Grants for £1,000 or more were listed in the accounts and were categorised as follows:

Culture and environmental – 8 grants totalling £7,000

Beneficiaries were Royal Opera House (£3,000), Chicken Shed Theatre (£1,500) and Jewish Arts Festival (£1,000). Four small grants totalled £1,500.

Education – 17 grants totalling £196,000

World ORT received 7 grants totalling £89,000. Other beneficiaries included Treehouse Trust (£50,000), Haifa University (£15,000), British Friends of Haifa University (£14,000 in total), RNIB – Sunshine House School (£10,000), British ORT (£5,000), Friends of Lubavitch (£3,000) and Youth Aliyah (£1,000). Seven small donations totalled £3,800.

Medical research – 9 grants totalling £334,000

Haifa University – Maritime Studies received 2 grants totalling £171,000. Two

other substaintial donations were made to Ray Tye Medical Foundation (£64,000). Other beneficiaries were Hatter Institute & Centre for Cardiology (£60,000 in three donations), Haifa University – Behaviour Research Centre (£16,000), Weizmann Institute and National Institute for Epilepsy (£10,000 each), FMRC (£2,000 in two donations) and BF Assaf Harofeh Medical Centre (£1,000). One small donation totalled £250.

Applications

Unsolicited applications will not be considered.

The Charles Hayward Foundation

Welfare and health, medical research, overseas

£1.8 million (2003)

Beneficial area Most grants are made in the UK.

Hayward House, 45 Harrington Gardens, London SW7 4JU

Tel. 020 7370 7063/7067

Website www. charleshaywardfoundation.org.uk

Correspondent David Brown, Administrator

Trustees *A D Owen, chair; I F Donald; Sir William Asscher; Mrs J M Chamberlain; Sir Jack Hayward; Mrs S J Heath; B D Insch; J N van Leuven; Miss A T Rogers; Ms J Streather.*

Charity Commission no. 1078969

Information available Good guidelines for applicants. Annual report and accounts with grants list and brief description of the purpose of each grant.

Summary

With very wide interests, a relatively modest income and a history of making many more small grants than is now the case, this foundation reports that only one in ten applications results in a grant.

General

Sir Charles Hayward used his personal fortune to establish and endow two charitable trusts, the Hayward Foundation and the Charles Hayward Trust. The two charities were combined in 2000, to become the Charles Hayward Foundation.

Grantmaking

In 2003 the foundation had assets amounting to £44 million and an income of £2.6 million.Grants totalled £1.8 million and were categorised as follows:

Youth and early intervention: 22 grants totalling £347,000

Grants included: £35,000 to Youth at Risk – London, the final instalment of three grants towards programmes in Young Offender Institutes; £25,000 to Who Cares? Trust – London towards measuring the educational progress of young people in care; £20,000 to Links – Northumberland towards the Foyer Project in Hexham; £15,000 to Bridge to Cross Charitable Trust – Monmouthsire towards building works for a youth drop-in centre in Abergavenny; £10,000 each to Birmingham Clubs for Young People towards upgrading fire escapes and fire protection at Billberry Hill Centre and Devon Youth Association towards tools and equipment for a motor mechanics project for young people; and £6,400 to Mutley Greenbank Trust – Devon towards refurbishment of a hall for an out-of-school club.

Medical research: 15 grants totalling £337,000

Grants included: £50,000 to Imperial College of Science and Technology – London; £33,000 to Research into Ageing towards research on the response of elderly muscle to training at university of Edinburgh; £30,000 to National Tremor Foundation – Essex, the first of three payments towards research on olfactory function; £24,000 to Clinical Research Trust UK, the second of two payments towards the development of a diagnostic test for Alzheimer's disease; £20,000 to Children's Liver Disease Foundation – Birmingham, the final of three payments into research on steroid use following liver surgery; and £12,000 to Cambridge Arthritis Research Endeavour, the second of three payments towards research on the cause of soft tissue rheumatism.

Arts, preservation & environment: 14 grants totalling £266,000

Grants included: £50,000 to Royal Geographical Society – London towards the cost of a lift; £45,000 to King's College London towards the restoration of a mosaic floor; £25,000 to Number 8 – Pershore Community and Arts centre towards rebuilding and renovation costs; £10,000 to Plantlife – Wiltshire towards the purchase of land; and £9,000 to Tricycle Theatre Company – London, towards the cost of a disabled lift.

Elderly: 11 grants totalling £149,000

Grants included: £25,000 to St Mary's Convent and Nursing Home – Chiswick towards helping the home comply with care standards; £18,000 to Crossroads – Broxtowe, the second of three grants towards additional care attendant hours; £15,000 to Deal Centre for the Retired – Kent towards the extension of the day centre; £10,000 to Abbeyfield Great Missenden towards the expansion of Abbeyfield House; £7,000 to Age Concern – Carmarthen, the second of two grants towards shopping services for the elderly.

Special needs: 11 grants totalling £148,000

Grants included: £25,000 to Children's Trust – Tadworth towards the extension to St Margaret's School; £20,000 to Derwen College – Shropshire towards new student accommodation for the College for the Disabled; £12,000 to the Association for Rehabilitation and Oral Skills – Malvern towards national training in Facial Oral Tract therapy; £10,000 to British Library of Tape Recordings – London towards the expansion of the Listening Books Scheme; £5,000 to Hebron Trust – Norfolk towards increased capacity at the Rehabilitation Centre for Women.

Overseas projects: 9 grants totalling £117,000

Grants included £40,000 to Royal Commonwealth Ex-services League towards medical funds and maize mills to benefit communities in Commonwealth countries; £15,000 to Kaloko Trust towards equipment costs for HIV/AIDS care and education programmes; £10,000 to St Philip's Church – London towards building a school in Luang Phabang; £4,500 to Leprosy Mission – Peterborough towards health education in East Delhi.

General welfare & social change: 9 grants totalling £106,000

Grants included £23,000 to Worcester and Malvern Woman's Aid towards furnishings and equipment; £20,000 to Maternity Alliance – London towards the costs of moving to new premises; £10,000 to EC Roberts Centre – Portsmouth towards the expansion of its family centre; and £7,100 to Longridge Road Under 8s Centre – London towards refurbishment work.

Community: 7 grants totalling £88,000

Grants included: £20,000 to Rothbury Jubilee Hall – Northumberland towards refurbishment costs; £10,000 to Bottesford VC Hall – Nottingham towards rebuilding costs; and £5,000 to Burbage Institute – Derbyshire towards the renovation of the village hall.

Hospices: 3 grants totalling £60,000

Grants were £25,000 to Hartlepool and District Hospice towards the costs of building a new day hospice; £20,000 to Primrose Hospice – Bromsgrove towards extension costs; and £15,000 to Woodlands Hospice – Liverpool towards constructing an out-patient annexe.

There were 53 small grants made totalling £100,000 ranging from £350 to Simpson House – Edinburgh towards equipment for the Sunflower Project to £5,000 to Moray Flood Relief Fund. 'Miscellaneous'; grants to 27 organisations totalled £49,000

Guidelines for applicants

(These programmes include the small grants scheme referred to above.)

The foundation runs a number of grantmaking programmes, which include one for medical research, a community grants programme and a programme for the elderly.

Where we operate

Geographical targeting

Our area of operation for our main grants programme is the UK. We do not target particular regions. We consider the quality of projects more important than their geographical location. Nevertheless, we also recognise that London organisations in particular are well served by charitable trusts.

We also have an overseas grants programme which makes grants to UK-registered charities which undertake projects in the undeveloped world.

Socio-economic targeting

Although we consider levels of socio-economic deprivation in an area are an important factor in determining the value of a project, more important criteria for our grantmaking are innovation, excellence and the development of new services and activities.

Activities to which funds may be allocated

We predominately fund capital costs, although in the area of medical research, project funding is the norm. Elsewhere, project funding may be offered for start-up or development activities where these are not part of the on-going revenue requirement of the organisation.

We place great emphasis on funding projects that are developmental or innovative. We would like to enable things to happen that would not otherwise happen. We prefer funding a project in its early stages rather than finishing off an already well supported appeal.

We also value projects that are preventive or provide early intervention. Our preferred area of impact is at the community and neighbourhood level.

We also wish to promote good practice. We would like to help with the development of solutions to society's problems and help to expand the take-up of these solutions where they are most needed.

Size and scope of grants

Typically £1,000 to £20,000. From time to time, we may make larger grants to fund projects of an exceptional nature which show outstanding potential.

Where agreed, project funding may be for up to a maximum of three years in duration, and will be tapered downwards if appropriate.

Our funding areas

We have recently reviewed our grant-making policy [August 2003] in order to focus on a narrower range of activities. A number of areas are now excluded.

Art, preservation and the environment

We would like to concentrate our grantmaking on the following:
- industrial heritage
- conservation and preservation of pictures, manuscripts and artefacts
- purchase of land or reclamation of recently purchased land to be used for nature reserves or inner-city gardens, parks etc., where these will be maintained in perpetuity
- conservation of gardens.

The fund will not consider:
- community arts troupes
- community arts centres

- endangered species
- environmental conservation
- animal rescue
- art and history workshops
- fellowships and academic education
- opera and ballet
- artistic productions.

Community facilities

We will support a limited number of projects providing community facilities. We will only support those facilities which provide services that meet basic needs and will accommodate new programmes of social inclusion and participation. The foundation will consider:

- capital costs of community centres and village halls
- capital costs of community facilities provided by churches and faith groups
- capital costs for Citizen's Advice Bureaux
- rescue organisations.

Funding will not be considered for:

- existing parks, playgrounds and recreation facilities
- sports clubs and sports facilities
- community transport
- refugees and asylum seekers.

The Elderly

In this policy area we wish to fund improvement of quality of life. We are particularly interested in seeking out programmes which show some creativity in improving the quality of life of elderly people. We wish to focus on:

- expansion or improvements to elderly care homes, sheltered and supported accommodation
- support for elderly in the community– advice and helplines, home maintenance schemes and home care, respite care homes and luncheon clubs. Informal day care or social and recreational activities– except those contracted by government
- schemes to alleviate isolation and depression in the elderly.

Where it has been shown that some elderly ethnic groups do not receive the services they need, we may seek to redress this balance.

The following areas are excluded:

- almshouses
- meals on wheels
- lifelong learning.

Medical research

In this area, we will focus on near-patient based research, which can show an immediate benefit to patients and is of direct clinical relevance. We will also consider bioengineering projects of immediate benefit to quality of life. We will also consider some research on what works in preventative health or complementary medicine.

The exclusions will be:

- drug research
- genetic research
- basic research
- animal research
- longitudinal studies.

Early intervention

We will continue funding in this area with particular emphasis on the following:

- services to families
- support for parenting
- services for children
- help for families suffering from domestic violence
- support for families in temporary accommodation
- early substance abuse prevention, diet and safety programmes.

The following are exclusions:

- early years education
- recovery from trauma
- research on early intervention with regard to pregnancy and birth.

Hospices

We will continue to fund the capital costs of in-patient day care, domiciliary care and training within hospices. We may also provide start-up project funding for new hospice or domiciliary services in new areas. Children's hospices are now included.

Criminal justice

We would like to support:

- alternatives to custody
- victim support services
- schemes to help prisoners maintain links with their families and be better parents
- accommodation and support for offenders on release
- rehabilitation of offenders.

We will occasionally fund prison reform activities.

The following is excluded:

- welfare of prisoners and their families.

Overseas

We will accept applications for projects in the undeveloped world. We favour high impact projects that have immediate results. We will only fund overseas projects through UK registered charities, which must be able to provide an adequate monitoring function for the grant. We will consider the following areas:

- clean water and sanitation
- basic health education programmes
- cure and rehabilitation from disease and disability
- youth at risk, orphans and street children
- basic training in farming skills and income generation.

The following are exclusions:

- overseas disability awareness
- HIV and AIDS
- victims of famine, war and disaster

- basic education
- gap years, electives or project visits overseas.

Special needs

We will fund the following:

- organisations that support those with physical and learning disabilities, where the services provided are not a statutory duty
- charities providing advice and support for those with rare or marginalised conditions
- capital costs of non-educational aspects of special schools
- training establishments and sheltered employment for the disabled.

The following are excluded:

- disability access and mobility
- disability advice, advocacy and awareness
- disability recreation
- social firms.

Youth at risk

We will continue with the following categories in this area:

- crime prevention schemes
- diversionary projects
- youth mentoring programmes
- community service and volunteering
- remedial education
- employment
- youth work
- uniformed organisations in areas of high socio-economic deprivations
- integrated housing, support and training projects for young people at risk (Foyers)
- programmes to promote responsibility in young people at risk.

The following areas are exclusions:

- youth recreation
- children in care
- fostering and adoption
- support and counselling.

Other areas

We may wish to consider projects outside our main areas of interest when such projects develop novel interventions into society's ills or address causes which are rare or unpopular.

Exclusions

Grants are not made for:

- academic chairs
- bursaries
- church restoration
- computers
- education
- endowment funds
- environmental and animal sciences
- fund-raising activities
- general repairs
- non-medical academic research
- paying off loans

- revenue funding or core costs, general funding, continuing funding and replacement funding
- replacement of government or lottery funding or activities primarily the responsibility of central or local government or any other responsible body
- travel, outings or holidays.

The foundation no longer makes grants for the following:

- homelessness
- mental health
- welfare
- addiction
- social change and research
- citizen organising or citizenship programmes.

Applications

Applications should be made in writing to the administrator, although applicants may telephone to discuss their project before submitting a formal application. It is generally best to start by sending a short résumé of the project, together with a set of your latest audited accounts. The trust will advise if more information is required.

All applications will receive an acknowledgement. However, as there is often a waiting list, and trustees meet only four times a year (usually in January, April, July and October) to consider applications, it may be several months before a decision is made.

Please note that there are always many more applications than the foundation are able to fund; on average, one in twenty applications are approved. Applicants are advised to read the full guidelines very carefully, as inappropriate applications waste time.

Information required:

- the official name of the organisation and its location;
- the name and position of person submitting the application, together with a contact telephone number and address;
- a description of your present work and the priorities you are addressing– quantify the scale of your operation: how many people do you help and how;
- a description of the project you are undertaking, detailing the number of people and groups who will benefit and how: specify how life will be improved for the target group;
- a breakdown of the costs for the full project. Capital and revenue costs should be kept separate: for a capital

project include only information on the capital costs;
- a breakdown of the funds raised to date towards your target, separating capital and revenue, where applicable– include the amount of any of your own funds or reserves going into the project, and also any money you intend to borrow: specify the amount of money you still need for capital and revenue;
- a timetable for the project: when it will start and be finished.

In addition, for overseas projects, briefly describe the political and economic situation in the country where the project will be located. Explain how this may impact the project.

Please enclose a recent set of full audited accounts. If there are connected organisations, include their accounts also.

(For projects in the UK) If applicable and relevant to the size of the project, please also provide further information, as follows:

- a summary of how you are going to evaluate the success of the project, and how you will report this back to us;
- an annual report;
- references, recommendations or letters of support;
- explanation of how you will fund the ongoing costs of your project;
- floor plans, drawings or pictures (no larger than A3).

For overseas projects the additional information suggested, where relevant and applicable, is:

- an annual report and full set of audited account;s
- explanation of how the ongoing costs of the project will be funded;
- a list of any other funders who are considering making significant contributions;
- a prospectus or business plan for the project;
- progress of any planning or statutory requirements for your project to succeed.

The Headley Trust

Arts, heritage, welfare, development
£3.1 million (2003)
Beneficial area Unrestricted.

Allington House, 1st Floor, 150 Victoria Street, London SW1E 5AE
Tel. 020 7410 0330 **Fax** 020 7410 0332
Email info@sfct.org.uk
Correspondent Michael Pattison, Director
Trustees *Sir Timothy Sainsbury; Lady Susan Sainsbury; T J Sainsbury; J R Benson; Miss Judith Portrait.*
Charity Commission no. 266620
Information available Annual report and accounts were provided by the trust.

Summary

This is one of the Sainsbury Family Charitable Trusts which share a joint administration. Like the others, it is primarily proactive, aiming to choose its own grantees, and its 2003 annual report states that 'proposals are generally invited by the trustees or initiated at their request'. The extent to which readers should in general be deterred by this is discussed in the separate entry, under the Sainsbury name, for the group as a whole.

In this particular case, the statement and the general sentiment that unsolicited applications are unlikely to be successful seems to be contradicted in the same document where, under the 'health and social welfare' heading the trust notes that 'the trustees will consider homelessness projects [...]'

The trust has a particular interest in the arts and in artistic and architectural heritage and has made big grants to museums, galleries, libraries and theatres. Though there were relatively few of these in 2003, they will probably reappear from time to time.

There are ongoing programmes for the repair of cathedrals and medieval churches. The trust also supports a range of social welfare issues. Its support for activities in developing countries is focused on sub-Saharan anglophone countries and on central and eastern Europe.

There is a small Aids for Disabled Fund.

General

The settlor of this trust is Sir Timothy Sainsbury. His co-trustees include his wife, eldest son and legal adviser.

Staff include Michael Pattison (director, as of all the Sainsbury family charities) and Hester Marriott, executive.

In words used by many of the Sainsbury charities, 'the trustees prefer to support innovative schemes that can be successfully replicated or become self-sustaining'. In this case they continue to add: 'The trustees also support a number of arts and environmental developments of national or regional significance.' However the accompanying list of grants now uses the term 'heritage' in place of 'environment' and this is probably the more accurate term.

There are good introductions to the list of new grants in the annual reports, under each of the charity's headings, explaining the policies and practices concerned.

Grants approved in 2003 were categorised with the number of grants and their value as follows:

Arts and heritage (UK)	96	£1,189,000
Arts and heritage (overseas)	9	£124,000
Developing countries	10	£172,500
Education	12	£324,000
Health and social welfare	124	£695,500
Total	251	£2,505,000

Arts and heritage, UK

The trustees respond to a wide and eclectic variety of building conservation or heritage projects in the UK. They also support regional museums with revenue costs or the purchase of unusual or exceptional artefacts and in general aim to promote an increase in educational access to museums and galleries. Trustees are interested in notable archeological projects.

The largest grants were £100,000 each made to Somerset House Trust towards the 'Free Time' programme for children and towards new signage, banners and orientation leaflets, and St Paul's Cathedral Foundation, under the cathedrals programme (see below), towards the restoration of the south front.

Other major beneficiaries were Holley Martlew Archaeological Foundation (£90,000), Bowes Museum Trust (£50,000), Crafts Study Centre Trust (£40,000), Oglander Roman Trust (£25,000), Rural Crafts Report (£20,000) and Stained Glass Museum Trust (£10,000).

There were eight small grants of £5,000 or under, including those to Ashmolean Museum, Glyndebourne Festival Opera, Norwich Cathedral Trust and Weald & Downland Open Air Museum.

There are two separate budgets for churches. The first is a 'cathedrals' budget (also applied to large churches), which totalled £285,000 in 2003, for restoration or repair work to the fabric of cathedrals and large churches of exceptional architectural merit. Trustees do not normally provide funding for modern amenities, organ repair or restoration, or choral scholarships.

As well as St Paul's Cathedral Foundation, mentioned above, support in 2003 was also given to Hereford Cathedral Perpetual Trust (£50,000), Boxgrove Priory Trust and Gloucester Cathedral (£35,000 each), Worcester Cathedral Appeal Trust (£30,000), St Albans Cathedral Trust (£25,000) and St Paul's – Deptford (£10,000).

There is also a programme for parish churches, with grants of up to around £3,000 made on the advice of an expert. They totalled £143,000 in 2003, and were made to 59 churches in the dioceses of Durham, Lincoln, Ripon & Leeds, Peterborough, Salisbury and Southwell:

Funding for fabric repair and restoration is considered for pre-16th century churches of exceptional architectural merit in rural villages which are poor or sparsely populated. This is achieved through a process of review, diocese by diocese. Urban churches are not eligible, and funding is available for fabric only (including windows) and not for refurbishment or for construction of church halls or other modern amenities.

Arts and heritage, overseas

Trustees support art conservation projects of outstanding artistic or architectural importance; particularly the restoration of buildings, statuary or paintings, primarily in the countries of central and eastern Europe. They seek out reputable local non-governmental organisations as partners in these countries. They are also willing to consider archaeological projects in the region.

Beneficiaries in 2003 were: World Monuments Fund towards emergency stabilisation and repairs to the Voskopoje churches in Albania (£40,000); Lithuanian National Commission for UNESCO towards the restoration of Uzutrakis Manor Park at Trakai (£25,000); Pinczow Regional Museum towards the restoration of the Pinczow Synagogue Frescoes in Poland (£20,000); McDonald Institute for Archaeological Research towards the excavation and recording of Ziyaret in Turkey (£15,000); and Friends of Aphrodisias Trust towards the fundraising efforts of the trust to support conservation work in Aphrodisias, Turkey (£10,000). Small grants were made to British Friends of the Art Museums of Israel and Guggenheim UK Charity Trust.

Developing countries

The trustees' primary geographical areas of interest are sub-Saharan anglophone Africa, and central and eastern Europe (except the Visegrad Four), the Baltic States and the former Soviet Union. Priority project areas are:

- water/sanitation: e.g. providing access to safe, potable water for disadvantaged communities, preserving areas of culturally or ecologically important swampland or marshland, improving urban or rural sanitary conditions and promoting the better use of water;
- environment: e.g. preserving natural woodland, promoting better use of wood stocks for fuel or construction;
- education and literacy: e.g. improving the quality of education and levels of literacy standards for underprivileged adults or children through training, materials, construction;
- healthcare: e.g. improving standards of health, (particularly reproductive) and assisting people with disabilities to lead a more fulfilled life;
- community and voluntary sector development: e.g. projects which provide training, support and information to assist the development of community groups and local charities.

Trustees will also consider volunteer-based emergency appeals and projects.

Beneficiaries during 2003 included: A Rocha Trust towards the international programme of development work (£30,000); ActionAid towards improving the effectiveness of local NGOs in the rural region of Brong Ahofa, Ghana (£22,000); Ashden Awards for Sustainable Energy towards the administrative costs of the awards for 2004 (£20,000); and HealthProm towards its three-year programme of reproductive healthcare training in an area of Uzbekistan (£7,500).

Education

The trustees' main area of interest is in providing bursary support, particularly for artistic or technical skills training. The bursaries are awarded to institutions for postgraduate study except in exceptional circumstances. They also aim to provide performing opportunities for talented young artists, as well as opportunities to participate in the performing/creative arts for young people who are disadvantaged or disabled.

Beneficiaries included BBC Symphony Orchestra (£75,000), Voices Foundation (£40,000), Edinburgh College of Art (£30,000) and English National Ballet (£21,000).

Health and social welfare

Trustees give priority to social welfare projects, particularly charities helping carers of an ill or disabled relative, and those that support elderly people of limited means. They will consider applications which deal with educational (e.g. literacy) and psychological support for pre-school children and their families. They continue to see parenting education and parenting support programme as a priority. The trustees will consider homelessness projects, particularly for older people, and are interested in care and support for families with autistic children.

This programme is unusual for a Sainsbury trust in specifically welcoming proposals or applications in specified fields.

Beneficiaries in 2003 included: Home-Start UK towards the cost of employing a regional consultant to develop new parent support schemes (£90,000); Changing Faces to employ a head of healthcare development (£60,000); Ormiston Children & Families Trust towards employing a worker to develop support for fathers in Suffolk and Essex (£35,000); Mary Hare Foundation towards the PACE appeal (£20,000); Voluntary Service Belfast towards the cost of new premises (£15,000); and Deafway to help convert an existing residential unit into a house for independent living (£10,000).

Organisations receiving grants of less than £5,000 – of which there were 38 – included both large national charities such as Cancer Research UK and small local groups like St John at Hackney Community Space.

Aids for Disabled Fund

The trustees make a number of small grants to appropriate charities, agencies and local authorities to provide aids for disabled individuals. These are awarded for a range of aids and equipment, including, but not limited to, the following:

- specially adapted computer systems for the partially blind;
- voice-activated computers for sufferers of spinal injuries;
- stair lifts and wheelchairs for people with restricted mobility.

Grants totalling £27,000 were made from this fund in 2003.

Applications

For information on the small Aids for Disabled Fund, ring the trust on 020 7410 0330.

Otherwise, see the guidance for applicants in the entry for the Sainsbury Family Charitable Trusts. A single application will be considered for support by all the trusts in the group.

However, for this as for many of the trusts, 'proposals are generally invited by the trustees or initiated at their request. Unsolicited applications are discouraged and are unlikely to be successful, even if they fall within an area in which the trustees are interested'.

The Health Foundation (formerly The PPP Foundation)

Health care and public health research, training and development

£12 million (2003)

Beneficial area Unrestricted.

90 Long Acre, London WC2E 9RA

Tel. 020 7257 8000 **Fax** 020 7257 8001

Email awards@health.org.uk

Website www.health.org.uk

Correspondent Stephen Thornton, Chief Executive

Trustees *Sir David Carter, chair; Bernard Asher; Prof. Yvonne Carter; Prof. Richard Cooke; Prof. Ram Gidoomal; Prof. Brian Pentecost; Michael Sayers; Dr Elizabeth Vallance; Prof. Klim McPherson; Prof. John Savill; John Roques.*

Charity Commission no. 286967

Information available Annual report and accounts provided by the foundation.

The Health Foundation is an independent charity that aims to improve health and the quality of healthcare in the UK.

It is the largest charitable foundation of its kind in the UK and spends around £15 million every year. It works in partnership with others to ensure that the learning generated from its work helps to shape future health policy and practice.

Since the last edition of this guide was published, the foundation has

undertaken a major strategic review of its grantmaking activities. All of its work is now structured around the following strategic aims:

- Developing leaders to improve health and healthcare services
- Engaging patients for better health and healthcare outcomes
- Engaging clinicians in quality improvement
- Supporting organisational efforts to improve quality and performance in health and healthcare services
- Building the knowledge base for quality and performance improvement.

Award schemes are constantly changing, please see the foundation's website for further details.

Applications

The fund does not accept unsolicited applications for grants.

The Heart of England Community Foundation

General

£600,000 (2002/03)

Beneficial area The city of Coventry and Warwickshire.

Aldermoor House, PO Box 227, Aldermoor Lane, Coventry CV3 1LT

Tel. 024 7688 4386 **Fax** 024 7688 4726

Email info@heartofenglandcf.co.uk

Website www.heartofenglandcf.co.uk

Correspondent Ms Kate Mulkern, Director

Trustees *Peter Deeley, chair; John Atkinson; Mrs Margaret Backhouse; Laurie Cooke; Andrew Corner; Stewart Fergusson; Donald Hunter; Mrs Dorette McAuslan; Peter Shearing; Ms Sue Tyler.*

Charity Commission no. 1045304

Information available Information was provided by the trust.

This foundation aims to raise and distribute funds for the benefit of the local community in Warwickshire and the city of Coventry. It intends to do this by:

- building a lasting source of charitable money and knowledge, so as to be able to respond strategically to the changing needs of the local communities;
- providing a comprehensive service to donors; managing their funds and donations in accordance with agreed objectives; making their giving in the community effective and creative;
- making grants to a wide range of voluntary and community groups on the basis of researched needs and evaluated results;
- forging links with business, voluntary and statutory sectors and using the trust's knowledge and contacts to promote a better understanding of community needs.

The general fund will give priority to groups or activities aimed at improving the quality of life and opportunity among groups who are disadvantaged by poverty, disability or other factors, and at creating and supporting social and economic development. The trustees will be looking for groups or projects which:

(a) foster a sense of pride and achievement through self-help and voluntary effort;

(b) aim to enhance the abilities of community and voluntary organisations assisting in social and economic development and regeneration;

(c) directly benefit small neighbourhood groups, particularly those from areas experiencing the greatest disadvantage;

(d) address the problems of crime and nuisance, and of fear of crime and nuisance, afflicting vulnerable communities;

(e) address the problem of young people including: homelessness; problems associated with the misuse of drugs; problems arising from behavioural difficulties or exposure to criminality or the need for vocational training; or for guidance around parenthood or health issues;

(f) support community care, to groups including: older people; people with physical disabilities; people with learning difficulties; or people with mental disabilities;

(g) assist the provision of counselling and guidance. For example, helplines or face-to-face counselling activities concerned with sexual abuse, drug abuse, mental health, or other traumatic or excessively difficult situations;

(h) tackle isolation, including rural isolation, ethnic exclusion, or stigmatising illnesses or disabilities.

In 2002/03 the trust had assets of £1.1 million and a total income of £1.2 million. This was the first year that it received donations totalling more than £1 million. Grants were made to 365 organisations from 15 funds, totalling £600,000. The origins of these donations could be broken down as follows:

Central government	£452,000
Trusts	£107,000
Companies	£28,000
Local government	£11,000
Individuals	£2,500

Nearly half of the trust's funds (£258,000) were given through the Local Network Fund for Children and Young People. Beneficiaries from this fund included Spring Playgroup to extend the capacity of the group and Coventry Crusaders to offer young people professional basketball coaching (£7,000 each), Atherstone Youth Marching Band for new instruments and Relate Rugby and North-East Warwickshire for a counselling service for children who have witnessed domestic violence (£6,000 each).

Other beneficiaries included William Batchelor Gardening Club to allow residents of high-rise flats to create 'gardens in the sky' (£5,000), Vietnamese Community Support Group to create a contact group (£4,000), Stratford Renal Unit Volunteers to develop a newsletter for patients and their families (£2,000), WATCH to give women training opportunities by funding childcare (£1,000), Southam Gymnastics for safety mats (£750), Age Concern – Leamington Spa for a minibus service (£500), Bhandan Ladies Group to provide opportunities for ladies to meet outside the home (£400) and Norton Lyndsey Wednesday Club for taking older people on a coach trip (£250).

Exclusions

Grants will not usually be considered for the following:

- general and major fundraising;
- individuals;
- educational institutions except where the institution or project is aimed at the relief of disadvantage;
- promotion of religious causes except where the institution or the project is aimed at relief of disadvantage;
- medical research;
- organisations with no permanent presence in the beneficial area;
- animal welfare;
- political activity;

- organisations with substantial reserves relative to turnover;
- sports clubs except where the institution or the project is aimed at relief of disadvantage;
- salaries and other core costs.

Only one grant will be given to an organisation in any one year from the foundation.

Applications

In writing to the correspondent. Organisations are encouraged to telephone the foundation to discuss their project in advance of applying.

The Heathcoat Trust

Welfare, local causes

£740,000 to organisations and individuals (2003/04)

Beneficial area Tiverton, Devon and Cornwall.

The Factory, Tiverton, Devon EX16 5LL

Tel. 01884 254949 (Ext. 296)

Correspondent E W Summers, Secretary

Trustees *Sir Ian Heathcoat Amory; M J Gratton; Mrs B Hill; J Smith; Mrs N J Green.*

Charity Commission no. 203367

Information available Full accounts were on file at the Charity Commission.

The trust makes over 100 grants a year to organisations, most of them for less than £1,000, and nearly all to local causes, centred on the Tiverton area. Other grants are made to individuals, employees and pensioners of the Heathcoat group of companies. Educational grants are given to children of employees or pensioners of the Heathcoat group of companies. Also to local students attending schools and colleges in Tiverton, or beyond if courses are not available locally.

In 2003/04, the trust had an income of £472,000; a slight increase on the previous year. Grants to organisations and individuals increased to £740,000.

Beneficiaries are likely to remain the same each year within the Tiverton area. These include Tiverton High School, Tiverton MS Society, INVOLVE (Tiverton Volunteer Centre) and Tiverton & District Scout Council.

Applications

In writing to the correspondent. There are application forms for certain education grants.

The Hedley Foundation

Youth, health, welfare

£929,000 (2002/03)
Beneficial area UK.

9 Dowgate Hill, London EC4R 2SU
Tel. 020 7489 8076 **Fax** 020 7489 8997
Website www.hedleyfoundation.org.uk
Correspondent Mrs Mary Kitto, Appeals Secretary
Trustees *J F Rodwell, chair; C H Parish; P R Holcroft; G R Broke; P G Chamberlin; Miss L B Wace.*
Charity Commission no. 262933
Information available 'Criteria for Grants' leaflet. Accounts and brief report. Full and informative grants lists.

Summary

Grants are mostly made for amounts between £1,000 and £5,000, with £15,000 as a usual maximum. Most are for capital costs such as new buildings or equipment, though they can be for general funding and occasionally for a period of up to three years. However the trust is not keen to support revenue or core funding.

Beneficiaries are often local health and welfare charities for young or disabled people, but local branches of national charities are also supported.

In 2002/03 grants were made to 250 organisations totalling £929,000.

General

The foundation continues to describe its criteria for grants as follows:

- Young people: their education, training, health, development and welfare (currently about half the foundation's budget).
- Churches and local community centres: new construction or adaptation for community use.
- Disabled people and the terminally ill: provision of specialist equipment and support for carers.
- Medical charities: the provision of specialist medical equipment.

Grants are for specific projects only, mostly one-off but a limited number of recurring grants for up to three years. Grants are normally between £1,000 and £5,000.

The great majority of grants are one-off, and are not repeated within 18 months.

An unusual feature of the list is that each award has against it the initials of an individual trustee, and the trust has said that 'trustees individually have visited many charities to which the foundation has made grants'. They do not appear to specialise, either geographically or by type of charity.

The largest grants of £15,000 each were made to Farms for City Children, United World Colleges and Weston Spirit, the latter being the first of two grants. Other larger grants of £10,000 each were made to AMBER, Bedford School Trust, English National Opera, Fairbridge, Lord Mayor's Appeal, Maggie's Cancer Caring Centre, Ocean Youth Trust (North East), Outward Bound Trust, St Luke's Hospital for the Clergy, Taste for Adventure Centre and Treloar Trust.

Other more typical grants were made to beneficiaries including 999 Club, Autism Initiatives, Haven House Foundation, Moorfields Eye Hospital, Shooting Star Trust and World Conservation Monitoring Trust (£5,000 each), Adventure Sailing Trust Limited, Children's Heart Foundation, National Kidney Research Foundation and Sick Children's Trust (£4,000 each), Abbeyfield Society Limited, Edinburgh Young Carers Project and Wingate Special Children's Trust (£3,000 each), Crimebeat – Cheshire, Deafway, Morning Star Trust and Tullochan Trust (£2,000 each) and Council for Music in Hospitals, Friends of Kent Churches and Wildlife Trust Cumbria.

Comment

This foundation shows an unusual and intriguing combination of a very long list of small awards, and also evidence of a highly active body of trustees.

Exclusions

Grants are made only to UK registered charities.

No grants to:

- overseas charities;
- individuals, under any circumstances;
- national and very large appeals;
- vehicles and transport.

Applications

Applications should be made in writing to Mrs M Kitto, appeals secretary.

The trustees meet about every eight weeks, so applications receive prompt attention. They should be accompanied by the latest available accounts, and a note of the present state of the appeal and its future prospects; in the case of buildings, it should also include an illustration or drawing and details of planning status. The foundation also states that video tapes are particularly welcome and will be returned.

Although Hedley staff are prepared to deal with questions from applicants, consulting the website will normally answer 90 per cent of them and save both time and money.

For community schemes it would be helpful to have a brief description of the community, its history, present make-up and aspirations, what is going for and against it and so on to put flesh on the application.

Trustees individually have visited many charities to which the foundation might make or have made grants.

Help a London Child

Children and young people

£731,000 (2003)
Beneficial area London, specifically the 95.8 Capital FM transmission area.

c/o Capital Radio, 30 Leicester Square, London WC2H 7LA
Tel. 020 7766 6203/6536 **Fax** 020 7766 6195
Email halc@capitalradio.com
Website www.capitalfm.com/helpalondonchild
Correspondent Rich Hornsell, Allocations Manager
Trustees *David Briggs; David Mansfield; Bill Midgley; Peter Williams; Paul Soames.*
Charity Commission no. 1091657
Information available Annual report and accounts, full grants list, application forms and guidelines.

Summary

HALC aims to give opportunities to the Capital's children and young people who:

- experience poverty and disadvantage;
- have/are experiencing abuse, neglect, homelessness, violence, crime;
- have an illness or disability.

HALC encourages applications from organisations working with children and young people, up to and including the age of 18, in the Greater London area who fit into one or more of the categories in our funder statement above.

Applications are assessed by an independent panel from London's voluntary sector who then make their recommendations to our trustees. Grants given include those to help fund: play and special needs equipment; sports and leisure activities; youth clubs; refuge and homelessness projects; activity breaks in the UK; health projects; and educational programmes; playgroups.

Help a London Child (HALC) raises all the money it allocates. It does this through a combination of activities, including the HALC weekend at Easter, charity balls and treks as well as through ongoing fundraising activities throughout the year. It has two rounds of funding per year. In 2003 it made 524 grants totalling £731,000. The maximum grant is £3,000.

HALC also runs a Christmas appeal which helps children and their families by giving out toys and food. In 2004, 50,000 children and families were provided with a quality toy for Christmas or food hampers.

Guidelines for applicants

The seven categories of organisations HALC funds are:

- community groups;
- playgroups;
- refuge/homelessness projects;
- social/leisure groups;
- special needs/health projects;
- youth;
- language and literacy.

The HALC panel look most favourably on projects that directly benefit children.

HALC invites applications from any group who has a written constitution and child protection policy as well as a management committee. If you are not a registered charity, you can still apply, but you must have your application endorsed by a registered group willing to accept the grant on your behalf.

Reapplications are encouraged. Organisations can be funded repeatedly for three years or more as long as they can show new aspects of the project and particularly, how the previous grant has enabled the project to develop. Organisations applying for a fourth year in a row will be given less priority than other applicants.

Where appropriate, applicants are advised to show how the project would maintain funding in future years if a repeat application were not successful.

Please be realistic in the amount you request from HALC – the average grant given in the first round of funding in 2004 was £1,678.

HALC will consider funding:

- sessional posts;
- capital costs, for example play, sports and special needs equipment;
- key core running costs, for example rent, project telephone bills, postage costs;
- projects run by local branches of national/regional organisations;
- trips or holidays in the UK;
- construction costs only for safety surfacing, storage and installation of equipment;
- volunteer costs;
- booklets, publications and information leaflets targeted at children and young people.

Grants from the first round of funding in 2004

Community groups – 32 grants

- Playschemes and activities organised by, and equipment for: community centres, after-school clubs, residents' associations, adventure playgrounds.
- Cultural activities and projects addressing the needs of children from local ethnic communities.
- London branches of welfare groups (i.e. Gingerbread, Homestart, WelCare).

Language and literacy projects – 8 grants

- Groups addressing non-statutory educational needs such as local branches of Volunteer Reading Help.
- Supplementary and mother tongue schools.

Playgroups and toy libraries – 10 grants

- Projects offering primary play facilities to children from disadvantaged backgrounds ages five and under.

Refuge/homeless projects – 6 grants

- Organisations running refuges for children affected by domestic violence (i.e. London Women's Aid and refuge groups).
- Projects focusing on homeless families with young children, and youth homelessness.

Social/leisure groups – 19 grants

- Arts, drama, music, and sports clubs for less advantaged young people.

Special needs/health projects –- 33 grants

- Equipment, activities and playschemes for groups supporting children and young people with disabilities and/or special needs.
- Projects for young people dealing with health issues (i.e. alcohol, drug and physical abuse, bullying, sexual health).

Youth – 12 grants

- Clubs and projects focused on young people aged 11 to 18.

Exclusions

HALC will not fund:

- individual children or families;
- retrospective funding;
- statutory funding e.g schools and hospitals;
- salaried posts;
- deficit funding;
- medical research;
- purchase of minibuses;
- trips abroad;
- distribution to other organisations;
- distribution to individuals;
- religious activities;
- political groups;
- general structural changes to buildings;
- projects which are part of a larger charity organisation and not separately constituted;
- core funding for a national or regional charity.

Applications

Grants are awarded twice a year, with closing dates in June for funding starting in October, and October for funding starting in February. For a copy of the 2005 application form and guidelines please send an A4 sae (28p) to:

Help a London Child 2005 Applications
Capital Radio
30 Leicester Square
London
WC2H 7LA

We encourage applicants to call the office should they have any questions before filling in the form. After the closing date the applications then go to an independent panel of experts from London's voluntary sector. For the June 2005 deadline, applicants will then be informed of the panels decisions in writing in the following October.

The charity continues to actively seek applications and is running 'Meet the Funder' sessions (where staff can go through the application form one-to-one with potential applicants) in each London borough. Those interested should contact their local CVS or HALC on the number above.

Capital Charities also run the following appeals through Capital Radio Group's stations across the UK. These are:

- 'Help a South Wales Child' at Red Dragon FM,
- 'Help a Local Child' in Sussex at Southern FM,
- 'Help a Local Child' in Kent at Invicta FM,
- 'Help a Local Child' in Hampshire at Power FM,
- 'Help a Local Child' in the West Midlands at BRMB FM
- 'Help a Local Child' in Oxfordshire at FOX FM
- '21st Century Kids' in Nottingham, Manchester and Newcastle at 106 Century FM, 105.4 Century FM and 100–102 Century FM.

Similarly, these branches of the charity seek to allocate grants to children and young people who experience disadvantage in the above regions and cities.

Please contact Annabel Durling at Capital Charities on 020 7766 6536 for more details, or email annabel.durling@capitalradiogroup.com

Help the Aged

Welfare, for older people

£6.4 million to organisations and individuals (2003/04)
Beneficial area UK.

207–221 Pentonville Road, London
N1 9UZ

Tel. 020 7278 1114 **Fax** 020 7278 1116
Email info@helptheaged.org.uk
Website www.helptheaged.org.uk
Correspondent Michael Lake, Director General

Trustees *John D Mather, chair; Henry Bowrey; Dr Beverley Castleton; Jo Connell; Anna Coote; June Crown; Brian Fox; Prof. Leslie Iversen; Prof. Oliver James; William Keates; Rosemary Kelly; Trevor Larman; William Menzies-Wilson; Michael Roberts; Kevin Williams; Christopher Woodbridge; Angus Young.*

Charity Commission no. 272786
Information available Report and accounts. Grants, guidance and project fundraising information.

Summary

The most important form of support for other charities by Help the Aged is best described as 'support in kind'. For example, its staff carry out training fundraising for 'other UK charities which share the objectives of Help the Aged'.

Help is, nevertheless, also given in the more traditional form of grants. In 2003/04, grants rose to £6.4 million – almost three-fold the total in 2001/02. However, as no further breakdown concerning grant giving in 2003/04 was avaialble, we repeat the last information we were provided with.

Generally small, and made through four departments or schemes, grants in 2001/02 were categorised as follows:

- Community support programme (£1,346,000)
- Special projects department (£235,000)
- Minibus scheme (£395,000)
- Local distributions by local committees (£293,000)

There are also extensive grantmaking programmes overseas, not covered here.

General

Help the Aged's website as at February 2005, stated that it is 'currently running a very much reduced grant making programme', although grants are still available under its 'Speaking Up for Our Age' programme. As no further details regarding this reduction in grant making were given, to provide some idea of the types of projects previously funded, we repeat information pertaining to 2001/02 below.

Help the Aged 'is primarily a fundraising organisation'. The charity raises money, some of which is given in grants,

through its Community Services division. They are usually small, and go to community-based groups for projects such as building and equipping day centres, setting up lunch clubs or buying minibuses, under a range of programmes and schemes, as follows, with figures for 2001/02 (note that these summary figures vary slightly from those used in the more detailed descriptions of grant programmes later in this entry.)

Community support general grants (£1,346,000)

We give support to community groups through advice, information, training and in grants. In deciding where we can give support two factors will be uppermost, namely that the projects in question

1. meet needs that have been defined by older people themselves
2. clearly target disadvantage.

Help the Aged is unique in combining development advice, grantmaking and project fundraising, and in providing these services free of charge.

We may be able to offer:
- help with developing your service, and in setting goals and standards for it
- help with setting up a group and with constitutions
- advice on developing a business plan
- advice on involving older people, and in running a group
- advice on fundraising
- advice on legal requirements
- advice on certain technical matters such as vehicle specs
- grants, whether revenue or capital, to develop a service
- grants for capital projects.

It may well be that the best way we can help, given the limited funds available, will be through advice or information to your organisation. [...] In the case of larger projects, such as significant capital programmes, our involvement could be considerable and spread over a period of time. In these situations, we ask then that organisations take part in a full feasibility study. [...]

We may agree that the best way of helping your project may be to second one of our regional development officers to you for a period of their time. They are trained fundraisers, and their expertise can help you turn your project into reality.

Criteria for supporting projects
Any project which we assist must meet all the following criteria:
- Be able to demonstration that the highest percentage of their use is by older people or their carers
- Be managed by properly constituted voluntary organisations, or those working

towards that status. Charitable status is not strictly necessary

- Reach local communities and target vulnerable or disadvantaged older people
- Produce evidence that older people have been identified or support this particular step forward, and will be involved in its development
- Meet a need where there is a clearly defined gap in available services and opportunities
- Have a clear idea of what you are trying to achieve, so that later on we can see together how much has been achieved
- Have a clear idea of how you are going to build on what you have achieved and keep it going
- Be able to demonstrate that assistance is towards a new project or service, or a development of an existing one.

Not more than three applications will be considered within a five-year period. Revenue grants will normally be available for a maximum of three years and in partnership with other funders.

Projects recently supported include:

- Advocacy projects
- Social research
- Conferences and events
- Assistance with mobility, sometimes involving minibuses and other forms of transport
- Daily living activities, such as day care centres and lunch clubs
- Hospices
- Refurbishment costs
- Home care support.

£1.3 million was given in grants under this scheme in 2001/02, categorised as follows:

Specialist care services	£605,000
Projects for preserving independence	£89,000
Advice/information/advocacy/research	£193,000
Access to buildings	£237,000
Access to transport	£58,000
Access to opportunities	£59,000
Empowerment	£62,000
Other	£43,000

The 293 new grant awards in 2001/02 ranged from around £100 to more than £30,000 (£36,000 over three years to Age Concern Ceredigion to expand a rural lunch club service in isolated rural areas). Only 22 other grants were for more than £10,000.

Some examples of the recipients included Northcall in North Yorkshire (£260 for equipment); ExtraCare Trust, West Midlands (£4,000 for a greenhouse for the gardening club); Trowbridge Shopmobility (£9,000 for power scooters); and Buttershaw Christian Family Centre (£1,800 for kitchen equipment). Larger grants included £15,000 each for Bristol Salvation Army, Age Concerns in West Glamorgan and in Spelthorne, the CAN homelessness team

in Northampton and Holborn Community Association.

The grants in England were geographically very uneven, with the south of England receiving 49% of the money and the Midlands and north of England 32%. Half of this latter amount was in Yorkshire (16%), with only very small amounts going to to the north east, the north west or the West Midlands (3% each). Wales received a high 14% and Scotland a low 6%.

There is a separate grants programme for Northern Ireland of about £40,000 a year.

Minibus grants (£286,000)

Help the Aged has an excellent programme in which it obtains and converts minibuses for local groups, at a lower cost than they would have to pay individually, In some cases, however, the local group will still need some assistance to make the purchase, and in 2000/01 £286,000 was given in grants for this purpose. The grants lists show a wide range of institutions including day centres, Age Concerns, Shopmobility and Care and Repair schemes, MIND groups and community transport schemes.

The grants can be quite large, if locally earmarked funds are available – say from a legacy, for example, with two groups receiving almost £40,000 (Cheadle Live at Home and Gullane Day Centre). Most grants, though, were for amounts between £500 and £5,000.

The older homelessness programme (£235,000)

These grants totalled £235,000 in 2001/02 and were made as part of the charity's programme development. The major beneficiaries included St Mungo's in London (£50,000) and the Salvation Army in Bristol (£23,000).

Grants from local Help the Aged Committees (£293,000)

Some local committees, tens rather than hundreds of them, raise money specifically for other local charities helping older people. The resulting grants totalled £293,000 in 2001/02.

Miscellaneous (£236,000)

Headed 'Director General Miscellaneous', these included £200,000 for the Oxford Centre on Ageing and £25,000 for 'British Commonwealth Ex-servicemen'.

Exclusions

- Funding for loans, or to reduce deficits already incurred by projects, or to make up a shortfall due to underbidding for a service contract;
- commercial companies or statutory agencies;
- organisations artificially created as trusts, designed to meet the needs of community care proposals or to realise European funding;
- holidays;
- residential or nursing homes, except to support independent living of older people and where the benefits extend to the wider community;
- registered social landlords except where there is a clearly defined project focusing on a vulnerable group, for example, homeless older people.

Grants towards individuals, outings, general entertainment, leisure clubs and festive celebrations are generally excluded except where they may be supported with funds specifically donated to us for that particular purpose or within a geographical area.

Applications

In the first instance contact the regional distributions department on 020 7253 0253 or by fax on 020 7239 1849. The distributions committee meets approximately every other month, usually in March, June, September and December. In between meetings, grants can be agreed for up to £5,000, but only out of funds earmaked for specific local areas or subjects.

The Hertfordshire Community Foundation

General

£512,000 (2002/03)

Beneficial area Hertfordshire.

Sylvia Adams House, 24 The Common, Hatfield, Hertfordshire AL10 ONB

Tel. 01707 251351 **Fax** 01707 251133

Email hcf@care4free.net

Website www.hertscf.org.uk

Correspondent Christine Mills, Grants Officer

Trustees *Stuart Lewis, chair; Roy Bain; Kate Bellinis; Betty Globe; Caroline*

McCaffrey; June Street; Richard Walduck; James Barham; David Cansdale; John Usher; John Peters; Christopher Laing; Bill Tudor John.

Charity Commission no. 299438

Information available Annual review was provided by the trust.

Launched in 1989, the foundation is one of a growing number of community trusts in the UK, which supports and provides funds to local charities and voluntary groups which serve the local community and benefit the lives of the people they serve.

Since the foundation commissioned the research and publication of *Causes for Concern – Spotlight on Hidden Community Needs in Hertfordshire*, four priority areas for grantmaking have been identified:

- disadvantaged children and families;
- activities and opportunities for young people;
- access to education, training and employment;
- the quality of life of older people.

The foundation is also able to support a wide range of charitable activities, in and around Hertfordshire. The trust advises therefore that it is always worth contacting them to discuss the project, in case they can help or direct you to someone else who can.

The trust also manages a growing number of funds on behalf of local donors. Each has its own remit, reflecting the donor's particular charitable interests and concerns. It has, for example, managed the Key Fund, an ESF initiative to help disadvantaged groups into employment, which finished in December 2003.

Major grants are given for both revenue and capital costs, but not usually long-term funding or as part of a large building project. The maximum grant is usually £5,000 as a one-off payment, or £15,000 over three years, but grants are on average smaller than this. Project grants are for up to £500 for specific items to help a group or project to start or develop, e.g. for training or tools. Small grants for disadvantaged children of up to £200 for urgent needs, and individual grants for young people within very specific areas.

In 2002/03 its assets stood at £2 million and it had an income of £821,000. Grants totalled £512,000 and were broken down as follows:

Children and families

– Donations included: £4,500 to Home-Start – East Hertfordshire; £3,000 each to CommonSense – St Albans and Watford TurnAround; £2,000 to Relate Hertfordshire Central; £1,500 to East Hertfordshire Community Playbus Association; £1,000 to Connections Ltd – Watford; £780 to Hertford Heath Primary School; and £500 to Playbox – North Hertfordshire.

Young people

– Grants included: £5,500 to Stortford Outreach and Resettlement Project – East Hertfordshire; £5,000 to Hertfordshire Young Homeless Group; £2,000 to Live Music Now!; £1,500 to Colne Valley Special Sailors; £1,000 to Rookery Youth Project; £500 each to Harpenden Graffiti Project and Hertford Music Festival Society; and £450 to Idance Foundation.

The key fund

– These donations were given to local community groups to help people who are disadvantaged in the labour market. Grants included: £10,000 each to Courtyard Arts, Dacorum Volunteer Bureau, Industrial Therapy Organisation – South Oxhey and Women's Information and Support Services; £9,300 to Diva – Broxbourne Asian Group; £7,500 to Hertfordshire and Bedfordshire Pastoral Foundation; £5,000 to Youth Matters; £2,900 to Highfield Mother and Toddler Group – Dacorum; £1,800 to ASCEND – South Oxhey; and £600 to Dacorum Mencap Friendship Scheme.

Older people

– Grants included: £3,000 each to Beaumont Centre – Cheshunt and Parkinson's Disease Society – Watford; £2,500 to Alzheimer's Society – North Hertfordshire and Stevenage; £1,200 to Broxbourne Friendship Club; £500 each to Polish Over 60's Club – Letchworth and University of the Third Age – Welwyn Hatfield.

Local communities

– Donations included: £6,000 to St Albans Asian Ladies' Bereavement Network; £4,900 to Carers in Hertfordshire; £3,600 to Diva – Broxbourne; £2,000 each to St Lawrence Church – Bovingdon and St Mary and St Joseph Church – Boxmoor; £1,500 to Hertfordshire and Eastern Region ME Support; £1,000 to Peace Hospice; £900 to Pemberton Club – St Albans; and

£240 to Hertfordshire and Bedfordshire Lupus Group.

Exclusions

No grants are made towards:

- UK or general appeals, or those with no specific Hertfordshire focus
- statutory or public bodies, or to replace withdrawn statutory funding
- religious or political causes, medical research, holidays, overseas travel or full-time education
- individuals, except within the terms of special funds, e.g. the Children's Fund.

Applications

An informal discussion with one of the grants staff is encouraged at an early stage. If appropriate, an application form will be issued. Major grants are considered quarterly, with deadlines at the end of February, May, August and November. Other requests are considered when received. Please refer to the foundations website at: www.hertscf.org.uk for further details.

Alan Edward Higgs Charity

Child welfare

£954,000 (2002/03)

Beneficial area Within 25 miles of the centre of Coventry only.

5 Queen Victoria Road, Coventry CV1 3JL

Tel. 024 7622 1311

Email clerk@higgstrust.org.uk

Correspondent The Clerk

Trustees *P J Davis; M F Knatchbull-Hugessen; Sir Derek Higgs.*

Charity Commission no. 509367

Information available Annual report and accounts were provided by the trust.

Grants are made to benefit 'wholly or mainly the inhabitants of the area within 25 miles of the centre of Coventry'. The main activity supported is 'the promotion of child welfare, and particularly the welfare of underprivileged children'.

The charity says:

It is the aim of the trustees to reach as wide a selection of the community as possible within the geographical limitations. They are happy to receive applications for grants from local bodies or associations and from national organisations which can show that any grant from the charity would be used to benefit persons resident within the geographical area. [...] the increasing range and diversity of donations continue to be welcomed.

The charity has told these editors that it is becoming more proactive in its grantmaking.

In 2002/03 it had assets of £21 million and an income of £981,000. Grants totalling £954,000 were made to 102 charities, of which 50 had also been supported in the previous year.

By far the largest grant was £364,000 to Alan Higgs Centre Trust, towards start-up costs; £45,000 to Coventry and Warwickshire Awards Trusts, to support the core costs of the Midland Sports Centre and Centre AT7; £30,000 each to Acorn's Children's Hospice Trust, towards core costs and Common Purpose, to fund the 'Your Turn' programme promoting citizenship for young people from ten Coventry schools; £25,000 to Warwick Arts Centre, to provide personal development in four primary schools in south east Coventry; £21,000 to Royal Midland Counties Home for the Disabled; £20,000 each to Belgrade Theatre, for the capital fund for the redevelopment of the theatre and St Martin in the Bull Ring, towards the capital fund to redevelop the hall complex; £18,000 to Family Holiday Association, to fund holidays for families in the Coventry area; and £16,000 to Coventry School Education Trust to provide bursaries for eight students.

Grants of £10,000 each included those to Autism West Midlands, Myton Hamlet Hospice, RNIB and Young Homeless Project.

Exclusions

Applications from individuals are not entertained. No grants for the funding of services usually provided by statutory services, medical research, travel outside the UK or evangelical or worship activities.

Applications

In writing to the clerk to the trustees, along with:

- a copy of the latest audited accounts;
- charity number (if registered);
- a detailed description of the local activities for the benefit of which the grant would be applied;
- the specific purpose for which the grant is sought;

- a copy of the organisation's policy that ensures the protection of young or vulnerable people and a clear description of how it is implemented and monitored.

The Hilden Charitable Fund

Minorities, overseas, penal, homelessness, general

£412,000 (2002/03)

Beneficial area UK and developing countries.

34 North End Road, London W14 0SH

Tel. 020 7603 1525 **Fax** 020 7603 1525

Email hildencharity@hotmail.com

Website www.hildencharitablefund.org.uk

Correspondent Rodney Hedley, Secretary

Trustees Ms M E Baxter; Mrs M G Duncan; A J M Rampton; Mrs A M A Rampton; Ms C S L Rampton; Dr D S Rampton; Mrs G J S Rampton; J R A Rampton; Dr M B H Rampton; Prof. C H Rodeck; Mrs E K Rodeck; H B Wood; C H Younger.

Charity Commission no. 232591

Information available Full accounts were provided by the trust. Detailed information and guidelines are available on the website.

The main interests of the trust are:

- homelessness (particularly amongst the young);
- minorities and race relations;
- penal affairs;
- overseas countries.

It also has a summer playscheme programme, which gives grants of up to £1,000. There is a preference for organisations working with refugees and minority ethnic groups in this programme. Across the main categories, there are no stated preferences although the fund does have priorities for specific types of work which change from time to time.

Grants are usually of up to £5,000 each and can be for capital or revenue purposes. They are rarely given to 'well-funded national charities' as it prefers to support work at a community level. However, the fund makes an annual

donation to Scottish Community Foundation, which makes donations to Scotttish charities at their discretion in the name of this fund; Scottish organisations should apply for funding through these means.

The only programme which has actual guides is the funding for overseas projects, which are as follows:

The types of applications sought by trustees

1. In supporting overseas development, the trustees wish to hear from projects which focus on community development, education and health.
2. Funds are available for capital and revenue funding. The funding programme is designed to help small and medium sized initiatives.
3. Trustees will consider applications from countries within the developing world. At present applications from Ghana, Ethiopia, Tanzania, South Africa and Bangladesh are particularly welcome.
4. In supporting community development, education and health initiatives. Trustees will particularly welcome projects that address the needs and potential of girls and women.
5. Where possible, the trustees would like to fund a number of projects in one geographical area. In funding projects, the trustees will be interested in projects which develop the capacity of local people.
6. Trustees will be pleased to hear from UK non governmental organisations/charities and hope that UK NGOs/charities will encourage their local partners, if appropriate, to apply directly to Hilden for grant aid.

Applicants should provide:

A. Evidence of commitment amongst local people and communities to the proposed work programme.
B. A coherent plan of how the work is going to be carried out together with relevant budgets. Project budgets should be presented in the context of the overall income and expenditure of the applicant NGO/charity.
C. A plan of how the work is going to be maintained and developed in the future by involving relevant agencies and attracting money and resources.
D. An explanation of why the local project seeks the help of a UK agency.
E. Details of local costs (e.g. salaries of state-employed teachers and medical personnel, cost of vehicles, petrol etc.) and notes of any problems over exchange rates or inflation.
F. An account of the political, economic, religious and cultural situation in the country/area.

G. A comment on the extent to which the project can rely on government and local state funding in the country concerned.

H. Details of monitoring and evaluation.

Essential:

for projects not based in the UK you should send details/information on the following:

1. Your latest annual accounts and annual report.
2. Your grant request in UK £.
3. Details of UK £ and local currency exchange rate.
4. Details of your non-profit/charity status.
5. Details of any UK charity link.
6. Details of any local reference e.g. British Embassy.
7. Please ensure you address the criteria A-H listed above.

In 2002/03 it had assets of £9.6 million and an income of £422,000. The management, administration and support costs, including the costs of generating its income, was very high at £162,000 and accounted for 38% of the trust's income for the year. After this, grants were made to 108 organisations of the 488 applicants and totalled £412,000, giving a success rate of less than 25%. They were broken down as follows:

Homelessness – 15 grants totalling £62,000

These grants went to day centres, advice and resettlement help, night shelters and street support services. The only beneficiary outside of these categories was Furniture Now in Lewes which received £3,500.

The largest grants were £6,000 to Big Issue in the North and £5,000 each to Hull Homelessness and Rootless Project, Leeds Simon Community, Newark Emmaus Trust, South Shropshire Young Persons Housing Project, St Theresa's Project – Peterborough, Warrington Action for Homeless and West Lancashire Crisis and Information Centre. Other beneficiaries included Manna House – Kendal (£4,400), Ace of Clubs – Clapham (£2,700) and Rectory Road Church – Stoke Newington (£1,300).

Minorities – 27 grants totalling £121,000

Grants were made generally within this category, with a large number for the running costs of providing welfare support, English language classes and assisting community self help amongst asylum seekers and refugees, the needs of detainees and the encouragement of greater take-up by ethnic minorities.

The largest grants were £12,000 to Joint Council for the Welfare of Immigrants (Immigrants Aid Trust), £8,000 to Detention Advice Service, £5,200 to Bangladesh Welfare Association in Middlesex and £5,000 each to Bangladesh Community Development – West Midlands, Beauchamp Lodge Settlement – Paddington, Chinese Information and Advice Centre – London, Guild of Psychotherapists, Haslar Visitor's Group, Somali Advisory Bureau – Westminster, Spitalfields City Farm and West Indian Ex-Servicemen's Association.

Other beneficiaries included Islington African Project (£4,000), Isla Hispana (£3,500), Women Against Rape (£3,000), Alliance for African Assistance (£2,000) and Essex Learning and Advice Centre (£1,000).

Penal – 13 grants totalling £62,000

Grants were made for educational and vocational workshops in prisons, to support the families of prisoners and for ex-offender resettlement programmes, as well as advice and support services to inmates.

The largest grants were £6,000 to Prisoners Advice and Care Trust – Dartmouth and £5,000 each to Breakout – Lowestoft, Dance United, Howard League for Penal Reform, Kestrel Theatre Company, Partners of Prisoners and Families – Manchester, Prisoners Advice and Care Trust – Pentonville, Prisoners Families and Friends Service – South London, Stepping Stones and WISH (Women in Special Hospitals).

The remaining beneficiaries were Providing Ex-Offenders with Positive Learning Environments (£4,500), London Shakespeare Workshop (£3,500) and Safe Ground (£2,500).

Overseas development – 23 grants totalling £108,000

Grants were made in Africa, Asia and Central and South America. The largest were £11,000 to Child Advocacy International - Cameroon for improvements at Bamenda Hospital and a programme for the treatment of Burkitt's Lymphoma, £10,000 each to Intermediate Technology Development Group – Bangladesh for an extensive micro-credit and business skill training project and Tanzania Development Trust for refurbishment and revenue support in schools, £7,500 to Womenkind Worldwide to explore the needs of women's groups in Bolivia (with a further £6,600 for work on domestic violence issues in Peru) and £6,000 each to Farm Africa to provide agricultural education in two schools in the Babati region of Tanzania, Fulshaind Village Trust – Bangladesh and Tamale Diocesan Development Group – Ghana for a community development project.

Other beneficiaries included Allavida (£5,000), Ons Plek Street Children Project – South Africa for its services for street girls (£3,000), Rural Community Development Organisation – Nepal to rebuild a village after a flood (£2,500), Wulugu Trust to improve schools in northern Ghana (£2,000) and Education for Democracy in South Africa to set up a library in a township in Cape Town (£1,500).

Other – 5 grants totalling £13,000

The largest of these was of £5,000 and went to Thames Community Foundation. The other four grants were of £2,000 each and went to Haringey Young Musicians, Integration Trust, National Association for Colitis and Crohn's Disease Association and Royal Air Force Prisoners of War Memorial Trust.

Scotland – 1 grant of £32,000

The only grant went to Scottish Community Foundation to pass on to other organisations. During the year, it gave 40 grants of £150 to £1,500 from the fund to self-help women's and families' groups and ethnic minorities amongst other causes.

The accounts stated under this category that no grants were made in Wales or Northern Ireland during the year. This was due to the low number of applications it received.

Playschemes – 24 grants totalling £15,000

The success rate for this scheme was 80%, with organisations working with refugee and immigrant communities given priority. Most of the projects supported were in Greater London.

Exclusions

No grants to or on behalf of individuals and no circular appeals.

Applications

For overseas grants: please see details in the guidelines above.

For Scottish organisations: Applications need to be submitted on a form available from Scottish Community Foundation at 126 Canongate, Edinburgh EH8 8DD (telephone: 0131 524 0300). Further information and application forms can be found at www.scottishcommunityfoundation. com).

For playscheme grants: Applicants should request a Summer Play Scheme Form.

For all other applications: Applications must be submitted with the two page summary form available from the trust; any appeals received without this form will be treated as a general enquiry and not considered for a grant. This form is available on the website or directly from the trust. The completed form should be returned with an annual report and accounts, projected income and expenditure for the current financial year and full details of how the project will be managed and administered. These are considered quarterly.

Lady Hind Trust

General

£315,000 (2003)

Beneficial area England and Wales only, with a preference for Nottinghamshire and Norfolk.

c/o Berryman Shacklock, Par House, Friar Lane, Nottingham NG1 6DN

Tel. 0115 945 3700

Correspondent W F Whysall, Trustee

Trustees *C W L Barratt; T H Farr; N R Savory; W F Whysall.*

Charity Commission no. 208877

Information available Full accounts were provided by the trust.

This trust makes mainly one-off grants for general charitable purposes, with some preference for supporting health and disability-related charities. It has similar criteria to, and the same trustees as, Charles Littlewood Hill Trust.

In 2003 the trust had assets of £8.3 million, which generated an income of £298,000. The management and administration expenses included £19,000 in stockbrokers' fees to a firm one of the trustees is a partner in. Whilst wholly legal, these editors always regret such payments unless, in the words of the Charity Commission, 'there is no realistic alternative'. Grants totalled £315,000. Those of £1,000 or more were broken down as follows (with £30,000 being given in smaller grants across all three areas):

Nottinghamshire – 59 grants totalling £142,000.

This category included two large grants, £10,000 each to Fundays in Nottinghamshire and Monty Hind Club. Other beneficiaries included Nottinghamshire Multiple Sclerosis Therapy Centre Limited (£7,500), Framework Housing Association, NSPCC – Nottinghamshire and Winged Fellowship Trust (£5,000 each), DARE and Southwell Care Project (£3,000 each), Emmanuel House Day Centre and Nottingham Counselling Service (£2,000 each), Woolaton Centre Project (£1,500) and East Midlands Open Minds, Literacy Volunteers, Outward Bound Trust, Phoenix Farm Methodist Church and St John's Community Outreach Group (£1,000 each).

Norfolk – 25 grants totalling £67,000

Beneficiaries included Church of St Peter and Paul – Heydon (£6,750), 2nd Reedham Scout Group (£6,000), Heritage House, Norfolk Churches Trust, Royal Norfolk Regimental Museum and Swannington Church (£5,000 each), Norfolk Family Mediation Service (£4,000), Nancy Oldfield Trust (£3,000), Matthew Project – Norwich (£2,500), Hamlet Centre Trust (£2,000) and Army Benevolent Fund – Norfolk, Aylsham High School, Hethersett Old Hall School and Sargent Cancer Fund for Children – Norfolk (£1,000 each).

Elsewhere – 51 grants totalling £73,000

This category included the largest grant made in the year, £12,000 to The Thiepval Project. Other beneficiaries included Juvenile Diabetes Research Foundation (£3,000), Cancer BACUP and National Society for Epilepsy (£2,500 each), East Anglia Children's Hospices (£2,000) and Alzheimer's Society, Breakthrough Breast Cancer, British Polio Fellowship, Crimestoppers Trust, Demand, Headway, Marie Curie Cancer Care, Meningitis Research Foundation, Nightstop UK, Parkinson's Disease Society and Young Minds (£1,000 each).

Exclusions

Grants are seldom made for parish church appeals unless they are within Nottinghamshire. Applications from individuals are not considered.

Applications

Applications, in writing and with latest accounts, must be submitted at least one month in advance of meetings in March, July and November. Unsuccessful applicants are not notified.

Historic Churches Preservation Trust (with the Incorporated Church Building Society)

Historic churches

£2 million (2003)

Beneficial area England and Wales.

31 Newbury Street, London EC1A 7HU

Tel. 020 7600 6090 **Fax** 020 7796 2442

Email director@historicchurches.org.uk

Website www.historicchurches.org.uk

Correspondent James Blott, Director

Trustees *Michael Hoare, chair; Archbishop of Canterbury; Archbishop of York; Sarah Bracher; Robin Cotton; Lady Harman; Stephen Johnston; Ian Lockhart; Major Iain Radford; The Very Revd Henry Stapleton; Philip Venning; Iain Wilkie; Antony Wedgwood.*

Charity Commission no. 207402

Information available Guidelines for applicants. Annual report and accounts with full grants list and review of the year's activities. Half-yearly Review magazine. Detailed website.

Summary

Over 300 grants and loans are normally made each year towards the upkeep of fine Christian churches in England and Wales, although this number has reduced in recent years. They normally start at £1,000, but there is also a programme of 'cornerstone' grants (formerly 'millennium' grants) for up to £50,000. Loans are also given, usually in combination with a grant.

General

This is a fundraising charity which helps any recognised Christian denomination, and also administers the smaller Incorporated Church Building Society which can only help Anglican churches.

To be helped by these charities, non Anglican churches must be over 100 years old, although the Incorporated Church Building Society can help Anglican churches of any age, as well as new churches being built. Money is donated or loaned towards fabric repairs on churches where the parish church council has insufficient funds. From 2004, the charity is offering limited grants for new facilities in churches, including facilities to make the building compliant with the requirements of the Disability Discrimination Act.

The criteria on which applications are judged now takes account of factors other than just the quality of the building, including the scale of the financial challenge to the community, relative to the resources available to it; the urgency of the project; the integration of the church with its community (including the use of the building for other than religious services); the wealth and fundraising potential of the area in which the church is situated and the effort that the community has made or intends to make to raise funds.

In 2003 the trust's income totalled £1.3 million, of which £825,000 came from donations. Grants totalled £2 million with £81,000 given in loans. The charity has been deliberately reducing its reserves since 2000.

Support to 304 churches was approved in 2003, £328,000 of it in the form of 'millennium' grants and £288,000 in 'cornerstone' grants. A total of £1.8 million in grants was made from the HCPT General Fund. Grants made from the ICBS General Fund totalled £200,000.

The major awards were to the churches of Deptford – St Paul (£75,000), St Leonards – Christ Church & St Mary Magdalene (£55,000), Kilburn – St Augustine (£50,000), Shalfleet – St Michael the Archangel (£40,000), Birstall – St Peter (£35,000), Gospel Oak – St Martin and Strethall – St Mary the Virgin (£30,000 each), Harlington – St Peter and St Paul (£25,000) and Lelant – St Uny (£20,000).

The very many smaller grants and loans were typically between £1,000 and £5,000.

Exclusions

The HCPT and ICBS will not fund:

- new amenities (other than worship area enlargement)
- church clocks
- furniture and fittings
- organ repair
- murals
- monuments
- decoration (except after repairs)
- churchyards and walls

- work that has already been started or completed
- non-Anglican churches less than 100 years old.

Churches must be open for public worship.

Applications

To help you check whether your project is likely to be eligible for a grant a short questionnaire is available on the trust's website, after which you can download an application form. This is done so that applicants are not put to the trouble of completing a form, only to find that their church or project does not qualify.

Hobson Charity Ltd

Social welfare, education

About £1 million (2003/04)
Beneficial area UK.

21 Bryanston Street, Marble Arch, London W1A 4NH
Tel. 020 7495 5599
Correspondent Mrs Deborah Clarke, Trustee & Secretary
Trustees *R F Hobson; Mrs P M Hobson; Sir Donald Gosling; Mrs Deborah Clarke.*
Charity Commission no. 326839
Information available Accounts are on file at the Charity Commission.

In 2003/04 the trust had an income of £650,000 (£29,000 in 2002/03) and a total expenditure of £1.1 million. Grants totalled around £1 million and were made from both income and capital funds. Income and expenditure totals vary from year to year. No further information was available.

Previous beneficiaries include John Grooms Association for the Disabled, Westminster Council Christmas Appeal Building Trust, Samuel Johnson Prize, CSV People for People, Churchill College Archives Fund, Health Foundation, Prince's Trust, Oriel College, White Ensign Association, British School of Osteopathy, Neil and Anne Benson Charity, British Sports Trust, Keeper of the Green, Terrence Higgins Trust, Hilda Laing Care Centre, Royal Albert Hall Trust, Royal Ballet, David Shepherd Foundation and Wooden Spoon Society.

Comment

Despite ample warning, and their obligation to the contrary, the Charity Commission were unable to give us sight of this trust's accounts.

Applications

In writing to the correspondent.

The Jane Hodge Foundation

Medicine, education, religion, mainly in Wales

£1.1 million (2002/03)
Beneficial area Unrestricted, but with a preference for Wales.

Ty-Gwyn, Lisvane Road, Lisvane, Cardiff CF14 0SG
Tel. 029 2076 6521
Correspondent Mrs Margaret Cason, Secretary
Trustees *Sir Julian Hodge; Lady Moira Hodge; Teresa Hodge; Robert Hodge; Joyce Harrison; Derrek Jones; Ian Davies; Margaret Cason.*
Charity Commission no. 216053
Information available Annual report and accounts. List of 50 largest grants.

General

This is Wales' largest grantmaking trust, a total of 278 grants were made in 2002/03. Support is also given to a few charities working in developing countries. There is a strong Roman Catholic religious element in some of the grantmaking, but this can include support for multi-faith initiatives.

Much of the money goes on a few major and often long-term ongoing local commitments in South Wales.

The foundation has general charitable objectives, but states a particular interest in the following areas:

- the encouragement of medical and surgical studies and research, and in particular the study of and research in connection with the causes, diagnosis, treatment and cure of cancer, poliomyelitis and tuberculosis and diseases affecting children;
- the general advancement of surgical science;
- the advancement of education;
- the advancement of religion.

In 2002/03 the foundation had assets of over £25 million and an income of £806,000. Grants totalled £1.1 million. Some beneficiaries received more than one grant during the year.

Grants were distributed under the following headings (figures for 2001/02 in brackets):

	No.	Amount	
Medical	51	£212,000	(67£218,000)
Educational	74	£371,000	(80 £177,000)
Religious	57	£272,000	(57£133,000)
Other	96	£208,000	(105£261,000)
Total	278	£1.1 million	(309£788,000)

The accounts listed the top 50 grants made in the year. Of these 11 were of £10,000 or more: Cardiff Business School (£204,000), Pontprennau Methodist Church (£165,000), Faceup and George Thomas Memorial Trust Limited (£50,000 each), University of Wales – Swansea and Red Dragon Radio Trust (£25,000 each), Carmelite Education Trust (£19,000) and Augustine Care, St David's Foundation and St Joseph's Society for Foreign Missions and Sherman Theatre (£10,000 each).

Examples of smaller grants include LATCH (£8,000), Race Equality First (£7,000), Age Concern Cymru, Canine Partners for Independence, Centre for European Studies, Centre for Research and Development in Catholic Education, Children's Hospital in Wales Appeal Limited, Danybryn Leonard Cheshire Home, Fransiscan Friars of the Atonement, National Children's Bureau, Shelter Cymru, Swansea Urology Cancer Fund and Tredegarville Baptist Church (£5,000 each), Diocese of Portsmouth – Jersey Catholic Education Fund (£4,000), Cardiff Institute for the Blind (£3,250) and Gurkha Welfare Trust, Samaritans – Bridgend and Welsh Heritage Schools Initiative (£3,000 each).

Exclusions

The foundation makes grants to registered or exempt charities only. No grants to individuals.

Applications

In writing to the correspondent. The foundation says that every application is acknowledged, despite the volume of requests.

Sir Harold Hood's Charitable Trust

Roman Catholic

£457,000 (2002/03)

Beneficial area Worldwide.

31 Avenue Road, St John's Wood, London NW8 6BS

Tel. 020 7722 9088

Correspondent Sir Harold Hood, Trustee

Trustees *Sir Harold J Hood; Mrs Margaret Gresslin; Revd James Hood; Mrs A M True; Nicholas True; John P Wall.*

Charity Commission no. 225870

Information available Accounts and annual report were provided by the trust.

The trust supports Roman Catholic charities, giving grants of between £2,000 and £33,000.

In 2002/03 it had assets of £7 million and an income of £498,000. Grants were made to 66 organisations totalling £457,000.

Most grants are made to organisations that receive regular donations, although in 2002/03 there were 21 beneficiaries who had not been supported in the previous year. Regular beneficiaries receive roughly the same amount each year.

The largest grant, as in the previous year, was £33,000 to PACT. Other grants of £10,000 or more were made to Archdiocese of Westminster (£25,000), National Catholic Fund and Craig Lodge Trust (£20,000 each), Duchess of Leeds Foundation and Hospital of St John & St Elizabeth (£18,000 each), Downside Settlement (£16,000), Diocese of Brentwood (£15,000), and Youth 2000, Royal Navy Catholic Charity and Coming Home Appeal – Clapham (£10,000 each).

More typical grants included those to Venerable English College – Rome, Hope Hospital – Cambridge and Redemptorists Zimbabwe (£8,000 each), Cardinal Hulme Centre and St Joseph's Pastoral Centre – Hendon (£7,000 each), Sacred Heart Church – Holloway, Diocese of Hexham & Newcastle – Jarrow, St Elizabeth's Home – Much Hadham and Langsyde School – South Africa (£6,000 each), St Francis' Leprosy Guide, Handmaids of Mary – Clapham and Diocese of Aberdeen (£5,000 each),

Apostleship of the Sea, House Aid – Bosnia and Westminster Cathedral (£4,000 each), St Mary & St Finnan – Glenfinnan, St Simon & St Jude – Ulshaw and St Gregory's Charitable Trust – Downside (£3,000 each) and Franciscan Friars and Sacred Heart Convent School (£2,000 each).

Exclusions

No grants for individuals.

Applications

In writing to the correspondent. Applications are considered in November and need to be received by September.

The Housing Associations Charitable Trust (Hact)

Housing and related social need

£600,000 (2004)

Beneficial area UK.

78 Quaker Street, London E1 6SW

Tel. 020 7247 7800 **Fax** 020 7247 2212

Email hact@hact.org.uk

Website www.hact.org.uk

Correspondent Heather Petch, Director

Trustees *Rev. David Walker, chair; Peter Stevenson; Saifuddin Ahmed; Trevor Hendy; Wayne Morris; Dawn Stephenson; Daoud Zaaroura; Gavin Cansfield; Sue Regan; Julian Corner; Omar Faruk*

Charity Commission no. 1096829

Information available Full information, including detailed guidelines and advice sheets for applicants, annual report, accounts and annual review were provided by the trust.

Summary

This is a national housing organisation and its grantmaking is just one part of a broader programme of activities designed to test and develop solutions to housing issues concerning groups on the margins of mainstream provision. It is not an endowed trust, but raises money from other organisations, statutory and charitable, that value its expertise in this highly complex area of need.

It is an 'involved' grantmaker, often bringing its own ideas and support to the activities that it funds.

General

Hact is a development agency and venture funder focusing on current and emerging issues particularly those concerning marginalised groups and people needing support... every year we enable organisations and projects [...] to resolve a myriad of housing problems thanks to our grants, networking experience and ability to influence policy.

Grantmaking is just one activity of the association, which is largely a development organisation, and many of the grants are made in direct support of these programmes.

Grant guidelines

The charity describes its grantmaking as follows.

Hact's framework for funding

Two themes underpin hact's activity and provide a broad framework for our projects and programmes:

- Independent Living – promoting the well-being and quality of life of individuals and their ability to live independently.
- Community – promoting mutual support, interdependence and enhancing the health and well-being of communities.

Hact's grant giving role

Grant giving is an integral part of our work to develop and promote housing solutions for people on the margins. Most of our programmes include a grant fund. However other elements of our work, such as training and research, have an equally important role in achieving our aims.

Why we provide grants

We primarily give grants to test new housing solutions or to increase the capacity of organisations, such as refugee community organisations and small providers of housing support. The success of funded projects is measured through hact's monitoring and evaluation systems. Independent evaluation of programmes overall, strengthens hact's ability to learn from our work. This learning is shared widely so as to influence policy and practice.

How much money will hact give?

Grants up to £25,000 a year can be made depending on the grant programme. The size of grant will be discussed as part of the assessment process and we will also try to advise on other funding options.

Hact can sometimes provide grants for up to three years.

Hact does not have an open grant fund so applications are only considered if they meet the criteria of one of our programmes. Funding limitations inevitably mean that good applications are not always successful. In addition, hact's grant funds are often part of a project designed to generate learning. Therefore we are often looking for a good mix of different types of projects and in different geographical areas.

Current funding activity and priorities

1. Hact Refugee Housing Development Fund

(Mainly England, Wales and Northern Ireland but consideration will be given to applications from Scotland by liaising with our sister organisation, The Lintel Trust)

Through its Refugee Housing Development Fund, Hact provides grants, mainly in dispersal areas, to develop housing and related projects, to encourage joint working and to increase the capacity of refugee community organisations.

Since the late 1980s Hact has given over £1.3 million to refugee community organisations to enable them to develop vital housing related projects.

In particular the fund will be used for activities that:

- improve access to housing and related services to encourage refugee communities to settle in dispersal areas;
- encourage cooperation and partnership working between refugee groups and housing providers to help refugees find and access decent and appropriate housing and explore new ways of responding to their needs;
- strengthen the capacity of new refugee community groups or established organisations enabling them to respond more effectively to relevant needs.

The success of funded projects is measured through independent evaluation and the learning widely disseminated.

Grants from the Refugee Housing Development Fund are intended for:

- user-led refugee community organisations;
- other voluntary organisations, including housing providers, who are working in partnerships with RCOs or who can demonstrate a high level of refugee involvement;
- services which are used mainly by people who have received a positive decision (refugee status or leave to remain);
- projects based in or providing services in dispersal areas (London and South East based projects are welcome to apply, though the fund is targeted mainly at areas of dispersal).

Grants of up to £25,000 will be given for one year.

2. Hact Supported Living Programme

We provide grants to small providers to help them to develop their capacity to meet the requirements of Supporting People and to secure sustainable futures.

Grants also provide opportunities for testing out solutions. External evaluation and wide dissemination of the learning will ensure that the grants benefit not only those receiving them, but also the wider sector.

We have one fund open for applications:

The Make it Happen Fund. This small grants fund is targeted at small organisations that provide front-line housing support services funded through Supporting People. The purpose of this fund is to enable small providers to undertake a specific piece of work that builds their organisation's capacity to meet the requirements of Supporting People.

Round 1 of the Make it Happen Fund closed on 17th August 2004.

Round 2 of the Make it Happen Fund will open early in 2005 [7th February]. If you would be interested in receiving information about this grant, please email Vicky Evans at vicky.evans@hact.org.uk or call 020 7247 7800.

3. Development work

Hact is also interested in supporting pilot projects or feasibility studies that relate to areas of work where Hact may develop programmes in future. Contact Hact to discuss any proposals because support is dependent on funding availability.

Decisions on Funding

Grants up to £10,000

Decisions on applications up to £5,000 can usually be made within three weeks of receiving all the details requested by Hact. Decisions on grants and loans between £5,000 and £10,000 will be made by a delegated Hact trustee and may therefore take a little longer.

Grants over £10,000

These applications must be submitted to a trust meeting for decision. The trust meets six times a year. Normally it is necessary for completed application forms to be received at least two months prior to a trust meeting to allow time for staff to complete a full assessment of your application.

Contacts

Refugee Programme

Azim El-Hassan, refugee programme manager: azim@hact.org.uk
Tel: 020 7458 1172

Hact Supporting Living Programme

Judy Lowe, supported living programme manager: judy.lowe@hact.org.uk
Tel: 020 7458 1171

Andrew Van Doorn – head of programmes:
andrew.vandoorn@hact.org.uk

Vicky Evans – programme manager:
vicky.evans@hact.org.uk

Grants in 2003

In 2003 the trust had an income of £1 million, largely from donations including those from the Henry Smith Charity [which also has an entry here] and the European Refugee Fund. During the year Hact gave grants totalling £662,000 to 41 projects. Some of the beneficiaries and projects mentioned below were given grants through programmes that are no longer running.

Grants now form an integral part of programme activity linked to other forms of capacity building support, networking, research, training and dissemination activity. Grants expenditure in 2003 included:

- 13 grants totalling £306,000 to address the housing needs of older people, including year one support for most of the cohort of 18 services that are a part of the Henry Smith Charity funded older people's programme;
- a grant of £15,000 to Homeless Link towards the costs of developing the Coalition for Older Homeless People which is funded in partnership with Help the Aged. This aims to take forward the learning and recommendations of the older homeless programme which hact ran jointly with Help the Aged until 2003;

- 13 grants totalling £240,000 for the refugee housing development initiatives including projects designed to enhance the capacity of refugee community organisations to influence and engage in the development of housing policy and practice, particularly in areas of dispersal;
- 10 small grants (under £5,000) totalling £31,000, which were the final grants in our 2001–2003 programme to assist small groups preparing for 'Supporting People'.

The largest grants during the year were made to the Lintel Trust, Hact's Scottish partner, which received £47,000, and Care and Repair England, which received £41,000. Other beneficiaries included the 1990 Trust, Fold Housing Association, London Rebuilding Society, Refugee & Asylum Seeker Advocacy Project, Refugee Action Liverpool, Somali Women's Group of Manchester and Coventry Refugee Centre (£25,000 each), Sefton Pensioners' Advocacy Centre (£24,000), Devon & Cornwall Refugee Support Council (£22,000), WASSR (£16,000), Homeless Link (£15,000), Family Housing Association Ltd – Wales (£12,000), Age Concern Northumberland (£10,000), National Energy Action (£8,000), Wandsworth Women's Aid (£5,000), Jericho Project (£4,000), Isle of Wight Social Audit Partnership (£1,500) and the Churches Key Project (£700).

Exclusions

No grants to:

- projects which are eligible for statutory funding, including furniture and building costs of housing schemes;
- ongoing revenue funding, including items which would normally be included in an organisation's annual budget;
- individuals;
- well-resourced organisations.

Applications

The trust says that it is committed to making the process of applying for funding as straightforward as possible.

The application process is as follows:

- act sends you an application pack;
- you read the grant guidelines and decide whether your project fits;
- you complete and return the form;
- at any point you can phone or e-mail the grants team for advice or clarification.

The decision-making process is as follows:

- Hact receives and acknowledges your application;
- it is assessed by a member of the grants and programme team;

Please remember that every application must be linked to one of the priority areas listed.

Potential applicants are invited to contact the programme team for further help and guidance:

Head of programmes – Andrew von Doorn

Programme officer – Vicky Evans

The grantmaking committee meets in February, April, June, September, October and December.

The Reta Lila Howard Foundation

Children, arts, environment

£750,000 (2002/03)

Beneficial area UK and Republic of Ireland.

Jamestown Investments Ltd, 4 Felstead Gardens, Ferry Street, London E14 3BS

Tel. 020 7537 1118

Email jamestown@btinternet.com

Correspondent The Company Secretary

Trustees *Tamara Rebanks; Charles Burnett; Pilar Bauta; Kim Dalglish; Sarah Mitchell; Melissa Murdoch; Gregg Weston; Willard Weston.*

Charity Commission no. 1041634

Information available Accounts were on file at the Charity Commission, without a list of grants, which was provided separately by the foundation.

The founder of this trust had an interest in children's charities and the trust's grantmaking focus is 'to support a few innovative projects that benefit children up to the age of 16 within the British Isles'. Funds are directed to selected projects, 'to support the education of young people or to ameliorate their physical and emotional environment'. In practice the trust also supports arts and environmental organisations. Donations are given over a finite period, with the aim that the project can be self-supporting when funding has ended.

In 2002/03 the trust had assets of £9.8 million and an income of £316,000. The level of grantmaking increased to that of several years ago, with grants totalling £750,000 in 2002/03. The annual report does not include a grants list, however, a list of beneficiaries for 2002/03 was provided by the foundation on request.

There were 23 grants made during the financial year to April 2003. With the exception of three smaller grants, they ranged fom £20,000 to £75,000.

The larger grants were made to the Tree Council and Farms for City Children (£75,000 each), Positive Parenting Publications (£53,000), National Museums and Galleries of Wales (£50,000), Contemporary Dance Trust (£45,000) and The Soil Association (£44,000).

Other beneficiaries included Wildlife Hospital Trust and Health Education Trust (£40,000 each), Countryside Education Trust (£36,000), National Youth Orchestra of Scotland (£30,000), Theatre in Health and Education (£25,000), Arts in Regeneration and West Wales Eco-Centre (£20,000 each).

The three smaller grants were made to Bibles for Children (£11,000), Barnados (£10,000) and ISS (£5,000).

In July 2003 the foundation made a further 20 grants totalling £478,000, perhaps accounting for all grant expenditure in the 2003/04 financial year.

Exclusions

Grants are not given to individuals, organisations which are not registered charities, or towards operating expenses, budget deficits, (sole) capital projects, annual charitable appeals, general endowment funds, fundraising drives or events, conferences, or student aid.

Applications

The trust states that it does not accept unsolicited applications, since the trustees seek out and support projects they are interested in.

The HSA Charitable Trust

Healthcare, medical research

£1.1 million (2003)
Beneficial area UK.

Hambleden House, Waterloo Court, Andover, Hampshire SP10 1LQ

Tel. 01264 353 211 **Fax** 01264 342625

Website www.hsa.co.uk

Correspondent Sir Guy Acland, Administrator

Trustees *Mrs Carolyn Lemon, chair; Maj. Gen. B Pennicott; K F Richardson; K Piggott; I M Maude.*

Charity Commission no. 263521

Information available Annual report and accounts. Guidance notes for applicants.

This charity is funded by the mutually owned HSA Group Limited which committed itself to giving 1% of its gross annual turnover for charitable activities, two-thirds of which is distributed through this trust. About one-fifth of the trust's expenditure is committed to the HSA Scholarship Awards programme – a field not covered in this entry. The charity describes its grantmaking as follows:

While the trust is committed to providing financial support for a wide range of deserving medical causes, it is particularly concerned to support those medical charitable organisations that are likely to benefit a substantial number of HSA contributors.

During 2000 the trustees undertook a review of the trust and have adopted a revised policy for grantmaking for the period 2001–2006. The current policy is to fund projects in the following specific areas [scholarships excluded. Ed.].:

- Help the Hospices and the hospice movement
- St John Ambulance
- Treatment of children with disabilities or sickness
- Treatment of people with medical illness
- Treatment of people with mental illness, mental handicap or learning difficulties
- Medical research [primarily through Action Medical Research. Ed.].

Grants are made for core, capital and project costs, and normally range from £500 to £10,000.

The charity does not normally make grants to very large national charities which enjoy wide support.

Grants in 2003

By far the largest grant in the year was £200,000 to Great Ormond Street Hospital for Sick Children. Other grants over £50,000 each were £88,000 to the Brain Research Trust, £96,000 to Action Medical Research and £70,000 to Royal Bournemouth Hospital.

Other beneficiaries included Countess of Brecknock Hospice and the Genesis Appeal (£25,000 each), Bassetlaw Hospice of the Good Shepherd (£15,000), Wessex Children's Hospice Trust – Naomi House (£13,000), CLIC, Forces Against Cancer, Headway – Devon, National Meningitis Trust, Research Council for Complementary Medicine, Sense and Tuberous Sclerosis Association (£10,000 each), the Shooting Star Trust Children's Hospice (£7,000), Taunton Opportunity Group (£6,000) and the National Centre for Young People with Epilepsy and the Schizophrenia Association of Great Britian (£5,000 each).

Exclusions

Applicants, other than those for scholarships, must have charitable status.

Other than for scholarships, there are no grants for individuals.

Applicant organisations must be based in the UK.

The trustees of the charity which receives the grant must have clear responsibility for the work which is being funded.

The trust does not normally make grants to:

- non-charitable umbrella organisations, such as most 'friends' groups
- charities whose operational area extends outside the UK
- very large national charities which enjoy wide support.

Applications

Trustee meetings are held four times a year: March, June, September and December.

There is no standard application form as we believe that this can be too restrictive. Applications should be made in writing to the correspondent above. There is some basic information that we would be grateful if you could provide and we ask you to confine your application to two sides of A4 paper.

Background

Please tell us what sort of organisation you are (i.e. what your legal status is) and its general aims and objectives. Are you part of a larger national organisation, and if so what is its name?

Project

Please give us an outline of the proposed project, including:

- its specific aims and objectives;
- how the project is to be organised and by whom;
- where the project is to take place;
- when it will start and how long it will take;
- whom it is intended to benefit and how many.

Finance

Please state how much money you need and for what purpose (e.g. equipment, building works, research, running costs, etc.) In addition state clearly how much you are asking the HSA Charitable Trust for and when you require it. We would also like to know which other funders you have approached and with what success. If you will need funding beyond the period of the proposed grant where is it to come from?

Evaluation

Please tell us how you will know whether the project has succeeded. In particular, what are the measurable specific objectives and how will you publicise the outcome of the project to other interested parties?

Attachments required

You must include:

- the most recent set of your annual accounts– if your accounts show apparently large reserves, attach a note explaining why you hold them and why they cannot be used to fund the project for which you are seeking funds;
- your most recent annual report;
- a detailed budget for the project.

The Albert Hunt Trust

Welfare

£1 million (2001/02)
Beneficial area UK.

Coutts & Co., Trustee Department, 440 Strand, London WC2R 0QS

Tel. 020 7663 6814 **Fax** 020 7663 6794

Correspondent Steve Harvey, Senior Trust Manager

Trustees *Coutts & Co; R J Collis; Mrs B McGuire.*

Charity Commission no. 277318

Information available Accounts were on file at the Charity Commission.

Summary

A very large number of modest grants are given to a wide range of organisations, both national and local, each year. Most grants are for between £1,000 and £2,000 and many seem to go to new beneficiaries. There are perhaps 50 awards for £5,000 or slightly more each year and these tend to go to regularly supported, national charities.

Grantmaking in 2001/02

In 2001/02 the trust had assets of £36.7 million and an income of almost £1.2 million. The grantmaking capacity of the trust has increased in recent years following the death of Miss M K Coyle, a long-standing trustee, who bequeathed £17 million from her estate to the trust.

The trust made 255 grants during the year, almost half of which were made to new recipients. The largest grants were made to Martin House Children's Hospice, Stockdales, Robert Owen Foundation and Wirral Autistic Society (£30,000 each).

Beneficiaries receiving £10,000 each included Acorn Village Trust, Birmingham St Mary's Hospice, Night Stop Stockport & Trafford and The Passage. Recipients of £5,000 included Action for Blind People, Church Housing Trust, Little Sisters of the Poor, Notting Hill Housing Trust, Society of St James and YMCA.

Most grants were for £2,000, with beneficiaries including 870 House, Apex Charitable Trust Limited, Compass, Gingerbread, League of Welldoers, Pembrokeshire Sibling Group, Seaview Project, Respite Association and Wiltshire Air Ambulance Appeal.

In 2003/04 the trust had a total expenditure of £1 million. Unfortunately, although submitted by the trust to the Charity Commission, the accounts for that year had not made it to the public files for inspection.

Exclusions

No grants for research or overseas work.

Applications

The correspondent states that no unsolicited correspondence will be acknowledged, unless an application receives favourable consideration. Trustees meet in March, July and November although appeals are considered on an ongoing basis.

The Hunter Foundation

Education, children
See below
Beneficial area Scotland.

Marathon House, Olympic Business Park, Drybridge Road, Dundonald, Ayrshire KA2 9AE

Correspondent Tom Hunter, Trustee

Trustees *Tom Hunter, chair; Marion Hunter; Jim McMahon; Robert Glennie; Vartan Gregorian.*

Scottish Charity no. SCO27532

Information available Information taken from the foundation's website.

The following limited information is taken from the foundation's website. There is little information available on how much an individual organisation or charity could hope to receive.

The Hunter Foundation (THF) is a venture philanthropy that invests in enterprise and educational initiatives aimed largely at children.

Our overarching aim is to help support the development of a more enterprising and ultimately entrepreneurial society in Scotland by funding projects of national import in this arena.

THF is funded by Tom and Marion Hunter and has an independent board of trustees whose responsibility it is to ensure that all funds are targeted to best effect in this arena.

As in private equity, THF takes a proactive role in all of the investments it makes in order to ensure maximum impact from the funding provided.

In general THF only funds projects capable of national implementation and that will, or are likely to make a major contribution to the national economic and social well-being of Scotland.

Since its formation in 1998 The Hunter Foundation has invested in excess of £13.5m into major enterprise and educational programmes including the Schools Enterprise Programme, The Hunter Centre for Entrepreneurship and

'Determined to Succeed' where THF is investing £2 million on a matched basis with the Scottish Executive to fund a number of new programmes across Scotland.

Applications

In writing to the correspondent.

The Huntingdon Foundation

Jewish education

See below

Beneficial area Jewish communities in the UK.

Forframe House, 35–37 Brent Street, London NW4 2EF

Tel. 020 8202 2282

Correspondent Mrs S Perl, Secretary

Trustees *Benjamin Perl, chair; S Perl; Mrs S Perl; Mrs R Perl.*

Charity Commission no. 286504

Information available Annual report and accounts, lacking the required grants list, are on file at the Charity Commission.

The trust defines its principal activity as 'the establishment and continued support of Jewish schools'. In recent years two new Jewish schools in London have been established, and it has also been involved with 'a major project in conjunction with a well known British university …[to] provide business and teaching degree graduate courses for Jewish students'. The foundation says it also supports Orthodox Jewish higher education establishments in the U.S.

In 2003/04 the trust had an income of £1.1 million and a total expenditure of £807,000. Further information for this year was not available.

Comment

There was no response to repeated written requests for a copy of the most recent annual report and accounts, despite the requirement to provide these on demand.

Despite ample warning, and their obligation to the contrary, the Charity Commission were unable to give us sight of this trust's accounts.

Applications

In writing to the correspondent.

Hurdale Charity Limited

Jewish

£1.2 million (2002/03)
Beneficial area Worldwide.

162 Osbaldeston Road, London N16 6NJ

Correspondent Abraham Oestreicher

Trustees *M Oestreicher; Mrs E Oestreicher; P Oestreicher; D Oestreicher; A Oestreicher; B Oestreicher.*

Charity Commission no. 276997

Information available Accounts were on file at the Charity Commission, but without a grants list.

The trust supports charitable activities mostly concerned with religion and education. Most of the support is given to Jewish organisations that are seen to uphold the Jewish way of life, both in the UK and overseas. In 2002/03 the trust had assets of £4 million, an income of £1.4 million and made 94 grants totalling £1.2 million.

There were 23 grants of over £1,000 each. Beneficaries included United Talmudical Associates Ltd (£205,000), Yeter Lev Jerusalem (£115,000), Mesifta (£154,000), Beer Yitzchok (£49,000), Ruzin Sadagura Trust (£35,000), Ora Vesimcha (£23,000), Yesodeh Hatorah School (£20,000), Rav Chesed Trust (£18,000) and Kollel Tiferes Shulem and Regentbrook Toras Chested Yeshiva (£10,000 each).

Beneficiaries of smaller grants included Alexander Usher Trust (£7,100), Beer Shmel Ltd (£6,000), Tomchei Share Zion (£5,000), MYA Charitable Trust and Medical Aid Trust (£2,000 each) and Kalev Gemach Ltd and Yeshivas Toras Moshe (£1,000 each).

Applications

In writing to the trustees.

This information is yet to be confirmed by the trust; the address matches that currently contained on the Charity Commission's register.

Impetus Trust

General, social welfare

Around £1.5 million each year
Beneficial area UK.

Hamilton House, Mabledon Place, London WC1H 9BB

Tel. 020 7953 0530 **Fax** 020 7554 8501

Email info@impetus.org.uk

Website www.impetus.org.uk

Correspondent Judith Brodie, Chief Executive

Trustees *Stephen Dawson, chair; Nat Sloane; Chris Mathias; Julia Middleton; Doug Miller; Michael Webber.*

Charity Commission no. 1094681

Information available Annual report, accounts, guidelines and further information taken from the trust's website.

Background

Impetus Trust was set up in 2002 and is believed to be the UK's first general venture philanthropy charitable fund. Its founders, Stephen Dawson (Chair) and Nat Sloane (Vice Chair), wanted to enable donors and charities to maximise their social return by creating an organisation and building an approach which would provide an impetus for:

- charities to make a step change in their performance
- donors to have confidence to give or give more
- people to bring their skills and experience to charities.

Impetus Trust has set itself a target of £3 million to raise for investment in charities in the first phase, and has already raised more than half this amount–sufficient to start the investment programme. Fundraising among members of the wider venture capital and business communities is continuing.

The Chief Executive, Judith Brodie, works closely with the Chair and Vice Chair, who continue to be actively involved.

The network of volunteer associates is being developed and we continue actively to seek charities that might benefit from the Impetus approach. We have charities at different stages in our screening and assessment process and have announced our first investment.

The Phase One objective is to prove that the Impetus approach works in practice, by building a successful track record with about 10 charities. This should be demonstrable within two to three years, at which point substantially larger funds will be raised, requiring a much higher profile and fundraising effort.

General

The trust also sets out its approach to working with the charities it will support, and the benefits to those charities; Impetus will:

- tackle the greatest need by focusing on: unfashionable, under-resourced sectors where management capacity needs strengthening; and, people-focused medium size UK-based charities with a minimum of three years operations
- maximise impact by selecting a small number of charities which: make a demonstrable difference to the lives of a substantial number of disadvantaged people; are capable of achieving high and sustainable impact; keenly want and need the distinctive investment package that we offer
- facilitate step change in these charities' performance with: three to five year funding of agreed core costs; capacity building; hands-on management support through monthly meetings and active monitoring.

As at October 2004, the trust had made a commitment of £400,000 over four years to Speaking Up!, an advocacy and support organisation for people with learning difficulties. Further beneficiaries will be announced as grants are made.

Selection criteria

The trust offers the following information on what it is looking for in potential grant recipients:

- charities that make a demonstrable, significant and sustainable difference to the lives of a substantial number of disadvantaged people
- charities at a critical stage in their strategic development–wanting to make a step change–and with an outline plan of how they might achieve it. These charities might be:
  - at a point where they could grow significantly
  - under performing and seeking to turn around their performance
  - viewing a merger or alliance as a potential and critical step in their development
- charities whose leadership keenly wants and needs the distinctive investment package that we offer (i.e. long term infrastructure funding plus capacity-building plus management support)
- charities with the following characteristics:
  - more than £250k and less than £10 million charitable income per year
  - operated and produced audited accounts for at least three years
  - HQ and a significant portion of its management in England and Wales

We are seeking to invest in 10–12 charities in our first two to three years, and have received about 150 approaches to date. In deciding which charities to invest in, we will also take the following into account:

- the quality of the leadership in the charity in relation to the step change proposed
- the value we think Impetus could add
- what is special/distinctive about the charity and their prospects for success/ sustainability in the sector
- how the charity would fit in our portfolio of investments (we are aiming to have a diverse portfolio of charity investments)
- geography: we intend to provide at least 50% or our funds to support charities outside London and the south east
- Impetus's capacity to deliver (including our funding/time availability, location of charity etc.)

The Impetus commitment is to:
- provide long-term funding for core costs
- help to build capacity in our selected charities
- develop hands-on collaborative relationships with the charities we support

Our financial investment in charities is likely to be between £100,000 and £500,000 over a period of between three to five years. This is likely to be mostly in the form of grants but, for some charities, may include a loan or similar.

Exclusions

The trust will not consider charities which focus on the following:

- animals, culture or heritage rather than people;
- aiming to proselytise and convert people;
- substantially/exclusively working in the areas of research or advocacy (unless the impact on people's lives is demonstrable).

No grants to individuals.

Applications

First, please check our Selection Criteria (above) to establish your charity's eligibility. If you think you are eligible, and interested in Impetus' approach, then please read the guidelines below. We look forward to hearing from you.

Please note that, given the nature of our intended funding and high involvement of our approach, we will be highly selective, selecting only a total of 10–12 charities for investment over the next 2–3 years. We have already had over 150 approaches from charities.

Selection Process

Our selection process will have several stages, to enable us to identify how, where and why Impetus could add value to help your charity achieve a step change in its performance.

Screening

- if you believe your charity may be eligible, email/send us the following:
  - a letter outlining how you meet our selection criteria (and how you first heard of Impetus Trust)
  - a copy of your current strategic/ business plan
  - your latest audited accounts.
- we will consider the information provided and respond promptly (usually within two weeks). If you fit our criteria and we believe that your charity could become one of those we hope to work with, we will then ask your Chief Executive to meet us.
- we will need to get to know you and your charity a lot better. For example by understanding its:
  - mission and aims for beneficiaries
  - unique position in its sector
  - future objectives and aspirations
  - key challenges
  - financial profile.

This step may involve one or more meetings and visits to see your charity, and meet your trustees and management team.

We would then make the decision on whether the charity should be put before the Investment Committee for a decision to proceed to the next stage. We expect to take no longer than one month from the initial meeting with you until we make this decision.

Assessment – pre-investment

- if we establish mutually that there is a good fit between us, and our Investment Committee agrees, then we would want to delve into much more detail. For example, in order to commit long term funding we would want to:
  - review your business plan
  - assess and evaluate your future objectives
  - carry out a detailed assessment of the charity, its market, its risk profile and its prospects
  - meet and get comfortable with the senior management and trustees
  - identify the specific areas where Impetus would initially contribute
  - develop the funding schedule to support this plan

– agree the performance indicators to be monitored

– prepare a written agreement setting out the investment package and how we will work together.

- assuming no obstacles have arisen at this stage, then we will submit our funding recommendation to the Investment Committee for approval to invest.

Decision and post investment

- assuming approval, we will then finalise commitment agreements between us and initiate the partnership.

We expect to meet each of our selected charities on a monthly basis and to monitor progress rigorously. We do not however intend to take a seat on your Trustee Board although we may introduce someone with suitable experience if this is required.

- we would expect this whole process to take about four to six months.

In our experience, the considerable efforts involved to explore and prepare for a prospective investment are both vital and productive, enhancing the likelihood of long-term success and reducing the likelihood of major problems between us.

Our funding commitment over the 3–5 year period will be conditional on the charity's ongoing satisfactory performance.

If you have any questions regarding this process, please contact us.

The Isle of Anglesey Charitable Trust

General, in Anglesey

£331,000 (2002/03)

Beneficial area The Isle of Anglesey only.

Isle of Anglesey County Council, County Offices, Llangefni, Anglesey LL77 7TW

Tel. 01248 752603 **Fax** 01248 752696

Email gvwfi@anglesey.gov.uk

Correspondent David Elis-Williams, Treasurer

Trustee *Anglesey County Council.*

Charity Commission no. 1000818

Information available Information was provided by the trust.

The trust, independent in law from, but administered by, the Isle of Anglesey Borough Council was set up with an endowment from Shell (UK) Limited when the company ceased operating an oil terminal on Anglesey, according to the terms of the 1972 private Act of Parliament which had enabled the terminal to be set up in the first place.

The objects of the trust are 'to provide amenities and facilities for the general public benefit of persons resident in the Isle of Anglesey'.

In 2002/03 it had an income of £345,000 and gave grants totalling £331,000. An annual grant is made towards the running costs of Oriel Ynys Mon Gallery (£215,000 in 2002/03). A further £115,000 was made to 63 other organisations.

Grants are made within the following categories:

- Village hall running costs (£50,000 in 35 grants)
- Community and sporting facilities (£23,000 in 6 grants)
- Minor works to churches and chapels (£34,000 in 9 grants)
- Other grants (£8,600 in 13 grants)

Exclusions

No grants to individuals or projects based outside Anglesey.

Applications

In writing to the correspondent, following advertisements in the local press in February. The trust considers applications once a year.

Isle of Dogs Community Foundation

Regeneration, general

£866,000 (2003/04)

Beneficial area The Isle of Dogs (i.e. the pre-2002 wards of Blackwall and Millwall) in the London borough of Tower Hamlets.

Jack Dash House, 2 Lawn House Close, Isle of Dogs, London E14 9YQ

Tel. 020 7345 4444 **Fax** 020 7538 4671

Email tbetts@idcf.org

Website www.idcf.org

Correspondent Tracy Betts, Director

Trustees *Richard Heyes, chair; Sr Christine Frost; Mark Bensted; David Chesterton; Jonathan Davie; Adrian Greenwood; Helen Jenner; Zinnat Ahmed; Mohammad Shahid Ali; Heather Bird; Ric Papineau; Anthony Partington; Martin Young; Alan Amos; John Anderson; Gay Harrington: Mandy Boutwood; Dermot O'Brien.*

Charity Commission no. 802942

Information available Application form with guidelines, an annual report and accounts were provided by the trust. A consultation and baseline study on regenerating the Isle of Dogs was also published in September 2002.

Summary

This foundation aims to revive the community living in the shadow of London's Canary Wharf development. In 2004 its endowment stood at £4 million, derived from Single Regeneration Budget (SRB) funding received several years earlier. It has also received donations from major financial companies in the area–despite this, the foundation reports that its income, and therefore its grantmaking capacity, has reduced over the past few years.

Grantmaking focuses on three key areas:

- community development;
- education and youth;
- training and employment.

General

This community foundation's expansion has been rapid in recent years, largely due to SRB grants.

Guidelines for applicants

The Isle of Dogs Community Foundation (IDCF) was established in 1990 to address social need in the pre-May 2002 Millwall and Blackwall wards of the London Borough of Tower Hamlets. Its constitution creates a permanent partnership between the local business, statutory and voluntary sectors.

IDCF is a community foundation working to create confident and integrated communities on the Isle of Dogs, supporting local community needs through a constructive and responsive grant programme. We aim to be constantly abreast of changing needs within our area of benefit in order to identify where grant-making and influence can best help meet those most pressing needs.

Who Can Apply?

We invite applications from non-profit organisations that work within the area of benefit. Your organisation may be a registered charity, a voluntary or community organisation. You must have your own constitution and bank account as required under charity law. Your project must fit under one of the following headings:

The Focus of our grant giving:

Education

Assisting in raising the standards of achievement and aspirations of children and young people through the development of extra-curricular and 'after hours' activities

Training and employment

Initiatives for raising the level of employment through the provision of training.

Community development

Engaging the local population to work together as an integrated community.

What you can apply for:

Training

Applications up to £100 as a contribution toward the cost of training your staff or volunteers. Requests will be considered for short training courses, conferences, seminars etc.

Fast Track

Applications up to £800. These grants are awarded as a contribution towards purchasing equipment, social outings, and events etc.

Standard

Applications up to £10,000. These grants are awarded as a contribution towards salaries, running costs, capital works (to a maximum of 50%), feasibility studies etc. projects working in the

following categories:

- education;
- training and employment;
- community development.

Grants in 2003/04

In the standard of grants category, 19 donations were made totalling £106,000. Examples of grants made were as follows: £10,000 each to Island Advice towards a bi-lingual advice worker, Island Friends towards the co-ordinator of the Elders Project and SPLASH Youth towards a youth manager's post; £9,500 to Docklands Women's Group towards a co-ordinator's post; £8,000 to Island Neighbourhood Project towards a

support worker's post; £7,500 to St Matthias Conservation Trust towards the centre co-ordinator's post; £7,000 to SPACE towards funding the director's post; £5,000 to Mudchute Allotment Society towards security fencing; and £5,000 to TH Community Transport towards the costs of an access bus.

A total of 62 grants totalling £28,000 were made in the fast track scheme. Beneficiaries included the following: £800 each to Alpha Grove Playgroup towards rental costs and John Tucker Club towards Christmas activities; £520 to St John's Bingo Club towards rental costs; £500 to Docklands Outreach towards computer upgrades; £400 to Samuda Estate LMO towards the costs of a day trip; and £200 each to Harbinger School towards governor training and Young at Heart Club towards Christmas activities.

The grants list indicates that the same organisation can receive more than one small grant in any given year, and this appears to happen fairly often. In 2001/02, for example, Docklands Outreach received five grants totalling £2,100.

18 training grants were made totalling £1,700.

Exclusions

IDCF will not fund:

- individuals;
- projects with primarily religious activities;
- projects with primarily political activities;
- projects/activities that are a statutory service;
- activities that are the responsibility of the local or health authorities;
- activities that have already taken place.

Applications

Application procedures for the three types of grant awarded are as follows:

Training grants

By letter, no more than one page of A4.

Fast track grants

Through a two-page application form, available from the foundation.

Standard grants

After discussion with the director, by using the 'single application form' currently being piloted by some London funders. This is available from the foundation.

The grants committee meets every month, except August. Trustees consider the committees' standard grant

recommendations at meetings in January, March, May, July, September and November. Fast track and training grant applications do not go to the main board and these grants are usually paid shortly after the meeting.

The J J Charitable Trust

Environment, literacy

£659,000 (2003/04)

Beneficial area Unrestricted.

Allington House, 1st Floor, 150 Victoria Street, London SW1E 5AE

Tel. 020 7410 0330 **Fax** 020 7410 0332

Email info@sfct.org.uk

Correspondent Michael Pattison, Director

Trustees *Julian Sainsbury; Mark Sainsbury; Miss Judith Portrait.*

Charity Commission no. 1015792

Information available Good annual report and accounts, with full grants listing were provided by the trust.

Summary

This is one of the Sainsbury Family Charitable Trusts, which share a joint administration. They have a common approach to grantmaking which is described in the entry for the group as a whole.

This trust's main areas of interest are (with number and the value of grant approvals in 2003/04):

	No.	Amount
Literacy support	9	£268,000
Environment – UK	17	£231,000
Environment – overseas	7	£68,000
General	2	£46,000

A relatively small number of grants are made. Few of them are for less than £5,000 and occasional grants can be for more than £100,000. 'Proposals are generally invited by the trustees or initiated at their request. Unsolicited applications are discouraged and are unlikely to be successful, even if they fall within an area in which the trustees are interested.'

'The trustees prefer to support innovative schemes that can be successfully replicated or become self-sustaining.'

General

The settlor of this trust is Julian Sainsbury and he is still building up the endowment, with donations totalling around £3.5 million over the last two years alone.

The staff of the trust include Michael Pattison, director of all the trusts in the group, and Mark Woodruff, executive.

Grantmaking in 2003/04

Grants were made during the year totalling £659,000.

Literacy support

The trustees aim to help improve the effectiveness of literacy teaching in the primary and secondary education sector for children with general or specific learning difficulties, including dyslexia, and to do the same through agencies working with ex-offenders or those at risk of offending. They also seek to target help at those who have become disaffected from education and who now find themselves homeless or in prison.

Their selection of projects to support takes account of relevant government initiatives and on-going developments within the prison education system. The trustees seek projects that pilot new ideas for teaching and supporting people with specific learning difficulties, or provide demonstrations that are likely to be of wider interest. Given budget constraints within the education and criminal justice sectors, the trustees seek to support projects aiming to deliver cost-effective solutions.

Grants during the year included: £75,000 to Pooh Bear Reading Assistance Society towards the salary costs of a project and volunteer co-ordinator for new work in Hull's Bransholme estate; £50,000 to Depaul Trust towards the second year of the Digital Streets online magazine and literacy learning resource for young homeless people; £20,000 to Bristol Youth Education Service towards the second and third years of the Bristol Dyslexia Initiative; and £5,000 to Global Care Albania towards the salary of a training manager.

Environment – UK

Grants are made for environmental education, particularly supporting projects displaying practical ways of involving children and young adults. Trustees rarely support new educational resource packs in isolation from the actual process of learning and discovery. They are more interested in programmes which help pupils and teachers to develop a theme over time (such as renewable energy), perhaps combining IT resources for data gathering and communication, with exchange visits and the sharing of information and ideas between schools.

Trustees are particularly interested in projects that enable children and young people to develop a sense of ownership of the project over time, and that provide direct support to teachers to deliver exciting and high quality education in the classroom.

The trustees have begun to support projects that lie beyond the schools sector and focus on sustainable agriculture and bio-diversity. This involvement is likely to grow in future years.

The trustees are also interested in the potential for sustainable transport, energy efficiency and renewable energy in the wider society. In some cases trustees will consider funding research, but only where there is a clear practical application. Proposals are more likely to be considered when they are testing an idea, model or strategy in practice.

Grants during the year included: £36,000 to Ashden Awards for Sustainable Energy towards providing for a UK sustainable energy award and associated costs; £15,000 to Envision towards the third year of school environmental projects with 16 to 18 year olds in London; £6,000 to Centre for Sustainable Energy towards disseminating information to other organisations; and £600 to Liverpool City Environment Centre towards a feasibility study for an outdoor classroom and renewable energy demonstration facilities.

Environment – overseas

The trustees continue to support community based agricultural projects which aim to help people to help themselves in an environmentally sustainable way.

Beneficiaries included Tree Aid – Burkina Faso (£15,000), Oxfam (£10,000), Feedback Madagascar (£7,500) and New Venture – Himalayas (£1,500).

General

Two grants were made. They were: £26,000 to Future Trust towards the second and final year of an arts-based project for young people in Macedonia, and £20,000 to the Idea Store in Tower Hamlets towards the creation of a Learning Lab.

Applications

See the guidance for applicants in the entry for the Sainsbury Family Charitable Trusts. A single application will be considered for support by all the trusts in the group.

However, for this as for many of the trusts, 'proposals are generally invited by the trustees or initiated at their request. Unsolicited applications are discouraged and are unlikely to be successful, even if they fall within an area in which the trustees are interested'.

Jacobs Charitable Trust

Jewish charities, the arts

About £725,000 (2003/04)

Beneficial area Unrestricted.

9 Nottingham Terrace, London NW1 4QB

Tel. 020 7486 6323

Correspondent The Rt Hon Lord Jacobs, Chair

Trustees *Lord Jacobs, chair; Lady Jacobs.*

Charity Commission no. 264942

Information available Annual report and accounts were on file at the Charity Commission.

Lord Jacob's family owned the British School of Motoring, the largest driving school in the world, until 1990. He is best known as a prominent member and generous supporter of the Liberal and now the Liberal Democrat party (for which work he was knighted).

In 2003/04 the trust had an income of £668,000 and a total expenditure of £750,000, most of which is usually given in grants. No further information was available for the year.

The trust makes about 50 grants a year. Previous beneficiaries include Royal Opera House Trust, Jewish Care, Israel Philharminic Orchestra Foundation, Central Synagogue General Charities Fund, Imperial War Museum Trust, Royal National Theatre Board, Community Security Trust, Jewish Museum, British ORT, Council for Beautiful Israel, Jewish Learning Exchange, Hampstead Theatre Trust, United Synagogue and World Jewish Relief.

Comment

This trust is perhaps best regarded as a vehicle for the charitable donations of Lord and Lady Jacobs, rather than as an institution in its own right, as it has neither endowment, premises or staff.

Despite ample warning, and their obligation to the contrary, the Charity Commission were unable to give us sight of this trust's accounts.

Applications

In writing to the correspondent.

John James Bristol Foundation

Education, health, older people, general

£1.2 million (2002/03)
Beneficial area Bristol.

7 Clyde Road, Redland, Bristol BS6 6RG
Tel. 0117 923 9444 **Fax** 0117 923 9470
Correspondent Julia Norton, Administrator
Trustees *Joan Johnson; David Johnson; Elizabeth Chambers; Jacqueline Marsh; Michael Cansdale; John Evans; Andrew Jardine; Andrew Webley.*
Charity Commission no. 288417
Information available Accounts were provided by the trust for a fee of £5.

The trusts' main objectives concern the relief of poverty and sickness, particularly of older people, or the advancement of education amongst the inhabitants of the City of Bristol or any other purposes beneficial to its inhabitants.

In 2002/03 the trust had assets of £34 million and an income of £1.3 million. Grants totalled £1.2 million and were categorised as follows:

Health–43 grants totalling £684,000

Two large grants of £250,000 each were made to Bristol Urological Institute and Childrens' Hospice South West. Other beneficiaries in this category included Bristol University for bowel cancer research, as in the previous year (£55,000), Barnardos Bristol (£20,000), Dementia Care Trust and Marie Curie Cancer Care (£10,000 each), Victim Support (£8,000), Motability and Starlight Children's Foundation (£6,000 each), Church Housing Trust–Bristol and Community of the Sisters of the Church (£5,000 each), Off the Record (£4,000), ChildLine (£3,000), Bristol

Cyrenians and Hosanna House (£2,000 each) and Blackberry Hill Hospital, Clover House, One25 and Visually Handicapped Self Help (£1,000 each). Nine small grants were made totalling £5,000.

Education–61 grants totalling £435,000

There were three educational funds, with many of the beneficiaries receiving regular support: 10 grants totalling £280,000 were made from the Bristol Independent Schools' Bursary Fund, all but one for £30,000 and including those to Bristol Cathedral School, Clifton College, Colston's Girls' School, Red Maids' School and Redland High School. There were 30 Prizes and Awards made to local schools in Bristol from teh Bristol Schools Special Prizes fund, mainly for £3,000 each, with recipients including Ashton Park School, Brislington School, Bristol Grammar School, Cotham School, Henbury School, Speedwell Technology College, St Thomas More School and Withywood Community School. Other educational grants were made to a range of organisations, including Windmill Hill City Farm (£25,000), Opportunity Network LC (£14,000), the Scout County of Avon (£7,500), Wheels Project Ltd (£6,000), Florence Brown School (£2,500), Bethesda Independent Methodist Church (£2,000), No Way Trust Bristol (£1,500) and Avon Outward Bound Association (£1,000). Seven small grants of less than £1,000 were made totalling £4,000.

The Elderly–174 grants totalling £59,000

There were 162 grants of less than £1,000 each totalling £36,000, with many beneficiaries receiving regular support. Larger grants included those to Bristol Care and Repair (£9,000), Little Sisters of the Poor (£2,500) and Redcliffe Care, Dolphin Society and Grateful Society (£1,000 each).

General–12 grants totalling £11,000

Beneficiaries included Break and Relate (£2,000 each) and Bedminster & Knowle Credit Union, Bristol Citizens Advice Bureau and Canynges Society (£1,000 each). Seven small grants of less than £1,000 each totalled £4,000.

The foundation has also committed a further £2 million to local organisations in the future.

Exclusions

No grants to individuals.

Applications

The trustees meet quarterly in February, May, August and November to consider appeals received by 31 January, 30 April, 31 July and 31 October respectively. There is no application form, but appeals should be submitted to the administrator on no more that two sides of A4. These are then photocopied and circulated to the trustees prior to the meeting. Supporting information, sent by an applicant with their appeal, is available to the trustees at their meetings, and if further information is required it will be requested and a visit to the applicant may be made by a representative of the foundation.

The Jerusalem Trust

Promotion of Christianity

£2.7 million (2003)
Beneficial area Unrestricted.

Allington House, 1st Floor, 150 Victoria Street, London SW1E 5AE
Tel. 020 7410 0330 **Fax** 020 7410 0332
Email info@sfct.org.uk
Correspondent Michael Pattison, Director
Trustees *Sir Timothy Sainsbury; Lady Susan Sainsbury; Dr V E Hartley Booth; Canon Gordon Bridger.*
Charity Commission no. 285696
Information available Annual report and accounts with full grants listing were provided by the trust.

Summary

This is one of the Sainsbury Family Charitable Trusts, which share a joint administration. Their approach to grantmaking have aspects in common which are described in the entry for the group as a whole. The trust is primarily proactive, aiming to choose its own grantees, and it discourages unsolicited applications.

The trust supports a wide range of evangelical organisations, across a broad though usually moderate spectrum of Christian activity.

The number and value of grant approvals in 2003 were categorised as follows:

	No.	Amount
Christian evangelism and mission work (UK)	55	£917,000
Christian media	10	£333,000
Christian education	23	£1,125,000
Christian evangelism/relief work overseas	24	£530,000
Christian art	6	£79,000

General

The income of the trust in 2003 was £2.7 million. Its staff include Michael Pattison, director and Mrs B Cass, executive.

The annual report uses wording that changes little from year to year, but there is full information on both the recipients and purposes of the grants:

Christian evangelism and mission work (UK)

Trustees are particularly interested in Christian projects which develop new ways of working with children and young people and projects which promote Christian marriage and family life. They are also interested in church planting and evangelistic projects and those which undertake Christian work with prisoners, ex-prisoners and their families.

Beneficiaries during 2003 included: Church Pastoral Aid Society towards the Children's Evangelism Initiative (£105,000); Feltham Prison Chaplaincy towards the costs of a new community chaplaincy project in south and west London (£70,000); The Message Trust towards the Eden Harpurhey project (£50,000); Prison Fellowship England & Wales towards the salary costs of a worker for the Compass project at HMP Highpoint (£45,000); Christians in Sport towards the costs of Regional Student Co-ordinators (£30,000); Prison Fellowship Scotland towards a field officer for the Sycamore Project (£20,000); and Oasis Charitable Trust towards the administration of the Faithworks Award (£10,000).

There were 25 grants for amounts of less than £5,000, with beneficiaries including Chrysalis Arts Trust, Joshua Generation, National Prayer Breakfast, Scripture Gift Mission and Youth With a Mission.

Christians in the media

Trustees are particularly interested in supporting training and networking projects for Christians working professionally in all areas of the media and for those considering media careers.

As in previous years, most of the money under this heading goes to the associated Jerusalem Productions (£250,000). Other beneficiaries included: The Bible Channel towards core costs and training (£22,000); Churches Advisory Council for Local Broadcasting towards its annual conference (£10,000); and Innovista towards filming and editing equipment for a training centre in Eurasia (£8,000).

Christian education

Trustees are particularly interested in the development of Christian school curriculum resource materials for RE and other subjects, the support, training and retention of Christian teachers in all subjects and lay training.

The main beneficiary was the Stapleford Centre in Nottingham, which received £361,000 in total during the year, £225,000 of which was for core costs. The remainder was for the administration of a grant and a bursary scheme and for consultancy costs. Four other large grants were made in this category. They were to: Evangelical Alliance towards bursaries for UK and overseas students (£150,000); CARE for Education, mainly towards a sex education project for 11 to 14 year olds (£108,000); Diocese of Guildford towards Christ's College, a new church school (£100,000); BBC Reading Fellowship towards the second phase of Foundations21, a major internet-based programme to promote adult Christian discipleship (£100,000).

Other grants were made to Prayer for the Nations (£38,000), BBC Religion (£25,000), Teach First (£15,000) and Catholic Evangelisation Services (£10,000).

Christian evangelism and relief work overseas

Trustees are particularly interested in proposals for indigenous training centres, the provision of Christian literature in central and eastern Europe and Anglophone Africa and support for Christian organisations working with HIV/AIDS.

Two large grants were made, to Coventry Cathedral International Centre for Reconciliation towards core costs (£105,000), and to the Tear Fund, towards HIV/AIDS, education, agriculture and community projects in Sudan, Chad, Nigeria and Turkmenistan (£100,000).

Other grants included those to Church Mission Society (£75,000), European Evangelical Alliance (£45,000), Slum Outreach Ministries – Nairobi (£15,000) and Nserester Orphanage – Uganda (£9,000).

Christian art

Trustees mainly focus on a small number of pro-active commissions of works of art for places of worship.

Grant recipients included: BibleLands towards the art exhibition 'Presence: Images of Christ for the third millennium', a series of linked exhibitions and installations in six cathedrals in Britain during 2004 (£36,000); All Saints Church – New Longton towards the cost of a mural and related improvements to the church (£10,000); and St Andrew's Church – Richmond towards the 'Man of Sorrow' installation (£7,000).

Exclusions

Trustees do not normally make grants towards building or repair work for churches. Grants are not normally made to individuals.

Applications

See the guidance for applicants in the entry for the Sainsbury Family Charitable Trusts. A single application will be considered for support by all the trusts in the group.

However, for this as for many of the trusts, 'proposals are generally invited by the trustees or initiated at their request. Unsolicited applications are discouraged and are unlikely to be successful, even if they fall within an area in which the trustees are interested'.

The Jerwood Foundation and the Jerwood Charity (formerly Charitable Foundation)

The arts

Around £4 million (2003)

Beneficial area UK, but with a limited special interest in UK organisations operating in Nepal.

22 Fitzroy Square, London W1T 6EN

Tel. 020 7388 6287

Email roanne.dods@jerwood.org

Website www.jerwood.org.uk

Correspondent Roanne Dods, Director

Trustees *The Jerwood Foundation: Alan Grieve, chair; Dr Peter Marxer; Dr Peter Marxer Jnr. The Jerwood Charity: Andrew Knight, chair; Edward Paul, Vice-chair; Viscount Chilston; Lady Harlech; Dr Kerry Parton; Julia Wharton; Anthony Palmer; Barbara Kalman; Tim Eyles.*

Charity Commission no. 1074036

Information available Guidelines for applicants and an annual report for both bodies, with summarised financial information and separately available financial statements for the charitable foundation, were provided by the trust. (As the Jerwood Foundation is not a UK-registered charity, it has no UK obligation to supply accounts.)

Summary

The Jerwood Foundation, established in 1977 and not a UK charity, funds capital projects in its own name. It also provides the means for the Jerwood Charity (renamed in 2004 to further distinguish it from the foundation) to support revenue projects.

The two organisations, though legally separate, operate as one and are described as such in this entry.

The funding of arts initiatives is their main activity, with educational support being concerned mostly with those starting their artistic working life. There are minor conservation and environmental strands.

Both capital and revenue grants are made. In 2003 grants totalled around £4 million. In addition the foundation and the charity initiate a wide range of artistic projects on their own. In most cases, their involvement with the causes they support is close, going well beyond simply matters of funding. A characteristic of much that they support is the use of the Jerwood name by the resulting institutions or programmes.

General

The foundation and the charity derive from a fortune made by an Englishman, John Jerwood, who became a key player in the Japanese cultured pearl industry.

Although there are excellent annual reports, no accounts are available for the Jerwood Foundation, the senior of the two organisations and the source of the funds for both, as it is not a charity and is not therefore bound by charitable disclosure requirements.

The organisations describe themselves as follows:

The Jerwood Foundation is dedicated to imaginative and responsible funding and sponsorship of the arts, education, design, conservation, medicine, engineering, science and other areas of human endeavour and excellence.

Alan Grieve, the present Chairman and Director of the Jerwood Foundation, has been involved with the foundation since its establishment in 1977. He was the legal adviser and confidant of John Jerwood and was involved with his business and private affairs for more than 25 years. He was also a director of John Jerwood's international trading company.

Formerly the senior partner of city solicitors, Taylor Joynson Garrett (now Taylor Wessing), Alan Grieve now devotes substantially the whole of his working life to the foundation. The foundation is based at its representative office in Fitzroy Square, London W1, where a small and dedicated staff manage the UK affairs of the Jerwood Charity and the Jerwood Foundation.

The foundation council and Alan Grieve have identified a particular role in supporting young people who have demonstrated achievement, commitment and excellence, particularly in the performing arts. The visual and performing arts are an industry capable of making important contributions to this country's success and reputation in the world. It is the mission of the foundation to recognise and support young people, mainly between twenty and thirty-five, whose careers can be uplifted at a critical time to the benefit of the individuals and the institutions they represent. Examples are the financial support which is given to young

actors, dancers, choreographers, playwrights, filmmakers, singers and others in the performing and visual arts, as well as to young engineers, chemists and doctors.

The council of the foundation believes that in a rapidly changing social and global economic environment it is important to support the far-reaching benefits conferred by a rich cultural life. Britain needs to support her artists and other young people who contribute to creating a vibrant cultural scene.

The foundation seeks to make grants which will produce tangible and visible results, having an influence and effect beyond the immediate recipient of the grant. The Jerwood Foundation is not merely a passive recipient of requests for grants, but actively researches new areas to support and it also develops its own initiatives. Frequently, it is able to develop and add value to applications, so that there is greater benefit to the individual or institution. As it is a private foundation unhindered by bureaucracy and committees, it is able to make speedy decisions, which can be of great value when funding demands arise.

Jerwood in 2003

The following statement from the foundation's chairman, Alan Grieve, explains the foundation's and the charity's activities in 2003:

It is encouraging to be able to report that during 2003 our portfolio of market investments has achieved growth of some 22%, and our other assets and investments in our balance sheet have also recorded improved valuations.

The other major event for us during 2003 has been the start of a permanent but expendable endowment for the Jerwood Charitable Foundation, now renamed the Jerwood Charity. During the year we made a capital grant to the Jerwood Charity of £5 million which has been invested by its trustees.

During the last five years (1999–2003) the foundation has made capital and revenue grants of an average annual total of £4.75 million. These have included major grants to The Royal Court Theatre (£3.7 million) and The Royal College of Physicians in London (£2 million). Although we are continuing our policy of holding back our capital and revenue grants in order to consolidate and strengthen our funds, we intend to increase the endowment of the Jerwood Charity.

The Jerwood Charity

It is very pleasing for me to see the charity under its new Chairman, Andrew Knight, and its own trustees, extend its range of activities and ensure the continuance of our aspiration for high achievement, excellence and innovation. These are fully reported by both

Andrew Knight and the Director, Roanne Dods. The Jerwood Foundation and its Council remain keenly interested and supportive of the charity and will encourage the symbiosis of the foundation, the charity and the Jerwood Space. The memento to John Jerwood has been translated into a recognition and strong credibility for the quality of the work which we support.

The Jerwood Space

The Jerwood Space celebrated its fifth anniversary by opening its new space – known as The Glasshouse. Adjoining the Gallery and covering part of the Courtyard, it provides year-round al fresco dining and hospitality space. The architects, Satellite Design Workshop, have created a simple and impressive structure which complements the original scheme and at the same time enables the kitchen block to be extended and to create an Art Wall for the latest Jerwood Commissions: a series of huge high-quality digital prints by young artists. The first of these was Paul McDevitt's Merge.

Our building was once again part of the architectural showcase London Open House, this time leading seven other venues with Dancing Houses, specially commissioned site-specific dance performances.

The Space has continued its established policy of providing performers and choreographers with highly subsidised rehearsal space in which to make their work. The 'Robin Hood' principle was maintained, with commercial theatre companies paying the market rate for hire of space while only taking a quarter of the available time. Out of 350 different organisations or individuals using the Jerwood Space this year, over half of them were subsidised with a 50%–85% reduction in fees. It is worth restating that the Space is now able to operate mainly from its own income generation, with a reduced subsidy from the Jerwood Foundation and with no call on public-sector monies.

The range of artists using the building is as diverse as ever, with young performers working alongside seasoned actors (such as those performing in Trevor Nunn's Young Vic production of Skellig) and young directors and choreographers benefiting from the experience of established actors and dancers from film, television and theatre.

It is tremendously gratifying to see artists whose reputations have grown during the life of the Space return in 2003: dancers Russell Maliphant and George Piper Dances; directors Thea Sharrock and Josie Rourke. It was equally pleasing to welcome innovative companies like Improbable Theatre and regional visitors such as the new Lichfield Garrick Theatre and Birmingham Stage Company, alongside regular users like the Young Vic and Donmar Warehouse.

During the year the Jerwood Artists Platform firmly established itself in the Gallery, alongside the Jerwood Sculpture, Painting and Drawing Prizes.

The Jerwood Collection Centre at the Wordsworth Trust

I am pleased to report that we have now completed the full grant in favour of the Wordsworth Trust. Construction work started in February 2003 and the roof of the Collection Centre was completed in December [2003]. The building will be unobtrusive but make a clear architectural statement. The drystone-walling so typical of the Lake District is being undertaken with the craftsmen's patience and skill. With the benefit of a dedicated professional team, led by the architects Benson+Forsyth, and the inspiration of the Director Dr Robert Woof, the new building will take its place within the heritage Wordsworth Centre. I know that logistical plans are well advanced to bring together the collection of some 50,000 letters, books, manuscripts, paintings and drawings into the new Jerwood Centre.

The Royal College of Physicians

The Healing Environment

During the second half of the year we were invited to sponsor, with the Arts Council and the College, this new book illustrated in full colour which comprises commissioned chapters and selected papers organised by the Centre for Medical Humanities, Royal Free and University College Medical School, London. The book provides a clear conceptual framework for understanding the healing environment and underlines the real contribution that the arts can make to the inner environment of feelings and perceptions of those on a path of physical or mental healing.

Arts, education and medicine are at the forefront of all that we do. The publication of The Healing Environment embraces all three. In recent years we have sponsored art, music, opera and drama in prisons. I believe there is common ground in this book with a shared purpose of enlightening, educating and healing through the arts. We are very pleased, and are rewarded ourselves, to be the principal sponsor of this groundbreaking, learned and stimulating publication by the Royal College of Physicians.

Art Collections

We have continued to develop both our art and sculpture collections but regrettably, and to some extent anticipated by my Statement last year, the planning and other difficulties in relation to Witley Court persuaded us that we should terminate our association with English Heritage at this site. We are well advanced in discussions which, I believe, will provide in the next few months a wonderful new setting for our Sculpture Park. It will include the work of young sculptors and be open to a wide and appreciative audience.

The Jerwood Name

The name Jerwood is now borne by theatres, libraries, art galleries, rehearsal studios, education centres, a concert hall, as well as by other places. It is also carried proudly by the Sea Cadets' offshore training ship. It may be that the strength of the name coupled with the successful and tangible activities of the Jerwood Charity have enhanced our credibility and, in turn, our effectiveness. I should certainly like to think that this is the case but it must be for others to judge. Together with the charity we would hope to push out boundaries, take risks (preferably with our eyes open), and avoid committees and introspective self-assessment.

Our style is based on strong enquiry and diligence prior to any grant and the expectation of tangible results unfettered by bureaucracy. We seek creative leadership, often of one individual, and effective partnerships.

I believe very strongly that resources and talent should go to achievement, be it institutional or individual, and not to excessive criticism and the ever increasing flow of paper.

Guidelines for applicants

The Jerwood funding guidelines are described as follows:

Introduction

The Jerwood Charity is a United Kingdom charity registered in 1999. It is supported financially and with other resources by the Jerwood Foundation, a private foundation established in 1977 by the late John Jerwood.

The Jerwood Charity is now responsible for revenue awards, donations and sponsorship in the United Kingdom which were previously undertaken by the Jerwood Foundation itself.

It is dedicated to funding and sponsorship of the visual and performing arts and education in the widest sense. It will continue to allocate a proportion of funding to conservation, environment, medicine, science and engineering.

The charity shares with the Jerwood Foundation a dedication to imaginative and responsible funding and sponsorship in areas of human endeavour and excellence which foster and enrich the fabric of society.

Please read the guidelines through carefully. Applications are accepted by post only. Please do not e-mail your application and please note that we are not able to fund individuals.

Funding policy

In every case the charity seeks to secure tangible and visible results from its grants and sponsorships. Influence and effect beyond the immediate recipient of a grant is encouraged. The Jerwood Charity aims to be active in identifying and creating new projects for sponsorship.

We aim to monitor chosen projects closely and sympathetically, and are keen to seek recognition of the charity's support.

Our strategy is to support outstanding national institutions while at the same time being prepared to provide seed corn finance and financial support at the early stages of an initiative when other grantmaking bodies might not be able or willing to act. The charity may wish to be sole sponsor (subject to financial considerations) or to provide partnership funding.

In particular the Jerwood Charity seeks to develop support and reward for young people who have demonstrated achievement and excellence, and who will benefit from a final lift to launch their careers. This special role is intended to open the way for young achievers and give them the opportunity to flourish.

The Jerwood Charity has the benefit of association with capital projects of the Jerwood Foundation. These include the Jerwood Space, the Jerwood Theatres at the Royal Court Theatre and the Jerwood Gallery at the Natural History Museum. The support for these initiatives by the Jerwood Foundation will be a factor when considering any applications.

Although the charity normally funds projects based within the United Kingdom, it will also consider a small number of applications from UK organisations operating overseas, especially within Nepal.

The Jerwood Charity will not merely be a passive recipient of requests for grants but will also identify areas to support and develop projects with potential beneficiaries.

We regret that inevitably there will be applications which will have to be refused, even if they fit within our funding priorities, as a result of the large number of applications we receive.

Current areas of interest

The Jerwood Charity has certain primary fields of interest, although these are constantly being reviewed and developed. All applicants should carefully read the exclusions before preparing an application.

The Arts

The charity is a major sponsor of all areas of the performing and visual arts. We are particularly interested in projects which involve rewards for excellence and the encouragement and recognition of outstanding talent and high standards, or which enable an organisation to become viable and self financing.

We rarely sponsor single performances or arts events, such as festivals, nor do we make grants towards the running or core costs of established arts organisations. We do not fund individuals.

The charity is active in support of conservation of the artistic and architectural heritage. However, we do not make grants towards building restoration projects.

Education

The charity aims to support projects which are educational in the widest sense. Currently, preference is given to initiatives benefiting young people who have completed school and university or other similar further education and are continuing their vocational and educational development.

We regret that we are unable to make grants to cover course fees or maintenance for individuals. We do not contribute to fundraising appeals by individuals. We do not contribute to fundraising appeals by individual schools or colleges, nor, except in very rare instances will the charity fund bursaries for a school or other institution.

Other Fields

The Jerwood Charity retains a small allocation for projects and award schemes within the fields of science, engineering, environment and conservation. The Jerwood Charity will continue its support of the Jerwood Salters Award for Chemistry and will be supporting new initiatives such as the Jerwood Business and Conservation Initiative in association with the Wildlife and Conservation Research Unit at Oxford University.

Jerwood prizes/awards

The Jerwood Charity will continue to fund and monitor established awards such as the Jerwood Painting Prize, Jerwood Applied Arts Awards with the Crafts Council, the Jerwood Choreography Awards with the Arts Council of England and Dance Umbrella, the Season of New Playwrights at the Royal Court Theatre and the Jerwood Art Commissions. The charity will also develop new schemes which will reflect the foundation's objective to support talent and excellence in our areas of interest.

Types of grants

The charity makes revenue donations on a 'one off' basis. There is a strong element of challenge funding, whereby the charity will make a grant provided the recipient or other interested party, such as central Government or Local Authority can match the remaining shortfall. The charity will rarely commit to funding over a fixed number of years, yet will be prepared in many cases to maintain support if consistency will secure better results, and the partnership is successful and producing good results.

Applications are made and assessed throughout the year. They are normally assessed initially by the Jerwood Charity's staff, with the help of expert advisers where appropriate. Final decisions are made by the board of trustees; every effort will be made to achieve speedy decisions.

Applications will be acknowledged. Decisions can normally be expected within six weeks and will be notified immediately. In view of the number of appeals we receive, detailed reasons for the rejection of an application are not generally given.

Grants will vary between the lower range of up to £10,000 (often plus or minus £5,000) and more substantial grants in excess of £10,000 and up to £50,000. There should be no expectation of grant level as all applications will be assessed on merit and need.

Exclusions

The Jerwood Charity will not consider applications on behalf of:

- individuals;
- building or capital costs (including purchase of equipment);
- projects in the fields of religion or sport;
- animal rights or welfare;
- general fundraising appeals which are likely to have wide public appeal;
- appeals to establish endowment funds for other charities;
- appeals for matching funding for Big Lottery Fund applications;
- grants for the running and core costs of voluntary bodies;
- projects which are of mainly local appeal or identified with a locality;
- medical research without current clinical applications and benefits;
- social welfare, particularly where it may be considered a government or local authority responsibility;
- retrospective awards.

The trustees may, where there are very exceptional circumstances, decide to waive the exclusions.

Applications

Applications should be by letter, outlining the aims and objectives of the organisation and the specific project for which assistance is sought. With the application the charity needs:

- a detailed budget for the project, identifying administrative, management and central costs;
- details of funding already in place for the project, including any other trusts or sources which are being or have been approached for funds: if funding is not in place, the foundation requires details of how the applicant plans to secure the remaining funding;
- details of the management and staffing structure, including trustees;
- the most recent annual report and audited accounts of the organisation, together with current management accounts if relevant to the project.

The charity may wish to enter into discussions and/or correspondence with the applicant which may result in modification and/or development of the project or scheme. Any such discussion will in no way commit the Jerwood Charity to funding that application.

As the charity receives a large number of applications, it regrets that it is not possible to have preliminary meetings to discuss possible support before a written application is made.

As at November 2004, the foundation stated that it is unable to consider unsolicited applications–prospective applicants should contact the foundation for up-to-date information.

Jewish Child's Day

Jewish children in need or with special needs

£369,000 (2002/03)

Beneficial area Worldwide.

5th Floor, 707 High Road, North Finchley, London N12 0BT

Tel. 020 8446 8804 **Fax** 020 8446 7370

Email info@jewishchildsday.co.uk

Website www.jewishchildsday.co.uk

Correspondent P Shaw, Executive Director

Trustee *The National Council.*

Charity Commission no. 209266

Information available Full accounts were provided by the trust.

The trust was established in 1947 to encourage Jewish children in the UK to help less fortunate Jewish children who were survivors of the Nazi holocaust. Now it supports projects benefiting Jewish children in the UK or overseas. It disburses funds raised itself through appeals.

In 2002/03 it had assets of £549,000 and an income of £524,000. Grants were made totalling £369,000. By far the largest grant was £62,000 to Manchester Jewish Federation. Other large grants were £32,000 to Give-A-Kid-A-Break, £30,000 to Micha Society for Deaf Children in Tel Aviv, £10,300 to Youth Aliya and £10,000 to Israel Sport Centre for the Disabled.

Other beneficiaries included Hamifal Educational Children's Homes (£9,900), Chernobyl (£8,000), British Friends of

Rambam Medical Centre, Nitzan, Saffa Institute and Eliya (£7,000 each), Side by Side Kids Ltd, Har Friends of Hematology and Shema (£5,000 each) British Friends of Laniado Hospital (£4,000), Merseyside Jewish Community Care (£700) and Anva (£500).

Exclusions

Individuals are not supported. Grants are not given towards general services, building or maintenance of property or staff salaries. No grants are made in response to general appeals from large UK organisations or to smaller bodies working in fields other than those set out above.

Applications

There is an application form which needs to be submitted together with a copy of the latest annual report and accounts and any supporting information. The trustees meet to consider applications twice a year, usually in March and September/ October; applications should be submitted two months earlier.

The trust states 'if you require any advice as to the eligibility of your application or assistance in preparing it please do not hesitate to contact us and we shall be happy to help'.

The Joffe Charitable Trust

Development policy, projects in developing countries

£400,000 (2002/03)

Beneficial area Mainly developing countries.

Liddington Manor, The Street, Liddington, Swindon SN4 0HD

Tel. 01793 790203

Correspondent Joel Joffe, Trustee

Trustees *Lady V L Joffe; Lord Joffe.*

Charity Commission no. 270299

Information available Annual report and accounts were provided by the trust.

Summary

About 25 grants are made every year, almost all to organisations concerned with support for developing countries

and dealing with such issues as human rights, the prevention of conflict and the relief of poverty. They are usually one-off, and generally for amounts up to £50,000.

General

This is a personal family trust, without staff or premises of its own. Lord Joffe is a former chairman of Oxfam and the Giving Campaign. The policy of the trust is described as follows in the annual report for 2002/03: 'The trustees have an ongoing relationship with a large number of charities and their decisions on which to support at any one time are based on their assessment of the quality of leadership and the impact that the initiatives which they support are likely to have'.

Guidelines for applicants

The trust offers the following information on its grantmaking aims and objectives:

1. Primary focus:
   Alleviation of poverty and protection/ advancement of human rights in the developing world (poverty for this purpose could include some forms of suffering such as mental or physical disability and lack of education).

Secondary focus:
   The support of individuals in the voluntary sector anywhere in the world who we judge are likely to make a real difference in alleviating poverty, advancing human rights and increasing the efficiency and effectiveness of the voluntary sector.

   2. Essential criteria in agreeing grants:
- Leadership
- Clear and narrow focus
- Clear objectives
- Value for money
- Effective financial controls
- Grants must aim to make a significant difference to the organisation and cause
- Sustainability
- Replicability/scaling up
- Campaigning potential.

3. Likely exclusions:
- Humanitarian assistance
- Large charities except perhaps for important projects which might not otherwise happen
- The arts
- Charities likely to exclusively benefit causes in the developed world.

4. Annual grant allocation:
- Approximately £500,000 per year
- Up to £50,000 of this may be set aside for applications which might not fall within the above but which the trustees feel they would like to support.

5. Favourable indicators in assessing grant applications:

- Support by other funders which I respect, e.g. financial assessment by DFID or the Community Fund or more generally the Joseph Rowntree Trust
- If the grant can help to scale up other grants to the charity in question
- Imaginative but realistic initiatives even though they may carry a risk of failure.

6. Core costs:

We will be sympathetic to applications for core costs which fit within the above criteria.

7. Unsuccessful applications:

Unfortunately, it is not possible to acknowledge unsuccessful applications due to a lack of resources, nor will reasons for the application being turned down be given.

Grants in 2002/03

The trust made 34 grants worth £400,000 in total in 2002/03. The largest grant, as in 2000/01, was made to Basic Needs UK, a charity supporting the development of improved mental health care and provision in, at present, India, Sri Lanka, Ghana, Tanzania and Uganda (£70,000).

Other large grants were made to the Institute for Philanthropy (£30,000), Oxford University Department for Continuing Education, Open University Foundation and InterRights (£25,000), People's Family Law Centre – South Africa (£20,000), One World Linking Organisation and Forestry Fund (£15,000 each), Quaker Peace Studies Trust (£13,000), Community Links Trust Limited and Hearing Conservation Council (£12,500 each) and Hantam Community Education Trust – South Africa, Kurdish Human Rights Project, Students' Partnership Worldwide, Witts University (South Africa) Charitable Trust – UK, PiggyBankKids and Centre for Innovation in Voluntary Action (£10,000 each).

Other beneficiaries included Norfolk Education and Action for Development (£7,500), Maradadi – South Africa (£6,500), Project Trust – Scotland and World Development Movement Trust (£5,000 each), Jewish Helping Hand Crèche – Soweto (£4,000), Soil Association and Forgotten Africa (£2,500 each) and TANZED (£1,500).

Exclusions

See above.

Applications

In writing to the correspondent, although the trust has previously stated that its resources are largely committed for the foreseeable future.

Unfortunately, due to limited resources, unsuccessful applications cannot be acknowledged.

The Elton John Aids Foundation

HIV/AIDS welfare and prevention

£3.8 million (2003)

Beneficial area UK and overseas.

1 Blythe Road, London W14 0HG

Tel. 020 7603 9996 **Fax** 020 7348 4848

Email admin@ejafuk.com

Website www.ejafuk.com

Correspondent Robert Key, Executive Director

Trustees *Sir Elton John, chair; Nigel Roberts, treasurer; Robert Key; John Scott; David Furnish; Lynette Jackson; Neil Tennant; Frank Presland; Anne Aslett; Marguerite Littman; Johnny Bergius; James Locke.*

Charity Commission no. 1017336

Information available Accounts and very brief annual report available from the foundation for £5. Funding criteria and application procedure.

Summary

Grants are given in both the UK and overseas, to organisations providing services for people affected by HIV/AIDS and for AIDS prevention education programmes. There are two funds each for UK and international grants, one for small grants (of up to £6,000), the other for larger grants, usually up to a maximum of £50,000. Around two thirds of the grant total is spent on international grants each year.

General

The foundation was established in 1993 by Elton John, who serves as its chairman. Its income each year is in the form of donations and there is no substantial endowment. In 2003 the foundation had an income of about £3.5 million.

The foundation describes its mission as:

to improve the quality of life of people living with HIV and AIDS by seeking out and financing service orientated projects that help to alleviate physical, emotional and financial suffering caused by AIDS. The foundation continues to fund preventative education programmes and initiatives that help to stop the spread of the HIV virus.

The foundation produces separate guidelines, for the UK and for international grants, from which the following excerpts have been taken.

UK funding criteria

The foundation has two distinct UK and international grant-making funds:

- General grants fund (over £6,000)
- Small grants fund (up to and including £6,000)

United Kingdom General Fund (over £6,000)

Who is eligible to apply?

Any registered charity involved in work specifically to benefit people infected/affected by HIV/AIDS and providing services within the UK and Eire.

Criteria for funding

The remit of the foundation is to help alleviate the physical, mental and financial hardship of those living with HIV/AIDS by funding direct care services and preventative education programmes. The foundation will consider applications that meet a recognised, demonstrable need in the light of changes in the epidemiology of HIV/AIDS. Clear aims and objectives, practical indicators and relevant monitoring and evaluation should be integral to any project proposal.

United Kingdom Small Grants Fund (up to and including £6,000)

This fund provides a response mechanism for local HIV/AIDS initiatives and is designed for use by registered charities to design and implement HIV/AIDS prevention and care activities in the UK and Eire,

International funding criteria

Who is eligible to apply?

Any not-for-profit organisation that is running programme(s) specifically to benefit those infected or affected by HIV/AIDS in the following programme countries may apply for funding:

Africa: Botswana, Kenya, Lesotho, Malawi, Mozambique, Namibia, Rwanda, South Africa, Swaziland, Tanzania, Uganda, Zambia.

Asia: Bangladesh, Cambodia, India, Nepal and Thailand.

Latin America: Mexico.

South America: Brazil, Chile.

Europe: Romania, Russian Federation, Ukraine.

Criteria for funding

The foundation will consider applications designed to alleviate physical, emotional or financial hardship caused by HIV/AIDS, as well as prevention/education projects aimed at those at risk of the disease, which meet a recognised, demonstrable need. Clear aims and objectives; practical indicators for work-in-progress, and relevant monitoring and evaluation of the results should all be integral to any project proposal. Please note: all funding will be awarded on a yearly basis, up to a maximum of three years.

EJAF is keen to encourage community based projects which:

- promote awareness of individual and collective vulnerability to HIV/AIDS
- ensure active participation by a broad and representative group of community members
- build capacity and ensure sustainability
- maximise use of community resources
- liaise with other sectors to avoid duplication and ensure a co-ordinated response to HIV.

Exclusions

For both UK and international grants the foundation will not fund:

- capital costs;
- conferences or educational courses;
- drug treatment costs;
- individual grants;
- repatriation costs;
- research programmes;
- retrospective funding.

Applications

Potential applicants should obtain a copy of the appropriate guidelines, either for the UK or international grants, by emailing admin@ejafuk.com

Organisations applying to the foundation for funds must provide full information about their work, including their objectives and evaluation plan. Those applying to either fund should include a copy of the latest annual report or accounts as well as a 'Certificate of Charity/NGO Registration' [There is actually no such document available from the Commission. No doubt a print out of the relevant page from the Charity Commission's website will do. Ed.]

Applicants to either general fund should enclose the following supporting information:

- constitution or memorandum and articles of association;
- budget relating to the application;
- latest audited accounts;
- financial management and accounting procedure;
- latest annual report
- two independent written references on your organisation/project.

There are three grants rounds during the year. Currently the closing dates are 31 March, 31 July and 30 November.

The Jones 1986 Charitable Trust

General

£482,000 (2002/03)

Beneficial area UK, mostly Nottinghamshire.

Blythens, Haydn House, 309–329 Haydn Road, Sherwood, Nottingham NG5 1HG

Tel. 0115 960 7111 **Fax** 0115 969 1313

Email raheason@blythens.co.uk

Correspondent Robert Andrew Heason, Trustee

Trustees R A Heason; R B Stringfellow.

Charity Commission no. 327176

Information available Annual report and accounts were provided by the trust.

The charity was established in 1986 with very wide charitable purposes. The trustees primarily support causes in the Nottingham area and the list of beneficiaries remains largely unchanged from year to year. Much of the money goes to charities assisting disabled people, or for medical research into disabilities.

In 2002/03 it had assets of £2.7 million and an income of £534,000 from donations and investments. Grants were made to 22 organisations totalling £482,000. Grants were broken down as follows:

Medical research – 3 grants totalling £177,000

The largest grant made during the year, as in the previous year, was to Nottingham University, which received £155,000 for Nottingham Health Authority. The other beneficiaries in this area were Headway (National Head Injuries Association) which received £12,000, and Nottinghamshire Leukaemia Appeal which received £10,000.

Relief of sickness or disability: generally – 5 grants totalling £57,000

Beneficiaries in this category were Winged Fellowship (£17,000), The New Appeals Organisation for the City and County of Nottingham (£15,000), Nottingham Deaf Society (£10,000), Long Eaton Society for Mentally Handicapped Children and Adults (£9,000) and Prince of Paste Anglers (£6,000).

Welfare of the young – 2 grants totalling £55,000

The two beneficiaries were Nottinghamshire Scouts, which received

£50,000, and the Nottinghamshire Battalion of the Boys Brigade, which received £5,000.

Education – 3 grants totalling £42,000

The three educational establishments to receive grants were Rutland House School (£30,000), Yeoman Park School (£10,000) and Nottingham University (£2,000).

Relief of poverty – 2 grants totalling £42,000

The two beneficiaries were Framework Housing Association (£24,000) and Scope (£18,000).

Relief of sickness or disability: young – 2 grants totalling £41,000

The main beneficiary in this category was Cope Children's Trust, which received £40,000. A further £1,000 was awarded to Chernobyl Children's Lifeline.

Welfare of the aged – 2 grants totalling £35,000

Beneficiaries were Age Concern Nottinghamshire (£25,000) and Radford Care Group (£10,000).

Purposes beneficial to the community – 3 grants totalling £33,000

Beneficiaries were Ruddington Framework Knitters Museum (£20,000), Kirkby Community Advice Centre (£10,000) and Bramcote Village Hall (£3,000).

Exclusions

No grants to individuals.

Applications

The trustees identify their own target charities and do not wish to receive applications.

The Jordan Charitable Foundation

General

£317,000 (2003)

Beneficial area Unrestricted, with strong local interests in Herefordshire and the Scottish Highlands.

Rawlinson and Hunter, Eagle House, 110 Jermyn Street, London SW1Y 6RH

Tel. 020 7451 9000 **Fax** 020 7451 9090

Email chris.hawley@rawlinson-hunter. com

Correspondent Chris Hawley, Secretary

Trustees *Sir Ronald Miller; Sir George Russell; Ralph Stockwell; Snowport Ltd; Parkdove Ltd.*

Charity Commission no. 1051507

Information available Full accounts were provided by the trust.

Summary

The trust does contribute to the core funding of some charities but this represents a fairly small proportion of its charitable spending. The real aim of the trustees is to seek larger, more meaningful projects to support, including the refurbishment of buildings used for charitable purposes and the provision of essential medical or other equipment.

Funds are given towards welfare causes, including the welfare of animals and plantlife. Although the trust had an unrestricted beneficial area, virtually all of its grants are made in the UK, particularly Herefordshire and the Scottish Highlands. There were no overseas beneficiaries during 20003. Smaller recurrent grants are made to a broad range of UK charities.

General

In 2003 it had assets of £30 million and an income of £861,000. The costs of generating the funds and administration expenses were £190,000. Grants were made to 61 organisations totalling £317,000. Many recipients of grants had also been supported in previous years.

The beneficiary of the largest grant was CLD Youth Counselling Trust, receiving £36,000. Other larger grants of £20,000 or more were to Hereford Cathedral Perpetual Trust (£30,000), League of Friends of Tenbury Hospital (£25,000)

and Migrating Salmon Foundation (£20,000). The accounts contained no analysis regarding what aspects of the organisations' work were being funded.

Among the other beneficiaries in the Scottish Highlands were National Trust for Scotland, Sutherland Schools Pipe Band – Golspie and Sutherland Young Carer Project (£5,000 each) and Dunrobin Castle Piping Championship (£500).

Other grants in Herefordshire included those to Herefordshire Lifestyles (£12,000), Herefordshire Headway (£10,000), Herefordshire Growing Point (£2,000) and Herefordshire Victim Support (£1,000).

Other beneficiaries included People's Advocacy Network (£7,500), St John's Ambulance (£7,000), Age Concern – England, Cancer Research UK, Eating Disorder Association, Marie Curie Cancer Care, Police Rehabilitation Trust and the Royal Welsh Agricultural Society (£5,000 each), Abbeyfield Hereford Society Limited, National Art Collections Fund, National Canine Defence League, Riding for the Disabled, Samaritans and Stroke Association (£3,000), ASPIRE, British Lung Foundation, Society for the Welfare of Horses and Ponies and Wildfowl & Wetlands Trust (£2,000) and Children's Hospice Association – Scotland and REGAIN (£1,000 each).

Applications

In writing to the correspondent.

The Kay Kendall Leukaemia Fund

Research into leukaemia

£978,000 (2003/04)

Beneficial area Unrestricted.

Allington House, 1st Floor, 150 Victoria Street, London SW1E 5AE

Tel. 020 7410 0330 **Fax** 020 7410 0332

Email info@sfct.org.uk

Correspondent Michael Pattison, Director

Trustees *Judith Portrait; T J Sainsbury; Christopher Stone.*

Charity Commission no. 290772

Information available Excellent annual report and accounts were provided by the trust.

This is one of the Sainsbury Family Charitable Trusts, which share a joint administration. They have a common approach to grantmaking which is described in the entry for the group as a whole.

This trust is solely concerned with funding research into the causes and treatment of leukaemia, which is done on the advice of an expert advisory panel. The work is well described in the annual report as follows:

Policies and Guidelines for Awarding Grants

Trustees keep their grantmaking policies under regular review. The guidelines currently applied are as follows:

1. Grants will be awarded for research on aspects of leukaemia and for relevant studies on related haematological malignancies.

2. Grants will also be awarded for the support of programmes associated with the care of patients with leukaemia subject to the conditions laid out below.

3. Requests for capital grants for leukaemia research laboratories or for clinical facilities for leukaemia will be considered either alone or in conjunction with proposals for the support of research and/or patient management.

4. Requests for single large items of equipment will be considered.

5. Preference will be given to proposals which are close to application to the care of leukaemia patients or to the prevention of leukaemia and related diseases.

6. Requests for support for basic science programmes may be considered but are likely to be funded only in exceptional cases. Project grant proposals or other small requests are not normally eligible.

7. Clinical trials will not be supported.

8. Grants are usually awarded to give additional support to programmes already underway, the aim being to further strengthen activities which are already of high quality. It follows that the KKLF will accept proposals from groups which already have support from other agencies.

9. The trustees will consider proposals from both UK and non-UK based organisations. Proposals from the latter must involve some degree of collaboration with UK colleagues.

10. Circular appeals for general support are not accepted.

11. Research grants are normally awarded for programmes of five years' duration. Support may be awarded for three years in the first instance with the final two years being dependent upon a review of progress over the first three years.

12. Programme grants may be renewed once for a period of up to five years. The maximum period of funding will be ten years. It is intended that the KKLF funding should not be the 'core' funding of any research group. Applicants should state clearly how their proposal relates to their core funding.

13. It is hoped that recipients of KKLF grants will try to ensure that support from other agencies is not withdrawn as a consequence of funding having been given by the KKLF.

14. Support for the costs of clinical care may be requested but this is normally permitted for a fixed term only (two to five years). A written assurance that the recruiting costs will be taken over at the end of the period by the appropriate Health Authority or NHS Trust will be a condition of awarding the grant.

Grants in 2003/04

During the year the fund made grants to eight beneficiaries totalling just over £978,000, although the amount approved, to be paid over a number of years in some cases, was almost £1.7 million. The largest grants were made to:

University of Manchester – £587,000

A five-year grant for a research programme using an immunotherapeutic approach aimed at the treatment of B-cell malignancies.

Imperial College School of Medicine, Hammersmith Hospital – £346,000 in total

A junior KKLF fellowship award of £187,000 was made for a three-year research project to study the relationship between particular genetic mutations in Down's syndrome children and their greatly increased risk of developing specific types of leukaemia.

A junior KKLF fellowship award of £160,000 was made for a three-year research project to investigate how the packaged structure of chromatin influences normal differentiations or leads to malignant transformation by

oncogenes in plasma cells leading to Multiple Myeloma.

University of Birmingham – £250,000

A further three-year grant towards a large-scale epidemiological study on survivors of childhood cancer, the British Childhood Cancer Survivor Study.

Applications

See above.

The Kennedy Charitable Foundation

Roman Catholic ministries, general, especially in the west of Ireland

£982,000 (2001/02)

Beneficial area Unrestricted, but mainly Ireland with a preference for County Mayo and County Sligo.

12th Floor, Bank House, Charlotte Street, Manchester M1 4ET

Tel. 0161 455 8380 **Fax** 0161 829 3803

Correspondent Alan Pye

Trustees *Patrick Kennedy; Kathleen Kennedy; John Kennedy; Brown Street Nominees Ltd; Patrick Joseph; Francis Kennedy.*

Charity Commission no. 1052001

Information available Accounts were on file at the Charity Commission, without an analysis of grantmaking.

General

The trust has no permanent endowment and is funded by donations. Its income for 2001/02 was £420,000 (£1.8 million in 2000/01). Grants are predominantly made to organisations connected with the Roman Catholic faith, mainly in Ireland.

Grants

In 2001/02 the trust made 88 grants totalling £982,000. The largest beneficiary, as in the previous year, was the Newman Institute in County Mayo, Ireland, which received two large grants totalling £550,000.

There were 13 grants that ranged from £10,000 to £50,000, with beneficiaries including Restoration Ministries – Belfast (£50,000), Dominican Order – Ireland (£27,500), Diocese of Elphin (£20,000), Mayo Emigrant Liaison Committee (£16,000), Diocese of Hexham and Newcastle (£12,000) and the Rainbow Family Trust (£10,000).

Other beneficiaries included Diocese of Anchonry (£8,000), Diocese of Salford (£3,000), Leukaemia Trust (£2,500), Northwest Hospice (£1,000), Friends of Rotunda (£750) and HCPT Pilgrimage Trust (£500).

In both 2002/03 and 2003/04 the trust's income and expenditure decreased – in 2003/04 total expenditure was £431,000. Unfortunately, although submitted by the trust to the Charity Commission, the accounts for these years had not made it to the public files for inspection.

Applications

In writing to the correspondent, but the foundation says that 'unsolicited applications are not accepted'.

Keren Association

Jewish, education, general

£3 million (2002/03)

Beneficial area UK.

136 Clapham Common, London E5 9AG

Correspondent Mrs S Englander, Trustee

Trustees *E Englander, chair; Mrs S Englander; P N Englander; S Z Englander; B Englander; J S Englander; Mrs H Z Weiss; Mrs N Weiss.*

Charity Commission no. 313119

Information available Accounts were on file at the Charity Commission, without a list of grants.

This trust has general charitable purposes, supporting the advancement of education and the provision of religious instruction and training in traditional Judaism.

In 2002/03 it had an income of £3.4 million and a total expenditure of £3.7 million. Grants were made totalling around £3 million. Further information for this year was not available.

Applications

In writing to the correspondent.

This entry was not confirmed by the charity, but the information was correct according to the Charity Commission.

The Peter Kershaw Trust

Medical research, education, social welfare

£318,000 (2002/03)
Beneficial area Manchester and the surrounding district only.

22 Ashworth Park, Knutsford, Cheshire WA16 9DE
Tel. 01565 651086
Email bryan_peak@compuserve.com
Correspondent Bryan Peak, Secretary
Trustees *H F Kershaw; M L Rushbrooke; R P Kershaw; H W E Thompson; D Tully.*
Charity Commission no. 268934
Information available Information was provided by the trust.

'The principal activities of the trust continue to be those of funding medical research, grants to medical and other institutions and to schools in respect of bursaries.'

In 2002/03 the trust had assets of £6 million, and an income of £303,000. Grants were made totalling £318,000.

Beneficiaries included: Old Moat Youth Outreach Project (£20,000), Withington High School for Girls (£18,000), Henshaw Society for the Blind and Burnage Multi-Agency Group (£15,000 each), Sycamore Project, Manchester YMCA, Contact, Independent Options – Stockport and Signpost Stockport for Carers (£10,000 each).

Exclusions

No grants to individuals or for building projects.

Applications

In writing to the correspondent, however the trust is always oversubscribed.

King George's Fund for Sailors

The welfare of seafarers

£1.8 million (2003)
Beneficial area UK and Commonwealth.

8 Hatherley Street, London SW1P 2YY
Tel. 020 7932 0000 **Fax** 020 7932 0095
Email seafarers@kgfs.org.uk
Website www.kgfs.org.uk
Correspondent Commodore Barry Bryant, Director General
Trustee *The General Council, of which Vice Admiral The Hon. Sir Nicholas Hill-Norton is Chair and Captain D C Glass is Deputy Chairman.*
Charity Commission no. 226446
Information available Annual report, accounts, annual review and full grants list were provided by the trust. The website is informative, but mainly promotional.

Summary

The fund makes grants, often recurrent, for a wide but little-changing range of seafarer's charities. Grants range from a few hundred pounds to several hundred thousand.

General

The fund was set up in 1917 as a central fundraising organisation to support other seafarers charities. It has a large and very costly fundraising operation (see below), with a network of volunteer area committees backed by professional staff, but almost half of its income comes from the interest and dividends on its investments.

Grantmaking in 2003

While most organisations appear regularly in the grants lists from year to year, amounts can vary substantially, and the fund makes special awards to help with major capital or development programmes, in addition to its more regular subventions.

Grants in 2003 were categorised as follows (with 2002 awards in brackets):

Hospitals, rest homes, rehabilitation centres, homes for the aged, etc.: £290,000 in 25 grants (£393,000 in 28 grants)

Major beneficiaries were the Ex-Services Mental Welfare Society £50,000

(£50,000), Royal Alfred Seafarers Society £50,000 (£44,000) and Scottish Veterans' Residences £45,000 (£20,000).

Children's homes, training ships, schools, scholarships and bursaries: £377,000 in 15 grants (£410,000 in 18 grants)

The largest grant, of £70,000, was for the Royal Merchant Navy School Foundation.

Funds supporting needy seafarers or their dependants: £906,000 in 17 grants (£1,031,000 in 21 grants)

The major beneficiaries were the Shipwrecked Fishermen and Mariners Society, £404,000 (£354,000) and SSAFA Forces Help £104,000 (£111,000).

Missions, clubs, societies and associations: £166,000 in six grants (£195,000 in seven grants)

The largest grant was to the Royal National Mission to Deep Sea Fishermen, for £85,000 (£100,000).

Fundraising costs

The remarkably high fundraising costs that have been reported over the years are as follows:

Donations, legacies and events		*... of which, fundraising costs were:*
1990	–	40%
1991	£2.2 million	27%
1992	£1.5 million	32%
1993	£1.1 million	44%
1994	£2.1 million	28%
1995	£829,000	54%
1996	£1 million	69%
1997	£2.1 million	31%
1998	£1.5 million	44%
1999	£1 million	68%
2000	£1.5 million	47%
2001	£1.7 million	43% (51% if exceptional restructuring costs are included)
2002	£1.5 million	46%
2003	£1.6 million	45%

In an effort to address these high fundraising costs, the fund has recently had a consultancy firm carry out an audit of its fundraising operation. The conclusion was that significant growth was needed in the fund's charitable income. As a result a professional fundraiser was appointed to overhaul the fundraising operation and to pursue new income streams. Hopefully the result should be more funds and reduced costs.

The strategy is part of a more general plan to modernise the fund and make it more relevant, with new activities as well as fulfilling its more traditional obligations.

Exclusions

The fund does not make any grants directly to individuals but rather helps other organisations which do this.

However, the fund may be able to advise in particular cases about a suitable organisation to approach. Full details of such organisations are to be found in A Guide to Grants for Individuals in Need, published by DSC.

Applications

Applications from organisations should be addressed to 'the director, finance and grants'. Trustees meet in July and November.

The King's Fund (King Edward's Hospital Fund for London)

Health and health care, especially in London

£1.7 million (2004)

Beneficial area London.

11–13 Cavendish Square, London W1G 0AN

Tel. 020 7307 2495 **Fax** 020 7307 2621

Email grants@kingsfund.org.uk

Website www.kingsfund.org.uk

Correspondent The Funding and development deparetment

Trustee *The management committee under the authority of the president and general council, including Sir Cyril Chantler, chair.*

Charity Commission no. 207401

Information available information is available on the fund's website.

The King's Fund is a leading independent health care charity, set up in 1897 by the Prince of Wales, later King Edward VII, to support the improvement of the health of Londoners and health care in London. Today it fulfils this mission through a range of activities, including research and policy analysis as well as grantmaking – which accounts for about one-quarter of its charitable expenditure. In 2004 the fund had assets amounting to £124 million. It had an income of £8.3 million. Grants totalled £1.7 million.

A new programme for funding and development in London

During 2005 the King's Fund are going to take a new approach to their role as a giver of grants to improve health in London. In June it will launch its new *Partners for Health in London Programme,/i>. Over the next few years this will focus funding and development efforts on four specific areas where health needs are still unmet, where there is scope to improve services and share learning.*

The four strands to the programme will be end of life care, sexual health, mental health advocacy and integrated healthcare (supporting choice across conventional and complimentary practice). The new programme will offer funding – more than £1 million to be shared annually between these areas – as well as development support for organisations involved in improving health through work in these areas. The King's Fund aims to become a more active partner in developing new ways of working.

On top of this the organisation plans to invest around half a million pounds in strategic funding (at its own initiative) for work beyond the specific strands in this new programme.

Please consult the fund's website for further details.

The Mary Kinross Charitable Trust

Mental health, community development, penal affairs

About £500,000 (2003/04)

Beneficial area UK.

36 Grove Avenue, Moseley, Birmingham B13 9RY

Correspondent Fiona Adams, Trustee

Trustees *Elizabeth Shields, chair; Fiona Adams; Neil E Cross; H Jon Foulds; Robert McDougall.*

Charity Commission no. 212206

Information available Annual reports and accounts were on file at the Charity Commission.

This trust prefers to work mainly with a group of charities with which it develops a close connection, led by at least one of the trustees.

The trust describes its grant policy as follows:

Trustees wish to continue the policy of the founder which was to to use the trust income to support a few carefully researched projects, rather than to make many small grants. At least one trustee takes responsibility for ensuring the trust's close involvement with organisations to which major grants are made. The fields of work chosen reflect the particular interests and knowledge of trustees.

For the organisations we support, we are able to pay core office costs which often enable staff to apply to other sources of funding.

Unfortunately we have to disappoint the great majority of applicants who nevertheless continue to send appeal letters. Because they work from home, trustees do not welcome telephone calls from applicants soliciting funds.

In 2003/04 it had an income of £719,000 and a total expenditure of £510,000, most of which was probably given in grants. No further information was available for the year.

Comment

Despite ample warning, and their obligation to the contrary, the Charity Commission were unable to give us sight of this trust's accounts.

Exclusions

No grants to individuals.

Applications

'Neither written applications nor telephone calls are welcome. There is no application form or timetable and procedure for assessing applications.' Trustees meet quarterly.

Ernest Kleinwort Charitable Trust

General

£1.2 million (2002/03)

Beneficial area UK and overseas, especially Sussex.

PO Box 191, 10 Fenchurch Street, London EC3M 3LB

Tel. 020 7475 6246

Correspondent Nick Kerr-Shepard, Secretary

Trustees *Kleinwort Benson Trustees Ltd; Madeleine, Lady Kleinwort; R M Ewing; S M Robertson; Sir Christopher Lever; Sir Richard Kleinwort.*

Charity Commission no. 229665

Information available Annual report and accounts.

The trust makes about 250 grants a year, widely spread and for amounts ranging from between £100 and £40,000. More than half of the money goes to Sussex-based charities. Most grants are in the following fields:

- youth
- disability and care for the elderly
- wildlife and conservation
- medical research.

The trust says that its current policy is 'to consider all written applications from registered charities, but only successful applicants are notified of the trustees' decision.

'Support is principally given to charities working in the fields of wildlife and environmental conservation (national and international) and charities operating in the county of Sussex. In approved cases, the trustees will provide assistance towards start–up or capital costs and ongoing expenses. This may take the form of a grant for say three years following which support may be withdrawn to enable the resources to be devoted to other projects. The trustees do not normally respond favourably to appeals from individuals, nor to those from small local charities e.g. individual churches, village halls, etc. where there is no specific connection.'

In 2002/03 the trust had assets of £32 million and an income of £1.3 million. Grants totalled £1.2 million. Many of the beneficiaries had been supported in previous years. Grants were categorised as follows:

Wildlife and conservation

A total of 46 grants totalling £256,000, were made in this category with most going to international charities. The major awards included: £28,000 to Tusk Trust; £20,000 each to Global Canopy Programme and WWF UK; £15,000 to Berkeley Reafforestation Trust; £12,000 to Woodland Trust; and £10,000 each to Earthwatch Europe and Fauna and Flora International.

Donations for the benefit of Sussex were £2,000 each to British and Irish Hardwoods Improvement Programme and Murray Downland Trust; £1,100 to International Tree Foundation; £1,000 to Sussex Farming and Wildlife Advisory Group; and £450 each to Cuckfield Museum and Weald and Downland Open Air Museum.

Disabled/handicapped treatment and care

There were 62 grants totalling £224,000. Of these, 52 donations amounting to £195,000 were made for the benefit of Sussex. Larger donations included: £38,000 to East Sussex Disability Association; £25,000 to Friends of Glyne Gap School; £15,000 to Agape Trust; and £10,000 each to Disability Fund and St Anthony's School Trust.

Smaller grants included: £7,500 to Disabilities Trust; £5,000 to Impact Foundation; £3,000 to Friends of Chailey Heritage; £2,100 to West Sussex Association for the Disabled; £2,000 to Sussex Lantern; £1,500 each to Mid Sussex Community Support Association and West Sussex Deaf and Hard of Hearing Association; £1,000 each to MIND – Hove and Brighton and Talking Newspaper Association; £750 to Leyden House Trust; £600 to Hamilton Lodge Brighton Limited; £450 to Sussex Autistic Society; and £300 Sussex ME/ CFS Society.

Care of the elderly

There were 15 grants totalling £46,000. Of these, Sussex accounted for all but two grants. The largest grants were £10,000 each to Abbeyfield Eastbourne Society Ltd and Age Concern – East Sussex. Other donations made in Sussex included: £3,500 to Age Concern – Burgess Hill; £2,000 to Contact the Elderly; £1,800 to Age Concern – Hassocks and District; £750 each to James Bradford Almshouses' Trust and Sussex Housing and Care; and £450 to RUKBA.

General welfare and social problems

There were 21 grants in this category, all but three of them in Sussex, totalling £42,000. The major awards were £25,000 to Voluntary Services Overseas, £15,000 to Merlin and £10,000 to Gingerbread.

Smaller donations in Sussex included: £4,000 to Mid Sussex Volunteering; £3,000 to Newhaven Volunteer Bureau; £2,000 to Ravenscourt; £1,500 to Brighton and Hove Unwaged, Advice and Rights Centre; £1,000 to Miracles; £750 to Burgess Hill District Lions Club; and £450 to Children's Family Trust.

Hospices for the benefit of Sussex

Five donations were made totalling £46,000. Grants were £20,000 to Martlets Hospice, £15,000 to St Wilfrid's Hospice, £7,500 to St Catherine's Hospice, £2,300 to Heatherley Cheshire Home and £1,500 to St Peter and St James' Hospice and Continuing Care Centre.

Medical research

In total 39 grants were made amounting to £134,000, including 18 grants worth £58,000 in Sussex. Donations included: £20,000 to Prostate Cancer Charity; £10,000 to Westcare UK; £9,000 to Theodora Children's Trust; £5,000 to Education for Choice; £3,000 to Square Smile; £1,500 to Foundation for the Study of Infant Deaths; £1,000 to Middlesex University; £500 to Pain Relief Foundation; £300 to Wosbey Foundation; and £200 to Spinal Research.

Reproductive health care

There were four grants totalling £67,000, including £30,000 each to Marie Stopes International and Population Concern. Other donations were £6,000 to Jamaica Family Planning Association and £750 to Family Planning Association – South East England Region.

Youth care

There were 51 donations totalling £205,000, with £112,000 of this going to 38 organisations in Sussex. Larger donations in this category included: £40,000 to Stowe School Foundation Appeal; £21,000 to Sussex Clubs for Young People; £20,000 to Prince's Trust; £16,000 to Raleigh International; and £10,000 each to Fairbridge and St Joseph's Catholic Primary School.

Other donations, made for the benefit of Sussex, included: £7,000 to Tideway Community School and Sixth Form Centre; £3,800 to Stafford House; £2,500 to Burgess Hill Girl Guide Hall Committee; £1,500 to Brighton and Hove Parents and Children Group; £1,000 each to Fair Play for Children and St Peter's Brighton Choral Foundation; £750 to Haywards Heath District Scout Council; £500 to Woodcraft Folk; and £300 each Brighton College, Sussex Army Cadet Force and Sussex Supreme Twirlers.

Miscellaneous

There were 31 miscellaneous donations totalling £123,000, of which £35,000 were made for the benefit of Sussex. Grants in this category included: £10,000 each to CVS and Jubilee Appeal for Commonwealth Veterans; £5,000 to Sussex Heritage Trust; £2,000 each to Chichester Bell Tower Project and Parish of St Mary the Virgin – Shipley; £1,500 each to Cuckfield Society and Eastbourne Care and Repair; £1,000 to Cuckfield Parochial Church Council; £600 to Royal Life Saving Society – Sussex Branch; and £450 each to Mid Sussex Choir and Sussex Historic Churches Trust.

Exclusions

Individuals and local charities outside Sussex are normally excluded.

Applications

In writing to the correspondent, enclosing a copy of the most recent annual report and financial statements. Trustees meet in March and October, but applications are considered throughout the year, normally within two to three months of receipt. Only successful applicants are notified of the trustees' decision.

The Sir James Knott Trust

General

£926,000 (2002/03)

Beneficial area Northumberland, County Durham (including Hartlepool) and Tyne and Wear.

16–18 Hood Street, Newcastle upon Tyne NE1 6JQ

Tel. 0191 230 4016 **Fax** 0191 230 4016

Email info@knott-trust.co.uk

Correspondent Vivien Stapley, Secretary

Trustees *Viscount Ridley; Mark Cornwall-Jones; Prof. Oliver James; Charles Baker-Cresswell.*

Charity Commission no. 1001363

Information available Annual report and accounts were provided by the trust.

The trust makes a very large number of small grants to a wide range of charities in the north east of England, about one-third of them to organisations also supported in the previous year.

The trust describes its grantmaking as follows:

Grants are normally only made to registered charities specifically operating in or for the benefit of the north east of England [with the exception of] Darlington, Stockton-on-Tees, Middlesbrough, Redcar and Cleveland.

Grants will commonly be in response to appeals in support of the welfare of the young, the elderly, seamen's and service charities, the disabled and disadvantaged, as well as education and training, medical care and research, historic buildings and the environment, music and the arts.

In 2002/03 the trust made 346 grants, comprising of 225 over £1,000 and 121 under £1,000 each. They were made in response to 632 applications, so that more than half of all applications resulted in a grant, though probably not all for the full amount requested.

During the year funds were distributed geographically as follows:

	Total £	%	No. of grants
Tyne & Wear	£359,000	38.8	144
Northumberland	£267,000	28.5	85
Durham	£152,000	16.4	59
North East general	£120,000	12.9	47
Other	£31,500	3.4	11

Funds were distributed in the following categories (as the trust states, these figures are approximate as there are numerous overlaps between categories. A new categorisation system will be adoped in subsequent years):

	Total £	%	No. of grants
Community welfare	£347,000	37.4	116
Youth/children	£205,000	22.1	96
Handicapped	£87,000	9.4	44
Heritage/museums	£72,000	7.8	15
Service charities	£50,000	5.4	14
Education/ expeditions	£48,000	5.2	17
Arts	£43,000	4.7	17
Conservation/ horticultural	£23,000	2.5	5
Maritime charities	£19,000	2.0	8
Elderly	£13,500	1.5	6
Medical	£13,000	1.4	6
Housing/homeless	£6,000	0.6	2

Larger grants included those to: Newcastle Diocesan Board of Finance (£21,000 in total), Bell View (Belford) Ltd – Northumberland (£20,000), Durham Diocesan Board of Finance and Northumbria Historic Churches Trust (£15,000 each) and Northumberland Wildlife Trust and Durham Association of Clubs for Young People (£10,000 each).

Other beneficiaries included: YMCA – North Eastern Division (£8,000), Lynemouth Community Trust (£7,000), Adventure Youth Sea Training – Hartlepool and Newcastle CVS (£5,000 each), North Northumberland Day Hospice (£4,000), Age Concern – Gateshead and Pennywell Neighbourhood Centre – Sunderland (£3,000 each), Samaritans – Hartlepool,

Samaritans – Sunderland and Upper Teesdale Agricultural Support Services (£2,000 each) and Alzheimer's Society – Newcastle, Barnardos – Newcastle and Northgate Hospital League of Friends (£1,000 each).

Beneficiaries receiving less than £1,000 each included: Berwick Autism Support Group, Cot Death Society North East, Gateshead Pre-School Learning Alliance, Multi-Cultural Information Centre – Newcastle and Owton Manor Baptist Church – Newcastle.

The trust also supported numerous citizens advice bureaux, guide associations and sea cadet branches.

Exclusions

No applications are considered from individuals, from non-registered charities or to replace funding withdrawn by local authorities. Grants are only made to charities from within the north east of England, and from UK charities either operating within, or where work may be expected to be of benefit to, the north east of England.

Applications

In writing to the correspondent, giving a brief description of the need, with relevant consideration to the following points:

- What type of organisation are you and how do you benefit the community?
- How are you organised and managed? How many staff/volunteers do you have?
- Are you a registered charity? If so, provide your registered number, if not you will need to submit the name and registered number of a charity which is prepared to administer funds on your behalf.
- What relationship, if any, do you have with similar or umbrella organisations?
- What is your main funding source?
- A description of the project you are currently fundraising for, the cost, how much would you like considered and when it is required.
- Who else have you approached and what response have you had?
- Have you applied to the Community Fund?
- Enclose a copy of your latest trustee report and accounts (if you are a new organisation then provide a copy of your latest bank statement).

Not all the questions/points may apply to you, but they give an idea of what the trustees may ask when considering applications. Trustees may contact applicants for further information.

Trustees normally meet in spring, summer and autumn. Applications need to be submitted up to two months in advance.

The Kobler Trust

Arts, Jewish, medical

£346,000 (2002/03)
Beneficial area UK.

Lewis Silkin, 12 Gough Square, London EC4A 3DW
Tel. 020 7074 8087
Correspondent Ms J L Evans, Trustee
Trustees *A Xuereb; A H Stone; Ms J L Evans; J W Israelsohn.*
Charity Commission no. 275237
Information available Full accounts were on file at the Charity Commission.

In 2002/03 the trust had assets of £3.5 million and an income of £184,000. Grants totalling £346,000 were given to 56 organisations, 23 of which were supported in the previous year.

The largest grant was £100,000 to Christopher Place. Other grants included those to Halle Conarts School (£30,000), Condon String Quartet and Tricycle (£25,000 each), Pavillion Opera (£12,000), Hearing Concern (£11,000), CRUSAID and Jewish Care (£5,000 each), Awkwright Scholarship (£4,500), Royal Academy of Arts (£3,500), Delamere Forest School, King's Cross Homelessness and Youth at Risk (£2,000 each) and Bognor Fun Bus (£1,000).

Exclusions

Grants are only given to individuals in exceptional circumstances.

Applications

In writing to the correspondent.

The Kreitman Foundation

Education, culture, the environment, health and welfare, Jewish charities

£486,000 (2002/03)
Beneficial area UK, USA and Israel.

Citroen Wells, Devonshire House, 1 Devonshire Street, London W1W 5DR
Tel. 020 7304 2000 **Fax** 020 7304 2020
Email cw@citroenwells.co.uk
Correspondent Gordon Smith
Trustees *Mrs S I Kreitman; N R Kreitman; R A Kreitman.*
Charity Commission no. 261195
Information available Annual report and accounts were provided by the trust.

The trust states that it supports 'projects in the field of education, culture, the environment, health and welfare'. In practice, many grants are also made to Jewish organisations.

In 2002/03 the trust had an income of £926,000 from assets worth £23.2 million. Grants were made totalling £486,000.

Grants in 2002/03

During the year the foundation made over 30 awards, ranging from large grants to small-scale gifts to community organisations.

The major grants relating to the year under review were as follows:

The foundation made a donation of £100,000 to the Durrell Wildlife Conservation Trust to help fund the construction of a new bat house at Jersey zoo. A donation of £60,000 was made to the Ashmolean Museum to provide funding of £35,000 to equip a new Indian sculpture and metalwork store in the Department of Eastern Art, and £25,000 to cover a year's salary for a Departmental Research Fellow working on a catalogue of the museum's Gandahara and related sculpture collections.

The foundation entered into a three-year commitment of £20,000 per year to Help the Aged to provide Mobile Medicare Units in India. This will help bring essential healthcare to older people in rural areas of India. Other three-year commitments entered into were to provide total funding of £51,000 to support Centrepoint in its work to provide a new internet cafe and social room at Camberwell Foyer; £22,500 pledged to the London Symphony Orchestra to fund LSO Discovery department's work in the community; and £15,000 to Sobell House Hospice Charity.

Other major grants were £50,000 to the Ancient India and Iran Trust; £30,000 to the University of Washington in respect of the Friends of the Early Buddhist Manuscript Project Fund; £25,000 to the NSPCC towards the Paedophile Special Investigation Service; and £13,700 to the Central Registry of Information on Looted Cultural Property 1933–1945, which is under the auspices of the Oxford Centre for Hebrew and Jewish Studies.

The foundation continued to support the following institutions: Kreitman School of Advanced Graduate Studies at Ben Gurion University, Tate Gallery Foundation and the Ben Gurion Graduate Fellowships.

Other beneficiaries during the year included Royal Academy Trust (£10,000), Friends of the Donmar Warehouse and the Scottish Poetry Library (£5,000 each), Almeida Theatre Company (£3,500) and the British Friends of the Israel Philharmonic Orchestra (£1,000).

Exclusions

No grants to individuals.

Applications

Grants are only given to charities of which the trustees have a personal knowledge. The trust is unable to respond to applications.

The Laidlaw Youth Project

Children and young people

£1 million (2004)
Beneficial area Scotland.

Abbey House, 83 Princes Street, Edinburgh EH2 2ER
Tel. 0131 247 6801 **Fax** 0131 247 6710
Email mmcginn@abbeyoffices.com
Website www.laidlawyouthproject.org
Correspondent Maureen McGinn, Chief Executive
Information available Information is available on the organisation's website.

Summary

This new organisation was established by Irvine Laidlaw, one of Scotland's richest men, as a vehicle for his charitable donations. It began operating in January

2004, initially as a one-year pilot project, with a view to continuing if its approach is a success. Its original focus was projects in Scotland aimed at children and young people which operate as collaborative activities, or as a befriending or mentoring project. Funding of up to £75,000 is available but average awards are closer to £30,000. It will continue to operate in 2005 with a similar level of funding but with an additional focus on education.

General

The following information is taken from the charity's website:

What is the Laidlaw Youth Project?

The Laidlaw Youth Project is aimed at translating good ideas for collaborative working into reality through encouragement and funding. These projects must be aimed at supporting vulnerable children and/or young people in Scotland.

The project has been set up through the donation of £1 million from Irvine Laidlaw (now Lord Laidlaw) and a contribution of £250,000 from the Scottish Executive, announced by Jack McConnell, First Minister, in November 2003.

Similar levels of funding should be available in 2005, but around 50% will be set aside for continuation funding of a number of existing projects to enable relationships to be developed between the funder and recipient charities.

Guidelines

Applications

All requests for funding will be expected to demonstrate need and also explain how these will deliver improved services for vulnerable children and young people in Scotland aged up to 23.

We are willing to consider the following:
- Partnership applications to improve service delivery (two or more organisations, at least one of which should be a registered charity).
- Applications with a proposal for capacity building.
- Applications from a single organisation or more than one organisation for funding of mentoring (and /or befriending) services. Where we use the term 'mentoring', this can be taken to include befriending as well.

Applicant bodies

We will accept applications from voluntary sector and public organisations. Applications from private sector bodies working in partnership with a charity or public sector body will be considered.

Where the application is for joint working, it must be accompanied by evidence of the other partners' willingness to participate in the activity for which funding is being sought. The application should also explain what role partners will play. We will expect a senior executive from each partner to be appointed as 'responsible owners' of the joint working proposal.

Organisations' operations do not need to be solely based in Scotland but they do need to deliver support to vulnerable children and young people in Scotland.

What we see as a priority

We will prioritise bids because we know that the total amount of funding sought will exceed the overall budget available. We will give priority to proposals which focus on improving outcomes for the most disadvantaged, and excluded children and young people. This will include young homeless people; cared for children and those leaving care; young carers; those at risk of offending or ex offenders; and the young unemployed. This list is not exhaustive nor is it set out in any particular order; but it is offered to demonstrate an intention to focus aid on areas of greatest need.

In addition, we will give priority to befriending and mentoring schemes which involve continuing support after major assistance/help/intervention. We are also likely to give priority to applications intended to deliver strategic improvements to befriending and mentoring services across Scotland.

Overall, we will give priority to proposals which use partnership working and/or mentoring to deliver improved continuity of care for the client groups.
- All applications need to show how their proposals will deliver improved continuity of support from end to end within the system for the individual young people involved.

What we will not fund

We will not fund applications where the bid is largely for capital (refurbishing accommodation, contributing towards buying: buildings; motor vehicles; or boats).

We wish to concentrate most of our funding in the pilot year so we are unlikely to offer funding for periods longer than 12 months (although we accept that some projects starting now will run into 2005). We may consider funding longer pieces of work but these will be the exception (and form a very small minority) because we need to review the Laidlaw Youth Project itself at the end of the first year.

We will not fund individuals. We are unable to fund posts in local authorities.

We are unlikely to fund one-off events such as seminars and conferences for staff involved in service delivery.

Because of the anticipated pressure on funds, we may also prioritise support for mentoring and befriending around schemes for the most disadvantaged young people. So mentoring of the general school age population or young people in general is unlikely to be funded.

Timescales

We are willing to offer revenue funding (for up to 12 months). We will also be prepared to offer funding for specific packages of work lasting up to 12 months. Because we cannot be clear about the future direction of the Laidlaw Project at this point (and are unable to commit for longer periods than 12 months), applications will need clearly to demonstrate an exit strategy for the end of funding.

Funding limits

We had over £1 million to spend in 2004. In order to be able to fund a range of proposals, we have set an upper limit of £75,000 for any single piece of work or scheme. There is no lower limit. However, we expect the average award to be around £25,000 (plus an additional sum to pay for evaluation). That could be the sole funding or could be a contribution towards a piece of work costing more than that. We will not require match funding as a condition of funding but we will be interested to hear about other possible funders.

We will also limit the funding of any single organisation to £75,000: for example, if a charity submits a series of proposals, then we would provide no more than £75,000 of support in total. The same may apply to a charity which is involved in a number of partnership bids, even if it is not the lead partner in every one; in such circumstances, we will examine each case on its merits, as it is not our intention to discourage joint working.

Coverage

We are willing to fund organisations working in any part of Scotland. We expect the client groups to be children and young people in Scotland. We are willing to support local organisations as well as national ones. Where pieces of work have a local focus (e.g. clients are drawn from, or activities based in, a disadvantaged neighbourhood), we will be interested to hear whether there might be any positive outcomes for the wider community, as well as the young clients.

Evaluation of support

We will expect to see evidence that applicants have considered not only how improved outcomes will be achieved but also how they will be measured. We will set aside financial support to cover the costs of evaluation. Evaluation costs can be included in budgets for applications. That might be carried out externally, when appropriate; for example, for some of the largest pieces of work. We expect to agree evaluation arrangements with applicants as a condition of funding. However, we are likely to ask for some surveying of clients as part of all final evaluation packages.

Other issues

As part of our objective is to learn about what works, we expect to have some contact with the activities we fund throughout the year. This will not lead to onerous demands on bodies involved. But it may involve some visits and/or meetings with lead contacts and, where possible and appropriate, some clients.

Reporting arrangements – we may require some interim reports on larger pieces of work. We expect to agree reporting and contact arrangements as a condition of funding.

Grants in 2004

The following are examples of projects supported during the year taken from Laidlaw's website, which does not include the amount given to each project:

Befriending and mentoring projects

- **Aberdeen Foyer: Supported Move-On Project**
  Aberdeen Foyer provides supported accommodation to 70 disadvantaged 16–25 year olds in Aberdeen/Aberdeenshire. While staying in the Foyer, support is provided through the individual action planning process to enable young people to move on to independent living.
  In addition the Foyer Move-On initiative provides a mentoring/befriending service to help those young people with the practicalities of independent living such as moving into a new home, establishing social networks and encouraging them to continue with employment/training. The befrienders are mainly volunteers although there are two members of staff working on this project – one in Aberdeen and one in North Aberdeenshire. The Laidlaw Youth Project has played a large part in funding this service whose aim is to help 25–30 young people per year in transition.

- **Crossroads Young Carer's Project, Sutherland**
  This is a local charity, which offers support to children with caring responsibilities. Many clients are referrals from social work. The Project uses outreach workers to travel to some of the young carers, to take them for breaks out of the caring situation, to meet with their peers and others involved in the project, to have fun, and to feel more part of the project.
  The workers are providing a supportive framework, developing existing good

practice between agencies, providing a range of support to the young carers and empowering them to realise their full potential, by giving them the same opportunities as their peers.

Funds from Laidlaw Youth Project are being used to allow this scheme to make more effective use of existing sessional and outreach workers to befriend and offer a more reliable service to the children who have caring responsibilities.

- **LINK ± East Fife Mental Health Adolescent Befriending Project**
  LINK – the East Fife Mental Health Adult Befriending Project launched the Adolescent Project in January 2003. The project works with 12–18 year olds with mental health issues in East Fife who have a Key Worker from Playfield House, Stratheden. Playfield receive on average 35 new referrals a month.
  The young people currently in the project have a variety of mental health issues, including; - suicide attempts, self-harm, eating disorders, Aspergers, ADHD, depression, Autism etc. These are often combined with other problems in their lives, such as alcohol, drugs, sexual abuse, school refusal, dyslexia, bullying, family breakdown and pregnancy.
  Laidlaw Youth Project funding is providing core support for six months. This will enable LINK to consolidate existing services and expanding into the Levenmouth area, as this has been identified as an area of high need.

Other partnership projects

- **Citylife, Edinburgh**
  This pilot project is for teenage mums who are no longer in education, are unemployed and live in the Wester Hailes and Sighthill areas of Edinburgh. These are areas of social and economic deprivation with teenage pregnancies in the Wester Hailes area four times the city average. Citylife is aware of the challenges and difficulties facing many teenage mums and is developing this project to provide support and befriending. The project will consist of group sessions twice a week.
  One session will be a mums and baby/toddler group where mums can meet together, interact and play with their children plus take part in some practical workshops, e.g. infant massage, story telling. Some workshops will be reinforced with outings to encourage outdoor activities. Other sessions will take the form of parenting courses and specialist workshops for teenage mums, covering topics such as children's health, child development, nutrition, healthy eating, benefits, and budgeting.
  One Parent Families Scotland, local community dieticians and other agencies

will facilitate the specialist workshops and resources while Citylife staff will co-ordinate activities and provide ongoing friendship and support to help the mums with practical issues.

- **Hope To Oban (H2O) with Oban Youth Café; Atlantis Leisure; and Stramash:`Detached Youth Worker pilot.'**
  Oban faces problems of remoteness and unemployment. As jobs for school leavers diminish, along with opportunities to become self reliant, an increasing number of young people are on the street and in danger of becoming 'at risk'.
  This project funding will increase the contact between the existing youth workers of H2O and the Oban Youth Café with the young people in and around the Oban Youth Café and to develop and extend further mentoring and guidance. It will allow the Youth Café to open for longer periods of time which will improve the deliverance of mentoring and guidance to the target group. This part of the project is jointly co-ordinated by Oban Youth Café and H2O
  The rest of the funding is for a new pilot initiative. Currently, many young people at risk are unable to access sport activities in the town although they do gather outside the buildings. A youth worker on the street will work with this group to assist them in accessing sport and other services that are available. The worker will also advise Atlantis Leisure, a community enterprise, on how to tailor its services to meet the needs of young people who are at risk. This part of the project will be co-ordinated by H2O who will also mentor and train the person appointed.

- **The Tullochan Trust with Haldane Regeneration Strategy Group (HRSG): Early Intervention Employability Mentoring Project**
  The Tullochan Trust has operated since 1998 in West Dunbartonshire but has worked intensively in Haldane, a recognised area of multiple deprivation, since 2001.
  They are providing a mentoring and support service for 56 young people aged between 16 and 20 years of age who are living 'chaotic' lifestyles. The project involves the use of Outdoor Education – residentials and single days, specialised workshops, sessions led by partner organisations and Community Action. The intensity of support varies depending on the needs and ability of the individual, this will range from weekly through to monthly support. The young people have regular assessment meetings with mentors – these meeting are used to work on basic skills like communication and confidence building. The regularity of the meetings again, will range from

weekly to monthly, as need determines. The pilot project will initially run for 1 year and continue if the tracking and evaluation process indicates the project has had a positive effect on the young people's lives.

At the time of writing (February 2005) the project was not accepting formal applications, but was welcoming informal discussions about potential projects it might be interested in. Contact the project directly for up-to-date information on its plans for continuation and future funding programmes

Exclusions

See above. No grants to individuals or capital projects.

Applications

In writing to the correspondent, although at the time of writing formal applications were not being accepted. Informal discussions about potential future projects were, however, being welcomed: 'We will be pleased to hear from bodies that have spotted opportunities for improving the way that services and support are delivered'.

grants are for amounts between £1,000 and £5,000, and are generally made to meet small capital requirements. There are modest regular annual payments to national charities, large and small, as well as to local causes both in the UK and overseas.

General

The annual report for 2002/03 has a good description of the trust's activities during the year:

The gross income of the charity was £1,168,000. Charitable donations of £1,037,000 were made [during the year].

The trust's principle activity is its grant-making programme. There has been no change in the trustees' grant-making priorities over the course of the year which continue to be to support a wide range of charities working to relieve poverty in its broadest sense both in the UK and overseas.

As indicated in previous reports, the trustees have been making a conscious effort to match charitable giving as closely as possible with income and it is therefore pleasing to report that this year charitable giving rose by £86,000 or 9%, amounting to 88.7% of total income compared to 73.7% the previous year. 315 grants, ranging in size

from £150 to £60,000, make up the total of £1,037,000.

In the UK grant recipients include organisations working with children, young people and the elderly, with the homeless, those with physical, mental or learning disabilities, while overseas there is a preference for supporting capacity building projects which will help to produce long-term solutions to the problems faced by countries in the developing world. The 25 grants of £10,000 and above were as shown in the table below.

In addition a grant of £60,000 was made to the Reculver Trust, which now owns the property occupied by the Beatrice Laing Trust and the other Laing Family Trusts administered along side it, and Echoes of Service received a total of £28,000 in four tranches towards ite evangelical missionary work.

The grants listed above totalled £418,000 (£290,000 in 2002), accounting for 40.3% (30.5%) of total charitable giving. Despite the increase in the number of larger grants awarded and in the percentage of the total charitable expenditure which they represent, the trustees continue to make a number of relatively modest annual grants towards the core funding of a selection of national organisations working in the priority areas mentioned above and remain committed to

The Beatrice Laing Trust

Relief of poverty and distress

£1 million (2002/03)

Beneficial area UK and overseas.

33 Bunns Lane, Mill Hill, London NW7 2DX

Tel. 020 8238 8890 **Fax** 020 8238 8897

Correspondent Miss Elizabeth Harley

Trustees Sir Maurice Laing; Sir Martin Laing; David E Laing; Christopher M Laing; John H Laing; Charles Laing; Paula Blacker.

Charity Commission no. 211884

Information available Good annual report and accounts.

Information available See the entry on the Laing Family Foundations for the work of the group as a whole.

Summary

This Laing trust concentrates particularly on small grants for the relief of poverty and distress. Most of the more than 350

THE BEATRICE LAING TRUST
25 grants of £10,000 and above

Purley Park Trust	£20,000	towards first phase of redevelopment of a residential home for adults with learning difficulties in Reading
SENSE International	£20,000	1st of 3 grants towards development of work in Romania
The Grange Centre – Leatherhead	£20,000	towards conversion of ambulance garage into new flats for disabled people
National Centre for Young People with Epilepsy	£20,000	towards multi-sensory room for Jubilee House
Winged Fellowship Trust	£20,000	towards redevelopment of Sandpipers, a holiday centre for disabled people in Southport
Treloar Trust	£19,000	towards the cost of equipping a flat within the new Independent Living Accomodation Unit
Africa Now	£15,000	2nd of 3 grants towards Land and Water Management Programme in western Kenya
British Red Cross Society	£15,000	final tranche of £50,000 grant to Southern Africa Regional Water & Sanitation Programme
Friends of Bedford Child Development Centre	£15,000	towards building extension
Isabel Hospice – Welwyn Garden City	£15,000	1st of 3 grants towards salary of Benefits Advisor
NSPCC	£15,000	final tranche of £50,000 grant towards development of Mansfield Special Investigation Service
Book Aid International	£13,000	towards Somaliland programme
Voluntary Service Overseas	£13,000	last of 4 grants towards a programme addressing issues of disability and disadvantage in Kenya
Boys and Girls Welfare Society	£10,000	towards phase 2 of building development programme at Bridge College for disabled young people in Stockport
David Gresham House – Abbeyfield North Downs Extra Care	£10,000	towards extention of David Gresham House in Surrey
E C Roberts Centre	£10,000	towards purchase and refurbishment of premises for provision of family support services in Portsmouth
International Service	£10,000	1st of 3 grants towards Women's Income Generation Project in Burkina Faso
King Edward's School Witley Education Trust	£10,000	to Bursary Fund
MERLIN (Medical Emergency Relief International)	£10,000	2nd of 3 grants towards strengthening the administrative base in the UK
NACRO	£10,000	1st of 2 further grants towards Education & Training Awards Scheme
Oxfam	£10,000	1st of 3 grants to 'You Are Here' programme
Resources for Autism	£10,000	towards fitting out of new resource centre for people with autism, their families and carers in Finchley
Riders for Health	£10,000	2nd of 3 grants towards cost of employing a fundraiser
The Greenbank Project	£10,000	towards refurbishment of education and training base to support disabled people on Merseyside

their programme of support for small local organisations working to relieve poverty in their own communities. These grants are usually made to meet capital rather then revenue requirements and rarely amount to more than a few hundred pounds; nevertheless, we are often told that they have made a significant difference, not simply in terms of their monetary value but also in the encouragement which they offer to local people. The trustees seek to ensure that the grants cover a broad geographical area, although the greater proportion of applications come from London and the south-east. As ever the total number of grants made represents only a very small percentage of the number of appeals received and in an effort to attract more focused applications the trustees are considering launching a website next year.

Management and administration costs amounted to £64,000, a rise of £12,000 (22.5%) on the previous year. This represented 5.5% of the total income. It should be noted that no attempt has been made to allocate any management or administrative costs to support costs, although it is likely that the vast proportion of these costs are actually incurred in the course of assessing applications etc.

Grants in 2001/02 were categorised as follows:

	No.	Amount
Health and medicine	133	£397,000
Social welfare	121	£265,000
Overseas aid	34	£152,000
Child and youth	35	£92,000
Religion	17	£47,000

This list shows a substantial reduction in the proportion of grants for child and youth causes.

The smaller grants are widely spread. The following are a random selection: Home Start Bassetlaw (£2,000); Youth Scotland (£1,250); Dial Swansea (£500); Vision Aid (£5,000); Spinal Injuries Association (£1,250); Action Aid (£1,750); Woodcroft Evangelical Church (£1,000); North Bristol Advice Centre (£2,000); Contact the Elderly (£1,000); and Shelter (£5,000).

Exclusions

No grants to individuals; no travel grants; no educational grants.

Applications

One application only is needed to apply to this or the Kirby Laing Foundation, Maurice Laing Foundation or Maurice and Hilda Laing Charitable Trust. Multiple applications will still only elicit a single reply; even then applicants are asked to accept non-response as a negative reply on behalf of all these trusts, unless a stamped addressed envelope is enclosed. Applications are considered monthly.

These trusts make strenuous efforts to keep their overhead costs to a minimum. As they also make a very large number of grants each year, in proportion to their income the staff must rely almost entirely on the written applications submitted in selecting appeals to go forward to the trustees. Each application should contain all the information needed to allow such a decision to be reached, in as short and straightforward a way as possible. Specifically, each application should say:

- what the money is for;
- how much is needed;
- how much has already been found;
- where the rest is to come from.

Unless there is reasonable assurance on the last point the grant is unlikely to be recommended.

The Kirby Laing Foundation

Health, welfare, Christian religion, general

£1.4 million (2003)

Beneficial area Unrestricted.

33 Bunns Lane, Mill Hill, London NW7 2DX

Tel. 020 8238 8890 **Fax** 020 8238 8897
Correspondent Miss Elizabeth Harley
Trustees *Sir Kirby Laing; Lady Isobel Laing; David E Laing; Simon Webley.*
Charity Commission no. 264299
Information available Report and accounts with analysed grants list showing all grants of £5,000 and above. The report explains the largest grants.

Information available See the entry on the Laing Family Foundations for the work of the group as a whole.

Summary

Along with the other Laing family trusts, this is a general grantmaker, with a Christian orientation and awarding almost all kinds of grants, few of them very large. It is unusual in the group for having a small number of artistic and cultural grants.

General

The foundation is administered alongside, and shares its 3 staff with, the Beatrice Laing Trust and the Maurice and Hilda Laing Charitable Trust. An application to any one of these three trusts, collectively known as the Laing Family Trusts, is treated as an application to all although, after the initial 'sorting' process, applications considered suitable for further consideration by the Kirby Laing Foundation follow the foundation's own administrative and decision making process.

In 2003 the foundation had assets amounting to £37 million and an income of £1.3 million. Grants totalled £1.4 million.

Grantmaking

2003 grants over £5,000 each were categorised as follows, shown below with examples of grants:

Children and youth, including education (5 grants totalling £31,000)

Beneficiaries were Youth Sport Trust (£10,000), Prince's Trust (£6,000) and Ace Centre Advisory Trust, Peper Harow Foundation and University of Oxford (£5,000 each).

Cultural and environmental (17 grants totalling £143,000)

Beneficiaries over £10,000 each were Royal Academy Trust (£25,000), Chetham's School of Music (£20,000) and British Architectural Library Trust, Chicken Shed Theatre Company, Stagecoach Youth Theatre – York and London Academy of Music and Dramatic Arts (£10,000).

Health and medicine (22 grants totalling £506,000)

The first instalments of two major new grants were released in 2003 – £200,000 to Plymouth Hospitals NHS Trust towards the building of a new library at Derriford Hospital and £100,000 towards the Royal Society of Medicine's Bicentenary Appeal.

Other grants were in the range of £5,000 and £25,000. Beneficiaries included John Grooms Association for Disabled People (£25,000), Macintyre Care and National Society for Epilepsy (£20,000 each), Royal College of Surgeons of England (£17,500), Rose Road Association, Royal Marsden Hospital Cancer Campaign and Sick Children's Trust (£10,000 each), Institute of Orthopaedics Oswestry (£7,500) and Brain Research Trust Institute of Neurology, Cancer Research

UK and Muscular Dystrophy Campaign (£5,000 each).

Overseas aid (12 grants totalling £83,000)

Beneficiaries in this category included Medical Emergency Relief International, Orbis and Tearfund (£10,000 each), Impact (£9,200), Ockenden International (£7,500), Dhaka Ahsania Mission (£6,500) and Armonia UK Trust, Farm Africa, Find Your Feet, Leprosy Mission and Village Service Trust (£5,000 each).

Religion (24 grants totalling £344,000)

There were 11 grants made of £10,000 or more. Beneficiaries were Lee Abbey Development Project – north Devon, Norwich Cathedral Trust and Sat-7 (£50,000 each), Crusaders (£30,000), St John's College – Nottingham (£25,000), British Youth for Christ (£15,000), Coventry Cathedral, Ifes Trust, Middle East Media, Riding Lights Theatre Company and Salvation Army UK HQ (£10,000 each).

Other beneficiaries included Stephen's Children (£7,500), Bible Society (£6,000), Church Mission Society (£5,500) and A Rocha Trust, Church Army, St John's Wood Church and Trans World Radio (£5,000 each).

Social welfare (9 grants totalling £78,000)

Grants included those to Toynbee Hall (£20,000), Dictune Trust, Norfolk Millennium Trust for Carers and the Brendoncare Foundation Development Trust (£10,000 each), Church Housing Trust (£7,500), Howard League for Penal Reform and Sir Oswald Stoll Foundation (£5,000 each)

121 smaller grants in the range of £50 and £4,000 were distributed by the Charities Aid Foundation and totalled £210,000.

Exclusions

No grants to individuals; no travel grants; no educational grants. The foundation rarely gives grants for the running costs of local organisations.

Applications

One application only is needed to apply to this or the Beatrice Laing Trust or Maurice and Hilda Laing Charitable Trust. Multiple applications will still only elicit a single reply. These trusts make strenuous efforts to keep their overhead costs to a minimum. As they also make a very large number of grants each year, in proportion to their income, the staff must rely almost entirely on the

written applications submitted in selecting appeals to go forward to the trustees.

Each application should contain all the information needed to allow such a decision to be reached, in as short and straightforward a way as possible. Specifically, each application should say: what the money is for; how much is needed; how much has already been found; where the rest is to come from.

Unless there is reasonable assurance on the last point the grant is unlikely to be recommended. The trust ask applicants, in the interest of reducing costs, to accept a non-response as a negative reply; if more is sought, a stamped addressed envelope must be sent with the application. Decisions are made on an ongoing basis.

Maurice and Hilda Laing Charitable Trust

Promotion of Christianity, relief of need

£1.7 million (2003)

Beneficial area UK and overseas.

33 Bunns Lane, Mill Hill, London NW7 2DX

Tel. 020 8238 8890 **Fax** 020 8238 8897

Correspondent Miss Elizabeth Harley

Trustees *Sir Maurice Laing; Lady Hilda Laing; Peter Harper; Robert M Harley; Thomas D Parr; Ewan Harper; John H Laing; Stephen Ludlow.*

Charity Commission no. 1058109

Information available Report and accounts with analysed grants list showing all grants of £5,000 and above. The report explains the largest grants.

Information available See the entry on the Laing Family Foundations for the work of the group as a whole.

Summary

The trust is mainly concerned 'with the advancement of Christian faith and values through evangelistic, education and media activities, both at home and overseas'. However the relief of need activities of Christian charities are widely supported.

General

The foundation is administered alongside the Beatrice Laing Trust and the Kirby Laing Foundation. An application to any one of these four trusts, collectively known as the Laing Family Trusts, is treated as an application to all although, after the initial 'sorting' process, applications considered suitable for further consideration by the Maurice and Hilda Laing Foundation follow the foundation's own administrative and decision making process.

Over 100 grants are made annually, ranging from a few hundred pounds to hundreds of thousands. They are probably (to judge by the precedent of other trusts in the group) of a wide range of types, from one-off awards, through multi-year projects to ongoing annual support.

In 2003 the trust had assets of almost £35 million. It had an income of £1.4 million and made grants totalling £1.7 million.

Grantmaking

Grantmaking policy has been set out as follows:

The trust has identified three main areas of giving:

Advancement of the Christian religion

Priorities are

- evangelistic activities intended to spread the gospel message, both in the UK and overseas.
- religious education, from primary school to postgraduate level.
- projects designed to promote Christian ethics/family life especially among young people.

Relief of poverty in the UK

Support for projects in this category is usually confined to those with a Christian basis to avoid overlap with the Maurice Laing Foundation, i.e. to projects where Christian faith is being manifested through practical action to help those in need. Preference will be given to projects of a practical nature rather than to research projects.

Priorities include projects run by churches or Christian organisations to help

- disadvantaged children
- the homeless
- elderly/disabled

particularly in inner city areas.

Relief of poverty overseas

Many beneficiaries will have a Christian foundation but this requirement is not exclusive in this category. Any overseas project aimed at relieving poverty is eligible but particular priorities are:

- work with children in need
- projects addressing problems such as HIV/AIDS through work to promote family values, improve women's heath and basic education etc.

Grantmaking policy and practice is well reviewed and illustrated in the annual reports. That for 2003 includes the following: The greater proportion of grants continue to be made to organisations seeking to advance Christian faith and values through evangelistic, educational and media activities at home and abroad.

Major grants in this area included the final instalment (£250,000) of a grant to the Lambeth Fund, towards evangelistic initiatives undertaken by the former Archbishop of Canterbury, £125,000 each to Church Schools Company and the Diocese of Liverpool Board of Education towards the establishment of church sponsored city academies in Lambeth and Liverpool respectively (both projects have been pledged a total of £500,000 over four years). The trustees' commitment to promoting Christian values in education can also be seen in the grant of £30,000 to the Stapleford Centre towards the development of in-service and distance learning courses for teachers.

The 2003 grants over £5,000 each were classified as follows, shown with examples of grants in each category.

Child and youth (6 grants totalling £290,000)

Aside from the two grants made to Church Schools Company and the Diocese of Liverpool Board of Education, described above, beneficiaries were Spurgeon's child care (£15,000), Children's Society and NCH Action for Children (£10,000) and The Frank Buttle Trust (£5,000)

Health and medicine (2 grants totalling £99,000)

Beneficiaries were John Grooms Association for Disabled People (£50,000) and Dorothy Kerin Trust (£49,000).

Overseas aid (22 grants totalling £191,000)

Grants in this category were in the range of £5,000 to £25,000. Beneficiaries included Topsy Foundation (£25,000), St Matthew's Children's Fund (£15,500), Y

Care International (£15,000), CAFOD (£11,000), Oxfam, Release International and UNICEF (£10,000 each), Viva Network (£7,500) and Childhope UK, Nazareth House Children's Home and Street Child Africa (£5,000 each).

Religion – church building (3 grants totalling £20,000)

Grants went to Coventry Cathedral (£10,000) and St Joseph's Church – Chasetown and St Vincent de Paul Church – Isleworth (£5,000 each).

Christain media (1 grant of £50,000)

The sole beneficiary was SAT-7.

Community outreach (6 grants totalling £65,000)

Beneficiaries were Prison Fellowship England and Wales (£25,000), Hope UK (£20,000) and Church Action on Homelessness in London, Gold Hill Baptist Church, Schools Outreach and Stepping Stones Trust (£5,000 each).

Religion – overseas (8 grants totalling £167,000)

A grant of £100,000 was made to World Faiths Development Dialogue. Other beneficiaries included Operation Mobilisation (£12,500), Anglican Church of Tanzania and Luis Palau Evangelistic Association Europe (£10,000 each), Haggai Institute (£6,000) and Evangelical Theological College – Ethiopia (£2,000).

Religion – home (22 grants totalling £610,000)

In addition to the grants to Lambeth Fund and Stableford Centre described above, the 20 other grants in this category ranged from £5,000 to £25,000. Beneficiaries included Alpha International, Bible Reading Fellowship, St John's College – Nottingham and Restoring Hope in our Church (£25,000 each), Scripture Union (£20,000), Oasis Charitable Trust, Philo Trust and Soul Survivor (£10,000 each), Fusion (£10,000), Time for God (£6,000) and Message Trust (£5,000).

Social welfare (4 grants totalling £45,000)

Beneficiaries were Shaftesbury Society (£25,000), Springboard Charitable Trust (£10,000) and Churches National Housing Coalition and Kainos Community (£5,000 each).

In addition a further 55 smaller grants of between £200 and £4,000 were distributed through the Charities Aid Foundation. These totalled £110,000. Other donations totalled £45,000.

Exclusions

No grants to groups or individuals for the purpose of education, travel, attendance at conferences or participation in overseas exchange programmes. No grants towards church restoration or repair.

Applications

The trust is administered alongside the Beatrice Laing Trust and the Kirby Laing Foundation. None of the trusts issue application forms and an application to one is seen as an application to all. In general the trusts rarely make grants towards the running costs of local organisations, which they feel have to be raised from local sources.

An application for a grant towards a specific capital project should be in the form of a short letter giving details of the project, its total cost, the amount raised and some indication of how it is to be financed.

A copy of the organisation's latest annual report and accounts, together with a stamped addressed envelope, should be enclosed. Unless a stamped addressed envelope is enclosed applicants are asked to accept non-response as a negative reply. Trustees meet quarterly to consider applications for larger grants (above £10,000). Applications for smaller amounts are considered on an ongoing basis.

The Laing Family Foundations

General

About £6.1 million (2003/04)

Beneficial area UK and overseas.

33 Bunns Lane, Mill Hill, London NW7 2DX

Tel. 020 8238 8890 **Fax** 020 8238 8897

Correspondent Miss Elizabeth Harley

Information available Excellent information available on the individual trusts.

The following trusts (except the Rufford Maurice Laing Foundation) are administered from a common office in north London and an application to one is seen as an application to all. However, they have different funding patterns and each has its own entry. They are:

- The Kirby Laing Foundation;
- The Rufford Maurice Laing Foundation;
- The Beatrice Laing Trust;
- The Maurice and Hilda Laing Charitable Trust.

There is an evangelical Christian background to the group, but collectively the grants lists cover most fields of welfare and health as well as the promotion of Christianity, at home and overseas. Support for medical research, of the scientific sort is limited, and there is no general support for the arts (though one trust has a limited interest in this field).

Over 1,000 grants a year are made. Though many of them are small, very large grants can also be made.

Most of the grants are for national organisations, big or small, with only limited support for local organisations or local branches of the larger networks.

Two of the trusts have strong specialist interests:

- advancement of Christianity: the Maurice and Hilda Laing Charitable Trust;
- small local grants for welfare and disability: the Beatrice Laing Trust.

Trustees, even those who are elderly, are much involved in the grantmaking process, and take a personal interest in many of the larger projects supported.

The trusts do not normally act collectively.

The general application requirements are set out below. These will suffice for all except specialist applications, the details for which are found in the 'applications' section of the relevant entries.

Exclusions

No grants to groups or individuals for the purpose of education, travel, attendance at conferences or participation in overseas exchange programmes.

In general the trusts rarely make grants towards the running costs of local organisations, which they feel have to be raised from within the local community.

Applications

None of the trusts issue application forms and an application to one is seen as an application to all.

An application for a grant towards a specific capital project should be in the form of a short letter giving details of the project, its total cost, the amount raised and some indication of how it is to be financed.

A copy of the organisation's latest annual report and accounts, together with a stamped addressed envelope, should be enclosed. Unless an sae is enclosed applicants are asked to accept non-response as a negative reply. Applications for small amounts are considered on an ongoing basis.

Lambeth Endowed Charities

Education, welfare

£859,000 to organisations (2003)
Beneficial area London borough of Lambeth.

127 Kennington Road, London SE11 6SF
Tel. 020 7735 1925 **Fax** 020 7735 7048
Correspondent The Director and Clerk
Trustee *14 co-optive trustees and governors, and two representative trustees and two representative governors appointed by Lambeth Borough Council. Dr C Gerada, Chair, Hayle's Charity. B R Holland, Chair, Walcot Charities.*
Charity Commission no. 206462
Information available Full accounts were provided by the trust.

The Lambeth Endowed Charities, with roots dating back to the 17th century, is an 'umbrella' title for what are now three charities: the Walcot Educational Foundation, Hayle's Charity and the Walcot Non-Educational Charity.

In 2003 just over £1 million was distributed in grants across the three charities. Of this £859,000 was given in grants to 324 organisations, with the remainder going to individuals.

The charities produce a leaflet for applicants, which includes the following information:

Who can apply?

Applications are considered from a wide range of organisations as well as from students and individuals with urgent needs. Typical applicants include schools, children and youth projects, community centres, pensioners' projects, counselling and advice centres, disability projects, medical and health projects, and employment and training schemes.

Types of grants

Voluntary-aided schools

The scheme of the Walcot Education Foundation makes special provision for the 20 voluntary-aided schools in the area of benefit. Grants towards the maintenance and insurance costs of these schools are made each year.

All Lambeth Schools

In addition, grants can be made to both voluntary-aided schools and non voluntary-aided schools as outlined:

'One-off' grants—applications for specific requirements that bring additional benefit are considered at grants meetings.

The small grants programme for schools

At the beginning of each year the trustees set aside funds for the following requirements, which may be applied for at any time and may be made in addition to a 'one-off' grant for a specific requirement.

Head's discretionary fund

To help with school uniform, personal hardship and other emergency costs to support pupils.

School journey grants

To assist with the cost of field trips and residential study breaks.

Extracurricular training

To support additional activities in schools such as music, artists-in-residence, after school sports, and home/school initiatives.

School support projects

To assist groups and projects involved with the arts, multimedia, sports and sciences to organise workshops and develop initiatives in schools.

Projects and organisations

'One-off' grants: applications for specific requirements—social or educational—are considered at grant meetings.

The small grants programme for youth and community groups

At the begnning of each year the trustees set aside funds for the folowing requirements, which may be applied for at any time and may be made in addition to a 'one off' grant for a specific requirement.

Parties/cultural celebrations

Grants can be made to groups organising parties for children, older and disabled people.

Play schemes

Grants can be made for Easter and summer play schemes.

Group holidays/outings

Grants can be made to support coach outings, day trips and holidays for people with disabilities and long-term illness, older people and families in need.

Equipment, facilities and urgent needs

There are a limited number of grants available for projects and organisations in this category.

The annual report 2003 listed all grants over £1,000 and contained the following information for each charity.

The Walcot Educational Foundation (£317,000 to organisations)

The Walcot Educational Foundation provides funds to support the education of young people aged under 30 who live in the borough of Lambeth. The term 'education' is given a wide interpretation and can include employment, recreational, social and physical training, as well as vocational training and academic studies.

The Scheme of the foundation makes special provision for voluntary-aided schools in Lambeth and grants towards the maintenance and insurance costs of these schools are made each year. Grants can also be made to other schools and educational projects in the borough.

At the beginning of each year, the governors set aside funds for recurring requirements, for which applications may be made at any time during the year. This is known as the 'Small Grants Programme'. Grants are limited but extensive, providing for school hardship funds, school journeys, school support workshops, cultural festivities and youth development activities. Grants to students and families in need also take up a significant proportion of the charity's resources.

Most grants under the Voluntary-Aided Schools heading were for Southwark Diocese and Board of Education maintenance and service agreements. Beneficiaries included: Holy Trinity C of E Primary School (four grants totalling £47,000); St Martin-in-the-Fields High School (three grants totalling £34,000); St Saviour's C of E Primary School (two grants totalling £23,000); Charles Edward Brooke School received (two grants totalling £20,000); Archbishop Michael Ramsey Technology College (two grants totalling £16,000); and Immanuel & St Andrew C of E Primary School (two grants totalling £15,000).

Beneficiaries under the 'Other schools' category included: Lambeth Education Business Partnership towards an Easter revision scheme (£15,000); Henry Cavendish Primary School PTA towards

outdoor seating and a canopy (£10,000); Granton Primary School towards dance classes (£5,000); Henry Fawcett Parent School Association towards a playship and playground improvements (£2,800); and Waldorf School of SW London towards the salary of a Eurythmy Therapist.

Beneficiaries under the 'Projects & organisations' category included: Amicus Vision towards the salary of a community development worker and the Community Zone towards running costs (£15,000 each); 198 Galley towards building/roof refurbishment, Centre for Young Musicians towards its bursary fund, High Trees Community Development Trust towards the costs of the centre's manager and Thessaly Community Project towards building costs (£10,000 each); Young Vic Company Limited towards a schools theatre production (£9,000) Lewin Pre-School towards running costs (£8,000); Christ Church North Brixton – 110 Foyer Project towards equipment and storage costs; Clapham Youth Centre towards a student worker placement and Lambeth E-Learning Foundation towards staff costs (£6,000 each); Pyramid Youth Development Project towards video/film equiment (£5,500); Fairbridge towards a youth training programme, South Island Children's Workshop towards salary costs and Trees for London towards community consultation/tree planting events (£5,000 each); Gasworks Gallery towards a gallery/artists in schools programme and Lansdowne Youth Centre towards dance group running costs (£3,000 each); Southbank Sinfonia towards instruments/equipment for school visits (£2,500); Great Lake Region Cultural Association and Women Being Concern (£2,000 each); Lynk Reach Ltd towards school poetry workshops (£1,500); and Hern Hill Harriers towards athletics programmes in schools and Thames Festival Trust towards carnival workshops for schools (£1,000 each).

The Walcot Non-Educational Charity (£23,000 to organisations)

This is a sister charity to the Walcot Educational Foundation and receives its funds directly from the foundation. The charity's aims are 'to relieve either generally or individually persons resident in the area of benefit who are in conditions of need, hardship or distress'.

The largest grants went to: Streatham Drop-in Centre towards a co-ordinator's salary (£6,000); and Age Concern towards ITC office equipment, Lambeth Carers towards office relocation costs,

Lambeth Mencap towards advocacy project running costs and Together in Notre Dame towards the salary of a community development worker (£5,000 each).

Hayle's Charity (£103,000 to organisations)

The trustees welcome applications from small local groups who may find it difficult to raise money elsewhere.

Gants were all for £5,000 or less and included those to: Action on Addiction and Home-Start – Lambeth towards volunteer training and support (£5,000 each); the British Home and Sangayi Association (£3,000 each); Broadway towards IT equipment and St Giles Trust towards Breakfast Project salary costs (£2,000 each); Adage IT Community Project towards rent, equipment and start-up costs (£1,500); and Arts Interest Group towards gallery trips for people who are disabled, London Marriage Guidance towards post-natal depression group running costs and Westminister Pastoral Foundation towards a counselling service for Lambeth residents (£1,000 each).

Exclusions

Beneficiaries must be residents of the London borough of Lambeth.

- UK charities – the Lambeth Endowed Charities do not normally make grants in response to general appeals from UK charities, especially where similar needs are being met by local projects. However, consideration may be given if you can show how its work relates specifically to Lambeth residents.
- Revenue funding – normally, the trustees will not consider revenue funding. However, occasionally they are prepared to make a large grant which will be paid in instalments over a two- or three-year period. Priority will be given to small local projects. Applicants for such funding will need to show how any balance of funds required can be raised and that alternative sources of funding can be found in the future.
- Statutory sources – no grants may be made where funds from statutory sources can be obtained.
- Debts – no grants may be made to meet the costs of debts already incurred.

Applications

All applications must be made on an application form, available on request from the office. Applicants are welcome to contact the office for further information and advice on how to apply.

The trustees meet quarterly, usually in early March, June, October and December, and applications must be received at least six weeks before the date of the relevant meeting. Please ring the office to check deadlines for applications.

Once your application has been received you will be contacted by the director or the fieldworker, who will usually arrange to visit your project to discuss your application in more detail. Successful applicants must report on how a grant has been used within 12 months.

The John and Rosemary Lancaster Charitable Foundation

Christian causes

£1.7 million (2002/03)

Beneficial area UK, with a local interest in Clitheroe.

c/o Text House, 152 Edisford Road, Clitheroe BB7 2LA

Tel. 01200 444404

Correspondent Mrs R Lancaster, Chair

Trustees Mrs R Lancaster, chair; J E Lancaster; S J Lancaster; J R Broadhurst.

Charity Commission no. 1066850

Information available Annual report and accounts on file at the Charity Commission.

General

The trust came into operation in 1997 'to promote the spreading of the Christian message'. The trust stated that it would prefer not to be included in this guide as it does not seek unsolicited requests (these being 'just a waste of time') and the annual report repeats this view, stating: 'Donations and funding are made at the absolute discretion of the trustees. However the administrative structure of the charity does not allow for the consideration of unsolicited funding.'

The bulk of its income continues to come in the form of donated (then sold)

shares in Ultraframe plc, a company of which one of the trustees is a director. In 2002/03 its income was £6.5 million. Grants of £1,000 or more were made during the year to 24 organisations totalling £1.7 million. An undisclosed number of smaller grants were also made totalling £4,000.

The largest grant, as in the previous year, was to Mission Aviation Fellowship, which received £405,000 (£1.3 million in 2001/02). Other beneficiaries of large grants in 2002/03 that received grants in the previous year include Message to Schools (£212,000), Oasis Charitable Trust (£200,000), New Generation Music and Mission (£138,000), Sparrows Interest (£92,000) and Love and Joy Ministries (£72,000). Other large grants to new beneficiaries went to Message Trust (£293,000), Festival Manchester (£150,000) and MIC (£36,000).

Other beneficiaries included Life Education Centre, Skills for Living and Cross Roads Trust (£5,000 each), Open Doors and Real Christmas (£2,000 each) and Bible Society, Mayor of Clitheroe Welfare Fund and Stoneyhurst Charity Golf (1,000 each).

The 2002/03 accounts also note the approval of two substantial donations which were yet to be paid to local projects, namely £2 million to Trinity Partnership towards the development of Clitheroe Arts Centre, and £3.5 million to fund the restoration of Clitheroe Civic Hall.

Comment

There was no response to repeated written requests for a copy of the most recent annual report and accounts, despite the legal requirement to provide these on demand.

Applications

The trust has previously stated: 'We do not consider applications made to us from organisations or people unconnected with us. All our donations are instigated because of personal associations. Unsolicited mail is, sadly, a waste of the organisation's resources.'

The Allen Lane Foundation

Unpopular causes

£580,000 (2003/04)

Beneficial area UK, and a small programme in Ireland.

90 The Mount, York YO24 1AR

Tel. 01904 613223 **Fax** 01904 613133

Email info@allenlane.org.uk

Website www.allenlane.org.uk

Correspondent Heather Swailes, Executive Secretary

Trustees *Clare Morpurgo; John Hughes; Christine Teale; Zoe Teale; Guy Dehn; Juliet Walker; Jane Walsh; Fredrica Teale.*

Charity Commission no. 248031

Information available Full guidelines and detailed annual report and accounts, all available on the foundation's website.

Summary

The foundation makes around 100 modest grants each year. They go to small organisations, in unpopular and little-supported fields, such as conflict resolution, reform of the penal system and policy and welfare work with refugee and asylum seekers.

Although no grants are given for work in the London area, and most grants go to small local initiatives, the trust does seek to fund work that has the potential of being of more than purely local significance.

About three-quarters of the applications received fall outside the foundation's clear and specific guidelines, reprinted below, and are therefore refused, although in 2003/04 the foundation reports a drop in refusals, largely due to 'getting the message across' about its policies and guidelines. About one-third of the appropriate applications result in a grant, though not necessarily for the full amount requested.

Background

The Allen Lane Foundation is a grant-making trust set up in 1966 by the late Sir Allen Lane, founder of Penguin Books, to support general charitable causes. The foundation has no connection now with the publishing company, but four of the trustees are members of the founder's family. Its endowment was valued at nearly £14.7 million at the end of March 2004 and the trustees awarded grants totalling £500,720 in the UK and €32,725 in the

Republic of Ireland in the financial year 2003/04. The foundation is a member of the Association of Charitable Foundations.

The trustees of the Allen Lane Foundation wish to fund the kind of work where it can make a lasting difference to people's lives, rather than alleviating a problem or disadvantage temporarily. At the same time we particularly wish to fund work which either focuses on unpopular beneficiary groups, or provides services which are open to everyone.

As the foundation's resources are modest, we generally fund smaller organisations where our grants can have more impact. We currently make grants in the UK and, for a limited programme concerned with penal reform, in the Republic of Ireland.

Guidelines for applicants

If you are not sure whether your work fits with our priorities you can always ring the foundation's office for advice.

Where do grants go?

The foundation makes grants for work all over the United Kingdom but not overseas. The foundation gives priority to work outside London and this means that grants are not made for work which only takes place within Greater London.

The foundation tries to target about 80% of its total giving at work that is of more than local significance (for example, covering a city, county, region or the whole country) and about 20% on local projects. Apart from a small programme in the Republic of Ireland, the foundation does not make any grants overseas. The programme in the Republic of Ireland is only for work in prisons, on penal reform or with offenders or ex-offenders.

What kind of work does the foundation fund?

The broad areas of work which are priorities for the foundation include:
- the provision of advice, information and advocacy (generalist services, or targeted at one or more of the priority groups listed below)
- community development
- neighbourhood mediation, conflict resolution and alternatives to violence
- research and education aimed at changing public attitudes or policy
- social welfare aimed at making a long-term difference and empowering users.

The size of grants (which are modest) are particularly appropriate for start-up funding of smaller projects, grants for equipment, training for staff or volunteers, small evaluations or one-off projects. But these are only given as examples – not an exhaustive list.

Grants can be made for project costs, or core costs. As the grants are small it is rare for an application for salaries to be appropriate, but a contribution to other core costs may be suitable. While recognising that on-going, tried and tested projects continue to need support, the foundation is always interested in unusual, imaginative or innovative projects.

Who does the foundation wish to benefit from the work it funds?

The foundation makes grants to organisations whose work it believes to be unpopular in UK society today.

Priority groups include:
- refugees and asylum-seekers*
- people from black and ethnic minority communities
- those experiencing mental health problems
- those experiencing violence or abuse
- offenders and ex-offenders
- gay, lesbian or bi-sexual people
- travellers
- older people.

(* The foundation does not have the resources to assess or monitor grants to local refugee community groups and applications from local groups will not normally be eligible. Priority will be given to groups working at a national or regional level.)

The foundation makes grants for:
- work where the users come from one or more of these groups or
- work which is open to everyone.

The foundation almost never makes grants for work with specific beneficiary groups who are not among its priorities. If you think your clients or users are an unpopular group but they are not mentioned above, you can always ring the Executive Secretary for clarification. But if your work helps only a particular group that is not among our priorities an application is very unlikely to be successful.

What size?

For local projects grants are normally between £250 and £3,000.

For projects of more than local significance grants are normally between £2,000 and £10,000.

Grants are usually single payments but may sometimes be for up to three consecutive years. Grants over several years will not normally exceed £5,000 in total for local work or £15,000 in total for work on a wider scale.

The foundation occasionally makes single grants of as much as £10,000 but only for work which has more than local significance.

Who can apply?

- registered charities
- other organisations which are not charities but which seek funding for a charitable project.

The foundation wishes to make grants which will make a significant impact and, as the grants are relatively small, priority is given to organisations of a modest size. The foundation rarely makes grants to:
- local organisations with an income of more than about £100,000
- organisations working on a more than local scale with an income of more than £250,000 per annum.

To be eligible you should be able to answer yes to the following questions. If the answer to any of these questions is no you should not consider making an application.

For all applicants:
- does your work take place in the UK or the Republic of Ireland?
- does your work take place outside Greater London?
- if your work relates to a local area – for example a town, village or local community, was your income last year less than £100,000?
- if your work covers a wider area – a county, region or nation, was your income last year less than £250,000?
- are you confident that your application is not subject to any of the exclusions listed?

Additionally, for applicants to the Ireland Programme only:
- does your work relate to prisons or penal reform or offenders or ex-offenders?

The Ireland Programme

The foundation has a small funding programme in Ireland which focuses on penal reform and work with offenders and ex-offenders. Trustees expect to spend approximately £40,000 per annum in this programme. Applications should be made in the same way as applications for the UK programme, except that the budget should be presented in euro.

Annual report 2003/04

The annual report is the most detailed for any trust of this size and is available in full on the website. Only a few introductory paragraphs are reprinted here.

Activities

During the year we received 755 applications and agreed 126 new grants totalling £501,720 in the UK and €32,725 in the Republic of Ireland *[the actual total grant figure for the year listed in the financial summary is around £580,000 after* adjustments - Ed.]. A list of all grants, together with a detailed analysis can be found in the Annual Review. From these figures it can be seen that the number of applications received far exceeds the foundation's resources. But many of the applications did not match the foundation's criteria and over 80% of the applications received were rejected. The foundation continues to publicise its policy and priorities as widely as possible, to reduce the number of inappropriate applications, and to this end some 430 copies of the guidelines were distributed by post or email during the year. We hope to save both the applicants' time, and our own, by making our priorities clear. It seems that having the guidelines available on the website has begun to have an impact. We are pleased that we continue to receive many applications for interesting and valuable work. The foundation would have no reason to exist if there were not good organisations ready to use our resources to further their work.

Charlotte Fraser legacy

Following the receipt of this legacy we agreed that it would be spent on a relatively small number of grants which would be larger than the foundation normally makes and that we would seek out a handful of exceptional recipients, rather than simply responding to applications in the foundation's usual way. Expenditure of the original legacy (of £126,795) continued this year with three grants totalling £65,000 which were made to the Campaign for Freedom of Information, Ruhama and one individual [see below]

Grants in 2003/04

Everyone: open to all – 26 grants totalling £112,000

Beneficiaries in this general category included: Centre for Corporate Accountability for work on a Safety and Conviction database (£12,000 over three years); Food Ethics Council for an agri-food research project (£10,000); Greenhouse – Bangor towards core costs of the community resource centre (£7,000 over two years); Speakeasy Advice Centre – Cardiff towards the core costs of providing free legal advice (£6,000 over three years); South & West Lancashire Food Bank towards core costs (£5,000 over two years); West Midlands Rural Support Network for the cost of producing promotional leaflets and Builth Wells Community Support for core costs (£3,000 each); Cleveland Housing Advice Centre for the core costs of welfare benefits advice work (£2,000); and West Plymouth Credit Union for publicity costs (£1,300).

People experiencing violence or abuse – 21 grants totalling £97,000

Beneficiaries included: Voice UK for core costs supporting adults with learning disabilities who have been abused (£15,000 over three years); Conflict Trauma Resource Centre – Belfast towards core costs of this organisation operating throughout Northern Ireland (£10,000 over two years); Lighthouse – Hull towards outreach work with women working in prostitution (£5,000 over two years); Survivors UK towards the core costs of this organisation working with men who have been sexually abused (£5,000); Blaenau Gwent Domestic Abuse Service towards core costs (£3,000 over two years); Life Centre – Chichester for the core costs of working with survivors of rape and sexual abuse (£2,000); and Women's Aid – Radnorshire towards the costs of a computer and a printer (£1,500).

Offenders and ex-offenders – 7 and 2 grants totalling £36,000 and €33,000 respectively

Beneficiaries included: Bedford Row Family Project – Limerick for an inter-agency collaboration project for prisoners and their families (€18,000); Irish Penal Reform Trust towards the organisation's communications strategy (€15,000); Restorative Justice Consortium towards employing an administrator (£12,000 over two years); HOPE towards core costs of work with prisoners and their families (£5,000); PEOPLE towards pre-release courses for life sentence prisoners in Somerset (£4,000); and Prison Phoenix Trust to extend yoga lessons and practice to prisons in Ireland (£2,000).

Older people – 15 grants totalling £61,000

Beneficiaries included: Shropshire Reminiscence for a salary and newsletter costs (£10,000 over three years); Clydebank Asbestos Group towards core costs (£5,000); Ainsdale Community Care Programme for care costs for the programme in Southport (£4,000 over two years); Ely & District Volunteering Centre for the Helping Hands Gardening and Decorating Project (£3,000 over two years); Young at Heart towards a healthy eating initiative for older people in Balerno, Edinburgh (£3,000); Alzheimer's Society Derwentshire Branch for core costs (£2,000).

People with mental health problems – 19 grants totalling £59,000

Beneficiaries included: Volunteers Plus to help mental health service users become volunteers (£6,000); Mind Crawley and Horsham for core costs (£5,000 over two years); Manic Depression Fellowship Scotland for a self-management course (£5,000); Mental Health Action Group – Sheffield towards core costs (£3,000 over two years); Act First to provide mental health awareness training direct from service users to agencies in the North West (£3,000); Make a Life to set up a support and activity group for mental health services users in Newton Abbot (£2,000); Time Out for the running costs of a lunch club for a user-led mental health group in Hungerford (£1,000 over two years); and Reflections – South Denbighshire towards core costs (£750).

Black & minority ethnic communities – 12 grants totalling £44,500

Beneficiaries included: Arid Lands & Sustainable Communities Trust for the dissemination of the Learning by Growing Project (£6,000); Monitoring Group towards the cost of working to support victims of rural racial harassment (£5,000); Fatima Women's Association for start-up and running costs of this ethnic minority women's organisation in Oldham (£4,000 over two years); Millen Advice Point towards employing an administrator in Swindon (£2,000); and Sathi Asian Men's Group towards enabling the group to extend its opening times for men in Bolton with mental health problems (£1,500 over two years).

Refugees and asylum seekers – 14 grants totalling £44,000

Beneficiaries included: Student Action for Refugees for core costs (£6,000 over three years); Yorkshire & Humberside Refugee Support Centre for start-up costs of a county-wide mental health support for refugee/asylum seekers (£6,000); Slough Refugee Support towards the costs of an administrator's post (£4,000 over two years); Derby Refugee Advice Centre towards core costs (£3,000); National Coalition of Anti-Deportation Campaigns for improving their website design (£2,500); Liverpool Great Lakes Community Association towards the costs of training events (£2,000); and Citizens Advice Gosport for training a volunteer to work at Haslar Removal Centre (£1,300).

Travellers – 4 grants totalling £26,500

Beneficiaries were: Irish Traveller Movement in Britain towards core costs (£12,000 over three years); Cardiff Gypsy & Traveller Project towards training (£6,000 over two years); Travellers Aid Trust for conference costs and publicity (£4,500); and Leeds Gypsy & Traveller Exchange for core costs (£4,000 over two years).

Gay, lesbian and bi-sexual people – 5 grants totalling £20,500

Beneficiaries were: Safra Project for research and to provide information on the treatment of lesbian, gay, bisexual and transgender people in Muslim countries (£10,000); Pink Parents UK towards volunteer training, co-ordinator costs and running costs (£3,500); Colchester Gay Switchboard for a pilot scheme to combine switchboards in East Anglia and Gay & Lesbian Friend Helpline – Gloucestershire towards the cost of work reaching older gay and lesbian people (£3,000 each); and Basildon and Thurrock Friend for training costs and core costs involved in running the Lesbian, Gay and Bisexual Helpline (£1,000).

Charlotte Fraser Legacy

Three grants were made from this legacy in the course of the year. Trustees wished to use the funds to make larger grants than the foundation is usually able to do. The beneficiaries were:

Ruhama – £30,000

This women's organisation in Dublin works primarily with women in prostitution. However, it has recently found an increasing need to address the problem of human trafficking, particularly of young women brought to Ireland and forced to work in prostitution. As well as working directly with women in this situation, Ruhama has also been working to raise awareness of the problem among the public, and other agencies such as the Garda. The grant contributed to the costs of this work.

Campaign for Freedom of Information – £25,000

This grant contributed to the cost of research carried out by the Campaign for example looking at how Freedom of Information legislation works in practice in other countries and the lessons which can be learnt from their experience.

Marian Partington – £10,000

This grant enabled Marian Partington to continue preparing and writing a book exploring themes of restorative justice, forgiveness and salvaging the sacred. The book arises from her experience of the murder of her sister Lucy Partington by Frederick West.

Comment

Though relatively small, this foundation is of exceptional interest in that its grants reach a group of charities whose names are otherwise seldom seen by these editors when working through the grants lists of other trusts.

Exclusions

The foundation does not currently make grants for:

- academic research;
- addiction, alcohol or drug abuse;
- animal welfare or animal rights;
- arts or cultural or language projects or festivals;
- work with children and young people;
- disability issues;
- endowments or contributions to other grant-making bodies;
- holidays or holiday playschemes, sports and recreation;
- housing and homelessness;
- individuals;
- large appeals from charities which enjoy widespread public support;
- medical care, hospices and medical research;
- museums or galleries;
- overseas travel;
- private and/or mainstream education;
- promotion of sectarian religion;
- publications;
- purchase costs of property, building or refurbishment;
- restoration or conservation of historic buildings or sites;
- vehicle purchase;
- work which the trustees believe is rightly the responsibility of the state;
- work outside the United Kingdom;
- work which will already have taken place before a grant is agreed;
- work by local organisations with an income of more than £100,000 per annum or those working over a wider area with an income of more than £250,000.

Conflicts of Interest

The foundation will not normally make grants to organisations which receive funding (directly or indirectly) from commercial sources where conflicts of interest for the organisation and its work are likely to arise.

Applications

Applications can be made at any time and are processed throughout the year.

Applicants should plan well ahead to allow sufficient time for applications to be assessed. If we are unable to help we will usually be able to give you a decision within a few weeks, but grants are allocated at meetings of the trustees which are held three times a year so it may be as long as four months before a final, positive decision is made.

We do not make grants retrospectively – for work, such as a particular event, which will have happened before a decision is made by trustees.

We announce closing dates for each trustees' meeting on our website and in correspondence. These simply indicate that an application received after that date may be too late to be assessed for that meeting (although if it were good enough, it might be taken to the next trustees' meeting after that). Applicants are urged not to wait until the last minute before a closing date to apply.

There is no formal application form but when sending in an application we ask you to complete the registration form at the end of this guide and return it with your application.

An application should be no more than 4 sides of A4 but the project budget may be on extra pages. It should be accompanied by your last Annual Report and Accounts if you produce such documents and the budget for the whole organisation (if this is different from the project budget) for the current year.

The application should answer the following questions:

- What are the aims of your organisation as a whole?
- How do you try to achieve these aims?
- How many paid staff or volunteers work for your organisation?
- Why is yours an unpopular cause or beneficiary group?
- What do you want our grant to help you do and how will you do it?
- What difference would a grant make to your work?
- How much will the work cost?
- Are you asking the foundation to meet the whole cost?
- What other sources of funding are you approaching?
- How will you know if the work has been successful?
- How will the work, and the way it is done, promote equal opportunities? If you do not think equal opportunities are relevant to your work please say why.

If further information is needed this will be requested by the Executive Secretary and a visit may be arranged when the application can be discussed in more detail. All applications should be made to the Executive Secretary, at the foundation's office, and not sent to individual trustees. If you have any queries about making an application you are encouraged to phone the Executive Secretary for clarification.

The LankellyChase Foundation

Social welfare, community development, arts, heritage, penal affairs, mental health

Around £5 million

Beneficial area UK.

2 The Court, High Street, Harwell, Didcot, Oxfordshire OX11 0ED

Tel. 01235 820044 **Fax** 01235 820044

Website www.lankellychase.org.uk

Correspondent Peter Kilgarriff

Trustees *Shirley Turner, chair; Ann Stannard; Dodie Carter; Leo Fraser-Mackenzie; Gordon Halcrow; Victoria Hoskins; Shameem Malooq; Elizabeth Moore; Simon Raybould; Sandy Robertson; Abdul Shakoor; Nicholas Tatman.*

Charity Commission no. 1107583

Information available Guidelines were provided by the foundation.

This charity, an amalgamation of The Chase Charity and the Lankelly Foundation was registered with the Charity Commission in January 2005. The guidelines are largely reprinted below.

Background

The Chase Charity and the Lankelly Foundation were established through the generosity of two separate entrepreneurs who successively developed a complex of property companies which operated in and around London. The Chase Charity was founded in 1962 and the Lankelly Foundation six years later. Both of the founders in turn asked Calton Younger to administer their trusts, a duty which he performed with compassion and creativity for 27 years.

During this time the policies and practices of both trusts developed as society changed but from the early days, with the encouragement of the founders, both groups of trustees reached out to the most isolated in our society. As time went by the two trusts adopted similar grant-making policies, whilst recognising that their differences of scale and emphasis were positive qualities; they reflected, particularly in the case of the Chase Charity, the founders' love of England's heritage and the arts, and these differences caught the attention of different needy groups, enabling the trusts to be more effective together than if they operated separately.

After so many years of working together, jointly employing the staff team, the two trusts have now resolved that they should take the next natural step and amalgamate to form the LankellyChase foundation. The two constituent parts bring with them all their history and characteristics into the new unified Foundation and the trustees welcome the future opportunities this brings. They recognise the many challenges which face our society and look forward to being able to respond to some of them, bringing a new clarity and focus to the care and staff personal involvement which have marked their work in the past.

Guidelines

What we support

We support work that has a recognisable charitable purpose.

We intend to concentrate upon smaller charities, many of whom will have only a local or regional remit. We will consider applications from large national charities but support will be rare and limited.

We look for user involvement as well as the proper use and support of volunteers and you will have to provide evidence of sound management and a commitment to equal opportunities.

We recognize that the black voluntary sector and minority ethnic groups have particular needs and we welcome applications from such organisations working within our priority areas.

We want our grants to be effective, to achieve something which otherwise would not happen, or to sustain something which otherwise might fail.

We do not make grants to replace funds that have been withdrawn from statutory sources, or consider applications to replace time expired grants from the Big Lottery or any National Lottery Board.

Where we work

Unless otherwise stated in the individual programme sections, we do not generally support organisations or work based in London or Northern Ireland.

Throughout the rest of the UK we aim to treat different geographical areas fairly and welcome applications from groups who feel isolated by their location.

For the next four years our main programmes are:

- Arts
- Breaking the cycle
- Developing communities
- Free and quiet minds
- Heritage
- Offenders and society.

In addition, the trustees have decided to develop a limited programme to support organisations working with refugees and asylum seekers.

The arts

The foundation recognises and values the contribution made by the arts to the mental and physical health of the nation. The trustees wish to encourage access to the arts, in particular amongst those who historically have been least able to participate, such as those in rural areas or with special needs. They also wish to support those who aim to realise their artistic ability.

The trustees have three distinct programmes of work and the information set out below is guided by the foundation's determination to promote access for those who seek it and personal excellence for those who work for it; also, in the light of the many problems communities face (referred to under our Developing Communities programme), the trustees wish to encourage those of different generations to come together through participation in and enjoyment of the arts.

Arts and special needs

Applications are encouraged from charities promoting arts activities for people with special needs.

Dance

Charities delivering dance to people of any age, ability or limiting circumstance; for instance, requests from charities offering dance in prisons are equally as welcome as from those offering it to the elderly or those in rural areas.

Transgenerational work with communities

The foundation will consider requests which promote activities bringing together all ages in a community, whether urban or rural; an example of this would be a community play.

Conditions:

Preference will be given to projects working with those in greatest financial, physical or mental need. The foundation welcomes applications from black and minority ethnic groups and from charities working with refugees and asylum seekers. The foundation looks favourably on work in rural areas; the trustees will accept applications for revenue or capital needs; the limit to the latter being £20,000, with the overall appeal amounting to no more than £0.5m.

The pursuit of excellence

The foundation runs two award schemes, one for music and the other for glass. Music: The Kirckman Concert Society Ltd started in 1963 and is principally funded by the foundation. Its aim is to give concert platform experience to promising young musicians. The scheme is not open to general application. Glass: The foundation funds an annual award through Central Saint Martins College of Art and Design. This is open to students taking the Postgraduate course in Fine Art and Glass at the College.

Breaking the cycle

We wish to support projects working to break cycles of abuse, violence, poverty and exclusion through work with families, children and/or young people.

Families and domestic abuse

We will consider projects that aim to break cycles of abuse and violence in families marginalised because of living in environments of multiple deprivation. These can include:
- domestic violence outreach projects
- rape and sexual abuse services
- work with women and young people in prostitution
- support to help local organisations develop domestic violence perpetrator programmes for non-convicted men.

Children

We will look for projects helping children over 5 years of age who are at risk of being marginalised because of living in environments of multiple deprivation.

Examples of work we would consider funding could be:
- work with children who have experience of living with domestic violence
- work to help children with developmental or behavioural problems, (not related to medically diagnosed conditions)
- work that promotes child protection.

Young people

We will look for projects providing opportunities for vulnerable young people marginalised by behavioural problems and/or personal issues, and who are living in environments of multiple deprivation.

Our focus will be:
- projects offering a range of activities to enhance educational achievement, life skills or employment opportunities to disaffected young people, especially those excluded from school
- preventive work with homeless young people in areas of rural deprivation

- enabling young people to take responsibility for their own projects.

We also run an annual Summer Playscheme small grants programme from February to May. Please see our website lankellychase.org.uk for details and an application form.

In this programme:
- we will only work with registered charities
- we will look for user involvement as well as the proper use and support of volunteers
- preference will be given to community based initiatives to meet local needs
- we will consider core costs to help small organisations sustain proven services
- we welcome applications from black and minority ethnic voluntary groups meeting cultural needs while promoting integration.

In addition to the general exclusions, in this area of work we will not support:
- capital expenditure
- supplementary education
- locally based groups in Greater London area
- projects working exclusively with substance misuse/drug rehabilitation services and drug education
- mediation or bereavement counselling
- mainstream activities of local organisations which are part of a wider network of others doing similar work e.g. Crossroads, Homestart Childcare, nurseries, pre-school and after-school clubs.

Developing communities

The foundation recognises that some communities face multiple problems that can lead to cycles of disadvantage and social exclusion. However within these communities there are individuals and organisations with the skills and talents that can transform people's lives and bring about positive social change.

The Developing Communities grants programme has been established to assist the process of building a more inclusive society and invites applications from organisations providing a range of activities that are:
- community controlled and managed
- responsive to the needs of all sections of their community
- working in partnership with other voluntary and statutory agencies to tackle the needs of their community in a holistic way
- seeking to develop sustainable funding strategies to enable them to participate in the long term development of their community providing opportunities for all to fulfil their potential
- seeking to create new employment opportunities that generate real wealth within communities.

The trustees recognise that community can be defined by area (neighbourhood based organisations) and by identity (including people with special needs, young people, older people, black and minority ethnic groups and refugees/asylum seekers).

Size and scale of grants

Revenue: Grants will normally be available for 1–3 years with an exceptional consideration for 5 years if a clear sustainable strategy can be demonstrated.

Capital: Grants of up to £50,000 to:
- help acquire an asset
- adapt existing assets (building)
- purchase equipment.

Applicants seeking capital grants must demonstrate the organisation's ability to generate long-term income from the acquisition of the asset or equipment.

Supporting community enterprise

Within this priority area the trustees, in September 2003, established a three year grants programme for full members of the Development Trust Association. The aim is to help smaller development trusts grow their enterprise activities, to help them increase trading for social purposes and make a bigger impact in their communities. The full guidelines are available on the LankellyChase website or the Development Trust Association website (dta.org.uk).

Free and quiet minds

Mental ill health can affect any person of any age and cause great distress, not only to those who endure it but also to their friends and families. It respects neither financial, national, sexual nor physical circumstances. There are many charities carrying out excellent work across the spectrum and the foundation has chosen to focus on two areas only of this broad field.

Black and minority ethnic groups

The Foundation recognises that over the years, those from black and minority ethnic groups have, for whatever reason, not had the same access to treatment as their peers in the white community; nor have they necessarily had the opportunity to shape the sort of care which they would choose for themselves.

Therefore, the foundation welcomes applications from charities led by black or minority ethnic groups, wishing to provide services to those from black and minority ethnic backgrounds who are experiencing or recovering from a mental illness and to those who care for people with mental ill health.

Psychiatric care

Men and women entering the psychiatric system lose much of what they previously might have taken for granted. Those who find themselves in secure hospitals or medium secure psychiatric units, particularly women, often have only limited access to alternative forms of therapy, exercise, arts activities or other activities which may improve their health or the conditions in which they find themselves.

The foundation seeks to work with charities focussing on people confined in secure hospitals or medium secure psychiatric units; charities working in the field of the arts would be particularly welcome.

Conditions: For both these areas, the foundation will only work with registered charities;

It will not consider applications from those based in Greater London (except under exceptional circumstances) or Northern Ireland.

It will not consider projects working exclusively with substance misuse/ drug rehabilitation services and drug education.

It will give grants for either revenue or capital needs.

Heritage

The LankellyChase foundation will support a programme of work with three main elements recognising the important role that heritage buildings play in a local community:

Rural parish churches

Grade 1 Listed Buildings located in a village with a population of less than 1,000 people. Evidence of local support is essential.

Grant range: Capital grants to a maximum of £3,000.

Almshouses

Priority will be given to applications from almshouses, in rural areas, that are of architectural merit and historical interest, providing accommodation to older people who are in housing and financial need. The appeal must take into account the mobility needs of residents and conform to the regulations of the Disability Discrimination Act.

Grant range: Capital grants to a maximum of £5,000.

Historic buildings

To consider applications from organisations managing buildings of architectural merit and historic interest that are used by and accessible to the community (including people with disabilities in accordance with the Disability Discrimination Act). Buildings in rural areas will be given priority. The level of community use and the involvement in the management of the organisation will be an important element in the assessment of the application.

Grant range: Capital grants to a maximum of £10,000.

In addition to the above eligibility criteria all applicants will need to be registered charities or have been granted exempt status.

No grants for capital appeals in excess of £500,000.

Offenders and society

The foundation seeks to strengthen voluntary and community sector agencies. Its aim is to encourage effective partnerships with our prison and probation services which are designed to reduce offending behaviour and its impact on children, families and the wider community.

This work will chiefly be carried out in two geographical regions, the eastern region and the south west region.

In the eastern region, our partnership with the Ormiston Trust and the Prison Service is now in its third year and this will continue for a further four years. The aims of this partnership is to support the children and families of prisoners by:

improving facilities and services in all of the area's prisons;

promoting better understanding of the problems faced by children who have a family member in prison within the schools and communities in which they live.

This work is managed by the Ormiston Children and Families Trust but it is designed to support other agencies involved in similar work within the region.

In the south west region, the foundation is embarking upon a new three year partnership with the Tudor Trust which is designed to support small voluntary and community agencies working with National Offender Management Service (NOMS) to resettle offenders and reduce re-offending. It will include a joint grants programme to support:

Services for those in prison that are aimed at improving the chance of successful resettlement, e.g. assistance towards finding employment and suitable accommodation upon release, education, arts, advice and mentoring projects which increase self-esteem and self-knowledge.

Services for the children and partners of prisoners which ameliorate the experience of visiting in prison, help to sustain family ties and reduce re-offending (e.g. schemes which support the involvement of family members in sentence planning, particularly where addiction to alcohol or drugs has been associated with criminal behaviour).

Services based in local communities which support those leaving prison or those serving community sentences.

These two programmes form the core of the foundation's work with offenders and their families. Our aim is to show that such regional collaboration can produce real improvements in service provision and provide longer term examples which influence policy-makers. We intend to carefully monitor and evaluate both programmes.

The foundation's grants outside these two regions will be limited to:

- New approaches in the resettlement of offenders or the support of detained refugees or asylum seekers. These must be able to show that they may be replicable, e.g. through the active involvement of large national charities which intend to promote developments elsewhere.
- Projects which are designed to strengthen the voluntary and community sector so that it is more able to meet the needs of black minority ethnic prisoners and their families.
- Projects which involve prisoners in the arts, principally dance or drama, with a view to strengthening self-esteem and self-understanding. Final performances must be open to partners and family members.
- Projects from the Greater London area may apply, within these parameters.

Special programme – refugees and asylum seekers

For various reasons, some refugees and asylum seekers in the UK are currently experiencing considerable difficulties. Therefore, for a limited period, the foundation has decided to consider applications from registered charities who are:

1. Working to prevent or tackle destitution amongst asylum seekers.
2. Working to strengthen the infrastructure of small, emerging, voluntary refugee groups, through the provision of training or practical support.
3. Providing a range of services to promote integration into the wider community

The foundation will not be able to help individual BME groups, except where they are working in the ways set out above or where they come within the trustees other priority areas.

Exclusions

In addition to exclusions specifically mentioned in our current programmes, we do not support:

- access to buildings;
- advancement of religion;
- after school and homework clubs;
- animal charities;
- breakfast clubs;
- bursaries and scholarships;
- child befriending schemes;
- circular appeals;
- expeditions/overseas travel;
- festivals;
- formal education including schools, colleges and universities;
- general counselling;
- holidays/holiday centres;

• hospitals and hospices;
• individual youth clubs;
• individuals - including students;
• medical care;
• medical research;
• mother and toddler groups/playgroups;
• museums/galleries;
• organisations working with particular medical conditions;
• other grant making organisations;
• research;
• sport;
• work that has already taken place;
• work which is primarily the responsibility of central or local government, education or health authorities.

Applications

Applications may be submitted at any time but you should be aware that the programmes are often over subscribed.

The trustees meet twice during each quarter but agendas are planned well ahead and you should expect a period of 6 months between an initial application and formal consideration by the trustees. All letters receive a written answer and we attempt to reply to all correspondence within one month.

During this period there may be further correspondence and telephone conversations. A member of staff, and possibly a trustee, will visit your organisation to discuss your application in detail. Should the visit be successful, the member of staff will act as an advocate on your behalf at the trustee meeting. You will be notified of the trustees' decision as soon as possible and, if a grant is agreed, of the conditions that have been attached to its release.

Your initial letter should answer the following questions:
• Who are you, where are you, what do you do?
• How much money do you need to raise and what is it for?
• How soon do you need it?
• Who else have you asked to help?
• What support have you already attracted?
• How will you measure success?

You should attach:
• brief information about the origins and current company/charitable status of your organisation;
• a copy of your most recent annual report and full audited accounts;
• an itemised income and expenditure budget for your organisation;
• an itemised income and expenditure budget for the work to be funded;
• equal opportunities policy;
• child and vulnerable adult protection policies;
• any additional information requested in the individual priority sections.

Only postal applications are accepted.

The Carole & Geoffrey Lawson Foundation

Jewish, child welfare, poverty, arts, education

£450,000 (2001/02)

Beneficial area UK.

Stilemans, Munstead, Godalming, Surrey GU8 4AB

Tel. 01483 420757

Correspondent Geoffrey Lawson, Trustee

Trustees *Geoffrey C H Lawson; Hon. Carole Lawson; Harold I Connick.*

Charity Commission no. 801751

Information available Accounts were on file at the Charity Commission.

This trust has general charitable purposes, particularly supporting Jewish organisations. Beneficiaries require a good track record and should be concerned with child welfare, relief of poverty and advancement of education and the arts. It particularly supports rebuilding work at Covent Garden.

In 2001/02 the trust had assets of £634,000 and a total income of £465,000. There were 17 grants made totalling £450,000.

By far the largest grant, as in previous years, was £135,000 to World ORT Trust. Other large donations went to Haste (£75,000) and Royal Opera House (£56,000).

Other grants were made to Heart and Stroke Endeavour (£25,000), Dulwich Picture Gallery (£15,000), Sylvan Charitable Trust (£7,000) and New Israel Opera (£5,000).

In 2003/04 the trust had a total expenditure of £532,000. Unfortunately, although submitted by the trust to the Charity Commission, the accounts for that year had not made it to the public files for inspection.

Exclusions

No grants to local charities or individuals.

Applications

In writing to the correspondent.

The Leathersellers' Company Charitable Fund

General

£1.1 million (2002/03)

Beneficial area UK, particularly London.

15 St Helen's Place, London EC3A 6DQ

Tel. 020 7330 1444 **Fax** 020 7330 1445

Email enquiries@leathersellers.co.uk

Website www.leathersellers.co.uk

Correspondent Mrs Penny Burtwell, Charities Administrator

Trustee *'The Warden and Society of the Mystery and Art of the Leathersellers of the City of London.'*

Charity Commission no. 278072

Information available Annual report and accounts on file at the Charity Commission, or available from the trust for a 'copying charge' of £25.

Summary

About 150 grants to institutions are made each year. Most funds are disbursed in ongoing annual donations or recurrent grants, mostly for between £10,000 and £50,000, to a largely fixed list of beneficiaries. There are around 80 grants for under £5,000 made each year, and some of these may go to new beneficiaries.

General

The trust had an income of £1.2 million from investments worth £29.3 million in 2003.

Its annual report describes its grantmaking policy as follows:

The policy of the trustees is to provide support to registered charities associated with the Leathersellers' Company, the leather and hide trades, education in leather technology and for the welfare of poor and sick former workers in the industry and their dependants. Thereafter financial support is provided to registered charities, with priority given to those based in London.

It also states that it is their policy to give at least £1 million each year, and defines the type of grant it makes as set out below.

Three types of grants are given:

- single grants.
- guaranteed annual grants – a fixed annual sum paid for a set period (usually four years).
- recurrent annual grants – fixed or variable annual payments made for an undefined period or variable annual sums paid for a fixed period.

In addition the fund provides management services free of charge (recurrent annual gifts-in-kind) to charities connected to the Leathersellers' Company).

Grants in 2002/03

The trust categorised its grants in 2002/03 as follows (with 2001/02 figures in brackets):

Grants by type		No.	Amount	
Single	£128,000	90	(£273,000	80%)
Guaranteed annual	£755,000	84	(£716,000	73%)
Recurrent	£157,000	4	(£155,000	10%)

Grants by charitable sector				
Education and sciences	£404,000	38%	(£386,000	34%)
Children and youth	£220,000	21%	(£185,000	16%)
Relief of those in need	£181,000	17%	(£292,000	25%)
Arts	£106,000	10%	(£101,000	9%)
Medicine and health	£45,000	4%	(£54,000	5%)
Disabled	£44,000	4%	(£54,000	5%)
Environment	£15,000	2%	(£15,000	1%)
The church	£14,000	1%	£37,000	3%)
Other	£28,000	3%	(£26,000	2%)

There were 164 grants to institutions, as well as 43 grants to individuals. 61 of these, accounting for almost 90% of the money spent, were for £5,000 or over and were included in the grants list.

Grants were led by £105,000 to Leathersellers Company Universities Exhibitions. Other larger grants included £64,000 to Colfe's Education Foundation, £52,000 to BSLT – University College Northampton, £50,000 to Prendergast School, £40,000 to Rainbow Trust, £35,000 to Centrepoint Soho, £30,000 to ChildLine, £25,000 to London College of Fashion, £22,000 to Leather Conservation Centre, £20,000 to Holbourne Museum – Bath, £15,000 each to Whitechapel Mission and Woodland Centre Trust, £13,000 to Youth at Risk and £10,000 each to Aidis Trust, Respond, Royal Botanic Gardens and Turning Point.

Grants of £5,000 each included those to Action for Kids Charitable Trust, Africa Education Trust, Historic Churches Preservation Trust, Homeshare, Kiloran Trust and New Avenues Youth and Community Project.

Applications

In writing to the correspondent. The fund does not publish guidelines due to the wide range of causes it supports. Applicants should send a one-page letter describing their background and explaining what funds they require and their purpose. If interested, the charity will then request further information or conduct a visit as appropriate. Penny Burtwell, the charities administrator, is happy to speak to potential applicants before they write in and can be contacted by telephone on 020 7330 1444.

The William Leech Charity

Health and welfare in the north east of England, overseas aid

£429,000 (2002/03)

Beneficial area Northumberland, Tyne and Wear, Durham and overseas.

RC Diocese of Hexham and Newcastle, St Vincent's Diocesan Offices, St Cuthbert's House, West Road, Newcastle upon Tyne NE15 7PY

Tel. 0191 243 3300 **Fax** 0191 243 3309

Correspondent Mrs Kathleen M Smith, Secretary

Trustees *R E Leech, chair; Prof. P Baylis; C Davies; A Gifford; R D Leech; N Sherlock; D Stabler; B Wallace.*

Charity Commission no. 265491

Information available Annual report and accounts were on file at the Charity Commission.

Awards are mostly one-off grants for amounts up to £1,000. The usual maximum grant is for £5,000, though a small number of charities are assisted with larger amounts every year. The charity has a strong presumption in favour of work that is carried out with a high level of voluntary input.

The charity also makes crisis loans (often to churches) and 'challenge grants' which match other funding £1 for £1.

Roughly one-third of the income is used to support research projects at the University of Newcastle, while a separate Lady Leech Fund awards grants to the value of about £40,000 a year 'to charities with a local connection assisting projects in underdeveloped areas in the world with special emphasis on the third world'.

The charity, established in 1972, had an income of £526,000 in 2002/03, mostly from its investments and the rent from its properties, the original endowment of the charity.

Extracts from the guidelines read as follows:

The following paragraphs are the present policies as to grants. These policies are not formal directions from the settlor, but they have his goodwill and will not be changed without careful consideration.

Geographical area

Grants are normally made to organisations for work in the counties of Northumberland, Tyne and Wear and Durham. Grants for other areas are sometimes made if there is a substantial connection with the Settlor or a local organisation.

University of Newcastle-upon-Tyne

... A substantial part of the income (at present one third) is granted [...] for readerships or research lectureships [...] For research in medicine and related sciences, including medical engineering.

Before his death the settlor wished it to be known that he was firm in his belief that mental attitudes can affect physical health and recovery from illness, and that it would be appreciated if some of the research could be targeted in this direction.

Preferred categories

... To encourage local and community spirited people to create and sustain interest in voluntary charitable work.

- Organisations in which a high proportion [at least two thirds] of the work is undertaken by voluntary unpaid workers. (See 'Volunteer Support Programme' below.)
- Organisations with a close connection to the settlor, or with districts in which William Leech (Builders) Ltd, built houses during the time when the Settlor was active in business.
- Organisations with an active Christian involvement.
- Organisations working in deprived areas for the benefit of local people, especially those which encourage people to help themselves.
- Organisations doing practical new work and putting new ideas into action.

The settlor also said 'I would fully support independent boys' and girls' clubs, YMCA,

YWCA, Scouts, Guides (Boys Brigade) and Christian youth clubs and Christian teaching colleges.'

Low priority categories

'I would avoid clubs etc. who receive substantial grants or donations from local councils or the government. I do not regard them as charities because they are subsidised.' (Sir William Leech.) *[See also 'exclusions' below. Ed.]*

Crisis loans

Where an organisation (often but not exclusively a church) is faced with an unexpected crisis a loan may be made in place of a grant. This is usually in order to allow them to get on with the building work, avoiding inflation costs. Loans are normally repayable over 5 years by annual instalments. Maximum loan £10,000. There are standard conditions.

Challenge grants

Where an organisation is raising funds by individual personal effort, the trustees are often willing to match £1 for £1. There are standard conditions.

Size of grants
- Large number of £250 to £1,000 grants plus pump-priming £50 to £100 grants, in the belief that a small amount can give considerable encouragement to the type of organisation we wish to support.
- Larger grants of up to £5,000 for new projects. In appropriate cases we will promise future support for up to three years to allow a project to get off the ground.
- About one third of our income after the university allocation will be set aside for occasional large grants of £50,000 to £150,000 to major local appeals. In this case it will normally be a condition of support that part of a project will be specifically named in honour of the Settlor.

Volunteer Support Programme

Volunteer Support Programme is an additional grants programme to assist volunteers in registered charities where at least two-thirds of the charitable work (excluding admin and fundraising) is done by volunteers. Likely grants will be in the region of £250 to £500.

Lady Leech Fund guidelines

This fund has an income of around £40,000 per annum, which is to be distributed to developing third world projects which have, if possible, a strong connection with our area (Northumberland, Tyne and Wear and Durham). Grants will probably be up to about £5,000, and would be payable to a registered charity (not individual). In suitable cases grants could be extended up to three years.

The ideal arrangement would be for someone whose home is in our area, but is actually working with the project overseas. An annual written report would be expected.

In 2002/03 the trust's expenditure was reduced significantly on the previous year to £469,000 (£1.5 million in 2001/02). It is likely that most of the trust's expenditure was spent on grants during the year. Unfortunately, no further information was available for the year.

Comment

There was no response to repeated written requests for a copy of the most recent annual report and accounts, despite the requirement to provide these on demand.

Despite ample warning, and their obligation to the contrary, the Charity Commission were unable to give us sight of this trust's accounts.

Exclusions

The following will not generally receive grants. The chair and secretary are instructed to reject them without reference to the trustees unless there are special circumstances:

- community centres and similar (exceptionally, those in remote country areas may be supported)
- running expenses of youth clubs (as opposed to capital projects)
- running expenses of churches (this includes normal repairs, but churches engaged in social work, or using their buildings largely for 'outside' purposes, may be supported)
- sport
- the arts
- individuals or students
- organisations which have been supported in the last 12 months (it would be exceptional to support an organisation in two successive years, unless we had promised such support in advance)
- holidays, travel, outings
- minibuses (unless over 10,000 miles a year is expected)
- schools
- housing associations.

Applications

A full written application to the correspondent is required. Appeals are considered at bi-monthly meetings.

Investigation process for applications
- Low priority: none.
- Proposed grant up to £1,000 or loan up to £10,000: written application only.
- Proposed grant of £1,001 to £10,000: one or more trustees must enquire further.

- Proposed grant of over £10,000: full papers must be circulated to the trustees to be discussed and approved.

For 'Volunteer Support Programme' grants, an application should consist of a one-page letter identifying the following as a minimum:

- the organisation's name and charity number
- the name and address of correspondent
- the project's aims, progress, funds raised to date and how much is still required, and for what
- numbers of paid workers, annual salary costs and total administration overheads, plus numbers of unpaid volunteers.

The Kennedy Leigh Charitable Trust

Jewish charities, general
£1.1 million (2002/03)
Beneficial area Israel and UK.

Ort House, 126 Albert Street, London NW1 7NE
Tel. 020 7267 6500 **Fax** 020 7267 6332
Email naomi@klct.org
Correspondent Naomi Shoffman, Administrator
Trustees G Goldkorn, chair; Mrs Lesley D Berman; Leila I Foux; Carole Berman Sujo; Angela L Sorkin; Michele Foux; M Sorkin.
Charity Commission no. 288293
Information available Annual report and accounts on file at the Charity Commission.

The trust's endowment of £18.6 million produced an income of £1 million in 2002/03. Grants totalled £1.1 million.

The trust's objects require three-quarters of its grant-making funds to be distributed to charitable institutions within Israel, with the remainder being distributed in the UK and elsewhere. The trust's 'mission statement' reads as follows:

The trust will support projects and causes which will improve and enrich the lives of all parts of society, not least those of the young, the needy, the disadvantaged and the underprivileged. In meeting its objectives the trust expects to become involved in a wide range of activities. The trust is able to provide several forms of support and will consider the funding of capital projects, set-up costs and bridging running costs. The trust is non-political and non-religious in nature.

The beneficiaries of new and continuing donations in Israel were: the Assocation for Children at Risk, Council for a Beautiful Israel – Tel Hashomer Hospital, Professor Feurstein International Centre for the Enhancement of Learning Potential, the Hebrew University of Jerusalem, Israel Tennis Centres, Magen David Adom, MAKSAM Centres, T'lalim, the Technion Institute – Haifa, United Jewish Israel Appeal and Zichron Menachem.

Exclusions

No grants for individuals.

Applications

'None considered. Funds fully committed for all non-Israel distributions.'

The Leigh Trust

Drug and alcohol rehabilitation, criminal justice, asylum seekers, racial equality

£353,000 (2002/03)
Beneficial area Unrestricted, but with some apparent London interest.

Clive Marks and Company, 1st Floor, Lynton House, 7–12 Tavistock Square, London WC1H 9LT

Tel. 020 7388 3577 **Fax** 020 7388 3570

Correspondent The Trustees

Trustees Hon. David Bernstein; Dr R M E Stone; Caroline Moorehead.

Charity Commission no. 275372

Information available Annual report and accounts on file at the Charity Commission.

The Leigh Trust was established in 1976. In 2002/03 the trust had assets of £2.3 million and an income of £81,000. The current policy is to distribute investment revenue and a proportion of capital gains.

Its guidelines say:

The trust makes grants to a variety of registered charities concerned with:
- drug and alcohol rehabilitation
- criminal justice
- asylum seekers/racial equality.

The trustees can respond favourably to very few applicants.

Grants were categorised by the trust as follows:

Addiction	£55,000
Asylum seekers/racial equality	£178,000
Children/youth	£10,000
Community	£15,000
Criminal justice	£55,000
Interfaith and religion	£7,500
General	£12,000
Racial equality	£20,000

The trust gave 32 grants in 2002/03. Over two-thirds, of the recipients had received a grant in the previous year, often for the same amount and purpose.

Grants included £25,000 each to Chemical Dependency Centre; £20,000 each to Clouds, Ethiopian Refugee Association – Haringey, ICAR and Jewish Council for Racial Equality; £15,000 to Joint Council for the Welfare of Immigrants; £12,000 to Children's Music Workshop; £10,000 each to Focus, Inquest Charitable Trust, Waltham Centre YMCA and Slough Refugee Support; £7,500 to Brighton Islamic Mission; £5,000 to National Association for Women Facing Childbirth in Detention; and £1,000 to Yisal Allon Educational Trust.

Exclusions

The trust does not make grants to individuals.

Applications

Initial applications should be made in writing to the registered office of the trust.

Organisations should enclose the most recent audited accounts, a registered charity number, a cash flow statement for the next 12 months, and a stamped addressed envelope.

Applicants should state clearly on one side of A4 what their charity does and what they are requesting funding for. They should provide a detailed budget and show other sources of funding for the project. The charity may be requested to complete an application form. It is likely that an officer of the trust will wish to visit the project before any grant is made. Trustees' meetings are held quarterly.

The Leverhulme Trust

Scholarships for education and research

£25 million (2003)
Beneficial area UK and developing countries.

1 Pemberton Row, London EC4A 3BG

Tel. 020 7822 6938 **Fax** 020 7822 5084

Email enquiries@leverhulme.org.uk

Website www.leverhulme.org.uk

Correspondent Prof. Sir Richard Brook, Director

Trustees Sir Michael Angus, chair; N W A Fitzgerald; Sir Michael Perry; Dr J I W Anderson; Dr A S Ganguly; Clive Butler.

Charity Commission no. 288371

Information available Detailed annual 'Guide to Applicants', and an annual report, available from the trust. Full information on the website.

Grants are made to institutions for specific research undertakings, for schemes of international academic interchange and, exceptionally, for education.

In 2003 grants were made totalling £25 million. Unfortunately, further information for this year was not available.

In 2002 it had a total expenditure of £26.7 million. There were 403 grants made during the year totalling £25.9 million, comprising £21.9 million in 170 grants as a direct result of trustees' decisions, and £4 million in 233 grants made on the recommendations of the trust's Research Awards Advisory Committee (RAAC). The following information is taken from its 2002 Review of the Year:

The trust has translated its basic task, namely that of awarding scholarships for education and research, into a variety of specific activities. These can be best represented in terms of the different categories of award. In terms of research support, there are four main patterns of award, namely projects, fellowships, networks and prizes. Awards are additionally made for education.

Projects.
Grants for research projects are made in two major categories: responsive awards, i.e. where the choice of topic and research design lie entirely with the applicant, and the programme awards, where the research community is invited to send proposals built around themes put forward by the trustees.

239

Most awards in the first category are for less than £250,000; the programme awards are for sums up to £1,250,000.

The themes proposed by the trustees for the programme awards in 2002 were two, namely The Behaviour of Large, Complex Systems and The Movement of Peoples in the Modern World, which received 69 and 39 bids respectively. (In 2003 the two topics were The Changing Character of War and The Nature of Evidence.)

Fellowships.

The majority of fellowships are awarded by the RAAC. One fellowship scheme within the direct care of the trustees is that of the Major Research Fellowships in the humanities and social sciences. These awards provide typically two or three years of teaching replacement so that the award holders can conduct a piece of intensive and concentrated research around a theme of their choosing. 27 awards were made in response to 171 applications.

Networks.

The trustees have continued to place weight upon the value of building links between research groups as a means of ensuring progress where the interaction of different viewpoints is an important contributor to success. 30 awards were made during the year.

A scheme with analogous ambitions, namely, the building of links, but where the distance between the disciplines is more dramatic, is that of Artists in Residence. The 11 awards made during the year indicate that this relatively new scheme has already provided a splendid array of interactions.

Prizes.

The Philip Leverhulme Prizes seek to recognise younger research colleges (typically less than 36 years of age) whose research contribution has already led to recognition at an international level. 124 nominations were received for 24 awards across five disciplines. Each prize winner receives £50,000.

Education.

The trust has continued to make direct awards to colleges and academies for the most part for the support of students undertaking graduate level professional training in the fine and performing arts.

Previous beneficiaries include Nottingham University, Institute for Fiscal Studies – University of London, Bristol University, School of Advanced Study – University of London, London School of Economics, University of Warwick, University of Durham and University of Exeter.

Further information on these categories, and other general information, can be found on the trust's website.

Exclusions

The trust does not offer funding for any of the following:

- core funding for institutions;
- contributions to appeals;
- exhibitions;
- endowments;
- equipment, sites, buildings or other capital expenditure;
- conferences, workshops or symposia which are not directly related to research projects;
- making good withdrawals or deficiencies in public finance.

The trust does not usually support research in the following fields for grants made to institutions:

- social policy and welfare (especially action research);
- medicine (potential applicants in doubt should write to the Director);
- school education (in very exceptional circumstances, the Director may use his discretion to accept an application of particular significance, breadth and originality).

Applications

All applicants should first ask for the trust's current 'Guide to Applicants' brochure before attempting to submit an application. The website may also be consulted.

Lord Leverhulme's Charitable Trust

Welfare, education, arts, young people

About £548,000 (2002/03)

Beneficial area UK, especially Cheshire, Merseyside and surrounding areas.

Leverhulme Estate Office, Thornton Hough, Wirral CH63 1JD

Correspondent The Administrator

Trustees *A E H Heber-Percy; A H S Hannay.*

Charity Commission no. 212431

Information available Annual report and accounts on file at the Charity Commission.

There are two restricted funds within the trust. One generates income which is

paid to National Museums Liverpool for the trustees of the Lady Lever Art Gallery. The second is Lord Leverhulme's Youth Enterprise Scheme; the income from this sponsors young people in the Wirral and Cheshire areas who receive support from the Prince's Youth Business Trust.

In 2002/03 the trust had an income of £532,000 and a total expenditure of £598,000. No further information was available for the year.

Previous beneficiaries include Girl Guides Association, Cheshire Residential Home Trust, Alder Hey Rocking Horse Appeal, Birkenhead Youth Club, National Garden Scheme, Animals in War Memorial Fund, Holbourne Garden Scheme, Wirral Autistic Society, Groundwork Wirral, Knowsley START, 'Not Forgotten' Association, Volunteer Reading Help, British Red Cross Society, Liverpool Students Community Association, Liverpool One Parent Families, Mencap, Tranmere Community Project and North West Cancer Research Fund.

Comment

The trust refused to send a copy of its latest annual report and accounts, despite its obligations to do so.

Despite ample warning, and their obligation to the contrary, the Charity Commission were unable to give us sight of this trust's accounts.

Exclusions

No grants to non-charitable organisations.

Applications

By letter addressed to the trustees setting out details of the appeal, including the most recent accounts.

The Levy Foundation

Young people, elderly, health, medical research, Jewish charities

£736,000 (2002/03)

Beneficial area UK and Israel.

6 Camden High Street, Camden Town, London NW1 0JH

Tel. 020 7874 7200 **Fax** 020 7874 7206

Email administrator@levyfoundation.
org.uk

Correspondent Sue Nyfield, Grants
Manager

Trustees *Mrs Jane Jason; Peter L Levy;
Silas Krendel; Melanie Levy; Claudia
Giat.*

Charity Commission no. 245592

Information available Annual report
and accounts were provided by the trust.

The foundation has reduced the number
of grants it makes, down from the 87 for
1998/99 to 45 in 2000/01, 47 in 2001/02
and 44 in 2002/03.

Grants are probably made on a fairly
personal basis to organisations already
known to the trustees. However, 'the
trustees have been keen to encourage the
next generation of the family to become
involved in the trust and as part of an
overall review of the foundation, they are
considering new procedures for the
awarding of grants'.

Although at least some grants are a
result of trustees' prior knowledge of the
charitable world, the trust does not wish
to deter potential applicants from
applying and therefore being considered
once the new procedures are in place.
'All applications do go to the trustees'
meeting and unsolicited applications
have been funded in previous years.' The
annual report for 2002/03 notes a fairly
low success rate of one in 19
applications.

The annual report for 2002/03 gives the
following information:

In the last twelve months, the foundation
agreed 43 grants in support of both capital
and revenue needs. The foundation is a
generalist trust and has traditionally given to
charities serving the elderly, young people,
people with disabilities and people with ill
health. This year has seen a continued
commitment to the causes of health and
community care, social welfare, the elderly
and the young. Grants awarded varied from
one to three years.

The number of applications received in
the financial year 2002/03 was 820, slightly
up on the previous year when 796
applications were received. This year the
foundation has only been able to fund one
out of every nineteen applications it has
received.

The following table puts our grants for
2002/03 into broad categories.

Health and community care	£333,000	18 grants	45%
Social welfare	£182,000	6 grants	25%
Religion	£101,000	2 grants	14%
Arts, culture and sport in the community	£61,000	7 grants	8%
Education	£35,000	5 grants	5%
Other	£24,000	5 grants	3%
Total	£736,000	43 grants	100%

The trustees will rarely fund applications
for the promotion of the arts, culture and
sport except where the activity is used as a
vehicle for community development.

An analysis of the ages of the beneficiaries
of the foundation's grants shows that 33% of
funds were awarded to organisations serving
young people, while 30% of funds went to
organisations providing services aimed at
older people. The remaining 37% of funds
were for services to an unspecified age
group or not age related.

The annual report for 2002/03 shows 21
grants paid during that year, and 22
grants committed for 2003/04, with a
total value of £736,000. The major
beneficiaries, as in previous years, were
For Dementia (formerly Dementia Relief
Trust), which received £224,000, and
London Youth, which received £150,000.
A new beneficiary during the year was
Reform Foundation Trust, which
received £100,000.

Other notable beneficiaries were the
Cystic Fibrosis Trust, which received two
grants totalling £51,000, and Cystic
Fibrosis Holiday Fund, which received
two grants totalling £20,000. Both
organisations are regular beneficiaries of
the foundation.

Other grant recipients, some of whom
receive grants on a regular basis,
included English Blind Golf Association
(£40,000), Jewish Council for Racial
Equality (£21,000 in total), Bnei Arazim
(£16,000), Motivation, Norwood and
Byre Theatre (£10,000 each), Photovoice
(£10,000 in total), Friends of Israel
Education Trust and Jewish Museum
(£5,000 each), Cancer Research UK and
Romford Drum & Trumpet Corps
(£2,000 each) and Westminster Pastoral
Foundation (£1,000).

Exclusions

No grants to individuals, under any
circumstances.

Applications

In writing to the grants manager at any
time. 'The trust has always welcomed
enquiries and I personally am happy to
talk to any potential applicant.' (Sue
Nyfield, Grants Manager).

The Linbury Trust

Arts, heritage, social welfare, general

£6.5 million (2003/04)

Beneficial area Unrestricted.

Allington House, 1st Floor, 150 Victoria
Street, London SW1E 5AE

Tel. 020 7410 0330 **Fax** 020 7410 0332

Email info@sfct.org.uk

Correspondent Michael Pattison,
Director

Trustees *Lord Sainsbury of Preston
Candover; Lady Sainsbury; Sir Martin
Jacomb; Sir James Spooner.*

Charity Commission no. 287077

Information available Excellent annual
report and accounts, with full grants
listing, were provided by the trust.

Summary

This is one of the Sainsbury Family
Charitable Trusts, which share a joint
administration. They have a common
approach to grantmaking which is
described in the entry for the group as a
whole, and which is generally
discouraging to organisations not
already in contact with the trust
concerned, but some, including this one,
appear increasingly open to unsolicited
approaches.

Over time, much of the trust's money
has gone in major capital projects. It also
funds numerous revenue projects in the
following fields:

- arts;
- education;
- medical;
- developing countries and humanitarian aid;
- drug abuse;
- environment and heritage;
- social welfare.

General

This is the trust of Lord and Lady
Sainsbury of Preston Candover.

Much of its support in past years has
been for major capital projects such as
the National Gallery and the Royal
Opera House, as well as other museums
and galleries. It has a particular interest
in dance and dance education, Lady
Sainsbury being the well known ballerina
Anya Linden. The trust has pioneered
research funding of chronic fatigue
syndrome.

Though unsolicited applications are 'only successful occasionally [...] all applications in the listed fields are considered on their merits', and the trust has published a note on its 'grant giving policies and priorities', attached to recent annual report and accounts, and assuming some response to charities not already known to the trustees. It read as follows:

The Linbury Trust's grants are made over a very wide range of charities. The sums awarded may be small or may amount to many millions, either on a once-only basis or as a commitment over a number of years.

The trustees can make grants to any charity or for any charitable purpose. Their practice is to give grants only to charities, and only to organisations which supply full and up-to-date audited accounts and current budgets, and for work which they believe will be fully cost-effective.

Preferred causes are as follows (not in order of priority):

a. Disadvantaged young people, including those who are homeless or are in danger of becoming so, or who are drug abusers.

b. Specific medical causes which the trustees have adopted and where, in the trustees' opinion, inadequate research is currently undertaken, or inadequate treatment and understanding exists; for example, chronic fatigue syndrome. Medical causes to which these criteria do not apply are generally not supported. The trustees usually take specialist advice before making decisions.

c. Although general educational causes are not supported unless they cover the particular needs of those in a. or b., limited exceptions are made when the trustees have particular knowledge concerning specific educational appeals.

d. Appeals for the benefit of older people will be considered if the results can be shown to improve their quality of life directly and in a cost effective way, and particularly when the goal is to help people to continue living in their own homes.

e. National heritage appeals will be considered and, in particular, appeals for historic buildings and major arts institutions. Trustees occasionally make grants for initiatives to safeguard the natural environment.

f. Grants for overseas aid will be eligible, particularly in the field of education, in those causes where the need is particularly great and grants will be notably cost effective.

g. Grants for the visual arts, the performing arts and for education in the arts will be favourably considered where, in the opinion of the trustees, the aim is to produce work of the highest standard, and where long term benefits will result.

h. Grants for capital projects or 'one-off' grants for specific purposes will not normally be repeated or supplemented within four years of the original grant, and then only in exceptional circumstances.

The trust's staff include Michael Pattison, director of each of the trusts in the group, and Dr Patricia Morison and Mr P Lawford, administrators.

The annual reports are unusual in that they describe policies and give the totals for new grants approvals, while the grants lists show, not new approvals, but the actual payments made to each organisation. These are often the result of major grant decisions taken and reported in previous years.

New grant approvals in 2003/04 were classified as follows:

	Revenue	Capital	Total
Arts	£124,000	–	£124,000
Drug abuse	£164,000	–	£164,000
Education	£423,000	£99,000	£522,000
Environment and heritage	£460,000	£400,000	£860,000
Medical	£180,000	–	£180,000
Social welfare	£374,000	£100,000	£474,000
Developing countries and humanitarian aid	£258,000	–	£258,000

Annual report 2003/04

This section of the entry reprints the report's description of the trust's grantmaking under each heading, and also notes some of the major individual grant payments (not grant approvals) made in that year.

Arts – £219,000 paid during the year

The Linbury Trust has been a stalwart and influential supporter of excellence in the arts for over thirty years. The visual and performing arts are a particular focus of support. Among the leading institutions to have been benefited in that period are: the National Gallery, the Royal Opera House, Tate Britain, the Royal Ballet, Dulwich Picture Gallery, the Royal Academy of Arts and Sadler's Wells.

Linbury continues to be an active supporter of dance, making grants to help both large and small companies develop their work.

The Linbury Biennial Prize for Stage Design is a unique award, fostering young and emerging talent in the field of stage design in the UK. The ninth Linbury Biennial Prize was won in 2003 by a postgraduate in Theatre Design from Wimbledon School of Art.

There were three grants under this heading for more than £10,000. The largest was for the Biennial Prize, mentioned above, which was for £154,000. Smaller grants included those to Art Fund Services Ltd, Contemporary Dance Trust, London Symphony Orchestra and Walker Dance Park.

Medical – £79,000 paid during the year

For many years, the trust's main activity in the field of medicine has been to support research into Chronic Fatigue Syndrome. Given the progress made in this field, this programme has now been largely wound down.

When the trustees initiated their work in 1990, there was deep ignorance about the condition. This was combined with an almost total lack of credible research and very poor patient management.

In 2004 the situation has changed markedly for patients with CFS/ME, and this has been achieved in no little measure through the trust's efforts. Whilst fifty-odd research projects which have been funded have not explained the aetiology of CFS/ME, much good work has been done in the fields of virology, immunology and endocrinology, resulting in a significant increase in knowledge of the condition. Real progress has resulted from projects, funded by Linbury, in the areas of CFS in childhood and adolescence and in cognitive behaviour therapy.

Perhaps most importantly, the trustees have been responsible, with others, for moving CFS/ME up the Department of Health's agenda. By persuading Sir Kenneth Calman to set up the independent working party under the chairmanship of Professor Hutchinson in 1999, which resulted in the 2002 report to the Chief Medical Officer, Linbury has achieved a great deal.

Three grants over £10,000 each were made to the Institute of Neurology – University College London (£41,000), Guy's, King's and St Thomas's School of Medicine (£18,000) and St Bartholomew's Hospital and the Royal London School of Medicine (£15,000).

Drug abuse – £95,000 paid during the year

The trustees are well aware that the harmful consequences of substance misuse are inseparable from much of the charitable work which they support under the category of Social Welfare. However, they also set aside funds specifically for voluntary organisations operating in the front line of providing services to counteract the damage wreaked by drug abuse, particularly in the case of young people and their families.

Linbury is also prepared to fund research that may result in wide-ranging benefits.

During the year the trustees agreed to fund a project at the National Addiction Centre that will provide rigorous evidence-based assessment of the efficacy of auricular acupuncture as well as a complement to more conventional methods of treating addiction.

Four grants were made during the year to: Addaction, towards the cost of a youth worker in Hackney (£40,000); Re-Solv, towards the costs of making and distributing a video to schools throughout the UK on the dangers of solvent abuse (£30,000); Chooselife – Carmarthenshire, towards the salary of the family support worker (£20,000); and Chemical Dependency Centre (£5,000).

Education – £685,000 paid during the year

The first instalment was paid towards the long-term commitment in support of the Queen Elizabeth the Queen Mother Chair in History at the Institute of Historical Research, part of the University of London [£50,000]. The chair is held by Professor David Cannadine, who in January 2004 gave the inaugural lecture.

The Linbury Trust has also been a major supporter of education in the arts. The Royal Ballet School [£100,000], LAMDA [100,000], Dance City – Newcastle [£110,000], and the Rambert School of Ballet and Contemporary Dance [£105,000] benefited from Linbury's support during the year. The long-standing relationship with the British School at Rome continued with the award of the annual Sainsbury Scholarships in Painting and Sculpture [£53,000] to gifted young artists for up to two years' study in Rome.

The grant total paid during the year was made up of £336,000 for revenue costs and £349,000 for capital projects.

Environment and heritage – £1,865,000 paid during the year

The trust supports museums, art galleries and historic buildings on a highly selective basis, and will consider help with both capital expenditure and revenue projects.

The trustees made a minor grant, payable over several years, towards the endowment appeal of St George's Chapel Windsor. They also made significant new commitments to two museums. They agreed further support of £200,000 over three years to the British Empire and Commonwealth Museum in Bristol; this museum whose education work the trust has previously supported, opened to considerable critical acclaim two years ago. They also undertook to support the extension of the Sir John Soane's Museum in London.

Linbury is the lead donor to the Imperial War Museum for the creation of the Churchill Museum in the Cabinet War Rooms; the first instalment of this major grant was paid during the year [£750,000]. Further support was given to the Ashmolean Museum in Oxford to advance the design for its development programme [£425,000].

The Museum of London's new temporary exhibitions gallery, the Linbury Galleries, opened in 2003 with a successful exhibition of London in the 1920s. The trust has provided grants in excess of £1.2 million towards the creation and opening of new space. Linbury, together with other Sainsbury Family Charitable Trusts and J Sainsbury plc, has also supported the Museum of London's work to establish the Sainsbury Archive, which will be an important resource for British commercial history.

Social welfare – £810,000 paid during the year

Within this major category, the trustees take particular interest in charities working with severely disadvantaged and under-achieving young people. The trust remains interested to hear about innovative and effective programmes designed to help young people to break free from the nexus of low aspirations, antisocial behaviour and crime which are so often the product of long-term economic deprivation and family breakdown.

Several charities continued to receive support to expand their work with young people who either are, or were recently, in custody, on the margins of the criminal justice system, or without a permanent home. These included the Depaul Trust [£75,000], Fairbridge [£125,000], the Foundation Training Company [£45,000], Second Chance [£60,000] and Trail-blazers [£50,000].

The Samaritans were awarded a grant [£17,000] to research and develop the use of text messaging as an up-to-date way of reaching, in particular, the vulnerable young people whom the Samaritans seek to help.

Improving the quality of life for older people and helping them to remain independent remains a separate area of interest within this overall category. Among the first-time beneficiaries was the Arts Interest Group [£22,000], a charity which makes it feasible for elderly and disabled people to visit London art galleries and museums.

Developing countries and humanitarian aid – £758,000 paid during the year

Palestine remains a primary area of interest to trustees; significant grants were made both to the St John of Jerusalem Eye Hospital [£200,000] and, continuing the

support given over several years, to the Al Quds Medical Foundation [£100,000].

The trust reserves some funds each year for responses to humanitarian disasters; this year assistance was given to MERLIN for work in Palestine [£20,000] and to both FARM-Africa [£25,000] and SOS Sahel for work in Ethiopia [less than £10,000].

The trust continued its long-running programme of support for postgraduate scholarships at the University of Cape Town, which enable the students to spend a year at the universities of either Oxford, Bristol or Sheffield. This programme is now being wound down.

A first-time beneficiary was Buskaid [£10,000], a music school teaching stringed instruments in Soweto, which achieves remarkable results with children many of whom come from very disadvantaged family circumstance.

Following recent tragic events in Asia, it is likely that the trust will be making a contribution to the relief effort in the region, which will no doubt be described in the 2004/05 annual report.

Applications

See the guidance for applicants in the entry for the Sainsbury Family Charitable Trusts. A single application will be considered for support by all the trusts in the group.

However, 'because of the trustees' pro-active approach, unsolicited applications are only successful occasionally, although all applications in the listed fields are considered on their merits'.

Enid Linder Foundation

Health, welfare, general

£323,000 (2003/04)

Beneficial area Unrestricted.

1 Snowhill, London EC1A 2DH

Tel. 020 7651 1700

Correspondent Tim Cripps, Secretary

Trustees *Jack Ladeveze; Audrey Ladeveze; M Butler; G Huntly; C Cook.*

Charity Commission no. 267509

Information available Annual report and accounts on file at the Charity Commission.

Summary

Usually around 100 grants are made each year (although only 25 were made in 2003/04), most of them in the range £1,000 to £5,000. There are often no more than ten new grants each year, with most money going to a mixed group of regularly supported beneficiaries, mainly in the field of health, particularly that of children and disabled people. Local (normally London and the south), national and international charities are supported.

General

In 2003/04 the foundation had assets amounting to almost £11 million. Its income of £396,000 all came from investment income from its assets. It spent £323,000 on grants which it categorised as follows:

General charitable causes	£248,000
Teaching hospitals and universities	£75,000

The largest grants made over £10,000 each were: £80,000 to Royal College of Surgeons; £25,000 to Cancer Research; £24,000 to Imperial College; £20,000 each the Egg Appeal – Royal Theatre Bath and Victoria and Albert Museum; and £15,000 to Médecins Sans Frontières.

Grants of £10,000 each went to Cystic Fibrosis, Leukaemia Research, Liver Research and National Children's Orchestra. Other beneficiaries included Beatrix Potter Society (£7,000), Institute of Child Health (£6,000) and Kidscape and Phyllis Tuckwell Hospice (£5,000 each),

Applications

In writing to the correspondent.

Lloyds TSB Foundation for the Channel Islands

General

About £1 million (2004)
Beneficial area The Channel Islands.

PO Box 160, 25 New Street, St Helier, Jersey JE4 8RG

Tel. 01534 503052 **Fax** 01534 864570

Email foundationci@Lloydstsb-offshore. com
Website www.ltsbfoundationci.org
Correspondent David Beaugeard, Executive Director

Trustees *Mrs Celia Jeune, chair; Andrew Ozanne, deputy chair; David Christopher; Wendy Hurford; Edward Le Maistre; Peter Mourant; David Watkins; Diana Rowland.*

Charity Commission no. 327113

Information available Information was taken from the foundation's website.

This is the smallest of the four Lloyds TSB Foundations described in this book (each one wholly independent of the others). Like those others, this charity also supports local communities.

The foundation's mission is to 'support and work in partnership with charitable organisations which help people, especially those who are disadvantaged or disabled, to play a fuller role in communities throughout the Channel Islands'.

Since its inception in 1985 the foundation has donated in excess of £5 million to charities in the Channel Islands. Its income for 2004 was £966,000.

The foundation primarily allocates its funds through charitable organisations to support local communities, helping people to improve their quality of life.

The trustees are keen to support organisations which contribute to local community life at the grass-roots level. The trustees are also keen to encourage the infrastructure of the voluntary sector and encourage applications for operational costs. This includes salary costs, which may be funded over two or three years, and training and education for managers and staff.

Donations for one-off projects are generally in the region of £2,500 to £25,000, but there is no minimum amount set by the trustees. Applications for larger amounts will be considered where there is a wider benefit.

The trustees generally make donations towards specific items rather than making contributions to large appeals for e.g. building costs. The majority of donations are made on a "one off" basis. Successful applicants are advised to leave at least one year before reapplying.

Social Partnership Initiative

The initiative is designed to encourage real working partnerships to be set up between the voluntary sector and the relevant States departments, to stimulate the voluntary sector into seeking out opportunities to develop new services, increase knowledge and key skills.

Please refer to the trust's website for further guidelines and areas of special interest.

In 2004 larger grants included: £80,000 to Families in Recovery Trust towards the salary and operational costs of the Jersey Addiction Group residential and rehabilitation centre; £57,000 to NSPCC towards a community development project; £50,000 to Guernsey Cheshire Homes towards the salary costs of two nurses; £30,000 each to Diabetes Action Jersey towards the costs of the project liaison officer for the second year of the Island-wide screening research programme and Jersey Focus on Mental Health towards the salary costs of the care manager; £25,000 each to Channel Island Air Search towards replacement aircraft engine and Guernsey Women's Refuge towards operational costs; £20,000 each to Aids Care Education & Training towards operational costs and St. Mary's Community Centre and Boys Brigade towards the renovation of the Community Centre; and £10,000 to Jersey Scout Associaton towards operational costs.

Exclusions

No grants for:

- Organisations which are not recognised charities.
- Activities which are primarily the responsibility of the Insular authorities in the Islands or some other responsible body.
- Activities which collect funds to give to other charities, individuals or other organisations.
- Animal welfare.
- Corporate subscription or membership of a charity.
- Endowment Funds.
- Environment - conserving and protecting plants and animals, geography and scenery.
- Expeditions or overseas travel.
- Fabric appeals for places of worship.
- Fund-raising events or activities.
- Hospitals and medical centres (except for projects which are clearly additional to statutory responsibilities).
- Individuals, including students.
- Loans or business finance.
- Promotion of religion.
- Schools and colleges (except for projects that will benefit disabled students and are clearly additional to statutory responsibilities).
- Sponsorship or marketing appeals.
- International appeals – trustees may from time to time consider a limited number of applications from UK registered charities working abroad.

Applications

An application form and guidelines are available from the administrator or from the foundation's website. All applications are reviewed on a continual basis. The trustees meet three times a year to approve donations. Decision making processes can therefore take up to four months. Applications up to £5,000 are normally assessed within one month and all applicants are informed of the outcome of their application.

Lloyds TSB Foundation for England and Wales

Social and community needs, education and training

£20 million (2004)

Beneficial area England and Wales.

3rd Floor, 4 St Dunstan's Hill, London EC3R 8UL

Tel. 0870 411 1223 **Fax** 0870 411 1224

Minicom 0870 411 1225

Email guidelines@lloydstsbfoundations.org.uk

Website www.lloydstsbfoundations.org.uk

Correspondent Kathleen Duncan, Director General

Trustees *Prof. Sir Robert Boyd, chair; Prof. Murray Stewart; Vicki Andrew; Prof. Claire Chilvers; Ann Curno; Irene Evison; John Hughes; Anne Parker; Jane Raimes; Gareth Roberts; Karamjit Singh; Colin Webb.*

Charity Commission no. 327114

Information available Guidelines for applicants. Excellent annual review. Annual report and accounts. Report on impact assessment. Good website.

Summary

The Lloyds TSB Foundation for England and Wales is one of the UK's largest grantmaking trusts. Grants are made to underfunded charities that work to improve the lives of people in local communities, especially those who are disadvantaged or disabled. There are four foundations – one each for:

England and Wales; Scotland; Northern Ireland; and the Channel Islands [each has an individual entry here]. In lieu of dividend on their shareholding, the independent foundations receive 1% of the group's pre-tax profits, averaged over three years. The foundation for England and Wales receives 72% of the income and has donated over £150 million since 1997. Covenanted income for 2004 was £22.7 million (down from £42 million in 2003) and it gave 2,960 grants, totalling £20.4 million.

We are one of the few grant-making trusts with trustees and staff in nine English regions and Wales and our regional structure enables us to respond effectively to local priority needs. Our funding supports charities working in the fields of social and community needs and education and training, and we welcome applications from all sections of the community.

The foundation has three programmes:

- the Community programme (about 85% of the grant total);
- the Collaborative programme (about 10% of the grant total);
- the New Initiatives programme (about 5% of the grants total).

Guidelines 2005

Guiding principles

A number of fundamental guiding principles underpin the work of the foundation and the way in which we work to fulfil our mission.

- We pursue an independent, philanthropic and generalist approach to grant-making.
- We maintain a local presence in each of the regions of England and in Wales.
- We support charities which contribute to local community life at the grassroots level.
- We aim to promote capacity building, and strategic and collaborative working within the voluntary sector.
- We strive to demonstrate best practice, including equality of opportunity, in the ways in which we work.
- We aim to work in ways that are open, transparent and non-bureaucratic.

In order to reach people in local communities we have trustees and staff based in each of the regions of England, and in Wales. Most of our funds (some 75%) are given to charities working at a local or regional level, and we decide the regions' budgets on the basis of population, taking account of deprivation. Our regional structure enables us to respond effectively to priority local needs. A smaller but significant proportion of our income is given to charities that benefit people across the whole of England and Wales.

We encourage innovation and new ideas but also recognise the need for core funding to enable tried and tested ways of working to continue. In 2004 66% of our funding was given for core funding, including salary costs.

We welcome and encourage contact from potential applicants at the earliest stage of preparation of an application to the foundation as we have specific priorities within the regions and for the England and Wales-wide grants programmes. [Full contact details are available at any time from the central office in London, or below].

What are our funding programmes?

We have three programmes of grant-making into which the guidelines fit. These may be applied for regionally or nationally, depending on the geographical coverage of the work – we will advise you on which programme would be most appropriate for your application. The majority of applications will come within the Community programme.

1. Community programme

This is our mainstream grants programme; the vast majority of applications fall within this programme – 88.5% of the funds distributed in 2004.

Details of particular current priorities in the regions and the England and Wales-wide Community Programmes are available from our regional offices, Central Office or from our website.

2. Collaborative programme

The trustees believe the foundation is well-placed to facilitate new ways of working in the sector and to promote the exchange of ideas, knowledge and good practice.

The trustees are keen to identify and support collaborative work (organisations working together) within the sector and with public agencies where appropriate, and have set aside funds specifically for this purpose. We generally take a pro-active approach to identify collaborative funding opportunities.

The kind of work we wish to support includes: projects enhancing co-ordination, co-operation and collaboration between charities to improve the sector's effectiveness, and the evaluation of work undertaken.

In addition to the cash funding for grants made in this programme, foundation staff may also be able to make a contribution of time and expertise to the project, such as membership of a Steering Group. This will vary from grant to grant, and will be discussed with you at an early stage.

In 2004, approximately 7% of the funds were distributed through this programme.

3. New initiatives

A proportion of the foundation's income is set aside to support new initiatives which demonstrate innovation, and where there is a clear intention to extend successfully piloted projects across England and Wales as a whole.

In 2004, approximately 3.5% of the funds were distributed through this programme.

Contact the England and Wales grants team for further details.

Looking ahead to 2006

The Community Programme will continue with approximately two-thirds of the foundation's grant-making budget, responding to local, regional and national needs, with a focus on identified priorities.

From 2006 we will launch a series of Thematic Programmes, with one-third of the foundation's grant-making budget. The first of these will build on the Collaborative Programme and during 2005 we will consult on other potential themes.

From 2006 the New Initiatives Programme will no longer be a specific programme in its current format.

We will publish our guidelines for 2006 in November 2005.

What will we fund?

The trustees' policy is to support underfunded charities so people, especially disadvantaged or disabled people, can play a fuller role in the community. We support a wide range of activities which fall within the broad areas of social and community needs and education and training.

The trustees regularly review changing social needs and will from time to time identify and support specific areas to focus on within their overall aims. In 2005 we continue to have a particular interest in supporting charities working in the three fields below. These apply to all three programmes.

- Family support
- Challenging disadvantage and discrimination
- Helping to make the voluntary sector more effective.

The following types of activity are generally eligible for consideration, but this list is not exhaustive and should be used only as a guide. Please ring us if you are unsure whether your application will be eligible.

- Advice services for people in any kind of need.
- Activities which encourage people to participate in and make a positive contribution to life in their community.
- Community centres and activities for disadvantaged or disabled people of any age.
- Services and support for people with disabilities and their carers.
- Services and support for people with physical or mental health needs.

- Activities which encourage disadvantaged or disabled people to participate in cultural activities.
- Lifelong learning.
- Reading and writing skills.
- Pre-school education.
- Promoting skills that people need to live independently.
- Training for disabled people, including training for the workplace.
- Training for disadvantaged people, to improve their chances of getting a job.

Details of particular current priorities in the regions and the England and Wales-wide programmes are available from our regional offices, central office or from our website.

Size and duration of grants, and grant requirements

Most of our grants (approximately 75%) are one-off payments but we also consider granting money over two years. We have a policy of reducing the level of support in the second year. We are happy for you to use our grant to attract funding from elsewhere.

We have a monitoring and evaluation policy. Full details are provided at the time the grant is approved. The following is a summary. We require acknowledgement of receipt from all grant recipients, and confirmation that the grant will be used for the purpose specified by the trustees.

If you receive a grant over two years you will be required to fill in a monitoring and evaluation form so the trustees can review progress. If they judge this to be satisfactory they will approve the release of the second payment.

If you receive a one-off grant of more than £5,000, we may ask that you fill in a monitoring and evaluation form, and a member of our staff may visit you to see how your work has progressed. This helps us understand the impact of our grants and helps develop future policy. If you receive a one-off grant of up to £5,000, we may telephone you as part of our monitoring procedures.

For grants made under the Collaborative programme there is a greater emphasis on the monitoring and evaluation process.

Under the Community Programme for work at local or regional level, the average grant in 2004 was £5,800. There is no minimum grant, and we encourage applications for small sums where there will be real benefit to people in local communities. For England and Wales-wide work, the average grant in 2004 was £15,100.

Grantmaking in 2004

A total of 4,810 requests for funding were received in 2004. The success rate is generally high (57%).

As a grassroots funder, the foundation allocates the majority of the grant-making budget (75%) to the nine regions and Wales. To ensure that we meet need rather than demand, each regional budget is based on the region's population, weighted for social deprivation. We distributed £16.3 million regionally, compared with £16.6 million in 2003.

Our core programme, the Community Programme, accounted for the majority – 2,851 grants were made totalling £18 million. The average regional Community Programme grant was £5,770. The average England and Wales-wide Community Programme grant was £15,140.

Through the Collaborative Programme, which enables our regional managers to work in a more strategic and pro-active manner, we made a further 69 grants totalling £1.5 million. By volume, the majority (53%) of our regional grants, across both programmes, were for amounts of £5,000 or less. By value, the majority fell into the range of £5,001–£10,000, amounting to £8.7 million. This reflects the foundation's position as primarily a provider of small to medium level grants. A small number of grants (328) were for amounts in excess of £10,000, totalling £6.2 million.

Grants in 2004 were broken down as follows:

East of England	£1.2 million (208 grants)
East Midlands	£1.4 million (245)
Greater London	£1.8 million (330)
North east	£1.3 million (188)
North west	£3 million (407)
South east	£1.3 million (203)
South west	£1.3 million (260)
Wales	£1.4 million (222)
West Midlands	£1.9 million (330)
Yorkshire	£2 million (346)
England and Wales-wide	£3.9 million (223)
New initiative grants	£688,000 (35)
International	£175,000 (5)

This section gives details of the offices along with details of their objectives for 2005.

England and Wales-wide Focus

Lloyds TSB Foundation for England & Wales
3rd Floor
4 St. Dunstan's Hill
London
EC3R 8UL
Tel: 0870 411 1223

Manager, England and Wales: Birgitta Clift

Grants Officers, England and Wales: Jude Stevens and Damien Wilson

The trustees will be prioritising grants within the following areas:

- Refugees and Asylum Seekers including increasing access to advice and information for refugees and asylum seekers.

- Supporting Diversity and Inclusion for charities working with people from black and minority ethnic (BME) including support for smaller charities covering England and Wales working with BME groups and also encouraging mainstream established charities to look at their policies and practices around inclusion.
- Capacity Building for charities including supporting charities so that they can better define and achieve their objectives, engage in consultation and planning, manage projects, develop the skills of individuals within the organisation and take part in partnerships. The Trustees will prioritise support for charities with an income of less than £100,000.

East Of England region

Lloyds TSB Foundation: East of England
Lloyds TSB Bank
28–34 Risbygate Street
Bury St Edmunds
Suffolk
IP33 3AH
Tel: 01284 750168

Regional Manager, East of England: Sue Denning

Regional Trustee, East of England: Professor Clair Chilvers

Looking forward to 2005 we plan to give special attention to:

- older people and carers in coastal and rural areas, particularly but not exclusively, Tendring, North Norfolk, West Norfolk, Waveney and Great Yarmouth
- lone parent families in urban areas, particularly Harlow, Peterborough, Stevenage and Basildon
- capacity building in the black and minority ethnic (BME) sector.

East Midlands region

Lloyds TSB Bank
PO Box 510
11 Low Pavement
Nottingham
NG1 7DF
Tel: 0115 958 8745

Regional Manager, East Midlands: Gary Beharrell

Regional Trustee, East of England: Professor Claire Chilvers

Looking forward to 2005 we plan to:

- help increase the capacity of organisations on the Lincolnshire coast to successfully apply for funding

- increase the number of successful applications received from BME groups
- encourage applications from voluntary groups providing services and support to rural communities, in particular the Peak District and Lincolnshire.
- encourage organisations to diversify their income streams and work collaboratively to reduce costs.

Greater London region

Lloyds TSB Foundation Greater London regional office
PO Box 46156
3rd Floor
4 St Dunstan's Hill
London
EC3R 8WQ
Tel: 020 7398 1728

Regional Manager, Greater London: John Aldridge

Regional Trustee, Greater London: Ann Curno

Looking forward to 2005 we plan to:

- sustain our commitment to BME communities with at least 50% of our funding going to support them
- support work which assists refugees and asylum seekers
- encourage activities and education for vulnerable young people.
- enable socially excluded groups, disabled people, those with mental health problems, those struggling with addiction, and ex-offenders to access education and employment training.

North East region

Lloyds TSB Foundation: North East
Lloyds TSB Bank
PO Box 779
Newcastle upon Tyne
NE99 1YJ
Tel: 0191 261 8433

Regional Manager, North East: Peter Ellis

Regional trustee, North East: Vicki Andrew

Looking forward to 2005 we plan to:

- target rural communities affected by issues of isolation and poor transport
- target areas with high levels of social need
- work with older people and with the groups that help them as they get older
- work with projects helping refugees and asylum seekers integrate into their new environment in the North East

North West region

Lloyds TSB Foundation: North West
Lloyds TSB Bank
Unit M8 The Gateway
89 Sankey Street
Warrington
WA1 1SR
Tel: 01925 234177

Regional Manager, North West: David Kay

Regional Trustee: Anne Parker

Looking forward to 2005 we plan to:

- encourage increased opportunities for the delivery of help and advice in rural communities
- support social cohesion across the region.
- encourage organisations to achieve quality assurance standards.

South East region

Lloyds TSB Bank
4 West Street
Havant
PO9 1PE
Tel: 023 9248 0774

Regional Manager, South East: John Paton

Regional trustee, South East: John Hughes

Looking forward to 2005 we plan to give special attention to:

- those areas in the region with the greatest need with a particular emphasis on small charities
- supporting BME voluntary groups.
- supporting people returning to the community.

South West region

Lloyds TSB Foundation: South West
Lloyds TSB Bank
Sedgemoor House
Deangate Avenue
Taunton
TA1 2UF
Tel: 01823 444032

Regional Manager, South West: Rodney Thorne

Regional Trustee: Jane Raimes

Looking forward to 2005 we plan to:

- encourage charities to undertake formal evaluation of their work.
- assist with the assimilation of refugees and asylum seekers in the region.
- encourage the establishment and further development of voluntary sector forums.

- support the establishment and formal constitution of the South West Funders Forum.

Wales

Lloyds TSB Bank
Black Horse House
Phoenix Way
Swansea Enterprise Park
Swansea
SA7 9EQ
Tel: 01792 314005

Manager, Wales: Mike Lewis

Trustee: Irene Evison

Looking forward to 2005 we plan to:

- develop support in the field of community regeneration across Wales
- support rural based organisations, particularly those working with disadvantaged or disabled people and to support cultural and language activities
- support employment and training opportunities for those marginalised in society
- support health and well-being initiatives within vulnerable communities.

West Midlands region

Lloyds TSB Bank
40 Gaolgate Street
Stafford
ST16 2NS
Tel: 01785 247488

Regional Manager, West Midlands: Karen Argyle

Regional Trustee, West Midlands: Gareth Roberts

Looking forward to 2005 we plan to:

- provide support to the most deprived areas in the region, in particular Sandwell, Walsall, Newcastle under Lyme, Tamworth and Coventry.
- improve both the quality and the number of applications received from BME groups.
- encourage older people to live more independent lives by providing support to them and their carers.

Yorkshire region

Lloyds TSB Bank
St Helen's Square
York
YO1 8QW
Tel: 01904 628 200

Regional Manager, Yorkshire: Stephen Robinson

Regional Trustee, Yorkshire: Gareth Roberts

Looking forward to 2005 we plan to:

- maintain the number of and value of grants awarded to South Yorkshire
- increase support for groups of disabled people.
- support rural outreach projects.

Exclusions

So much work needs support within the community that we have had to exclude some activities. The main areas that we do not normally help are:

- Organisations which are not recognised charities are normally considered to be outside our guidelines. The Charity Commission's guidance states that if an organisation has charitable aims then it must apply to the Commission for registration. One exception is if the income of such an organisation is less than a certain amount, as specified by law (£1,000 a year at the time of going to print). In this case you are normally eligible to apply to us. For further information about registration ring the Charity Commission helpline on 0870 333 0123 or go to their website: www.charitycommission.gov.uk
- Activities which a statutory body is responsible for.
- Activities which collect funds to give to other charities or to individuals or to other organisations.
- Animal welfare.
- Corporate subscriptions or membership of a charity.
- Endowment funds.
- Environment - conserving and protecting plants and animals, geography and scenery.
- Expeditions or overseas travel.
- Fabric appeals for places of worship - including capital projects to comply with the Disability Discrimination Act.
- Fundraising events or activities.
- Hospitals and medical centres.
- Loans or business finance.
- Promoting religion.
- Schools and colleges – On an exceptional basis, applications may be eligible from a school which is a charity in its own right, and which caters exclusively for children with special needs. Please ask for further information if you think your school might be eligible.
- Universities - mainstream teaching activities. The trustees may from time to time consider funding projects based at Universities which fall within the foundation's guidelines.
- Sponsorship or marketing appeals.
- International - The trustees may from time to time consider a limited number of applications from UK-registered charities working overseas. A two-year International Funding Project runs throughout 2004

and 2005 and no new applications can be considered at this time. Please refer to our website or ask for further information.

We do not generally fund building projects, but may consider support for a specific aspect of such projects, e.g. equipment or furnishings.

If you are not sure if your application is within our guidelines, please contact a member of our staff for advice before you fill in the application form.

Applications

We have an application form which you can obtain from any member of the Foundation staff or from our website at www.lloydstsbfoundations.org.uk. You can return your form at any time, but you must send it by post. We will not accept forms that have been e-mailed or faxed.

We will guide you in completing your application in relation to how your proposal fits our current priorities in your region or across England and Wales, and how much money it would be realistic to request. If applicable, we will suggest the most appropriate aspect of your funding requirements for you to submit to us.

You will receive confirmation that we have received your application, usually within one week. We may then contact you, either to discuss aspects of the application on the telephone, or to arrange to visit you.

We ask for a copy of your most recent annual report and full accounts with your completed application form, together with a copy of a recent bank statement in order to verify the bank account details which you will also need to provide on the application form. For recently established organisations which have not yet produced a set of accounts, we ask instead for a projected cashflow and budget.

As part of the assessment process, the trustees ask for information about your commitment to equal opportunities.

We respond to all applications that we receive, so you will definitely be informed of the outcome of your application. The board of trustees meets every three months to approve grants so it usually takes up to three months for us to make decisions. Our staff will give you an indication of when you will hear the outcome.

We strongly advise that you contact us for guidance in the initial stages of your application, and well before you complete the application form.

This is particularly important if you are considering applying for funding over more than one year.

Lloyds TSB Foundation for Northern Ireland

Social and community need, education and training, scientific and medical research

£1.6 million (2003)

Beneficial area Northern Ireland.

The Gate Lodge, 73a Malone Road, Belfast BT9 6SB

Tel. 028 9038 2864 **Fax** 028 9038 2839

Email info@lloydstsbfoundationni.org

Website www.lloydstsbfoundationni.org

Correspondent Sandara Kelso-Robb, Executive Director

Trustees *Mrs Ann Shaw; Lady McCollum; Roy MacDougall; Mrs Brenda Callaghan; Mrs Breige Gadd; Mrs Dawn Livingstone; David Magill; Denis Wilson; Mrs Angela McShane; David Patton; Mrs Janice Doherty; Peter Morrow.*

Northern Irish Charity no. XN72216

Information available Annual review with accounts and guidelines for applicants were provided by the foundation.

Summary

This is the one of the four Lloyds TSB Foundations described in this book (each one wholly independent of the others). Like those others, this charity also supports local communities.

Most donations are said to be one-off, with a small number of commitments made over two or more years. The trustees say that they prefer to make donations towards specific items rather than contributions to large appeals, though the trust will consider core funding for small local charities.

Applications which help to develop voluntary sector infrastructure are encouraged. Donations are generally between £2,500 and £5,000, but probably can be larger.

Guidelines for applicants

The guidelines for applicants read as follows:

The foundation allocates its funds in support of the Northern Ireland community, to enable people, primarily those in need, to be active members of society and to improve their quality of life.

The overall policy of the charity is to support underfunded charities which enable people, especially disadvantaged or disabled people, to play a fuller role in the community.

The trustees are also keen to encourage the infrastructure of the voluntary sector and encourage applications for operational costs. This includes salary costs which may be supported over two or three years, and training and education for managers and staff.

Donations for one-off projects are generally in the region of £2,500 and £5,000, but there is no minimum. Applications for larger amounts will be considered where there is wider benefit.

The foundation has two main target areas to which it seeks to allocate funds
- Social and community needs
- Education and training.

Social and community needs

A wide range of activities are supported and the following are meant as a guide only.

Community services

Family centres, youth and older people's clubs, after school clubs, play schemes, help groups, childcare provision.

Advice services

Homelessness, addictions, bereavement, family guidance, money advice, helplines.

Disabled people

Residences, day centres, transport, carers, information and advice, advocacy.

Promotion of health

Information and advice, mental health, hospices, day care, home nursing, independent living for older people.

Civic responsibility

Juveniles at risk, crime prevention, promotion of volunteering, victim support, mediation, rehabilitation of offenders.

Cultural enrichment

Improving participation in and access to the arts and national heritage for disadvantaged and disabled people.

Education and training

The objective is to enhance educational opportunities for disadvantaged and disabled people of all ages.
- Projects which help socially excluded people develop their potential and secure employment.
- Employment training (for disabled and disadvantaged people).
- Promotion of life skills, independent living skills for disabled people.

- Enhancing education for disabled young people, pre school education, literacy skills (where no other support is available).

In 2003 the foundation made 275 grants worth £1.6 million, averaging £5,900 each.

They were broken down geographically as follows:

Belfast	£899,000 (127 grants)
Londonderry	£195,000 (23)
County Antrim	£159,000 (29)
County Armagh	£90,000 (21)
County Down	£98,000 (24)
County Fermanagh	£37,000 (12)
County Londonderry	£45,000 (14)
County Tyrone	£80,000 (17)
Great Britain	£37,000 (8)

Multiple Awards included: £30,000 to NI Children's Hospice towards the salary of 'Head of Home'; £16,000 to Simon Community Northern Ireland towards the 'Outspoken' project; £10,000 to Action Cancer towards the Mobile Detection Unit Rural Communities Scheme; £7,500 to Action MS towards the Care Advice Project; £5,000 to Fivemiletown Community Development Association to support three projects; £4,000 to Nexus Institute – Belfast towards the salary of an outreach counsellor; £3,500 to Cancer Lifeline towards counselling and heating costs; £2,600 to Hope UK to support running costs; and £1,000 to Strand Presbyterian Church towards the cost of a youth worker.

Exclusions

No support for:
- organisations which are not recognised as charities by the Inland Revenue;
- individuals, including students;
- animal welfare;
- environmental projects, including projects which deal with geographic and scenic issues–however the trustees may consider projects that improve the living conditions of disadvantaged individuals and groups;
- activities which are normally the responsibility of central or local government or some other responsible body;
- schools, universities and colleges (except for projects specifically to benefit disabled people);
- hospitals and medical centres;
- sponsorship or marketing appeals;
- fabric appeals for places of worship;
- promotion of religion;
- activities which collect funds for subsequent redistribution to others;
- endowment funds;
- fundraising events or activities;

- corporate affiliation or membership of a charity;
- loans or business finance;
- expeditions or overseas travel (except for projects specifically benefiting disadvantaged young people from Northern Ireland);
- construction of and extensions to buildings.

'The trustees may from time to time consider a limited number of applications from NI based charities working overseas. However we are currently only supporting charities which we approach ourselves and cannot accept unsolicited applications for overseas work.'

Applications

Application is on a form available from the foundation, which says 'Please bear in mind that the trustees will only see your application form together with one additional page of supporting text.

The information requested includes: registered charity number and evidence of tax-exempt status, a brief description of the activities of the charity, details of the project for which the grant is sought, details of overall funding needed for the project, including a breakdown, what funds have already been raised, how the remaining funds will be raised, trustees' report and full audited or independently examined accounts.

Trustees meet quarterly to review applications.

Lloyds TSB Foundation for Scotland

Social and community needs, education and training, scientific, medical and social research

£7.3 million (2003)

Beneficial area Scotland and overseas.

Riverside House, 502 Gorgie Road, Edinburgh EH11 3AF

Tel. 0870 902 1201 **Fax** 0870 902 1202

Email enquiries@fundingthefuture.org.uk

Website www.fundingthefuture.org.uk

Correspondent Andrew Muirhead, Chief Executive

Trustees *Revd Norman Drummond, chair; Prof. Sir Michael Bond; Mrs Sandra E Brydon; Mrs Fiona Crighton; Ms Rani Dhir; Revd Ronald Ferguson; Ms Elaine Ross; Ms Susan Robinson; Prof. Joyce Lishman.*

Scottish Charity no. SC009481

Information available Criteria, priorities and principles booklet. Exemplary annual reviews and application packs. Full report and accounts. Comprehensive information is also available on the foundation's fine website.

Summary

The foundation allocates its funds in support of the Scottish community, to enable people, primarily those in need, to be active members of society. Although the majority of awards are for local charities, the foundation does consider larger appeals where benefit is provided across Scotland. There is no minimum or maximum sum granted, with awards ranging from a few hundred to tens of thousands of pounds.

Lloyds TSB Foundation for Scotland not only offers support under the main grant scheme but also provides funding under two other grant schemes:

- Capacity Building Grant scheme;
- Partnership Drugs Initiative.

About two in three grants are for amounts between £2,000 and £10,000. Most are one-off, but grants can be spread over two or three years. Capital, running and project costs can all be supported.

In 2003 the foundation had assets of £1.9 million and an income of £8.2 million. Grants were made totalling £7.3 million.

Background

The foundation was formed in 1986 as one of four independent trusts established by the then TSB Group. Collectively they receive 1% of the bank's pre-tax profits for distribution. The Foundation for Scotland receives 19% of this amount. Since the merger between Lloyds Bank and the TSB Group in December 1995, and in common with the Foundations for England and Wales, Northern Ireland and the Channel Islands, income to this foundation has grown significantly.

This foundation has also developed partnerships with other bodies, including the Scottish Executive, for particular programmes and £750,000 of its income came from such sources in 2003.

There are 17 staff including six grant assessors and two capacity building grant co-ordinators.

Besides its regular programme of 'surgeries' throughout Scotland, the foundation also runs an annual forum at which all applicants, whether successful or not, are invited to discuss their views of the foundation's work.

Lloyds TSB staff can claim £400 annually for fundraising or for volunteering their time. In 2003 this initiative raised £845,000 for charities in Scotland with 636 members of staff claiming matched giving grants.

Grantmaking practice

The foundation's own excellent descriptions of its grantmaking are reprinted in full below, following a few brief introductory notes.

Multi-year awards

Future year commitments are restricted to 30% of the next year's projected income and 15% of the following year's projected income. Grants given over several years are often tapered i.e. the grant is reduced each year. The trust also states: 'smaller charities that are more fragile have priority on multi-year awards, as larger more sophisticated applicant groups arguably have the machinery to enable them to make applications on a regular basis, and are consequently better able to win resources'.

Success rates

The foundation estimates that about 40% of applications are successful, but that collectively they only get, on average, one-third to a half as much money as they had requested.

Reasons for rejection

The foundation has published the following note on this:

The trustees regret that demands made on the foundation's funds always outstrip the funds available and this means that many good applications, whilst meeting criteria, cannot be supported. Owing to the high quality of applications in general, there is often a narrow margin between success and failure.

In assessing past applications, there were a few recurring features in those which were unsuccessful:

- Lack of clear plans for other fundraising.
- Insufficient detail on potential benefits a project would create.
- 'All or nothing' requests for large appeals. (The foundation would prefer to see a part-funding option.)
- Inadequate explanation about the financial position of an applicant, e.g. policy on reserves, reasons for changes in level of costs year on year, etc.
- No clear strategy on safety/security, particularly important where a group are working with children or vulnerable adults, or engaged in transport.
- Multi-year funding:
  - Lack of strategy for the period beyond which funding was being sought.
  - Vague objectives.

It should be stressed that applications are generally of a very high quality, however applicants may find the above to be a helpful checklist.

Earlier, but still useful, advice is as follows:

In particular the foundation emphasises the following, to be remembered when completing the application form:

- Keep it simple – be concise and direct;
- Stress the difference our support will make – facts and figures are important;
- Always provide a detailed breakdown of costs;
- Tell us about other fundraising – we will be particularly interested to learn of local community fundraising as well as approaches to other charitable trusts;
- It is essential that objectives relating to revenue funding are 'SMART' – Specific, Measurable, Achievable, Realistic and Testing.

Criteria, Priorities and Principles 2003–05

Principles

The undernoted principles will apply to all applications and priority support will be considered for projects demonstrating one or more of the following which:

- Encourage empowerment by consulting and involving users.
- Help and encourage independent living and development of life skills.
- Provide new and continuing opportunities for personal enrichment and quality of life, e.g. skills training across all age bands.
- Collect information through contacts or research to establish, consolidate and promote good practice and develop policy.
- Represent and promote the needs of people through advocacy, advice,

information and support. In particular for people with mental health problems, physical and learning disabilities and the elderly.

- Demonstrate a collaborative approach by networking with other agencies/providers to avoid duplication of services.
- Demonstrate equality of opportunity.
- Promote anti-racism and discourage anti-social behaviour.
- Demonstrate good evaluation and monitoring procedures.
- Adopt preventive measures and stimulate early intervention programmes.
- Encourage the involvement of volunteers.
- Recognise cultural diversity and particular needs that may arise.
- Demonstrate care for the safety of children and vulnerable adults – in particular SCRO/disclosure checks on all volunteers/staff.

General Criteria

The trustees of the foundation are focused on the needs of disadvantaged and marginalised people throughout Scotland. Funds are allocated to recognised charities which primarily help people to be active members of society and improve their quality of life. Criteria have been set by the trustees in a way which attempts to include a wide variety of charitable activity.

Only applications which fit the criteria will be assessed for funding support. As demand for funding often outstrips supply, applications which fall within the foundation's priority areas – as listed below – will rank above those fulfilling the general criteria only.

- The board of trustees is particularly keen to receive applications seeking to address the needs of minority groups working within the published criteria. The foundation is also sensitive to the special circumstances arising from rural deprivation.
- The trustees are keen to support innovative projects but recognise the value of established services. Both approaches are seen as having equal value and will be considered for support on the merit of individual projects.
- Both capital and revenue funding will be considered. Applicants are advised to consider the average award amounts noted in the annual review. This may help to form an expectation of the level of funding which the foundation may provide.

Social and Community Needs

Community Activities

After school clubs; youth clubs; clubs for the elderly; family centres; playgroups/ nurseries (operating in areas of deprivation); community centres; village halls; arts and drama projects (which concentrate on the

disabled and disadvantaged); volunteering; self-help groups.

Crisis and Advice Services

Homelessness; addictions; family guidance; bereavement; counselling; befriending; money advice; women's aid.

Disabled People

Day centres; residential accommodation; advice and support; transport.

Health Issues

Information and advice; mental health; hospices; day care for the elderly; support for carers.

Civic Responsibility

Crime prevention; offenders and their families; at risk/hard to reach young people; promotion of good citizenship.

Education and Training

Development of Potential

Guiding young people to develop their potential; improve literacy skills; build self-confidence and self-esteem; assist individuals into further education.

Employment

Assisting individuals to obtain employment with particular emphasis on young people; training which will provide disadvantaged and disabled people with employment opportunities.

Life Skills and Independent Living

Particular interest in young people; the elderly; and those mentally or physically disadvantaged.

Research – Scientific, Medical and Social

The board will from time to time make funding available for research purposes. Grants will be made in partnership with research bodies, pursuing aspects of work agreed by the trustees, displaying a rigorous assessment/review process for dealing with research applications. Such bodies are encouraged to contact the chief executive of the foundation prior to submitting a formal proposal.

The foundation will not consider research applications other than as part of an agreed partnership arrangement.

Priorities 2003–05

Every three years the trustees establish priorities from within the general criteria. Priority support will be considered for projects which include any of the following:

Children – projects which:

- Provide a safe place where children can talk about their worries/concerns/ emotional issues e.g. children's counsellors or therapeutic services.
- Create a safe environment for children to have the opportunity to play together.

- Build self-esteem and self-confidence which will enhance life changes and experiences for children, and/or broaden their horizons through opportunities which they may not currently have, e.g. life skills projects/drama/art.
- Promote peer support and advocacy giving children a voice and encouraging empowerment.
- Support for children as young carers and their siblings (including siblings of special needs children).

Young People – projects which:

- Value young people by listening to them and addressing their problems.
- Show evidence of young people's involvement by including them in decision making.
- Work with hard–to–reach young people who do not include themselves in organised youth work.
- Support detached and outreach work which reaches the most vulnerable young people in our society.
- Promote accreditation of young people by recognising their contribution through involvement as a volunteer or as a service user, thus building self-esteem.

Ageing Population – projects which:

- Represent and promote the needs and wellbeing of older people through advocacy, advice or support. Encourage inclusion and reduce isolation.
- Support older people who provide direct services, i.e. work done by older people for older people.
- Support inter-generational projects or themes which strengthen contact across generations and cultural divides.
- Help and encourage independence and independent living.

Parenting – projects which:

- Promote parenting skills which help with understanding and responding to children's social, emotional and development needs.
- Encourage male participation by promoting the importance of the role of fathers and their active involvement in the lives of their children.
- Support opportunities which allow families to take part in ordinary family life, e.g. outings/holidays (within the UK).

Physical and Mental Disability – projects which:

- Improve the quality of life for disabled people by promoting independence and raising awareness of disability.
- Assist people with learning disabilities, sensory impairments and users of mental health services.

Support for People at Risk – projects which:

- Establish support networks to assist homeless people back into mainstream society.
- Provide information, advice and raise awareness of homelessness services.
- Work with people living in supported/ temporary accommodation.
- Provide advice, support, or accommodation to sufferers of domestic abuse and their children.
- Provide support to people suffering abuse from bullying or anti-social behaviour.

Substance Misuse – projects which:

- Focus on early intervention, including education and alternative activities, aimed at building awareness and minimising harm.
- Provide support, advice, and information to people whose lives are affected by the misuse of drugs, alcohol, or volatile substances, e.g. solvents.

Development of People and Resource – charities which:

- Are umbrella organisations working with charities focused on our priority areas to improve operational efficiencies and assist with the development of access to funding.
- Work within our priority areas by assisting the development of staff and volunteers as well as the skills of user groups.
- Operate as community centres/village halls by providing physical facilities for the benefit of groups working within our priority areas.

Grant schemes

Standard grants scheme

The Standard Grant Scheme is our main grant programme and it is through this programme that the majority of charities are introduced to the foundation. In particular we fund local community organisations where our funding will make a real difference.

Over the past twelve months we have approved applications by 433 recognised charities in Scotland (about 50% of those who applied). All sorts of charities receive funding from this scheme – no charity is too small to be considered. Our primary interest is in local charities working at the grassroots but we are also keen to fund charities which make a difference on a national level.

In order to assess your eligibility, please look at our Criteria, Priorities and Principles for 2003 – 2005. Our priority areas are updated every three years in consultation with the voluntary sector in Scotland.

If you would like to talk to someone about your application or the sorts of projects that we fund, we hold surgeries all over the country where you can meet a member of

our assessment team. Last year we held more than 80 surgeries across the length and breadth of Scotland.

The capacity building grant programme

This programme is designed to support growth and development activities and address short term skill gaps in the voluntary sector in Scotland by providing funding for voluntary organisations to access a panel of independent consultants. The consultants are experienced in the voluntary sector and can assist in resolving many of today's issues affecting charities. The panel of consultants has skills in areas such as:

- financial management
- fundraising planning
- good governance
- information technology
- marketing
- strategic planning
- staff development.

The foundation issues a separate note for applicants interested in this programme. Some of its contents are as follows:

We anticipate considerable interest in this programme, and we are unlikely to be able to meet all requests... The primary aim of the present programme is 'capacity building' – that is, helping organisations to create and sustain services which have value for the community, to use their resources efficiently and effectively and to maintain good working relationships with their committees, staff, volunteers, other agencies, the users of their services and the public in general. Applications for fundraising alone will therefore attract a lower priority than those where the fundraising element is one part of a much wider strategic area which meets this criteria.

[The programme] is particularly interested in supporting recognised charities whose focus is on social and community needs [see 'general criteria' section above for more details, Ed.].

You can apply for a capacity building grant at the same time as submitting an application for a standard grant.

For further details on how to apply, see 'applications' section.

In 2003, 87 charities in Scotland benefited from Capacity Building, with a total of almost £300,000 allocated.

Partnership Drugs Initiative

The Partnership Drugs Initiative (PDI) is a strategic funding programme that promotes voluntary sector work with vulnerable children and young people affected by substance misuse. With the continued support of our partners, The Scottish Executive and Atlantic Philanthropies, we work with Drug Action Teams and local charities to make a difference to the lives of children and young people affected by substance misuse.

Our target groups are:
- Children and young people in families in which parents misuse drugs and/or alcohol.
- Pre-teen children who are at higher risk of developing problem substance misuse.
- Young people who are developing or have established problem substance misuse.

The PDI promotes partnership between agencies to ensure a holistic approach to meeting the needs of vulnerable young people and their families. Funding awards are made directly to the voluntary organisation but the applications should be channelled through the local Drug Action Team.

One of the main aims of the PDI is to contribute to establishing 'what works' in tackling the problems of substance misuse.

In 2003 £1.3 million was invested in 18 grants.

The overseas programme

The Overseas Programme was initiated in 2003, when trustees recognised the difficulties that Scottish charities have in getting funding for overseas work.

During its inaugural year the scheme has awarded funds to 23 Scottish charities working abroad, with grants ranging from £2,000 to £40,000. The foundation is the biggest independent funder of overseas projects in Scotland.

Exclusions

The trustees regret they cannot support all fields of voluntary and charitable activity. To focus funding on the foundation's priority areas, the following purposes will not be considered:

- organisations which are not recognised as a charity by the Inland Revenue/Charity Commission;
- individuals – including students;
- animal welfare;
- environment – projects entirely of an environmental nature e.g. geographic and scenic, conservation and protection of flora and fauna;
- mainstream activities and statutory requirements of schools, universities and colleges;
- mainstream activities and statutory requirements of hospitals and medical centres;
- sponsorship or marketing appeals;

- activities which collect funds for subsequent redistribution to others;
- the establishment/preservation of endowment funds;
- expeditions or overseas travel;
- building projects for places of worship, other than where such buildings provide accommodation to community groups;
- building projects for visitor centres, heritage centres, museums and theatres;
- historic restoration;
- retrospective funding;
- the one year rule – applicants will not be eligible for further consideration until at least one year has elapsed from their original application. In the case of a multi-year award having been granted, no further application will be considered until 12 months has elapsed from the final scheduled payment, e.g. an organisation granted a three-year award in April 2003 may not re-apply until April 2006.

Applications

Application forms for all grants schemes, complete with comprehensive guidance notes, are available from the foundation. These can be requested by telephone, by e-mail, or through the website. Foundation staff are always willing to provide additional help.

Surgery dates for all the schemes are finalised in December of the preceding year and details can be obtained from the foundation after that date.

Standard grant scheme process

Before submitting an application, information and advice can be assessed through surgeries, visits, telephone or e-mail contact. Once submitted, applications are allocated to an assessor. The assessor will contact you, either by telephone or personal visit to discuss the application. The assessor's report is then presented to the assessment team which meet weekly. The team puts forward recommendations to the trustees. The trustees consider applications at their board meetings which are held every two months. Closing dates for applications are usually 12 weeks before each board meeting. Applicants will be notified of the decision within 14 days of the meeting.

One-off awards

Progress reports should be sent within a year of receiving the grant. Review visits will be carried out upon at least 50% of

these awards. You can re-apply 12 months after the original award date.

Multi-year awards

One month before each payment is due, a progress report will be requested. The report should include objectives for the coming year and a copy of the most recent audited accounts. Following receipt of the report, an evaluation visit will take place and if this is satisfactory the next payment will be issued. You can re-apply 12 months after the final payment is scheduled.

The capacity-building grant process

The application procedure differs from the standard scheme. Every potential applicant is visited by one of the programme co-ordinators for exploratory talks before applications are submitted. Applications are dealt with by a team of consultants before recommendations are given to the trustees. The trustees meet three times a year. Closing dates for applications are usually 20 weeks prior to board meetings. If successful a consultant will contact you to complete an agreement and action plan; once this has been signed the grant will be given and the consultant will commence the work as agreed. More details on this process can be found the trust's annual review or on the website.

The foundation's literature also includes helpful tips on filling in the application.

Partnership drugs initiative

Contact your local Drug Action Team or the PDI Programme Manager to discuss your proposal. They will also be able to advise you of the deadline for submitting your application.

Further infomration is available from Rachel Sunderland, the PDI Programme Manager on 0870 902 1201 or by e-mail at rs@ltsbfoundationforscotland.org.uk. Contact information on local Drug Action Teams is available at www.drugmisuse.isdscotland.org/index.shtml

Overseas grant programme

Contact the trust for further details.

The Lolev Charitable Trust

Jewish

See below
Beneficial area Worldwide.

14a Gilda Crescent, London N16 6JP
Correspondent A Tager, Trustee
Trustees *A Tager; E Tager; M Tager.*
Charity Commission no. 326249
Information available Accounts are on file at the Charity Commission.

The objects of the charity are the relief of the sick and needy and the support of Orthodox Jewish education.

In 2003 the trust's income and expenditure increased dramatically by around £1 million on the previous year to £1.8 million. No further information was available for the year, however, most of its income has previously been from donations, with almost all being then distributed in grants

Previous beneficiaries include Yeshivat Knesset Hagdola, Or Avraham, Yad Harashaz, Chajdey Shalom, Ateres Chachomin, Ezer Nissuin Fund, Zidit Shov, Mishcan Rephael, Mifal Oseh Chayil and Talmud Torah RMA.

Applications

In writing to the correspondent.

The London Marathon Charitable Trust

Sport, recreation and leisure

£1.2 million (2002/03)
Beneficial area London and any area where London Marathon stages an event (City of Birmingham, South Northamptonshire and, from 2005 City of Liverpool).

2 The Square, Richmond, Surrey TW9 1DY
Tel. 020 8940 0102 **Fax** 020 8940 5798
Email lmct@ffleach.co.uk
Correspondent David Golton

Trustees *Sir James Swaffield, chair; John Austin; Geoff Clarke; James Clarke; John Disley; Eileen Gray; Sir Eddie Kulukundis; Dame Mary Peters; Bryan Smith; Joyce Smith; Richard Sumray; Lord Patrick Carter; Sir Rodney Walker.*
Charity Commission no. 283813
Information available Full accounts and guidelines were provided by the trust.

This trust was formed to distribute the surplus income from the London Marathon to much-needed recreational facilities in the city. Grants are made in London and any area where London Marathon stages an event including City of Birmingham, South Northamptonshire and, from 2005 City of Liverpool.

Its funds are raised from the money the organisers receive for the marathon itself (as well as the Hydroactive Challenges for Women in London, Birmingham and Liverpool and Adidas Flora London Half Marathons in Silverstone and Liverpool) from entries, sponsorship and the like. This totals around £1.5 million a year and is available in grants from the trust. (The trust has no connection to the fundraising efforts of the individuals involved in the race, who raise around £30 million each year for their chosen good causes.)

Grants have been for amounts up to £350,000 and are made in all the London boroughs to fund (or part-fund) the development of a wide variety of sports and recreational facilities for local people of all ages and sporting abilities. Grants have been made towards sports equipment for schools, ramps and lifts to help people with disabilities enjoy sport, the establishment of play areas and nature trails and improvements to existing leisure facilities.

In 2002/03 the trust had assets of £5.2 million. Total income was £2 million, of which £1.8 million came from the trading subsidiary. Grants were made to 40 organisations totalling £1.2 million.

A total of £272,000 was given to London Borough Councils. This consisted of £60,000 to Sutton, £45,000 to Tower Hamlets, £40,000 to Haringey, £26,000 to Southwark, £25,000 to Ealing, £21,000 to Lewisham, £10,000 to Wandsworth, £8,600 to Waltham Forest, £7,000 to Wandsworth and £5,000 each to Ealing and Hackney.

By far the largest grants were £350,000 to National Playing Fields Association and £106,000 to London Playing Fields Society. Other beneficiaries included

Battersea Ironsides Sports Club and the Royal Parks (£45,000 each), Sport Aid (£40,000), Tower Hill Improvement Trust (£30,000), Disabled Sailing Centre (£24,000) and Joseph Court Tenants and Residents Association (£20,000).

In 2004, the trust gave its first grant outside London to the City of Birmingham for the provision of pool lifts for the disabled at swimming pools across the city.

Exclusions

Grants cannot be made to 'closed' clubs or schools, unless the facility is available for regular public use. No grants are made for recurring or revenue costs. Individuals are not supported.

Applications

On a form available from the correspondent. The trustees meet once a year; the closing date is usually the end of August.

The Lord's Taverners

Minibuses and sports equipment for people with disabilities, cricket

£2.7 million (2004)
Beneficial area UK.

10 Buckingham Place, London SW1E 6HX
Tel. 020 7821 2828 **Fax** 020 7821 2829
Email hq@lordstaverners.org
Website www.lordstaverners.org
Correspondent Nicky Atkinson, Foundation Manager
Trustee *The Council of The Lord's Taverners comprising Richard Groom, Chair, and 17 others.*
Charity Commission no. 306054
Information available Annual report and accounts. Guidelines for applicants available from website.

Summary

The charity's aim is 'to give young people, particularly those with special needs, a sporting chance':

- by providing incentives to play cricket in schools and clubs (The Lord's Taverners is accredited by The

England and Wales Cricket Board (ECB) as the official National Charity for recreational cricket;

- by encouraging young people with special needs to participate in sporting activitie;s
- by supplying minibuses to special needs organisations
- by creating recreational facilities in conjunction with the National Playing Fields Association.

General

This is a sports-based fundraising charity, supported by a network of voluntary fundraising committees around the country which organise a range of events. In 2004 it had an income of £5.6 million, mainly as a result of fundraising activities, but also from donations, subscriptions and investments. Grants were made during the year totalling £2.7 million.

Grants in 2004 were allocated in the following categories:

- cricket £700,000
- minibuses £1.7 million
- sport and recreation for young people with special needs £320,000

In addition £30,000 a year is given to the National Playing Fields Association.

Guidelines for applicants

Youth Cricket

'To encourage youth participation at the grass roots level of the game by way of providing a variety of cricket equipment bags. Awarding grants towards the cost of non turf pitches, practice ends and netting. Also the funding or sponsoring of a variety of regional and national competitions for youth cricket.'

Lord's Taverners Minibuses

Specially adapted minibuses are donated to schools, homes and organisations which look after youngsters under the age of 25 who have special needs and/or disabilities. A contribution of a minimum of £8,000 towards the cost of the vehicle is required from the recipient organisations. There is currently a two year waiting list. There is also a Fast Track option with a six month waiting list for a contribution of a minimum of £16,000. The average cost of an adapted minibus is approximately £32,000 (depending on specifications).

The Lord's Taverners will provide either:

(i) a 15 or 17 seat standard minibus (not converted to take wheelchairs); or

(ii) a 13 seat minibus with a semi-automatic under floor tail-lift which will carry up to 4 wheelchairs; or

(iii) a 16 seat minibus with a semi-automatic under floor tail-lift which will carry up to 5 wheelchairs.

A contribution is required from the recipient organisation as 'it demonstrates that you are able to raise funds to maintain the vehicle once you have received it, as costs about £4,000 per year to run; you will treat it with respect as you will have invested in it.'

The minibus committee meets quarterly and applicants will be informed as soon as possible on the outcome of their request.

Sport & Recreation for Young People with Special Needs

Funds for sports related equipment and facilities are granted to organisations to encourage youngsters (under the age of 25 years) with physical or mental disabilities to participate in sporting and recreational activities within a group environment. Grants do not normally exceed £5,000.

Exclusions

Youth cricket

 The following is not normally grant aided:

- building or renovation of pavilions_
- sight screens
- bowling machines
- mowers/rollers
- overseas tours
- clothing.

Sport for young people with special needs

The following will not normally be considered for a grant:

- capital costs
- general grants
- running costs including salaries
- individuals (although applications will be considered for equipment to enable an individual to participate in a team/group recreational activity)
- holidays/overseas tours.

Minibuses

Homes, schools and organisations catering for young people with special needs under the age of 25 years, are entitled to only one minibus per location, although applications are accepted for a replacement.

Applications

Cricket grants are normally considered by the foundation on the recommendation of the ECB and the necessary application forms are available from local county cricket boards.

The foundation committee meets quarterly to review applications for grant aid. All applications must be presented on the appropriate application forms and should be submitted to the foundation secretary no later than one month before the foundation committee meeting.

Application forms with detailed application instructions are available from the foundation secretary or on the website.

The Lotus Foundation

Children and families, women, animal protection, addiction recovery, education

£250,000 (2004)

Beneficial area UK, especially London and Surrey; occasionally overseas.

90 Jermyn Street, London SW1Y 6JD

Email bridget@lotusfoundation.com

Website www.lotusfoundation.com

Correspondent Mrs B Starkey, Trustee

Trustees *Mrs B Starkey; R Starkey; Mrs E Turner.*

Charity Commission no. 1070111

Information available Information was provided by the trust.

This trust was established in 1998 and aims to make grants to other established and newly-formed charities. The primary objectives of the trust are 'to offer financial aid and assistance to facilitate family and child welfare, women's issues, animal protection, addiction recovery and education'.

In 2004 grants totalled £250,000. Beneficiaries in 2003 included: Lil' Angel Bunny Foundation (£12,000), Visions of Glory (£10,000), Disability Challengers (£5,000), Noah's Ark Children's Hospice, the Beacon Appeal and Drugs Abuse Resistance Education (£2,000 each), The House of St Barnabas Soho, Mayday

Trust and SAIL (£1,000 each) and London Wildcare (£500).

Exclusions

No response to circular appeals. No grants to individuals, non-registered charities, charities working outside of the foundation's areas of interest, or for research purposes.

Applications

In writing to the correspondent. Initial enquiries by e-mail are welcome. Otherwise, give a brief outline of the work, amount required and project/programme to benefit. The trustees prefer applications which are simple and economically prepared rather than glossy 'prestige' and mail sorted brochures.

Note: In order to reduce administration costs and concentrate its efforts on the charitable work at hand, unsolicited requests will no longer be acknowledged by the foundation.

John Lyon's Charity

Children and young people in north and west London

£3.1 million (2003/04)

Beneficial area The London boroughs of Barnet, Brent, Camden, Ealing, Kensington and Chelsea, Hammersmith and Fulham, Harrow and the Cities of London and Westminster.

45 Pont Street, London SW1X 0BX

Tel. 020 7591 3330 **Fax** 020 7589 0807

Email info@johnlyonscharity.org.uk

Website www.johnlyonscharity.org.uk

Correspondent The Grants Office

Trustees *The keepers and governors of the possessions revenues and goods of the Free Grammar School of John Lyon. Grants committee: Nick Stuart, chair; Prof. D M P Mingos; Mrs G Baker; F Singer.*

Charity Commission no. 237725

Information available Full information is available on the charity's website.

This is one of the largest local educational charities in the country, supporting both formal and informal educational activities of every sort. Its budgets vary greatly from year to year for historical reasons, and from one part of its beneficial area to another. There are, however, significant cross-borough grants.

Background

The charity began in the late 16th century when John Lyon donated his 48 acre Maida Vale farm as an endowment for the upkeep of two roads from London to Harrow and Kenton. In 1991, the charity was given discretion to use the revenue from the endowment to benefit the inhabitants of the London boroughs through which these roads passed.

The charity is an independent branch of the larger Harrow Foundation which also governs Harrow and John Lyon schools. It is advised in one part of its grantmaking by Julia Kaufmann, formerly a director of BBC Children in Need.

General

The charity makes over 60 substantial new grants a year, for amounts normally between £2,000 and £50,000 and there are a further 50 or so for amounts of £2,000 or less under its 'small grants scheme'. Few grants are recurrent, though the larger awards may be for periods of up to three years.

The largest grants tend to be in the form of support for ongoing bursary and scholarship programmes, and then support for capital projects.

Guidelines for applicants

John Lyon's Charity, 'enhancing the conditions of life and improving the life-chances of young people through education,' gives grants to groups and organisations for the benefit of children and young adults who are resident in the London boroughs listed above. Grants are made in consultation with these local authorities.

We give grants:

- to support education and training, particularly for young adults;
- to broaden horizons and encourage an appreciation of the value of cultural diversity through activities such as dance, drama, music, creative writing and the visual arts;
- to provide childcare, support for parents, and help where parental support is lacking;
- to enhance recreation through sport, youth clubs and playschemes;
- to help young people achieve their full potential;
- to promote youth issues;
- to develop new opportunities for young people.

Some fixed-term grants may be eligible for renewal, depending on changing circumstances, records of achievement, and the availability of funds.

What we fund:

- capital costs (e.g. equipment, furniture etc);
- revenue costs (e.g. salaries, running costs).

The maximum length of any grant is normally three years. There are no strict limits on the amount of a grant that may be awarded.

Monitoring projects

A recurrent feature of both local and national projects aimed at children and young people is the precariousness and instability of their funding. We need you to explain to us what kind of help you need.

Because we need to learn from the experience of those who receive grants we expect reports on the progress of each project. Without this feedback, examples of good practice and valuable initiatives can be lost.

The information we get back from supported projects will also help shape future policy.

The size and scope of any evaluation exercise will be related to the level of grant.

Grantmaking in 2003/04

During the year the charity made 138 new grants totalling £3.1 million. It gives the following review of some of the activities it has recently funded:

Resourcing the Arts in Schools
ACAVA (Association for Cultural Advancement through Visual Art) provides visual arts services including studios for professional artists. The charity was the original funder of First Base, ACAVA's pioneering scheme that provides free studio spaces for young artists. Support is now provided for ACAVA's Sculptors-in-Schools programme [£96,000 over three years] developed in partnership with Hammersmith & Fulham LEA Arts Team. The scheme complements the charity's existing support for the Arts Team's rolling programme of dance residencies in schools.

University of the Arts London (formerly The London Institute), the consortium of the capital's leading art and design schools, has combined with the Specialist Schools Trust to deliver Resourcing Creativity [£40,000 per year for three years], a project to develop innovative approaches to arts education in Specialist Arts Colleges. Artists engage in long-term projects with schools.

There is access to art facilities and out of hours art classes at the University as well as work placements, an exhibition space for pupils' artwork, and guidance on career opportunities in the arts. The programme is run in tandem with the Government's Widening Participation initiative to encourage a wider range of applicants to higher education.

Support has been provided for Transforming Children through Singing, a programme for primary schools organised by the Voices Foundation [£10,000]. The approach emphasises pitch matching, hand signs and awareness of rhythm, pulse, patterns and phrasing introduced through songs and games. There are simple call and response games at nursery level, working up with older children to songs in three or four parts and to more complex exercises involving hand signs. The curriculum is "embedded" in schools through a teacher-training programme.

Composing for Kids is organised by SPNM, the Society for the Promotion of New Music [£7,500 per year for two years from the charity]. Emerging composers are paired with primary schools and there is an annual national composition project, Sound Inventors.

Museums and Galleries

Our policy is for the arts to be at the centre of provision for young people—and not only in schools. London's great arts institutions are increasingly involving young people. Enthralled children and their key workers gathered around pictures from the superb national collection are a common feature at the National Gallery. The Gallery's Line of Vision programme, supported by the charity [£20,000 per year for three years], targets children in care and introduces them to the pleasures of appreciating and making art.

At the Royal Academy of Arts, sixth-formers can treat Britain's oldest fine arts institution as a 'home from home'. Indifference is overcome through AttRAct [£25,000 per year for two years], an access programme designed to appeal directly to young people. There are private views, free membership of the Young Friends of the Academy, a transport stipend for visitors from the outer boroughs, a life-drawing programme, and sessions exploring career opportunities in the visual arts. A liaison group of A-Level art students steers the programme. The project builds on the popularity of the John Lyon Open Evenings based on major exhibitions that attracted over 1,000 students.

The charity has supported the ice rink at Somerset House and is now a major backer of the summer Family Free Time event which opens up Somerset House and the art collections to schools, community groups and families [£50,000 towards both activities]. Artists are selected from around

the world and the diverse performers attract an equally diverse audience. In the courtyard children race between the fountains to the next activity.

With the support of the charity and other funders Wigmore Hall Education reaches out to school children through music projects based on a rich programme of artistic performances. There are masterclasses, pre-concert talks, study days, teacher training and a Chamber Tots series for pre-school children. The charity has also contributed to the refurbishment of the Bechstein Education Room, part of Wigmore's Second Century Appeal to 'bring the Hall up to date with 21st Century standards' [£25,000 in total].

Subsidising Theatre Tickets for Young People

In London's theatres the core audience is middle-aged. Of those using concessionary tickets the majority are over 60. How to encourage a theatre going habit among young people? One way is to sell tickets at affordable prices. The charity funds ticket subsidies for young people at Hampstead Theatre [£15,000], access to West End shows for disadvantaged families through the Mousetrap Foundation [£6,000], and has contributed to the low-cost ticket scheme at the National Theatre [£5,000] which is part of an attempt to broaden the National Theatre audience base.

New Writing

Over the years a stream of professional writers, actors and directors have passed though the Young Writers' Programme at the Royal Court Theatre. The charity has funded a series of projects at the Court. Metropolis (1995), Class (1998), Playwrights at Work (2002) and Rampage (2003) all received critical acclaim as well as producing "graduates" who have gone on to work in the theatre and media. Support is now being provided for Critical Mass [£20,000 per year for two years], a programme of writing groups, tutorials, script selection, rehearsal and production aimed at encouraging the involvement of black and inner city young people. The aim is to redress the imbalance where London's diverse culture is under-represented in the arts. The project draws on a network of young writers and will culminate in a professional showcase—a series of authentic and entertaining stage pictures of life in the capital for the appreciation of everyone, especially school-age audiences.

Around the Boroughs

In Camden the charity matched the support of the Council for the ever-popular annual Camden Schools Music Festival at the Royal Albert Hall [£4,000]. There has been similar support for school concerts organised by Westminster Choral Society and Hootdrum [£8,000 per year for three years], an "urban

drumming" programme for schools and youth clubs.

Arts Depot in Barnet is a purpose built arts centre comprising a studio theatre, an art gallery and educational, rehearsal and workshop spaces. As well as capital support, the charity has pledged help for the education programme that includes Youth Theatre and Continuing Education, Arts Learning Ladder, Schools Outreach and Visual Art Education [£20,000 for capital costs and £20,000 per year for three years as revenue funding].

In Brent, Granville Youth Arts and Training Centre is on the South Kilburn Estate, one of the most disadvantaged neighbourhoods in the charity's area. It is owned and managed by the Council Youth Service. Security is tight. But despite the steel doors and scruffy exterior, Granville houses well-equipped dance and music studios and the charity has helped to renovate and equip the video production suite [£10,000].

Training the Professional Artists of the Future

Since 1882, the Royal College of Music has provided musical training of the highest standard. The charity funds bursaries for students and helps with student performances that take place daily and are free of charge [£20,000 per year for three years]. English National Ballet School provides intensive classical ballet training for 16–19 year olds who are completing their preparation for a professional career. The School has close links with the English National Ballet. Support has been provided to enable the School to offer places to talented students who cannot afford the fees [£20,000]. Funds for distribution as bursaries and scholarships to students from low income backgrounds and who are residing in the charity's beneficial area have also been provided to the Foundation for Young Musicians [£12,000], Friends of Drama Centre London [£6,000] and the London Academy of Music and Dramatic Art [£42,000 in total], one of the world's leading drama schools. The charity's donation to the Campaign for LAMDA to enable them to move into new and expanded premises has been recognised by the naming of a rehearsal studio 'The John Lyon Studio'.

Other beneficiaries during the year included Holland Park School–Kensington & Chelsea (£90,000 over three years for youth work), Brent Youth Service (£40,000 for a small grants programme), Featherstone High School (£20,000 for a music/media recording studio), Westminster Play Association (£15,000 per year for three years towards running costs) and Contact a Family (£10,000 per year for three years for running costs).

Small grants ranging from £300 to £2,500 included those to Brentside High School, Edgware Junior School, Foundling Museum, Royal Humane Society, Imperial College, Mayor's Thames Festival, Teenage Cancer Trust, Workshops for the Imagination and Young Pavement Artist Competition.

Exclusions

The charity cannot give grants:

- to individuals;
- for research, unless it is action research designed to lead directly to the advancement of practical activities in the community;
- for feasibility studies;
- for medical care and resources;
- in response to general charitable appeals, unless they can be shown to be of specific benefit to children and young people in one or more of the geographical areas listed;
- as direct replacements for the withdrawal of funds by statutory authorities for activities which are primarily the responsibility of central or local government;
- to umbrella organisations to distribute to projects which are already in receipt of funds from the charity;
- for the promotion of religion or politics;
- for telephone helplines;
- as core funding for national charities;
- for advice and information services;
- to Housing Associations.

Applications

You should put in a letter the following information:

- a summary of the main purpose of the project;
- details of the overall amount requested;
- over what time scale;
- some indication of how funds from the charity would be allocated.

If your first proposal is assessed positively, you will be sent an application form. This must be completed and returned (not by e-mail or fax) by the deadline date in order for your project to be considered for funding.

The grants committee meets three times a year, in March, June and November. Closing dates are about two months in advance of these meetings.

The M B Foundation

General

Around £550,000 (2002/03)

Beneficial area Some preference for Greater Manchester.

Newhaven Business Park, Barton Lane, Eccles, Manchester M30 0HH

Tel. 0161 787 7898 **Fax** 0161 707 8582

Correspondent The Trustees

Trustees *Rabbi W Kaufman; Rabbi M Bamberger.*

Charity Commission no. 222104

Information available Accounts were on file at the Charity Commission, without a list of grants.

In 2002/03 the foundation had an income of £1.4 million and a total expenditure of £612,000. Grants totalled around £550,000. Unfortunately, no further details were available on the size or number of beneficiaries for this year, or in any previous year. We have not been able to obtain any information on its work, other than it supports general and educational causes.

Applications

In writing to the correspondent, although the trust states that its funds are already committed.

The M K Charitable Trust (formerly the Mendel Kaufman Charitable Trust)

Jewish charities

Around £450,000 (2003/04)

Beneficial area UK, especially the north east of England.

c/o Cohen Arnold & Co., 1075 Finchley Road, Regent Street, Temple Fortune, London N11 0PU

Tel. 020 8731 0777

Correspondent Mr Swartz

Trustees *Z M Kaufman; C S Kaufman; S Kaufman; A Piller; D Katz.*

Charity Commission no. 260439

Information available Information was on file at the Charity Commission.

This trust, formerly known as the Mendel Kaufman Charitable Trust, does not list the recipients of any of its grants. However, the trust said some years ago that it 'supports Jewish organisations, with a preference for the north east of England, especially the Gateshead area'.

In 2003/04 the trust had an income of £623,000 and a total expenditure of £584,000. Grants were made totalling around £450,000. No further information was available.

Comment

There was no response to written requests for a copy of the most recent acounts, despite the trust's obligation to provide these on demand

Applications

In writing to the correspondent.

The Mackintosh Foundation

Performing arts, general

£385,000 (2002/03)

Beneficial area UK, with an interest in western Scotland, and overseas.

1 Bedford Square, London WC1B 3RB

Tel. 020 7637 8866 **Fax** 020 7436 2683

Correspondent Nicholas Mackintosh, Appeals Director

Trustees *Sir Cameron Mackintosh, chair; Nicholas Mackintosh; Nicholas Allott; D Michael Rose; Patricia Macnaughton; Alain Boublil; Robert Nobel.*

Charity Commission no. 327751

Information available Information was provided by the trust.

In 2002/03 the foundation had an income of £948,000 mostly in donations from Sir Cameron Mackintosh, the settlor. Grants to 214 organisations were made totalling £385,000.

A brief history of the foundation

During the 14 years it was set up, the foundation has made over 3,500 separate grants (including repeats) totalling over £15 million to over 1,100 different charities. It has endowed Oxford University at a cost of well over £1 million with a fund known as *The Cameron Mackintosh Fund for Contemporary Theatre*, part of which has been used to set up a visiting professorship of contemporary theatre at the university. It also provided a fund of £1 million over a period of 10 years to the Royal National Theatre, for revivals of classical stage productions under the auspices of the RNT. It has provided financial support to a number of projects in the United States [...] This includes a major grant of US$1.5 million over 5 years to the Alliance of New American Musicals to foster, encourage and promote the creation and production of new dramatico-musical plays by American writers and artists. the foundation also paid £500,000 of 'partnership funding' over 5 years in respect of selected applications by theatres and others under the *Art Council's Arts for Everyone* scheme.

The foundation classifies its grants in the following way:

- Theatre and the performing arts
  - Theatre companies and buildings
  - Promotion of new theatrical works and classical music repertoire
  - Theatrical training and education
  - theatre-related pastoral care
- The homeless
- Children and education
- Medical
- Community projects
- The environment
- Overseas.

Grants in 2002/03

Grants were distributed by size as follows (with figures for the previous year in brackets):

	2002/03	2001/02
£150,000–£199,999	–	(1)
£100,000–£149,999	–	(1)
£50,000–£99,999	1	(–)
£20,000–£49,999	1	(1)
£10,000–£19,999	5	(10)
£5,000–£9,999	12	(17)
£1,000–£4,999	79	(149)
Less than £1,000	116	(110)

Exclusions

Religious or political activities are not supported. Apart from the foundation's drama award and some exceptions, applications from individuals are discouraged.

Applications

In writing to the correspondent. The trustees meet in May and November in plenary session, but a grants committee meets weekly to consider grants of up to £10,000.

The MacRobert Trust

General

£754,000 (2002/03)

Beneficial area UK, mainly Scotland.

Cromar, Tarland, Aboyne, Aberdeenshire AB34 4UD

Tel. 01339 881444

Website www.themacroberttrust.org.uk

Correspondent Air Comm. R W Joseph, Administrator

Trustees *R M Sherriff, chair; Mrs C J Cuthbert; Keith Davis; D M Heughan; J Mackie; W G Morrison; Group Capt. D A Needham; A M Summers; Mrs J C Swan; H B Woodd.*

Scottish Charity no. SC031346

Information available Accounts costing an excessive £25. Good website featuring guidelines and a full grants list.

Summary

The trust was established on 6 April 2001 when the assets of the no longer operating MacRobert Trusts, a collection of four charitable trusts and two holding companies were merged into the new, single MacRobert Trust. The merging of these trusts has led to a decrease in management and administration cost and a general increase in grantmaking.

The trust has assets totalling around £50 million, comprising of Douneside House (a holiday country house for serving and retired officers of the armed forces and their families) and an estate of 1,700 acres of woodland and 5,300 acres of farmland and associated residential properties let by the trust. The surplus income generated from these assets, following management and administration costs, is donated in grants.

Guidelines for applicants

Guidelines, available on the trust's website, say:

Grants are given to recognised charities UK-wide, but with a preference for Scotland.

The major categories under which the trustees consider support are:

- science and technology
- youth (especially uniformed and similar groups)
- services and sea
- ex-service hospitals and homes
- disability
- education
- community welfare

The other categories the trust will consider are:

- agriculture and horticulture
- arts and music
- medical care
- Tarland and Deeside.

The trustees look for clear, realistic and attainable aims. Grants vary but most lie between £5,000 and £10,000. Occasionally the trustees make a recurring grant of up to three years.

The trustees recognise the need to assist voluntary organisations which need funds to complement those already received from central government and local authority sources. However, this is not to say that the trust makes a grant where statutory bodies fail to provide.

The trustees are prepared to make core/revenue grants where appropriate but favour projects.

The trustees recognise that, at present, experiment and innovation are much more difficult to fund and the trust's role in funding them the more significant.

Grantmaking in 2002/03

During the year the trust made grants totalling £754,000 (£580,000 in 2001/02). Grants were broken down as follows:

Agriculture and horticulture: 9 grants totalling £114,000

The largest grant made was to Royal Highland & Agricultural Society of Scotland, which received £100,000. Other beneficiaries included Royal Northern Countryside Initiative (£4,000), Farmers' Company Charitable Fund (£2,000), Kintore Pipe Band and Macaulay Institute (£1,000 each) and Jacob Sheep Society (£250).

Services and sea: 9 grants totalling £54,000

Beneficiaries included Sailors' Soldiers' Airmen's Centres (£15,000), British Commonwealth Ex-Services League and Sailors' Families Society (£10,000 each), Not Forgotten Association (£5,000), Scottish Society for Employment of Ex-Regular Sailors, Soldier and Airmen (£500) and Royal British Legion (£250).

Youth: 11 grants totalling £47,000

Beneficiaries included YMCA – Scottish National Council (£10,500 in total), Fairbridge in Scotland (£10,000), Aberdeen International Youth Festival (£5,000), Commonwealth Youth Exchange Council (£4,000), Guide Association and Scout Association – Scottish Headquarters (£2,000 each) and Children 1st – Aberdeen Touch of Tartan Ball (£500).

Education: 7 grants totalling £47,000

Other beneficiaries included 'educational grants', probably for individual students (£27,500), Dyslexia in Scotland (£5,000), Business Dynamics (£4,000), Industrial Society (£3,000) and Munlochy Educational Trust Fund (£250).

Medical care: 7 grants totalling £38,000

Four larger grants were made, to Archie Foundation, Barbara Stewart Cancer Trust and Leukaemia Research Fund (£10,000 each) and Anthony Noble Trust – Scotland (£7,500). Small grants were made to Marie Curie Cancer Care (£600 in total) and Cancer Research (£25).

Disabled and handicapped: 5 grants totalling £33,500

Beneficiaries were Royal Institute for the Blind and Sense – Scotland branches (£10,000 each), Scope (£7,500), Noah's Ark (£5,000) and Hospitalfield Organic Produce Enterprise Trust (£1,000).

Arts and music: 7 grants totalling £22,000

Beneficiaries included Scottish Borders Community Orchestra (£7,500), Ulster Orchestra Society Limited (£5,000), Haddo House Choral & Operatic Society (£4,500) and Jura Music Festival (£250).

Tarland and Deeside: 7 grants totalling £13,500

Beneficiaries included Scotland's Gardens' Scheme (£1,500), St Moluag's Church Fabric Fund – Tarland (£900), Tarland Development Group (£400), Riding for the Disabled Association (£250) and Aboyne Highland Games (£100).

Science and technology: 2 grants totalling £12,000

The two grants were made to Royal Academy of Engineering Leadership Awards (£7,500) and the Royal Institution (£4,500).

Ex-services hospitals and homes: 1 grant for £8,000

The beneficiary this year was Sir Oswald Stoll Foundation, which received £8,000. Previous beneficiaries include Scottish Veterans' Residencies and King Edward VII Hospital for Officers.

The trust also made non-monetary donations to the Royal Air Force Benevolent Fund for Alastrean House, which it leases from the MacRobert Trust, totalling £140,000, Tarland Golf Club (£5,000) and Scottish Agricultural College – Walton Farm (£4,000). Further grants were also made to Douneside House (£98,000), Alastrean House (£50,000) and the Horticulture/Gamekeeping Training Scheme (£47,000).

Comment

The charge of £25 for a copy of the annual report and accounts is excessive, although from an applicant's point of view, the relevant information is available on the trust's clear and simple website.

Exclusions

Grants are not normally provided for:

- religious organisations (but not including youth/community services provided by them, or projects of general benefit to the whole community);
- organisations based outside the UK;
- individuals;
- endowment or memorial funds;
- general appeals or mail shots;
- political organisations;
- student bodies (as opposed to universities);
- fee-paying schools (apart from an educational grants scheme for children who are at, or need to attend, a Scottish independent secondary school and for which a grant application is made through the headteacher);
- expeditions;
- retrospective grants;
- departments within a university (unless the appeal gains the support of, and is channelled through, the principal).

Applications

The application form and full guidelines can be downloaded from the website, although applications must be posted.

The trustees meet to consider applications twice a year in March and October. To be considered, applications must be received for the March meeting by the end of October previously and for the October meeting by early June previously.

Applicants are informed of the trustees' decision, and if successful, payments are made immediately after each meeting.

The Manifold Trust

Historic buildings, environmental conservation, general

£1.2 million (2003)
Beneficial area UK.

Shottesbrooke House, Maidenhead SL6 3SW

Fax 01628 820159
Correspondent Miss Christine Gilbertson, Trustee

Trustees *Sir John Smith; Lady Smith; Miss Christine Gilbertson.*

Charity Commission no. 229501

Information available Annual report and accounts, and full grants list, were provided by the trust.

Summary

Most funding is for the preservation of historic buildings, particularly churches, the latter being done mainly through block grants to the Historic Churches Preservation Trust and the Council for the Care of Churches.

Most grants are for amounts between £400 and £5,000, but can be considerably higher.

General

In 2003 the trust's income was £998,000. The total overspend of £468,000 represented about 3.8% of the assets of the charity, so there is not likely to be a sudden decline in its grantmaking – especially as most of these assets are in the form of property and therefore not subject, as yet, to the recent rapid decline in both the value and the earning power of other kinds of investment.

During 2003 the trust made 256 grants. The trust has offered the following comments about the applications it receives:

- We favour humble causes. A letter stands a better chance of success with us than does a glossy brochure.
- We do not like to see high administrative expenditure, particularly fundraising expenditure.
- We are also put off by the use of jargon.
- We dislike contributing to endowments.

The trust gives the following information about its support for churches, including church bells:

Churches seeking money for structural repairs should not apply. The trust does indeed provide money for such churches, and is keen to do so, but it is not equipped to compare their relative merits. Accordingly it makes a block grant instead to the Historic Churches Preservation Trust [featured elsewhere in this resource] and to the equivalent body in Scotland, the Scottish Churches Architectural Heritage Trust, 15 North Bank St, The Mound, Edinburgh EH1 2LP, and also to the Council for the Care of Churches, Church House, Great Smith Street, London SW1P 3NZ.

The trust is also very keen to help churches bring into use again bells which have not been rung for many years, and to augment old peals of less than six bells. Applications for grants for this purpose should be made, not to the Manifold Trust, but to Ian Oram Esq., The Cottage, School Hill, Warnham, Horsham RH12 3QN who acts for the Bells Restoration Funds Committee of the Central Council of Church Bellringers. He advises the trust on these matters.

Grants in 2003

During the year the trust paid 256 grants totalling £1,201,000, apportioned roughly as follows:

For repairs to churches and their contents	42%
For preserving the environment	21%
For preserving historic ships	13%
For education, research and the arts	12%
For repairs to other historic buildings	10%
Other causes	2%

In all, 44% of the grants were for £1,000 or less, and 7% were for £10,000 or more. In total, £238,000 was given to the Historic Churches Preservation Trust, £209,000 to the Lichfield and Hatherton Canals Restoration Trust and £150,000 to the HMS Warrior Preservation Trust.

Other beneficiaries included Magdalene College (£39,000 in total), Hampshire & Wight Trust for Marine Archaeology (£30,000), Airfields Environment Trust, Georgian Group, Inland Waterways Association and Rural Housing Trust (£10,000 each), Dudley, St Thomas & St Luke PCC (£8,000); Avoncroft Museum of Buildings (£7,500); Royal Society of Arts, King Edward VII's Hospital, Moray Society, Kennet & Avon Canal Trust and Alfold PCC (£5,000 each), Bacton PCC (£4,000), St Neot PCC and Shrewsbury & Newport Canals Trust (£3,000 each), St John's Church – Templecorran and the Royal School of Needlework (£2,500 each), Cotswold Canals Trust and Churchill College (£2,000 each), Friends of Watlington Library, Tusk Trust, Centre for Alternative Technology, Scottish Native Woods and Friends of the Earth (£1,000 each) and Suzy Lamplugh Trust, Bramford Road Methodist Church, Windsor & Eton Choral Society and World Owl Trust (£500 each).

Comment

Contrary to the practices of many other trusts and foundations, this admirable trust seeks to spend its money, rather than to increase or even maintain its endowment. 'The grants made by the trust normally exceed its income, the trustees believing that it is better to meet the present need of other charities than to reserve money for the future.'

Exclusions

The trust does not give grants to churches for 'improvements'; nor, with regret, to individuals for any purpose.

Applications

The trust has no full-time staff. Therefore, general enquiries, and applications for grants, should be made in writing only, by post or by fax, and not by telephone. The trust does not issue application forms; applicants should please:

- describe the cause or project;
- state how much money it is hoped to raise;
- if the appeal is for a specific project: state also (a) how much it will cost (b) how much of this cost will come from the applicant charity's existing funds (c) how much has already been received or promised from other sources (d) how much is therefore still being sought;
- list sources of funds to which application has been or is intended to be made (for example local authorities, or quasi-governmental sources, such as the National Lottery);
- if the project involves conservation of a building, send a photograph of it – a snapshot will do – and a note (or pamphlet) about its history;
- send a copy, if it is not too bulky, of the charity's latest income and expenditure account and balance sheet.

Applications are considered twice a month, and a reply is sent to most applicants (whether successful or not) who have written a letter rather than sent a circular.

Marchig Animal Welfare Trust

Animal welfare

£825,000 (2003)

Beneficial area Worldwide.

PO Box 9422, Carnwath ML11 8YG

Tel. 01555 840991 **Fax** 01555 840991

Email info@marchigtrust.org

Website www.marchigawt.org

Correspondent Les Ward, Managing Trustee

Trustees *Madame Jeanne Marchig; Les Ward; Bill Jordan.*

Charity Commission no. 802133

Information available Full accounts and an information leaflet were provided by the trust. Further information is available via the website.

The objects of the trust are to protect animals and to promote and encourage practical work in preventing cruelty. There are no restrictions on the geographical area of work, types of grants or potential applicants, but all applications must be related to animal welfare and be of direct benefit to animals. Projects supported by the trust have included mobile spay/neuter clinics, alternatives to the use of animals in research, poster campaigns, anti-poaching programmes, establishment of veterinary hospitals, clinics and animal sanctuaries.

As well as giving grants, the trust also makes Marchig Animal Welfare Trust Awards. These awards, which take the form of a financial donation in support of the winner's animal welfare work, are given in either of the following two categories: (a) The development of an alternative method to the use of animals in experimental procedures and the practical implementation of such an alternative resulting in a significant reduction in the number of animals used in experimental procedures; (b) Practical work in the field of animal welfare resulting in significant improvements for animals either nationally or internationally.

The trust has increased its grantmaking significantly over the past couple of years. In 2003 the trust had an income of £508,000 and made grants totalling £825,000 (in 2002 this figure was around £100,000).

Grants in 2004

The trust's website gives many examples of projects that have been supported worldwide recently, although the amounts awarded are not given. They include:

- Advocates for Animals, UK: support for investigative report into pet shops;
- Amigos dos Gatos do Algarve, Portugal: feral cat neutering programme;
- Animal Care Land, India, sterilisation and rabies vaccination programme for stray dogs in Tirupati, India;
- Blue Cross of India: animal birth control programmes in Chennai and Kanchipuram;
- Brooke Hospital, UK: establishment of a second Mobile Veterinary Team in the Nile Delta region of Egypt;
- Colne Valley Animal Rescue, UK: construction of shelter perimeter fence;
- Compassion Unlimited Plus Action, India: sterilisation and vaccination programme for stray dogs in the municipality limits surrounding the city of Bangalore, India;
- Costa Blanca Feral Cat Trust, UK: sterilisation of feral and abandoned cats in the Costa Brava area;
- Cotton Tails Rescue, UK: support for neutering expenses;
- Dog Rescue Centre, Samui Thailand: support for the construction of kennels;
- Fethiye Friends of Animals Association, Turkey: ongoing support for static and mobile clinics, including the purchase and establishment of the first mobile clinic for Istanbul;
- Foundation for the Protection of Community Dogs, Romania: for the purchase of a mobile veterinary clinic.

Exclusions

Applications which fail to meet the above criteria will be rejected. Additionally, those relating to: educational studies or other courses; expeditions; payment of salaries; support of conferences and meetings; and activities that are not totally animal welfare related.

Applications

On an application form available from the correspondent or via the website.

The Jim Marshall Charitable Trust

General

Around £300,000 a year

Beneficial area Milton keynes area only.

Simpson Wreford and Co, 62 Beresford Street, London SE18 6BG

Tel. 020 8854 9552

Email carl@simpsonwreford.co.uk

Correspondent Carl Graham

Trustees J C Marshall; K W J Saunders; B Charlton; S B Marshall; L Hack.

Charity Commission no. 328118

Information available Accounts were on file at the Charity Commission.

Established in 1989 by the founder of Marshall Amplification plc, this trust supports organisations concerned with children, young people, families and people who are sick or have disabilities. Grants are also made directly to individuals. The trust deed lists Buckinghamshire Association of Boys' Clubs, London Federation of Boys' Clubs, Macintyre Homes, Variety Club Children's Charity and Wavedon All Music Plan as specific, but not exclusive, beneficiaries.

In 2002 the trust had assets of £424,000. During this year there was a significant increase in its income to £1.7 million (2001: £302,000) due to a donation received of this amount. Grants for the year totalled £1.3 million. This was an unusually high figure for the charity and the correspondent stated that in the future, funds for grant distribution will probably be around £300,000.

The main project supported in the year was £1.1 million to the Phoenix Lodge Hospice and Respite Care Centre. The aim was to build and manage facilities for young adults with life limiting conditions. The trustees of that charity have decided however that this is now not a viable project. Consequently the trustees of the Jim Marshall Charitable Trust have requested that the money be

repaid in order that funds may be donated to other cause(s).

Other beneficiaries during the year included Bedford Amateur Boxing Club, Grand Order of Water Rats and London Youth (£25,000 each), Chaucer Clinic (£20,000), Luton and Bedfordshire Youth Association (£15,000), David Berglas Foundation for Youth and S.O.S (£5,000 each), The Stables (£3,000), Coda Club and Hilton Ball (£2,000 each) and Centre for Integrated Living and Willen Hospice (£1,000 each). Miscellaneous grants under £1,000 each totalled £6,000. Five individuals were also supported.

Comment

There was no response to repeated written requests for a copy of the most recent annual report and accounts, despite the requirement to provide these on demand. It may be the case that none more recent have been produced, as the latest on file at the Charity Commission are for 2002.

Applications

In writing to the correspondent at any time.

Marshall's Charity

Parsonage and church improvements

£550,000 (2003)

Beneficial area England and Wales.

Marshall House, 66 Newcomen Street, London SE1 1YT

Tel. 020 7407 2979 **Fax** 020 7403 3969

Email grantoffice@marshalls.org.uk

Website www.marshalls.org.uk

Correspondent Richard Goatcher, Clerk to the Trustees

Trustees D M Lang, chair; Mrs A Nicholson; W E McConnell; B S Perryer; M J Dudding; R W P Brice; A G H Stocks; C P Stenning; C G Bird; S Clark; Mrs G M F Issac; W D Eason; J Hammant; J A N Heawood.

Charity Commission no. 206780

Information available Accounts were provided by the trust.

The charity supports parsonage buildings throughout England and Wales, helps with the upkeep of churches in Kent,

Surrey and Lincolnshire (Church of England only), supports the parish of Christ Church, Southwark and makes grants for education to Marshall's Educational Foundation. Special consideration is given to parishes in urban priority areas. Projects must cost more that £3,500, and the charity will not contribute more than 50% of the project.

In 2003 it had assets of £14.7 million, held in property rather than shares. This produced an income of £1.1 million. Grants were made totalling £520,000.

Exclusions

No grants to churches outside the counties of Kent, Surrey and Lincolnshire, as defined in 1855.

Applications

To the correspondent in writing. Trustees meet in January, April, July and October. Applications need to be sent by the end of January, April, July and October for consideration at the next meeting.

John Martin's Charity

Religious activity, relief-in-need, education

£589,000 (2002/03)
Beneficial area The town of Evesham only.

16 Queen's Road, Evesham, Worcestershire WR11 4JP
Tel. 01386 765440 **Fax** 01386 765340
Email enquiries@johnmartins.org.uk
Website www.johnmartins.org.uk
Correspondent Phil Woodcock, Clerk
Trustees N J Lamb, chair; J K Icke, vice Chair; Revd J Bomyer; Revd B Collins; A W Bennett; Mrs J Turner; G Robbins; Revd R Armitage; J H Smith; R G Gould; C Scorse; R G Emson; Mrs D Raphael; Mrs F S Smith.
Charity Commission no. 527473
Information available Information was provided by the trust.

Grants are available for:

- propagation of the Christian gospel – the charity helps with the expenses of designated local clergy, PCCs and St

Andrew's Church of England First School in Hampton;
- promotion of education – grants are made to all state schools and the college in Evesham to support special needs education, in additional to considering other educational projects;
- individual students – people aged 16 to 50 may apply for educational grants to support further and higher educational or vocational studies;
- miscellaneous education awards – given for music, arts and education visits, together with support with school uniforms;
- relief in need of individuals and organisations – grants are made for the benefit of children, single parent families, people with disabilities and people who have fallen on hard times for a variety of circumstances beyond their control. An annual heating allowance is made to older people on limited incomes and those who benefit are invited to outings to the seaside and pantomimes.

Any unspent income at the end of the financial year can be used for the relief of conditions arising from health problems or medical needs either within the town of Evesham or certain designated villages.

In 2002/03 the charity had assets of £14 million and an income of £719,000. Grants were made to 43 organisations totalling £589,000. The largest grant was £15,000 to St Richard's Hospice. Other beneficiaries included MIND and Riverside Shop Mobility (£6,000 each), ExtraCare (£5,200) and Citizens Advice and Evesham Adventure Playground (£5,000 each).

All the schools within the town received grants of varying amounts, for assistance with special educational needs. The largest donations were £12,000 to Evesham High School and £10,000 to Prince Henry's High School.

Exclusions

No grants for the payment of rates or taxes, or otherwise to replace statutory benefits.

Applications

On a form available from the correspondent on request. Initial telephone calls are welcomed. The trustees normally meet on the second and fourth Thursday in each month, with one meeting in June and December. The charity can make urgent grants in exceptional circumstances. Applicants for education grants should supply an

sae and may obtain details of deadlines from the charity.

Mayfair Charities Ltd

Orthodox Judaism

£4 million (2002/03)
Beneficial area UK and overseas.

Freshwater House, 158–162 Shaftesbury Avenue, London WC2H 8HR
Tel. 020 7836 1555
Email mark.jenner@highdorn.co.uk
Correspondent Mark Jenner, Secretary
Trustees B S E Freshwater, chair; D Davis.
Charity Commission no. 255281
Information available Annual report and accounts, of some complexity, with a separate grants list provided by the trust.

The trust had assets of around £63 million in 2002/03, generating an income of £4.8 million. Many of the assets are in the form of property or of subsidiary trading companies. During the year grants were made to organisations totalling almost £4 million. The review of the year explains the trust's current focus:

In recent years, the [trustees] have decided to support certain major projects which during the year under review and subsequently, have received substantial financial grants from the company. At the present time the trustees have entered into commitments for the financial support of colleges and institutions which would absorb approximately £7 million over the next five years.

In previous years substantial donations have been made to the connected Raphael Freshwater Memorial Association and Beth Jacob Grammar School for Girls. Many organisations receive on-going support.

Grants in 2003

The trust provided a separate list of 400 donations of £500 or more made in the nine months up to the end of 2003. The list shows that all but a few grants were made to Orthodox Jewish institutions in the UK, and also, probably to a lesser extent, in Israel and Poland, and reflect the trust's focus on making several large donations to certain major projects.

Substantial grants were made to SOFT (£569,000), Merkaz Lechinuch Torani (£558,000), Ohr Someach Institutions (£553,000), Beth Jacob Grammar School for Girls (£505,000), Meshech Chochma Ohr Yehoshua (£188,000) and Kollel Chibas Yerushalayim (£185,000).

Comment

The trust appears to be largely a vehicle for the philanthropic activities of property investor B S E Freshwater, who is closely connected with the management of some of the major beneficiary organisations.

Applications

In writing to the correspondent.

The Medlock Charitable Trust

Education, health, welfare

£920,000 (2002/03)

Beneficial area Overwhelmingly the areas of Bath and Boston in Lincolnshire.

St George's Lodge, 33 Oldfield Road, Bath BA2 3ND

Tel. 01225 428221 **Fax** 01225 789262

Correspondent David Medlock, Trustee

Trustees *Leonard Medlock; Brenda Medlock; David Medlock; P H Carr.*

Charity Commission no. 326927

Information available Accounts were provided by the trust.

The trust's endowment of £23 million produced an investment income of £1.4 million in 2002/03, with a further £76,000 coming from donations. It is close to meeting its target of distributing at least £1 million in grants each year.

Grantmaking

The trust describes its grantmaking policy as follows:

The trustees have identified the City of Bath and the borough of Boston as the principal but not exclusive areas in which the charity is and will be proactive. These areas have been specifically chosen as the founder of the charity has strong connections with the City of Bath, the home of the charity, and has family connections of long standing with the borough of Boston.

To date the charity has supported and funded a number of projects in these areas by making substantial grants. These grants have been made to fund projects in the areas of education, medicine, research and social services all for the benefit of the local community. During the year, the trustees also receive many applications for assistance from many diverse areas in the United Kingdom. These are all considered sympathetically.

Grants in 2002/03

The trust gave a breakdown of its grants, but using quite general headings that in some cases it is difficult to ascribe individual grants to. However the table does make clear the strong emphasis on education (2001/02 figures are given in brackets):

	2002/03	2001/02
Education	£411,000	£535,000
Local community	£395,000	£165,000
Charitable trusts	£114,000	£205,000

In 2002/03 the trust received 615 applications and made 179 grants totalling £920,000. There were 34 beneficiaries who had received grants in the previous year.

The largest grant during the year was made to the Research Institute for the Care of the Elderly, which received a grant of £100,000 and was not supported in the previous year.

Other larger grants included those to Royal United Hospital – Bath for their Forever Friends Appeal and the University of Bristol (£50,000 each), SS Great Britain Trust (£40,000), St Thomas' Church of England Primary School (£29,000), Centenary Pre-School (£25,000), Summerfield School (£21,000), British Urological Society, Off the Record and William Lovell School Fund (£20,000 each).

Other beneficiaries included Bath Festivals Trust (£15,000), National Eye Research Centre (£12,500), Gurkha Welfare Trust (£12,000), British Stammering Association, Greater Bristol Foundation and Zion Methodist Church (£10,000 each), Withywood Community School (£8,000), Thomas Keble School (£7,000), Kingsdon Manor School (£6,000), BANES Sports Development, Lincolnshire Community Foundation and the Wey Valley School (£5,000 each), Karnataka Parents' Association (£4,000), St Mary's Church of England Primary School (£3,000), Mayor of Boston Charity Fund and Temple Primary School (£2,000 each) and 93rd (City of Bath) Squadron Air Training Corps, Combe Down Holiday Trust, Dorset Trust, Cruse Bereavement Care,

Radio Link and Friends of Bristol Oncology Centre (£1,000 each).

There were 20 small grants of less than £1,000 each, with beneficiaries including Bath Disabled Companions Club, Cancer Research Campaign, Stepping Stones Pre-School, Children's Hospice South West, Derby Deaf Children Society, Charter Trustees of the City of Bath and Trevor Bayliss Foundation.

Exclusions

No grants to individuals or students.

Applications

In writing to the correspondent.

Mental Health Foundation

Mental health and learning disability research

£322,000 (2002/03)

Beneficial area UK.

83 Victoria Street, London SW1H 0HW

Tel. 020 7802 0300 **Fax** 020 7802 0301

Email mhf@mhf.org.uk

Website www.mentalhealth.org.uk

Correspondent The Trustees

Trustees *Christopher S Martin, chair; Jane Carter; Abel Hadden; Prof. Rachel Jenkins; Dr Zenobia Nadirshaw; Giles Ridley; Philippa Russell; David Sachon; Daphne Statham; Lady Weston; Michael O'Connor; Prof. Stephen Platt; Andrew Wetherell.*

Charity Commission no. 801130

Information available Accounts, but without a list of grants, were provided by the foundation.

The mission of the foundation is to generate new understanding, knowledge, support and services which are exemplary and replicable. These should promote emotional wellbeing and improve the lives of people with mental health issues and/or with learning disabilities. The foundation's objectives are to:

- increase knowledge and understanding about mental health across society;
- combat the stigma associated with mental distress;

- improve policy and practice in the field of mental health and learning disabilities;
- empower users and carers;
- build the confidence and competence of people working in the mental health/learning difficult field;
- influence governments on issues relating to mental health/learning disability policies, practices and services.

Much of this work is carried out by the foundation itself. However, the 2001/02 accounts stated the following, under the heading 'Grant making policy': 'The foundation has an internal process for identifying areas of work where it can make a useful contribution. For some projects this will involve the funding of other organisations through a grants programme. The foundation identifies such organisations through a tendering process. Organisations awarded a grant work to an agreed contact, which specifies the conditions. The monitoring of satisfactory delivery of the contract is in the first instance the responsibility of the project/programme manager.'

In 2002/03 the foundation had assets of £1.5 million. Total income was £3.9 million, mostly comprised of donations, gifts, legacies, charitable trading, fundraising events and grants from statutory sources and Community Fund. Total expenditure totalled £3.2 million, included £322,000 in grants, although details of these were not included in the accounts.

Exclusions

No grants for:

- individual hardship, education and training;
- travel;
- attendance at conferences;
- capital;
- expenses such as vehicles or property;
- general appeals;
- general running costs;
- overseas events.

Applications

Please contact the foundation offices for current grant priorities, guidelines and closing dates.

The Mercers' Charitable Foundation

General welfare, elderly, conservation, arts, Christian faith activities, educational institutions

£10 million budgeted (2003/04)

Beneficial area UK; strong preference for London and the West Midlands, 'slight' preference for south east England and Norfolk.

Mercers' Hall, Ironmonger Lane, London EC2V 8ME

Tel. 020 7726 4991 **Fax** 020 7600 1158

Email katherinep@mercers.co.uk

Website www.mercers.co.uk

Correspondent Katherine Payne, Grants Manager

Trustee *The Mercers' Company.*

Charity Commission no. 326340

Information available Full information was provided by the trust. Full details also on the website.

The Mercers' Company has several trusts, the main one being the Mercers' Charitable Foundation. All trusts are administered centrally and should be considered as one.

Charitable expenditure has increased sharply over the past few years (£4.7 million in 2001/02, £7.2 million in 2002/03), with grants up to £10 million in 2003/04.

Around half this amount is used for the major grants programme, which awards grants of £50,000 or more to organisations with which the Mercers' Company has an existing relationship, with unsolicited applications unlikely to be successful. The other half of the budget is given over to the main committees, which are largely reactive and are open to applications. The main committees and categories are:

Charity – medical welfare, general welfare, disabled, youth and elderly

Education – institutional grants to schools, colleges, educational projects with a particular emphasis on the 'state maintained' sector in London and the West Midlands

Education bursaries – grants to parents of pupils in their last two years of compulsory education at fee paying independent schools and to some

courses in higher education *(see The Educational Grants Directory, published by Directory of Social Change, for details)*

Heritage and Arts – material (or fabric) conservation and refurbishment, wildlife and environment conservation, library and archive conservation, performing and visual arts

Church – support for cathedrals, churches with a Mercers' Company connection and general appeals to promote the Christian faith (appeals for grants for fabric restoration are not normally entertained as an annual grant is made for this purpose to the Historic Churches Preservation Trust).

There is also a small grants programme, with grants for £2,000 or less in the Charity and Education categories and £1,000 or less in the Church and Heritage and Arts categories.

In all cases, the trustees are looking to assess whether an organisation is well managed and has its finances in order; that the proposed project has been well planned and will meet an identified need and that the organisation's procedures are in line with good practice.

Grantmaking in 2002/03

Grants to institutions

During the year 1,685 written applications were received from charities of which 48% (808) received a grant. The average grant was £8,045. However, it should be noted that 16 grants within the trustees' major grants programme (which involve grants larger than £50,000) accounted for £3.68 million of the amounts paid to institutions of £6.5 million. Major grants are made to organisations only after a detailed scrutiny and assessment of the proposal and are usually paid over instalments of two or three years. The trustees continued to give significant support to smaller, grassroots organisations.

The following is a selection of beneficiaries, all of whom received grants during the year, with the purpose of the grant:

- St Paul's Schools' Foundation – £1 million: the foundation supports two schools; the grant was made towards the restricted funds for rebuilding proposals, an expanding bursaries programme and outreach community programmes at both schools.
- Brendoncare Foundation – £500,000: towards the redevelopment of Stildon Care Home, East Grinstead.
- Gresham College Trust and the Greham Professors – £270,000:

towards the cost of the programme of lectures concerning 'issues of current interest to the City'.

- Walsall Academy – £150,000: the final instalment of £1 million over three years towards the cost of construction of a City Academy, which was opened in September 2003.
- Barts and the London, Queen Mary's School of Medicine & Dentistry – £100,000: the second of three instalments towards the Refugee Doctors Programme, a training course to enable refugee doctors to requalify within the NHS.
- Holy Trinity & St Silas CE Primary School, Camden – £70,000: towards the development of the school's ICT resources and the improvement of the play area.
- Natural History Museum – £50,000: the second of three instalments towards the Darwin Centre's outreach programme.
- The Royal Institution of Great Britain – £40,000: towards the development costs of an educational website.
- Phoenix Secondary & Primary School, Tower Hamlets – £30,000: towards the playground development for this special school.

Beneficiaries receiving £10,000 or less included London Nautical School – Lambeth, Harmeny Education Trust – Northumberland, E-Learning Foundation, Royal Liverpool Philharmonic, Book Aid International, Gurkha Welfare Trust, Down's Syndrome Association, Hearing Dogs for Deaf People, Hospice Care Kenya, Woodlands Hospice Charitable Trust – Liverpool, Nightstop UK and Dulwich Picture Gallery.

Exclusions

The company does not respond to circular (mail shot) appeals, nor does it provide sponsorship. Generally, funds are only available to charities registered with the Charity Commission or exempt from registration. Other likely exclusions are

- ongoing salary costs (although start up salary costs may be considered)
- running costs, utility bills (but reasonable core costs for new service provision is acceptable)
- capital fundraising where the new building should be funded by statutory bodies such as DfES or NHS
- animal welfare charities
- endowment appeals
- mother tongue language classes (English language classes will be considered)

- refurbishment/maintenance of village halls
- community groups outside London
- organisations that have received a grant in the last three years
- organisations that give grants (there is a separate block grants programme)
- organisations where the umbrella organisation has been supported (e.g. almshouse association)
- branches of national charities (although more sympathetic if they are in London).

Applications

Initial applications should be in the form of a letter (no more than two sides of A4), giving details of the charity, its activities, and the proposed project, with some idea of costs, and sent to the grants manager. Please note that this should be accompanied by a copy of the latest audited accounts. The company's grants department staff are happy to give advice. Qualifying applicants will then be sent an application form and guidelines.

The charity committee meets every six weeks; other committees meet quarterly.

The Merchant Taylors' Company Charities Fund

Education, church, medicine, general

£322,000 (2002/03)

Beneficial area UK.

30 Threadneedle Street, London EC2R 8JB

Tel. 020 7450 4440

Website www.merchanttaylors.co.uk

Correspondent Michael Brent, Clerk to the Trustees

Trustee *The Master and Warden of the Merchant Taylor's Company.*

Charity Commission no. 1069124

Information available Information was provided by the trust.

Grants are considered for the arts, social care and community development, disability, the elderly, poverty, medical studies and research, chemical dependency, homelessness, children, and

education, with priority for special needs.

In 2002/03 the trust had an income of £372,000 and made grants totalling £322,000, broken down as follows:

Educational awards

Grants totalling £143,000 included money for training awards, prizes and other awards made via nine schools associated with Merchant Taylors' Company. The schools include Merchant Taylors' School Northwood, Merchant Taylors' School for Boys and Girls – Crosby, St Helen's Girl's School – Northwood, Wolverhampton Grammar School, Foyle & Londonderry College and Willingford School – Oxford.

Training awards

Grants were made to five organisations totalling £30,000. They went to Textile Conservation Centre (£10,000), Federation of Merchant Taylors for bursaries (£7,500), Guildhall School of Music (£3,500), Mansfield House Settlement for Outward Bound and Sail Training Association fees (£2,600) and Toynbee Hall (£1,500).

Church and clergy

Grants to five organisations totalled £5,000. These were £2,000 to St Helen's Church – Bishopgate, £1,000 each to Friends of St Paul's Cathedral and St Margaret's Church – Lee and £500 each to St Michael's – Cornhill and St Paul's Church Swanley & St Peter's Huxtable.

Medical aid

One grant of £5,000 went to Disability Partnership.

Miscellaneous

Grants totalled £43,000, including £10,000 to South East London Economic Development Agency, £6,100 to Farms for City Children, £5,000 each to Church Housing Trust and New Economic Foundation, £3,900 to Belcanto London Academy, £3,500 to CHICKS and £1,000 each to London Bridge Museum and VSO.

Livery and freemen fund

Grants were made to six organisations from this designated fund; £11,000 to Groundwork Southwark, £10,000 to Homestart, £5,500 to Alone in London, £4,500 to Charterhouse in Southwark, £4,400 to St Saviour's and St Olave's

School and £1,800 to Hope and Homes for Children

Millennium fund

Three grants were made totalling £59,000 including £18,000 each to the London School of Fashion and St Martins.

Applications

In writing to the correspondent.

Millennium Stadium Charitable Trust

Sport, the arts, community and the environment

£850,000 (Jan 2002–Nov 2003)
Beneficial area Wales.

c/o Fusion, The Coal Exchange, Mount Stuart Square, Cardiff CF10 5ED

Tel. 029 2049 4963 **Fax** 029 2049 4964

Email louise@fusionuk.org.uk

Website www.millenniumstadium.com

Correspondent Louise Edwards, Trust Officer

Trustees *Tom Jones, chair; Simon White; Edmond Fivet; Elise Stewart; David Rees; Tony Mahoney; Michael John; Wendy Williams; Peredur Jenkins.*

Charity Commission no. 1086596

Information available Information was provided by the trust.

The trust was established by an agreement between the Millennium Commission and the Millennium Stadium plc. Its income is generated through a 25p levy on every ticket purchased for public events at the stadium.

Its objective is 'to improve the quality of life in the Welsh community via Welsh sport, art, language, culture, music and folklore and does so by the issuing of two types of grants in: 'Activate' and 'Traws Cymru – Across Wales'.

'Activate' aims to provide funding for new or existing projects in Wales that demonstrate the capacity to develop and educate people by sustainable means, within the areas of sport, the arts, community or the environment.

'Traws Cymru' aims to foster greater understanding and friendship among the people of Wales by supporting projects that bring groups together through sporting or cultural exchanges. Exchanges can be one-way or two-way, as long as two groups are involved.

Funding for both schemes is available to voluntary, non-profit and charitable organisations as well as local authorities for non-core activities. There is no upper or lower age limit for participants. Applicants are invited to make a case as to why they should be given a grant and what impact it would have on their organisation. Grants are split into three categories:

- National: available to national organisations delivering projects Wales-wide, up to a maximum of £20,000;
- Regional: for projects covering a county, up to a maximum of £10,000;
- Local: for projects serving a town or city, up to a maximum of £2,000.

While all organisations will be considered on their merit, priority will be given to organisations that provide for people who are disadvantaged by age, gender, disability, ethnicity or social and economic circumstances.

Since the trust's inception beneficiaries have included:

National organisations

Dragons Rugby Trust, Welsh Hockey Union, FAW Trust, Reactivate, Welsh Netball Association, Welsh Womens Rugby Union and The Soil Association (£20,000 each); Athletics Association of Wales (£16,000); SNAP Cymru, Welsh Deaf Rugby Union, Welsh Badminton and Community Dance Wales (£10,000); Surf Living Association of Wales and Prince's Trust Cymru (£8,000 each); Welsh Lacrosse Association (£6,000); WGU Golf Development and Boys and Girls Clubs of Wales (£5,000 each) and Welsh Jazz Society (£2,000 each).

Regional organisations

Rhondda Cynon Taff Community Arts, Blaenau Gwent County Council and Horizon (£10,000 each); Theatr Gwynedd, Mind in the Vale of Glamorgan, Holyhead Studio Project and Bridgend County Borough Council (£5,000 each); Sure Start Merthyr Tydfil and Brecon Mountain Rescue (£3,500 each); and Clyne Riding Disabled Club (£2,000).

Local organisations

Llanerchymedd Youth Club (£4,000); Clwb Ffermwyr Ifanc Penmynydd (£2,500); Durand Primary School, Dulais Valley Partnership, Cwmbran Centre, Penmaenmawr Phoenix Football Club, Shore FM, Llandaf North U16 Girls Rugby and Local Aid – Swansea (£2,000 each); Kimnel Bay Girls Football Club (£1,000); and Troedyrhiw After School Klub (£800).

Eligible costs include: A new project or activity, travel costs, equipment, purchasing musical instruments, coaching, tuition fees, training fees, exchange programmes.

Ineligble costs: Day to day running costs, grants to fund other organisations, retrospective requests, requests from individuals, requests which do not directly benefit people in Wales, requests from applicants who have already applied to the trust in the same financial year.

Comment

As this book was going to press new accounts for the financial year 2003/04 were received by the Charity Commission showing a more modest total expenditure of £474,000.

Contact the trust directly for up-to-date information on its programmes.

Exclusions

No grants to individuals, local authorities for core activities (non-core activities can be supported) or organisations without a constitution that states it is not-for-profit, voluntary or charitable.

Applications

On an application form available from the correspondent or by downloading from the website. Organisations may only submit one application per financial year (April–May) and should allow approximately three months for notification of a decision. The trustees meet at certain times throughout the year to assess applications. Applicants are asked to contact the correspondent for the next deadline.

Milton Keynes Community Foundation

Welfare, arts

£425,000 (2002/03)

Beneficial area Milton Keynes unitary authority.

Acorn House, 381 Midsummer Boulevard, Central Milton Keynes MK9 3HP

Tel. 01908 690276 **Fax** 01908 233635

Email information@ mkcommunityfoundation.co.uk

Website www.mkcommunityfoundation. co.uk

Correspondent The Grants Manager

Trustees *Francesca Skelton, chair; Peter Kara; Judith Hooper; Stephen Cowdrill; Eleanor Millburn; Elspeth Tudor Price; Michael Murray; Bernard Stewart; Ruth Stone; Peter Selvey; Stephen Norrish; Susan Mallalieu; Richard Brown; Dorothy Cooper; Roger Kitchen; Andrea Pickerin; Dominic Newbould; Linda Breaden.*

Charity Commission no. 295107

Information available Information was taken from the trust's website.

The foundation is a local grantmaking charity that helps to improve the quality of life for people living within the Unitary Authority Area of Milton Keynes. The trust awards over one hundred grants each year to local voluntary organisation and charities, supporting projects that benefit the whole community, including people with special needs and other disabilities, children and youth, older people and projects that develop the artistic and cultural life of the city.

The foundation helps to build stronger communities by encouraging local giving and raises a majority of its funds through a membership scheme, supported by local people and companies who make an annual donation.

In 2002/03 the trust received 178 requests for applications totalling £1.4 million. Grants totalling £425,000 were awarded supporting a total of 108 community projects. Grants categories are as follows:

Small grants

Sums up to £1,500 are made monthly, for example to give groups access to valuable funding for a specific project or piece of equipment.

Donations included: £1,500 each to Ernest Fryer House to provide a leisure and recreation room for the 34 residents, Little Tinkers to help start up a new pre–school and Milton Keynes Mind for the Steps Project to design and construct a sundial sculpture; £1,400 to Tennis Works Club to provide a year–round junior tennis programme that operates out of curriculum time; £1,000 to Falconhurst Combined School PTA for dance and music workshops; £970 to Bow Brickhill Parent and Toddler Group to replace safety matting for babies and toddlers; £500 to Education Centre for the Organ Fund to recondition and install a pipe organ; and £250 to Milton Keynes Mencap Society to hold a fund day for people with learning disabilities.

General grants

Grants of up to £7,500 are made five times a year to groups who require funding for larger projects and may include the buying of equipment, small building works, short-term projects and one-off training courses.

Grants included: £7,500 each to Girlguiding Milton Keynes to purchase equipment for a kitchen area, Loughton Baptist Church to refurbish the community centre and Milton Keynes Play Association for the first stage of developing an outward bound centre at Emberton Park; £7,300 to BTCV to deliver a programme of practical conservation projects for young people; £7,000 each to MacIntrye Care to redevelop the coffee shop and Milton Keynes Wheelwright Project to purchase tools and equipment; and £3,400 to Morrlands Centre Fundraising to part fund two projects celebrating the 25th anniversary of the centre.

Arts Fund grants

Grants are available for up to £7,500 and are made five times a year for those involved in the whole spectrum of local arts initiatives that are of community benefit.

Donations included: £5,000 each to Cornelius and Jones to produce a new show adapting Hoffman's fairytale The Nutcracker, Electric Cabaret to create a physical theatre show in public places, Living Archive to develop the young people's films workshop and Music Makers of Milton Keynes towards a community production of My Fair Lady; £3,000 to Milton Keynes Racial Equality Council to help finance the cost of producing a cultural event including a community theatre performance in Milton Keynes; and £2,800 to Milton Keynes Community Mediation to cover the costs of mediators to attend the Mediation UK Conference in Sheffield.

Development grants

Up to £25,000 per year for three successive years are available for innovative and creative projects that develop a group's activity in supporting local people and are considered annually. Core costs may be included but an application must show what will happen to the project at the end of the term, for example it will have completed its work or become self-funding. These grants are considered annually.

Examples of previous projects that have received funding include £73,000 to Milton Keynes Racial Equality Council to employ a new development worker and £49,000 to MKCVO for an information centre for voluntary sector groups.

The foundation also has funding available from the Local Network Fund which is aimed at making a difference to the lives of children and young people living in poverty or at a disadvantage. It supports small voluntary and community groups working with young people aged 0–9 years old. Grants available are for between £250 to £7,000. Application packs are available from the LNF Call Centre on 0845 113 0161.

Exclusions

Grants are normally not given to proposals chiefly focused upon the following:

- sponsorship and fundraising events;
- contributions to major appeals;
- projects outside the beneficial area;
- political groups;
- projects connected with promoting a religious message of any kind;
- work which should be funded by health and local authorities or government grants aid;
- retrospective grants, nor grants to pay off deficits.

Applications

Application forms and guidelines are available on the website or can be requested by telephoning the office. The grants staff can be contacted to assist with any queries or help with applications.

The Monument Trust

Arts, health and welfare (especially AIDS), environment, general

£3.2 million (2003/04)

Beneficial area Unrestricted, but UK in practice.

Allington House, 1st Floor, 150 Victoria Street, London SW1E 5AE

Tel. 020 7410 0330 **Fax** 020 7410 0332

Email info@sfct.org.uk

Correspondent Michael Pattison, Director

Trustees S Grimshaw; Linda Heathcoat-Amory; R H Gurney; Sir Anthony Tennant.

Charity Commission no. 242575

Information available Annual report and accounts, with a good listing of grants but minimal analysis of grantmaking policy, were provided by the trust.

Summary

This is one of the Sainsbury Family Charitable Trusts, which share a joint administration, but are otherwise independent of each other. They have a common approach to grantmaking which is described in the entry for the group as a whole. In this case the trust notes that: 'proposals are generally invited by the trustees or initiated at their request. Unsolicited applications are discouraged and are unlikely to succeed, even if they fall within an area in which the trustees are interested'.

The trust's main areas of interest are (with number and the value of grant approvals in 2003/04):

	No.	Total
Health and community care	26	£779,500
The arts	12	£644,000
AIDS	8	£563,000
Social development	13	£837,000
General	5	£108,000
The environment	8	£269,500
Total	72	£3,201,000

The following is the only indication of the policies of the trust, beyond what can be deduced from the grants approved: 'The trustees prefer to help prove new ideas or methods that can be replicated widely or become self-sustaining. They also continue to support a number of arts and environmental projects of national or regional importance.'

Grants in 2003/04

Health and community care

There were 10 grants of more than £10,000 each, the largest of which was £190,000 to Coram Family towards a development worker and family support worker to consolidate a pilot in Southwark. Other grants included: £80,000 over two years to SUN at Bow towards two trainee development workers; £60,000 to Community Service Volunteers towards a pilot scheme to test the use of volunteers to provide daily contact with children on the Child Protection Register; and £25,000 to King's College London towards the Sir Roy Griffiths Memorial Chair.

A further 17 grants of £10,000 or less were made in this category.

The arts

There were four grants of more than £10,000, the largest of which was £500,000 over three years to Kelvingrove Art Gallery & Museum towards its redevelopment. Other grants were: £75,000 over three years to Edward James Foundation towards bursaries; £15,000 to National Youth Theatre of Great Britain for bursaries; and £12,000 to Royal Scottish National Orchestra towards Soundstation.

A further eight grants of £10,000 or less were made.

AIDS

There were seven grants over £10,000, the largest of which was £175,000 over two years to Terrence Higgins Trust towards the Lighthouse King's project. Other grants included: £70,000 over two years to University of Liverpool Department of Pharmacology & Therapeutics for research; and £15,000 to Waverley Care – Edinburgh towards the provision or respite care at Milestone House.

One grant of £10,000 or less were also made in this category.

Social development

Twelve grants over £10,000 were made in this category, the largest of which was £158,000 over three years to Judge Institute of Management, University of Cambridge towards staff costs for the Masters programme. Other grants included: £112,000 to Airborne Initiative to employ two additional keyworkers; £85,000 over three years to CharityBank to support the establishment of a funding brokerage service for community enterprise; and £26,000 to

Helix Arts towards a new arts project in the Oswald Unit at HM Young Offenders Institute Castington.

One further grant of £3,000 was made in this category.

General

Two larger grants of £50,000 each were made to Millennium Library Trust towards the extension of the Everyman Millennium Library project, and for the Sainsbury Archive towards the associated costs of preparing the archive for transfer to the Museum of London.

A further three grants of £10,000 or less were also made in this category.

The environment

Three larger grants were made in this category. They were: £110,000 over three years to Painshill Park Trust to employ a project manager to prepare and implement the final phase of restoration; £90,000 over three years to Chelsea Physic Garden towards employing a taxonomist and its education programme; and £50,000 to the Dean and Chapter of Norwich towards essential repairs on the medieval Ethelbert Gate.

A further five grants were made for less than £10,000 each.

Exclusions

Grants are not normally made to individuals.

Applications

See the guidance for applicants in the entry for the Sainsbury Family Charitable Trusts. A single application will be considered for support by all the trusts in the group.

However, for this as for many of the trusts: 'proposals are generally invited by the trustees or initiated at their request. Unsolicited applications are discouraged and are unlikely to be successful, even if they fall within an area in which the trustees are interested.'

The Henry Moore Foundation

Fine arts, in particular sculpture, drawing and printmaking

£499,000 (2003/04)

Beneficial area UK and overseas.

Dane Tree House, Perry Green, Much Hadham, Hertfordshire SG10 6EE

Tel. 01279 843333

Website www.henry-moore-fdn.co.uk

Correspondent Timothy Llewellyn, Director

Trustees *Sir Ewen Fergusson, chair; Dawn Ades; David Ansbro; Malcolm Baker; Marianne Brouwer; Prof. Andrew Causey; James Joll; Simon Keswick; Greville Worthington; Henry Wrong.*

Charity Commission no. 271370

Information available Annual review magazine available on the foundation's website.

The foundation was established in 1977 to advance the education of the public by the promotion of their appreciation of the fine arts and in particular the works of Henry Moore. It concentrates its support on sculpture. The aims of the foundation are achieved through specific projects initiated within the foundation both at Perry Green and in Leeds, particularly exhibitions and publications, and by giving grant aid to other suitable enterprises.

The Henry Moore Foundation's grant-making programme has been revised to provide additional financial resources to support the work of living artists and contemporary art practice. Special consideration will be given to projects outside London and to venues with limited opportunities to show contemporary art. Other long-standing categories supporting historic and contemporary sculpture will remain in the programme, including post-doctoral research fellowships assisting outstanding young scholars; exhibitions, providing financial support for established public galleries and agencies towards all aspects of exhibition making in the field, and grants for conferences, workshops and lecture series.

Grants are usually restricted to the following categories:

- Exhibitions (established galleries only) – to support all aspects of exhibition making
- Commissions to make new work – temporary or permanent, indoors or out

- 'Challenge Fund' – seed money to encourage ambitious projects and other sources of funds
- Publications – exhibition catalogues and other publications in the field
- Conferences, workshops, symposia and lecture series
- Fellowships for artists at appropriate institutions
- Post-doctoral research fellowships for art historians at British universities – advertised annually
- Bursaries for post-graduate students of fine art or art history at appropriate UK institutions – advertised annually.

As a result of the foundation's grant making review, some categories of grant have been suspended and new categories have been introduced. The category 'capital grants' has now been suspended, as has museum acquisitions, public art and conservation, except in very exceptional circumstances.

Grantmaking

In 2003/04 the foundation had an income of £3.7 million and spent £2.6 million on funding the Moore institutions and their exhibitions, projects and research. In addition, £499,000 was spent on grants to other organisations. The value of the individual grants was not disclosed by the foundation, but the annual review listed and grouped the grants awarded as follows:

Fellowships for artists

'After consulting widely with artists and host institutions, we have remodelled our fellowships for artists. In future the foundation will consider applications jointly from an artist and an institution for a fellowship of £12,000 over a six month period. As fellowships will thus be tied to the academic year, as they have often been in the past, applications may be made at any time and the number of fellowships awarded will depend on the resources available in any year.' Three artists received fellowships during 2004.

Post-doctoral research fellowships

'Fellowships of £15,000 to develop publications are now awarded for one year to scholars who have recently completed PhD degrees. Scholars requiring additional time may re-apply.' There were eight post-doctoral research fellowships in 2004.

Research projects

Two research projects were supported in the year.

Support for post-graduate students

'Support under this category will be revised to offer bursaries of between £500 and £1,500 to post-graduate students of fine art history at British institutions to help fund special research or creative projects. An open competition will be held each winter.'

Conferences, lectures and workshops

Four were supported during the year.

Publications

'Funding in this category has now been increased to encourage applications for financial support for catalogues of contemporary work.' Seven projects were supported during the year.

Exhibitions

41 exhibitions were supported in 2003/04.

Exclusions

The foundation does not give grants to individual applicants, nor does it provide revenue expenditure.

Applications

In writing to the director. The guidelines state that all applicants should cover the following:

- the aims and functions of the organisation;
- the precise purpose for which a grant is sought;
- the amount required and details of how that figure is arrived at;
- details of efforts made to find other sources of income, whether any firm commitments have been received, and what others are hoped for;
- details of the budget for the scheme and how the scheme will be monitored.

Applications are usually considered at quarterly meetings of the donations sub-committee, which makes recommendations to the management committee of the trustees. Applications should not be made by telephone or in person.

John Moores Foundation

Social welfare in Merseyside and Northern Ireland, emergency relief overseas

£756,000 (2002/03)

Beneficial area Merseyside (plus Skelmersdale, Ellesmere Port and Halton), Northern Ireland, South Africa, overseas.

7th Floor, Gostins Building, 32–36 Hanover Street, Liverpool L1 4LN

Tel. 0151 707 6077 **Fax** 0151 707 6066

Email jmf@dial.pipex.com

Website www.jmf.org.uk

Correspondent Tara Parveen, Grants Director

Trustees *Barnaby Moores; Mrs Jane Moores; Sister M McAleese; Peter Bassey.*

Charity Commission no. 253481

Information available Information was provided by the trust.

Summary

At least 75% of grants are for £5,000 or less and go to charities based in the areas set out above, though no unsolicited requests for funding in South Africa will be considered. Grants are made for both revenue and capital purposes; about one-quarter are revenue grants for two or three years. About two in five applications from Merseyside and Northern Ireland result in a grant.

General

The trust had an income of £884,000 in 2002/03 from investments worth about £13 million. The foundation says of its grantmaking:

During the last 20 years the trustees have confined their giving to five main categories:

- Merseyside
- Northern Ireland
- South Africa
- world crisis
- one-off exceptional grants that interest trustees.

1. Merseyside is the first concern of trustees.
2. Northern Ireland would normally receive about 10%.
3. Post-apartheid South Africa has very great needs in literacy and health, particularly as they affect women and children. The trustees remain committed to making a realistic contribution to these areas but only to projects known to or initiated by trustees because of the difficulties of monitoring overseas projects. Trustees do not respond to unsolicited applications from South African projects.
4. World crisis tends to include man-made or natural disasters such as famine, flood or earthquake which by definition need large one-off grants to prevent loss of life. These donations are normally made to one of the big aid agencies such as British Red Cross.
5. Occasional one-off exceptional grants are rare and unspecified and are to causes that interest trustees.

Trustees do not respond to unsolicited applications requests in categories 3, 4 and 5.

Grant making is mainly directed towards new and/or small organisations in the area of Merseyside (including Skelmersdale, Ellesmere Port and Halton) and in Northern Ireland, who work with disadvantaged or marginalised people and who find it more than usually difficult to raise money from other sources. Preference is given to organisations seeking funding for projects which fall within the foundation's target areas for giving which are:

- women including girls
- black and ethnic minority organisations
- race gender and disability awareness
- advice and information to alleviate poverty
- second chance learning
- grass roots community groups.

And, in Merseyside only:

- people with disabilities
- carers
- support and training for voluntary organisations
- homeless people
- childcare
- complementary therapies.

The trust's separate policy leaflets for Merseyside and Northern Ireland provide more in-depth details of work the foundation will consider funding. Part of this information is reprinted below:

Purposes for which grants are given

The foundation makes grants for:

- running costs
- help towards salaries
- one-off project costs
- equipment.

And, in Merseyside only:

- help towards minor building refurbishment.

Size of grants

In Merseyside

The size of grant varies, but in general over 75% of grants are £5,000 or less.

In Northern Ireland

The size of grant varies, but no grants are for more than £5,000. Very few grants are given for more than one year.

The trust also defines some interests of current concern in its Merseyside programme, as follows:

The arrival of new refugees in Merseyside and the outcome of the Macpherson Report (Stephen Lawrence Inquiry) confirm that community groups will have to respond differently to meet new, special and existing needs. To assist groups meet such needs the trustees took the decision to introduce experimental funding in the following areas:

People in crisis

Projects that increase the participation of refugees in full community life will be given priority and grants will only be given for work directly involving:

- emergency support to incoming refugees including the provision and development of specialist legal advice on resettlement.
- local projects working towards the integration of refugees in community life including basic education, training, health, cultural, general social welfare, and schemes that target excluded people within the refugee community as well as initiatives that enable them to meet their own needs.

Co-operative working/trust building

Projects that address the 'causes' are a priority while less emphasis will be given to the 'symptoms'. To address this concern grants will be given for work directly involving:

- local trust building initiatives to encourage co-operation and joint working between different community and voluntary groups – projects which break down barriers.
- support for non-black community groups who are developing and implementing culturally sensitive policies.
- the provision of advice, information and assistance with individual advocacy.

Applicants must demonstrate that the proposal is led and supported by their organisation, and is open to all those who wish to join it or make use of the services offered.

Grants in 2002/03

The trust made 124 grants, categorised as follows (those for 2001/02, where comparable, in brackets):

Merseyside

	No.	Total	No.	Total
Advice	4	£96,000	(6)	(£118,000)
Black/racial minority	11	£40,000	(6)	(£33,000)
Carers/childcare	16	£77,000	(12)	(£50,000)
Community organisations	14	£92,000	(6)	(£31,000)
Complementary therapy	-	-	(-)	(-)
Cooperative work/trust building	1	£5,000	(-)	(-)
Disability	8	£25,000	(8)	(£25,000)
Homelessness	5	£32,000	(6)	(£37,000)
Refugees/asylum seekers	3	£6,000	(4)	(£13,000)
Second chance learning	5	£36,000	(3)	(£30,000)
Social welfare	19	£79,000	(12)	(£36,000)
Training for community groups	3	£16,000	(1)	(£4,000)
Unemployed people	-	-	(1)	(£10,000)
Women	11	£59,000	(7)	(£37,000)
Total	100	£563,000	(72)	(£425,000)

Northern Ireland

	No.	Total	No.	Total
Advice	3	£12,000	(2)	(£10,000)
Black/racial minority	1	£5,000	(1)	(£5,000)
Community organisations	6	£25,000	(9)	(£33,000)
Disabled people	1	£1,000	(-)	(-)
Second chance learning	2	£6,000	(1)	(£5,000)
Social welfare	2	£10,000	(2)	(£10,000)
Training	-	-	(1)	(£5,000)
Women	5	£21,000	(9)	(£28,000)
Total	20	£80,000	(25)	(£96,000)

International

	No.	Total	No.	Total
International	4	£113,000	(6)	(£156,000)

The trust also provided the following information:

During the year 2002/03, 271 written applications were received (315 in 2001/02), of which 166 were from Merseyside, 46 from Northern Ireland and 59 from other areas.

124 grants were made totalling £756,000 (compared with 103 grants totalling £678,000 in 2001/02). Of these, 35 were revenue grants of more than one year. 71% of grants given were for £5,000 or less, of which 20% were for £1,000 or less.

The largest grant during the year, as in the previous year, was made to Merseyside Information & Advice Project, which received £56,000 towards running costs. Other beneficiaries on Merseyside and in Northern Ireland included: Salvation Army – Bootle towards installing a platform lift (£25,000); Health @ Work – Merseyside for the cost of setting up and running a Voluntary Counselling and Support service (£20,000); Sheila Kay Fund – Merseyside towards running costs (£15,000); Bronte Youth & Community Centre – Liverpool towards running costs (£12,500); Big Issue in the North towards running costs of the Premier Drugs Service for homeless people in Liverpool (£10,000); Strand Creche – Bootle towards running costs (£9,000); Zero Centre – Wirral towards salary costs (£7,500); Liverpool Family Service Unit towards the cost of a daycare service for under-5s (£7,000); Knowsley

Play Resource Centre for a contribution towards salary costs (£6,000); Colin Community Groups Association – Belfast towards running costs of the advice centre (£5,000); Creggan Pre-School & Training Association – Derry towards salary costs (£4,000); Croxteth & Gillmoss Community Federation – Liverpool towards salary costs (£3,000); Liverpool Six Community Association towards running costs (£2,000); Trojans Youth & Community Development Group – Derry towards the costs of recruiting and training volunteers, and Home-Start Antrim District towards the cost of installing a stair lift (£1,000 each).

Three organisations received grants for work in South Africa. They were UNICEF Southern African Appeal (£50,000), Women's Education Fund for Southern Africa (£40,000) and Craft Association (£23,000).

Exclusions

The foundation does not give grants for:

- individuals;
- academic or medical research;
- animal charities;
- arts, heritage or local history projects;
- new buildings;
- churches for church-based or church-run activities (although community groups running activities in church premises which come within the foundation's policy guidelines will be considered);
- children and young people, except via the South Moss Foundation (administered by JMF);
- conservation and the environment;
- employment creation schemes;
- festivals;
- holidays, expeditions and outings;
- medicine or health;
- national organisations or organisations based outside of Merseyside or Northern Ireland, even if working within those areas;
- overseas projects, unless initiated by the foundation;
- schools, universities or colleges;
- sponsorship, including fundraising events;
- sport;
- statutory bodies;
- vehicles;
- victims of crime – other than rape crisis and domestic violence projects.

Applications

Applications should be in writing and accompanied by an application form, copies of which are obtainable from the foundation. Before submitting an application, please make sure that your project does not fall into one of the excluded areas. Separate policy leaflets providing guidance for applicants in Merseyside and Northern Ireland are available. If you are unsure or you would like to discuss your application, please telephone the foundation's office.

Applications are expected to contain the following information:

- a description of your organisation, its work and existing sources of funding;
- a description of the project for which you are applying for funds;
- detailed costings of the project, including details of funds already raised or applied for if any;
- details of how the project will benefit people within the foundation's target groups.

Applicants should also send if possible:

- latest accounts;
- latest annual report;
- list of management committee members;
- equal opportunities policy.

Most groups who apply for funding are visited, but the foundation may simply telephone for more information. Trustees meet five to six times a year and all applications are acknowledged.

The Peter Moores Foundation

The arts, particularly opera, social welfare

Around £10 million (2002/03)
Beneficial area UK and Barbados.

c/o Wallwork, Nelson & Johnson, Chandler House, 7 Ferry Road, Riversway, Preston, Lancashire PR2 2YH

Tel. 01772 430000 **Fax** 01772 430012

Email moores@pmf.org.uk

Website www.pmf.org.uk

Correspondent Lesley Mills, Administrator

Trustees *Michael Johnstone; Peter Egerton-Warburton; Eileen Ainscough; Ludmilla Andrew; Countess of Harewood; Nicholas Payne; Kirsten Suenson-Taylor.*

Charity Commission no. 258224

Information available Annual report and accounts, without a full list of grants, are on file at the Charity Commission.

Summary

The foundation concentrates on supporting opera and other forms of music, and the opera-connected Compton Verney House project which receives over one-third of the available funds. Peter Moores himself worked professionally in opera.

General

Grants are made in the fields of fine art (including Compton Verney House), music (performance and recording), training, health, youth, race relations, heritage, social welfare and the environment. The foundation also focuses its work in Barbados through the Peter Moores Barbados Trust.

In 2002/03 the foundation had an income of £10.9 million and a total expenditure of £10.7 million, most of which is likely to have been given in grants. No further information was available on the distribution of funds during the year.

In previous years the following opera companies have been supported on a large scale: English National Opera, Almeida Opera, Welsh National Opera, Rossini Opera Festival and Wildbad and Garsington Opera. The foundation has also been involved in the establishment of the Saïd Business School at Oxford University and has supported the Venice in Peril appeal.

The foundation's website has information on many of the organisation's that receive or have received support.

Comment

There was no response to repeated written requests for a copy of the most recent annual report and accounts, despite the requirement to provide these on demand.

Despite ample warning, and their obligation to the contrary, the Charity Commission were unable to give us sight of this trust's accounts.

Applications

In writing to the correspondent, but applicants should be aware that the foundation has previously stated that it 'will normally support projects which come to the attention of its patron or trustees through their interests or special knowledge. General applications for

sponsorship are not encouraged and are unlikely to succeed.

The J P Morgan Foundations

Education

£529,000 (2003)

Beneficial area UK, with a special interest in Islington, Havering, east London, Bournemouth, Edinburgh and Glasgow.

10 Aldermanbury, London EC2V 7RF
Tel. 020 7325 8771 **Fax** 020 7325 8195
Email duncan.grant@jpmorganfleming.com
Correspondent Duncan Grant, Director

Trustees *J P Morgan Fleming Marketing Ltd, who have appointed the following managing committee: Mark Garvin, chair; Duncan Grant; Edward Banks; Richard Chambers; Catherine Eardley; Stephanie Emery; Richard Kaye; Carol Lake; Carole Machell; Duncan MacIntyre; Michael Ridley; Maria Ryan; Jonathan White; Dorcas Williams.*

Charity Commission no. 291617

Information available Annual report and accounts were provided by the trusts.

Summary

Formerly the Save and Prosper Educational Trust, the educational trust is now part of J P Morgan Fleming Asset Management. Originally founded in 1974, the trust was established as part of a tax-avoiding school fees planning service. Further recruitment of parents into the scheme was stopped by the Charity Commission a few years ago and the corresponding income for this trust will diminish to zero by the year 2014.

However, another charity, the J P Morgan Fleming Foundation, is being built up as the old one declines. This entry covers both charities, which now operate simply as J P Morgan Foundations.

In 2003 the educational trust, currently the larger of the two, had an income of £532,000. The income for the smaller foundation was £143,000.

Grantmaking policies

Guidelines for the trust have previously been described by the trust as follows, and these principles still appear to apply.

Support is for UK-based educational projects, with an emphasis on special needs, which generally fit into one of the following categories:

- Special needs education including youngsters disadvantaged by disability, background or lack of opportunity.
- Giving something back to the community by way of children's projects that offer education and training that widen the opportunities for youngsters, particularly those children who are in trouble or 'at risk'.
- Primary and secondary schools, universities and museums.
- Supporting school age children and students in all art forms, helping them to gain access to the arts and to better appreciate them.
- Generally, we do not give support direct to individuals but some scholarships and bursaries are made to organisations supporting educational fees and maintenance.
- New and innovative ways of advancing education in the UK.
- J P Morgan Fleming Foundation has a modest unrestricted portion of its budget that is generally used for donations to children's charities.

Grants in 2003

The foundations' areas of giving were as follows (shown with percentage of giving in brackets):

- Community development and human services (42%)
- Primary and secondary education (27%)
- Arts and culture (31%)

Communities where funds were directed (shown with percentage of giving in brackets):

- London and east London (59%)
- Havering/Romford (16%)
- Bournemouth (11%)
- Edinburgh (9%)
- Glasgow (5%)

The trust also says the following about grants:

In 2003 the focus shifted to 'an inch wide and a mile deep' approach to grant making.
JPMorgan, through its charities wishes to deepen good partnerships with the local community. This is reflected in supporting fewer projects than in 2002 but with larger awards over a longer period of time.

In 2003 the sum of £600,000 was allocated in 89 grants of which £529,000 was paid.

Many of the grants were annual awards or part of multi-year awards. There were 26 larger grants, made by both charities, for £10,000 or more. These included: £25,000 each to Bournemouth Symphony Orchestra to fund the Primary Schools Project in Bournemouth and Poole and Duke of Edinburgh Award to fund work in London, Edinburgh and Glasgow; £21,000 to Royal Academy Trust to fund a life drawing education project; £20,000 to Royal Scottish Academy of Music and Drama to fund the development of a major primary school music project in Glasgow and Edinburgh; £17,000 to Fryent Primary School to support a 'hard to reach' youngsters project at the school; £15,000 each to CEDC to support a school club project for children with 'challenging behaviour', First Step to fund core costs of the special needs playgroup, Harmeny Education Trust to support the instruction and equipment costs, RNIB – Redhill College to support the Soundscape Project and Youth at Risk to fund the Coaching for Community project in High Wycombe; and £13,000 to Bart's City Life Saver to support tarining courses.

Beneficiaries of grants of £10,000 each included: Barnardos to support the Blackfird Brae School in Edinburgh; Family Welfare Association to fund a student advisor with the Education Grants Advisory Service; Glyndebourne Productions Ltd to support the education department with its work in Lewes, Brighton and Thanet; Hackney Education Action Zone to support Turkish speaking pupils at Hackney Free and Parochial School; Harold Hill Youth Motocross to fund training and equipment purchase for the motorcycle project; Newton's Primary School to fund tuition and instuments for a music project; Roundhouse Trust to fund the educational Co-ordinator Project; St Francis' Hospice to fund the education programme in specialist palliative care; and Who Cares Trust to fund a pilot school project in Bournemouth.

Other grants include: £7,500 to NCH to fund an Early Intervention Project in north Romford schools; £6,000 to New Platform to fund a video and resource pack for a schools' teenage pregnancy project; £5,500 each to London Borough of Havering to fund Saturday arts workshops and summer library shows and St Paul's Girls' School to fund a half fee bursary for a young person from Tower Hamlets; £5,000 each to Camden Alcoholics Support Association to part fund an employment training worker, Community Foundation for Tyne & Wear and Northumberland to fund a training project for 'at risk' young people, Hanley Crouch Community Association to fund a play worker for after school and holiday play projects, Museum of Garden History to part fund the education officer and YWCA Vineries Project to part fund education work with teenage mothers at its Dagenham Centre; £4,000 to City of London Festival to support schools' work with the festival; £2,500 to Great Ormond Street Hospital Trust to fund IT equipment for the hospital school and Lordship Lane Primary School to part fund tuition and instrument costs for a music project and Museum of Fulham Palace towards the costs of the education officer; £2,000 to Kith and Kids to support the Two for One volunteer project, Northwold Primary School to fund tennis development at the school and October Gallery to fund the education department; £1,000 each to Bridgewater School to fund a lap-top computer for the special needs department and Phoenix Secondary and Primary School to subsidise travel for an educational visit and Wysing Arts to support the education department; and £500 to Scottish European Education Trust to fund a primary school quiz.

Exclusions

Projects not usually supported include:

- open appeals from national charities;
- building appeals;
- charity gala nights and similar events;
- appeals by individuals for study grants, travel scholarships or charity sponsorships.

Applications

To apply for funding please write a brief letter (not more than two sides of A4) to Duncan Grant, the director. Please avoid bulky items such as cassettes in the original request.

Please set out your reasons for applying along with an indication of the level of funding required. There is no application form or specific closing dates for initial inquiries. Applications are always acknowledged, and will be reviewed within eight weeks. We will contact you within this time if we can take your applications forward.

Final approval for funding must come from trustees who meet four times a year, in January, March, July and October.

If your application is unsuccessful we suggest you wait at least a year before re-applying.

The Mulberry Trust

General

£608,000 (2002/03)

Beneficial area UK, with an interest in Harlow, Essex and surrounding areas, including London.

Messrs Farrer & Co, 66 Lincoln's Inn Fields, London WC2A 3LH

Tel. 020 7242 2022

Correspondent Ms Cheryl Boyce

Trustees *John G Marks; Mrs Ann M Marks; Charles F Woodhouse; Timothy J Marks.*

Charity Commission no. 263296

Information available Accounts on file at the Charity Commission.

Summary

Around 100 grants are made each year, most being for amounts of £5,000 or less. Grants go to a wide range of causes, with both local institutions, including hospices and universities, and national charities receiving funding. Around half the grants seem to go to regularly supported recipients.

General

In 2002/03 the trust had an income of £773,000, including £602,000 from a gift of shares. Investments were worth £4.9 million. The accounts listed 74 grants of £500 or more. There was a mix of new and previously supported organisations.

The largest grants were £65,000 to University of Cambridge and £50,000 each to Essex Community Foundation and Harlow Poors Chaity – Alms Houses.

There were 19 further grants for £10,000 or over. Beneficiaries included Credit Action, Pioneer Sailing Trust and University of Nottingham (£25,000 each), Bayswater, Foundation for Church Leadership and Institute and Leadership Institute (£20,000 each) and Church Housing Trust and Jubilee Plus (£10,000 each).

Other beneficiaries included Relationship Foundation and Jefford Weller Bugatti Trust (£6,000), Relationship Foundation and Jefford Weller Charitable Trust (£5,000 each), North Lakeland Hospice at Home (£3,000), Churchgate School – Harlow and Spadework (£2,000 each) and Action for Blind People, Elimination of Leukaemia Fund and Salvation Army (£1,000 each).

Grants unlisted in the accounts were made to 26 organisations and totalled £10,000.

Applications

The trust has stated that it 'will not, as a matter of policy, consider applications which are unsolicited'.

The National Art Collections Fund

Acquisition of works of art by museums and galleries

£4.4 million (2003)
Beneficial area UK.

Millais House, 7 Cromwell Place, London SW7 2JN

Tel. 020 7225 4800 **Fax** 020 7225 4848

Email grants@artfund.org

Website www.artfund.org

Correspondent Mary Yule, Director of Grants

Trustees *David Verey, chair; David Barrie, director; Paul Zuckerman, treasurer; Dr Wendy Baron; Sir Geoffrey de Bellaigue; William Govett; Prof. Michael Kauffmann; Dr David Landau; John Mallet; Dr Jennifer Montagu; Prof. Lord Refrew of Kaimsthorn; Charles Sebag-Montefiore; Anthony Snow; Timothy Stevens; The Hon. Felicity Waley-Cohen; Prof. Sir Christopher White.*

Charity Commission no. 209174

Information available Annual report and accounts were provided by the fund. An annual review, with accounts, which gives a full illustrated record of all works assisted is also available, as is the leaflet 'Information for Grant Applicants'. Informative website.

Increasingly known as simply the Art Fund, this fundraising and membership charity makes over 100 grants to museums and galleries all around the

UK to subsidise the purchase of works of art of all kinds. The grants usually form part of a funding package put together to acquire a particular work.

There is no upper or lower limit to the level of grant assistance, but the range is normally £1,000 to £20,000; however, larger grants are also made. In 2003 the income of the fund came mainly from legacies (£1.3 million), members' subscriptions (£2.2 million) and from income on the charity's investments (£1.3 million). During the year the fund made grants to 103 organisations and institutions totalling £4.4 million.

Nine institutions received grants of £100,000 or more in support of exhibitions and aquisitions. These were the British Museum (£542,000), National Galleries of Scotland (£530,000), Victoria & Albert Museum (£449,000), National Museum of Photography, Film & Television (£342,000), Ashmolean Museum (£303,000), Fitzwilliam Museum (£234,000), Tate Gallery (£182,000); Perth Museum and Art Gallery and Braintree District Museum (£100,000) each.

Other beneficiaries included the National Portrait Gallery (£89,000), National Museums and Galleries of Wales (£87,000), Jersey Museum (£60,000), Abbott Hall Art Gallery – Kendal (£40,000), Leeds Museums and Galleries (£34,000), Manchester Art Gallery (£32,000), Northamptonshire Record Office (£20,000), Gallery of Modern Art – Glasgow (£16,000), Royal Marines Museum – Southsea (£15,000), Victoria Art Gallery – Bath (£12,000), Lincoln City and County Museum (£10,000), Moyses Hall Museum – Bury St Edmunds (£9,000), Harris Museum and Art Gallery – Preston (£7,000), Aberdeen Art Gallery (£6,000), Doncaster Museum and Art Gallery (£5,000) and the School of Art Gallery and Museum – Aberystwyth (£4,000).

Grants of less than £4,000 each were made to 45 institutions totalling £102,000.

Exclusions

Grants are restricted to institutions which have a permanent exhibition space, are open to the public and registered with the Museums, Libraries and Archives Council.

Applications

To the correspondent. A basic information leaflet is available for applicants, and an application form.

Applicants are expected to have approached other sources of help, and, except in very special circumstances, museums are expected to make a contribution to the purchase from their own funds.

The trustees meet monthly, apart from January and August. Meeting dates are available from the Grants Office, and the deadline for applications is two weeks before the meeting.

Nemoral Ltd

Orthodox Jewish causes

£439,000 (2002/03)
Beneficial area Worldwide.

13–17 New Burlington Place, Regent Street, London W1X 2JP

Tel. 020 7734 1362

Correspondent The Trustees

Trustees *C D Schlaff; M Gross; Mrs Z Schlaff; Mrs R Gross; Michael Saberski.*

Charity Commission no. 262270

Information available Accounts were provided by the trust, although with a limited annual report.

The trust supports the Orthodox Jewish community in the UK and abroad. In 2002/03 it had assets of £732,000, which generated an income of £32,000. Grants were made totalling £439,000, a significant decrease on previous years. After other expenses, there was a deficit for the year of £411,000. In the previous year, there was an income of £81,000, a grant total of £355,000 and a deficit of £279,000; there was no explanation in the accounts as to why this situation is occurring.

The largest grants were £69,000 each to British Friends of Chazon Ish and Yeshivat Kollel Avrechim Breslov, £64,000 to Ostrowce Institutions, £63,000 to Kahal Chasidei Bobov, £54,000 to United Talmudical Association and £50,000 to Chevrath Torah Veyirah.

Other beneficiaries included Talmud Torah Komemiut (£15,000), Yeshivat Shaar Hashamayim (£10,000), Beis Medrash Govoha (£6,000), Chevras Oneg Shabbos Viyom Tov (£4,000), Friends of Bobov Foundation (£3,500), Beis Ruzhin Trust and Congregation Tiferes Shulem (£2,000 each) and Society of Friends of Torah (£1,500).

Applications

In writing to the correspondent.

Network for Social Change

Third world debt, environment, human rights, peace, arts

£926,000 (2002/03)

Beneficial area UK and overseas.

BM 2063, London WC1N 3XX

Email thenetwork@gn.apc.org

Correspondent Tish McCrory, Administrator

Trustees *Ingrid Broad; Prue Hardwick; Doro Marden; Jen McClelland; Philip Sanders; Jonathan Smith; Martin Stamp; Giles Wright.*

Charity Commission no. 295237

Information available Annual report and accounts.

Summary

Network for Social Change, formerly the Network Foundation, is a group of philanthropic individuals who have come together to support progressive causes. Grants, for up to £15,000, typically go to organisations addressing such issues as environmental sustainability and economic and social justice.

In each year a new major and longer-term project may also be initiated.

'Projects funded by the Network for Social Change are all researched and sponsored by members; unsolicited applications are not considered.'

General

In 2002/03 the Network's income was £895,000, and it made grants totalling £926,000. It described its year's work as follows:

There is an annual funding cycle, in which grants to a maximum per project of £15,000 are made into the categories listed below and focus on projects which are likely to effect social change, whether by example, publicity, lobbying or other legal and charitable means. The Network supports projects which redistribute wealth to those in need, promote human rights, safeguard the earth's resources, promote peace and non-

violence and alternative healthy living options.

A summary of the pools are as follows:

	No.	Total
peace and security	9	£99,000
green planet	9	£80,000
arts for change	8	£74,000
equity & poverty	8	£66,000
health and wholeness	5	£58,000
social justice	5	£42,000

Smaller grants are also made four times each year, and involve members researching and circulating projects which they intend to fund personally. A meeting is then held where other members are given the opportunity to hear about the projects and choose whether to support them. During the year, 39 projects were supported through this process to a total sum of £156,000.

Larger grants, usually spread over several years, can be made where a group of Network members join together to co-ordinate the most effective means of bringing about social change in one particular field.

Current projects are one focussing on localisation (rather than globalisation), and 'Smart Justice', aimed at reducing the number of prisoners in UK prisons. Past major projects have been Jubilee 2000, the campaign for international debt relief, and nuclear policy research carried out by the Oxford Research Group.

Grants in 2002/03

With the accounts was a list of the 50 largest donations. Those receiving £15,000 or more were as follows:

Jubilee Plus	£109,000
Prison Reform Trust	£108,000
Oxford Research Group	£43,000
New Economics Group	£40,000
Friends of the Earth Trust	£29,500
Millennium Debate	£22,500
British American Security Information Council	£22,000
Partnership for Growth	£21,000
The Gaia Foundation	£19,500
Sustain: The Alliance for Better Food and Farming	£18,000
Kurdish Human Rights Project	£18,000
The Juneberry Trust	£15,500
ASH (Action on Smoking and Health)	£15,500
Photovoice	£15,000

Smaller grants over £1,000 each included those to Scottish Centre for Non-Violence, Scientists for Global Responsibility, People & Planet Trust, Save the Children Fund, Kids Company, Ecological Foundation and Paddington Development Trust.

Applications

The network chooses the projects it wishes to support and does not solicit applications. Unsolicited applications cannot expect to receive a reply.

Information for potential members is provided by contacting the Network for Social Change at the address below.

The Frances and Augustus Newman Foundation

Medical research and equipment

£530,000 (2002/03)

Beneficial area UK and overseas.

c/o Baker Tilly (Chartered Accountants), 3rd Floor, 1 Georges Square, Bristol BS1 6BP

Tel. 0117 945 2000 **Fax** 0117 945 2001

Email hazel.palfreyman@bakertilly.co.uk

Correspondent Hazel Palfreyman

Trustees *Sir Rodney Sweetnam, Chair; Lord Rathcavan; John L Williams.*

Charity Commission no. 277964

Information available Annual report and accounts were provided by the trust.

The foundation aims to advance the work of medical professionals working in teaching hospitals and academic units, mostly (but not exclusively) funding medical research projects and equipment, including Fellowships of the Royal College of Surgeons of England. Grants range from £2,000 to £45,000 a year and can be given for up to three years.

In 2002/03 the foundation had assets of £9.5 million and an income of £437,000. Grants totalled £530,000 and were categorised as follows:

UK ongoing research	£220,000
UK 'one-off'	£140,000
Research fellowships awarded through the Royal College of Surgeons	£160,000
Overseas	£11,000

Ongoing research grants went to nine organisations and included £40,000 to the Royal Hospitals – Belfast, £37,000 to Muscular Dystrophy Campaign, £32,000 to St Thomas' Hospital, £17,000 to Royal College of Surgeons, and £8,000 to Queen Elizabeth's Foundation for Disabled People.

UK one-off grants went to eight organisations and included £40,000 to Royal College of Surgeons, £38,000 to University of Cambridge, £25,000 to University of Liverpool, £16,000 to

University of Bristol, £5,000 to St Wilfrid's Hospice and £3,000 to the Peace Hospice.

Research fellowships of £40,000 each were given in London, Bristol, Sheffield and Southampton for research into bowel disorders, the function of mucus in the voice box, artificial hip loosening and the mechanisms of inflamation in hay fever respectively.

As in the previous year, the only overseas grant went to Paracare Association of Palm Beach Inc, this year for £11,000.

Exclusions

Applications are not normally accepted from overseas. Requests from other charities seeking funds to supplement their own general funds to support medical research in a particular field are seldom supported.

Applications

Applications should include a detailed protocol and costing and be sent to the secretary. They may then be peer-reviewed. The trustees meet in June and December each year and applications must be received at the latest by the end of April or October respectively. The foundation awards for surgical research fellowships should be addressed to the Royal College of Surgeons of England which evaluates each application.

The North British Hotel Trust

Welfare, health

£331,000 (2003/04)

Beneficial area UK, but mainly Scotland.

1 Queen Charlotte Lane, Edinburgh EH6 6BL

Tel. 0131 554 7173

Correspondent The Trustees

Trustees *W G Crerar, chair; I C Fraser; Dr R L Frew; J R M MacQueen; P Crerar; G Brown.*

Charity Commission no. 221335

Information available Perfunctory annual report, accounts, uncategorised grants list.

The trust makes over 50 grants a year. Giving is concentrated in areas where the North British Trust Hotels company operates (a holding of shares in that company constitutes the charity's endowment). It is possible that the trust operates as the recipient of applications addressed to the company's hotels. There are over 20 such hotels in Scotland, covering much of the country.

There are also four hotels in England, with grants being made close to those in Scarborough, Harrogate and Barnby Moor in Yorkshire.

Most identifiable grants are for welfare purposes, especially those benefiting older or disabled people, or for health.

In 2003/04 the trust had assets of £5.8 million and an income of £369,000. Grants totalling £331,000 were made during the year, the largest of which were £100,000 each to Duke of Edinburgh Award Scheme and Eden Court Theatre, £25,000 to Scottish Youth Hostels Association, £18,000 to Old Peoples' Welfare Association, £15,000 to Royal National MOD – Oban, £12,000 to Scarborough Homeless and £10,000 to Scottish Chamber Orchestra.

Other beneficiaries included Music in Hospitals (£7,000), Atholl Centre – Pitlochry (£6,500), Barnardo's – Blackford Brae Project (£5,000), Down's Syndrome Scotland (£3,000), Oban Youth and Community Centre (£2,000), West Lothian Ramblers Association (£1,000) and RNIB (£500).

Exclusions

No grants to individuals.

Applications

An application form is available from the correspondent.

The Northern Rock Foundation

Disadvantaged people

£19.3 million (planned for 2005)

Beneficial area Cumbria, Northumberland, Tyne and Wear, County Durham and the Tees Valley.

The Old Chapel, Woodbine Road, Gosforth, Newcastle upon Tyne NE3 1DD

Tel. 0191 284 8412 **Fax** 0191 284 8413

Minicom 0191 284 5411

Email generaloffice@nr-foundation.org.uk

Website www.nr-foundation.org.uk

Correspondent Fiona Ellis, Director

Trustees *Leo Finn, chair; David Chapman; Barbara Dennis; David Faulkner; Tony Henfrey; Charles Howick; Chris Jobe; Lorna Moran; Frank Nicholson; Dorothy Russell; Julie Shipley.*

Charity Commission no. 1063906

Information available Excellent report, accounts, newsletter, guidelines and application forms, all available on the foundation's website.

Summary

The aim of the foundation is to help those who are disadvantaged in society in the North East of England (Northumberland, Tyne and Wear, County Durham and the Tees Valley) and Cumbria.

The foundation receives its income under a covenant from Northern Rock plc, which transfers 5% of its pre-tax profits to the foundation each year.

Grants may be made for limited capital, core or project funding and for one, two, three or more years. The foundation also offers loans.

It has seven grant programmes (launched in January 2003) which reflect its current priorities:

- prevention (of local and regional social decline);
- regeneration (through local initiatives);
- exploration and experiment;
- aspiration (cultural, environmental, heritage and sporting activities);
- better sector;
- basics (day to day services);
- capital (scheme for cultural organisations).

Although there is no longer a separate small grants programme, the foundation still offers a much more rapid response for applications for amounts under £15,000.

There is an extensive, detailed review of the foundation's activities during its first five years of existence (1998 to 2002) which can be downloaded from its website.

General

The foundation is endowed with the right to 5% of the pre-tax profits of Northern Rock plc., formerly a mutually owned organisation. The company's profits have been rising, and along with them, therefore, the income of this foundation. Grantmaking through the main programmes has steadily increased: in 2003 the total was £17 million; in 2004 it was £17.3 million. In 2005 planned spending on grantmaking is £19.3 million. In 2003 the foundation's trustees agreed to allocate £10 million from their reserves for special initiatives: in that year they supported a £1.8 million training programme, and in 2004 they allocated £4.2 million to a programme designed to prevent prisoners re-offending, and £4 million on a scheme to tackle domestic abuse.

The foundation operates a range of grant programmes, described below, but also undertakes initiatives of its own (including a voluntary sector training programme run in association with Directory of Social Change).

There are also a small number of 'exceptional' grants, outside the guidelines, and these may be large. In 2003, for example, just four 'exceptional' grants were made, including: £100,000 to BALTIC towards activities at the centre for contemporary art in Gateshead, and £90,000 over three years to AbilityNet to establish a North East and Cumbrian IT support resource for disabled people.

As the foundation is continuing with programmes initiated in 2003, some of the following information is repeated from the last edition:

Guidelines for applicants

Our primary purpose is to help disadvantaged people. We mean by this disadvantage due to:

- age–for example, young people and old people;
- disability;
- displacement –for example, refugees, asylum seekers, survivors of domestic violence;
- the collapse of industry or other employment providers;
- geography–where people live may affect their ability to get basic services, to work together for mutual benefit or to enjoy a healthy and fulfilled life;
- prejudice and discrimination, for example, against gay men and lesbians or black and minority ethnic people.

We would prefer to assist by responding to people's own views of what needs to be done and equipping them, financially, to make changes themselves. We are much less interested in outside providers and umbrella bodies but we will respond if they present an excellent argument for our

support and demonstrate a strong contribution to our objectives.

All our grant programmes except Aspiration are specifically aimed at tackling disadvantage. Aspiration is different – it is for everyone whatever their circumstances.

Where will we fund projects?

We have decide to concentrate our efforts on Cumbria, Northumberland, County Durham, Tyne and Wear (Gateshead, Newcastle upon Tyne, North Tyneside, South Tyneside and Sunderland) and the Tees Valley (Darlington, Hartlepool, Middlesbrough, Redcar and Cleveland and Stockton on Tees).

What do we want to do?

We want to support projects which directly and clearly fulfil one of the following seven programmes. Please resist the temptation to try to squeeze into the programmes if your plan does not really fit.

What kind of grants do we give?

We offer core support, project grants and capital grants. Under certain circumstances we may make loans or invest in organisations in other ways.

What sort of organisations can apply?

You should be a properly constituted organisation. You do not have to be a registered charity but the purpose for which you are applying must be charitable according to law and you must be allowed by your constitution to take on the task you propose. You need to show us that you are capable of carrying out the proposal you put to us. You are more likely to be successful if your organisation is led by or has strong representation of the people you are trying to help.

How much can you apply for?

You should apply for what you need to do the job. We have a policy of funding fewer applicants properly rather than giving many smaller grants. Your programme manager will, if necessary, go through your budget with you to see if it is sound and to test whether you could manage with less if we cannot offer all you need. We encourage you to apply to other funders as well as us since we cannot often fund the whole cost of a project.

Our trustees meet five times a year and aim to spend approximately the same amount at each meeting. In 2003, 20% of the number of grants awarded were for £10,000 or less. We gave 343 grants in the year. The average grant size (excluding one-off special grants), was £43,577.

Small organisations, i.e. those with an annual expenditure of less than £25,000,

are unlikely to receive a grant of more than £15,000 towards core or project costs. This is because we doubt that extremely rapid growth will have good results for the organisation.

NB. Fast Track: if you apply for £15,000 or less we can process the application more quickly if necessary.

Can you hold more than one grant at a time?

We would rather you did not become too dependent on us for the bulk of your income so we discourage organisations from asking for too many grants to run at the same time. But we take a sensible and practical view: if your organisation serves different groups of people in different ways you can talk to a programme manager and see if another bid might be possible.

No foundation can do everything. We have listed the things we never do elsewhere [see Exclusions]. You should read our list of exclusions before applying to make sure that your organisation and the project you propose are not automatically excluded.

Programmes

Prevention

Actions which stop social problems from developing or worsening.

We want to fund projects or organisations that work to prevent a decline in the quality of life of people affected by neighbourhood problems or broader discrimination. We believe that there are some key factors that lead to a decline in community life. Here are the ones on which we want to concentrate:

- persistent crime;
- prejudice and discrimination;
- high rates of teenage pregnancy;
- the difficulties of providing good parenting;
- substance misuse and abuse;
- environmental decay;
- youth disaffection;
- inadequate facilities for local groups to meet including community centres and village halls.

We know that some smaller groups may lack the experience and skills to gather information, manage projects and articulate their needs to others who might be able to help them. We will provide additional financial help to buy in extra expertise if needed.

While we believe that medical care and disease prevention are best left to others, we will support the promotion of general good health and well-being, for example, through schemes to encourage better dietary habits, and sporting activities in pursuit of health and fitness.

We will be looking for a clear understanding of the issue or problem you want to tackle, an argument as to why your approach is likely to help and a good plan to run, adjust and reflect on your activities.

Regeneration

Local initiatives which improve the economic prospects of an area or a community of interest.

We want to help people and communities to become economically more stable. That may mean the creation of more social businesses or money to help development trusts. It may mean looking at alternative ways of providing local jobs, facilities and services. We will consider training programmes and schemes that help people in an area acquire skills or confidence to re-enter the workplace. We are interested in supporting projects both in urban and rural areas that clearly help towards the economic development of the place. This may include capital grants for buildings or equipment where there is clear economic benefit.

Generally we will favour projects based in a particular area over those taking a broader approach. You will need to describe the place in which you are working and tell us why its economy needs rebuilding. You will need to show us that you have thought about how to ensure that any money we provide is spent as locally as possible. The request to us must be for something that is charitable though you do not have to be a registered charity to apply. If you, or we, are unsure about the charitable status of your proposal we will take advice from the Charity Commission.

Exploration and experiment

Researching, trying out, thinking, finding new ideas or ways to address social problems.

We would like applicants to be clearer about when they are trying out a new idea and when they are simply looking for money to sustain one that they already know works. We will treat real attempts to try out new ideas quite differently. We will encourage experiment, and acknowledge that new ideas do not always work. We realise that introducing a successful idea into a new area is also an experiment. We will be looking for ways to learn what works and what does not. Plans to tell others about what you learn will be essential to a successful application. Any research must have a practical application.

Examples – action research into new ways of treating persistent offenders, practical research into the causes of disadvantage or social problems.

Aspiration

Assistance to arts, environmental, heritage and sporting charities which raise the profile of our area and make it a better place in which to live and enjoy life.

We will help organisations that provide enjoyable and stimulating activities of the highest quality to the widest population in our area. Examples include:
- arts projects;
- museums;
- environmental or outdoor amenities;
- heritage sites;
- charitable sports clubs.

We will want to look at the quality of the experience you offer and to be confident that you have thought about how to make your facility or activity available to as many people as possible. Sometimes activities will be, by their nature or because of the place in which they happen, restricted to fewer participants. We will, nevertheless, fund such projects from time to time. We will look at the overall distribution of our grants to make sure that we offer a wide variety of grants in different places and for the benefit of different people.

Capital

Support for significant, ambitious and high-quality proposals for new or refurbished buildings for arts, environmental, heritage or sporting organisations. We are interested in both the activities inside the building and the quality of its design.

Better sector

Making the sector more capable of helping itself and others, articulating its needs and fighting its corner.

We believe that the people affected by social disadvantage are in the best position to judge what is needed to improve things. But they sometimes need outside advice or help from well-skilled countywide or regional bodies. These umbrella groups provide the training, advice and support that can enable smaller organisations to develop and thrive. We want to help them to provide a better service. We are particularly interested in organisations that promote quality both in their own work and as an example to others. We will also use this part of our budget to support other training initiatives and programmes, of our own making or suggested by others.

Basics

Not every project has to be about changing circumstances: sometimes people just need more of what services or help they are already receiving. We want to help organisations that add high-quality services and assistance to people over and above what statutory authorities provide.

Because there are so many people in need of this help and so many organisations to serve them, we have to set some priorities. They are:

- in the field of disability, projects designed to benefit people with mental health issues or learning disabilities;
- projects that help people to retain independence, remain in their own homes and benefit from the work of advocacy services;
- carers' organisations;
- refuges and other support for survivors of domestic violence;
- money, debt and welfare advice, establishing credit unions and other schemes to help people with limited means to manage their money.

Grantmaking in 2003

During the year the foundation made grants totalling £18.7 million. It received 1,146 grant applications–of these 32% were ineligible (around 367). Of the 779 eligible applications that were put to the trustees, 343 were successful (58%) – a further 218 were pending at the end of the year. The funds were allocated as follows:

Prevention	£3,866,000
Better Sector	£3,563,000
Basics	£3,234,000
Aspiration	£2,568,000
Regeneration	£2,364,000
Buildings to Inspire and Delight	£2,318,000
Exploration	£547,000

Beneficiaries in 2003 included the following:

Project North East – £1,837,000 over three years to provide a programme of infrastructure support, building upon the skills of the voluntary and community sector throughout the North East (special project).

Directory of Social Change – £360,000 towards training for workers and management committee members managing voluntary organisations and community groups in the North East.

The Alnwick Garden Trust – £250,000 towards building the world's biggest wooden treehouse in the garden in Northumberland.

Institute for Public Policy Research – £180,000 over three years to establish IPPR North, a policy and research think tank in the North East.

Mobex North East – £103,000 over three years towards the project director's salary for this organisation working with disadvantaged people.

Wigton Youth Station – £96,000 over two years towards extending the opening hours by employing more sessional workers in Barrow-in-Furness, Cumbria.

Dodgy Clutch Theatre Company – £90,000 over three years to support a creative team to plan large-scale events in the North East.

The Art Studio – £82,000 over three years towards staffing costs for the studio in Sunderland, supporting people with mental health problems through creative activities.

Trimdon 2000 Ltd – £79,000 over three years to employ a manager for a community regeneration project in Trimdon Village, County Durham.

Grantmaking in 2004

During 2004 the foundation's grantmaking rose to £24.5 million. The funds were allocated as follows (these figures are provisional at the time of writing):

Prevention	£4,014,000
Regeneration	£3,084,000
Basics	£2,960,000
Aspiration	£2,558,000
Capital	£2,249,000
Better Sector	£1,482,000
Exceptional	£520,000
Exploration	£457,000
Total programmes	£17,324,000
Loans	£968,000
Special projects	£8,173,000
Total investment	£26,465,000

Beneficiaries in 2004 included the following:

Aquila Housing Association – £1,867,000 over five years to establish a domestic abuse rapid response service for Gateshead (special project).

Acumen Community Enterprise Development Trust Limited – £750,000 over three years towards core funding for a new community enterprise trust in Easington in County Durham.

North East Theatre Trust Ltd – £350,000 over two years to extend and refurbish Live Theatre premises in Newcastle.

Brinkburn Music – £150,000 over three years towards the cost of Brinkburn Music Festival in Northumberland.

Action to Regenerate Community Trust – £85,000 over two years to employ a director to develop the organisation's 'Listening Matters' model for supporting community action in the North East.

Monster Productions – £68,000 over three years towards researching, developing and performing theatre for children under four in the North East.

12 Villages Community Network – £15,000 towards providing creative learning opportunities in community venues for village residents in County Durham.

South Bank Women's Centre – £8,000 to assist with the sustainability of this organisation in Redcar and Cleveland.

Baseline – £2,000 to access the help of a consultant to improve the management of the project.

Seaton Delaval and Holywell Community Forum – £1,500 providing activities for young people to prevent anti-social behaviour.

Planned for 2005

The foundation's planned spending for 2005 (£19.3 million) has been allocated as follows:

Prevention	£5,000,000
Basics	£3,285,000
Regeneration	£3,000,000
Aspiration	£2,850,000
Capital Grants	£2,000,000
Better Sector	£1,950,000
Exploration	£700,000

These are only preliminary figures, as the actual figures are likely to rise in each category. The foundation is also considering 'activities outside its operating area'.

Exclusions

There are certain organisations, projects and proposals that the foundation will not consider.

It states that it spends the equivalent of several small grants saying 'no' to inappropriate applications each year.

If you or your project fall into one of these categories please do not apply to the foundation:

- organisations which do not have purposes recognised as charitable in law;
- charities which appear to us to have excessive unrestricted or free reserves (up to 12 months' expenditure is normally acceptable), or are in serious deficit;
- national charities which do not have a regional office or other representation in the North East;
- grantmaking bodies seeking to distribute grants on our behalf;
- open ended funding agreements;
- general appeals, sponsorship and marketing appeals;
- corporate applications for founder membership of a charity;
- retrospective grants;
- replacement of statutory funding;
- activities primarily the responsibility of central or local government or health authorities;
- individuals and organisations that distribute funds to individuals;
- animal welfare;
- mainstream educational activity, schools and educational establishments;
- medical research, hospitals, hospices and medical centres;
- medical treatments and therapies including art therapy;
- fabric appeals for places of worship;
- promotion of religion;
- expeditions or overseas travel;
- minibuses, other vehicles and transport schemes except where they are a small and integral part of a larger scheme;
- holidays and outings;
- playgrounds and play equipment;
- private clubs or those with such restricted membership as to make them not charitable;
- capital bids purely towards compliance with the Disability Discrimination Act;
- amateur arts organisations;
- musical instruments;
- sports kit and equipment.

Applications

Applications must be made on the foundation's application form, available from its website. This comes with full instructions and guidance. There are separate forms for applications for less than £15,000 and more than £15,000. In brief, each form has to be accompanied by:

- a brief supporting statement (not more than two pages);
- current budget and recent management accounts;
- most recent annual report and accounts (or equivalent for very small organisations);
- the 'objects' and 'dissolution' parts of your constitution;
- your budget for the project, how much you are asking for and how you hope to get the rest.

The brief supporting statement needs to cover:

- your organisation and its qualifications for taking on this project;
- the need for the project, its importance, scale and urgency;
- what you plan to do and how;
- the level of user involvement at all stages;
- how you will measure its success and learn from your experience, if appropriate;
- the timetable for the project;
- how, if appropriate, you would continue when a grant expires.

Information should be accurate and comprehensive. If something essential is missing the foundation will ask you to supply it and therefore the processing of your application will be delayed.

Your application will be acknowledged and the foundation will let you know straight away if it is ineligible. If it is eligible, you will be told which staff member will assess it.

There should normally be a response within four months (for applications for less than £15,000, two months).

'Please remember that all foundations receive many more requests than they can help. Undoubtedly we will have to turn down many good applications.'

The Northwood Charitable Trust

Medical research, health, welfare, general

Around £1.5 million (2003/04)

Beneficial area Scotland, especially Dundee and Tayside.

22 Meadowside, Dundee DD1 1LN

Tel. 01382 201534 **Fax** 01382 227654

Correspondent Brian McKernie, Secretary

Trustees *Brian Harold Thomson; Andrew Francis Thomson; Lewis Murray Thomson.*

Scottish Charity no. SC014487

Information available Brief annual report and accounts, with a list of the 50 largest donations only, available from the trust for £10.

The Northwood Trust is connected to the D C Thomson Charitable Trust, D C Thomson & Company and the Thomson family. It was established by Eric V Thomson in 1972 and has received additional funding from other members of the family.

The brief annual report notes that 'the trustees have adopted the principle of giving priority to assisting Dundee and Tayside based charities' and says 'unsolicited applications for donations are not encouraged and will not normally be acknowledged'. Other than this there is little indication of the trust's grantmaking policy, beyond what can be deduced from the partial, uncategorised grants lists, and there was no review of the trust's grantmaking in previous reports.

Grants total around £1.5 million each year. No recent information was available.

Previous beneficiaries include Brittle Bone Society, Couple Counselling Tayside, Dundee Age Concern, Dundee Repertory Theatre, Dundee Samaritans, Macmillan Cancer Relief – Scotland, Tayside Association for the Deaf, Tayside Orthopaedic and Rehabilitation Technology Centre and Tenovus Medical Projects.

Applications

The trust's funds are fully committed and it states that no applications will be considered or acknowledged.

The Norwich Town Close Estate Charity

Education in and near Norwich

£515,000 to organisations and individuals (2002/03)

Beneficial area Within a 20-mile radius of the Guildhall of the city of Norwich.

10 Golden Dog Lane, Magdalen Street, Norwich NR3 1BP

Tel. 01603 621023 **Fax** 01603 767025

Correspondent David Walker, Clerk

Trustees *M G Quinton, chair; N B Q Back; P J Colby; T C Eaton; R E T Gurney; A P Hansell; J S Livock; H W Watson; R H Pearson; A B Shaw; R G Round; D Fullman; Mrs S Gale; Lady J Hopwood; P R Blanchflower; Mrs B Ferris.*

Charity Commission no. 235678

Information available Full accounts were on file at the Charity Commission.

Only charities based within a 20 mile radius of Norwich and carrying out educational activities will be supported by the charity.

In 2002/03 the trust had assets of £13.7 million and an income of £641,000. Grants to organisations and individuals totalled £515,000, and were broken down as follows:

	2002/03	2001/02
Education	£55,000	£69,000
Pensions	£137,000	£88,000
Television licences	£4,000	£4,000
Relief-in-need	£4,000	–
Doughty's hospital residents' maintence	–	£1,000
Other bodies	£315,000	£303,000

Donations categorised as 'other bodies' above £10,000 were: £50,000 to Academy Trust for costs associated with the conversion of Howes Garage into a training school; £29,000 to Friends of Earlham Early Years Centre as match funding; £25,000 to Whitlingham Charitable Trust for costs of providing a visitors centre; £18,000 each to Relate, Norfolk, Waveney and West Suffolk for the costs of establishing a project to counter domestic violence and to Wherry Yacht Charter Trust for crew training; and £16,000 to Association of Parents, Friends and Teachers of Angel Road Middle School, Attleborough High School Charitable Trust for the cost of a mini-bus.

Grants of £10,000 or less included: £10,000 each to Costessey High School towards costs of becoming a specialist school, How Hill Trust to increase the value of the educational endowment fund and Norfolk and Norwich Festival for the production of Everyman Morality Play; £8,000 to Dean and Chapter of Norwich Catherdral for the cost of an exhibition; £5,000 to Norwich City Historical Trust to acquire memorabila; £1,500 each to Mid-Norfolk Youth for Christ for running costs and Chaplaincy at UEA for a computer; and £1,000 to Ranworth First School Friends Association for a play area and equipment.

Exclusions

No grants to: individuals who are not Freemen (or dependants of Freemen) of the city of Norwich; charities more than 20 miles from Norwich; or charities which are not educational. Revenue funding for educational charities is not generally given.

Applications

After a preliminary enquiry, in writing to the clerk.

'When submitting an application the following points should be borne in mind:

- Brevity is a virtue. If too much written material is submitted there is a risk that it may not all be assimilated.
- The trustees like to have details of any other financial support secured.
- An indication should be given of the amount that is being sought and also how that figure is arrived at.
- The trustees will not reimburse expenditure already incurred.
- Nor, generally speaking will the trustees pay running costs, e.g. salaries.'

The Nuffield Foundation

Education, child protection, family law and justice, access to justice

£5.6 million (2004)

Beneficial area UK and Commonwealth.

28 Bedford Square, London WC1B 3EG

Tel. 020 7631 0566 **Fax** 020 7232 4877

Website www.nuffieldfoundation.org

Correspondent The Trustees

Trustees *Baroness O'Neill, chair; Sir Tony Atkinson; Prof. Genevra Richardson; Prof. Lord Robert May; Prof. Sir Michael Rutter; Mrs Anne Sofer; Dr Peter Doyle.*

Charity Commission no. 206601

Information available Excellent annual report and accounts and annual review; detailed guidelines for applicants (summarised below, but all potential applicants should see a full copy).

Summary

'Project grants', from £5,000 to over £200,000, are made to organisations and institutions to support research, developmental or experimental projects that meet a practical or policy need.

The foundation's grants areas are

- supporting research and innovation that will bring about beneficial social chang;e
- development of research and professional capacity, especially in the sciences and the social sciences, targeted at people in the early stages of their careers.

Programmes in early 2005 were:

- Child protection, family law and justice;
- Access to justice;
- Older people and their families;
- Open door (miscellaneous);
- Education;
- Commonwealth.

In addition the foundation runs a number of grant programmes that have specific objectives (for example: science bursaries for schools and colleges; undergraduate science research bursaries; starter grants for newly appointed lecturers in science, engineering and mathematics; the Oliver Bird PhD Studentships in Rheumatic Disease Resarch; the Social Science Small Grants scheme; and the New Career Development Scheme for post-doctoral social scientists and their senior partners. Details and application forms are available from the foundation or from its website. These are for individuals and so not featured in this entry.

The foundation also has two major in-house projects: the Nuffield Council on Bioethics and the Nuffield Curriculum Centre (see website for further details). Neither of these are covered in this entry. Extensive publicity and information work is also carried out directly by the foundation.

In 2004 the foundation had assets amounting to £202 million and an income of £7.5 million. Grants totalled £5.6 million including those for individuals.

General

The aims of the foundation are described in broad terms as follows:

Lord Nuffield wanted his foundation to 'advance social well being', particularly research and practical experiment. The foundation aims to achieve this by supporting work which will bring about improvements in society, and which is founded on careful reflection and informed by objective and reliable evidence.

Grants for organisations

About half the foundation's expenditure is on what it calls 'project grants'. These range in size from £5,000 to over £200,000. Some grants are for research, others support practical innovation or development, often in voluntary sector organisations. In both cases the preference is for work 'that has wide significance, beyond the local or routine. The foundation looks to support projects that are imaginative and innovative, take a thoughtful and rigorous approach to problems, and have the potential to influence policy or practice'.

There are three areas of special interest and they are described below. In addition, the Open Door programme is used to fund projects that lie outside these areas of interest – or span boundaries between them – and that Address the general aims of the foundation.

Around 60 project grants are made each year, varying between four and twenty grants in each area. Full details of how to apply are given in the guide 'How to Apply for a project grant 2004/5', which is available from the foundation or from its website. Decisions are made at trustees' meetings, which are held quarterly. The first stage in applying for a project grant is to submit a short outline proposal.

Applying for a project grant

At 16 pages, the guide for applicants 'How to apply for a project grant', is so long that it cannot be reproduced here in full. Readers are referred to the website, given above. Some of the general guidance for project grant applications reads as follows:

Through its project grants the foundation seeks to fund self-contained projects that are:

- Innovative – the trustees are keen to fund work work that has a clear element of originality. They will not fund routine research, nor the mere repetition of existing work.
- Practical – the trustees look for outcomes that will influence practice directly or that can be translated into policy or practice in the short or medium term.
- Generalisable – the trustees will not consider proposals of purely local interest but seek to fund work that will be widely applicable.
- Reflective – the trustees look for evidence that applicants have thought carefully about how to judge whether the work undertaken is successful or not.

Not all projects meet all these criteria, but the great majority meet most of them.

Research projects must have implications for practice or policy in the short or medium term. The trustees will not normally support research that simply advances knowledge, which is properly the domain of the Research Councils.

Development projects are broadly of two kinds. Some involve trying something new. Such projects must be of more than local interest. They must have the potential to be widely applied, either directly or as a model which others can follow. Evaluation must be carefully considered, as must the dissemination of the findings.

Others involve some facility that will be of practical value. The range of possible projects is wide and could include, for example, written materials, or a physical device. Again, such developments should be of general rather than local interest and the trustees will look for evidence that applicants have carefully considered how the information can be disseminated. Some element of evaluation is also desirable.

The foundation is particularly interested in dissemination of project findings to practitioners and sees this as important activity in its own right. It encourages grant applications to include provision for this in the planning of projects, and is willing to consider applications for supplementary grants for this purpose.

Programmes

The first four areas (child protection, family law and justice; access to justice; older people and their families; open door) are supported through project grants, with a uniform set of criteria.

Child protection, family law and justice

This programme supports work to help ensure that the legal and institutional framework is best adapted to meet the needs of children and families. Grants in this areas are considered by a separate specialist committee, whose members include academics in law, psychiatry and social work research, and practitioners in law, social work and relevant voluntary organisations. The committee is interested in a broad range of topics that go beyond child protection in a narrow sense, and in practical developments as well as research.

Particular interests include (but are not limited to):

- the development of an integrated system of family justice, including work drawing attention to the anomalies and obstructions in the present system.
- the roles and training needs of professionals in the system, including those that may contribute to the new family court welfare system, family mediation or other support services for the family jurisdictions.
- interdisciplinary work in family law, including other government policies with implications for families.
- children at risk or in need, including 'looked after' children but also a much broader range of children who might benefit from support.
- broader provision for children in need, for instance the education of looked after children (considered jointly with the foundation's Education programme).
- placement and planning for children, including adoption (special guidelines are available in this area).
- children aged 16 or over who leave care.
- contact following separation or divorce, including the movement of children and child abduction.
- legal and financial aspects of divorce or separation (following marriage or cohabitation) and their aftermath. This includes studies of family finances following divorce, the new ancillary relief procedures, and pensions.
- marriage and divorce in minority ethnic communities, including expectations and practices of specific communities and changes in these over time.
- children in the legal system, for example, child witnesses.
- policing and risk management that affects children, including the risk management of 'dangerous men'.

Where a proposal is for a research study, the committee is interested in the dispassionate examination of evidence. It notes that evidence is likely to be different in different cases, for different types of children and families, and is more likely to support work that takes this approach.

There were 13 new grants in 2003 totalling £626,000, including the following:

- £99,000 to Department of General Practice and Primary Care – Barts and the London Hospital, towards 'the Prevention of Domestic Violence: a pilot study in primary care'.
- £70,000 to Parentline Plus, Family Rights Group and Family Welfare Association, towards a shared Family Policy Officer for a joint development project
- £64,000 to Policy Research Bureau, towards developing principal research and management capacity at the bureau.
- £33,000 to the Immigration Law Practitioners' Association, towards 'Working with Children Subject to Immigration Controls: guidelines for best practice'.
- £10,000 to One Plus One, towards web-based information about the legal differences between married and cohabiting relationships.
- £5,000 to British Association for Adoption and Fostering, to promote the importance of improving adoption services for Scottish children and reviewing adoption legislation.

Access to justice

The foundation has long had an interest in the area of access to justice. Our current objectives in this area are:

- to promote developments in the legal system that will improve its accessibility to all people.
- to promote wider access to legal services and advice and a better understanding of the obstacles to access to justice.
- to fund research and promote developments in alternative dispute resolution.
- to help promote a greater knowledge of the rights and duties of the individual, including those of the European citizen.
- to examine the implications of new human rights' obligations on civil (not criminal) justice.
- to help promote a greater public understanding of the role of law in society and of the legal system.

Replacement or core funding of existing services (such as law centres) will not be considered. Projects on penal policy, drugs, policing, crime prevention, criminal or environmental law will not normally be supported under the 'Access to justice' area of special interest unless they fulfil one of the objectives set out above.

There were 14 new grants in 2002 totalling £751,000, including the following:

- £164,000 to Mind, towards establishing local advice surgeries for mental health service users.
- £72,000 to Federation of Information and Advice Centres, towards the cost to voluntary organisations of achieving the Legal Service Commission Quality Mark.
- £60,000 to Prisoners' Advice Service, towards a racial discrimination development project.
- £40,000 to Scottish Consumer Council towards 'Modernising the Civil Justice System in Scotland: a series of seminars to explore issues and the way forward'.
- £10,000 to Law Centre NI, towards legal advice needs for people with mental health problems.

Older people and their families

The foundation wishes to fund work that starts from the perspectives, needs and interests of the older person and his or her family, rather than those of service providers. It is interested in projects that will enhance individual autonomy and choice and that recognise variation in preferences and provision.

The foundation is keen to support work that brings an international comparative perspective to bear, and is particularly interested in fostering work that considers European as well as other countries' perspectives.

As with all its areas of grant making, the foundation is interested in a wide range of topics. Issues that might be of interest include:

- The financial circumstances of elderly people and economic planning for later life. This might include planning for long-term care, pensions and insurance, (including private as well as state provision), pension splitting on divorce, intergenerational transfers and so on. It is particularly interested in projects that recognise the complex relationship between state, private and family provision.
- Family solidarity and family obligations, including projects focussing on caring responsibilities between generations; their implications for the labour market; legal and social obligations; changing relationships as a result of family change; and ways of supporting family ties.
- Autonomy and decision-making in later life, including socio-legal matters such as competence, powers of attorney, conflicts of interest, advance directives and so on. The foundation wishes to foster work that

improves autonomy as well as social responsibilities of older people.

- Retirement, work and citizenship, including the diverse positions of older people in employment; retirement and employments rights; and activities that promote active citizenship for elderly people.

The foundation is interested in innovative schemes that support interaction between professionals, informal carers and health and social workers, and notes that there may be particular scope for European comparisons here. Projects that address the relationship between health and social care will not be considered if they are routine research projects on aspects of service provision.

The foundation will not make grants for the following:

- support for mainstream academic or medical training;
- medical or biological research into ageing, disability, dementia or mental illness;
- housing or transport unless there is direct bearing on one of the topics above.

In 2003 major grants included:

- £96,000 to Pensions Policy Institute, towards evaluating long-term policy reform options in the UK pension system.
- £74,000 to Personal Social Services Research Unit, London School of Economics/Nuffield Community Research Unit, University of Leicester, towards 'Paying for Long-term Care for Older People in the UK'.
- £35,000 to Third Age Employment Network, to enable the Equality and diversity forum to build on its dual role and to employ a part-time researcher/manager for 12 months.
- £30,000 to Community Transport Association towards mobility and inclusive transport.
- £28,000 to Dementia Voice, towards investigating 'enabling' domestic environments for people with dementia.

Open Door

The foundation keeps an "open door" to proposals of exceptional merit for research projects or practical innovations outside its special areas of interest, or to projects that span areas of interest. These must have some bearing on our widest charitable object—'the advancement of social well-being'.

Subjects of interest include, but are not limited to: work on poverty, disadvantage, social welfare, disability, and work that crosses boundaries between our areas of special interest (for instance, learning and social provision; law and society; science and education).

Trustees are also especially interested in work that objectively examines current or proposed statutory arrangements, as independent funding can play a key role here. Through the Open Door, the foundation may also identify emerging areas that justify more sustained attention.

In 2003 there were 15 new grants, totalling £841,000 and led by the following:

- £233,000 to SGDP Centre – Institute of Psychiatry, towards research into the effects of early deprivation on long-term adjustment.
- £99,000 to Department of Psychology – Goldsmiths College, towards research into enhancing the effectiveness of video identification evidence.
- £97,000 to Policy Studies Institute, towards research into the impact of labour market deregulation on employees.
- £54,000 to National Centre for Social Research, towards research into family life and atypical working hours.
- £33,000 to Association of Commonwealth Universities, towards the development of a retired academics matching service.
- £12,000 to Daycare Trust, towards a briefing paper on family life and informal care.
- £5,800 to Institute of Governance, Public Policy and Social Research – Queen's University Belfast, for an online Research Bank for Northern Ireland.

Education

The foundation is focussing support in education on areas with which Nuffield has become identified. Building on strength was an underlying principle of our recent reassessment of short to medium term priorities for the education programme. We want to identify and help develop good work which is happening in these areas:

- education 14–19;
- speech and language difficulties;
- assessment;
- curriculum policy and practice.

Whilst we are no longer accepting unsolicited grant applications, we are open to considering exploratory work in the areas above. Email education@nuffieldfoundation.org if you have an idea you would like us to consider.

Commonwealth programme

The Nuffield Commonwealth Programme supports initiatives to bring about long-term inprovements in health, education and civil

justice in Eastern and Southern Africa and to foster North-South partnerships.

The programme is unusual amongst sources of funding of overseas work. Firstly it directly supports the development of service delivery and secondly it actively seeks partnerships between UK-based and southern organisations, where the UK-based partner is providing more than money, monitoring and moral support. It focuses on projects that improve services through development of the expertise and experience of practitioners and policy makers, and where active involvement from the UK-based organisation will increase the initiative's effectiveness.

Change is at the heart of each project supported under the programme – at individual, community, organisational and societal level. Recognising that achieving lasting change takes a long time, the programme supports only a small number of projects, but over an extended period, usually five years.

The programme makes grants every two years.

Major grants between 2000–2003 included:

- £284,000 to hospice Africa UK, towards developing palliative care in Africa.
- £250,000 to Department of Forensic Medicine – Dundee University, towards medico-legal training for professionals assisting women and child victims of violence in South Africa,
- £199,000 to Department of Medical Microbiology – University College London, towards developing the expertise of biomedical health professionals in Tanzania.
- £96,000 to Riders for Health, towards specialised training in preventative maintenance and driving skills training.

Exclusions

The trustees will not consider the following:

- general appeals;
- buildings or capital costs;
- projects which are mainly of local interest ;
- research that is mainly of theoretical interest;
- day to day running costs or accommodation needs;
- the provision of health or social services;
- grants to replace statutory funding;
- healthcare (outside mental health);
- the arts;
- religion;
- museums, exhibitions, performances;

- sports and recreation;
- conservation, heritage or environmental projects;
- animal rights or welfare;
- attendance at conferences;
- expeditions, travel, adventure/holiday projects;
- business or job creation projects;
- academic journals;
- medical research (other than in rheumatism and arthritis research).

Grants are not made for the following purposes except when the activity is part of a project that is otherwise acceptable:

- work for degrees or other qualifications;
- production of films, videos or television programmes;
- purchase of equipment, including computers.

Applications

If you are thinking of making an application, you must first send a written outline proposal. A member of staff will then advise you whether the proposal comes within the trustees' terms of reference and whether there are any particular questions or issues you should consider. The outline should describe:

- the issue or problem you wish to address;
- the expected outcome(s);
- what will happen in the course of the project;
- (for research projects) an outline of the methods to be employed;
- an outline of the budget and the timetable.

The outline must not exceed three sides of A4, but you are welcome to include additional supporting information about yourself and your organisation. If you are advised to proceed with a full application, the staff member dealing with your proposal may suggest a meeting or, if matters are straightforward, may advise you to proceed straight to a full application. Extensive guidance on the preparation of full applications, too long to be summarised here, is available from the foundation and is published on its excellent website.

The Nuffield Trust

Research and policy studies in health

£243,000 (2003/04)

Beneficial area UK.

59 New Cavendish Street, London W1G 7LP

Tel. 020 7631 8450 **Fax** 020 7631 8451

Email mail@nuffieldtrust.org.uk

Website www.nuffieldtrust.org.uk

Correspondent John Wyn Owen, Secretary

Trustees *Sir Denis Pereira Gray, chair; Prof. Sir Leszek Borysiewicz; Prof. Sir Keith Peters; Dame Fiona Caldicott; Sir Christopher France; Lord Carlile; Baroness Cox; Prof. Don Detmer*

Charity Commission no. 209201

Information available Annual report is available on the trust's website.

General

The grants of this trust, not to be confused with the Nuffield Foundation, are generally made for work commissioned by the trust or arising out of its policy seminars and programmes. Currently, no unsolicited applications are supported.

The work is centred at present on four areas:

- health policy futures;
- the changing role of the state in health care;
- public health;
- quality.

In 2003/04 the trust had assets amounting to £55 million and an income of £1.7 million.

Grants 2003/04

The trust's annual report stated that the difficult economic and financial climate of the last few years had severely limited its ability to make grants. In the year only four grants were made totalling £243,000. Projects supported were Policy Futures for UK Health (£171,000), Quality of Health Care in the UK (£65,000), Annual Public Health Forum 2004 (£5,000) and European Conference on Health Economics (£1,000).

Exclusions

Grants are not awarded to individuals for personal studies, nor to meet the core costs of other organisations.

Applications

At their March 2004 meeting, the trustees reviewed the prospects for grant-making in the light of the actual and projected financial position of the trust and decided that the suspension on unsolicited grant applications should be extended indefinitely. This policy will however be reviewed periodically.

When grants were available, extensive guidance notes were available on the trust's website. Potential applicants should view this to see if grants are available, and if so how to apply.

Oglesby Trust

General

£500,000 per year

Beneficial area The north west of England.

PO Box 336, Altrincham, Cheshire WA14 3XD

Email oglesbycharitabletrust@ bruntwood.co.uk

Website www.oglesbycharitabletrust.co. uk

Correspondent The Trustees

Trustees *Jean Oglesby; Michael Oglesby; Robert Kilson; Roger Groarke; Kate Vokes; Jane Oglesby.*

Charity Commission no. 1026669

Information available See the website, as above.

This relatively new grantmaking trust offers the following information:

The trust has been set up to support a broad spectrum of charitable activities reflecting the beliefs and interests of the founding trustee family.

It is accepted that the trust will be relatively modest in its resources and the trustees will be seeking to place its funds where they can have a real and measurable impact. It is realised that there already exist a large number of charitable and government backed organisations operating across all fields and it is not our intention to compete with or supplement these.

The trustees will be looking to form associations with bodies with whom they might become involved either on a one-off basis or over a period of time. Financial support will be relatively low during this early period and will gradually grow over the ensuing years as the trust expands.

The funding of the trust comes from annual contributions from Bruntwood Estates Ltd., a north west based property company owned by the founding trustees which in 2003 had a net worth of £145 million.

The trust income is £500,000 per annum and grants each year will be made of around this figure, the maximum grant to any one project to date has been £50,000 and generally will be between £5,000 and £20,000.

In order that we can be confident that any donations are making a real difference there is an application process that must be followed. There are two processes, for larger and smaller funds.

The trustees have toiled long and hard to put together the funds which are going into the trust. They will expect the recipients to understand their value and so to extend a similar level of care in its use.

Who do we help?

The trustees will be looking to work with organisations that can demonstrate that the funds are making a real difference rather than being absorbed into an anonymous pool, no matter how significant the end result may appear to be. Although all donations may not fall under this heading it will certainly be the case that this will apply in the majority of instances.

The trust will only be looking to be involved with organisations that both demonstrate the highest standards of propriety and sound business sense in the activities. This does not mean high overheads but does mean focused use of funds where they are needed.

The trust would prefer to see the item that they are funding being operated as an individual project which can be ring-fenced as far as possible. Activities will be preferred that are not a part of current core operations and can be demonstrated to make a real difference as opposed to supplementing existing operations.

The activities of the applicant must be primarily based in the North West of England

The following are the fields the trust will be looking to support:

- Artistic development both on an individual and group level;
- Educational grants and building projects;
- Environmental improvement projects;
- Improving the life and welfare of the underprivileged where possible by the encouragement of self-help;
- Medical aid and research.

The Smaller Donations–Acorn Fund

We do have a fund set aside each year for smaller donations, we call this our Acorn Fund, and donations for this will be between £200 and £1,000. This fund is now

administered in conjunction with the Community Foundation for Greater Manchester–contact 0161 214 0951 for an application form.

Exclusions

The trust will not support:

- activities, which collect funds for redistribution to other charities;
- animal charities;
- charities whose principal operation area is outside the UK;
- church and all fabric appeals;
- conferences;
- conservation of buildings;
- continuing running costs of organisation;
- costs of employing fundraisers;
- expeditions;
- general sports unless strongly associated with a disadvantaged group;
- holidays;
- individuals;
- large National charities enjoying wide spread support;
- loans or business finance;
- religion;
- routine staff training;
- sectarian religions;
- sponsorship and marketing appeals.

Applications

Wherever possible the trustees will be looking for a proper financial plan prepared by the applicant. This should contain clear and measurable goals, which will be reviewed at regular intervals by the parties. In cases where the applicant does not possess either the skills or the resources to prepare these, the trust may be prepared to assist. It must be clearly understood that everyone must buy into these objectives at all times.

In order that we can assess all applications from a similar basis, we ask that you complete the Stage 1 Application Form. We undertake to respond to this in a maximum of 4 weeks. If this response is positive then you will be required to complete a more detailed form under Stage 2. The forms can either be printed from the website or downloaded so that they can be completed electronically.

Finally in most cases the trustees will wish to interview the applicant at their place of operation or project site both prior to the granting of funds and during the lifetime of the project to monitor the progress.

The P F Charitable Trust

General, particularly arts/heritage, health, welfare, education

£5.6 million (2002/03)

Beneficial area Unrestricted, with local interests in Oxfordshire and Scotland.

Ely House, 37 Dover Street, London W1S 4NJ

Correspondent D H Pocknee, Secretary, or Geoffrey Fincham

Trustees *Robert Fleming; Valentine P Fleming; Philip Fleming; Rory D Fleming.*

Charity Commission no. 220124

Information available Brief annual report and accounts; grants list covers top 50 grants only.

The trust states that its policy is to 'continue to make a substantial number of small grants to charitable organisations both on a one-off and recurring basis'.

In 2002/03 it had assets amounting to £75 million and an income of £1.9 million. Grants totalled £5.6 million and went to 'a wide variety of UK charitable causes'. The 50 largest donations – those of £10,000 or more – are lised in the acocunts. These account for over 80% of the total value.

By far the largest grant was £2.2 million to St Paul's Cathedral Foundation for the cleaning and restoration of the interior. There were six other grants made of £100,000 or more: £500,000 to the Oxford University Boat Club Trust towards the new boat house project; £333,000 to the Fleming-Wyfold Art Foundation towards the maintenance and running costs of the art foundation; £250,000 to Alnwick Garden towards development costs; £115,000 to Marie Curie Cancer Care for nursing services in Oxfordshire and Argyllshire; and £100,000 each to CAF, Oxford Children's Hospital towards building costs and Sir John Soane's Museum towards property costs.

Other larger grants included £60,000 to Isaac Newton Institute for Mathematical Science and £50,000 each to Watlington Hospital Charitable Trust, Maggie's Centre – Inverness, Prince's Trust and Scottish Community Foundation.

Remaining listed grants were mainly for either £25,000, £20,000 or £10,000 each and included those to British Sporting

Arts Trust, Covent Garden Cancer Research Trust, Help the Hospices, Historic Churches Preservation Trust, Nettlebed Community Fund, Lorn Counselling Service, Purley Park Trust, Roundhouse Project, Seven Springs Play and Support Centre and University of Cape Town Trust.

Exclusions

No grants to individuals or non-registered charities.

Applications

Applications to the correspondent in writing. Trustees usually meet monthly to consider applications and approve grants.

The Parthenon Trust

Humanitarian assistance, third world development, medical research, treatment and care, assistance for the disadvantaged, general

£4.5 million (2003)

Beneficial area Unrestricted.

Saint-Nicolas 9, 2000 Neuchatel

Tel. 00 41 32 724 8130 **Fax** 00 41 32 724 8131

Correspondent John E Whittaker, Secretary

Trustees *Geraldine Whittaker, chair; Dr J M Darmady; Prof. C N Hales.*

Charity Commission no. 1051467

Information available Annual report and accounts.

Summary

The giving is international, with the organisations, as well as the activities, being based in a number of countries.

Unusually for such a large trust, as a general rule 'grants are [...] not earmarked for expenditure on specific projects'.

Many beneficiaries are regularly supported and new recipients usually account for only a modest proportion of the total awarded in a given year.

Although geographically distant for UK charities, the trust is not

unapproachable: 'Applicants are urged to approach the secretary informally before submitting their applications'.

General

The trust is funded by donations 'from a privately endowed foundation based overseas', to a value of £9 million in 2003. Parthenon itself has no endowment and very modest expenditure on administration (around £40,000 to £50,000). In 2003 the trust's level of expenditure dropped considerably to £5.9 million (£11.9 million in 2002). It is likely that grants during the year totalled around £4.5 million, although this could not be confirmed [see below].

Though a UK-registered charity, the trust is based in Switzerland, the home of the chair, Geraldine Whittaker and the secretary, her husband John Whittaker. Dr Darmady is a retired consultant paediatrician and Professor Hales is professor of clinical biochemistry at Cambridge University.

The trust provides a note describing its work as follows:

Trustees' policy is primarily the relief of hardship and the advancement of health (though other charitable causes will be considered). The trustees are particularly interested in helping:
- children in need
- refugees
- famine victims.

They are also interested in helping the aged, the homeless and the long-term unemployed and in supporting longer-term development in the third world.

The trustees are interested in supporting medical research, in areas which appear to be underfunded in relation to the likelihood of achieving progress. They are also interested in supporting patient care, hospices and rehabilitation: and in helping the disabled (including the blind, the deaf and the mentally and physically handicapped).

As a general rule, grants are made to officially approved charitable or non-profit organisations and are not earmarked for expenditure on specific projects.

Some further points were added by the trust to help in writing this entry. On the issue of what is most likely to affect the chances of success of a particular application, the trust noted:

Inter alia, Parthenon tries to assess the cost-effectiveness of potential grantees in relation to that of other organisations seeking to achieve similar objects. (It is however recognised that a high expense ratio is not necessarily evidence of low cost-

effectiveness). The fact that a potential grantee had unnecessarily expensive accommodation would tell against it.

Great importance is attached to the quality of potential grantees' management and to peer ratings – what do other charities think of a potential grantee?

If it is appropriate for a potential grantee to make use of volunteers, how successful has it been in recruiting them?

Finally, the fact that a medical research application had been submitted or endorsed by a major medical research charity which specialised in the field in question would obviously improve its chances of success, as would favourable reports from referees.

Further on core costs:

Parthenon is entirely willing to make grants for this purpose and in any case its grants are to a large extent capable of being so used, since most of them are made for 'general purposes'. Parthenon's response to the social investment initiatives is that, as a pure grant-giver, it cannot play a proactive role, but that it is willing to consider funding requests.

Grants

Unfortunately the trust's most recent accounts at the time of writing (those for 2003) were 'missing' from the trust's file at the Charity Commission, even though they had been received there. This made obtaining up-to-date information difficult.

The trust has previously made substantial grants to organisations including UNICEF, Save the Children, Médecins sans Frontières (UK), Cancer Research Campaign, Association Voix Libres, EORTC (European Organisation for Research and Treatment of Cancer Foundation), British Red Cross, Fundacion Promotora del Desarrollo de la Boquilla, Prince of Wales International Business Leaders Forum, Action Against Hunger UK and the People's Committee of Son-La Province – Vietnam.

Parthenon does not confine its giving to English-speaking charities. For example, it has supported a Swiss organisation working with underprivileged people in Bolivia (Association Voix Libres) and the Catholic University of Louvain, a long-standing beneficiary.

More modest grants in recent years include those made to Population Council, Special Olympics Belgium, ECHO International Health Services, SOS Children's Villages of India, Ahli Arab Hospital, Gaza, Centre Européen Juif d'Information, Fondation Charcot, a Belgian organisation for research into

Multiple Sclerosis and Nutrition Third World.

Exclusions

No grants for individuals, scientific/ geographical expeditions or projects which promote religious beliefs.

Applications

Anyone proposing to submit an application should telephone the secretary. Unsolicited written applications are not normally acknowledged.

The Patrick Charitable Trust

General, with a particular interest in Muscular Dystrophy

£1.4 million (proposed in 2004/05)

Beneficial area UK, with a special interest in the Midlands.

The Lakeside Centre, 180 Lifford Lane, Kings Norton, Birmingham B30 3NU

Correspondent J A Patrick, Chair

Trustees *J A Patrick, chair; M V Patrick; Mrs H P Cole; W Bond-Williams; N C Duckitt; G Wem.*

Charity Commission no. 213849

Information available Accounts and annual report were provided by the trust.

Joseph Patrick lived in Worcestershire when he established the trust in 1962 for general charitable purposes, although there is some preference for charities that tackle Muscular Dystrophy and its effects. Grants can be one-off or ongoing.

In 2003/04 the trust had assets of £7.4 million and an income of £548,000. Grants were made to 43 organisations during the year totalling £246,000, although this is likely to increase significantly in the next financial year (see below).

Grantmaking in 2003/04

The following chairman's report, describing the trust's activities during the year, is taken from the annual report:

The trustees are delighted to report that as the trust approaches its 43rd year, they have

been able to make further significant donations together with future commitments to the charitable sector.

Muscular Dystrophy and its subsidiary charity, the Joseph Patrick Trust, continue to be major beneficiaries this year. The trustees have been able to add a further £40,000 towards its loan to contribute to the defining research programme for Duchenne Muscular Dystrophy. The trustees are conscious that the time scale is very flexible for this research, however, by guaranteeing the funding through the loan to Muscular Dystrophy, their Research Committee know that there is a designated grant available. To date the loan amounts to £540,000, on which Muscular Dystrophy have been able to earn additional interest of £36,000.

The Patrick Cancer Information Centre at the Queen Elizabeth Hospital in Birmingham has been extended to double its size thanks to the trust's grant of £22,000. The trustees would like to record their thanks to Joyce McLoughlin and her team for their dedication to providing vital information to patients experiencing cancer.

The trustees have provided a grant to Acorns Hospice for the Memorial Gardens of £25,000 that will form part of their new Worcester Hospice. The garden will be named in memory of Andrew Patrick, who passed away from Muscular Dystrophy at the age of 13, in whose memory the Patrick Trust was founded.

A wide range of smaller donations have been made to help charities involved in disability and the disadvantaged.

The trustees have continued to give selective support to some areas of the arts sector. As previously, Birmingham Royal Ballet has been a significant beneficiary and this year the trust was able to support David Bintley's new ballet, 'Beauty and the Beast', with a £25,000 donation. Thanks to an Arts Council initiative, the trustees were able to ensure that Birmingham Royal Ballet toured smaller theatres in the South West of England. The trust took particular interest in their visit to the Hall for Cornwall in Truro.

In the education field, the trust continues to support Imagineering [£25,000], with their innovative ideas for encouraging young people to take an interest in engineering and technology. As this country's industrial heritage continues to decline, it is increasingly important that young people realise that manufacturing is just as vital to the economy as the service sector.

The trustees continue their support of Green College, Oxford, giving a grant of £30,000 towards the renovation of the exterior of the historic Observatory building.

Other beneficiaries included: the Orchid Ball which was held in Scotland in aid of Muscular Dystrophy (£6,000); Golden Freeway children's charity to provide computers and a dedicated internet

service provider for five youngsters in the West Midlands (£5,500); Birmingham Hippodrome Development Trust for the cost of 70 youngsters from various hospitals to see Cinderella at the theatre (£3,000); St Mary's Hospice – Birmingham towards care for terminally and seriously ill patients and to provide visits to patients homes (£2,500); Willow Trust to provide day visits on canal boats maintained by the trust for seriously ill and disabled adults and children (£1,000); Royal Birmingham Society of Artists towards the sponsorship of a fundraising dinner (£500); and Coventry City Farm (£250).

The trust has also published details of its proposed donations in the financial year 2004/05 amounting to £1.4 million. These future donations include a £600,000 loan instalment to Muscular Dystrophy, £350,000 to Oundle School Foundation for the Sci-Tec Centre, £125,000 to the Patrick Foundation, £111,000 to Belgrade Theatre – Coventry, £40,000 to the Joseph Patrick Trust and £10,000 to Gloucester Cathedral for disabled access.

Exclusions

No grants to individuals.

Applications

In writing to the correspondent at any time, although it should be noted that the trust's substantial future commitments may mean there are little funds for new applications.

The Peacock Charitable Trust

Medical research, disability, general

£1.8 million (2002/03)

Beneficial area UK.

c/o Charities Aid Foundation, Kings Hill, West Malling, Kent ME19 4TA

Tel. 01732 520081 **Fax** 01732 520001

Email bdavis@cafonline.org

Correspondent Mrs Barbara Davis

Trustees *W M Peacock; Mrs S Peacock; C H Peacock; K R Burgin.*

Charity Commission no. 257655

Information available Annual report and accounts, including a full list of grants, but without a narrative report.

Summary

The trust gives between 120 and 150 grants each year, many of them recurrent and towards the running costs of the organisations concerned. They are concentrated on medical and health charities, disability and some youth work.

Many of the larger, repeating grants go to well known national charities.

General

This family trust was administered personally by Mr and Mrs Peacock for almost 35 years, with the assistance of Mr D Wallace who prepared reports on the majority of applicants to the trust for presentation to the trustees. Mr Wallace has now retired, and the administration is now carried out by the Charities Aid Foundation. No changes to grantmaking policy or practice are expected.

Grantmaking in 2002/03

During the year the trust made 125 grants totalling £1.8 million (£2.4 million in 2001/02). Grants ranged from £500 to £110,000, although most were for between £2,000 and £25,000. All but £183,000 of the grant total in 2002/03 went to organisations also supported in the previous year.

The larger grants were made to Cancer Research UK (£110,000), Fairbridge (£100,000), Marie Curie Cancer Care (£85,000), Royal Hospital for Neuro Disability (£75,000), Cancer BACUP (£60,000), Cancer Relief Macmillan Fund, Jubilee Sailing Trust and St Wilfred's Hospice (£50,000 each), Queen Elizabeth's Foundation for Disabled People (£42,000), Action for M.E., British Heart Foundation and YMCA England (£40,000 each); all received similar amounts during the previous year.

Other beneficiaries included the Iris Fund (£35,000), Epsom Rheumatology Research Fund (£30,000), Alzheimer's Research Trust (£25,000), Addaction and Prostate Cancer Charity (£20,000 each), Prince's Trust (£18,000), Sound Seekers (£15,000), Wey & Arun Canal Trust and Talking Newspaper Association of the UK (£12,000 each) and Army Benevolent Fund, Population Concern, Research into Ageing, Sail Training Association and Sight Savers International (£10,000 each).

Smaller grants included those to Alzheimer's Disease Society (£9,000), DeafPLUS, Marine Conservation Society, Neurofibromatosis Association and Woodlands Trust (£8,000 each), Disabled Sport England and Wimbledon Guild of Social Welfare (£7,000 each), Cancer Support Dudley and Not Forgotten Association (£6,000 each), British Deaf Association, Research Council for Complementary Medicine and Sussex Clubs for Young People (£5,000 each), ADAPT Trust, Centrepoint – Soho and St Tiggywinkles Wildlife Hospital (£4,000 each), Bendon Care Foundation Development Fund (£3,000), Chichester Cathedral Restoration & Development Trust, Mayflower Sail Training Society and Victim Support – Merton (£2,000 each) and Pelican Trust Foundation (£500).

The trust has said that, in line with the founder's lifelong enthusiasm for sailing, it has an interest in supporting charities which involve disabled people in sailing activities.

The trust also says that many of the repeated grants go towards the running costs of organisations, in recognition of the fact that charities need, and sometimes lack, continuity. It says its newer grants are often for capital purposes. Some of its recent grants have also helped organisations to pay off their debts.

Comment

The accounts properly note that trustee K R Burgin was paid the sum of £6,450 (£2,350 in 2001/02) for accountancy services. Nevertheless these editors prefer trustees to be unremunerated unless, in the words of the Charity Commission, 'there is no realistic alternative'.

Exclusions

No donations are made to individuals and only in rare cases are additions made to the list of charities already being supported.

Applications

In 2003 the trust stated that its funds were fully committed, and with the big reduction in interest rates it was unlikely to be able to help any new causes. This is the case for 2004 and the trust requests that no unsolicited applications be sent.

The Dowager Countess Eleanor Peel Trust

Medical research, general

£462,000 (2002/03)

Beneficial area UK, with an apparent interest in the Lancaster area.

Sceptre Court, 40 Tower Hill, London EC3N 4DX

Tel. 020 7423 8000 **Fax** 020 7423 8001

Email lvalner@trowers.com

Correspondent L H Valner, Secretary/ Trustee

Trustees *J W Parkinson, chair; R M Parkinson; Anthony G Trower; R L Rothwell Jackson; L H Valner.*

Charity Commission no. 214684

Information available Full accounts were provided by the trust.

The trustees' 2002/03 report reads as follows:

The trustees meet on at least three occasions each year. All applications for grants are vetted by the secretary or the chairman and the secretary. Any applications rejected at this stage are listed in the agenda for the next trustees' meeting with the reason for rejection. Applications for consideration at the trustees' meetings are presented with a report and summary of the financial statements for the last complete year.

Grantmaking policy

(a) General
The trustees prefer to support specific projects rather than general operating expenses. They regret that, due to the number of applications they receive, they are not normally able to support small local charities with gross income of less than £25,000 pa. The trustees scrutinise the financial position of applicants, and those with Income Accounts showing substantial surpluses are unlikely to be supported. Applications from individuals are not accepted.

(b) Applications for medical research grants
The trustees have been receiving an increased number of requests for grants towards medical research as well as their other commitments. Therefore a new

research reserve account was established in the year [2002/03] to promote a fair and efficient distribution of funds at their disposal to support medical research.

During the year £106,000 was contributed to the account to provide medical research grants.

Applications for medical research grants are categorised, as appropriate, for a 'minor grant' (£5,000 or less) or a 'major grant' (greater than £5,000 per annum for a defined research project for one to three years). Applications to be considered for a major grant are assessed en bloc annually at the trustees' March meeting. Applications are competitive and are met from funds set aside for this purpose.

In 2002/03 the trust had assets of £10.5 million, which generated an income of £533,000. Grants were made to 70 organisations totalling £462,000, all of whom have received grants from the trust in the past (the 2002/03 accounts lists all organisations that have previously received multiple grants from the trust). Although 31 charities are specified in the trust deed, none received a grant during the year.

The largest grant during the year was made to the University of Edinburgh, which received a grant of £105,000. Other beneficiaries receiving grants of £10,000 or more were Peel Studentship Trust – University of Lancaster (£75,000), Peel Medical Research Trust (£49,000), Imperial College University of London (£30,000), Church of England Clergy Stipend Trust (£20,000), Samantha Dickson Research Trust and YMCA Lancaster & District (£10,000 each).

With the exception of a small annual donation of £100 to East Meon Parochial Church Council, all other grants were for between £1,000 and £7,500.

Beneficiaries included Age Concern – England (£7,500), British Commonwealth Ex-Services League, Disabled Living and Iris Fund for Prevention of Blindness (£5,000 each), International Spinal Research Trust, Lancaster Royal Grammar School – Peel Further Education Award and Police Convalescence & Rehabilitation Trust (£3,000 each), St Margaret's Somerset Hospice and Sight Concern – Bedfordshire (£2,500 each), Voluntary Service – Belfast, Karten CTEC Centre and Guideposts Trust Ltd (£2,000 each), House of St Barnabas – Soho (£1,500) and Association of the Mentally Infirm Elderly, Christian Help in Partnership, Cornerstone Community – Belfast, Crossroads – West Lancashire, Lonsdale District Carers and Soundaround (£1,000 each).

Comment

Trustees are paid for their services and received a total of £20,000 in 2002/03, as well as being reimbursed £6,000 for expenses relating to travel, hotel and secretarial expenditure on behalf of the trust. The trust also purchases investment management and secretarial services from businesses with which two of the trustees, J W Parkinson and L H Valner, are connected. These received £36,000 and £44,000 respectively in 2002/03.

It is the view of these editors that experienced and competent voluntary trustees can be found for the rewarding task of giving away someone else's money, who do not need to be paid for this. Nor do the editors feel that it is desirable to place a charity's commercial business with bodies connected to the trustees, unless, in the words of the Charity Commission, 'there is no realistic alternative'.

Exclusions

No grants to children's charities, individuals or charitable bodies substantially under the control of central or local government.

Applications

In writing to the correspondent.

The following information is required for applications for medical research:

- a general outline of the aim, objectives and direction of the research project;
- details of the institution where the research will be carried out and by whom;
- outline of the costs and of funding required for the project and details of any funds already in hand;
- as with all applications to the trust, the annual report and accounts of the charity/institution should be enclosed.

Where the application is received well in advance of the trustees' March meeting, an update of any changes to the application or the project may be required nearer to the time.

A brief (and not too technical) annual report on the progress of each project supported with a major grant is requested from the research team.

The Performing Right Society Foundation

Music

£1.2 million (2003)
Beneficial area UK.

29–33 Berners Street, London W1T 3AB
Tel. 020 7306 4044 **Fax** 020 7306 4814
Email ben.lane@prsfoundation.co.uk
Website www.prsfoundation.co.uk
Correspondent Ben Lane, Applications Coordinator
Trustees *David Bedford; Marcus Davey; Anne Dudley; Nigel Elderton; Anthony Mackintosh; Michael Noonan; John Sweeney.*
Charity Commission no. 1080837
Information available Information was provided by the trust. Additional information taken from the website.

Background

The foundation was set up by the Performing Right Society (PRS), which has been supporting new music since 1953 by reacting to applications for support as and when they arrived. In 1999, PRS established a taskforce to determine the best way to continue to support new music in the UK, which resulted in the launch, in 2000, of an independent foundation to support new music of any genre.

General

The foundation offers the following review of its main objective and activities:

The principle objective of the Performing Right Society Foundation (PRSF) is to provide funds to support, sustain and further the creation and performance of new music in the UK, and increase the public's appreciation of, and education in, new music.

The foundation is an artistically driven organisation which aims to promote and support the creation and performance of all genres of music and to help people enjoy and understand the new music they experience. In order to energise the new music landscape in the UK, PRSF directs its support towards creatively adventurous and pioneering musical activity.

In just over four years [2000–2004], PRSF has successfully funded over 1,000 new music initiatives, to the tune of nearly £5 million. Its funding and partnership activities have enabled many groundbreaking collaborations and projects. In addition, PRSF actively supports new music projects throughout the UK, which help to inspire musical creativity in young people.

Since its launch at Abbey Road studios in March 2000, the foundation has gone from strength to strength, quickly establishing itself as a model of good practice within the arts funding system – widely praised for its culture of efficiency, easy access and fast decision making and for its free advice service for potential applicants.

This open-door culture and flexibility has contributed to the breadth of PRSF's outreach. Statistics revealed at the 2002 PRS AGM showed that the foundation has successfully supported and communicated with an excellent geographical spread of projects and a genuinely diverse range of genres.

Grantmaking in 2003

The foundation has several funding schemes, including Festivals, Live Connections, New Works, Performance Groups and Special Projects.

During the year the foundation made 327 grants from its various schemes to organisations totalling £1.2 million. Grants ranged from £140 to £44,000.

Beneficiaries receiving more than £10,000 each included: Visiting Arts for the Creative Collaborations in Music Awards 2003/04 (£44,000); City of Birmingham Symphony Orchestra for the Cultural Diversity and Harmony project (£28,000); The Kashmir Club and Scottish Traditional Music Trust (£20,000 each); Community Music Limited and Guildhall School of Music and Drama for the Connect Professional Apprentice Scheme (£15,000 each); Beverley & East Riding Folk Festival for the Coming of Age project (£14,000); and Northern Ireland Music Industry Commission (£12,000).

Grants for £10,000 each included those to the Royal Festival Hall, Showcase Scotland, Greenwich and Docklands Festivals, 20,000 Voices, Generator North East, Urban Development, Tomorrow's Warriors Ltd and Chicken Shed Theatre Company. Grants for either £8,000 or £7,500 included those to Bath Festival Trust, Music Theatre Wales, Serious Events Limited, British Music Information Centre, Futuresonic, Birmingham Contemporary Music Group and Leeds Music Promotions.

Other beneficiaries included Drake Music Project Scotland (£7,000), Dundee City Council Education Department and Homemade Music Ltd (£6,000 each), Oxford Contemporary Music (£5,500),

Cambridge Folk Festival, Cheltenham International Jazz Festival and Greenwich Theatre (£5,000 each), Ear to the Ground, Hebrides Ensemble and Leeds College of Music – Leeds International Jazz Conference (£4,000 each), Pure Media UK, Harlequin and Laptop Jams (£3,000 each), Future World Funk (£2,500), Vale of Glamorgan Festival of Music and Umbrella Melts (£2,000 each), Soma Recordings Ltd, Rhythms of the World, the Jazzhearts, Ensemble Eleven and Lancashire Life Morecambe Band (£1,000 each), Exmoor Singers in London (£750) and Welsh Amateur Music Federation (£250).

Exclusions

The foundation will not offer funding for:

- individuals;
- recordings/demos;
- college fees (except for scholarships for those studying composition/songwriting at a post-graduate level);
- musical equipment or instruments.

Applications

On an application form available to download from the foundation's website, or by telephoning the foundation. The application forms for each programme also include full guidelines for applicants.

Deadlines for applications vary from programme to programme. Contact the foundation for further information.

The foundation stresses that it funds NEW music.

The Jack Petchey Foundation

Young people in east London and west Essex

£7 million (2005)

Beneficial area East London, west Essex, and from 2005 all north London boroughs.

Exchange House, 13–14 Clements Court, Clements Lane, Ilford, Essex IG1 2QY

Tel. 020 8252 8000 **Fax** 020 8477 1088

Email mail@jackpetcheyfoundation.org.uk

Website www.jackpetcheyfoundation.org.uk

Correspondent Andrew Billington, Director

Trustees *Ron Mills; Ray Rantell; Graham Adams; Barbara Staines.*

Charity Commission no. 1076886

Information available Annual report and accounts are available from the foundation's website. Its website also includes guidelines, application forms and good general information about the foundation.

The foundation's website provides full information on its activities. It states:

The Jack Petchey Foundation, established in 1999, gives grants to programmes and projects that benefit young people aged 11 – 25. The foundation is eager to help young people take advantage of opportunities and play their full part in society.

Grants are given through different programmes including: Achievement Award Scheme, Leader Award Scheme, Projects Grants and Sponsorship.

Grants of over £13 million have been given since the foundation was established.

Areas of Interest:

East London and West Essex are the core areas of the foundation – (Barking & Dagenham, Brentwood, Epping Forest, Hackney, Harlow, Havering, Newham, Redbridge, Tower Hamlets, Thurrock, Uttlesford, Waltham Forest). Recent additions include all north London boroughs.

From mid-2006 the foundation will offer grants in boroughs south of the River Thames.

There are four main methods of grant support:

1. Achievement Awards
2. Project Grants
3. Leaders Awards
4. Sponsorship

1. Achievement Awards (£1,600,000 for 2005)

Jack Petchey Achievement Awards are given to young people (mainly between 11 and 25 years of age) who make a wholehearted contribution to their club, school, group or community.

The recipient is given a framed Certificate of Achievement to keep and £200 (£300 in schools and colleges) to spend on a community/club project of their choice. (Grants cannot be used by the winners themselves, but must be spent on their club/school or projects that benefit others.) In other words, Achievement Awards can be worth £2,400 a year to a club/school or community project.

The Award Scheme is run through clubs, schools and community projects in east and north London and west Essex. Grants are channelled through these organisations, so applications must be made by club leaders, teachers, community managers etc. (If your club is associated with Essex Association of Boys Clubs or Community Links please contact them first.)

2. Project Grants (£4,000,000 for 2005)
In addition to Achievement Awards, the foundation gives Project Grants. The value is normally between £500 and £50,000. The catchment area for Project Grants is east and north London and west Essex and the projects must benefit young people.

Are you eligible?
You can apply if you are a registered charity or a group with charitable purposes. If you are not a registered charity or school, you will need to give us some extra information. (You can apply for a grant even if you are not a registered charity as long as your group has charitable purposes. In this case you should send us a copy of your constitution or set of rules which should set out the following: the group's name and objectives; how the governing body is elected or appointed; what will happen to the assets if the group ceases to function; the organisation's bank details and who is authorised to sign cheques; and names, addresses and phone numbers of two independent referees.)

Financial information
Please attach to your application the following financial information: your organisation's most recent annual report and full accounts; a budget plan for the project; and any other information you think will help.

What we do support?
The foundation is likely to support:
- programmes in east London, north London and west Essex that benefit young people;
- organisations and charities that promote involvement and personal responsibility within society;
- clubs and youth groups that demonstrate that they are enabling individuals to achieve their potential, take control of their lives and contribute to society as a whole;
- the training of youth leaders;
- projects that assist young people to overcome problems that prevent them reaching their potential–these may include addiction, homelessness and ill health;
- projects that help develop self-esteem through involving young people in sport and other worthwhile activities;
- youth organisations, Scouts, Sea Cadets, Police Cadets, Guides, Army Cadets, etc;
- schools and other training establishments so that they can provide a better service

to young people (care is taken not to give grants where statutory funding is available);
- volunteer projects;
- schemes that tackle the problems faced by young people from ethnic minority groups;
- projects where there is match funding or demonstrable support from those involved with the organisation.

3. Leaders Awards (£500,000 for 2005)
Jack Petchey Leader Awards are linked to the Jack Petchey Achievement Award Scheme.

Awards are given to adults who have demonstrated, in an outstanding way, an ability to encourage and motivate young people aged 11–25 in east London, north London or west Essex.

The scheme is open to youth leaders, school teachers, community leaders, volunteer leaders, sports coaches and any other adults who have regular contact with young people.

Any school or club participating in the Achievement Award Scheme can nominate a 'leader'. It works best when young people, leaders/teachers/volunteers are involved in choosing an adult for this award (worth £1,000).

The foundation can supply a Nomination box and Internal School/Club Nomination forms.

When the school/club has chosen their 'leader' another formal form must be sent to the Jack Petchey Foundation.

Awards winners will be: invited to an Annual Leaders Presentation ceremony; presented with a gilt medallion; and given a cheque for £1,000 to be spent on a community/school/club project of their choice.

4. Sponsorship (£168,000 for 2005)
The Jack Petchey Foundation will consider sponsoring young people (usually 11–25 years old) living in east London, north London or west Essex who are undertaking projects, or participating in events, that will benefit other people or specific charities.

Before completing the sponsorship form, please check the following points:
- do you live in the foundation's area (east or north London/west Essex)?;
- does the project benefit other people (charity/school/community project?);
- will each applicant raise at least £200 from other sources?;
- participants over 25 may seek sponsorship if they are raising money for youth projects in east London or west Essex;
- brief details and, where appropriate, a budget for the project should be attached to the sponsorship form;
- the attached form should normally be carefully completed by the young person concerned (not the adult leader or

parent). A short letter should be attached to each form explaining why the applicant is taking part;
- if a group is applying for sponsorship, their forms should be submitted together with a covering note from the leader or teacher.

The normal support from the foundation will be £200 (maximum of 10 participants for a single event).

Note to Youth Leader and Teachers: if your club is associated with London Youth, Community Links or Essex Association of Boys' Clubs, please contact them first.

Grants and Awards in 2004
Achievement Awards
Recipients of Achievement Awards in 2004 included Barking & Dagenham Befrienders Educational Project, BATTS Table Tennis Club, Elm Park Twirlers, Paradise Zone, Sahara Communities Abroad, South Essex Thurrock Netball Association and Youth Create.

Project Grants
Beneficiaries in 2004 included the London Borough of Tower Hamlets, which received £395,000. Other beneficiaries included: London Youth (£56,000), Scouts and Sea Cadets (£50,000 each), NSPCC (£25,000), Dyslexia Institute (£19,000), Eastside Youth Leaders Academy (£10,000) and Addaction (£5,000).

Leader Awards
Recipients of these awards include individuals from organisations such as: A Space, which runs an after-school club and a healthy eating programme for young people; Cubitt Town Youth Project, where the recipient works as a full-time drug and sexual health worker in the Isle of Dogs area; Epping Forest District Council, where the youth officer was nominated directly by the Jack Petchey Foundation for his work; and Hornchurch & Upminster Sea Cadets.

Sponsorship
During the year the foundation offered sponsorships to the value of £48,000. These grants supported 'gap' years and fundraising initiatives undertaken by young people.

The foundation has also agreed in principal to sponsor a new school in Hackney under the Government's City Academy Programme. The school is likely to cost up to £30 million, with the foundation contributing £2 million. The school to be called the Petchey Academy, is scheduled to open in 2006.

Exclusions

The foundation will not accept applications:

- from applicants who have applied within the previous 12 months;
- that directly replace statutory funding;
- from individuals or for the benefit of one individual (unless under a sponsorship scheme);
- for work that has already taken place;
- which do not directly benefit people in the UK;
- for medical research;
- for animal welfare;
- for endowment funds;
- that are part of general appeals or circulars;
- organisations that do not positively welcome young people from different races, religions and cultures.

The foundation is also unlikely to support:

- building or major refurbishment projects:
- conferences and seminars;
- projects where the main purpose is to promote religious beliefs.

Applications

Application forms for each of the grant schemes are available from the foundation and can be downloaded from its website. There are no deadlines for applications but they should be made in 'good time' before the money is needed. The foundation holds monthly management meetings and aims to give a decision within six weeks.

The Pilgrim Trust

Social welfare, art and learning, preservation of buildings

£1.6 million (2003)

Beneficial area UK, but not the Channel Islands and the Isle of Man.

Cowley House, 9 Little College Street, London SW1P 3SH

Tel. 020 7222 4723 **Fax** 020 7976 0461

Email georgina.nayler@thepilgrimtrust.org.uk

Website www.thepilgrimtrust.org.uk

Correspondent Miss Georgina Nayler, Director

Trustees *Lady Jay, chair; Sir Richard Carew Pole; Neil MacGregor; Nicolas Barker; Lord Bingham; Dame Ruth Runciman; Eugenie Turton; Lord Cobbold.*

Charity Commission no. 206602

Information available Guidelines for applicants and excellent annual report and accounts.

Summary

As has been reported in its previous annual reports, during 2001 and 2002 the trust suffered a substantial drop in the value of its investments. In 2003 it had assets amounting to £46 million and an income of £1.8 million. In 2003 it received 930 applications from which 95 awards were made totalling £1.6 million; an average grant of £16,000. Very few grants are for more than £60,000. There is a small grants fund for applications of £5,000 or less.

Grants can be one-off, or, less frequently in the future than in the past, for up to three years, and can be for core or programme costs.

Background

Edward Harkness of New York founded the Pilgrim Trust in 1930 by endowing it with a capital sum of just over £2 million. The donor 'was prompted by his admiration for what Great Britain had done in the 1914–18 war, and by his ties of affection for the land from which he drew his descent'. He desired that the gift should be used to give grants for some of the country's more urgent needs and to promote her future well being.

General

Applications from all parts of the UK are welcomed.

Trustees particularly welcome collaboration between organisations to achieve their joint aims.

Grants may be offered for more than one financial year, but the trustees are reluctant to make recurring grants for more than three years.

Trustees run a small grants fund and have set aside an annual sum of £200,000 for applications for £5,000 or less.

Guidelines for applicants

Social welfare

- Projects that assist people involved in crime or in alcohol or drug misuse to change their lives and find new opportunities.
- Projects concerned with the employment, support or housing of those with mental illness.
- Projects in prisons and projects providing alternatives to custody that will give new opportunities to offenders and will so assist rehabilitation.
- Projects for young people who are looked after by local authorities in residential or in foster care and for those leaving that care, to help them into education, training and employment.
- Trustees may seek out projects concerned with the welfare and integration of refugees and asylum seekers within the UK. They have decided, however, that they themselves will identify those projects to which they wish to contribute. They will NOT consider unsolicited applications.

Art and learning

- The promotion of scholarship, academic research, cataloguing and conservation within museums, galleries, libraries and archives, particularly those outside London. Grants may not be given direct to individuals but must be made to a charitable or public organisation.
- Trustees do not exclude acquisitions for collections, but funds for this are strictly limited.

Preservation

- Preservation of particular architectural or historical features on historic buildings or the conservation of individual monuments or structures that are of importance to the surrounding environment, including buildings designed for public performance. Trustees will not normally contribute to major restorations or repairs unless a discrete element of the project can be clearly identified as appropriate for the trust to support.
- Projects that seek to give a new use to buildings that are of outstanding architectural or historic interest.
- The preparation and dissemination of architectural or historical research about buildings and designed landscapes and their importance to the community.
- Cataloguing and conservation of records associated with archaeology, marine archaeology, historic buildings and designed landscapes.

Places of worship

The trust makes annual block grants for the repair of the fabric of historic churches of any denomination to the Historic Churches Preservation Trust for Churches in England and Wales (020 7736 3054) and to the Scottish Churches Architectural Heritage Trust (0131 225 8644). Applications should be made directly to the appropriate body. Churches in Northern Ireland should apply to the trust directly.

Projects to develop new facilities within a church or the re-ordering for liturgical purposes will not be supported.

Conservation of historic contents

The trust makes an annual block grant to the Council for the Care of Churches (020 7898 1866) for the conservation of historic contents (organs, bells, glass and monuments etc.) and important structures and monuments in church yards for places of worship of all denominations. Applications should be addressed directly to the Council. Churches in Northern Ireland should apply to the trust directly.

Grantmaking in 2003

Grants were broken down as follows, shown with examples of grants in each category.

Social welfare

Projects in prison's alternatives to custody – five grants totalling £121,000

Grants included £45,000 to Wish towards a community link worker, £40,000 to Lancaster and District YMCA towards the 'Wise Up' Project for young offenders, £20,000 to Revolving Doors Agency towards the 'Young People, Mental Health and Offending' project and £6,100 to Post Adoption Centre towards counselling work with birth mothers in prison.

Support for people with mental illness – 14 grants totalling £181,000

Grants included £21,000 to Next Steps – Malton to appoint a coordinator, £20,000 each to 42nd Street – Manchester towards employing a director and Action for Children in Conflict towards the haven project in Liverpool to support and counsel traumatised young refugees and asylum seekers, £19,000 to Mind in Taunton and West Somerset towards the Likeminds' mentoring project, £17,000 to Winchester Alliance for Mental Health

towards the Winchester Community Recycling Partnership, £12,000 to Mosaic Clubhouse – Balham towards employing a senior support worker, £10,000 each to Core Arts – London towards a support coordinator and Forth Sector – Edinburgh towards an IT course and £7,400 to the Second Step Housing Association – Bristol towards the 'Horizons' mentoring project.

Projects for looking after young people – four projects totalling £102,000

Grants were £47,000 to East London Foster Carers towards a pilot project to employ an educational support worker, £25,000 to the Caldecott Foundation, £20,000 to Who Cares? Trust – London towards the 'Getting the most from Education' project and £10,000 to Move On towards the Housing Education Team.

Drug and alcohol misuse – 11 grants totalling £677,000

Grants included £75,000 to JP Getty Trust towards the appointment of an Addictions Advisor, £28,000 to Hull Lighthouse Project towards a part-time outreach worker to support women involved with prostitution and drugs, £25,000 to Addaction towards the Maya Project aftercare and resettlement programme, £20,000 to Cranstoun Drug Services towards the work of the referral and assessment team for the residential and treatment programme, £17,000 to Torridge Addiction Action Group – Devon towards a volunteer coordinator and £15,000 each to Axe Street Project – Barking towards an IT/administration worker and PANDA towards a part-time volunteer coordinator.

Preservation

Secular – 8 grants totalling £106,000

Grants included £16,000 to Sion Mills Building Preservation Trust towards ongoing costs, £20,000 to Great Hospital – Norwich towards fabric repairs to the Derlyngton Tower, £15,000 to St Austell China Clay Museum towards the repair of Mica Drags and £10,000 each to Dawn Sailing Barge towards the repair costs and Mausolea and Monuments Trust towards office costs.

Places of worship – 12 grants totalling £422,000

The two largest grants were £160,000 to Council for the Care of Churches and £120,000 to Historic Churches Preservation Trust. Other beneficiaries included Bristol Cathedral (£25,000), Sheffield Cathedral (£20,000), Liverpool Old Hebrew Congregation and Southwark Cathedral (£15,000 each),

Dunluce Parish Church – Bushmills and Hereford Cathedral (£10,000 each) and Ripon Cathedral (£2,000).

Miscellaneous – 2 grants totalling £20,000

Grants of £10,000 each went to Cytal Apt towards the salary costs of a development officer and PMSA Edinburgh.

Arts and learning

Conservation and cataloguing – 9 grants totalling £162,000

Grants included £60,000 to Bowes Museum County Durham towards the employment of a textiles conservator, £20,000 to the Type Museum towards the funding of a curator; £15,000 to Barmouth Sailors' Institute towards the display of artefacts from the Bronze Bell Wreck, £10,000 each to London Metropolitan Archives towards the conservation of Consistory Court Wills 1751–1858 and Sybil Campbell Library – London towards a conservation project and £8,000 to Staffordshire University towards the cataloguing of the Iris Strange Collection.

Research and scholarship – 3 grants totalling £53,000

Grants were £24,000 to Chatham Historic Dockyard Trust towards new research into ship timbers found under the Wheelwrights' shop at Chatham, £11,000 to Sheffield Regional Archive Center to employ a researcher for the PMSA National Recording Project Sheffield and South Yorkshire and £8,000 to St John's College – Nottinghamshire towards the completion of the 'Images of Salvation' CD.

During the year 17 small grants were distributed totalling £121,000.

Exclusions

The purpose of the application must be charitable. Normally applications will only be considered from UK-registered charities except where the applicant is exempt from registration, is a recognised public body or is registered as a Friendly Society.

The project must be based within the UK. Organisations from the Channel Islands and the Isle of Man are not eligible to apply. No grants can be made to private individuals.

Currently, the Pilgrim Trust does not make grants for:

- major capital projects and major appeals, particularly where 'partnership' funding is required and where any contribution from the

Pilgrim Trust would not make a significant difference;

- activities that the trustees consider to be primarily the responsibility of central or local government;
- medical research, hospices, residential homes for the elderly and people with learning disabilities;
- projects which offer training or employment for people with learning disabilities;
- projects for people with physical disabilities and schemes specifically to give access to public buildings for people with physical disabilities;
- drop-in centres, unless the specific work within the centre falls within one of the trustees' current priorities, youth and sports clubs, travel or adventure projects, community centres or children's play groups;
- drop-in centres or hostels for people who are homeless;
- re-ordering of churches or places of worship for wider community use;
- education, assistance to individuals for degree or post-degree work, school, university and college development ;
- trips abroad;
- one-off events such as exhibitions, festivals, seminars, conferences and theatrical and musical productions;
- commissioning of new works of art;
- general appeals.

Applications

An application form, and guidelines for applicants, are available from the correspondent or the trust's website.

- You can make an application at any time during the year. The full board of trustees meets quarterly, normally in late January, April, July and October. Applications will normally be placed before trustees at the next quarterly meeting following submission, so long as the application and all the necessary supporting information is received at least six weeks before the date of that meeting.
- You should read the guidelines carefully to make sure that your organisation and your project is eligible. You should then complete the application form, which is attached to the guidelines, and send it to the trust with all the relevant supporting information from the checklist at the end of the form.
- You must include details of your organisation's bank account, the latest audited accounts and annual report, a budget for the project and details of other sources of funding. Your application will not be considered

without your organisation's audited accounts.

- If the application does not fall within the trustees' current priorities, you will be informed within two weeks of the submission. All eligible applications will be acknowledged within two weeks and any necessary further information requested.
- Trustees run a small grants fund and have set aside an annual sum of £100,000 for applications of £5,000 or less. These applications normally require less detailed assessment, whereas a site visit or meeting may be required for larger applications. Applicants for sums of less than £5,000 should include the names of two referees from organisations with whom they work.
- For larger projects, the average grant from the Pilgrim Trust is in the region of £20,000.

The full guidelines for applicants and the application form are available to download in PDF format.

The Pilkington Charities Fund

Welfare, health

£511,000 (2002/03)
Beneficial area Unrestricted, but with a strong preference for Merseyside.

Rathbones, Port of Liverpool Building, Pier Head, Liverpool L3 1NW
Tel. 0151 236 6666 **Fax** 0151 243 7003
Correspondent The Trustees
Trustees *Neil Pilkington Jones; Mrs Jennifer Jones; Arnold Philip Pilkington.*
Charity Commission no. 225911
Information available Annual report and accounts were provided by the trust.

Summary

The fund's grants are divided between social welfare in Merseyside and national welfare, disability, medical research and overseas aid charities. A small proportion is reserved for the benefit of present or former employees of the Pilkington glass company.

Grants are awarded twice a year, in October and April. Most range from £1,000 to £5,000, though larger grants for up to £100,000 are sometimes made,

and typically go to national or international charities.

General

In 2002/03 total funds of £9 million generated most of the trust's £475,000 income. Grants were made to 78 organisations totalling £421,000, with a further £60,000 being given to C&A Pilkington Trust Fund, and £30,000 given to St Helens Village Appeal for 'specific projects'.

During the financial year there were two rounds of grant distribution, with just three organisations receiving grants in both rounds. Most local beneficiaries have also received grants in previous years. Although about half the grant total goes to national charities, especially those concerned with health and disability, about two-thirds of these are based on Merseyside.

Larger grants during the year were made to Psychiatry Research Trust (£40,000), Refugee Council (£30,000), Oxfam (£25,000), Liverpool Personal Service Society (£25,000 in total), Liverpool School of Tropical Medicine (£20,000), Cancer Research Campaign (£13,000), Home Start – St Helens (£12,000 in total), Arthritis Research Campaign, Tomorrow's People (formerly Getting Merseyside Working), Social Partnership – Transit Programme and Willowbrook Hospice (£10,000 each).

Other beneficiaries include Home Start – South Sefton (£8,000 in total), Age Concern – St Helens, Children at Risk Foundation, Derma Trust, Merseyside Drugs Council, Terence Higgins Trust and West Lancashire Women's Refuge (£5,000 each), British Liver Trust (£4,500), Traidcraft (£4,000), Angels International, Changing Faces, Orrell Park and District Community Association and Youth at Risk (£3,000 each), Big Issue North West, Toxteth Citizen's Advice Bureau, Liverpool Royal School for the Blind, Toxteth Tabernacle Baptist Church Level 3 and WRVS – St Helens (£2,000 each) and ADFAM National, Arthritis Care, Harvest Trust, Sefton Children's Holiday Fund, Walton Youth Project and Who Cares? Trust (£1,000 each).

Exclusions

Grants are only made to registered charities. No grants to individuals.

Applications

In writing to the correspondent. Applications should include charity registration number, a copy of the latest accounts and details of the project for which support is sought.

Polden-Puckham Charitable Foundation

Peace and security, ecological issues, social change

£300,000 (2002/03)

Beneficial area UK and overseas.

BM PPCF, London WC1N 3XX

Email ppcf@btinternet.com

Website www.polden-puckham.org.uk

Correspondent Jagdish Patel, Secretary

Trustees *Carol Freeman; David Gillett; Harriet Gillett; Jenepher Gordon; Heather Swailes; Anthony Wilson.*

Charity Commission no. 1003024

Information available Full accounts and information for applicants were provided by the trust.

This foundation supports 'projects that change values and attitudes, that promote equity and social justice, and that develop radical alternatives to current economic and social structures', giving towards:

Our underlying approach
  In its work PPCF aims to support projects that change values and attitudes, that promote equity and social justice, and that develop radical alternatives to current economic and social structures. It gives particular consideration to small pioneering headquarters organisations.

Peace and security
  Development of ways of resolving international and internal conflicts peacefully, and of removing the causes of conflict.

Ecological sustainability
  Work which tackles the underlying pressures and conditions leading towards global environmental breakdown; particularly initiatives which promote sustainable living.

Other issues
  PPCF also supports human rights and women's issues where it is related to policy changes and to peace and ecological issues. PPCF also has a long-standing link with the Society of Friends and has supported the work of Quaker groups.

It prefers to make grants available to small, pioneering organisations which find it difficult to attract funds from other sources. Due to this emphasis, grants are often for long periods and may be given towards core costs. The average grant size for new applicants is £2,500.

In 2002/03 the trust made grants totalling around £300,000. Beneficiaries included, Sustain (£9,000), Soil Association (£8,000), Transnational Institute (£5,000), Small World Action (£4,000), World Information Service on Energy (£1,000).

Exclusions

The trust does not support: individuals; travel bursaries (including overseas placements and expeditions); study; academic research; capital projects (e.g. building projects or purchase of nature reserves); community or local projects (except innovative prototypes for widespread application); general appeals; or organisations based overseas.

Applications

The trustees meet twice a year in spring and autumn; applications should be submitted by 15 February and 15 September respectively. Decisions can occasionally be made on smaller grants between these meetings. The foundation will not send replies to applications outside its area of interest. Up-to-date guidelines will be sent on receipt of an sae.

Applications should be no longer than two pages and should include the following:

- a short outline of the project, its aims and methods to be used;
- the amount requested (normally between £500 and £5,000 over one to three years), the names of other funders and possible funders, and expected sources of funding after termination of PPCF funding;
- information on how the project is to be monitored, evaluated, and publicised;
- background details of the key persons in the organisation.

Please also supply:

- latest set of audited accounts;
- a detailed budget of the project;
- list of trustees or board of management;
- names of two referees;
- charity registration number;
- annual report.

The foundation strongly recommends that potential applicants should view their website. Applications outside of the trust's criteria will not receive a reply.

The Porter Foundation

Jewish charities, environment, arts, general

£1.3 million (2002/03)

Beneficial area Israel and the UK.

Southgate Chambers, 37 Southgate Street, Winchester, Hampshire SO23 9EH

Tel. 01962 849684 **Fax** 01962 854400

Email theporterfoundation@btinternet.com

Correspondent Paul Williams, Director

Trustees *Dame Shirley Porter; Sir Leslie Porter; Steven Porter; David Brecher; Abbey Castle.*

Charity Commission no. 261194

Information available Brief guidelines for applicants, reprinted below. Annual report and accounts.

Summary

This foundation has cut back on the number of beneficiaries during recent years and is making fewer, larger grants, mainly to the connected Porter environmental centre at Tel Aviv University and to other causes in Israel. These accounted for 90% of the grants by value in 2002/03.

General

The foundation was set up in 1970 by Sir Leslie Porter and Dame Shirley Porter, a former leader of Westminster City Council and daughter of Sir John Cohen, the founder of Tesco.

Its aim is to support 'projects in the fields of education, culture, the environment, health and welfare which encourage excellence, efficiency and innovation and which enhance the quality of people's lives'.

The following review of the foundation's acitivities in 2002/03 is taken from that year's accounts:

The Porter Foundation is continuing the process of transforming itself from a general purpose charitable vehicle giving small grants to a wide range of organisations, to a more focused environmental/educational charity, dispensing the greater part of its income through a small number of strategic partner organisations.

The reason for this is two-fold:

- Like most charitable foundations, the Porter Foundation's annual income has contracted in recent years due to market conditions and changes in the tax regime relating to charities.
- The trustees believe that more impact can be derived from concentrating resources in order to 'make a difference' than spreading them thinly across a wide range of causes.

The Porter Foundation's main strategic partner for the next five years will be Tel Aviv University, through the construction and development of the Porter School for Environmental Studies (PSES). PSES is planned as an interdisciplinary centre of excellence to generate practical solutions to intractable environmental issues. Israel is an ideal centre for such research, being sited at the junction of three continents and having first-hand experience of the dangers of rapid, uncontrolled industrial development.

The school is to be housed in a specially designed eco-building and is planned to be the first building in the Middle East that generates all its energy needs with zero emissions. The building will be the home of a series of integrated, multi-faculty research teams, embracing architecture, exact and life sciences and law among others.

The PSES will also engage in environmental outreach activity with other charitable organisations that share its aims and values.

The long term aim is to make the school the hub of a number of partnerships with similar world-class centres of academic excellence, both in the UK and worldwide.

The foundation will continue to support the Daniel Amichai Nautical Centre in Tel Aviv, an educational facility for young people throughout Israel, linked to the state school system.

The Royal Academy continues to be the major beneficiary in the cultural sector. A limited number of community awards continue to be given, usually to organisations with links to the foundation over a number of years.

The foundation's guidelines say that 'grants can be made for capital projects or for specific programmes or activities with a measurable end result. Grants will not be made on a recurring annual basis, or to cover general running costs. There is no maximum grant. Matching funding applications are welcomed.'

In 2002/03 assets stood at £28 million, generating an income of £1.1 million. A total of almost £1.3 million was given in donations. As described above, the majority of the money was given to Tel Aviv University Trust, which received £795,000 in 20 instalments for the Porter School for Environmental Studies. JPAIME also received a total of £207,000 in three instalments, presumably for the Daniel Amichai Nautical Centre.

The other significant beneficiaries during the year, as in previous years, were Royal Academy Trust (£75,000), UJIA (£66,000 in total) and New Israel Fund (£41,000 in total).

The remaining beneficiaries were a mixture of Jewish organisations based in the UK and Israel, and other UK organisations. These included National Portrait Gallery (£16,000), Imperial War Museum (£15,000), Oxford Centre for Hebrew and Jewish Studies (£11,000 in total), English Chamber Orchestra (£5,000), British Friends of Art Museums of Israel (£4,000 in total) and British Friends for a Beautiful Israel, Jewish Care and World ORT (£1,000 each).

There were also a further 14 donations of less than £1,000 each made to organisations totalling £3,400.

Comment

It seems unlikely that substantial grants are given in response to unsolicited applications from organisations not previously known to the trustees.

Exclusions

The foundation makes grants only to registered charitable organisations or to organisations with charitable objects that are exempt from the requirement for charitable registration.

Grants will not be made to:

- general appeals such as direct mail circulars;
- charities which redistribute funds to other charities;
- third-party organisations raising money on behalf of other charities;
- to cover general running costs.

No grants are made to individuals.

Applications

- An initial letter summarising your application, together with basic costings and background details on your organisation – such as the annual report and accounts – should be sent to the director. Speculative approaches containing expensive publicity material are not encouraged.
- If your proposal falls within the foundation's current funding criteria you may be contacted for further information, including perhaps a visit from the foundation staff. There is no need to fill out an application form.
- Applications fulfilling the criteria will be considered by the trustees, who meet three times a year, usually in March, July and November.
- You will hear shortly after the meeting whether your application has been successful. Unfortunately, it is not possible to acknowledge all unsolicited applications (unless a stamped, addressed envelope is enclosed). If you do not hear from the foundation, you can assume that your application has been unsuccessful.
- Due to limits on funds available, some excellent projects may have to be refused a grant. In such a case the trustees may invite the applicant to re-apply in a future financial year, without giving a commitment to fund.

The J E Posnansky Charitable Trust

Jewish charities, health, welfare

£515,000 (2002/03)

Beneficial area UK and overseas.

c/o Siedd & Co., 673 Finchley Road, London NW2 2JP

Tel. 020 7431 0909

Correspondent The Trustees

Trustees *Lord Mishcon; Philip A Cohen; Gillian Raffles; Anthony Victor Posnansky; P A Mishcon; E J Feather; N S Ponansky.*

Charity Commission no. 210416

Information available Accounts were on file at the Charity Commission.

The trust gives mainly to Jewish charities, although grants are also made to social welfare and health charities.

In 2002/03 the trust had an income of £197,000 generated from assets of £3.6 million. Grants totalling £515,000 were given to 97 organisations.

There were two large grants made during the year: £96,000 to Action Aid and £85,000 to British Council of the Shaare Zedek. Other larger grants included £32,000 to World Jewish Relief, £30,000 to UK Friends of Magen David Adom, £25,000 to JPAIME, £20,000 to Friends of Alyn, £15,000 to British Wizo, £14,000 to Jewish Care and £13,000 each to Friends of Hebrew University of Jerusalem and Norwood Ltd.

Other beneficiaries included New Israel Fund and United Kingdom Jewish Aid and International Development (£5,000 each), Terence Higgins Trust and Sick Children's Trust (£2,500 each), Help the Aged and St Luke's Hospice (£1,000 each), RNIB (£500) and Abbeyfield Eastbourne Society Ltd (£50).

Exclusions

No grants to individuals.

Applications

In writing to the correspondent. The trustees meet in May.

The Prince of Wales's Charitable Foundation

See below

£1.9 million (2003/04)

Beneficial area UK.

The Prince of Wales's Office, St James's Palace, London SW1A 1BS

Tel. 020 7930 4832 **Fax** 020 7930 0119

Correspondent David Hutson

Trustees *Sir Michael Peat; Philip Reid; Kevin Knott; Hon. Lord Rothschild.*

Charity Commission no. 277540

Information available Accounts were provided by the trust.

The foundation principally continues to support charitable bodies and purposes in which The Prince of Wales has a particular interest.

In 2003/04 the foundation had assets amounting to £4 million. It had an income of £1.9 million from covenants and investments. The foundation has two wholly owned subsidiaries, Duchy Originals Ltd and A G Carrick Ltd, from which most of its income is derived. Grants to 87 organisations totalled £1.9 million, including nearly £1 million in support of charities in which the Prince has a particular interest (such as the Prince of Wales's Phoenix Trust, the Prince of Wales's Foundation for Intgrated Health and Prince's Foundation). Of these the latter received

£246,000 from restricted funds. A number of other donations were made from restricted funds totalling £794,000, mainly in the field of culture. Restricted funds also met the majority of the costs of the second Prince of Wales's Education Summer School and its annual grant of US$90,000 to the United World Colleges.

Grants were broken down into the following classifications:

Category	2004	2003
Animals	–	£2,250
Armed services	£3,000	£21,500
Children and youth	–	£200
Community	£30,000	£30,000
Culture	£289,000	£29,000
Education	£269,000	£199,000
Environment – built and natural	£642,000	£577,00
Heritage	£9,000	£38,000
Hospices and hospitals	£82,000	£50,000
Medical welfare	£448,000	£516,000
Overseas aid	£6,000	£41,000
Religion	£8,000	–
Restoration of churches and cathedrals	£20,000	£38,000
Social welfare	£136,000	£23,000
Total	£1.9 million	£1.6 million

Grants made over £10,000 each were listed in the accounts. Beneficiaries from the general fund included: The Prince's Foundation (£301,000); The Prince of Wales's Foundation for Integrated Health (£202,000), Prince of Wales's Phoenix Trust (£200,000); Soil Association (£65,000); English Farming & Food Partnerships (£50,000), English College Foundation (£31,000), Business in the Community (£30,000), St Luke's Hospice and Joseph Weld and Trimar Hospice Trust (£18,000 each) and Mihai Foundation and FARA Foundation (£13,000 each).

Exclusions

No grants to individuals.

Applications

In writing to the correspondent, with full details of the project including financial data.

Mr and Mrs J A Pye's Charitable Settlement

General

£564,000 (2003/04)

Beneficial area UK, with a special interest in the Oxford area and, to a

lesser extent, in Reading, Cheltenham and Bristol.

c/o Mercer & Hole Chartered Accountants, International Press Centre, 76 Shoe Lane, London EC4A 3JB

Tel. 020 7353 1597 **Fax** 020 7353 1748

Correspondent D Tallon, Trustee

Trustees *G C Pye; J S Stubbings; D S Tallon.*

Charity Commission no. 242677

Information available Accounts were provided by the trust.

The charity was endowed by the Pye family of Oxford, although G C Pye is the sole remaining family trustee. The trust is administered by Mercer & Hole, whose partner David Tallon is an active and concerned trustee.

In 2003/04 the endowment of £10.2 million generated an income of £634,000 (largely through a particularly successful property investment).

Grantmaking

The trust's grantmaking policy and general criteria are reprinted here unchanged from previous years:

In making grants the trustees seek to continue the settlor's interests while expanding them to encompass other causes.

The following list is by no means exhaustive and is given for guidance only:

- Environmental – this subject particularly deals with organic farming matters, conservation generally and health-related matters such as pollution research and some wildlife protection.
- Adult health and care – especially causes supporting the following: post–natal depression, schizophrenia, mental health generally and research into the main causes of early death.
- Children's health and care – for physical, mental and learning disabilities, respite breaks etc.
- Youth organisations – particularly projects encouraging self reliance or dealing with social deprivation.
- Education – nursery, primary, secondary or higher/institutions (not individuals).
- Regional causes around Oxford, Reading, Cheltenham and Bristol – under this category the trustees will consider academic and arts projects.

The overall policy of the trustees is to support underfunded charities in their fields of interest in order to assist those charities to play a fuller role in the community. Unfortunately, due to the demands made it is not possible to support all applications even though they may meet the charity's criteria. However, the trustees particularly recognise the difficulty many smaller charities experience in obtaining core funding in order to operate efficiently in today's demanding environment.

The trust has previously estimated that, at best, less than one in eight requests for grants is successful.

In the year under review [2003/04], grants amounting to £564,000 (compared with £552,000 in the previous year) have been made to 256 charities (173 in the previous year) concerned with nutritional and medical research, mental health, education, child welfare, conservation and the arts as well as national and local needs in various fields.

During the year, only 11 grants were for £10,000 or more, with just another 14 for amounts above £3,000. More than two-thirds of grants were for £250 or £500 and a few new beneficiaries received more than £500. However, in financial terms, more than half of the money goes in larger grants to a small group of charities that have been supported for many years. During the year, these were led by:

	2003/04	(2002/03)
Elm Farm Research Centre	£123,000	(£123,000)
Music @ Oxford	£73,000	(£80,000)
University College, Oxford	£50,000	(£50,000)
Magdalen College School, Oxford	£30,000	(£30,000)
Harris Manchester College, Oxford	£20,000	(£20,000)
Plan International UK	£15,000	(£7,500)
Radcliffe Medical Foundation	£15,000	(£15,000)
Oxfordshire Community Foundation	£12,500	(£22,000)
Association for Post Natal Illness	£12,000	(£12,500)
The Philharmonia Orchestra	£11,500	(–)
London International Piano Competition	£10,000	(£10,000)

By contrast, over half of the 65 grants of £500 were awarded to charities which had not been supported in the previous year. These included Barton Training Trust, Bliss, Bristol Mind, Bobath Centre, Crimestopper Trust, Elmfield School for Deaf Children, Home Start, Marine Conservation Society, Oxfordshire Playbus, Purley Park Trust, Soil Association, Willow Trust and Well Women Information.

The grants lists are not categorised. However the charity suggests that the following headings reflect the general emphasis of its grantmaking:

- Environmental
- Oxford/arts
- Oxford/education
- Adult health and care
- Oxford/health research
- Children's health and care
- Oxford generally.

The charity also provides loans (from its revenue rather than its capital) as well as grants. In 2003/04 the amount loaned ranged from £1,000 to £100,000. There

were 14 loans made during the year totalling £262,000, with most loan recipients having been supported in previous years.

Exclusions

Applications will not normally be considered in relation to:

- organisations which are not registered charities;
- activities which are primarily the responsibility of central or local government;
- appeals for funds for subsequent redistribution to other charities–this would also preclude appeals from the larger national charities;
- endowment funds;
- fabric appeals for places of worship, other than in [Oxford, Reading, Cheltenham and Bristol];
- fundraising events;
- hospitals and medical centres (except for projects which are clearly additional to statutory responsibilities);
- overseas appeals;
- promotion of religion.

Applications

There are no application forms but the following information is essential:

- registered charity number or evidence of an organisation's tax exempt status;
- brief description of the activities of the charity;
- the names of the trustees and chief officers (NB more important than patrons);
- details of the purpose of the application and where funds will be put to use;
- details of the funds already raised and the proposals for how remaining funds are to be raised;
- the latest trustees report and full audited or independently examined accounts (which must comply with Charity Commission guidelines and requirements).

Applications can be made at any time, with the trustees meeting quarterly to take decisions. Any decision can therefore take up to four months before it is finally taken. However, all applicants are informed of the outcome of their applications and all applications are acknowledged. Telephone contact will usually be counterproductive, as the trust only wishes to respond to written applications.

Queen Mary's Roehampton Trust

War disabled ex-service people and their dependants
£480,000 (2003/04)
Beneficial area UK.

13 St George's Road, Wallington, Surrey SM6 0AS

Tel. 020 8395 9980 **Fax** 020 8255 1457

Email alanbaker13@hotmail.com

Correspondent Alan H Baker, Clerk to the Trustees

Trustees *Maj. Gen. R P Craig, chair; Dr J Watkinson, Vice-Chair; J J Macnamara; Col. S D Brewis; Col. A W Davis; Brig. A K Dixon; R R Holland; Dr J G Paterson; R D Wilson; S R Gallop; Mrs S Freeth; Baroness Emerton.*

Charity Commission no. 211715

Information available Guidance sheet and application pro-forma. Good annual report and accounts.

The trust had an income of £499,000 in 2003/04, from its endowment worth about £10 million. Grants are made for welfare activities and for building work to a wide range of ex-service welfare charities. The trust describes its grantmaking as follows:

The trust makes approximately 40 awards a year, totalling about £480,000. About half of this amount represents 'block' grants made to ex-service charities to support their welfare expenditure on beneficiaries. This includes welfare grants to those in need of help and such things as the provision of holidays and the supply of television sets for housebound ex-service men and widows. The other half is spent mainly in assisting with the modernisation of nursing homes and other accommodation provided specifically for disabled ex-service people and their widows.

2003/04 grants were divided as follows:

	No.	Amount
Welfare grants	25	£252,000
Building schemes	15	£180,000
New buildings	3	£45,000
Other	2	£3,500

Most recipient organisations feature regularly in the grants lists. However, the amounts awarded usually vary from year to year, and are for specific purposes rather than in the form of ongoing annual payments. Grants ranged from £1,000 to £40,000

About half of the grants were for amounts of £10,000 or more; beneficiaries included: £40,000 to Army Benevolent Fund; £35,000 to the Haig Homes; £25,000 each to the Royal Naval Benevolent Trust, the Royal Patriotic Fund Corporation and Scottish Veterans' Garden City Association; £20,000 to Broughton House; £15,000 to the Royal British Legion and the Ex-services Mental Welfare Society; and £10,000 each to Burma Star Association, Bournemouth War Memorial Homes, Chaseley Trust, the 'Not Forgotten' Association and Scottish Veterans' Residences.

Exclusions

No grants to individuals.

Applications

(In writing to the correspondent (seven copies), to be submitted in April or September annually. Details must be given of the number of war disabled and their widows assisted during a recent period of 12 months. In the case of nursing/residential homes, information concerning occupancy will be required under a number of headings (complement, residents, respite holidays, waiting list). Three copies of the latest annual report and accounts should be enclosed).

The Queen's Silver Jubilee Trust

See below

Around £2 million (2002/03)
Beneficial area UK.

The Prince's Trust, 17–18 Park Square East, London NW1 4LH
Tel. 020 7543 7463 **Fax** 020 7543 1306
Email nicola.brentnall@princes-trust.org.uk
Correspondent Nicola Brentnall
Trustees Sir Robin Janvrin; Sir Willian Castell; Stephen Hall; Peter Mimpriss; Sir John Riddell.
Charity Commission no. 272373
Information available Accounts are on file at the Charity Commission.

This trust was founded with the proceeds of an annual appeal launched in 1976, which, when it closed, had accumulated a fund of around £13 million. Its assets now stand at around £35 million.

The objects of the trust are:

- advancement of education;
- relief in need;
- assistance of children, young people, older people and the advancement of their physical, mental and spiritual welfare;
- provision of facilities for recreation or other leisure time occupation;
- advancement of other exclusively charitable purposes for the benefit of the community.

In 2002/03 it had an income of £1.2 million and a total expenditure of £2.4 million, most of which is likely to have been given in grants. A substantial grant may have been given to the Prince's Trust, as in the previous year when a £4 million donation was made.

Other previous beneficiaries include Prince of Wales – Business Leaders Forum, Nation's Trust, Liverpool Community Spirit, Prince's Foundation, Medi Memorial Peace Garden Project, Dyslexic Computer Training, Swaziland Work Camps Association, Chaverim and Winged Fellowship Trust.

Comment

Despite ample warning, and their obligation to the contrary, the Charity Commission were unable to give us sight of this trust's accounts.

Applications

Potential applicants are advised to enquire with the trust first to check whether it is open to applications. While it aims to respond to all applicants, the level of administration involved does not always allow this.

Trustees meet twice a year.

Rachel Charitable Trust

General, Jewish in the UK and Europe

About £3 million (2002/03)
Beneficial area UK and Europe.

c/o 5 Wigmore Street, London W1U 1PB
Correspondent The Trustees

Trustees L Noe; Mrs S D Noe; J Joseph.
Charity Commission no. 276441
Information available Accounts are on file at the Charity Commission.

In 2002/03 the trust had an income of £1.6 million and a total expenditure of £3.3 million. Grants were made totalling around £3 million. No further information was available for the year.

Previous beneficiaries include the Yeshiva Ohel Shimon Trust, which has received donations of up to £1 million. Other recent beneficiaries include Yeshiva Shaarei Torah Manchester, Encounter – Jewish Outreach Network, Project Seed, Cometville Limited, Shaarei Zedek Hospital, Jewish Learning Exchange, Chosen Mishpat Centre, Gertner Charitable Trust, Hertsmere Jewish Primary School, British Friends of Shuut Ami, Shomrei Hachomot Jerusalem, Manchester Jewish Grammar School, London Millennium Bikeathon, Children's Hospital Trust Fund and Friends of Sanz Institution.

Comment

Despite ample warning, and their obligation to the contrary, the Charity Commission were unable to give us sight of this trust's accounts.

Applications

In writing to the correspondent.

The Rank Foundation

Christian communication, youth, education, general

£4.8 million (2003)
Beneficial area UK.

PO Box 2862, Whitnash, Leamington Spa CV31 2YH
Tel. 01926 744550 **Fax** 01926 744550
Email sheila.gent@rankfoundation.com
Website www.rankfoundation.com
Correspondent Mrs Sheila Gent, Grants administrator
Trustees F A R Packard, chair; M D Abrahams; J A Cave; A E Cowen; M E T Davies; Mrs L G Fox; J R Newton; V A L Powell; Lord Shuttleworth; D R W Silk; Earl St Aldwyn; Hon. Mrs C Twiston-Davies; Mrs L C Onslow.

Charity Commission no. 276976

Information available Excellent reports and accounts.

Summary

This a heavily proactive foundation, with offices around the country, and much of whose grants are committed to ongoing programmes; because of this only about one in four of the unsolicited appeals are supported.

It concentrates exclusively on:

- the promotion of Christian principles through film and other media;
- encouraging and developing leadership amongst young people;
- supporting disadvantaged young people and those frail or lonely through old age or disability.

Large grants are typically part of a three or five year commitment and very seldom result from an unsolicited application.

Small grants (less than £5,000) are usually one off. Local charities are unlikely to get recurrent funding or multi-year awards.

Currently, around one in four applications result in a grant.

General

The charity was established in 1953 by the late Lord and Lady Rank (the founders). It was one of a number established by the founders at that time and to which they gifted their controlling interest in The Rank Group plc (formerly The Rank Organisation plc), best known as a film production company, though this was but one of its commercial interests.

The Rank trusts and foundations all share a Christian ethos.

The main office of the foundation is in Bushey, Hertfordshire, but grant applications are handled through the Leamington address given above.

In 2003 the foundation had an income of £7.8 million and made grants across various programmes totalling £4.7 million, including £1.9 million to the Foundation for Christian Communication. Grants were broken down by category as follows:

	Number of grants	£
Promotion of Christian religion	1	£1.9 million
Youth (including education)	153	£2.8 million
Community care programme	337	£2.1 million

General appeals

The Directors of the Rank Foundation see many examples of imaginative work at local level, some of which can be greatly encouraged by modest financial help from sources outside the local community.

The Directors take into account the level of local support that can realistically be expected and whether a small grant from the foundation will bring an initiative to a successful conclusion.

In considering unsolicited appeals, The Rank Foundation will tend towards projects where there are relatively small, attainable targets and they place great importance on clear evidence of local support. The directors also take into account whether it is likely that any grant that they make will be put to immediate use–we are unlikely to make a grant towards a large appeal at an early stage in the programme.

Youth work

In interpreting this objective, the directors take a broad view and include work with young people that is designed to involve them in decisions which affect their future and to foster in them attitudes which will make them more useful members of society. The directors subscribe wholeheartedly to the views of the founders that young people are the seedcorn for the future wellbeing of our society and that they should be encouraged to develop to the full extent of their potential. The directors have decided that the funds available to them would be best used in firstly identifying worthy projects and then funding them on a meaningful basis over a number of years. It has also been agreed that an integral part of the process should be careful monitoring and these have been the bases upon which funding has been committed.

There are four programmes in this category which are open to applications, and one, Rank Leadership Scheme, where unsolicited applications will not be considered. The four open programmes (with details of grants made in 2003) are:

Youth or adult? (39 grants were made to partner organisations totalling £1.2 million)

This is a five-year, degree-qualifying scheme which enables on-the-job training of young leaders who are experienced but unqualified. It is important that the host agency ensures that this work is integral to their core programme, involving the young people in the design, development and implementation of the programme and activities. This works in conjunction with the YMCA George Williams College and covers a Foundation Studies Certificate to a BA Degree in Informal and Community Education.

The programme is run in partnership with youth organisations. The total funding through each partner is typically between £100,000 and £200,000, paid over a number of years. Partner organisations are varied, with recipients in 2003 including YMCA George Williams College (£156,000), Federation of London Youth Clubs (£61,000), JUMP (£34,000), Lancashire Youth Association (£31,000), Energy and Vision (£20,000) and Children's Society (£4,100).

Investing in success (14 organisations received £609,000)

... builds upon partnerships which have been developed over the years with a number of established organisations.

The foundation lists five key expectations after it has agreed to fund a project, which are: involvement in project staff selection; membership of any project management team or support group; reasonable and regular access to the project; regular written progress reports and an annual report and financial summary; attendance at a regular evaluation coference organised by the foundation.

The beneficiaries included People at Work Unit (£113,000), Dundee Drugs and AIDS Project (£55,000), Rural Media Company (£50,000), Waterloo Adult and Youth Project (£40,000) and Space Place (£20,000).

Rank Volunteer (Gap) Awards (Five organisations received £361,000)

... encourages full time volunteering in organisations with which the foundation is already working, either during the period between school and further education or during a period of unemployment.

This scheme is for young people aged 17–24 and is operated directly by the foundation. Beneficiaries included Gap Year Project (£195,000), Cumbria Youth Alliance (£56,000) and VSU Youth in Action (£195,000)

Key Worker scheme (13 posts supported at the cost of £278,000)

... a number of strategic posts are supported within organisations with which the foundation has worked for some time and where qualified workers with specialist skills are often needed. This is particularly so in training up young apprentice leaders in areas such as the outdoors, enterprise and employment and in formal and informal education initiatives.

Organisatons supported were Prince's Trust – Cymru (£40,000), London Youth Support Trust (£30,000), Outward

Bound Trust (£27,000), Iona Community (£20,000) and Fleetwood Gymnasium Boy's Club (£10,000).

Community Care Programme

The foundation has continued its support for frail, elderly and disabled people in rural areas and to help individuals to overcome the effects of their disabilities and thereby improve the quality of their lives. The foundation has continued its support for national dementia organisations and for organisations that help carers.

Disabled

There were 106 grants made in this category totalling £785,000, ranging from £250 to £35,000. This included 33 grants of £10,000 or more, with beneficiaries including Winged Opportunities Without Limits (£35,000), Fellowship Trust (£26,000), Children's Society (£20,000), Bacup Trust (£15,000) and Abilitynet (£10,000)

Community service

There were 156 grants made totalling £787,000, ranging from under £200 to £60,000, although most grants in this major programme are for £2,000 or less. There were 24 grants of £10,000 or more. Beneficiaries included Prince's Trust and Business in the Community (£60,000 each), Airborne Initiative and Emmaus (£30,000 each), Depaul Trust (£25,000), Voices for the Child in Care (£20,000), Safe in the City (£15,000) and National Galleries of Scotland (£10,000).

Elderly

Grants to 42 organisations totalled £389,000. Of grants made, 18 were for £10,000 or more and included those to Age Concern –Devon (£30,000), RSAS – Age Care (£25,000), Deafway (£20,000) and Invalids at Home and Take a Break (£10,000 each).

Special projects

The foundation has established a new category aimed at dealing with issues of poverty, homelessness, drugs and crime prevention and the rehabilitation of young offenders. We continue to support organisations like the Foundation Training Company and CFAR, working in prisons and immediately post release, helping create opportunities that prevent reoffending, whilst actively encouraging positive changes in legislation. The foundation is also working on community regeneration projects, investigating ways and means to encourage greater community cohesion in areas ravaged by crime, racial violence and the impact of hard drugs.

Contact the trust for further information on this category before submitting an application.

Medicine

Grants were made to 10 organisations totalling £159,000. Beneficiaries included Help the Hospices (£100,000), Dr Kershaw's Hospice (£20,000), Royal College of Surgeons of England (£3,000) and St John's Ambulance – Suffolk (£2,000).

The foundation has changed its policy on funding hospices. Applications should now be made through Help the Hospices who consider applications and make recommendations to trust.

Promotion of Christian religion

One large grant of £1.9 million was made to the foundation's subsidiary, The Foundation for Christian Communication as part of a substantial and continuing commitment. This is not an open programme and unsolicited applications will not be considered.

Comment

As the statutory youth services have dissolved, this foundation's active programmes have been remarkably important in holding together parts of the youth movement. The foundation is remarkable for its devolved nature, with most of its senior staff dispersed around the country and with its grants wholly lacking the London and south of England focus that is general among trusts.

Exclusions

Grants to registered charities only. Appeals from individuals or appeals from registered charities on behalf of named individuals will not be considered; neither will appeals from overseas or from UK-based organisations where the object of the appeal is overseas.

In an endeavour to contain the calls made upon the foundation to a realistic level, the directors have continued with their policy of not, in general, making grants to projects involved with:

- agriculture and farming;
- cathedrals and churches (except where community facilities are involved);
- culture;
- university and school building and bursary funds;
- medical research.

Applications

Applications should be addressed to the general appeals office at the address below.

There is no formal application form, but for administrative purposes it is helpful if the actual appeal letter can be kept to one or two sides of A4, which can be supported by reports, etc. General appeals, including unsolicited appeals relating to youth projects, should include:

- charity registration number;
- full details of project and total cost involved;
- amount already raised;
- the most recent audited set of accounts.

Preliminary enquiries are welcomed. Unsolicited appeals are considered quarterly (see below). All appeals are acknowledged and applicants advised as to when they will be considered. The trustees meet quarterly in March, June, September and December.

The Joseph Rank Trust

The Methodist Church, Christian-based social work

£1.7 million (2004)

Beneficial area UK and Ireland.

11a Station Road West, Oxted, Surrey RH8 9EE

Tel. 01883 717919 **Fax** 01883 717919

Email secretary@ranktrust.org

Website www.ranktrust.org

Correspondent John A Wheeler

Trustees *Colin Rank, chair; Revd David Cruise; Revd Paul Hulme; Gay Moon; Sue Warner; James Rank; Michael Shortt; J Anthony Reddall; Revd Dr R John Tudor.*

Charity Commission no. 1093844

Information available Full and clear accounts and grants lists with an excellent annual report were provided by the trust.

Summary

Up to 60% of the trust's grants are for the maintenance and improvement of Methodist churches. Most of the remainder is for a range of welfare activities, especially for youth and generally but not always carried on by Methodist or other church-based organisations.

Only a small number of new beneficiary organisations are supported each year. In recent years the trustees have been active in implementing the aims identified in a review of the trust's activities in 2001, including being more proactive in the approach to grant giving. As a result the likelihood of grants being made in response to unsolicited appeals will further diminish.

General

This is a Christian-based trust particularly interested in initiatives established by Christians to meet social needs. It grew out of a number of trusts initiated by Joseph Rank, but is separate to the Rank Foundation. At the end of 2002 the Joseph Rank Benevolent Trust ceased operations, with its assets being transferred to the Joseph Rank Trust. Effectively the procedure was a name change.

The trust's areas of interest

The directors have identified two main areas of interest, as follows:

1. The adaptation of Methodist Church properties with a view to providing improved facilities for use both by the church itself and in its work in the community in which it is based.
2. Work with young people.

In the case of work on Methodist Church properties, the directors only consider applications that are put forward for their consideration by either the Property Committee of the Church, which is based in Manchester, or the London Committee, which is based at Central Hall, Westminster. The directors do not consider applications put forward by individual churches.

In the case of work with young people, the directors work mainly with the Youth Department of the Methodist Church or with The Rank Foundation, a charity established by J. Arthur (Lord) Rank, a son of the Founder. That being the case, it is seldom possible to offer support to unsolicited appeals received for that area of work.

In considering all appeals, the directors take into account the primary objective of the trust, which is to advance the Christian faith.

After earmarking funds to support their main areas of interest the directors are prepared to consider other unsolicited appeals, although resources remaining to support such appeals are limited. Unsolicited appeals are selected for consideration by the directors that demonstrate, in their view, a

Christian approach to the practical, educational and spiritual needs of people.

Grants in 2004

During the year the trust made 105 grants totalling £1.7 million (£2.6 million in the previous year. Grants were categorised as follows (with 2003 figures in brackets):

	2004	**(2003)**
Church property schemes	£891,000 51%	£1.6 million 63%
Youth projects	£551,000 32%	£560,000 21%
Community service	£189,000 11%	£268,000 10%
Religion – education	£55,000 3%	£65,000 3%
Elderly people	£32,000 1.8%	£49,000 1.9%
Health and healing	£10,000 0.6%	—
Disabled people	£2,000 0.1%	£23,000 0.9%

The trust also showed the geographical distribution of grants:

North East	£354,000	20%
Ireland	£230,000	13%
Midlands	£195,000	11%
Anglia	£185,000	11%
North West	£180,000	10%
South West	£121,000	7%
London	£107,000	6%
Wales	£86,000	5%
South East	£84,000	5%
Scotland	£48,000	3%
South Central	£25,000	1%
National	£115,000	7%

Church property schemes

There were 40 grants made in this category. The two largest grants were of £50,000 each to Christ Church – Pendle and Trinity Methodist Church – East Grinstead. Other churches to receive support included Ashdon Methodist Church – Preston, Calvert Memorial Church – Hastings, Killarney Methodist Church, Petts Wood Methodist Church, Tadcaster Methodist Church and Wingrave Methodist Church – Aylesbury. Most grants were for between £10,000 and £40,000.

Youth projects

There were 35 youth projects in total funded during the year. Projects were categorised as general, Methodist Church, 'Youth or Adult' and 'Investing in Success'.

In the general section the largest grant was £20,000 to Forest YMCA of East London towards ecumenical liaison and development work (this represents the final year of a three year commitment). Other beneficiaries included East Belfast WIRE Project (£7,900), Soul in the City (£10,000), Blackrock Youth Centre (£7,000), Carrickfergus Methodist Church (£5,000) and St Giles Trust (£2,500).

Youth projects identified and monitored by the Methodist Church went to Highwoods Methodist Church – Colchester (£47,000), Bramford Road Methodist Church – Ipswich (£27,000) and Furnival Burngreave Community

Projects and Penrith Methodist Church (£25,000 each).

Under 'Youth or Adult?', eight grants were made totalling £217,000. Grants were made to projects which combined training for individual youth workers with project development. Recipients included All Saints Church – Pontefract (£43,000), Mid-Norfolk Youth for Christ (£39,000), Joss Street Hall Association – Invergordon (£38,000), Alliance Youth Works – Coleraine (£32,000) and YMCA George Williams College (£23,000),

Three grants were made under 'Investing in Success'. They were to Birmingham Asbury Methodist Circuit (£55,000), Campitor Limited – Wakefield (£31,000) and Amelia Trust Farm – Vale of Glamorgan (£30,000).

Community service

There were 23 grants made, most of which were instalments of multi-year awards. Larger grants included: £25,000 to St Martin's Centre for Health and Healing towards funding the post of director; £20,000 to Merseyfest towards fostering links between the Christian churches on Merseyside and the communities in which they are based; and £15,000 to Nehemiah Project towards employment costs of a mentor/trainer helping recovering addicts to gain employment skills.

Smaller grants included £10,000 to Family Service Unit – Sheffield, £9,000 to Spires, £7,800 to Addiction Recovery Foundation, £7,000 to CBA Projects Limited, £5,000 to Beulah Scotland, £4,000 to St Michael's York Trust and £3,000 to Gloucestershire Community Chaplaincy.

Religious education

The five beneficiaries were: £35,000 to Alpha International towards an advertising campaign to raise national awareness of the Alpha Course; £8,000 to Gloucestershire University; £4,800 Friends International; and £2,000 to Parish of Christ Church – Newtown.

Disabled, elderly, health

The seven grants from these three categories were £10,000 to Methodist Ministers' Pension Scheme, £9,000 to RADICLE, £5,000 each Bakers' Benevolent Fund and Southwark Churches Care, £3,000 to Contact the Elderly and £2,000 to Community Link-up.

Exclusions

No grants to individuals, for charities on behalf of individuals, or for unregistered organisations.

303

Applications

'On-going commitments, combined with the fact that the directors are taking an increasingly active role in identifying projects to support, means that uncommitted funds are limited and it is seldom possible to make grants in response to unsolicited appeals.'

'If applicants consider that their work might fall within the areas of interest of the trust the following basic information is required:

- charity name and charity registration number;
- an outline of the project for which funding is sought;
- details of the TOTAL amount required to fund the project in its entirety;
- details of the amount already raised, or irrevocably committed, towards the target;
- a copy of the most recent annual report and audited accounts.

'Applicants should endeavour to set out the essential details of a project on no more than two sides of A4 paper, with more detailed information being presented in the form of appendices. In general, it is not helpful to include video or audio cassettes.'

'In normal circumstances, papers received before the middle of February, May, August and November will be considered in March, June, September and December respectively.

'All appeals are acknowledged and the applicants advised that if they do not receive a reply by a specified date it has not been possible for the directors to make a grant.'

The Märit and Hans Rausing Charitable Foundation

National heritage, children, medical research, nature preservation

£795,000 (2003)
Beneficial area UK and worldwide.

39 Sloane Street, London SW1X 9LP
Tel. 020 7235 9560 **Fax** 020 7235 9580

Correspondent Lesley Dean, Secretary
Trustees *Peter A Hetherington; Prof. Anthony R Mellows; Philippa F Blake-Roberts; Sir Edward Cazalet.*
Charity Commission no. 1059714
Information available Full accounts were provided by the trust.

Information available

The trustees will only consider applications for grants in the following fields.

English national heritage

With a preference for:

- conservation and improvement of collections;
- the mounting of exhibitions;
- the increase of public access;

(buildings and general running costs will not be considered).

Children's charities (not individual cases)

- helping particularly gifted children to develop;
- the protection of children from cruelty and abuse;
- the prevention and alleviation of suffering and distress of disabled children.

Medical

- Medical research and medical equipment.

Nature conservation

- The conservation and preservation of wildlife in the countryside in the England.

In 2003 the trust gave £795,000 in grants to organisations in the UK and overseas. The largest grant was made to Lund University in Sweden, which received £301,000. The other overseas grant was made to the International Reconstructive Plastic Surgery (Ghana) Project, which received £25,000.

UK grants were made to 42 organisations (totalling £469,000), only two of which received grants in the previous year (these were Dame Vera Lynn Trust for Children with Cerebral Palsy and Uplands Community College, both receiving £25,000 in 2003).

Other beneficiaries included the Restoration of Appearance and Function Trust and the Weizmann Institute Foundation (£50,000 each), British Association of Adoption & Fostering

(£25,000), St George's Hospital Medical School (£20,000), Philharmonia Orchestra and South Downs Planetarium Trust (£15,000 each), Down's Syndrome Trust and the Royal College of Surgeons (£10,000 each), Action Research and Listening Books (£5,000 each), Industrial Trust (£4,000), Brainwave (£3,000), Sobell House Hospice Charity (£2,000), Barn Owl Trust (£1,000) and Sticky Fingers Playgroup (Wadhurst) (£300).

Exclusions

No grants to individuals. No deficit funding.

Applications

In writing to the trustees (but note that the foundation, which is lightly staffed, already reports that it is receiving an 'overwhelming' number of applications).

The Lisbet Rausing Charitable Fund

Humanities and social science research

£1.6 million (2003)
Beneficial area Unrestricted.

39 Sloane Street, London SW1X 9LP
Tel. 020 7838 7105 **Fax** 020 7235 9580
Email led@arcticnet.com
Correspondent Lesley Dean, Administrator
Trustees *Dr Lisbet Rausing; Dr Sigrid Rausing; Prof. Peter Baldwin.*
Charity Commission no. 1090750
Information available Basic accounts were provided by the trust.

In July 2002 the fund commited £20 million over 10 years to the School of Oriental and African Studies (SOAS) to fund the Hans Rausing Endangered Languages Project.

The project comprises three elements: a documentation programme, which awards grants annually through an international panel for research and documentation worldwide, an archive programme and an academic programme.

In 2003 the language project received an instalment of just over £1 million. There was also one other beneficiary during the year, Fauna and Flora International, which received £611,000.

Applications

'The parameters of our fund do not permit us to consider unsolicited applications. The trustees decide on the purpose and recipients of grants with the help of specialist advice and, if they decide to invite applications within a specific programme, arrangements will be made for appropriate publicity'.

The trustees regret that it will not be possible for them to enter into correspondence on these arrangements.

The Sigrid Rausing Trust

Human rights, women's rights, minority and indigenous rights, social and environmental advocacy

£10.3 million (2004)

Beneficial area Unrestricted.

Eardley House, 4 Uxbridge House, London W8 7SY

Tel. 020 7908 9870 **Fax** 020 7908 9879

Email srtrust@arcticnet.com

Website www.sigrid-rausing-trust.org

Correspondent Jo Andrews, Director

Trustees *Sigrid Rausing; Joshua Mailman; Robert Bernstein; Susan Hitch*

Charity Commission no. 1046769

Information available Brief policy guidelines. Annual report and accounts with list of grants.

Summary

This is a UK-based foundation but the larger grants are given on a wholly international basis. The medium and smaller awards are more often for UK organisations. The trust states that it aims to increase its grant giving to around £15 million by the end of 2006. It does not generally accept unsolicited applications, but there is an open pre-application process, with details on the website.

Work is in the following fields (with number of grants and amounts for 2004):

	No.	Amount
Human rights	27	£4.2 million
Women's rights	23	£2.2 million
Minority and Indigenous Rights	9	£736,000
Social & environmental advocacy	30	£2.9 million
Small Grants	21	£160,000

Guidelines for applicants

The trust offers the following guidelines to its work:

The Sigrid Rausing Trust takes as its guiding framework the Universal Declaration of Human Rights adopted by the United Nations in 1948. The preamble of the Declaration begins with these words: 'Whereas recognition of the inherent dignity and of the equal and inalienable rights of all members of the human family is the foundation of freedom, justice and peace in the world.' The funding categories below are all human rights orientated, and aim to form a coherent framework for the work of the Trust.

The trust's funding is divided into sections as follows:
Human Rights
Research, Support and Advocacy
Women's Rights Advocacy
Social and Economic Participation
Implementation of Rights
Minority Rights
Marginalised Indigenous and Minority People
Lesbian and Gay Rights
Refugees and Migrants
Social and Environmental Advocacy
Corporate and Institutional Accountability
Environmental Justice
Labour Rights

Most of the work of the Trust is in the field of International Human Rights. The Trustees take a particular interest in Women's Rights, and review all applications with regard to their impact on women, in addition to the stated aims of the application. They are interested in lasting social change, and in forming long-term partnerships with the organisations the Trust supports.

All organisations that contact the Trust, where their aims fall within the guidelines, will be carefully considered. Due to the number of applications and the rigorous criteria imposed by the Trustees and Director, it is not possible for all to receive an invitation to apply.

Grants in 2004

During 2004 a total of £10.3 million was distributed in grants.

Human rights

Of grants made in this category, donations were led by £800,000 for Human Rights Watch, which also received £900,000 in the previous year. Other grants included £500,000 to Amnesty International, £350,000 to Human Rights in China, £300,000 to International Crisis Group, £250,000 to the Fund for Global Human Rights, and £200,000 for International Centre for Transitional Justice, £150,000 each to Article 19, Institute for War and Peace Reporting, Interights, £137,000 for Anti-Slavery International, £125,000 for the Children's Legal Centre

Women's Rights.

The largest grants in this category were £275,000 to Womankind Worldwide, and £250,000 to Mama Cash. Other grants included £170,000 to Women Living Under Muslim Laws, £150,000 each to The Hestia Fund and Television Trust for the Environment, £125,000 to Asylum Aid and £120,000 to Camfed, £110,000 to Oxfam. £100,000 each to the Center for Reproductive Rights, African Women's Development Fund, Akina Mama Wa Afrika and Rainbo

The environment

There was a grant of £275,000 to Pesticide Action Network, £250,000 to Global Witness, £160,000 to the European Environmental Bureau, £150,000 each to Global Green Grants, Blacksmith Institute, Intermediate Technology Development Group, the International Institute for Environment and Development and the New World Foundation. Other grants included £135,000 to Chemical Reaction £130,000 to FERN, £125,000 to Friends of the Earth International and the International Rivers Network. £75,000 to Fauna and Flora International, and £50,000 to The Corner House.

Minority and Indigenous Rights

This included a grant of £150,000 to the European Roma Rights Center, £120,000 each to ASTRAEA and International Lesbian and Gay Association, £100,000 to Kurdish Human Rights, £75,000 to the Minority Rights Group and £50,000 for Bail for Immigration Detainees.

Small Grants

Grants included: £10,000 each to the Iraq Body Count Project, Widow's Rights International, Scottish Native Woods, Recontre pour La Paix in Congo, Project Parity, Women in Politics Support Unit, Zimbabwe, Detention Advice Service, London and £5,000 each for the Centre for Civic Initiatives, Azerbaijan, High Weald AONB, the Lydia Project, the Jewish Museum.

Exclusions

No grants are made to individuals.

Applications

In writing to the correspondent, but unsolicited applications cannot normally be considered or acknowledged. There is a very simple initial two-page application form for invited applicants.

The Rayne Foundation

Education, medicine and health, the arts, social welfare, general

£1.3 million (2002/03)
Beneficial area UK.

Carlton House, 33 Robert Adam Street, London W1U 3HR

Tel. 020 7487 9637

Website www.raynefoundation.org.uk

Correspondent The Director

Trustees R A Rayne, chair; Lord Claus Moser; Lord Tom Bridges; Lady Jane Rayne; Prof. Dame Margaret Turner-Warwick.

Charity Commission no. 216291

Information available Annual report and accounts.

The foundation's assets of £41 million produced an income of £1.5 million in 2002/03. The normal grant size is £5,000–£20,000 and may be paid over more than one year.

The foundation describes its aims as:

- helping the most vulnerable or disadvantaged individuals in society, especially children, young people and the elderly;
- supporting work of national importance;
- providing direct benefits or services to people;
- acheiving excellence at all levels;
- supporting neglected causes;
- levering funding from other sources.

Arts

We support all types of art and culture in the arts sector.

Our current areas of special interest in the arts sector are:

- Building projects for performance/ display/conservation facilities (but not building maintenance or repairs);
- Specialist arts-education organisations or the education department of general arts organisations which help children and young people with the transition between the different levels of formal education.

We are unlikely to support applications for performances, temporary exhibitions or festivals.

Education

We support education (at all levels, formal and informal). We believe it is important that people achieve high levels of attainment and that their education is well-rounded.

Our current areas of special interest in the education sector are:

- Bursaries towards student fees or maintenance grants offered by individual university departments and academic institutes for study leading to a taught post-graduate degree, particularly in subjects which are part of recognised emerging research areas. We will not accept applications from or in respect of individual students.
- Encouraging participation by individuals with special physical, learning or emotional needs to take part in structured year out placements organised by charities. We will not accept direct applications from individuals, but only jointly with the charity.
- Support towards the costs (fees or maintenance) of retraining in the UK of refugees who are professionally qualified abroad (although we will not accept applications from or in respect of individuals).

We do not support building projects or equipment at maintained secondary or primary schools, or at any nursery or pre-school.

Health/welfare

We support projects to improve the health of people and to support the development of medical treatment. We wish to support important health or medical areas which are less well-supported by other funders.

We are not structured to support health/ medical research projects directly. We may support specific health/medical research projects, especially those of clear benefit to patients, through other medical research charities, usually only if they are members of the Association of Medical Research Charities (or if they

demonstrate they meet standards equivalent to the Association's Guidelines on Good Research Practice). All charities funded must have the proper infrastructure to evaluate and monitor the research carried out.

Our current areas of special interest in the health/medicine sector are:

- The provision of medical and healthcare for homeless people which involves ways to increase active participation by homeless people in their health.
- Research into the longer-term and broader consequences of specific interventions (e.g. intensive rehabilitation or improved hearing in children or recognition of communication defects etc). For obvious practical reasons the outcome of many types of surgical and medical treatments are often assessed in fairly narrow terms over relatively short periods of time. However, research into the longer term and broader consequences in terms of quality of life, independent employability, self-worth, participation and achievement are less rigorously assessed.

We are unlikely to support the following:

- large medical, research or health related building projects

(although we may fund more modest building projects);

- medical, research or health-related equipment;
- NHS patient treatment;
- undergraduate studies;
- individual bursaries for elective students;
- direct support to medical research projects.

Social welfare

We support all types of social welfare and development work. We are very keen to support new ideas to help solve problems, though we are prepared to consider proposals which are more simply about helping people in need.

We are not currently planning to identify any areas of special interest in the social welfare and development sector.

Grants in 2002/03

there were 244 grants paid to organisations. The annual report included a list of all grants over £10,000. They were broken down as follows, shown here with examples of grants in each category.

Arts – £293,000

There were five grants of £25,000 each made to Imperial War Museum, Kelvingrove Refurbishment Appeal, National Museum and Galleries on Merseyside, Old Vic Theatre Trust and the Rayne Trust. Other beneficiries inlcuded National Gallery (£20,000), Crafts Study Centre (£15,000), London Symphony Orchestra, National Youth Theatre of Great Britain, Shakespeare Schools Festival and Wigmore Hall Trust (£10,000 each).

Education – £85,000

Grants went to Chetham's School of Music (£25,000), Byam Shaw School of Ary (£20,000), University of Bristol (£15,000), 21st Century Trust and British ORT (£13,000 each).

Health and medicine – £430,000

By far the largest donation was £250,000 to University of Edinburgh Development Services. Other beneficiaries included Academy of Medical Sciences and Stoke Mandeville Hospital Charitable Fund (£25,000), Royal Society of Medicine (£20,000) and Abbeyfield Nottingham, British Dyslexia Association, Mental Health Foundation and University of Cape Town Trust (£10,000 each)

Social welfare – £389,000

The beneficiaries of the two largest grants were Jerusalem Foundation (£52,000) and the Rayne Trust (£50,000). Other beneficiaries included Lansdowne House Alcohol Recovery Unit (£30,000), New Israel Fund (£23,000), Council for Assisting Refugee Academics (£22,000), Caldecott Foundation and Westlon Housing Association (£20,000 each), Union Chapel Project (£15,000), Student Partnership Worldwide (£12,000) and Drug and Alcohol Foundation, English Pen, Northamptonshire Association of Youth Clubs and Samaritans (£10,000 each).

Exclusions

No grants to individuals.

Applications

'Charities whose proposals meet all the Foundation's aims and which fall within one or more of the sectors we support are asked to send a letter of application to the director, on no more than four sides of A4 (please do not include an sae). Please include a copy of the full annual report and accounts, but no other enclosure is required at this stage. The letter should clearly explain how the work will meet all our aims, including:

- what the charity does, why this work is needed and who will benefit;
- summary of objectives, timetable and how you measure success;
- identify who is responsible for leading the work and their experience;
- showing how the charity will be viable during and after the work;
- summarising the costs and the income/deficit of the work;
- request a specific sum and indicate how any shortfall will be funded;
- give the name and contact details of up to two unconnected referees.

Please do not email or fax applications to us. They will not be accepted. Applications may be submitted at any time. There are no deadlines.

The Sir James Reckitt Charity

Society of Friends (Quakers), general

£594,000 to organisations (2003)

Beneficial area Hull and the East Riding of Yorkshire, UK and occasional support of Red Cross or Quaker work overseas.

7 Derrymore Road, Willerby, East Yorkshire HU10 6ES

Tel. 01482 655861

Email jim@derrymore.karoo.co.uk

Website www.sirjamesreckitt.co.uk

Correspondent J McGlashan, Administrator

Trustee *J H Holt, chair and 13 others, mainly descendants of the founder.*

Charity Commission no. 225356

Information available Guidelines for applicants. Report and accounts provided by the trust.

Summary

The charity gives grants to a wide range of local charities in Hull and the East Riding of Yorkshire as well as to some national charities. Quaker organisations and those in line with Quaker beliefs are supported, and there is an emphasis on the broad category of 'social work'. At least half of the charity's grants are awarded over a period of years and many organisations are regular recipients. It has a list of regular beneficiaries which it supports on an annual basis, although the recipients are informed that the grant may end at any time at the discretion of the trustees. Most grants are for £5,000 or less.

General

In 2003 the charity had assets of almost £16 million, an income of £676,000 and it gave £632,000 in grants, mainly to organisations, with £28,000 to individuals.

In accordance with the wishes of the founder, the trust gives priority to:

- purposes in all localities connected with the Society of Friends (Quakers)
- purposes connected with Hull and the East Riding of Yorkshire.

Other areas of support are charities, both national and regional, particularly those concerned with current social issues, and whose work extends to the Hull area.

International causes are considered in exceptional circumstances, such as major disasters, with support usually being channelled through Society of Friends or British Red Cross Society.

Support for new projects which have not yet gained charitable status is usually channelled through an existing registered charity.

Appeals from individual Quakers need the support of their local monthly meeting. Appeals from other individuals are usually only considered from residents of Hull and the East Riding of Yorkshire.

Support is not given to causes of a warlike or political nature.

The guidelines also state that the trustees will not normally consider a further appeal from an organisation not on the subscription list if a grant has been paid in the previous two years.

Grants in 2003

Grants were made in the following categories:

Social work – grants to 112 organisations totalling £210,000

The largest grant in this category was £20,000 to British Red Cross. Other grants included Doorsteps of Hull (£9,600), Sobriety Project (£6,300), Hull CVS (£5,800), Hull Independent Housing Aid Centre (£5,000), Calvery Trust (£3,200), Hull and East Yorkshire Mind (£2,900), Citizen's Advice – Hull,

East Yorkshire CVS (£2,300), Intermediate Technology, Listening Books and Ulster Quaker Service Committee (£2,100 each), FARM Africa and LEAP Confronting Conflict (£2,000 each), Mental Health Foundation and Centre 88 (£1,800), Alone in London, Mobility Trust and Hull Compact Limited (£1,500 each), Children and Family Action in Withernsea (£1,300), Quaker Social Action (£1,100) and British Executive Services Overseas, Cherry Tree Community Association, Crisis Pregnancy Centre, Hull Jewish Community Care, Mental Health Action Group and Prisoners Abroad and Smart Move (£1,000 each).

Payments under £1,000 each were made to 38 organisations totalling £22,000.

Education – 19 grants totalling £122,000

There were eight grants made of over £10,000 each. Beneficiaries were Ackworth School (£16,000), Leighton Park School (£14,000) and Hymers College, Mount School, Saffron Walden School, Sibford School, Sidcot School and Bootham School (£11,000 each). Other beneficiaries included Hull University Development Fund (£8,000), Endeavour Training (£2,000) and Field Studies Council (£1,200).

Payments under £1,000 each were made to five organisations totalling £122,000.

Medical – grants to 30 organisations totalling £107,000

There were three grants were made of £10,000 or more to: the re-treat (£18,000); Dove House Hospice (£17,000); and the Artificial Heart Foundation (£10,000). Other beneficiaries included Action for ME (£5,100), Cornerhouse (£4,500), Yorkshire Cancer Research (£3,400), British Deaf Association (£2,600), British Home for the Incurables (£2,400), Martin House Children's Hospice (£2,000), National Hospital for Neurology and Neurosurgery (£1,500) and Stroke Association (£1,100).

Payments under £1,000 each were made to seven organisations totalling £4,100.

Religion – grants to 31 organisations totalling £105,000

By far the largest grant in this category was £55,000 to British Yearly Meeting. Other beneficiaries included Woodbrooke College (£10,000), Holy Trinity Church Appeal Hull and Responding to Conflict (£5,000 each), Pickering & Hull Monthly Meeting

(£2,100), Yorkshire Friends Holiday School (£2,000), Friends Fellowship of Healing (£1,700), North Somerset and Wiltshire Monthly Meeting (£1,500) and West Midlands Quaker Peace Education Project and York Minster Fund (£1,000 each).

Payments under £1,000 each were made to 11 organisations totalling £5,900.

Children – 15 grants to organisations totalling £25,000

Beneficiaries included Humber Pre School Learning Alliance (£5,000), Kids Hull Family Centre (£4,600), Barnardos (£3,200), Hull Children's Adventure Playground Association (£1,500) and Starlight Children's Foundation (£1,000).

Payments under £1,000 each were made to six organisations totalling £3,300.

Youth – grants to 16 organisations totalling £18,000

Beneficiaries included Humberside County Scout Group (£2,600), Humberside Youth Association Limited (£2,000), Hull Sea Cadets (£1,600), Rhema Youth Works (£1,500) and Hull Kingston Scouts, Jubilee Sailing Trust and National Association of Clubs for Young People (£1,000 each).

Payments under £1,000 each were made to six organisations totalling £2,700.

Elderly – grants to 6 organisations totalling £10,000

Beneficiaries included Abbeyfield Beverly Society Limited (£3,900), Age Concern Hull (£2,000) and Yorkshire Friends Housing Society (£1,000).

One unlisted payment of £500 was also made.

Environment – grants to 5 organisations totalling £4,400

Listed beneficiaries were Yorkshire Wildlife Trust (£1,900) and Withernsea Millennium Green Trust (£1,000).

Payments under £1,000 each were made to three organisations totalling £1,500.

Further monies were distributed to individuals under the categories of social work (£15,000) and youth (£14,000).

Exclusions

Grants are normally made only to registered charities. Local organisations outside the Hull area are not supported, unless their work has regional implications. Grants are not normally

made to individuals other than Quakers and residents of Hull and the East Riding of Yorkshire.

Applications

In writing to the correspondent, giving details of the project, the costs involved and the benefits it will bring. Guidelines are available on request.

Applications are measured against the charity's guidelines and decisions are taken at the twice-yearly meeting of trustees.

The Christopher H R Reeves Charitable Trust

Food allergies, disability

£326,000 (2003)

Beneficial area UK.

Hinwick Lodge, Nr Wellingborough, Northamptonshire NN29 7JQ

Tel. 01234 781090 **Fax** 01234 781090

Correspondent E M Reeves, Trustee

Trustees *E M Reeves; V Reeves; M Kennedy.*

Charity Commission no. 266877

Information available Information was provided by the trust.

The trust states that it is 'holding about 75% of its income and capital for application in the limited area of food allergy and related matters. Nearly all the income in this section has already been committed to Allergy Research and Environmental Health at King's College, London and to the production and distribution of a database of research references under the title of Allergy and Environmental Medicine Database'.

New appeals related to food allergy and intolerance are invited and a response will be made to applicants.

The remaining 25% of the trust's income and capital will be held for general donations. The main area of interest is in disability. Donations will largely be made to charities already associated with the trust. Only successful applicants will receive a response.

In 2003 the trust had assets of £3.5 million generating a low income of £121,000. Grants were made to 35 beneficiaries totalling £326,000.

The largest grants were made to Family Action in our Region (FAIR) (£200,000 in total) of which the trustees of this trust are also trustees.

Other beneficiaries included RNIB (£50,000), Rare Breeds Survival Trust (£10,000), St John Ambulance, Timespan and the Solicitors' Benevolent Fund (£2,000 each) and Cancer Research UK, Mayday Trust, Clergy Orphan Corporation and Project Charitable Trust (£1,000 each).

Exclusions

No grants for: individuals; overseas travel and expeditions; animal charities; church/community hall/school appeals outside the north Bedfordshire area; overseas aid; children's charities; drugs/alcohol charities; mental health charities; or education.

Applications

In writing to the correspondent, including a copy of the latest annual report and accounts. Trustees meet five times a year in March, May, July, September and November. Only successful applicants will receive a reply.

Reuben Brothers Foundation

Healthcare, education, general
See below
Beneficial area UK and overseas.

6th Floor, 42–43 Upper Berkeley Street, London W1H 5QL
Tel. 020 7972 0094 **Fax** 020 7972 0097
Email rbfoundation@motcomb.co.uk
Correspondent Malcolm Robin Turner, Trustee
Trustees *David Reuben; Simon Reuben; Malcolm Robin Turner*
Charity Commission no. 1094130
Information available Limited information available.

Summary

This relatively new trust was established in 2002 as an outlet for the charitable giving of billionaire property investors David and Simon Reuben. Robin Turner,

the third trustee of the foundation and its main correspondent, is the director of Motcomb Estates Ltd, the company that deals solely with the Reuben brothers' property portfolio.

General

The foundation was endowed by the brothers with a donation of $100 million (£54.1 million), with the income generated to be given to a range of charitable causes, particularly to healthcare organisations and for educational purposes. It is likely that organisations in India and Iraq, where the brothers have their roots, may benefit as well as organisations in the UK.

Unfortunately the foundation's first accounts for the 18-month period up to the end of December 2003, although submitted by the foundation, were not available to view in the public files at the Charity Commission.

Applications

In writing to the correspondent, although the trust has stated that applications are by invitation only.

The Richmond Parish Lands Charity

General, in Richmond, Surrey
£606,000 to organisations (2003/04)

Beneficial area Richmond, Kew, North Sheen, East Sheen, Ham, Petersham and Mortlake.

The Vestry House, 21 Paradise Road, Richmond, Surrey TW9 1SA
Tel. 020 8948 5701
Website www.rplc.org.uk
Correspondent Mrs Penny Rkaina, Clerk to the trustees
Trustees *The Mayor ex-officio of Richmond; three nominated by the borough of Richmond (not necessarily councillors or officials); five nominated by local voluntary organisations; up to five co-opted.*
Charity Commission no. 200069

Information available Detailed annual report and accounts, guidelines, including a clear map of the area of benefit, and application forms.

Established in 1786, the charity supports a wide range of causes in some parts of the borough of Richmond-upon-Thames, as outlined above. It makes around 100 revenue grants each year for between £500 and £15,000. At least two in three of the organisations have been supported in the previous year, although the trustees prefer not to make commitments for ongoing funding. The charity can make a few grants for capital purposes, in the same range as the revenue grants, each year.

In 2003/04 the charity had assets of £46 million, which produced a gross income of £1.4 million. After expenditure of £961,000, including property expenses and support costs, a total of £606,000 was given in grants to 124 organisations.

Grants were classified in the following fields, with totals for 2003/04 (2002/03 figures shown in brackets):

The relief of poverty	£114,000	(£132,000)
Social and medical welfare	£123,000	(£131,000)
Mental health and learning disability	£68,000	(£67,000)
Physical disability	£12,000	(£15,500)
Youth/sport	£35,000	(£63,000)
Music and the arts	£22,000	(£13,000)
Welfare of the elderly	£97,000	(£99,000)
Education projects	£128,000	(£112,000)
Education fund	£79,000	(£85,000)
Community centres/general	£94,000	(£103,000)

This includes £77,000 that was awarded to individuals from the charity's education fund; £33,000 in heating vouchers to older people through its WARM campaign, and £55,000 in small grants to individuals in severe need.

In 2001 the charity implemented a four-year plan to take forward the priorities identified through its 'review of need'. The three priorities were:

- the needs of young people
- Mortlake
- housing and accommodation.

Grants ranged from £53 up to £45,000, though most were between £500 and £5,000. Beneficiaries of the largest grants were: MIND – Vineyard project (£45,000); Richmond CAB (£35,000); Care Leavers' Support (£20,000); SPEAR (£19,000); Age Concern and Mortlake Community Association (£18,000 each); Cambrian Centre – core costs, Crossroads and Integrated Neurological Services (£16,000 each); Princess Alice Hospice and Richmond Adult and Community College – HALO scheme (£15,000 each); Cambrian Centre – youth club and Richmond Music Trust

(£12,000 each); and Addiction Support and Care Agency, Orange Tree Theatre, Orleans House Gallery – Stables Education Centre and Richmond Good Neighbours – general support (£10,000 each).

Exclusions

Projects and organisations located outside the benefit area, unless it can be demonstrated that a substantial number of residents from the benefit area will gain from their work. UK charities (even if based in the benefit area), except for that part of their work which caters specifically for the area.

Applications

If you would like some clarification on whether your organisation would qualify for a grant, please contact the charity (020 8948 5701) who will be able to give you guidance. You will also be given an application form. You may also download an application form and relevant details from the charity's website.

When you send in your application form be sure that you have filled in all sections and that you have enclosed all the documents requested. If your organisation or project is new, you will probably need to write a covering letter giving relevant background and explanation.

On receipt of your application the clerk to the trustees will evaluate it and may wish to ask further questions before submitting it to the trustees for their consideration. You may be assured that all eligible applications will be put before the trustees.

Trustees' meetings are held eight times a year, when eligible applications received 14 days beforehand are considered. A schedule of meetings and deadlines is provided in the guidance pack and on the website. They may decide that they need further information before they can make a decision regarding a grant. You will be advised by letter within 10 days of the meeting whether or not your application has been successful. If you wish to know before that you may of course telephone the clerk.

Ridgesave Limited

General, education

£660,000 (2001/02)
Beneficial area UK.

c/o 1075 Finchley Road, London NW11 0PU
Correspondent The Trustees
Trustees J L Weiss; Mrs H Z Weiss; E Englander.
Charity Commission no. 288020
Information available Annual report and accounts on file at the Charity Commission, but without a list of grants.

This trust was set up to support organisations for education or other general charitable purposes. In 2002/03 the charity had an income of £611,000 and a total expenditure of £787,000. This information was taken from the Charity Commission database, unfortunately this was not available to view in the public files. In 2001/02 the trust had assets of £3 million and an income of £607,000.

Grants totalled £660,000. No further information was available, as unfortunately a grants list was not included in the accounts.

Applications

In writing to the correspondent.

The Robertson Trust

General, in Scotland

£6 million (2002/03)
Beneficial area Scotland.

85 Berkeley Street, Glasgow G3 7DX
Tel. 0141 221 3151 **Fax** 0141 221 0744
Email admin@therobertsontrust.org.uk
Website www.therobertsontrust.org.uk
Correspondent Sir Lachlan Maclean, Secretary
Trustees Ian J G Good, chair; Thomas M Lawrie; Sir Lachlan Maclean; Richard J A Hunter; David D Stevenson; Mrs Barbara M Kelly.
Scottish Charity no. SC002970
Information available Annual report and accounts. Annual review. Guidelines for applicants. Biannual newsletter.

Summary

A wide range of organisations are supported each year, with grants of all sizes, although more than half the grant total reported above was spent in one of the four priority areas:

- care;
- education;
- medical charities
- drug prevention and treatment.

During 2000/01 a small grants programme was created to allow smaller charities to apply for one-off donations of up to £3,000 for a particular project or activity. Outside this programme, there is no set minimum or maximum grant size.

General

The trust was established in 1961 by the Robertson sisters, who inherited a controlling interest in a couple of whisky companies (now the Edrington Group) from their father and wished to ensure the dividend income from the shares would be given to charitable purposes.

In 2002/03 the trust had an income of £6.7 million from assets of £235 million. Most of the assets are still in the form of shares in the private Edrington Group (which is controlled by the trust) and which cannot be freely sold under the terms of the trust.

Guidelines for the trust read as follows:

The trustees have currently identified four priority areas for funding which are:

Care

Examples include residential homes and day care centres for older people, charities supporting people with disabilities or mental health problems, services for people who are homeless and family support groups.

Drug prevention and treatment

For example drug and alcohol rehabilitation and/or education programmes, projects working with children who are at risk of misusing drugs and services working with recovering drug addicts to assist them back into training and employment.

Education

This includes schools, colleges or other projects for children and young people with special needs, support for capital developments at further education establishments and informal community-based education activities.

Medical

Examples include hospices, cancer relief charities and charities supporting people with medical conditions such as diabetes or asthma.

These priority areas account for a minimum of 40% of the trust's expenditure each year but applications will be considered from most fields of charitable activity.

The Robertson Trust currently disburses £6 million a year. There are no minimum or maximum donations. The trust does operate a small grant scheme for smaller charities to apply for one-off donations of up to £3,000 to support a particular project or activity.

The trust prefers to offer a contribution towards the total funds required for both capital and revenue requests. Core funding or specific project costs will be considered and may be for a maximum period of three years. As an example revenue grants towards salary costs average between £5,000–10,000 a year. Significant donations over £50,000 are usually only considered in the trust's priority areas. An organisation considering applying for a major donation is advised to telephone the trust beforehand for an informal discussion.

In 2002/03, out of 782 applicants, 470 grants, totalling £6 million, were awarded in the following areas:

Care	£1.6 million (180 grants)
Drugs	£521,000 (9)
Educational	£1.6 million (71)
Medical	£1 million (15)
Animal welfare	£63,000 (8)
Arts, culture and heritage	£205,000 (48)
Community	£742,000 (117)
Environment	£147,000 (12)
Sport	£150,000 (10)

Grants were also broken down by size, as follows:

up to £1,000	60
£1,001–£5,000	180
£5,001–£10,000	150
£10,001–£20,000	55
over £20,000	25

There were 11 grants made over £100,000 each.

The main donation in the education category was £362,726 to Robertson Scholarship Trust to fund the bursary award scheme. The trust also made donations to Angus College (£200,000) and Kibble Education and Care Centre, Lauder College Centenary Trust (£100,000 each).

In the medical category, the main donation of £550,000 went to University of Strathclyde for the Laboratory of Electronic Sterilisation Technologies, £250,000 to the Ninewells Cancer Campaign for a Photon Radio Surgery System and £100,000 each to University of Dundee for a Virtual Reality Simulation Laboratory and University of Aberdeen for a flow Cyclometer in support of Ophthalmology Development.

In the drug abuse category the trust provided funding of £379,000 to University of Glasgow – Centre for Drug Misuse for research into the prevention and treatment of drug addiction in Scotland.

In the care category a donation of £204,000 was made to Children's Hospice Association Scotland for the building of Robin House in Balloch.

Exclusions

The trust does not support:

- individuals or organisations which are not recognised as charities by the Inland Revenue or the Charity Commission;
- general appeals or circulars, including contributions to endowment funds;
- local charities whose work takes place outside Scotland;
- projects which are exclusively or primarily intended to promote political beliefs;
- organisations which have applied within the last 12 months;
- students or organisations for personal study, travel, or for expeditions, whether in Scotland or not.

The trust is unlikely to support:

- projects which are properly the subject of statutory funding;
- projects which collect funds to distribute to others.

Applications

(The trust does not have an application form. It invites application by letter to enable applicants to express themselves in their own words without the restrictions of set questions. However, there are certain details which you will need to include to enable the trust to make an informed decision on whether or not to fund an organisation.

- A brief description of the organisation.
- A description of the project – what do you want to do, where will it take place and how will the work be managed?
- How do you know there is a need for this work?
- What will be the benefits of the work?
- How do you intend to monitor and evaluate the work so that you know whether or not you have been successful?
- What is the income and expenditure budget for the piece of work, including details of funds already raised and other sources being approached?

In addition the trust will require a copy of your most recent annual report and full accounts. If the request is for a donation towards salary costs, a job description will also be required.

The trustees meet every two months in May, July, September, November, February and March. You are advised to submit your application as soon as it is ready and it would be unusual to have to wait more than three months for a decision. You may be contacted for more information or to arrange an assessment visit).

Mrs L D Rope Third Charitable Settlement

General

Around £1 million (2003/04)

Beneficial area UK and overseas, with a particular interest in Suffolk.

Crag Farm, Boyton, Near Woodbridge, Suffolk IP12 3LH

Tel. 01473 288 987 (office hours)
Fax 01473 217182

Correspondent Crispin M Rope, Trustee

Trustees *C M Rope; P H Jolly.*

Charity Commission no. 290533

Information available Annual report and accounts are on file at the Charity Commission.

Summary

This trust is based near Ipswich, and takes a keen interest in helping people from its local area. Most of the funds are already committed to projects it has initiated itself, or to ongoing relationships. Unfortunately, only about one in ten applications to this trust can be successful.

Guidelines

The trust produces detailed guidelines for applicants, from which the main points are as follows:

Our charitable trust was founded in 1984. We are based near Ipswich, in Suffolk, and take a keen interest in helping people from our local area, although we do also help other charities and individuals throughout the UK and overseas.

Roughly 75% of our grants are used to develop our own projects each year but there are funds left over for people who write in to us.

Our priorities

'Our trust deed gives the following descriptions:

Relief of Poverty

Support for a number of causes and individuals where the trustees have longer term knowledge and experience, particularly those both in the UK and in the Third World who are little catered for by other charities ... or are in particularly deprived areas. ...

Education

Support for a proposed airship museum; support for Catholic schools in the general area of Ipswich; and projects relating to the interaction of mathematics and physical science with philosophy.

Religion

Support for the Roman Catholic religion and ecumenical work, both generally and for specific institutions connected historically with the families of William Oliver Jolly and his wife Alice and their descendants.

General

Public and other charitable purposes in the general region of south east Suffolk and in particular the parish of Kesgrave and the areas surrounding it, including Ipswich.

Our trustees' judgement is based on a desire to help where it is most needed, particularly those charities and individuals who find it hard to find funding from other sources or who come from the more deprived areas.

Successful unsolicited applications to the charity usually display a combination of the following features:

- Size: The trustees very much prefer to encourage charities that work at 'grassroots' level within their community. Such charities are unlikely to have benefited greatly from grant funding from local, national (including funds from the National Lottery) or European authorities. They are also less likely to be as wealthy in comparison with other charities that attract popular support on a national basis. The charities assisted usually cannot afford to pay for the professional help other charities may use to raise funds.
- Volunteers: The trustees prefer applications from charities that are able to show they have a committed and proportionately large volunteer force.
- Administration: The less a charity spends on paying for its own administration, particularly as far as staff salaries are concerned, the more it is likely to be considered by the trustees.

- Areas of interest: Charities with the above characteristics that work in any of the following areas:

  – Helping people who struggle to live on very little income, including the homeless.
  – Helping people who live in deprived inner city and rural areas of the UK, particularly young people who lack the opportunities that may be available elsewhere.
  – Helping charities in our immediate local area of south east Suffolk.
  – Helping to support family life.
  – Helping disabled people.
  – Helping Roman Catholic charities and ecumenical projects.

Grants made to charities outside the primary beneficial area of south east Suffolk are usually one-off and small in scale (in the range between £100 to £750).

Unlike many trusts, we can consider helping people on a personal basis. We give priority, as we do with charities, to people struggling to live on little income, with an emphasis on those from our local area.

In 2003/04 the trust had an income of £2.4 million and a total expenditure of £1.1 million. Grants were made totalling around £1 million. Unfortunately, no further information was available for this year.

Recent projects

The trust's recent major beneficiaries and long-term projects, for amounts up to £80,000, include the following: Roman Catholic Diocese of East Anglia, for funding of building work on Voluntary Aided Schools and to support introduction of pension scheme for Diocesan Priests; Science/Human Dimension Project, Jesus College, Cambridge was designed to improve public awareness of important philosophical and general implications of developments in science and mathematics; Westminster Diocese – Depaul Trust, to fund a project to encourage the greater use of volunteers by the Depaul Trust itself and more generally; CAFOD, for which the trustees continue to concentrate overseas giving on specific projects with which they have a long term relationship and on CAFOD projects; Kesgrave Town Council – Pavilion, towards the construction of a pavilion for the new youth football ground; Hope House Suffolk, for a project to house four young people who are disabled and require constant care.

The trust usually makes many small grants, with previous beneficiaries including Ipswich Crossroads, Lowestoft

Volunteer Bureau, Reality at Work in Scotland and Anti-Slavery International.

Comment

Despite ample warning, and their obligation to the contrary, the Charity Commission were unable to give us sight of this trust's accounts.

Exclusions

The following are the main exclusions for unsolicited applications (further information on these can be found in the guidelines):

- national charities;
- replacement of statutory funding;
- requests for core funding;
- buildings;
- medical research/health care, except in the immediate local area;
- students, except for a few overseas postgraduate science students in the last stages of their studies;
- schools, except in the local area;
- environmental charities and animal welfare;
- the arts;
- 'matched' funding except on a small scale;
- individuals – repayment of debts.

Applications

Please send a concise letter (preferably one side of A4) explaining the main details of your request. Please always send your most recent accounts and a budgeted breakdown of the sum you are looking to raise. The trust will also need to know whether you have applied to other funding sources and whether you have been successful elsewhere. Your application should say who your trustees are and include a daytime telephone number. Individuals should write a concise letter including details of household income and expenses, daytime telephone number and the name of at least one personal referee.

The Rose Foundation

Grants for building projects

£939,000 (2002/03)

Beneficial area In and around London.

28 Crawford Street, London W1H 1LN

Tel. 020 7262 1155 **Fax** 020 7724 2044

Correspondent Martin Rose, Trustee

Trustees *Martin Rose; Alan Rose; John Rose; Paul Rose.*

Charity Commission no. 274875

Information available Annual report and accounts were provided by the trust.

Established in 1977, the foundation supports charities requiring assistance for their building projects, giving small grants to benefit as large a number of people as possible rather than large grants to small specific groups. The foundation applied to the Charity Commission to modernise its trust deed in 2002, which was to make it more applicable to how the foundation operates rather than to change how it works.

Grants are made towards small self-contained schemes of less than £200,000 in or around London and range from £5,000 to £15,000 each. Previously the trust has given up to £30,000, but reduced this figure to keep to its spirit of giving a large number of smaller grants despite the decline of the stock market in recent years. Projects should commence between January and June, with the applications submitted by the end of the preceding March to allow sufficient time for the foundation to become involved with the design and construction process to ensure economy of cost and effectiveness in design (although the advice is purely for guidance with all final decisions on the project being made by the applicant).

In 2002/03 the foundation had assets of £23 million and an income of £798,000. Grants to 63 organisations were made totalling £939,000.

Grants were led by £330,000 to Ability UK and £194,000 to New Amsterdam Charitable Foundation.

Other grants were in the range of £1,000 to £30,000 and included: £30,000 to Brighton College; £23,000 to Ravenstone Primary School; £22,000 each to the British Community Trust – Peru and Rheumatology Discretionary Fund; £21,000 to the Spires Centre; £20,000 to Hammerson Home Charitable Trust; £18,000 to University College School; £10,000 each to Ace of Clubs, Canonbury School Foundation, Museum of London, Royal Academy of Arts, St Martin-in-the-Fields Almshouse and Westminster Eduction Action Zone; £8,500 to Norwood Ltd; £8,000 to Royal National Theatre; £7,500 to Edgware Masorti Synagogue; £5,000 to the Peter Pan Trust; £2,000 to World Jewish Relief.

Unlisted smaller grants went to 24 organisations totalling £5,400.

Exclusions

The foundation can support any type of building project (decoration, construction, repairs, extensions, adaptations) but not the provision of equipment (such as computers, transportation and so on). Items connected with the finishes, such as carpets, curtains, wallpaper and so on, should ideally comprise a part of the project not financed by the foundation.

Applications

In writing to the correspondent. Applications should be received by the end of March for building projects starting between January and August of the following year, with final decisions usually made in mid-June. The trustees meet formally three times a year, and consult informally on a constant basis.

The Rothschild Foundation

Arts, culture, general

£507,000 (2002/03)

Beneficial area Unrestricted, with a special interest in Buckinghamshire.

The Dairy, Queen Street, Waddesdon, Aylesbury, Buckinghamshire HP18 0JW

Tel. 01296 653235 **Fax** 01296 651142

Email fiona.sinclair@nationaltrust.org.uk

Correspondent Fiona Sinclair

Trustees *Sir Edward Cazalet; Lord Rothschild; Lady Rothschild; Hannah Rothschild; SJP Trustee Company Ltd.*

Charity Commission no. 230159

Information available Annual report and accounts, without an analysis of grants.

General

This foundation was set up in 1956 by James Armand de Rothschild, of the Rothschild banking dynasty, for general charitable purposes. In 2000 the foundation also established a Buckinghamshire small grants programme to provide support for projects and activities within the county.

In 2002/03 assets stood at £23.5 million, generating a very low return of £255,000;

donations of £681,000 brought the foundation's total income to £936,000. Grants were made during the year totalling £507,000.

Grants in 2002/03

Grants during the year were broken down in the foundation's accounts into several categories, the names of which changed slightly from the previous year, although the general focus remains the same, with heritage the main priority. Apart from two large donations, no grant was for more than £15,000.

Arts, heritage and culture – £376,000

The two largest donations, as in the previous year, were made in this category. The foundation made a grant of £200,000 to the National Trust for the restoration of Waddesdon Manor near Aylesbury, a project which has received substantial support in recent years, and which during 2002/03 accounted for almost 40% of the foundation's grant total. This stately manor was built by the great-uncle of the foundation's settlor, Baron Ferdinand de Rothschild, to house his vast collection of 18th century art and furniture. It was donated to the National Trust in 1957 with the management being overseen by Lord Jacob Rothschild. As in the previous year the other large donation was made to Butrint Foundation (£90,000) for the restoration and development of the Butrint archeological site in Southern Albania. Other beneficiaries included Whitley Laing Foundation (£15,000), Artists on Film (£12,000), Burlington Magazine and Royal Academy Trust (£10,000 each), Anglo-Israel Association (£6,000), Unicorn Children's Theatre (£5,000), Bodleian Library (£4,000) and British Friends of Israel Philharmonic, English Chamber Orchestra and Music Society and Venice in Peril (£1,000 each). Smaller donations totalled £540.

Buckinghamshire small grants programme – £66,600

Twelve grants were made in this category to a range of organisations including British Wheelchair Sports Foundation and Iain Rennie Hospice at Home (£10,000 each), Ryder-Cheshire Volunteers (£9,000), PACT (£8,000), Chearsley Under Fives Pre-School and Waddesdon Village Hall Committee (£5,000 each) and Friends of Stoke Mandeville Hospital and Cuddington Church of England School (£2,000 each).

Health and social care – £55,000

Beneficiaries included British Agency for Adoption and Fostering, Louisa Cottages Charity Trust and Shelter (£10,000 each), Friends of Seva Mandir and

National Tenants Resource Centre (£2,000 each), After Adoption and Cancerbacup (£1,000 each) and Medicins du Monde Health, Starlight Foundation and Winfield Trust (£500 each). Smaller donations totalled £2,400.

Education and recreation – £8,600

Four beneficiaries were listed: Oxford Iris Murdoch Appeal and Reeds School Foundation Appeal (£2,500 each), Royal Academy of Music Development (£2,000), Sir John Plum Fellowship Fund (£1,000). Smaller grants totalled £590.

Animals – £1,100

One grant, to Canine Partners (£1,000), was listed, with probably one further donation of £100 being made.

About one-quarter of recipients received a grant in the previous year and probably do so on an annual basis.

Applications

In writing to the correspondent. Applications are considered at half-yearly meetings.

The Rowan Charitable Trust

Overseas aid, social welfare, general

£397,000 (2002/03)
Beneficial area UK, especially Merseyside, and overseas.

c/o Morley Tippett, White Park Barn, Loseley Park, Guildford GU3 1HS

Tel. 01483 575193

Correspondent Emma Harries

Trustees C R Jones; Mrs H E Russell.

Charity Commission no. 242678

Information available Information was provided by the trust.

Summary

The trust gives two-thirds of its money to overseas projects and one-third to social welfare projects in the UK. Up to and sometimes over 100 grants are made a year. They are rarely for more than £25,000 and most for between £1,000 and £10,000. Larger grants often go to charities with which the trust has an existing connection. Smaller one-off grants, sometimes repeated, go to a variety of beneficiaries, including many campaigning groups.

General

In 2002/03 the trust had assets of £4.9 million and an income of £473,000.

The trust's guidelines are as follows:

The trust gives two thirds of its money to overseas projects and one third to UK based projects. It gives a mix of one-off grants and recurrent ones. It has regularly given grants to a limited number of large national organisations and development agencies, but also gives smaller grants to much smaller organisations and locally based projects.

The trust will support advocacy and challenges to powerful economic forces, on behalf of the poor, the powerless or the left out, especially if they themselves are enabled to participate in articulating a vision of economic justice.

UK Grants Programme

The trust focuses on projects on Merseyside which will benefit disadvantaged groups and neighbourhoods in such spheres as:
- housing and homelessness
- social and community care
- community development
- education
- employment/unemployment
- aftercare
- welfare rights
- human rights.

Overseas projects

The trust focuses on projects which will benefit disadvantaged groups and communities in such spheres as:
- agriculture – especially crop and livestock production and settlement schemes
- community development – especially appropriate technology and village industries
- health – especially preventative medicine, water supplies, blindness
- environmental – especially protecting and sustaining ecological systems at risk
- human rights – especially of women, children and disabled
- conflict resolution and reconciliation
- fair trade – especially relating to primary producers and workers.

For both UK and overseas projects:

The trustees are interested in projects which:
- involve the local community in the planning and implementation
- invest in people through training and enabling
- have a holistic concern for all aspects of life [...]

In 2002/03 grants totalled £397,000. These are outlined below.

Overseas projects: £266,000 in 57 grants

There were four grants of £10,000 or more: Christian Aid and ITDG (£50,000 each) and Church Mission Society and Rurcon Communications (£10,000 each). Other grants included CMS – Agriculture and Theology Project (£8,000 each), Banana Link (£6,000), Fairtrade Foundation, Mildmay Mission Hospital, Mines Advisory Group, Traidcraft, UK Food Group and World Development Movement Trust (£5,000 each), Baby Milk Action, Foundation for International Environmental Law and Development, New Israel Fund and Sound Seekers (£3,000 each), ADD, Hospice Care Kenya, Minority Rights Group International, Responding to Conflict, Sight Savers and Y Care International (£2,000 each), Inter Care (£1,500) and Books Abroad, Legal Assistance Abroad, Teso Development Trust and Work Aid (£1,000 each).

UK projects: £132,000 in 33 grants

There was one grant made over £10,000 – £15,000 to Children's Society. Other beneficiaries included Barnardos, Family Service Units and Merseyside and Regions Churches Ecumenical Assembly (£8,000), Refugee Council (£7,000), Employment Opportunities and Social Partnership (£4,000 each), Community Integrated Care, Crossroads Caring for Carers, National Playbus Association and Terrence Higgins Trust (£3,000 each), Aidis Trust and National Autistic Society (£2,000 each), YMCA England (£1,500) and Disability Law Service and Knowsley START (£1,000 each).

Exclusions

The trust does not give grants for:
- individuals;
- buildings, building work or office equipment (including IT hardware);
- academic research and medical research or equipment;
- expeditions;
- bursaries or scholarships;
- vehicle purchases;
- animal welfare charities.

Applications

In writing to the correspondent. No application forms are issued.

Applications should include:
- a brief description (two sides of A4 paper) of, and a budget for, the work for which the grant is sought;

- the organisation's annual report and accounts (this is essential).

The applications need to provide the trustees with information about:

- the aims and objectives of the organisation;
- its structure and organisational capacity;
- what the funds are being requested for and how much is being requested;
- how progress of the work will be monitored and evaluated.

Trustees meet twice a year. The closing dates for applications are 30 June and 15 December.

'Unfortunately the volume of applications received precludes acknowledgement on receipt or notifying unsuccessful applicants. The trust emphasises that it is unable to make donations to applicants who are not, or do not have links with, a UK-registered charity.'

The Joseph Rowntree Charitable Trust

Peace, democracy, racial justice, corporate responsibility

£4.9 million (2003)

Beneficial area UK, Republic of Ireland and South Africa.

The Garden House, Water End, York YO30 6WQ

Tel. 01904 627810 **Fax** 01904 651990

Email info@jrct.org.uk

Website www.jrct.org.uk

Correspondent Stephen Pittam, Trust Secretary

Trustees *Andrew Gunn, chair; Ruth McCarthy; Tom Allport; Margaret Bryan; Helen Carmichael; Peter Coltman; Christine Davis; Marion McNaughton; Beverley Meeson; Emily Miles; Roger Morton; Susan Seymour; David Shutt; Imran Tyabji.*

Charity Commission no. 210037

Information available Annual report and accounts were provided by the trust. Detailed and up-to-date information on funding programmes is available on the website.

Summary

Up to 200 grants are made each year, ranging in size from a few hundred pounds to over £100,000, and from one-off to three-year grants, sometimes further renewed. They are very often to meet the core costs of the organisations concerned. Grants cover, at present, the following areas:

- Peace: work that promotes the nonviolent resolution of conflict, including work on the arms trade, the creation of a culture of peace, developing effective peacebuilding measures and supporting the right to conscientious objection to military service.
- Democratic process: work which strengthens democracy, upholds the rights of the citizen and encourages people to take their democratic rights and obligations seriously and to exercise them in ways that make them real.
- Racial justice: work which promotes racial justice in all parts of society, including empowering black and minority ethnic people to engage in decision making and policy development, and work which monitors and challenges racism and racial injustice whether relating to colour or culture.
- Corporate responsibility: work aimed at improving the impact of business on society, particularly through the statutory regulation of business in the public interest and the monitoring of business practice in specific companies or industry sectors.
- Quaker concerns: work that helps to deepen the spiritual life of the society of Friends or that develops Quaker responses to problems of our time.
- Ireland (north and south): work that nurtures the democratic process, fosters a culture of equality and human rights, addresses issues of poverty and social exclusion, and promotes dialogue, understanding and co-operation across religious, racial and political divides.
- South Africa: work that promotes a just and peaceful South Africa, particularly through the reduction of rural poverty and addressing the problems of violent conflict at all levels of society.

General

All trustees are members of the Religious Society of Friends (Quakers).

The trust made 124 grants in 2003 totalling £4.9 million, ranging from £436 to £350,000. Over 70% of beneficiaries had been supported by the trust in previous years. Many grants are multi-year awards and in some cases support continues over many years – not surprisingly given the limited number of organisations taking a lead in some of the fields in which it operates. Perhaps because of the limited number of grants made, the trust is often able to develop a close working relationship with the organisations that it supports.

In 2003 it received 694 applications, 131 being successful. This may be due to the fact that it operates in fields where there are relatively few other trust funders, such as work for peace, democracy and justice.

The staff of the trust include:

Stephen Pittam, trust secretary

Juliet Prager, deputy trust secretary

Nick Perks, assistant trust secretary

Maureen Grant, development officer.

Guidelines for applicants

The trust offers the following information about its grant programmes, with additional information on grants added by the editor.

We make grants mainly for work in Britain. A small number of grants are made to (mainly) Brussels–based organisations working to influence EU policy in the trust's fields of interest. Outside Britain, we make grants only for work towards peace, justice and reconciliation in South Africa and in Ireland (north and south).

Many JRCT funded projects share these features:

- The work is about removing problems through radical solutions, and not about making the problems easier to live with.
- There is a clear sense of objectives, and of how to achieve them.
- The work is innovative and imaginative.
- It is clear that the grant has a good chance of making a difference.

We try to maintain an adventurous approach to funding. Where appropriate, we are willing to take risks and fund unpopular causes which may not always fall neatly into one of the programme areas listed below.

Peace – £695,000

Joseph Rowntree hoped that his trust would 'sound a clear note with regard to the great scourges of humanity, especially with regard to war'. As part of the Quaker tradition, the JRCT is committed to the creation of a peaceful world, and the creation of a culture of peace.

The trust recognises that complex phenomena create peace and war. Joseph Rowntree wanted to seek out the underlying causes of weakness or evil rather than remedying 'more superficial manifestations'. The trust believes that long-term approaches to create peace are usually more effective than short-term fixes. We are idealistic, but recognise that pragmatism is often more effective than purity.

Much of our work on corporate responsibility, racial justice and democracy, in Ireland (north and south) and South Africa, is already aimed at these underlying causes in order to create a culture of peace, accountability and democracy. Under the heading of 'Peace', we anticipate funding groups or organisations that are working to influence the behaviour and thinking of the public, and of people in powerful positions including those working in the military, national governments and international organisations.

We wish to support organisations or individuals who promote values similar to our own when working towards peace. We would not fund those who advocate aggressive military solutions to conflicts.

We wish to fund organisations or individuals who can identify the strategic steps needed towards achieving peace. We hope to evaluate grant applications in terms of the extent to which the work proposed will ultimately advance the cause of peace and nonviolence.

We are particularly interested in funding organisations or individuals who are working on:

- control or elimination of specific forms of warfare and the arms trade
- influencing appropriate agencies to take or promote peaceful choices to prevent violent conflict or its recurrence
- the practicalities and improved effectiveness of peace building and conflict resolution
- the creation of a culture of peace
- pacifism and conscientious objection to military service.

We will not fund:

- work on interpersonal violence, domestic violence, or violence against children
- work focused solely on local situations
- work which focuses on the immediate effect of conflict on victims
- research which is more theoretical than practical, or which is not aimed at making change happen
- work focused more exclusively on other governments' policy than on that of the UK, unless the work is on pacifism or conscientious objection to military service
- work which seems only to 'preach to the converted'.

Location of work

We are most likely to fund individuals and organisations working in the UK and Ireland and (if the organisation is working on influencing an international institution such as the EU, NATO or the UN) the rest of Europe.

The largest donations of over £10,000 each included: £111,000 over three years to Nuclear Information Service towards education work; £56,000 over three years to University of Bradford, Department of Peace Studies towards the research and dissemination of a project New Weapons and New Threats; £50,000 over three months to Campaign Against the Arms Trade/TREAT to a research programme; £50,000 over one year to Landmine Action towards emergency core and project costs; £32,000 over 6 months to BASIC/ISIS/Saferworld – a joint project Conflict in Iraq – concerns and consequences; £15,000 over one year to British Pugwash Trust – Nuclear Weapons Awareness Programme; and £12,000 over one year to Hawthorn Press, towards publishing a book on peace journalism.

Racial justice – £857,000

1. National programme

The trust seeks to promote racial justice and equality of opportunity as a basis for a harmonious multi-racial, multi-ethnic society in the UK.

The trust seeks to work towards this aim through all its grantmaking fields, in addition to its specialist racial justice programme.

The Racial Justice programme area works at three levels:

- Local – West Yorkshire (see below)
- National – focusing on England, Wales, Scotland and Ireland (work in Northern Ireland is funded through a separate programme
- European.

An important test of all applications to this programme area is whether they are promoting racial justice. The trust is keen to encourage communication and co-operation between different racial groups.

The trust welcomes applications from black and ethnic minority groups and from multi-racial groups, and encourages and looks for involvement of black and ethnic minority people at all levels of the projects and organisations it supports.

At national level, the trust supports projects working to:

- promote issues of racial justice with policy shapers, decision makers and opinion formers
- encourage black and ethnic minority people/black-led organisations to contribute to policy development on the basis of their experience in meeting needs; and to participate at planning and decision making levels
- monitor and challenge racism and racial injustice whether relating to colour or culture

- explore and advocate ways to eliminate racial violence and harrassment.

At European level, the trust expects that work undertaken on an EU-wide basis will be funded from sources in several EU member states. The trust supports projects working to:

- promote awareness amongst policy makers and within the European institutions of the need to protect the human rights of minority communities, asylum seekers and migrants
- research and disseminate information concerning current EU policies and their impact on minority communities
- provide a forum for NGOs from all EU countries to share experiences on matters relating to race and immigration and to build alliances on shared interests
- work for a more accountable and open process for developing EU policy in relation to race and immigration.

The largest grants were: £150,000 over three years to Runnymede Trust towards core costs; £96,000 over three years to Migration Policy Group to cover core costs; £64,000 over two years to NMP Anti Racist Trust towards the core costs of Black Racial Attacks Independent Network; £40,000 over 8 months to York Travellers Trust towards core costs; £15,000 over one year to Institute of Race Relations towards a European Race Audit; £13,000 over 15 months to George Padmore Institute towards publishing catalogues of international book fairs of radical, black and third world books; £12,000 over six months to Pakistani Community Centre – Oldham towards a discrimination and racism initiative; and £12,000 over one year to Runnymede Trust towards the UK Race in Europe Network.

Refugees and asylum-seekers – limited funds are available to support work on asylum and refugee issues. The trust supports projects and individuals working on:

- current policies on refugees and asylum-seekers
- the likely future direction of asylum policy in the UK and EU and into how this might be influenced to create a rational and humane policy benefiting both migrant and settled communities.

Work in this area is likely to be focused on research and dissemination of information linked with strategies for making an impact on policy. The trust does not fund pure academic research.

Grants under the refugee and asylum programme included: £86,000 over three years to Asylum Aid towards the costs of a research and policy officer; £50,000 over one year to Institute for Public Policy Research towards asylum and immigration in the UK and Europe;

£30,000 over one year to Bail for Immigration Detainees towards research and policy work; and £10,000 over six months to Northern Refugee Centre, an emergency grant for the continued employment of the information and resource worker.

2. West Yorkshire programme

Grants are awarded to projects that are imaginative, innovative and able to demonstrate that they are likely to make a difference.

The grants may range from a few hundred pounds to a maximum of £15,000 per year for three years, and might be for an event, a small research project, a worker's salary or for running costs.

The trust is interested in supporting work which meets most of the following criteria:

- it will help a group identify areas for developing and strengthening their organisation so that it may carry out its aim effectively
- it will empower a community or communities to take action in order to challenge racial injustices
- it will have long term impact
- it will be sensitive to issues of cultural identity but will facilitate growth and development
- it will promote equal opportunities and reflect this in its practices.

Grants in the West Yorkshire programme included: £44,000 over three years to South Leeds Elderly Group towards the salary costs of a part-time development worker; £30,000 over three years to Leeds Asylum Seekers' Support Network towards the the English at Home scheme; £23,000 over two years to United Caribbean Association towards the costs of a part-time staff development officer; £15,000 over one year to Keighley Voluntary Services towards the Racial Justice & Community Cohesion Project; £5,000 over two years to Bradford Resource Centre & Community Statistics Project towards anti-racist work in schools; and £3,700 to Afrikan Curriculum Development Association towards publishing books to develop and promote publishing skills within the black community in Leeds.

Democratic process – £817,000

The trust's current work on democracy is rooted in Rowntree's concern that his philanthropy should 'change the face of England' (sic).

Change remains the keynote of our approach to democracy today: change to bring about a greater understanding of democratic culture and of the [mutual] responsibilities of democratic process throughout the United Kingdom; change to counter abuses of power. Our funding has focused on work in the following areas:

- the nuts and bolts of a new constitutional settlement, to tackle the weaknesses which result from our unwritten constitution
- legal provision for freedom of information
- the argument for a Human Rights Act; discussion of its content; work to raise awareness of its significance; monitoring its implementation
- the importance of local democracy as a counter to centralisation of power
- ways to tackle the politicisation of the civil service
- independent scrutiny of proposed legislation
- the right relationship between the executive and the judiciary
- alternatives to the present 'first past the post' electoral system
- the need to protect and enhance civil liberties
- how to rectify the perception that people are subjects, rather than citizens with concomitant rights and obligations.

In the recent past the trust has been able to support many of the major UK research and educational initiatives aimed at addressing these issues.

The trust recognises that these central provisions are necessary but not sufficient preconditions for a fully democratic culture. The trust wishes to fund work which encourages people to take seriously their democratic rights and obligations, exercising them in ways that make them real rather than merely theoretical. This may be achieved through educational work, or other kinds of 'bottom up' initiatives.

Now that there is a Human Rights Act on the statute book, the trust is concerned to see that its provisions are used to enforce the human rights of people who are without privilege, rather than simply by those who are well-connected and know how to 'work the system'.

Applications to the trust should demonstrate clearly how the work is likely to make an impact. The trust is unlikely to support purely academic work in this area.

The largest grants were: £159,000 over three years to Campaign for Freedom of Information towards core costs; £90,000 over five years to Francesca Klug towards promoting the values of human rights in the UK; £75,000 over two years to National Alliance of Women's Organisations towards core costs; £75,000 over three years to openDemocracy towards core editorial costs; £72,000 to Hansard Society towards the costs of employing a director of the Parliament and Government programme; £60,000 over three years to Institute of Welsh Affairs towards core costs; £20,000 to Statewatch, a supplementary grant for core costs; and £10,000 over two years to Constitution Unit towards a research proposal.

Ireland – £757,000

1. Programme in Northern Ireland

The trust seeks to support charitable work which promotes justice and equality within the social and political structures of society. Almost all the trust's grant making takes place within the UK. Over the last twenty years a significant programme of work has been supported in Northern Ireland.

Currently the trust's programme supports projects and individuals working to:

- promote new ideas to sustain the democratic process and democratic accountability
- encourage accountability, openness and responsiveness in government, government agencies and the civil service
- build new community structures to enable citizens to participate in the democratic process
- protect and enhance civil liberties and human rights
- promote dialogue, understanding and co-operation across political and religious divides
- challenge sectarianism
- promote non-violence and creative ways to handle conflict
- celebrate difference and value pluralism
- tackle poverty, inequality and social exclusion
- address contentious issues and develop new thinking on how to resolve these
- explore new ideas about the future social, economic and political relationships within the island of Ireland, between Britain and Ireland, and within the European Union.

The trust is interested in supporting work which addresses the root causes of the conflict in Northern Ireland and which is aimed at influencing policy. Much of the trust's work has been directed towards providing infrastructure, technical assistance and support for those working at a local level. A strong focus of the trust's programme has been on women's initiatives working in the areas outlined above. The trust will need to be convinced that other funds such as those from statutory agencies and the European Union are not available for work which it funds.

The largest grants in the Northern Ireland category were: £114,000 over three years to Springfield Inter-Community Development Project towards a research project; £60,000 over two years to Committee on Administration of Justice towards core costs; £30,000 over one year to Democratic Dialogue towards core costs;

317

£30,000 over six months to One Small Step Campaign towards core costs for the campaign to encourage peace and reconciliation in Northern Ireland; £25,000 over one year to St Columb's Park House towards a project Negotiating Change: Sharing and Conflict Amelioration in Derry/Londonderry; £15,000 over two years to PAKT Lurgan towards its Active Citizenship Programme; and £13,000 over one year to Spirit of Enniskillen Trust towards its Building Diversity and Citizenship programme.

2. Programme in the Republic of Ireland

The trust seeks to support charitable work which promotes justice and equality within the social and political structures of society. The trust has operated in Ireland (Republic) since 1994.

The trust's programme supports organisations and individuals working to:
- promote new ideas to nurture the democratic process, democratic accountability, and active citizenship
- foster a culture of equality and human rights, and monitor the government's record in implementing internationally recognised standards in human rights
- promote dialogue, understanding and co-operation across religious, racial and political divides; celebrate difference and challenge sectarianism
- safeguard the rights, and address the needs of minorities including travellers and the emerging communities of refugees and asylum seekers; and promote concepts of pluralism and racial justice with policy shapers, decision makers and opinion formers
- encourage accountability, openness and responsiveness in government, government agencies and the civil service
- address issues of poverty, inequality and social exclusion, in areas where there is little community infrastructure; and support those who campaign to make these issues a priority of government programmes and policies
- address contentious issues and develop new thinking on how to resolve these
- promote non-violence and sponsor creative ways to handle conflict
- explore new ideas about the future social, economic and political development of the island, north and south.

The trust is keen to support initiatives which can make a difference. The limited size of our resources, together with our interest in influencing policy, has tended to result in support being offered to organisations working at a national level. However, the trust is open to consider creative and innovative initiatives at a local level, particularly from organisations working

outside of Dublin, and especially where local initiatives can demonstrate national relevance.

Grants can range from a few hundred euros to in excess of €100,000 over three years. The trust is able to offer only a small number of the larger strategic grants, which are aimed at raising the effectiveness and profile of key organisations, and at encouraging organisational development. The trust will need to be convinced that funds from other sources, particularly statutory agencies and the European Union, are not available for proposals it receives.

Grants included: £168,000 over two years to TASC towards 'The Democracy Commission'; £65,000 over three years to Irish Penal Reform Trust towards core costs; £45,000 over two years to Action from Ireland for core costs; £30,000 over 18 months to Migrant Information Centre towards core costs; £20,000 to Community Workers Co-operative towards its media, communication and information project; and £20,000 over 12 months to LIR Anti-Racism Programme towards the salary and project costs of a part-time worker.

South Africa – £355,000

The trust has made grants in South Africa for over 30 years.

Following a review and consultation during 2002/03, we have decided to fund work in a single area. We now consider applications only for work in KwaZulu Natal.

Our key concerns are poverty, inequality and conflict. In today's South Africa these are complex and interrelated issues. We will consider funding work in urban or peri-urban areas, but we prioritise work in rural areas. We also recognise that women suffer disproportionately from both poverty and violence and we prioritise funding to organisations that uphold, promote and demonstrate gender equality.

We like to fund work that:
- addresses the root causes of problems, rather than making problems easier to live with
- is long-term and collaborative, and which builds on and develops resources and partnerships
- which is innovative and imaginative, and does not easily attract funding from other sources
- where the grant would make a significant difference to your organisation.

For example, proposals that we would consider funding include:
- work which promotes community participation, local government accountability, and local implementation of national policies
- work that supports communities, community organisations or social

movements to: access resources and rights, or explore new economic, social and/or environmental approaches to development which promote equality, human rights and injustice
- long-term programmes in specific communities to address problems of endemic violence
- organisations that help unions, advice offices, paralegals or other groups working directly with rural people
- the development and promotion of proven models or tools of peacebuilding as accessible, replicable resources
- advocacy or policy work, on a local, provincial or national level, on issues related to rural poverty and inequality, land reform, conflict and violence.

We believe that work in South Africa should acknowledge the devastating impact of HIV/AIDS. We do not generally fund specific HIV/AIDS projects. We do expect our programme and the groups that we fund to play a part in addressing the challenge of HIV/AIDS.

This policy covers the period from 2004 to 2008. We recognise that, in the changing context of transition and transformation in South Africa, we may need to amend the policy from time to time.

In addition to the general exclusions, the trust will not consider applications:
- from UK-based organisations for work in (or in connection with) South Africa
- From organisations based elsewhere in Africa.

Grants (shown here in Rands) included: R750,000 over 12 months to Alliance for Children's Entitlement to Social Security towards widening the reach of social assistance; R511,000 over 12 months to Centre for Rural Legal Studies towards its Legal Literacy Education Project; R400,000 over two years to South African History Archive towards its Freedom of Information programme R256,000 over two years to Riviersonderend Advice and Development Centre towards ongoing advice work; R250,000 over 12 months to Quaker Peace Centre for core costs; R200,000 over two years to Sex Worker Education and Advocacy Taskforce (SWEAT) towards the costs of a research worker; and R100,000 over three years to Inclusive and Affirming Ministries for a video project.

Corporate responsibility – £815,000

In recent years the position of business in society has received a great deal more attention. Few boards of public companies now argue that they are accountable only to their shareholders and only for their financial stewardship. Campaigning organisations have increasingly challenged the business community to operate in a more just, sustainable and transparent way. Many groups in society, including investors, consumer groups, trade associations and consultants, are assisting an evolution of business practices and reporting. Although progress has been patchy, and this process has not so far addressed the position of companies whose core business does harm to society, the direction of change is clearly set. In view of this, the trust does not see itself as continuing to fund mainstream work in this area.

However, the trust believes that there is a continuing role for individuals and organisations within civil society to provide independent monitoring and analysis of these developments, give voice to the concerns of under-represented or marginalised stakeholders, and act as a source of radical ideas.

The trust is particularly interested in funding:
- work towards improved statutory regulation of business in the public interest, at a UK or a European level
- monitoring of business practice in specific companies or industry sectors. The trust is concerned that the business practices of all companies should respect human rights and not give rise to injustice or suffering.

The trust will give serious consideration to applications for:
- work to support individual employees or those adversely affected by the actions of corporate bodies to hold those bodies to account in the wider public interest; this does not include claims for financial compensation or other forms of personal redress
- work illuminating conflicts between the use of resources and how the cost of that use is allocated. Our aim is to achieve transparency and mutual responsibility between business, government and citizens as producers and consumers.

As in all its programmes, the trust will not fund academic research and can only fund work that is legally charitable. The trust prefers to support work which will not easily attract funds from elsewhere and which has a good chance of making a meaningful, long-term difference.

The trust welcomes the development of products and services that enable consumers and investors to express their support for more responsible and sustainable business practice. Many existing ethical products are now commercially viable and new products and markets will continue to develop. The trust is therefore unlikely to make further grants to promote ethical investment or ethical consumption and will consider applications only where there is a clear case for charitable funding.

Grants included: £168,000 over two years to Centre for Corporate Accountability towards core funding; £85,000 over three years to Pesticide Action Network UK towards information and regulation of pesticide use and exposure; £60,000 over three years to Corporate Watch towards core costs; £22,000 over one year to CORE Coalition towards core funding; £21,000 over one year to Norfolk Education and Action for Development towards the 'Just Business' project; £17,000 over one year to Green Audit towards CERRIE committee work; £60,000 over two years to PressWise towards the employment of a development worker; and £41,000 over one year to Public Services International Research Unit towards work around the OECD Anti-bribery Convention.

Quaker concerns – £516,000

The trust seeks to foster the development of what Joseph Rowntree, in the trust's founding memorandum, called a 'powerful Quaker ministry', interpreted as inclusively as possible. This may include practical ways to deepen the spiritual life of Friends or developing Quaker responses to problems of our time.

Trustees see the lives of individual Friends and Meetings, and their wider community, as interdependent. Primarily, this programme area supports work designed to strengthen the Society of Friends but which is less likely to attract funds from other sources. This could include support for innovative approaches to the development of Quaker life and thought.

Who can apply
Trustees will consider applications from Britain Yearly Meeting, from local Meetings, or from other Quaker organisations in Britain. Applications from individuals are also welcomed.

Each application will be considered carefully, in the light of the general application requirements.

In addition, trustees will consider:
- the way in which a concern has been developed and tested
- the prospective benefit of the project to Friends and the wider society
- the relationship between the proposed project and other work within the Society
- other funds available to the applicant.

What we will not fund
As well as the general exclusions, trustees will not generally make grants for:
- the core work and management of the Society of Friends, either centrally or in local Meetings
- work that is in danger of being 'laid down' due to lack of funds.

Grants included: £149,000 over two years to Quaker Council for European Affairs towards core funding; £350,000 over three years to Woodbrooke Quaker Study Centre towards its education programme; and £21,000 over three years to Young Friends General Meeting towards core/employment costs.

Exclusions

Generally, the trust does not make grants for:
- work in larger, older national charities which have an established constituency of supporters;
- general appeals;
- local work (except in Northern Ireland or the Republic, or parts of Yorkshire);
- building, buying or repairing buildings;
- providing care for elderly people, children, people with learning difficulties, people with physical disabilities, or people using mental health services;
- work in mainstream education, including schools and academic or medical research;
- work on housing and homelessness;
- travel or adventure projects;
- business development or job creation;
- paying off debts;
- work which should be funded by the state, or has been in the recent past;
- work which has already been done;
- work which tries to make a problem easier to live with, rather than getting to the root of it;
- the personal benefit of individuals in need;
- the arts, except where they are used in the context of the kinds of work which the trust does support.

The trust can only support work which is legally charitable.

Refer also to the relevant policy sheets summarised above and available in full on the trust's website, which explain more about what the trust may or may not make grants for.

Applications

The trust expects all applicants to have made themselves familiar with the relevant funding programmes, summarised above but set out in full on the website and available in leaflet form.

They then require a letter and a completed registration form (also on the website). The details expected in the letter are set out in detail on the website and leaflet, at a length too great to be reprinted here.

There is a deadline for receipt of applications of around ten weeks before the meeting of trustees. It is helpful if applications arrive well before the deadline. Occasionally it is possible to deal with applications which arrive after the deadline, but there have to be exceptional reasons for this to be considered. There are earlier deadlines for applications to the South Africa programme.

The trust has moved to a system of three (rather than four) grant-making cycles a year.

Contact the trust for up-to-date information on deadlines.

The Joseph Rowntree Foundation

Research and development in social policy

£4.7 million (2003)

Beneficial area UK, with some preference for York.

The Homestead, 40 Water End, York YO30 6WP

Tel. 01904 629241 **Fax** 01904 620072

Email info@jrf.org.uk

Website www.jrf.org.uk

Correspondent Lord Richard Best, Director

Trustees *Sir William Utting, chair; Debby Ounsted; Dame Ann Bowtell; Catherine Graham-Harrison; Susan Hartshorne; Ashok Jashapara; Robert Maxwell; Bharat Mehta; Nigel Naish; Tony Stoller.*

Charity Commission no. 210169

Information available Full and exemplary information available from the foundation's website.

Summary

The foundation initiates, manages and pays for an extensive social research programme. It does not normally respond to unsolicited applications and many of its programmes issue formal and detailed requests for proposals. However modest proposals for minor gap-filling pieces of work in the foundation's fields of interest may

sometimes be handled less formally and more rapidly.

The general fields of work are:

- housing;
- social policy;
- social care.

The foundation also makes some grants locally in and around York, and directly manages or initiates innovative and exciting housing schemes.

General

This is not a conventional grantmaking foundation. It supports research, of a rigorous kind, usually carried out in universities or research institutes, but also has a wide range of other activities not necessarily involving grants of any kind.

During 2003 the foundation spent £4.7 million (£6 million in 2002) on its various activities, including its Research and Development Committees, grants to charities in York and other projects.

The annual review for 2004 reflects on 100 years of grantmaking for the foundation:

This year marks the centenary of the act of philanthropy that gave rise to the Joseph Rowntree Foundation and to its independent sister organisations, the Joseph Rowntree Charitable Trust and the Joseph Rowntree Reform Trust. The decision reached by 'JR' to devote a substantial part of the fortune amassed from his confectionary business in trusts to further the causes of social justice and human brotherhood was a remarkable act of generosity in itself. But the far-sightedness of his vision and the compelling terms in which he explained the guiding purpose of his bequest are no less impressive. Rightly surmising that the public were more likely to support appeals from soup kitchens and other palliative responses to deprivation, Joseph proposed that his money should be used to uncover the roots of social disadvantage. In the words of his founding memorandum for the three trusts: 'The need of seeking to search out the underlying causes of weakness or evil in the community, rather than of remedying their more superficial manifestations, is a need which I expect will remain throughout the continuance of the trusts.'

The task set for Rowntree Trustees of promoting social change and the 'right measures of human achievement' seems no less daunting at the start of the twenty-first century than it must have done 100 years ago. Social 'weakness' and 'evil' today assume different forms to the miseries of destitution and slum housing that Joseph knew in York, and on which his son, Seebohm, published a memorable study

(Poverty: A study in town life). The wealth and comforts of life in contemporary Britain are on a scale that he would have found it hard to imagine. But when a substantial minority of the population, including disproportionate numbers among the young and old, are palpabley excluded from the fruits of national prosperity, the continuing relevance of our search for social justice and change based on objective evidence is beyond doubt.

The organisation that is now JRF began its life as a custodian of New Earswick, the model village that Joseph established as a practical answer to the abysmal living conditions that Seebohm had catalogued in central York. The Joseph Rowntree Housing Trust (JRHT), administered as part of the foundation, is today a registered social landlord responsible not only for a much expanded village, but also a number of other developments and care homes for older and disabled people. Its record of innovation includes pioneering 'part-buy, part-rent' flexible tenure schemes and the first, fully accessible 'Lifetime Homes' as well as Hartrigg Oaks, Britain's first Continuing Care Retirement Community that opened six years ago. In that tradition, JRHT has become the City of York Council's chosen partner to develop 'Derwenthorpe', a new, mixed-tenure community of 540 homes on the east side of the city. If planning permission is granted this year, it will not only help to tackle the increasingly serious housing shortages in York, but also demonstrate our commitment to high-quality housing, sustainable communities and environmentally sensitive development.

It does not require a hundred years to demonstrate that the process of achieving social improvement through greater knowledge and understanding is a slow one. The impact and influence of most JRF projects can best be characterised as 'dripping on the stone', rather than sudden alterations in policy or practice. Alongside our achievements, it is pleasing to note the start of new research programmes during 2003/04, including topical work on immigration and inclusion, as well as the instigation of an independent commission to examine the governance of public services. Our policy and practice development programmes have also gathered pace, reinforcing the messages from research on topics as varied as easing housing shortages, long-term care for older people and the changing role of backbench councillors in local authorities. After a number of years when falling world stock markets have eroded the value of the foundation's endowment, it is also encouraging to report a modest recovery. Low interest rates and other factors have exerted continuing pressures on our income, but the level of expenditure agreed for

2004, following a 12% reduction, should now prove sustainable in years to come.

Research programmes

The foundation describes its programmes in considerable depth on its website. The following is an overview of the foundation's research. It would not be worthwhile to approach the foundation on the basis of the information in this entry on its own.

How the foundation works

The foundation does not make grants: those supported are considered partners in a common enterprise. The foundation takes a close interest in each project from the outset, often bringing together an advisory group to give guidance on a project, and taking an active role in the dissemination of the project's findings to bring about policy and practice change. foundation staff oversee the progress of individual projects within the programme and act as a point of contact throughout.

As a general rule, the foundation aims to provide full financial support rather than being one of a number of funders. However, where the involvement of another organisation would help the project achieve its aims, joint funding may be considered.

How work gets funded

The foundation is keen to fund a variety of different kinds of projects, depending on the state of knowledge about a particular topic.

- The majority of proposals are canvassed under broad programme themes, or through specific briefs using the JRF website, email notification, direct mail, and, occasionally, advertisements.
- In addition, JRF sometimes commissions work directly.
- Occasionally we will consider proposals arising from an unsolicited approach.

The foundation does not have a preference for methodology but it must be appropriate for the question.

The foundation likes to be outward looking in its approach and encourages user groups and community-based groups to apply for funding where appropriate. If the proposal is for a research project the project team must include people with knowledge, experience and research skills to carry out a successful research project.

Who decides which projects are approved?

Once received, a proposal passes through three stages of scrutiny:

- the project management team, which assesses whether the proposal fits within the foundation's current priorities and is technically adequate;
- the Committee, which considers and decides between competing proposals

and makes funding recommendations to trustees; and
- JRF trustees, who make the final decision.

Programmes and projects

Experience has convinced us that we are likely to have greater impact on changing policy and practice through supporting programmes of work. The majority of the projects supported by the foundation are part of a broader programme. The forms of the programmes vary and proposers should read the guidance on current priorities carefully.

Programmes often have a specialist adviser and sometimes an advisory committee drawing in expertise from relevant fields. They advise on the priorities and progress of the programmes as a whole, and on issues concerning dissemination, but assessing individual proposals remains the task of the committees.

Exclusions

With the exception of funds for particular projects in York and the surrounding area, the foundation does not generally support:

- projects outside the topics within its current priorities;
- development projects which are not innovative;
- development projects from which no general lessons can be drawn;
- general appeals, for example from national charities;
- core or revenue funding, including grants for buildings or equipment;
- conferences and other events, websites or publications, unless they are linked with work which the foundation is already supporting;
- grants to replace withdrawn or expired statutory funding, or to make up deficits already incurred;
- educational bursaries or sponsorship for individuals for research or further education and training courses;
- grants or sponsorship for individuals in need;
- work that falls within the responsibility of statutory bodies.

Applications

The detailed guidelines from the foundation are quoted extensively below as a general guide to good practice for these kind of applications.

Initial enquiries: The foundation's staff are happy to give advice to those uncertain about the relevance of a proposal for the foundation, or the form in which it should be presented. Proposers are advised to obtain a copy of the most recent Research and

Development information before making a proposal (www.jrf.org.uk or, if no access to internet, call 01904 629241). A draft proposal or short outline covering the main headings identified below, received early, is welcome and usually better than a telephone call. These should be sent to The Research Director, Joseph Rowntree Foundation, The Homestead, 40 Water End, York YO30 6WP (Tel: 01904 629241).

The form of the proposal: The foundation does not have an application form for proposals but does require them to follow a standard format. You should provide two unbound copies of the proposal presented as follows:

- a succinct but clear proposal of a maximum 3,000 words;
- a summary of the proposal of not more than 600 words;
- completed copies of the foundation's project budget forms, with supporting details;
- a curriculum vitae for the project proposer (and worker/s if known).

Any proposal not submitted in this way may be returned for revision and thus delayed for consideration by the relevant committee.

The required structure of proposals is the same whether you are making an unsolicited proposal or responding to a particular programme of work.

What should the proposal cover?

Title

Give the project a short, explanatory title.

Background

This section should explain the reasons for undertaking the project. You must place the proposed piece of work in the context of existing knowledge and practice, demonstrating a familiarity with the field and the relationship of your proposal to relevant recent or current work being carried out by others.

You should also explain the extent to which the new project will relate to or build upon previous work. Demonstration projects must give details about the innovative nature of the work and the evidence that such a development is likely to be beneficial. Projects concerned to transfer good practice from one setting to another must also provide evidence that the practice is based on a sound assessment of 'what works'. Research proposals should indicate what gaps in knowledge the proposed project seeks to fill.

Aims

You must clearly state the aims of the proposal.

Policy relevance

You must draw out the policy or practice implications of the proposed work. Be as explicit as possible about the scale and nature of the policy or practice questions your project will address and also the timeliness of the proposal.

Methods

You must state clearly the methods to be adopted and why they are appropriate. This principle applies to both practice- and research-based work. Those proposing research projects should include details of the approach to be adopted; the way in which the work would be pursued (e.g. how samples for either qualitative or quantitative work would be chosen, numbers involved, methods of analysis). Demonstration and other development projects need to provide details of the work to be carried out and show how the activities would be monitored and evaluated.

Timetable

You must provide a schedule setting out the elements of the work to be done. This should cover what activities will be carried out, when they will occur, how they relate to other activities and how long they will take. You must allow time within your schedule to complete the required outputs (usually a 'findings' and an accessible report). The foundation gives close attention to ensuring that projects are completed on time (elements of funding may be withheld in the event of delays).

Staffing

Those submitting the proposal should include a curriculum vitae detailing their qualifications, experience and any relevant publications. Similar details should be included for other key workers, where known. You should also provide information about the current and likely future commitments of staff who will be working on the project and the ways in which they would fit the additional work in with existing commitments. Any known or possible additional facilitation expenses for disabled people on the team should be included in the budget.

Dates for submissions

Dates when applications need to be received in order to be considered by the next cycle of committee and trustee meetings are shown on www.jrf.org.uk

Joseph Rowntree Reform Trust Limited

Political reform, social justice, where ineligible for charitable funding

£954,000 (2003)

Beneficial area Mainly UK.

The Garden House, Water End, York YO30 6WQ

Tel. 01904 625744 **Fax** 01904 651502

Email info@jrrt.org.uk

Website www.jrrt.org.uk

Correspondent Tina Walker, Trust Secretary

Trustees *Directors: Archy Kirkwood MP, chair; Professor Lord (Trevor) Smith of Clifton; Christine Day; Pam Giddy; Dr Christopher Greenfield; Diana Scott; Lord (David) Shutt; Paedar Cremin; Mandy Cormack.*

Information available An excellent leaflet including applications procedures and grant details, largely reprinted below; annual report and accounts; also a brief history of the trust entitled Trusting in Change, A Story of Reform, published 1998.

Summary

The trust, which is not a charity and therefore pays tax on its income, makes grants for non-charitable campaigning, political and otherwise, overwhelmingly in Britain. It does not support causes that can be funded by charitable fundraising or charitable foundations

Perhaps half of the support goes to the Liberal Democrat Party, though all kinds of liberal causes are supported. Grants for other organisations, or individuals, can be of all sizes from £250 up to hundreds of thousands of pounds.

From the trust's present capital of around £30 million, there is a grant budget of about £750,000 each year.

General

The trust was established in 1904 as the Joseph Rowntree Social Service Trust. It is one of three trusts set up by Joseph Rowntree, a Quaker businessman with a lifelong concern for the alleviation of poverty and other great social ills of his and future days. The three trusts are all entirely independent of each other.

Though the trust is probably best known for its continuing support, in the name of political diversity, of the Liberal Democrat Party and its predecessors, it has supported liberal thought and activity in almost every political party in Britain.

The trust's work goes beyond parliamentary politics. It played an important part in the great development of British pressure groups in the 1970s – it was an early and major supporter of Amnesty, for example – and in recent years it has been the biggest supporter, in financial terms, of Charter 88 and the movement for constitutional change of which it is part. It is now showing an increasing interest in the development of regional autonomy in England.

The trust's information leaflet explains that:

...it differs from almost every other trust in the UK in that it is not a charity [the other similar organisation is the smaller Barrow Cadbury Trust. Ed.]. Charities must not have political objectives. They may engage in political activity in pursuit of their charitable aims, but those aims must not in themselves be political.

By contrast, this trust is a limited company which pays tax on its income. It is therefore free to give grants for political purposes; to promote political reform and constitutional change as well as the interests of social justice. It does so by funding campaigning organisations and individuals who have reform as their objective, and since it remains one of the very few sources of funds of any significance in the UK which can do this, it reserves its support for those projects which are ineligible for charitable funding.

Aims

The trust's principal concern is the continuity of reform within the democratic system. It seeks to foster creative intervention by anticipating and brokering change within the body politic – identifying the points where the minimum amount of thrust will have the maximum effect when directed as accurately and efficiently as possible.

Always aiming for good value from the projects it supports, the trust looks for those ideas whose time has come, or is about to come, and offers small amounts of money (as well as sometimes quite large amounts) at the moment when it judges that the most positive results can be achieved.

The trust aims to correct imbalances of power; strengthening the hand of individuals, groups and organisations who are striving for reform. It rarely funds projects outside the UK, directing most of its resources towards campaigning activity in this country, and will not fund research or any other charitable activity.

Political grants

The trust is not committed to the policies of any one political party, and has supported individual politicians or groups promoting new ideas and policies from all the major parties in the UK. Grants are not normally given towards the administrative or other core costs of party organisations. Direct party support has, however, been given when trustees have judged that particular political developments should be fostered, especially those central to a healthy democratic process such as constitutional and electoral reform.

In general, the trust's political grants aim to encourage a positive exchange of views and ideas among those involved in the political process, to redress the balance of financial inequality between the parties and to stimulate radical change.

Social justice

The trust has helped a large number of non-party pressure groups and other organisations which are ineligible for charitable funding, but which need assistance for particular purposes in the short term (the trust will not normally provide long-term funding). Such groups need not all be national organisations, but the national relevance of local campaigns is a crucial factor that the directors will consider.

Personal awards

Lastly, the trust operates a personal awards scheme to support a limited number of effective individuals.

Grants in 2002

In 2002 the sum of £505,000 was given in political grants and £449,000 for other purposes.

The political grants were headed by £500,000 to the Liberal Democrats.

The largest grants for other purposes were £129,000 for the Campaign for English Regions. Other larger grants included £53,000 to Searchlight, £49,000 to North East Constitutional Convention, £38,000 to Britain in Europe, £29,000 to Fawcett Society, £21,000 to Campaign for Yorkshire and £13,000 to Conservatives for Change.

Exclusions

The trust will not fund research or any other charitable activity. It rarely funds projects outside the UK.

Applications

'The process of applying for a grant is straightforward. There are no application forms. Applicants should simply write by post or email to the trust secretary, succinctly outlining the nature of the project and what it hopes to achieve, and enclosing a budget and any other supporting documents where appropriate.

'Proposals are judged on their merits within the prevailing social, political and economic climate, so beyond the broad aims outlined above there cannot be any advance guidance about which areas of activity the trust is likely to support, the amount of funding which might be available or for how long.'

Trust staff make an initial assessment and can reject inappropriate applications. Those which pass this first stage are considered in greater detail but may still be rejected by the trust's office. All staff rejections are reported to the directors at their next meeting, when those applications which have survived the preliminary vetting are submitted to the directors for decision.

The meetings take place in March, June, September and December. Applications must be submitted at least one month in advance of the meeting dates. Applicants should consult the trust's website or contact the office to find out about forthcoming application deadlines.

A system of small grants, up to £3,000, also operates between quarterly meetings. Such grants must be agreed by three directors, including the chair, and applications can be considered at any time. In exceptional circumstances, larger grants may also be agreed at any time, but only by the unanimous support of all the directors.

Royal British Legion

Service

£1.9 million to organisations (2003)

Beneficial area UK, excluding Scotland.

48 Pall Mall, London SW1Y 5JY
Tel. 020 7973 7200 **Fax** 020 7973 7399
Website www.britishlegion.org.uk
Correspondent The Grants Department
Trustees J G H Champ, chair; J J Brookes; C W Broughton; T B Buckby; I P Cannell; R I Glendinning; J Hawthornthwaite; M Hammond; E R Jobson; J H Lawrence; A I V Lyon; N Rogers; D P Smith; R E Swabey; J A Tedder; M E W Tidman; J B Tuckey; J E Williamson.
Charity Commission no. 219279
Information available Full accounts and information is available on the Legion's website.

The welfare of men and women who have served in the armed forces by providing grants to individuals and service organisations. It tends to support the same charities each year.

In 2003 it had assets of £143 million and an income of £65.3 million. Total expenditure was £54.5 million, most of which was spent on its own services. Grants to organisations totalled £1.8 million, with a further £8.1 million given in grants to individuals (further information can be found in *A Guide to Grants for Individuals in Need*, also published by Directory of Social Change).

Beneficiaries during the year, as in previous years, were the Officers' Association (£1 million), Royal British Legion Industries Ltd (£335,000), Haig Homes and Ex-Service Mental Welfare Association (£100,000 each), Ex-Service Fellowship Centres (£50,000), Alcohol Recovery Project (£41,000), Royal Commonwealth Ex-Services League (£29,000), 'Not Forgotten Association' (£20,000), Community Housing and Therapy (£18,000), British Ex-Services Wheelchair Sports Association (£16,000), COBSEO Project (£12,000) and Earl Haig Fund – Scotland and Montecillo Trust (£10,000 each). Five other organisations received smaller grants totalling £16,000.

Although the Legion's grantmaking focus is narrow in terms of the kind of organisations it will support, and the same organisations receive support each year, it does state: 'grants to other charities are made against applications for support, after scrutiny by the trustees of the applicant's current financial position and the business plan put forward in support of the application.'

Exclusions

Funding is not given to people who have served with the Women's Land Army, National or Auxiliary Fire Service, Civil Defence organisations, or NAAFI.

Applications

Societies should apply in writing to the secretary of the Benevolent and Strategy Committee.

The Rubin Foundation

Jewish charities, general

£787,000 (2002/03)

Beneficial area UK and overseas.

The Pentland Centre, Squires Lane, Finchley, London N3 2QL

Tel. 020 8346 2600 **Fax** 020 8349 2300

Email amcmillan@pentland.com

Correspondent Allison McMillan, Secretary

Trustees *Alison Mosheim; Angela Rubin; R Stephen Rubin; Carolyn Kubetz; Andrew Rubin.*

Charity Commission no. 327062

Information available Annual report and accounts on file at the Charity Commission.

This foundation is closely connected with Pentland Group Ltd (*see the Guide to UK Company Giving, published by Directory of Social Change*), with two trustees being on the board of directors of that company. The foundation's income comes in the form of an annual payment of between £200,000 and £300,000 from the company. Grants are then made using that income, and also funds from capital held by the foundation. In 2002/03 grants were made totalling £787,000.

In 2002/03 there were 27 grants for £1,000 or more, mainly going to Jewish charities. The largest grant, as in the previous year, was made to United Jewish Israel Appeal, which received £251,000. Another substantial grant of £250,000 was made to the new Churchill Museum at the Cabinet War Rooms.

Of the remaining 25 beneficiaries, 10 had been supported in the previous year. These were the Reform Foundation Trust (£61,000), Community Security Trust (£40,000), Chai Cancercare (£25,000), Jewish Care (£17,000), West

London Synagogue of British Jews and Norwood (formerly Norwood Ravenswood) (£15,000 each), Jewish Association of Business Ethics (£10,000), Royal Opera House Foundation (£7,000), Council of Christians and Jews (£5,000) and Institute for Jewish Policy Research (£1,000).

New beneficiaries during the year included the University of Oxford (£25,000), Trialogue Educational Trust (£15,000), London Jewish Cultural Centre (£10,000) and Jewish Child's Day, World Jewish Relief and National Sports Medicine Institute of the United Kingdom (£1,000 each).

Small grants of less than £1,000 each totalled £6,500.

Applications

The foundation has previously stated that 'grants are only given to people related to our business', such as charities known to members of the Rubin family and those associated with Pentland Group Ltd. Unsolicited applications are very unlikely to succeed.

The Rufford Maurice Laing Foundation

Nature conservation, sustainable development, environment, general

£2 million (2002/03)

Beneficial area Developing countries, UK.

5th Floor, Babmaes House, 2 Babmaes Street, London SW1Y 6RF

Tel. 020 7925 2582 **Fax** 020 7925 2583

Email kenny@rufford.org

Website www.rufford.org

Correspondent Terry Kenny, Director

Trustees *C R F Barbour; A Gavazzi; A J Johnson; J H Laing; M I T Smailes; Sir Maurice Laing; D Edwards.*

Charity Commission no. 326163

Information available Annual report and accounts, useful information on its website.

Summary

At least £2 million is donated each year, two-thirds of which goes to charities involved in nature conservation, environmental and sustainable development projects in non-first world countries (17 out of the 21 largest grants were made in these areas in 2002/03). Larger grants, of £50,000, tend to go to these areas. Charities working in other fields such as health and welfare (especially children) are also supported, but are more likely to receive amounts under £20,000.

Over half the grants awarded are for amounts of under £10,000 and are often for between £1,000 and £2,000. These go to a wide range of organisations, covering most fields of charity.

General

This foundation is another trust deriving from the Laing building fortune, though it does not share a common administration with the other Laing trusts. The original trust was established in 1982 by John Hedley Laing, who is also a trustee of the Whitley Laing Foundation and has previously been a trustee of WWF-UK, Conservation International and the Wildlife Protection Society of India. In 2002/03 the foundation had an income of £2.4 million, almost all from its investments then worth around £58 million.

In August 2003 the Rufford Foundation and the Maurice Laing Foundation merged to form this trust, which is essentially a name change as its objects and focus remain the same. The merger will not affect any charities currently supported by either of the organisations.

Grantmaking

The foundation's website contains the following information on its programmes:

The Major Grants Programme

This programme supports registered charities whose work is concerned with nature conservation, the environment and sustainable development, with approximately half of the foundation's funding going to these areas. This programme's remit also supports projects in the field of HIV/AIDS and our giving is facilitated via the Elton John AIDS Foundation. Within this programme, we tend to concentrate on projects in non-first world countries.

The Small Grants Programme

Many other causes are supported through this programme, especially in the field of social welfare. Grants in this category are available up to £5,000 for projects run by UK registered charities.

Rufford Small Grants for Nature Conservation

The foundation supports and runs this programme in association with the Whitley Laing Foundation. These grants of up to £5,000 are aimed at small conservation programmes and pilot projects and are not designed to be a small part of a large undertaking. Awards are available to individuals and small groups.

Guidelines for applicants

The website also contains the following helpful information for applicants:

1. What grants are available?

   Grants are available within [the] three categories.

2. Are there funds available now?

   There are only limited funds currently available due to our existing commitments. Only projects which meet our criteria in full are eligible, so please ensure that this is the case before you apply.

3. How long does it take for applications to be processed and responded to?

   We strive to respond to all applications within 4 weeks of receipt. Please do not telephone us, we will contact you!

4. Are there any time limits or 'closing dates' for applications?

   No. Applications are accepted throughout the year.

5. Is there a grant minimum?

   The minimum grant awarded is £500.

6. What is the maximum grant awarded?

   There is no set maximum, however, usually no gift in excess of £5,000 is granted for any non-conservation/ environmental projects. Moreover, even in this sector new gifts are unlikely to be in excess of £5,000– £10,000.

7. If a charity has been refused funding, is there an appeals procedure?

   Whilst we sympathetically consider all applications which meet with our criteria, with limited funds available it is not possible to either give reasons why applications are not successful or enter into any dialogue or correspondence regarding projects which have been refused funding.

8. If our application is not successful, may we reapply at a later date?

   As long as the application meets with all our criteria, reapplications can be made a minimum of 12 months after the initial application. Applications which fail to meet our criteria are rejected and informed.

For grants of £5,000 and below

One-off grants falling within this category are made at the discretion of the trust director and trust administrator on the basis of written information received from the prospective donee, which must include a copy of their latest accounts and annual report. The grants are subsequently ratified by all trustees.

For grants of between £5,000 and £20,000

As above with the exception that at least one trustee must approve the grant.

For grants of £20,000 and above

Prior to a recommendation being made to the trustees, a staff member will visit the organisation concerned. This is particularly the case for organisations new to the foundation. The grants are made with the approval of the majority of trustees. In the case of a recurring grant a full progress report is required from the project to be viewed at the trustees' bi-annual meetings.

Grants in 2002/03

During the year 121 grants were made totalling £2 million. The foundation's annual report contained the following information on the largest 21 grants during the year:

- £371,000 to Whitley Laing Foundation, made to cover:

  – 68 Rufford Small Grants of up to £5,000 each,

  – Sponsorship of the Whitley Award,

  – Rufford Postgraduate Programme,

  – Contributions towards administration costs.

- £250,000 to Elton John AIDS Foundation. This grant was divided amongst 17 charities working worldwide in this field running projects to support highly vulnerable, marginalised groups and young people living with or at risk of HIV/AIDS. The individuals grants ranged from £1,500 to £38,000.

- £148,000 to Conservation International. This grant was allocated to CI's Transfrontier Conservation Area (TFCA) Unit in order for them to develop a range of TFCA advocacy and facilitation initiatives in South Africa, Botswana, Namibia and Angola.

- £121,500 to TRAFFIC International. This grant covered a number of international projects based in the developing world and a proportion was allocated for development of the organisation as a whole.

- £94,000 to WWF-UK. This grant supported a number of their international campaigns including a series of pilot programmes to help WWF intensify its activities by concentrating on fewer, larger, more ambitious programmes of environmental work.

- £66,000 to Fauna & Flora International, as a contribution towards the core costs of the organisation.

- £66,000 to Peace Parks Foundation. This grant was split between a National TFCA Technical Advisor for Namibia, a facilitator for Limpop/ Shashe TFCA and a fundraiser for Peace Parks Foundation. Through the work of those in these positions the promotion of the conservation of biological diversity and the development of economic prosperity in southern Africa will be greatly assisted.

- £51,500 to Attivecomeprima. This Italian charitable organisation offers a global concept of support for the person facing the cancer experience, including psychological, psycho-physical, medical and creative activities. The grant covered a percentage of their core and fundraising costs.

- £50,000 to EIA Charitable Trust. This grant was made towards the budget of the extended campaign to protect the ozone layer, focusing on the illegal trade in chemicals harmful to the ozone layer, largely in developing countries.

- £50,000 to Global Canopy Foundation. This grant was made to support the core costs of this organisation which seeks to link existing and new projects studying the world's forest canopies into one integrated global programme of research, education and conservation.

- £50,000 to Royal Society for the Protection of Birds. This grant was made to support proposals to tackle the ongoing problem of illegal bird killing in Mediterranean countries, specifically Cyprus and Greece.

- £50,000 to Institute of Zoology. This grant contributed towards the compilation and production of the 2003 IUCN Red Lists and associated data analysis. The IUCN Red List is the world's most comprehensive inventory of the global conservation status of species.
- £50,000 to Southern African Wildlife College. The grant was made towards providing natural heritage managers for Africa, particularly in protected areas, with the motivation and relevant skills to manage their areas and associated wildlife populations in a sustainable and culturally acceptable manner in cooperation with stakeholders.
- £50,000 to IMPACT Foundation. IMPACT aims to combat needless disability through disease because of a lack of knowledge or shortage of medical service. This grant was made for two of IMPACT's programmes: the purchase of an ambulance and generator for the Floating Hospital – Bangladesh, and the FAITH Project in Metro Manila.
- £48,000 to Tusk Trust. The trust aims to provide practical support to conserve areas of natural habitat for the benefit of both wildlife and the surrounding communities. This grant was made towards the core costs of the trust and the Dian Fossey gorilla project in Rwanda.
- £41,500 to Compassion in World Farming Trust. This grant helped to fund the production of various materials to support their campaign to bring an end to battery and enriched cages for hens.
- £37,500 to Wildlife Protection Society of India. This grant was allocated to WPSI's Legal Programme, the Tiger Poaching & Trade Investigation Project and the Van Gujjar Resettlement Project, as well as a percentage of the running costs and infrastructure requirements. The WPSI has been receiving support from the foundation for many years.
- £30,000 to Global Action Plan. The grant was made towards Ergo, a lifestyle magazine and consumer guide to sustainable living, aimed at individuals with an interest in how their lives have an impact on the environment, and also a fundraising post at the charity.
- £30,000 to Wildlife Trust of India. WTI has a set of programmes which look comprehensively at conservation issues in India through a team of professionals that include wildlife

biologists, veterinarians, lawyers and communication specialists among others. The WTI has received on-going support from the foundation, and in 2002/03 received this grant towards core costs.

- £25,000 to Disasters & Emergency Committee. This grant was given to the umbrella organisation to support the Southern African Crisis Appeal.
- £22,000 to Environmental Justice Foundation. The EJF partners groups working on a diversity of issues including marine conservation, sustainable agriculture and the trade in endangered wildlife. In 2002/03 the foundation provided support for an international shrimp campaign that aims to raise public, corporate and political awareness of the serious ecological and social issues linked to global production of farmed and wild shrimp.

A total of 16 out of the above 21 beneficiaries were supported in the previous year, with some being regular beneficiaries. Interestingly, several of the grants listed above were for 'core costs', 'running costs' and salaries.

As well as the above mentioned grants, £100,000 was given to Charities Aid Foundation for further distribution on behalf of individual trustees of the Rufford Maurice Laing Foundation. This further distribution included grants to schools, colleges and welfare organisations.

Beneficiaries receiving more typical grants included Farms for City Children, Help the Aged and Samaritans (£20,000 each), Nobody's Children and University of Cambridge (£10,000 each), Down's Syndrome Educational Trust and University of Exeter (£5,000 each), Blind British Sport, Good Shepherd Project and Second Chance (£2,000 each), Dial UK and Medical Engineering Resource Unit (£1,500 each), Children in Distress, Mental Aid Projects and Uphill Ski Club (£1,000 each) and Horn Aid UK and Walk the Walk (£500 each).

Comment

In 2002/03, support costs and management and administration charges totalled £335,000, 16.75% of the total amount spent on grants.

Exclusions

The foundation cannot consider proposals for:

- building or construction projects;
- non-charitable organisations;
- grants to individuals;

- projects which seek to exclusively benefit local communities, such as playgroups, youth clubs, luncheon clubs and so on;
- loans;
- endowment funds;
- general appeals or circulars;
- student conservation expeditions.

Applications

For Major Grants Programme, contact Terry Kenny. For Small Grants Programme, contact Sian Venturotti. All applications must be received by post and meet the following criteria:

- All applicants must be charities registered in the UK.

Applications must include:

- a comprehensive plan outlining the project for which funding is being sought;
- a full budget;
- a covering letter with contact details;
- a copy of the charity's most recent accounts;
- a copy of the latest annual report (if available).

Applications are assessed monthly. Gifts over £5,000 will be considered at trustees' meetings held twice a year. Each application is assessed individually and while the trust strives to respond quickly, it only has one full-time member of staff, so please be patient. Any incomplete applications received, or applications which fail to meet with the trust's criteria, as outlined above, will immediately be rejected.

After a grant has been made, the organisations running the project will be asked for a progress report. Visits may also be made to some of the larger organisations.

For Rufford Small Grants for Nature Conservation, contact Josh Cole by e-mail only at josh@rufford.org.

The Saddlers' Company Charitable Fund

General

£303,000 (2003/04)

Beneficial area UK, but mainly England in practice.

Saddlers' Hall, 40 Gutter Lane, London
EC2V 6BR

Tel. 020 7726 8661/6 **Fax** 020 7600 0386

Email clerk@saddlersco.co.uk

Website www.saddlersco.co.uk

Correspondent W S Brereton-Martin,
Clerk

Trustee *The Saddlers' Company. The
company is directed by the court of
assistants consisting of the master, three
wardens, a number of past masters and up
to four junior assistants. There shall be a
minimum of 12 and a maximum of 24.*

Charity Commission no. 261962

Information available Annual report
and acounts were provided by the trust.

The trust supports many of the same
charities each year such as Alleyn's
School and Riding for the Disabled.
After making these allocations, about
one quarter of the remaining money is
allocated to major UK charities working
in all charitable sectors, and about three
quarters for responding to specific
charitable appeals in support of people
with disabilities, which are received
throughout the year.

The trustees have focused on aiding
smaller charities assisting people with
disabilities since 1996. This policy is
being continued. To meet the trust's
policy, members of the livery are asked
to visit a charity local to them and
report on the charity's suitability to
receive a grant. This is then considered
by a grant committee whose
recommendations are passed on to the
trustees.

In 2003/04 the trust had assets of
£7.5 million and a total income of
£521,000. Grants were made totalling
£303,000, broken down as follows:

category	2003/2004	(2002/2003)
City of London	£10,000	(£3,000)
Saddlery trade	£12,000	(£7,000)
Equestrian	£35,000	(£40,000)
Education	£140,000	(£154,000)
General charitable purposes	£25,000	(£13,000)
Charities for people with disabilities	£81,000	(£86,000)

The accounts listed all grants over
£1,000, broken down into the relevant
programmes, as follows:

City of London

Beneficiaries included St Paul's
Cathedral (£1,000).

Saddlery trade

Beneficiaries included Museum of
Leathercraft (£2,000) and Walsall
Leather Museum (£1,000).

Equestrian

Beneficiaries included British Horse
Society (£24,000) and Combined
Services Equitation Association (£2,000).

Education

By far the largest grant made during the
year was £130,000 to Alleyn's School for
Saddlers' Scholarships, a regular
beneficiary. Other recipients of large
grants were Nottingham Trent
University (£4,000) and City & Guilds
(£3,000).

General charitable activity

Beneficiaries included Royal British
Legion (£1,700) and Leather
Conservation Centre (£9,000).

*General charitable activity – charities for
people with disabilities*

There was a large grant to a regular
beneficiary under this category, £28,000
to Riding for the Disabled. Grants of
£1,200 each went to 27 organisations
including Dreams Come True, RoRo
Sailing Project, Queen Alexandra
College, Across (Southend), West Suffolk
Headway, PSS Caring for the
Generations, Dressability and Growing
Places. Other beneficiaries included
KIDS London (£1,500) and Visually
Handicapped Self Help and Company of
Hackney Carriage Drivers (£1,000 each).

Exclusions

No grants to individuals.

Applications

In writing to the correspondent. Grants
are made in January and July, following
trustees' meetings. Charities are asked to
submit reports at the end of the
following year on their continuing
activities and the use of any grant
received.

The Sainsbury Family Charitable Trusts

See individual trusts

About £55 million (2003/04)
Beneficial area See individual trusts.

Allington House 1st Floor, 150 Victoria
Street, London SW1E 5AE

Tel. 020 7410 0330 **Fax** 020 7410 0332

Email info@sfct.co.uk

Correspondent Michael Pattison,
Director

Trustee

These trusts, listed in the box below,
each have their own entries (except for
the four smallest which are described at
the end of this entry). However they are
administered together and it is said that
'an application to one is taken as an
application to all'.

Their grantmaking ranges from the
largest to the smallest scale, including
massive long-term support for major
institutions such as the National Gallery
or the Sainsbury Centre for Mental
Health as well as for a range of specific
issues ranging from autism to the
environmental effects of aviation. There
is an office with over 30 staff and a large
number of specialist advisers.

However, even collectively, the trusts do
not form a generalist grantmaking
organisation; though active in most
fields of charitable activity, it is usually
within particular and often quite
specialised parts of each sector.

Most of the trusts use a similar formula
to describe their grantmaking:

'Proposals are generally invited by the
trustees or initiated at their request.
Unsolicited applications are discouraged
and are unlikely to succeed, even if they
fall within an area in which the trustees
are interested. The trustees prefer to
support innovative schemes that can be
successfully replicated or become self-
sustaining.'

A typical programme might have the
following elements:

- support for a major, long-term
  research initiative, whether academic

THE SAINSBURY FAMILY TRUSTS
(with totals of grant payments or approvals
for the most recent year available):

Gatsby Foundation	£33,300,000
Linbury Trust	£6,500,000
Monument Trust	£3,200,000
Headley Trust	£3,100,000
Jerusalem Trust	£2,700,000
Kay Kendall Leukaemia Fund	£978,000
J J Charitable Trust	£659,000
Ashden Trust	£650,000
Three Guineas Trust	£639,000
Tedworth Trust	£595,000
Glass-House Trust	£572,000
Woodward Trust	£467,000
Staples Trust	£425,000
Alan & Babette Sainsbury Trust	£375,000
True Colours Trust	£278,000
Mark Leonard Trust	£201,000
Indigo Trust	£160,000
Elizabeth Clark Trust	£145,000
Total	**£54,945,000**

or in the form of an action research programme;

- support for specialised national groups promoting good practice in the field concerned;
- grants for a few service delivery organisations, often small and local, and addressing the most severe aspects of the issues involved.

In these editor's view, charities that are indeed developing new ideas and approaches would be most unwise to assume that the Sainsbury trusts will automatically get to hear of this.

'Applications' are probably not the best way forward – indeed they are a poor form of art generally, and may perhaps be best avoided except where specifically requested. More sensible might be to write briefly and say what is being done or planned, on the assumption that, if one or more of the trusts is indeed interested in that area of work, they will want to know about what you are doing. A telephone call to do the same is fine. Staff are polite, but wary of people seeking to talk about money rather than issues.

More generally, the trusts are involved in a number of networks, with which they maintain long-term contact. Charities doing work relevant to the interests of these trusts may find that if they are not a part of these networks (which may not be inclusive and most of which are probably London-based) they may get limited Sainsbury attention.

The most inappropriate approach would often be from a fundraiser. Staff, and in many cases trustees, are knowledgeable and experienced in their fields, and expect to talk to others in the same position.

Most of the trusts do fund ongoing service delivery, but generally infrequently and usually on a modest scale. For such grants it is not clear how they choose this play scheme or that wildlife trust. To them, these may be small and relatively unimportant decisions, and they may rely on trustees or staff simply coming across something suitable, or on recommendations through what they have called their 'usual networks'.

Collective support

The trusts sometimes act collectively, with support for the same organisations from a number of the trusts.

In 2003/04 organisations that appeared in more than one grants list included Royal Ballet School and National Portrait Gallery, and also Ashden Awards for Sustainable Energy.

It is not clear to the outsider whether such cross-trust support is the result of interaction at trustee or at officer level, or both. However it does seem that there is such a thing as being 'in' with the group of trusts as a whole – a cause of occasional resentment by those who see the Sainsbury trusts, perhaps entirely wrongly, as being something of a closed shop.

The smaller Sainsbury family trusts

The True Colours Trust (CC no. 1089893)

Special needs, sensory disabilities and impairments, palliative care, young carers, HIV/Aids.

Grant total: £278,000 (2003/04)

Trustees: Miss L A Sainsbury; D M Flynn.

Established in 2001, this is the newest of the 18 Sainsbury family charitable trusts. It is interested in supporting:

- services for people with special needs;
- hearing impairment in children and adults;
- speech and language disorders;
- hospice and palliative care for children;
- services which support young careers;
- support for people with HIV/Aids in Africa.

The 2003/04 accounts included the following statement, which appears to be generic across the Sainsbury trusts:

Grants are likely to be made to a small number of pilot projects which have the potential to develop into larger programmes. The trustees are also likely to consider support for projects that assist in raising awareness and the development of high quality educational materials. The trustees prefer to support innovative schemes that can be successfully replicated or become self-sustaining.

Proposals are generally invited by the trustees or initiated at their request. Unsolicited applications are not encouraged and are unlikely to be successful. Grants are not normally made to individuals.

In 2003/04 it had assets of £755,000 and an income of £41,000. In total 76 grants were approved totalling £278,000, broken down as follows:

Special needs – 2 grants totalling £139,000

Children's Express received £79,000 towards an action research project for children who are deaf to produce an overview of the experience to gain personal development and skills in journalism, research, running a project and teamwork. National Blind Children's Society was given £60,000 to produce set texts as part of the CustomEyes programme.

Children and young careers

No grants were approved during the year under this category, although there were three grants paid which were approved, and accounted for, in the previous financial year.

HIV/Aids in Africa – 1 grant of £10,000

This went to Nairobi Hospice towards a palliative care training programme.

Small grants for disadvantaged children – 72 grants totalling £76,000

The majority of grants in this category were of less than £1,000 each; 58 such grants were made totalling £11,000. Larger grants included £10,000 each to Coleraine and District Riding for Disabled Association towards new premises and Maplewood School for a new hydrotherapy pool, £8,000 to Special Toys Educational Postal Service for switches and specially adapted toys for use by 50 children, £5,000 to Jessie May Trust for palliative care, £4,000 to Park Lane Special School for a sensory lighting system, £2,000 to Chester and Ellesmere Port Young Carers Project for the holiday programme and £1,000 to Winkleigh Pre-School for resources.

General – 1 grant of £30,000

This went to BBC World Service Trust to assist in raising awareness of Down's Syndrome in Russia.

The Mark Leonard Trust (CC no. 1040323)

Environmental education, youth, general. Grant total: £201,000 (2003/04)

Trustees: Mrs Z Sainsbury; Miss Judith Portrait; J J Sainsbury; Mark Sainsbury.

This trust mostly supports environmental causes and youth work, although it also gives towards general charitable purposes. The following descriptions of its more specific work are taken from its 2003/04 annual report:

Environment

Grants are made for environmental education, particularly to support projects displaying practical ways of involving children and young adults. The trustees rarely support new educational resource packs in isolation from the actual process of learning and discovering. They are more interested in programmes which help pupils and teachers to develop a theme over time (such as renewable energy), perhaps combining IT resources for data gathering and communication, with exchange visits and the sharing of information and ideas between schools.

The trustees are particularly interested in projects that enable children and young people to develop a sense of ownership of the project over time, and that provide direct support to teachers to deliver exciting and high quality education in the classroom.

The trustees are also interested in the potential for sustainable transport, energy efficiency and renewable energy in the wider society. In some cases the trustees will consider funding research, but only where there is a clear practical application. Proposals are more likely to be considered when they are testing an idea, model or strategy in practice.

Youth work

The trustees aim to help projects that support the rehabilitation of young people who have become marginalised and involved in antisocial or criminal activities. They wish to apply their grants to overcome social exclusion. They are also interested in extending and adding value to the existing use of school buildings, enhancing links between schools and the community, and encouraging greater involvement of parents, school leavers and volunteers in extracurricular activities.

The accounts also include the following statement:

Proposals are generally invited by the trustees or initiated at their request. Unsolicited applications are not encouraged and are unlikely to be successful, even if they fall within an area in which the trustees are interested. The trustees' objective is to support innovative schemes with seed funding, leading projects to achieve sustainability and successful replication. Grants are not normally made to individuals.

In 2003/04 it had asset of £8.5 million and an income of £881,000. Grants were approved totalling £201,000, broken down as follows:

Environment – 14 grants totalling £111,000

The largest grants were £22,000 to Ashden Awards for Sustainable Energy and £21,000 to Building Exploratory for a new exhibition room on construction and regeneration in Hackney. Other grants included £10,000 to Transport 2000 Trust for core costs, £9,600 to Green Light Trust to set-up a forest schools programme in the East of England, £7,000 to Walworth Garden Farm for a part-time community education coordinator, £4,000 to

Sustrans for the national development and dissemination of Travel Smart Initiative pilots and activities, £3,500 to Cyclists' Touring Club for a web-based cycling information facility, £600 to Liverpool City Environment Centre for a feasibility study for an outdoor classroom and renewable energy demonstration facilities.

Youth work – 9 grants totalling £77,000

The largest were £14,000 to WorldWide Volunteering for Young People towards enabling a free postal service for youth volunteering opportunities and £10,000 each to Energy and Vision for a schools education worker, Resonance 104.4FM for training and outreach posts and the employment of a business development officer, Shout! towards a mentor coordinator working with performance arts amongst young people at risk of teenage pregnancy or gun crime in Tottenham and Street Dreams towards salary costs.

Other grants were £7,000 to Children's Express for the photojournalism component of a nine-month media course for children in Islington, £5,900 to Groundwork Leeds for two pilot environmental and social learning courses for 13 to 14 year olds and £5,000 each to The Bridge for a training video for people working with young people at risk from drug or alcohol dependency and Hampton Trust for a peer mentoring project amongst teenagers in south east Hampshire.

General – 3 grants totalling £28,000

These went to London Borough of Tower Hamlets towards the creation of a Learning Lab at Whitechapel Idea Store (£20,000), Play Ball for All towards the indigenous production of low cost leather footballs for promoting health and fitness amongst young people in sub-Saharan Africa (£5,800) and St Nicholas's Church – New Romney for emergency repairs (£2,000).

The Indigo Trust (CC no. 1075920)

Offenders, core skills, homelessness, women.   Grant total: £160,000 (2003/04)

Trustees: Miss F E Sainsbury; C T S Stone; Miss J S Stone

The following information is taken from the 2003/04 annual report:

During the year, the trustees have continued to support projects in the following areas of interest:

- improvement of education, learning and mental health care in young offenders institutions and prisons

- supporting the development of core skills, especially literacy, in children, women and disadvantaged groups
- homelessness, particularly among young people and ex-armed services personnel
- women's issues, particularly raising awareness of domestic violence.

Grants are likely to be made to a small number of pilot projects which have the potential to develop into larger programmes. The trustees are also likely to consider support for projects that assist in raising awareness and the development of high quality educational materials. The trustees prefer to support innovative schemes that can be successfully replicated or become self-sustaining.

Proposals are generally invited by the trustees or initiated at their request. Unsolicited applications are not encouraged and are unlikely to be successful. Grants are not normally made to individuals.

In 2003/04 it had assets of £2.4 million and an income of £2.6 million, almost all of which came from donations received. Grants were approved to four organisations totalling £180,000. These were categorised under four separate headings, which did not include the homelessness category from the previous year.

Clean Break Theatre Company received £35,000 in the Young Offenders category. This was for the 'Women and Anger' anger management programme for women who are prisoners, ex-offenders or detained under the Mental Health Act.

Women's Education in Building was given £42,000 in the Women's Issues category, for teaching costs for a pilot English course for Somali women.

Refugees into Jobs received £93,000 in the Literacy and Basic Skills category. This was for an access to work scheme for refugee teachers in West London.

Under the General category, Ashden Awards for Sustainable Energy received £10,000 towards its 2004 awards.

The Elizabeth Clark Charitable Trust (CC no. 265206)

Palliative care.
                    Grant total: £145,000 (2003/04)

Trustees: Miss Judith Portrait; Dr Jane Davy; Dr Gillian Ford.

This is now the smallest of the 18 Sainsbury Family Charitable Trusts. The administrators tell us that the trustees have now decided how to allocate its remaining funds and the trustees will therefore not be considering any further applications. It describes its work as follows in the 2003/04 annual report:

Trustees are free to apply funds for any charitable purpose. Bearing in mind the settlor's wish to bring about improvements in nursing, the trustees have decided to concentrate on supporting development of good practice in palliative care. Trustees do not generally support capital or revenue appeals from hospices and research bodies nor make grants to individuals. They have a proactive approach to their grantmaking and unsolicited appeals are unlikely to succeed, particularly now that the resources of the charity are predominately earmarked for a single programme as discussed below under 'Review of the Years.

The following text is taken from the 'Review of the Year' section:

Breathlessness is a major symptom for many patients with end-stage disease. For some time [the] trustees have been keen to support an innovative breathlessness project, and this year they approved a grant to Addenbrooke's NHS Trust (now Cambridge University Hospitals NHS Foundation Trust) of £120,000 over two years towards a pilot for a community-based, multidisciplinary breathlessness service for both cancer and non-cancer patients.

As noted in previous annual reports, the trustees are supporting a major project at the University of Sheffield Department of Palliative Medicine. This project aims to design and test a general assessment and referral tool for palliative care which can be used in all care settings. Trustees consider that progress in the concluding stages of the first phrase of this project has been good. Trustees plan to look at the case for supporting a second phrase in due course, and are unlikely to make other significant awards until they have decided whether to offer further support to this project.

In 2003/04 it had assets of £472,000 and an income of £27,000. Grants totalled £145,000. Aside from the £120,000 to Addenbrooke's NHS Trust, £25,000 went to St Michael's Hospice.

Exclusions

No grants are normally given to individuals by many of the trusts (though a number of them fund bursary schemes and the like operated by other organisations).

Applications

See above.

The Alan and Babette Sainsbury Charitable Fund

General

£376,000 (2003/04)

Beneficial area Worldwide.

Allington House, 1st Floor, 150 Victoria Street, London SW1E 5AE

Tel. 020 7410 0330 **Fax** 020 7410 0332

Email info@sfct.org.uk

Correspondent Michael Pattison, Director

Trustees *The Hon. Simon Sainsbury; Miss Judith Portrait.*

Charity Commission no. 292930

Information available Full accounts were provided by the trust.

Summary

This is one of the Sainsbury Family Charitable Trusts, which share a joint administration. They have a common approach to grantmaking which is described in the entry for the group as a whole.

This trust's main areas of interest are (with number and the value of grant approvals in 2003/04):

	no.	approved
Health and social welfare	10	£185,000
The arts	3	£99,000
Education	1	£75,000
General	1	£30,000
Overseas	1	£10,000
Scientific and medical research	1	£1,000

General

The late Lord Sainsbury of Drury Lane was the settlor of this trust. Its assets in 2003/04 stood at £10.1 million, generating an income of £558,000. Grants were paid during the year totalling £376,000.

Staff involved in its work include Michael Pattison, director of all the trusts in the group, Patricia Morison and Victoria Hornby.

The following information about the trust's grantmaking in 2003/04 is taken from the annual report.

The trustees concentrate their resources on a small number of programmes which are built on themes of the trust's earlier grantmaking. At present these include support for ethnic minority and refugee groups, community-based mental health initiatives, human rights and encouraging participation in the arts.

Grants

The largest grants during the year were made to: Evelyn Oldfield Unit towards the cost of leadership training in west London and the development of a support programme for small refugee groups in Manchester (£110,000); and Pestalozzi Children's Village Trust towards the costs of educating disadvantaged children (£75,000).

Other beneficiaries included: Islington Music Centre (£50,000), Ashden Awards for Sustainable Energy (£30,000), Medical Foundation for the Care of Victims of Torture (£40,000), Student Action for Refugees (£20,000), World ORT (£10,000) and Nightingale House (£5,000).

Exclusions

Grants are not normally made to individuals.

Applications

See the guidance for applicants in the entry for the Sainsbury Family Charitable Trusts. A single application will be considered for support by all the trusts in the group. However, please see comments above regarding the selection of beneficiaries.

The Robert and Lisa Sainsbury Charitable Trust

See below

£2.1 million (2001/02)

Beneficial area Unrestricted.

c/o Horwarth Clark Whitehill, 25 New Street Square, London EC4A 3LN

Tel. 020 7353 1577 **Fax** 020 7583 1720

Email david.walker@horwath.co.uk

Correspondent David Walker, Director

Trustees *Lady Lisa Sainsbury; Christopher Stone; Stephanie Dale; Dominic Flynn; Gilla Harris; Judith Portrait; John Rosenheim.*

Charity Commission no. 276923

Information available Accounts, with a brief report.

The trust's objects are 'the advancement of education in art, the humanities and other branches of learning in the UK and elsewhere'. It primarily supports the Sainsbury artistic institutions at the University of East Anglia in Norwich.

In 2001/02 it had an income of £1.8 million, mainly from grants and donations, and made grants totalling £2.1 million. Although the annual report for 2001/02 continues to say that 'grants have been made to a wide range of charities', there were in fact only 10 awards listed, and two of them accounted for most of the grant total.

The largest were to the University (£1.3 million for the acquisition of works of art and for a special exhibition) and NW London Hospital – NHS Trust (£500,000).

The other beneficiaries were Sainsbury Institute for the Study of Japanese Arts and Culture (£108,000), Dean and Chapter of the Cathedral of Norwich (£97,000), Trinity Hospice (£35,000), Dominican Missions (£7,000), Demelza House Children's Hospice (£1,500) and British Museum Society, London Welsh Male Voice Choir and Nurses Welfare (£1,000 each). Grants for less than £1,000 each totalled £4,500.

This is not one of the jointly administered Sainsbury Family Charitable Trusts, though much of its funding has in the past come from the Gatsby Foundation, which is.

In 2002/03 the trust had a total expenditure of £1.3 million. Unfortunately, no further information was available for the year.

Comment

Despite ample warning, and their obligation to the contrary, the Charity Commission were unable to give us sight of this trust's recent accounts.

Exclusions

No grants to individuals.

Applications

In writing to the correspondent.

Basil Samuel Charitable Trust

General

£404,000 (2002/03)

Beneficial area UK and overseas.

c/o Great Portland Estates Plc, Knighton House, 56 Mortimer Street, London W1N 8BD

Tel. 020 7580 3040

Correspondent Mrs Coral Samuel, Trustee

Trustee *Coral Samuel.*

Charity Commission no. 206579

Information available Accounts were provided by the trust.

The trust describes its policy as making 'a limited number of grants of £25,000 or more to medical, socially supportive, educational and cultural charities plus a number of smaller donations to other charities'. The larger awards are often part of ongoing support, while the remainder are more typically one-off awards for between £5,000 and £10,000.

In 2002/03 the trust had an income of £355,000. Grants were made to 25 organisations totalling £404,000. Thirteen organisations received grants in the previous year, including the largest beneficiary, CST, which received £60,000 in 2002/03.

Other beneficiaries included Somerset House Arts Fund, the Old Vic Theatre Trust and Jewish Care (£50,000 each), Macmillan Cancer Relief (£30,000), Museum of London (£25,000), Help the Hospices and Attingham Trust (£10,000 each), Meningitis Trust, Countryside Foundation for Education and Royal Star & Garter Home (£5,000 each), Commonwealth Jewish Trust (£2,000) and Wellbeing (£1,000).

Exclusions

Grants are given to registered charities only.

Applications

In writing to the correspondent. 'The trustees meet on a formal basis annually and regularly on an informal basis to discuss proposals for individual donations.'

The Sandra Charitable Trust

Health, social welfare, animal welfare

£376,000 to organisations (2002/03)

Beneficial area UK, with a slight preference for the south east of England.

Moore Stephens, St Paul's House, Warwick Lane, London EC4P 4BN

Tel. 020 7248 4499

Correspondent K Lawrence

Trustees *Richard Moore; M Macfayden.*

Charity Commission no. 327492

Information available Full accounts were provided by the trust.

The trust's review of activities states that 'beneficiaries included nurses, charities involved in animal welfare and research, environmental protection, relief of poverty and youth development'.

In 2002/03 it had assets of £10.7 million, which generated an income of £391,000. Expenses which, included costs of generating funds and administration, were extremely low at £1,000. Grants were made to organisations totalling £376,000, with a further £56,000 being given in 108 grants to nurses.

The largest grants were £44,000 to National Sports Medicine Institute of the UK, £38,000 to SPARKS, £20,000 each to Barnardos and Florence Nightingale Foundation and £10,000 each to Museum of Garden History and Treloar.

Grants in the south east of England included £5,000 each to Dorchester Abbey Restoration Campaign and Shaftesbury Homes & Arethusa, £4,500 to Dulwich Picture Gallery, £3,000 to St Mary–le–bow Church – London, £2,200 to West London Action for Children, £2,000 to Berkshire Medical Heritage Centre and £1,000 each to Oxford Radcliffe Hospital's Charitable Fund and South East Cancer Help Centre.

Donations elsewhere included £9,800 to Youth Sport Trust, £5,000 each to Civic Trust and Health Unlimited, £3,000 each to Anti–Slavery International, Charlie Waller Memorial Trust, Multiple Sclerosis Society and Students Exploring Marriage, £2,000 each to Asthma Research, Development Trust, Haven Trust, National Library for the Blind and Royal Life Saving Society UK and £1,000 each to Child Bereavement Trust, Hope

& Homes for Children, Readathon and Woodland Heritage.

Exclusions

No grants to individuals other than nurses.

Applications

The trust states that 'unsolicited applications are not requested, as the trustees prefer to support charities whose work they have researched ... funds are largely committed'.

The Schreib Trust

Jewish, general

£450,000 (2002/03)
Beneficial area UK.

147 Stamford Hill, London N16 5LG
Tel. 020 8802 5492
Correspondent Mrs R Niederman, Trustee
Trustees *Mrs I Schreiber; J Schreiber; A Green; Mrs R Niederman.*
Charity Commission no. 275240
Information available Basic accounts were on file at the Charity Commission, without a list of grants or a full narrative report.

It is difficult to glean an enormous amount of information about this trust's grant-giving policies as only brief accounts were on file at the Charity Commission. Although the trust's objects are general, it lists its particular priorities as relief of poverty and advancement of religious education. In practice, the trust may only support Jewish organisations.

In 2002/03 the trust made grants totalling around £450,000, although it is not known who received the money or what size the grants were. (In 1999/2000 the trust made grants totalling £2.1 million, which appears to have been all of its endowment. The trust's income is now mainly from donations, most of which is then distributed as grants.)

Comment

There was no response to repeated written requests for a copy of the most recent annual report and accounts, despite the

legal requirement to provide these on demand.

Applications

In writing to the correspondent.

Schroder Charity Trust

Medical, international relief, social welfare, heritage, environment, arts

£442,000 (2002)
Beneficial area UK, occasionally overseas.

31–45 Gresham Street, London EC2V 7QA
Tel. 020 7698 6578
Correspondent Mrs S Robertson, Secretary
Trustees *Directors: Mrs C L Fitzalan Howard; Mrs C B Mallinckrodt; B L Schroder; T B Schroder; Mrs L K E Schroder-Fane; Mrs J Schroder.*
Charity Commission no. 214050
Information available Accounts had been filed with the Charity Commission up to 2003, but were only available to view in the public files up to 2002.

This trust makes grants towards medical charities, international relief, social welfare, heritage, environment and the arts. Preference is given to UK-registered charities and charities in which the Schroder family has a special interest.

In 2003 the trust had an income of £702,000 and a total expenditure of £560,000, this information was taken from the Charity Commission, no further information was available for this year. In 2003 it had assets of £3.3 million, an income of £641,000 and made 128 grants totalling £442,000.

By far the largest donation was £200,000 to St Paul's Cathedral Foundation. There were four other grants of £10,000 or more: £50,000 to Durham High School for Girls; £30,000 to Columba Centre; and £10,000 each to Cord Blood Charity and Old People's Home.

Other beneficiaries included Anthony Nolan Bone Marrow Trust (£5,500), Atlantic Education Project, CAF, English National Ballet and Game Conservancy Trust (£5,000 each), Air League

Educational Trust (£1,500), Alzheimer's Society, Brainwave, Cancer Relief Macmillan Fund, National Maritime Museum and RUKBA (£1,000 each) and Action on Addiction, British Lung Foundation, Drugscope, Help the Aged, National Eye Research Centre and Water Aid (£500 each).

Following the sale of the investment banking arm of Schroder plc in 2000, the Schroder Charity Trust is no longer a vehicle for the company's charitable giving. Consequently, the scale and culture of the trust has changed. We were advised that: 'The charitable giving policy is now reactive rather than a proactive ethos and is concentrated on specific family projects and appeals received personally (e.g. at home) by the directors of the trust.'

Exclusions

No grants to individuals.

Applications

In writing to correspondent, at any time. Trustees meet every six months to consider appeals.

The Francis C Scott Charitable Trust

Disadvantaged young people in Cumbria and north Lancashire

£1.2 million (2002/03)
Beneficial area Cumbria and north Lancashire, comprising the towns of Lancaster, Morecambe, Heysham and Camford.

Suite 3, Sand Aire House, Kendal, Cumbria LA9 4UJ
Tel. 01539 741610 **Fax** 01539 741611
Email info@fcsct.org.uk
Website www.fcsct.org.uk
Correspondent Chris Batten, Director
Trustees *Mrs S E Bagot, chair; R W Sykes; D Shaw; Miss M M Scott; F A Scott; W Dobie; I H Pirnie; F J R Boddy; C C Spedding.*
Charity Commission no. 232131
Information available Information was provided by the trust.

This trust supports registered charities addressing community deprivation in Cumbria and north Lancashire. In autumn 2003 the trust undertook a strategic review of its grant-making policies. It is principally concerned with meeting the needs of young people from 0–19 years. It seeks to target its funds where they can be most effective and can make a real difference to people's lives.

The trust will continue to support the following areas of particular interest:

- family work to support children and their carers in the age range 0 to 8 years;
- youth work with young people of 13–19 years, including leader training;
- finding meaningful ways to support 10–13 year olds through the 'transition years'

The trust welcomes and actively seeks funding partnerships with other grantmakers and service providers to enable the development of projects within Cumbria and Lancashire. Grants are usually in the range of £1,000 to £15,000. It will provide both capital and revenue grants, typically covering no more than 3 years duration.

In 2002/03 grants to 102 organisations totalled £1.2 million and were broken down by the trust as follows:

Young people	£437,000 (29 grants)
Families and children, women and men	£370,000 (24)
Disabled, chronically ill and elderly	£167,000 (25)
Communities and charity support	£130,000 (16)
Other	£56,000 (8)

Exclusions

No grants to individuals or non-registered charities. No grants for church restoration, medical appeals, expeditions or scholarships. No applications are accepted from schools.

It is unusual for trustees to support UK charities with local operations or projects.

Applications

The trust is always pleased to hear from charities who need help. If an organisation thinks that it may come within the trust's criteria it is invited to write to the director to request an application form. Initial applications should be made on the trust's standard form which should be completed and returned with the latest set of accounts.

The trust welcomes potential applicants to telephone the director or one of his colleagues for an informal discussion before submitting an application.

Grants below £5,000 are decided on a monthly basis with larger appeals going to the full trustees' meetings in March, July and November.

The whole process of application to receipt of a grant may take up to four months. An application form is available from the correspondent and should be returned with the latest set of audited accounts.

The Scottish Community Foundation

Community development, general

£862,000 (2002/03)
Beneficial area Scotland.

126 Canongate, Edinburgh EH8 8DD
Tel. 0131 524 0300 **Fax** 0131 524 0325
Website www. scottishcommunityfoundation.com
Correspondent Giles Ruck, Chief Executive
Trustees *Rev'd Bobby Anderson; Alastair Balfour; Anne Boyd; Hamish Buchan; Alastair Dempster; Michael Gray; Iain Johnston; Helen Mackie; George Menzies; Martin Sime; Graeme Simmers.*
Scottish Charity no. SC022910
Information available Information was provided by the trust.

The Scottish Community Foundation spent over £860,000 on grants in 2002/03. Of this amount, roughly 40% or £330,000 was earmarked for specific statutory or lottery grant programmes including Millennium Awards for individuals, while around £530,000 was spent on general community grants. The foundation makes small grants, of up to £5,000, for community groups in Scotland. In common with other community foundations, it makes grants from various sources – both public and private – as well as having its own endowment with which it distributes money. The endowment was already relatively high, amounting to a little over £1.3 million in 2003.

The foundation provided the following general information:

Since our creation in 1996 we have distributed over £7 million in grants across Scotland. Through a range of programmes we have supported constituted community groups and individuals working to improve their own life and enhance their communities.

At this time we are only able to support constituted community groups as grants for individual awardees – Chase Youth Awards and You and Yours Community Awards – have reached their limits. We hope to be in a position to restart these programmes within the next year. Please visit our website for further information.

For community groups, so long as your project fits the eligibility criteria detailed in each sector and your group has a formal constitution then we will be delighted to hear your idea and receive an application under one of the Community Grants or Women's Fund grant programmes. If you want to confirm your organisation's eligibility or sound out your idea, then please call us.

New large scale developmental grants
A new programme has been introduced called the New Opportunities Fund Fair Share programme which will make large scale developmental and capacity building grants for selected communities.

Community grants
Community grants are one-of sums of up to £5,000. The purpose of these grants is to assist charities and groups improving the quality of life and life chances in Scotland. This funding is directed at local groups and charities, often where the project is initiated by members of the local community.

Specific grants
The Women's Fund raises funds for community organisations supporting women's personal development or involvement in their community.

Fair Share is an initiative designed to target lottery money at those parts of the UK that have not received their fair share of lottery funds in the past.

Exclusions

The community grants programme will not fund non-constituted community groups.

Applications

'There are no closing dates for applications. Decisions for main grants will be made approximately three months from the receipt of application. Decisions for the small grants programme will be made within four weeks of receipt of application. 'If you would like an application form, more information or advice, please contact the foundation and we will give you any further help we can. 'Guidelines are available to help you complete the application form. 'We cannot assess groups for a grant without sight of their constitution (or other founding deed) and up-to-date accounts. Please ensure you include these when returning your application form to avoid any delay in processing your application. 'If you would like us to acknowledge safe receipt of your application please address, stamp and return the postcard.'

The Samuel Sebba Charitable Trust

Jewish causes

£961,000 (2002/03)

Beneficial area UK and Israel.

Clive Marks and Company, 1st Floor, Lynton House, 7–12 Tavistock Square, London WC1H 9LT

Tel. 020 7388 3577 **Fax** 020 7388 3570

Correspondent Clive M Marks, Trustee

Trustees *Leigh Sebba; Stanley Sebba; Leslie Sebba; Victor Klein; Clive M Marks.*

Charity Commission no. 253351

Information available Annual report and accounts on file at the Charity Commission.

Summary

The trust makes grants, normally of £5,000, to Jewish organisations as well as a few non-Jewish ones. Its annual report says that unsolicited applications are unlikely to succeed.

General

In 2002/03 the trust had an income of £719,000 from investments worth £36 million. The trust outlines its policy as follows:

The principal aims of the trust are to support a wide range of registered charities and to encompass many areas of the Jewish community, particularly those involved in learning and teaching of the Jewish faith, its history, as well as the training of Rabbis, teachers, lay-leaders and counsellors.

The trust will from time to time fund a small number of specialist consultants to advise charities on their internal structure,

budgeting, staff training, as well as future planning and efficiency.

Monitoring can be carried out when recommended by a small research team who are available to attend site visits, this facility enables the trust to support efficient and effective charities, giving them the confidence for on-going support.

Future developments

The trustees will be concentrating principally on four areas:

- general communal matters including youth clubs and community centres;
- Jewish education, Jewish schools and training of future Rabbis;
- hospices and aged;
- medical aid and hospitals.

Grants in 2002/03

Grants were categorised by the trust as follows (with figures for 2001/02 in brackets):

Education	£374,000	(£521,000)
Medical	£249,000	(£72,000)
Community	£241,000	(£94,000)
Hospice and aged	£36,000	(£8,500)
Interfaith	£30,000	(–)
Arts	£18,000	(£21,000)
Children/youth	£12,000	(£20,000)
Preventative medicine	£1,500	(–)
Total	£961,500	(£736,500)

The trust made 77 grants for £5,000 or more and a number of smaller grants totalling £131,500. Most listed grants were for £5,000 and just under half of the beneficiaries had received a grant in the previous year. The largest grant went to Neurim, a home for people with severe disabilities (£100,000). There were six further substantial grants, going to the following beneficiaries: Multiple Sclerosis Society (£80,000), British Council of Shaare Zedek Medical Centre (£72,000), British Friends of Haifa University and Multiple Sclerosis Trust (£50,000 each), Friends of Bar Ilan University (£25,000), Jerusalem Academy Trust (£20,000),

Other grants were made to beneficiaries including Coventry Cathedral and Riding for the Disabled.

Comment

Unfortunately, there is no narrative review of the charitable activities, nor are the grants analysed and explained as the law requires.

Exclusions

No grants to individuals.

Applications

Organisations applying must provide proof of need, they must forward the

most recent audited accounts, a registered charity number, and most importantly a cash flow statement for the next 12 months. All applications should have a stamped addressed envelope attached. It is also important that the actual request for funds must be concise and preferably summarised on one side of A4.

Because of ongoing support to so many organisations already known to the trust, it is likely that unsolicited applications will, for the foreseeable future, be unsuccessful.

The Severn Trent Water Charitable Trust

Relief of poverty, money advice, debt counselling

£579,000 designated to organisations (2002/03)

Beneficial area The area covered by Severn Trent Water Ltd, which stretches from Wales to east Leicestershire and from the Humber estuary down to the Bristol Channel.

Emmanuel Court, 12–14 Mill Street, Sutton Coldfield, West Midlands B72 1TJ

Tel. 0121 355 7766 **Fax** 0121 354 8485

Email office@sttf.org.uk

Website www.sttf.org.uk

Correspondent S Braley, Director

Trustees *Dr Derek W Harris, chair; John R A Crabtree; Mrs L Pusey; Mrs Edna Sadler; Roy Simpson; Mrs Mary Milton; Mrs Sheila Barrow; Andrew D Peet; David Vaughan.*

Charity Commission no. 1064005

Information available Information was provided by the trust.

The trustees operate two grant programmes:

1) For individuals and families in hardship. Grants are one-off and structured to make a significant difference to the individual's life.

2) For organisations to facilitate or develop money advice and debt counselling work.

The trust was established by Severn Trent Water Ltd in 1997 with £2 million to help those in financial need or hardship meet the cost of water bills. It will also help with other household costs if it can be demonstrated that it will help towards future financial stability or make a significant improvement to the recipient's circumstances.

Grants are given to organisations in the area to improve or expand money advice/debt counselling to eligible people. The organisation must be able to demonstrate that a project is likely to benefit customers of Severn Trent Water Ltd.

Grants are available for both revenue and/or capital expenditure and can be for up to three years. Organisations seeking revenue funding of more than one year must be able to prove that the project will be able to continue to achieve its objectives and deliver a quality service with no additional funding. The continuation of funding beyond one year will always be subject to satisfactory project performance and availability of funding. Recipients will be required to report on the progress of the project. The funding will be made quarterly in advance. Capital purchases must normally be made within three months of the grant award. Grants of up to £90,000 for a project have been provided.

All recipient organisations will be required to provide an end of year report detailing project achievements. The trust may require the provision of further information to help publicise the work of the trust.

In 2002/03 the trust had an income of £2.6 million and a total expenditure of £2.4 million, of which £1.7 million was designated to individuals. A further £350,000 was designated to organisations for money advice/debt counselling services. During this year, the trust developed areas of special interest in order to target funding. Organisations seeking support are advised to contact the trust to find out what the target area is before applying.

Applications for small capital grants such as training aids/computer equipment can be submitted up to a maximum of £1,500.

Applications

On a form available from the correspondent. Further details can be found on the website.

ShareGift (the Orr Mackintosh Foundation)

General, but see below

£1.5 million (2002/03)

Beneficial area Unrestricted.

46 Grosvenor Street, London W1K 3HN

Tel. 020 7337 0501

Website www.sharegift.org

Correspondent Bridget Roe, Director

Trustees *Viscount Mackintosh of Halifax; Charles Moore; Matthew Orr.*

Charity Commission no. 1052686

Information available Leaflets and website. Annual report and accounts.

Summary

Creating an entirely new flow of money to charities, this organisation pools donations of shares, often small and inconvenient or unwanted, until it has enough money to make substantial grants.

The charity makes donations at its own discretion, but is guided in doing so by suggestions from people who donate shares or help ShareGift in other ways.

Grants are normally made to the general funds of the charity concerned, rather than for specific projects.

No grants are given in response to applications by charities.

General

Launched in 1996, this charity was developed by Claire Nowak, a former city investment manager, now Viscountess Mackintosh and chief executive of the charity, and Matthew Orr, a stockbroker whose firm, Killik and Co., provides free of charge many of the required technical services as well as office space.

The scheme is based on the fact that many people own small parcels of shares, for a variety of reasons, such as popularly advertised flotations of companies and as the result of take-overs and mergers. In what is still largely a paper-based share registration system, these shareholdings are often a considerable nuisance, needing some know-how to handle but being of too little value to justify paying professional fees to have this done.

ShareGift will accept the relevant share certificates, with minimum hassle for the donor, and sell them at no cost to the charity by bulking together batches of similar certificates from a number of donors. The donor is able is able to get full charitable tax relief on the gift.

The bulk of ShareGift's funds are generated by working directly with companies and individual shareholders. Fundrasing charities can also work with ShareGift. These generally find it uneconomic to manage their own internal system for handling donations of unwanted share certificates (or even, in some cases, any donations of shares) but if they can persuade their supporters to send these to ShareGift, they can be sure that (providing these donors identify the charity they support) they will get a donation from ShareGift's trustees.

Other donors simply send in gifts of shares without suggesting a charity or cause to benefit, being primarily motivated by disposing of a nuisance shareholding.

Grantmaking

Grants are made only to charities that have been suggested by the individuals and organisations that help create ShareGift's income. For larger gifts of shares, and where there is a definite charitable nomination, the amount of the grant will normally follow closely the value of the shareholding. Where the value of the shares is very small, ShareGift may well make up the amount from its 'pool' of undesignated funds at least to its usual minimum of a few hundreds of pounds. However all this is entirely at the discretion of the trustees; no particular charity has any entitlement to a grant.

A total of 228 donations totalling £1.5 million were made to 187 organisations in 2002/03, of these 33 were for amounts of £10,000 or more. Grants included: £310,000 to the Leys School; £98,000 to the Prince's Trust; £57,000 to NSPCC; £55,000 to the Royal Star and Garter Home; £53,000 to Christian Blind Mission; £50,000 to Help the Hospices; £47,000 to Wycombe Royal Grammar School Foundation; £41,000 to UNICEF UK; £30,000 to RNIB; £27,000 to Oxfam; £26,000 to Cancer Research UK; £25,000 to National Literacy Trust; £20,000 each to Barnardos, Macmillan Cancer Relief, RSPCA, Scope and Victim Support; £15,000 each to Dreams Come True Charity, Weston Spirit and Whizz Kidz and £10,000 each to British Heart

Foundation, Get Up and Give Appeal, National Trust NCH, North Ayrshire Women's Aid, St Barnabas Hospice and Youth Sport Trust.

Exclusions

Grants to UK registered charities only.

Applications

No applications can be considered. Charities wishing to benefit from the scheme should contact ShareGift to discuss how they might promote the concept to their and everyone else's advantage.

The Sheepdrove Trust

Environment, education

£750,000 (2003)

Beneficial area UK, but especially north Lambeth – London

2 Methley Street, London SE11 4AJ

Correspondent Ms J E Kindersley

Trustees *Mrs Juliet E Kindersley; Peter D Kindersley; Mrs Harriet R Treuille; Barnabas G Kindersley.*

Charity Commission no. 328369

Information available Annual report and accounts were provided by the trust.

The work of the charity is described as follows:

The trustees' interests are directed towards organic farming and, when possible, they prefer to initiate projects which increase sustainability, bio-diversity and organic farming, such as research into organic seed production and nutrition. For example, they donate to the Soil Association, Elm Farm Research Centre, Forum for the Future, Pesticides Action Network and HDRA. They have sponsored educational research in the past and support a small educational venture on the internet. They also support the Newbury Spring Music Festival.

The trustees try and support applications from Lambeth where appropriate. For example they donate to Kid's Company, Roots and Shoots and Kensington Summer Project on a long term basis.

The trust is endowed with money made by the Dorling Kindersley publishing enterprise, but the trust's holding of shares in the company was sold in 2000, when the endowment was valued at £18 million.

In 2003 the trust had an income of £1.1 million. Grants were made totalling £750,000. Previous beneficiaries also include the Hawk and Owl Trust, British Trust for Ornithology, Kids Company and Roots and Shoots.

Exclusions

No grants to students or other individuals, nor for building projects or medical research.

Applications

In writing to the correspondent.

The Sheffield Church Burgesses Trust

Church, general

£1.1 million (2002/03)

Beneficial area Sheffield.

c/o Wrigleys, 3rd Floor, Fountain Precinct, Balm Green, Sheffield S1 2JA

Tel. 0114 267 5594 **Fax** 0114 276 3176

Correspondent G J Smallman

Trustees *P W Lee; Canon Dr G Tolley; D L Fletcher; J F W Peters; S McK Hamilton; Prof. G D Sims; N J A Hutton; S A P Hunter; A G Johnson; D F Booker; M P W Lee; I G Walker.*

Charity Commission no. 221284

Information available Information was provided by the trust.

The trust supports general charitable causes in Sheffield, Sheffield Cathedral and the Sheffield city Anglican parishes. It favours pump priming grants and is keen to be an enabler, rather than a long term funder, of new projects. The trust expects to make a major contribution to a current appeal by Sheffield Cathedral and is bearing that in mind in its present pattern of grantmaking. Funding is also provided for the Church Burgesses Educational Foundation.

In 2003 the trust had assets of £24 million and an income of £1.8 million. The amount transferred to the Church Burgesses Educational Foundation was £230,000. Grants totalled £1.1 million and were broken down as follows:

- Ecclesiastical grants to institutions totalled £528,000 and were broken down into three categories:

- Church building grants (£278,000), previous beneficiaries include Holy Trinity Millhouses, St Chad's – Woodseats, St Mark's – Mosborough, St Mary's – Walkley and Wadsley Parish Church.

- Central deanery stipend support grants (£169,000).

- Other grants – other ecclesiastical grants were made totalling £81,000. Previous beneficiaries include CBA Projects Limited, Hillsborough and Wadsley Bridge – Church Army and St Lawrence – DATIC running costs.

- Cathedral expenditure (£404,000)

  This included £66,000 towards cathedral projects and an annual grant of £293,000.

- General charitable grants to institutions (£159,000 to 84 causes)

  Beneficiaries included Bradfield Festival of Music, CBA Projects Ltd, Christians Against Poverty, C.R.U.S.E and Gleadless Valley Methodist.

- Ecclesiastical grants to clergy (£6,300)

  Grants were for clergy working expenses and support grants.

Applications

In writing to the correspondent. The trustees meet in January, April, July and October.

Sherburn House Charity

Welfare and the relief of need

£532,000 (2002/03)

Beneficial area The ancient Diocese of Durham (the north east of England between the rivers Tweed and Tees).

Ramsey House, Sherburn House, Durham DH1 2SE

Tel. 0191 372 2551

Email sphallett@sherburnhouse.org

Website www.sherburnhouse.org

Correspondent Stephen Hallett, Chief Officer

Trustees *Canon G Miller; Margaret Bozic; William Brooks; David Forbes; Dorothy Hale; Mary Hawgood; Lindsay Perks; Leslie B Smith; Ron Wilson; Gene Hill; Peter Thompson; Margaret L Rushford; Ian Stewart; Steve Laverick.*

Charity Commission no. 217652

Information available Annual report and accounts were provided by the trust.

This is a new grantmaker, formed from a reorganisation of Christ's Hospital in Sherburn, itself an active charity since 1181. Primarily a housing and residential care charity, it started making grants in the summer of 1998. Funding must be to 'relieve need, hardship or distress'.

There is a single sheet of guidelines which notes the following areas of interest:

- health (including mental health)
- learning disabilities
- physical disabilities
- substance abuse
- community needs
- homelessness
- special needs
- effects of long-term unemployment.

'We adopt no specific priorities but we do prefer applications from locally based or managed organisations within the beneficial area'.

Unusually and usefully, the grants lists show the amount asked for by each of the successful applicants. The figures suggest that most successful applicants for amounts up to £5,000 received the full amount requested but that larger applications were often scaled down, and for the largest amounts scaled down severely.

In 2002/03 the charity had assets of £18 million and an income of £1.8 million. Grants totalling £532,000 were given to 99 organisations, ranging from £500 to £15,000. They were classified geographically as follows, showing the number and value of grants:

	No.	Amount
Region wide	8	£39,500
Northumberland	22	£120,000
Newcastle upon Tyne	15	£55,000
Sunderland	7	£38,000
Gateshead	5	£22,000
North Tyneside	3	£17,500
South Tyneside	3	£17,000
County Durham	17	£104,000
Darlington	8	£43,000
Hartlepool	5	£15,000
Stockton	7	£44,000

Beneficiaries included Wansbeck Citizen's Advice Bureau, The Toby Henderson Trust, Caring Hands Charity and Westhelp (£15,000 each), Blyth Valley Citizen's Advice Bureau and St Mary & St Peter's Community Project (£12,000 each), Newcastle Society for the Blind, Trinity House Social Centre and Clarences Community Shop (£10,000 each), Salvation Army – Shakespeare House and Darlington Nightstop (£7,000 each), Baseline, Hendon Young People's Project, After Adoption, Red Hall

Partnership and Cleveland Alzheimer's Residential Centre Ltd (£5,000 each), North Farm Residents and Community Association and Durham City and District Credit Union (£4,000 each), Darlington Bond Scheme and ADDvance (£3,000 each).

Smaller grants included those to Newsham Over 60's Club, Sunderland Deaf Society, The Gotcha Group, Dyspraxia Foundation and Women's Freedom Group.

Exclusions

No support for:

- organisations which have substantial reserves or are in serious deficit;
- grantmaking bodies seeking to distribute grants on the charity's behalf;
- activities which are the responsibility of central/local government or other statutory body;
- fabric appeals for places of worship per se;
- fabric appeals for halls except those which demonstrate service/activities for the whole community;
- fundraising events or activities;
- general appeals;
- sponsorship;
- expeditions or overseas travel;
- mainstream educational activity;
- national charities except those which have a strong representation within the stated area;
- hospitals and medical centres (except hospices);
- retrospective grants;
- organisations who have received a grant or have been refused a grant within the preceding two years;
- those who do not fully complete the application form.

Applications

On the application forms available from the correspondent. This is a straightforward four-page document. Applications for summer activities should ideally be submitted by the beginning of April to allow the charity to give an answer well before the summer.

The Archie Sherman Charitable Trust

Jewish charities, education, arts, general

£1.6 million (2002/03)

Beneficial area UK and overseas.

27 Berkeley House, Hay Hill, London W1J 8NS

Tel. 020 7493 1904 **Fax** 020 7499 1470

Email trust@sherman.co.uk

Correspondent Michael Gee, Trustee

Trustees *Michael J Gee; Allan H S Morgenthau; E A Charles.*

Charity Commission no. 256893

Information available Annual report and accounts, with no narrative review of charitable activity or explanation of grants.

General

Most of the funds go to Jewish causes, particularly for education or welfare, many of which receive ongoing support, typically more than £20,000 a year each. A few arts organisations are similarly supported. The smaller one-off grants, mostly for £500 or £1,000, are made mainly to arts and children's charities and are frequently repeated from year to year. The trust has previously been reported as saying that it was committed to a considerable number of long-term projects with payments spread over as much as six years.

In 2002/03 an income of £1.4 million was generated from assets worth £16.2 million. The trust made 52 grants totalling just over £1.6 million, with some organisations receiving more than one grant during the year, and some recurrent from the previous year.

Grants in 2002/03

Grants were divided into the following categories during the year

Education and training	£526,000
Overseas aid	£276,000
General charitable purposes	£350,000
Medical, health and sickness	£200,000
Economic/community development	£125,000
Arts and culture	£81,000
Relief of poverty	£1,000

By far the largest grant was £500,000 to London Jewish Cultural Centre. Other grants over £100,000 each were £125,000 to Rosalyn and Nicholas Springer Charitable Trust, £141,000 to Diana and

Allan Morgenthau Charitable Trust and £101,000 to the Tel Aviv Foundation.

Other beneficiaries included Jacqueline and Michael Gee Charitable Trust (£84,000), Jewish Care and Nightingale House (£50,000 each), Friends of Jaffa (£49,000), UJIA (£36,000), Norwood Ltd (£26,000), Royal Academy of Arts (£25,000), the Royal Opera House (£20,000), Community Security Trust and Jerusalem Foundation (£10,000 each).

Applications

In writing to the correspondent. Trustees meet every month except August and December.

The Shetland Charitable Trust

Social welfare, art and recreation, environment and amenity

£14 million (2002/03)

Beneficial area Shetland only.

22–24 North Road, Lerwick, Shetland ZE1 0NQ

Tel. 01595 744991 **Fax** 01595 690206

Email mail.charitable.trust@sic.shetland. gov.uk

Correspondent Jeff Goddard, Finance Controller

Trustee *24 trustees, being the elected Shetland councillors (acting as individuals), the Lord Lieutenant and the Headmaster of Anderson High School. The chair is Bill Manson.*

Scottish Charity no. SC027025

Information available Generally exemplary reports and accounts, available from the trust for the reasonable charge of £2.

The original trust was established in 1976 with 'disturbance receipts' from the operators of the Sullom Voe oil terminal. As a clause in the trust deed prevented it from accumulating income beyond 21 years from its inception, in 1997 most of its assets were transferred to a newly established Shetland Islands Council Charitable Trust, which is identical to the old trust except for the omission of the prohibition on accumulating income. This has now been renamed Shetland Charitable Trust.

The trust was run by the Shetland Islands Council until 2002. The trust is currently administered by its own separate staff.

In 2002/03 the trust had assets of £195 million with an income of £11.6 million and grants totalling £13.5 million.

The funds are used to create and sustain a wide range of facilities for the islands, largely by funding further trusts as the following breakdown shows (with their 2002/03 grant totals):

Shetland Welfare Trust – day care and running costs	(£2.7 million)
Shetland Recreational Trust	(£2.4 million)
Isleburgh Trust	(£1.3 million)
Shetland Amenity Trust	(£1 million)
Christmas Grants to Pensioners	(£881,000)
Shetlands Arts Trust	(£524,000)
Independance at Home Scheme Grants	(£394,000)
Voluntary Bodies	(£288,000)
Shetland Recreational Trust – special projects	(£286,000)
Specialist Aids & Social Assistance	(£261,000)
Shetland Recreational Trust – West Mainland Leisure Centre	(£190,000)
Walter and Joan Gray Eventide Home – running costs	(£181,000)
Shetland Alcohol Trust	(£152,000)
Shetland Citizens Advice Bureau	(£135,000)
Other grants totalled	£2.8 million.

Exclusions

Funds can only be used to benefit the inhabitants of Shetland.

Applications

Applications are only accepted from Sheltland-based charities. The trustees meet every six to eight weeks.

SHINE (Support and Help in Education)

Education of children and young people

£539,000 (2003/04) see below

Beneficial area Greater London and Manchester.

1 Cheam Road, Ewell Village, Surrey KT17 1SP

Tel. 020 8393 1880 **Fax** 020 8394 2570

Email info@shinetrust.org.uk

Website www.shinetrust.org.uk

Correspondent Stephen Shields or Ruth Dwyer

Trustees *Gavin Boyle, chair; David Blood; Gerry Boyle; Peter Harrison; Mark Heffernan (founder); Christian Hore; Jim O'Neill; John Phizackerley; Richard Rothwell; Dr Caroline Whalley.*

Charity Commission no. 1082777

Information available Annual report and accounts. Good website.

Summary

SHINE makes a small number of large multi-year grants, usually for amounts over £20,000, to partner organisations working with underachieving 7–18 year olds from disadvantaged areas in Greater London. SHINE says it generally searches proactively for projects to fund, although guidelines for organisations are available on its website.

In the 2003/04 financial year the trust had assets of almost £4 million and an income of £3.3 million. Grants totalled £539,000. (In April 2004 the trustees committed a further £926,000 in grant awards. Details will be included in the 2004/05 accounts).

General

In 2005 the charity stated:

SHINE has spent the last four years researching, developing and testing educational projects enabling us to identify areas where we can make a difference and find out what really works. Currently, we are *replicating* some of our projects which have been delivering measurable educational benefits, so that more children, either in the one borough, or across a number of London boroughs can benefit. We are also piloting the replication of a select number of our projects in Manchester.

This doesn't mean we've stopped searching – our grants team are constantly seeking new and innovative projects to fund. However, our priority in the immediate future is to fund more of what we know works.

The charity describes its work as follows:

SHINE is a dynamic young charity set up to fund educational support programmes for children and young people from the most disadvantaged parts of Greater London. We focus on value for money investment and proven educational impact. We believe that we can support effective intervention in the lives of children and young people by:
- finding sound organisations to fund;
- developing solid proposals with them which have measurable educational outcomes;
- rigorously monitoring and evaluating all funded projects, establishing the exact

impact on raising educational achievement levels; and
- replicating successful projects elsewhere.

In order to achieve this we will fund only organisations and projects that meet our essential criteria below.

Organisations

We will consider funding organisations which can demonstrate that they are:
- well managed
- in a healthy financial position
- working with other local agencies, particularly schools and local authorities
- providing venues and services which are open and accessible to all
- led by staff who have a high level of experience and competency.

Projects

We wish to fund projects which have the following key elements:
- the main focus is on educational subjects, especially promoting literacy, numeracy and science
- content and methodology will excite and engage participants, making creative use of IT where appropriate
- there are clear and measurable target educational outcomes – principally this will mean linking to standardised tests (at primary level) and GCSEs or a recognised equivalent (at secondary level)
- a significant number of children/young people will be supported
- these children/young people themselves want to improve their situation
- the project will be sufficiently long term to support sustainable improvement
- families of participants are linked to the project in a way which supports their child's learning
- there is appropriate use of volunteers
- the project budget represents value for money.

SHINE wishes to build long term relationships and partnerships with the organisations we fund, therefore the majority of our grants are in excess of £20,000. We fund new start ups, pilots and development or replication of projects. We will also fund core costs.

Grants in 2003/04

The following awards were comitted during the year:

CATZ Clubs	£95,000
Millfields School	£80,000
Community Service Volunteers	£55,000
St Paul's and Latymer Schools and Hammersmith & Fulham LEA	£51,000
Shaftesbury Homes & Arethusa	£50,000
Youth Culture TeleVision	£50,000
Peper Harow	£38,000
AXIS Educational Trust	£36,000
All Nations Centre	£25,000
Springboard for Children	£25,000
Cambridge University & Hackney Learning Trust	£19,000
LIFT: Learning for Life with Technology	£15,000

Exclusions

Shine will not fund:
- the direct replacement of statutory funding;
- schools or other educational establishments, except where funding is for activities which are clearly additional;
- short term programmes;
- programmes targeted at specific subject or beneficiary groups;
- parenting programmes, where the primary focus is the parent rather than the child;
- activities promoting particular political or religious beliefs;
- projects taking place outside Greater London, except projects that are part of SHINE's replication programme.

Applications

All potential applicants must initially speak to a member of the grants team by telephoning 020 8393 1880. The trustees meet about three times a year, but not at fixed intervals.

The Shirley Foundation

Autism

£5 million (2003/04)
Beneficial area UK.

North Lea House, 66 Northfield End, Henley-on-Thames, Oxfordshire RG9 2BE
Tel. 01491 579004 **Fax** 01491 574995
Email steve@steveshirley.com
Website www.steveshirley.com/tsf
Correspondent Elizabeth Lake, Administrator
Trustees *Dame Stephanie Shirley, chair; Prof. Eve Johnstone; Michael Robert Macfadyen; Anne McCartney Menzies.*
Charity Commission no. 1097135
Information available Accounts and report available from the trust.

Summary

There has been a re-ordering of this foundation's priorities, after six years in which over £50 million has been committed to charitable activities.

Our investment so far has split approximately 30% into Information Technology projects and 70% to support research and service development in the field of Autism Spectrum Disorders (ASD). With the exception of our existing significant ongoing commitment to the Oxford Internet Institute, the trustees have decided that our future focus will be mainly on ASD and, within that, on larger projects that can clearly have strategic impact on the sector as a whole. We are particularly keen to support collaborative medical research to explore the causes of autism and to use our influence and funding to lever extra resources for this area.

Most of the annual grant total goes to organisations with which the foundation has close connections or at least an established relationship. The foundation no longer publishes guidelines and says 'applicants should note that with £5 million in grants planned from 2003/04 onwards, current resources are fully committed'.

General

The foundation was established by Dame Stephanie (Steve) Shirley, a business technology pioneer.

Dame Shirley describes the work and achievements of the foundation in her report for 2003/04:

It is my pleasure to report on our eighth year of operation, which included the transfer of all activities from the original foundation (No. 1057662) to the incorporated foundation (No. 1097135) on 23 July 2003. For good form, the trustee board reiterated the Mission:
'Facilitation and support of pioneering projects with strategic impact in the field of Autism Spectrum Disorders, with particular emphasis on medical research'.
Adverse stock market conditions meant that (with one exception) no new projects were undertaken or old ones extended. Of the steady stream of unsolicited applications, we ignored those that were totally outside our remit but responded, albeit negatively, to all individual and relevant applicants, often suggesting appropriate contacts and potential funders. With expenditure focussed on already-committed projects, there was time to promote our philanthropic aims for the sector and we achieved excellent exposure in the media including acknowledgement of my personal contributions by the Chancellor of the Exchequer at 11 Downing Street in January 2004.
The exception was a development and revision of the medical research project for which we provided seedcorn support last year. Pioneered by two English and two American universities, this project has been successfully subsumed, at a reduced but

more realistic level, into the US National Alliance for Autism Research (NAAR). This currently funds some 150 researchers in over 70 establishments worldwide (including UK) and is partnered with government and other funders.

NAAR seeks to incorporate in the UK and elsewhere and has therefore taken over this foundation's initial work towards a medical research charity in this country. To demonstrate NAAR's intent to globalise and to inform the fundraising which has become our prime input, I have accepted a position on NAAR's trustee board on a year by year basis. We have also contracted the services of an experienced consultant to advise on fundraising worldwide and represent this foundation in the US.

Ongoing support

In November 2003 we noted with pleasure the opening of the secondary unit of the Ysgol Plas Brondyffryn School for children with autism; so were doubly disappointed when the Brondyffryn Trust Board collapsed early in 2004. Many activities will continue but this corporate disbanding underlines how difficult it is for diverse bodies to work co-operatively.

During the year our projects at Nottingham University and PEACH successfully concluded.

We continued our support of Birmingham University's web-based certificate in caring for people with autism; Resources for Autism's Expert Witness service; Oxford University's study of sleep disorders in children with autism and a study at Cambridge University of the prevalence of autism in primary schools.

Also during the year, Autism Cymru organised a series of training sessions across Wales and planned its first international conference for 500 practitioners and parents in Cardiff in May 2004. Shortlisted last year for 'Best New Charity in the UK', its chief executive, Hugh Morgan, has now been shortlisted by the Charity Finance magazine for the 2004 Charity Awards 'For Excellence in Leadership and Management'. Jane Hutt, Minister for Health and Social Services in Wales, recently endorsed our investment in this national charity:

'The work of Autism Cymru would not have been possible without the funding, established three years, from The Shirley Foundation. I commend both The Shirley Foundation and Autism Cymru for their hard work and dedication to improving the lives of people with autistic spectrum disorders and the contribution which Autism Cymru is making to the development of an autism strategy in Wales.'

With funding from Autism Cymru and others, the autismconnect website is now freestanding (apart from a few fees from this foundation) and making modest progress under its editor Adam Feinstein.

In November 2003 I spoke at the Wirral Autistic Society's AGM held at Giles Shirley Hall:

'This building now provides a truly innovatory service for eleven adults with autism that, due to the skilful design, can be shared with the general public without loss of privacy for those in our care. They enjoy individual ensuite rooms, grouped into four flats, each with communal living space. The building also houses a community hall, with kitchen facilities, a state-of-the-art IT suite with 20 work stations and a small heritage centre, where touch screen computers provide an opportunity to study the history of the village. The hall and computer suite are available for hire.'

Giles Shirley Hall has made a significant improvement, not only to the appearance of the village, but also to the lives of the villagers and surrounding community. What for many years was a dilapidated and derelict eyesore, has now been restored to a magnificent focal point of architectural interest, which has injected new life into the village. The hall is used on Tuesdays as a Computer Club for young people with Asperger's Syndrome, on Wednesdays for line dancing classes, on Thursdays for IT Open Access and on Fridays for Senior Citizens' luncheons. In addition to this, the hall and/or the IT suite is used by local companies for conferences, training events etc.

'Without The Shirley Foundation's massive support and generosity, this project would not have been possible and a wonderful opportunity to provide resources for people with autism and to regenerate community life would have been missed.'
Michael Hatton, Chief Executive, Wirral Autistic Society

March 2004 had The Kingwood Trust and I speaking at the launch to the All-Party Parliamentary Group for Autism in the House of Commons of the report by Housing Options Tomorrow's Big Problem which the foundation initiated and sponsored.

I have also spoken to complement our support of the Foundation for People with Learning Disabilities, part of The Mental Health Foundation, and its report Why Are We Here? published in April 2004 as part of a national training initiative to raise awareness among support staff of the spiritual needs of people with learning disabilities.

'...People with learning disabilities need to be supported to find their own way to find the answers to the questions about life.'
Pat Charlesworth, Advisory Committee
'The Shirley Foundation's support has enabled the Foundation for People with Learning Disabilities to fund two ground-breaking pieces of research addressing the spiritual and religious needs of people with learning disabilities and to disseminate the

findings widely. The rights of people with learning disabilities have been overlooked for too long and this work has enabled us to create a national profile for this important issue.'
Dr Andrew McCulloch, Chief Executive, Foundation for People with Learning Disabilities

Prior's Court School currently has 59 pupils with autism aged 5–19 who also have moderate to severe learning disabilities. The foundation-funded PhD study of the impact of art on the school's pupils is proving to be a leader in its field. We continue to hold the freehold (let at a rose rent) but in December 2003 the school became fully independent operationally.

'It is a humbling experience to attend reviews and have parents turn to us and say thank you for giving us the son/daughter we never thought we would have. To see students who start at Prior's Court School with very difficult behaviours and the inability to interact with anyone becoming less anxious, coping with difficult situations and beginning to play appropriately is a reward in itself. One of our younger students would not hold eye contact, which many with autism find difficult, after a few months he was able to look at everyone when spoken to, his family were amazed! Another Mum thanked us for enabling her to take her son to the supermarket without having to worry about him taking things off the shelf and eating them. All these things seem so small but if you have lived with someone with autism every little achievement is celebrated. I am a qualified nurse and all through my nursing profession I have not had such a rewarding job as working at Prior's Court School. I would like to take this opportunity to thank The Shirley Foundation for the opportunity and their support.'
Lynda Whiley, Head of Millington House
'Support from the Shirley Foundation has meant that Prior's Court School can thrive as a truly unique and inspirational educational establishment and centre of excellence in the field of autism. We are privileged with a firm basis with which to adapt to the commercial environment to continue the vision and dream of our founder Steve Shirley.'
Robert Hubbard, Chief Executive, Prior's Court School

Seminal work is in hand dealing with the transition to adult services, in particular to The Kingwood Trust.

Now that the foundation has concluded its very first project, The Kingwood Trust, I should like to comment on what has been achieved there. As other parents have had to do, I started this trust to support my own son Giles because there were no suitable services available for him. I financed it, ran it in predecessor mode and chaired its board of trustees for many years. It took 7 years for the organisation to become eligible for charitable status, so 17 years in total for it to become freestanding. Today, led by Ann Macfadyen, it is poised for the next phase of its development and currently supports 37 adults in the Thames Valley area whose needs challenge existing services.

The support of The Shirley Foundation, and of Dame Stephanie and her husband personally, has been key to all that The Kingwood Trust has been able to achieve for people with autism. Their determination to give their son a life in the community was the basis and inspiration for the subsequent work of the trust. Dame Stephanie founded The Kingwood Trust in 1994. This start up not only included bringing three large properties into use (subsequently gifted to the trust), and funding the set up of its office in Henley, but also a huge commitment in personal time and energy.

Dame Stephanie was Chair of the Trust for its first five years. Her work encompassed putting together a multi-talented Trustee Board, publicising the work of the Trust, launching the Trust's fundraising, and persuading a distinguished group of influential people to serve as Patrons of the Trust.

From 1999, when Lady Hornby took over as Chair, The Shirley Foundation has provided, over a five year period, the vital financial support to sustain the operation of The Kingwood Trust as its activity has grown. As this period ends, the trust is now carrying out enough funded support work to sustain its infrastructure costs and be financially independent.

The Kingwood Trust is now celebrating its tenth year of operation, a period which has seen it pioneer a number of new ways of enabling adults with autism and learning disabilities to achieve a real life in their community. The trust would like to express its gratitude to Dame Stephanie and The Shirley Foundation for all that they have done to make this possible.'

Keith Hasted, The Kingwood Trust

Summary

Apart from the annual grant to the Oxford Internet Institute, the year's focus was again Autism Spectrum Disorders with, by extension, learning disability. Despite the curtailment of its grant-making, the foundation has facilitated a number of positive developments in the sector, not least by its emphasis on medical research. Future work is likely to concentrate on infrastructure support, especially fundraising, for NAAR's global research targeted to determine the causes of autism by 2014 and to halve the global costs of the disorder by 2020.

Exclusions

No grants to individuals, or for non autism-specific work.

Applications

In writing (less than two pages) or by e-mail to the correspondent.

Trustees meet quarterly but there are no set times at which applications should be made. However it should be noted that the trust states that funds are currently fully committed.

Shlomo Memorial Fund Limited

Jewish causes

Around £1.5 million (2002/03)
Beneficial area Worldwide.

Cohen Arnold & Co., New Burlington House, 1075 Finchley Road, London NW11 0PU

Tel. 020 8731 0777 **Fax** 020 8731 0778
Correspondent I Lopian, Secretary
Trustees *E Kleineman; G Nadel; I D Lopian; H Y Hoffner; M S Lebanon Weisfish; A Toporowitz.*
Charity Commission no. 278973
Information available Annual report and accounts on file at the Charity Commission.

This trust's income is mainly comprised of Gift Aid donations from its subsidiaries, which it utilises in making grants to Jewish charities. In 2002/03 the trust had an income of £1.8 million and a total expenditure of £2.1 million. Grants were made totalling around £1.5 million. No further information was available.

Comment

There was no response to repeated written requests for a copy of the most recent annual report and accounts, despite the requirement to provide these on demand.

Applications

In writing to the correspondent.

The Henry Smith Charity

Social welfare, older people, disability, health, medical research

£19 million (2003)
Beneficial area UK. Specific local programmes in east and west Sussex, Hampshire, Kent, Gloucestershire, Leicestershire, Suffolk and Surrey.

5 Chancery Lane, Clifford's Inn, London EC4A 1BU

Tel. 020 7320 6884 **Fax** 020 7320 3842
Website www.henrysmithcharity.org.uk
Correspondent Richard Hopgood, Director
Trustees *Julian Sheffield, chair; Mrs A E Allen; Lord Egremont; Countess of Euston; Mrs C Godman Law; Marilyn J Gallyer; J D Hambro; Lord Hamilton of Dalzell; T D Holland-Martin; Sir John James; G E Lee-Steere; M Lowther; T J Millington-Drake; Mark Newton; Ronnie Norman; P W Smallridge; P W Urquhart; Mrs Diana Barran.*
Charity Commission no. 230102
Information available Annual report and accounts available on the charity's website.

The Henry Smith Charity was founded in 1628 with the objects of relieving and where possible releasing people from need and suffering. These objects continue in the grant making policy today. The Henry Smith Charity makes grants totalling over £20 million per annum for a wide range of purposes across the UK, funded from investments.

In 2003 the charity had assets amounting to £572 million and an income of £23 million.

There are three types of grant made:

- 'Special list' grants – grants made on a one-off basis which relate to a specific project for which applicants have requested support. This could include purchase/ refurbishment of a building, purchase of specialist equipment, other similar capital expenditure, or one year's running costs.
- 'General list' grants – annual grants made for more than one year, and up to three years. They are usually for a specific item in the applicant's budget such as a salary, or towards the costs of a particular project. Grants can be used for core costs.

- 'Small grants' – grants are given to organisations with an annual income of less than £150,000. Applications can be made for grants between £500 to £10,000. Grants can be for one-off capital items such as equipment purchase; these grants must be used within six months of being awarded. Grants can also be towards one year's running costs. Grants are one-off payments although repeat applications can be considered.

Small grants in the traditional counties are made made upon the recommendation of individual trustees living in those counties. There is a separate programme for the rest of the UK.

The charity also awards 'major' grants. These consist of a programme of grants in a specially selected area. Their aim is to make a significant impact in the chosen field. These grants are not open to application.

Grants, other than for the small grant schemes, are generally large. Few are for less than £20,000 and some are for £100,000 or more. There seems to be a general maximum of about £200,000.

Programme areas

The trustees use the following programme areas to classify their grants:

Hospitals and Medical Care

Projects providing residential care or health care for those who are sick or in need, and projects which provide outreach services such as home care support. Services operated by the NHS will not normally be funded.

Hospices and palliative care

Projects providing residential care or health care for those who are sick or in need, and projects which provide outreach services such as home care support.

Medical research

Specific medical research projects will be considered, although the Charity does not normally fund cancer research. Generally, only applications from recognised 'Centres of Excellence' will be considered (see separate guidelines).

Disability

Projects which are specifically aimed at the rehabilitation and training of the disabled can be considered.

Elderly

Projects for the relief of the elderly, such as housing or support services. Projects which can be considered are residential care or health care for those who are sick or in need, emotional support such as befriending services and day care centres. Preference will be given to projects in needy areas.

Young people

Projects that provide support to young people at risk particularly those living in areas of considerable deprivation.

Drugs and alcohol

Projects aimed at the support and rehabilitation of people with drug and/or alcohol problems, as well as those to support people at risk of developing such problems, will be considered.

Community service

Projects that provide support for communities in areas of considerable deprivation including ethnic minority groups. This could include projects providing employment for the disadvantaged, shelter and necessities of life such as furniture for the homeless, or work with offenders.

Family services

Projects which provide support to families at risk.

Homeless

Projects providing practical support for the homeless and those at risk of homelessness.

Holidays for children

Projects which provide holidays or outings for children from areas of considerable deprivation or children with a disability, aged 13 or under. For more information on this programme please call our Information Line on 020 7320 6277.

Grants in 2003

'Special', 'general' and small grants paid in 2003 were broken down geographically as follows:

National	26%
London	13%
South east	13%
North west	9%
North east	8%
Yorkshire	6%
South west	5%
Wales	5%
West Midlands	5%
Eastern	4%
Scotland	3%
East Midlands	2%
Northern Ireland	1%

Standard grants

A total of 594 grants totalling £17.4 million were paid from the 'general' and 'special' lists. These were broken down as follows:

Young people	£3.1 million
Community service	£2.8 million
Multiple disability	£2.3 million
Mental disability	£1.9 million
Elderly	£1.4 million
Homeless	£1.1 million
Medical research	£1.1 million
Family support services	£829,000
Physical disability	£780,00
Drugs and alcohol	£558,000
Hospices and palliative care	£518,000
Hospitals and medical care	£308,000
Ethnic minorities	£240,000
Counselling	£191,000
Rehabilitation of offenders	£180,000
Refugees	£88,000

The following is taken from the 2003 trustees' report:

The trustees have again awarded a grant (£375,000 to the housing charity HACT to identify projects meeting the various housing needs of the elderly, particularly involving the rural elderly, those suffering from senile dementia and minority ethnic elderly.

A number of other substantial grants were awarded during the year:

£250,000 to Hull Community Church towards the cost of a new building to house a wide range of community projects and services for the disadvantaged.

- £200,000 to the Mary Hare School for the Deaf towards the development of a performing arts conference and education centre for deaf people.
- £200,000 to the University of Oxford for a new magnetoencapholgrahic facility to develop neuro imaging to analyse brain activity in children suffering from autistic spectrum disorders (the first such facility within the UK).
- £180,000 over three years to School-Home Support Service UK to help it roll out its work in supporting school children and their families across London and five regional centres
- £150,000 over three years to Guy's and St Thomas's NHS Trust towards the research costs of a multi-disciplinary project on vascular damage and systemic inflammation (a condition responsible for the death of many critically ill patients who have the potential for making a full recovery if successfully treated).
- £150,000 over three years to the Hospice of the Valleys (South Wales) as a continuation grant towards its core costs in supporting terminally ill patients in their homes, their carers and loved ones by offering cancer care, terminal care and bereavement support groups.

Grant schemes in 2003.

The grants – and the grantees – come in all shapes and sizes and cover a very wide spectrum of need. The photographs show some of the work we are funding, but we identify below some grants where we feel our money has helped achieve real and sustainable advances or is funding something deeply unglamorous but essential:

- A grant of £100,000 was awarded to the British Urological Institute towards a new research centre for urological diseases, including incontinence (a Cinderella subject from a funding perspective, but covering very common conditions).
- A grant of £60,000 over 3 years was awarded to the Hepatitis C Trust towards the cost of a website and helpline. The Trust is the only charity working exclusively on Hepatitis C, which according to some experts is of "epidemic" proportions.
- A grant of £30,000 to the Anna Freud Centre (as the final year of a three year grant) to set up the Parent-Infant Project for mothers who fail to bond with their babies. The project has developed a clinical assessment tool which systematically examines parent-infant interactions to identify those relationships where the infant may be at risk. The system will be adapted for use by primary tier professionals such as GPs and health visitors.
- A grant of £10,000 to Age Concern Wolverhampton (as the final year of a three year grant of £45,000) towards the cost of a Partnership and Resource Development Worker, who has strengthened relationships with the local authority and put the charity in a far more sustainable financial position (following severe financial difficulties in the late 90's).
- A grant of £30,000 to Community Campus (as the final year of a three year grant) to a project which trains vulnerable young people in Middlesbrough and Stockton in building trade skills through the renovation of inner city houses. Many of the young people then become tenants. Community Campus now houses 80 young people and earns 65% of its income from statutory sources.
- A grant of £10,000 to DIVA (Newcastle's Domestic Violence Forum) as the final year of a three year grant towards the cost of an Asian Issues Worker to develop this work in the Asian community. The charity has attracted funding from statutory sources to ensure that this work continues on sensitive issues and develops training for others.

Small grants

£1.4 million was spent on small grants in 2003, comprising £1.3 million on grant in the 'traditional counties' with which the charity has a historic connection and £0.2 million under a scheme for the rest of the UK.

The 'traditional' counties are:

Gloucestershire
Hampshire
Kent
Leicestershire
Suffolk
Surrey
East Sussex
West Sussex.

Medical research guidelines

From 1 October 2004 support in this field is now given to projects which are potentially connected to the other grant making of the Henry Smith Charity and which focus on particular beneficiaries and where the research is intended to improve the quality of patients lives. Consideration will also be given to pathfinder research where a practical application is envisaged.

The key areas are:

Mental Health

For example (but not restricted to):

- Alzheimer's/dementia;
- autism;
- depression;
- drug and alcohol addiction;
- schizophrenia;
- self-harm;
- suicide.

Physical Disability

For example (but not restricted to):

- arthritis;
- diseases of the eye and ear;
- spinal conditions;
- skin diseases;
- burns.

Health of the poor, elderly or vulnerable

As well as research into causes and treatments this could also include preventative studies or the development of treatments which might be more accessible to the poor or more tailored to their needs.

For example (but not restricted to):

- dementia;
- depression;
- drug and alcohol addiction;
- hepatitis/cirrhosis;
- incontinence;
- infant mortality;
- respiratory conditions such as TB.

Exclusions

What will not normally be considered for funding

- Arts or educational projects, except those specifically for the rehabilitation and/or training of the disabled, prisoners or young people at risk of offending.
- Leisure or recreational activities, except those specifically and solely for the rehabilitation and/or training of the disabled, or holidays and outings for children from areas of considerable deprivation or children with a disability.
- Evironmental projects.
- Projects which promote a particular religion.
- Community centres, except those in areas of considerable deprivation, where those served are primarily in special need of help (for example, the elderly, those prone to drug or alcohol abuse or the homeless), and where the staff involved in the project have professional qualifications.
- Capital appeals for places of worship.
- Youth clubs, except those situated in areas of considerable deprivation.
- Playgrounds, except where a substantial element of need is involved, for example, disabled children or children in an area of considerable deprivation.
- Local authorities.
- Umbrella or grant-making organisations
- Universities and colleges, and grant maintained, private or local education authority schools or their Parent Teachers Associations, except if those schools are for students with special needs.
- Charities applying on behalf of individuals.
- General requests for donations.
- Running costs under £10,000 per annum except as specified under the Small Grants Programme.
- Professional associations and training of professionals.
- Projects which are abroad, even though the charity is based in the UK.
- Expeditions or overseas travel.
- Campaigning organisations or citizens advice projects or projects providing legal advice.
- Community transport projects.
- General counselling projects, except those in areas of considerable deprivation and with a clearly defined client group.

Applications
Special and General List application guidelines

There is no application form, but trustees suggest that the following guidelines be used:

Applications should be no longer than four A4 sides, and should incorporate a short (half page) summary

Applications should also include a detailed budget for the project and the applicant's most recent audited accounts. If those accounts show a significant surplus or deficit of income, please explain how this has arisen.

Applications should:

a. State clearly who they are, what they do and whom they seek to help.

b. Give the applicant's status, e.g., registered charity.

c. Describe clearly the project for which the grant is sought answering the following questions: What is the aim of the project and why is it needed? What practical results will it produce? How many people will benefit from it? What stage has the project reached so far? How will you ensure that it is cost-effective?

d. If the request is for a salary, enclose a job description.

e. If the request is for medical research, please see separate guidelines.

f. Explain how the project will be monitored, evaluated and, how its results will be disseminated.

g. State what funds have already been raised for the project, and name any other sources of funding applied for.

h. Explain where on-going funding (if required) will be obtained when the charity's grant has been used.

i. If the request is for revenue funding for a specific item, please state the amount sought.

j. Give the names and addresses of two independent referees.

Applications can be submitted at any time during the year. A letter acknowledging the application will be sent within two weeks of receipt.

Summaries of applications which are within the charity's objects and current policy are sent to the trustees.

If there is sufficient support for an application, one of the charity's visitors will be asked to prepare a report which usually involves a visit.

Applications for medical research projects are subject to independent peer review.

Trustees meet quarterly, in March, June, September and December to consider applications.

Applicants whose appeals have been considered at those meetings will be informed in writing of the trustees' decision within two weeks of the meeting.

Applicants who are unsuccessful are required to wait a minimum of six months from the date of notification before reapplying.

Applicants whose appeals are outside the charity's objects and/or current policy will be notified within four weeks of receipt of application.

Small Grants Programme application guidelines

Applications from the Counties with which the Charity has a traditional connection (Gloucestershire, Hampshire, Kent, Leicestershire, Suffolk, Surrey, East Sussex and West Sussex), are under the aegis of a particular Trustee who is resident in that County.

Applicants from these counties should complete an application form and should also include a detailed budget for the project and the most recent annual report/audited accounts.

Applications are considered by the County Trustee and recommendations for grants are subject to approval when the Trustees meet in March, June, September and December.

For further information or to receive an application form through the post, please call our Information Line on (020) 7320 6434.

Other Areas:

Applications from areas outside of the traditional counties can be submitted at any time during the year; they are processed fortnightly and are sent to the trustees of the Small Grants Committee.

If there is sufficient support, the grant is approved and the applicant is informed by telephone. All applicants will be sent a letter within four weeks of receipt of their application.

Applicants who are unsuccessful are required to wait a minimum of six months from the date of notification before reapplying.

The trustees do not require applicants to use a special application form, but suggest that the following guidelines be used:

1. Applications should be no longer than two A4 sides.

2. Applications should also include a detailed budget for the project and the applicant's most recent annual report/ audited accounts. If those accounts show a significant surplus or deficit of income, please explain.

3. Applications should:

a. State clearly who they are, what they do and whom they seek to help.

b. Give the applicant's status, e.g., registered charity.

c. Describe clearly the project for which the grant is sought answering the following questions: What is the aim of the project and why is it needed? What practical results will it produce? How many people will benefit from it?

d. State what funds have already been raised for the project, and name any other sources of funding applied for.

e. Ask, whenever possible, for a specific amount.

f. Give the names and addresses of two independent referees.

Please keep the application as simple as possible and avoid the use of technical terms, acronyms and jargon. Please do not send videos or CD Roms as unfortunately we do not have the facilities to watch them.

Medical research

The trustees do not require applicants to use a special application form.

In addition to requirements listed in the standard guidelines for applications to the General or Special list please include a full scientific proposal which should use the following standard headings:

- background.
- aims/objectives.
- study design
- methods
- statistics
- conclusion
- list of any publications relating to the project.

Please incorporate a clear summary of the project in layman's terms (no more than a single side of A4).

Please include a CV of the lead researcher.

The Scientific Proposal will be sent out for independent peer review.

Please give details of what other funding has been sought and with what result.

Please give an explanation if no other funding has been sought.

In making the preliminary assessment the following considerations will be made:

Whether the locus of the proposed research is a centre of excellence and those overseeing the research are eminent in their fields.

The potential practical benefit of the research in terms of, if appropriate, patient treatment and the alleviation of suffering.

The prospects that the research will either produce such benefits within the timescale of the project or enable a much larger project which is likely to be picked up by larger, more specialised funders such as MRC or Wellcome.

Whether the research could be funded elsewhere (i.e. by one of the larger funders) or whether funding at Smiths may potentially determine whether the research proceeds or not (because, for example, the research is at too early a stage or its subject/condition too 'unattractive' to attract a larger funder).

Funding will normally be for up to 3 years but could be considered up to a maximum of 5 years to enable a project to be completed or developed, following a second peer review after an appropriate period to evaluate both what has been achieved and the case for further work and funding.

The Sobell Foundation

Jewish charities, health and welfare

£2.6 million (2002/03)

Beneficial area England, Wales and Israel.

PO Box 2137, Shepton Mallet, Somerset BA4 6YA

Tel. 01749 813135 **Fax** 01749 813136

Email enquiries@sobellfoundation.org. uk

Website www.sobellfoundation.org.uk

Correspondent Mrs Penelope Jane Newton

Trustees *Mrs Susan Lacroix; Roger K Lewis; Mrs Andrea Gaie Scouller.*

Charity Commission no. 274369

Information available Annual report and accounts were provided by the trust.

Summary

Grants are made each year to 'small national or local charities' in England, Wales, Israel and Commonwealth of Independent States (C.I.S.). They are generally for between £500 and £10,000 each, although perhaps ten grants for £50,000 or over are made in most years,

for welfare or health causes (not research), specifically for:

- people who are sick;
- adults and children with physical and mental disabilities;
- older people;
- children;
- homelessness.

Probably over half the grants by value are to Jewish organisations, mainly in Britain but also in Israel.

Note that no grants are made in Scotland or Northern Ireland.

General

The foundation was established by Sir Michael Sobell in 1977 and 'grants tend to be made in line with his interests which are principally causes benefiting children, the sick, elderly, needy and disabled. In following these interests, the trustees aim to achieve a balance between Jewish charities (in the UK and Israel) and non-Jewish charities in England and Wales.' The trust's guidelines for applicants include the following:

We will only consider applications from charities registered with the Charity Commission, or charities that hold a Certificate of Exemption from the Inland Revenue. Overseas applicants must supply the details of a UK registered charity through which grants can be channelled on their behalf.

We concentrate our funding on small national or local charities; the trustees are unlikely to support large national charities which enjoy wide support.

We restrict our funding on a geographical basis to the following countries: England, Wales, Israel and C.I.S. We will only accept applications from charities based in these countries for projects and activities within these countries.

Areas covered: England, Wales, Israel, C.I.S

- Medical care and treatment, including respite care and hospices
- Care for physically and mentally disabled adults and children
- Education and training for physically and mentally disabled adults and children
- Care and support of the elderly
- Care and support for children
- Homelessness.

Areas covered: Israel only

- Immigrant absorption
- Co-existence projects
- Higher education.

In 2002/03 the foundation had assets of £41 million (£52 million in 2001/02) and a total income of £2.9 million. Around 500 grants were made totalling £2.6 million, with some organisations receiving more than one grant during the year.

The accounts stated: The trustees have charitable commitments for 2003/04 of £1,2 million and commitments of approximately £587,000 due for the years 2004/05 through to 2007/08 and have set themselves targets for future commitments. Funds set aside to meet the commitment for the Sobell House Hospice of £1 million are to be paid from capital. £526,000 was paid during 2001/02, £374,000 paid during 2002/03 with the balance of £100,000 carried forward and paid in April 2003.

The main beneficiary, as in the previous year, was Sobell House Hospice Charity, which received £374,000 in two grants. Other beneficiaries receiving £50,000 or more included Tel Aviv Foundation (£124,000 in total), United Jewish Israel Appeal (£120,000 in total), St George's Hospital Medical School (£84,000 in total), New Israel Fund (£71,000 in total), Barnardos (£62,000), Norwood, Dorothy House Foundation Ltd, Friends of the Bar Ilan University, Brain Research Trust and Prior's Court School Appeal (£50,000 each) and Jerusalem Foundation (£50,000 in total).

Other larger grants included those to the National Heart and Lung Institute (£40,000 in total), Friends of Ilan (£35,000), Jewish Museum London (£25,000), CBF World Jewish Relief (£20,000), Hornsey Trust for Handicapped Children (£18,000), NSPCC (£15,000), JNF Charitable Trust (£13,000), International Spinal Research (£12,000) and Muscular Dystrophy Campaign, Queen Alexandra College, Jewish Deaf Association, Depaul Trust, Fair Trials Abroad Trust and Kidsactive (£10,000 each).

Smaller grants included those to the Bracken Trust, Cancer Resource Centre, Befriending Network, Samaritans, Devon Community Foundation and UK Friends of AWIS (£5,000 each), Yakar Educational Foundation (£4,000), Prospect Foundation Ltd, Colon Cancer Concern, Rethink Disability and National Pyramid Trust (£3,000 each), Tripscope, National Eye Research Centre, Torfaen Opportunity Group and Rainbow Trust Children's Charity (£2,000 each) and Maidstone Crossroads Scheme, Baby Life Support Systems, Tower Hamlets Old People's Welfare Trust, Oneg Shabbos Youth Club Trust, Youth Aliyah Child Rescue, Newhaven Volunteer Bureau, Commonwealth

Jewish Trust and Old Windsor Day Centre (£1,000 each).

Exclusions

No grants to individuals. Only registered charities or organisations registered with the Inland Revenue should apply.

Applications

Applications should be made in writing to the administrator using the application form obtainable from the foundation or printable from its website.

The application form asks you about your organisation and your proposal for funding. It should be accompanied by:

- an income and expenditure budget;
- current year's summary income and expenditure budget for the organisation;
- most recent annual report;
- most recent full accounts
- Inland Revenue certificate of exemption (if applicable).

It will generally be two to three months before applicants are notified of the trustees' decision.

Trustees meet every three to four months and major grants are considered at these meetings. Requests for smaller amounts may be dealt with on a more frequent basis.

Most applications are dealt with on an ongoing basis, and there are no deadlines for the receipt of applications.

The Souter Charitable Trust

Christian evangelism, welfare

£1.1 million (2002/03)

Beneficial area UK, but with a preference for Scotland; overseas.

PO Box 7412, Perth PH1 5YX

Tel. 01738 634745 **Fax** 01738 636662

Correspondent Ramsay Gillies, Secretary

Trustees *Brian Souter; Betty Souter; Mrs Ann Allen.*

Scottish Charity no. SC029998

Information available An information sheet was provided by the trust. Annual report and accounts are available from the trust for £10.

This trust is funded by donations from Scottish businessman Brian Souter, one of the founders of the Stagecoach transport company. It gives the following account of its policies:

Our stated policy is to assist 'projects engaged in the relief of human suffering in the UK or overseas, particularly those with a Christian emphasis'. We tend not to get involved with research or capital funding, but would be more likely to provide a contribution towards the revenue costs of a project. Applications for building projects, personal educational requirements or personal expeditions are specifically excluded.

Most grants are one-off payments of £1,000 or less; a small number of projects receive support over three years. The grants list indicates a specific interest in the support of marriage and parenting issues, and it has a preference for funding revenue rather than capital costs.

In 2002/03, 291 grants were paid out, of which three-quarters were for £1,000 or less. Over 30% of the total was accounted for by one grant, of £360,000, to Alpha International, an Anglican evangelical movement based in Knightsbridge, London which had received £400,000 in the previous year. Other large grants were made to the Church of the Nazarene (£95,000), Operation Mobilisation (£65,000) and Sargent Cancer Care (£50,000).

At least six of the 12 largest grants were to specifically Scottish charities, including £50,000 for Schools Enterprise Scotland and £32,000 to Scripture Union Scotland.

Smaller grants have previously been made to Prince's Trust – Scotland, Highland Theological College and Turning Point Scotland.

Exclusions

Building projects, personal education grants and expeditions are not supported.

Applications

In writing to the correspondent. Please keep applications brief and no more than two sides of A4 paper: if appropriate, please send audited accounts, but do not send brochures, business plans, videos and so on. The trust states that it will request more information if necessary. The trustees meet at least every two months, and all applications will be acknowledged in due course, whether successful or not. A stamped addressed envelope would be appreciated. Subsequent applications should not be made within a year of the initial submission.

The South East London Community Foundation

Community activities

£3.2 million (2003/04)

Beneficial area The London boroughs of Lambeth, Southwark, Lewisham, Greenwich, Bromley and Bexley (plus other areas depending on the programme – contact the foundation for details).

Room 6, Winchester House, 11 Cranmer Road, London SW9 6EJ

Tel. 020 7582 5117 **Fax** 020 7582 4020

Email enquiries@selcf.org.uk

Website www.selcf.org.uk

Correspondent G Williamson, Secretary

Trustees *S I Aziz; P Davenport; G Davies; L Garner; P Jefferson Smith; C Lindsay; J C Roberts; A Sawyerr; C Souter; K Thomas; G Williamson.*

Charity Commission no. 1091263

Information available Annual report and accounts were provided by the trust.

The foundation is primarily the local distributor of funds from a number of government programmes under a variety of different schemes. The money it distributed in 2003/04 increased dramatically on the previous year:

The foundation has expanded further in its second year operating as a company. Total grants awarded were £3,164,000 compared to £1,943,000 [in 2002/03], a 63% increase, and expenditure, mainly in support of the grant giving, was £352,000, a 29% increase over the previous year [....]

The year has been one of achievement of the charity's objects, building on the foundation laid in previous years. The foundation's reputation as a capable grant distributor and community supporter has been further enhanced by the quality and efficiency of the team of grant officers. The 776 grants awarded are the 'tip of the iceberg' compared with the number of assessments and support visits made. This has no doubt helped us secure two new contracts: the 'Partners in Time – Key Fund', awarding grants in the London Borough of Greenwich, and the New Cross Gate New Deal for Communities. The contract from Southwark Alliance has been continued for a further two years and the Local Network Fund contract agreed for a further two years.

We have also continued our 'Financial Intelligence Communities' outreach work providing one-to-one and group financial training to newly formed, hard to reach communities, enhancing their development and financial skills. In addition we have provided well received Child Protection Training with the support of the Local Network Fund for many groups in South East London.

The foundation makes grants that are:
A: Wholly within the foundation's own discretion, or;
B: In partnership with bodies that provide them. The practice that has been established as most effective is:

- the foundation and the fund provider agree strategic objectives for the grant making;
- the foundation advertises grant rounds, receives and assesses bids and recommends grants;
- a panel comprising mainly of representatives of the fund provider or set up by the foundation itself, agree to the grant;
- to ensure conformity with our trust deed, a committee of the foundation's trustees confirm the grants.

Current programmes

Neighbourhood Renewal Community Chest – Lambeth, Greenwich and Lewisham (and Southwark)

The purpose of the grants made in Lambeth, Greenwich and Lewisham are to contribute to regeneration by encouraging greater involvement in local community activities; improving the management of local community activities and organisations; improving the local neighbourhood; to better understand cultural diversity and promote racial harmony. Grants range from £50 to £50,000; grants up to £1,000 can be fast tracked. Projects in Southwark are funded according to the following themes: educational achievement, health & well-being, housing, environment & community safety, children & young people, employment & enterprise.

Deadlines in 2005:

3rd June

2nd September

2nd December

Community Learning Chest

Grants are available from £50 to £2,000 for learning and development activities in Lambeth, Lewisham, Southwark and Greenwich. Applications can be made at any time.

Healthy Communities Fund

Grants are available for up to £5,000 to promote health improvement and reduce health inequalities in Lewisham only. Deadlines for applications were yet to be announced at the time of writing– contact the foundation for up-to-date information.

Local Network Fund for Children & Young People

Grants are available for up to £7,000 in Lambeth, Lewisham, Southwark, Greenwich, Bexley and Bromley to improve the lives of disadvantaged children or young people (aged up to 19). Ring 08451 130161 for an application form.

Upcoming deadlines:

1st July 2005

30th September 2005

13th January 2006

Deptford Challenge Trust

Grants are available for up to £30,000 in Deptford for projects or activities that meet local needs and benefit the local community. Projects that strengthen self-help are encouraged. Priority's given to projects that bring different groups (age group or ethnicity) together to help build a sense of shared community. Small grants are also available for up to £5,000. The closing date for applications is 31st December 2005

NDC New Cross Gate

Up to £5,000 is available to support community projects in the New Cross Gate area (a leaflet is available stating the exact area). Upcoming deadlines are September 2005 and January 2006– contact the foundation for up-to-date information on later deadlines.

Sport Relief Grants

Grants are available for up to £5,000 for sporting activities that help people who are experiencing difficulties in their lives; bring different communities together; or increase access to sport for people that are excluded or isolated. Applications can be made any time until September 2006. Eligible areas are Westminster,

City of London, Camden, Islington, Kensington & Chelsea, Croydon, Southwark, Greenwich, Lewisham, Lambeth, Bexley and Bromley.

Exclusions

No grants for individuals (except for the Community Learning Chest), political groups or activities which promote religion.

Applications

Application forms for the various programmes are available from the foundation.

The South Yorkshire Community Foundation

General

£1.1 million (2002/03)

Beneficial area South Yorkshire wide, with specific reference to Barnsley, Doncaster, Rotherham, Sheffield.

Clay Street, Sheffield S9 2PF

Tel. 0114 242 4294 **Fax** 0114 242 4605

Email grants@sycf.org.uk

Website www.sycf.org.uk

Correspondent Richard Clarke, Director

Trustees *Martin P W Lee, chair; Christopher J Jewitt; David Clark; Martin J W Venning; Pauline Acklam; Isadora Aiken; Narendra Bajaria; Anthony G Green; Timothy M Greenacre; Galen Ives; Brian P Last; Michael J Mallett; James Ogley; Joseph Rowntree; Lady Sykes; Roger Viner; Maureen Shah.*

Charity Commission no. 517714

Information available Application form and guidelines. Annual review and accounts.

The South Yorkshire Community Foundation, launched in 1986, specialises in funding small community and voluntary groups within the south Yorkshire area. It particularly supports projects and groups that work with communities facing poverty and/or discrimination. Priority is also given to small and medium sized groups which find it hard to raise money elsewhere.

Projects funded include those which help local people in need, such as people who may be homeless, ill, disabled or older, and community life, such as nursery care, arts and culture, nature and heritage and sport. Applicants do not have to be a registered charity but do have to have a charitable purpose. As well as running its own programme, the foundation also makes grants on behalf of its donors.

In 2002/03 the foundation had assets of £1.1 million and an income of £1.5 million. Grants totalled £1.1 million. Unfortunately, a full list of beneficiaries was not available. The trust did, however, supply a summary of its main grant programmes and examples of beneficiaries from each. These are as follows:

South Yorkshire-wide area

Local Network Fund for Children and Young People

Grants between £250 and £7,000 are available for small groups working with children and young people, up to the age of 19, for projects which meet one for the four themes:

- 'Isolation and access – projects that help children who may feel isolated or alone, or have trouble accessing services.
- 'Aspirations and experiences – projects that give children experiences, or help them achieve goals that other children may take for granted.
- 'Economic disadvantage – projects that help families to improve their living standards and cope with difficulties that come from being on low incomes.
- 'Children's voices – projects that give children and young people the chance to express their opinions and give advice in matters that concern them.'

Application forms are available through a national call centre: 0845 1130 161. Completed forms are sent to the foundation for processing.

Beneficiaries included the Yemeni Youth Association – Sheffield (£7,000), Canklow Crusaders Junior Football Club – Rotherham (£6,000), Grimethorpe Activity Zone – Barnsley (£6,500) and Doncaster Youths with Asperger Syndrome Project (£5,000),

Small Grants Programme

These grants are intended for smaller, less well-resourced groups from across South Yorkshire, where small amounts of funding can make a real difference.

The majority of grants are one-off payments of between £50 and £1,000 (up to £1,500 in exceptional circumstances).

Beneficiaries included Get Sorted Music Academy – Rotherham (£1,000), Safe @ Last – Sheffield (£980), Grimethorpe Pentecostal Church – Barnsley (£930) and Doncaster Chinese Women's Group (£570).

Sheffield area

Sheffield First for Health Small Grants Fund

This fund provides grants of between £50 and £600 for new community groups with a health focus or for established groups to develop new, health-related activities.

Beneficiaries included Sheffield Fibromyalgia Self Help Group (£600) and Sheffield Forum of Self Help Groups (£500).

Neighbourhood Renewal Community Chest for Sheffield

Grants of between £50 and £5,000 are provided for small community groups, looking to improve their neighbourhood, who are working with people facing poverty and/or disadvantage.

Beneficiaries included Owls Trust Allstars (£4,800) and Lai Yin Association (£2,100).

Neighbourhood Renewal Community Learning Chest for Sheffield

Grants of up to £5,000 are provided for community groups involved in regenerating their local neighbourhood. Grants of up to £500 are also provided to individuals involved in neighbourhood renewal.

Beneficiaries included Roshni Asian Women's Resource Centre (£4,800).

The foundation also runs a grant programme called Community Champions for volunteers working with or in community groups. Further information can be found on the foundation's website or by contacting the Grants Team on 0114 242 4294.

Exclusions

Each grant programme has its own exclusions. Please consult the website or contact the foundation for more information. General exclusions include private membership clubs, political campaigns or programmes that discriminate participation based upon religion, race, ethnicity or other grounds.

Applications

Applications are made by completing a simple form, available with the grant programme closing dates, from the foundation. Initial enquiries can be made by email, telephone or fax. Applications are reviewed on a six-weekly basis by panels of local volunteers.

The main foundation grant programmes have four closing dates per year – the end of February, May, August and November.

The W F Southall Trust

Quaker, general

Around £300,000 (2003/04)

Beneficial area UK and overseas.

c/o Rutters Solicitors, 2 Bimport, Shaftesbury, Dorset SP7 8AY

Tel. 01747 852377 **Fax** 01747 851989

Email southall@rutterslaw.co.uk

Correspondent Stephen T Rutter, Secretary

Trustees *Donald Southall, chair; Joanna Engelkamp; Claire Greaves; Mark Holtom; Daphne Maw; Christopher Southall; Annette Wallis.*

Charity Commission no. 218371

Information available Information was provided by the trust.

This trust prefers to support smaller charities where the grant will make a more significant difference. Areas of work supported are: Society of Friends; peace and reconciliation; alcohol, drug abuse and penal affairs; environmental action; homelessness; community action; and overseas development. Grants currently total between £250,000 and £300,000 a year.

In 2003/04 the trust had assets of £6.9 million and an income of £514,000, including an extraordinary gift to capital of £250,000. Grants were made to 104 organisations totalling £281,000. Those over £2,000 each were listed in the accounts and were broken down as follows:

Quaker and Society of Friends – 14 grants totalling £103,000

A substantial grant of £50,000 went to Britain Yearly Meeting. Other grants included £16,000 to Woodbrooke College, £7,500 to Friends World Committee for Consultation, £6,000 to Friends Schools Joint Bursary Scheme and £5,000 to Leaveners.

Peace and reconciliation – 15 grants totalling £54,000

The largest grant in this category was £20,000 to Quaker Peace Studies – Bradford University. Other grants included £6,000 to Friends Schools Joint Bursary Scheme; £5,000 each to International Voluntary Services and Peacemakers UK, £4,000 each to Leap Confronting Conflicts and Responding to Conflict and £2,500 to Scottish Centre for Nonviolence.

Alcohol and drug abuse/penal affairs – 9 grants

The only listed grant was £2,500 to Inside Out Trust.

Environmental action – 9 grants totalling £19,000

Listed grants in this category were £5,000 to Green Light Trust and £3,000 to Worcestershire Wildlife Trust.

Homelessness – 4 grants totalling £13,000

Beneficiaries were £5,000 to Quaker Social Action, £3,000 to St Mungos, £2,500 to Quaker Homeless Action and £2,000 to Alone in London.

Community Action – 26 grants totalling £39,000

Listed grants were £3,500 to Refugee Council, £3,000 to Corrymeela Community and £2,500 to Toynbee Hall.

Overseas development – 24 grants totalling £33,000

Listed grants were £6,500 to Oxfam and £2,500 to Tree Aid.

Exclusions

No grants to individuals or large national charities.

Applications

In writing to, or e-mailing, the correspondent requesting an application form. Applications are considered in February/March and November. Applications received between meetings are considered at the next meeting.

The Sovereign Health Care Charitable Trust (formerly known as The Charities Fund)

Health, Disability

£354,000 (2003)
Beneficial area UK.

Royal Standard House, 26 Manningham Lane, Bradford, West Yorkshire BD1 3DN

Tel. 01274 729472 **Fax** 01274 722252

Email charitiesfund@ sovereignhealthcare.co.uk

Correspondent The Secretary

Trustees G McGowan; J Hellawell; M Austin; D Child; S N Johnson; M S Bower; C M Hudson; D J Lewis; Mrs S E Berry.

Charity Commission no. 1079024

Information available Information was provided by the trust.

This trust is funded by donations received under the Gift Aid scheme from the investment income of The Hospital Fund of Bradford. Its objects are to provide amenities for hospital patients and to make grants to charities 'for the relief and assistance of needy sick and elderly people'.

In 2003 it had assets of £174,000 and an income of £308,000, from Gift Aid. Grants totalled £354,000 and were broken down as follows:

Grants to hospitals	£19,000
Grants to associations and institutions	£315,000
Nurses' training grant	£20,000

The largest grant was £50,000 to Bradford Can Appeal. Other large grants of £10,000 or more included those to Marie Curie Cancer Care and Sue Ryder Foundation (£12,000 each) and Lord Mayor's Appeal and Team of the Year Awards (£10,000 each).

Grants under £10,000 each included those to St Gemma's Hospice (£6,000), Bradford Society for Mentally Handicapped Children, National Heart Research and Yorkshire Air Ambulance (£5,000 each), British Epilepsy Association and Martin House Hospice (£3,500 each), Christians Against Poverty (£3,000), Kirkwood Hospice, Sargeant Cancer Care for Children and The Bradford Soup Run (£2,500 each), Alzheimer's Society, International Glaucoma and MS Therapy Centres (£1,500 each) and Barnardo's, DeafBlind UK and Shelter (£1,000 each).

Exclusions

No grants to individuals.

Applications

In writing to the correspondent.

SPARKS Charity (Sport Aiding Medical Research For Kids)

Medical research

£797,000 (2003/04)
Beneficial area UK.

Linden House, Ashdown Road, Forest Row, East Sussex RH18 5BN

Tel. 01342 825 390

Email info@sparks.org.uk

Website www.sparks.org.uk

Correspondent Renny Leach, Medical Research Consultant

Trustees T Brooke-Taylor; Sir T Brooking; H Edmeades; M Higgins; J Hill; M Kelly; D Metcalfe; D Mills; R Uttley; A Walker; S Waugh; J Wilkinson.

Charity Commission no. 1003825

Information available Information was on file at the Charity Commission.

SPARKS supports medical research related to the prenatal period and the early years of life. Altough it funds research across all therapeutic areas, research must be aimed at providing a therapeutic intervention which will make a significant contribution to reducing mortality or relieving the condition, disease or disability in question. The charity will only support research which is likely to have a clear clinical application in the near future. therefore grant applications for routine basic research which is unlikely to have clinical application within ten years will not be considered.

Funded research takes the form of project grants of up to three years in length with a clearly definable subject area and outcome, or for equipment grants for use within a specific research proposal. Pilot projects of short duration to test a concept in preparation for a full application will also be considered.

Funding for a clearly justified grant application including all salary, consumable and equipment components is not likely to exceed £45,000 per year.

In 2003/04 the charity had assets of £424,000 and an income of almost £2 million, mainly from fundraising events. Seven grants totalled £797,000. Beneficiaries were: Institute of Child Health (three grants of £139,000, £45,000 and £10,000), University College Hospital London (£199,000), University of Aberdeen (£132,000), University of Southampton (£110,000) and Guys & St Thomas' Hospital (£86,000).

Exclusions

The charity is unable to consider:

- applications which are concurrently submitted to other funding bodies;
- grants for further education, for example, MSc/PhD course fees;
- grants towards service provision or audit studies;
- grants for work undertaken outside the UK;
- grants towards 'top up' funding for work supported by other funding bodies;
- grants to other charities.

Applications

Prior to submitting a full application, all applicants are required to complete an outline proposal form which is available from Renny Leach. Suitable applicants will be sent an application form (by email in Word format) and a copy of the relating terms and conditions.

All completed applications are assessed by full peer review, firstly by independent external referees and then by the SPARKS Medical Advisory Committee.

The Spitalfields Market Community Trust

See below

See below

Beneficial area The London borough of Tower Hamlets, especially Bethnal Green.

Attlee House, 28 Commercial Street, London E1 6LR

Tel. 020 7247 6689 **Fax** 020 7247 8748

Email smct.org@virgin.net

Correspondent Tim Budgen

Trustees *Stella Currie, chair; Jusna Begum; Sue Brown; Ghulam Mortuza; Ala Uddin.*

Charity Commission no. 1004003

Information available See below

Founded in 1991 as a limited company (then called Startaid Ltd), the trust was established as part of the 'planning gain' arrangements accompanying the development of what had been Spitalfields fruit and vegetable market. The trust received £3.75 million from Spitalfields Development Ltd (the developers of the site) and £1.25 million from the City of London Corporation (freeholders of the site). All directors of the trust have local connections.

In early 2005 the trust's office had a voicemail message stating that the trust is 'no longer awarding grants'. It is unclear whether this message was referring to the end of a particular grant round, a complete change of policy or if the trust was being wound up. No-one from the trust was available to clarify the situation, despite leaving several messages on the answer machine for a return call. It would appear from information on the Charity Commission's database, however, that its funds are all but expended, with the trust also having a dwindling income. It would, therefore, seem to be the case that the predictions made by the trust in previous years about the exhaustion of funds has been realised.

From the previous edition:

The trust was established in 1991 and over the last ten years has distributed over £6.5 million in grants. Initially the directors only made grants from income. However with a reduction in interest rates, the income dropped significantly. To enable the trust to

continue to make an impact in the area, it was decided to make distributions from capital. This policy is reviewed each year but obviously if it continues for any length of time, it will lead to a reduction in the trust's capital and to the eventual exhaustion of the trust's funds.

The trust has also previously stated that: 'the priorities of the trust continue to be reviewed. Amongst the issues being considered are the depletion of trust funds and future of the trust itself. A major consultation exercise is planned to inform the trust's forward strategy.'

The Charity Commission has also received a correspondence from the trust notifying them of a change to its trust deed. It seems, therefore, that applications to the trust would be fruitless.

Applications

See general section.

Foundation for Sport and the Arts

Sport, the arts

£4 million (2003/04)

Beneficial area UK.

PO Box 20, Liverpool L13 1HB

Tel. 0151 259 5505 **Fax** 0151 230 0664

Email info@thefsa.net

Website www.thefsa.net

Correspondent Richard Boardley, Secretary

Trustees *Sir Tim Rice, chair; Lord Brabazon; Dame Janet Baker; Sir Christopher Chataway; Lord Faulkner; Clive Lloyd; Lord Grantchester; Steve Roberts; Gary Speakman; Baroness McIntosh of Hudnall.*

Information available Annual report and accounts and guidelines for applicants.

The foundation was formed in July 1991 to channel funds generated by the football pools into sport and the arts. Following the demise, at the end of March 2004, of the agreement with the government whereby that funding was committed, Spotechplc, the owner of Littlewoods pools, had undertaken to continue its support.

The grants and loans offered by the trustees of the foundation aim to support and promote sport and the arts at every level of attainment to pursue their interests in these fields. Trustees are particularly keen to ensure that young people are given the opportunity to take part in and enjoy activities which can engage them for life.

In 2003/04 the foundation had assets of £26 million and an income of £2.6 million. Grants totalled almost £4 million.

Grant criteria

We look to support a wide range of activities where there is clear beneficial impact across the community. Our particular goal at this time is to encourage active participation by young people.

We look for evidence of active fund raising, and the involvement and commitment of local people in trying to help themselves, where an award of up to £40,000 can make the difference between success and failure.

Apart from professional football and horse racing, most socially inclusive sport is considered. Support for the arts covers the widest spectrum of activity.

Applications

Full guidelines can be downloaded from the foundation's website. All applications should be made on the questionnaire which can be also be downloaded. This should be printed out, completed and returned, with all relevant associated documents. Alternatively guidelines and questionnaires are available on request.

The Spring Harvest Charitable Trust

The promotion of Christianity

£750,000 (2002/03)

Beneficial area UK and overseas.

14 Horsted Square, Bellbrook Industrial Estate, Uckfield, East Sussex TN22 1QG
Tel. 01825 746510 **Fax** 01825 769141
Email theclerk@shct.springharvest.org
Correspondent The Clerk to the Trustees
Trustees *J S Richardson, chair; I C Coffey; C A M Sinclair; Faith Forster.*
Charity Commission no. 1042041
Information available Annual report available from the trust for an 'administration fee' of £25.

Registered as a charity in 1994, this trust seeks to 'equip the Church for action'. The main focus of the trust's grantmaking is evangelism and compassion, both within the UK and overseas.

In 2002/03 the trust had an income of £650,000 and a total expenditure of £879,000. Grants totalled around £750,000, a figure that seems to largely remain constant each year.

Previous beneficiaries include Tear Fund, Eurovangelism, Oasis Trust, Signpost International, Release International, British Youth for Christ, Care for the Family, Lambeth Fund, Scripture Union International, World Evangelical Fellowship, Bulgarian Evangelical Theological Institute, Saltmine Children's Theatre Company, Keswick Convention Trust, Prison Fellowship, Hackney Marsh Partnership, Traidcraft Exchange, International Needs UK, Southampton Action for Employment and World in Need, Caring for Life, Friends in the West, Joshua Generation, Links International and Oxford Centre for Mission Studies.

Comment

Accounts are available from the trust for £25, an unrealistic amount to spend on the accounts of a single trust.

Applications

In writing to the correspondent, although the trust states that all funds are allocated for 2005.

St James's Place Foundation

Children and young people with special needs

About £615,000 (2003)

Beneficial area UK.

St James's Place House, Dollar Street, Cirencester, Gloucestershire GL7 2AQ
Tel. 01285 640302 **Fax** 01285 640436
Email gail.mitchell-briggs@sjp.co.uk
Correspondent Gail Mitchell-Briggs, Secretary
Trustees *Malcolm Cooper-Smith; Sir Mark Weinberg; Mike Wilson; David Bellamy.*

Charity Commission no. 1031456
Information available Annual report and accounts are on file at the Charity Commission.

Summary

Established in 1992 to provide employees at the parent company with a motivation to undertake fundraising activities, this foundation was supported entirely from donations from members of the company for the first seven years of its life. The company views the efforts of its employees as important in terms of both raising funds for a much needed cause and improving the community spirit in the workplace. The foundation's management committee is comprised of one member of each of its branches and one member of head office, to keep the sense of community spirit within the workplace. Employees have jumped out of planes, run and cycled through deserts and climbed mountains. Since 1999, the funds raised through these activities have been matched pound-for-pound by the company as corporate donations.

The foundation selects one theme that it will support. The current theme has been 'Cherishing the Children', which supports young people who are aged 25 or under who have a physical or mental disability or who have a life-threatening or degenerative illness. Organisations must have at least 75% of its users meet this criteria to be considered. Beneficiaries must be registered/ recognised charities or special needs schools. When this category was first selected for the theme (1996–1998), it was aimed at pre-teen children, with the age range first extended to 17 years old in 1999, and then to 25 from January 2003.

The following criteria are stated to be true of any theme the trust runs:

- 'Applicants should be well-established registered charities with a proven track record, which have worthwhile objectives and are run efficiently and economically. Applications from individuals will not be considered.
- 'Applications should be in respect of tangible projects or equipment with visible end results.
- 'The project should help as many people as possible or, where this is not applicable, have a major impact on the lives of those helped.
- 'UK only.'

In addition to this, grants can be made by the local branches of the parent company, to a maximum of £2,500 each, for general charitable purposes. A small

351

number of grants are also made outside the current theme, although these are usually as recurrent grants applicable to the theme at the time and matching the money raised by employees of the parent company undertaking a major fundraising activity.

In 2003 the foundation had an income £1.2 million, including corporate donations, and a total expenditure of £665,000, most of which is given in grants. No further information was available for the year.

Grantmaking policy

Recommendations for grants to be paid under the current theme are made on a quarterly basis by the managing committee to the trustees for approval.

The decision mechanism of the foundation for the distribution of the corporate donation to worthy causes is different from other funds raised. It was agreed between the managing committee and the trustees, that funds from the corporate donation should be used to fund larger projects not limited to the foundation's theme 'Cherishing the Children', and not limited to the UK.

The major beneficiary so far of the corporate donations since 2000 has been Hope & Homes for Children, a UK-based charity that provides homes for children in war torn and disaster areas of the world, primarily in Eastern Europe and Africa.

There is an intention to donate up to a further £180,000 to the Variety Club Children's Charity to sponsor a further nine Sunshine Coaches at locations throughout the UK, which is expected to happen by the end of 2004.

Recent beneficiaries

The foundation makes around 100 grants each year under the 'Cherishing the Children' theme. As well as Hope & Homes for Children and the Variety Club Children's Charity, recent beneficiaries include Hope House Children's Hospice – Oswestry, Diabetes UK – Wirral Junior Branch, Spring Centre – Gloucester, Paternoster School – Cirencester, Elms Bank Community High Special School – Manchester, Seven Springs (Cotswolds) Play & Support Centre, Alder Hey Children's Hospital Rocking Horse Appeal – Liverpool, Cystic Fibrosis Trust, Sussex Autistic Society, Child and Sound – London and Birmingham Institute for the Deaf.

Other grants

In addition to the grants made under our current theme of 'Cherishing the Children', a number of additional smaller grants, up to a

maximum of £2,500 each, have been made by the foundation during the year. The beneficiaries of these grants were selected by the regional offices of St James's Place Capital plc, rather than by the managing committee, in order to promote more local interest in the foundation through the country.

Beneficiaries included Ryan Abraham Equipment Fund, Manic Depression Fellowship, Big Brothers and Sisters Edinburgh, World Vision, Child Victims of Crime, Dreams Comes True, St Mark's Hospital, Kingfisher Trust, Mulberry Bush School Limited, Winchester Young Carers, Rainbow Hospice, Access Partnership and Life Education Centres.

Comment

Despite ample warning, and their obligation to the contrary, the Charity Commission were unable to give us sight of this trust's accounts.

Exclusions

The foundation will not consider applications in relation to holidays. It has a policy of not considering an application from any charity within two years of giving a grant.

The trust does not provide support for:

- political, sectarian, religious and cultural organisations
- research projects
- sponsorship or advertising
- building projects, running costs, administration or salaries.

Applications

All applications must be submitted on a fully completed application form and be accompanied by the latest audited report and accounts, together with any supporting explanatory documents as appropriate. The trustees meet quarterly.

St Katharine & Shadwell Trust

Education, training, general

£482,000 (2002/03)

Beneficial area The St Katharine & Shadwell wards in the borough of Tower Hamlets.

PO Box 1779, London E1W 2BY

Tel. 020 7782 6962 **Fax** 020 7782 6963

Correspondent Jenny Dawes, Director

Trustees *The trust is run by a board of governors: Sir Robin Mountfield, chair; Lucky Begum; Maj. Gen. Geoffrey Field; Sir David Hardy; Les Hinton; Mary Nepstad; Jane Reed; Richard Roberts; Cllr Abdul Shukur; Eric Sorensen; Revd Ronald Swan; Peter Rimmer; Dan Jones; Vaughan Williams; Cllr Shafiqul Haque; Ranu Miah; Angela O'Phanoll.*

Charity Commission no. 1001047

Information available Full accounts and annual report were provided by the trust.

The trust was created in 1990 by Wapping Neighbourhood and News International, the latter making a £3.5 million donation to the trust in 1991. It was set up to improve the quality of life of residents of the St Katharine and Shadwell wards in the borough of Tower Hamlets. Whilst principally a grant-making trust, it is designed to offer a framework for partnerships between business, residents, the local authority and voluntary organisations.

The trust is also administering Neighbourhood Renewal/Community Chest for all Tower Hamlets but below focuses mainly on the work of the trust (excluding Neighbourhood Renewal or Community Chest projects).

The board of governors who administer the trust's work includes local residents, councillors from the local authority and representatives from local business, namely News International, who also donate office space to the trust.

Designed to meet the changing needs of the future, its objectives include:

- the promotion of education and learning, including training in employment skills;
- the provision of facilities for recreation or other leisure-time occupations;
- the relief of poverty and sickness;
- the advancement of public education in the arts;
- the provision of housing accommodation for people who are in need or have physical or mental disabilities;
- the relief of unemployment;
- urban regeneration.

Up to and including 2005, priority is given to the education and training of children and adults with a particular emphasis on literacy projects. Applications relating to activities for pensioners or events that can bring together different sections of the community will also be considered.

When the trust was established in 1990, it only awarded grants to unsolicited applications. However, the board decided that there were certain areas of need where a single grant was an insufficient response and as a result have developed a series of special project grants. These are given for projects initiated by the trust, of particular importance in meeting the trust's current priorities or in which the trust has been involved in ways other than the gift of money.

In 2002 the trust had assets of £6 million and a total income of £692,000. Grants amounted to £482,000, broken down as follows:

Education and training – 23 grants totalling £107,000

Shaw Trust, formerly Working Support (£15,000), Leyton Orient Community Sports Programme (£10,000); Tower Hamlets Playgroups and Under 5s Association (£5,000 each); Shadwell Basin Outdoor Activity Centre and Children's Music Workshop (£6,000 each).

Recreation and leisure for older people – 6 grants totalling £13,000

Tower Hamlets Community Transport (£10,000); Wapping Community Group (£1,000) and Glamis Tenants and Residents Association (£750).

Activities to bring together different sections of the community and promote harmony – 3 grants totalling £7,800

Bangladesh Youth Movement (£1,000); Golden Moon Youth Project (£1,000) and Chinese Association of Tower Hamlets (£867).

Neighbourhood Renewal/ Community Chest – 23 grants totalling £76,000

(£5,000 each to) Barkentine Management Team, Eastern Theatre, On the One, SHEHAB and to Wapping Pensioners Action Group (£1,254).

There was also a special project grant for recreation and leisure of £7,200 for coach hire for summer outings for older people.

Exclusions

The charity does not normally fund expenditure involving ongoing salary or premises costs or donations to general fundraising appeals. School pupils under 16, full-time students on postgraduate courses or gap-year travel are not normally supported.

Organisations and individuals who wish to apply for grants are welcome to contact the charity's office by letter or telephone for further information and advice. The office is usually open on Tuesday and Wednesday mornings and Thursday.

Applications

Standard application forms are used for both Neighbourhood Renewal and Community Chest.

Applications to the trust, excluding above–do not use application forms. Applicants are asked to write a letter giving details of their request and of their organisation. Applicants are usually visited by the director, and grant decisions are made by the governors who meet four times a year, although urgent requests for small grants may be considered at any time. Successful applicants are asked to help the trust monitor its work by making a simple report on how the grant was spent and how effective the trust's contribution really was.

The Staples Trust

Development, environment, women's issues

£425,000 (2003/04)

Beneficial area Overseas, UK.

Allington House, 1st Floor, 150 Victoria Street, London SW1E 5AE

Tel. 020 7410 0330 **Fax** 020 7410 0332

Email info@sfct.org.uk

Correspondent Michael Pattison, Director

Trustees *Jessica Sainsbury; Peter Frankopan; James Sainsbury; Alex Sainsbury; Judith Portrait.*

Charity Commission no. 1010656

Information available Excellent annual report and accounts were provided by the trust.

Summary

This is one of the Sainsbury Family Charitable Trusts, which share a joint administration. They have a common approach to grantmaking which is described in the entry for the group as a whole.

This trust's main areas of interest are (with number and the value of grant approvals in 2003/04):

	No.	Amount
Overseas development	8	£108,000
Environment	9	£277,000
Women's issues	4	£44,000
Frankopan fund	9	£26,000
General	5	£135,000

General

This is the trust of Jessica Sainsbury and its trustees include her husband and her two brothers who lead the **Tedworth** and **Glass-House** trusts (see separate entries).

Its staff include Michael Pattison, who is director of each of the Sainsbury Family Trusts, and Hester Marriott, executive.

The trust offers the standard Sainsbury description of its grantmaking practice: 'Proposals are generally invited by the trustees or initiated at their request. Unsolicited applications are discouraged and are unlikely to be successful, even if they fall within an area in which the trustees are interested. The trustees prefer to support innovative schemes that can be successfully replicated or become self-sustaining'.

There is probably a special interest in Croatia, but this does not dominate grantmaking in central and eastern Europe.

Grants in 2003/04

Grants were paid during the year totalling £425,000 (grants approved totalled £590,000). The rest of this entry is taken from the 2003/04 annual report, with examples of individual approved grants.

Overseas development

Trustees' priorities in this category are projects which contribute to the empowerment of women, the rights of indigenous people, improved shelter and housing, income-generation in disadvantaged communities and sustainable agriculture and forestry.

Trustees are particularly interested to support development projects which take account of environmental sustainability and, in many cases, the environmental and developmental benefits of the project are of equal importance.

Grants were made to: Pragya to extend the training element of a programme to cultivate wild plants in order to ensure the sustainability of these species in the Indian Himalayan region (£21,000); Protimos Educational Trust towards core costs (£20,000); World Development Movement Trust towards the cost of producing educational materials and maintaining contact with other partner groups overseas (£15,000); and Foundation for Central Asian Development towards rehabilitation and micro-finance initiatives in Afghanistan, particularly to provide wool and supplies for carpet production by women (£12,000) Grants of £10,000 each were given to: Small World Action Projects towards the use of participatory video to give voice to disadvantaged and dispossessed communities, both in the UK and overseas; CAFOD towards post-war humanitarian work in Iraq; Cambridge Female Education Trust towards the cost of micro-finance scheme for young Zimbabwean women entrepreneurs; and Peace Direct towards core costs.

Environment

Projects are supported in developing countries, central and eastern Europe and the UK. Grants are approved for renewable energy technology, training and skills upgrading and, occasionally, research.

In central and eastern Europe, trustees are interested in providing training opportunities for community/business leaders and policy makers and in contributing to the process of skill-sharing and information exchange.

In the UK, trustees aim to help communities protect, maintain and improve areas of land and to support work aimed at informing rural conservation policy.

Grants were made to: Ashden Awards for Sustainable Energy to fund the annual awards (£52,000); CEE Bankwatch Network towards core costs (£45,000); Non-Profit Enterprise Sustainability & Enterprise Team towards helping environmental NGOs in Cambodia, and Women's Environmental Network towards core costs (£40,000 each); Envolve to cover support for local environmental action groups in Bath, Fauna & Flora International towards a project to help conserve the Cardamom Mountain Forest complex in Cambodia and Intermediate Technology Development Group Ltd towards a

project to introduce gravity ropeways in the Mustang district in Western Nepal (£30,000 each).

Women's issues

Trustees are willing to consider projects in the UK and overseas, focussing mainly on domestic violence and women's rights./Q>

The four beneficiaries were: Trinity Centre towards the expansion of the TRYangle domestic violence project (£20,000); Women's Library towards core and projects costs (£15,000); Foundation for Women's Health, Research and Development towards the costs of a meeting in Nigeria (£7,000); and Domestic Violence Intervention Project towards relocation costs (£2,500).

Frankopan Fund

Trustees have established a fund to assist exceptionally talented postgraduate students primarily from Croatia to further or complete their studies (in any discipline) in the UK.

Grants ranging from £500 to £6,000 were made to nine individuals.

General

Four beneficiaries in this category received grants for £10,000 each; they were: Brain & Spine Foundation, Cambridge University Development Office, Jesus College and the Victoria and Albert Museum. £5,000 was also awarded to the National Association of People Abused in Childhood.

Exclusions

Normally, no grants to individuals.

Applications

See the guidance for applicants in the entry for the Sainsbury Family Charitable Trusts. A single application will be considered for support by all the trusts in the group.

However, for this as for many of the trusts, 'proposals are generally invited by the trustees or initiated at their request. Unsolicited applications are discouraged and are unlikely to be successful, even if they fall within an area in which the trustees are interested'. See also the text above.

The Starfish Trust

Sickness, medical

£304,000 (2003/04)

Beneficial area Within a 25-mile radius of Bristol.

PO Box 213, Patchway, Bristol BS32 4YY

Tel. 0117 970 1756 **Fax** 0117 970 1756

Correspondent Robert N Woodward

Trustees *Charles E Dobson; Mary Dobson.*

Charity Commission no. 800203

Information available Full accounts were provided by the trust.

Priority is given to appeals from individuals and charitable organisations living or based within a 25-mile radius of central Bristol in the following areas:

- direct assistance to people who are disabled;
- direct assistance to people for the relief of illness or disease;
- medical research and welfare in the above areas.

In 2002/03 it had assets of almost £2 million, which generated an income of £109,000. Grants were made totalling £304,000 million (£1.2 million in the previous year, due to an exceptional donation made from reserves).

A total of 26 grants were made during the year. Major beneficiaries were Burton Hill School (£100,000 in three grants) and Rainbow House Rehabilitation Centre for Children (£86,000).

Other beneficiaries included Centre for Deaf People (£40,000 in three grants), Cruse Bereavement Care and Muscular Dystrophy Campaign (£5,000 each), Bristol Care and Repair (£3,500), Stepping Out Charity (£3,000 in two grants), Disability Aid Fund (£1,900), Listening Books (£1,500), Shelter (£600), Aidis Trust (£500) and North Somerset Council (£250).

Exclusions

Individuals and charitable organisations outside a 25-mile radius of Bristol or not working in the areas defined above.

Applications

In writing to the correspondent.

The Steel Charitable Trust

Health, welfare, general

£950,000 (2002/03)

Beneficial area UK and overseas, with a local interest in Luton and the surrounding area.

Bullimores, 3 Boutport Street, Barnstaple, Devon EX31 1RH

Tel. 01271 375257 **Fax** 01271 323121

Correspondent The Secretary

Trustees N E W Wright, chair; A W Hawkins; J A Childs; J A Maddox.

Charity Commission no. 272384

Information available Full accounts were provided by the trust.

The aim of the trust is to make grants to a wide range of general charitable purposes, at the trustees' discretion, concentrating mainly on the fields of culture and recreation, medical research, health, social services, environment and preservation and international aid.

In 2002/03 the trust has assets of £18 million and an income of £788,000. Management and administration costs totalled £45,000, including a payment of £28,000 to a firm of accountants in which one of the trustees is a partner. Whilst wholly legal, these editors always regret such payments unless, in the words of the Charity Commission, 'there is no realistic alternative'.

Grants to 100 organisations totalled £950,000 (a reduction from £1.3 million in 2001/02) and were broken down as follows:

	2002/03		2001/02	
	No.	Total	No.	Total
Social services	31	£293,000	112	£387,000
Health	16	£152,000	16	£208,000
Medical research	7	£70,000	28	£138,000
Environment and preservation	26	£247,000	22	£99,000
Culture and recreation	16	£151,000	32	£135,000
International aid activity	4	£37,000	4	£33,000
Memorial grants	1	£150,000	2	£300,000
Total	100	£950,000	216	£1,300,000

In total 11 grants for £20,000 or over were awarded either in the Luton area or to UK–wide charities. Two-thirds were awarded to the same beneficiaries as in the previous year, including one of the largest donations of £100,000 to Pasque Hospice for the Pasque and Keech Cottage Hospices.

The trust deed allows for grants to be given to any charitable body but particularly to 7 specified in the deed of settlement. All of these received large grants in 2002/03, as follows:

- Imperial Cancer Research Fund (£25,000)
- The Salvation Army (£25,000)
- National Deaf Children's Society (£25,000)
- The Donkey Sanctuary (£20,000)
- PDSA, Luton (£20,000)
- International League for the Protection of Horses (£20,000)
- Friends of St Mary's Church, Luton (£20,000).

Large new grants went to the following:

- Bushmead Church (£150,000)
- Cancer Research UK (£25,000)
- SSAFA (£20,000)
- Fairbridge (£20,000).

Other grants ranged from £250 to £15,000, with most between £1,000 and £2,000. The majority of the beneficiaries were located in the southern half of England. Organisations to received some of the larger donations included: Historic Churches Preservation Trust to help preserve, repair, maintain, improve and reconstruct UK churches and PDSA for maintaining a full Pet Aid Scheme in Luton (£15,000 each); Bedfordshire and Luton Community Foundation towards the establishment funding, CARE Fund – Blackerton to redevelop an old farm house into a hotel providing work opportunities for adults with special needs and Macmillan Cancer Relief – Luton and Bedfordshire towards a new cancer treatment, care day and outpatient unit (£10,000 each); Luton Churches Education Trust towards the Safe and Sound Project (£8,000); King's College Hospital Charitable Trust to purchase equipment (£5,000); Hertfordshire Breast Unit Appeal to build a unit at the QEII Hospital in Welwyn Garden City (£4,000); and Luton Music Club towards the 2002/03 series (£3,000).

Recipients who received grants of £1,000 and £2,000 included: Bedfordshire Crossroads for office and administration costs of the charity, Cambridge Handel Opera Group towards the production of Handel's Serse and ChildLine to increase the number of counsellors and counselling supervisors in the Bedfordshire area (£2,000 each); and Arthritis Research Campaign towards tissue engineering research project at Univeristy of Bristol, Bedford Community Rights Centre to alleviate poverty and regenerate local economy by giving advice and advocacy and Luton Accommodation and Move On Project Ltd to provide resettlement support and advice to 16–25 year olds at risk of homelessness (£1,000 each).

Beneficiaries of less than £1,000 included: Gloucestershire Resource Centre to rejuvenate part of the city works site for local community benefit (£750); Bath Recital Artists' Trust towards the purchase of a rehearsal piano, Farming and Wildlife Advisory Group for the Devon Hedge Competition 2003 and Luton and Bedford Youth Association to an organisation helping young people to achieve their potential (£500 each); and CVS for Blaby District towards a mental health awareness event (£250).

Exclusions

Individuals, students and expeditions are not supported.

Applications

In writing to the correspondent, including:

- statement of purpose for which the grant is required;
- full latest accounts showing all other sources of funding;
- statement of existing funding for the purpose of the grant application.

Applications are not acknowledged. Grants are made at the end of January, April, July and October.

Stevenson Family's Charitable Trust

Education, mainly Oxford and Cambridge universities, general

£401,000 (2002/03)

Beneficial area Unrestricted.

33 St Mary Axe, London EC3A 8LL

Tel. 020 7342 2630

Correspondent Hugh A Stevenson, Trustee

Trustees Hugh A Stevenson; Mrs Catherine M Stevenson; Sir Jeremy F Lever.

Charity Commission no. 327148

Information available Annual report and accounts.

This is the family trust of Hugh and Catherine Stevenson. A well known City of London figure, Mr Stevenson was formerly the chairman of Mercury Asset

Management, one of London's largest investment management companies. He is chairman of Equitas and a director of Standard Life.

The trust is operated personally with no premises or salaried staff of its own and is probably best seen simply as the vehicle for the personal donations of Mr and Mrs Stevenson, rather than as an institution with an independent existence.

The pattern of donations is for a number of large and often one-off donations accounting for most of the grants by value, and a group of small grants of £5,000 or less, sometimes for as little as £120. In 2002/03 the trust made grants totalling £401,000 (£859,000 in 2001/02).

The main grant in 2002/03 as in the previous year was to Trustees of the University College Old Members Trust which received £200,000. Other beneficiaries of large grants were National Gallery Trust (£50,000), Foundling Museum (£25,000), Macmillan County Durham and St Paul's Cathedral Foundation (£20,000), Great Ormond Street Hospital Children's Charity (£17,500), St Michael and All Angels – Sunninghill (£15,000), Moorfields Eye Hospital International Children's Eye Centre Appeal and Berkshire County Blind Society (£10,000 each).

Smaller grants included those to Royal Opera House Foundation (£7,000), University of Cape Town Trust (£6,600), Windsor Festival Society (£2,500), Royal National Theatre (£2,000), Art Fund (£1,500), Chandler Centre and Salvation Army (£1,000 each), Kingston Hospital Cancer Unit Appeal and Ethiopiaid (£500 each) and Abbeyfield Society – Eastbourne (£250).

Applications

'No unsolicited applications can be considered as the charity's funds are required to support purposes chosen by the trustees.'

The Stewards' Company Limited (incorporating the J W Laing Trust and the J W Laing Biblical Scholarship Trust)

Christian evangelism, general

£5.8 million (2002/03)
Beneficial area Unrestricted.

124 Wells Road, Bath BA2 3AH
Tel. 01225 427236 **Fax** 01225 427278
Email stewardsco@stewards.co.uk
Correspondent Brian John Chapman, Secretary
Trustee *Twenty directors, chaired by J G McEwen.*
Charity Commission no. 234558
Information available Annual report and accounts, listing the top 50 grants.

The charity supports Christian evangelism, especially but not exclusively that of Christian Brethren assemblies (different to those of the 'Exclusive' or 'Plymouth' Brethren). The work is described as follows:

This charitable company's main activities are to act as owner or custodian trustee of various charitable properties, mainly used as places of worship and situated either in the UK or overseas and to act as administrative trustee of a number of Christian charitable trusts.

The two major such trusts are the J W Laing Trust and the J W Laing Biblical Scholarship Trust. There are also 11 smaller ones.

The trust describes its objects as being:

[...]the advancement of religion in any matter which shall be charitable, and in particular by the furtherance of the Gospel of God and education in the Holy Scriptures, and the relief of the poor.

Its grantmaking policy is described as follows:

The trust takes into account the financial resources of the charities, the efforts made

by members of such charities to maximise their own funding, including where appropriate sacrificial giving by themselves and their members, and the assessed value of the work of such charities consistent with the objective of the main grant-making charities [i.e. Stewards Company, Laing Trust and Laing Scholarship: Ed.].

In 2002/03 it had assets of £98 million and an income of £3.9 million. Grants were made totalling £5.8 million and were broken down as follows:

Overseas	£3.1 million
Home	£2.1 million
Charitable organisations and objects	£594,000

During 2002/03 a total of 289 grants were paid to insitutions. The accounts only include the 50 largest grants. Beneficiaries receiving £100,000 or more, with some receiving support each year, were:

Myrtlefield Trust	£1 million
Echoes of Service	£828,000
Beatrice Laing Trust	£594,000
UCCF	£501,000
Scripture Gift Mission	£280,000
Counties	£260,000
Retired Missionary Aid Fund	£150,000
Interlink	£125,000

Other beneficiaries listed included MCF (£50,000), London Bible College (£42,000), Medical Missionary News (£80,000), IFES (£80,000), Belfast Bible College (£68,000) and Gospel Literature Outreach (£55,000).

A total of £79,000 was also distributed to 61 individuals.

Applications

In writing to the correspondent.

The Sir Halley Stewart Trust

Medical, social and religious research

£875,000 (budgeted for 2004/05)
Beneficial area Unrestricted, but mainly UK and south and west Africa in practice.

22 Earith Rd, Willingham, Cambridge CB4 5LS
Tel. 01954 260707 **Fax** 01954 260707
Website www.sirhalleystewart.org
Correspondent Mrs Sue West
Trustees *Prof. John Lennard Jones, chair; Dr Duncan Stewart; William P Kirkman; Lord Stewartby; George Russell; Prof.*

Phyllida Parsloe (Chair of social committee); Miss Barbara Clapham; Prof. J Wyatt; Michael Ross Collins; Brian Allpress; Prof. Philip Whitfield; Prof. C Hallett; Revd Lord Griffiths (Chair of religious committee); Dr A Caroline Berry; Prof. Gordon Willcock (Chair of medical committee).

Charity Commission no. 208491

Information available Full information available on the trust's website.

Background

The trust was established in 1924 by Sir Halley Stewart, a non-conformist minister, politician and later businessman and philanthropist. He endowed the charity and established its founding principles.

Summary

There are three grant programmes within this Christian-based organisation, each with a separate grants committee. Something around £250,000 is usually spent on each programme a year.

- medical;
- social and educational;
- religious.

Payments are normally made to institutions in support of the salaries of individuals and their research. The trustees prefer to support innovative and imaginative people – often promising young researchers – with whom they can develop a direct relationship. Sometimes a contribution towards the expenses of a project is given. Grants are normally limited to two or three years but are sometimes extended.

Perhaps because of its location, there appears to be a higher representation of beneficiaries from Cambridge organisations than from anywhere else (though the trust says that this is not the result of any deliberate policy).

General

The trust describes its grantmaking as follows:

The trust has a Christian basis and is concerned with the development of body, mind and spirit, a just environment, and international goodwill. To this end it supports projects in religious, social, educational and medical fields.

The trust aims to promote and assist innovative research activities or pioneering developments with a view to making such work self-supporting. It emphasises prevention rather than alleviation of human suffering.

Grants are usually in the form of a salary. The trustees prefer to support innovative and imaginative people–often promising young researchers–with whom they can develop a direct relationship. Sometimes a contribution towards the expenses of a project are given.

Grants are normally limited to 2 or 3 years, but are sometimes extended. Applicants should be sure that any proposal fits the trust's current priority areas.

Small individual grants are sometimes given to projects falling within the current priority areas.

The trustees have selected certain areas of special interest which are currently treated as priorities.

Religious

The trust is committed to advancing Christian religion. The trustees' particular interests are:

- Theological training in cases where there is special and specific need (e.g. in Africa or Eastern Europe).
- Teaching in the UK about Christianity, outside the formal education system.
- Encouragement of specific groups of people (e.g. the elderly, people with disability, students in higher education, those from ethnically mixed communities...) to explore their spiritual needs and strengths.
- To encourage appropriate people to develop their skills in communicating the Christian message through the media.

Anyone contemplating approaching the trust for support in this field is strongly advised to make a preliminary enquiry before submitting an application.

Social and Educational

Applications are welcomed for research and development projects which will have a direct impact on the conditions of a particular group of people, as well as having wider implications. The trustees are particularly interested in:

- Innovative projects which attempt to prevent and resolve conflicts, promote reconciliation and increase understanding within families and across racial, cultural, class, religious and professional divides.
- Innovative projects which attempt to help people 'move beyond disadvantage'. These may be concerned with youth employment; the social and family aspects of youth crime; the rehabilitation of offenders; homelessness; refugees or race relations.
- Projects which attempt to address the needs of vulnerable people in imaginative ways.
- Innovative projects overseas, particularly in Burkina Faso, Mali and South Africa, which are aimed at community development.

Medical

Projects should be simple, not molecular, and capable of clinical application within 5–10 years, and they may include a social or ethical element. Non-medical trustees should be able to understand the application and appreciate the value of the work. Projects may be of a type unlikely to receive support from Research Councils or large research-funding charities. The trustees particularly welcome applications concerned with:

- Problems associated with the elderly such as Alzheimer's Disease, nutrition, osteoporosis and incontinence.
- The prevention of disease and disability in children.
- The prevention, diagnosis and treatment of tropical infectious and parasitic diseases.
- Innovative projects, involving any discipline, which are likely to improve health care.
- Ethical problems arising from advances in medical practice.

In 2003/04 the trust had assets of £20.5 million and an income £1 million. Grants were made totalling £771,000. In 2004/05 the trust plans to spend £875,000 on grantmaking.

Recent grants

Religious

Recent beneficiaries include: Centre for Jewish Christian Relations – Cambridge, for scholarships to enable two students from Eastern and Central Europe to attend the centre, which promotes Jewish-Christian dialogue and understanding (£40,000 over two years); Mercian Trust, for the salary costs of a Community Chaplain for the North Staffordshire Community Chaplaincy Project aimed at breaking the cycle of re-offending, working in HMP Shrewsbury (£30,000 over three years); The Edinburgh Centre for Muslim-Christian Studies, for the salary costs for Director of Studies for this independent centre promoting greater understanding between the Christian and Muslim faiths (£22,000 for one year); and Evangelical Contribution on Northern Ireland (ECONI), for dissemination costs of ECONI's Thinking Biblically, Building Peace strategy to church leaders throughout Northern Ireland (£5,000).

Social and educational

Recent beneficiaries include: Outside Chance, for the introduction of pre-release programmes for young offenders in HM Young Offenders Institute Norwich (£38,500 over three years);

357

Conflict and Change – London, for a development worker and additional project costs for a new Muslim Mediation Service (£34,000 over 18 months); The Ark Trust – Edinburgh, to support the provision of volunteering opportunities for homeless people with complex needs by running a launderette as part of an holistic approach. The grant covers salary costs of the volunteer development worker, volunteer expenses and training costs (£25,000); and AfriKids, for a salary for two key workers involved in the development of a Street Children Project in Bolgatanga, Northern Ghana (£15,000 over three years).

Medical

Recent beneficiaries include: University of Nottingham, Faculty of Medicine and Health Sciences, for a research study to develop a novel test for MRSA, and funding to support a PhD student (£50,000 over three years); St Mark's Hospital & Academic Institute, Biomaterials & Tissue Engineering Group, Harrow, for a student to work on the development of a device for guided tissue regeneration of fistulae in Crohn's disease (£37,500 over two years); King's College London, Institute of Psychiatry at The Maudsley, for a six-month epidemiological study to investigate whether patients with psychotic disorders are at increased risk of osteoporotic fractures (£18,500); and University of Wales College of Medicine, for consumables for research aiming to identify the active immunomodulatory component(s) of honey, and investigate the mechanism of action of these components (£10,000).

Exclusions

The trust will be unable to help with funding for any of the following :

- general appeals of any kind;
- personal education fees or fees for taught courses–unless connected with research which falls within our current priority areas;
- educational or 'gap' year travel projects;
- the purchase, erection or conversion of buildings;
- capital costs;
- running costs of established organisations;
- university overhead charges.

The trustees do not favour grantmaking to enable the completion of a project or PhD.

Applications

The application should come, in the first instance, from the individual concerned, rather than the 'host' organisation. Applications can be received throughout the year and will be considered for the next available meeting. Assessment can take several weeks, so applicants should allow for this when submitting their proposals (which should not be faxed or e-mailed). The trust states that it reserves the right to close an agenda once a suitable number of proposals have been received.

The following is reprinted from the trust's own material:

How to apply to us for a grant

'First make sure that your project falls within the trust's current areas of interest. Check the trust's website for the latest information. If you are in doubt, a quick telephone call to the trust office is welcomed.

'There is no formal application form. Applicants should write to the administrator with a short description of the proposed work. We need to know exactly what you plan to do with the grant, where you will be doing the work, how much money you will need and approximately how long the work should take. You need to state what you believe will be the benefit of your work and how the findings will be disseminated. Development projects should indicate where they hope to obtain future funding after the trust's support has ended. Where appropriate it is helpful to include: a CV or job description, a copy of the annual report and accounts.

'If we cannot help you we will let you know. It is worth pointing out that we receive many applications for support, and although your work may fit the objects of the trust, we may not necessarily be able to help you.

'If it is decided to take your application further, it will be seen by those trustees who are most interested in that particular field. Please note that this process may take several weeks. You may be asked for more details at this stage. These trustees may then recommend that the application be considered at a full trustees' meeting at which final decisions are made.'

Full trustees' meetings are held three times a year, in February, June and October.

Other advice

The following guidance for trustees should also be helpful for applicants:

The trust should seek to fund the unfashionable and unpopular.

Points to be borne in mind when assessing an application:

Does it fit with the objects of the trust and fall within one of the current priority areas?

How much funding is requested?

What exactly will the money be used for?

Where will the work be done?

How long will it take?

What will be the benefit of the work? Within what time frame?

How will the findings be disseminated?

The Stobart Newlands Charitable Trust

Christian causes

£875,000 (2003)
Beneficial area UK.

Mill Croft, Hesket Newmarket, Wigton, Cumbria CA7 8HP

Tel. 01697 478261

Correspondent Mrs M Stobart, Trustee

Trustees *R J Stobart; M Stobart; R A Stobart; P J Stobart; L E Rigg.*

Charity Commission no. 328464

Information available Annual report and accounts were provided by the trust.

This family trust makes up to 50 grants a year, nearly all on a recurring basis to Christian religious and missionary bodies. Unsolicited applications are most unlikely to succeed.

The trustees are directors and shareholders of J Stobart and Sons Ltd, which is the source of almost all its income. In 2003 its income was £655,000. Grants were made during the year totalling £875,000.

As in previous years, over half the total spent on grants was given to three organisations. These are Mission Aviation Fellowship (£200,000), Operation Mobilisation (£160,000), and World Vision (£152,000).

Other beneficiaries of larger grants over £10,000 each included Tear Fund (£35,000), Every Home Crusade and Way to Life (£30,000 each), London City Mission (£28,000), Open Air Mission

(£27,000), Logos Ministries (£21,000), Living Well Trust (£17,000), CUMNISCU (£15,000), Faith Mission (£13,000) and Scripture Gift Mission and Teen Challenge (£10,000 each).

Small grants under £1,000 to organisations totalled £5,500.

Exclusions

No grants for individuals.

Applications

Unsolicited applications are most unlikely to be successful.

The Stoller Charitable Trust

Medical, children, general

£468,000 (2002/03)

Beneficial area UK, with a preference for the Greater Manchester area.

PO Box 164, Manchester M24 1XA

Tel. 0161 653 3849 **Fax** 0161 653 6874

Email alison.sct@tiscali.co.uk

Correspondent Alison M Ford, Secretary

Trustees *Norman K Stoller, chair; Roger Gould; Jan Fidler; Sheila M Stoller.*

Charity Commission no. 285415

Information available Basic accounts, with a separate grants list, were provided by the trust.

The trust supports a wide variety of charitable causes, but with particular emphasis on those which are local, medically-related or supportive of children. There is a bias towards charities in Greater Manchester where the trust is based. It also endeavours to maintain a balance between regular and occasional donations and between the few large and many smaller ones.

In 2002/03 the trust had assets of £4.8 million and an income of £212,000, down significantly on the previous year, when the trust received donations alone of £485,000 compared to just £20 in 2002/03. Despite this drop in income, the trust is still maintaining the same level of awards. During the year grants were made totalling £468,000 (£442,000 in 2001/02). The trust made 180 grants, with a few organisations receiving more

than one grant during the year, and 27 organisations receiving grants on a regular basis.

Grants can be considered for buildings, capital costs, projects, research costs, recurring costs and start-up costs. As well as one-off grants, funding may also be given for up to three years.

As in the previous year, the recipient of the largest amount of money was The Message, which received £70,000 in total in four awards. The Message is a Christian organisation based in Manchester working with disaffected young people in the Greater Manchester area. Grants were made for its Eden projects and Festival: Manchester, a free faith-based event combining music and extreme sports with community service and social action projects.

Other beneficiaries receiving £10,000 or more were St John Ambulance (£32,000 in total), Prince's Trust (£26,000 in total), Emmaus Bolton and Chetham's School of Music (£25,000 each), Broughton House (£25,000 in total), Shrievalty Trust (£24,000), United Learning Trust (£20,000), Royal Northern College of Music Awards Fund (£11,000 in total) and International Society (£10,000).

Beneficiaries receiving grants of £1,000 or less included: Groundwork Oldham & Rochdale, Shelter, Lady Taverners in the North West, Oldham Independent Housing Aid Centre, Macmillan Cancer Relief, Genesis Appeal, Manchester Cathedral and St Anne's Hospice (£1,000 each), CARE Hand in Hand Appeal, Manchester Dog's Home, Blue Coat School, Institute for the Special Child, Children's Liver Disease Foundation, Holiday Aid for Romanian Children and Disability Aid Fund (£500 each), Rotary Club of Windermere, National Autistic Society, National Playing Fields Association, The Furniture Station, National Police Community Trust, Sight Savers International, Derma Trust, Seagull Trust and Headway (£250 each) and Portico Library and Art Gallery and Pennine Pen Animal Rescue Centre (£100 each).

Regular beneficiaries of the trust, most of whom received £500 or £1,000, include: Salvation Army, Norwood, Save the Children Fund, NSPCC, Christie's Hospital & Holt Radium Institute, Adventure Farm Trust, SENSE and Big Issue in the North.

Exclusions

No grants to individuals.

Applications

In writing to the correspondent. Applications need to be received by February, May, August or November and the trustees meet in March, June, September and December.

The Stone Ashdown Charitable Trust

Equality and discrimination

£472,000 (2002/03)

Beneficial area UK, mainly London, and, to a limited extent, overseas.

4th Floor, Barkat House, 116–118 Finchley Road, London NW3 5HT

Tel. 020 7472 6060

Correspondent The Grants Manager

Trustees *Richard Stone; Lutfur Ali; Leroy Logan.*

Charity Commission no. 298722

Information available Accounts were on file at the Charity Commission.

The Stone Ashdown Trust was created in 2000 from the Joe Stone Charitable Trust, re-named Stone Ashdown, and with funding from the Lord Ashdown Charitable Settlement, which continues to carry out its own programmes and has a separate entry. The trust received a donation of £4 million from the Lord Ashdown Charitable Settlement in 2000/01, its first year of operation, which accounted for almost all its income. In 2002/03 it had assets of £2.4 million and an income of £239,000. Grants totalled £472,000.

The new trust describes its origins as follows:

The new trust describes its origins as follows:
  The Stone Ashdown Trust was set up in the year 2000. It brings together two grant making programmes.
  One is from the Joe Stone Charitable Trust which takes its name from Dr Joe Stone (later Lord Stone of Hendon).
  The other grants programme is from the charitable trust set up by Joe Stone's brother, Arnold Silverstone (later Lord Ashdown of Chelwood).
  The new trust continues those grants of the Ashdown programme that are concerned with:
• Equalities, especially racial justice.

- Interfaith dialogue and action, especially between Muslims and Jews.
- Jewish organisations with a progressive approach, and with programmes which work with people from other communities.
- Organisations that work with people likely to experience discrimination, especially where the discrimination results in difficulties in accessing grants from other sources. Most of these organisations which are supported by the trust are black-led or with a black majority of clients and on the management committee.

Grantmaking

The trustees have skill and expertise in the areas of activity of the trust. Unfortunately, with falls in the stock market no applications from new beneficiaries can be considered. The trust does not have the staff to acknowledge any unsolicited applications.

Grants in 2002/03

Relief of Poverty – £39,000 in 8 grants

There were two grants of £10,000 each to Maxilla Nursery Centre and Paddington Development Trust. Other beneficiaries included Queens Park Family Support Unit (£5,000), War on Want (£3,000) and Westminster Association for Mental Health (£250).

Advancement of education – £8,800 in 7 grants

Beneficiaries included Ebury Bridge Youth Club (£4,500), Brooksby Melton College (£1,000), United Examining Board (£750) and Hawkins Woodfield Foundation (£400).

Inter-religious dialogue – £17,000 in 2 grants

Grants were £15,000 to School of Oriental and African Studies and £2,000 to Brighton Islamic Mission.

Asylum and immigration – £17,000 in 4 grants

Grants were £9,000 to Westminster Diocese Refugee Service (£9,000), Paddington Law Centre (£4,000), Detainees Support Help Unit (£3,000) and Christian Life Centre (£580).

Black and minority ethnic voluntary sector support – £111,000 in 24 grants

The five largest grants were £20,000 to 1990 Trust, £15,000 to Yaa Asantewaa

Arts and Community Centre and £10,000 each to Black Training and Enterprise Group, Ebony Steel Band Trust and Siri Behavioural Health. Other beneficiaries included Claudia Jones Organisation (£5,000), Yemeni Community Centre (£3,000), Respect Trust (£2,000), Sickle Cell Society (£1,000) and Nubian Life Resource Centre (£250).

Promoting equalities and anti-racism – £227,000 in 32 grants

Larger grants included £25,000 each to Civil Liberties Trust and Community Links, £15,000 to Uniting Britain Trust, £12,000 to Inquest Charitable Trust and £10,000 to Runnymede Trust. Other beneficiaries included Toynbee Hall (£8,500), Antidote (£6,000), Avenues Youth Project, Black Police Association Charitable Trust and Kensington and Chelsea Community History Group (£5,000), Union of Jewish Students (£3,000), Indian-Jewish Association (£1,000) and Refugee Education Training and Support (£250).

Outward-looking Judaism in the UK – £27,000 in 8 grants

Beneficiaries included Leo Baeck College (£6,500), Union of Jewish Students (£2,500), Liberal Jewish Synagogue – Women Rabbis Network (£1,000), Jewish Radio Trust and Jewish Museum (£100).

Other – £36,000 in 4 grants

Grants were £20,000 to Stephen Spender Memorial Trust, £10,000 to Paddington Farm Trust, £5,000 to Community Accountancy Self Help and £1,000 to Meanwhile Gardens Community Association.

Exclusions

The trust does not generally support individuals.

Applications

The trustees are no longer likely to respond to unsolicited applications.

Stratford upon Avon Town Trust

Education, welfare, general

£1.3 million (2002/03)

Beneficial area Stratford upon Avon.

14 Rother Street, Stratford-upon-Avon, Warwickshire CV32 6LU

Correspondent Richard Eggington, Chief Executive

Trustees Dr N Woodward, chair; Cllr S Beese; Cllr D Barker; Mrs V Harris; Prof. I Heggie; Mrs J Holder; Mrs Rosemary Hyde; Cllr S Price; Cllr V Seaman; Mrs Carole Taylor.

Charity Commission no. 1088521

Information available Full accounts were provided by the trust.

This new trust was created in May 2001 after an investigation by the Charity Commission into the workings of two long-standing trusts in the town, The College Estate Charity and The Guild Estate Charity. It was found that the town council, which acted as trustees for the previous trusts, were using the funds for social benefit but as an extension of the council's own work rather than as identifiable charitable expenditure. The creation of this new trust is intended to clarify the charity expenditure produced by these charitable funds. Income is pigeon-holed proportionally against the trust which would have received it under the old circumstances and donated accordingly. A payment of 36% of the old College Estate Charity's income is made to King Edward VI Grammar School in keeping with the terms of the original trust deed.

The trust has general charitable purposes with the Stratford-upon-Avon council area. Its objectives are:

- relief of need, hardship and distress;
- relief of sickness, disability, old age and infirmity;
- support of facilities for education, including the advancement of learning and knowledge;
- support for recreations and other leisure-time facilities;
- advancement of the Christian religion.

As well as being a grantmaker, the trust owns a civic hall, bandstand, chapel and a fountain celebrating the town's 800th anniversary.

In 2002/03 the trust had assets of £37 million, which generated a healthy income of £2.6 million. Grants were made to 103 organisations and totalled £1.3 million. A further £409,000 was spent on upkeep of its assets, mostly the civic hall. It also spent £435,000 on management and administration.

By far the largest grant, as usual, went to King Edward VI Grammar School and was for £522,000. There were 30 other grants of £10,000 or more, including £59,000 to Citizen's Advice Bureau, £54,000 to Stratford in Bloom, £50,000 each to Friends of Shakespeare's Church, £36,000 to Stratford-upon-Avon College, £33,000 to Stratford-upon-Avon High School, £22,000 each to Thomas Jolyffe Primary School and Shakespeare Birthplace Trust, £20,000 each to Stratford and District MENCAP and Community Flute Festival, £16,000 to Friends of Stratford Shopmobility and £10,000 each to Stratford Music Festival and Royal Shakespeare Theatre Summer Education Programme.

Other beneficiaries included Young Enterprise (£4,500), the Mayor's Fund (£3,000), Escape Workshop (£2,000) and Stratford Choral Society, Trailblazers Youth Club and Witness Service Stratford (£1,000 each).

Applications

In writing to the correspondent.

The W O Street Charitable Foundation

Education, disability, young people, social welfare

About £300,000 (2003)

Beneficial area UK, with local interests in the north west of England and Jersey.

c/o Barclays Bank Trust Company Ltd, PO Box 15, Osborne Court, Gadbrook Park, Rudheath, Northwich CW9 7UE

Tel. 01606 313173

Email eandt-info@barclays.co.uk

Correspondent Miss M Bertenshaw, Trust Officer

Trustees Barclays Bank Trust Co. Ltd; A Paines.

Charity Commission no. 267127

Information available Annual report and accounts are on file at the Charity Commission.

The trust make about 90 grants each year with a usual maximum limit of £10,000. Most grants are for £5,000 or less, and mainly go to UK welfare and disability charities.

In considering grants the trustees pay close regard to the wishes of the late Mr Street who had particular interests in education, relief of poverty, the relief of persons with financial difficulties (particularly the aged, blind and disabled) and the relief of ill health or sickness and social welfare generally. Special support is given to the North West of England and to Jersey.

The trustees have selected a limited number of educational projects to which significant grants are being given over a shortish period (usually no more than three years) to enable the projects to find their feet. The trustees are keeping this policy under review but it is likely that a programme of supporting projects of this nature will be sustained (at least for the foreseeable future). As a result the trustees will not be able to devote so much of their resources as they have in the past to smaller 'one-off' grants.

In 2002/03 the trust had a total expenditure of £450,000. Unfortunately, although submitted by the trust to the Charity Commission, the accounts for that year had not made it to the public files for inspection.

Previous beneficiaries include Action for Kids Charitable Trust, Addaction, Bury Crossroads, Bury Hospice, Buxton for Youth, Craven Trust, Crossroads, Cumbria Deaf Association, Disability Initiative, Edinburgh and Leith Age Concern, Heart of England Care, Independent Schools Information Service, Lifeline Project, Museum of Science and Industry in Manchester, Network – the Whitby Resource Centre, Prince's Trust, Sick Children's Trust, Sussex Autistic Society and YMCA – West Bromich and District.

Comment

There was no response to repeated written requests for a copy of the most recent annual report and accounts, despite the requirement to provide these on demand.

Exclusions

No grants towards:

- schools, colleges or universities;
- running or core costs;
- religion or church buildings;

- medical research;
- animal welfare;
- hospices;
- overseas projects or charities;
- NHS trusts.

Applications directly from individuals are not considered.

Applications

In writing to the correspondent. Trustees aim to consider appeals on a quarterly basis, at the end of January, April, July and October.

The Bernard Sunley Charitable Foundation

General

£1.5 million (2002/03)

Beneficial area Unrestricted, but mainly southern England.

20 Berkeley Square, London W1J 6LH

Tel. 020 7408 2198 **Fax** 020 7499 5859

Correspondent Dr Brian Martin, Director

Trustees *John B Sunley; Mrs Joan M Tice; Mrs Bella Sunley; Sir Donald Gosling.*

Charity Commission no. 213362

Information available Very brief guidelines for applicants. Brief report and accounts, with a good, categorised list of grant payments, and a description of the purposes of the 50 largest of them. There is no information on the number or value of new multi-year awards.

Summary

This is one of the few big trusts that will, in principle, fund any kind of charitable activity in the UK, and which offers no information on the criteria by which one application is preferred to another. No doubt as a consequence of this, the charity receives many applications, only about one in ten of which can be funded. Grants range in size from several hundred thousand pounds down to less than £1,000, although most grants will be for less than £10,000. The long-noted bias towards the southern half of England continued in 2002/03, more notably amongst the larger grants.

As well as making grants for capital purposes, donations are also made for endowments, scholarship funds, research programmes and for core funding.

Background

The foundation continues to have fairly high investment management costs; in 2002/03 these costs amounted to £254,000, or 10.5% of investment income. Management and administration costs were very low at £16,000, although 'support costs' totalled £168,000, or £483 per grant made.

All four trustees have held their posts since at least 1984. John B Sunley is the son of the founder Bernard Sunley and is a former chairman of Sunley Holding plc and a council member of Business for Sterling (an organisation opposed to Britain's joining the euro currency area). Joan Tice and Bella Sunley are both members of the founding family. The only external trustee is Sir Donald Gosling, founder of NCP car parks and one of Britain's wealthiest men [see also the Gosling Foundation Limited, described elsewhere].

In 2002/03 the trust had assets of £51 million. Income during the year totalled £5.5 million (£2.5 million in 2001/02), which included £2.4 million from investments and £2.9 million in Gift Aid from the trust's trading subsidiary.

Grants were classified as follows (social welfare is a new category, and overseas grants are allocated to the relevant category:

	2002/03	1960–2003
Children and youth	£294,000	£7.4 million
Health	£219,000	£17.4 million
Elderly	£211,000	£7.1 million
Community	£206,000	£10 million
Environment and animals	£184,000	£2.6 million
Social welfare	£169,000	£169,000
Arts	£47,000	£6.3 million
Education	£45,000	£15 million
Religion	£35,000	£3.5 million
Service charities	£26,000	£1.3 million
Professional and public bodies	£23,000	£2.2 million
Overseas	–	£2.4 million
Total	£1,459,000	£75.4 million

Grantmaking in 2002/03

The trust gives the following review of activities during the year:

During the year, the trustees approved 348 grants totalling, in value, £1,459,000, which compares with 348 grants at a total value of £2,643,000 in [2001/02]. Grant payments totalling £1,528,000 were made.

50 grants, each for £5,000 or more, were approved during the year, and these are listed within the various categories below. In each case, the charity and the purpose of the grant is listed. The total value of these grants was £1,021,550, which represented 70% by value of all grants approved during the year. In addition, the foundation approved a further 298 grants, each of less than £5,000.

Beneficiaries included:

Children and youth

- Oxford Kilburn Club (£40,000 towards the cost of refurbishing the clubhouse);
- Prince's Trust (£31,000 to fund the Sunley Business Programme in Kent);
- Caldecott Community – Kent (£25,000 towards the cost of building a new senior school);
- YMCA – Ashford (£10,000 towards the cost of a youth worker);
- Sea Cadets – Twickenham (£8,000 for core funding);
- Canterbury Diocesan Board of Finance (£5,500 for Archbishop George's Youth Fund);
- Amber Foundation (£5,000 for core funding);
- British Sports Trust (£5,000 for core funding);
- Extern (£5,000 towards the cost of a new football pitch at Kinnahalla);
- Sports Aid Trust (£5,000 for core costs).

Health

- Demelza House Children's Hospice – Kent (£54,000 for core funding);
- National Hospital for Neurology (£50,000 towards the cost of a European Dementia Research Centre);
- SeeAbility (£20,000 towards building costs for new centre at Honiton in Devon);
- Dame Vera Lynn Trust for Children with Cerebral Palsy (£12,000 for core funding);
- Pilgrims Hospices in East Kent (£10,000 for major refurbishment works at Canterbury);
- WellBeing (£10,000 for core funding);
- Great Ormond Street Children's Hospital (£9,000 for core funding);
- Ryder-Cheshire Foundation (£9,000 to part fund staff costs);
- Colon Cancer Concern (£5,000 for core costs).

Elderly

- Central & Cecil Housing Trust (£150,000 towards refurbishing the Woodlands Centre in Merton);
- Age Concern – Canterbury (£50,000 towards the purchase of their freehold site);
- Age Concern – Kingston upon Thames (£5,000 towards rebuilding works at their existing centre).

Community

- Thames Valley & Chiltern Air Ambulance (£30,000 for core funding);
- Community of St Paul, Turkana – north Kenya (£20,000 to fund a water drilling project);
- Christ Church Community Centre, South Nuffield – Surrey (£5,000 towards building costs);
- CRASH (£5,000 towards building costs);
- CRISIS (£5,000 for core funding);
- Kent People's Trust (£5,000 for core funding);
- Rural Development Trust, Anantapur – India (£5,000 for core finding).

Environment and animals

- The Wildlife Trust (£60,000 for the Sunley Wildlife Fund);
- Forum for the Future (£50,000 to fund a director for a course of Sustainable Investment);
- British Horse Society (£31,000 for building works at Hickstead);
- Brooke Hospital for Animals (£22,000 to fund new water boreholes and medicines for their work in Afghanistan);
- International League for the Protection of Horses (£8,000 for core funding).

Social welfare

- Deafblind UK (£100,000 for core funding);
- Winged Fellowship Trust (£20,000 towards extending the Sandpipers, Southport Centre).

Arts

- Cromarty Arts Centre (£10,000 towards restoring a listed building);
- Heritage Information Trust (£10,000 to set up a web-based information database);
- Deal Music Festival (£9,000 for core funding);
- Bluebell Railway Preservation Trust (£5,000 towards a marketing campaign).

Education

- Moulton Primary School – Northampton (£15,000 towards a new library);
- Sir Roger Manwood's School – Sandwich (£10,000 towards a new music centre);
- Lloyds Officer Cadet Scholarship (£5,000 for a scholarship).

Religion

- St Mary the Virgin, East Haddon – Northants (£8,000 towards the church restoration fund);
- St Lawrence the Martyr, Godmersham – Kent (£5,000 for building works);
- St Mary, Balham – South East London (£5,000 towards funding a new community centre);
- St Mary, Chilham – Kent (£5,000 for fabric repairs);
- Sweet Turf Christian Centre, Netherton – West Midlands (£5,000 towards funding a new centre).

Service charities

- White Ensign Association (£20,000 for core funding).

Professional and public bodies

- Town and Country Planning Association (£20,000 for core funding).

Smaller grants

As with the larger grants, smaller grants were made to a wide and diverse range of organisations. Most of the smaller grants were for between £1,000 and £3,000.

Beneficiaries across all categories included: National Literacy Trust, Long Buckby Junior School – Northampton, Canterbury Festival, Fenlan Archaeological Trust, British Embassy Church of St George – Madrid, Buckmore Park Activity Centre – Chatham, Church Army – Cardiff, Trinity United Reformed Church – Blackburn, Chooselife – Llanelli, Weir Baptist Church – Lancashire, Community Action Furness – Cumbria, Voluntary Organisation for the Uplifting of Children, YMCA – Birmingham, Sandwell Young Carers, Grange Day Centre – Newcastle, South & Vale Carers Centre – Didcot, East Suffolk Association for the Blind, Tramps Fund and Ex-Services Mental Welfare Society.

Exclusions

'We would reiterate that we do not make grants to individuals; we still receive several such applications each week. This bar on individuals applies equally to those people taking part in a project sponsored by a charity such as VSO, Duke of Edinburgh Award Scheme, Trekforce, Scouts and Girl Guides, etc., or in the case of the latter two to specific units of these youth movements.'

Applications

'Appeals are considered regularly, but we would emphasise that we are only able to make grants to registered charities [but see above. Ed.] and not to individuals. There is no application form, but the covering letter to the Director should give details as to the points below, and should be accompanied by the latest approved report and accounts.'

The details requested are as follows:

- A description of what the charity does and what its objectives are.
- An explanation of the need and purpose of the project for which the grant is required.
- How much will the project cost? The costings should be itemised and supported with quotations etc. as necessary.
- The size of grant requested.
- How much has already been raised and from whom. How is it planned to raise the shortfall?

- If applicable, how the running costs of the project will be met, once the project is established.
- Any other documentation that the applicant feels will help to support or explain the appeal.

Sutton Coldfield Municipal Charities

Relief of need, education, general

£794,000 to organisations (2002/03)

Beneficial area The former borough of Sutton Coldfield, comprising three electoral wards: New Hall, Vesey and Four Oaks.

Lingard House, Fox Hollies Road, Sutton Coldfield, West Midlands B76 2RJ

Tel. 0121 351 2262 **Fax** 0121 313 0651

Correspondent Andrew MacFarlane, Clerk to the Trustees

Trustees Dr Nigel Cooper, chair; Jean Millington; Rodney Kettel; John Gray; Cllr David Roy; John Slater; Alfred David Owen; Cllr J Whorwood; Sue Bailey; Cllr Susanna McCorry; Mr John Jordan; Revd J Langstaff; Mrs J Rothwell; Mr D Grove; M I Waltho.

Charity Commission no. 218627

Information available Good annual report with plenty of information including a full grants list showing the purposes of the awards, listed by charity objective was provided by the trust.

Summary

About 65 grants are made each year to schools and other organisations in the Sutton Coldfield area, as well as many grants to individuals, mostly for school clothing. Grants range from a few hundred pounds to around £100,000.

General

The charity, which is one of the largest and oldest local trusts in the country, was set up by Royal Charter in 1528. In terms of assets, income and grantmaking capacity it ranks within the top 2% of UK charities. The trust states:

The objectives of the charity are:

- to help the aged, the sick, those with disabilities and the poor

- to support facilities for recreation and leisure occupations
- to promote the arts and advance religion
- the repair of historic buildings
- the advancement of education through grants to schools and individuals for fees, maintenance, clothing and equipment.

These objects are achieved by:

- providing almshouses
- making grants
- providing school clothing vouchers.

Applicants have to submit detailed information about their proposed projects and are encouraged to meet the charities' staff to discuss these.

Applicants are usually visited by members of staff who provide the trustees with extensive background information.

If a grant is awarded, this should normally be used within one year.

Grantmaking

Over 600 grant applications were received [in 2002/03] from individuals and organisations. Some requests cannot be considered, particularly if the applicant is based outside the area of benefit. There are a few exceptions if an organisation provides significant benefits to Sutton's residents that cannot be met from local sources. These include hospices and some national medical charities.

The charity's officers present applications to the grants committee, which meets eight or nine times per year. Officers act as 'advocates' in these circumstances, presenting evidence gained from visits, meetings, documents and accounts. The committee sometimes defers applications if it needs further information. Otherwise, the trustees decide whether to grant a request in full, to make a reduced award, or decline the application. If the recommended award exceeds £20,000 it is referred to the board of trustees for a decision. (School Clothing Grants are an exception, being approved en bloc by the grants committee.) There is careful monitoring of how awards are spent and the trustees evaluate the impact of their grants. To ensure that awards are used for their allocated purpose, payments are usually made on receipt of suppliers' invoices, or, in the case of school clothing grants, by issuing vouchers redeemable at designated suppliers.

The charity welcomes initial contacts from individuals and organisations interested in making applications. Officers will always advise on the best way to design a grant request and to ensure that the necessary range of information is available to the trustees.

In 2002/03 the trust had assets of £28 million, which generated an income of £1.5 million. Grants were made totalling £794,000, broken down as follows:

Grants to help the aged, sick, those with disabilities and the poor

A total of £186,000 in grants was made for this purpose to individuals and organisations. Grants to organisations ranged from £260 to Mere Green Elderly Luncheon Club for Christmas celebrations to £90,000 over three years to Sutton Coldfield Cancer Support Centre to cover accommodation costs. Other beneficiaries included: KIDS West Midlands for building improvements (£33,000); Norman Laud Association towards ground rent at Elmscote Drive (£16,000); Heart Care – Sutton Coldfield Unit to purchase five exercise bikes and two rowing machines (£6,500); and Edward's Trust for new carpets and a security camera (£4,000). Grants of less than £500, often for Christmas celebrations, included those to Brampton Hall Community Association, Heron Court Warden Scheme, Tanners Close Residents and Elmscote Drive Sheltered Housing Scheme. Grants were also made to 34 individuals and ranged from £100 to £2,800 [see *A Guide to Grants for Individuals in Need*, also published by the Directory of Social Change].

Grants to support facilities for recreational and leisure occupations

Seven grants were made totalling £54,000. They were to: Sutton Coldfield Recreational Trust for club house renovations and grounds maintenance (£20,000); Chester Road Brigades for a replacement minibus (£17,000); Walmley Sports Alliance to refurbish the clubhouse and grounds maintenance (£10,000); Sutton Coldfield West District Scout Council to set up a new Explorer Scout Unit (£2,500); Sutton Sailing Club for an outboard motor for a safety boat (£2,000); Girl Guiding – Trinity Division for resource packs for Brownie units (£1,500); and Boldmere S & S Falcons Football Club for a secure storage facility (£1,000).

Miscellaneous and community projects

Five grants were made under this heading totalling £53,000. They were to: Banners Gate Jubilee Play Forum for the provision of play equipment for children with disabilities (£30,000); Churchill Parade Action Group for operating costs of a CCTV system for two years (£9,500); Relate – Sutton Coldfield to cover deficits for a two year period (£6,500); Churches Together – Sutton Coldfield to finance community lunches and participation in the carnival for two years (£5,000); and Second Thoughts for a laptop computer and display panels (£2,000).

Grants to promote the arts and advance religion

£281,000 was made in six grants. Three large grants were made to: Chester Road Baptist Church and St James CE Church for renovations and refurbishments (£100,000 each); and Holy Trinity RC Church for refurbishment of the church conference centre (£60,000). The other three grants were to: Falcon Lodge Methodist Church to resurface a car park and replace security rails (£11,000); Sutton Coldfield Philharmonic Society towards expenses for concerts and Four Oaks Methodist Church for repairs and redecoration (£5,000 each).

Advancement of education (through grants for maintenance and equipment)

Grants were made to eight organisations totalling £217,000. They were to: Sutton Coldfield Grammar School for Girls to extend the library and convert a foyer into a study room (£60,000); Longmoor School to create a sensory garden in the grounds (£50,000); Coppice Primary School for a networked portable computer system (£40,000); St Joseph's RC Primary School to extend the playground and for play equipment and Walmley Junior School for IT equipment and furnishings for a new IT suite (£20,000 each); Hill West Infant School for computer equipment and a digital camera (£19,000); Four Oaks Cluster Group of Schools for a joint project with other schools (£6,000); and Trinity Play Centre for half its annual rent (£2,000). There was also an educational grant made and five individual sponsorships, and school clothing grants totalling £25,000 [see the *Educational Grants Directory*, also published by the Directory of Social Change].

Exclusions

No awards are given to individuals or organisations outside the area of benefit, unless the organisations are providing essential services in the area.

Applications

In writing to the correspondent. The following applies to applications from groups and organisations.

There are no forms, so applicants may provide information in a format which is most convenient for them but they must include the following:

- a brief description of the organisation, its objects and its history;
- the number of members/users, their age range and any membership fees paid;
- a full account of the purpose of the project for which a grant is requested;
- accurate costs, showing reasonable estimates from a range of sources where appropriate and including VAT if payable–no additional sums will be granted if estimates prove to be inaccurate;
- other sources of funding–these must be shown;
- sixteen copies of the latest audited accounts or, for very small organisations, copies of bank statements. Notes of explanation may be included; for example, if accounts show a balance set aside for a particular project applicants may wish to point this out.

Receipt of applications is not normally acknowledged unless a stamped addressed envelope is sent with the application.

Applications may be submitted at any time. The grants committee meets eight or nine times a year. Requests for grants over £20,000 must be approved by the board of trustees, who meet four times a year.

At all stages, staff at the charities will give assistance to those making applications. For example, projects and applications can be discussed, either at the charity's office or on site. Advice about deadlines for submitting applications can also be given.

(There are application forms for individuals, who must obtain them from the charity.)

The Sutton Trust

Education

£1.6 million (2003)

Beneficial area UK only.

111 Upper Richmond Road, Putney, London SW15 2TJ

Tel. 020 8788 3223 **Fax** 020 8788 3993

Email emma@suttontrust.com

Website www.suttontrust.com

Correspondent Emma Claridge, Projects Officer

Trustees *Sir Peter Lampl; Karen Lampl; Glyn Morris.*

Charity Commission no. 1067197

Information available Informative annual review, separate annual accounts. Website with application details.

Summary

The trust funds projects which provide educational opportunities for able young people from non-privileged backgrounds. The projects range from early years for children up to 3 years of age, through schooling to further and higher education, including research projects. There is an emphasis on innovative start-up projects that have the scope to benefit large numbers in the future.

The trust welcomes exploratory telephone calls from organisations seeking to be active in its field.

General

The Sutton Trust was established in 1997 with the aim of providing educational opportunities for children and young people from non-privileged backgrounds, and has achieved a considerable amount in its field in this short period. In 2003 it had an income of £2.2 million. Grants totalled £1.6 million.

Grantmaking

The trust describes its grantmaking as follows:

The Sutton trust focuses on the following areas:

- access to university, including summer schools, teacher weeks, and outreach
- the open access research scheme at the Belvedere School – Liverpool
- specialist schools
- independent state school partnerships
- early years and parenting
- primary and secondary school enrichment projects.

What is funded?

The Sutton Trust was founded to provide educational opportunities for children and young people from non-privileged backgrounds, with a particular emphasis on recognising the needs and raising the aspirations of the academically able. The trust welcomes applications in these areas, particularly for innovative projects, pilot schemes or new research.

In particular the Sutton Trust funds projects in the following specific areas:

- access to university for under-represented groups;
- the development of able children, including independent/state school partnerships;
- enriching early learning for the under-three age group, including the involvement of parents in stimulating their children's early development;
- research and analysis surrounding these issues.

Most funding goes to educational institutions e.g. schools, FE colleges, universities. Applications from other groups that organise formal education projects or undertake educational research are also welcome. The trust only funds projects that are based in the UK. Project funding is usually provided for one year, in the first instance.

The trust is committed to finding and funding new and exciting projects in all areas of our work, seeking to stimulate debate and improve the educational experiences for young people. We welcome any proposals which fall within our guidelines, especially from the maintained sector.

Grants in 2003

The trust funds educational projects for children from pre-school to university, although most of the money at present goes to projects involving older students. Grants in 2003 were broken down by the trust as follows:

University projects	£545,000
Open Access	£510,000
Research	£250,000
Schools	£232,000
Early years	£66,000
Miscellaneous	£32,000

Details of current programmes within each of these categories follow.

University projects

At present, the trust supports six Sutton Trust Summer Schools (at Bristol, Cambridge, Nottingham, St Andrew's, Durham and Oxford universities) and two teacher summer schools alongside a wide range of other schemes aimed at encouraging non-privileged students to attend university. Other established schemes include an annual A-level Saturday school at the London School of Economics, an ancient Egyptology summer school with UCL and the British Museum and a health care summer school with the University of Southampton. New projects for 2005 include a four-year ambassador programme with the Oxford Access Scheme and a medicine summer school with UCL and the Royal Free Hospital.

Grants ranged from £1,100 to £118,000.

Open Access

This scheme has been in operation at the Belvedere School, Liverpool, since September 2000, and is explained and described in the trust's annual review as follows:

Although only seven percent of the population attend independent schools, 85 of the top 100 schools are independent. The Open Access scheme is designed to allow able children to attend independent day schools, regardless of their families' financial background, so that all places are awarded purely on merit. There is no limit to the number of funded places under the scheme.

Research

Recent research undertaken or funded by the trust includes an analysis of government match-funding schemes, MORI surveys of teachers, students and parents and an analysis of university admissions. 'The trust is keen to analyse research previously undertaken and to conduct follow-up research into this and into the effectiveness of the schemes run by the trust. Research is an area in which the Sutton Trust would like to expand its interests, and we would welcome proposals for appropriate work with a practical aim.'

Individual grants ranged from £870 to £52,000.

Schools

The trust funds various 'master classes' for primary school children and projects which aim to raise aspirations, develop intellectual skills and encourage students to continue to higher education. It also funds a number of independent/state school partnerships in partnership with the DfES, and is committed to supporting four specialist schools a year in conjunction with the Specialist Schools Trust. The trust generally only funds specialist schools in the London area.

Grants ranged from £1,000 to £25,000.

Early years

The trust supports schemes designed to support parents in difficult circumstances dealing with the challenges of early years and to encourage early learning in under-threes through the involvement of parents; the trust also contributed to research into the first 12 months of life.

Grants ranged from £900 to £10,500

Exclusions

No support for:

- individuals
- scholarships
- assisted places replacement schemes or independent school fees;
- sports projects
- capital projects, including equipment, building work etc
- general appeals
- arts projects, including music
- projects outside the UK.

Applications

Before making a formal application, applicants are advised to write in with a brief outline of a project or to make an exploratory call to discuss their project.

The Sutton Trust does not have a standard application form. Instead they ask for a two-page description of the project, including, where relevant:

Background

- what sort of organisation you are (legal status, date established, size and structure);
- your general aims and objectives;
- details of any affiliations to other organisations.

Project

An outline of the proposed project, including:

- specific aims and objectives;
- how the project is to be organised and by whom;
- where the project will take place;
- any anticipated problems in set up and operation of the project;
- when it will start and how long it will take.

Finance

In addition, please provide a detailed budget, including:

- itemised costs of the project, indicating the funding you are requesting from us;
- when the funds are required;
- which other funders you have approached and with what success;
- if you will need funding beyond the period of the grant, where it is to come from.

Benefits

- what are the anticipated results of the work will be;
- the number and age group of the people who will benefit;

- how you will attract and involve the young people you aim to benefit.

Evaluation

- how you will know whether the project has succeeded;
- the measurable specific objectives;
- how you will publicise the outcome of the project to other interested parties.

The Charles and Elsie Sykes Trust

General

£328,000 (2003)

Beneficial area UK, with a preference for Yorkshire, and overseas.

6 North Park Road, Harrogate, Yorkshire HG1 5PA

Correspondent Mrs Judith M Long, Secretary

Trustees *John Ward, chair; Mrs Anne E Brownlie; Martin P Coultas; Mrs G Mary Dance; John Horrocks; R Barry Kay; Dr Michael D Moore; Michael G H Garnett; Dr Michael W McEvoy.*

Charity Commission no. 206926

Information available Accounts and full grants list were provided by the trust.

The trust outlines its grant-making policy in its annual report. It has two main strands. Under the first it considers applications received. Preference is given to applications from Yorkshire, although many are received from outside the region that are unlikely to be successful, as are those which are received from individuals or without examined or audited accounts.

The trustees have previously stated that they welcome the availability to the public of information about charities and the mode of applications to them but nevertheless regret the receipt of so many unsuitable applications, which cause wasted time to all parties. (Less than 10% of applications to the trust are likely to be successful.)

Under a second strand, the trust makes annual donations to a number of registered charities (upon annual production of satisfactory accounts) where regular support is perceived to be 'desirable and proper'. The trustees note

with regret the failure of a number of those charities on the 'annual' list to provide proper information about their accounts.

In 2003 it had assets of £8.9 million, an income of £350,000 and made grants totalling £328,000. A wide range of causes are supported, and the trustees have sub-committees to consider both medical and non-medical grants.

Annual grants during the year totalled £171,000. Special (or one-off) grants totalled £157,000. The trust provided the following breakdown of the categories supported, and number of grants made:

	Amount	no.
Social and moral welfare	£53,000	32
Children and youth	£37,000	18
Medical research	£36,000	22
Disabled and physically handicapped	£26,500	14
Medical welfare	£22,500	13
Older people's welfare	£18,000	11
Mental health and mentally handicapped	£14,000	9
Cultural and environmental heritage	£9,500	4
Sundry	£8,000	7
Hospices and hospitals	£6,500	3
Blind and partially sighted	£3,000	3
Deaf, hard of hearing and speech impaired	£1,000	1
Education	£1,000	1

The three largest grants were made to: Harrogate & District Hospital towards the MRI Scanner Appeal and for the provision of ancillary equipment (£50,000); Royal Northern College of Music – Manchester as a follow-up to a earlier grant (£20,000); and Marrick Priory – Richmond, North Yorkshire for the upgrade and development of facilities for the disabled at the outdoor education centre for young people (£15,000).

Other beneficiaries included University of Cambridge Department of Medicine (£6,000), Christians Against Poverty – Bradford, Gateway Centre – York, Martin House – Wetherby and the Selby Abbey Appeal (£5,000 each), Harrogate Hospital Radio Society (£4,000), Motor Neurone – Northampton and York Minster (£3,000 each), Motability – Harlow and the Whitby Resource Centre (£2,500 each), Alzheimer's Research Trust – Cambridge, Breast Cancer Campaign, Diabetes UK and In Kind Direct (£2,000 each).

Exclusions

The following applicants are unlikely to be successful: individuals; local organisations not in the north of England; and recently-established charities. Non-registered charities are not considered.

Applications

Applications from registered charities may be made with full details and an sae to the above address. Applications without up-to-date audited or examined accounts will not be considered. The trust regrets that it cannot conduct correspondence with applicants.

The Tajtelbaum Charitable Trust

Jewish, welfare

About £500,000 (2002/03)

Beneficial area Generally UK and Israel.

17 Western Avenue, London NW11 9EH

Correspondent Mrs I Tajtelbaum, Trustee

Trustees *Mrs I Tajtelbaum; I Tajtelbaum; M Tajtelbaum; E Tajtelbaum; E Jaswon; H Frydenson.*

Charity Commission no. 273184

Information available Accounts were on file at the Charity Commission but without a list of grants.

The trust makes grants to orthodox synagogues and Jewish educational establishments, and to homes for older people and hospitals, generally in the UK and Israel.

In 2002/03 the trust had an income of £1.7 million, a significant increase on the previous year, mainly derived from rental income and Gift Aid donations. Grants totalled around £500,000. Unfortunately no further information was available on the size or number of beneficiaries for this year.

Previous beneficiaries have included Friends of Arad, Friends of Horim, Gur Trust and Huntingdon Foundation.

Applications

In writing to the correspondent.

The Talbot Village Trust

General

£345,000 (2002)

Beneficial area The boroughs of Bournemouth, Christchurch and Poole; the districts of east Dorset and Purbeck.

Dickinson Manser, 5 Parkstone Road, Poole, Dorset BH15 2NL

Tel. 01202 673071

Email garycox@dickinsonmanser.co.uk

Correspondent Gary S Cox, Clerk

Trustees *Sir Thomas Lees, chair; Henry Plunkett-Ernle-Erle-Drax; Sir George Meyrick; Sir Thomas Salt; James Fleming; Christopher Lees.*

Charity Commission no. 249349

Information available Accounts are on file at the Charity Commission.

As well as making grants, this trust also gives extensive support to charities in the form of loans. In addition, the charity owns and manages land and property at Talbot Village, Bournemouth, including almshouses which it maintains through an associated trust. There is a strong property focus to much of the trust's work.

The trust had an income of £1.3 million in 2002, half of which came from rents, and had assets worth £25 million. Grants to 34 organisations totalled £345,000, of which many were given for capital works and improvements.

The largest grant by far was £90,000 to Poole Deanery Synod to support the Deanery Youth Worker Project. Other large donations included: £50,000 to Julia Perks Foundation for the building of a children's hospice and respite care centre; £40,000 to Townsend Youth Partnership for a purpose built youth centre; £30,000 to Clouds to finance the Working for Recovery Programme; £35,000 each to Dorset Community Action for the Morden Village Hall Project and Friends of Dolphin Trips for Disabled to purchase a new generation dolphin boat; £25,000 each to Ringwood Waldorf School to build three pre-school kindergarten rooms and St Marks School to enlarge the school hall; and £15,000 to Bournemouth and Poole Sea Cadets to purchase new boats and HQ building.

Grants of £10,000 or below included: £10,000 each to Bournemouth Youth Services and East Howe Youth Centre,

both to focus on youth projects; £8,000 to Christchurch Scouts for fitting out costs for the scouts centre; £6,000 to Dorset County Council for the Arts and Health Project; £5,000 to South Wessex Indutrial Project for equipment for the Duke of Edinburgh Award Scheme; £2,000 to Wimborne Methodist Church for removable staging for the church and hall; £1,700 to 20th Christchurch Scout Group to replace the driveway and fencing at the scout hut; and £1,300 to Parkstone Sports and Arts Centre to install security cameras.

Comment

Despite ample warning, and their obligation to the contrary, the Charity Commission were unable to give us sight of this trust's recent accounts.

Exclusions

No grants for individuals.

Applications

In writing to the correspondent.

The David Tannen Charitable Trust

Jewish

£769,000 (2002/03)

Beneficial area UK.

Sutherland House, 70–78 West Hendon Broadway, London NW9 7BT

Tel. 020 8202 1066 **Fax** 020 8202 1469

Correspondent J M Miller, Trustee

Trustees *J M Miller; S Jacobowitz.*

Charity Commission no. 280392

Information available Accounts were on file at the Charity Commission.

The trust makes grants for the advancement of the Jewish religion. In 2002/03 the trust had assets totalling £11 million and an income of £1.6 million. Grants were made totalling £769,000.

By far the largest grants were £175,000 to Gevurath Ari Torah Academy Trust and £100,000 to Cosmos Bela Limited. Other large grants included those to Kahal Chassidim Bobov (£86,000), Lelov (£55,000), Academy and TT Trust (£50,000), Friends of Yeshiva Ohr

Elchanan (£30,000), Atereth Israel Rabinical College and Bnei Torah Movement (£25,000 each), Craven Walks Charitable Trust (£15,000) and Altereth Yehoshua Charity, Helenslea Charity Limited and Yeshivs Toldos Aharon (£10,000 each).

Beneficiaries receiving under £10,000 included Friends of Beis Yisrael Trust (£9,000), Bais Yakov Institutions (£7,000), Finchley Road Synagogue and WST Charity Limited (£5,000 each), Hendon Adath Yisroel Congregation (£4,000), Beis Hamedrash Hendon Trust (£2,000) and Beth Matityahu, Chai Lifeline Cancer Care and Golders Green Kollel (£1,000 each).

Applications

In writing to the correspondent.

The Tedworth Charitable Trust

Parenting, child welfare and development, general

£595,000 (2003/04)

Beneficial area Unrestricted, but UK in practice.

Allington House, 1st Floor, 150 Victoria Street, London SW1E 5AE

Tel. 020 7410 0330 **Fax** 020 7410 0332

Email info@sfct.org.uk

Correspondent Michael Pattison, Director

Trustees *James Sainsbury; Mrs Margaret Sainsbury; Alexander Sainsbury; Jessica Sainsbury; Miss Judith Portrait.*

Charity Commission no. 328524

Information available Annual report and accounts, with good information on grants but none on grantmaking policy, were provided by the trust.

Summary

This is one of the Sainsbury Family Charitable Trusts, which share a joint administration. They have a common approach to grantmaking which is described in the entry for the group as a whole.

This trust's main areas of interest are (with number and the value of grant approvals in 2003/04):

	No.	Amount
Parenting, family welfare and child development	10	£304,000
General	7	£178,000
Arts & the environment	6	£113,000

As with most Sainsbury trusts, grants for local activities are heavily concentrated in the southern half of England.

General

This is the trust of James Sainsbury and the trustees include his brother and sisters, who each have their own foundations.

Staff include Michael Pattison, director of all the Sainsbury trusts, and Hester Marriott, executive. As with some other of the Sainsbury trusts there is no indication of policy or practice beyond the following:

Proposals are generally invited by the the trustees or initiated at their request. Unsolicited applications are discouraged and are unlikely to be successful, even if they fall within an area in which the trustees are interested. The trustees prefer to support innovative schemes that can be successfully replicated or become self-sustaining.

Grants in 2003/04

Parenting, family welfare and child development

The major commitment was for continuing support to the Families, Children and Childcare project of the Royal Free Hospital and the Department of Education at Oxford University (£152,000). The other beneficiaries were: Home-Start UK, towards staff salaries and publications (£50,000); University of Reading, towards the core costs of the Winnicott Research Unit (£22,000); National Family and Parenting Institute, towards the salary of a policy, research and development officer for the Family Friendly Britain Campaign (£18,000); Thomas Coram Research Unit, towards therapeutic group support for primary school children with emotional and/or behavioural difficulties (£17,000); Parenting Education and Support Forum, towards the part-time salary of a research and development director (£16,000); William Tynedale Primary School, towards therapeutic group support for primary school children with emotional and/or behavioural difficulties (£11,000); The Small School, to employ a writer in residence to focus on environmental issues with pupils and the local community (£9,000); and Coram Family and International Initiative UK (£5,000 each).

General

The main grant was made to Worcester College, Oxford towards the endowment appeal (£125,000). Other beneficiaries were: Dartington Hall Trust, towards the major capital redevelopment of Schumacher College (£20,000); ActionAid (£10,000); Sengwer Indigenous Development Project (£8,000); Centre for Attachment-based Psychoanalytic Psychotherapy (£7,500); Unitree Foundation – Poland (£7,000); and Trinity Hospice, towards an individual's fundraising trek (£400).

Arts & the environment

Grants were made to: Ashden Awards for Sustainable Energy, to fund an annual award for outstanding small-scale renewable energy projects in the UK and in developing countries (£40,000); Navdanya International Centre for Sustainable Living in India, towards core costs (£30,000); Environmental Research Association Ltd, towards core costs and the production of an anthology of craft-related articles (£26,000); Royal Academy of Music, to provide bursary support for a student (£10,000); University of Reading, for a bursary for a student (£4,000); and Cornwall Arts Centre Trust, towards the Carn to Cove programme of rural events (£3,000).

Exclusions

Grants are not normally made to individuals.

Applications

See the guidance for applicants in the entry for the Sainsbury Family Charitable Trusts. A single application will be considered for support by all the trusts in the group.

However, for this as for many of the trusts, 'proposals are generally invited by the trustees or initiated at their request. Unsolicited applications are discouraged and are unlikely to be successful, even if they fall within an area in which the trustees are interested'.

Tees Valley Community Foundation (formerly Cleveland Community Foundation)

General

£1.5 million (2002/03)

Beneficial area The former county of Cleveland, being the local authority areas of Hartlepool, Middlesbrough, Redcar, Cleveland and Stockton-on-Tees.

Southlands Business Centre, Ormesby Road, Middlesbrough TS3 0HB

Tel. 01642 314200 **Fax** 01642 313700

Email info@teesvalleyfoundation.org

Website www.teesvalleyfoundation.org

Correspondent Kevin Ryan, Director

Trustees *Dr Tony Gillham, chair; Margaret Fay; John Foster; Chris Hope; Marjory Houseman; Alan Kitching; Kate Macnaught; Sir Ronald Norman; Jack Ord; Robert Sale; Pat Sole; Michael Stewart; Ian Collinson; Geoffrey Crute; John Redhead; John Sparke; John Bennett; Pam Taylor.*

Charity Commission no. 700568

Information available Information was provided by the trust.

The foundation gives support to organisations and groups working to support a wide range of community needs, including those working with people who are disabled, ethnic groups and 'talented' musicians.

Support is also given to youth clubs, sports centres, community partnerships, crime prevention and training within voluntary organisations.

In 2002/03 the foundation had assets of £6.2 million. It had an income of £1.1 million, mainly from donations, grants and gifts. Grants totalled £1.5 million and were disbursed through the following programmes:

Teesside Youth Fund

This fund distributed 12 grants totalling £11,000 to organisations working with young people who are disadvantaged or disaffected. Grants ranged from £500 to £2,500.

The Pursuit of Excellence Scheme which is part of the Teesside Youth Fund, supports individuals who are excelling in their chosen field and who are in need of financial assistance to achieve their aims. The foundation looks for those who are likely to reach national and/or international prominence in a sporting or artistic endeavor. The scheme distributed 22 grants totalling £7,900. Grants ranged from £200 to £500.

Teeside TEC Distribution Fund

A total of £655,000 was distributed by this fund in 35 grants.

The Cleveland Fund

A total of £71,000 was distributed in 53 grants to a wide range of organisations. Grants ranged from £1,000 to £5,000.

The Teesside Power Fund

This fund distributed 10 grants totalling £11,000 to groups supporting residents living within the nine wards in the Teesside Power Station region. Grants ranged from £1,000 to £2,000.

Global Grants

This new scheme provides small grants to support activities that may improve the employment prospects of any unemployed persons, or those under threat of redundancy and resident in Tees Valley. Grants can support activities other than training, such as those that increase confidence, motivation and interpersonal skills. Grants can be made to individuals between 31 and 64 who have not finally retired.

A scheme for individuals between 16 and 30 is available through The Prince's Trust who can be contacted on 0190 478 8488.

Evening Gazette Making a Difference Fund

This new fund prioritises projects that address the issue of disadvantage, projects fulfilling a need not already being met and projects aimed at improving the social environment.

The foundation continues to administer two government-funded schemes.

The Local Network Fund

This programme supports local voluntary and community groups working with disadvantaged children and young people up to the age of 19. Grants range from £250 to £7,000. The fund distributed 65 grants totalling £333,000. For further details or an application form contact the Local Network Fund National Call Centre on 0845 113 0161.

Redcar & Cleveland and Middlesbrough

Neighbourhood Renewal Community Chest Programme/ Community Learning Chest

The objective of this programme is to contribute to and enhance the regeneration of disadvantaged areas of Redcar & Cleveland and Middlesbrough by stimulating and supporting community activity. It is hoped that local people become involved in improving their communities and neighbourhoods. Local criteria are set and decisions are made by panels of community representatives. Grants are available ranging from £50 to £5,000. Redcar & Cleveland Community Chest distributed 53 grants totalling £143,000. Redcar & Cleveland Community Learning Chest distributed 15 grants totalling £34,000. Middlesborough Community Chest distributed 52 grants totalling £188,000. Middlesborough Community Learning Chest distributed 15 grants totalling £46,000.

Exclusions

No grants for major fundraising appeals, sponsored events, promotion of religion, holidays or social outings. Each fund has separate exclusions; contact the foundation for further details.

Applications

Guidelines and application forms are available from the foundation for each of its funds and on its website, with the exception of the Local Network Fund which can be obtained from its call centre. Staff at the foundation are happy to help applicants with form completion although on government funds the foundation employs outreach providers for this task. Grants officers may telephone or visit applicants to obtain sufficient additional information before considering the application. Each application is considered against the criteria of the fund detailed in the guidelines. Normally decisions are made within three months.

Each fund has its own distribution committee. The frequency and dates of each meeting vary for each fund and information can be found on the website.

The Sir Jules Thorn Charitable Trust

Medical research, medicine, small grants for humanitarian charities

£1.8 million (2003)
Beneficial area UK.

24 Manchester Square, London
W1U 3TH

Tel. 020 7487 5851 **Fax** 020 7224 3976

Email info@julesthorntrust.org.uk

Website www.julesthorntrust.org.uk

Correspondent David H Richings, Director

Trustees *Ann Rylands, chair; Christopher Sporborg; Prof. Frederick V Flynn; Sir Bruce MacPhail; Nicholas Wilson; Mrs N V Pearcey; Mrs E S Charal; William Sporborg; Prof. Sir Ravinder N Maini.*

Charity Commission no. 233838

Information available Excellent website, with full descriptions of grantmaking programmes and clear guidelines for applicants. Good annual report and accounts (not on the website).

Summary

The trust has four regular grant programmes (with 2003 expenditures):

- medical research projects (£1,208,000, 8 new projects);
- medically-related projects (£313,500, 4 projects);
- special projects (£108,000, 2 new awards);
- single donations (£175,500, 646 awards).

The medical research projects must have strong clinical relevance. They may meet the salaries of research workers, but this is done only in the context of an approved project, i.e. they are not fellowships or studentships per se.

Research into AIDS and cancer is not covered and grants are made to institutions and not to individuals or for joint funding of projects with other grantmakers.

With the exception of the fourth programme, grants can be large. Within the medical research programme, one award was for £996,000, but this was for a special scheme.

The main funding scheme for medical research, and the annual 'special grants' programme are not open to unsolicited applications.

The small grants programme is quite different, with several hundred grants across a wide variety of humanitarian fields, and with a reported success rate of about two in every three applications.

General

The trust has an endowment of about £72 million, generating an income, before capital losses or gains, of £2.3 million in 2003. Investment management fees of £141,000 were a modest 5.6% of this amount.

'Seed corn' grants are for up to 12 months and most project grants are for between one and three years. The trust is a member of the Association of Medical Research Charities, whose high standards, such as those for full peer review, it must therefore meet or exceed. It is helped in this by an expert Medical Advisory Committee.

A recent innovation is the annual Sir Jules Thorn Award of up to £1 million to 'support an outstanding young research group at one of the top UK medical schools invited to bid'. This support can be spread over five or more years.

The 'special grants' programme, for which up to £500,000 can be allocated each year depending on the resources available, is in a field chosen by the trustees and for which unsolicited applications are not invited.

The trust's excellent website gives a comprehensive description of its grant programmes, as follows:

The trust was established in 1964 by Sir Jules Thorn. It makes grants for medical research and for humanitarian purposes.

Its primary interest is in the field of medicine, where grants are awarded to universities and hospitals in the United Kingdom to support clinical research, with modest donations provided also for medically related purposes.

Outside of medicine some funds are allocated for donations to humanitarian appeals and to special projects but on a lesser scale than the commitment for medical research.

Grants for medical research

When he founded the trust, Sir Jules Thorn was concerned that his endowment should be used to alleviate the suffering of patients, and to aid diagnosis. These themes are central to the trustees' policy in awarding grants.

Criteria

- Clinical relevance
  The work should be likely to bring benefit to patients in the short term. Priority is given to research which could have clinical applicability within 5 years.
- Importance and priority
  The condition under investigation should be an important problem which affects a substantial number of people, and thus carries a heavy economic cost to the nation.
- Originality
  Applicants must be able to demonstrate the originality of their hypothesis. High quality science will be expected.
- Methodology
  A clear and convincing plan of investigation will be a prerequisite.
- The research team
  It will be expected that the investigators will have an established first class track record in the field of research with which their project is concerned, and will be well versed in the techniques to be employed.
- Cost
  The applicants will need to demonstrate that their cost estimates are fully justified. The trust does not fund overheads (bench fees), and will not meet consumables costs which qualify for reimbursement from the NHS 'Culyer' budget.

If potential applicants have doubts about whether their project meets these criteria they should contact the trust.

Types of award

Research grants are made within one of two schemes.

- Sir Jules Thorn Award for Biomedical Research
  One award of up to £1 million is made annually for a programme of work which may extend over a period of up to 5 or more years, and is judged to be at the leading edge of international science. This scheme is available only to Medical Schools invited to submit applications. It is NOT available for unsolicited bids.
- Seed Corn Fund
  Research investigators in UK universities are eligible to apply for grants of not more than £10,000 each for a period of up to one year. The fund is designed to provide a flexible, quick-response, source of grant support at the point of entry to the research market, enabling preliminary data essential for subsequent research to be obtained. The trust's normal exclusions apply. Proposals to assist with basic work will not be considered unless the applicant is able to demonstrate clearly how the transition to clinical application will be achieved within five years of the subsequent research commencing. The fund is limited and is closed if the resources allocated in a particular year are fully allocated.

Registration of controlled trials

The trust supplies data on all properly controlled clinical trials which it funds, to the register maintained by Current Controlled Trials Limited. It considers that the availability of information about such trials is in the best interests of patients, researchers, and other funding bodies.

Commercial exploitation of research

The trust requires each institution receiving its research grants to enter into a legal agreement to share any income arising from the subsequent commercial exploitation of the research.

Examples of research which has been funded by the trust

- Sir Jules Thorn Award for Biomedical Research

The award is made following competitive bids from invited UK medical schools and postgraduate biomedical institutes. In 2002 University of Manchester in conjunction with Hope Hospital was the successful bid, with £996,000 over four years being awarded for a project investigating inflammation in ischaemic brain damage.

How applications are assessed

- The trust operates a policy of peer review for all applications.
- The scientific merit of submissions is assessed by an eminent Medical Advisory Committee, which makes recommendations to the trustees as to whether grants should be awarded.
- At the discretion of the committee, the opinion of expert reviewers may be sought.
- Wherever possible, feedback will be given to applicants who are unsuccessful. It is possible, however, that an application may fail, not because of inherent shortcomings but because resource constraints oblige the Medical Advisory Committee to prioritise proposals and to select a limited number to receive awards.

[For 'exclusions' and 'how to apply' see the relevant sections below.]

Medically-related donations

The trustees endeavour to allocate some funds each year for medicine generally, in addition to their primary commitment to medical research. They keep in mind Sir Jules Thorn's concern to alleviate the suffering of patients and to aid diagnosis.

The resources available are limited–rarely more than £300,000 in total–so this scheme is not a source of substantial funding for capital projects. Depending on the appeals received the trustees may allocate the total fund in any one year to just one project, or divide it between several deserving appeals.

[For 'How to apply', see below.]

Small single donations programme

Sir Jules Thorn was a great humanitarian and whilst his endowment was provided primarily for medicine and medical research, he was content for some funds to be allocated to appeals of a humanitarian nature.

Accordingly, the trustees earmark some resources each year for such purposes but the amount available is strictly limited. The trust receives many more appeals than it can support with a grant. Each case is treated on its merits and the trustees' policy is to spread the funds as widely as possible. As a consequence, the trust can offer only relatively small donations, usually for amounts of between £100 and £750. Requests are considered for contributions to core funding, or for specific projects, but this programme does not provide substantial sums for capital projects.

(The word 'humanitarian' might possibly mislead. As used here, it refers to direct health and welfare activities, rather than to primarily campaigning activities. Practical help for, say, the homeless might be supported but, for example, a campaign to stop the UK arms trade would probably not.)

In any one year the trust may make as many as six hundred or more donations to a very wide range of appeals (see below).

[For 'exclusions' and 'applications', see below.]

Special projects

The trust has an interesting 'special projects' programme, described as follows:

At the trustees' discretion, funds are allocated annually to one 'special project' linked to a theme determined by the trustees. The total award is normally for a maximum of £500,000, but may be spread between several projects related to the same theme.

This programme is not available for unsolicited bids. Applications may be submitted only upon specific invitation from the trust.

Past 'special projects' have been for:
- The deaf and hard of hearing
- Psychiatric nursing
- The geriatric community
- Youth at risk
- Hospitals and accident and emergency services
- Museum education
- Library development
- Hospice and respite care.

Grants in 2003

Good examples of these are included in the material from the trust reprinted above. The largest single award was for £970,000 to University of Edinburgh,

Department of Medicine towards reseach into cell therapy for lung disorders. Other grants for medical research included those to University of Leicester (£98,000), University of Southampton (£92,000) and Quenn Mary's School of Medicine & Dentistry (£80,000).

Three medically-related projects received ad-hoc support from the trust during the year. These were Motor Neurone Disease Association (£200,000). Robert Jones & Agnes Hunt Orthopaedic Hospital (£100,000) and Digestive Disorders Foundation (£13,500).

The special projects for the year were Children's Adventure Farm Trust (£62,000), Family Holiday Association (£50,000) and ASBAH Leeds & Bradford (£39,500).

Small single donations were made as follows:

Amount	Number	Total
Over £1,000 (Sport Aid Trust)	1	£2,500
Of £1,000	5	£5,000
Between £1,000 and £650	15	£11,000
Between £650 and £500	34	£20,500
Of £500	111	£55,500
Of £400	78	£31,200
Between £300 and £250	143	£43,000
Of £200 or less	50	£9,000

Recent beneficiaries of small donations included Barts Cancer Centre of Excellence, Iain Rennie Hospice at Home, St Dunstan's, Royal Blind Asylum and School, Centrepoint, Hull Homeless and Rootless Project, Scottish Veterans' Residences, Sussex Autistic Society, Action for Kids, Brain & Spine Foundation, Caring for Life, Donna Louise Trust, Epilepsy Outlook, High Blood Pressure Foundation, Liverpool Voluntary Society for the Blind, Ro Ro Sailing Project, Stepping Stones, Wirral Autistic Society, British Stammering Association, East Belfast Mission, Luton Shopmobility, North Liverpool Security Project, Aintree Hospitals NHS Trust, Diabetes UK, Roundabout and Support Dogs.

Comment

This is an impressive institution. The main research programmes, making a relatively small number of large grants, seems likely to be more effective than other comparable programmes from other trusts which spread their money around much more widely.

The small grants programme is also impressive though in almost an opposite way. By keeping the size of the awards down, the trust ensures that applicants, most of them from small or very small charities, have a high chance of success and a smaller risk of the disheartening refusals that are very often their lot.

Exclusions

Medically-related grants to UK universities and hospitals

The trust does not fund:

- research which is considered unlikely to provide clinical benefit within five years;
- research which could reasonably be expected to be supported by a disease-specific funder, unless there is a convincing reason why the trust has been approached;
- research into cancer or AIDS, for the sole reason that they are relatively well funded elsewhere;
- 'top up' grants for ongoing projects;
- research which will also involve other funders, apart from the institution itself;
- individuals–except in the context of a project undertaken by an approved institution which is in receipt of a grant from the trust;
- research or data collection overseas;
- third parties raising resources to fund research themselves;
- research institutions which are not registered charities.

Unless stated specifically elsewhere, the trust does not have a current programme to support any of the following:

- PhD scholarships–other than in the context of an approved project submitted by the holder of a funded post at an approved institution;
- intercalcated BSc degrees;
- travelling fellowships;
- student elective periods of study in the UK or abroad;
- fellowships and bursaries.

Potential applicants should ensure that their requirements do not fall within one of the excluded categories. In the event of doubt, please contact the trust.

Smaller donations programme

It is not possible for the trust to make donations in the following categories.

- To beneficiaries who do not have registered charity status. Thus individuals are among those excluded. Regrettably the trust cannot respond to requests for financial help from or on behalf of individuals in distress.
- To overseas organisations, or to organisations based in the UK who use their funds for charitable purposes overseas.
- To organisations raising money for medical or medically-related research.
- For the purchase of raffle tickets.
- To denominational beneficiaries.
- For church restorations or repairs.

- Where support has been given within the previous two years.

Applications
For medical research

Enquiries

- Before considering an approach to the trust, potential applicants should check that their research meets the trust's policy criteria, and is not proscribed by its exclusions.
- Investigators who wish to apply for 'seed corn' funding should contact the trust.
- Invariably demand for grants exceeds the supply of funding. From time to time the trust is obliged to impose a moratorium on the submission of new applications. Potential applicants should contact the trust for current information on the availability of funding.

Applications

- If the trust is able to accept new applications for 'seed corn' grants, a letter of invitation enclosing detailed guidance on the structure and information required will be sent to applicants.
- All applications will be acknowledged and the likely timescale for assessment will be advised.

Medically-related donations

Appeals are considered by the trustees at their meetings in April and November each year.

There is no specific application form. Proposals should be submitted to the trust's director and should cover the following areas.

- The background to the appeal, including any brochures and feasibility assessment.
- Information about the applicant, which must be an institution having charitable status. Applications from individuals cannot be considered.
- Details of the appeal, including the total sum being raised, donations or pledges already received, and the plans for securing the remainder. Time scales for implementation should be given.

Potential applicants who wish to establish whether their appeal would fit the criteria should contact the trust.

Smaller donations programme

There are no specific dates for submitting applications. Appeals may be made at any time and will be considered

by the trustees as soon as possible, depending on volume.

There is no special application form. Applicants should submit their appeal to the director, and ensure that they cover the following matters, briefly:

- the nature and objectives of the charity (a brochure is helpful);
- the reason for the appeal;
- how much is being raised in total and from what sources (including the charity's own reserves);
- the gap to be bridged;
- a short financial budget - the last report and accounts should accompany the application.

Appeals by e-mail cannot be accepted.

All applicants will be advised of the outcome as soon as possible. Successful applicants should note that it is not necessary to include the trust on databases for receipt of newsletters and other mailings.

The Three Guineas Trust

Autism

£639,000 (2003/04)

Beneficial area Unrestricted.

Allington House, 1st Floor, 150 Victoria Street, London SW1E 5AE

Tel. 020 7410 0330 **Fax** 020 7410 0332

Email info@sfct.org.uk

Correspondent Michael Pattison, Director

Trustees *Clare Sainsbury; Christopher Stone; Miss Judith Portrait.*

Charity Commission no. 1059652

Information available Good annual report and accounts, with full grants listing, were provided by the trust.

This is one of the Sainsbury Family Charitable Trusts, which share a joint administration. They have a common approach to grantmaking which is described in the entry for the group as a whole.

It is the trust of Clare Sainsbury, and its present interest is in autism and the related Asperger's Syndrome, but its grantmaking may increase and its interests widen in future years, as explained in the annual report. During the past few years the trust has received around £7 million in donations and gifts from the settlor.

Scope of grantmaking

The trustees do not at present wish to invite applications, except in the field of autism and Asperger's Syndrome, where they will examine unsolicited proposals alongside those that result from their own research and contacts with expert individuals and organisations in this field. The trustees prefer to support innovative schemes that can be successfully replicated or become self-sustaining. The trustees are also keen that, wherever possible, schemes supporting adults and teens on the autistic spectrum should include clients/service users in decision-making.

There is a specific fund to enable people in developing countries to hire autism practitioners from the UK to deliver practical, one-off training courses for professionals and parents in countries which have little current provision for autistic children and adults.

The main beneficiary during the year was the National Autistic Society, which received £265,000 in total, mostly towards the salary and associated costs of the national programme co-ordinator of the HELP programme, and the officer and administrator in Scotland, but also towards setting up a local and national resource called Public Autism Research Information System (PARIS).

There were 19 other grants made during the year. Including those to Autism West Midlands (£70,000), Lothian Autistic Society (£40,000), Full of Life (£20,000), Autistic Society Greater Manchester Area (£10,000) and Autism Bedfordshire (£2,000).

Exclusions

No grants for individuals.

Applications

See the guidance for applicants in the entry for the Sainsbury Family Charitable Trusts. A single application will be considered for support by all the trusts in the group.

However, for this as for many of the trusts, other than in the field of autism, 'proposals are generally invited by the trustees or initiated at their request. Unsolicited applications are discouraged and are unlikely to be successful, even if they fall within an area in which the trustees are interested'.

The Tolkien Trust

Christian – especially Catholic, welfare, general

About £600,000 (2002/03)

Beneficial area UK, with a preference for Oxfordshire.

Manches Solicitors, 3 Worcester Street, Oxford OX1 2PZ

Tel. 01865 722106 **Fax** 01865 813687

Correspondent Mrs Cathleen Blackburn

Trustees *John Tolkien; Christopher Tolkien; Priscilla Tolkien.*

Charity Commission no. 273615

Information available Accounts are on file at the Charity Commission.

The trust's main assets are the copyright in certain works of J R R Tolkien. This provides the trust with its income, and although there is no permanent endowment, there should always be an income from book royalties during the period of copyright. Recent film treatments of Tolkien's work, and the financial benefits that such things bring, has boosted the income and expediture of the trust significantly.

In 2002/03 the trust's income rose by £1 million on the previous year to almost £1.3 million. Total expenditure increased to £685,000, most of which is likely to have been awarded in grants.

There appears to be a preference for Christian organisations, especially Catholic, then welfare and organisations in Oxfordshire. Many of the trust's beneficiaries, both UK-wide and local, seem to receive grants each year.

Previous beneficiaries include Find Your Feet Ltd, Catholic Housing Aid Society, St Anthony's RC Headington, Bodleian Library, St Anthony's RC Church – Littlemore, Oxford Marriage Care, Tablet Trust, Wrexham Concern Trust, Agenda Magazine, Aldeburgh Poetry Trust, Editions Charitable Trust, Friends of Earth Trust Limited and Mold and District Life Group.

Comment

Despite ample warning, and their obligation to the contrary, the Charity Commission were unable to give us sight of this trust's accounts.

Exclusions

No support for non-registered charities.

Applications

In writing to the correspondent.

The Tompkins Foundation

Health, welfare

£538,000 (2002/03)

Beneficial area UK.

7 Belgrave Square, London SW1X 8PH

Tel. 020 7235 9322 **Fax** 020 7259 5129

Correspondent Richard Geoffrey Morris

Trustees *Elizabeth Tompkins, patron; Peter Vaines; Susan Floyd.*

Charity Commission no. 281405

Information available Full accounts were on file at the Charity Commission.

The foundation was established in 1980. Its objects are as follows:

- the advancement of education, learning and religion;
- the provision of facilities for recreation and other purposes beneficial to the community.

In 2002/03 the trust had assets of £8.2 million and an income of £562,000. Grants totalled £538,000, ranging from £500 to £100,000. Many of the beneficiaries supported had received donations in previous years. Recipients included: Foundation of Nursing Studies (£100,000); International Centre, SSAFA, St Mary's Coronary Flow Trust and St Mary's Hospital Trustees (£50,000 each); Chicken Shed Theatre (£25,000), Leonard Cheshire Foundation (£20,000), Anna Freud Centre (£15,000), Bristol Cathedral (£10,000), CTBF Enterprises (£2,500) and City of London Police Federation Rupert Fund (£500).

Exclusions

No grants to individuals.

Applications

The trust makes a substantial proportion of its grants to organisations previously supported and does not seek further applications.

The Triangle Trust (1949) Fund

Health, welfare, education

£455,000 (in grants to organisations, 2002/03)

Beneficial area UK.

28 Great James Street, London
WC1N 3EY

Tel. 020 7831 5942 **Fax** 020 7831 5942

Email triang@triangletrust.org

Correspondent Jill Hailey, Secretary

Trustees *Mrs Melanie Burfitt, chair; Mrs J Turner; Dr Marjorie Walker; M Powell; R Kathoke; Nicholas Crawshaw.*

Charity Commission no. 222860

Information available Annual report and accounts were provided by the trust.

Summary

The trust makes grants to organisations mostly for amounts between £1,000 and £5,000, but it also supports a small number of causes with larger amounts. The trust seeks out its own projects to support, and also responds to a probably limited number of unsolicited applications, which must fall into the guidelines featured in this entry.

General

In 2002/03 the trust had assets totalling £11.5 million and an income of £479,000. Grants were made to 75 organisations totalling £455,000.

The trust gives a proportion of its money to individuals in need (£56,000 to 107 individuals in 2002/03), mostly former employees of the pharmaceutical industry or their dependants (its founder was chairman of Glaxo Laboratories). The rest is given in grants to organisations, which the trust prefers to seek out proactively for itself. The trust does, however, issue guidelines and has recently introduced an application form, which implies that at least some unsolicited applications do result in grants. The trust's guidelines on this read as follows:

Trustees prefer to initiate their own projects for funding, and do not normally respond to unsolicited applications. Applications will usually only be accepted from registered charities, and projects submitted must fall within one of the areas of priority funding and pass an additional test (see below).

The annual report for 2002/03 describes the trust's grantmaking as follows:

Long and short term collaborative projects with organisations and charities have continued. Trustees have also made grants towards core costs of supported charities. Areas of activity included disabled, elderly, carers and disadvantaged people, and educational costs to give those who would otherwise be unemployed a chance of entering the workplace. Emphasis on the homeless has been scaled back. Trustees have added an overarching objective of integrating or reintegrating individuals into society through projects and charities supported

Grants in 2002/03

There were 12 beneficiaries of £10,000 or more, the largest being the University of London (£66,500). Other larger grants were made to Family Welfare Association (£52,500 in total), Dundee City Council (£20,000), Leicester City Link (£15,000), South Yorkshire Probation Service (£14,000), BACO (£12,000), Mobility Trust and BEAT (£11,000 each), and Advance Housing and Support, Headway Essex, Seven Springs Play Centre and the Cedar School (£10,000 each).

Beneficiaries of £5,000 or less included Age Concern Berkshire, Carmarthen and East Cheshire, Alzheimers Society Penrith, Cancer Resource Centre, Habitat for Humanity, Hull Hostel Forum, Lothian Centre for Integrated Living, National Youth Orchestra, Pancreatitis Support Network, Matthew Trust and Wallasey Welfare Advice.

Exclusions

- Overseas charities or projects outside the UK;
- charities for the promotion of religion;
- medical research;
- environmental, wildlife or heritage appeals.

Applications

Organisations should apply using the trust's application form, available from the correspondent. This should be returned to the trust by post. The accompanying guidance states that 'trustees prefer to initiate their own projects for funding, and do not normally respond to unsolicited applications'.

Trust for London (see also the City Parochial Foundation)

Social welfare in London

£951,000 (2003)

Beneficial area The Metropolitan Police District of London and the City of London.

6 Middle Street, London EC1A 7PH

Tel. 020 7606 6145 **Fax** 020 7600 1866

Email info@cityparochial.org.uk

Website www.cityparochial.org.uk/tfl

Correspondent Mr Bharat Mehta, Clerk to the Trustees

Trustees *The trustee of Trust for London is City Parochial Foundation, whose trustees are: Ms Maggie Baxter, Chair; Nigel Pantling, Vice Chair; Prof. Julian Franks; Peter Williams; Ms Elahe Panahi; Charles Edward Lord; Ian David Luder; Archdeacon of London; Peter Dale; Mrs Gillian Roberts; Prof. Gerald Manners; John Barnes; Miles Barber; John Muir; Mrs Jyoti Munsiff; Mrs Lynda Stevens; Albert Tucker; Ms Jane Wilmot; Cllr Raj Chandarana.*

Charity Commission no. 294710

Information available Leaflet on policies and procedures, annual report and an annual grants review. Materials are available in a range of formats, including Braille and audiotape.

Summary

The trust was established in 1986 with an expendable endowment of £10 million derived from the proceeds of sales of the Greater London Council's assets.

It shares its administration and trustees with the City Parochial Foundation, which has a separate entry. In 2003 the trust had an income of £631,000; grants were made totalling £951,000.

Grant guidelines 2002–2006

We will fund and, where appropriate, work with new and emerging small voluntary organisations that benefit people and communities in London.

A group is 'small' if it is made up of volunteers or members and has no more than the equivalent of two full-time paid staff.

An organisation applying for funding should:

- benefit local people and communities in London
- be charitable, but not necessarily a registered charity
- help local communities to identify and tackle local problems
- do work that might be used to teach others
- be set up by local people and communities to help themselves
- be open to all members of their community
- be set up to tackle a specific issue.

All organisations approaching us for help must:

- have a constitution or a set of rules that govern their activities
- be run by a group of people who may be called the trustees or the management committee
- operate their own bank or building society account
- be able to provide financial statements for the last year.

What we provide funding for
We will fund:

- identify needs and delivering services
- gaining access to training opportunities
- organise meetings, conferences, seminars and events which identify problems, raise awareness, explore solutions, or promote good practice.

The costs our funding can cover
Our funding can be used to cover everyday costs and overheads; one-off capital costs for building equipment; and the costs of paying for sessional and part-time staff.

We are particularly keen to fund work with:

- Black, Asian and minority ethnic community organisations;
- organisations providing creative educational activities for children and young people;
- refugee and migrant groups; and
- self-help groups.

Grants in 2003/04

The trust's grantmaking period runs from May to January each year. Grants are made within the following categories (with the allocated percentage during the period in brackets):

Black, Asian and minority ethnic community organisations (11%)

Recent beneficiaries include: Havering Asian Social and Welfare Association, towards the salary and costs of a development worker to work with older women (£15,000 over two years); Wise Thoughts, towards the organisation's rent (£10,000 over two years); Kollun – Tower Hamlets, towards rental costs and the salary costs of a project manager (£8,000 over two years); Mann Saffer – Ealing, towards the costs of one-to-one counselling, complimentary therapy and administration costs (£7,000); Grace Women's Organisation – Hackney, towards renting training rooms (£5,000); and Feltham Asian Women's Group – Hounslow, towards the running costs of the organisation (£2,500).

Educational activities for children and young people (25%)

Beneficiaries include: Greenwich Mandarin and Supplementary School, towards the salary costs of the head teacher and coordinator, volunteers' expenses and training, teaching materials and running costs (£14,000 over two years); Croydon School for Arabic and Kurdish Studies, towards teachers' salaries and rent (£10,000); Cabinda Community Association – Haringey, towards the cost of mother tongue and supplementary classes (£8,000 over two years); Horwood Estate Bangla School – Tower Hamlets, towards rent and teaching materials (£6,000); Canal Museum Trust – Islington, towards the costs of creating a new interactive exhibition area focusing on canal horses (£5,000); and Christ Family Assembly Supplementary School – Lewisham, towards rent and running costs (£2,500).

Refugees and migrant groups (28%)

Recent beneficiaries include: Hispanic Welfare Association – Waltham Forest, towards the salary of a part-time outreach worker and running costs (£14,000); Somali Teachers Association – Ealing, towards salary costs of a part-time coordinator (£10,000); All Afghan Association – Ealing, towards the premises costs of the organisation (£7,500); Great Nile Trust – Hackney, towards rent and running costs (£6,000); Watanzania Tuinuate Group – Redbridge, towards rent and running costs (£4,000); and African Youth Development – Lewisham, to develop cultural education activities for young people (£2,500).

Self-help groups (14%)

Recent beneficiaries include: Safra, towards its publication and running costs (£20,000); Sebbon Street Exchange – Islington, towards the salary costs of a part-time administrator (£11,000); Southwark Homeless Information Project, towards rent, publishing and print costs (£10,000); Stoned Arts – Brent, towards the rent and running costs of the organisation (£7,000); North Kensington Women's Textiles Workshop – Kensington & Chelsea, towards the salaries of part-time tutors for sewing classes (£4,000); and Southwark Explorers Club, towards transport and administrative expenses (£3,500).

Disabled people's organisations (2%)

Recent beneficiaries include: African and Caribbean Children with Learning Difficulties Foundation – Lambeth, towards rental costs (£8,500); Somali Disability Association – Brent, towards the rent and running costs of the organisation (£7,000); African and Caribbean Disablement Association – Waltham Forest, towards the purchase of equipment and running costs (£5,000); and Venturers Drama Group, to meet the production costs of a play for people with visual impairment (£2,500).

The trust also made a donation of £153,000 to its own initiative, the Resource Unit for Supplementary and Mother Tongue Schools, which operates across London, towards the salary and general costs of the unit's director. Another of the trust's own initiatives, the Refugee Communities History Project, received £15,000. These initiatives accounted for 20% of donations.

Exclusions

The trust will not fund:

- distribution by umbrella bodies
- general appeals.
- holiday play schemes.
- individual members of the public.
- major expenses for buying or building premises.
- part of a full-time salary.
- replacing spending cuts made by local or central government.
- research.
- trips abroad.

Applications

We do not send out application forms. The first thing you should do is read these guidelines and check that your organisation and the work you want us to fund fits into our grantmaking priorities detailed above.

Stage 1

If you feel that your work does fit the guidelines you should send us written details of your planned work and funding needs (on no more than two sides of A4 paper) along with:

- your organisation's constitution.
- your most recent financial accounts.
- your most recent annual report.

Or

telephone a field officer at the foundation to talk about your work and the funding you are looking for.

Stage 2

If we feel that your planned work fits into our grantmaking priorities, a field officer will arrange to meet you to discuss it further.

Stage 3

Once you and the field officer agree about what you should apply for, he or she will give you an application form to fill in. The field officer will go through the form with you to make sure that you understand what information we need. We must receive your full application form before the relevant deadlines listed below.

Stage 4

The field officer will present this application to the grants committee, which will make the final decision about funding your application.

Stage 5

You will be told about the decision in writing after the foundation's trustee board meeting.

Our field officers are here to help you to apply for funding. If you would like to discuss your proposal before writing to us, please ring us on 020 7606 6145.

When you should apply

The application process takes quite a long time, so you need to contact us at least three months before the relevant deadline. The grants committee meets four times a year, in March, June, September and December. The deadlines for receiving your completed applications are:

31 January for the March meeting

15 April for the June Meeting

31 July for the September Meeting

15 October for the December Meeting.

The Trusthouse Charitable Foundation

General

£1.9 million (2002/03)

Beneficial area Unrestricted, but mainly UK.

5 Chancery Lane, Clifford's Inn, London EC4A 1BU

Tel. 020 7320 6996 **Fax** 020 7320 3842

Correspondent Richard Hopgood

Trustees *Sir Richard Carew Pole, chair; Sir Jeremy Beecham; Baron Bernstein of Craigwell; Baroness Cox of Queensbury; Earl of Gainsborough; Duke of Marlborough; The Hon. Mrs Olga Polizzi; Sir Hugh Rossi; Lady Stevenson; Baroness Hogg; Anthony Peel.*

Charity Commission no. 1063945

Information available Annual report and accounts and new guidelines for applicants were provided by the trust.

General

The trust makes at least 300 grants a year, most of which are for £5,000 or less. In 2002/03 it made 330, with no general payments being for more than £50,000. The accounts noted an early payment of £382,000 to Moorfields Eye Hospital in London, part of an initial £500,000 instalment of a £1 million grant. The second instalment of £500,000 is to be paid on commencement of building works.

The recipients of all but the 50 largest grants are not disclosed, presumably on the grounds that the £818,000 in 280 grants involved was 'not material'. There were 52 grant payments for £10,000 or more, accounting for £1.1 million or nearly 58% of the grant total.

Grants in 2002/03

Grants were categorised into fields such as 'aged', 'arts', 'homeless' and 'youth training', although the trust does have a wide general grantmaking policy.

After the substantial payment to Moorfields Eye Hospital, the largest grants were made to Eton College and University of East Anglia (£50,000 each). Other larger grants include those to Barts & The London NHS Trust (£30,000), Siobhan Davies Dance Company and LAMDA (£25,000 each), Lady Margaret Beaufort Institute of Theology and Abbeyfield Society Ltd

(Eastbourne) (£20,000 each) and Pallant House Gallery Appeal, Woodland Trust, National Galleries of Scotland and Carers UK (£15,000 each).

Recipients of grants of £10,000 each included Brendoncare Foundation Development Trust, Contemporary Arts Society, Young Vic Theatre, Bryson House, Rainbow Trust Children's Charity, Prison Fellowship England and Wales, Purley Park Trust, Gurkha Welfare Trust, St Martin-in-the-Fields Social Care Unit, British Lung Foundation, Operation Smile and Oxfordshire Association for Young People.

New guidelines for applicants

In July 2004 the trust issued formal guidelines as a result of a policy review. The trust states that the guidelines do not totally preclude projects which fall outside the categories detailed, but such projects are much less likely to be funded.

Projects within the UK

The trustees will consider applications from anywhere in the UK, especially those concerned with areas of deprivation.

Broad priorities are

- Healthcare and disability;
- Community support;
- Education and the arts.

Healthcare and disability

The trustees will consider applications in respect of:

- Physical and mental disability: projects involving rehabilitation (including related art and sports programmes); projects particularly for ex-service men and women (including former employees of the emergency services); projects for children (including holidays).
- Hospices and palliative care: projects involving the start-up or piloting of new services; the provision of domiciliary care; the training and education of palliative care specialists, volunteers and carers; the refurbishment of premises; the provision of equipment (excluding in all cases services or costs which are normally funded from statutory sources).
- Medicine: support services (e.g. specialist medical helplines) for those suffering from chronic (e.g. dementia) or terminal conditions; special equipment (not available on the NHS) for the chronically or terminally ill at home.

Community support

The trustees will consider applications in respect of:

- Community: the support of carers; projects in deprived communities (including those recommended by

Community Foundations); projects addressing financial exclusion; the provision of sporting facilities or equipment in deprived areas.

- Drugs and alcohol: the rehabilitation of substance misusers.
- Elderly: projects addressing isolation and loneliness (e.g. befriending schemes); domiciliary support (e.g. respite for carers); restricted residential improvements.
- Ex-offenders: projects working with prisoners and ex-offenders to enhance their living skills and reduce the risk of re-offending.
- Young people: projects which build the confidence, life skills and employment skills of young people in severe need.

Education and the arts
The trustees will consider applications in respect of:

- Arts: projects which enable the disabled and people living in areas of need and poverty to participate in the performance arts and to experience artistic excellence in the performing arts; projects which encourage and give opportunities to young talented people whose circumstances might otherwise deny them.
- Education: projects which help children at risk of exclusion or with exceptionally challenging behaviour to realise their educational potential (e.g. through special support in mainstream education or through special educational provision); projects which encourage and give opportunities to young talented people whose exceptional circumstances might otherwise deny them access to further/higher education.
- Heritage: community projects (excluding large capital appeals) which restore and bring back into use heritage properties and resources, particularly in areas of need and poverty.

Projects outside the UK
The trustees will also consider applications from charities based in the UK which undertake healthcare, health education and community projects in developing countries, including Central Europe and the former Soviet Union; and projects supporting other charitable work in developing countries. The foundation currently spends around 5% of its grants budget on overseas projects.

Types of grant
The foundation currently makes over 300 grants a year, of which the majority are small grants (averaging £3,000). A small number of larger grants (i.e. over £25,000) are awarded each year.

The foundation will in future offer grants under two separate schemes:

- the Small Grant Scheme offers grants of up to £10,000 to organisations with annual incomes below £150,000 p.a. for one-off purposes (e.g. equipment, small capital works etc.) within the priorities set out above, where the grant is needed and will be spent within six months of receipt. Applicants seeking a grant under this scheme should complete form A for Small Grant Applications. (Small grants will not normally be awarded to large national organisations, but applications from local branches for local projects will be considered.)
- the Larger Grant Scheme offers grants of over £10,000 (up to a maximum of £30,000 over three years for revenue grants and up to £50,000 for capital projects) within the priorities set out above.

Applications for revenue grants towards the salary of individual posts will only be considered in respect of specific projects. Capital grants will not normally be offered to very large capital projects (e.g. over £1 m), but individual and discrete elements of very large projects may be considered.

Applicants seeking a grant under this scheme should complete form B for Larger Grant Applications.

Exclusions
The foundation will not normally support foreign charities, except those which are based in the UK and are operating overseas. The foundation does not give grants to other grantmaking bodies.

Applications
On application forms A or B available on written request to the correspondent, which can be submitted at any time during the year. Please note the foundation does not accept telephone requests.

Summaries of applications which are within the foundation's objects and guidelines are sent to the trustees with advice. If there is sufficient support, the application will be submitted to a meeting of the grants committee for a decision.

If a grant of more than £10,000 is under consideration, an assessment visit will be made by one of the staff or an independent assessor.

The grants committee meets quarterly to consider supported applications. Applicants whose appeals have been considered at those meetings will be informed in writing of the trustees' decision within two weeks of the meeting.

Applicants who are unsuccessful are required to wait a minimum of six months from the date of notification before reapplying.

Applicants whose appeals are outside the foundation's objects or current policy will be notified within four weeks of receipt.

The Tubney Charitable Trust

Conservation of the natural environment, welfare of farmed animals
£3.3 million (2003/04)

Beneficial area UK and International (see below).

First Floor, Front Wing, 30–31 Friar Street, Reading RG1 1DX

Tel. 0118 958 6100 **Fax** 0118 959 4400

Email info@tubney.org.uk

Website www.tubney.org.uk

Correspondent Ms Sarah Ridley, Executive Director

Trustees *Jonathan Burchfield; Terry Collins; Jim Kennedy; René Olivieri.*

Charity Commission no. 1061480

Information available Annual report and accounts. Excellent website.

The trust was created in 1997 by Mr Miles Blackwell. Following the deaths in August 2001 of Miles and his wife, Briony the trust has grown substantially in size. In 2003/04 it had assets of £35 million and an income of £16 million, mainly comprised of a one-off donation.

In accordance with the wishes of the founders, the trust has a limited life and is gradually spending down its endowment over an expected eight to ten year period.

Given the trust's short lifespan, the charity seeks to support sustainable, high-quality projects that deliver a long-term impact.

During the first half of 2004 the trust's grantmaking was on hold while it underwent a strategy review. The outcome of this was a narrowing-down of its work into two primary programmes. The trust's open grant making programme now focuses on the:

- Conservation of the natural environment of the UK through achievement of Biodiversity Action Plan targets.
- Improvement of the welfare of farmed animals both in the UK and internationally.

The trust is particularly interested in projects which:

- Provide long-term gains which fully justify the costs and risks.
- Involve collaboration, bringing independent organisations together into cooperative networks.
- Avoid duplication of work by building on the pre-existing knowledge and experience of the applicant or others.
- Take advantage of and augment existing frameworks.
- Leverage other funding.
- Incorporate rigorous monitoring and evaluation and disseminate the knowledge and experience gained.

In addition, the trustees may from time to time establish new initiatives in these or other areas and invite applications of special interest to them.

Guidelines

Conservation of the natural environment programme

Aim

The trust aims to support high-quality projects that will deliver a

long-term impact on the protection and enhancement of the natural environment of the UK through the achievement of UK Biodiversity Action Plan targets (www.ukbap.org.uk).

What

The trust supports projects and organisations that fulfil all of the following criteria:

- Make measurable, significant and sustainable contributions to the achievement of targets outlined in the UK Biodiversity Action Plan for habitats and species.
- Reflect and respond to the current situation and impending changes affecting the natural environment and its conservation.
- Take holistic approaches to nature conservation. For example, landscape scale approaches, enlarging important sites or linking fragmented habitats.
- Incorporate rigorous monitoring and evaluation and disseminate the knowledge and experience gained.
- Provide long-term biodiversity gains which fully justify the costs and risks.

How

The trust likes to support projects and organisations that demonstrate some or all of the following:

- Involve collaboration, bringing independent organisations together into cooperative networks.
- Avoid duplication of work by building on the pre-existing knowledge and experience of the applicant or others (e.g. extending and enhancing pilot programmes).
- Take advantage of and augment existing frameworks (e.g. SSSI designations, agri-environment schemes, etc.).
- Provide public access in balance with the conservation objectives.
- Build on existing environmental initiatives, such as extending nature reserves or developing further projects already achieving gains for biodiversity.
- Seek to develop new techniques or approaches where the design of these is based on current knowledge and best practice.
- Link conservation of priority habitats or species to farming in a sustainable fashion.
- Leverage other funding.

Specific guidance is available for applications dealing with:

- land acquisition
- land owner advisory projects
- species projects.

Welfare of farmed animals programme

Aim

The trust aims to support high-quality projects that have a long-term impact on the improvement of the welfare of farmed animals (all animals bred and reared for the production of food or other products) both in the UK and internationally.

What

The trust supports projects and organisations that fulfil all of the following criteria:

- Achieve demonstrable improvement in the welfare of farmed animals.
- Reflect and respond to the current situation and impending changes affecting the welfare of farmed animals.
- Incorporate rigorous monitoring and evaluation and disseminate the knowledge and experience gained.
- Provide long-term gains in the welfare of farmed animals which fully justify the costs and risks.

How

The trust likes to support projects and organisations that demonstrate some or all of the following:

- Involve collaboration, bringing independent organisations together into cooperative networks.
- Avoid duplication of work by building on the pre-existing knowledge and experience of the applicant or others (e.g. extending and enhancing pilot programmes).
- Take advantage of and augment existing frameworks (e.g. food quality schemes, animal welfare standards and food premium schemes, etc.).
- Translate scientific knowledge of animal welfare into practice.
- Seek to develop new techniques or approaches where the design of these is based on current knowledge and best practice.
- Ensure best practice amongst relevant groups, e.g. farmers, vets, food producers, retailers, consumers etc.
- Create demonstrable changes in public behaviour that result in improvement in the welfare of farmed animals.
- Promote positive links between agriculture, animal welfare and nature conservation.
- Leverage other funding.

Capital costs and revenue costs

The trust supports both capital and revenue costs. However, grants are not made towards capital projects (i.e. buildings and refurbishment costs) unless they are part of a larger project that falls clearly within the aims of the trust. Items of equipment are also unlikely to be funded unless they are part of a wider proposal. The trust does not support endowments.

Minimum and maximum levels of funding

The trust does not consider applications for under £30,000. Since the trust wants to support significant projects that have long-term impact, a maximum level of support has not been set. Applicants should ask for the funding that their project needs. However, please bear in mind that the trust's funds are finite.

All budgets will be carefully scrutinised and must contain detailed itemisations of costs as well as a well-reasoned rationale for expenditures. It must be clearly identified where any grant monies from the trust will be applied.

Funding periods

The trust does not have minimum or maximum periods of funding. The trust wants to support high-quality projects that deliver long-term impact, but these projects must be sustainable without on-going support from the trust.

Alternative funding

While the trust does not have specific matching requirements, it is highly unlikely that an applicant's entire project will be supported. The trust expects that other relevant sources of funding will be explored. Applicants should describe their fundraising strategy, the rationale for their approach to the trust and the likelihood of leveraging funding from other sources.

Exclusions

No grants for:

- individuals.
- non-UK charities.
- expeditions, fieldwork and postgraduate study.
- projects that replace statutory funding and provision.
- retrospective funding.
- projects for which the primary purposes are pure research, publications, conferences, public lectures, curriculum development or the development of websites.
- projects where a significant portion of the expected benefit is job creation or community engagement.
- general fund-raising appeals, deficit-financing or fund-raising costs.
- building construction and renovation or transport purchase where these are a primary objective.
- proposals for which applications have been made to the trust in the previous 12 months.
- permanent endowments.

Specific environmental exclusions:

- urban regeneration schemes.
- horticultural therapy.
- recycling or waste reduction projects.
- playground and school grounds improvements.
- projects for which the promotion of the cultural, historic, or scenic value of the natural environment, or its role as an educational and community amenity, are the primary objectives.
- campaigning where this is a primary objective.

Specific animal welfare exclusions:

- animals bred previously for the production of food or other products which are now kept within collections, etc. with no intention of use of those products.
- animals kept on farms with the intention of using them to assist in farm management, for example cats, sheepdogs, draught animals.
- farm animals kept outside agricultural settings as pets, for example pigs.
- zoos.
- animal rescue centres and hospitals where the primary beneficiaries are not farmed animals.
- welfare issues arising from use of animals in scientific research or commercial product development.
- welfare issues arising from the use of animals in sports.
- campaigns and education about animal welfare issues where these do not clearly lead to measurable improvements in the welfare of farmed animals.

Applications

The trust has a rolling, two stage application process. Eligible applicants must submit an initial application using the online application facility, available through the trust's website. A hard copy of the initial application form is available, if online submission is not possible. Applicants will be informed within two months of the receipt of an initial application as to whether they will be invited to submit a more detailed, second stage application. Detailed applications may only be submitted by invitation.

The trust will contact those applicants invited to submit a detailed application, to discuss the application. In addition, the applicant may be asked to visit the trust, or the trust may visit the project. The trust will assess the application and the applicant will be informed of the trustees' decision within six months of receipt of a completed detailed application.

The trust provides advice and guidance for all applicants to help them to increase their chances of being successful with their application. Applicants are therefore encouraged to contact the trust at any stage of the application process should they require assistance with submitting an application.

The Tudor Trust

Welfare, general

£22.1 million (2003/04)

Beneficial area UK and sub-Saharan Africa.

7 Ladbroke Grove, London W11 3BD

Tel. 020 7727 8522

Website www.tudortrust.org.uk

Correspondent The Trustees

Trustees Mrs Mary Graves; Mrs Helen Dunwell; Dr Desmond Graves; Mrs Penelope Buckler*; Christopher Graves* (also the present director of the trust); Ray Anstice; Mrs Catherine Antcliff; Mrs Louise Collins; Mrs Elizabeth Crawshaw; Matt Dunwell*; James Long*; Ben Dunwell*; Frances Runacres; Monica Barlow* (asterisks indicate membership of the grantmaking trustee committee).

Charity Commission no. 1105580

Information available Excellent annual report and accounts were provided by the trust. Website also includes full guidelines for applicants.

Summary

The trust meets a range of both capital and revenue needs, notably including related building costs, for voluntary and community groups. Grants can be of all sizes, but most are for amounts between £20,000 and £50,000, very often to be paid over a period of two or three years.

Much larger grants can be made, but these are more likely to be the result of proactive work by the trust.

Grants for work outside the UK are targeted and proactive, and therefore applications are not sought for this aspect of the trust's work.

Background

The trust was founded in 1955 by Sir Godfrey Mitchell who endowed it with shares in the Wimpey building company (making this one of the extraordinary number of major trusts with their origins in the building industry). The shareholdings have now been wholly diversified, with investments valued at £270 million in March 2004.

The trust spends from both income and capital, and has so far maintained its levels of grantmaking despite reductions in both income and, to a greater extent, in the value of its investment portfolio.

The trustees include a substantial number of family members, including

Christopher Graves who is also the director of the trust.

Grants committees meet every three weeks and are made up of both trustees and staff (though grants are the overall responsibility of the trustee committee which also itself considers some of the more substantial grants).

General

Grant approvals are categorised as follows:

	No.	2003/04
Youth	105	£2,883,000
Older people	56	£1,458,000
Community	149	£4,040,000
Relationships	112	£2,690,000
Housing	65	£1,991,000
Mental health	91	£2,819,000
Substance misuse	45	£1,543,000
Learning	43	£1,170,000
Financial security	38	£1,363,000
Criminal justice	44	£1,543,000
Overseas	28	£644,000
Total	776	£22,144,000

The staffing is modest for an organisation spending this amount of money and doing so through 700 to 800 grants a year. The 'support costs' of the grantmaking activity represent just 3.9% of the grant total. In part this may be made possible by a substantial degree of voluntary input from trustees.

Review of Grantmaking Activities 2003/04

The following is taken from the annual report:

The new guidelines and website have been well received. A total of 3,583 applications from organisations were received during the year. After careful initial consideration, involving trustees and staff, 920 of these were developed and put forward for discussion by one of the grants committees. Of these, 776 received grants. This compares with the 2,500 applications resulting in 700 grant allocations in the previous year.

The way we record new applications differs slightly from previous years, so direct comparisons may be misleading. However it is quite clear that there has been a substantial rise in approaches to the trust. A good number of these fall within the remit and are strong applications. It is of some concern to us that the trust is unable to support so many of them. However, as a trust with a broad remit, Tudor is looking for new ideas and ways of doing things and we naturally invite a wide range of applicants to contact us. The grants lists demonstrate the variety of work and organisations that we fund. We will continue to review the efficacy of this approach to grant making.

Tudor aims to be a thoughtful funder. The small team strives for efficiency and in this it

is supported by trustees who meet regularly. We continue to monitor the time it takes to consider applications. During the year, it typically took around three months to make a decision on an application, although complex applications requiring extended dialogue can take much longer. Timely funding is an important part of Tudor's work. We continue to review how this is best achieved whilst maintaining administrative costs at around 5% of grant commitments totals.

The appointment of two new grants officers in the previous year and a grants team assistant earlier this year has built Tudor's capacity to work increasingly closely with our applicants. Advice on the eligibility of projects and assistance in developing applications is readily available. We remain keen to respond imaginatively to organisations' real concerns in order to achieve significant long-term change.

The introduction of the new 'Gifts' database and a grants classification system which combines recent work by the Association of Charitable Foundations with our own remit-based system now allows more flexible reporting. Tudor committed £22.1 million during the year (2002/03: £16 million). This is a welcome return to former levels of giving after the exceptional dip in 2003. Encouragingly, each of the nine new remit headings were well represented.

The trust targets areas of work where there is considerable need. We therefore consider it justified for the trust to use its expendable endowment in addressing this need, even if this is likely to diminish the underlying value of the trust fund. Although a budget figure of £20 million was set at the beginning of the year there was an understanding that this might increase if the new funding guidelines encouraged a wealth of strong applications. This is, in fact, what happened.

Within our limited resources we have tried to fund each successful application realistically, whether they are asking for relatively small or large amounts, so that the project has sufficient funds to work effectively. At the beginning of the year the board of trustees encouraged the grants committees to allow the average size of grant to increase without reducing the number of applications to be considered. It is therefore encouraging to note that the average commitment during the year rose to £28,500 (2002/03: £22,800). This trend is set to continue in the coming year, assisted by a modest reduction in the number of grants likely to be given. The trust made 776 grants this year but we anticipate around 650 will be more sustainable in future years.

Guidelines for applicants

The following information is taken from funding guidelines released in October 2004. A new edition of the guidelines was due to be released in April 2005 (see below for a summary). Contact the trust directly or check its website for up-to-date information.

Tudor aims to help break cycles of disadvantage and dependency. Preventing people from being drawn into these cycles is crucially important too. We are therefore interested in supporting projects that increase people's capacity to cope, build their confidence and vision and give them greater control over their future. By supporting an independent and vibrant voluntary sector we hope to unlock the potential that exists within communities, providing new opportunities to achieve lasting change.

Areas of Support

Youth: encouraging confident participation

Young people who are:
- aged between 9–25;
- at risk.

Projects involving:
- detached youth work;
- centres and meeting places where young people participate in decision-making;
- peer education and peer mentoring;
- support for disaffected young men;
- youth organisations which offer counselling for young people.

Older people: supporting sociability and independence

Older people who are:
- isolated;
- living with dementia.

Projects involving:
- intergenerational work;
- new ways of caring for people with dementia;
- service for ethnic minority communities.

Community: renewing the social fabric

People who are:
- living in disadvantaged communities;
- living in marginalised areas;
- experiencing social exclusion.

Projects involving:
- community resources and centres set up and run by local people;
- community managed green spaces in urban areas;
- Gypsy/Traveller communities;
- support for refugees recently granted leave to stay.

Relationships: improving relationships in communities, schools and families

People who are:
- isolated, lonely or just managing;
- in families under stress;
- affected by domestic violence, especially children.

Projects involving:
- work with parents, especially fathers;
- contact centres
- work with perpetrators of domestic violence;
- domestic violence outreach services.

Housing: prevention and routes out of homelessness

People who are:
- homeless or at risk of becoming homeless;
- young and vulnerable.

Projects involving:
- prevention of homelessness or family conciliation;
- homeless families;
- user participation/user-led work;
- resettlement and on-going support;
- affordable housing in remote areas.

Health: Mental health: positive approaches to mental health

People who have:
- mental health difficulties;
- a personality disorder;
- a brain injury;
- an eating disorder or who self-harm.

Projects involving:
- promotion of children's emotional wellbeing;
- self-help or user-led work;
- crisis services;
- services for ethnic minorities;
- social firms.

Health: Substance misuse: programmes for prevention and rehabilitation

People who are:
- young and at risk;
- misusing drugs, alcohol or solvents;
- families/carers of misusers;
- substance misusers with mental health difficulties.

Projects involving:
- peer education schemes;
- self-help;
- services for ethnic minorities;
- residential centres for parents with young children;
- complementary therapies.

Learning: new learning opportunities

People who are:
- needing extra support in their learning;
- missing out on education.

Projects involving:
- home/school/community links;
- alternatives for those not attending school.

Financial security: routes out of poverty

People who are:
- excluded from mainstream financial services;
- only just managing.

Projects involving:
- financial literacy
- integrated money advice and budgeting schemes;
- community credit schemes;
- community finance.

Criminal justice: reducing offending and promoting rehabilitation

People who are:
- young and at risk of offending;
- families/friends of offenders;
- offenders at pre/post release stage;
- mentally/personality disordered offenders.

Projects involving:
- alternatives to custody;
- accommodation;
- strengthening family relationships/visiting;
- therapeutic regimes/interventions;
- routes to employment.

How we fund

Social problems are frequently complex and difficult to resolve. Projects focusing their work in these areas will sometimes have unpredictable outcomes and timescales. Uncertainties are to be expected and risk taking is an integral part of our grant making. We aim to be a responsive and supportive funder by being straightforward, accessible and flexible. We are keen to respond imaginatively to organisations' real concerns in order to achieve significant, long term change. New thinking about familiar problems is welcomed.

Who we fund

The trustees particularly want to work with smaller, under-resourced organisations which are people centred and provide direct services. We may also consider exceptional projects from larger organisations which address Tudor's aims in imaginative ways.

What we fund

Projects meeting Tudor's aims by addressing the issues can be considered for support provided they have a charitable purpose. However our resources are limited and only a proportion of applications can be funded. The trustees have therefore drawn up priorities for their grant making. The Grants Team can advise organisations on the eligibility of projects and assist applicants in developing their applications for consideration by the trustees.

The trustees read applications brought to the grant making committees in detail. In

taking final decisions the trustees have to make difficult judgements. Of the many good applications presented only some can be offered funding.

Grants in 2003/04

Since this trust was last researched its annual report now includes a geographical breakdown of where grants were made and their value. There is also now a comprehensive grants list included in the report, with an explanation of the purpose of every grant over £10,000 and its duration.

Geographical Spread

Tudor has maintained its policy of making grants across a broad spectrum of need throughout the UK. We are now able to report on the geographical location of the projects we have supported rather than the address of the organisation's head office. It would be unwise to draw strategic conclusions from variations in geographical spread from year to year. It is perhaps worth noting that projects in the South West received considerable support this year, with 11% of our funds going to projects in this area. We also renewed our commitment to funding in Northern Ireland again this year after the dip in both the number and value of grants made in 2003.

Grants made by region, by value in 2003/04

Region	No. of grants	Value of grants	%
East Midlands	29	£538,000	2
Eastern	44	£1,306,000	6
London	199	£6,131,000	28
North East	37	£1,117,000	5
North West	82	£2,441,000	11
Northern Ireland	25	£741,000	3
Scotland	58	£1,494,000	7
South East	66	£1,922,000	9
South West	80	£2,379,000	11
Wales	23	£644,000	3
West Midlands	40	£912,000	4
Yorkshire & the Humber	64	£1,755,000	8
Rest of the World	29	£765,000	3
Total	776	£22,145,000	100

Funding for Greater London continues to be significant with over £6 million going to London-based projects. Once again the boroughs with high levels of disadvantage feature strongly.

London boroughs receiving most funding in 2003/04

Borough	No. of grants	Value of grants
Islington	16	£730,000
Tower Hamlets	22	£729,000
Lambeth	20	£609,000
Camden	20	£555,000
Westminster	13	£505,000
Kensington & Chelsea	16	£450,000

Tudor remains committed to reaching parts of the country which are under-represented in the receipt of grants. We now attend some carefully selected 'meet the funder' events in order to talk to potential applicants. Visiting a range of the projects we fund, or are considering funding, not only helps us to gauge the quality of the project but gives us a better sense of the strength and variety of the local voluntary sector. We continue to build our visiting capacity, having visited 204 projects in 2003/04 (2002/03: 173).

The inclusion of a full, classified list of grants in the trust's annual report now enables the reader to appreciate the scale of its work throughout the UK. Examples of beneficiaries and grants made in each of its programmes are as follows:

Community

- Hull Community Church – £100,000 for a new, larger community building to replace the the current premises housing various charitable projects in Hull;
- Federation of City Farms & Community Gardens – £90,000 over three years for the core costs of an organisation which supports, promotes and represents city farms and community gardens throughout the UK;
- Employability Forum – £75,000 over three years to help refugees integrate more fully into the UK, particularly within a work environment;
- Fiveways – £60,000 for a joint project with Mid Wales Housing Association to build a multi-voluntary agency office based in Llandrindod Wells;
- South Leeds Elderly and Community Group – £50,000 for the refurbishment of a new Healthy Living Centre in Leeds;
- Number One Community Project – £40,000 over two years for the salary of the project manager for a community centre in Derby;
- Shantallow Community Residents' Association – £30,000 over two years towards the salary of a new coordinator to develop community based services and activities in the Greater Shantallow area of Derry, Northern Ireland;
- Trust Project – £24,000 over two years for the development of this new organisation for women involved in prostitution in South London;
- Worsley Mesnes South Community Action Group – £15,000 towards the cost of fitting out and furnishing a new community centre in Wigan;
- Croxteth & Gilmoss Community Federation – £10,000 towards the salary of the executive officer post of a community project in Liverpool.

Beneficiaries of less than £10,000 included Lancashire Global Education

Centre (£9,000), Brookfield Spaceplace (£8,000), Flower and Dean Estate (£5,000), Dingle Multi-Agency Centre Ltd (£3,000) and Grange Residents Group (£1,000).

Criminal Justice

- Community Links for Ex-Offenders – £100,000 over two years for running and salary costs of a new organisation, supporting offenders at the pre- and post-release stage, encouraging them to make a positive contribution to their local community;
- Pakistani Resource Centre – £91,000 over three years for the salary of the chief executive officer for an organisation working with the South Asian community in Manchester around welfare rights, criminal justice and mental health;
- Action for Prisoners' Families – £70,000 over three years for the core costs of a national federation of services supporting the families of prisoners;
- Prisoners Abroad – £50,000 over two years for core costs, including salaries, to support offenders in prisons abroad and their families at home in the UK;
- Shannon Trust – £40,000 over two years for the running costs of a reading scheme in prisons throughout the UK;
- Contact Cheshire Support Group – £30,000 towards start-up costs of a visitors' centre at HM Women's Prison, Styal;
- Open College of the Arts – £20,000 over two years towards a pilot scheme providing distance learning art courses for prisoners;
- Prison Phoenix Trust – £15,000 towards the running costs of yoga and meditation workshops in prisons;
- Ebony Steelband Trust – £10,000 for steelpan workshops to be held in the young offenders section of two London prisons.

There were five smaller grants made to Dialogue Trust (£8,000), Feltham Community Association (£5,000) and Mellow Yellow Information Services (£3,000).

Financial Security

- Citizens Advice Bureau: Vale Royal – £90,000 over three years for a new financial literacy advisor post in Northwich, Cheshire;
- Wessex Reinvestment Trust – £80,000 over two years for the salary of a loans manager to provide a wide range of affordable loan finance to small businesses and social enterprises;

- Barnsley Credit Union – £50,000 over two years towards the salary of a debt worker for a money advice and budgeting service;
- Portsmouth Area Regeneration Trust – £40,000 over two years for running costs to support PART's charitable activities as a community development finance institution;
- Who Cares? Trust – £30,000 for the production and distribution of a CD on financial literacy for young people in care;
- Just Credit Union Ltd – £20,000 over three years for the development of a rural credit union in Shropshire;
- Citizens Advice Bureau: Port Talbot – £16,000 over two years for the salary of a young person's advisor providing CAB advice at a local youth centre;
- Citizens Advice Bureau: Selby – £10,000 for the salary of a rural outreach worker in Yorkshire.

Out of 38 grants in this category, over half were made to Citizens Advice Bureaux around the UK, however grants are not made towards their core work.

Housing

- Centrepoint Soho – £120,000 over three years for salaries to strengthen services for young care leavers across London;
- Big Issue Foundation – £90,000 over three years for regional managers' salaries to support local, regional and national development and growth;
- YMCA: Birkenhead – £60,000 over two years for the executive director's post during a rebuilding programme;
- Save the Family Trust Ltd – £50,000 over two years for a new full-time settlement and outreach worker to support homeless families in securing permanent accommodation in Chester and North Wales;
- Doorstep Homeless Families Project – £40,000 over two years for a family development worker at a centre for homeless families in North West London;
- Poole Housing Forum – £30,000 over three years for a project worker at the Poole Accommodation and Support Scheme providing practical support for homeless people;
- Crisis Fareshare South Yorkshire – £20,000 over two years for the running costs of a food distribution service;
- Nightstop Southampton – £10,000 over two years for the running costs of a nightstop service to provide short-term accommodation to homeless young people.

Smaller grants included those to Acton Homeless Concern and Streetwise Opera (£5,000 each), Wycombe Rent Deposit (£4,000) and Advocates for the Homeless (£3,000).

Learning

- Real Action – £90,000 over three years towards the running costs of literacy projects for children, teenagers and adults at the organisation's base in Queen's Park and at other venues in North Paddington, London;
- Resource Unit for Supplementary and Mother Tongue Schools – £75,000 over three years for the training and support of supplementary schools in North London;
- West Bromwich African Caribbean Resource Centre – £60,000 over two years for the salary of the manager of the African Caribbean Education Support Service;
- Family Nurturing Network – £50,000 over two years for the Family Connections and/or Dinosaur school projects in Oxfordshire, for children with emotional and behaviour projects;
- School Home Support – £40,000 over two years for core costs to support a period of consolidation following merger and rapid expansion;
- Binoh of Manchester – £30,000 over two years for the salary of a youth outreach worker to support young people excluded or at risk of exclusion from Jewish schools in Manchester;
- Cookstown & District Women's Group – £15,000 for the refurbishment of the Positive Steps Learning Centre, a community education centre in County Tyrone;
- Living Well Trust – £10,000 for a pilot project in Carlisle, working with young people who have voluntarily excluded themselves from school.

Smaller grants included those to Silai for Skills (£8,000), Mile Project (£6,000), Multi-Cultural Education & Youth (£5,000) and Centre for Innovation (£3,000).

Mental Health

- Home Farm Trust Ltd – £150,000 towards the cost of building and equipping a purpose built six-person residential unit in Hertfordshire, supporting people who have learning disabilities who have developed dementia;
- Restormel Association of Mental Health – £70,000 over three years to continue and develop the Rural Community Link Project managing

self-help drop-in and craft groups for people with mental health problems in isolated villages in the Cornish borough of Restormel;
- Young Minds Trust – £60,000 over two years for the salary of a deputy director for an organisation promoting the mental health of young people;
- WAND – £40,000 over two years towards the post of a manager for an advocacy service for people with mental health problems in North Devon;
- Brent Adolescent Centre – £30,000 over 18 months to cover the shortfall in income at a specialist mental health service for young people who would not generally access mainstream services;
- Prevention of Professional Abuse Network – £10,000 for the core costs of an organisation which addresses abuse by professionals working in the health care and social work fields.

Smaller grants included those to Mind – Taunton & West Somerset (£7,000), Headway – Ipswich & East Suffolk (£5,000), Resources for Autism (£3,000) and Friendship Centre Moldgreen (£2,000).

Older People

- Abbeyfield Epping Society Ltd – £150,000 towards the capital costs of building and extension to Cunningham House to provide specialist dementia care;
- St Mary's Convent and Nursing Home – £100,000 for the upgrading of residential and nursing facilities in Chiswick, London for elderly people;
- Abbeyfield Paisley Society – £75,000 towards the capital costs of a nine-bed dementia unit for older people at a new care home and day centre in Paisley;
- Foleshill Multi-Cultural Open Forum – £50,000 over two years towards the salary of a social worker and the running costs of the Foleshill Elders Group in Coventry;
- North Essex Advocacy Teams – £40,000 over two years for running costs to maintain and expand an advocacy service for vulnerable older people living at home and in residential care;
- Answer – £30,000 for the building costs of a new day centre in Whitburn, West Lothian for older people. particularly those with dementia, mental health problems or depressive illnesses;
- Yemeni Elderly in Small Heath & Sparkbrook – £10,000 over two years

for volunteer training and expenses for work with Yemeni elders in Birmingham.

Smaller grants included those made to Lynemouth Day Centre (£7,500), Acredale House Day Centre (£6,000), Latin America Golden Years Club (£5,000), and Vassall Elderly Project (£3,000).

Overseas

- Resources Oriented Development Initiatives – £76,000 over two years for a prisoner rehabilitation programme in Kenya, using sustainable agriculture;
- Chikukwa Ecological Land Use Community Trust – £30,000 over three years for the running costs of a sustainable agriculture training centre in Zimbabwe;
- Gaia Foundation – £15,000 for the development phase of the Earth Community Network;
- Young & Elderly in Society – £10,000 for the production of a training manual and training on sustainable agriculture with three women's groups in Uganda.

Small grants included those to St Jude Family Projects (£7,000), Royal Higher Education Society (£4,000 - staff grant) and Afghan Reading Project (£2,000 - staff grant).

Relationships

- St John's Diocesan Home – £130,000 for the purchase or refurbishment of a property which will allow St John's to extend and improve residential services for children who have been at risk of abuse or violence;
- Caldecott Foundation – £75,000 over three years towards the salaries and running costs of the Throughcare Service supporting children through the process of leaving a therapeutic community school;
- Cornwall Domestic Violence Forum – £60,000 over two years towards the costs of a Men and Relationships Programme in Cornwall, for perpetrators of domestic violence;
- Knowle West Development Trust – £50,000 over three years for the running costs of the Social Services Project supporting families in Bristol;
- Schoolhouse Education Project – £30,000 over two years for the expansion of youth and family counselling in 10 schools in Greenwich and Lewisham;
- Inquest – £20,000 over two years for a caseworker to provide a specialist advice and support service to bereaved

families dealing with the inquest system;

- Midlothian Women's Aid – £10,000 over two years for an outreach worker at a women's refuge, to support women and children living in the community.

Most of the smaller grants in this category were made to Homestart schemes around the UK. Others included those to Family Mediation Highland (£9,000), Blaenau Gwent Domestic Abuse Services (£5,000) and Henry Spink Foundation (£2,000 - staff grant).

Substance Misuse

- Adfam National – £90,000 over three years for the Road to Release family support project at Holloway prison;
- Drugline Lancashire Ltd – £75,000 over three years for the development of a volunteer programme, including accredited training in drugs work;
- Kenward Trust – £50,000 for a new wing including detox facility at this residential drug/alcohol rehabilitation centre near Maidstone, Kent;
- Fast Forward Positive Lifestyles Ltd – £40,000 over two years to involve marginalised young people as volunteer drugs educators, based in Edinburgh;
- Liverpool Social Partnership in Drugs Prevention – £30,000 over two years for the Fixers Project, which trains unemployed people as community drug workers;
- Addiction Rehabilitation Centre – £20,000 emergency funding for a day rehabilitation programme for substance misusers in Manchester;
- Open Road Visions Ltd – £10,000 towards the purchase of new premises for their centre for substance misusers in Colchester.

Four smaller grants were made to Addicted Women and Youth Outreach (£7,000), Alleyway Trust (£6,000), York Alcohol Advice Service (£5,500) and Crime Reduction Initiatives (£2,000 - staff grant).

Youth

- Attlee Foundation – £100,000 for a new youth and community centre in Spitalfields, London;
- Muslim Youth Helpline – £60,000 over three years for the salary of a director for a new national helpline for troubled young Muslims;
- Straight Talking Project – £50,000 over two years for the running costs of a peer mentoring project working with young people aged 13 to 16 focusing

on the realities of teenage pregnancy and parenthood;

- Felixstowe Youth Development Group – £40,000 over two years for the salary of a project manager for an open access drop-in centre for young people;
- Ayr Churches Together – £30,000 over three years for The Ark, a new alcohol-free drop-in centre/club for young people in Ayr;
- Kingswood Bus Project – £20,000 over two years towards the salaries of youth workers for a mobile youth project visiting villages in South Gloucestershire;
- Waverley Youth Project – £10,000 over two years for the running costs of three evening youth groups in Surrey, taking referrals from other agencies.

Smaller grants included those to Devon Youth Association (£9,000), Campden and District Peelers Trust (£8,000), Soul's Harbour Pentecostal Church (£7,000), Linden Church Trust (£6,500), Durham City Centre Youth Project (£2,500) and Northolme Residents' Association (£1,500).

Applying for funding from the Tudor Trust in 2005/06

The following was provided by the trust as a summary of its grantmaking policy over the next couple of years - full revised guidelines were due April 2005:

The Tudor Trust was 50 in March 2005. In its first 50 years it has given over £430 million in grants. During its Golden Jubliee year the trustees have decided to review Tudor's previous work as part of continuing discussions to inform its future direction. To help achieve this, the trust will contain its funding during 2005/06 so that it can concentrate on developing its plans for April 2006.

- For one year, from 1 April 2005 to 31 March 2006, the Tudor Trust will only consider applications from organisations which were awarded a grant by Tudor in the previous five years (to qualify, the grant committee letter must be dated on or after 1 April 2000).
- Projects will only be considered if they meet current funding priorities. These are contained in Tudor's funding guidelines. Even applications which appear to fall within the trustees' current priorities may be rejected after an initial assessment; unfortunately Tudor does not have the resources to fund all good projects and has to be selective at an early stage.
- The Tudor Trust will only fund one project at a time for any organisation. New projects can only be put forward once support for a previous project has expired

(usually 12 months after the date of the last payment).

Please do not apply unless you are sure you are eligible. If in doubt, please contact the Tudor Trust for advice on 020 7727 8522.

Comment

The practice of trustees meeting every three weeks to consider applications alongside the grants team, rather than working primarily from written reports which often refer to discussions or visits many weeks earlier, is a model of good practice.

The trust has also addressed suggestions made in the last edition of this guide regarding improvements to its annual report. Happily the report now contains a comprehensive list of grants, the purpose for which they were made and over how many years. Geographical distribution of funds is also illustrated. These inclusions serve to fully illustrate the extent of the trust's support throughout the voluntary sector and its obvious impact.

Exclusions

This exclusions list details what we do not fund at the moment. In some cases we will consider a certain type of project if it fits under one remit, but not another. For example, while we don't fund counselling under our Health or Relationships remits, youth organisations offering counselling for young people are a current priority under our Youth remit. If you are in any doubt about whether we would consider your application, please contact us for advice.

So unless specifically mentioned in our current priorities, we are unable to consider for funding:

- individuals – including students
- statutory authorities
- larger national charities enjoying widespread support
- organisations whose main purpose is working with:
  - people with a learning disability
  - people with a physical disability
  - people with a physical illness
  - people with a sensory impairment
  - people with an Autistic Spectrum Disorder
- the core work of:
  - advice & information giving organisations including CABx
  - Community foundations
  - Councils for voluntary Service

– infrastructure organisations

– Volunteer bureaux or centres

- projects whose main focus is:

Community

- community transport
- playgrounds/play equipment
- promotion of volunteering
- summer schemes
- under 5's provision and children's centres
- village and church halls

Criminal justice

- crime prevention
- victims of crime and abuse

Health

- carers
- counselling
- hospitals & hospices
- medical care
- medical research

Learning

- adult learning
- after school and homework clubs
- breakfast clubs
- bursaries and scholarships
- employment training
- mainstream schools and colleges
- IT training centres
- mother tongue classes/cultural activities
- research
- universities

Relationships

- adoption services
- bereavement
- counselling

Other

- animal charities
- arts
- conferences and events
- conservation of buildings, flora & fauna
- endowment appeals
- expeditions/overseas travel/activities promoting
- personal development
- holidays/holiday centres
- publications
- promotion of religion
- museums/places of entertainment/ leisure clubs
- scouts, guides and other uniformed youth groups
- social enterprise
- sport
- Projects overseas:

Tudor currently runs a proactive, targeted programme of funding promoting sustainable agriculture in sub-Saharan Africa. We cannot consider any new applications from overseas projects.

Applications

Please note that from 1 April 2005 to 31 March 2006 the Tudor Trust is only considering applications from organisations which have received a grant from the trust in the previous five years. Contact the trust directly to check eligibility.

Tudor does not use an application form. Please send your application by post. Applications cannot be accepted as faxes or e-mails.

Please address applications to 'The Trustees'. We acknowledge all applications.

There are no deadlines for sending us your project proposals. All applications are assessed on a rolling programme.

Tudor wants to reach a clear understanding of the people and the ideas behind a project proposal. We exist to make grants not to create paperwork. However, the trustees need a certain minimum level of information to be able to make decisions. Tudor's staff aims to help applicants provide that information.

Please read through the points below carefully before making an application. If you still have questions about how to apply, or need more guidance or information once you have read these guidelines, please phone us on 020 7727 8522. We will be happy to call you back if necessary.

Application process

All applications go through an initial assessment process (which involves a trustee) and applicants will be quickly informed if Tudor cannot consider their proposal. This may happen to some applications even though they appear to fall within the trustees' current priorities. Unfortunately insufficient resources mean we have to be selective even at this early stage.

The Grants Team will help develop those applications likely to go to one of the grant making committees of trustees. As far as possible, the same Grants Officer will stay in touch with your organisation throughout the process. The Grants Officer will contact you for more details, if they are needed, in writing or by telephone. Projects may also be visited by a trustee or member of staff.

Tudor tries to consider grant applications quickly. We aim to make a decision on most applications within 12 weeks. This is not a hard and fast rule – in exceptional circumstances a decision can be made more quickly, and complex applications can of course take longer to assess.

Currently the trustees meet every three weeks to consider applications through a Grants Committee and trustee Committee. The trustees see most of the papers you provide with your application. They will discuss your application in detail and usually make an immediate decision on funding. Occasionally they may request further information or an assessment visit. The trustees have to make difficult decisions, which can seldom be reviewed.

The Grants Officer will send you a letter with the trustees' final decision. If a grant has been approved this will include straightforward terms for its release.

The trustees are always interested to hear how your work progresses. We try to build supportive relationships with organisations. Your proposal should outline your objectives and how you will know you have achieved them. We expect a clear report about the way the project is developing. What to include in this report will also form part of the terms attached to the grant. A trustee or a member of staff may also visit your organisation during the course of a grant to see how things are going.

Types of funding available

We can consider applications for core costs, project costs, building and equipment costs, and any other costs crucial to your work.

Funding may initially be for a period of up to three years. Alternative finance schemes (including loan funding) can occasionally be considered. Retrospective funding is not available.

It is important that your organisation applies for what it actually needs. We are looking for applications that are realistic but also allow you to work effectively. The Trustees need to understand what your project aims to achieve, and what it is likely to cost, even if Tudor cannot cover all the funding. It is important for you to tell us what money you have raised so far and what other ideas you have for raising funds.

The average grant awarded in 2003/04 was for £28,500, and most of our grants lie between £10,000 and £60,000. We also make a substantial number of grants for amounts between £1,000 and £10,000 (we do not usually make grants of less than £1,000) and some grants over the £100,000 level each year.

What to include in a full application

Set out below is some of the information you might like to consider including in your application. However the Trustees are keen for you to describe the project in your own words in a way that suits you. They welcome photographs and other materials describing your work, especially if they are easily photocopied.

- A brief summary of your proposal: as part of your introductory letter you could include a brief outline of your organisation, what you aim to achieve and the costs involved.
- What you do: a brief history and description of current work of the whole organisation, including numbers of staff, volunteers and beneficiaries involved.
- Why you are seeking the Trust's help: a more detailed description of the project/proposals/area of work for which funding is requested. For example, you could say what the need is, who will benefit and how, what activities will take place and what services you want to provide. Information on opening hours or a weekly timetable, the project's catchment area, maps and details of the population you are serving are all helpful.
- Who will benefit: estimates of numbers of different people involved or likely to be involved in your project and how you will assess its success and the quality of the services provided.
- Who else is involved: numbers of staff and volunteers involved in the project for which you are seeking funding. If you are applying for funding for a specific post please include a job description.
- Similar organisations: how does your work complement other projects in the area? Is there an opportunity to work with them?
- How much it will cost: an annual breakdown of the costs of the project over the whole period you are asking funding for. For revenue costs this might be core organisational costs, salaries, premises costs, activities and training. For capital costs, these might include building costs, VAT, fees, furniture and equipment.
- Where you are seeking funding: details of where else you have applied or intend to apply for funding, including grants already promised or received.
- When you need the funding: an approximate start date for the project and for how many years it is initially planned to run.

- Building and refurbishment projects: A3/A4 drawings of building plans and details of lease arrangements and planning permissions. Budgets showing how you will meet the ongoing costs of running the new/extended/refurbished building are generally required.
- Please include in your application:
- your charity number (if you are a registered charity),
- a copy of your constitution/governing document or information on how your group operates (if you are not a registered charity)
- an income and expenditure budget for the whole organisation for the current year. If your organisation is a subsidiary please send both sets of financial information, and
- a copy of your most recent annual report and accounts (or a copy of a recent financial/bank statement if the organisation is too new to have annual accounts).

Tudor does not use an application form. Please send your application by post.

Re-applying for funding

Tudor will normally just fund one project at a time for any organisation. New projects can only be put forward for funding once the Trust's support for a previous project has expired.

If your organisation has previously received a refusal from Tudor you are asked not to re-apply for at least twelve months from that date.

If you are already receiving revenue funding from Tudor and would like to apply for further funding for the same project, you should contact us well before the end of the funding period.

The Douglas Turner Trust

General

£411,000 (2001/02)

Beneficial area West Midlands, particularly Birmingham; UK.

1 The Yew Trees, High Street, Henley-in-Arden B95 5BN

Tel. 01564 793085

Correspondent J E Dyke, Trust Administrator

Trustees *W S Ellis; D P Pearson; T J Lunt; Sir Christopher Stuart White.*

Charity Commission no. 227892

Information available Accounts were on file at the Charity Commission.

The trust makes grants and loans to registered charities, mostly in the West Midlands. Most of the income is used to support charities on an annual basis, providing they can prove their need for continuing support. Grants are made to a variety of charities, most of which are local social welfare organisations. Awards are typically in the range of £1,000 to £5,000 but go as high as £40,000.

In 2001/02 the trust had assets of £12 million and an income of £432,000. Grants were made to 81 organisations totalling £411,000.

The largest grants were £40,000 to Age Concern – Birmingham for the TV fund and £30,000 to Acorns Children's Hospice. Other large grants were £18,000 to Christian Aid, £15,000 to Merlin for the India Earthquake Appeal and as an annual donation and £10,000 each to British Red Cross, Compton Hospice, Historic Churches Preservation Trust, Royal Academy of Arts, St Luke's Hospital for the Clergy, St Martin's Renewal Campaign and St Mary's Hospice.

Other beneficiaries included MSA (£7,000), Birmingham City Mission (£6,500), 870 House and Foundation for Conductive Education (£5,000 each), Asian Welfare Association (£2,000), Action Force Volunteers and Dodford Children's Holiday Farm (£1,000 each), Boys Brigade 39th Company (£750) and Birmingham Music Festival (£500).

In 2002/03 the trust had a total expenditure of £405,000. Unfortunately, although submitted by the trust to the Charity Commission, the accounts for that year had not made it to the public files for inspection.

Exclusions

No grants to individuals or non-registered charities.

Applications

In writing to the correspondent with a copy of your latest annual report and accounts. There are no application forms. The trustees meet in February, May, August and October to consider applications, which should be submitted in the month prior to each meeting. Telephone enquiries may be made before submitting an appeal.

Trustees of Tzedakah

Jewish, welfare

About £400,000 (2002/03)
Beneficial area UK.

Brentmead House, Britannia Road, London N12 9RU

Tel. 020 8446 6767

Correspondent C Hollander

Trustee *Trustees of Tzedakah Ltd.*

Charity Commission no. 251897

Information available Accounts are on file at the Charity Commission.

The objectives of this charity are:

- the relief of poverty.
- advancement of education.
- advancement of religion.
- such other charitable purposes, causes or projects as the trustees see fit.

It makes a small number of large grants and a large number of small grants to meet these aims.

In 2002/03 the trust had an income of £455,000 and a total expenditure of £473,000. Grants were made totalling about £400,000. Unfortunately, no further details were available for this year.

Previous beneficiaries include Gevuras Ari Torah Academy, Telz Institutions, Friends of Or Someach, Friends of Poneviez Yeshiva, Hasmonean Girls School, Woodstock Sinclair Trust, Torah Temimoh, Lubavitch Foundation, Hendon Adath Yisroel Synagogue, Menorah Foundation School, Beis Yisroel Trust Fund, BSD Trust Fund, Mayim Rabim Schotz Yeshivas, Menorah Primary School, CWCT Trust Fund, Marie Curie Cancer Care and Acdut Aid Society.

Comment

There was no response to repeated written requests for a copy of the most recent annual report and accounts, despite the requirement to provide these on demand.

Despite ample warning, and their obligation to the contrary, the Charity Commission were unable to give us sight of this trust's accounts.

Exclusions

Grants only to registered charities. No grants to individuals.

Applications

This trust states that it does not respond to unsolicited applications.

The Underwood Trust

General

£408,000 (2002/03)
Beneficial area Wiltshire and Scotland and UK-wide.

32 Haymarket, London SW1Y 4TP

Website www.theunderwoodtrust.org.uk

Correspondent Antony P Cox, Manager

Trustees *Robin Clark; Patricia Clark; Jack C Taylor.*

Charity Commission no. 266164

Information available Information was taken from the trust's website.

'The trust currently supports UK registered charities and other offical charitable organisations which benefit society nationally or locally in Wiltshire and Scotland.

'The Trust anticipates the annual investment income available for grant making for the next few years will be around £500,000. However the trust has given and intends to continue to give annual support to a number of charities of around £250,000. Hence this only leaves around £250,000 available for new applications each year.

'In the current year applications are invited at a level between £15,000 and £25,000. Grants are normally only made for one year, although this may cover a project lasting over a longer period. As you will appreciate this will only result in around 15 grants being made in the year from the applications received.

'If you see larger grants on the donation list it is likely that these are part of the trust's annual support or as a proactive intervention by the trustees, rather than from an application. Please do not ask for amounts larger than £25,000 as these will not be considered.'

During the financial year ending April 2004, the trustees distributed a large amount of the accumulated reserves. Consequently, funds held by the trust are at a very low level. Due to the fact that the income of the trust does not rise evenly during the year, the trustees forecast they will have no available funds before January 2005. The trustees are unable to consider any new applications in this period, as only donations previously committed will be given support.

Grants are categorised under the following headings:

- Medicine and health
- Welfare
- The environment
- Education and sciences
- The arts.

In 2002/03 the trust had an income of £538,000 and gave grants totalling £408,000. According to the trust's website (accessed July 2004), in the last financial year the following major grants were made:

Medicine and health

In total nine grants were made amounting to £86,000. Donations included £25,000 to National Eye Research Centre, £10,000 each to British Stammering Association, Prospect Foundation Limited and Restoration of Appearance and Function Trust, £5,000 to Evolution Appeal – Swindon and £1,000 to Highland Hospice.

Welfare

Grants totalling £122,000 were made to 11 organisations. Donations included £25,000 to Centrepoint, £19,000 to Crime Concern, £12,000 to Wiltshire Blind Association, £10,000 each to Counsel and Care, Police Foundation, Wiltshire and Swindon Community Foundation and Windmill Hill City Farm, £5,000 to Youth Action Wiltshire and £1,000 to The Story of Christmas.

The environment

In total nine donations were made totalling £107,000. Grants included £35,000 to Friends of the Earth Trust Limited, £25,000 to Aigas Trust, £10,000 each to Game Conservancy Scottish Research Trust, St James Conservation Trust and Wiltshire Wildlife Trust, £5,000 to Princes Foundation and £1,000 each to Game Conservancy Trust and RSPB.

Education and sciences

In total four grants were made amounting to £43,000. These were £22,000 to Guildhall School Trust, £10,000 each to Childnet International and Farms for City Children and £1,000 to Countryside Foundation.

The arts

A total of five grants were made each for £10,000. Beneficiaries were International Musician's Seminar, London Philharmonic Orchestra, Music For Youth, Royal Overseas League Golden Jubilee Trust and Scottish Opera.

Exclusions

No grants to:

- individuals directly.
- political activities.
- commercial ventures or publications.
- the purchase of vehicles including minibuses.
- overseas travel or holidays.
- retrospective grants or loans.
- direct replacement of statutory funding or activities that are primarily the responsibility of central or local government.
- large capital, endowment or widely distributed appeals.

Applications

In July 2004 the trust stated on their website that:

'The trust will not consider any new applications in the period April 2004 to January 2005'.

In any event, all applicants should review the guidance on the trust's website and complete the application form which can be found on there.

Unemployed Voluntary Action Fund

Voluntary projects engaging unemployed people as volunteers

£1.4 million (2002/03)

Beneficial area Scotland.

Comely Park House, 80 New Row, Dunfermline, Fife KY12 7EJ

Tel. 01383 620780 **Fax** 01383 626129

Email uvaf@uvaf.co.uk

Website www.uvaf.org.uk

Correspondent Mrs Sandra Carter, Chief Executive

Trustees *Susan Elsley, Convener; Farkhanda Chaudhry; Philomena de Lima; Carol Downie; Susan Elsley; John*

Hawthorne; John Knox; Stuart McGregor; Laurie Naumann; Jonathan Squire.

Scottish Charity no. SC005229

Information available Full accounts, report and review were provided by the trust.

The fund has the following aims:

- overcoming social exclusion through providing opportunities for unemployed people to volunteer
- introducing 'purpose' through volunteering for people with higher support needs
- promoting job readiness through volunteering
- promoting racial equality and reducing racial disadvantage through funding and benefiting ethnic minority groups
- providing opportunities for volunteering, for its intrinsic value, which are inclusive
- assisting projects in the fields of health, social and community development which tackle social exclusion across Scotland.

Projects must aim to meet needs in one or more of the fields of social and community development or health. The voluntary activity must develop a service which will positively assist those involved as volunteers and its beneficiaries. Projects should show how they will:

- combat exclusion by reducing isolation, improving communication and increasing self-worth and independence
- provide ongoing, regular, structured voluntary work
- enhance and improve skills which promote job readiness, educational opportunities and personal development.

The application should show evidence of the need for the service and assess realistically what measurable change can be achieved.

In 2002/03 the fund had assets of £59,000 and an income of £1.6 million, of which £872,000 was received in 'grant–as–aid' from The Scottish Executive to distribute to local projects which create opportunities for volunteering primarily for people not in work, £500,000 was received from the Ethnic Minority Grant Scheme (EMGS) to promote racial equality and reduce racial disadvantage, £250,000 for Valuing Volunteers, and a total of £20,000 was recieved from the Community Fund and Lloyds TSB Charitable Foundation towards action research. Grants totalled

£1.4 million and were broken down as follow:

Major grants programme – 36 grants totalling £709,000

Grants are given for three years. Organisations receiving their first payment included: SOLVE (Volunteers with Higher Support Needs – Clydesdale) to develop and support opportunities for people with higher needs, as a result of mental health difficulties, disabilities or behavioural problems to volunteer (£28,000); Ark Trust for a volunteer co–ordinator helping to involve people who are homeless as volunteers and provide appropriate support and training for personal development (£26,000); Tullochan Trust for the Haldane Volunteer Project in West Dunbartonshire to involve volunteers in activities with children in one–to–one and group settings which promote inclusion and job readiness (£22,000); Gorebridge Health and Regeneration Project to establish a day club for older people who are socially isolated (£20,000); Dyslexia Scotwest to involve volunteers in developing a helpline and resource bank (£14,000); and East Neuk Resource Group Inititative to involve volunteers in an outreach support project (£13,000).

Small grants scheme – 13 grants totalling £36,000

'For some organisations a small grant in the range of £1,500 to £5,000 provides a timely injection of funds to pilot a new project and to assess the elements to develop it further. These include improving management skills as well as the services volunteers will be involved in.'

Beneficiaries in 2002/03 included: Headway Falkirk to establish the activities of the organisation (£5,000); Contact a Family to extend a network of volunteer representatives (£4,600); Starter Packs Angus to assist homeless people going into new tenancies (£3,100); Maryhill Community Health Project to involve volunteers in promoting positive health and reducing stress (£2,700); Glenboig Neighbourhood House – Coatbridge to provide training and develop the role of volunteers in a community cyber cafe (£2,300); and Reachout Stoke Club – Inverclyde to invlove volunteers in a variety of roles to support people with poor mental health (£1,800).

Supplementary grants – 2 grants totalling £1,500

Beneficiaries were Living Memory Association (£1,000) and Dyslexia Scotwest (£500).

Training bursary scheme – 11 grants totalling £10,000

Recipients in this category are generally in the first year of funding in the main grants programme. Beneficiaries in the year included: Dove Centre – Edinburgh (£1,600); Shopmobility – Moray (£1,500); Yorkhill Family Bereavement Service – Glasgow (£1,300); Muslim Women's Resource Centre – Glasgow (£1,000); Living Memory Association (£890); Dundee International Women's Centre (£740); Highland Community Care Forum (£530); and Ark Trust – Edinburgh (£290).

Ethnic minority grants scheme – 94 grants totalling £443,000

These grants are administered by the fund on the behalf of The Scottish Executive and are given to voluntary organisations in Scotland for projects designed to reduce discrimination and promote racial equality in the fields of employment, education, health, social welfare and law. In addition to the 20 main grants (awarded over five years), 65 small and capacity building grants were made. Donations were broken down as follows:

Main grants scheme

Beneficiaries included: Glasgow YMCA and LINKnet Mentoring Fife (£23,000 each); AMINA: Muslim Women's Resource Centre – Glasgow (£15,000); STILLS Ltd – Edinburgh (£14,000); NVA Europe Ltd: The Hidden Gardens (£6,500); and Castlemilk Churches Together Refugee Project (£5,400).

Small grants scheme

Recipients included: Communities United – Glasgow and Dundee Khawateen Group (£5,000 each); Taleem Trust – Glasgow (£4,200); Mutilcultural – Fife (£3,700); Association of Chinese Parents – Glasgow (£3,100); and All Pakistan Women's Association – Edinburgh (£2,900).

Capacity building grants

Beneficiaries included: AMINA: Muslim Women's Resource Centre – Glasgow, Dundee International Women's Centre and Radio Awaz (£2,000 each); REACH Community Health Project – Glasgow and Refugees' Action Group – Glasgow (£1,800 each); Multi Ethnic Aberdeen Limited (£1,600); African Women's Group – Aberdeen (£1,400); and Edinburgh Indian Association (£1,300).

Exclusions

Schemes which cannot be considered include exhibitions, arts clubs and performances; business co-operatives; credit unions; food co-operatives; out-of-school care; housing and hostel welfare; formal educational or vocational courses and skills and training; clean-ups and one-off projects; holidays and camps; conservation schemes; building projects, including playgrounds; social clubs; sports centres and sports activities; campaigning and political activities.

Applications

In writing to the correspondent. The trustees meet quarterly.

United Trusts

General

£598,000 (2002/03)

Beneficial area Mainly North West England.

PO Box 14, 8 Nelson Road, Edge Hill, Liverpool L69 7AA

Tel. 0151 709 8252 **Fax** 0151 708 5621

Email information@unitedtrusts.org.uk

Website www.unitedtrusts.org.uk

Correspondent John Hugh Pritchard

Trustee *Up to 20 people elected by members.*

Charity Commission no. 327579

Information available Annual report and accounts were provided by the trust.

The trusts promote tax-free charitable giving (mainly but not exclusively payroll giving) through the formation and development of workplace controlled charitable funds (called workplace trusts), and local citizen controlled charitable funds (called local trust funds) for distribution through United Trusts within the donor-designated local areas.

Grants are given to benefit charities serving within the local communities concerned. Potentially all charities are eligible, including in some areas grants for the relief of individual cases of poverty and hardship (these are routed through 'umbrella charities'). United Trusts is not in itself a payroll-giving agency charity. Services are supplied in association with United Way, Charities Aid Foundation and all payroll-giving agency charities.

In 2002/03 the trust had an income of £745,000 and made grants totalling £598,000.

The distributions by local United Trusts Funds during the year was as follows:

Merseyside	£81,000
Lancashire	£1,500
Greater Manchester	£4,500
Cheshire	£2,500
Cumbria	£500
Other	£167,000
Total	£257,000

The breakdown of distributions by United Trusts Workplace Trusts during the year was as follows:

Merseyside	£227,000
Cumbria	£49,500
Greater Manchester	£8,500
Lancashire	£15,000
Cheshire	£17,000
Other	£24,500
Total	£341,500

Information on individual beneficiaries was not available.

Exclusions

Grants to individuals, called 'people for people funds', are made through 'umbrella charities' in cases where the government does not feel it has a responsibility.

Applications

It is requested that applications from Merseyside charities should be made to the secretary of the local United Trust Fund or Workplace Trust concerned if the address is known.

UnLtd (Foundation for Social Entrepreneurs)

Social enterprise

£2 million (2003/04)

Beneficial area UK

123 Whitecross Street, Islington, London EC1Y 8JJ

Tel. 020 7566 1100 **Fax** 020 75661101

Email info@unltd.org.uk

Website www.unltd.org.uk

Trustees *Jeremy Oppenheim, chair; James Cornford; Laurence Demarco; Liz Firth; Kate Kirkland; Adele Blakebrough; Michael Norton; Tanya Pein; Christopher Smallwood; Martyn Williams; John*

Brown; Anthony Freeling; Louise
Willington.

Charity Commission no. 1090393

Information available Full information
is available on the trust's website.

Summary

This organisation is unique in this
publication in that it exists to make
grants to individuals to undertake social
initiatives. In effect it makes grants for
the start-up costs of new organisations
and community groups to enterprising
individuals who need support to
implement their ideas and projects for
improving their communities.

It was established in 2000 by seven
partner organisations: Ashoka,
Changemakers, Comic Relief,
Community Action Network, Scarman
Trust, School for Social Entrepreneurs
and Senscot. In 2003 the Millennium
Commission invested £100 million in the
organisation after a competitive process
in which UnLtd was successful.

Its prime objective is to distribute
Millennium Awards to social
entrepreneurs. These awards are funded
by the income generated from the
endowment which is held by the
Millennium Awards Trust of which
UnLtd is the sole trustee.

General

The organisation gives the following full
information about its awards:

What are UnLtd Awards?

A complete package of support

UnLtd's Millennium Awards provide practical
and financial support to social entrepreneurs
in the UK – people who have both the ideas
and the commitment to develop projects
which will benefit their community.

We know that there are thousands of
people who have the ideas and the vision to
make a real difference. We also know that
many of them need encouragement and
support, contact with others just like them,
and access to training to help them grow
and give their projects the best chance of
success.

That's why you don't just get money from
UnLtd. If you win an award you will get a
complete package of support designed just
for you, in addition to the financial support.

Levels of award

UnLtd currently offers two levels of award:
Level 1: Awards of between £500 and
£5,000 (expected average of £2,000)
Level 2: Awards of between £10,000 and
£20,000 (expected average of £15,000)

Level 1 Awards are designed to help make
new ideas become real projects. UnLtd gives
out 1,000 Level 1 Awards each year across
the UK. Level 1 Awards are aimed at
individuals or informal groups of people who
want to set up new projects in their spare
time. The money is to help with the running
costs of the project.

Level 2 Awards support projects that are
already developed or pay for the living
expenses of award winners to help them
devote more time to their projects. These
awards are given out once in the spring and
once in the winter.

It is people who are important to UnLtd –
which is why we only offer support to
individuals. We do not support organisations.

Where the money comes from

UnLtd Millennium Awards are funded by the
income from a legacy of £100 million
granted by the Millennium Commission. This
legacy is carefully invested so that the
income can be obtained for awards for the
future - this is what is called a permanent
endowment.

The Millennium Commission is the only
distributor of lottery funds to good causes
who some time ago decided to provide
awards to individuals. Around 25,000 of
these have been made so far and they have
been so successful that they decided to
provide the legacy to UnLtd to carry on this
work for the future.

Level 1

Level 1 Awards are aimed at individuals or
informal groups of people who want to set
up new projects in their spare time. The
money is to help with the running costs of
the project. At Level 1 you can apply for an
award of between £500 and £5,000, (with
an average award size of £2,000). These
awards are for people who:

- have an idea for a project which will
  benefit their community;
- have thought about how they will run their
  project;
- have some evidence that there is a need
  for their project;
- will learn a new skill from carrying out
  their project.

Above all, UnLtd wants to support people
who have the energy and commitment to
develop their project and whilst doing it, will
have the opportunity to increase their skills
and vision. The award can be used for the
things you need to start or develop your
project: materials, equipment, renting rooms
for meetings and so on.

Level 2

Level 2 Awards support projects that are
already developed, or pay for the living
expenses of award winners to help them
devote more time to their projects. UnLtd

has Level 2 Awards of between £10,000 to
£20,000 to give out each year across the
UK. The average size of a Level 2 Award is
likely to be £15,000. These awards are for:

- people who have a powerful idea for a
  project;
- people whose projects will be sustainable
  after the UnLtd award has finished;
- projects which have the potential to
  operate on a wider scale or be replicated
  in other parts of the UK;
- people who have the vision commitment
  to make the project work;
- people who have knowledge of similar
  initiatives or work.

Level 2 Awards are given out in two phases
each year, once in the spring and once in
the winter. For further details on the Level 2
Awards process, and how to apply, please
contact your local UnLtd office who will be
able to advise you when to apply and explain
the application process in more detail.

Review of 2003/04

The following information is taken from
the 2003/04 annual report and accounts
of UnLtd, in which the organisation
provides comprehensive details and
analysis of its activities during the year.

In the annual report for the year 2002/03
UnLtd published its overarching objectives
for the year ended 31 March 2004. These
were:

- to establish the organisational
  infrastructure to deliver the objectives of
  the organisation;
- to make 1,000 Level 1 Awards and 50
  Level 2 Awards;
- to conduct a pilot of the Millennium
  Awards Fellowship Programme;
- to start a programme of research.

The main achievements for the year are:
The year 1 April 2003 to 31 March 2004
is the third year in the life of the Foundation
for Social Entrepreneurs. Given that the
endowment was received on 27 February
2003, this year is effectively the first year of
operations. In the previous financial year, six
country and regional offices became
operational and in the last quarter of 2002/
03 105 Level 1 Awards were made and 5
Level 2 Awards were made.

Awards applications and analysis

In [2003/04] 1,490 applications were
received. Of these applications, 477 Level 1
Awards (861 Award winners) and 34 Level 2
Awards have been made. In total
£1,950,000 was expended on Awards.
Award payments are made in a minimum of
two instalments. The processing time of six
weeks to deal with applications was met with
few exceptions. During the year substantially
larger than expected volumes of applications

were received therefore resources had to be devoted to processing these. This accounts for the marginal reduction in Level 1 Awards made compared to the target. For the same reason applications were not invited for Level 2 Awards until slightly later in the year.

For both Level 1 and Level 2 Awards

During this period approximately 5,000 Level 1 application packs were distributed, either directly to enquirers, at funding fairs and by other organisations.

At Level 1 there were 1,404 applications received; of which, 477 were awarded to 861 individuals.

At Level 2 there were 86 applications received; of, which 34 were successful.

Ratio of successful to unsuccessful:
- 34% at Level 1
- 40% at Level 2

Note that the Level 2 Awards given during this period were part of the pilot of the Level 2 competition and therefore applications were not widely encouraged, resulting in a higher success ratio. We would expect a lower success ratio at Level 2 in future years, due to the higher level of competition and lower amount of awards.

Processing information

The average time to process applications from date of receipt till date of the final decision by the Awards Committee was six weeks. This figure can rise to a maximum of 10 weeks during August and Christmas periods, when there are no award rounds.

Average time taken to process grant claims from receipt to payment:

UnLtd's finance department runs award payments at the end of each month. For an award winner to receive payment they must have submitted all relevant paperwork (e.g. references, signed contract, bank and payment detail forms and police checks where appropriate). The amount of time this can take varies as it is the responsibility of the award winner (and their referees) to provide this information to UnLtd: it has taken 6 months for some award winner to be ready for payment whilst other take only a month. The average time taken for this process is approximately 2 months.

Plans for 2004/05

Funding:

UnLtd Millennium Awards Scheme – core funding is now in place for the awards scheme into perpetuity – the income of the Millennium Awards Trust. The Foundation for Social Entrepreneurs is committed to raising additional sums to fund more awards and has met with early success in 2004/05:

Scotland

Scotland UnLtd has negotiated additional funds for awards for the next three years totalling £615,000 from ESF. This is to reinforce the existing Level 2 award programme and extend it more effectively to the Highlands and Islands.

North Yorkshire

North Yorkshire County Council have agreed to provide a total of £225,000 over the next two years so that UnLtd can extend its awards programme to support individuals promoting social enterprises in rural areas.

South East

A partnership between UnLtd, Social Firms South East and Development Trusts Association is to receive £95,000 over three years to provide a joined up initiation and response support service to those pursuing the development of social enterprise in the South East.

London

UnLtd has been granted £78,000 over one year from the New Deal for Communities to fund 25 awards in a deprived area of South London.

The Awards Scheme will be continued across the UK from 6 office locations (London, Birmingham, Bradford, Cardiff, Belfast and Edinburgh).

Regional offices

Head Office/London Office:
123 Whitecross Street
Islington
London
EC1Y 8JJ
Telephone: 020 7566 1100
Fax: 020 7566 1101
Email: info@unltd.org.uk

Birmingham Office:
Unit G2
The Ground Floor
The Arch
48–52 Floodgate Street
Birmingham
B5 5SL
Telephone: 0121 766 4570

Bradford Office:
Second Floor
Highpoint Building
Westgate
Bradford
BD1 2TT
Telephone: 01274 750630

North Yorkshire Office:
PO Box 82
Whitby
YO21 2WT
Telephone: 01287 660011

Northern Ireland Office:
Room 70/71
Scottish Mutual Building
16 Donegal Square South
Belfast
BT1 5JG
Telephone: 028 9024 4007

Scotland UnLtd Office:
54 Manor Place
Edinburgh
EH3 7EH
Telephone: 0131 226 7333

Wales Office:
Fourth Floor
Baltic House
Mount Stuart Square
Cardiff
CF10 5FH
Telephone: 029 2048 4811

Applications
Level 1

If you would like to apply for a Level 1 Award, the first step is to complete the eligibility questionnaire [via the website]. If you have completed the questionnaire and your answers met our criteria, the next step is to contact your local office to discuss your idea in more detail, and request an application form.

If you have not yet completed the questionnaire, please do so. This will help you find out if you should apply for an award. If after completing the questionnaire you find you are not eligible, you may wish to discuss the reasons with your local office.

London

If you are from London and would like to apply for a Level 1 Award you should attend one of our surgery days before you submit your application. There, you will be able to find out more about UnLtd's work, have the opportunity to discuss your application with us and find out whether your proposal is likely to be successful.

To book a place on a surgery please call Habibur Rahman on 0845 850 1122. We hold these surgeries every month.

Level 2

To find out more about our Level 2 Awards, please contact your regional office who may invite you to attend a seminar prior to submitting your application.

North Yorkshire

If you live in North Yorkshire, you can apply for a Level 2 Award throughout the year.

Scotland
If you live in Scotland, please see the UnLtd Scotland website, www.scotlandunltd.com, for further information on how to apply.

The Valentine Charitable Trust

Welfare and the environment

£500,000 (2002/03)
Beneficial area Dorset.

Preston & Redman, Hinton House, Hinton Road, Bournemouth, Dorset BH1 2EN

Tel. 01202 292424

Correspondent D J E Neville-Jones, Trustee

Trustees *D J E Neville-Jones; S F Neville-Jones; Mrs P B N Walker; N E N Neville-Jones.*

Charity Commission no. 1001782

Information available Accounts were on file at the Charity Commission.

The trust's objects are to provide amenities and facilities for the benefit of the public, which are not provided for from public funds. It also wishes to support the protection and safeguarding of the countryside and wildlife, and the control and reduction of pollution.

In 2002/03 the trust had an income of £857,000. Grants totalled around £500,000 for the year. Grants have previously been made to British Red Cross Appeals, Broadstone Methodist Church, Relate – Dorset, Army Benevolent Fund, Marine Conservation Society, Motability, SSAFA and Samaritans.

Exclusions

No grants to individuals.

Applications

In writing to the correspondent.

John and Lucille van Geest Foundation

Medical research, healthcare, general

£694,000 (2002/03)
Beneficial area UK and overseas, with a special interest in south Lincolnshire and adjoining areas.

42 Pinchbeck Road, Spalding, Lincolnshire PE11 1QF

Correspondent S R Coltman, Trustee

Trustees *Lucille van Geest; Hilary P Marlowe; Stuart R Coltman; Tonie Gibson.*

Charity Commission no. 1001279

Information available Annual report and accounts were provided by the trust.

The foundation had an income of £731,000 in 2002/03, from its investments then worth just under £16 million. The trustees' grantmaking policy is set out as follows in the annual report:

The charity's funds available for making grants will normally be applied by the trustees:

In providing financial support to charitable bodies concerned with the following areas of medical research:

- brain damage (Alzheimer's disease, Huntingdon's disease, Parkinson's disease, strokes etc.)
- cancer
- heart disease
- lung disease
- sight and/or hearing loss.

In providing financial support to charitable bodies concerned with the welfare of people in need through illness, infirmity or social circumstances, in particular the welfare of older people and of children who reside in South Lincolnshire and adjoining areas and who:

- have brain damage or a mental illness
- have cancer
- have a heart disease
- have lung disease
- have sight and/or hearing loss
- have disfigurement through injury
- are physically disabled
- are bedridden
- are terminally ill
- are at-risk

and to charitable bodies concerned with the welfare of victims of natural disasters and man-made disasters.

Grants in 2002/03 were broken down as follows (with figures for 2001/02 in brackets):

	No.	Amount	
Medical research	6	£268,000	(7 £348,000)
Health/social welfare	24	£399,000	(18 £417,000)
Emergency relief	1	£28,000	(1 £10,000)
Education	1	£10,000	(–)

The grants for medical research were headed by two large awards, for Nottingham Trent University and the Orchid Cancer Appeal (£100,000 each). Both these recipients had also been supported in 2001/02. Other beneficiaries were Action Research (£28,000), Cystic Fibrosis Trust (£20,000) and Alzheimer's Research Trust and Diabetes UK (£10,000 each).

By far the largest grant in the health and social welfare category was for £170,000 and went to DeafBlind UK, also the major beneficiary in the previous year. Other grants were in the range of £2,500 to £27,000. Beneficiaries included Huntingdon's Disease Association (£27,000), Motor Neurone Disease Association (£20,000), Whizz Kidz (£16,000), British Heart Foundation (£15,000), Calibre (£10,000), Kesteven Blind Society (£7,000), Changing Faces, National Benevolent Fund for the Aged and West Norfolk Hospice (£5,000 each) and Blind Outdoor Leisure Development and Prostate Cancer Fund (£2,500). A number of the grants in this category went to recipients that had been supported in the previous year

For education, Marshfields School received £10,000. The emergency relief grant went to the British Red Cross (£28,000).

Exclusions

No grants to individuals.

Applications

In writing to the correspondent, but only other charities engaged in areas of work to which the trustees' policy extends are considered. Telephone calls are not welcome. The trustees meet three to four times a year to consider applications, but there are no set dates. Every applicant will receive a reply.

The Vardy Foundation

Christian causes, education in the north east of England, general

£606,000 to organisations and individuals (2001/02)

Beneficial area UK with a preference for north east England, overseas.

Houghton House, Emperor Way, Doxford International Business Park, Sunderland SR3 3XR

Tel. 0191 525 3000

Email foundation@regvardy.com

Correspondent Sir Peter Vardy, Chair of the Trustees

Trustees *Sir Peter Vardy, chair; Mrs M B Vardy.*

Charity Commission no. 328415

Information available Account were on file at the Charity Commission.

The trust was set up in 1989 with general charitable objectives. In 2001/02 it had assets of £9.7 million and an income of £2.4 million, mainly due to a donation of £2 million from the foundation's settlors. Grants were made to organisations and individuals totalling £606,000.

The trustee's report lists just five major beneficiaries. These were: Alpha Partners and University of Sunderland (£100,000 each), Healing Hands (£80,000), County Durham Foundation (£45,000) and Bolivian Community Project (£25,000).

In 2002/03 it has an income of £2.5 million and a total expenditure of £1.5 million. Unfortunately, although submitted by the trust to the Charity Commission, the accounts for that year had not made it to the public files for inspection.

Applications

In writing to the correspondent.

The Variety Club Children's Charity

Children's charities

£2.6 million to organisations (2003)

Beneficial area UK.

Variety Club House, 93 Bayham Street, London NW1 0AG

Tel. 020 7428 8100

Website www.varietyclub.org.uk

Correspondent The Company Secretary

Trustees *Hugo Amaya-Torres; Jarvis Astaire; Hedy-Joy Babani; John Barnett; Philip Burley; Stephen Crown; Raymond Curtis; Manuel Fontenla Novoa; Richard Freeman; Anthony Harris; Tony Hatch; Richard Harrington; Russell Kahn; Paul Lawrence; Kenneth Mustoe; Ronnie Nathan; Rod Natkiel; John Ratcliff; Angela Rippon; Lionel Rosenblatt; Pamela Sinclair; John Webber.*

Charity Commission no. 209259

Information available Annual report and accounts

Summary

The charity raises money and then provides Sunshine Coaches, mobility aids or general grants to help those:

- with mental, physical or sensory disabilities;
- with behavioural or psychological disturbances;
- suffering through distress, abuse or neglect.

General grants are described as follows:

'Applications can be made from non-profit making groups and organisations working with children under the physical age of 19. In general, consideration is given to funding specific items of equipment that are for the direct use of sick, disabled and disadvantaged children.'

'There is no upper or lower limit on the level of grant, but most grants are for less than £5,000. Many requests are for small sums under £500.'

General

The background to this important grantmaker is given in the box overleaf. The income in 2003 was £9.4 million.

The money funds four programmes:

Sunshine Coaches [£2.3 million in 2003]

Sunshine Coaches offer children the chance to explore a bigger, better world. The now familiar white minibuses were launched in 1962, and almost 40 years later over 4,000 have been presented by the Variety Club Children's Charity—many with generous support from the corporate sector.

In 2003, 98 coaches (each costing about £25,000) were supplied to children's hospitals and hospices, and to organisations 'striving to improve the quality of life for young people'.

The Easy Riders Wheelchair Programme [£12,000 to one organisation]

[This] has a simple goal: to give disabled children a better life. Founded in 1988, Easy Riders have given custom-designed wheelchairs, trikes and buggies to over 2,170 children who are contending with a wide range of disabilities.

93 electric wheelchairs, buggies and trikes were given in 2003.

Variety at Work

Created in the 1960s, Variety at Work is the special part of the charity, which exists purely to give children wonderful experiences, rather than raise money. Its aim is simple – to bring happiness to as many youngsters as possible, so that they can look forward to magical moments. This is achieved by providing entertainment and experiences for them through all sorts of spectacular events throughout the country, all year long.

Appeals [£202,000 in 87 grants to organisations]

Each week over 50 appeals arrive at the Variety Club office from individuals desperate for their quality of life to be improved to institutions desperate to maintain and improve the services their provide for disadvantaged children. Grants are given to hospitals, hospices, special projects and therapy pools, play annexes, sensory rooms, communicators and toys.

In addition to money given to specific projects, Variety gives many gifts to disadvantaged youngsters. Every Christmas our Toy Fund sends over 25,000 gifts, games and toys to children who would otherwise have no present of any kind.

Other help includes payments towards house adaptations which enable children to stay at home and be cared for by their families instead of going into institutions, computers to enable disabled children to communicate and sensory room equipment which provides lights and sounds which can

THE HISTORY OF THE VARIETY CLUB

The club's website has the following interesting account of the origins of the charity:

The roots of the Variety Club of Great Britain go back to 1927 when, in Pittsburgh, United States, a group of 11 men–all friends–and involved in show business set up a social club. They rented a small room in the William Penn Hotel for their new club, which they named the Variety Club, as all its members were drawn from various branches of the show business world.

On Christmas Eve 1928 a one-month-old baby was abandoned on a seat in the Sheridan Square Theatre in Pittsburgh, Pennsylvania, with a note pinned to her dress, which read as follows:

'Please take care of my baby. Her name is Catherine. I can no longer take care of her. I have eight others. My husband is out of work. She was born on Thanksgiving Day. I have always heard of the goodness of show business people and pray to God that you will look after her' (signed, 'A heartbroken mother').

When all efforts by the police and local newspapers failed to locate the parents, the theatre's 11 club members decided to underwrite the infant's support and education.

The subsequent publicity surrounding Catherine and her benefactors attracted many other show business people anxious to help. Before long Catherine had more clothes and toys than any child could possibly need.

Naturally the Club members had no trouble finding other disadvantaged children to benefit from the extra gifts and while the generous show business world donated presents to Catherine, the Club continued to supply a growing number of children with much-needed presents. As a result, by the time Catherine was adopted at the age of five, the Club that she had effectively started was well on the way to becoming a recognised children's charity.

It was not long before the Variety Club decided to actively raise funds for its adopted cause of disadvantaged children. The first fund-raising event of the Club was held under a Circus Big Top, which is why the circus vernacular is used within the Club structure world-wide.

The Variety Club of Great Britain–or Tent 36–was set up by two Americans: Robert S Wolff, chairman of RKO, who became the club's first Chief Barker, and C J Latta of ABC Cinemas/Warner Brothers. It was formed at an inaugural dinner at the Savoy in October 1949 and by the end of 1950 had already raised nearly £10,000.

From the start, Tent 36–like the Variety Club as a whole–consisted of a group of charitable individuals and companies, the majority of whom were related to show business and were happy to give large sums of money for the cause–sometimes as straightforward cash donations and sometimes through their support for the Club's auctions and raffles with donated items. The Club numbered a formidable array of film producers, agents and celebrities within its ranks, all of whom were eager to give their time and services –free of charge–to help towards making the increasingly varied and wide ranging fundraising events as successful as possible.

Variety Club of Great Britain, along with the other members of Variety Club International, has long been characterised as 'the Heart of Show Business'. Its membership over the years is drawn in large measure from the multi-faceted world of entertainment and the leisure industries.

stimulate or calm children when they are in despair.

Variety's Appeals Committee, which includes specialist advisers in medicine, social work, physiotherapy and building work, meet regularly to consider a wide range of requests–many of which can be heart-rending.

Computer grants

These are referred to in the guidelines on the charity's website as a separate heading but do not appear in the 2003 annual report, so this may be either a small or a new programme.

Grants in 2001

The grants list does not distinguish between cash grants and the value of gifts of Sunshine Coaches. There were 111 grants of between £5,000 and £36,000 listed in the accounts.

Exclusions

For grants to organisations: trips abroad; medical treatment or research; administrative or salary costs; maintenance or ongoing costs; repayment of loans; distribution to other organisations; computers for mainstream schools or non-disabled children; basic cost of a family vehicle and non-specific appeals.

Applications

There are application forms for each programme, available from the charity or through its website.

Wales Council for Voluntary Action

Local community, volunteering, social welfare, environment, regeneration

£18.8 million (2003/04)

Beneficial area Wales.

Baltic House, Mount Stuart Square, Cardiff CF10 5FH

Tel. 0870 607 1666 **Fax** 029 2043 1701

Minicom 029 2043 1702

Email help@wcva.org.uk

Website www.wcva.org.uk

Correspondent Graham Benfield, Chief Executive

Trustees *Tom Jones, chair; Margaret Jervis, Vice Chair; Douglas E Morris, Treasurer; and 36 other board members.*

Charity Commission no. 218093

Information available Information was taken from the trust's annual report and accounts for 2003/04, and from its website.

Wales Council for Voluntary Action (WCVA) represents, supports and campaigns for the voluntary sector in Wales by undertaking research on policy, providing information and training, and administering a range of grant programmes on behalf of various bodies including charitable trusts, the Millennium Commission, the National Assembly for Wales, the Big Lottery Fund and the European Structural Funds. Although it only administers funds for other bodies and has no funds of its own, it merits inclusion here due to the diverse nature of the schemes and the amounts of money involved.

In 2003/04 WCVA awarded £18.8 million to over 3,500 projects across Wales – more than double the total amount given in grants and number of projects supported in the previous year. This continued significant increase in direct charitable expenditure is largely due to the uptake of the Communities First Trust Fund in its final year of phase one. 2,457 grassroots projects where supported by the fund in 2003/04, investing £6.6 million in local community action in some of Wales' most excluded communities.

Grant Programmes

The schemes detailed below are those currently open to application at the time of writing (February 2005). However, as new rounds of grantmaking are announced periodically and an additional £20 million of funding for voluntary sector activity was notified in 2003/04, the following information should be used as a guide only. For up-to-date information on each scheme contact WCVA before applying.

Enfys (Rainbow)

WCVA is managing the scheme in partnership with the Environment Agency, the Prince's Trust and Environment Wales. The scheme aims to award 365 grants between 2001 and 2005. These will include:

- Process grants: 200 grants up to £5,000 each for activities such as feasibility studies or establishing partnerships).
- Community grants: 140 grants up to £25,000 each for community led initiatives enabling disadvantaged communities in particular to develop large scale projects.
- Partnership grants: 25 grants up to £100,000 each for substantial projects that demonstrate true partnership between public, private and voluntary organisations.

Enfys has so far awarded funding totaling £5.3 million to 282 projects across Wales.

You will be advised of the date of the Panel at which your application will be reviewed upon acknowledgment of the receipt of your application.

Further guidance on submitting an application can be obtained from Katie Burgess on 01492 539803; email kburgess@wcva.org.uk

Support and advice is available from Prince's Trust Cymru Development Officers by contacting 01492 539803.

The application form is available from the Big Lottery Fund by phoning 08450 000 122.

Social Risk Fund

The scheme will provide community and voluntary groups with easy and speedy access to European funding. WCVA has drawn a package of funds together from the European Social Fund, under the Objective 1 and Objective 3 programmes and from the National Assembly for Wales.

This means the scheme will be able to approve 100% grants for eligible project costs. Grants of up to £10,000 are available for eligible projects that cost no more than £10,000 in total. There are no set deadlines for applications so your group can apply for funding at anytime during the lifetime of the scheme (April 2004–March 2007). WCVA aims to make the assessment process as quick as possible so that you should hear whether your group's completed application is successful within 30 working days of receipt of all information required for assessment.

Grants are available for voluntary and community groups that can show how their project will contribute to longer term economic regeneration, through raising skills levels and increasing access to, and widening participation in education, training and employment for specific target groups. The fund aims to help develop projects that combat social exclusion, and help identified target groups towards employment or to gain new skills, in order to increase the opportunities for employment.

The fund will support small community and voluntary groups that are developing new projects that, for example:

- Improve the quality of life for the target groups or their local community/ environment.
- Combat social exclusion.
- Develop and strengthen local networks and groups that aim to help the target groups back into the work place or help them improve or gain skills in order to become more employable.
- Provide support for community businesses and co-operatives

Please note that the examples given are for illustrative purposes only – your group may come up with other kinds of projects that fit with the fund's overall objectives

To be eligible to apply for a grant under the Social Risk Fund your organisation must meet the following basic criteria:

- You must be a legally constituted organisation.
- You must be independent of government and private sectors.
- You must be a community-based/ voluntary organisation.
- Your annual gross income must be £100,000 or less.
- You must have a written equal opportunities statement or demonstrate that you are working towards adopting an equal opportunities statement.
- The people your project seeks to support must be aged between 16 and 64.
- Your project must take place in Wales.

Before completing your application, we advise you to contact a WCVA European funding advisor based in your local area and to read the guidelines for applications carefully:

Aaron Walters
North Wales WCVA, 13 Wynnstay Road
Colwyn Bay
Conwy
LL29 8NB
Tel: 01492 539816
Fax: 01492 539801

Ingela Mann
Mid Wales WCVA, Ladywell House
Newtown
Powys
SY16 1JB
Tel: 01686 611053
Fax: 01686 627863

Iestyn Evans
South Wales WCVA, Maritime Offices
Woodland Terrace
Pontypridd
Cardiff
CF37 1DZ
Tel: 01443 485640
Fax: 029 2043 1701

All Wales:
WCVA, Baltic House
Mount Stuart Square
Cardiff
CF10 5FH
Tel: 029 2043 1752
Fax: 029 2043 1701

Or by email at the general address for the fund: socialrisk@wcva.org.uk

Volunteering in Wales Fund

Volunteering in Wales is a grant scheme targeted at volunteers. Supported by the Welsh Assembly Government, selected projects can be grant assisted for up to three years. Grants of up to a maximum of £25,000 in the first year, £12,500 in the second year, and £6,250 in the third year are possible.

The scheme supports projects whose aims are mainly achieved by volunteers; that recruit and place volunteers; that develop good practice in volunteering; or that encourage activities in areas where volunteering is less well developed. Any constituted voluntary organisation working, or planning to work in Wales is eligible to apply.

This scheme came to a close at the end of 2004, with all funds being allocated. However, WCVA was expecting a decision from the Welsh Assembly in March 2005 about additional funding for a further round of the scheme. If this is to go ahead, which as at February 2005 seemed unlikely, it is anticipated that the deadline for applications will again be in December. Call 0870 607 1666 for up-to-date information.

Communities First Trust Fund

Communities First is a Welsh Assembly Government regeneration programme targeted on the most deprived communities in Wales. The trust fund is the first major initiative of the Communities First Support Network, funded by The Welsh Assembly Government and administered by WCVA. Following completion of the final year of phase one in 2004, the fund has been extended for a further three years.

- £9 million has been provided over three years by The Welsh Assembly Government;
- £20,000 has been allocated to each of the 139 Communities First electoral wards and 'communities of interest' with smaller pockets of deprivation at sub-ward level attracting £10,000, in each year;
- Applications may be made at any time and grants of up to 100% can be awarded.

The purpose of the scheme is to support any type of activity that involves local people, through small community organisations, that benefits their community. The activities must provide some measure of economic, environmental, social or cultural benefit for people living in a Communities First area. The fund is described as "red tape busting" and is intended to provide easy to access resources for local groups.

What is the Communities First Support Network?

The Communities First Support Network is a partnership of eight key national community development and regeneration organisations across the voluntary and community sector supported by the Welsh Assembly Government. The network members are Black Voluntary Sector Network, Community Action Network, Community Development Cymru, Development Trusts Association Wales, Groundwork Wales, Menter a Busnes, Wales Co-operative Centre and WCVA.

How much can I apply for?

Each Communities First electoral ward and 'community of interest' has £20,000 allocated to it for each of the three years of the scheme with smaller pockets of deprivation at sub-ward level attracting £10,000 in each year. Applications in excess of £5,000 will not be considered and no group will be eligible to access more than £5,000 in any financial year. Grants of up to 100% may be awarded however groups are encouraged to apply for part funding for their project and seek the additional funding they require from other sources. Groups are eligible to apply to the trust fund if they have an outstanding end of project report from a previous trust fund grant, however any grant awarded will not be paid to the group until the previous grant has been accounted for.

Who can not apply to the fund?

The rules of the trust fund prevent the following groups/individuals from applying:

- Communities First Partnerships;
- referees, however the group the referee is employed by may apply provided they use a different nominated referee;
- national organisations, unless the group is a local branch with local management/accountability arrangements and bank account;
- town and community councils;
- other statutory organisations;
- schools – however the school PTA/ Friends may apply to the trust fund provided the funding is not to carry out improvements to the building or grounds or is to provide equipment or educational trips, which could reasonably be expected to be provided by the Local Education Authority.

This scheme is open and on-going. For more information or an application pack contact the Communities First Helpdesk free on 0800 587 8898, email: enquiries@communitiesfirst.info or visit the website: www.communitiesfirst.info for up-to-date information.

Mental Health Grants Scheme

The Local Mental Health grants scheme is set up to support and enhance the voluntary sector contribution to the care of people experiencing mental health problems, and their families and carers, in Wales. It is funded under the National Assembly for Wales Mental Illness Strategy.

The scheme provides funding for local services that enable people experiencing mental health problems, and their families and carers, to live as independent and fulfilled lives in the community as possible. The scheme also supports local mental health development services throughout Wales that support voluntary organisations, user groups, and family and carer groups.

The scheme is open to existing grant recipients under the 1998–2002 LMHGS and funding is allocated on a three year rolling programme. This scheme has been rolled over to the 2005/06 financial year.

Millennium Volunteers

Millennium Volunteers is an UK wide programme for young people who are interested or involved in volunteering. The purpose of the programme is to promote and recognise a sustained commitment by young people aged 16–24 to voluntary activity which makes a clear impact on the community.

In Wales the programme is managed by the National Co-ordinating Group, a partnership between the Wales Council for Voluntary Action, the Wales Youth Agency and the Council for Wales Voluntary Youth Service. Applications can be made from between £50 to £7,000 to cover volunteers' costs. There is no restriction on the number of applications that can be made.

The Millennium Volunteers programme aims to:

- offer challenging and interesting volunteering opportunities
- enable young people to acquire new skills and knowledge and develop personally
- increase recognition of volunteering by young people in the community
- set a standard for volunteering opportunities in Wales
- make a positive impact within local communities
- encourage ownership of the programme by young people.

FIVE reasons why you should involve young people in your organisation:

- because they bring new ideas and enthusiasms
- they have a different perspective
- to broaden your reach
- to change the profile of your organisation
- to improve your impact.

If your organisation could benefit from involving young people as volunteers you can apply to us for a grant of £50–£7,000 to develop youth volunteering.

FIVE reasons why you should become a MV if you are between 16–24:

- to have new experience
- to make new friends
- to develop skills
- to improve your job prospects
- to have fun! (and get the t-shirt/cap/ Award of Excellence!)

If you would like to become a MV and join a project in your area, contact the nearest Local Co-ordinating Partner (LCP) – details are listed on the WCVA website. The LCP will help you to identify volunteering which best matches your interests.

Future MV Advisory Panel meetings together with closing dates are listed below.

Meeting date	Closing date
29 June 2005	10 June 2005
14 Sept 2005	26 August 2005
25 January 2006	6 January 2006

All funding has come from the Welsh Assembly Government.

Strategic Recycling Scheme

WCVA has launched a new recycling grant scheme which will see almost £30 million invested in reducing the amount of waste produced in Welsh communities.

The Strategic Recycling Scheme (SRS) has been set up to fund partnership-based projects across Wales in areas such as re-use, recycling and composting.

Grants of up to £1.5 million are available for projects designed to create wealth from waste and which meet the following priorities:

1. To increase the amount and range of materials diverted away from final disposal.

2. To increase the number of households participating in waste recycling, re-use and composting projects.

3. To develop sustainability in communities.

The preferred approach is partnership working between the public, private and community sectors and all applications must involve the local authority.

WCVA Chief Executive Graham Benfield OBE commented: 'The SRS allows communities to access resources and build the partnerships needed in achieving high re-use, recycling and composting participation.

The money will go a long way to developing local initiatives to reduce the amount of municipal waste, creating a better local environment now and in the future.'

SRS is a rolling grant programme where funding applications may be submitted at any time.

For further information and to request the SRS guidance notes and application form, contact the SRS administrator Gwyneth Jones on 01492 539806 or email gjones@wcva.org.uk.

There may be other schemes on the horizon for 2005 and beyond, depending on external sources of funding. Call the WCVA Helpdesk on 0870 607 1666 for the latest information on any new schemes.

Exclusions

Grants are made to constituted voluntary organisations only.

Applications

There are separate application forms for each scheme (see details for each scheme above). Contact WCVA on 0870 607 1666, or visit its website, for further information.

Sir Siegmund Warburg's Voluntary Settlement

Medicine and education

£619,000 (2003/04)

Beneficial area UK, especially London.

33 St Mary Axe, London EC3 8LL

Correspondent Robin R Jessel, Secretary

Trustees *Hugh A Stevenson, chair; Doris E Wasserman; Dr Michael J Harding; Christopher Purvis.*

Charity Commission no. 286719

Information available Annual report and accounts were provided by the trust.

In 2003/04 this trust, which primarily funds medical research, had assets of over £11 million and an income of £362,000. Grants to 10 organisations totalled £619,000, broken down as follows:

Health and medicine – 4 grants totalling £505,000

By far the largest grant was £481,000 to ICH (UCL) new Century Cohort Study. Other donations were £10,000 each to Changing Faces and Deafway for a residential home for deaf people with mental problems and £4,900 to Queen Mary and Westfield College towards the investigation of dynein in a model of motor neurone disease.

Culture and the arts–2 grant totalling £50,000

Grants were £45,000 to Royal Academy of Arts and £5,000 to Paintings in Hospitals.

Education – 5 grants totalling £63,000

Grants were £45,000 to Institute for Jewish Policy Research, £2,500 to Island Trust and £1,000 to St Paul's Girls' School. King Edward's School, Whitley – Warburg Science School received two grants; an annual grant of £7,500 and £6,900 towards a scholarship.

Exclusions

No grants to individuals.

Applications

In writing to the correspondent.

The Waterside Trust

Christian causes, welfare

£1 million (2003)

Beneficial area Unrestricted, but mainly UK.

56 Palmerston Place, Edinburgh EH12 5AY

Tel. 0131 225 6366 **Fax** 0131 220 1041

Email robert@mccp.co.uk

Correspondent Robert Clark

Trustee *Irvine Bay Trustee Company.*

Scottish Charity no. SC003232

Information available Annual report and accounts were provided by the trust.

This trust is believed to be one expression of the philanthropy of the Brenninkmeyer family. Long term fundraisers will remember organisations such as the Marble Arch Trust. The family always sought the minimum of publicity for their energetic and much admired work and it may be that the increasing calls in England for transparency for such bodies were one reason why those trusts were closed down and some of the work rebased in Scotland. However, the Kulika Trust, at least, has remained an active and well known grantmaker.

Though the family's Catholic interests were always apparent, the range of their philanthropic interests have been wide and enterprising over the years.

It had been expected that this trust would no longer be making grants on a scale previously seen over the past few years, with its reserves being spent and it subsequently relying on its income from donations to distribute as grants. In fact, donations to the charity have remained significant, with £1 million being received in 2003, all of which was distributed as grants.

It is the intention of the trust to distribute all of its annual income. Grants will now be smaller and made to more organisations, and few, if any, will be for work overseas.

There is no information about grantmaking policy or practice in the annual reports but the trust has said it gives grants 'to improve the lives of disadvantaged people' and has supplied the following further information on its policy:

Grants are made to organisations which provide adult Christian formation and pastoral care, offer educational and recreational activities for disadvantaged young people and young offenders, provide care and support for the elderly and deprived families, and organisations engaged in community development. Ethics and Church management and finance are also areas of interest.

The trust no longer appears to have an interest in the field of genetics.

In 2003 it made 119 grants (from 761 applications) totalling £1 million to 98 organisations. With one notable exception, no single grant was for more than £32,000, and most were for £10,000 or less.

The main beneficiary during the year was Derwent Charitable Consultancy, a connected organisation (Waterside trustee D J Burnstone is also a director of the consultancy) which aims to 'improve the management of charities and help charities in the most effective use of their resources', which received four grants totalling £213,000 – one of which was for £185,000, another, for £20,000, was listed as being for 'adviser's fees'.

Other beneficiaries receiving multiple grants during the year were: Catholic Children's Society for various projects and local branches (£47,000 in total); National Catholic Fund for a salary, a symposium and a conference (£38,500); Heythrop College for its Institute for Religion, Ethics and Public Life, a conference and student sponsorships (£34,000 in total); Students Exploring Marriage Trust towards its expansion into Cardiff (£23,500 in total); Scottish Marriage Care for a salary and a summer course (£22,000 in total); Westminster Catholic Diocese for a salary and a secondment (£22,000 in total); Maryvale Institute for bursaries and an evangelisation and basic skills project (£18,000 in total); Prison Fellowship England and Wales for its Sycamore Tree programme (£17,000 in total); Time for Families for support groups and a summer course (£11,500); and Kulika Charitable Trust – Uganda (£6,000 in total).

Single grants included those to Child Welfare and Adoption Society – Uganda (£32,000), Sarum College Trust (£22,000), Caritas Social Action (£20,000), Church of the English Martyrs – Streatham (£15,000), St Cuthbert's Care – Hexham & Newcastle Catholic

Diocese (£12,000), Carmel Care Trust and SPACE Project – Berwick upon Tweed (£10,000 each), Jennyruth Workshops Ltd – Ripon (£7,500), Depaul Trust (£5,000), Stapleford Centre (£3,000), Uganda Development Services and Special Educational Needs Families Support Group (£2,000 each) and Franciscan International Study Centre and Basildon Village Hall (£1,000 each).

Comment

The accounts for the Waterside Trust note that D J Burnstone, a director of its trustees, Irvine Bay Trustee Company, who have the final approval of grants and loans, is also a director of one of the trust's bankers, Matlock Bank Limited. DSC always regrets such connections unless, in the words of the Charity Commission, 'there is no realistic alternative' and unless the nature of this need is explained in the annual report.

Exclusions

No grants to:

- individuals.
- environmental projects.
- construction costs or purchase of buildings.
- arts organisations.
- conservation groups.
- endowment appeals.
- major research projects.

Applications

In writing to the correspondent, for consideration on an ongoing basis.

The Wates Foundation

'Support of the disadvantaged', especially close to south London

£1.6 million (2003/04)

Beneficial area Greater London within the M25 corridor with a preference for south London.

Wates House, Station Approach, Leatherhead, Surrey KT22 7SW

Tel. 01372 861000 **Fax** 01372 861252

Email director@watesfoundation.org.uk

Website www.watesfoundation.org.uk

Correspondent The Director

Trustees *Jane Wates, chair; Susan Wates; Ann Ritchie; Michael Wates; Clare Price; William Wates; Nick Edwards. (The grants committee of the foundation also includes other members of the Wates family.)*

Charity Commission no. 247941

Information available Excellent reports and accounts, including guidance for applicants, all on the particularly clear and simple website.

Summary

This trust has assets in excess of £31 million and an annual income of over £1.6 million, all of which is distributed in grants. The grant total has been increasing year on year (the foundation stated that £1.7 million was distributed in 2004/05). The foundation makes about 60 major grants and about 30 small grants a year to registered charities in Greater London, usually in one of the following fields:

- community support and development
- ethnic minority and immigrant communities
- 'Foundations of Society'
- arts, heritage and the environment.

The foundation also has 'areas of special focus'. Currently these are the criminal justice system and substance abuse and alternative therapies.

There is an emphasis on outcomes and performance measurement.

Grantmaking

Programme areas

Foundation grants are articulated in five broad programme areas each of which has specific aims set by the trustees. These aims, which are reviewed regularly, are the criteria against which trustees assess the relevance and potential impact of outcomes that a grant applicant proposes to achieve with the help of a foundation grant.

Note: The foundations grant-making programmes are current until March 2006. The trustees will be conducting a strategic review before that date and it is anticipated that there will be a closer definition of some programmes and deletion of others.

Community support & development

Aims

To support activities facilitating access to and delivery of community services to those in need.

To help develop the capacity of community organisations to deliver their services better.

Typical projects

The delivery of services, therapies and facilities such as housing and housing advice, counselling and training to persons such as the homeless, young persons generally, those unemployed, disadvantaged women, people of all ages in care, the disabled and the mentally ill. Community capacity building projects such as training, core and infrastructure funding and promotion of standards such as quality assurance.

Aid to ethnic and immigrant communities

Aims

To support activities promoting equality of access and the status of ethnic and immigrant communities in society.

To foster cultural, racial and religious cohesion in local communities.

Typical projects:

Those delivering education, training and employment, counselling, information and advice, healthcare and therapies and other support to single and multi-ethnic or immigrant communities, including access to English where it is not a first language.

Foundations of society

Aim

To support activities relating to citizenship, health, religion and education that will foster moral qualities and intellectual skills and enable beneficiaries to develop as responsible members of society.

Typical projects:

Those promoting citizenship values, sexual and mental health services and education, intellectual access, moral and spiritual well being and understanding within society.

Arts, heritage and the environment

Aim

To contribute to mainstream culture through the Arts, the conservation and promotion of the national heritage, and the rural and urban environment.

Typical projects

Those providing performing and visual arts to the public in general and the disadvantaged specifically, and schemes to raise public awareness and

understanding of the national heritage and secure it for posterity. Activities that conserve and regenerate the natural and built environments through education, training and works.

Areas of special focus

Aim

To support areas of charitable endeavour that the Trustees from time to time identify as deserving of particular emphasis.

Current areas of focus:

- Criminal justice system.

Projects include crime diversion, custody in prison and care and support on release.

- Substance abuse and alternative therapies.

Mainstream substance abuse projects including: research dealing with causation, remedial therapies and related factors such as mental health; alternative or complementary therapy projects; and projects addressing groups whose cultures, customs or language might limit access to therapies.

Many foundation funded projects share these features:

- The work is about providing solutions to problems rather than making them more bearable.
- There is a clear sense of objectives, and of how to achieve them.
- The work may be innovative in a pioneering or risky sense.
- A grant has a good chance of making a difference.

Range and types of grant

The foundation makes grants in two financial categories – small grants and large grants.

SMALL GRANTS FUND

From April 2004, the foundation allocates £150,000 a year to small one-off grants of less than £10,000. It is expected that most of these grants will be of the order of £5,000. Grants may be towards a project or activity.

Applicants for grants under the Small Grants Fund must be registered charities and have an income of less than £50,000 in the twelve months before the application.

Decisions on applications under this fund are taken out of committee and can be expected within three working weeks.

New applications will not normally be considered from previously successful

applicants within 24 months of the completion of a previous grant period.'

LARGE GRANTS FUND

Our large grants are either one-off payments or a grant covering a number of years. Grants may be towards a specific project or to cover core costs such as revenue (salaries), infrastructure development and capacity building, training or service provision.

The Grants Committee considers applications to the Large Grants Fund at one of the three annual grants meetings: July, November & March. Following the initial assessment process, applicants proceeding to the formal application stage are told for which grants meeting agenda their application has been scheduled.

New applications will not be considered from previously successful applicants within 24 months of a one-off grant payment or from the end of the periodic grant period.'

One-off grants

A one-off grant is unlikely to exceed £15,000.

Periodic grants

Our periodic grants range from £10,000 up to £60,000, but are typically of the order of £30,000 to £50,000 depending on the nature of the project and the number of years.

The maximum period of support is three years.

Periodic grants are subject to tapering instalments such that there is a maximum payment in one year with lower payments in each of the other years. The maximum in any one year is presently £25,000, but is typically of the order of £20,000 to £22,000.

Grants 2003/04

Grants by programme area:

	Number	Amount
Community support & development	71 grants	£649,000
Aid to ethnic & immigrant communities	13 grants	£143,000
Foundations of society	34 grants	£383,000
Arts, heritage & the environment	8 grants	£58,000
Areas of special focus	27 grants	£266,000

Annual report 2003/04

Analysis

Over 620 applications were received this year of which 87.3% were rejected. The foundation's trustees made 81 new grants totalling £1.6 million, a 7% increase in value on last year. This is a further consolidation of the trustees' wish to make fewer but larger grants. Some 50% of all new grants are now over three years with more than 20% of awards between £40,000 and £60,000 and 47% exceeding £20,000.

A number of our grants this year have been made as a pro-active joint venture with other funders early in the application stage. This approach has clear benefits to applicants when building a funding package and is something that we wish to develop further. We were also able to use our grant to the Surrey Care Trust 'Swingbridge' project to unlock an additional sum of money for the Trust under a landfill tax scheme. Again, this kind of partnership benefited all concerned.

Geographically, the focus of the foundation's grant making is now firmly in the Greater London area particularly south of the River Thames. Of the 81 new awards in 2003/04, 60 (74%) were in London. The 37 grants to organisations in South London represent 46% of the total of the new awards and over 47% of the value.

Twelve new grants (15%) were in the Southeast including Surrey reflecting the fact that Andrew Wates was High Sheriff of Surrey over the period. As noted in the chairman's report, the trustees have altered their funding guidelines this year to exclude the areas of Surrey and Kent outside the M25 unless the applicants are sponsored by a member of the Wates family. Six 'national' grants went to organisations with a focus in London but whose work extends beyond the capital.

New grants in 2003/04

Community support and development (39 grants totalling £744,000)

The largest grants in this category were £52,000 to Quaker Social Action – East London towards the cost of developing the Odd Jobs project, a social enterprise to provide training and employment; £48,000 to Bellingham Community Project, South London towards the salary of an assistant manager (outreach & communities) at the new community centre in the Lewisham/ Catford area; £45,000 each to Dorset Road Community Project – South London towards the salary of the project co-ordinator for this community project in Stockwell, Lambeth Women's Aid – South London towards the salary of a new senior outreach worker's post working with victims of domestic and sexual violence and Surrey Springboard – Dorking towards the salaries of the vocational training team leaders for this charity working with the unemployed; £42,000 to Meridian Money Advice – Greenwich towards the core costs of a debt and welfare benefit advice project; £41,000 to Ladder to the Moon, South London towards core costs of delivering a strategic development plan for this community theatre project in Wandsworth &

District and £40,000 each to Family Friends – North London towards the cost of an operations manager for this pro-active family support service in London, Home-Start Croydon towards the salary of the volunteer co-ordinator in the north of the borough and St Peter's Church, South London towards the salary of the manager of the InSpire Community Centre in Walworth.

Other beneficiaries included Bethwin Road Playground Project – Camberwell (£29,000), Copleston Centre – Peckham (£25,000); Knights' Youth Centre – Lambeth (£23,000), Cancer Care – Dorset and Social Property Trust (£5,000 each), ACEVO – UK (£4,000), London Sports Forum for Disabled People (£500) Eastwick Junior School – Surrey (£100).

Ethnic and immigrant communities (8 grants totalling £218,000)

Grants in this category were: £45,000 to African Youth Trust – Islington & Hackney towards the salaries of the director and administrative assistant, Brunswick & Wentworth Community Centre – East London towards the costs of a youth project in the Spitalfields area; £39,000 to Lewisham Multi Lingual Advice Service towards the core costs of this organisation facilitating access to ethnic communities; £37,000 to Kurdish Cultural Centre – London towards the salary of the centre's manager; £36,000 to SHARE Community/ Mushkil Aasaan – South London towards core costs of a scheme training young Asian girls with disabilities and learning difficulties in Battersea and Tooting; £9,100 to Oxygen, Kingston towards the costs of a Korean community development project in the New Malden area; £5,000 to Company of Angels – South London towards a series of workshops in Lambeth working with young Albanians; and £2,000 to Chatsworth Baptist Church – South London towards an ethnic minorities Language Partners training scheme in Merton.

Foundations of society (19 grants totalling £406,000)

The largest grants in this category were: £50,000 to Deptford Youth Forum – South London towards core costs of a new post in the New Expressions project; £49,000 to Barnardo's Windermere Centre – South London towards the costs of the chief instructor at this West Norwood vocational training centre; £45,000 to Leap Confronting Conflict – North London towards the Quarrel Shop project; £44,000 to Arvon Foundation – London towards an education officer's post for this charity promoting creative writing skills for children; £42,000 to Maternity Alliance Educational & Research Trust, London towards the costs of a pregnancy support project for Gypsy and Traveller women; £40,000 to Lifetrain Trust – Surrey towards the Right Trax youth education and

support project in four Surrey schools; and £33,000 to Young Vic Theatre – South London towards the costs of the teaching, participation & research project in Southwark & Lambeth.

Other beneficiaries included: Fairbridge, South London (£21,000), Colon Cancer Concern – London (£15,000), Federation of London Youth Clubs (£10,000), Farms for City Children – Devon and Vassall Ward Youth Project – South London (£5,000 each), London Children's Ballet (£2,000), Joint Girls and Boys Brigade Band – Norbury (£500).

Arts, heritage & the environment (4 grants totalling £41,000)

Grants in this category were: £30,000 to The Museum of Garden History – Lambeth; £10,000 to St Martin in the Fields – London towards the cost of the business plan for the Crypt Appeal; £500 to Blue Elephant Theatre – South London towards running costs; and £400 to Daintynak Performing School – Ladywell towards a summer school programme.

Areas of special focus (11 grants totalling £197,000)

Grants in this category were; £45,000 each to Creative & Supportive Trust – Camden towards the costs of an education co-ordinator for the female ex-offenders education project and Stepping Stones Trust – South London towards the costs of an operations manager of this Christian-based charity supporting ex-offenders on release; £36,000 to St Botolph's Project, East London towards the costs of a support worker for a street drinkers project; £30,000 to London Action Trust – Greater London towards the NewLIFE project, helping ex-offenders into work; £15,000 to High Sheriff's Award – Surrey towards the cost of setting up this new awards scheme to support crime prevention projects; £12,000 to Irene Taylor Trust – London towards the cost of a 12-months research project into the impact of arts-based projects on female offenders at HMP &YOI Bullwood Hall; £8,000 to Unit for the Arts & Offenders towards the costs of establishing two new information web sites for crime diversion in the community projects and arts opportunities for ex-offenders; £5,000 to Charlie Waller Memorial Trust towards the Beating the Blues project in HMYOI & RC Reading; £900 to HMP High Down – Surrey towards the cost of publishing poetry from an offenders art and writing exhibition; and £120 to HMP Woodhill – Greater London towards the cost of books for a human rights study project.

Exclusions

The foundation does not support: organisations that are not registered charities unless in the process of registering; any work that is not legally charitable, including that of political parties or political lobbying; any work that is a statutory responsibility whether fulfilled or not; sponsorship of individuals for any purpose; applications from large, well-established or national charities, umbrella organsations; other grant making bodies; any building project including the repair of churches and church appeals; capital purchases such as IT equipment or furniture; disaster relief appeals; specific medical conditions or disabilities; sporting, social or other fundraising events; animal welfare organisations; foreign travel including expeditions; conferences; projects where the activity takes place overseas and projects outside the Greater London area. Applications from charities in those parts of Surrey and Kent outside the M25 will only be considered if they are initiated or endorsed by a member of the Wates family.

Applications

Although the foundation's grants committee meets three times a year in March, July and November, initial applications to the foundation are accepted at any time on a rolling basis. A reply can normally be expected within 14 working days.

There is no time limit set before unsuccessful applicants might re-apply, but a telephone call to the foundation office is advisable in the circumstances.

The formal process of preparing an application and undertaking visits for an application that goes forward to one of the three meetings generally starts up to three months ahead of the meeting date.

Initial applications should be in the form of a letter on no more than four A4 pages. Additional publicity material, pamphlets, newspaper cuttings or reviews will not be read.

An initial application should address the following questions: Who you are and what you do; what you want to do: an outline of the project, where it will be delivered, over what time scale and how; what is the budget for the project and to whom you have applied for funds; why you are the right organisation to carry out the work; who will do the work and what training or accreditation they will have; how the work will involve those you seek to benefit; what difference you hope to achieve and how you intend to measure it

• How you will monitor and ensure the quality of the work undertaken.

A budgetary breakdown may be attached additional to the four-page limit. Budgets covering more than one year should include elements for inflation. Salary costs should identify NI costs.

Letters should be accompanied by signed copies of your most recent annual report and accounts.

The next stage

All requests for support are rigorously filtered before an invitation to apply using our application questionnaire may be issued. On average, 93% of applications to the Foundation are rejected.

Final point

Although we have a small staff, we are happy for potential applicants to ring us up and discuss funding opportunities or seek clarification if you are in doubt about whether you are eligible under our guidelines: this often saves on nugatory correspondence.

Please note that the foundation office is closed on Fridays and all public holidays.

The Wellcome Trust

Biomedical research, history of medicine, biomedical ethics, public engagement with science

£395 million (2003)
Beneficial area UK and overseas.

Wellcome Building, 183 Euston Road, London NW1 2BE
Tel. 020 7611 8545
Email grantenquiries@wellcome.ac.uk
Website www.wellcome.ac.uk
Correspondent Rebecca Christou, Grants Information Officer
Trustees Sir Dominic Cadbury, chair; Prof. Sir Michael Rutter; Prof. Julian Jack; Prof. Christopher R W Edwards; Prof. Martin Bobrow; Prof. Adrian Bird; Prof. Jean Thomas; Edward Walker-Arnott; Alistair Ross Goobey.
Charity Commission no. 210183
Information available Extensive information is available from the marketing department and is accessible through the trust's website.

Summary

With assets worth around £10 billion and grants in 2003 of £395 million, the Wellcome Trust is the second largest grantmaker described in this resource, and the largest biomedical funding charity in the world.

General

Established in 1936 by the entrepreneur and philanthropist Sir Henry Wellcome, the Trust, an endowed charity, will spend about £3 billion in the next five years supporting biomedical research and related activities in the UK and overseas; 85 per cent of this will be spent in the UK.

The trust funds 'blue skies' research as well as more applied clinical research. It also actively supports the translation of research findings for medical benefit.

Reflecting the profound impact today's research will have on society, the trust also seeks to raise awareness of the medical, ethical and social implications of research.

As an endowed charity, the trust is independent of governmental or commercial concerns. It takes a long-term, balanced perspective, and forms national and global partnerships to work towards health benefits for all.

Perhaps best known for funding the UK's contribution to the international Human Genome Project, a groundbreaking project to produce a genetic 'book' of humankind, the trust's continuing support of the HGP has propelled the UK to the forefront of the genomic revolution.

Today the trust supports more than 6,000 researchers worldwide and is not only able to develop the skills and experience of gifted individuals, but also form important alliances with government and industry in order to maximise the value of the research it funds. For example:

• The trust has been responsible for a number of world-class developments, including the largest sequencing and biological computing site in Europe–the Wellcome Trust Genome Campus. This campus houses the Sanger Institute which is contributing a third of the sequence data to the Human Genome Project.

• The trust has worked with the UK government to modernise research infrastructure in UK universities after years of neglect, contributing £525 million to the Joint Infrastructure Fund and Science Research Investment Fund initiatives.

• Together with 14 pharmaceutical and technology companies, it established a public-private initiative–the SNP consortium–with the aim of identifying genetic variations in DNA that make individuals relatively sensitive or resistant to disease.

• In collaboration with the NHS and universities, the trust is stimulating clinical research in the UK, by funding five new Clinical Research Facilities. In this initiative around £18 million has been awarded in order to translate research knowledge into patient care.

- Overseas, the trust conducts pioneering research in HIV/AIDS, malaria and other major killer diseases. For example, in 1997 it established the Africa Centre in KwaZulu Natal.
- The Wellcome Wing is an innovative new 'theatre of science' which has been built at the Science Museum in London. This, alongside six other regional science centres in the UK, illustrates the trust's commitment to engaging the public in medical science.

The trust has experienced unprecedented growth over the past 15 years, at a time of revolutionary advances in biomedical science. Its asset base increased from £1 billion in the mid 1980s to a figure of £10 billion today.

The charity's fortunes have been greatly enhanced through an astute investment programme which manages assets across a variety of investments including equities, securities and property, including some of the most desirable residential properties in London.

Its scientific research programmes are too extensive and too specialised to be summarised or reviewed in this entry, but potential applicants should note that the trust is concerned primarily with medical science, at the highest levels, and is not normally a funder of service-delivering or campaigning charities even in the fields of health and medicine.

Some non-scientific readers of this book may be interested in two relatively minor areas of grantmaking:

- history of medicine research;
- medicine in society programme.

These are described below, after brief information on the scale and direction of the main research grant programmes.

Scientific grants

The trust classified its new awards in 2002/03 and 2001/02 as follows:

	2002/03 £ million	2001/02 £ million
Genetics	£92.2	£105.8
Career support	£76.3	£86.2
Science Research Investment Fund	£71.5	£43.2
Neurosciences	£32.6	£30.3
Joint Infrastructure Fund	£28.3	£27.2
Infection and immunity	£27.3	£27.1
Molecular and cell	£23.4	£36.1
Physiology and pharmacology	£20.4	£38.2
International	£17.1	£28.6
Other infrastructure	£15.0	£1.1
Tropical medicine and infectious diseases	£14.4	£15.3
Population studies	£9.7	£14.9
Other	£7.5	£5.8
History of medicine	£6.8	£5.9
Translation activities	£6.4	£4.5

Public engagement with science	£4.2	£1.7
Equipment	£3.3	£6.8
Cardiovascular initiatives	£2.8	£0.7
Biomedical ethics	£2.0	£1.6
Collaborative awards	——	£2.9
Supplementation of Grants	£15.2	£4.9
Less grants awarded and no longer required	(£15.8)	(£10.3)
Less grants to subsidiaries	(£65.6)	(£59.9)
Total grants awarded	£395.0	£418.6

Although grants are generally awarded in support of particular individuals the award is normally made to the host institution. Small grants may be awarded directly to individuals for the purpose of travel and for developing the public understanding of science.

The major beneficiary institutions were as follows:

	2002/03 £ million	2001/02 £ million
University College London	£42.1	£46.2
University of Oxford	£33.6	£52.4
University of Cambridge	£29.6	£32.5
King's College London	£29.2	£15.9
Imperial College of Science, Technology and Medicine	£25.9	£25.2
University of Glasgow	£19.8	£10.5
University of Edinburgh	£19.1	£36.3
Structural Genome Consortium	£18.0	——
University of Manchester Institute of Science and Technology	£15.7	£1.1
University of Sheffield	£12.9	£4.4
University of Leeds	£12.6	£3.7
University of York	£11.1	£5.1
University of Dundee	£9.0	£17.5
University of Bristol	£6.2	£9.6
University of Manchester	£6.1	£11.7
University of Newcastle upon Tyne	£5.6	£6.7
University of East Anglia	£5.6	£2.1
Cardiff University	£5.6	£1.4
London School of Hygiene and Tropical Medicine	£4.3	£8.5
University of Birmingham	£4.3	£6.3
University of Warrington	£4.2	£11.9
Medical Research Council	£3.0	£1.6
Kenya Medical Research Institute – Kenya	£2.9	£0.2
University of Leicester	£2.5	£14.0
University of Warwick	£2.4	£1.3
Africa Centre for Health and Population Studies – South Africa	£2.2	£6.5
University of Nottingham	£2.2	£2.9
Queen Mary and Westfield College	£2.2	£0.9
City University, London	£1.9	£0.2
University of Southampton	£1.8	£1.8
University of Aberdeen	£1.8	£1.8
University of Wale College of Medicine	£1.6	£3.1
University of Bath	£1.5	£2.2
University of Kent	£1.5	£0.8
University of Cape Town – South Africa	£1.4	£0.7
Queens University, Belfast	£1.4	£0.5
Hungarian Academy of Science – Hungary	£1.2	£0.9
St George's Hospital Medical School	£1.1	£4.3
University of Durham	£1.1	£1.0
Birkbeck College London	£1.1	£2.1
University of Wales, Bangor	£1.0	£0.2
University of Tartu – Estonia	£1.0	——
University of Reading	£1.0	£0.4
University of Exeter	£1.0	£3.5
University of Witwatersrand – South Africa	£0.9	£0.1
University of St Andrews	£0.8	£1.4
University of Strathclyde	£0.8	£0.4
Royal Veterinary College	£0.8	£0.5
National Centre of Biological Science – India	£0.7	£0.9
University of Aston	£0.7	——

History of medicine

The trust supports research in medical history in UK universities, as well as in Wellcome Units for the History of Medicine at three UK universities and in the Wellcome Trust Centre for the History of Medicine at University College London.

Public engagement projects

The History of Medicine Grants Panel has set aside part of its annual budget to fund public engagement projects. The trust does not wish to be prescriptive with this scheme, with all approaches considered. Applications may involve, for example, television, radio, exhibitions, theatre, websites, educational resources, lecture and debate series, so long as the overriding principle is either:

- to provide greater contributions to general history coverage and the promotion of history of medicine; or
- to promote historical research in a manner that stimulates an informed dialogue between researchers, policy makers and the wider public with the aim of raising awareness and understanding of biomedical science.

Projects involving links between historians of medicine and biomedical scientists/clinicians that stimulate an informed debate around current health and research issues are particularly encouraged, for example animal experimentation, genetics, cloning and stem-cell research. In addition, projects that utilise the rich resources within the Wellcome Library are also encouraged.

Grants will not be available to contribute towards acquisitions of artefacts to be displayed in museums.

Eligibility

Applications are invited from a wide range of organisations, including charitable bodies and other not-for-profit organisations. Applications are also accepted from commercial companies who would otherwise not be able to undertake the proposed work as it would not be considered commercially viable. Academics, clinicians, science writers or other individuals are also eligible to apply. The proposed activity must take place in the UK.

Preliminary application procedure

Preliminary applications should be made in writing at least six weeks before the official deadline and should include:

- a brief CV and full publication list;
- details of proposed activity (maximum two page);

- approximate cost of proposal broken down into salaries, equipment and project running costs.

Full applications should be submitted by 1 March, 1 August and 1 December of each year. These deadlines are strictly adhered to and applicants are strongly advised to submit their completed proposals at least one week beforehand.

Contact
Grants Section (History of Medicine)
Tel: 020 7611 7202/8231
Fax: 020 7611 8254
E-mail: hom@wellcome.ac.uk

Grants in 2002/03

In 2002/03, Exeter and Warwick [Universities] were the first recipients of the Wellcome Trust's new Strategic Awards in the History of Medicine, providing large-scale, long-term (five-year) support for clusters of medical historians working on a common theme. Previously, long-term support has focused on Wellcome Units in the History of Medicine, which gave little scope for burgeoning new groups to develop further.

The £700,000 award to [University of Exeter] will support research on interplay between nature and nurture in health and disease from 1850 to the present day, including environmental and occupational respiratory diseases, and the history of gender, sexuality and the family.

The £600,000 grant to [University of Warwick plus a researcher at the University of Leicester] will support research on the social history of medicine and medical practice in early modern Europe and in the UK over the past two centuries.

The awards provide support for research, core administrative support, postgraduate teaching and outreach work.

Two Enhancement Awards – lower-level support without the need for a single research theme – were made in 2002/03, to groups at Oxford Brookes University and the universities of Durham and Newcastle upon Tyne. Both types of award provide important opportunities for centres to develop their research capacity in the history of medicine – an area in which the trust has long played a critical role in the UK.

Medicine in Society programme

This covers two fields:

Research in biomedical ethics

The biomedical ethics research programme funds research into the social, ethical and public policy consequences of advances in biomedicine. In 2002/03 awards in this area totalled £2 million – roughly the same is awarded each year.

Public engagement with science

The trust funds research in the public engagement with science and provides support for public communication initiatives. In 2002/03 awards in this area totalled £4.2 million, a significant increase on previous years as a result of recent new initiatives.

The two programmes in this field are Society Awards and the ReDiscover science centres and museums initiative. They are described as follows:

Society Awards

These awards are targeted, time-limited calls for research and activity in specified areas. These awards are available to support research or larger scale activities that aim to make a significant impact– ideally of nationwide importance–on public engagement with science and its related issues.

Pre-application workshops will be offered to those interested in applying to the Engaging Science grants programme.

Scope/subject boundaries

The current themes, for which applications are still being invited, are:

- *Young people's education (two years)*

To introduce interesting new ideas in science education and boost teachers' confidence in handling socioscientific issues.

- *Broadening access (one year)*

To promote dialogue among new audiences on the impact of biomedical science on their lives.

- *sciart*

To encourage artists and other creative professionals to explore biomedical subjects and themes in their work within the public arena.

The scheme is open to:

- mediators and practitioners (e.g. science centre staff, science communicators, artists, educators, health professionals etc.);
- academics (e.g. biomedical scientists, historians, social scientists or ethicists).

Projects are funded for a maximum of three years and might include:

- academic research or larger-scale activities in any of the three themed areas; or

Activities such as:

- workshops,
- talks and discussions in public venues;
- drama and art projects for a variety of different audiences and age groups;

- conferences and seminars that disseminate academic findings to a broader audience.

Eligibility criteria: For research projects

- Applicants must normally hold an established academic post in a UK or Republic of Ireland university or other institution of higher education.
- Where the proposed principal investigator is not funded by a higher education funding council or acceptable equivalent, they may apply for their salary as long as there is a sponsor who holds an established academic post in a UK or Republic of Ireland university or other institution of higher education whose source of salary is acceptable to the trust.
- The head of department must guarantee that the principal investigator will have access to the necessary resources.

Research proposals can be accepted from some charitable bodies and other not-for-profit organisations, where they will be undertaking the work directly, provided the organisation has been checked for eligibility to hold trust grants. It is not possible to give grants to other organisations to be redistributed.

Eligibility criteria: For activities

- Applications are accepted from a range of organisations, including academic institutions, charitable bodies and other not-for-profit organisations.
- Applications will also be accepted from commercial companies who would not otherwise be able to undertake the proposed work and where outputs would not be considered for commercial funding.
- Applicants must be based in the UK and the activity must take place in the UK.
- Grants will normally be awarded to organisations rather than individuals. Applicants will be encouraged to apply through an organisation. If this is not possible, individuals can apply but they must demonstrate a strong track record in the area of their application.

Eligibility assessment

If this is an organisation's first application to the trust, an eligibility assessment will be carried out. A copy of the organisation's articles of association and audited accounts from the previous year must be submitted for the assessment. Applications will not proceed until these checks have been completed. For further information, email: engagingscience@wellcome.ac.uk.

How to apply

- Applications will be invited by specified deadlines twice a year and will be subject to review by referees.
- Funding decisions will be made by an expert panel.
- The deadlines for applications in 2004 were 1 June and 1 September.
- Decisions will be made up to four months after receipt of applications.

ReDiscover

ReDiscover will bring new life to science by offering grants to UK science centres and museums to renew, replace, refresh or redevelop exhibition space.

ReDiscover is a joint venture between the Millennium Commission, the Wellcome Trust and the Wolfson Foundation to support science education and engagement with the public.

The fund has a total of £33 million available which is being awarded over four funding rounds. In the first round, nine awards totalling £3.8 million were made. Decisions on the second round will be made early in 2004.

New Information for Rounds 3 and 4

Prospective applicants should be aware that deadlines have passed.

Round 3

Deadline for applications: (1 March 2004)

Announcement of awards: August 2004

Round 4

Deadline for applications: 1 October 2004

Announcement of awards: March 2005

ReDiscover funds, which form up to 75 per cent of the total project cost, should be spent by December 2005. As such, we would expect applications to Round 3 would be for larger more complex projects, similar to those funded in Rounds 1 and 2. Round 4 however, will be for short duration projects only.

In addition to applications covering the full spectrum of science, including technology and engineering, we would like to encourage applications that have a biomedical focus.

Eligibility

Awards will only be made to organisations that fulfil all of the following eligibility criteria:

- present science and technology exhibitions to the public;
- be charitable or not-for-profit and have a formally registered constitution;

- be a continuous operation throughout the year with permanently employed staff;
- attract a minimum of 30,000 visitors per annum;
- have been in operation for at least one year at the date of application;
- be financially viable;
- be based in the UK;
- be able to demonstrate that at least 25 per cent partnership funding has been secured. This can be in the form of an in kind donation.

Please note that if your organisation does not fulfil all of the eligibility criteria listed above your application will not be taken forward.

Application procedure

An application form and a set of guidelines are available to download as PDF documents. Applicants must refer to these guidelines before completing an application form. Please note that details covered on the form will include:

- project objectives including the details of the intended audience;
- the educational potential;
- amount requested from ReDiscover;
- total project costs with a full budget breakdown of all elements e.g. design costs, essential project-related building work;
- details of partnership funding;
- the beneficial effect that the project will have upon the viability of your organisation;
- evaluation and dissemination.

Where essential building works are required as part of the proposal applicants will be asked to supply additional supporting information.

Grants in 2002/03

The following projects/organisations received grants in the first round:

Techniquest – Cardiff (£927,000) – an exhibition with 35 new interactive exhibits designed to stimulate awareness of the link between science and music. 'Musiquest' will also feature equipment to support educational programmes and a flexible performance area for musical activities, science demonstrations and concerts.

At-Bristol (£923,000) – the redevelopment of the first floor of Explore At-Bristol including a new 'Live Science' exhibition. Among other developments, the Curiosity Zone Gallery will be extended and grouped into the new themed areas of light, sound, electricity and magnetism, vortices and perception. Accessibility to

the Imaginarium planetarium will also be improved.

Discovery Museum – Newcastle (£554,000) – the creation of a four-part exhibition, the centrepiece of which will be the first steam turbine-powered vessel, the Turbinia. Discovery Stations will feature games and experiments based on scientific principles. Top Tyneside Innovations will honour three key Tyneside inventors and new Education, Resource and Activity Modules will provide hands-on activities.

Glasgow Science Centre (£360,000) – the upgrading of the Science Show Theatre and the creation of 'Enviroscan' which will include an Auto Weather Station linked to schools and educational projects, a Climate Change Theatre and the Clyde Monitoring Exhibit which will collect and feed back data on the River Clyde.

Museum of Science and Industry – Manchester (£250,000) – 'Manchester Science' will be a new exhibition celebrating the work of eminent Manchester scientists, Dalton, Rutherford, Joule and Lovell. Three key themed areas will cover Historical Manchester Science, Contemporary Manchester Science and 'What Do You Think?' – an interactive area designed to encourage debate, questioning and feedback.

Ulster Folk and Transport Museum – Hollywood, Northern Ireland (£231,000) – the redevelopment of the existing 'Flight Experience' exhibition in line with the Centennial of Flight 2003. In addition, a new gallery space will include an air traffic control station, interactive aircraft parts and models and a flight simulator.

Look Out Discovery Centre – Bracknell (£231,000) – the enhancement of the educational provisions of the centre through new and refurbished exhibits around the themes of water and woodlands. These will include 'The Stream' – a centrepiece exhibit of flowing water and movable obstacles and dams, and a three metre tall vortex of water.

Hunterian Museum and Art Gallery – Glasgow (£225,000) – the establishment of 'Re-discover Kelvin', a range of new interactive exhibits to interpret and display Kelvin's collection of scientific instruments and principle works. The development will include new lecture demonstration apparatus; associated education programmes and easier access to the exhibit.

Scottish Seabird Centre – North Berwick (£120,000)

The installation of a live satellite-linked camera from the visitor centre to the remote island archipelago of St Kilda. Visitors will be able to observe the island's large puffin population and marine visitors such as whales, dolphins and basking sharks. An additional camera will give visual access to the underwater antics of seabirds and seals.

For further information please contact:

Ms Debbie Vincent
Grants Administrator
Medicine in Society
The Wellcome Trust
183 Euston Road
London NW1 2BE
Tel: 020 7611 7347
E-mail: rediscover@wellcome.ac.uk

Comment

The commitment, energy and enterprise of this trust, at least in the aspects of its work that are accessible to the lay observer, continue to impress.

Exclusions

The trust does not normally consider support for the extension of professional education or experience, the care of patients or clinical trials.

Contributions are not made towards overheads and not normally towards office expenses.

The trust does not supplement support provided by other funding bodies, nor does it donate funds for other charities to use, nor does it respond to general appeals.

For policy on funding cancer research (and other funding policies) please refer to 'Research Funding Policies' on the website (www.wellcome.ac.uk/en/1/biopolcan.html).

Applications

Applicants are advised, in the first instance, to contact the grants section by telephone for further relevant information or to make a preliminary application in writing.

A preliminary application should include:

- brief details of the proposed research (one A4 page maximum);
- a note of existing funding from all sources, including the source of the applicant's salary funding;
- a brief curriculum vitae;

- a list of relevant publications and an approximate costing.

The quality of the proposed research is not judged at this stage.

If applicants are eligible to apply, they are sent a full application form. A preliminary application can be submitted at any time, other than those for special schemes and initiatives with advertised closing dates.

For UK-based project or programme grants a preliminary application is not necessary and an application form can be obtained via the trust's website.

The trust has many funding schemes and therefore potential applicants are advised to refer to the website for information on meeting dates and application deadlines.

The Welton Foundation

Medical research, music, general

£524,000 (2003/04)

Beneficial area UK.

33 St Mary Axe, London EC3A 8LL
Tel. 020 7280 2800
Email robin.jessel@intraforum.net
Correspondent Robin R Jessel, Secretary
Trustees D B Vaughan; H A Stevenson; Prof. J Newsom-Davis.
Charity Commission no. 245319
Information available Accounts and report.

Summary

The foundation describes its general grantmaking policy thus:

The objective of the foundation is to provide financial support to other charities at the absolute discretion of the trustees. As a discretionary trust the foundation has no fixed policy for making grants. The current policy of the trustees is in the main to support charitable causes in the fields of health and medicine, but they can exercise their discretion to make donations to any other charities

General

In 2003/04 the foundation had assets of £6.5 million generating an income of £295,000. Grants were made during the

year totalling £524,000 (£193,000 in the previous year),

Grants were made to 35 organisations during the year under the following categories:

Health and medicine (14 grants – £314,000)

A substantial grant of £150,000 was made to Academy of Medical Sciences, Other larger grants were £60,000 to Epilepsy Research Foundation and £48,000 to Digestive Disorders Foundation. Other beneficiaries included University of Oxford – Department of Clinical Neurology (£15,000), Changing Faces (£10,000), Brendoncare Foundation Development Trust and USL Middlesex Hospital (£5,000 each), Oxford Children's Hospital Campaign (£2,000), Cancer Relief Macmillan Fund and Home Farm Trust (£1,000 each).

Community development (1 grant of £2,000)

The sole beneficiary was Bramford Road Methodist Church Community Centre.

Conservation/heritage (4 grants – £23,000)

Grants went to Friends of Benjamin Franklin House (£10,000), Bowes Museum and World Monuments Fund in Britain (£5,000 each) and Shoreditch Church (£3,000).

Culture and arts (6 grants – £20,000)

Beneficiaries in this category included: British Youth Opera (£5,000), New Orange Tree Theatre (£4,000), Academy of St Mary's Wimbledon (£3,000), City Chamber Choir (£1,500).

Disability (2 grants – £79,000)

A substantial grant of £76,000 was made to Aidis Trust. Roy Kinnear Charitable Foundation received £2,500.

Education and training – (7 grants – £84,000)

A substantial grant of £60,000 went to Kidscape. Other beneficiaries included Fairbridge, Joint Educational Trust and Peper Harrow Foundation (£5,000 each), Atlantic College (£2,500) and Frank Hodgson Memeorial Fund (£1,000).

Services charities (1 grant of £5,000)

The sole beneficiary was Royal Airforces Association.

Exclusions

Grants only to registered charities, and not in response to general appeals.

Applications

In writing to the secretary, stating: what the charity does; what specific project the money is needed for, giving as much detail as possible; how much money is needed; the source of any other funding.

Due to the number of appeals received, the foundation only replies to those that are successful.

The Westminster Foundation

General

£1.7 million (2003)

Beneficial area UK, and local interests in central London (SW1 and W1 and immediate environs), the north west of England, especially rural Lancashire and the Chester area, and the Sutherland area of Scotland.

70 Grosvenor Street, London W1K 3JP

Tel. 020 7408 0988 **Fax** 020 7312 6244

Correspondent Colin Redman, Secretary

Trustees *The Duke of Westminster, chair; J H M Newsum; R M Moyse.*

Charity Commission no. 267618

Information available Annual report and accounts were provided by the trust, without a full report or explanation of grants made.

The foundation makes almost 200 grants a year, mainly for welfare and educational causes, but with substantial support for conservation and rather less for medicine and the arts. Grants appear to be all for UK causes and perhaps half by number, though less by value, are in the areas of special interest given above.

Though grants can be every large, all but a handful are usually for amounts of not more than £60,000 and most are between £5,000 and just a few hundred pounds. About half of the beneficiaries were also supported in previous years.

The foundation has previously noted that: 'It is usual that the trustees have knowledge of, or connection with, those charities which are successful applicants.

The trustees tend to support caring causes and not research.'

This is assumed to be a largely personal trust, created by the present duke. He is well known in the charity world for his active personal involvement in many organisations, and no doubt a significant number of the regular beneficiaries are organisations with which he has developed a personal connection that goes beyond grantmaking.

In 2003 it had assets of £25 million and a total income of £2.3 million, largely due to it receiving donations totalling £1.7 million. Management and administration fees amounted to £50,000. Grants were made to 176 organisations and totalled £1.7 million. They were broken down as follows:

Youth – 17 grants totalling £173,000

NSPCC – Northwest Major Appeal received £100,000. Other grants over £10,000 each were £24,000 to Chester Youth Club and £13,000 each to Kidscape and Youth Sport Trust.

Other grants included £8,000 to the Timothy Trust, £5,000 to Farms for the City, £2,500 to Pimlico Family Workshop Toy Library, £2,000 to the Honeypot Charity, £1,000 to Armourers and Brasiers Gauntlet Trust, £500 to Chester and District Scout Association and £50 to Weston Spirit.

Education – 15 grants totalling £410,000

The two largest grants were £155,000 to University of Cambridge and £100,000 to University of Liverpool. Other large grants included £55,000 to Royal United Services Institute for Defence, £33,000 to Training for Life Limited, £24,000 to Teach First, £17,000 to Foundation of Nursing Studies and £12,000 to Investment Property Forum Education Trust.

Medical – 32 grants totalling £139,000

In this category there were five grants of £10,000 or more: £28,000 to Dyslexia Institute, £25,000 to Royal Marsden Cancer Campaign, £12,000 to Arthritis Care and £10,000 to British Cancer Help Centre and Woodlands Hospice.

Other grants included £7,800 to Commonwealth Society for the Deaf, £6,000 to British Kidney Patient Association, £5,000 to St Lazarus Charitable Trust, £4,200 to Florence Nightingale Foundation, £2,500 to

Countess of Chester Hospital, £2,000 to King Edward VII's Hospital for Officers, £1,500 to Cancer Research, £1,000 each to British Heart Foundation, Middlesex Hospital Radio Fund and National Osteoporosis Society and £500 to Trinity Hospice.

Arts – 19 grants totalling £210,000

The six largest grants of £10,000 or more were £100,000 to Armed Forces Memorial Appeal, £50,000 to the Tank Museum and £10,000 each to Army Benevolent Society, Churchill Museum Appeal, English Sinfonia and Royal Opera House.

Other grants included £4,600 to Live Music Now!, £2,000 each to Chester Archaeological Society and Friends of the Chester Military Museum, £1,000 each to City of Chester Band and the Royal Society of Arts, £500 to Dunrobin Pipig Championship and £250 each to Grosvenor Museum Society and Sutherland Pipe Band.

Social and welfare – 65 grants totalling £538,000

There were 15 grants of over £10,000 in this category with the Extra-Care Charitable Trust receiving the largest of £100,000. Other larger grants included £50,000 to Forum for the Future, £30,000 to Business in the Community, £25,600 to the Not Forgotten Association, £22,660 to Royal Agricultural Society for the Commonwealth, £20,000 Cardinal Hume Centre, Centrepoint Soho, Passage 2000 and St Mungo's Community Housing, £17,082 to Burma Star Association, £11,691 to Inter-Faith Network for UK and £10,000 to Esther Benjamin Trust.

Other grants included £8,900 to the Arvon Foundation, £7,700 to Trekforce Expedition, £5,000 each to Gurkha Welfare Trust, NCH Lache Family Centre and National Cycle Network Centre Appeal, £3,700 to Voices Foundation, £2,500 to the Lord Mayor of Westminster's Christmas Appeal, £1,300 to Community Foundation for Greater Manchester, £1,000 each to Bolton Community Transport and Furniture Services, Chester Council for Voluntary Service, Dial House, Northwest Community Business Association, Sunderland Care and Repair and White Ensign Association Ltd, £350 to Variety Club, £250 to Lairg Community Association and £90 to Riding for the Disabled.

Exclusions

Only registered charities will be considered; charitable status applied for, or pending, is not sufficient. No grants to individuals, 'holiday' charities, student expeditions, or research projects.

Applications

In writing to the secretary, enclosing an up-to-date set of accounts, together with a brief history of the project to date, and the current need.

The Westminster Foundation for Democracy

Strengthening democracy overseas

£3 million (2002/03)

Beneficial area Outside the UK.

2nd Floor, 125 Pall Mall, London SW1Y 5EA

Tel. 020 7930 0408 **Fax** 020 7930 0449

Email wfd@wfd.org

Website www.wfd.org

Correspondent David French, Chief executive

Trustees *Mike Gapes MP, chair; Nik Gowing; Michael Moore MP; Michael Trend MP; Michael Aaronson; Georgina Ashworth; Nicola Duckworth; Mary Kaldor; Elfyn Llwyd MP; Patrick Smith; Frances D'Souza; Caroline Spelman MP; Richard Spring MP; Gisela Stuart MP.*

Information available Annual report and accounts, information leaflets and details of projects supported are available from the foundation.

Summary

The foundation gives grants, seldom for more than £30,000 and often for less than £10,000, for projects to support democracy anywhere in the world, but its work is concentrated in Central and Eastern Europe, in the former Soviet Union and in anglophone Africa.

Half the grants are channelled through the UK political parties.

General

The foundation receives almost all its money from the government, but it makes its own decisions about the projects to be supported. In 2002/03 grants were made totalling just over £3 million. It describes its policies as follows:

WFD funds a wide range of organisations and projects that aim to build pluralist democratic institutions abroad, such as:
- political parties;
- parliaments or other representative institutions;
- legal reform;
- human rights groups;
- independent media;
- women's organisations and projects;
- other political non-governmental organisations;
- election systems or administration;
- trades unions.

It will give preference to projects which contain clear action plans, designed to achieve concrete results; those whose effects will be lasting; and to building up organisations which can be self-sustaining, rather than encouraging continuing dependence on outside assistance.

The following is David French, the Chief Executive's introduction to the 2002/03 annual review, which gives a good picture of how the foundation operates and its plans for the future:

The foundation is an independent agency sponsored by the Foreign and Commonwealth Office (FCO). Yet it is structured and operates on a cross-party, political basis: half its work (in financial terms) is delivered through the Westminster political parties, developing party-to-party relationships across the political spectrum in the interests of promoting thriving, multi-party democracies. This unusual mix, combined with the foundation's interests in supporting parliamentary, civil society and other non-partisan initiatives, gives it a position and capacity to operate in ways matched by few other organisations in the world.

When we began, earlier this year, to formulate a new strategic direction for the foundation it quickly became clear to us that we should build on these distinguishing strengths, while contributing to the FCO's objectives of promoting democracy and the rule of law internationally.

The strategy approved by the board of governors in July 2003 is based on the vision of achieving sustainable political change in emerging democracies. It is centred on the foundation's capacity to design and deliver coordinated party-to-party political development programmes in the countries in which it chooses to work. This

political work will continue to be complemented by non-partisan initiatives; and our emphasis in future will be to bring together these interests in programmes which will enable the foundation to make a multi-dimensional impact over time in the countries in which it is active.

Geographically, the foundation will strengthen its commitment to working in two regions. Having undertaken much successful work in central and eastern Europe over its first decade, including a wide range of projects in countries which have joined the European Union, we shall concentrate our interests on the Eastern neighbours of an enlarged EU. We shall also continue and strengthen our commitment to democracy-building in Africa, focusing mainly on the sub-Saharan region, where again WFD has made a range of significant contributions in recent years. While we shall maintain an overall balance between the volume of work in these two regions, we shall also be devoting limited resources to exploring the opportunities to develop a third area of focus, in the Islamic world. Beyond these geographical interests we shall retain a limited facility, within specified criteria, to continue making small grants in other regions where a special case can be made.

The foundation's new strategy anticipates the development of country-based programmes. Once we have committed to working in a country we shall expect to maintain a sustained interest in it over a number of years, with Westminster parties and the foundation's central teams making contributions to the development of our work in the country. Countries will be chosen according to clearly defined criteria, while the shape of each programme will reflect the local interests and opportunities. Understanding the characteristics and influences in each locality will be an essential prerequisite of all our work. Wherever we work, the development of political party initiatives will be the norm, complemented by parlimentary and civil society work appropriate to local circumstances.

WFD's methodology will correspondingly develop to support the strategy. Achieving the highest standards of transparency and thoroughness both in the formulation of programmes and in their evaluation is important to us. Developments in the foundation's operational and grant-making practice will seek to strengthen its relationships with funders such as the Department for International Development, the UN Development Programme and the EU and with FCO itself. The foundation will look to substantial growth in its funding, since we are ambitious to build on the reputation we have established over our first decade; and we recognise the immense field of opportunity open to us.

While the new strategy builds on the successes of the past, these changes represent a major shift in the method and style for the foundation, and of course this will have a direct impact on the projects we can support. The foundation was active in 46 countries last year. We expect substantially to reduce this number over the next two years as we increase our commitment, and impact, in fewer locations.

Exclusions

The foundation does not fund:

- conferences;
- research;
- educational scholarships;
- cultural, health or social projects.

Applications

In writing to the correspondent. Applicants are advised first to check the website, which has detailed guidelines for applications, including guidance on budget costings. Project evaluations are part of the conditions of assistance from the foundation.

Potential applicants can also consider seeking advice in the first instance from the international office of a UK political party with corresponding aspirations.

Trustees normally meet quarterly at the end of January, April, July and October.

The Garfield Weston Foundation

General

£36 million (2002/03)

Beneficial area UK.

Weston Centre, 10 Grosvenor Street, London W1K 4QY

Tel. 020 7399 6565 **Fax** 020 7399 6588

Email fhare@wittington-investments.co.uk

Website www.garfieldweston.org

Correspondent Fiona Hare, Administrator

Trustees *Guy Weston, chair; Galen Weston; Miriam Burnett; Eliza Mitchell; Nancy Baron; Camilla Dalglish; Jana R Khayat; Anna C Hobhouse; George G Weston; Sophia Mason.*

Charity Commission no. 230260

Information available Excellent descriptive annual report and accounts with grants analysis and a full list of grants.

Summary

The huge foundation makes about 1,500 one-off grants a year, typically for amounts anywhere between £3,000 and £1 million. Perhaps helped by the fact that the income of the foundation has been rising rapidly, about half of all appeals result in a grant, though not necessarily for the full amount requested. Awards are regularly made in almost all fields except overseas aid and animal welfare.

Probably more than 85% of the money, and an even higher proportion for the largest grants, is for capital or endowment projects.

The published 'criteria' for grantmaking, reported below, are in the most general terms. Compared to the general run of trusts described in this book, there are relatively few grants to unconventional causes, or for campaigning or representational activities, and more for institutions such as independent schools and charities connected with private hospitals. Nevertheless almost all kinds of charitable activity, including the radical, are supported to some extent, except that there are very few grants to major charities with high levels of fundraising costs.

The foundation is one of the few which can consider very large grants. The largest grant in 2002/03 was for £3.5 million (to the Thrombosis Research Institute).

The charity's ten trustees (all family members) are backed by a very modest staff, but nevertheless the foundation aims to deal with applications within three months of their being received – an unusually prompt response time.

In 2002/03 the foundation had assets standing at £2.3 billion. It's income amounted to almost £29 million. Grants totalled £36 million.

Grantmaking

The trust describes as follows the criteria by which applications are assessed.

- The financial viability of the organisation.
- The degree of need for the project requiring funding.
- The amount spent on administration and fundraising as compared to the charitable activities.
- The ability to raise sufficient funding to meet the appeal target.
- Whether the aims of the organisation meet the trustees' aspirations.
- Whether the organisation has the right priorities.
- Where possible, the ability of the organisation to meet its goals.

There were ten grants made for £1 million or more. Beneficiaries were Thrombosis Research Institute London (£3.5 million), Royal Marsden Hospital Charity (£2 million) and Oxford Brookes University School of Health Care, National Gallery, Roundhouse Trust, Royal Marsden Hospital Charity, Royal Society, Specialist Schools Trust, University of Edinburgh, University of York – CNAP and Welsh National Opera (£1 million each).

It is the practice of the foundation to make single, one-off grants. However the grants lists show that a few beneficiaries are supported in consecutive years, and occasionally for even longer.

Grants by sector

The annual reports describe the purposes of some of the larger grants under each of the headings listed above, but for most awards there is only a list of the recipient organisations with no indication of the purpose.

THE GARFIELD WESTON FOUNDATION
Grants in 2002/03

	2002/03		(2001/02)		(2000/01)	
	Value	No	(Value)	(No.)	(Value)	(No.)
Education	£8.7m	156	(£6.2m 134)		(£13.5m 171)	
Health	£12m	90	(£4.4 m 88)		(£7.8m 134)	
Welfare	£3.5m	232	(£4.8 m 265)		(£5m340)	
Religion	£3.9m	442	(£3.7m 422)		(£3.8m 431)	
Arts	£3.8m	64	(£8.5m 84)		(£3.8m 90)	
Youth	£2.4m	147	(£2.9m 197)		(£2m 215)	
Environment	£0.8m	26	(£0.3 m 31)		(£1m42)	
Community	£0.7m	152	(£0.9m 149)		(£0.6m 167)	
Mental health	£0.7m	50	(£1m 67)		(£0.6m57)	
Other	£0.3m	12	(£0.2m 12)		(£0.5m 29)	
TOTAL	£37m	1351	(£33m 1449)		(£38.9m1,682)	

Education

There were three grants of £1 million each in this category. The Royal Society received support towards the refurbishment and redevelopment of their Grade 1 listed Carlton House Terrace premises and continued support was given to the Specialist Schools Trust (formerly the Technology Colleges Trust) and York University towards the work of the Centre for Novel Agricultural Products.

Almost all other large grants listed in the annual report were for capital projects, such as those to Royal Academy of Music (£256,000) and Yehudi Menuhin School, National Centre for Young People with Epilepsy, Portland College and Treloar Trust (£250,000 each).

Awards divide into three groups:

- to universities, often for research centres and other causes which 'reach out to the wider public'
- to schools and colleges, both fee paying and state sector, and usually for unspecified purposes
- to educational charities and museums.

Health/mental health

Most large grants, at least where the purpose was identifiable, were for capital projects. These include the four grants made over £1 million. Following the assitance provided over a number of years the trustees provided a major grant of £3.5 million to the Thrombosis Research Institute towards upgrading equipment and development work. The Royal Marsden received £2 million towards major capital development. Grants of £1 million each went to University of Edinburgh towards its new Research Institute for Medical Cell Biology and Oxford Brookes Univeristy towards its new School of Health Care building.

Grants of £250,000 each were provided to the University of Newcastle for a clinical research facility, Moorfields Eye Hospital for a new centre for children, the National Hospital for Neurology and Neurodisability for the first European Dementia Research Centre, the University of Oxford for a new Cardiovascular Clinical Research Facility and the Liver Group at Imperial College for research into the creation of an artificial liver.

Medical research beneficiaries included Action Research which received £300,000. This was divided between an investigation into the causes and effects of epilepsy at the Institute of Neurology at University College London and research into molecular pathways of cell death in motor neurone regeneration at Sheffield University.

Regional hospitals and hospices around the country continued to benefit from funding at various levels, as organisations providing research, information and support into a wide range of conditions. A £50,000 grant went to the British Homeopathic Association towards a new post at Liverpool University, to encourage the development of homeopathy as a fully integrated part of the British national healthcare system.

Welfare and community

These are two separate headings in the accounts but there is considerable overlap between them.

A major grant of £500,000 went to the British Commonwealth Ex-services League towards its Jubilee Appeal for Commonwealth Veterans.

Age Concern's national office received a grant of £150,000 for their Volunteer Development programme. Grants to other charities working with older people included £100,000 each to Abbeyfield Society to help them extend their Integrated Care Programme, Brendoncare Foundation towards the redevelopment of their residential care home in East Grinstead and Central and Cecil Housing Trust for a capital rebuild in Merton and £50,000 to the Lady Margaret Hungerford Chrity towards the refurbishment of their almshouses.

Support was given to several projects working with young offenders – a grant of £100,000 went to the Centre for Adolescent Rehabilitation. The Rehabilitation of Addicts in Prison Trust also received £100,000. The Princes Trust received £50,000 for its project to help young people referred by the criminal justice system to help increase their social and educational skills.

Grants to benefit people with disabilities included £100,000 each to Leonard Cheshire and Sue Ryder towards the cost of providing purpose-built living facilities and £50,000 towards the Royal National Institute for Deaf People for renovation costs and for developing skills and activities for deaf people with severe learning disabilities.

A grant of £50,000 was distributed to Faith Together in Leeds towards the renovation costs and the provision of a new meeting space. Many of the organisations supported under 'community' applied for help with upgrading facilities and providing disabled access.

Religion

This heading refers mainly to church maintenance and restoration. Grants ranged from the £500,000 each donated to Peterborough Cathedral Development and Preservation Trust and Wells Cathedral to about 300 grants for local churches, for amounts under £10,000 each.

The arts

There were two major grants of £1 million each to Welsh National Opera to support its ongoing work and National Gallery towards the creation of a new reception and visitor information spaces. A grant of £250,000 was donated to the Arnolfini centre towards the planned expansion of its premises. The Royal National Theatre received £150,000 towards an initiative aimed at attracting new audiences. Support has been given to charities dealing with the whole range of the arts, including opera, dramatic theatre, galleries and music. A number of grants have also been made to youth theatre and educational projects.

Environment

The largest grant was £250,000 to the Marine Stewardship Council for their Sea into the Future appeal, a major public campaign to raise money for the world's seafood resources. The sum of £200,000 was donated to Game Conservancy Trust towards their conservation research work.

Grants ranging from £500 to £30,000 were made to support Wildlife Trusts, canal restorations, forestry management, village greens, city farms and Groundwork projects.

Youth

The grants in this category reflect the trustees' interest in ensuring that adequate provision is made for youth acrivities to take place in a safe environment and one which also meets the interests and needs of young people.

A grant of £1 million went to the Roundhouse towards refurbishment costs. The sum of £250,000 was donated to Girl Guiding UK for improvements to its residential training facilities. There were three organisation in receipt of £100,000 each including the Attlee Foundation towards establishing a multi-purpose youth and community centre with sports facilities and Urdd Gobaith

Cymru towards new accommodation, a sports centre and a heritage centre.

Exclusions

Support cannot be considered for organisations or groups which are not UK registered charities. Applications from individuals or for individual research or study or from organisations outside the UK cannot be considered. The trustees do not support animal welfare charities.

Charities are asked not to re-apply within a 12-month period of an appeal to the foundation, whether they have received a grant or not.

Applications

All applications are considered on an individual basis by a committee of trustees. From time to time, more information about a charity or a visit to the project might be requested. Trustees meet monthly and there is no deadline for applications, which are considered in order of receipt. It normally takes three or four months for an application to be processed. All applicants are notified of the outcome by letter.

Grants are normally made by means of a single payment and the foundation does not normally commit to forward funding.

All applications are asked to include the following information:

- the charity's registration number
- a copy of the most recent report and audited accounts
- an outline description of the charity's activities
- a synopsis of the project requiring funding, with details of who will benefit
- a financial plan
- details of current and proposed fundraising.

Note that the administrator, Fiona Hare, is the same person as the Fiona Foster whose name was given in previous editions of this book.

The Will Charitable Trust

Environment/ conservation, cancer care, blindness, mental disability

£449,000 (2002/03)

Beneficial area UK and overseas.

Farrer & Co Solicitors, 65–66 Lincoln's Inn Fields, London WC2A 3LH

Tel. 01932 724148 (Sunbury office)

Email willcharitabletrust@yahoo.co.uk

Correspondent The Trustees

Trustees *H N Henshaw, chair; P Andras; A McDonald.*

Charity Commission no. 801682

Information available Annual report and accounts.

Summary

Grants, usually between £10,000 and £30,000 'to substantial organisations having proven records of successful work in their fields of operation', and one-off grants to local or county-wide organisations, in the following fields:

- woodland and conservation
- cancer
- blindness
- mental handicap.

General

The trust describes its policy as follows:

The trust provides financial assistance to charitable organisations whose activities fall within the following categories, mainly within the United Kingdom:

a) Conservation of the countryside in Britain, including its flora and fauna

b) Care of and services for people suffering from cancer and their families

c) Care of blind people and the prevention and cure of blindness

d) The provision of residential care for mentally handicapped people in communities making a lifelong commitment to provide a family environment and the maximum choice of activities and lifestyles.

A proportion of the trust's income is devoted to assistance in other fields, but this is reserved for causes which have come to the attention of individual trustees and which the trustees regard as deserving. It is only in exceptional circumstances that the trustees will respond favourably to requests from

organisations whose activities fall outside the categories listed above.

It is unlikely that applications relating to academic or research projects will be successful. The trustees recognise the importance of research, but lack the resources and expertise required to judge its relevance and value.

The grants in 2002/03 were categorised as follows:

	No.	Amount
Woodland and other conservation	9	£103,000
Care of mentally handicapped people	9	£98,000
Care of the blind; prevention/cure of blindness	11	£115,000
Care of cancer patients	7	£102,000

The only grants outside these headings were to the Almshouse Association (£5,000) and Jubilee Appeal for Commonwealth Veterans (£2,000). Also, as in the previous year Sherborne Abbey Tower Vault Appeal (£20,000) and King George's Fund for Sailors (£5,000).

The grants lists show that many of the major beneficiaries are supported regularly. However the trust has decided that at this time it is inappropriate to make grant commitments for more than two years.

Beneficiaries in 2001/02 included the following.

Woodland and conservation

BTCV and Royal Horticultural Society (£15,000 each). Six county wildlife trusts were supported.

Care of mentally handicapped people

Home Farm Trust (£15,000), Acorn Village, Camphill Village Trust and Kent Autistic Society (£10,000 each) and Orchard Vale (£8,000).

Care of the blind, prevention of, or cure of blindness

Sense, Sightsavers and RNIB (£15,000 each), Derbyshire Association for the Blind and Henshaw's Society for the Blind (£10,000 each) and Newcastle Society for the Blind (£4,500).

Care of cancer patients

Macmillan Cancer Relief and Marie Curie Cancer Centre (£25,000 each), Help the Hospices (£15,000), Earl Mountbatten Hospice (£10,000) and Council for Music in Hospitals (£7,000).

There were no geographically identifiable grants outside England in any of the last three years.

The charity notes that it is typically only able to respond positively to about one in seven of the applications that it receives.

Exclusions

Grants are only given to registered charities.

Applications

The grants administrator is Ian McIntosh who has an office in Sunbury, Middlesex. Telephone enquiries should be made to him on 01932 724148. Unless advised to the contrary, applications should be submitted in writing to the correspondent at the address above. There are no application forms. The trust normally distributes income twice yearly. Grants are made in March to organisations whose activities fall within the fields of blindness and mental handicapped with applications to be received by 31 January at the latest. Grants are made in October to organisations operating within the fields of conservation and cancer, with applications to be received by 31 August at the latest.

The H D H Wills 1965 Charitable Trust

Environment, general

£613,000 (2002/03)
Beneficial area UK and Ireland.

Henley Knapp Barn, Fulwell, Chipping Norton, Oxfordshire OX7 4EN

Tel. 01608 678051 **Fax** 01608 678052

Email willsct@ukonline.co.uk

Correspondent Mrs Wendy Cooper, Trust Secretary

Trustees *John Carson; The Lord Killearn; Lady E H Wills; Dr Catherine Wills; Liell Francklin.*

Charity Commission no. 244610

Information available Annual report and accounts.

Summary

The trust runs three separate funds with a combined income of about £700,000, and, for about 85% of this, with different areas of grantmaking in different years, on a seven-year cycle.

In 2002/03 grants were for the preservation of wildlife (as in the previous year). In 2003/04 the money will go a single connected charity, the Ditchley Foundation and in both 2004/

05 and 2005/06 grants will be at the trustees' discretion.

In every year nearly £100,000 is available for unrestricted grantmaking and is at present disbursed in a very large number of small grants to new beneficiaries.

General

The trust has been endowed by the family of Sir David Wills – from a fortune derived largely from the tobacco company of that name – and had assets of £28 million in 2003.

The three funds it operates are the Martin Wills Fund (£564,000 income in 2002/03, restricted in most years), the General Fund (£94,000 and unrestricted), and the Knockando Church Fund (restricted solely for the upkeep of this church in Morayshire and amounting to just £4,000).

The General Fund

Donations from the General Fund are made for general charitable purposes, and have in the past included substantial amounts to the Ditchley Foundation and the Sandford St Martin Trust, both created by Sir David Wills. However in the last few years it has been used for the very extensive small grants programme.

There were 123 grants made in 2002/03 totalling £68,500. There were two grants for £5,000, two for £2,000 and 10 for £1,000. All other grants were for either £500 or £250 each.

So far as can be seen – and the uncategorised grants lists do not make this easy to determine – none of the recipients had also been supported in the previous year. This would be expected given the ban on reapplication noted under 'applications' below.

Almost all kinds of charities appear to be supported, though there seems to be the greatest interest in charities in and around Oxfordshire or the Cotswolds, and in those working with young people.

The grants are well spread around the country, with Scotland, perhaps, coming nearest to being over represented. A small proportion of the grants are for charities working overseas.

The larger grants were made to Sandford St Martin PCC – Parish Hall and St Peter's Church – Ousden (£5,000 each), Trustees of George Crofton's Discretionary Trust and University of Cambridge Centre for Brain Repair (£2,000 each). Beneficiaries receiving £1,000 each included Elgin Museum, Handicapped Anglers' Trust, National

Portrait Trust and Wimbledon College Development Campaign.

The eclectic list of beneficiaries receiving either £500 or £250 included Africa Educational Trust, Beulah Scotland, Children's Adventure Farm Trust, East Belfast Mission, Haven Trust, Gosforth Sea Cadets, Little Sisters of the Poor, Music in Country Churches, Royal School for the Blind – Liverpool, Sea Cadets – Ellesmere Port, Bradford Police Club for Young People, Coventry City Farm, Hack Horse Farm, Prisoners Abroad, Samaritans – Cambridge, Weston Spirit and Unravel Mills.

The Martin Wills Fund

The trust notes that the income of the Martin Wills Fund is donated as follows in seven-year cycles – 2003/04 is the fifth year of the present cycle:

Fifth year: Ditchley Foundation (2003/04), which was set up by Sir David Wills in 1965 as a conference centre to discuss topics of mutual Anglo/American interest.

Sixth and seventh years: Charities at the trustees' discretion, being charities which reflect the trustees' particular interests (2004/05 and 2005/06).

First year (of new cycle): Magdalen College, Oxford (2006/07), a college at which many family members have been educated.

Second year: Rendcomb College, Gloucestershire (2007/08), set up by Sir David Wills' father, Noel Hamilton Wills, in 1920 as a college for underprivileged Gloucestershire boys.

Third and fourth years: Any registered charity dedicated or primarily dedicated to the preservation of wildlife (2008/09 and 2009/10), which was of particular interest to the late Martin Wills.

In 2002/03 the fund made donations totalling £541,000. Beneficiaries of the fund (wildlife charities) during the year included Martin Wills Wildlife Maintenance Trust (£325,000 in total), Spey Fishery Board (£84,000 in total), University of Oxford (£50,000 in total), Tusk Trust (£40,000 in total), AfriCat Foundation (£20,000 in total), Barn Owl Trust, North Atlantic Salmon Fund and British Butterfly Conservation (£5,000 each) and Migratory Salmon Foundation (£1,000).

Exclusions

No grants to individuals or national charities.

Applications

In writing to the correspondent. The trust considers small appeals monthly and large ones bi-annually from the Martin Wills Fund. Only one application from a given charity will be considered in any one 18-month period.

The Harold Hyam Wingate Foundation

Jewish, medical, research, education, the arts, general

£412,000 (2002/03)

Beneficial area Mainly UK.

2nd Floor, 20–22 Stukeley Street, London WC2B 5LR

Email karen.marshall@act.tt

Website www.wingate.org.uk

Correspondent Karen Marshall, Trust Administrator

Trustees *R C Wingate; A J Wingate; R H Cassen; D L Wingate; W J Wingate; J Drori.*

Charity Commission no. 264114

Information available Accounts and annual report, guidelines available on website.

This foundation is involved in the support of Jewish life and learning, as well as being committed to funding the arts, medical research, health, education and projects addressing social exclusion. The trustees favour projects which they feel are unlikely to attract sponsorship from commercial sources. Capital projects are sometimes supported, but on a highly-selective basis.

The trust also administers The Wingate Scholarships which makes grants to young people with outstanding potential for educational research. (For further information, see *The Educational Grants Directory, also published by DSC.*)

In 2002/03 the foundation had assets of £11.3 million, generating an income of £459,000. Grants were made to 68 organisations totalling £412,000. Scholarships totalled £369,000.

During the year funds were allocated as follows:

Jewish life and learning	24%
Performing arts	24%
Education and social exclusion	19%
Music	17%
Literary prizes	7%
Medical research	5%
Development projects	4%

Jewish life and learning

By their selection of projects, institutions and activities which they would support, the trustees' aspiration is to encourage Jewish cultural, academic and educational life in a manner that enhances the Jewish contribution to the life of the wider community.

In particular, applications are invited from academic institutions specialising in Jewish subjects and from bodies promoting Jewish culture, including museums, libraries and literary publications.

Applications are also welcomed from organisations able to demonstrate a record in inter-faith dialogue, in promotion of reconciliation between Jews in Israel and their Arab neighbours and the encouragement of liberal values in both communities.

Performing arts (excluding music)

The foundation has been a consistant supporter of the performing arts. The trustees intend to maintain that policy with particular emphasis on financial support for not-for-profit companies with a record of artistic excellence that require additional funding not available from public sources or commercial sponsorship. [This can enable them] to broaden their repertoire or develop work of potentially outstanding interest which cannot be funded from usual sources.

Assistance will also be considered for training and professional development for creative talent or technical professions. In exceptional cases, the trustees will consider capital grants towards schemes for buildings or equipment.

Education and social exclusion

The foundation recognises that there are already considerable public resources allocated to these two areas. However, it will be willing to consider support for projects which may not qualify for public funding or attract other major funding bodies. Contributions towards the running expenses or projects for a strictly limited period will be considered, and in certain cases, applications for contributions towards capital projects.

Eligible projects would ideally be innovative, focus on the disadvantaged and have lasting effects. Alternatively they should consist of work (e.g. action research, pilot schemes) that would lead to such projects, and preferably they should also be capable of replication if successful.

UK projects which the foundation has supported in the past include those providing for vulnerable children, the education of children who have autism, homeless children, deaf adults, disabled artists, outreach work of arts organisation and help for ex-offenders.

Music

The trustees recognise that music is seriously under-funded in the UK and will consider applications for support in those areas of music performance and education which do not readily attract backing from commercial sponsors or other funding bodies, or which are not eligible for public funding. Priority will be directed towards supporting the work or education of musicians based in, or wishing to study in the UK, but by no means exclusively so. An important criterion will be whether, in the opinion of the trustees, the funding sought will make a significant difference to the applicant's prospects.

The foundation will be prepared to consider applications for support for on-going expenses and will be willing to consider such support for a period of up to three years. Priority will be given to those organisations which give opportunities to young professionals and to education projects for young people as well as for new adult audiences. This would include direct assistance as well as funding for organisations which promote their work or performance, and support for master-classes. Exceptionally, the foundation will be prepared to consider applications for capital development projects.

The foundation reserves the right to draw up particular priorities for a given year such as support for aspiring conductors, young composers, amateur choral work, or the musical education of young people and/or adults.

Development projects

Applications are welcome from organisations working in developing countries for projects in any of the foundation's priority fields, including music and the arts that satisfy the criteria. It will be willing to consider support for projects which may not qualify for public funding or attract other major funding bodies. However, the foundation would welcome applications to address the particular problems of water supply.

Projects supported in the past have included education for secluded castes in India, training for classical musicians in South Africa, and water supply in Africa.

Medical research

This covers projects that involve the systematic acquisition of new data to test a hypothesis. Assistance may be sought for research expenses (equipment and/or consumables) or for support for personnel. The trustees encourage applications for research that is of clear clinical relevance, covering areas such as, but not only, epidemiology, clinical physiology and pathophysiology, diagnosis and therapeutics. Applications for support for 'basic' science areas such as genetics and molecular biology are less likely to receive support.

There is no set format for applications, but in general, these should address the following issues:

- background and relevant past work;
- hypothesis, including clinical relevance;
- research plan;
- data analysis;
- support required;
- justification of required support;
- key literature reference (a maximum of 20 is suggested);
- curriculum vitae of the applicant and others named in the application. Complete bibliographs are not required; publication totals (peer review papers, reviews, book chapters) will suffice, except that complete references should be given for four peer review publications.

Health care

This category covers grants to support the establishment of additional health care resources. Typical projects include the cost of providing disgnosis techniques of therapies not otherwise available, patient support services or care facilities. Applicants are warned that it is not the policy of the trustees to fund health care that should normally be provided by the NHS. Applications should be supported by evidence that the proposal refers to services or facilities of proven value.

Beneficiaries during 2002/03 included World Ort Union (£34,000), Soho Theatre (£30,000), Little Angel Theatre (£25,000), Oxford Centre for Hebrew and Jewish Studies (£20,000), English Touring Opera (£15,000), English National Opera (£12,000), Anne Frank Trust UK, Institute of Jewish Studies and Jerusalem Foundation (£10,000 each), Alzheimer's Disease International, Gabrieli Trust and Voice for the Child in Care (£5,000 each), British Youth Opera (£3,000), National Children's Bureau (£2,000) and Attlee Foundation and Mousetrap Foundation (£1,000 each).

Exclusions

No grants to individuals. The Wingate Scholarship Fund, for students over the age of 24, is separately administered by Faith Clark at the above address. Obtain details direct from her or from The Educational Grants Directory.

The trustees will not normally consider donations to the general funds of large charitable bodies, wishing instead to focus support on specific projects.

Applications

In writing to the correspondent, giving financial statements where possible. Applications are only acknowledged if a stamped addressed envelope is enclosed or if the application is successful. They are considered about every three months.

The Wixamtree Trust

General

£602,000 (2003/04)

Beneficial area Primarily Bedfordshire.

c/o CCAS, 80 Croydon Road, Elmers End, Beckenham, Kent BR3 4DF

Tel. 020 8658 8902 **Fax** 020 8658 3292

Email wixamtree@ccas.globalnet.co.uk

Correspondent Paul Patten, Administrator

Trustees *S C Whitbread; Mrs J M Whitbread; H F Whitbread; C E S Whitbread; N G McMullen; I A D Pilkington.*

Charity Commission no. 210089

Information available Accounts were provided by the trust.

This trust funds any registered charities based or operating within Bedfordshire.

In 2003/04 the trust had assets of £17 million and received an income of £504,000 from its investments during the year. Applications were received from 315 organisations during the year and grants totalling £602,000 were awarded to 100 of these.

By far the largest grant was £100,000 to Moggerhanger House Preservation Trust. Other grants of £10,000 or more each were: £30,000 each to Emmaus Village – Carlton and Reach Out Projects, £20,000 to St Andrew's Church, £15,000 each to Fowlmere Nature Reserve and NCH Action for Children and £10,000 each to All Saints Preservation Trust, Animal Health Trust, Bedfordshire Crimebeat, Chelmsford Cathedral Chapter Appeal Fund, Hinwick Hall College, Household Cavalry Museum Trust, Luton Law Centre, Philharmonia Orchestra for the

Stepping Stones project, St John Ambulance, St Peter's Church – Sharnbrook and Glen Urquhart High School for a minibus appeal.

Beneficiaries of smaller grants included Cardigan PCC (£8,500), Bedfordshire Festival of Music, Speech and Drama, Contact the Elderly, Flittabus Community Transport, Marie Curie Cancer Care, Relate, Sandy Upper School – Classroom of the Future project and Sight Concern Bedfordshire (£5,000 each), Bedford Volunteer Bureau, Kempston East Methodist Church and HomeStart Bedford (£3,000 each), Complete Works Theatre Company (£2,200), Biggleswade and Sandy Gateway Club, Hospice at Home Volunteers, Ivinghoe Project and Wilshamstead Village Hall (£2,000 each), Kempston East Methodist Church and Association for Spina Bifida and Hydrocephalus (£1,500) and Cambridge Music Festival, Deafblind UK, Everyman Support Group, Happy Days Children's Charity and People's Dispensary for Sick Animals (£1,000 each).

Exclusions

No grants to non-registered charities, individuals or overseas projects.

Applications

On a form available from the correspondent. The trustees meet in January, April, July and October. An application form is available by e-mail and all requests for support must be accompanied by a current report and accounts where available.

The Wolfson Family Charitable Trust

Jewish charities

£3 million (2002/03)

Beneficial area Israel and UK.

8 Queen Anne Street, London W1G 9LD

Tel. 020 7323 5730 **Fax** 020 7323 3241

Correspondent Dr Victoria Harrison, Secretary

Trustees *Lord Wolfson of Marylebone; Lady Wolfson; Mrs Janet Wolfson de Botton; M D Paisner; Prof. Barrie Jay; Sir Eric Ash; Sir Bernard Rix.*

Charity Commission no. 228382

Information available Annual report and accounts were provided by the trust.

Summary

The trust gives a relatively small number of often very large grants, mostly to institutions in Israel, in the fields of science, medical research, health, welfare and, to a lesser extent, arts and humanities.

Much of the trust's future income is already committed to long-term projects.

The trust shares offices and administration with the much larger Wolfson Foundation, and an application to one may be considered by the other.

General

The trust operates on a large scale and over an extended time frame, often having sharp changes in the level of new commitments each year.

There is a 'three year rolling plan of grants' which, as a general policy, 'are given to act as a catalyst, to back excellence and talent and to provide support for promising future projects which may currently be underfunded, particularly for research, renovation and equipment'.

In 2002/03 the trust had assets of £44 million which generated an income of £2.5 million. Several large new awards were committed but not paid during the period of the accounts. Grants were made during the year totalling £3 million.

Grantmaking in 2002/03

The following is the list of grants paid during the year:

Science, technology and medical research – £1.7 million

- Tel Aviv University, £438,000 for a new computer and software engineering building;
- Israeli Centre for Digital Information Services (Tel Aviv University), £375,000 for computer hardware and related equipment to Israeli universities;
- Technion – Israel Institute of Technology, £250,000 for equipment for the study of cellular proteins/ cancer immunology;
- Weizmann Institute of Science, £200,000 for the renovation and extension of the Wolfson building;
- The Hebrew University of Jerusalem, £200,000 for three teaching and three research laboratories;

- Ben Gurion University, £117,000 to update the thermal imaging laboratory;
- Bar Ilan University, £75,000 for equipment for the Institute of Superconductivity;
- Hadassah Medical Organisation, £50,000 towards research in the gene therapy institute.

Health and welfare –- £869,000

- Soroka Medical Centre, Beer Sheva, £250,000 for an MRI scanner for the Department of Radiology;
- Hadassah Medical Organisation, £190,000 for four intensive care beds;
- Rabin Medical Centre, £125,000 for equipment for the Department of Obstetrics and Gynaecology;
- Magen David Adom, £104,000 for two ambulances and a defibrillator;
- Rabin Medical Centre, £100,000 for new MRI systems for the imaging department on Beilinson campus;
- Yad Sarah, Jerusalem, £50,000 for a wheelchair and alarms;
- Shaare Zedek Medical Centre, £50,000 for an electrophysiology system for cardiology department and CT scanner.

Education – £332,000

- Jews Free School, £300,000 for Technical laboratories;
- Ben Gurion University, £32,000 for the Herzog Centre archive.

Arts and humanities – £107,000

- The Jerusalem Foundation, £100,000 for landscaping (£50,000) and to equip the resource centre at Bernard Bloomfield Science Museum (£50,000);
- Hebrew University, £7,000.

The trust also notes that it has agreed future commitments totalling £7.2 million.

Exclusions

Grants are not made to individuals.

Applications

The trust shares its application procedure with the Wolfson Foundation. A brief explanatory letter, with organisation and project details, including costs and current shortfalls, will elicit an up-to-date set of guidelines in return, if the charity is able to consider the project concerned.

The Wolfson Foundation

Medical and scientific research, education, health and welfare, heritage, arts

£31 million (2003/04)

Beneficial area Mainly UK, but also Israel.

8 Queen Anne Street, London W1G 9LD

Tel. 020 7323 5730 **Fax** 020 7323 3241

Correspondent Dr Victoria Harrison, Executive secretary

Trustees *Lord Wolfson of Marylebone, chair; Lady Wolfson; Lord Quirk; Lord Quinton; Sir Eric Ash; Sir Derek Roberts; Lord McColl; Lord Turnberg; Mrs Janet Wolfson de Botton; Mrs Laura Wolfson Townsley; Sir David Weatherall.*

Charity Commission no. 206495

Information available Annual report and accounts, with a much improved description of major grants but weak on grantmaking policy and practice. Guidelines for applicants.

Summary

Grants are for buildings and equipment, but not for revenue or project costs, in three major areas:

- medical research and health care;
- science, technology and education;
- arts and the humanities.

Grants can be very large; few are for amounts of less than £5,000.

The foundation shares offices and administration with the smaller Wolfson Family Charitable Trust, and an application to one may be considered by the other.

Background

This very large family foundation had investments of £602 million and an income of £34 million in 2003/04. It is a family foundation endowed from the fortune created by Sir Isaac Wolfson through the Great Universal Stores company. Grants were made totalling £31 million.

Guidelines for applicants

The trust offers the following information for applicants:

The major areas supported by the trustees are:

- Medical research and healthcare, especially the prevention of disease and the care and treatment of sick, disadvantaged and disabled people.
- Science, technology and education, particularly where the benefits may accrue to the development of industry, commerce and teaching in the UK.
- Arts and the humanities, including libraries, museums, galleries, the visual arts and historic buildings.

The trustees make grants for:

- Capital projects, towards the cost of a new building or extension, or for renovating existing ones.
- Equipment for specific purposes and/or furnishings and fittings.

Grantmaking in 2003/04

This was described as follows:

As a general policy, grants are given to act as a catalyst, to back excellence and talent and to provide support for promising future projects which may currently be underfunded, particularly for renovation and equipment. There is a continued emphasis on science, technology, medicine, health care, education and the visual arts.

Trustees make awards twice each year and are advised by panels comprising trustees and specialists which meet before the main board meetings. As well as assessing the merits of the applicants proposals and their congruence with the foundation's aims and priorities, appraisal criteria include: value and quality, standing of leading applicants, business participation, aesthetics, review of accounts, financial viability and adequate provision for ongoing costs and maintenance.

Priorities include the renovation of historic buildings, libraries, support for preventive medicine, programmes for people with special needs, the visual arts and education. Grants are made to universities for student accommodation, equipment for research, new buildings and renovations. Awards for university research are normally made under the umbrella of designated programmes in which vice-chancellors are invited to participate. All applications are assessed by expert external reviewers.

Medicine research and health care

This remained the area receiving the largest proportion of the foundation's funds, mainly through grants for capital infrastructure supporting top quality research at British universities.

An award of £2 million was made to fund a floor in the new Manchester Interdisciplinary Biocentre following a joint application from UMIST and the University of Manchester. Grants were also made for an Imaging Unit at the University of Cambridge's Stem Cell Biology Unit (£1.5 million) and toward extending the Jodrell Laboratory at the Royal Botanic Gardens – Kew (£1.25 million)

Five major awards were made in the general area of neuroscience for: the Wolfson Institute for Clinical and Cognitive Neuroscience at the University of Wales – Bangor (£1.25 million); one of the country's first magnetoencephalography imaging facilities at York (£1.2 million); the Laboratory for Cellular Imaging in Hearing Research at UCL (£1 million); the Wolfson Centre for Brain Development and Function at Birkbeck College (£800,000); and an MIR scanner for the National Society for Epilepsy (£500,000).

Additional medical research projects each received £500,000: Addenbrooke's Hospital (Cambridge Breast Unit) and the Universties of Bristol (Centre for Life Course and Epidemiology), Newcastle (Laboratories for Musculoskeletal Research) and Surrey (Centre for Translatinal Research).

In the area of medical education, the major award was for a lecture theatre at the University of Birmingham's Medical School (£1.5 million). Awards were also made to three hospitals (each having a research or educational element): Oxford Children's Hospital (£500,000 for its oncology ward), Sunderland Royal Hospital (£200,000 for its education centre) and the Royal Hospital for Sick Children – Edinburgh (£190,000 for surgical equipment).

The trustees continued their programmes for people with special needs and hospices. Thirty-eight grants totalling over £1.3 million were made to organisations in the area of special needs. Fifteen grants totalling over £750,000 were made for palliative care projects, including £75,000 per annum over three years for Wolfson Bursaries for the training of hospice/palliative care medical staff, in a programme administered by Help the Hospices.

Science education and research

Trustees made major awards to the University of Oxford (£1.5 million towards the bioinformatics floors in the new Structural Bioinformatics Unit) and to the Natural History Museum (£400,000 toward medical entomology laboratories for research into tropical diseases in the Darwin Centre).

The Royal Society/Wolfson Foundation Laboratory refurbishment programme (administered by the Royal Society) continued into its sixth year, with awards focussing particularly on nanotechnology. Trustees agrees to extend the programme for a further four years at a level of £2.5 million per annum.

The merit awards programme for high performing academics – another programme administered by the Royal Society and jointly funded with the government (the Department of Trade and Industry) – continued into its third year. Grants were made to 22 academics at 15 universities.

Awards were also made under the first round of ReDiscover, a programme for the renewal of science museums and centres, funded jointly with the Wellcome Trust and the Millennium Commission.

Arts and humanities

The major award during the year was toward the construction of a Centre for Conservation at the British Library (£600,000). Another leading library – the John Rylands Library in Manchester – was awarded £200,000 for an exhibition gallery.

Fourteen awards (ranging in size from £210,000 to £1,500) were made under the second year of the joint programme with the Department for Culture, Media and Sport for the renovation of museums and galleries.

The trustees also made a number of awards for the performing arts, notably £195,000 for renovation work at Usher Hall in Edinburgh, £100,000 for improvements to the exterior of the National Theatre and £100,000 for a practice room in the new library and performance research centre at the Royak Academy of Music.

Education

Four awards were made for student accommodation or teaching facilities at Oxford and Cambridge colleges, including £180,000 toward four rooms in a new student accommodation block at Wolfson College – Oxford.

Smaller grants

Description and examples of smaller grants made, those for less than £50,000, are as follows:

THE WOLFSON FOUNDATION Summary of grants in 2003/04	Amount
Science & Technology (including medical research)	£24.3 million
Arts & Humanities	£1.9 million
Education (including higher education buildings, schools and science/medical education)	£4.6 million
Health and Welfare (including hospices and special needs)	£2.1 million
£32.9 million in total (less £1.6 million relinquished grants)	

Education

Medical education and learned societies

One grant was made under £50,000. Royal College of Surgeons of England received £33,000 for audio visual equipment for a lecture theatre.

Intercalated awards

These awards support selected medical students to take a year out of their medical training for an additional science-based degree. Grants ranged from £4,000 to £16,000 to each institution, and were made to students at 19 institutions including University of Manchester, University of Glasgow, St George's Hospital Medical School, University of Wales College of Medicine and University of Aberdeen.

Higher education buildings

Smaller grants were £40,000 to Queen Mary College – University of London for the restoration of the Octagon Reading Room and £25,000 to Green College – Oxford for the restoration of Radcliffe Observatory.

Schools programme

Grants to 52 secondary schools ranged from £5,400 to £50,000.

Individual educational projects

Four grants were made, all of which were for smaller amounts. Grants were £15,000 to Girlguiding UK for its National Leadership Training Centres, £10,000 to Farms for City Children – Devon towards the costs of renovating Nethercott House, £100 to University of Westminster and £50 to London School of Economics.

Arts and humanities

Libraries

Two grants were made under £50,000 each: £25,000 to Oxford Literary and Debating Union Trust towards the restoration of Oxford Union Library; £10,000 to Toynbee Hall towards refurbishment work to create a library and reading room.

Churches, chapels and synagogues

Over 70 grants were made for repair work to the historic fabric of listed buildings. Grants were between £2,000 and £4,000.

Cathedrals

Grants were £25,000 to Worcester Cathedral, £20,000 to Bristol Cathedral, £15,000 to Lincoln Cathedral and £10,000 each to Portsmouth Cathedral and St Patrick's Cathedral – Armagh.

Other historic buildings

Grants of £5,000 each were made to Aylesford Priory for the restoration of its gatehouse and Lamp of Lothian Collegiate Trust – Haddington for the refurbishment of Poldrate Mill.

Museums and galleries

A grant of £30,000 was made to Brading Roman Villa – Isle of Wight.

Music and ballet projects

Two grants under £50,000 went to Yehudi Menuhin School – Surrey and Central School of Ballet.

Theatres

One grant under £50,000 was made to Theatre Royal – Bury St Edmonds.

Individual arts and humanities projects

Eight grants were made in the range of £3,700 to £50,000. Grants included £50,000 to Battle of Britain Monument Committee for a monument to commemorate the Battle of Britain, £20,000 to Roy Jenkins Memorial Scholarships for a scholarship for a British Student and £5,000 to Second World War Experience Centre – Leeds for equipment for the conservation of records.

Wolfson History Prizes

These prizes, awarded annually, aim to promote and encourage standards of excellence in the writing of history for the general public. Two awards were made of £15,000 and £10,000.

Health and welfare

Special needs

Grants were made to 38 organisations in this category, 31 of which received £50,000 or less. They were for building work or equipment, and included £50,000 to Leonard Cheshire Foundation – Hertfordshire, £30,000 to Treloar Trust – Hampshire, £25,000 each to Orpheus Centre – Surrey and Portland College – Mansfield, £18,000 to National Autistic Society – South Yorkshire, £10,000 each to British Red Cross – Warwickshire, London Youth and Scarborough and District Search and Rescue Team and £5,000 to Little Heath School – Essex.

Hospices/palliative care

Grants were made to 13 organisation in this category, 9 hospices received grants in the range of £5,000 and £50,000.

Exclusions

Overheads, running or administrative costs, VAT or professional fees; non-specific appeals (including circulars), endowment funds or conduit organisations; costs of meetings, exhibitions, concerts, expeditions, etc.; the purchase of land; research involving live animals; film or video production.

Applications

Before submitting an application please write to enquire whether your project is eligible, enclosing a copy of the organisation's audited accounts for the previous two years.

If a project is eligible, further details of the application process will be provided.

The Charles Wolfson Charitable Trust

Medical research, health, education, Jewish charities, general

Around £3 million (2002/03)

Beneficial area UK, Israel.

c/o 129 Battenhall Road, Worcester WR5 2BU

Correspondent Mrs Cynthia Crawford

Trustees *Lord Wolfson of Sunningdale; Simon Wolfson; John Franks; Andrew Wolfson.*

Charity Commission no. 238043

Information available Annual report and accounts were on file at the Charity Commission.

Summary

Generally large grants are made, with NHS or teaching hospitals getting about two-thirds of the grant total. Most of the remainder goes to specifically Jewish welfare or educational charities. About 30 small grants are made to a rather more varied list of beneficiaries. This trust is not connected, at least directly, with the Wolfson Foundation. It is unusual in its concentration on property investment and the annual reports include a convincing defence of this policy.

Grantmaking

In 2002/03 the trust had both an income and total expenditure of around £3.5 million, most of which is likely to have been given is grants. No further information was available for the year.

The trust makes grants only 'to registered charities or to hospitals and schools [...] especially for capital or fixed term projects'. Unusually, the charity has from time to time bought buildings to make them available to other charities so that effectively the income foregone can be seen as a donation to the charity concerned (and it is identified as such in the accounts).

There is no information on how beneficiaries are selected. Although some grants are in very specialist fields, there is no indication that professional advice is sought, let alone the use of the peer review process that is widely regarded as necessary for evaluating specialist proposals. It seems likely that most grants are made to organisations that have developed personal links with the trustees.

Previous beneficiaries include Northwick Park NHS hospital Children's Centre, Kings College – London University, Princess Royal NHS Hospital – Telford, Royal West Sussex NHS Trust, Worthing and Southlands NHS Trust, Huntingdon Foundation (Orthodox Jewish), Margaret Thatcher Fund, AISH Hatorah, Community Service Volunteers and Nightingale House Home for Aged Jews.

Comment

Despite ample warning, and their obligation to the contrary, the Charity Commission were unable to give us sight of this trust's accounts.

Exclusions

It is not the policy of the trust to make grants to individuals or to charities for running costs.

Applications

In writing to the correspondent. Grants are made in response to applications, and while all applications will be considered, the trustees cannot undertake to notify all unsuccessful applicants, because of the volume of appeals received.

The Woodward Charitable Trust

General

£467,000 (2003)

Beneficial area Unrestricted.

Allington House, 1st Floor, 150 Victoria Street, London SW1E 5AE

Tel. 020 7410 0330 **Fax** 020 7410 0332

Email contact@woodwardcharitabletrust.org.uk

Website www.woodwardcharitabletrust.org.uk

Correspondent Michael Pattison, Director

Trustees *Camilla Woodward; Shaun A Woodward MP; Miss Judith Portrait.*

Charity Commission no. 299963

Information available Annual report and accounts were provided by the trust. There is also a simple, clear website.

Summary

This is one of the Sainsbury Family Charitable Trusts which share a joint administration but it operates quite differently to most others in this group in that it gives a large number of small grants in response to open application.

The value and number of grants in 2003 were categorised as follows:

	No.	Amount
Arts	6	£216,000
Community and social welfare	39	£107,000
Disability and health	8	£64,500
Education	6	£67,500
Environment	2	£1,000
Miscellaneous grants	2	£11,000

Policies

Trustees award three types of grant:
- Major grants between £10,000 and £50,000 (no more than three made per year, usually within areas a – e below.
- Small grants between £100 and £5,000 (around 20 – 30 grants made each year, within a – g below.
- Children's summer scheme grants between £500 and £2,000 (generally about 10 to 15 grants are made each year.

The trustees favour small scale, locally based initiatives. Funding is primarily for one-off projects, but the trustees are willing to consider core costs. The main areas of grantmaking in the future are likely to be:

a) Homelessness, especially affecting women, refugee groups, and covering facilities such as women's refuges;

b) Prisons and prisoners, with particular emphasis on post-release help and on families of prisoners;

c) Travellers;

d) Addiction, including projects tackling the social exclusion elements and preventative programmes;

e) Arts outreach work by local groups, particularly in fields which do not attract funding from other Sainsbury Family Charitable Trusts.

Trustees may also consider:

f) Disability projects;

g) Environmental projects, especially with a strong education element, provided they are distinctive and not merely a part of current fashion.

Potential applicants are encouraged to telephone the administrator to discuss their work if they think it might apply to the trustees' criteria.

Grantmaking

The trust does make a small number of large grants to organisations already known to the trustees. There were just three of these apparent in 2002/03 but they accounted for over half of the grant total. The largest grant, as in previous years, was to English National Opera (£200,000); the other large grants were made to Bowel Cancer Research (£50,000) and Dragon School Trust Ltd (£25,000).

Apart from £15,000 to Trialogue Educational Trust, all other grants were for £10,000 or less, and mostly for under £5,000.

Other beneficiaries included Oxfordshire Association for Young People (£10,000), Community Links (£8,000), Unicorn Theatre and Caldecott Foundation (£5,000 each), Tools for Self Reliance – Milton Keynes (£3,000), Bangladesh Welfare Association in Middlesex, Helping Hands Community Trust and Child Psychotherapy Trust (£2,000 each) and Girls Workshop, Tiny Tots Community Playgroup, Wirral Swallows and Amazons Adventure Group and York Student Community Action (£1,000 each).

Exclusions

The trustees are unable to respond to: standard appeals; general appeals from large national charities; requests for small contributions to large appeals; medical research; individuals; student support; course fees; expedition costs; hospices; parish facilities; homework clubs; overseas projects.

Applications

On simple application forms available from the trust, or downloadable from the website. Potential applicants are invited to telephone Karin Hooper in advance to discuss the advisability of making an application.

Main grants are allocated following trustees' meetings in January and July each year, with the exception of summer schemes, which are considered at the beginning of May each year. All application forms are assessed on arrival and if additional information is required you will be contacted further. Applicants must make sure the trust receives a project budget and audited accounts.

The website has a most useful diary of trustees' meetings and of the cut-off dates for applications.

Yorkshire Dales Millennium Trust

Conservation and environmental regeneration

Around £600,000 (2003/04)
Beneficial area The Yorkshire Dales.

The Old Post Office, Main Street, Clapham, Lancaster, North Yorkshire LA2 8DP

Tel. 01524 251002 **Fax** 01524 251150

Email info@ydmt.org

Website www.ydmt.org

Correspondent Iain Oag, Director

Trustees *Lord Shuttleworth, chair; Roger Stott; Dorothy Fairburn; Brian Braithwaite-Exley; Heather Jane Hancock; Colin Speakman; Marquess of Hartington; David Anthony Welton Joy; Jane Roberts; Joseph Joshua Pearlman; Robin Grove-White; Steve Macaré; David Rees-Jones; Hazel Waters; Judith Donovan; Peter Charlesworth.*

Charity Commission no. 1061687

Information available Information was provided by the trust. It also has a new website.

This trust's patron is HRH The Prince of Wales and the role of the trust is to distribute money to organisations, communities and individuals in the Yorkshire Dales. Its first year of grant-making was 1998/99.

The trust makes grants towards the conservation and regeneration of the natural and built heritage and community life of the Yorkshire Dales. It supports, for example, planting new and restoring old woods, the restoration of dry stone walls and field barns, conservation of historical features and community projects.

As well as voluntary organisations and community groups, beneficiaries include farmers and other individuals, Yorkshire Dales National Park Authority, estates, National Trust, parish councils, district councils and English Nature.

The trust makes grants to applicants for up to 70% of their project costs. For every project it supports the trust can pull in matching funding from other sources.

In 2003/04 it had both an income and a total expenditure of around £1 million. Its income is derived from donations and gifts from other organisations such as Rural Development Commission, European Regional Development Fund and Environment Agency. Grants totalled £600,000, with the remainder being spent on fundraising and management/administration costs.

Applications

In writing to the correspondent.

The Zochonis Charitable Trust

General

£1.4 million (2003/04)
Beneficial area UK, particularly Greater Manchester, and overseas, particularly Africa.

Cobbetts, Ship Canal House, 98 King Street, Manchester M2 4WB

Tel. 0845 165 5270

Correspondent The Trustees

Trustees *John Zochonis; Richard B James; Archibald G Calder; Joseph J Swift.*

Charity Commission no. 274769

Information available Very brief annual report and accounts with an uncategorised grants list.

This trust had an annual income of £1.3 million in 2003/04. Grants totalled £1.4 million.

The trust distributes around 95 grants a year. In 2003/04 the amounts ranged from £500 to £125,000, but most were for smaller amounts. Grants do not appear to be ongoing, but charities with an established relationship with the trust are supported intermittently, if not regularly, over many years.

The beneficiaries of the six largest grants were: Altrincham Grammar School for Girls (£125,000) and BESO, Greater Manchester Shrievalty Police Trust, Henshaw's Society for Blind People, MENCAP and National Missing Persons Helpline (£50,000 each).

Grants of £25,000 each were made to nine organisations, including Children's Adventure Farm Trust, Church Housing Trust, Emmaus Bolton, Genesis Appeal, Manchester YMCA, Police Rehabilitation Trust, Relate and St John's Ambulance.

Other beneficiaries included CARE, North West Lung Centre and Specialist Schools Trust (£20,000 each), Orbis (£15,000), Wood Street Mission (£10,000), Autistic Society of Greater Manchester (£7,500) and Addiction Rehabilitation Centre, Catholic Children's Society, Children Today, Christ Church Landmark and Friends 0f Africa (£5,000 each).

Exclusions

No grants for individuals.

Applications

In writing to the correspondent.

Community Foundation Network

Community Foundation Network is the national association for local community foundations in the UK, supporting local organisations. Each community foundation is an independent charity, and the larger of them, in bold, have their own entries. However the movement as a whole is increasingly important, and they share common features. Among other things, they all aim to build permanent endowment funds from local donors, often with striking but varying levels of success.

Community foundations also channel funds on behalf of companies and other agencies which recognise that they have detailed knowledge of local needs. In particular, in England most of them are the local agents for the government's Local Network Fund.

The foundations are increasingly called on to help deliver short-term programmes and emergency assistance on behalf of other grantmakers as well.

Community foundations already exist in most parts of the UK and new ones are being established all the time. At present, around 82% of the English regions are covered, along with all of Scotland, Wales and Northern Ireland. Community Foundation Network estimates that around 90% of the UK population have access to a community foundation.

A list of all current community foundations, with contact details follows below. Many are still at early stages of development, while others are well established grantmaking foundations. Those in bold have their own, separate entries in this book.

Bedfordshire and Luton Community Foundation
BRCC Offices
The Barn, Buttercup Farm
Hockliffe Road
Tebworth
LU7 9QA
Tel: 01525 878142
Fax: 01525 878142
Contact: Mark West (Director)
Email: mark.west@cleghorn.co.uk
Website: www.communityfoundations
    .org.uk/blcf

Berkshire Community Foundation
Arlington Business Park
Theale
Reading
RG7 4SA
Tel: 01189 303021
Fax: 01189 304933
Contact: Robin Draper (Director)
Email: bcf@patrol.i-way.co.uk
Website: www.berksfoundation.org.uk

The Birmingham Foundation
St Peter's Urban Village Trust
Bridge Road
Saltley
Birmingham
B8 3TE
Tel: 0121 326 6886
Fax: 0121 328 8575
Contact: Harvey Mansfield (Director)
Email: team@bhamfoundation.co.uk
Website: www.bhamfoundation.co.uk

Community Foundation for Bournemouth, Dorset and Poole
549 Christchurch Road
Boscombe
Bournemouth
Dorset
BH1 4AH
Tel: 01202 720347
Contact: Lorraine Dabner
Email: bdpfoundation@btconnect.com

The Buckinghamshire Foundation
Unit 4 Farmbrough Close
Stocklake Park
Aylesbury
HP20 1DQ
Tel: 01296 330134
Fax: 01296 330158
Contact: Mike Sparks (Director)
Email: info@thebucksfoundation.org.uk
Website: www.thebucksfoundation.org.uk

Community Foundation for Calderdale
Room 158
D Mill
Dean Clough Industrial Park
Halifax
HX3 5AX
Tel: 01422 349700
Fax: 01422 350017
Contact: Steve Duncan (Acting Director)
Email: enquiries@ccfound.co.uk
Website: www.ccfound.co.uk

Cambridgeshire Community Foundation
St Johns Innovation Centre
Cowley Road
Cambridge
Cambridge
CB4 0WS
Tel: 07941 226 778
Contact: Jane Darlington (Director)
Email: jane@cambscf.org.uk
Website: www.cambscf.org.uk

Cornwall Community Foundation
The Orchard
Market Street
Launceston
Cornwall
PL15 8AU
Tel: 01566 779333
Contact: Andrew Middleton (Director)
Email: andrew.middleton@cornwall
    foundation.com
Website: www.cornwallfoundation.com

The Craven Trust (covers Keighley, Sedbergh, Grassington, Barnoldswick and the Trough of Bowland)
c/o Hon Secretary, Mrs Linda Lee
4 Halsteads Way
Steeton
Keighley
BD60 6SN
Email: info@craventrust.org.uk
Website: www.craventrust.org.uk

Cumbria Community Foundation
Unit 6b
Lakeland Business Park
Cockermouth
CA13 0QT
Tel: 01900 825760
Fax: 01900 826527
Contact: Andrew Beeforth (Director)
Email: Enquiries@cumbriafoundation.org
Website: www.cumbriafoundation.org

Dacorum Community Trust
48 High Street
Hemel Hempstead
HP1 3AF
Tel: 01442 231396
Contact: Margaret Kingston
    (Administrator)
Email: mk@dctrust.org.uk
Website: www.dctrust.org.uk

Derbyshire Community Foundation
The Old Nursery
University of Derby
Chevin Avenue
Mickleover
DERBY
DE3 5GX
Tel: 01332 592050
Fax: 01332 592200
Contact: Rachael Grime (Executive
    Director)
Email: info@derbyshirecommunity
    foundation.co.uk
Website: www.derbyshirecommunity
    foundation.co.uk

Devon Community Foundation
The Island
Lowman Green
Tiverton
Devon
EX16 4LA
Tel: 01884 235887
Fax: 01884 243824
Contact: Melanie McLoughlin (General
    Manager)
Email: admin@devoncf.com
Website: www.devoncf.com

County Durham Foundation (includes Darlington)
Jordan House
Forster Business Centre
Finchale Road
Durham
DH1 5HL
Tel: 0191 383 0055
Fax: 0191 383 2969
Contact: Gillian Stacey (Director)
Email: info@countydurhamfoundation
    .co.uk
Website: www.countydurhamfoundation
    .co.uk

Essex Community Foundation
52A Moulsham Street
Chelmsford
Essex
CM2 0JA
Tel: 01245 355947
Fax: 01245 251151
Contact: Laura Warren (Chief Executive)
Email: general@essexcf.org.uk
Website: www.essexcommunityfoundation
    .org.uk

The Fermanagh Trust
34a East Bridge Street
Enniskillen
Co. Fermanagh
BT74 7BT
Tel: 028 6632 0210
Fax: 028 6632 0230
Contact: Lauri McCusker (Director)
Email: fermanaghtrust@talk21.com

Finsbury Park Community Trust
Park Gate House
306 Seven Sisters Road
London
N4 2AG
Tel: 020 8211 0121
Fax: 020 8211 0234
Contact: Debra Hilton
Email: fpct@fpct.org.uk
Website: www.fpct.org.uk

Gloucestershire Community Foundation
c/o British Energy Plc
Barnett Way
Barnwood
Gloucester
GL4 3RS
Tel: 01452 656385
Fax: 01452 654164
Contact: Darien Parkes(Director)
Email: darien.parkes@british-energy.com

Greater Bristol Foundation (covers Bristol, North Somerset, South Gloucestershire, Bath and North East Somerset)
Royal Oak House
Royal Oak Avenue
Bristol
BS1 4GB
Tel: 0117 989 7700
Fax: 0117 989 7701
Contact: Helen Moss (Director)
Email: info@gbf.org.uk
Website: www.gbf.org.uk

The Community Foundation for Greater Manchester
Beswick House
Beswick Row
Manchester
M4 4LE
Tel: 0161 214 0940
Fax: 0161 214 0941
Contact: Nick Massey (Director)
Email: enquiries@commmunityfoundation
    .co.uk
Website: www.communityfoundation.co.uk

Community Foundation for Hampshire and the Isle of Wight
Beaconsfield House
Andover Road
Winchester
Hampshire
SO22 6AT
Tel: 01962 857374
Fax: 01962 841160
Contact: Neil Sumpter(Co-ordinator)
Email: info@hantscf.org.uk

Heart of England Community Foundation (Coventry & Warwickshire)Aldermoor House
P O Box 227
Coventry
West Midlands
CV3 1LT
Tel: 024 7688 3416
Fax: 024 7688 3097
Contact: Jennie Bryce (Acting Director)
Email: info@heartofenglandcf.co.uk
Website: www.heartofenglandcf.co.uk

Herefordshire Community Foundation
The Fred Bulmer Centre
Wall Street
Hereford
HR4 9HP
Tel: 01432 272550
Contact: David Barclay (Director)
Email: daveandpam.barclay@ukgateway.net

Hertfordshire Community Foundation
(includes areas of Barnet)
Sylvia Adams House
24 The Common
Hatfield
Hertfordshire
AL10 0NB
Tel: 01707 251351
Fax: 01707 251133
Contact: Tony Gilbert (Director)
Email: info@hertscf.org.uk
Website: www.hertscf.org.uk

Hull & East Yorkshire Community
Foundation
c/o Hull Community Investment Fund
Hull Cityventures
48 Queen Street
Hull
HU1 1UU
Tel: 01482 320021
Fax: 01482 329189
Contact: Nigel Mills
Email: nigelm@citycompanies.co.uk

Isle of Dogs Community Foundation
Jack Dash House
2 Lawn House Close
London
E14 9YQ
Tel: 020 7345 4444
Fax: 020 7538 4671
Contact: Tracey Betts (Director)
Email: tbetts@idcf
Website: www.idcf.org

Kent Community Foundation (includes
Medway)
Office 23
Evegate Park Barn
Evegate
Smeeth
Ashford
TN25 6SX
Tel: 01303 814500
Fax: 01303 815150
Contact: Iain McArthur (Chief Executive)
Email: admin.kcf@btopenworld.com
Website: www.kentcf.org.uk

Community Foundation for Leeds
1st Floor
6 Lisbon Square
Leeds
LS1 4LY
Tel: 0113 242 2425
Fax: 0113 242 2432
Contact: Sally-Anne Greenfield (Chief
Executive)
Email: info@leedscommunityfoundation
.org.uk
Website: www.leedscommunityfoundation
.org.uk

Leicestershire, Leicester & Rutland
Community Foundation
The Beaumont Enterprise Centre
72 Boston Road
Leicester
LE4 1HB
Tel: 0116 229 3088
Fax: 0116 235 1844
Contact: Nicola Dalby (Director)
Email: admin@llrcommunityfoundation
.org.uk

Lincolnshire Community Foundation
4 Mill House
Carre Street
Sleaford
Lincolnshire
NG34 7TW
Tel: 01529 305825
Fax: 01529 305825
Contact: Gordon Hunter
Email: info@lincolnshirecf.org
Website: www.lincolnshirecf.org

London North East Community
Foundation
PO Box 77
Ilford
Essex
IG1 1EB
Tel: 020 8554 7922
Contact: Phil Miller
Email: teleos.training@btinternet.com

Community Foundation for Merseyside
(formerly the Sefton Community
Foundation)
c/o Alliance & Leicester
T169 1st Floor Ops
Bridle Road
Bootle
GIR 0AA
Tel: 0151 966 4604
Fax: 0151 966 3384
Contact: Dave Roberts (Executive Director)
Email: info@cfmerseyside.org.uk
Website: www.cfmerseyside.org.uk

Milton Keynes Community Foundation
Acorn House
381 Midsummer Boulevard
Central Milton Keynes
MK9 3HP
United Kingdom
Tel: 01908 690276
Fax: 01908 233635
Contact: Julia Seal (Chief Executive)
Email: information@mkcommunity
foundation.co.uk
Website: www.mkcommunityfoundation
.co.uk

Norfolk Community Foundation
109 Dereham Road
Easton
Norwich
Norfolk
NR9 5ES
Tel: 01603 882138
Contact: Kate Kingdon (Director)
Email: katekingdon@norfolkfoundation
.com

Northamptonshire Community
Foundation
Suite 14
Burlington House
369 Wellingborough Road
Northampton
NN1 4EU
Tel: 01604 230033
Fax: 01604 639780
Contact: Tina Matthew (Director)
Email: northantscf@btconnect.com

**Community Foundation for Northern
Ireland**
Community House
Citylink Business Park
6a Albert Street
Belfast
BT12 4HQ
Tel: 028 9024 5927
Fax: 028 9032 9839
Contact: Avila Kilmurray (Director)
Email: info@communityfoundationni.org
Website: www.communityfoundationni.org

North West London Community
Foundation
Central Depot (Unit 4)
Forward Drive
Harrow
Middlesex
HA3 8NT
Tel: 020 8424 1167
Fax: 020 8909 1407
Contact: Ron Swain (Director)
Email: director@nwlondoncf.org.uk

Nottinghamshire Community Foundation
Cedar House
Ransom Wood Business Park
Southwell Road West
Mansfield
Nottinghamshire
NG21 0HJ
Tel: 01623 636365
Fax: 01623 620204
Contact: Rowena Morrell (Director)
Email:
    enquiries@nottscommunityfoundation
    .org.uk
Website: www.nottscommunityfoundation
    .org.uk

O-Regen
Paradox Centre
3 Ching Way
Chingford
London
E4 8YE
Tel: 020 8501 9900
Fax: 020 8501 9922
Contact: Julian Martin (Director)
Email: info@o-regen.co.uk
Website: www.o-regen.co.uk

Oxfordshire Community Foundation
Vanbrugh House
20 St Michael's Street
Oxford
OX1 2EB
Tel: 01865 798666
Fax: 01865 245385
Contact: Emma Tracy (Director)
Email: ocf@oxfordshire.org
Website: www.oxfordshire.org

Community Foundation in Powys
Sefton House
Middleton Street
Llandrindod Wells
Powys
LD1 5DG
Tel: 01597 822110
Fax: 01597 825846
Contact: Harvey Rose (Chief Executive)
Email: harvey.cfip@virgin.net
Website: www.cfip.org.uk

Royal Docks Trust London
37 Rushey Green
Catford
London
SE6 4AF
Tel: 01322 226336
Website: www.royaldockstrust.org

Community Foundation for Shropshire
and Telford
Meeting Point House
Southwater Square
Telford
Shropshire
TF3 4H5
Tel: 01952 201858
Fax: 01952 210500
Contact: Mike Pugh (Director)
Email: contact@cfst.co.uk

St Katharine & Shadwell Trust
1 Pennington Street
London
E1W 2BY
Tel: 020 7782 6962
Fax: 020 7782 6963
Contact: Jenny Dawes (Director)
Email: enquiries@skst.org
Website: www.skst.org

The Scottish Community Foundation
126 Canongate
Edinburgh
EH8 8DD
Tel: 0131 524 0300
Fax: 0131 524 0329
Contact: Giles Ruck (Chief Executive)
Email: mail@scottishcommunityfoundation
    .com
Website: www.scottishcommunity
    foundation.com

Solihull Community Foundation
Block 33
Land Rover
Lode Lane
Solihull
B92 8NW
Tel: 0121 700 3934
Fax: 0121 700 9158
Contact: Robin Evans (Director)
Email: director@solihullcf.org
Website: www.solihullcf.org

Somerset Community Foundation
Unit 1, Baybrook Farm
Lower Godney
near Wells
Somerset
BA5 1RZ
Tel: 01458 833133
Fax: 01458 833395
Contact: Stella Elston (General manager)
Email: info@somersetcf.org.uk
Website: www.somersetcf.org.uk

**South East London Community
Foundation** (also covers parts of Central
London)
Room 6
Winchester House
11 Cranmer Road
London
SW9 6EJ
Tel: 020 7582 5117
Fax: 020 7582 4020
Contact: Lena Young (Director)
Email: enquiries@selcf.globalnet.co.uk
Website: www.selcf.com

South Yorkshire Community Foundation
Clay Street
Sheffield
S9 2PF
Tel: 0114 242 4857
Fax: 0114 242 4605
Contact: Richard Clarke (Director)
Email: info@sycf.org.uk
Website: www.sycf.org

Staffordshire Community Foundation
Oak Tree Cottage
Newton
Admaston
Rugeley
Staffordshire
Tel: 01889 500635
Contact: Peter Atkins
Email: pda60@hotmail.com
Website: http://www.staffscf.org

Stevenage Community Trust
c/o Astrium
Gunnels Wood Road
Stevenage
SG1 2AS
Tel: 01438 773368
Fax: 01438 773341
Contact: Pat Henry (Director)
Email: stevenagecommunitytrust@
    btopenworld.com
Website: www.stevenagecommunitytrust
    .org

Community Foundation for Suffolk
1 Cornhill
Ipswich
Ipswich
Suffolk
IP1 1AQ
Tel: 01473 251834
Fax: 01473 251848
Contact: Stephen Singleton (Director)
Email: stephen.singleton@ipswich-cvs
    .org.uk

Surrey Community Foundation
c/o Waverley Borough Council
The Burys
Godalming
Surrey
GU7 1HR
Contact: Wendy Varcoe
Email: wvarcoe@waverley.gov.uk

Sussex Community Foundation
c/o Action in Rural Sussex
Sussex House
212 High Street
Lewes
East Sussex
BN7 2 NH
Tel: 01273 407331
Fax: 01273 483109
Contact: Jeremy Leggett (Chair)
Email: jeremy-leggett@ruralsussex.org.uk

Tees Valley Community Foundation
(formerly the Cleveland Community
Foundation)
Southlands Business Centre
Ormesby Road
Middlesbrough
TS3 0HB
Tel: 01642 314200
Fax: 01642 313700
Contact: Kevin Ryan (Director)
Email: info@teesvalleyfoundation.org
Website: www.teesvalleyfoundation.org

Thames Community Foundation
NPL-Building 5-Room 112
Queens Road
Teddington
TW11 0LW
Tel: 020 8943 5525
Fax: 020 8943 2319
Contact: Nigel Hay (Business Development
    Director)
Email: tcf@thamescommunityfoundation
    .org.uk
Website: www.thamescommunity
    foundation.org.uk

Community Foundation serving Tyne & Wear and Northumberland
Cale Cross
156 Pilgrim Street
Newcastle upon Tyne
NE1 6SU
Tel: 0191 222 0945
Fax: 0191 230 0689
Contact: George Hepburn (Chief
    Executive)
Email: general@communityfoundation
    .org.uk
Website: www.communityfoundation
    .org.uk

The Community Foundation in Wales
(Sefydliad)
14-16 Merthyr Road
Whitchurch
Cardiff
CF4 1DG
Tel: 029 2052 0250
Fax: 029 2052 1250
Contact: Nigel Griffiths(Chief Executive)
Email: mail@cfiw.org.uk
Website: www.cfiw.org.uk

Community Foundation for Wiltshire & Swindon
48 New Park Street
Devizes
Wiltshire
SN10 1DS
Tel: 01380 729284
Fax: 01380 729772
Contact: Ruth Jones (Director)
Email: info@wscf.org.uk
Website: www.wscf.org.uk

Worcestershire Community Foundation
37 Ombersley Road
Worcester
WR3 7BP
Tel: 01905 25472
Contact: Martin Gallagher
Email: friel.gallagher@btinternet.com

York and North Yorkshire Community
Foundation
Primrose Hill
Buttercrambe Road
Stamford Bridge
York
YO41 1AW
Tel: 01759 377400
Fax: 01759 377401
Contact: Stephen Beyer (Director)
Email: office@ynycf.plus.com

Subject index

The following subject index begins with a list of categories used. The categories are very wide-ranging to keep the index as simple as possible. The *Grant-making Trusts* CD-ROM and the *trustfunding.org* website has a much more detailed search facility on the categories. There may be considerable overlap between the categories – for example, children and education, or older people and social welfare.

The list of categories is followed by the index itself. Before using the index, please note the following:

How the index was compiled

1. The index aims to reflect the most recent grant-making practice. It is therefore based on our interpretation of what each trust has actually given to, rather than what its policy statement says or its charitable objects allow it to do in principle. For example, where a trust states that it has general charitable purposes, but its grants list shows a strong preference for welfare, we index it under welfare.

2. We have tried to ensure that each trust has given significantly in the areas where it is indexed (usually at least £15,000). Thus small, apparently untypical grants have been ignored for index purposes.

3. The index has been complied from the latest information available to us.

Limitations

1. Policies may change; some more frequently than others.

2. Sometimes there will be a geographical restriction on a trust's grant giving which is not shown up in this index, or the trust may not give for the specific purposes you require under that heading. It is important to read each entry carefully. You will need to check:

(a) The trust gives in your geographical area of operation.

(b) The trust gives for the specific purposes you require.

(c) There is no other reason to prevent you making an application to this trust.

3. We have omitted the General category as the number of trusts included would make it unusable. It is also worth noting that one or two of the categories list almost half the trusts included in this guide.

Under no circumstances should the index be used as a simple mailing list. Remember that each trust is different and that often the policies or interests of a particular trust do not fit easily into the given categories. Each entry must be read individually before you send off an application. Indiscriminate applications are usually unsuccessful. They waste time and money and greatly annoy trusts.

The categories are as follows:

Arts and culture *page 425*

A very wide category including performing, written and visual arts, crafts, theatres, museums and galleries, heritage, architecture and archaeology.

Children and young people *page 426*

Mainly for welfare and welfare-related activities.

Community and economic development *page 427*

This includes employment.

Disadvantaged people *page 427*

This includes people who are: socially excluded; socially and economically disadvantaged; unemployed; homeless; offenders; victims of social/natural occurrences, including refugees and asylum seekers.

Education and training *page 428*

Environment and animals *page 429*

This includes agriculture and fishing, conservation, animal care, environmental education, transport and sustainable environment.

Housing *page 429*

Ill or disabled people *page 429*

This includes people who are ill, or who have physical or mental disabilities, or learning difficulties, or mental health problems.

Health *page 430*

This excludes medical research, which is listed separately.

Medical research *page 431*

Minority ethnic *page 432*

Older people *page 432*

Religion general *page 433*

This includes interfaith work and religious understanding.

Christianity *page 433*

Judaism *page 434*

Rights, law and conflict *page 434*

This includes citizen participation, conflict resolution, legal and advice services, rights, equity and justice.

Science and technology
page 434

Social science, policy and research *page 434*

Social welfare *page 435*

This is a very broad category covering community care and services, counselling and advice, social preventive schemes, community centres and activities.

Sport and recreation *page 436*

Voluntary sector capacity building *page 436*

Women *page 436*

Arts and culture

29th May 1961 Charitable Trust
Milly Apthorp Charitable Trust
Arbib Foundation
Ashden Charitable Trust
Lord Ashdown Charitable Trust
Band Trust
Barbour Trust
John Beckwith Charitable Trust
British Record Industry Trust
Britten-Pears Foundation
Audrey & Stanley Burton Charitable Trust
William A Cadbury Charitable Trust
CAF (Charities Aid Foundation)
Charities Advisory Trust
CHK Charities Limited
Clore Duffield Foundation
Clothworkers' Foundation and other Trusts
Colyer-Fergusson Charitable Trust
Community Foundation for Calderdale
Community Foundation for Greater Manchester
Community Foundation for Northern Ireland
Community Foundation Serving Tyne & Wear and Northumberland
Ernest Cook Trust
County Durham Foundation
Cripplegate Foundation
D'Oyly Carte Charitable Trust
Djanogly Foundation
Drapers' Charitable Fund
Dunard Fund
John Ellerman Foundation
Eranda Foundation
Esmée Fairbairn Foundation
Sir John Fisher Foundation
Foyle Foundation
Hugh Fraser Foundation
Gannochy Trust
Gatsby Charitable Foundation
Robert Gavron Charitable Trust
J Paul Getty Jr Charitable Trust
Simon Gibson Charitable Trust
Girdlers' Company Charitable Trust
Glass-House Trust
Goldsmiths' Company Charity
Great Britain Sasakawa Foundation
Greater Bristol Foundation
Grocers' Charity
Gulbenkian Foundation
Paul Hamlyn Foundation
Charles Hayward Foundation
Headley Trust
Heart of England Community Foundation
Hobson Charity Ltd
Reta Lila Howard Foundation

Jacobs Charitable Trust
Jerwood Foundation and Charity
Sir James Knott Trust
Kobler Trust
Kreitman Foundation
Kirby Laing Foundation
Leathersellers' Company Charitable Fund
Lord Leverhulme's Charitable Trust
Levy Foundation
Linbury Trust
Lloyds TSB Foundation for England and Wales
Lloyds TSB Foundation for Northern Ireland
Lloyds TSB Foundation for Scotland
London Marathon Charitable Trust
John Lyon's Charity
Mackintosh Foundation
MacRobert Trust
Manifold Trust
John Martin's Charity
Mercers' Charitable Foundation
Milton Keynes Community Foundation
Monument Trust
Henry Moore Foundation
Peter Moores Foundation
National Art Collections Fund
Network for Social Change
Northern Rock Foundation
P F Charitable Trust
Pilgrim Trust
Porter Foundation
Prince of Wales's Charitable Foundation
Mr and Mrs J A Pye's Charitable Settlement
Sigrid Rausing Trust
Rayne Foundation
Robertson Trust
Rose Foundation
Rothschild Foundation
Alan and Babette Sainsbury Charitable Fund
Robert and Lisa Sainsbury Charitable Trust
Basil Samuel Charitable Trust
Schroder Charity Trust
Archie Sherman Charitable Trust
Shetland Charitable Trust
Foundation for Sport and the Arts
St Katharine & Shadwell Trust
Steel Charitable Trust
Stevenson Family's Charitable Trust
Bernard Sunley Charitable Foundation
Sutton Coldfield Municipal Charities
Triangle Trust (1949) Fund
Trusthouse Charitable Foundation
Wates Foundation
Welton Foundation
Westminster Foundation
Garfield Weston Foundation
Harold Hyam Wingate Foundation

Children and young people

Community and economic development

AIM Foundation
Milly Apthorp Charitable Trust
Ashden Charitable Trust
Birmingham Foundation
Burdens Charitable Foundation
Barrow Cadbury Trust and the Barrow Cadbury Fund
CHK Charities Limited
Church Urban Fund
Coalfields Regeneration Trust
Community Foundation for Greater Manchester
Community Foundation for Northern Ireland
Community Foundation Serving Tyne & Wear and Northumberland
Community Foundation for Wiltshire & Swindon
Cripplegate Foundation
Cumbria Community Foundation
Diana, Princess of Wales Memorial Fund
Dulverton Trust
Esmée Fairbairn Foundation
Allan and Nesta Ferguson Charitable Settlement
Football Foundation
Four Acre Trust
Gatsby Charitable Foundation
J Paul Getty Jr Charitable Trust
Glass-House Trust
Greater Bristol Foundation
Grocers' Charity
Gulbenkian Foundation
Isle of Dogs Community Foundation
Mary Kinross Charitable Trust
Allen Lane Foundation
Lloyds TSB Foundation for England and Wales
John Moores Foundation
Northern Rock Foundation
P F Charitable Trust
Sigrid Rausing Trust
Sir James Reckitt Charity
Rowan Charitable Trust
Joseph Rowntree Charitable Trust
Scottish Community Foundation
Sherburn House Charity
Henry Smith Charity
South East London Community Foundation
South Yorkshire Community Foundation
St Katharine & Shadwell Trust
Tees Valley Community Foundation
Triangle Trust (1949) Fund
Tudor Trust

Wales Council for Voluntary Action
Waterside Trust
Wates Foundation
Westminster Foundation

Disadvantaged people

1989 Willan Charitable Trust
29th May 1961 Charitable Trust
Sylvia Adams Charitable Trust
AIM Foundation
Ajahma Charitable Trust
Alchemy Foundation
H B Allen Charitable Trust
Milly Apthorp Charitable Trust
Ashden Charitable Trust
Balint Family Charitable Trusts
Barbour Trust
Baring Foundation
John Beckwith Charitable Trust
Bedford Charity (Harpur Trust)
Booth Charities
Bromley Trust
William A Cadbury Charitable Trust
Barrow Cadbury Trust and the Barrow Cadbury Fund
CAF (Charities Aid Foundation)
Camelot Foundation
Sir John Cass's Foundation
Charities Advisory Trust
Church Urban Fund
City Parochial Foundation
Clothworkers' Foundation and other Trusts
Richard Cloudesley's Charity
Colyer-Fergusson Charitable Trust
Comic Relief
Community Foundation for Greater Manchester
Community Foundation for Northern Ireland
Community Foundation Serving Tyne & Wear and Northumberland
Ernest Cook Trust
County Durham Foundation
Cripplegate Foundation
Diana, Princess of Wales Memorial Fund
Drapers' Charitable Fund
EBM Charitable Trust
John Ellerman Foundation
Euro Charity Trust
Eveson Charitable Trust
Esmée Fairbairn Foundation
Fishmongers' Company's Charitable Trust
Hugh Fraser Foundation
Gatsby Charitable Foundation
J Paul Getty Jr Charitable Trust

Girdlers' Company Charitable Trust
Grand Charity of Freemasons
Greater Bristol Foundation
Grocers' Charity
H C D Memorial Fund
Hadley Trust
Paul Hamlyn Foundation
Hampton Fuel Allotment Charity
Haramead Trust
Peter Harrison Foundation
Charles Hayward Foundation
Help the Aged
Hilden Charitable Fund
Jane Hodge Foundation
Albert Hunt Trust
J J Charitable Trust
Jones 1986 Charitable Trust
King's Fund
Mary Kinross Charitable Trust
Sir James Knott Trust
Maurice and Hilda Laing Charitable Trust
Beatrice Laing Trust
Allen Lane Foundation
LankellyChase Foundation
Leathersellers' Company Charitable Fund
Leigh Trust
Levy Foundation
Linbury Trust
Enid Linder Foundation
Lloyds TSB Foundation for England and Wales
Lloyds TSB Foundation for Northern Ireland
Lloyds TSB Foundation for Scotland
John Lyon's Charity
Mackintosh Foundation
Mercers' Charitable Foundation
John Moores Foundation
Network for Social Change
North British Hotel Trust
Northern Rock Foundation
Nuffield Foundation
Parthenon Trust
Pilgrim Trust
Pilkington Charities Fund
Mr and Mrs J A Pye's Charitable Settlement
Rayne Foundation
Robertson Trust
Mrs L D Rope Third Charitable Settlement
Rowan Charitable Trust
Joseph Rowntree Charitable Trust
Alan and Babette Sainsbury Charitable Fund
Sandra Charitable Trust
Severn Trent Water Charitable Trust
Sherburn House Charity
Henry Smith Charity
Sobell Foundation

Education and training

Environment and animals

Housing

Ill or disabled people

Health

Medical research

Hugh Fraser Foundation
Joseph Strong Frazer Trust
Gatsby Charitable Foundation
Girdlers' Company Charitable Trust
Teresa Rosenbaum Golden Charitable Trust
Mike Gooley Trailfinders Charity
Grand Charity of Freemasons
Charles Hayward Foundation
Health Foundation
Hedley Foundation
Jane Hodge Foundation
Elton John Aids Foundation
Jones 1986 Charitable Trust
Kay Kendall Leukaemia Fund
Peter Kershaw Trust
Mary Kinross Charitable Trust
Ernest Kleinwort Charitable Trust
Kreitman Foundation
William Leech Charity
Kennedy Leigh Charitable Trust
Leigh Trust
Levy Foundation
Linbury Trust
Enid Linder Foundation
Lloyds TSB Foundation for Northern Ireland
Lloyds TSB Foundation for Scotland
Lotus Foundation
Mackintosh Foundation
Mental Health Foundation
Mercers' Charitable Foundation
Monument Trust
Peter Moores Foundation
Frances and Augustus Newman Foundation
North British Hotel Trust
Northwood Charitable Trust
Nuffield Foundation
P F Charitable Trust
Parthenon Trust
Peacock Charitable Trust
Dowager Countess Eleanor Peel Trust
Pilkington Charities Fund
Mr and Mrs J A Pye's Charitable Settlement
Rayne Foundation
Christopher H R Reeves Charitable Trust
Robertson Trust
Alan and Babette Sainsbury Charitable Fund
Archie Sherman Charitable Trust
Henry Smith Charity
SPARKS Charity
Starfish Trust
Steel Charitable Trust
Sir Halley Stewart Trust
Bernard Sunley Charitable Foundation
Charles and Elsie Sykes Trust
Sir Jules Thorn Charitable Trust
Trusthouse Charitable Foundation
John and Lucille van Geest Foundation

Sir Siegmund Warburg's Voluntary Settlement
Waterside Trust
Wates Foundation
Wellcome Trust
Welton Foundation
Garfield Weston Foundation
Will Charitable Trust
Harold Hyam Wingate Foundation
Charles Wolfson Charitable Trust
Wolfson Family Charitable Trust
Wolfson Foundation

Minority ethnic

CAF (Charities Aid Foundation)
Community Foundation Serving Tyne & Wear and Northumberland
Hilden Charitable Fund
Allen Lane Foundation
Levy Foundation
Lloyds TSB Foundation for England and Wales
Lloyds TSB Foundation for Scotland
John Moores Foundation
Northern Rock Foundation
Jack Petchey Foundation
Joseph Rowntree Charitable Trust
Alan and Babette Sainsbury Charitable Fund
Stone Ashdown Charitable Trust
Tudor Trust
Wates Foundation

Older people

29th May 1961 Charitable Trust
Alchemy Foundation
Allchurches Trust Ltd
H B Allen Charitable Trust
Viscount Amory's Charitable Trust
Milly Apthorp Charitable Trust
Lord Ashdown Charitable Trust
Balint Family Charitable Trusts
Band Trust
David and Frederick Barclay Foundation
Barnwood House Trust
Percy Bilton Charity
Booth Charities
Bridge House Trust
William A Cadbury Charitable Trust
Childwick Trust
Clore Duffield Foundation
Coalfields Regeneration Trust
Comic Relief
Community Foundation for Calderdale
Community Foundation for Merseyside
Community Foundation Serving Tyne & Wear and Northumberland

Cripplegate Foundation
Cumbria Community Foundation
Djanogly Foundation
Dulverton Trust
Dunhill Medical Trust
Sir John Eastwood Foundation
Maud Elkington Charitable Trust
Eveson Charitable Trust
Execution Charitable Trust
Esmée Fairbairn Foundation
Donald Forrester Trust
Hugh Fraser Foundation
Joseph Strong Frazer Trust
Girdlers' Company Charitable Trust
Gosling Foundation Limited
Grand Charity of Freemasons
Grocers' Charity
Charles Hayward Foundation
Headley Trust
Health Foundation
Heart of England Community Foundation
Help the Aged
Albert Hunt Trust
John James Bristol Foundation
Jones 1986 Charitable Trust
Ernest Kleinwort Charitable Trust
Sir James Knott Trust
Beatrice Laing Trust
Allen Lane Foundation
Levy Foundation
Linbury Trust
Lloyds TSB Foundation for England and Wales
Lloyds TSB Foundation for Scotland
Mercers' Charitable Foundation
Peter Moores Foundation
North British Hotel Trust
Northern Rock Foundation
Nuffield Foundation
P F Charitable Trust
Dowager Countess Eleanor Peel Trust
Pilkington Charities Fund
Mr and Mrs J A Pye's Charitable Settlement
Queen Mary's Roehampton Trust
Rank Foundation
Joseph Rank Trust
Rayne Foundation
Sir James Reckitt Charity
Robertson Trust
Rowan Charitable Trust
Scottish Community Foundation
Archie Sherman Charitable Trust
Henry Smith Charity
Sobell Foundation
Sovereign Health Care Charitable Trust
W O Street Charitable Foundation
Bernard Sunley Charitable Foundation
Sutton Coldfield Municipal Charities
Talbot Village Trust
Triangle Trust (1949) Fund

Tudor Trust
UnLtd (Foundation for Social Entrepreneurs)
John and Lucille van Geest Foundation
Waterside Trust
Garfield Weston Foundation
Wixamtree Trust

Religious activities (general)

Achiezer Association Ltd
Allchurches Trust Ltd
Alliance Family Foundation
Viscount Amory's Charitable Trust
Lord Ashdown Charitable Trust
AW Charitable Trust
Balint Family Charitable Trusts
Band Trust
Burdens Charitable Foundation
Audrey & Stanley Burton Charitable Trust
William A Cadbury Charitable Trust
Edward Cadbury Charitable Trust
Central Church Fund
Charitworth Limited
Charity Association Manchester Ltd
Childs Charitable Trust
Childwick Trust
Church Urban Fund
Clore Duffield Foundation
Clothworkers' Foundation and other Trusts
Richard Cloudesley's Charity
Clydpride Ltd
Joy Cohen Charitable Trust
Colyer-Fergusson Charitable Trust
Alice Ellen Cooper Dean Charitable Foundation
Itzchok Meyer Cymerman Trust Ltd
Debmar Benevolent Trust
Djanogly Foundation
Dulverton Trust
Englefield Charitable Trust
Entindale Ltd
Joseph Strong Frazer Trust
Gederville Ltd
Girdlers' Company Charitable Trust
Glencore Foundation for Education and Welfare
Goshen Trust
M & R Gross Charities Limited
Kathleen Hannay Memorial Charity
Maurice Hatter Foundation
Hedley Foundation
Jane Hodge Foundation
Sir Harold Hood's Charitable Trust

Huntingdon Foundation
Hurdale Charity Limited
Isle of Anglesey Charitable Trust
Jacobs Charitable Trust
Jerusalem Trust
Jewish Child's Day
Kennedy Charitable Foundation
Keren Association
Kobler Trust
Kreitman Foundation
Maurice and Hilda Laing Charitable Trust
Kirby Laing Foundation
Beatrice Laing Trust
John and Rosemary Lancaster Charitable Foundation
Carole & Geoffrey Lawson Foundation
Leathersellers' Company Charitable Fund
William Leech Charity
Kennedy Leigh Charitable Trust
Leigh Trust
Levy Foundation
Lolev Charitable Trust
M K Charitable Trust
Marshall's Charity
John Martin's Charity
Mayfair Charities Ltd
Mercers' Charitable Foundation
Merchant Taylors' Company Charities Fund
Peter Moores Foundation
Nemoral Ltd
J E Posnansky Charitable Trust
Rachel Charitable Trust
Rank Foundation
Sir James Reckitt Charity
Mrs L D Rope Third Charitable Settlement
Rothschild Foundation
Joseph Rowntree Charitable Trust
Rubin Foundation
Alan and Babette Sainsbury Charitable Fund
Basil Samuel Charitable Trust
Schreib Trust
Samuel Sebba Charitable Trust
Sheffield Church Burgesses Trust
Archie Sherman Charitable Trust
Shlomo Memorial Fund Limited
Sobell Foundation
Souter Charitable Trust
W F Southall Trust
Spring Harvest Charitable Trust
Stewards' Company Limited
Sir Halley Stewart Trust
Stobart Newlands Charitable Trust
Stone Ashdown Charitable Trust
Sutton Coldfield Municipal Charities
Tajtelbaum Charitable Trust
David Tannen Charitable Trust
Tolkien Trust

Tompkins Foundation
Trustees of Tzedakah
Underwood Trust
Vardy Foundation
Waterside Trust
Wates Foundation
Westminster Foundation
Garfield Weston Foundation
Harold Hyam Wingate Foundation
Wixamtree Trust
Charles Wolfson Charitable Trust
Wolfson Family Charitable Trust

Christianity

Allchurches Trust Ltd
Viscount Amory's Charitable Trust
Band Trust
Burdens Charitable Foundation
William A Cadbury Charitable Trust
Edward Cadbury Charitable Trust
Central Church Fund
Childs Charitable Trust
Church Urban Fund
Clothworkers' Foundation and other Trusts
Richard Cloudesley's Charity
Colyer-Fergusson Charitable Trust
Dulverton Trust
Englefield Charitable Trust
Girdlers' Company Charitable Trust
Goshen Trust
Kathleen Hannay Memorial Charity
Hedley Foundation
Jane Hodge Foundation
Sir Harold Hood's Charitable Trust
Isle of Anglesey Charitable Trust
Jerusalem Trust
Kennedy Charitable Foundation
Maurice and Hilda Laing Charitable Trust
Kirby Laing Foundation
Beatrice Laing Trust
John and Rosemary Lancaster Charitable Foundation
Leathersellers' Company Charitable Fund
William Leech Charity
Marshall's Charity
John Martin's Charity
Mercers' Charitable Foundation
Merchant Taylors' Company Charities Fund
Peter Moores Foundation
Rank Foundation
Sir James Reckitt Charity
Mrs L D Rope Third Charitable Settlement
Joseph Rowntree Charitable Trust
Sheffield Church Burgesses Trust

Souter Charitable Trust
W F Southall Trust
Spring Harvest Charitable Trust
Stewards' Company Limited
Sir Halley Stewart Trust
Stobart Newlands Charitable Trust
Sutton Coldfield Municipal Charities
Tolkien Trust
Vardy Foundation
Waterside Trust
Wates Foundation
Westminster Foundation
Wixamtree Trust

Judaism

Achiezer Association Ltd
Alliance Family Foundation
Lord Ashdown Charitable Trust
AW Charitable Trust
Balint Family Charitable Trusts
Audrey & Stanley Burton Charitable
    Trust
Charitworth Limited
Charity Association Manchester Ltd
Childwick Trust
Clore Duffield Foundation
Clydpride Ltd
Joy Cohen Charitable Trust
Itzchok Meyer Cymerman Trust Ltd
Debmar Benevolent Trust
Djanogly Foundation
Entindale Ltd
Gederville Ltd
Glencore Foundation for Education and
    Welfare
M & R Gross Charities Limited
Maurice Hatter Foundation
Huntingdon Foundation
Hurdale Charity Limited
Jacobs Charitable Trust
Jewish Child's Day
Keren Association
Kobler Trust
Kreitman Foundation
Carole & Geoffrey Lawson Foundation
Kennedy Leigh Charitable Trust
Levy Foundation
Lolev Charitable Trust
M K Charitable Trust
Mayfair Charities Ltd
Nemoral Ltd
J E Posnansky Charitable Trust
Rachel Charitable Trust
Rothschild Foundation
Rubin Foundation
Basil Samuel Charitable Trust
Schreib Trust
Samuel Sebba Charitable Trust
Archie Sherman Charitable Trust

Shlomo Memorial Fund Limited
Sobell Foundation
Tajtelbaum Charitable Trust
David Tannen Charitable Trust
Trustees of Tzedakah
Harold Hyam Wingate Foundation
Charles Wolfson Charitable Trust
Wolfson Family Charitable Trust

Rights, law and conflict

Ajahma Charitable Trust
Alchemy Foundation
Bridge House Trust
Bromley Trust
William A Cadbury Charitable Trust
Barrow Cadbury Trust and Barrow
    Cadbury Fund
Camelot Foundation
Charities Advisory Trust
Church Urban Fund
Comic Relief
Community Foundation for Northern
    Ireland
County Durham Foundation
Cripplegate Foundation
Diana, Princess of Wales Memorial Fund
Dulverton Trust
Allan and Nesta Ferguson Charitable
    Settlement
Gulbenkian Foundation
Paul Hamlyn Foundation
Charles Hayward Foundation
Heart of England Community
    Foundation
Hilden Charitable Fund
Allen Lane Foundation
Kennedy Leigh Charitable Trust
Leigh Trust
Levy Foundation
Lloyds TSB Foundation for England and
    Wales
Lloyds TSB Foundation for Scotland
John Martin's Charity
John Moores Foundation
Peter Moores Foundation
Network for Social Change
Northern Rock Foundation
Nuffield Foundation
Parthenon Trust
Polden-Puckham Charitable Foundation
Mr and Mrs J A Pye's Charitable
    Settlement
Sigrid Rausing Trust
Sir James Reckitt Charity
Rowan Charitable Trust
Joseph Rowntree Charitable Trust
Joseph Rowntree Reform Trust Limited

Alan and Babette Sainsbury Charitable
    Fund
Severn Trent Water Charitable Trust
South Yorkshire Community Foundation
W F Southall Trust
Staples Trust
Sir Halley Stewart Trust
Stone Ashdown Charitable Trust
Three Guineas Trust
Tudor Trust
Wates Foundation
Westminster Foundation for Democracy

Science and technology

Clothworkers' Foundation and other
    Trusts
Ernest Cook Trust
Esmée Fairbairn Foundation
Gatsby Charitable Foundation
Paul Hamlyn Foundation
Jerwood Foundation and Jerwood
    Charity
Leathersellers' Company Charitable
    Fund
Lloyds TSB Foundation for Northern
    Ireland
MacRobert Trust
Nuffield Foundation
Mrs L D Rope Third Charitable
    Settlement
Alan and Babette Sainsbury Charitable
    Fund
Underwood Trust
Wellcome Trust
Wolfson Family Charitable Trust
Wolfson Foundation

Social sciences, policy and research

CAF (Charities Aid Foundation)
Esmée Fairbairn Foundation
Gatsby Charitable Foundation
Robert Gavron Charitable Trust
Joffe Charitable Trust
Allen Lane Foundation
Leverhulme Trust
Levy Foundation
Nuffield Foundation
Lisbet Rausing Charitable Fund
Joseph Rowntree Charitable Trust
Joseph Rowntree Foundation
Wolfson Foundation

Social welfare

Sport and recreation

Voluntary sector capacity building

Women

Geographical index

The following geographical index aims to highlight when a trust gives preference for, or has a special interest in, a particular area: county, region, city, town or London Borough. Please note the following:

1. Before using this index please read the following and the introduction to the subject index on page 424. We must emphasise that this index:

   (a) should not be used as a simple mailing list, and

   (b) is not a substitute for detailed research.

When you have identified trusts, using this index, please read each entry carefully before making an application. Simply because a trust gives in your geographical area does not mean that it gives to your type of work.

2. Most trusts in this list are not restricted to one area, usually the geographical index indicates that the trust gives some priority for the area(s).

3. Trusts which give throughout England, Northern Ireland, Scotland and Wales have been excluded as have those which give throughout the UK, unless they have a particular interest in one or more locality.

4. Each section is ordered alphabetically according to the name of the trust.

The categories for the overseas and UK indices are as follows:

England

We have divided England into the following nine categories:

Some trusts may be found in more than one category due to them providing grants in more than one area i.e. those with a preference for northern England.

Overseas Categories

This includes trusts which support missionary organisations when they are also interested in social and economic development.

The Middle East has been listed separately. Please note that most of the trusts listed are primarily for the benefit of Jewish people and the advancement of the Jewish religion.

North East

1989 Willan Charitable Trust
Barbour Trust
Coalfields Regeneration Trust
County Durham Foundation
Sir James Knott Trust
William Leech Charity
Northern Rock Foundation
Sherburn House Charity
Tees Valley Community Foundation
Community Foundation Serving Tyne & Wear and Northumberland
Vardy Foundation

North West

Baring Foundation
Booth Charities
Coalfields Regeneration Trust
Community Foundation for Greater Manchester
Community Foundation for Merseyside
Cumbria Community Foundation
Sir John Fisher Foundation
Freshfield Foundation
Peter Kershaw Trust
Lord Leverhulme's Charitable Trust
London Marathon Charitable Trust
M B Foundation
John Moores Foundation
Northern Rock Foundation
Oglesby Trust
Dowager Countess Eleanor Peel Trust
Pilkington Charities Fund
Rowan Charitable Trust
Francis C Scott Charitable Trust
SHINE
Stoller Charitable Trust
W O Street Charitable Foundation
United Trusts
Westminster Foundation
Yorkshire Dales Millennium Trust
Zochonis Charitable Trust

Yorkshire and the Humber

Audrey & Stanley Burton Charitable Trust
Coalfields Regeneration Trust
Community Foundation for Calderdale
North British Hotel Trust
Sir James Reckitt Charity
Sheffield Church Burgesses Trust
South Yorkshire Community Foundation
Charles and Elsie Sykes Trust
Yorkshire Dales Millennium Trust

East Midlands

Coalfields Regeneration Trust
Ernest Cook Trust
Derbyshire Community Foundation
Sir John Eastwood Foundation
Maud Elkington Charitable Trust
Haramead Trust
Lady Hind Trust
Jones 1986 Charitable Trust
London Marathon Charitable Trust
Medlock Charitable Trust
Patrick Charitable Trust
Henry Smith Charity
John and Lucille van Geest Foundation

West Midlands

29th May 1961 Charitable Trust
Birmingham Foundation
William A Cadbury Charitable Trust
Edward Cadbury Charitable Trust
CHK Charities Limited
Coalfields Regeneration Trust
Baron Davenport's Charity
Eveson Charitable Trust
Heart of England Community Foundation
Alan Edward Higgs Charity
Jordan Charitable Foundation
London Marathon Charitable Trust
John Martin's Charity
Mercers' Charitable Foundation
Patrick Charitable Trust
W F Southall Trust
Stratford upon Avon Town Trust
Sutton Coldfield Municipal Charities
Douglas Turner Trust

Eastern England

Sylvia Adams Charitable Trust
AIM Foundation

Bedford Charity (Harpur Trust)
Essex Community Foundation
Essex Youth Trust
G C Gibson Charitable Trust
Simon Gibson Charitable Trust
Hertfordshire Community Foundation
Lady Hind Trust
Mercers' Charitable Foundation
Norwich Town Close Estate Charity
Jack Petchey Foundation
L D Rope Third Charitable Settlement
Henry Smith Charity
Steel Charitable Trust

South West

Viscount Amory's Charitable Trust
Baring Foundation
Barnwood House Trust
CHK Charities Limited
Community Foundation for Wiltshire & Swindon
Ernest Cook Trust
Alice Ellen Cooper Dean Charitable Foundation
Devon Community Foundation
Greater Bristol Foundation
Heathcoat Trust
John James Bristol Foundation
Medlock Charitable Trust
J P Morgan Foundations
Mr and Mrs J A Pye's Charitable Settlement
Henry Smith Charity
Starfish Trust
Talbot Village Trust
Underwood Trust
Valentine Charitable Trust

South East

Alice Trust
Arbib Foundation
CHK Charities Limited
Coalfields Regeneration Trust
Colyer-Fergusson Charitable Trust
Ernest Cook Trust
Englefield Charitable Trust
Peter Harrison Foundation
Ernest Kleinwort Charitable Trust
Mercers' Charitable Foundation
Milton Keynes Community Foundation
P F Charitable Trust
Peacock Charitable Trust
Mr and Mrs J A Pye's Charitable Settlement
Rothschild Foundation
Sandra Charitable Trust
Henry Smith Charity

Tolkien Trust

London

Milly Apthorp Charitable Trust
Baring Foundation
Bridge House Trust
Cadogan Charity
Campden Charities
Sir John Cass's Foundation
City Parochial Foundation
Richard Cloudesley's Charity
Cripplegate Foundation
Drapers' Charitable Fund
Fishmongers' Company's Charitable Trust
Girdlers' Company Charitable Trust
Goldsmiths' Company Charity
Hampton Fuel Allotment Charity
Help a London Child
Isle of Dogs Community Foundation
The King's Fund
Lambeth Endowed Charities
Leathersellers' Company Charitable Fund
London Marathon Charitable Trust
John Lyon's Charity
Mercers' Charitable Foundation
J P Morgan Foundations
Mulberry Trust
Peacock Charitable Trust
Jack Petchey Foundation
Richmond Parish Lands Charity
Rose Foundation
Saddlers' Company Charitable Fund
Sheepdrove Trust
SHINE
South East London Community Foundation
St Katharine & Shadwell Trust
Trust for London
Wates Foundation
Westminster Foundation

Channel Islands

W O Street Charitable Foundation
Lloyds TSB Foundation for the Channel Islands

Wales

Coalfields Regeneration Trust
G C Gibson Charitable Trust
Simon Gibson Charitable Trust

Alphabetical index

DUCHY COLLEGE
LIBRARY